# PRENTICE HALL
# WORLD HISTORY
## CONNECTIONS TO TODAY

# THE MODERN ERA

Elisabeth Gaynor Ellis and Anthony Esler
With Senior Consultant Burton F. Beers

PRENTICE HALL

# THE WORLD HISTORY TEAM

Core Team: Lynda Cloud, Kathryn Dix, Anne Falzone, Monduane Harris, Carol Leslie, Emily Rose, Frank Tangredi, Elizabeth Torjussen

Advertising and Promotion: Carol Leslie, Rip Odell

Art and Design: Laura Jane Bird, Paul Gagnon, Monduane Harris, AnnMarie Roselli, Gerry Schrenck, Kira Thaler

Computer Test Bank Technology: Greg Myers, Cleasta Wilburn

Editorial: Tom Barber, Jim Doris, Anne Falzone, Nancy Gilbert, Mary Ann Gundersen, Barbara Harrigan, Rick Hickox, Naomi Kisch, Marion Osterberg, Kirsten Richert, Luess Sampson-Lizotte, Amit Shah, Frank Tangredi

Manufacturing: Rhett Conklin, Matt McCabe

Marketing: Laura Asermily, Lynda Cloud

Media Resources: Martha Conway, Libby Forsyth, Vickie Menanteaux, Emily Rose

Pre-Press Production: Carol Barbara, Kathryn Dix, Annette Simmons

Production: Christina Burghard, Joan McCulley, Marilyn Stearns, Elizabeth Torjussen, Cynthia Weedel

Text Permissions: Doris Robinson

ISBN 0-13-434806-0

4 5 6 7 8 9 10    02 01 00 99

PRENTICE HALL
Upper Saddle River, New Jersey
Needham, Massachusetts

**ACKNOWLEDGMENTS**

Grateful acknowledgment is made to the following for permission to reprint copyrighted material:

Excerpt from "Requiem," translated by Robin Kemball, Copyright © 1974 by Robin Kemball, from *Selected Poems* by Anna Akhmatova, edited and translated by Walter Arndt. Reprinted by permission of **Ardis**. Excerpt from "No Time" by Nguyen Sa, from *A Thousand Years of Vietnamese Poetry*, translated by Nguyen Ngoc Bich with Burton Raffel and W. S. Merwin, edited by Nguyen Ngoc Bich. Copyright © 1962,

1967, 1968, 1969, 1970, 1971, 1974 by The Asia Society, Inc. Reprinted by permission of Nguyen Ngoc **Bich**. From "A Doll's House," from *The Complete Major Prose Plays of Henrik Ibsen* by Henrik Ibsen, translated by Rolf Fjelde. Translation copyright © 1965, 1970, 1978 by Rolf Fjelde. Used by permission of **Dutton Signet, a division of Penguin Books USA Inc.** From "The Heirs of Stalin," from *The Collected Poems, 1952–1990*, Yevgeny Yevtushenko, edited by Albert C. Todd with the author and James Ragan. Copyright © 1991 by Henry Holt and Co. Reprinted by permission of **Henry Holt and Co.** From

*Casualties* (**Longmans**, 1970). Lines from "Year after year I have Watched," by Li Ch'ing Chao, translated by Kenneth Rexroth from *Love and the Turning Year: One Hundred More Poems from the Chinese* by Kenneth Rexroth. Copyright © 1970 by Kenneth Rexroth. Reprinted by permission of **New Directions Publishing Company**. Excerpts from "The Prologue" to *The Canterbury Tales* by Geoffrey Chaucer, translated by Nevill Coghill (Penguin Classics, 1951, Fourth revised edition, 1977), copyright © Nevill Coghill, 1951, 1958, 1960, 1975, 1977. Reprinted by permission of **Penguin Books Ltd.** Four

lines of "In Memory of W. B. Yeats," from *W. H. Auden: Collected Poems* by W. H. Auden. Copyright © 1940 and renewed 1968 by W. H. Auden. Reprinted by permission of **Random House, Inc.** and **Faber and Faber Limited.** From "We Crown Thee King" by Rabindranath Tagore from *The Hungry Stones and Other Stories*, published by The Macmillan Company, 1916. Reprinted by permission of **Simon & Schuster, Inc.** and **Macmillan Publishers Ltd.** Four lines

(Acknowledgments continue on page 685.)

# PRENTICE HALL
# WORLD HISTORY
## CONNECTIONS TO TODAY

# Authors

### Elisabeth Gaynor Ellis

Elisabeth Gaynor Ellis is a historian and writer. She is a co-author of *World Cultures: A Global Mosaic*. Ms. Ellis, a former social studies teacher and school administrator, has taught world cultures, Russian studies, and European history. She holds a B.A. from Smith College and an M.A. and M.S. from Columbia University.

### Senior Consultant
### Burton F. Beers

Burton F. Beers is Professor of History at North Carolina State University. He has taught European history, Asian history, and American history. Dr. Beers has published numerous articles in historical journals and several books, including *The Far East: A History of Western Impacts and Eastern Responses,* with Paul H. Clyde, and *World History: Patterns of Civilization*.

### Anthony Esler

Anthony Esler is Professor of History at the College of William and Mary. He received his Ph.D. from Duke University and received Fulbright Fellowships to study at the University of London and travel to Ivory Coast and Tanzania. Dr. Esler's books include *The Human Venture: A World History* and *The Western World: A History,* as well as seven historical novels.

### Diane Hart

Diane Hart is an education writer and consultant specializing in history and social studies. She is the author of several social studies textbooks as well as resource books for teachers including *Authentic Assessment: A Handbook for Educators*. A former teacher and Woodrow Wilson Fellow, she remains deeply involved in social studies education through her active involvement in both the National and California Councils for the Social Studies.

# Program Reviewers

## AREA SPECIALISTS

**Africa**  Abraham Kuranga, Department of History, Cincinnati State, Technical and Community College, Cincinnati, Ohio

**Ancient World**  Maud Gleason, Department of Classics, Stanford University, Palo Alto, California

**Chicano/a Studies**  Shirlene Soto, California State University, Northridge, California

**East Asia**  Burton F. Beers, Department of History, North Carolina State University, Raleigh, North Carolina

**Economics**  Richard Sylla, Department of Economics, Stern School of Business, New York University, New York, New York

**Medieval Europe**  Kathryn Reyerson, Department of History, University of Minnesota, Minneapolis, Minnesota

**Modern Europe**  Douglas Skopp, Department of History, State University of New York, Plattsburgh, New York

**Religion**  Michael Sells, Department of Religion, Haverford College, Haverford, Pennsylvania

**South Asia**  David Gilmartin, Department of History, North Carolina State University, Raleigh, North Carolina

Susan Wadley, Department of Anthropology, Syracuse University, Syracuse, New York

**Southwest Asia**  Linda T. Darling, Department of History, University of Arizona, Tucson, Arizona

**Women's History**  Lyn Reese, Women in the World: Curriculum Resource Project, Berkeley, California

# Program Reviewers
## Continued

# Contents

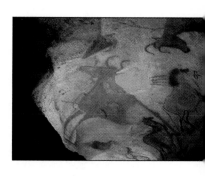

## THE BIG PICTURE

# UNIT 3  World Wars and Revolutions

## THE BIG PICTURE

## UNIT 5 Case Studies on Contemporary Issues

# Special Features

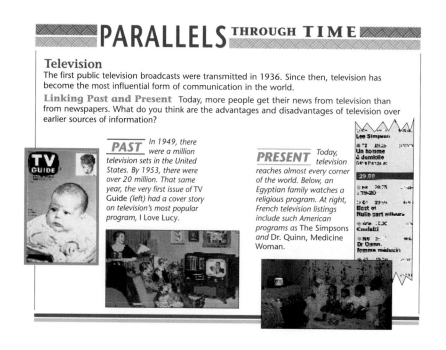

**PARALLELS THROUGH TIME**

**Television**
The first public television broadcasts were transmitted in 1936. Since then, television has become the most influential form of communication in the world.

**Linking Past and Present** Today, more people get their news from television than from newspapers. What do you think are the advantages and disadvantages of television over earlier sources of information?

**PAST** *In 1949, there were a million television sets in the United States. By 1953, there were over 20 million. That same year, the very first issue of TV Guide (left) had a cover story on television's most popular program, I Love Lucy.*

**PRESENT** *Today, television reaches almost every corner of the world. Below, an Egyptian family watches a religious program. At right, French television listings include such American programs as The Simpsons and Dr. Quinn, Medicine Woman.*

## Art History

▶ *Works of art reveal the talents and creativity of artists and artisans around the world.*

## World Literature

▶ *Literature selections offer insights into diverse world cultures throughout history.*

ART HISTORY

**Trade and Commerce Quilt** *This quilt, made around 1830 by Hannah S. Stokes, celebrates the bustling sea trade of that period. Its design includes rowboats, sailing ships, and the newly invented steamship. Quilting provided a creative outlet for women living in lonely stretches of rural America. A quilt like this one might take more than a year to complete.* **Art and Literature** *Art historians classify quilts as "folk art." What do you think this phrase means?*

# Skills for Success

# Charts, Graphs, and Time Lines

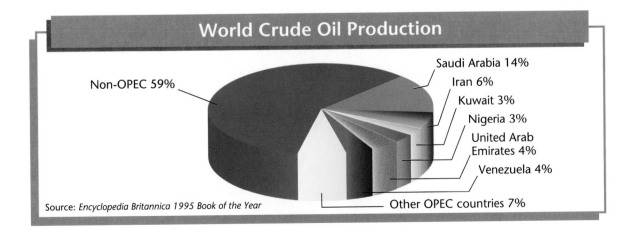

**World Crude Oil Production**

Non-OPEC 59%
Saudi Arabia 14%
Iran 6%
Kuwait 3%
Nigeria 3%
United Arab Emirates 4%
Venezuela 4%
Other OPEC countries 7%

Source: *Encyclopedia Britannica 1995 Book of the Year*

# Maps

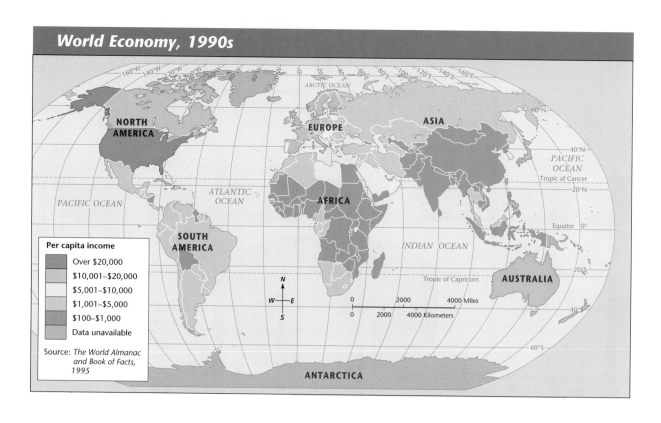

**World Economy, 1990s**

Per capita income
- Over $20,000
- $10,001–$20,000
- $5,001–$10,000
- $1,001–$5,000
- $100–$1,000
- Data unavailable

Source: *The World Almanac and Book of Facts, 1995*

# Documents

# About This Book

## *World History: Connections to Today, The Modern Era*

is organized into 5 units, made up of 20 chapters. The Table of Contents lists the units and chapters, special features and graphics, and the Reference Section at the back of the book.

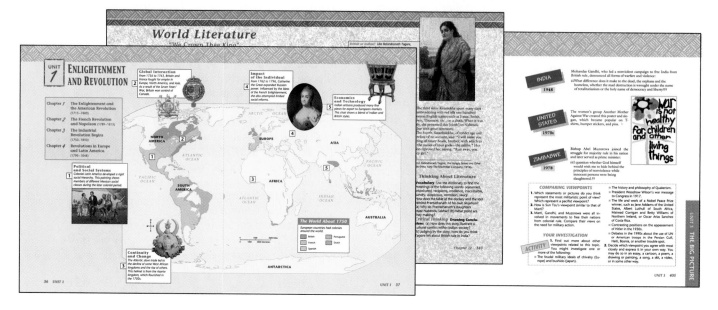

## IN UNITS 1–5

- **Unit Opener:** a two-page introduction that includes a map and illustrations.
- **World Literature:** a two-page literature excerpt from the time period of the unit.
- **The Big Picture:** a six-page wrap-up to each unit, including:
    - **Unit-in-Brief**, a short summary of each chapter in the unit;
    - **A Global View**, a thematic essay and timeline;
    - **You Decide**, a document-based look at an enduring global issue.
    - **Case Studies on Contemporary Issues:** a special 36-page unit that includes seven case studies on topics ranging from the fall of communism to civic participation and the growth of democracy.

## IN EACH CHAPTER

- **Chapter Opener:** a two-page introduction that includes a locator map, theme questions, and timeline.
- **Guide for Reading:** an introduction to each section, including questions to guide your reading and a list of vocabulary terms in the section.
- **Section Reviews:** questions at the end of each section that test your understanding of what you have read.

- **Issues for Today:** questions linking content in the chapter to enduring issues.
- **Global Connections:** historical notes that show how events and ideas are connected over time and place.
- **Maps, Graphs, and Charts:** graphics that provide essential information and also teach important critical thinking and graphics skills.
- **Chapter Review:** two pages that present a Skills for Success skill lesson and review your understanding of the chapter content, plus providing opportunities for critical thinking and activities.
- **Special Features:**
    **Parallels Through Time**, on links between past and present;
    **Art History**, presenting artistic masterpieces from around the world;
    **Up Close**, an in-depth look at an interesting person or event;
    **Cause-and-Effect Charts** on key historical developments;
    **Quick Study Charts**, providing graphic overviews of historical developments.

## REFERENCE SECTION

- Includes an Atlas, Glossary, Historical Documents, Literature and Science Connections, and an Index.

# Researching on the Internet

## The Internet and the World Wide Web

The **Internet** is a global computer network that began in the 1960s as a U. S. Department of Defense project linking university computer science departments. The Internet has since grown to include millions of business, governmental, educational, and individual computers around the world. The **World Wide Web**, or "the Web" for short, is a collection of linked electronic files. Using programs called browsers, Internet users can find out what files are available on the Web and then access those files.

## Searching the Internet

There are two basic ways to find information on the Internet. The first is to go directly to the Web site that contains the information you want. Each Web site has its own address, called a **URL**, or Universal Resource Locator. (For example, http://www.phschool.com is the URL of the Prentice Hall Web site.) Of course, this method only works if you know the appropriate URL. Also, Web sites sometimes change URLs or disappear altogether.

The second way is to search the Web for information on your chosen topic. Using a **search engine**, such as Infoseek or Yahoo!, you type the key words representing the topic you want to research. The search engine will then scan the Internet and list all of the Web sites with information on your topic.

Whichever method you choose, you will encounter Web sites containing **hyperlinks**. These appear on your screen as colored or underlined text or as icons. Hyperlinks act as doorways to other documents. When you click your mouse on hyperlinked text or graphics, an entirely new document appears on your screen. That document may come from the same computer as the Web site you just left, or from one thousands of miles away.

As you search the Internet, you should pay careful attention to the source of the information you find—is it from a government agency, or a university, or a private company, or an individual? Not all sources are equally accurate or reliable.

**Visit the Prentice Hall Home Page!**
*http://www.phschool.com*

## Tips for Successful Searches

- **Keep your search focused**. Because the Internet contains so much interesting and varied information, it is easy to "wander off" into other parts of the Internet and forget about the information that you are trying to locate. To avoid this, you should establish a specific research goal *before* you begin your Internet research.

- **Make bookmarks for your favorite Web sites.** A bookmark is a note to your computer to "remember" the location of the Web site. You can reach any bookmarked site from any other site with a simple click of your mouse.

- **Use specific key words.** If your key words are too general, your search might turn up thousands of Web sites. To search for information on the French Revolution, for example, the key words "French Revolution" are preferable to "history" or "France." Many search engines have useful tips on searching with key words.

- **Evaluate the quality of Internet information.** Not all of the information available on the Internet is appropriate for your research. Ask a teacher, parent, or librarian for help in evaluating the reliability and appropriateness of Web sites and information.

# The Big Picture

## FOCUS ON THEMES

Events that happened hundreds of years ago, or thousands of miles away, can have a powerful impact on our lives. Ancient Greeks pioneered democratic ideas that influenced the framers of our Constitution. American rock 'n' roll grew out of the music brought to North America by Africans in the time of slavery. Today, decisions made by a Brazilian planter, a Saudi Arabian oil minister, or a Japanese manufacturer can have a direct impact on our daily lives.

This textbook can help you understand how today's complex world came to be. To make the past easier to comprehend, this text emphasizes nine themes. They can help you to focus on key features of each society you read about. The nine themes are

- Continuity and Change
- Geography and History
- Political and Social Systems
- Religions and Value Systems
- Economics and Technology
- Diversity
- Impact of the Individual
- Global Interaction
- Art and Literature

In the following pages, you will learn what these themes are and how they can help you to understand world history.

Turn to the following pages in your textbook and identify how one or more of the themes listed above is highlighted on that page: page 126, page 481.

# CONTINUITY AND CHANGE

Human history is a story of change. Some changes are quick. For example, in 1532, Spanish conquerors toppled the vast Incan empire of Peru, transforming South America forever. Other changes take place over centuries, such as the spread of democratic ideas or the shifting role of women in many societies. While change is always happening, enduring traditions and concerns link people across time and place. In India, current politics are affected by a social system more than 3,000 years old. And the question of how to get a good education was as important to a youth in ancient Egypt, Rome, or China as it is to you.

**ACTIVITY**    Interview a parent or any other older acquaintance. Ask them to identify three ways in which your community or the world has changed in the last 25 years.

Migration has been taking place since the beginning of history. One of the most common migrations has been the movement from farming villages (left) to crowded industrial cities (right).

In the 1940s, the government of South Africa imposed apartheid, a system of strict racial separation. In the 1990s, apartheid was abolished, and Nelson Mandela, far right, became president of South Africa.

# GEOGRAPHY AND HISTORY

Geography influences the work people do, the clothes they wear, the food they eat, and how they travel. Since the time of the pharaohs, for example, Egyptians have used the Nile River to transport people and goods. But people also try to master their surroundings. They have built dams to control flooding and cut highways through rugged mountains. More recently, pollution and other environmental issues have caused heated debate. The uneven distribution of vital natural resources, such as oil or gold, is another way geography has helped to shape history.

With a partner, create a Geographic Profile for your local area. You might list location, climate, type of land, nearest waterways, plant and animal life, resources, and outstanding geographic features.

▷ Geography plays a key role in military strategy. Using knowledge of geographic conditions, the French general Napoleon Bonaparte seized control of the high ground to win the Battle of Austerlitz.

▷ The cutting down of tropical rain forests, like this one in Costa Rica, has become an urgent economic and environmental issue of our time.

▷ The Sahara is the world's largest desert. Since early times, it has served as a highway for trade and migration among widely separated African civilizations.

## Battle of Austerlitz, 1805

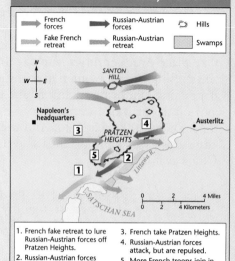

| | |
| --- | --- |
| → French forces | → Russian-Austrian forces |
| → Fake French retreat | → Russian-Austrian retreat |

⌒ Hills
▢ Swamps

1. French fake retreat to lure Russian-Austrian forces off Pratzen Heights.
2. Russian-Austrian forces chase French.
3. French take Pratzen Heights.
4. Russian-Austrian forces attack, but are repulsed.
5. More French troops join in to defeat Russian-Austrian forces.

### GEOGRAPHY AND HISTORY

In December 1805, Napoleon's forces fought a combined Russian-Austrian army at the Battle of Austerlitz. Thanks to Napoleon's superior leadership, his outnumbered troops won an outstanding victory.

1. **Location** On the map, locate (a) Austerlitz, (b) Pratzen Heights, (c) Satschan Sea, (d) Napoleon's headquarters.
2. **Movement** How were Napoleon's troops able to defeat the Russian-Austrian forces south of Pratzen Heights?
3. *Critical Thinking* **Making Generalizations** Why is control of the high ground important in a battle?

# POLITICAL AND SOCIAL SYSTEMS

Kings and queens, presidents and dictators, elected congresses and tribal councils—each society has a way to govern itself. A government tries to keep order within a society and protect it from outside threats. Societies have other important institutions, including the most basic one of all, the family. Social classes—which rank people based on wealth, ancestry, occupation, or education—are also important. Nobles, priests, merchants, workers, and slaves were common social classes in early societies. In addition, most societies have made sharp distinctions between the roles of women and men.

**ACTIVITY**  Draw a political cartoon describing a current political issue in your country, state, or community.

Modern democracy has its roots in the Greek city-state of Athens, left, where every adult male citizen was expected to take part in government. In 1994, Haitians celebrated a return to democratic government after years of military rule.

▶ A feudal social system is based on rigid classes and mutual obligations. This chart shows the feudal system developed in Japan in the 1100s.

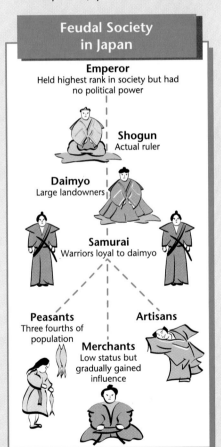

**Feudal Society in Japan**

**Emperor**
Held highest rank in society but had no political power

**Shogun**
Actual ruler

**Daimyo**
Large landowners

**Samurai**
Warriors loyal to daimyo

**Peasants**
Three fourths of population

**Artisans**

**Merchants**
Low status but gradually gained influence

▼ Describe the type of political system you think this cartoon represents.

PALOMO
Mexico City
MEXICO

Cartoonists & Writers Syndicate

CLAP CLAP CLAP CLAP CLAP CLAP CLAP CLAP CLAP CLAP CLAP

©Palomo

# RELIGIONS AND VALUE SYSTEMS

How was the world created? How can we tell right from wrong? What happens to us after death? Since early times, people have turned to religion for answers to such questions. Religious ideas—such as the belief in a single true God, shared by Jews, Christians, and Muslims—have exerted a powerful influence on human life. Other kinds of value systems have also shaped societies. The ancient Chinese thinker Confucius preached duty, respect for parents, and loyalty to the state. In the 1800s, a strict code of "middle-class values"—including hard work, thrift, and good manners—came to dominate western society. Through their religions and value systems, people define their vision of a good society.

**ACTIVITY**

Make a list of 10 values that you think are shared by most people in your community. Compare your list with those of others in the class.

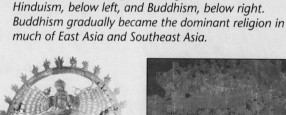

*Jesus, pictured at left, the founder of Christianity, was born in Palestine about 4 B.C. Today, Christianity is the most widely practiced religion in the world, with over a billion followers.*

*Sacred books help pass religious beliefs and values from one generation to the next. Above, a Jewish boy studies the Torah. Below, Muslim children learn to read the Quran.*

*Two major world religions emerged in India: Hinduism, below left, and Buddhism, below right. Buddhism gradually became the dominant religion in much of East Asia and Southeast Asia.*

# ECONOMICS AND TECHNOLOGY

Early humans lived by hunting animals and gathering plants. When people learned how to grow crops, they settled in farming villages. Thousands of years later, the steam engines of the Industrial Revolution created millions of factory jobs. These examples all show the impact of technology. Technology is often related to economic questions. Who controls vital resources? How are goods exchanged? Are people fairly rewarded for the work they do? Economic motives have forged trading networks, caused wars, and contributed to the rise or decline of nations.

**ACTIVITY** Skim through a recent news magazine. Locate two advertisements or articles that deal with advances in technology and two articles that deal with economic issues. Identify the topics addressed by each article in a one-sentence summary.

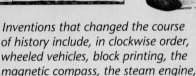

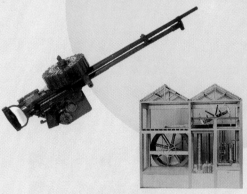

Inventions that changed the course of history include, in clockwise order, wheeled vehicles, block printing, the magnetic compass, the steam engine, and the automatic machine gun.

What do you think is the meaning of this cartoon?

One major economic trend of the past 50 years has been a sharp rise in the number of women who work outside the home.

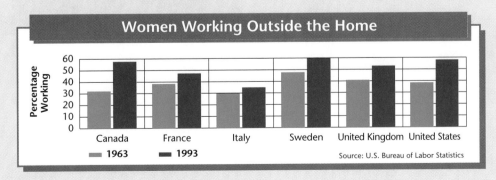

**Women Working Outside the Home**

Percentage Working

60
50
40
30
20
10
0

Canada    France    Italy    Sweden    United Kingdom    United States

■ 1963    ■ 1993

Source: U.S. Bureau of Labor Statistics

# DIVERSITY

How many languages can you think of? English, Spanish, and Japanese are easy. But what about Urdu, Quechua, Gaelic, or Wolof? Today, as in the past, the diversity of human culture is shown by the hundreds of languages people speak. Diversity is also reflected in religions, social systems, art, customs, and forms of government. Within each nation, there may also be a mix of cultures. India, for example, has 16 official languages and hundreds of other regional languages. While diversity has enriched human experience, cultural or ethnic differences can also lead to conflict.

**ACTIVITY**

Make a list of six examples that show diversity in your community. The list might include languages, religions, buildings, clothing styles, foods, or cultural events.

| Comparing Languages | | | | | |
|---|---|---|---|---|---|
| **English** | month | mother | new | night | nose | three |
| **German** | Monat | Mutter | neu | Nacht | Nase | drei |
| **Persian** | māh | mādar | nau | shab | bini | se |
| **Sanskrit** | mās | matar | nava | nakt | nās | trayas |
| **Spanish** | mes | madre | nuevo | noche | nariz | tres |
| **Swedish** | månad | moder | ny | natt | näsa | tre |

◄ *Many diverse languages—stretching from Western Europe to India—came from a common root. Word similarities show the relationship of these "Indo-European" languages.*

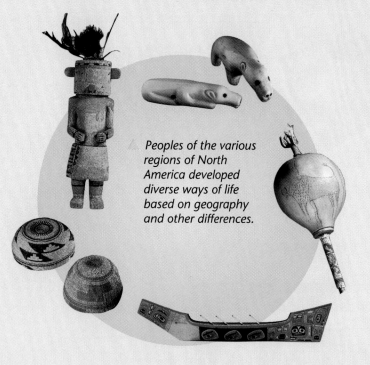

*Peoples of the various regions of North America developed diverse ways of life based on geography and other differences.*

▲ *Russia is the world's largest country, spanning both Europe and Asia. This drawing from the early 1800s shows the diverse peoples of Russia.*

# IMPACT OF THE INDIVIDUAL

Some people have such an impact on events that we remember them long after they die. Vietnam still honors the Trung sisters who fought against Chinese invaders nearly 2,000 years ago. In the 1400s, the voyages of Christopher Columbus and Vasco da Gama launched new patterns of world trade and conquest. The 1900s saw such important political leaders as Mohandas Gandhi, Adolf Hitler, Franklin Roosevelt, Mao Zedong, Juan and Eva Perón, Gamel Abdel Nasser, and Margaret Thatcher. For good or for ill, these individuals have shaped our world.

**ACTIVITY**

Skim the Index of this book (pages 661–684) and find three people whose names you recognize. Try to identify the reason that each of these people is famous. Then check your responses against the book.

Nearly 4,000 years ago, the Babylonian king Hammurabi became the first person in history to collect all the laws of one civilization into a single legal code.

In the 1300s, Mansa Musa built the West African kingdom of Mali into one of the most prosperous empires in the world.

As prime minister of India, Indira Gandhi led the world's largest democracy from 1966 to 1977 and again from 1980 until her assassination in 1984.

In the 1400s, Joan of Arc, a teenage peasant woman, led French troops to battle in an effort to liberate France from its English conquerors.

In the late 1800s, Polish-born chemist Marie Curie was one of the first scientists to conduct experiments in radioactivity.

Benjamin Franklin was an inventor, writer, diplomat, and political thinker whose ideas helped shape the young United States of America.

Simón Bolívar led the battle to liberate Venezuela, Ecuador, Bolivia, and other South American nations from Spanish rule in the early 1800s.

Jomo Kenyatta led the Kikuyu people in their struggle against British rule and, in 1963, became the first president of an independent Kenya.

# GLOBAL INTERACTION

Coffee was first grown in the 1300s in the Middle East. Two hundred years later, Portuguese settlers carried coffee beans to Brazil. Today, Brazil is the world's leading exporter of coffee. This is one example of global interaction. Nations may interact in many ways—through trade, through migration, or through war and conquest. When people traveled by oxcart or sailing ship, interaction was slow. Today, communication and transportation networks can instantly link all parts of the globe. Organizations such as the United Nations and the World Bank show the growing interdependence of the world.

Look through a current newspaper and find three articles concerning interaction between the United States and other countries. Locate these countries on the maps on pages 604–605.

How can a war in one part of the world affect people living in other parts of the world?

Starting in the 1400s, European powers gained outposts along the African coast. This ivory carving from Benin depicts Portuguese soldiers and was probably sold to them.

For 1,500 years, the city of Constantinople (present-day Istanbul, Turkey) was a center of world trade, attracting merchants from as far away as China and Britain.

# ART AND LITERATURE

From early times, people have created art and literature to reflect their lives and values. Stone by stone, Europeans of the Middle Ages raised soaring cathedrals dedicated to the glory of God. In West Africa, griots, or professional poets, recited ancient stories, preserving both histories and traditional folk tales. In the 1920s, the murals of the Mexican painter Diego Rivera depicted the history of Mexico and the lives of its people. Throughout this book, you will see what poems, stories, songs, paintings, sculpture, and architecture show us about other times and other places.

Skim through the pages of this book and find one example of painting, sculpture, or architecture that appeals to you. Freewrite a brief description of how you respond to it.

► *During the Renaissance, Italian artists such as Michelangelo developed new ways to represent humans in a realistic way. This statue of Moses is almost eight feet tall.*

▲ *Japanese paintings such as this one give us a detailed look at life during a time when Japan was isolated from the rest of the world.*

▼ *The ancient Chinese poem at left describes the emotions of parents whose children have gone off to war. Almost 2,500 years later, the German artist Käthe Kollwitz explored the same theme in her print* The Parents, *at right.*

> ❝My mother is saying,
> 'Alas, my young one
>     is on service;
> Day and night he gets
>     no sleep.
> Grant that he is being
>     careful of himself,
> So that he may come
>     back, and not be cast
>     away.'❞

# Connecting with Past Learnings
## Prehistory to Early Modern Times

To understand modern world history requires familiarity with the history of ancient and medieval times. Events, concepts, and relationships that began thousands of years ago continue to have an impact on contemporary times.

This unit serves as a review of key developments from prehistory to early modern times. It focuses on major trends and revolutionary ideas of earlier eras—trends and ideas that transformed people and their cultures in new ways. Highlights include the emergence of river valley civilizations, the cultures of Greece and Rome, the growth of empires and regional civilizations, and the upheavals of the Renaissance, Protestant Reformation, and Scientific Revolution, which rocked the western world and launched early modern times.

▼ *Zhou dynasty dragon head*

## PART I   EARLY CIVILIZATIONS

## PART II   EMPIRES OF THE ANCIENT WORLD

*Mayan figurine* ▶

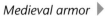
*Medieval armor* ▶

# Part III Regional Civilizations

# Part IV Early Modern Times

▲ *Philip II of Spain*

▼ *Astrolabe*

# Early Civilizations

## 1. TOWARD CIVILIZATION
### (PREHISTORY–3000 B.C.)

### Key Facts

- About 12,000 years ago, during the Neolithic period, or New Stone Age, people learned to farm.

- By about 5,000 years ago, the advances made by early farming communities led to the rise of civilizations.

- Historians define eight basic features common to most early civilizations: cities, well-organized central governments, complex religions, job specialization, social classes, arts and architecture, public works, and writing.

Historians call the earliest period of human history the Old Stone Age, or the Paleolithic age. This long period dates from the time of the first stone tool makers to about 10,000 B.C. Paleolithic people were **nomads,** moving from place to place to follow game animals and search for edible plants. They lived in small hunting and food-gathering bands of about 20 to 30 people.

Stone Age people learned to adapt to their environment for survival. Men and women made simple tools and weapons such as digging sticks, spears, and axes. They developed spoken language which let them cooperate as they worked. During the ice ages, people invented clothing and learned to build fires.

### The Growth of Farming

About 11,000 years ago, nomadic bands made a dramatic breakthrough. They learned to farm. By producing their own food, they could remain in one place. This change from nomadic to settled farming life ushered in the New Stone Age, or Neolithic age. Neolithic farmers settled in permanent villages.

Because people could now settle in one place, agriculture led to a growth in population. Village life also reshaped the roles of women and men. Heads of families formed a council of elders to make important decisions. Often, a village chief emerged. During times of want, warfare increased and some men gained status as warriors. These warriors had power over both women and other men. The status of women declined, though they did not lose all their influence or rights.

About 5,000 years ago, the advances made by early farming

| | 3000 B.C. | 2500 | 2000 |
|---|---|---|---|
| **AFRICA** | 3100 Menes unites Egypt | 2550 Great Pyramid and Sphinx at Giza | 2050 Middle Kingdom of Egypt begins |
| **THE AMERICAS** | 3200 Cultivation of maize and cotton | 2400 Temple platforms in Peru | 2000 Permanent towns in Valley of Mexico |
| **ASIA AND OCEANIA** | 3000 Sumerian city-states thrive | 2500 Indus Valley civilization | 2000 Development of Chinese writing |
| **EUROPE** | 3100 Skara Brae settlement | | 2000 Bronze Age in Europe |

communities led people to a new stage of development—the beginning of civilizations.

## Beginnings of Civilization

Historians define eight basic features common to most early civilizations: (1) cities, (2) well-organized central governments, (3) complex religions, (4) job specialization, (5) social classes, (6) arts and architecture, (7) public works, and (8) writing.

In Africa and Asia, the first cities grew after farmers began raising crops in fertile lands along river valleys. Rich soils and a reliable water source allowed farmers to produce surplus, or extra, crops. These surpluses helped populations to expand. As populations grew, some villages became cities.

**Organized governments.** The challenge of farming in a river valley contributed to the establishment of city governments. To control flooding and channel waters to fields, early farmers worked together. They built dikes, dug canals, and carved out irrigation ditches.

Such projects required leadership and well-organized governments. Some city governments grew powerful and complex. Over time, government bureaucracies grew. A **bureaucracy** is a system of managing government through departments run by appointed officials.

Social organization also became more complex. People were ranked in social classes according to their jobs. Priests and nobles were usually at the top. Next came wealthy merchants,

followed by **artisans,** or skilled craft workers. Below them stood the vast majority of people, peasant farmers. Slaves were at the lowest social level.

A critical new skill emerged—writing. Priests probably developed writing in order to record the amount of grain collected or other information. Early writing was made up of **pictograms,** or simple drawings showing the ideas represented.

### Review

1. **Identify** (a) Old Stone Age, (b) New Stone Age
2. **Define** (a) nomad, (b) bureaucracy, (c) artisan, (d) pictogram
3. What dramatic breakthrough allowed nomadic bands to settle in villages for the first time?

| 1500 | 1000 | 500 B.C. |
|---|---|---|

**1290–1224**
Reign of Ramses II

**1600**
Nubian kingdom established

**750–650**
Nubian rule over Egypt

**1400**
Rise of Olmec civilization

**850**
Chavín culture in Peru

**500**
Adena mounds in Ohio

**1650**
Shang dynasty in China

**1100**
Assyrians expand power

**539**
Persian empire created

**1700**
Height of Minoan civilization

**750**
Greeks colonize the Mediterranean

# 2. FIRST CIVILIZATIONS: AFRICA AND ASIA (3200 B.C.–500 B.C.)

## Key Facts

■ A rich civilization emerged in the valley of the Nile River in Egypt.

■ Independent Sumerian city-states developed in Mesopotamia, an area of fertile land between the Tigris and Euphrates rivers.

■ The Hebrews developed Judaism, a monotheistic religion based on the worship of one God.

▲ *Queen Nefertiti, wife of an Egyptian pharaoh*

The first civilizations took shape in the river valleys of North Africa, the Middle East, India, and China. Though they grew in isolation across a widely scattered area, they developed complex ways of life and beliefs that continue to affect our world today.

## Ancient Kingdoms of the Nile

More than 5,000 years ago, a rich farming civilization grew in the valley of the Nile River in Egypt. To control the Nile's annual floods, village people learned to cooperate. They built dikes, reservoirs, and irrigation ditches to channel the river and store water for the dry season. Eventually, these villages joined together into two kingdoms. About 3100 B.C., King Menes united these kingdoms, creating along the Nile the world's first unified state.

After Menes' reign, the history of ancient Egypt can be divided into three main periods: the Old Kingdom (about 2700 B.C.–2200 B.C.), the Middle Kingdom (about 2050 B.C.–1800 B.C.), and the New Kingdom (about 1550 B.C.–1100 B.C.).

During the Old Kingdom, **pharaohs** (FAIR ohz), or Egyptian rulers, organized a strong central state. They built majestic pyramids to serve as tombs. During the Middle and New Kingdoms, trade and warfare brought Egypt into contact with other civilizations. New ideas, customs, and technologies spread from one people to another in a process called **cultural diffusion**. Powerful New Kingdom pharaohs such as Queen Hatshepsut and Ramses II created a large empire that eventually reached the Euphrates River. After Ramses II, Egyptian power slowly declined.

## Egyptian Civilization

Egyptians worshipped many gods and goddesses. They also built tombs to preserve their bodies for the afterlife and filled them with items that they would need in their new lives.

Egyptian society was organized into classes. The pharaoh, who was considered both a god and a king, ruled at the top. Next came the nobles, who fought the pharaoh's wars. A tiny class of merchants and artisans developed. Farmers and slaves were at the bottom of society.

## City-States of Ancient Sumer

To the northeast of the Nile lies the Fertile Crescent, an arc of soil-rich land. More than 5,000 years ago, the independent city-states of Sumer grew along the Tigris and Euphrates rivers in a part of the Fertile Crescent called Mesopotamia. A **city-state** is a political unit made up of a city and the surrounding lands.

Control of the Tigris and Euphrates rivers was the key to the development of a civilization in Sumer. Villagers built dikes and irrigation ditches. Using clay bricks, Sumerians built **ziggurats,** or soaring pyramid-temples.

The city-states of Sumer often fought for control of land and water. War leaders gained importance and eventually became hereditary rulers. A social **hierarchy** (HI uh rahr kee), or system of ranks, emerged. The highest rank included the ruling family, leading officials, and high priests.

## Geography of the Ancient Middle East

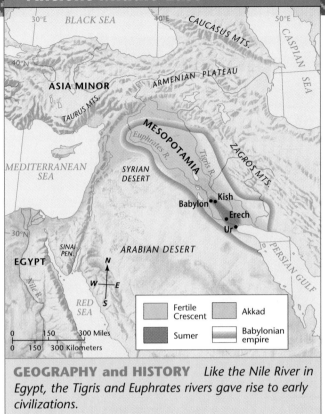

**GEOGRAPHY and HISTORY** *Like the Nile River in Egypt, the Tigris and Euphrates rivers gave rise to early civilizations.*

By 3200 B.C., Sumerians had invented the earliest form of writing, called **cuneiform** (kyoo NEE uh form). **Scribes,** or specially trained people who knew how to read and write, kept the records for the kingdom.

### Invaders, Traders, and Empire Builders

Mesopotamia's location at a geographical crossroads made it tempting to invaders, some of whom built great empires. An **empire** is a group of states or territories controlled by one ruler. Sargon, the ruler of Akkad, conquered the city-states of Sumer about 2300 B.C. He built the first empire known to history.

About 1790 B.C., Hammurabi (hah moo RAH bee), king of Babylon, brought much of

Mesopotamia under his control. He published a remarkable set of laws, the Code of Hammurabi. This code was the first major collection of laws in history. In 539 B.C., Persian armies overthrew Babylon.

Warfare and trade in Mesopotamia spread ideas and technology around the Mediterranean. Knowledge of iron-working became common. An Assyrian king founded one of the first libraries. The Phoenicians, famous as sailors and traders, created an alphabet. The Persians improved trade by encouraging the use of coins.

### The World of the Hebrews

Among the many peoples who occupied the Fertile Crescent were the Hebrews. According to the Torah, the Hebrews' most sacred text, they once lived in Mesopotamia. About 2000 B.C., they migrated into a region known as Canaan.

The early Hebrews developed Judaism, a **monotheistic** religion (based on the worship of one God). They recorded events and laws, such as the Ten Command-

ments, in the Torah. **Prophets,** or spiritual leaders, urged the Hebrews to obey God's law. They preached a strong code of **ethics,** or moral standards of behavior. They urged both personal morality and social justice, calling on the rich and powerful to protect the poor and weak.

By 1000 B.C., the Hebrews established the kingdom of Israel. A famous ruler, King Solomon, built a splendid temple dedicated to God, at Jerusalem. Eventually the kingdom split into two parts. A series of invading armies captured the Hebrew kingdoms.

During their captivity, the Hebrews became known as Jews. They lived under foreign rulers until about 2,000 years ago when many were forced to leave their homeland. This **diaspora** (di AS puhr uh), or scattering of people, sent Jews to different parts of the world. Wherever they settled, they maintained their traditions. Today, Judaism is considered one of the world's major religions for its unique contribution to religious thought.

### Review

1. **Identify**  (a) Nile River, (b) Fertile Crescent, (c) Mesopotamia, (d) Hebrews
2. **Define**  (a) pharoah, (b) cultural diffusion, (c) city-state, (d) ziggurat, (e) hierarchy, (f) cuneiform, (g) scribe, (h) empire, (i) monotheistic, (j) prophet, (k) ethics, (l) diaspora
3. Name two geographic locations where early civilizations developed.

## 3. EARLY CIVILIZATIONS IN INDIA AND CHINA
### (2500 B.C.–256 B.C.)

### Key Facts

- India's first civilization grew in the Indus River valley.
- The Aryans moved into the Indus Valley and built a new civilization along the Ganges River.
- During the Shang and Zhou Dynasties, the ancient Chinese made significant achievements in many areas.

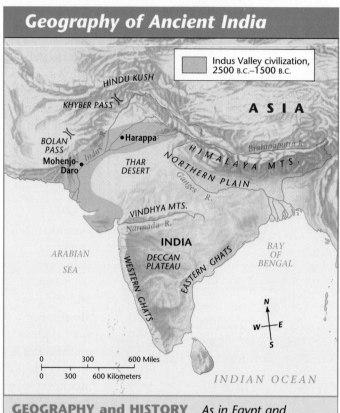

### Geography of Ancient India

Indus Valley civilization, 2500 B.C.–1500 B.C.

**GEOGRAPHY and HISTORY** *As in Egypt and Mesopotamia, the Indus Valley civilization grew up in a fertile river valley. Indus people built great cities and carried on farming and trade.*

As civilizations took shape in the Nile Valley and Fertile Crescent, people in India and China carved out their own civilizations. These grew along the fertile river valleys of Asia.

### Cities of the Indus Valley

India's first civilization emerged in the Indus River valley about 2500 B.C. The people of the Indus flourished there for 1,000 years, building a civilization that covered the largest area of any in ancient times. Its two main cities, Mohenjo-Daro and Harappa, were carefully planned. Each city was laid out in a grid pattern, with blocks larger than modern city blocks. Houses had complex plumbing systems, with baths, drains, and water chutes that led to underground sewers.

Most Indus people were farmers. Powerful leaders, perhaps priest-kings, made sure the cities had a steady supply of grain. Merchants and traders sailed with cargoes of cotton cloth, grain, copper, and pearls all the way to the cities of Sumer.

By 1750 B.C., the quality of life in Indus Valley cities was declining. Scholars think the final blow fell about 1500 B.C. with the arrival of nomadic people from the north. The newcomers were Aryans. With their horse-drawn chariots and superior weapons, they overran the cities and towns of the Indus region.

### Kingdoms of the Ganges

The Aryans were Indo-European people who migrated across Europe and Asia seeking water and pasture for their horses and cattle. Over many centuries, waves of Aryans traveled through the mountain passes into northwestern India. In time, Aryans spread eastward to the forests of the Ganges River basin. They made tools of iron and built walled cities. By 500 B.C., a new Indian civilization had emerged. It consisted of many rival kingdoms, though people shared a common culture.

Most of what we know about the Aryans comes from the Vedas, a collection of prayers, hymns, and other religious teachings. Aryan priests memorized and recited the Vedas for a thousand years before they were written down.

The Aryans divided people into social classes by occupation. The three basic groups were the priests; the warriors; and the herders, farmers, artisans, and merchants. Eventually, the Aryans added a fourth group—non-Aryans whom they had conquered. This group was at the lowest level of society. It included farm workers, servants, and other laborers. Over time, these divisions gave way to a more complex system of castes. **Castes** are social groups into which people are born and which they cannot leave.

Aryans were **polytheistic.** That is, they believed in many gods. As Aryan society developed and changed, people moved toward the notion of a single spiritual power beyond the many gods of the Vedas. They called this power **brahman** and believed it lived in all things. Some Aryans became **mystics,** or individuals who devote their lives to seeking spiritual truth.

## Early Civilizations in China

Long distances and physical barriers separated China from Egypt, the Middle East, and India. This isolation contributed to the Chinese belief that China was the center of the Earth and the sole source of civilization. This led the ancient Chinese to call their land the Middle Kingdom.

▲ *Zhou dynasty dragon head of bronze and gold*

Great barriers blocked the easy movement of the Chinese to the outside world. High mountains, brutal deserts, thick jungles, and the vast Pacific Ocean lay between China and the rest of the world. Still, the Chinese found ways to trade with neighboring peoples. In time, Chinese goods reached the Middle East and beyond.

Chinese history began in the Huang He Valley, where Neolithic people learned to farm. As in other places, the need to control the river through large water projects probably led to the rise of a strong central government.

**The Shang and Zhou Dynasties.** About 1650 B.C., a Chinese people called the Shang came to power in northern China. In 1027 B.C., the Zhou (JOH) people overthrew the Shang. The Zhou Dynasty lasted until 256 B.C. A **dynasty** is a ruling family. To justify their rebellion against the Shang, the Zhou Dynasty promoted the idea of the **Mandate of Heaven,** or the divine right to rule. Later, this idea expanded to explain the **dynastic cycle,** or the rise and fall of dynasties. If rulers became corrupt, the Chinese believed that Heaven withdrew its support, or mandate, and the dynasty fell.

By Shang times, the Chinese had developed complex religious beliefs. They prayed to many gods and nature spirits. Over time, Chinese religious practices came to center on respect for ancestors. The Chinese called on the spirits of their ancestors to bring good fortune to the family. The Chinese also believed the universe reflected a balance between two forces, yin and yang. Yin was linked to the Earth and female forces, while yang stood for Heaven and male forces.

During the Shang and Zhou periods, the Chinese studied the movement of the planets, recorded eclipses, and created an accurate calendar. They developed the art and technology of bronze making, silk making, and bookmaking. By 256 B.C., China was a large, wealthy, and highly developed center of civilization.

# Empires of the Ancient World

## 1. EMPIRES OF INDIA AND CHINA
### (600 B.C.–A.D. 550)

### Key Facts

- In ancient India, two major religions developed—Hinduism and Buddhism.
- Under the Maurya and Gupta empires, India grew into a center of trade.
- Shi Huangdi united all of China. Under the Han rulers who followed Shi Huangi, Chinese civilization made huge advances.

Between 600 B.C. and A.D. 550, strong, unified empires emerged in India and China. These civilizations set patterns in government, religion, and philosophy that influenced later cultures.

## Indian Religions, Indian Empires

Two major religions, Hinduism and Buddhism, grew in ancient India. Hinduism has no single founder and no single sacred text. It grew from the beliefs of the different groups who settled in India. Even so, all Hindus share certain basic beliefs. They believe that everything is part of the unchanging, all-powerful spiritual force called brahman. The most important Hindu gods represent aspects of brahman. The goal of life for Hindus is to achieve union with brahman. **Reincarnation** is the rebirth of the soul in another bodily form. Reincarnation allows people to work toward union with brahman through several lifetimes.

Another major religion, Buddhism, emerged in the 500s B.C.

While it shared many Hindu traditions, Buddhism differed from Hinduism. Buddhism's founder, Siddhartha Gautama, became known as the Buddha, which means the "Enlightened One." The Buddha taught that desire causes suffering. To overcome suffering people should rid themselves of desire. Buddhism's final goal was **nirvana,** or union with the universe and release from the cycle of rebirth.

**Powerful Empires of India.** For centuries, northern India was a battleground. Then, in 321 B.C., Chandragupta Maurya (chun druh GUP tuh MOW uhr yuh) forged the first great Indian empire. The Maurya dynasty eventually conquered much of India.

The most honored Maurya emperor was Chandragupta's grandson, Asoka. Turning his back

---

| 650 B.C. | 350 B.C. | 50 B.C. |
|---|---|---|

**AFRICA**

**500 B.C.**
Ironworking flourishes in Meroë

**146 B.C.**
Destruction of Carthage

**680 B.C.**
King Taharqa rules Nile Valley

**THE AMERICAS**

**700s B.C.**
Chavín gold carvings made

**400s B.C.**
Collapse of Olmec civilization

**ASIA AND OCEANIA**

**566 B.C.**
Buddha is born

**221 B.C.**
Shi Huangdi completes unification of China

**551 B.C.**
Confucius is born

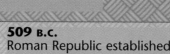

**EUROPE**

**509 B.C.**
Roman Republic established

**700s B.C.**
Rise of Greek city-states

**460 B.C.**
Age of Pericles begins

**323 B.C.**
Hellenistic age begins

on violent conquest, Asoka converted to Buddhism. He ruled by moral example. His rule brought peace and wealth. Asoka also paved the way for the spread of Buddhism throughout Asia.

After Asoka's death, rivals battled for power. Despite unrest, India developed into a center of world trade. Then, about 500 years after the Mauryas, the Gupta dynasty united much of India. Under the Guptas, who ruled from A.D. 320 to about 550, India enjoyed a golden age of peace and achievement.

Most Indians of that period were village peasants. Then, as today, the village and the family maintained order in daily life. The caste system also greatly influenced Indian society. Caste rules governed every part of life–including where people lived and how they earned a living.

Despite its inequalities, caste created a stable social order.

## Chinese Philosophy, Chinese Empires

China's most influential philosopher, Confucius, was born in 551 B.C. A brilliant scholar, Confucius took little interest in religious matters. He was concerned with social order and good government. He taught that harmony resulted when people accepted their place in society. He put **filial piety**, or respect for parents, above all other duties. Confucius' ideas came to influence every area of Chinese life and eventually spread to neighboring countries.

**Strong Rulers Unite China.** When the Zhou dynasty weakened, a powerful new ruler, Shi Huangdi, rose to unify all of China. He spent 20 years conquering the warring states. He built a strong government

and set the stage for China's classical age. His most remarkable and costly achievement was building the Great Wall.

After Shi Huangdi died, a new dynasty, the Han, was founded. It lasted from 206 B.C. to 220 A.D. Under Han rulers, the Chinese made huge advances in trade, government, technology, and the arts. The Silk Road, which eventually stretched 4,000 miles (6,400 km), linked China to civilizations of the Fertile Crescent. The Han empire brought 400 years of unity to China.

### Review
1. **Identify** (a) Siddhartha Gautama, (b) Confucius, (c) Shi Huangdi, (d) the Han Dynasty
2. **Define** (a) reincarnation, (b) nirvana, (c) filial piety
3. What are two basic teachings of Hinduism?

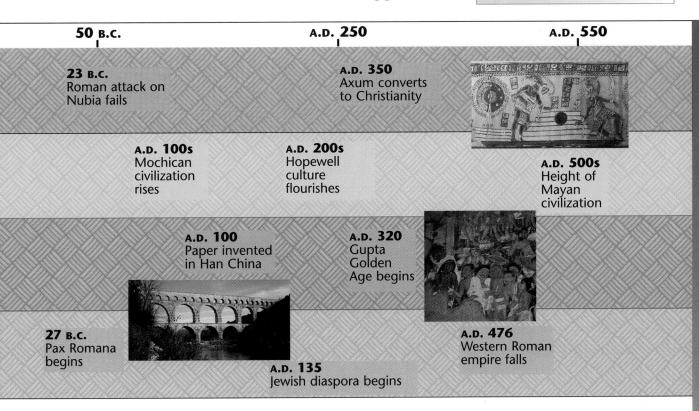

50 B.C.

A.D. **250**

A.D. **550**

**23 B.C.**
Roman attack on Nubia fails

A.D. **350**
Axum converts to Christianity

A.D. **100s**
Mochican civilization rises

A.D. **200s**
Hopewell culture flourishes

A.D. **500s**
Height of Mayan civilization

A.D. **100**
Paper invented in Han China

A.D. **320**
Gupta Golden Age begins

**27 B.C.**
Pax Romana begins

A.D. **476**
Western Roman empire falls

A.D. **135**
Jewish diaspora begins

# 2. ANCIENT GREECE
## (1750 B.C.–133 B.C.)

## Key Facts

- Through trading contacts, Minoan and Mycenaean culture borrowed many ideas from older civilizations.

- After the Persian Wars, democracy flourished in Athens.

- Guided by a belief in reason, Greek artists, writers, and philosophers used their genius to seek order in the universe.

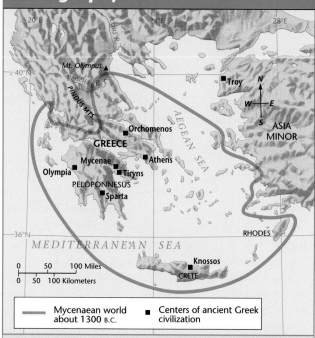

**Geography of Ancient Greece**

**GEOGRAPHY and HISTORY** *Islands in the Aegean Sea were home to the earliest Greek civilizations. Later, independent Greek city-states arose on the Greek mainland.*

Unlike many other civilizations, Greek civilization did not rise in a fertile river valley. Instead, it grew in a rugged corner of southeastern Europe. Over time, independent Greek city-states created a civilization that set a standard of excellence for later civilizations. Greek ideas about the universe, the individual, and government still live on in the world today.

## Early People of the Aegean

The island of Crete in the Aegean Sea was home to the Minoan people, the earliest civilization in the region. The Minoans were traders who set up outposts throughout the Aegean world and on the Greek mainland. Through contact with Egypt and Mesopotamia, this early people gained ideas and technology that they adapted to their own culture. Minoan civilization reached its height between about 1750 B.C.

and 1500 B.C. By about 1400 B.C., Minoan civilization had vanished. A natural disaster may have helped destroy these island people.

The Mycenaeans, another civilization of sea traders, soon dominated the Greek mainland and Crete. They thrived between about 1400 B.C. and 1200 B.C. The Mycenaeans, too, absorbed Egyptian and Mesopotamian ideas, which they passed on to later Greeks. They are best remembered for the Trojan War. The poet Homer described the conflict in his two epic poems, the *Iliad* and the *Odyssey.* These poems reveal much about the values and religion of the ancient Greeks. The heroes display honor and courage. Such ideals greatly influenced Greek culture. Three thousand years later, the

epics of Homer and the ideals of the ancient Greeks continue to inspire us.

## The Rise of Greek City-States

When Mycenaean civilization declined, the Greeks seemed to step backward. For centuries, Greeks lived in small, isolated farming villages. Eventually, they began to build many small city-states. However, they frequently warred among themselves. Despite their differences, Greeks shared a common culture, including their language, religion, and festivals. They became skilled sailors and traders. Eventually, Greek colonies took root all around the Mediterranean. Greek ideas and culture spread.

As their world expanded after 750 B.C., the Greeks evolved a unique version of the city-state, called the **polis.** Typically, Greeks built cities on two levels. On a hilltop stood the **acropolis** (uh KRAHP uh lihs), or hilltop city. There, the Greeks dedicated temples to the gods and goddesses. On flatter ground below lay the walled main city with its marketplace, theater, public buildings, and homes.

At first, the ruler of the polis was a king. A government in which a king or queen exercises central power is a **monarchy.** Slowly, power shifted to a class of noble landowners. The result was an **aristocracy,** or rule by a land-holding elite. As trade expanded, a new middle class of wealthy merchants, farmers, and artisans formed in some cities. They challenged the land-owning nobles for power and came to rule some city-states. The result was a form of government called an oligarchy. An **oligarchy** is government by a small, powerful elite, usually from the business class.

In the Greek city-state of Sparta, a warrior society took root. Spartan boys trained for military service. Girls exercised regularly. Because men were occupied with war, some women gained responsibilities such as running the family's estates. In contrast, the city-state of Athens, evolved into a **democracy,** or government by the people. By modern standards, Athenian democracy was quite limited. Only male citizens participated.

When the Persians threatened the Greeks, the city-states briefly joined together to defend themselves. After the Persian Wars, Athens thrived. Under the leadership of Pericles, a Greek statesman from 460 B.C. to 429 B.C., democracy and culture flourished. Athens became a **direct democracy.** That

▲ *Athena, goddess of wisdom*

is, a large number of male citizens took part in the day-to-day affairs of government. Athenian power and influence increased.

## The Glory That Was Greece

Greeks had great confidence in the power of the human mind. Many Greek artists, writers, and philosophers denied that events were caused by the gods. Instead they used observation and reason to find causes for what happened. Philosophers and teachers like Socrates, Plato, and Aristotle developed new ideas about truth, reason, justice, and government. People developed new styles of architecture, sculpture, and painting that reflected those ideas. Philosophers, poets, and dramatists set the standard for what later Europeans called the classic style.

**Alexander and the Hellenistic Age.** While the Greek city-states warred among themselves, King Philip of neighboring Macedonia built a superb army. Eventually, Philip controlled all of Greece. When he died, his 20-year-old son Alexander took the throne. In the next 12 years, this confident young man earned the title Alexander the Great. His conquests spread Greek civilization through the Mediterranean world and across the Middle East to the outskirts of India.

Alexander's conquests linked a vast area. He and his generals founded new cities. Greeks surged out of Greece to settle these new cities. In time, Greek culture blended with Persian, Egyptian, and Indian cultures to create the Hellenistic civilization. Art, science, mathematics, and philosophy flourished. The city of Alexandria became a center of learning. Even as Greek political power waned, Greek ideas about law, freedom, justice, and government came to dominate the Mediterranean world. This legacy influenced the civilizations of Rome and Western Europe.

### Review

1. **Identify** (a) Homer, (b) Pericles, (c) Alexander
2. **Define** (a) polis, (b) acropolis, (c) monarchy, (d) aristocracy, (e) oligarchy, (f) democracy, (g) direct democracy
3. What cultural ties united the Greek world?
4. How were Greek city-states governed?
5. Why did many Greek philosphers, writers, and authors reject the belief that events were caused by the whims of the gods?

# 3. ANCIENT ROME AND THE RISE OF CHRISTIANITY
## (509 B.C.–A.D. 476)

## Key Facts

- Conquest and diplomacy helped the Romans spread their rule from Spain to Egypt.
- During the Pax Romana, Roman emperors brought peace, order, and prosperity to the lands they controlled.
- Christianity, which began in Roman-held lands in the Middle East, spread throughout the Roman empire.

Rome expanded across the Mediterranean and grew into a huge, diverse empire. Rome's 1,000-year history had many lasting effects. Probably none was more important than the spread of key parts of the civilizations of Greece, Egypt, and the Fertile Crescent westward into Europe.

## The Roman World Takes Shape

Rome began as a small city-state in Italy. The Romans were an Indo-European people who settled along the Tiber River in small villages. Their neighbors, the Etruscans, ruled much of central Italy, including Rome. After the Romans threw out the hated Etruscan king in 509 B.C., they resolved never to be ruled by a monarch again. Instead, they set up a **republic,** a government in which

officials are chosen by the people. At first, the most powerful people in government were **patricians,** or members of the landholding upper class. Eventually, commoners, or **plebeians,** were also elected to the Roman Senate.

As Rome's political system changed, its armies expanded Roman power across Italy. By about 270 B.C., Rome occupied all of Italy. Rome's success was due partly to skillful diplomacy and partly to its efficient, well-disciplined army. Furthermore, Rome generally treated its defeated enemies with mercy. By 133 B.C., Roman power reached from Spain to Egypt.

## From Republic to Empire

Military victories put the Romans in control of busy trade routes. Incredible riches flooded into Rome from conquered lands. This new wealth, however, had disturbing consequences. Increased corruption and self-interest replaced virtues such as simplicity, hard work, and devotion to duty. Attempts to reform the system led to a backlash. For 100 years, Rome faced a series of civil wars.

Eventually, a powerful Roman general named Augustus restored order. Although he was not called a king, he exercised absolute power. Under Augustus, who ruled from 31 B.C. to A.D. 14, the 500-year-old republic came to an end. A new age dawned—the age of the Roman Empire.

As Rome's first emperor, Augustus helped the empire recover from the long period of unrest.

He laid the foundation for a stable government and undertook economic reforms. The 200-year span that began with Augustus ended with emperor Marcus Aurelius. It is known as the Pax Romana, or "Roman Peace." During this time, Roman emperors brought peace, order, unity, and prosperity to the lands under their control.

▲ **Roman Engineering** *Roman engineers built this bridge, road, and aqueduct across the Gardon River in France.*

## The Roman Achievement

Through war and conquest, Rome spread its civilization to distant lands. Yet the civilization that developed was not simply Roman. Rather, Rome acted as a bridge between the east and the west by borrowing and transforming Greek and Hellenistic achievements to produce Greco-Roman civilization.

The Romans greatly admired Greek culture. They took Greek ideas and adapted them to their own ways. Roman sculptors, for instance, used the Greek idea of realism to reveal an individual's character in each stone portrait. Roman architects improved on design elements such as the arch and the dome. Above all, Romans excelled as engineers. They built roads, bridges, aqueducts, and harbors throughout the empire. Many of these remained standing long after Rome fell.

Probably the greatest legacy of Rome was its commitment to the rule of law and to justice. These ideas still shape western civilization today. The rule of law fostered unity and stability. Roman law would become the basis for legal systems in Europe and Latin America.

## The Rise of Christianity

Early in the Pax Romana, a new religion, Christianity, sprang up in Roman-held lands in the Middle East. Its founder was a Jew named Jesus. Jesus was born around 4 B.C. in Bethlehem. He was prophesied to be the **messiah,** or savior sent by God to lead the Jews to freedom. The teachings of Jesus were firmly rooted in the Jewish religion. He believed in one God and accepted the Ten Commandments, laws that Jews believed God gave them.

At the same time, Jesus preached new beliefs. He called

himself the Son of God and taught that his mission was to bring salvation and eternal life to all of God's children—anyone who would believe in him. He extended the Jewish ideas of mercy and sympathy for the poor and helpless to include forgiveness and love for enemies.

To some Jews and Romans, Jesus was a dangerous troublemaker. Eventually, he was executed. But his disciples, or followers, believed that Jesus had risen from the dead, talked with them, and then ascended into heaven. Slowly, a few Jews accepted the teaching that Jesus was the messiah, or the Christ, from the Greek for "the anointed one." These people became the first Christians.

At first, Christianity remained a **sect,** or small group, within Judaism. Then Paul, a Jew from Asia Minor, set to work to spread the new faith to non-Jews. At first, Rome persecuted Christians. Nevertheless, Christians organized into a church and grew in strength. Eventually, Christianity reshaped Roman beliefs.

**The Long Decline.** After the death of the emperor Marcus Aurelius in A.D. 180, turmoil rocked the Roman Empire. Eventually, the empire split into two parts, east and west, each with its own ruler. In the west, a corrupt government, poverty and unemployment, and declining moral values contributed to the decline. Germanic peoples along the northern borders began to claim territory from the weakened empire. Then foreign invaders marched into Italy and, in

▲ **Jesus Healing a Woman** *This Roman mural depicts Jesus healing an afflicted woman.*

476, took over Rome itself. But the Roman empire did not disappear from the map. The eastern Roman empire prospered under the emperor Constantine. In time, the eastern Roman empire became known as Byzantium. It lasted for another 1,000 years.

### Review

1. **Identify** (a) Augustus, (b) Pax Romana, (c) Jesus
2. **Define** (a) republic, (b) patrician, (c) plebeian, (d) messiah, (e) sect
3. Why did Rome change from a republic to an empire ruled by an emperor?
4. Give an example of a Roman achievement that continues to influence western civilization today.
5. Describe the relationship between Christianity and Judaism.

# 4. CIVILIZATIONS OF THE AMERICAS
## (1400 B.C.–A.D. 1570)

## Key Facts

- Between A.D. 300 and 900, Mayan civilization flourished from southern Mexico through Central America. In the 1400s, the Aztecs conquered most of Mexico and built a highly developed civilization.

- By the 1500s, the Incas established a centralized government in Peru.

- Eight culture groups developed in North America. Their diverse ways of life were strongly influenced by geography.

The first American civilization, the Olmecs, began in the tropical forest along the Mexican Gulf Coast. Olmec society lasted from about 1400 B.C. to 500 B.C. Later, other advanced civilizations developed in Middle and South America, including those of the Mayas, Aztecs, and Incas. Diverse groups of people lived in North America.

## Civilizations of Middle America

The first settlers in the Americas were nomadic hunters who probably migrated across a land bridge between Siberia and Alaska. Gradually, they populated two vast continents. These early hunter-gatherers adapted to a variety of climates and resources. Between 8500 B.C. and 2000 B.C., Neolithic people in Mexico, or perhaps farther south, began to raise a variety of crops including corn, beans, and squash. They also learned to tame animals.

**The Mayas.** Although the Olmec civilization was the first in the Americas, more is known about the Mayan city-states of Central America. Mayan farmers cleared the rain forests to produce maize, or corn, to feed their cities. Mayan society was divided into social classes. Each city-state had its own ruling chief. Priests held great power. Towering pyramid temples and palaces served as sacrificial altars and burial places. The Mayas developed a hieroglyphic writing system and an accurate calendar. Today millions of people in Central America speak Mayan languages.

**The Aztecs.** Several hundred years after the decline of Mayan civilization, the Aztecs conquered most of Mexico. By 1500, the Aztec empire numbered about 30 million people. War brought immense wealth as well as power to the Aztecs. **Tribute,** or payment from conquered peoples, helped the Aztecs turn their capital into a magnificent city.

The Aztec developed a complex social structure with a single ruler or emperor at the top. A large class of priests performed the rituals and sacrifices needed to please the many Aztec gods. Conquered peoples often supplied both tribute and human sacrifices for Aztec religious rituals. As a result, the conquered people were unhappy and often rebelled. When armies from Spain later arrived, they found allies among the peoples who were ruled by the Aztecs.

▲ *Mayan potters fashioned clay figurines depicting people at all levels of society. Here, an aristocrat poses in his robes of state.*

## The World of the Incas

In South America for more than 2,000 years, civilizations rose and fell. Then in the 1400s, the Incas came down from the Andes mountains of Peru. Led by Pachacuti, a skilled warrior and leader, they rapidly conquered an empire that stretched 2,500 miles (4,000 km) down the Andes and along the Pacific coast. By the 1500s, the Incas of South America had established a centralized government in Peru, ruled by a god-king and a powerful class of priests.

The emperor had absolute power over the Inca empire. He claimed to be divine and lived in splendor. From the mountain capital at Cuzco, he ran an efficient government. His chain of command reached to every village. Specially trained officials kept records on quipus, collections of knotted colored strings, which probably noted dates and events as well as statistics.

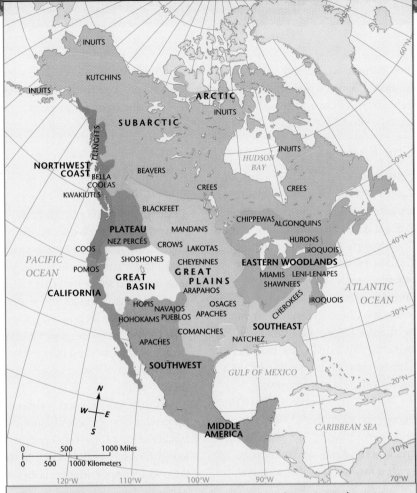

## North American Culture Areas About 1450

**GEOGRAPHY and HISTORY** As Native Americans spread out to populate North America, they developed varied cultures. The map shows culture areas in which tribes shared similar ways of life.

*pueblos* by the Spanish, of stone and adobe brick. At the center of their village life was the kiva. A **kiva** is a large underground chamber used for religious ceremonies. In the late 1100s, the Anasazi began to build housing complexes in the shadow of canyon walls. Cliffs offered protection from raiders. By the late 1200s, drought forced the Anasazi to abandon their cliff dwellings. Their traditions survive today among the Hopi and other Pueblo Indians.

Far to the east of the Anasazi, in the Mississippi and Ohio river valleys, other farming cultures emerged as early as 700 B.C. The Hopewell people left behind giant earthen mounds in many different shapes. Objects found in Hopewell mounds show evidence that they traded far and wide, from the Gulf of Mexico to the Great Lakes. By about A.D. 800, this culture was replaced by the Mississippians. These people grew corn and other crops. They built large towns and ceremonial centers. Their greatest center, Cahokia in present-day Illinois, housed as many as 40,000 people by about 1200.

The Incas worked to unite their conquered peoples. They imposed their own language, Quechua (KEHCH wuh), and religion on the people. They also created one of the great road systems in history. It was more extensive than even the roads that united the Roman empire. The Inca roads wound more than 12,000 miles (19,000 km) through mountains and deserts. In the 1500s, civil war broke out in the Inca empire. The fighting weakened the empire at the moment that Spanish invaders were about to arrive.

## Peoples of North America

Before 1500, many groups of Native Americans with diverse ways of life lived in North America. Eight culture groups lived in the Arctic, Northwest Coast, California, Great Basin, Southwest, Great Plains, Southeast, and Eastern Woodlands. These societies were strongly influenced by geography.

The best-known society of the desert southwest is that of the Anasazi. These resourceful people built large villages, later called

### Review

1. **Identify** (a) Olmecs, (b) Mayas, (c) Aztecs, (d) Incas, (e) Anasazis, (f) Mississippians
2. **Define** (a) tribute, (b) kiva
3. Who ruled the Mayan city-states?
4. Describe two steps the Incas took to unite their empire.

*Part II Empires of the Ancient World* **15**

# Regional Civilizations

## 1. THE RISE OF EUROPE
### (500–1300)

### Key Facts

- In the 800s, a ruler named Charlemagne temporarily reunited much of Europe. He revived learning and furthered the blending of German, Roman, and Christian traditions.

- Feudalism, the manor economy, and the Roman Catholic Church were dominant forces during the Middle Ages.

When Germanic peoples ended Roman rule in the West, they began to create a new civilization. Their culture differed greatly from that of the Romans. They had no cities and no written laws. Instead, they lived in small communities, ruled by elected kings whose chief role was to lead them in war. Europe became a fragmented, largely isolated region.

### The Early Middle Ages

Between 400 and 700, Germanic invaders carved Europe into small kingdoms. Then around 800, Western Europe had a moment of unity when Charlemagne (SHAHR luh mayn), or Charles the Great, built an empire reaching across France, Germany, and part of Italy. He revived learning, extended Christian civilization into northern Europe, and furthered the blending of German, Roman, and Christian traditions. He also set up a strong, efficient government.

After Charlemagne died in 814, his empire crumbled. A new wave of raiders overran Europe, plundering and looting. Kings and emperors proved too weak to maintain law and order. People needed to defend their homes and lands. In response to that basic need for protection, a new system, called feudalism, evolved.

### Feudalism and the Manor Economy

Under the system of **feudalism**, powerful local lords divided their large landholdings among the lesser lords. In exchange for land and protection, these lesser lords, or **vassals**, pledged service and loyalty to the greater lord. A lord granted his vassal a **fief** (FEEF), or estate. It included the peasants who worked the land. Feudalism gave a strict order to medieval society.

Feudal lords battled constantly for power. Many nobles trained from boyhood for a future occupation as a **knight**, or mounted warrior. In the later Middle Ages, knights adopted a

---

| | **500** | **750** | **1000** |
|---|---|---|---|
| **AFRICA** | | **600s** Islam spreads to North Africa | **800s** Ghana controls gold-salt trade |
| **THE AMERICAS** | | **600s** Mayan civilization thrives | **800s** Mississippian civilization flourishes |
| **ASIA AND OCEANIA** | **500s** Buddhism introduced to Japan | **622** Muhammad's hijra from Mecca to Medina | **960** Song dynasty in China |
| **EUROPE** | **500s** Byzantine empire reaches height | | **800** Charlemagne crowned emperor by pope |

code of conduct called **chivalry**. Chivalry required knights to be brave, loyal, and true to their word. In warfare, knights had to fight fairly and be generous to their enemies. Since warfare often meant seizing lands, lords fortified their homes to withstand attack. Medieval strongholds gradually became sprawling stone castles.

The heart of the medieval economy was the **manor**, or lord's estate. Most manors included one or more villages and surrounding lands. Most of the peasants on a manor were **serfs**, who were bound to the land. Peasants could not be bought and sold like enslaved people, but they spent their lives working for the lord of the manor. In return, the lord gave them the right to farm some land for themselves, as well as protection from invaders.

**The Medieval Church.** After the fall of Rome, the Christian Church split into eastern and western churches. The western church, headed by the pope, became known as the Roman Catholic Church. As the Church grew stronger and wealthier, it became the most powerful **secular**, or worldly, force in medieval Europe. Some Church leaders, including the pope, ruled over their own territories, like feudal lords. Eventually, the pope claimed to have authority over all secular rulers. The Church also controlled the spiritual lives of Christians throughout Europe.

**Economic Expansion and Change.** By the 1000s, advances in agriculture and commerce spurred economic revival throughout Europe. People used new iron plows to improve farming. New trade routes and goods increased

wealth. Merchants began to ask local lords for permission to set up towns to act as trade and manufacturing centers. Merchant **guilds**, or associations, came to dominate life in medieval towns. By 1300, Western Europe's economic revival was making momentous changes in medieval life.

> **Review**
> 1. **Identify** (a) Germanic tribes, (b) Charlemagne, (c) Roman Catholic Church
> 2. **Define** (a) feudalism, (b) vassal, (c) fief, (d) knight, (e) chivalry (f) manor, (g) serf, (h) secular, (i) guild
> 3. What effect did Charlemagne's rule have on Europe?
> 4. How was medieval society organized under feudalism?

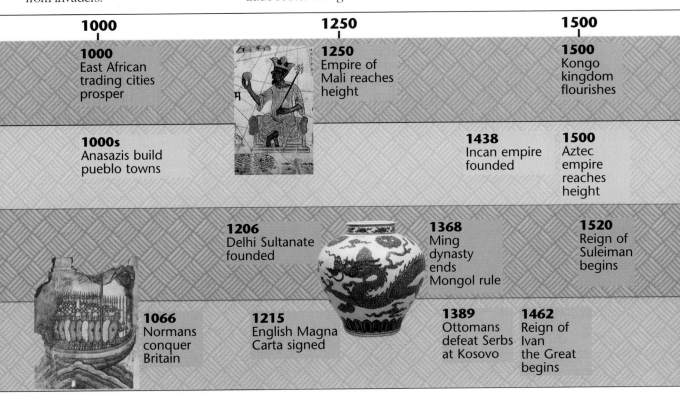

**1000**

**1000**
East African trading cities prosper

**1000s**
Anasazis build pueblo towns

**1250**

**1250**
Empire of Mali reaches height

**1500**

**1500**
Kongo kingdom flourishes

**1438**
Incan empire founded

**1500**
Aztec empire reaches height

**1206**
Delhi Sultanate founded

**1066**
Normans conquer Britain

**1215**
English Magna Carta signed

**1368**
Ming dynasty ends Mongol rule

**1389**
Ottomans defeat Serbs at Kosovo

**1520**
Reign of Suleiman begins

**1462**
Reign of Ivan the Great begins

*Part III Regional Civilizations* **17**

# 2. THE HIGH MIDDLE AGES
## (1050–1450)

### Key Facts

- During the High Middle Ages, feudal monarchs began to build a framework for the modern nation-state.
- European contacts with the Middle East during the Crusades revived interest in trade and exploration.
- Beginning in the 1300s, famine, plague, and war marked the decline of medieval Europe.

During the early Middle Ages, hundreds of feudal nobles ruled over territories of varying size. Most were loyal to a king or other overlord, but royal rulers had little power. During the High Middle Ages, feudal monarchs started to increase their power. Over many centuries, they built the framework for what would become the European nations of today.

## Growth of Royal Power in England

When William the Conqueror took the throne of England in 1066, he helped unify England and strengthen the monarchy. William's successors built a system of tax collecting. They also strengthened finances and law. Other English kings broadened the system of royal justice and developed the basis for English **common law,** or law that is common—the same—for all

people. An early jury system also developed. A **jury,** or group of men sworn to speak the truth, determined which cases should be brought to trial.

As the English kings strengthened the throne, they clashed with nobles and the Church. Out of those struggles came traditions of government that would influence the modern world. In the early 1200s, a group of nobles checked the growing power of the English kings. They forced King John to sign the Magna Carta, or great charter.

**The Magna Carta.** The Magna Carta contained two basic ideas that in the long run would shape government traditions in England. First, it said that the nobles had certain rights. Over time, the rights that had been granted to nobles applied to all English citizens. Second, the Magna Carta made clear that the monarch must obey the law. This included respecting the legal rights of the people. The king also agreed not to raise new taxes without first consulting his Great Council of lords and clergy. Eventually, the Great Council became the Parliament.

▲ **English Monarch and Parliament** In this scene, the king of England presides over Parliament. On either side of him are his vassals.

## The Holy Roman Empire and the Church

The Holy Roman Empire arose from the patchwork of Germanic states that formed after the death of Charlemagne. When a single ruler united the separate kingdoms, the pope crowned him "emperor." His successors took the title Holy Roman Emperor.

During the early Middle Ages, the Church had spread its influence across Europe. By the High Middle Ages, both

◀ **Imperial Crown** Holy Roman emperors first wore this jewel-encrusted gold crown around the late 900s.

popes and monarchs were extending their authority. Explosive conflicts erupted. Popes clashed with the Holy Roman emperors who ruled lands from Germany to Italy. Some conflicts arose over who would control appointments to high Church offices. Eventually, popes claimed the right to remove kings and emperors from the throne. Refusal to obey the Church could result in excommunication. **Excommunication** was a harsh penalty. It meant that someone could not receive the **sacraments,** or sacred rituals of the Church.

In the 1200s, the Roman Catholic Church reached its peak of power. However, after a French king engineered the election of a French pope, the papacy entered a period of decline.

## Europeans Look Outward

In 1050, Western Europe was barely emerging from isolation. However, several civilizations in the Middle East and Asia had long been major powers. Muslims, as believers in the Islamic faith are called, had built a great empire and created a major civilization. It reached from Spain across North Africa and the Middle East to the borders of India.

In the eastern Mediterranean, Byzantine civilization was a rival to Islam. The Byzantines were Christians. Then Muslim Turks invaded the Byzantine Empire. They also attacked Christian pilgrims to the Holy Land, or Palestine, in the Middle East. The Byzantine emperor asked the pope in Rome for help. Soon, thousands of Christian

▲ *Chartres Cathedral, France* About 1140, Medieval architects developed the Gothic style of architecture, exemplified by this cathedral.

knights from Europe, as well as armies of ordinary men and women, left for the Holy Land to fight the Muslims. They fought a series of **crusades,** or holy wars.

For 200 years, crusaders marched and fought. For a time they held parts of Palestine. The Crusades failed in their chief goal— the conquest of the Holy Land. Instead, they left a bitter legacy of religious hatred behind them. However, the Crusades increased European trade, heightened papal power, and increased the power of feudal monarchs. Contacts with the Muslim world also introduced Christians to regions they had never known existed.

**Learning, Literature, and the Arts.** As economic and political conditions improved in the High Middle Ages, a revival of learning took place. The Church wanted better-educated clergy. Royal rulers needed literate officials for their growing bureaucracies. Schools sprang up around the great cathedrals, eventually becoming the first universities. Ideas and texts that had originated in ancient Greece reached the universities through the

works of Muslim scholars. New writings began to appear in the **vernacular,** or everyday languages of ordinary people. Spain's great epic, *Poem of the Cid*, told of conflict with Islam. Famed Italian poet Dante Alighieri (DAHN tay al lee GYEH ree) wrote the *Divine Comedy*, an imaginary journey into hell and purgatory.

## A Time of Crisis

In the late Middle Ages a series of disasters struck. Bubonic plague, a disease spread by fleas on rats, raged throughout the world and eventually throughout Europe. Unsanitary conditions aided the spread of the disease, which was called the Black Death. One in three people died, more than in any war in history.

The plague brought social upheaval and plunged the European economy to a low ebb. Unable to provide sufficient comfort to people, the Church faced opposition and reform efforts. Famine and war added to the turmoil of the period. Western Europe would not fully recover from the effects of the Black Death for 100 years.

### Review
1. **Identify** (a) Magna Carta, (b) Holy Roman Empire, (c) Black Death
2. **Define** (a) common law, (b) jury, (c) excommunication, (d) sacrament, (e) crusade, (f) vernacular
3. What principles were established in the Magna Carta?
4. What were the results of the crusades?

# 3. The Byzantine Empire and Russia (330–1613)

## Key Facts

- After the fall of Rome, Greco-Roman heritage survived in the Byzantine empire.
- Traders and missionaries brought Byzantine culture and Eastern Orthodox Christianity to Russia and Eastern Europe.
- Invasions and migrations created a mix of ethnic and religious groups in Eastern Europe.

The fall of Rome left Europe divided. To the west, medieval civilization began to grow. To the east, the Roman empire survived as the Byzantine empire. Byzantine civilization later influenced Eastern Europe and Russia, bringing Greek culture as well as Eastern Orthodox Christianity to the Slavic people.

## The Byzantine Empire

As German invaders pounded the Roman empire in the west, emperors moved their base to the eastern Mediterranean. By 330, the emperor Constantine had rebuilt the Greek city of Byzantium. He renamed it Constantinople. In time, the eastern Roman empire became known as the Byzantine empire. During the Middle Ages, Constantinople thrived, controlling key trade routes that linked Europe and Asia. The Byzantine empire also protected Western Europe from invaders from the east.

**Justinian's Code.** The most famous Byzantine emperor was Justinian, who ruled from 527 to 565. He was aided by his wife Theodora. Justinian set up a commission to collect and organize the laws of ancient Rome. The result was known as Justinian's Code. By the 1100s, Justinian's Code had reached Western Europe, influencing the laws and principles of the Roman Catholic Church as well as medieval monarchs. The code thus preserved and spread the heritage of Roman law.

**Byzantine Christianity.** As in Western Europe, Christianity was important in the Byzantine empire. But a division grew between Byzantine Christians and Roman Catholics. In the Byzantine empire, the emperor controlled Church affairs, rejecting the pope's claim to authority over all Christians. Further, Byzantine clergy retained the right to marry. By 1054, a number of such controversies caused a **schism,** or permanent split, between the Eastern (Greek) Orthodox and Roman Catholic churches.

By the time of the schism, the Byzantine empire was declining. In 1453, Constantinople fell to the Ottoman Empire. The ancient Christian city, renamed Istanbul, eventually became a great center of Muslim culture.

**Byzantine heritage.** For 1,000 years, Byzantine civilization had thrived, blending Christian beliefs with Greek science, philosophy, arts, and literature. The Byzantines also expanded upon Roman achievements in engineering and law. When the empire fell in the 1400s, Greek scholars left Constantinople to teach at Italian universities. They took valuable Greek manuscripts to the West. They also took their knowledge of Greek and Byzantine culture. The work of these scholars contributed to the European cultural flowering known as the Renaissance.

◀ *An Influential Empress* *Theodora, seen in this mosaic carrying a church offering, encouraged her husband, Justinian, to protect women's rights.*

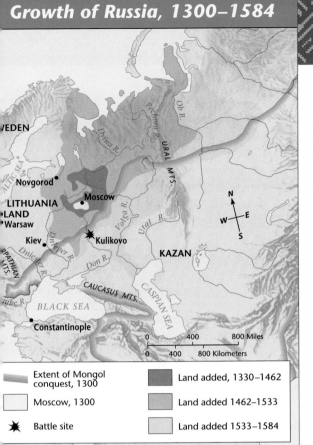

**Extent of Mongol conquest, 1300**

**Moscow, 1300**

★ **Battle site**

**Land added, 1330–1462**

**Land added 1462–1533**

**Land added 1533–1584**

**GEOGRAPHY and HISTORY** *Between 1300 and 1584, Russia grew from a small area around Moscow to a large territory.*

## The Rise of Russia

The early history of Russia began in the fertile area of present-day Ukraine. During Roman times, a people called the Slavs moved into southern Russia. Then, in the 700s and 800s, the Vikings began to travel on Russian rivers, trading and collecting tribute from the Slavs. The Vikings also traded with Constantinople. Eventually, the city of Kiev in the Ukraine became the center of the first Russian state. Kiev served as a vital trade center.

Trade brought Kiev into the Byzantine sphere of influence. Constantinople eventually sent missionaries to convert the Slavs to Christianity. About 863, two Greek monks adapted the Greek alphabet so they could translate the Bible into Slavic languages. This alphabet became the written script still used in Russia and Ukraine. With the adoption of Byzantine Christianity, Russians acquired a written language. A class of educated Russian priests grew. Russians adapted Byzantine religious art, music, and architecture.

**The Mongol Conquest.** In the early 1200s, the Mongols of central Asia overran land from China to Eastern Europe. Though they were fierce conquerors, the Mongols were generally tolerant rulers. But the absolute power of the Mongols served as a model for later Russian rulers. Mongol rule also cut Russia off from Western Europe at a time when Europeans were making rapid advances in the arts and sciences.

Eventually, the princes of Moscow gained power and defeated the Mongols. Between 1462 and 1505, Ivan III, known as Ivan the Great, brought much of northern Russia under his rule. He and his successors took the title **czar,** the Russian word for Caesar. Ivan III built the framework for absolute rule. His grandson, Ivan IV, further centralized royal power. He undercut the privileges of the nobles and bound the serfs to the land. Ivan IV introduced Russia to a tradition of extreme absolute power that earned him the title "Ivan the Terrible."

## Shaping Eastern Europe

In Eastern Europe, no single ethnic group dominated the region. An **ethnic group** is a large group of people who share the same language and cultural heritage. Over time, many groups settled in Eastern Europe. In the early Middle Ages, the Slavs came from Russia. Waves of Asian peoples moved into the area, among them the Huns, Avars, Bulgars, Khazars, and Magyars. Vikings and other Germanic people added to the mix.

Later, Byzantine missionaries carried Eastern Orthodox Christianity, as well as Byzantine culture, throughout the Balkans. At the same time, German knights and missionaries spread Roman Catholic Christianity to the area. In the late Middle Ages, Eastern Europe was a refuge for many Jewish settlers when Western European Christians persecuted them.

The result is a region of many peoples, languages, and cultural traditions. In this region, competing claims to territories have often produced turmoil.

### Review
1. **Identify** (a) Constantinople, (b) Justinian, (c) Kiev, (d) Ivan III
2. **Define** (a) schism, (b) czar, (c) ethnic group
3. Describe the legacy of Byzantine civilization
4. What element of Mongol rule continued to influence the Russian czars, even after they ousted the Mongols from Russia?

# 4. THE MUSLIM WORLD (622–1650)

## Key Facts

■ The religion of Islam emerged on the Arabian peninsula in the 600s.

■ Muslim civilization eventually created cultural ties among diverse peoples across three continents.

■ By the 1500s, the Mughals, Ottomans, and Safavids dominated the Muslim world.

In the 600s, a major religion, Islam, emerged in Arabia. Within a few years, Arabs spread Islam across a huge empire. The Arab empire eventually broke apart. Still, Islam continued to spread, creating shared traditions among diverse peoples. Islamic civilization opened routes for the transfer of goods, ideas, and technologies.

## Rise of Islam

Muhammad, the prophet of Islam, was born in Mecca in western Arabia about 570. According to Muslim belief, when Muhammad was about 40, he was called in a vision to become the messenger of God. He spent the rest of his life spreading Islam. Eventually, thousands of Arabs embraced the new religion.

Like Judaism and Christianity, Islam is monotheistic. Muslims believe in one all-powerful, compassionate God. All Muslims accept five basic duties, known as the Five Pillars of Islam. They include belief in one God, daily prayer, charity to the poor, fasting, and the **hajj,** or pilgrimage to Mecca. Muslims also hold that the Quran contains the sacred word of God and is the final authority on all matters. Over time Muslim scholars have applied the teachings of the Quran to every aspect of daily life. In this way, Islam is both a religion and a way of life.

## Islam Spreads

When Muhammad died in 632, Abu Bakr was elected the first **caliph,** or successor to Muhammad. He launched a breath-taking military campaign to conquer lands across the Byzantine and Persian empires. A key reason for the Arab's swift and wide-ranging conquests was their belief in the holiness of their faith and certainty of paradise for those who fell in battle.

A series of rulers led the conquests that carried Islam from the Atlantic to the Indus Valley. Eventually, the Abbassid dynasty moved the capital of Islam to Baghdad and ruled until 1258. Under the Abbassids, Baghdad

▲ **Open-Air Marketplace** *Muslim bazaars sold local goods as well as imports made available by a vast trading network.*

exceeded Constantinople in size and wealth. But as the 1200s drew to a close, the Arab empire had fragmented and fallen. Independent Muslim caliphates and states were scattered across North Africa and Spain, while Mongol converts to Islam ruled the Muslim Middle East.

## Golden Age of Muslim Civilization

The advancing Muslim empire united people from diverse cultures, blending the cultures of Arabs, Persians, Egyptians and other Africans, and Europeans. Muslim society was more open than that of medieval Europe. People could advance in society, especially through religious, scholarly, or military achievements. Muslim leaders imposed a tax on non-Muslims but allowed Christians, Jews, and others to practice their own faiths. Many non-Muslims converted to Islam. In later centuries, Turkish and Mongol converts helped spread Islam far across Asia.

Between 750 and 1350, Muslim merchants established a vast trading network. Islamic ideas, products, and technology spread across the Muslim world and beyond. Muslims pioneered the study of algebra, and made contributions in the fields of astronomy, philosophy, and literature. Muslims also made advances in medicine and surgery. Islamic art reached new heights. Artisans developed elaborate mosaics of abstract and geometric patterns. In the field of architecture, domed **mosques,** or houses of worship, came to dominate Muslim cities. Baghdad became a great Muslim center of learning.

## Muslims in India

About 1000, Turkish converts to Islam began raiding India. Then, in the late 1100s, a Muslim **sultan,** or ruler, defeated Hindu armies. He set up a capital in Delhi. His successors founded the Delhi sultanate, which lasted from 1206 to 1526.

Muslim rule brought changes to India. Widespread destruction of Buddhist monasteries contributed to the decline of Buddhism as a major religion in India. Many Hindus were killed. Some converted to Islam. Eventually, Muslim rulers grew more tolerant and Indian Muslims absorbed elements of Hindu culture.

In 1526, Turkish and Mongol invaders again

▲ *Jeweled gold canteen from the reign of Suleiman*

poured into India. At their head rode Babur. He swept away the remnants of the Delhi sultanate and set up the Mughal dynasty, which ruled from 1526 to 1857. In the late 1600s, economic hardship sparked revolts against the Mughal dynasty. Eventually, European traders began to work against the once-powerful Mughal empire.

## The Ottoman and Safavid Empires

While the Mughals ruled India, two other dynasties, the Ottomans and the Safavids dominated the Middle East and parts of Eastern Europe. All three empires owed much of their success to new weapons, including cannons and muskets.

**The Ottoman empire.** The Ottomans were Turkish-speaking nomadic people who had migrated from Central Asia. In the 1300s, they moved across Asia Minor and into the Balkans. In 1453, they captured Constantinople and renamed it Istanbul. The Ottoman empire was a powerful force for 500 years. Under the sultan Suleiman (soo lay mahn) who ruled from 1520 to 1566, the Ottoman empire enjoyed its golden age. At its height, the empire stretched from Hungary to Arabia and Mesopotamia and across North Africa. By the 1700s, European advances in commerce and military technology left the Ottomans behind.

**The Safavid empire.** By the 1500s, the Safavids (sah FAH

▲ *A Magificent Sultan* Europeans dubbed Suleiman "the Magificent" because of the spendor of his court. But they also admired his virtues as a ruler.

weedz), a Turkish-speaking Muslim dynasty, had united a strong empire in present-day Iran. Pressed between the Ottomans and the Mughals of India, the Safavids fought many wars. The outstanding Safavid ruler, Shah Abbas the Great, ruled from 1588 to 1629. Abbas revived the glory of ancient Persia. His capital became a center for the international silk trade. In the late 1700s, a new dynasty, the Qajars (kah JAHRZ) won control of Iran. They ruled until 1925.

### Review

1. **Identify** (a) Muhammad, (b) Baghdad, (c) Mughal dynasty, (d) Ottoman empire
2. **Define** (a) hajj, (b) caliph, (c) mosque, (d) sultan
3. What are some of the teachings of Islam?
4. How did Islam spread far beyond Arabia so quickly?

# 5. KINGDOMS AND TRADING STATES OF AFRICA
## (750 B.C.–A.D. 1586)

## Key Facts

- Between 800 and 1600, a series of powerful West African kingdoms controlled the rich Sahara trade route.
- Indian Ocean trade routes led to the growth of wealthy city-states along the East African coast.

Vast migrations of people have contributed to the rich diversity of African cultures. One such series of migrations, called the Bantu migrations, probably occurred because of changes in the environment. Over a period of a thousand years, Bantu peoples from West Africa moved south and east to populate most of southern Africa. Today as many as one third of Africans speak a language in the Bantu family.

## Early Civilizations of Africa

Long before the Bantu migrations, important civilizations rose and flourished in Africa. While ancient Egyptian civilization developed in Northern Africa, another civilization—called Nubia or Kush—took shape along the Nile to the south.

**The Kingdom of Nubia.** For 4,000 years, powerful kings and queens reigned over Nubia. From time to time the Egyptians to the north conquered the land, but Nubians always regained their independence. As a result of conquest and trade, Nubian rulers used many Egyptian traditions. By 500 B.C., Nubian rulers moved their capital to Meroë (MEHR uh wee), a thriving trade center. Meroë produced iron for tools and weapons. The city may have spread iron technology across the savanna lands into West Africa through its extensive trade. Finally, about A.D. 350, armies from the kingdom of Axum overran Nubia.

Unlike Nubia, North Africa and Egypt were ruled, for a time, by the Greeks and then the Romans. Under Roman rule, Christianity spread to the cities of North Africa. Islam eventually replaced Christianity as the main religion of the region. North Africa benefited from the blossoming of Muslim civilization. Linked into a global trade network, North African ports did a busy trade in grain, wine, fruit, ivory, and gold.

## Kingdoms of West Africa

By A.D. 100, settled farming villages on the western savannas of Africa were expanding. Soon trade networks linked the savanna to forest lands in the south and then sent goods across the Sahara. By A.D. 200, camels, brought to North Africa from Asia, had revolutionized trade across the Sahara. Camel caravans created new, profitable trade networks. Gold and salt were the major products. Gold was plentiful in present-day Ghana, Nigeria, and Senegal. North Africans sought gold for trade to Europeans. West Africans traded gold to North Africans for an equally valuable item, salt. People need salt in their diet to stay healthy, especially in hot, tropical areas.

▲ West African gold

**The Kingdom of Ghana.** By A.D. 800, the rulers of the Soninke people had united many farming villages to form  Ghana. The king controlled gold-salt trade routes in West Africa. So great was the flow of gold that Arab writers called Ghana "land of gold." Muslim merchants eventually established Islam in Ghana. When the empire of Ghana declined in the late 1100s, it was swallowed up by a new rising power, the kingdom of Mali.

**The Kingdom of Mali.** Mali emerged by 1250. It controlled both the gold-mining regions to the south and the salt supplies of the Sahara. The greatest emperor of Mali was Mansa Musa (MAHN sah MOO sah), who came to the throne in 1312. Musa expanded Mali's borders. A convert to Islam, Musa  journeyed to Mecca in 1324 to fulfill the hajj. Musa's pilgrimage forged new ties with Muslim states, and brought scholars and artists to Mali.

**The Kingdom of Songhai.** As Mali weakened in the 1400s, a new West African kingdom,

Songhai (SAWNG hī), arose. Songhai forged the largest state that had ever existed in West Africa. The kingdom controlled trade routes and wealthy cities like Timbuktu, a leading center of learning. Songhai prospered until about 1586. At that time, civil war and invasion weakened and splintered the empire.

## Trade Routes of East Africa

By the time the kingdom of Axum conquered Nubia about A.D. 330, Axum had long been an important trading center. Located southeast of Nubia, Axum linked trade routes between Africa, India, and the Mediterranean world. A powerful Axum king converted to Christianity in the 300s. At first, Christianity strengthened ties to the Mediterranean world. However, in the 600s, Islam came to dominate North Africa, leaving Axum an isolated island of Christianity. Axum slowly declined but its legacy survived in present-day Ethiopia.

As Axum declined, a string of trading cities gradually rose along the East African coast. Since ancient times, traders had visited this coast. In the 600s, Arab and Persian merchants set up Muslim communities under the protection of local African rulers. By 1000,

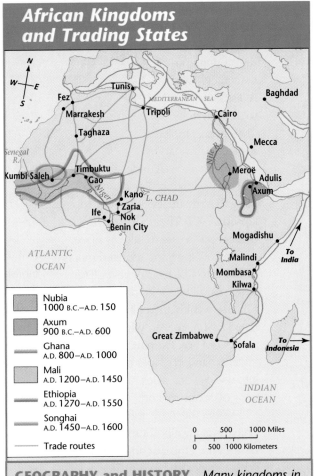

**African Kingdoms and Trading States**

Nubia
1000 B.C.–A.D. 150

Axum
900 B.C.–A.D. 600

Ghana
A.D. 800–A.D. 1000

Mali
A.D. 1200–A.D. 1450

Ethiopia
A.D. 1270–A.D. 1550

Songhai
A.D. 1450–A.D. 1600

Trade routes

0    500   1000 Miles
0   500  1000 Kilometers

**GEOGRAPHY and HISTORY** *Many kingdoms in East Africa and West Africa developed because of profitable trade with other lands.*

port cities were thriving from trade across the Indian Ocean.

## Many Peoples, Many Traditions

The ways of life of African societies varied greatly from place to place. Early African peoples hunted, farmed the land, fished along the coasts and rivers, or herded livestock. Farming peoples generally lived in tight-knit communities. Hunters and herders were often nomadic.

Across Africa, religious beliefs were varied and complex. Village Africans worshipped many gods and goddesses. Christianity and Islam also influenced peoples in some parts of Africa. Patterns of family life also varied. In some African groups, the **nuclear family** was typical, with parents and children living and working together. In other African communities, people lived in a joint family. Several generations shared the same complex of houses.

African societies preserved their histories and values through both oral and written literature. Oral traditions date back many centuries. In West Africa, **griots** (GREE ohs), or professional poets, recited ancient stories. They preserved both histories and traditional folk tales.

### Review

1. **Identify** (a) Bantu migrations (b) Nubia, (c) Ghana, (d) Mansa Musa, (e) Axum
2. **Define** (a) nuclear family, (b) griot
3. How did Nubian civilization prosper?
4. How did the gold-salt trade develop between West Africa and North Africa?

# 6. SPREAD OF CIVILIZATIONS IN EAST ASIA
## (500–1603)

### Key Facts

■ China expanded and grew rich under the powerful Tang and Song dynasties.

■ During the 1200s and 1300s, the Mongols ruled much of Asia. After the fall of the Mongols, the Ming restored Chinese culture and later imposed a policy of isolation.

■ During the 1100s, Japan created a feudal society ruled by powerful military lords.

After the Han dynasty collapsed in A.D. 220, China remained a divided land for nearly 400 years. Various Chinese dynasties rose and fell. Then in the 500s, China re-emerged as a united empire. For a short period the Sui dynasty ruled. Then a Sui general and his son, Tang Taizong, led a successful revolt and established their own dynasty, the Tang.

## Two Golden Ages of China

Under the rule of the Tang dynasty (618–907), China was restored to its earlier glory. Tang armies marched deep into Central Asia and surrounding regions. They forced neighboring lands to become **tributary states**. That is, while these states remained independent, their rulers had to acknowledge Chinese supremacy and send regular tribute to the Tang emperor. Tang rulers restored the bureaucracy. They redistributed land to the peasants. They also completed a system of canals to encourage internal trade and transportation. The Tang dynasty finally collapsed in 907. The Song dynasty soon rose to take its place.

In 960, the Song reunited much of China to rule for 319 years. The Song period was a golden age. Chinese wealth and culture dominated East Asia even when its armies did not. Farming and foreign trade expanded. Paper money came into use. Several cities had populations over one million.

Under the Tang and Song, China was a well-ordered society. Besides the emperor and the aristocratic families, the two main classes were the gentry and the peasantry. The gentry were wealthy landowners who valued scholarship more than physical labor. Most scholar-officials at court came from this class. The peasants worked the land. However, even peasants could move up in society through education and government service.

A rich economy supported the thriving culture of Tang and Song China. Prose and poetry

▲ Emperor Tang Taizong

flourished. Scholars produced works on philosophy, religion, and history. Painting and calligraphy became essential skills for the scholar-gentry.

## The Mongol and Ming Empires

In the early 1200s, the Mongols dominated Asia. They invaded China and finally toppled the Song dynasty in 1279. The Mongols established peace and order within their domains. Political stability set the stage for economic growth. Under the protection of the Mongols, trade flourished along the Silk Road and across Eurasia.

In 1368, a rebel Chinese army pushed the Mongols back beyond the Great Wall. A new dynasty, the Ming—meaning brilliant—sought to reassert Chinese greatness after years of foreign rule. The Ming restored the civil service exams. Confucian learning again became the road to success. Chinese cities were home to many industries and the economy thrived.

Early Ming rulers proudly sent Chinese fleets into distant waters. The Chinese admiral Zheng He (DZUH-NG HEH) commanded hundreds of vessels carrying 25,000 sailors during a series of expeditions. His goal was to promote trade and collect tribute. Zheng He's fleet explored all the way to the coasts of East Africa.

▲ Ming porcelain jar

**Emperor**
Held highest rank in society but had no political power

**Shogun**
Actual ruler

**Daimyo**
Large landowners

**Samurai**
Warriors loyal to daimyo

**Peasants**
Three fourths of population

**Artisans**

**Merchants**
Low status but gradually gained influence

**Korea.** As early as Han times, China extended its influence to peoples beyond the Middle Kingdom. To the northeast, Korea lay within the Chinese zone of influence. While Korea absorbed many Chinese traditions over the centuries, it also maintained its own identity. Koreans improved on a number of Chinese inventions. They advanced Chinese wood block printing techniques by creating moveable metal type to print books. They also created an alphabet for spoken sounds that was easier to use than Chinese characters. Its use led to an extremely high literacy rate in Korea.

## An Island Empire Emerges

Like Korea, Japan felt the powerful influence of Chinese civilization early in its history. At the same time, the Japanese continued to maintain their own distinct culture. The surrounding seas both protected and isolated Japan. While Japan was close enough to the mainland to learn from Korea and China, it was too far away for China to conquer.

By about A.D. 500, Japan's first and only dynasty—the Yamato—dominated Honshu, the largest Japanese island. In the early 600s, the Yamato dynasty sent young Japanese nobles to study in China. They returned to Japan spreading Chinese thought, technology, and

arts. For a time, the Japanese modeled much of their society on Chinese culture and government. Eventually, however, the Japanese chose to adopt some Chinese ways while discarding or changing others.

## Japan's Feudal Age

In theory, the emperor headed Japanese society. In fact, he was a powerless, though revered, figurehead. Real power lay in the hands of the **shogun**, or supreme military commander. He distributed lands to vassal lords who agreed to support him with their armies in time

of need. These great warrior lords were called **daimyo** (DĪ myoh). They, in turn, granted land to lesser warriors called **samurai,** meaning "those who serve." Samurai were the fighting aristocracy in the constant struggle for power. Japan had evolved into a feudal society.

In 1603, Tokugawa Ieyasu (toh kuh GAH wah ee YAY yah soo) founded the Tokugawa shogunate, which ruled Japan until 1868. The Tokugawas brought peace and stability to Japan. They imposed central government control on all of Japan and created a unified, orderly society. Trade flourished, merchants prospered, and prosperity contributed to a flowering of culture. Still, the shoguns were extremely conservative. They tried to preserve samurai virtues and ancient beliefs. This commitment would bring them into sharp conflict with the foreigners who arrived in the 1500s.

### Review
1. **Identify** (a) Tang, (b) Song, (c) Mongols, (d) Ming, (e) Tokugawa
2. **Define** (a) tributary state, (b) shogun, (c) daimyo, (d) samurai
3. How did the Tang and Song dynasties benefit China?
4. Who held the most power in feudal Japan?

## 1. THE RENAISSANCE AND REFORMATION
### (1300–1600)

### Key Facts

- The Renaissance was a period of cultural rebirth in the arts, literature, and learning.
- Reformers like Martin Luther and John Calvin challenged Church corruption and established the Protestant churches.
- During the Scientific Revolution, a new approach to science changed the way Europeans viewed the world.

Between the 1300s and 1500s, Europe went through a period of cultural rebirth. We call this period the Renaissance. During the same span of time, the Protestant Reformation and the Scientific Revolution changed European civilization.

### The Renaissance

The Renaissance was truly a "rebirth" of western culture. It began in Italy and spread to northern Europe. The Renaissance reached its highest expression in painting, sculpture, and architecture. Great artists such as Michelangelo and Leonardo da Vinci created modern styles in the arts. Writers such as Shakespeare advanced poetry and literature.

At the heart of the Italian Renaissance was an intellectual movement known as **humanism**. Based on the study of classical Greek and Roman cultures, humanism focused on worldly subjects. This focus contrasted sharply with the religious issues studied by medieval thinkers. Humanists believed that education should help people think in new ways. Humanism produced a new attitude toward culture, learning, and the world.

A key advance in technology was the development of printing in Europe. Printing spread Renaissance ideas throughout Europe. As books became more readily available, more people learned to read and write. People gained access to a broad range of knowledge and ideas. Presses churned out Bibles as well as books on topics from medicine and law to astrology, mining, and geography. In the 1500s, between 150 and 200 million books went into print.

### The Protestant Reformation

During the Renaissance, the Roman Catholic Church fell on

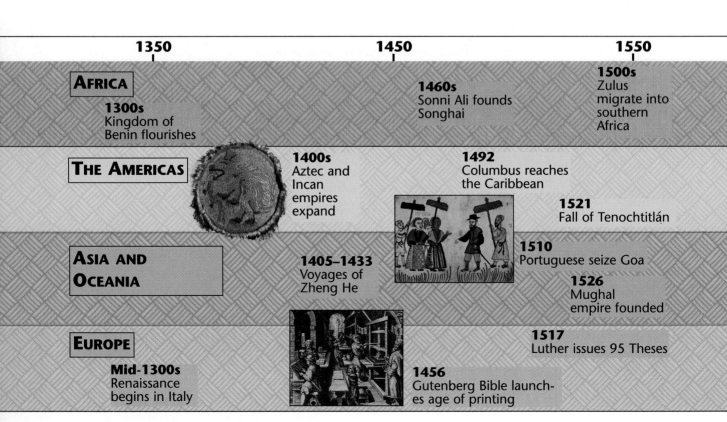

| | 1350 | 1450 | 1550 |
|---|---|---|---|

**AFRICA**
- **1300s** Kingdom of Benin flourishes
- **1460s** Sonni Ali founds Songhai
- **1500s** Zulus migrate into southern Africa

**THE AMERICAS**
- **1400s** Aztec and Incan empires expand
- **1492** Columbus reaches the Caribbean
- **1521** Fall of Tenochtitlán

**ASIA AND OCEANIA**
- **1405–1433** Voyages of Zheng He
- **1510** Portuguese seize Goa
- **1526** Mughal empire founded

**EUROPE**
- **Mid-1300s** Renaissance begins in Italy
- **1456** Gutenberg Bible launches age of printing
- **1517** Luther issues 95 Theses

hard times. Christians grew impatient with the corruption of the clergy and the worldliness of the Church. Then in 1517, a German monk and professor of theology named Martin Luther protested Church abuses. Luther rejected a number of Church doctrines. He believed that the Bible, and not the Church, was the sole source of religious truth. Eventually, Martin Luther and other reformers, such as John Calvin, broke away from the Church entirely. They founded modern Protestant churches.

As the Protestant Reformation grew, the Catholic Church began to reform itself. The increased religious zeal, however, led to widespread intolerance and persecution on both sides. Conflicts between Catholic and Protestant nations would shape European politics for centuries.

## The Scientific Revolution

Both the Renaissance and the Reformation looked to the past for models. In contrast, the profound change that took place in science in the 1500s pointed ahead. It brought a new way of thinking about the physical universe. We call that historic change the Scientific Revolution.

Despite the opposition of the Church, the new approach to science spread. This approach used observation and experimentation. Complex mathematical calculations converted observations and experiments into scientific laws. In time, this approach became known as the scientific method.

During the Scientific Revolution, scientists discovered many scientific laws for the first time.

Polish scholar Nicolaus Copernicus proposed a **heliocentric,** or sun-centered, model of the universe. In England, Isaac Newton used mathematics to show that a single force, **gravity,** keeps the planets in their orbits around the sun. Other discoveries in astronomy, chemistry, and medicine opened the way for further advances. These discoveries helped change the way Europeans viewed the world.

---

### Review
1. **Identify** (a) Renaissance, (c) Reformation, (d) Scientific Revolution
2. **Define** (a) humanism, (b) heliocentric, (c) gravity
3. How did humanism relate to the Renaissance?
4. What is the scientific method?

---

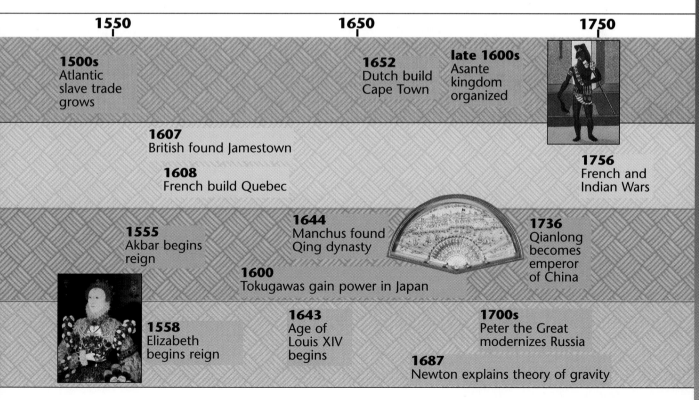

**1550**    **1650**    **1750**

**1500s**
Atlantic slave trade grows

**1652**
Dutch build Cape Town

**late 1600s**
Asante kingdom organized

**1607**
British found Jamestown

**1756**
French and Indian Wars

**1608**
French build Quebec

**1555**
Akbar begins reign

**1644**
Manchus found Qing dynasty

**1736**
Qianlong becomes emperor of China

**1600**
Tokugawas gain power in Japan

**1558**
Elizabeth begins reign

**1643**
Age of Louis XIV begins

**1700s**
Peter the Great modernizes Russia

**1687**
Newton explains theory of gravity

## 2. THE FIRST GLOBAL AGE: EUROPE AND ASIA (1415–1796)

### Key Facts

- The desire for spices led Europeans to seek control of the Indian Ocean trade network.

- Improvements in technology helped European explorers navigate the vast oceans of the world.

- By the late 1500s, the Dutch replaced the Portuguese as the major European power in Asia. In the 1700s, England and France vied for dominance.

▲ *Global Trade Network* Through trade with India and East Asia, European states grew wealthy and powerful.

Beginning in the 1500s, European powers gradually built trading empires in Asia. Thus began a period of increasing global interdependence that has continued to the present day.

### The Search for Spices

Today we take spices for granted. During the Middle Ages, spices from Asia brought huge profits. Asian goods and spices flowed to Europe along complex overland trade routes. Each time goods passed from one trader to another—from Muslim to Italian merchants—the prices increased. Europeans wanted to cut out the Muslim and Italian middlemen. They wanted direct access to the riches of Asia. By the late 1400s, this desire spurred Europeans to explore the oceans.

Improvements in technology helped Europeans conquer the vast oceans of the world. **Cartographers,** or map makers, created more accurate maps and sea charts. Europeans also learned to use the astrolabe. An **astrolabe** is an instrument developed by the ancient Greeks and perfected by the Arabs to determine latitude at sea. The Portuguese developed the **caravel,** a ship that combined the best elements of European, Arab, and Chinese sailing designs.

Portugal led the way in exploration. Portuguese ships explored the coast of West Africa. They rounded the Cape of Good Hope to reach the great spice ports of India. Eventually, they circled the globe. Portuguese voyages spurred other

▲ Astrolabe

European nations to seek a sea route to Asia. In 1492, Christopher Columbus convinced the king and queen of Spain that he could reach Southeast Asia by sailing west across the Atlantic. Columbus believed he had reached islands off the coast of East Asia. But Europeans soon realized that he had found a route to two continents previously unknown to them.

**Southeast Asia.** When European fleets reached Southeast Asia, they came to a world that had long before developed its own cultures and trading patterns. Sandwiched between China and India, Southeast Asia was strongly influenced by its two powerful neighbors. Over time, the distinctive cultures of Southeast Asia blended with elements from Indian and Chinese civilization. The key products of mainland Southeast Asia were spices including cloves, nutmeg, ginger, and pepper. Island Southeast Asia controlled the rich sea trade routes between India and China.

## European Footholds in Southeast Asia and India

When the Portuguese arrived in the Indian Ocean, their ships were small in size and number. Still, they had one great advantage: cannons. In less than 50 years, the Portuguese had seized cities and built military and trading outposts rimming the southern seas. For most of the 1500s, Portugal controlled the spice trade between Europe and Asia.

By the early 1600s, other Europeans were trying to replace the Portuguese in Asia. The Dutch were the first to challenge Portuguese fleets. By the late 1500s, Dutch warships and trading ships put them in the forefront of European commerce. Like the Portuguese, the Dutch used military force to further their trading goals. The Portuguese and Dutch set up bases on the coasts of Asia. Spain, however, took over the Philippines.

In the 1700s, the growing power of England and France contributed to a decline in the Dutch overseas trading empire. Unrest within Mughal India tempted French and English traders to take advantage of the rivalries between Indian princes. By the mid-1700s, the British and French were locked in a global power struggle that included India. A group of wealthy English merchants formed the British East India Company. They used British and Indian troops to drive the French from their trading posts. The Company often gained its ends, not only by military force, but by winning the backing of local Indian rulers. The activities of the British East India Company set the stage for the expanding British raj, or rule.

## Encounters in East Asia

The Europeans who reached East Asia in the 1500s often made a poor impression on their hosts. Portuguese sea traders who landed in China in 1514 had little to offer in exchange for silks and porcelains. European textiles, metalwork, and other goods were inferior to Chinese products. The Ming Chinese eventually allowed the Portuguese a trading post at Macao, near Canton. For many years, however, Europeans were allowed to trade only under strict supervision.

Unlike the Chinese, the Japanese at first welcomed western traders. In 1543, the Portuguese reached Japan. Later came the Spanish, Dutch, and English. They arrived at a time when strong daimyos were struggling for power. The Japanese quickly acquired western firearms. For a time, they opened their doors to Christian missionaries.

The Tokugawa shoguns, however, became increasingly hostile toward foreigners. After learning how Spain had seized the Philippines, they may have seen the newcomers, including the missionaries, as agents of an invading force. In response, they expelled foreign missionaries. By 1638, Japan was barred to all western merchants. The shoguns also outlawed the building of large ships to end foreign trade. They forbade Japanese to travel abroad. Each year, just one or two Dutch ships were permitted to trade. Japan maintained its policy of strict isolation for more than 200 years. Not until 1853 did Japan reopen contacts with the western world—and then only by force.

▲ Chinese fan showing foreign flags in Canton

### Review
1. **Identify**  Southeast Asia
2. **Define**  (a) cartographer, (b) astrolabe, (c) caravel
3. Why did Europeans seek a trade route to Asia?
4. Why did the Tokugawa policy toward foreigners change over time?

# 3. THE FIRST GLOBAL AGE: EUROPE, THE AMERICAS, AND AFRICA
## (1492–1750)

### Key Facts

- The arrival of Europeans in North and South America brought disaster to Native Americans.

- European powers built colonial empires in the Americas.

- Beginning in the 1400s, Europeans established trading outposts in Africa. Millions of slaves were imported from Africa to meet labor demands in American colonies.

During the age of exploration, European powers built colonial empires in the Americas and Africa. Not only did they bring into contact the peoples of Africa, Europe, and the Americas, but they began an exchange of plants, animals, institutions, values, and ideas that affects the world to this day.

## Conquest in the Americas

A flood of Spanish explorers, settlers, and missionaries followed Columbus to the Americas. Among the first Spaniards to arrive were conquistadors (kahn KEES tuh dohrz), or conquerors. Wherever they went they claimed the land and its people for their king and Church. In brutal struggles, the conquistadors overthrew the Aztec and Incan civilizations. Although Native Americans fought back, the pattern of conquest was repeated across the Americas. Meanwhile, another deadly invader was at work: disease. Europeans unknowingly carried diseases to which Native Americans had no immunity. These diseases spread rapidly, wiping out village after village.

An immediate result of Spanish conquest of the Americas was the flow of treasure to Spain. In the 1500s and early 1600s, treasure fleets sailed each year to Spain, loaded with gold and silver. The wealth of the Americas helped make Spain the most powerful country in Europe.

## Remaking the Americas

In order to build an American empire, the Spanish set out to impose their culture, language, religion, and way of life on millions of people. To Spain, winning souls for Christianity was as important as gaining land. Spanish soldiers helped Roman Catholic missionaries who built churches and worked to turn new converts into loyal subjects of Spain.

The Spanish also wanted a profitable empire. Sugar cane quickly became a key resource. However, sugar cane is grown on plantations, large estates run by an owner or the owner's overseer. Plantations needed large numbers of workers to be profitable. At first, Spanish monarchs gave the conquistadors encomiendas, or the right to demand labor or tribute from Native Americans in a particular area. The conquistadors used this system to enslave Native Americans under brutal conditions. Later, settlers imported millions of Africans and forced them to work as slaves.

Over the centuries, the Spanish colonies developed a unique culture. It combined European, Native American, and African traditions. The blending of diverse traditions changed people's lives throughout the Americas.

## Struggle for North America

In the 1500s and 1600s, France and England joined Spain in claiming parts of North America. Although North America did not yield gold treasure, tobacco plantations, fishing, and fur trading soon turned large profits.

**The French.** The French built their first permanent settlement in Quebec. Fur trappers and Catholic missionaries advanced into the wilderness. By the 1700s, French forts, missions, and trading posts stretched from Quebec to the Great Lakes and down the Mississippi River to Louisiana.

**The English.** The English built their first permanent colony at Jamestown, Virginia, in 1607. Throughout the 1600s and 1700s, individuals and groups of English settlers founded colonies. Many came seeking religious freedom. The English colonists needed workers to clear land and raise crops. A growing number of Africans were brought to the colonies and sold as slaves.

By the 1700s, Britain and

France had emerged as bitter rivals for power around the globe. The struggle came to a head when the Seven Years' War erupted in Europe and spread to North America. When it was over, the British had won control of Canada.

**Impact on Native Americans.** The arrival of European settlers in North America often brought disaster to Native Americans. As settlers claimed more land, Native Americans resisted. Bitter fighting resulted. Disease weakened or killed large numbers of Native Americans. Still, the cultural influence of Native Americans helped shape the emerging new society.

## Turbulent Centuries in Africa

The first encounters between Europeans and Africans took place in the 1400s. Europeans established trading forts along the western coast of Africa. Then, in the 1500s, Europeans began to view slaves as the most important item of African trade. For 300 years, the profitable Atlantic slave trade filled the demand for labor in Spain's American empire.

By the 1800s, when the overseas slave trade was finally stopped, an estimated 11 million enslaved Africans had reached the Americas. Another two million probably died under the brutal conditions of the voyage.

The slave trade drained countless women and men from West Africa. Some societies and small states disappeared. Other African states arose. Some new African states came to depend on the slave trade. One large state that arose in West Africa in the late 1600s was the Asante kingdom. The Asante traded gold and slaves for firearms.

## Changes in Europe

European exploration and trade between 1500 and 1700 brought major changes to the world. Columbus' arrival in the Americas sparked a vast global exchange of people, ideas, cultures, plants, animals, technology, and even disease. New foods, such as potatoes and corn, helped feed Europe's rapidly growing populations. The migration of millions of peoples led to an enormous transfer of ideas and technologies. Because this global exchange began with Columbus, we call it the Columbian exchange.

**A Commercial Revolution.** Expanded trade and the push for overseas empires spurred the growth of European **capitalism,** the investment of money to make a profit. **Entrepreneurs,** or enterprising merchants, organized, managed, and assumed the risks of doing business. European monarchs adopted new policies to strengthen their nation's economies. In the 1500s and 1600s, Europe emerged as a powerful new force on the world scene.

### Land Claims in the Americas About 1700

HUDSON BAY

Pelts

NEWFOUNDLAND

NEW FRANCE

Whale meat, fish

NOVA SCOTIA

ENGLISH COLONIES

LOUISIANA

Tobacco, grain

FLORIDA

ATLANTIC OCEAN

GULF OF MEXICO

BAHAMAS (Eng.)

MISSISSIPPI R.

Silver

MEXICO

WEST INDIES

Sugar, tobacco

CARIBBEAN SEA

PACIFIC OCEAN

GUIANA

Tobacco, cacao, hides

Gold

Silver

Amazon R.

BRAZIL

Sugar, tobacco, cotton

PERU

Copper, grain

Gold, diamonds

CHILE

Meat

Silver, hides

STRAIT OF MAGELLAN

N
W — E
S

0    750    1500 Miles
0   750   1500 Kilometers

**Land claims about 1700**

- Dutch
- English
- French
- Portuguese
- Spanish
- → Main exports

**GEOGRAPHY and HISTORY** *By the 1700s, European nations claimed vast stretches of land in both North and South America.*

### Review

1. **Identify** Columbian exchange
2. **Define** (a) conquistador, (b) plantation, (c) encomiendas, (d) capitalism, (e) entrepreneur
3. Name two effects of the Spanish conquest of the Americas.

## 4. THE AGE OF ABSOLUTISM (1550–1800)

### Key Facts

- European monarchs sought absolute power over their nations and peoples.
- Louis XIV achieved royal absolutism and helped France become the most powerful nation in Europe in the 1600s.

During the 1500s and 1600s, European monarchs worked to centralize their power. As they competed for overseas empires, the center of world civilization shifted to Europe.

### Extending Spanish Power

During the 1500s, Spain became the first modern European power. Thanks in part to silver from the Americas, Spanish kings were able to expand Spain's influence and strengthen the Catholic Church. Spain became the foremost power in Europe. Spanish kings became **absolute monarchs.** That is, they ruled with complete authority over the government and lives of the people. Absolute monarchs believed that they ruled by **divine right.** That is, the kings believed that their authority to rule came directly from God.

King Philip II of Spain fought many wars to increase Spanish Catholic power throughout the world. Over time, however, costly wars drained the wealth out of Spain almost as fast as it came in. By the late 1600s, France had replaced Spain as the most powerful nation in Europe.

### France Under Louis XIV

In the late 1500s, religious wars between French Protestants and the Catholic majority tore France apart. A series of kings sought to restore order. One man who promoted Catholic power was Cardinal Armand Richelieu, the chief minister of the king of France. Richelieu was determined to destroy the power of French nobles and French Protestants. He and his successors extended royal power and the interests of the Catholic church.

**King Louis XIV.** In 1643, five-year-old Louis XIV inherited the French throne. While still a teenager, he took over the government himself. Like his great-grandfather, Philip II of Spain, Louis believed in divine right. He took the sun as the symbol of his power and became known as the Sun King.

To increase royal power, Louis expanded the bureaucracy and appointed wealthy middle-class men to collect taxes. This helped tie the middle class to the monarchy. He poured vast resources into wars to gain more land and dominate Europe. Louis' European rivals, however, joined together to fight him. They hoped to maintain the **balance of power**, or the distribution of military and economic power that would prevent any one nation from dominating Europe.

Louis XIV ruled France with absolute authority for 72 years.

▲ *Salon de la Guerre, Versailles* *The Salon de la Guerre, or Hall of War, is a dazzling example of an ornate artistic style called baroque.*

During that time, French culture, manners, and customs became the standard for European taste. Louis built the immense palace of Versailles (ver sī), which housed at least 10,000 people. He spared no expense to make Versailles the most magnificent building in Europe.

## Triumph of Parliament in England

In contrast to France, England turned away from royal absolutism. From 1485 to 1603, England had been ruled by the Tudor dynasty. Although the Tudors believed in divine right, they recognized the value of good relations with Parliament in order to raise money and gain political support. However, when the English throne passed to the Stuarts, the ruling family of Scotland, trouble began. The Stuarts behaved as absolute monarchs. They clashed with Parliament and with a group of English Protestants called Puritans. When one Stuart king, Charles I, tried to arrest leaders of Parliament's House of Commons, civil war began.

**The English Civil War.** The civil war lasted from 1642 until 1649. When Parliamentary forces won, Charles I was tried and executed. This was a clear signal that in England, no ruler could claim absolute power or ignore the rule of law. For the next ten years, England would be a republic, known as the Commonwealth.

The new republic faced many problems. Supporters of Charles II, the uncrowned heir to the throne, attacked England. Puritans called for social reforms, angering the gentry. Eventually, a newly elected Parliament asked Charles II to return to England, restoring the monarchy. Still, Puritan ideas remained important. Years later, they would play an important role in shaping the United States of America.

**Limits on Royal Power.** Three years after the death of Charles II, Parliament invited his niece Mary and her husband William III of Orange, to become the rulers of England. Before they could be crowned, however, they had to agree to Parliament's demands. These demands became known as the English Bill of Rights. Under the Bill of Rights, England became a **limited monarchy,** a government in which a constitution or legislative body limits the monarch's powers. English rulers still had much power, but they agreed to obey the law and govern in partnership with Parliament.

## Absolute Monarchy in Russia

In the early 1600s, Russia was still a medieval state, untouched by the Renaissance and largely isolated from Western Europe. However, when Peter the Great took power in 1682, he set Russia on the road to becoming a great modern power. Using terror to enforce his absolute authority, he centralized royal power. Peter also pushed through social and economic reforms, imported Western technology, and built Russian military power.

By the mid-1700s, absolute

▲ Peter the Great shearing a beard to encourage men to shave and adopt European ways

monarchs ruled four of the five major European powers—Prussia, Austria, France, and Russia. Britain, with its strong Parliament, was the only exception. But new ideas would soon shatter the French monarchy, upset the balance of power, and revolutionize societies around the globe. That is the story of *The Modern Era.*

### Review

1. **Identify** (a) Louis XIV, (b) Puritans, (c) Stuarts, (d) Peter the Great
2. **Define** (a) absolute monarch, (b) divine right, (c) balance of power, (d) limited monarchy
3. Describe one way in which Louis XIV strengthened the power of the French monarchy.
4. Why did the Stuarts clash with Parliament?

# UNIT 1

# ENLIGHTENMENT AND REVOLUTION

### Global Interaction

**2** From 1756 to 1763, Britain and France fought for empire in Europe, North America, and Asia. As a result of the Seven Years' War, Britain won control of Canada.

NORTH AMERICA

ATLANTIC OCEAN

PACIFIC OCEAN

SOUTH AMERICA

### Political and Social Systems

**1** Colonial Latin America developed a rigid social hierarchy. This painting shows members of different Mexican social classes during the later colonial period.

N
W — E
S

### Continuity and Change

**3** The Atlantic slave trade led to the decline of some West African kingdoms and the rise of others. This helmet is from the Asante kingdom, which flourished in the 1700s.

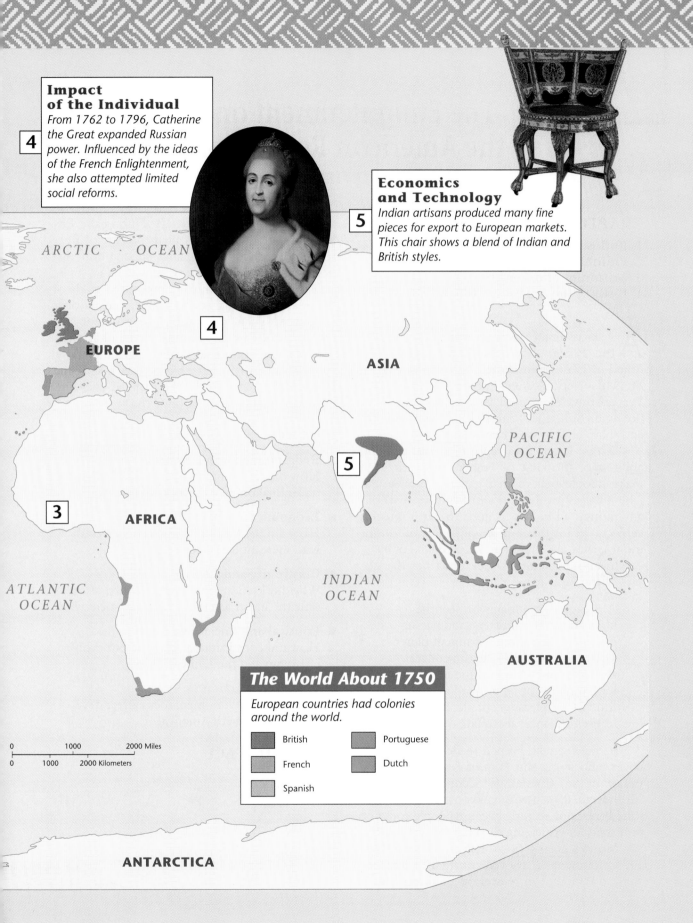

**Impact
of the Individual**

**4** From 1762 to 1796, Catherine the Great expanded Russian power. Influenced by the ideas of the French Enlightenment, she also attempted limited social reforms.

**Economics
and Technology**

**5** Indian artisans produced many fine pieces for export to European markets. This chair shows a blend of Indian and British styles.

ARCTIC · OCEAN

**EUROPE**

**4**

**ASIA**

**3**

**AFRICA**

PACIFIC
OCEAN

**5**

ATLANTIC
OCEAN

INDIAN
OCEAN

**AUSTRALIA**

**The World About 1750**

European countries had colonies around the world.

British

French

Spanish

Portuguese

Dutch

0      1000      2000 Miles
0   1000   2000 Kilometers

**ANTARCTICA**

# The Enlightenment and the American Revolution

## (1715–1800)

## CHAPTER OUTLINE

1 Philosophy in the Age of Reason
2 Enlightenment Ideas Spread
3 Britain at Mid-Century
4 Birth of the American Republic

All across France, readers smiled as they read the *Persian Letters*. This collection, published in 1721, commented on many aspects of French society. Readers knew that the authors, Persian travelers named Usbek and Rica, were not real. Still, the writers' humorous remarks and sharp criticisms of France hit home.

In one letter, Rica reports on the amazing abilities of the king of France, who can even make people believe that paper is money: "If [the king] is involved in a difficult war without any money, all he has to do is to get it into his subjects' heads that a piece of paper will do for money, they are immediately convinced of it."

In another letter, Usbek describes the nobles of the French court:

66A great lord is a man who sees the king, speaks to ministers, and has ancestors, debts, and government pensions. If, in addition, he can conceal the fact that he has nothing to do by looking busy, or by pretending to be fond of the pleasures of life, he thinks himself the most fortunate of men.99

It did not take French readers long to discover who wrote the *Persian Letters*. He was a minor noble, Charles de Secondat, Baron de Montesquieu (MAHN tehs kyoo). He had published the book secretly because people could be punished for criticizing the king or the Church.

Montesquieu's book helped usher in the Enlightenment, a movement that sought to shine the "light" of reason on traditional ideas about government and society. During the Enlightenment, sometimes called the Age of Reason, thinkers fought against superstition, ignorance, intolerance, and tyranny.

Enlightenment thinkers promoted goals of material well-being, social justice, and worldly happiness. Their ideas about government and society stood in sharp contrast to the old principles of divine-right rule, a rigid social hierarchy, and the promise of a better life in heaven. Since the 1700s, Enlightenment ideas have spread, challenging established traditions around the world.

**FOCUS ON** these questions as you read:

- **Religions and Value Systems**
  How did the Enlightenment challenge the traditional order in Europe?

- **Economics and Technology**
  How did the ideas of the physiocrats clash with mercantilist policy?

- **Continuity and Change**
  Why did Enlightenment ideas at first affect only the upper levels of European society?

- **Political and Social Systems**
  How did constitutional government evolve in Britain and the United States?

- **Global Interaction**
  How did Enlightenment ideas affect developments in North America?

## TIME AND PLACE

*A New View of the World* The first balloon flights in the late 1700s caused a sensation. By conquering gravity, balloons not only gave people a new perspective on the world but also inspired a new faith in the power of human reason. In this way, they are a perfect symbol for the European Age of Enlightenment, during which they were invented. ***Economics and Technology*** How would balloon flights provide a new perspective on the world?

## HUMANITIES LINK
*Art History* Jean-Antoine Houdon, *Voltaire* (page 41).
*Literature* In this chapter, you will encounter passages from the following works of literature: Baron de Montesquieu, *Persian Letters* (page 38); Alexander Pope, "Essay on Man" (page 40); Fanny Burney, *Evelina* (pages 58–59).

| 1707 England and Scotland unite | 1719 Defoe's *Robinson Crusoe* | 1748 Montesquieu's *The Spirit of the Laws* | 1762 Rousseau's *The Social Contract* | 1781 Joseph II of Austria grants religious toleration | 1783 Treaty of Paris ends American Revolution |
|---|---|---|---|---|---|

| 1700 | 1720 | 1740 | 1760 | 1780 | 1800 |
|---|---|---|---|---|---|

# 1 Philosophy in the Age of Reason

## Guide for Reading

- How was the Enlightenment linked to the Scientific Revolution?

- What ideas about government emerged during the Enlightenment?

- What economic ideas did Enlightenment thinkers support?

- **Vocabulary** *natural laws, social contract, natural rights, philosophe, physiocrat, laissez faire, free market*

66 Go, wondrous creature! mount where Science guides;
Go, measure earth, weigh air, and state the tides;
Instruct the planets in what orbs to run,
Correct old Time, and regulate the sun. 99

Those lines by the English poet Alexander Pope celebrated the successes of humans—the "wondrous creature"—in the Scientific Revolution. By the early 1700s, European thinkers felt that nothing was beyond the reach of the human mind. Using the methods of modern science, reformers set out to study human behavior and solve the problems of society.

## A World of Progress and Reason

The Enlightenment grew out of the Scientific Revolution of the 1500s and 1600s, with its amazing discoveries by thinkers like Copernicus and Newton. (See page 29.) In the 1700s, other scientists expanded European knowledge. Joseph Priestley and Antoine Lavoisier (ahn TWAHN lah vwah ZYAY), for example, built the framework for modern chemistry. Edward Jenner developed a vaccine against smallpox, a disease whose path of death spanned the centuries.

Scientific successes created great confidence in the power of reason. If people used reason to find laws that governed the physical world, why

not use reason to discover natural laws—laws that govern human nature? By applying scientific knowledge, inventors changed peoples' lives. Why not apply natural laws to change human society? Through the use of reason, insisted Enlightenment thinkers, they could solve every social, political, and economic problem. Heaven could be achieved here on Earth.

## Two Views of the Social Contract

In the 1600s, two English thinkers, Thomas Hobbes and John Locke, set forth ideas that were to become key to the Enlightenment. Both men lived through the upheavals that shook England early in the century. Yet they came to very different conclusions about human nature and the purpose and nature of government.

**"Nasty, brutish, and short."** Thomas Hobbes set out his ideas in a work titled *Leviathan.* Hobbes argued that people were naturally cruel, greedy, and selfish. If not strictly controlled, they would fight, rob, and oppress one another. Life in the "state of nature"—without laws or other control—would be "solitary, poor, nasty, brutish, and short."

To escape that "brutish" life, said Hobbes, people entered into a social contract, an agreement by which they gave up the state of nature for an organized society. Hobbes believed that only a powerful government could ensure an orderly society. Such a government was an absolute monarchy, which could impose order and compel obedience. Not surprisingly, Hobbes had supported the Stuart kings in their struggle against Parliament.

**Natural rights.** John Locke had a more optimistic view of human nature. People were basically reasonable and moral, he said. Further,

---

## GLOBAL 🌐 CONNECTIONS

Growing knowledge of other cultures enriched western thought. Enlightenment thinkers were drawn to the sages of China and the gurus, or religious thinkers of India, as well as to Greek and Roman philosophers. Some saw Native American sachems, or wisemen, as great sources of wisdom, closer to nature and natural truths than western thinkers.

they had natural rights, or rights that belonged to all humans from birth. These included the right to life, liberty, and property.

In *Two Treatises of Government,* Locke argued that people formed governments to protect their natural rights. The best kind of government, he said, had limited power and was accepted by all citizens. Thus, unlike Hobbes, Locke rejected absolute monarchy and sided with Parliament in its struggle against the Stuarts.

Locke then set out a radical idea. A government, he said, has an obligation to those it governs. If a government fails its obligations or violates people's natural rights, the people have the right to overthrow the government. This right to revolution would echo through Europe, in Britain's North American colonies, and around the world in the centuries that followed.

## *Montesquieu's* Spirit of the Laws

In the 1700s, France saw a flowering of Enlightenment thought. An early and influential thinker was the Baron de Montesquieu. Montesquieu studied the governments of Europe, from Italy to England. He read all he could about ancient and medieval Europe and learned about Chinese and Native American cultures. His sharp criticism of absolute monarchy opened the doors for later debate.

In 1748, Montesquieu published *The Spirit of the Laws.* In it, he discussed governments throughout history and wrote admiringly about Britain's limited monarchy. Montesquieu felt that the British had protected themselves against tyranny by dividing the functions and powers of government among three separate branches: the legislature, executive, and judiciary. (In fact, Montesquieu had misunderstood the British system, which did not separate powers in this way.) To him, the separation of powers was the best way to protect liberty.

Montesquieu also felt that each branch of government could serve as a check on the other two, an idea that we call checks and balances. Some 40 years after Montesquieu's book appeared in France, the ideas of separation of powers and checks and balances in government were written into the Constitution of the United States. (See page 57.)

**Voltaire** *Jean-Antoine Houdon, who lived from 1741 to 1828, was the greatest sculptor of his time. His work combined classical dignity with precise realism. In this statue, even though Voltaire is shown in the robes of ancient Rome, his face is starkly realistic. Houdon makes no effort to hide the ravages of old age on the features of the philosopher, who was 84 years old at the time the sculpture was begun.* **Art and Literature** *Classical Greek sculpture stressed ideals of perfect physical beauty. How do you think a classical Greek sculpture of Voltaire might differ from this one by Houdon?*

## *The World of the Philosophes*

In France, a group of Enlightenment thinkers applied the methods of science to better understand and improve society. These thinkers were called philosophes, which means "lovers of wisdom."

**Voltaire defends freedom of thought.** Probably the most famous philosophe was François-Marie Arouet, who took the name Voltaire. "My trade," said Voltaire, "is to say what I think," and he did so throughout his long, controversial life. Voltaire used biting wit as a weapon to expose the abuses of his day. He targeted corrupt officials and idle aristocrats. Barbs flew from his pen against inequality, injustice, and superstition. He detested the slave trade and deplored religious prejudice.

Voltaire's outspoken attacks offended the government and the Catholic Church. He was imprisoned and forced into exile. He saw his books censored and burned, but he continued to defend freedom of speech. "I do not agree with a word that you say," he supposedly declared, "but I will defend to the death your right to say it." (◪ See *You Decide*, "What Limits Should There Be on Freedom of Speech?" pages 134–135.)

**The Encyclopedia.** Another philosophe, Denis Diderot (dee DROH), labored some 25 years to produce a 28-volume *Encyclopedia*. As the editor of this huge work, Diderot did more than just gather articles on human knowledge. His purpose was "to change the general way of thinking" by explaining the new thinking on government, philosophy, and religion. Diderot's *Encyclopedia* included articles by leading thinkers of the day, including Montesquieu and Voltaire.

▲ *Diderot's* Encyclopedia

In their *Encyclopedia* articles, the philosophes denounced slavery, praised freedom of expression, and urged education for all. They attacked divine-right theory and traditional religions. Critics raised an outcry. The French government argued that the *Encyclopedia* was an attack on public morals, while the pope threatened to excommunicate Catholics who bought or read the volumes.

Despite efforts to ban the *Encyclopedia*, as many as 20,000 copies were printed between 1751 and 1789. This work did much to shape French public opinion in the mid-1700s. When translated into other languages, it helped spread Enlightenment ideas across Europe and into the Americas.

## Rousseau: A Controversial Figure

The most controversial philosophe was Jean-Jacques Rousseau (ZHAHN ZHAHK roo SOH). Rousseau was a strange, difficult man. Coming from a poor family, he never felt comfortable in the glittering social world of Enlightenment thinkers.

Rousseau believed that people in their natural state were basically good. This natural innocence, he felt, was corrupted by the evils of society, especially the unequal distribution of property. This view was later adopted by many reformers and revolutionaries.

In 1762, Rousseau set forth his ideas about government and society in *The Social Contract*. It begins: "Man is born free, and everywhere he is in chains." The chains, says Rousseau, are those of society, which controls the way people behave. He argues, however, that some social controls—control by a freely formed government, for example—are good, not evil. In consenting to form a government, he says, individuals choose to give up their self-interest in favor of the common good. Although people surrender their rights, they retain their freedom because the government is based on the consent of the governed.

Rousseau put his faith in the "general will," or the best conscience of the people. The good of the community as a whole, he said, should be placed above individual interests. He defined freedom as obedience to the law. Thus, unlike many Enlightenment thinkers who put the individual first, Rousseau felt that the individual should be subordinate to the community.

Rousseau has influenced political and social thinkers for more than 200 years. Woven through his work is a hatred of political and economic oppression. His ideas would help fan the flames of revolt in centuries to come.

## Limited "Natural Rights" for Women

The Enlightenment slogan "free and equal" did not apply to women. Women did have "natural rights," said the philosophes. But unlike the natural rights of men, these rights were limited to the areas of home and family.

## European Political Thinkers

| Thinker | Major Ideas | Quotation | Connections Today |
|---------|-------------|-----------|-------------------|
| **Thomas Hobbes**<br>*Leviathan*<br>(1651)<br> | People are driven by selfishness and greed. To avoid chaos, they give up their freedom to a government that will ensure order. Such a government must be strong and able to suppress rebellion. | "The condition of man [in the state of nature] . . . is a condition of war of everyone against everyone." | Hobbes's ideas have been used to justify absolute power. To some people today, Hobbes presents a bleak but true view of how people and governments behave. |
| **John Locke**<br>*Two Treatises of Government*<br>(1690)<br> | People have a natural right to life, liberty, and property. Rulers have a responsibility to protect those rights. People have the right to change a government that fails to do so. | "Men being . . . by nature all free, equal, and independent, no one can be put out of this estate and subjected to the political power of another without his own consent." | Locke's ideas influenced authors of U.S. Declaration of Independence and French revolutionaries in the 1790s. Later, people extended his ideas to include equality for women and others. |
| **Baron de Montesquieu**<br>*The Spirit of the Laws*<br>(1748)<br> | The powers of government should be separated into executive, legislative, and judicial branches, to prevent any one group from gaining too much power. | "In order to have . . . liberty, it is necessary that government be set up so that one man need not be afraid of another." | His ideas about separation of powers greatly influenced framers of U.S. Constitution. |
| **Jean-Jacques Rousseau**<br>*The Social Contract*<br>(1762)<br> | People are basically good but become corrupted by society. In an ideal society, people would make the laws and would obey them willingly. | "Only the general will can direct the energies of the state in a manner appropriate to the end for which it was founded, i.e., the common good." | Rousseau has been hailed as a champion of democracy for his idea that political authority lies with the people. But dictators have used his ideas about the "general will" to justify their programs. |

*Interpreting a Chart  Political and social philosophers thrived in Enlightenment Europe. Their ideas had a major impact throughout the world of their time and continue to influence developments today.  ■  Why did Montesquieu recommend separation of powers of government? How might Rousseau's ideas be used to justify dictatorship?*

By the mid-1700s, a small but growing number of women protested this view. They questioned the notion that women were by nature inferior to men and that men's domination of women was therefore part of "nature's plan." Germaine de Staël in France and Catharine Macaulay and Mary Wollstonecraft in England argued that women had been excluded from the social contract itself. Their arguments were ridiculed and often sharply condemned.

Wollstonecraft was the best known of the British female critics. She accepted that a woman's first duty was to be a good mother. At the same time, however, she felt that a woman should be able to decide what is in her own interest and should not be completely dependent on her husband. In 1792, Wollstonecraft published *A Vindication of the Rights of Woman*. In it, she called for the same education for girls and boys. Only education, she argued, could give women the tools they needed to participate equally with men in public life.

## New Economic Thinking

Other thinkers, the **physiocrats,** focused on economic reforms. Like the philosophes, physiocrats looked for natural laws to define a rational economic system.

**Laissez faire.** Physiocrats rejected mercantilism, which required government regulation to achieve a favorable balance of trade. Instead, they urged a policy of **laissez faire** (LEHS ay FAIR), allowing business to operate with little or no government interference. Unlike mercantilists, who called for acquiring gold and silver wealth through trade, the physiocrats claimed that real wealth came from making the land more productive. Extractive industries, they said, such as agriculture, mining, and logging, produced new wealth. While mercantilists had imposed tariffs, or taxes on foreign goods, to protect local manufacturing, physiocrats supported free trade and wanted to lift all tariffs.

**ISSUES For TODAY**

Laissez-faire economists argue that society would be better off if the government allowed business and the marketplace to operate without interference. What is the proper role of government in a nation's economy?

**Adam Smith.** British economist Adam Smith greatly admired the physiocrats. In his influential work, *The Wealth of Nations,* he argued that the **free market,** the natural forces of supply and demand, should be allowed to operate and regulate business. He tried to show how manufacturing, trade, wages, profits, and economic growth were all linked to the forces of supply and demand. Wherever there is a demand for goods or services, he said, suppliers will seek to meet it. They do so because of the economic rewards they can get from fulfilling the demand. A strong supporter of laissez faire, Smith believed that the marketplace was better off without any government regulation. At the same time, however, he did believe that government had a duty to protect society, administer justice, and provide public works.

Adam Smith's ideas would gain increasing influence as the Industrial Revolution spread across Europe and beyond. His emphasis on the free market and the law of supply and demand would help to shape immensely productive economies in the 1800s and 1900s.

## SECTION 1 REVIEW

1. **Identify** (a) Thomas Hobbes, (b) John Locke, (c) Baron de Montesquieu, (d) Voltaire, (e) Denis Diderot, (f) Jean-Jacques Rousseau, (g) Mary Wollstonecraft, (h) *The Wealth of Nations.*
2. **Define** (a) natural laws, (b) social contract, (c) natural rights, (d) philosophe, (e) physiocrat, (f) laissez faire, (g) free market.
3. How did the successes of the Scientific Revolution influence Enlightenment thinkers?
4. Describe the government favored by each of the following: (a) Hobbes, (b) Locke.
5. How were the physiocrats different from the mercantilists?
6. *Critical Thinking* **Defending a Position** Rousseau put the "general will"—the common good—over the interest of the individual. Do you agree with that position? Why or why not?
7. *ACTIVITY* Create a cartoon to illustrate the ideas of one or more of the philosophes you read about in this section.

# Enlightenment Ideas Spread

## Guide for Reading

- How did Enlightenment ideas pose a challenge to the established order?

- Why did some European rulers embrace Enlightenment ideas?

- What ideas influenced artists and writers of the Enlightenment?

- How did most people live during the Age of Reason?

- **Vocabulary** *salon, enlightened despot, baroque*

From France, Enlightenment ideas flowed across Europe, and beyond. Everywhere, thinkers examined traditional beliefs and customs in the light of reason and found them flawed. Even absolute monarchs experimented with Enlightenment ideas, although they drew back when it became clear that the changes called for by the philosophes might threaten the old order—that is, the established way of doing things.

## The Challenge of New Ideas

The ideas of the Enlightenment spread quickly through many levels of society. Educated people all over Europe eagerly read not only Diderot's *Encyclopedia* but also the small, cheap pamphlets that printers churned out on a broad range of issues. At the same time, middle-class men met to discuss the new ideas in the coffee-houses that were sprouting up in Europe's major cities.

*Spreading Enlightenment Ideas Printing presses helped carry the ideas of the philosophes to a growing literate middle class. Booksellers offered not only Diderot's massive* Encyclopedia *but also cheaper books and pamphlets on a range of issues. Here, customers examine the wares in a local bookshop.* **Continuity and Change** *How are ideas spread today?*

**Achieving a just society.** As Enlightenment ideas spread, people began to challenge the old ways. More and more, they saw the need for reform to achieve a just society.

During the Middle Ages, most Europeans had accepted without question a society based on divine-right rule, a strict class system, and a belief in heavenly reward for earthly suffering. In the Age of Reason, such ideas seemed unscientific and irrational. A just society, Enlightenment thinkers taught, should ensure material well-being, social justice, and happiness in this world.

**Censorship.** Government and Church authorities felt they had a sacred duty to defend the old order. They believed the old order had been set up by God. To protect against the attacks of the Enlightenment, they waged a war of censorship, banning and burning books and imprisoning writers. Some writers avoided the censors by having their books printed in the few countries, like the Netherlands, that allowed

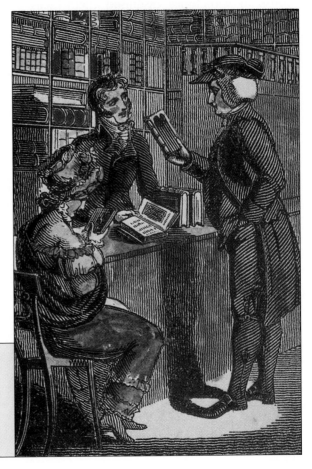

freedom of the press. Others published their books under a false name.

Writers like Montesquieu, Voltaire, and Rousseau sometimes disguised their ideas in works of fiction. You have already seen how Montesquieu mocked French society in the *Persian Letters.* The hero of Voltaire's humorous novel *Candide* travels across Europe and even to the Americas and the Middle East in search of "the best of all possible worlds." Voltaire slyly uses the tale to expose the corruption and hypocrisy of European society. Novels like *Candide* did not suggest specific reforms but did show readers the need for change.

## Salons

The new literature, the arts, science, and philosophy were regular topics of discussion in **salons,** informal social gatherings at which writers, artists, philosophers, and others exchanged ideas. The salon originated in the 1600s, when a group of noblewomen in Paris began inviting a few friends to their homes for poetry readings. Only the most witty, intelligent, and well-read people were invited to the salons.

By the 1700s, some middle-class women began holding salons. In the drawing rooms of these *salonières* (sah lohn YAIR), middle-class citizens could meet with the nobility on an equal footing to discuss and spread Enlightenment ideas.

## The Salon in the Rue Saint Honoré

In 1713, 14-year-old Marie-Thérèse Rodet was wed to François Geoffrin (zhehf RAN), 48. Everyone said it was a good match. Monsieur Geoffrin was a rich and well-respected manufacturer who would provide a comfortable life for his young wife.

The Geoffrins settled into a house on the Rue Saint Honoré (SAHN ahn oh RAY) in Paris. In the years that followed, Madame Geoffrin gave birth to two children and dutifully cared for her home and family. The pattern of her life seemed set forever—quiet and uneventful, without much intellectual excitement.

**A new world.** Then one day, a neighbor invited Madame Geoffrin to attend her salon. For the first time, the young woman heard the polished conversation of learned men and women. It opened the door to a new world.

Inspired, Madame Geoffrin eventually set up her own salon in the house on Rue Saint Honoré. She entertained poets and philosophers, artists and musicians. Her husband protested, but she would not give in. For years, he sat silent and ignored at the table while her guests dined and talked. One day, someone noticed that the old man was absent and inquired about him. "It was my husband," replied Madame Geoffrin. "He is dead."

**The *salonière*.** By 1750, Madame Geoffrin was a leading *salonière*. In her home, she brought together the brightest and most talented people of her day. On Mondays, Geoffrin welcomed artists and musicians. The young musical genius Wolfgang Amadeus Mozart played for her guests. On Wednesdays, philosophers and poets came for discussion and dispute. Diderot was a regular at the Wednesday dinners, and Madame Geoffrin donated large sums of money to support the *Encyclopedia*.

Even visiting monarchs paid their respects at what came to be called the "kingdom" of Rue Saint Honoré. Madame Geoffrin corresponded with Catherine II of Russia and Maria Theresa of Austria. Catherine was so eager to learn what was going on that she had spies report on the conversation at Geoffrin's salon.

**"Women ruled then."** *Salonières* like Madame Geoffrin were often not well educated themselves. They set up salons to learn from the conversations of educated men. The *salonières* were not intimidated by such men, however. While remaining gracious, they demanded high standards of discussion. Diderot commented:

> 66Women accustom us to discuss with charm and clearness the driest and thorniest subjects. . . . Hence we develop a particular method of explaining ourselves easily, and this method passes from conversation into style.99

By the end of the 1700s, the influence of women's salons had ended. Later, looking back, the celebrated court painter Elisabeth Vigée Lebrun observed: "Women ruled then."

## Enlightened Despots

Discussions of Enlightenment theories also enlivened the courts of Europe. Philosophes tried to convince European rulers to adopt their ideas. If they could "enlighten" the ruling classes, they thought, they could bring about reform. Some monarchs did accept Enlightenment ideas. They became enlightened despots, or absolute rulers who used their power to bring about political and social change.

**Frederick the Great.** As king of Prussia from 1740 to 1786, Frederick II exerted extremely tight control over his subjects. Still, he saw himself as the "first servant of the state," with a duty to work for the common good.

Frederick admired Voltaire and lured him to Berlin to develop a Prussian academy of science. When the king was not busy fighting wars, he had swamps drained and forced peasants to grow new crops such as the potato. He also had seed and tools distributed to peasants who had suffered in Prussia's wars. He tolerated religious differences, welcoming victims of religious persecution. "In my kingdom," he said, "everyone can go to heaven in his own fashion."

Frederick's reforms were directed mainly at making the Prussian government more efficient. He reorganized the civil service and simplified laws. But a "rationalized" bureaucracy also meant a stronger monarchy—and more power for Frederick himself. (★ See *Skills for Success,* page 60.)

**Catherine the Great.** Catherine II of Russia read the works of the philosophes and exchanged letters with Voltaire and Diderot. She praised Voltaire as someone who had "fought the united enemies of humankind: superstition, fanaticism, ignorance, trickery."

Catherine, who became empress in 1762, experimented with Enlightenment ideas. Early in her reign, she made limited reforms in law and government. She granted nobles a charter of rights and spoke out against serfdom. Still, like Frederick in Prussia, Catherine intended to give up no power. When a serf revolt broke out, she ruthlessly suppressed it. She also allied herself with the Russian nobles who opposed change. In the end, Catherine's contribution to Russia was not reform but an expanded empire.

**Joseph II.** The most radical enlightened despot was the Hapsburg emperor Joseph II, son and successor of Maria Theresa. An eager student of the Enlightenment, Joseph traveled in disguise among his subjects to learn of their problems. His efforts to improve their lives won him the nickname the "peasant emperor."

Maria Theresa had begun to modernize Austria's government. Joseph continued her reforms. He chose talented middle-class officials rather than nobles to head departments and imposed a range of political and legal reforms. Despite opposition, he granted toleration to Protestants and Jews in his Catholic empire. He ended censorship and attempted to bring the

Catholic Church under royal control. He sold the property of many monasteries and convents, which he saw as unproductive, and used the proceeds to build hospitals. Joseph even abolished serfdom. Like many of his reforms, however, this measure was canceled after his death.

## The Arts and Literature

In the 1600s and 1700s, the arts evolved to meet changing tastes. As in earlier periods, artists and composers had to please their patrons, the men and women who commissioned works from them or gave them jobs.

**Courtly art.** In the age of Louis XIV, courtly art and architecture were either in classical style, in the Greek and Roman tradition, or in the grand, complex style known as baroque. Baroque rooms were filled with gilded bronze, marble, and crystal. Baroque paintings were huge, colorful, and full of excitement. They glorified historic battles or the lives of saints. Such works matched the grandeur of European courts.

By the mid-1700s, architects and designers developed the rococo style. Unlike the heavy splendor of the baroque, rococo art was personal, refined, elegant, and charming. Furniture and tapestries featured delicate shells and flowers, as well as a European version of Chinese decorations. Portrait painters showed noble subjects in charming rural settings, surrounded by happy servants and pets.

**Middle-class audiences.** A new audience, the growing middle class, emerged with its own requirements. Successful merchants and town officials wanted their portraits painted, but without frills. They liked pictures of family life or realistic town or country scenes. Dutch painters such as Rembrandt van Rijn (REHM brant van RĪN) conferred great dignity on merchants and other ordinary, middle-class subjects.

**Trends in music.** New kinds of musical entertainment evolved in the baroque era. Ballets and operas—plays set to music—were performed at royal courts. Before long, opera houses sprang up from Italy to England to amuse the paying public. The music of the period followed ordered, structured forms well suited to the Age of Reason.

Among the towering musical figures of the period was Johann Sebastian Bach. A devout German Lutheran, Bach wrote complex and beautiful religious works for organ and choirs. Another German-born composer, George Frederick Handel, spent much of his life in England. There, he wrote the *Water Music* and other pieces for King George I, as well as many operas. His most celebrated work, the *Messiah,* combines instruments and voices. Today, it is a standard at Christmas and Easter concerts.

In 1762, a six-year-old prodigy, Wolfgang Amadeus Mozart, burst onto the European scene to gain instant celebrity as a composer and performer. In his brief life, the young man from Salzburg composed an amazing variety of music with remarkable speed. His brilliant operas, graceful symphonies, and moving religious music helped define the new style of classical composition. At age 35, Mozart died in poverty, leaving a musical legacy that thrives today.

**The novel.** By the 1700s, literature developed new forms and a wide new audience. Middle-class readers, for example, liked stories about their own times told in plain prose. One result was an outpouring of novels, long works of prose fiction.

A number of English novelists created popular works. Daniel Defoe wrote *Robinson Crusoe,* an exciting tale about a sailor ship-

*Throwing a Kiss* These delicate porcelains in the rococo style that developed in the 1700s show an aristocratic couple flirting. The man wears a long Chinese-style robe, called a banyan, that was in fashion among the nobility at the time. **Religions and Value Systems** What do the gestures of the two figures tell you about the manners of the aristocracy?

**Peasants Gathering Hay** *Enlightenment ideas did not change life for most Europeans. The vast majority continued to live in villages and work as farmers. Here, English peasants rake hay, which was used to feed farm animals during the winter.* **Political and Social Systems** *Based on the picture, what conclusion can you draw about the role of women on the farm?*

wrecked on a tropical island. Through hard work, his own wits, and the help of an islander whom he names Friday, Crusoe survives his ordeal. In *Pamela*, Samuel Richardson used a series of letters to tell a story about a servant girl. This technique was adopted by several other authors of the period. ( See *World Literature*, "Evelina," pages 58–59.)

### Lives of the Majority

Most Europeans were untouched by either courtly or middle-class culture. They remained what they had always been—peasants living in small rural villages. Their culture was based on centuries-old traditions that changed slowly.

**Conditions west and east.** Peasant life varied across Europe. Villages in Western Europe were relatively more prosperous than those in Eastern Europe. In the West, serfdom had largely disappeared. Instead, some peasants worked their own patches of land. Others were tenants of large landowners, paying a yearly rent for the land they farmed. Still others were day laborers who hired themselves out for the farm season.

In central and Eastern Europe, by contrast, serfdom was firmly rooted. In Russia, it spread and deepened in the 1700s. Peasants bound to the land owed labor services to their lords and could be bought and sold with the land. Russian landowners could also send serfs to labor in government mines or serve long terms as soldiers in the imperial armies.

**Old ways survive.** Despite advances, some echoes of serfdom survived in Western

Europe. In France, peasants still had to provide free labor, repairing roads and bridges after the spring floods just as their ancestors had done. In England, country squires had the right to hunt foxes across the plowed and planted fields of their tenants.

By the late 1700s, radical ideas about equality and social justice seeped into peasant villages. While some peasants eagerly sought to topple the old order, others resisted efforts to bring about change. In the 1800s, war and political upheaval as well as changing economic conditions would transform peasant life in Europe.

## SECTION 2 REVIEW

1. **Identify** (a) *Candide,* (b) Joseph II, (c) Johann Sebastian Bach, (d) George Frederick Handel, (e) Wolfgang Amadeus Mozart, (f) Daniel Defoe.
2. **Define** (a) salon, (b) enlightened despot, (c) baroque.
3. (a) Describe three ways in which Enlightenment ideas spread. (b) Why did those ideas threaten the old order?
4. What were the goals of enlightened despots?
5. How did courtly tastes differ from middle-class tastes?
6. How did peasant life vary across Europe?
7. *Critical Thinking* **Analyzing Information** (a) What did Frederick II mean when he said, "In my kingdom, everyone can go to heaven in his own fashion"? (b) How did his actions reflect that idea?
8. *ACTIVITY* Imagine that you are living in Paris during the 1700s. Organize a salon to discuss a "just society." Be sure to include supporters of both the old order and Enlightenment ideas among your guests.

# 3 Britain at Mid-Century

## Guide for Reading

- Why did Britain become a global power in the 1700s?
- What new political institutions emerged in Britain in the 1700s?
- What groups held political power in Britain?
- **Vocabulary** *constitutional government, prime minister*

66Foreign trade is . . . the honor of the kingdom, the noble profession of the merchant, . . . the supply of our wants, the employment of our poor, the improvement of our lands, the nursery of our [sailors], the walls of the kingdom, the means of our treasure, the sinews of our wars, the terror of our enemies.99

With words like these, English advocates of mercantilism preached their cause in the mid-1600s. Over the next century, Britain embraced this doctrine and built a colonial and commercial empire that reached around the world. It replaced Spain as the most successful European empire builder and outstripped the Netherlands as the foremost European trading nation. At the same time, Britain developed a constitutional monarchy, a political system somewhere between the absolute monarchies of the European continent and later democratic governments.

## Global Expansion

Why did Britain, a small island kingdom on the edge of Europe, rise to global prominence in the 1700s? Here, we can look at only a few reasons for its success.

**Geography.** England's location made it well placed to control trade during the Renaissance. In the 1500s and 1600s, English merchants sent ships across the world's oceans and planted outposts in the West Indies, North America, and India. From these tiny settlements, England would eventually build a global empire.

**Success in war.** In the 1700s, Britain was generally on the winning side in European conflicts. Each victory brought valuable rewards. By the Treaty of Utrecht, France gave Britain Nova Scotia and Newfoundland in North America. It also won a monopoly on the slave trade in Spanish America. The slave trade brought enormous wealth to British merchants, who invested their profits in other ventures. In 1763, the Treaty of Paris ending the Seven Years' War brought Britain all of French Canada. The British East India Company pushed the French out of India.

Unlike its European rivals, Britain had no large standing army. Instead, it built up its fleet. By 1763, Britain had a more powerful navy than its greatest rival, France. With its superior naval power, it was well able to protect its growing empire and trade.

**A favorable business climate.** England offered a more favorable climate to business and commerce than its European rivals. Although-

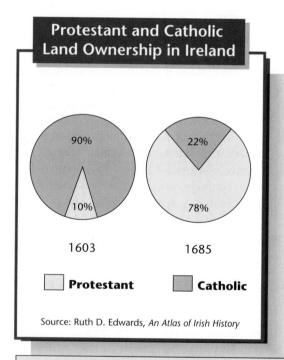

### Protestant and Catholic Land Ownership in Ireland

90% / 10% — 1603

22% / 78% — 1685

□ **Protestant**　■ **Catholic**

Source: Ruth D. Edwards, *An Atlas of Irish History*

*Interpreting a Chart* In the 1600s, England seized land from Irish Catholics and gave it to English and Scottish settlers, who were Protestants. By the end of the century, Protestants controlled most of Ireland.
■ *What percentage of Ireland's land was owned by Catholics in 1603? In 1685?*

**United Kingdom of Great Britain, 1707**

The Act of Union joined England and Scotland in the United Kingdom of Great Britain in 1707. The tiny kingdom of Wales had joined with England some 200 years earlier.

1. **Location** On the map, locate (a) Irish Sea, (b) Edinburgh, (c) London, (d) English Channel.
2. **Place** Which neighboring land was controlled by Britain but was not part of the United Kingdom in 1707?
3. *Critical Thinking* **Applying Information** How might it benefit England to join politically with its neighbors?

England followed mercantilist policies, it put fewer restrictions on trade than France did. Also, while British nobles, like most nobles in Europe, looked down on trade, some did engage in business activities.

**Union with Scotland.** At home, England grew by merging with neighboring Scotland. In 1707, the Act of Union united the two countries in the United Kingdom of Great Britain. The union brought economic advantages to both lands. It allowed trade to pass freely between England and Scotland, creating a larger market for farmers and manufacturers. Although many Scots resented the union, growing prosperity eventually made it more acceptable. The United Kingdom also included Wales.

**Ireland.** England had controlled Ireland since the 1100s. In the 1600s, English rulers tried to subdue Catholic Ireland by sending Protestants from England and Scotland to settle there. They gave Protestant settlers title to Irish Catholic lands.

The Irish fiercely resisted Protestant rule. When uprisings failed, repression increased. Catholics were forbidden to own weapons, marry non-Catholics, or serve as teachers.

## Growth of Constitutional Government

In the century following the establishment of the Bill of Rights (see page 35), three new political institutions arose in Britain: political parties, the cabinet, and the office of prime minister. The appearance of these institutions was part of the evolution of England's constitutional government—that is, a government whose power is defined and limited by law. Unlike the United States Constitution, which is a single written document, the British constitution is made up of all acts of Parliament over the centuries. It also includes documents such as the Magna Carta and Bill of Rights, as well as unwritten traditions that protect citizens' rights.

**Political parties.** Two political parties emerged in England in the late 1600s, Tories and Whigs. The conservative Tories were generally landed aristocrats who sought to preserve older traditions. They supported broad royal powers and a dominant Anglican Church. The Whigs backed more liberal policies. They were more likely to reflect urban business interests, support religious toleration for Protestants, and favor Parliament over the crown. For much of the 1700s, the Whigs dominated Parliament.

## Political Campaigns

Wherever there have been elections, there have also been election campaigns. Throughout history, politicians eager to win office have done whatever they could to win votes.

**Linking Past and Present**  What methods do candidates use to win votes in the United States today? Do you think any of the same methods were used in England in the 1700s? Explain.

**PAST**  Only men who owned land could vote in England during the 1700s. Even so, elections were a time of bustling activity. In this painting by the great British artist William Hogarth, campaigners try to win votes for their candidates outside a tavern.

**PRESENT**  In the United States today, political campaigns are elaborate affairs, and citizens participate in events like the convention (right) mainly through television. Candidates, such as Carol Moseley-Braun (far right), however, still go out to shake hands with their supporters.

These early political parties were unlike the party organizations that we know today. They represented cliques among the rich, powerful men who served as members of Parliament. Linked by family ties or personal agreements, members pooled their votes to advance their common interests. The modern political party, representing groups of voters and with a distinct platform, did not appear until the 1800s.

**The cabinet system.** The cabinet was another new feature of government. In 1714, the British throne passed by hereditary right to a German Protestant prince. George I spoke no English and relied on the leaders in Parliament to help him rule. Under George I, and his German-born son George II, a handful of parliamentary advisers set policy. They were called the cabinet because they met in a small room, or "cabinet."

In time, the cabinet gained official status. It was made up of leaders of the majority party in the House of Commons. The cabinet remained in power so long as it enjoyed the support of the Commons. If the Commons voted against a cabinet decision, the cabinet resigned. This cabinet system (also called a parliamentary system) was later adopted by other countries in Europe and elsewhere around the world.

**The prime minister.** Heading the cabinet was the prime minister. The prime minister was the leader of the majority party in Parliament and in time the chief official of the British government. From 1721 to 1742, the able Whig leader Robert Walpole molded the cabinet into a unified body, requiring all members to agree on major issues. Although the title was not yet used, Walpole is often called Britain's first prime minister.

## Politics and Society

The age of Walpole was a time of peace and prosperity. But even as Parliament and the cabinet assumed new powers, British government was far from democratic. Rather, it was an oligarchy—a government in which the ruling power belongs to a few people.

**The ruling elite.** In Britain as on the continent, landowning aristocrats were seen as the "natural" ruling class. The highest nobles held seats in the House of Lords. Other wealthy landowners, along with rich business leaders in the cities, controlled elections to the House of Commons. The right to vote was limited to a relatively few male property owners, and their votes were often openly bought.

**Other classes.** The lives of most people contrasted sharply with those of the ruling elite. The majority made a meager living from the land. In the 1700s, even that poor existence was threatened. Wealthy landowners bought up farms and took over common lands, evicting tenant farmers and small landowners. Many landless families drifted into towns, where they faced a harsh and desperate existence.

A small but growing middle class included successful merchants and manufacturers. They controlled affairs in the towns and cities. Some improved their social standing by marrying into the landed gentry. The middle class also produced talented inventors and entrepreneurs who helped usher in the Industrial Revolution. (See Chapter 3.)

## George III Reasserts Royal Power

In 1760, George III embarked on a 60-year reign. Unlike his father and grandfather, the new king was born in England. He spoke English and loved Britain. But George was eager to recover the powers the crown had lost. Following his mother's advice, "George, be a king!" he set out to reassert royal power. He wanted to end Whig domination, choose his own ministers, dissolve the cabinet system, and make the House of Commons follow his will.

**Personal rule.** Gradually, George found seats in Parliament for "the king's friends." Then, with their help, he set out to regain control of the government.

His troubles, however, began early in his reign. After the Seven Years' War, George and his ministers adopted a new policy: English colonists in North America must pay the costs of their own defense. When colonists protested, Parliament passed harsh measures to force them to obey. In 1775, these and other conflicts triggered the American Revolution—and disaster for Britain. (See Section 4.)

**Cabinet rule restored.** Britain's loss of its American colonies discredited the king. Increasingly, too, he suffered from bouts of mental illness. In the crisis of leadership that followed, cabinet rule was restored in 1788.

In the decades ahead, revolution engulfed France, and Napoleon Bonaparte's armies stormed across Europe, dragging Britain into long wars. During that time, the cabinet controlled the government. The British came to see the prime minister as their real political leader.

## SECTION 3 REVIEW

1. **Identify** (a) Act of Union, (b) Tories, (c) Whigs, (d) Robert Walpole, (e) George III.
2. **Define** (a) constitutional government, (b) prime minister.
3. How did each of the following contribute to Britain's rise to global prominence in the 1700s: (a) geography, (b) success in war, (c) attitudes toward business and commerce?
4. Who made up the ruling oligarchy in Britain?
5. *Critical Thinking* **Comparing** How does the parliamentary system of government that evolved in England differ from the modern American system of government?
6. *ACTIVITY* Make a diagram showing the relationship among the English crown, prime minister, cabinet, and Parliament.

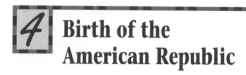

# 4 Birth of the American Republic

## Guide for Reading

- How were the 13 English colonies part of a global empire?

- Why did colonists come to resent British rule?

- How did Enlightenment ideas influence Americans?

- What was the global impact of the American Revolution?

Early in 1776, English colonists in North America eagerly read the newly published *Common Sense*. The pamphlet called on them to declare their independence from Britain. Its author, Tom Paine, a recent immigrant from England, wrote with passion under the cool banner of reason. "In the following pages," he declared, "I offer nothing more than simple facts, plain arguments, and common sense."

In *Common Sense*, Paine echoed the themes of the Enlightenment. He rejected ancient prejudice and tyranny, while appealing to reason, natural laws, and the promise of freedom. He wrote:

66 'Tis repugnant to reason, to the universal order of things, to all examples from former ages, to suppose that this Continent can long remain subject to any external power. 99

Colonists hotly debated Paine's arguments. As resentment of British policies grew, however, many came to agree with his radical ideas. Soon, they set out on the dangerous and uncertain road that led to independence from British rule.

## The 13 English Colonies

By 1750, a string of 13 prosperous colonies stretched along the eastern coast of North America. They were part of Britain's growing empire. Colonial cities such as Boston, New York, and Philadelphia were busy centers of commerce linking North America, the West Indies, Africa, and Europe. Colonial shipyards produced many vessels used in that global trade.

Britain applied mercantilist policies to its colonies. In the 1600s, Parliament had passed the Navigation Acts to regulate colonial trade and manufacturing. For the most part, these acts were not rigorously enforced. Smuggling was common and was not considered a crime by the colonists.

By mid-century, too, the colonies were home to diverse religions and ethnic groups. Social distinctions were more blurred than in Europe, although government and society were dominated by wealthy landowners and merchants. In politics as in much else, there was a good deal of free discussion. Colonists felt entitled to the rights of English citizens, and their colonial assemblies exercised much control over local affairs.

Ways of life differed from New England to the southern colonies. Still, colonists shared common values, respect for individual enterprise, and a growing self-confidence. They also had an increasing sense of their own destiny separate from Britain.

## Growing Discontent

After 1763, relations between Britain and the 13 colonies grew strained. The Seven Years' War, called the French and Indian War in North America, had drained the British treasury. King George III and his ministers thought that the colonists should help pay for the war and for the troops still stationed on the frontier. Britain began to enforce the long-neglected laws regulating colonial trade, and Parliament passed new laws to raise taxes from the colonies.

The British measures were not burdensome. Still, colonists bitterly resented what they saw as an attack on their rights. "No taxation without representation," they protested. Since they had no representatives in Parliament, they believed, Parliament had no right to tax them. While Parliament did repeal some of the

◀ *Teapot celebrating repeal of a British tax*

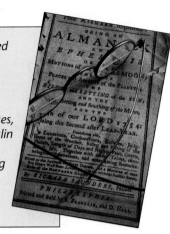

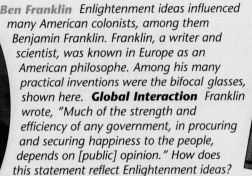

**Ben Franklin** Enlightenment ideas influenced many American colonists, among them Benjamin Franklin. Franklin, a writer and scientist, was known in Europe as an American philosophe. Among his many practical inventions were the bifocal glasses, shown here. **Global Interaction** Franklin wrote, "Much of the strength and efficiency of any government, in procuring and securing happiness to the people, depends on [public] opinion." How does this statement reflect Enlightenment ideas?

hated measures, in general, it asserted its right to tax.

**Early clashes.** A series of violent clashes intensified the crisis. In 1770, British soldiers in Boston opened fire on a crowd that was pelting them with stones and snowballs. Colonists called the death of five protesters the "Boston Massacre." In 1773, a handful of colonists staged the Boston Tea Party, hurling a cargo of recently arrived British tea into the harbor to protest a tax on tea. When Parliament passed harsh laws to punish Massachusetts, other colonies rallied to its support.

**Fighting begins.** In April 1775, the crisis exploded into war. The next month, as fighting spread, colonial leaders met in a Continental Congress to decide what action to take. Members included some extraordinary men: the radical yet fair-minded Boston lawyer John Adams, the Virginia planter and soldier George Washington, and such pillars of the American Enlightenment as Benjamin Franklin and Thomas Jefferson.

**Declaring independence.** The Congress set up a Continental Army, with George Washington in command. The following year, it took a momentous step, voting to declare independence from Britain. Young Thomas Jefferson drafted the Declaration of Independence, a document that clearly reflects the ideas of John Locke in lines such as these:

66We hold these truths to be self-evident, that all men are created equal, that they are endowed by their Creator with certain unalienable rights, that among these are life, liberty, and the pursuit of happiness. That to secure these rights, governments are instituted among men, deriving their just powers from the consent of the governed.99

The Declaration claimed that people had the right "to alter or abolish" unjust governments—a right to revolt. Jefferson carefully detailed the colonists' grievances against Britain. Because the king had trampled colonists' natural rights, he argued, the colonists had the right to rebel and set up a new government that would protect them. Aware of the risks involved, on July 4, 1776, American leaders adopted the Declaration, pledging "our lives, our fortunes, and our sacred honor" to the cause of the United States of America.

## The American Revolution

At first, the American cause looked bleak. The British had professional soldiers, a huge fleet, and plentiful money. They occupied most major American cities. Also, about a third of the colonists were Loyalists who supported Britain. Many others refused to fight for either side.

The Continental Congress had few military resources and little money to pay its soldiers. Still, colonists battling for independence had some advantages. They were fighting on their own ground for their farms and towns. Although the British held New York and Philadelphia, rebels controlled the countryside.

**The French alliance.** A turning point in the war came with the American triumph over

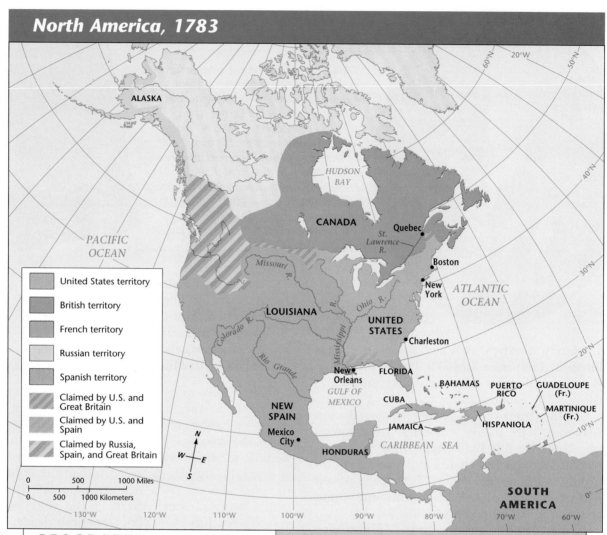

# North America, 1783

ALASKA

HUDSON BAY

PACIFIC OCEAN

CANADA

Quebec

St. Lawrence R.

Boston

New York

ATLANTIC OCEAN

Missouri R.

LOUISIANA

Ohio R.

UNITED STATES

Charleston

Colorado R.

Rio Grande

Mississippi R.

New Orleans

FLORIDA

BAHAMAS

PUERTO RICO

GUADELOUPE (Fr.)

GULF OF MEXICO

CUBA

MARTINIQUE (Fr.)

NEW SPAIN

Mexico City

JAMAICA

HISPANIOLA

CARIBBEAN SEA

HONDURAS

SOUTH AMERICA

**Legend:**
- United States territory
- British territory
- French territory
- Russian territory
- Spanish territory
- Claimed by U.S. and Great Britain
- Claimed by U.S. and Spain
- Claimed by Russia, Spain, and Great Britain

0   500   1000 Miles
0   500   1000 Kilometers

N S E W

## GEOGRAPHY AND HISTORY

*In the peace treaty ending the American Revolution, Britain recognized the United States as an independent nation, stretching from the Atlantic Ocean in the east to the Mississippi River in the west. Britain still controlled Canada, to the north of the new nation.*

**1. Location** *On the map, locate (a) United States, (b) Mississippi River, (c) Canada, (d) New Spain.*

**2. Region** *(a) Who claimed Louisiana in 1783? (b) Who claimed Alaska? (c) What area was claimed by Russia, Spain, and Great Britain?*

**3. Critical Thinking** *Solving Problems* *What methods might the nations shown on the map use to resolve conflicting land claims?*

the British in 1777 at the Battle of Saratoga. The victory convinced France to join the Americans against its old rival, Britain. The alliance brought the Americans desperately needed supplies, trained soldiers, and French warships. Spurred by the French example, the Netherlands and Spain soon added their support.

Hard times continued, however. In the brutal winter of 1777–1778, Continental troops at Valley Forge suffered from cold, hunger, and disease. Through this crisis and others, George Washington proved a patient, courageous, and determined leader able to hold the ragged army together.

**Treaty of Paris.** Finally in 1781, with the help of the French fleet, Washington forced the surrender of a British army at Yorktown, Virginia. With that defeat, the British war effort crumbled. Two years later, American, British, and French negotiators signed the Treaty of Paris ending the war. In it, Britain recognized the independence of the United States of America. It also accepted the new nation's western frontier as the Mississippi River.

## A New Constitution

A national government set up by a document that Americans called the Articles of Confederation was too weak to rule the new United States effectively. To address this problem, the nation's leaders gathered once more in Philadelphia. During the hot summer of 1787, they hammered out the Constitution of the United States. This framework for a strong, flexible government has adapted to changing conditions for more than 200 years.

**The impact of Enlightenment ideas.** The framers of the Constitution had absorbed the ideas of Locke, Montesquieu, and Rousseau and had studied history. They saw government in terms of a social contract entered into by "We the People of the United States." They provided not only for an elective legislature but also for an elected president rather than a hereditary monarch.

The Constitution created a federal republic, with power divided between the federal, or national, government and the states. A central feature of the new federal government was the separation of powers among the legislative, executive, and judicial branches, an idea borrowed directly from Montesquieu. Within that structure, each branch of government was provided with checks and balances on the other branches.

The Bill of Rights, the first 10 amendments to the Constitution, recognized the idea that people had basic rights that the government must protect. They included freedom of religion, speech, and the press, as well as the rights to trial by jury and to private property.

**Limited freedom.** In 1789, the Constitution became law. It set up a representative government with an elected legislature to reflect the wishes of the governed.

Yet most Americans at the time did not have the right to vote. Only white men who met certain property requirements could vote. Women could not cast a ballot. Nor could African Americans—enslaved *or* free—or Native Americans. It would take many years of struggle before the right to vote and equal protection under the law were extended to all adult Americans.

**Global impact.** Despite its limits, the Constitution of the United States created the most liberal government of its day. From the start, the new republic shone as a symbol of freedom to European countries and to Latin America. Its Constitution would be copied or adapted by many lands throughout the world.

The Enlightenment ideals that had inspired American colonists brought changes in Europe, too. In France in 1789, a revolution in the name of liberty and equality toppled the monarchy. Before long, other Europeans took up the cry for freedom. By the mid-1800s, most absolute monarchs across Europe would see their powers greatly reduced.

## SECTION 4 REVIEW

1. **Identify** (a) Navigation Acts, (b) Continental Congress, (c) George Washington, (d) Thomas Jefferson, (e) Battle of Saratoga, (f) Treaty of Paris of 1783, (g) Bill of Rights.
2. What role did the 13 colonies have in the British empire?
3. Explain why conflict between the colonists and Britain increased after 1763.
4. Give two examples of how Enlightenment ideas were reflected in each of the following: (a) the Declaration of Independence, (b) the Constitution of the United States.
5. How did the ideals of the American Revolution influence other nations?
6. *Critical Thinking* **Analyzing Information** In your own words, describe the idea of separation of powers. Then, give two examples of how your life would be different if the Constitution did not provide for separation of powers.
7. *ACTIVITY* Write a storybook for young children describing the causes, main events, and effects of the American Revolution.

# World Literature
## Evelina
### Fanny Burney

**Introduction** *One of England's first female novelists was Fanny Burney. In 1778, she published* Evelina, or The History of a Young Lady's Entrance Into the World. *It tells the story of a 16-year-old woman who is sent from her small rural village to visit London. In a series of letters home, Evelina tells of her adventures in the city. The novel gives us an interesting picture of upper-middle-class life. In the following passage, Evelina describes going to her first dance in London.*

LETTER X
EVELINA TO THE REV. MR. VILLARS
*Monday, April 4*

We are to go this evening to a private ball, given by Mrs. Stanley, a very fashionable lady of Mrs. Mirvan's acquaintance.

We have been *a-shopping* as Mrs. Mirvan calls it, all this morning, to buy silks, caps, gauzes, and so forth.

The shops are really very entertaining, especially the [textile dealers]; there seem to be six or seven men belonging to each shop; and every one took care by bowing and smirking, to be noticed. We were conducted from one to another, and carried from room to room with so much ceremony, that at first I was almost afraid to go on.

I thought I should never have chosen a silk: for they produced so many, I knew not what to fix upon; and they recommended them all so strongly, that I fancy they thought I only wanted persuasion to buy everything they showed me. And, indeed, they took so much trouble, that I was almost ashamed I could not.

At the [hat shop], the ladies we met were so much dressed, that I should rather have imagined they were making visits than purchases. But what most diverted me was, that we were more frequently served by men than by women; and such men! so [fussy], so affected! they seemed to understand every part of a woman's dress better than we do ourselves. . . .

The dispatch with which they work in these great shops is amazing, for they have promised me a complete suit of linen [by] the evening.

I have just had my hair dressed. You can't think how oddly my head feels; full of powder and black pins, and a great cushion on the top of it. I believe you would hardly know me, for my face looks quite different to what it did before my hair was dressed. When I shall be able to make use of a comb for myself I cannot tell; for my hair is so much entangled, *frizzled* they call it, that I fear it will be very difficult.

I am half afraid of this ball tonight; for, you know, I have never danced but at school; however, Miss Mirvan says there is nothing in it. Yet, I wish it was over.

Adieu, my dear Sir, pray excuse the wretched stuff I write; perhaps I may improve by being in this town, and then my letters will be less unworthy your reading. Meantime, I am,
Your dutiful and affectionate,
EVELINA

P. S. Poor Miss Mirvan cannot wear one of the caps she made, because they dress her hair too large for them.

LETTER XI
EVELINA TO THE REV. MR. VILLARS
*Tuesday, April 5*

We passed a most extraordinary evening. A *private* ball this was called, so I expected to have seen about four or five couples; but Lord! my dear sir, I believe I saw half the world! Two very large rooms were full of company; in one were cards for the elderly ladies, and in the other were the dancers. My mamma Mirvan, for she always calls me her child, said she would sit with Maria and me till we were provided with partners, and then join the card-players.

**Rich Women and Poor** *Lines between social classes were sharply drawn in London of the 1700s. Here, a wealthy Englishwoman and her daughters give money to a poor woman and her baby.* **Diversity** *How does clothing signal the difference between rich and poor in this painting?*

The gentlemen, as they passed and repassed, looked as if they thought we were quite at their disposal, and only waiting for the honor of their commands; and they sauntered about, in a careless indolent manner, as if with a view to keep us in suspense. I don't speak of this in regard to Miss Mirvan and myself only, but to the ladies in general; and I thought it so provoking, that I determined in my own mind that, far from honoring such airs, I would rather not dance at all, than with anyone who would seem to think me ready to accept the first partner who would condescend to take me.

Not long after, a young man, who for some time looked at us with a kind of negligent impertinence, advanced on tiptoe towards me; he had a set smile on his face, and his dress was so foppish, that I really believed he even wished to be stared at; and yet he was very ugly.

Bowing almost to the ground with a sort of swing, and waving his hand, with the greatest conceit, after a short and silly pause, he said, "Madam—may I presume?"—and stopped, offering to take my hand. I drew it back, but could scarce forbear laughing. "Allow me, Madam," he continued, affectedly breaking off every half moment, "the honor and happiness—if I am not so unhappy as to address you too late—to have the happiness and honor—"

Again he would have taken my hand; but, bowing my head, I begged to be excused, and turned to Miss Mirvan to conceal my laughter.

He then desired to know if I had already engaged myself to [dance with] some more fortunate man? I said No, and that I believed I should not dance at all. He would keep himself, he told me, disengaged, in hopes I should relent; and then, uttering some ridiculous speeches of sorrow and disappointment, though his face still wore the same invariable smile, he retreated.

Source: Fanny Burney, *Evelina, or The History of a Young Lady's Entrance Into the World* (New York: W.W. Norton & Company, 1965).

## Thinking About Literature

1. **Vocabulary** Use the dictionary to find the meanings of the following words: saunter, dispatch, indolent, provoke, condescend, foppish.
2. (a) What preparations does Evelina make for the ball? (b) Describe three things that she finds surprising or amusing.
3. What annoys Evelina about the behavior of the men at the ball?
4. *Critical Thinking* **Linking Past and Present** (a) Based on the excerpts, do you think that *Evelina* reflected the experiences of most middle-class young women of the 1700s? (b) Why would Burney's novel appeal to these young women? (c) Do similar stories appeal to young women today? Explain.

## CHAPTER REVIEW

### REVIEWING VOCABULARY

Select *five* vocabulary words from the chapter. Write each word on a separate slip of paper. Then, write the definition for each word on other slips of paper. Scramble the slips and exchange them with another student. Match the words with their definitions, and then check each other's results.

### REVIEWING FACTS

1. According to John Locke, what should happen if a government violates people's natural rights?
2. According to Adam Smith, how should wages and prices be regulated?
3. How did Enlightenment thinkers differ from medieval thinkers regarding a just society?
4. How did Eastern and Western Europe differ regarding serfdom?
5. What areas combined to form the United Kingdom of Great Britain?
6. What was the cabinet system?
7. How did taxation create tensions between the American colonies and the British government?
8. What idea from the Baron de Montesquieu was incorporated into the United States Constitution?

### REVIEWING CHAPTER THEMES

Review the "Focus On" questions at the start of this chapter. Then select *three* of those questions and answer them, using information from the chapter.

## SKILLS FOR SUCCESS    DISTINGUISHING FACTS FROM OPINIONS

When reading either primary or secondary sources, you must be able to distinguish facts from opinions. A **fact** is a statement that can be proved by reliable sources. An **opinion** is a judgment that reflects a person's beliefs or feelings. It may or may not be provable.

The passage at right is from a college textbook discussion of Frederick the Great of Prussia. Read the passage. Then, answer the following questions.

1. **Determine which statements are facts.**
   (a) List two statements about Frederick's economic policies that appear to be facts. (b) How could you prove that these are facts?

2. **Determine which statements are opinions.**
   (a) List two statements from the passage that are opinions. (b) How do you know that they are opinions?

3. **Determine how the writer uses facts to support his opinions.** What fact does the writer use to support his opinion that Frederick's policies as king produced "several economic absurdities"?

66Viewed as a general, diplomat, and the master mechanic of Prussian administration, Frederick the Great was efficient and successful, but he was scarcely enlightened. . . .

No physiocrat could have done more than Frederick to improve Prussian agriculture. From England he imported clover, crop rotation, and the iron plow, which turned up the soil more effectively than the old wooden share. . . .

Frederick, however, was hostile to the doctrine of laissez faire and cut imports to the bone to save money for the support of the army. His mercantilism . . . placed a staggering burden of taxation on his subjects and produced several economic absurdities. For instance, Frederick tried to make Prussia grow its own tobacco, for which the climate was not suited. . . .99

Source: Crane Brinton et al., *Modern Civilization* (Englewood Cliffs, NJ: Prentice Hall, 1967).

## CRITICAL THINKING

1. **Synthesizing Information** Write a sentence summarizing the major ideas of each of the following thinkers: (a) John Locke, (b) Baron de Montesquieu, (c) Voltaire, (d) Mary Wollstonecraft, (e) Adam Smith.

2. **Linking Past and Present** Today, we talk about human rights rather than natural rights. Describe a human rights issue that has recently been in the news.

3. **Predicting Consequences** What do you think would be the effects of Britain's repression of Catholics in Ireland?

4. **Analyzing Information** (a) What ideas about government do you think English settlers brought with them to the Americas in the 1600s and 1700s? (b) How might those ideas have contributed to the outbreak of the American Revolution?

## ANALYZING PRIMARY SOURCES

Use the quotation on page 55 to answer the following questions.

1. What three "unalienable rights" did the Declaration list?

2. According to the Declaration, what is the purpose of government?

3. What is the source of government power?

## FOR YOUR PORTFOLIO

**WRITING A DIARY ENTRY** Write a diary entry from the point of view of someone living in Western Europe or North America during the Age of Enlightenment. To begin, review the chapter and make a list of people, ideas, and events that you might comment on. Then choose a topic for your entry, such as the publication of an important book or an event you attended. Use outside resources to add to the information in the text. Then write your diary entry, including as many details as you can to make it "authentic." Finally, share your diary entry with the class. Explain why you chose the topic you did.

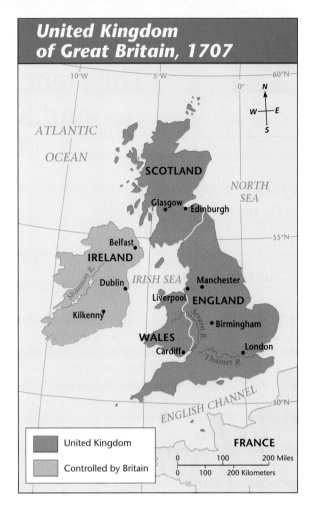

**United Kingdom of Great Britain, 1707**

## ANALYZING MAPS

Use the map to answer the following questions.

1. Which three areas made up the United Kingdom?

2. List one city in each of those three areas.

3. What was the relationship between Ireland and Britain?

**INTERNET ACTIVITY**

**WRITING A LETTER** Use the Internet to research one of the political thinkers described in the text. Then write a letter to him explaining why you think his ideas are or are not relevant in the present day.

# The French Revolution and Napoleon

## (1789–1815)

## CHAPTER OUTLINE

1 On the Eve of Revolution
2 Creating a New France
3 Radical Days
4 The Age of Napoleon Begins
5 The End of an Era

Rain pounded the Parisian suburb of Versailles on the morning of June 20, 1789. In the street, delegates to the National Assembly milled about outside their meeting hall. A notice on the door announced that King Louis XVI would speak to them on a future day. But why were the doors locked?

These middle-class men had been chosen as representatives to help the king solve France's financial crisis. But they had their own plans, too. They wanted sweeping reforms of a government sadly out of touch with its people. Already they had challenged the old order by insisting that nobles and clergy meet with them.

Perhaps that demand had pushed the king too far. Did the locked door mean that he was going to forbid them to meet altogether? The delegates stood in the rain, debating what to do next. One delegate suggested that they move their meeting to an indoor tennis court nearby.

They trooped off to the tennis court. Crowds of curious spectators pushed into the galleries. Jean-Joseph Mounier (moon YAY), a leading member of the Assembly, spoke up:

66Let us swear to God and our country never to separate and to meet wherever circumstances might require until we have established a sound and just constitution.99

As the delegates took the oath, the crowd in the gallery cheered. They sensed that they were witnessing a revolutionary moment.

The men who took the Tennis Court Oath were children of the Enlightenment who believed that the government could be rationally reformed. Like the delegates to the American Continental Congress in 1776, they pledged their lives to freeing their country from tyranny. They had no idea that they would help trigger an upheaval considerably more radical than the American Revolution. The French Revolution ultimately destroyed an absolute monarchy and disrupted a centuries-old social system.

Between 1789 and 1815, events in France upset the balance of power across all of Europe. Most historians see the French Revolution as a major turning point that helped usher in the modern era in European politics.

FOCUS ON these questions as you read:

- **Religions and Value Systems**
  What beliefs and attitudes inspired the leaders of the French Revolution?

- **Political and Social Systems**
  How did the French Revolution reshape social and political institutions?

- **Impact of the Individual**
  How did the rise of Napoleon Bonaparte create upheaval across Europe?

- **Continuity and Change**
  What were the temporary and lasting effects of the French Revolution?

## TIME AND PLACE

***Storming the Bastille*** For centuries, French kings jailed their enemies in the Bastille, an imposing fortress in Paris. Even the great philosopher Voltaire was once held there. Its heavy cannons, high towers, and thick walls symbolized the monarch's power. But on July 14, 1789, an angry mob seized the Bastille, shaking the monarchy to its roots. ***Political and Social Systems*** Compare this picture to the photograph on page 34. How do Versailles and the Bastille represent two sides of absolute monarchy?

## HUMANITIES LINK

***Art History*** Francisco Goya, *The Third of May, 1808* (page 84).
***Literature*** In this chapter, you will encounter passages from the following works of literature: William Wordsworth, *The Prelude* (pages 72 and 76); Edmund Burke, *Reflections on the Revolution in France* (page 72); Olympe de Gouges, *Declaration of the Rights of Woman* (page 77).

| 1789 French Revolution begins | 1793 Reign of Terror begins | 1799 Napoleon overthrows Directory | 1804 Napoleon becomes emperor | 1812 Napoleon invades Russia | 1815 Napoleon defeated at Waterloo |
|---|---|---|---|---|---|

| 1790 | 1795 | 1800 | 1805 | 1810 | 1815 |
|---|---|---|---|---|---|

# On the Eve of Revolution

## Guide for Reading

- What was the social structure of the old regime?

- Why did France face an economic crisis by 1789?

- Why did efforts at reform fail?

- **Vocabulary** *bourgeoisie, deficit spending*

On April 28, 1789, unrest exploded at the Réveillon (ray vay OHN) wallpaper factory in Paris. A rumor had spread that, though bread prices were soaring, the owner was planning to cut wages for his workers. Enraged workers then invaded the owner's home, leaving it in ruins.

Meanwhile, on the outskirts of the city, a group of nobles was enjoying an afternoon at the racetrack. Unaware of the trouble, they returned to Paris through the neighborhood of Réveillon's factory. An eyewitness told what happened as the aristocrats' carriages bumped through the streets:

> 66A troop of men stopped the people returning from the races . . . asking them whether they were for the nobles or the Third Estate [the common people] . . . insulting those it thought noble. They forced the women from their carriages and made them shout: 'Long live the Third Estate!'99

Though unpleasant, incidents like the Réveillon riots did not worry most aristocrats too much. Yes, France was facing a severe economic crisis. But a few financial reforms would certainly settle things. And rioters would get the hanging they deserved.

The nobles could not have been more wrong. The crisis went deeper than government finances. Reform would not be enough. By July, the hungry, unemployed, or poorly paid people of Paris had taken up arms. Their actions would push events further and faster than anyone could foresee.

## The Old Regime

In 1789, France, like the rest of Europe, still clung to an outdated social system that had emerged in the Middle Ages. Under this *ancien regime,* or old order, everyone in France belonged to one of three classes: the First Estate, made up of the clergy; the Second Estate, made up of the nobility; or the Third Estate, the vast majority of the population.

**The clergy.** In the Middle Ages, the Church had exerted great influence throughout Christian Europe. In 1789, the French clergy still enjoyed enormous wealth and privilege. They owned about 10 percent of the land, collected tithes, and paid no direct taxes to the state. High Church leaders such as bishops and abbots were usually nobles who lived very well. Parish priests, however, often came from humble origins and might be as poor as their peasant congregations.

The First Estate did provide social services. Nuns, monks, and priests ran schools, hospitals, and orphanages. But during the Enlightenment, philosophes targeted the Church for reform. They pointed to the idleness of some clergy, Church interference in politics, and its intolerance of dissent. In response, many clergy condemned the Enlightenment for undermining religion and moral order.

**Nobles.** The Second Estate was the titled nobility of French society. In the Middle Ages, noble knights had defended the land. In the 1600s, Richelieu and Louis XIV had crushed the nobles' military power but given them other rights—under strict royal control. Those rights included top jobs in government, the army, the courts, and the Church.

At Versailles, ambitious nobles vied for royal appointments, while idle courtiers enjoyed endless entertainments. Many nobles, however, lived far from the center of power. Though they owned land, they had little money income. As a result, they felt the pinch of trying to maintain their status in a period of rising prices.

Many nobles hated absolutism and resented the royal bureaucracy that employed middle-class men in positions once reserved for the aristocracy. They feared losing their traditional privileges, especially their freedom from paying taxes.

**The Third Estate.** In 1789, the Third Estate numbered about 27 million people, or 98 percent of the population. It was a diverse group. At the top sat the bourgeoisie (boor zhwah ZEE), or middle class. The bourgeoisie included the prosperous bankers, merchants, and manufacturers who propped up the French economy. It also included the officials who staffed the royal bureaucracy, as well as lawyers, doctors, journalists, professors, and skilled artisans.

The bulk of the Third Estate—9 out of 10 people in France—were rural peasants. Some were prosperous landowners who hired laborers to work for them. Others were tenant farmers or day laborers. Still others owed obligations to local nobles.

The poorest members of the Third Estate were city workers. They included apprentices, journeymen, and others who worked in industries such as printing or clothmaking. Many women and men earned a living as servants, stable hands, porters, construction workers, or street hawkers of everything from food to pots and pans. A large number were unemployed. To survive, some turned to begging or crime.

**Discontent.** From rich to poor, members of the Third Estate resented the privileges enjoyed by their social "betters." Wealthy bourgeois families could buy political office and even titles, but the best jobs were still reserved for nobles. Urban workers earned miserable wages. Even the smallest rise in the price of bread, their main food, might mean starvation.

Peasants were burdened by taxes on everything from land to soap to salt. Though technically free, many owed fees and services that dated to medieval times, such as the corvée (kohr VAY), unpaid labor to repair roads and bridges. Peasants were also incensed when nobles, hurt by rising prices, tried to reimpose old manor dues. Also, only nobles had the right to hunt game. Peasants were even forbidden to kill rabbits that ate their crops.

In towns and cities, Enlightenment ideas led people to question the ancien regime. Why, people demanded, should the first two estates have privileges at the expense of the majority? It did not meet the test of reason! Everywhere, the Third Estate called for the privileged classes to pay their share. In 1789, the Abbé Sieyès (syay

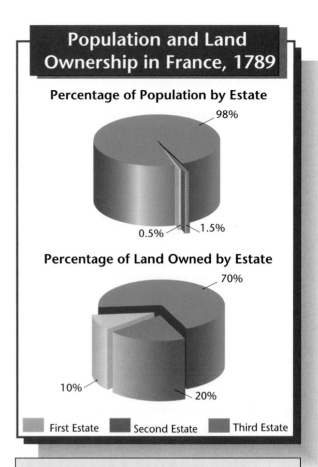

### Population and Land Ownership in France, 1789

**Percentage of Population by Estate**

98%

0.5%   1.5%

**Percentage of Land Owned by Estate**

70%

10%   20%

First Estate   Second Estate   Third Estate

*Interpreting a Graph* Inequalities among France's three estates were a leading cause of discontent. ■ Which estate included the fewest people? Which owned the most land? Based on these graphs, what reason did the Third Estate have to be discontented?

EHS), a member of the clergy, wrote a widely read pamphlet that asked:

66What is the Third Estate?
    EVERYTHING.
What has it been in the political order
    up to now? NOTHING.
What is it asking for? To become
    SOMETHING.99

### A Financial Crisis

Hand in hand with social unrest went a mushrooming financial crisis. The crisis was caused in part by years of deficit spending, that is, a government spending more money than it takes in. Louis XIV had left France deeply in debt. Wars like the Seven Years' War and the American Revolution strained the treasury even further. Costs generally had risen in the 1700s, and the lavish court soaked up millions. To bridge the gap between income and expenses, the government borrowed more and more money. By 1789, half its tax income went just to pay interest on this enormous debt.

To solve the financial crisis, the government would have to increase taxes, reduce expenses, or both. However, the nobles and clergy fiercely resisted any attempt to end their exemption from taxes.

**A crumbling economy.** Other economic woes added to the crisis. A general economic decline began in the 1770s. Then, in the late 1780s, bad harvests sent food prices soaring and brought hunger to poorer peasants and city dwellers.

Hard times and lack of food inflamed these people. In towns, people rioted, demanding bread. In the countryside, peasants began to attack the manor houses of the nobles. Arthur Young, an English visitor to France, witnessed the violence:

66 Everything conspires to render the present period in France critical: the [lack] of bread is terrible; accounts arrive every moment from the provinces of riots and disturbances, and calling in the military, to preserve the peace of the markets. 99

**Failure of reform.** The heirs of Louis XIV were not the right men to solve the crisis. Louis XV, who ruled from 1715 to 1774, pursued pleasure before serious business and ran up more debts. His grandson, Louis XVI, was well-meaning but weak and indecisive. He wisely chose Jacques Necker, a financial wizard, as an adviser. Necker urged the king to reduce court spending, reform government, and improve internal trade by abolishing tariffs that made trade costly. When Necker proposed taxing the First and Second estates, however, the nobles and high clergy forced the king to dismiss the would-be reformer.

As the crisis deepened, the pressure for reform mounted. Finally, the wealthy and powerful classes demanded that the king call the

*A Heavy Burden* In this cartoon, a priest and a nobleman stand on a stone that crushes a peasant. The words on the stone refer to taxes and other obligations that peasants traditionally owed to the government. *Political and Social Systems* What was the cartoonist saying about the relationship among France's three estates?

Estates General before making any changes. French kings had not summoned the Estates General for 175 years, fearing that nobles would try to recover the feudal powers that they had lost under absolute rule. To reform-minded nobles, the Estates General seemed to offer a chance to carry out changes like the Glorious Revolution in England. It would establish a constitution to bring the absolute monarch under the control of the nobles and guarantee their privileges.

## The King Takes Action

As 1788 closed, France tottered on the verge of bankruptcy. Bread riots were spreading, and nobles, fearful of taxes, were denouncing royal tyranny. A baffled Louis XVI finally summoned the Estates General to meet at Versailles in May 1789.

**The cahiers.** In preparation, Louis had all three estates prepare *cahiers* (kah YAY), or notebooks, listing their grievances. Many cahiers called for reforms such as fairer taxes, freedom of the press, or regular meetings of the Estates General. In one town, shoemakers denounced regulations that made leather so expensive they could not afford to make shoes. Some peasants demanded the right to kill animals that were destroying their crops. Servant girls in the city of Toulouse demanded the right to leave service when they wanted and that "after a girl has served her master for many years, she receive some reward for her service."

The cahiers testified to boiling class resentments. One called tax collectors "bloodsuckers of the nation who drink the tears of the unfortunate from goblets of gold." Another one of the cahiers condemned the courts of nobles as "vampires pumping the last drop of blood" from the people. Another complained that "20 million must live on half the wealth of France while the clergy . . . devour the other half."

**The Tennis Court Oath.** Delegates to the Estates General from the Third Estate were elected, though only propertied men could vote. Thus, they were mostly lawyers, middle-class officials, and writers. They were familiar

▲ Fan celebrating the Estates General

with the writings of Voltaire, Rousseau, and other philosophes and with the complaints in the cahiers. They went to Versailles, not only to solve the national financial crisis, but also to insist on reform.

From the beginning, the Estates General was deadlocked over the issue of voting. Traditionally, each estate had met separately and voted as a group. This system always allowed the First and Second estates to outvote the Third Estate two to one. The Third Estate wanted all three orders to meet together.

After weeks of stalemate, delegates of the Third Estate took a daring step. Saying that they represented the people of France, they transformed themselves into the National Assembly. They then invited members of the other estates to help them shape a constitution. A few days later, as you have read, the National Assembly found itself locked out of its meeting place. In fact, workers were just preparing the hall for a royal speech, but many delegates believed that the king intended to send them home. They then took the famous Tennis Court Oath, vowing not to disband until they had drawn up a constitution for France.

When some reform-minded clergy and nobles joined the National Assembly, Louis XVI grudgingly had to accept it. At the same time, royal troops gathered around Versailles and Paris. Rumor held that the king would dissolve the Assembly.

The crisis deepened in early July. The king, who had brought back Necker to help with the financial crisis, again dismissed the popular minister. Food shortages were also getting worse because of a disastrous 1788 harvest.

## Storming the Bastille

On July 14, Paris seized the spotlight from the National Assembly meeting in Versailles. The streets buzzed with rumors that royal troops were going to occupy the capital. More than 800 Parisians assembled outside the Bastille, a grim medieval fortress used as a prison for political and other prisoners. The crowd was demanding weapons and gunpowder believed to be stored there.

The commander of the Bastille refused to open the gates and opened fire on the crowd. In the battle that followed, many people were killed. Finally, the enraged mob broke through the defenses. They killed the commander and five guards and released a handful of prisoners, but found no weapons.

When told of the attack, Louis XVI asked, "Is it a revolt?" "No, sire," replied a noble, "It is a revolution." The storming of the Bastille quickly became a symbol of the French Revolution. Supporters saw it as a blow to tyranny, a step toward freedom. Today, the French still celebrate July 14 as Bastille Day, the French national holiday.

## SECTION 1 REVIEW

1. **Identify** (a) Jacques Necker, (b) cahiers, (c) National Assembly, (d) Bastille.
2. **Define** (a) bourgeoisie, (b) deficit spending.
3. (a) Describe the three estates of French society. (b) Why were members of each estate discontented with conditions in 1789?
4. What were the causes of the financial crisis that gripped France?
5. (a) Why did Louis XVI call the Estates General in 1789? (b) What were the results of this decision?
6. *Critical Thinking* **Applying Information** A French lawyer of the day wrote that Louis XVI "was too well intentioned not to try to remedy abuses that had shocked him, but he possessed neither the character nor the talents to control an impetuous nation in a situation that cried out for reform." (a) How does this description apply to the king's actions in 1789? (b) Do you think Louis XVI could have prevented the outbreak of revolution? Why or why not?
7. *ACTIVITY* Imagine that you belong to one of the following groups in 1789 France: nobles, high clergy, parish priests, the bourgeoisie, peasants, city workers. With two partners, write a cahier describing what you think is the chief problem facing the nation.

# 2 Creating a New France

## Guide for Reading

- How did popular uprisings contribute to the French Revolution?

- What political and social reforms emerged in the early stages of the revolution?

- How did people outside France respond to the revolution?

- **Vocabulary** *émigré, sans-culotte*

Excitement, wonder, and fear engulfed France as the revolution unfolded at home and spread abroad. Today, historians divide this revolutionary era into four phases. The moderate phase of the National Assembly (1789–1791) turned France into a constitutional monarchy. Then, a radical phase (1792–1794) of escalating violence led to a Reign of Terror. There followed a period of reaction against extremism, known as the Directory (1795–1799). Finally, the Age of Napoleon (1799–1815) consolidated many changes brought by the revolution. In this section, you will read about the moderate start of the French Revolution.

## Revolts in Paris and the Provinces

The political crisis of 1789 was punctuated by the worst famine in memory. Starving peasants roamed the countryside or flocked to the towns, where they swelled the ranks of the unemployed. As grain prices soared, even people with jobs had to spend up to 80 percent of their income on bread.

**The Great Fear.** In such desperate times, rumors ran wild, setting off what was later called the "Great Fear." Tales of marauders attacking villages and towns spread panic. Other rumors claimed that government troops were seizing peasant crops.

Inflamed by famine and fear, peasants unleashed their fury on nobles who were trying to reimpose medieval dues. Defiant peasants attacked the homes of nobles, burned old manor records, and stole grain from storehouses. The attacks died down after a time, but they demonstrated peasant anger with an unjust regime.

**Paris in arms.** Paris, too, was in turmoil. As the capital and chief city of France, it was the revolutionary center. Various factions competed for power. Moderates looked to the Marquis de Lafayette, the aristocratic "hero of two worlds" who had fought alongside George Washington in the American Revolution. Lafayette headed the National Guard, a largely middle-class militia organized in response to the arrival of royal troops in Paris. The Guard was the first group to don the tricolor, a red, white, and blue badge, which was eventually adopted as the national flag of France.

A more radical group, the Paris Commune, replaced the royalist government of the city. It could mobilize whole neighborhoods for protests or violent action to further the revolution. Newspapers and political clubs—many even more radical than the Commune—blossomed everywhere. Some demanded an end to monarchy and spread scandalous stories about the royal family and members of the court.

## Liberty, Equality, Fraternity

Peasant uprisings and the storming of the Bastille stampeded the National Assembly into action. On August 4, at a stormy all-night meeting, nobles in the National Assembly voted to end their privileges. They gave up their old manorial dues, their exclusive hunting rights, their special legal status, and their exemption from taxation.

**An end to special privilege.** "Feudalism is abolished," announced the weary delegates at 2 A.M. The president of the Assembly later wrote:

66 This has been a night for destruction and for public happiness. We may view this moment as the dawn of a new revolution, when all the burdens weighing on the people were abolished and France was truly reborn. 99

Were the votes on the night of August 4 voluntary? Contemporary observers and historians today note that the nobles gave up nothing that they had not already lost. In the months ahead, the National Assembly turned the reforms of

**Declaration of Rights** *The Marquis de Lafayette presented a first draft of the Declaration of the Rights of Man and the Citizen in July 1789. Lafayette had fought for American independence and was inspired by the ideals of the new United States. The final declaration, shown here, expresses the basic beliefs of the French Revolution in 17 articles.* **Religions and Value Systems** *How does this painting glorify the value of human rights?*

August 4 into law, meeting a key Enlightenment goal—the equality of all citizens before the law.

**Declaration of the Rights of Man.** In late August, as a first step toward writing a constitution, the Assembly issued the Declaration of the Rights of Man and the Citizen. The document was modeled in part on the American Declaration of Independence. All men, it announced, were "born and remain free and equal in rights." They enjoyed natural rights to "liberty, property, security, and resistance to oppression." Like Locke and the philosophes, it insisted that governments exist to protect the natural rights of citizens.

The Declaration further proclaimed that all male citizens were equal before the law. Each French man had an equal right to hold public office "with no distinction other than that of

*Sweet Dreams* Lavish tapestries and glittering chandeliers adorned the bedchamber of Queen Marie Antoinette at Versailles. Tales of her extravagance inflamed public anger against the queen. She even had a mock peasant village built on the ground of Versailles so that she and her ladies-in-waiting could play at being milkmaids. **Art and Literature** Compare this picture to the one on page 34. How are these two rooms similar in style?

their virtues and talents." In addition, the Declaration asserted freedom of religion and called for taxes to be levied according to ability to pay. Its principles were captured in the enduring slogan of the French Revolution, "Liberty, Equality, Fraternity."

Uncertain and hesitant, Louis XVI was slow to accept the reforms of the National Assembly. Parisians grew suspicious as more royal troops arrived. Nobles continued to enjoy gala banquets while people were starving. By autumn, anger again turned to action.

## Women March on Versailles

"Bread!" shouted the mob as it streamed down the road that led from Paris to Versailles.

"Bread!" In a driving rainstorm, they marched the entire 12 miles (19 km). They wanted to see the king and would not take no for an answer.

Angry mobs were not a new sight in France. What surprised many observers, however, was that this mob was made up of thousands of women. On October 5, they showed themselves as determined as the men who had stormed the Bastille three months earlier.

A group of rough-spoken market women burst into the palace at Versailles. A duchess later recalled the scene:

66The fishmonger women cried out that they wanted to speak to the king . . . and they could be calmed only by admitting a dozen of them to the presence of that unfortunate prince. His goodness disarmed them, and their opinions were so changed by the time they returned to their companions that they ran the risk of being the victims of their fury.99

**"We'll wring her neck!"** Much of the crowd's anger was directed at the queen, Marie Antoinette. She was the daughter of Maria Theresa, the Hapsburg empress of Austria. Ever since Marie Antoinette had married Louis, she had come under attack for being frivolous and extravagant. She eventually grew more serious and even advised the king to compromise with moderate reformers. Still, she remained a source of scandal. Enemies accused her of immorality. Early in the revolution, the radical press spread the story that she had answered the cries of hungry people for bread by saying "Let them eat cake." Though the story was untrue, it helped inflame public anger against Marie Antoinette.

"Death to the Austrian! We'll wring her neck!" shouted the women who stormed Versailles. "Tear out her heart, cut off her head, fry her liver and even then it won't be all over."

Lafayette and the National Guard eventually calmed the crowd. Still, the women would not leave Versailles until the king met their most important demand—to return with them to Paris. Not too happily, the king agreed.

**A triumphant procession.** The next morning, the crowd marched back to Paris, led by women perched on the barrels of seized cannon. They told bewildered spectators that they were bringing back to Paris "the baker, the baker's wife, and the baker's boy"—Louis XVI, Marie Antoinette, and their son. "Now we won't have to go so far/When we want to see our king," they sang. Crowds along the way cheered the king, who now wore the tricolor.

The royal family moved into the Tuileries (TWEE luh reez) palace. For the next three years, Louis was a virtual prisoner in his own capital.

The women of Paris would continue to take action during the revolution. Elisabeth Guenard, who sympathized with the royal cause, also understood what drove the women to Versailles. "You have to be a mother," she wrote, "and have heard your children ask for bread you cannot give them to know the level of despair to which this misfortune can bring you." ■

## A Time of Reform

The National Assembly soon followed the king to Paris. Its largely bourgeois members worked to draft a constitution and to solve the continuing financial crisis.

**Reorganizing the Church.** To pay off the huge government debt—much of it owed to the bourgeoisie—the Assembly voted to take over and sell Church lands. In an even more radical move, it put the French Catholic Church under state control. Under the Civil Constitution of the Clergy, issued in 1790, bishops and priests became elected, salaried officials. The Civil Constitution ended papal authority over the French Church and dissolved convents and monasteries.

Reaction was swift and angry. Many bishops and priests refused to accept the Civil Constitution. The pope condemned it. Large numbers of French peasants, who were basically conservative, also rejected the changes. When the government punished clergy who refused to

*To Versailles!* As famine gripped Paris, poor mothers did not have enough food for their children. On October 5, 1789, thousands of women decided to bring Louis XVI to Paris, where he could no longer ignore their suffering. **Continuity and Change** Based on this painting, in what ways do you think the march challenged traditional roles of women?

support the Civil Constitution, a huge gulf opened between revolutionaries in Paris and the peasantry in the provinces.

**A written constitution.** The National Assembly completed its main task by producing a constitution. The Constitution of 1791 set up a limited monarchy in place of the absolute monarchy that had ruled France for centuries. A new Legislative Assembly had the power to make laws, collect taxes, and decide on issues of war and peace. Lawmakers would be elected by tax-paying male citizens. Still, only about 50,000 men in a population of more than 27 million could qualify as candidates to run for the Assembly.

To make government more efficient, the constitution replaced the old provinces with 83 departments of roughly equal size. It abolished the old provincial courts and reformed laws. The middle-class framers of the constitution protected private property and supported free trade. They compensated nobles for land seized by the peasants, abolished guilds, and forbade city workers to organize labor unions.

To moderate reformers, the Constitution of 1791 seemed to complete the revolution. Reflecting Enlightenment goals, it ended Church interference in government and ensured equality before the law for all citizens. At the same time, it put power in the hands of men with the means and leisure to serve in government.

**The fateful flight.** Meanwhile, Marie Antoinette and others had been urging the king to escape their humiliating situation. In 1791, Louis finally gave in. One night in June, a large coach lumbered north from Paris toward the border. Inside sat the king disguised as a valet, the queen dressed as a governess, the royal children, and a loyal friend pretending to be their wealthy Russian employer.

When they stopped at a small town, a former soldier who had been stationed in Paris recognized Marie Antoinette. Louis's disguise was uncovered when someone held up the new revolutionary currency with the king's face on it.

The royal family was trundled back to Paris, to the insults of the crowds. The old shouts of "Long live the King!" were replaced by cries of "Long live the Nation!" To Parisians, the king's dash to the border showed he was a traitor to the revolution.

## Reaction Outside France

Events in France stirred debate all over Europe. Supporters of the Enlightenment applauded the reforms of the National Assembly. They saw the French experiment as the dawn of a new age for justice and equality. In his poem *The Prelude,* the English poet William Wordsworth later recalled how the start of the French Revolution stirred feelings of joy and hope:

66Bliss was it in that dawn to be alive,
   But to be young was very Heaven!99

**Widespread fears.** European rulers and nobles, however, denounced the French Revolution. They increased border patrols, fearing the spread of the "French plague." Fueling those fears were the horror stories that were told by émigrés (EHM ih grayz)—nobles, clergy, and others who had fled revolutionary France. Émigrés reported attacks on their privileges, property, religion, and even their lives. "Enlightened" rulers turned against French ideas. Catherine the Great of Russia burned Voltaire's letters and locked up her critics.

In Britain, Edmund Burke, who had defended the American Revolution, bitterly condemned revolutionaries in Paris. In *Reflections on the Revolution in France,* he predicted all too accurately that the revolution would become more violent:

66Plots and assassinations will be anticipated by preventive murder and preventive confiscation. . . . When ancient opinions and rules of life are taken away, the loss cannot possibly be estimated. From that moment we have no compass to govern us.99

**Threats from abroad.** Louis XVI's failed flight brought further hostile rumblings from abroad. In August 1791, the king of Prussia and the emperor of Austria—who was Marie Antoinette's brother—issued the Declaration of Pilnitz. In it, they threatened to intervene if necessary to protect the French monarchy.

The declaration may have been mostly bluff. But revolutionaries in France took the threat seriously and prepared for war. The revolution was about to enter a new, more radical phase.

## War at Home and Abroad

In October 1791, the newly elected Legislative Assembly took office. Faced with crises at home and abroad, it would survive for less than a year. Economic problems fed renewed turmoil. Assignats, the revolutionary currency, dropped in value, which caused prices to rise rapidly. Uncertainty about prices led to hoarding and additional food shortages.

**The sans-culottes.** In Paris and other cities, working-class men and women, called sans-culottes* (sanz kyoo LAHTZ), pushed the revolution into more radical action. By 1791, many sans-culottes demanded a republic. They also wanted the government to guarantee them a living wage.

The sans-culottes found support among radical leaders in the Legislative Assembly, especially the Jacobins. A revolutionary political club, the Jacobins were mostly middle-class lawyers or intellectuals. They used pamphleteers and sympathetic newspaper editors to advance the republican cause.

**From right to left.** Within the Legislative Assembly, hostile factions feuded for power. Members with similar views sat together in the meeting hall. On the right sat those who felt reform had gone far enough or even wanted to turn the clock back to 1788. In the center sat supporters of moderate reform. On the left sat the Jacobins and other republicans who wanted to abolish the monarchy and pushed for other radical changes. This seating arrangement led to the modern use of the terms *right*, *center*, and *left* to describe similar political positions.

**War on tyranny.** Groups on the left soon held the upper hand. In April 1792, the war of words between French revolutionaries and European monarchs moved onto the battlefield. Eager to spread the revolution and destroy tyranny abroad, the Legislative Assembly declared war first on Austria, then on Prussia, Britain, and other states. The great powers expected to win an easy victory against France, a land divided by revolution. In fact, the fighting that began in 1792 lasted on and off until 1815.

---

*Sans-culottes means "without culottes," the fancy knee-breeches worn by upper-class men. Shopkeepers, artisans, and other working-class men wore trousers, not culottes.

**Protecting the Revolution** "I guard the nation," says the inscription on this brass-and-ivory button, below. It showed the wearer's determination to defend the revolution from threats at home and abroad. Among the most ardent revolutionaries were the sans-culottes, like the young man at right. They would help push the revolution in a more radical and violent direction. **Political and Social Systems** How does this picture suggest that the sans-culottes were determined to protect the revolution?

*je garde la nation*

## SECTION 2 REVIEW

1. **Identify** (a) Great Fear, (b) Marquis de Lafayette, (c) tricolor, (d) Legislative Assembly, (e) Declaration of Pilnitz, (f) Jacobins.
2. **Define** (a) émigré, (b) sans-culotte.
3. What role did the people of Paris play in the French Revolution?
4. Describe two main ideas or reforms contained in each of the following: (a) the Declaration of the Rights of Man and the Citizen, (b) the Civil Constitution of the Clergy, (c) the Constitution of 1791.
5. (a) Why did some people outside France support the French Revolution? (b) Why did other people oppose it?
6. *Critical Thinking* **Comparing** Compare the women's march on Versailles to the storming of the Bastille in terms of goals and results.
7. *ACTIVITY* In a group of five or six students, write and perform a skit about *one* of the following events: the Great Fear; the night of August 4; the women's march on Versailles; the flight and capture of the royal family.

# 3 Radical Days

## Guide for Reading

- Why did the revolution become more radical?

- What was the Reign of Terror?

- How did the French Revolution change daily life?

- **Vocabulary** *suffrage, nationalism*

Someone who had left Paris in 1791 and returned in 1793 could have gotten lost. Almost 4,000 streets had new names. Louis XV Square was renamed the Square of the Revolution. King-of-Sicily Street, named for the brother of Louis XVI, had become the Rights of Man Street.

Renaming streets was one way that Jacobins tried to wipe out all traces of the old order. In 1793, the revolution entered a radical phase. For a year, France experienced one of the bloodiest regimes in its history as determined leaders sought to extend and preserve the revolution.

## *Downfall of the Monarchy*

War heightened tensions in Paris, especially as dismal news arrived from the front. Well-trained Prussian forces were cutting down raw French recruits. Royalist officers deserted the French army, joining émigrés and others seeking to restore the king to power.

**Outbreaks of violence.** Battle disasters inflamed revolutionaries who thought the king was in league with the invaders. A crowd of Parisians invaded the Tuileries on August 10, 1792, and slaughtered the king's guards. The royal family fled to the Legislative Assembly.

A month later, citizens attacked the prisons that were holding nobles and priests accused of political offenses. These prisoners were killed, along with many ordinary criminals. Historians have disagreed about the people who carried out the "September massacres." Some call them "bloodthirsty savages," while others argue that they were patriots defending France from its enemies. In fact, most were ordinary citizens fired to fury by real and imagined grievances.

**The French Republic.** Backed by Paris crowds, radicals took control of the Assembly. Radicals called for the election of a new legislative body, the National Convention. Suffrage, the right to vote, was to be extended to all male citizens, not just to property owners.

The Convention that met in September 1792 was a more radical body than earlier assemblies. It voted to abolish the monarchy and declare France a republic. Deputies then drew up a new constitution for France. The Jacobins, who controlled the Convention, set out to erase all traces of the old order. They seized lands of nobles and abolished titles of nobility. All French men and women were called "Citizen." Louis XVI became Citizen Capet, from the dynasty that ruled France in the Middle Ages.

**Death of a king and queen.** The Convention also put Louis XVI on trial as a traitor to France. The king was convicted by a single vote and sentenced to death. On a foggy morning in January 1793, Louis mounted a scaffold in a public square in Paris. He tried to speak, but his words were drowned out by a roll of drums. Moments later, the king was beheaded.

In October, Marie Antoinette was also executed. The popular press celebrated her death. "The Widow Capet," however, showed great dignity as she went to her death. Their son, the uncrowned Louis XVII, died of unknown causes in the dungeons of the revolution.

## *The Convention Under Siege*

By early 1793, danger threatened France on all sides. The country was at war with much of Europe, including Britain, the Netherlands, Spain, and Prussia. In the Vendée (vahn DAY) region of western France, royalists and priests led peasants in a rebellion against the government. In Paris, the sans-culottes demanded relief from food shortages and rising prices. The Convention itself was bitterly divided between Jacobins and a rival group, the Girondins.

ISSUES *For* TODAY

A complex blend of ideas and conditions led to the overthrow of the French monarchy. What circumstances can lead to revolution?

## Portraits in Wax

The custom of making wax sculptures of famous people dates to Roman times. Today, wax museums such as the legendary Madame Tussaud's in London or the Hollywood Wax Museum in Los Angeles remain popular tourist attractions.

**Linking Past and Present**  Why do you think wax museums have fascinated people for centuries?

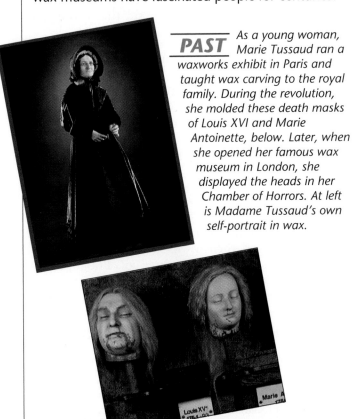

**PAST**  *As a young woman, Marie Tussaud ran a waxworks exhibit in Paris and taught wax carving to the royal family. During the revolution, she molded these death masks of Louis XVI and Marie Antoinette, below. Later, when she opened her famous wax museum in London, she displayed the heads in her Chamber of Horrors. At left is Madame Tussaud's own self-portrait in wax.*

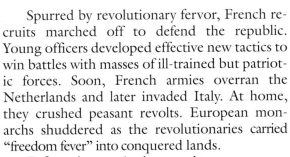

**PRESENT**

*Today, skilled artisans continue to produce lifelike wax sculptures of celebrities like Bill Cosby (above) and Arnold Schwarzenegger (right).*

**Committee of Public Safety.** To deal with the threats to France, the Convention created the Committee of Public Safety. The 12-member committee had almost absolute power as it battled to save the revolution. It prepared France for all-out war, ordering all citizens to join the war effort:

    66Young men shall go to battle. Married men shall forge arms and transport provisions. Women shall make tents and clothing and serve in hospitals. Children will make lint from old linen. And old men shall be brought to public places to arouse the courage of soldiers.99

Spurred by revolutionary fervor, French recruits marched off to defend the republic. Young officers developed effective new tactics to win battles with masses of ill-trained but patriotic forces. Soon, French armies overran the Netherlands and later invaded Italy. At home, they crushed peasant revolts. European monarchs shuddered as the revolutionaries carried "freedom fever" into conquered lands.

**Robespierre.** At home, the government battled counterrevolutionaries under the guiding hand of Maximilien Robespierre (ROHBZ pyair). Robespierre, a shrewd lawyer and politician, quickly rose to the leadership of the Committee of Public Safety. Among Jacobins, his selfless dedication to the revolution earned him the nickname "the incorruptible." Enemies called him a tyrant.

Robespierre had embraced Rousseau's idea of the general will. He promoted religious toleration and sought to abolish slavery. Though cold and humorless, he was popular with the sans-culottes, who hated the old regime as much as he. He believed that France could achieve a "republic of virtue" only through the use of terror. "Liberty cannot be secured," he cried, "unless criminals lose their heads."

**Reign of Terror.** Robespierre was a chief architect of the Reign of Terror, which lasted from about July 1793 to July 1794. Revolutionary courts conducted hasty trials. Spectators greeted death sentences with cries of "Hail the Republic!" or "Perish the traitors!"

Perhaps 40,000 people died during the Terror. About 15 percent were nobles and clergy. Another 15 percent were middle-class citizens, often moderates who had supported the revolution in 1789. The rest were peasants and sans-culottes involved in riots or revolts against the Republic. Many were executed, including victims of mistaken identity or false accusations by their neighbors. Many more were packed into hideous prisons, where deaths were common.

The engine of the Terror was the guillotine. Its fast-falling blade extinguished life instantly. A member of the legislature, Dr. Joseph Guillotin (GEE oh tan), had introduced it as a more humane method of beheading than the uncertain ax. But the guillotine quickly became a symbol of horror. William Wordsworth, who had welcomed the start of the revolution, turned in revulsion from the Terror:

> **❝**The Mother from the Cradle of her Babe,
> The Warrior from the Field, all perished, all,
> Friends, enemies, of all parties, ages, ranks,
> Head after head, and never heads enough
> For those that bade them fall.**❞**

Within a year, though, the Reign of Terror consumed its own. Weary of bloodshed and fearing for their own lives, the Convention turned on the Committee of Public Safety. Once the heads of Robespierre and other radicals fell, executions slowed down dramatically.

## Reaction and the Directory

In reaction to the Terror, the revolution entered a third stage. Moving away from the excesses of the Convention, moderates produced another constitution, the third since 1789. The Constitution of 1795 set up a five-man Directory

*The Guillotine  Early versions of the guillotine had been used for centuries. In the 1790s, though, it became a symbol of the Reign of Terror. Some people considered the guillotine humane because it worked swiftly and surely. Others were horrified because it made executions routine and simple, like a present-day assembly line.* **Economics and Technology** *What newer methods of capital punishment have been invented since the 1700s?*

and a two-house legislature elected by male citizens of property.

The Directory held power from 1795 to 1799. Weak but dictatorial, it faced growing discontent. Leaders lined their own pockets but failed to solve pressing problems. When rising bread prices stirred hungry sans-culottes to riot, the Directory quickly suppressed them.

As chaos threatened, politicians turned to a popular military hero, Napoleon Bonaparte. They planned to use him to advance their own goals—a bad miscalculation! Before long, Napoleon would outwit them all to become ruler of France.

## Women in the Revolution

As you have seen, women of all classes participated in the revolution from the very beginning. Working-class women demonstrated and fought in street battles. In Paris and elsewhere, women formed their own political clubs. A few, like Jeanne Roland, were noted leaders. Roland supported the revolution through her writings, her salon, and her influence on her husband, a government minister.

**Rights for women.** Many women were disappointed when the Declaration of the Rights of Man did not grant equal citizenship to women. Olympe de Gouges (oh LAMP duh GOOZH), a journalist, demanded equal rights in her *Declaration of the Rights of Woman*:

&& Woman is born free and her rights are the same as those of man. . . . All citizens, be they men or women, being equal in the state's eyes, must be equally eligible for all public offices, positions, and jobs. . . . [Women] have the right to go to the scaffold; they must also have the right to go to parliament. &&

Women did gain some rights. The government made divorce easier, a move aimed at weakening Church authority. It allowed women to inherit property, to undermine the tradition of nobles leaving large estates to their oldest sons. These reforms, like others, did not last long after Napoleon gained power.

**Setbacks.** As the revolution progressed, women's right to express their views in public came under fire. In 1793, a committee of the National Convention declared that women did not have "the moral and physical strength necessary to practice political rights." Women's revolutionary clubs were banned.

Among the many women who became victims of the Terror were republicans like Gouges and moderates like Roland. As she mounted the steps to the guillotine, Roland cried, "O liberty, what crimes are committed in your name!"

## Changes in Daily Life

By 1799, the 10-year-old French Revolution had dramatically changed France. It had dislodged the old social order, overthrown the monarchy, and brought the Church under state control.

New symbols such as the red "liberty caps" and the tricolor confirmed the liberty and equality of all male citizens. Elaborate fashions and powdered wigs gave way to the practical clothes and simple haircuts of the sans-culottes. To show their revolutionary spirit, enthusiastic parents gave their children names like Constitution, Republic, or August Tenth.

**Nationalism.** Revolution and war gave people a strong sense of national identity. In earlier times, people had felt loyalty to local authorities. As monarchs centralized power, loyalty shifted to the king or queen. Now, the government rallied sons and daughters of the revolution to defend the nation itself. Nationalism, an aggressive feeling of pride in and devotion to one's country, spread throughout France.

By 1793, France was a nation in arms. From the port city of Marseilles (mahr SAY), troops marched to a rousing new song:

&& Come, children of the fatherland,
The glorious day has arrived.
Against us the bloody banner
Of tyranny is raised.
To arms, citizens!
Join the battalions.
Let us march, let us march! &&

"La Marseillaise" (mahr say EHZ) would later become the French national anthem.

**Social reform.** Revolutionaries pushed for social reform, such as compulsory elementary education. The Convention set up state schools to replace religious ones and organized systems to help the poor or care for old soldiers and war widows. The government also abolished slavery in French West Indian colonies and extended religious toleration.

The Convention tried to de-Christianize France. It created a secular calendar with 1793 as the Year I of the new era of freedom. It banned many religious festivals, replacing them with secular celebrations. Huge public ceremonies boosted support for republican and nationalist ideals.

**The arts.** French arts moved toward a grand classical style that echoed the grandeur of ancient Rome. The leading artist of the period was Jacques Louis David (dah VEED). David immortalized such stirring events as the Tennis Court Oath and, later, the reign of Napoleon. (See the painting on page 79.) David's paintings helped shape the way future generations pictured the French Revolution.

## SECTION 3 REVIEW

1. **Identify** (a) Committee of Public Safety, (b) Maximilien Robespierre, (c) Directory, (d) Olympe de Gouges, (e) "La Marseillaise," (f) Jacques Louis David.
2. **Define** (a) suffrage, (b) nationalism.
3. (a) Why did revolutionaries fear that the revolution was in danger? (b) What was their response to that danger?
4. What were three results of the Reign of Terror?
5. Describe one effect of the French Revolution on each of the following: (a) daily life, (b) the arts, (c) the rights of women.
6. *Critical Thinking* **Defending a Position** Robespierre wrote, "Terror without virtue is fatal. Virtue without terror is powerless. Terror is nothing but prompt, severe, and unbending justice." Do you agree that the Reign of Terror was necessary to defend the republic? Why or why not?
7. *ACTIVITY* Create a poster that might have been used to support or oppose *one* of the following: the goals of the Jacobins; the execution of Louis XVI or Marie Antoinette; the policies of the Committee of Public Safety; French nationalism; equal rights for women.

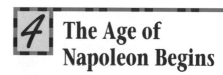

# 4 The Age of Napoleon Begins

## Guide for Reading

- How did Napoleon gain power?
- What role did Napoleon play in furthering the French Revolution?
- How did Napoleon build and defend his empire?
- **Vocabulary** *plebiscite, annex, blockade*

66 He was like an expert chess player, with the human race for an opponent, which he proposed to checkmate. 99

Thus did Madame Germaine de Staël (STAHL), a celebrated writer and intellectual, describe Napoleon Bonaparte. Napoleon himself expressed a humbler view of his rise to power. "Nothing has been simpler than my elevation," he once observed. "It is owing to the peculiarities of the time."

From 1799 to 1815, Napoleon would dominate France and Europe. A hero to some, an evil force to others, he gave his name to the final phase of the revolution—the age of Napoleon.

## *The Man From Corsica*

Napoleon Buonaparte (as he once spelled his name) was born on the French-ruled island of Corsica in the Mediterranean. His family were minor nobles, but had little money. At age nine, he was sent to France to be trained for a military career. When the revolution broke out, he was an ambitious 20-year-old lieutenant, eager to make a name for himself.

Napoleon favored the Jacobins and republican rule. However, he found the conflicting ideas and clashing personalities of the revolution confusing. He wrote his brother in 1793:

66 Since one must take sides, one might as well choose the side that is victorious, the side which devastates, loots, and burns. Considering the alternative, it is better to eat than be eaten. 99

*Napoleon Crossing the Alps* This portrait by Jacques Louis David glorifies Napoleon as a military hero. His fame as a general helped Napoleon become emperor. When a government is weak, he commented, the people look for a genius to save the country. Once they find him, "a great people, thronging around him, seems exultingly to proclaim, 'This is the man.'" **Impact of the Individual** Why do you think other French soldiers are barely visible in this painting?

**Early successes.** During the turmoil of the revolution, he rose quickly in the army. In December 1793, he drove British forces out of the French port of Toulon (too LOHN). He then went on to win several dazzling victories against the Austrians, capturing most of northern Italy and forcing the Hapsburg emperor to make peace. Hoping to disrupt British trade with India, he led a colorful expedition to Egypt in 1798. The Egyptian campaign proved disastrous, but Napoleon managed to hide stories of the worst losses from his admirers in France.

Success fed his ambition. By 1799, he moved from victorious general to political leader. That year, he helped overthrow the weak Directory and set up a three-man governing board, the Consulate. Another constitution was drawn up, but Napoleon soon took the title First Consul. In 1802, he had himself named consul for life.

GLOBAL CONNECTIONS

The Egyptian campaign was a military failure but a cultural success. Napoleon sent a commission of scientists, artists, and other scholars to collect extensive information on Egypt. Their work introduced Egyptian culture to Europe and launched a craze for Egyptian styles. More important, French troops discovered the Rosetta Stone. As you read, French scholar Jean Champollion was eventually able to use the Rosetta Stone to decipher ancient Egyptian hieroglyphics.

**A self-made emperor.** Two years later, Napoleon had accumulated enough power into his hands to take the title Emperor of the French. He invited the pope to preside over his coronation at Notre Dame cathedral in Paris. During the ceremony, however, Napoleon took the crown from the pope's hands and placed it on his own head. By this action, Napoleon meant to show that he owed his throne to no one but himself.

Yet at each step on his rise to power, Napoleon had held a plebiscite (PLEHB ih sīt), or ballot in which voters say yes or no to an issue. Each time, the French strongly supported him. To understand why, we must look at his policies.

## France Under Napoleon

During the consulate and empire, Napoleon consolidated power, strengthening the central government. Order, security, and efficiency replaced liberty, equality, and fraternity as the slogans of the new regime.

# CAUSE AND EFFECT

## Long-Term Causes

Corrupt, inconsistent, and insensitive leadership
Prosperous members of Third Estate resent privileges of First and Second estates
Spread of Enlightenment ideas

## Immediate Causes

Huge government debt
Poor harvests and rising price of bread
Failure of Louis XVI to accept financial reforms
Formation of National Assembly
Storming of Bastille

## THE FRENCH REVOLUTION

## Immediate Effects

France adopts its first written constitution
French feudalism ends
Declaration of the Rights of Man and the Citizen adopted
Monarchy abolished
Revolutionary France fights coalition of European powers
Reign of Terror

## Long-Term Effects

Napoleon gains power
Napoleonic Code established
French conquests spark nationalism
French public schools set up

## Connections Today

French people remain proud of Napoleon's glory days
French law reflects Napoleonic Code
Metric system, set up after revolution, in use worldwide
After centuries of power, French political and military influence declines in Europe

*Interpreting a Chart* Once it began, the French Revolution moved swiftly. Its long-term causes, however, had been building up for decades. ■ Why is the rise of Napoleon considered a long-term effect rather than an immediate effect?

**Reforms.** To restore prosperity, Napoleon modernized finance. He regulated the economy to control prices, encourage new industry, and build roads and canals. To ensure well-trained officials and military officers, he promoted a system of public schools under strict government control.

At the same time, Napoleon backed off from some social reforms of the revolution. He made peace with the Catholic Church in the Concordat of 1801. The Concordat kept the Church under state control but recognized religious freedom for Catholics. Revolutionaries who opposed the Church denounced the agreement, but Catholics welcomed it.

Napoleon won support across class lines. He encouraged émigrés to return, provided they took an oath of loyalty. Peasants were relieved when he recognized their right to lands they had bought from Church and nobles during the revolution. The middle class, who had benefited most from the revolution, approved Napoleon's economic reforms and the restoration of order after years of chaos. Napoleon also made all "careers open to talent," a popular policy among those who remembered the old aristocratic monopoly of power. Napoleon's chief opposition came from royalists on the right and republicans on the left.

**Napoleonic Code.** Among Napoleon's most lasting reforms was a new law code, popularly called the Napoleonic Code. It embodied Enlightenment principles such as the equality of all citizens before the law, religious toleration, and advancement based on merit.

But the Napoleonic Code undid some reforms of the French Revolution. Women, for example, lost most of their newly gained rights under the new code. The law considered women minors who could not exercise the rights of citizenship. Male heads of households regained complete authority over their wives and children. Again, Napoleon valued order and authority over individual rights.

## Subduing an Empire

From 1804 to 1814, Napoleon furthered his reputation on the battlefield. He successfully faced down the combined forces of the greatest European powers. Year after year, he marshaled the military might of France to field enormous armies. He took great risks and even suffered huge losses. "I grew up on the field of battle," he once said, "and a man such as I am cares little for the life of a million men." By 1810, his Grand Empire reached its greatest extent. "We are babes in the hands of a giant," sighed Czar Alexander I of Russia.

As a military leader, Napoleon valued rapid movements and made effective use of his large armies. He developed a new plan for each battle, so opposing generals could never anticipate what he would do next. His enemies paid tribute to his leadership. Napoleon's presence on the battlefield, said one, was "worth 40,000 troops." The map on the right highlights Napoleon's most celebrated strategic victory, the Battle of Austerlitz.

**The Grand Empire.** Napoleon redrew the map of Europe. He annexed, or added outright, some areas to France, including the Netherlands and Belgium as well as parts of Italy and Germany. He abolished the tottering Holy Roman Empire and created a 38-member Confederation of the Rhine under French protection. He cut Prussian territory in half, turning part of old Poland into the Grand Duchy of Warsaw. And he forced alliances on European powers from Madrid to Moscow. At various times, the rulers of Austria, Prussia, and Russia reluctantly signed treaties with the "Corsican upstart," as his enemies called him. (See the map on page 83.)

Napoleon put friends and family members on the thrones of Europe. He unseated the king of Spain and placed his own brother, Joseph Bonaparte, on the throne. Napoleon also divorced his wife, Josephine, to marry a Hapsburg princess, the niece of Marie Antoinette. He and his heirs could then claim kinship with the ancient ruling families of Europe.

**France versus Britain.** Britain alone remained outside Napoleon's European empire. With only a small army, Britain relied on its sea power to stop Napoleon's drive to rule the continent. In 1805, Napoleon prepared to invade England. But at the Battle of Trafalgar, fought off the southwest coast of Spain, British admiral Horatio Nelson smashed a French fleet. During the battle, Nelson was fatally shot by a French sniper but lived long enough to learn of the

## Battle of Austerlitz, 1805

1. French fake retreat to lure Russian-Austrian forces off Pratzen Heights.
2. Russian-Austrian forces chase French.
3. French take Pratzen Heights.
4. Russian-Austrian forces attack, but are repulsed.
5. More French troops join in to defeat Russian-Austrian forces.

### GEOGRAPHY AND HISTORY

In December 1805, Napoleon's forces fought a combined Russian-Austrian army at the Battle of Austerlitz. Thanks to Napoleon's superior leadership, his outnumbered troops won an outstanding victory.

1. **Location** On the map, locate (a) Austerlitz, (b) Pratzen Heights, (c) Satschan Sea, (d) Napoleon's headquarters.
2. **Movement** How were Napoleon's troops able to defeat the Russian-Austrian forces south of Pratzen Heights?
3. *Critical Thinking* **Making Generalizations** Why is control of the high ground important in a battle?

British victory. His last words were, "Thank God, I have done my duty."

With an invasion ruled out, Napoleon tried to strike at Britain's lifeblood, its commerce. He waged economic warfare through the Continental System, which closed European ports to British goods. Britain responded with its own blockade of European ports. A blockade involves shutting off ports to keep people or supplies from moving in or out. During their long struggle, both Britain and France seized neutral ships suspected of trading with the other side. British attacks on American ships sparked anger in the United States and eventually triggered the War of 1812.

**Successes and failures.** In the end, Napoleon's Continental System failed to bring Britain to its knees. Although British exports declined, its powerful navy kept open vital trade routes to the Americas and India. Meanwhile, restrictions on trade hurt Europe, created a scarcity of goods, and sent prices soaring. Resentful European merchants ignored Napoleon's ban on British goods and engaged in widespread smuggling.

Still, for years the French celebrated unforgettable successes. Napoleon's triumphs boosted French nationalism. Great victory parades filled the streets of Paris with cheering crowds. To this day the glory and grandeur of the age of Napoleon are a source of pride to many French citizens.

## SECTION 4 REVIEW

1. **Identify** (a) Consulate, (b) Concordat of 1801, (c) Napoleonic Code, (d) Battle of Trafalgar, (e) Confederation of the Rhine, (f) Continental System.
2. **Define** (a) plebiscite, (b) annex, (c) blockade.
3. (a) Describe Napoleon Bonaparte's rise to power. (b) Why did many French support him?
4. How did Napoleon's policies both extend and turn back the reforms of the French Revolution? Give examples.
5. (a) How did Napoleon come to dominate most of Europe? (b) Why did his efforts to subdue Britain fail?
6. *Critical Thinking* **Drawing Conclusions** Why do you think both royalists and republicans opposed Napoleon?
7. *ACTIVITY* Draw a political cartoon commenting on the rivalry between Britain and Napoleonic France, from either a British or French point of view.

# The End of an Era

## Guide for Reading

- What events led to Napoleon's downfall?
- What principles guided leaders at the Congress of Vienna?
- How did the Congress of Vienna seek to impose a new order on Europe?
- **Vocabulary** *guerrilla warfare, abdicate, legitimacy*

Napoleon watched the battle for the Russian city of Smolensk from a chair outside his tent. As fires lit up the walled city, he exclaimed;

"It's like Vesuvius erupting. Don't you think this is a beautiful sight?"

"Horrible, Sire," replied an aide.

"Bah!" snorted Napoleon. "Remember, gentlemen, what a Roman emperor said: 'The corpse of an enemy always smells sweet.'"

In 1812, Napoleon pursued his dream of empire by invading Russia. The campaign began a chain of events that eventually led to his downfall. Napoleon's final defeat brought an end to the era of the French Revolution.

## Challenges to Napoleon's Empire

Under Napoleon, French armies spread the ideas of the revolution across Europe. They backed liberal reforms in the lands they conquered. In some places, they helped install revolutionary governments that abolished titles of nobility, ended Church privileges, opened careers to men of talent, and ended serfdom and manorial dues. The Napoleonic Code, too, was carried across Europe. French occupation sometimes brought economic benefits as well, by reducing trade barriers and stimulating industry.

Yet Napoleon's successes contained the seeds of defeat. While nationalism spurred French armies to success, it worked against them, too. Many Europeans who welcomed the ideas of the French Revolution nevertheless saw Napoleon's armies as foreign oppressors. They

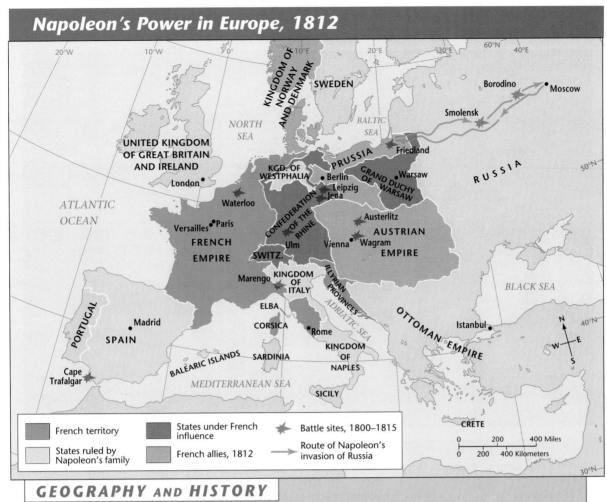

French territory

States ruled by Napoleon's family

States under French influence

French allies, 1812

Battle sites, 1800–1815

Route of Napoleon's invasion of Russia

## GEOGRAPHY AND HISTORY

By 1812, Napoleon had won battles throughout Europe. His victories, though, also sowed the seeds of his final defeat.

1. **Location** On the map, locate (a) Spain, (b) Moscow, (c) Confederation of the Rhine, (d) Cape Trafalgar.

2. **Interaction** What problems might geography create in Napoleon's effort to conquer Russia?

3. **Critical Thinking** **Synthesizing Information** Why was it important for France to build a strong navy at the time of Napoleon?

---

resented the Continental System and Napoleon's effort to impose French culture.

From Rome to Madrid to the Netherlands, nationalism unleashed revolts against France. In the German states, leaders encouraged national loyalty among German-speaking people to counter French influence.

**Resistance in Spain.** Resistance to foreign rule bled French occupying forces in Spain. In 1808, Napoleon replaced the king of Spain with his own brother, Joseph Bonaparte. He also introduced liberal reforms that sought to undermine the Spanish Catholic Church. But many Spaniards remained loyal to their former king and devoted to the Church. When they resisted the invaders, well-armed French forces responded with brutal repression. Far from crushing resistance, the French reaction further inflamed Spanish nationalism.

Spanish patriots conducted a campaign of guerrilla warfare, or hit-and-run raids, against the French. (In Spanish, *guerrilla* means "little war.") Small bands ambushed French supply trains or troops before melting into the countryside. These attacks kept large numbers of French soldiers tied down in Spain, when

**The Third of May, 1808** *This painting by the Spanish artist Francisco Goya shows the execution of Spaniards by Napoleon's troops. The man about to be shot throws out his arms, a martyr for the cause of liberty. The faceless French soldiers embody the inhumanity of war. Artists like Goya shifted away from the heroic, classical style of Jacques Louis David toward more emotional scenes.* **Art and Literature** *Why do you think Goya painted the scene as taking place at night? What effect does the lantern create?*

Napoleon needed them elsewhere. Eventually, the British sent an army under Arthur Wellesley, later the Duke of Wellington, to help the Spanish fight France.

**Defeat in Russia.** Despite revolts in Spain and elsewhere, Napoleon continued to seek new conquests. In 1812, Alexander I of Russia resigned from the Continental System. Napoleon responded by assembling his Grand Army. About 600,000 soldiers from France and other countries invaded Russia.

To avoid battles with Napoleon, the Russians retreated eastward, burning crops and villages as they went. This "scorched earth" policy left the French hungry and cold as winter came. Napoleon entered Moscow in September. He realized, though, that he could not feed and supply his army through the long Russian winter. In October, he turned homeward.

The 1,000-mile retreat from Moscow turned into a desperate battle for survival. The French general Michel Ney described the grim scene:

66The army marches covered in great snowflakes. The stragglers fall to the lances of the Cossacks. As for me, I cover the retreat. Behind files the army with broken ranks. It is a mob without purpose, famished, feverish. . . . General Famine and General Winter, rather than the Russian bullets, have conquered the Grand Army.99

Only about 100,000 soldiers of the once-proud Grand Army survived. Many died. Others deserted. Napoleon himself rushed back to Paris to raise a new force to defend France. His reputation for success, however, was shattered.

## Downfall of Napoleon

The disaster in Russia brought a new alliance of Russia, Britain, Austria, and Prussia against a weakened France. In 1813, they defeated Napoleon in the Battle of the Nations at Leipzig. The next year, as his enemies closed in on France, Napoleon abdicated, or stepped down from power. The victors exiled him to Elba, an island in the Mediterranean. They then recognized Louis XVIII, brother of Louis XVI, as king of France.

**Napoleon returns.** The restoration of Louis XVIII did not go smoothly. The Bourbon king agreed to accept the Napoleonic Code and honor the land settlements made during the revolution. However, many émigrés rushed back to France bent on revenge. An economic depression and the fear of a return to the old regime helped rekindle loyalty to Napoleon.

As the victorious allies gathered for a general peace conference in Vienna, Napoleon escaped his island exile and returned to France. Soldiers flocked to his banner. As citizens cheered Napoleon's advance, Louis XVIII fled. In March 1815, the emperor of the French entered Paris in triumph.

**Waterloo.** Napoleon's triumph was short-lived. His star soared for only 100 days, while the allies reassembled their forces. On June 18, 1815, the opposing armies met near the town of Waterloo in Belgium. British forces under the Duke of Wellington and a Prussian army commanded by General Blücher crushed the French in an agonizing day-long battle. Once again, Napoleon was forced to abdicate and go into exile on St. Helena, a lonely island in the South Atlantic. This time, he would never return.

**Legacy of Napoleon.** Napoleon died in 1821, but his legend lived on in France and around the world. His contemporaries as well as historians have long debated his legacy. Was he "the revolution on horseback," as he claimed? Or was he a traitor to the revolution?

No one, though, questions Napoleon's impact on France and on Europe. The Napoleonic Code consolidated many changes of the revolution. The France of Napoleon was a centralized state with a constitution. Elections were held with expanded, though limited, suffrage. Many more citizens had rights to property and access

*Retreat From Moscow* This British cartoon depicts Napoleon's retreat from Moscow. Hundreds of thousands of French soldiers died during their long trek across Russia's frozen landscape. **Global Interaction** Why do you think this cartoonist made light of the suffering of Napoleon's army?

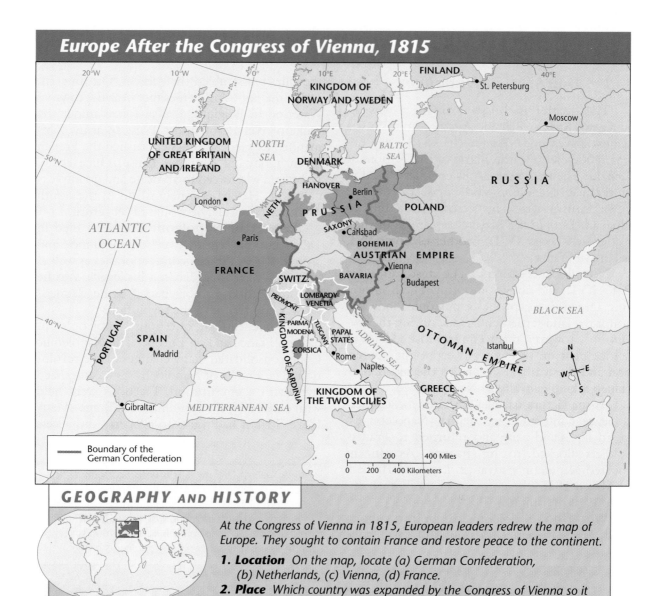

## Europe After the Congress of Vienna, 1815

Boundary of the
German Confederation

### GEOGRAPHY AND HISTORY

At the Congress of Vienna in 1815, European leaders redrew the map of
Europe. They sought to contain France and restore peace to the continent.

**1. Location** On the map, locate (a) German Confederation,
(b) Netherlands, (c) Vienna, (d) France.
**2. Place** Which country was expanded by the Congress of Vienna so it
could contain French ambitions to the north?
**3. Critical Thinking** **Comparing** Study the map on page 83. What new countries appeared after
the Congress of Vienna?

to education than under the old regime. Still,
French citizens lost many rights promised so fer-
vently by republicans during the Convention.

On the world stage, Napoleon's conquests
spread the ideas of the revolution. He failed to
make Europe into a French empire. Instead, he
sparked nationalist feeling across Europe. The
abolition of the Holy Roman Empire would
eventually help in creating a new Germany.
Napoleon also had a dramatic impact across the
Atlantic. In 1803, his decision to sell France's
vast Louisiana Territory to the American government doubled the size of the United States
and ushered in an age of American expansion.

## The Congress of Vienna

After Waterloo, diplomats and heads of state
again sat down at the Congress of Vienna. They
faced the monumental task of restoring stability
and order in Europe after 25 years of war.

**Glittering spectacle.** The Congress met
for 10 months, from September 1814 to June
1815. It was a brilliant gathering of European
leaders. Diplomats, courtiers, and royalty dined
and danced, attended concerts and ballets, and
enjoyed hunting parties and picnics arranged
by their host, Emperor Francis I of Austria. Beneath the glittering spectacle, paid spies slipped

in and out of rented palaces, anxious to find out who was saying what to whom.

**Serious work.** While the entertainment kept thousands of smaller players busy, the real work fell to Prince Clemens von Metternich of Austria, Czar Alexander I of Russia, and Lord Robert Castlereagh (KAS uhl ray) of Britain. Defeated France was also invited to send a representative to Vienna, Prince Maurice Talleyrand.

The chief goal of the Vienna decision makers was to create a lasting peace by establishing a balance of power and protecting the system of monarchy. Each of the leaders also pursued his own goals. Metternich, the dominant figure at the Congress, wanted to restore the *status quo* (Latin for "the way things are") of 1792. Alexander I urged a "holy alliance" of Christian monarchs to suppress future revolutions. Lord Castlereagh was determined to prevent a revival of French military power. The aged diplomat Talleyrand shrewdly played the other leaders against one another to get defeated France accepted as an equal partner.

## The Vienna Settlement

Despite clashes and controversies, the diplomats at Vienna finally worked out a framework for peace. Their decisions set the stage for European politics for the next 100 years.

**Balance of power.** The peacemakers redrew the map of Europe. (See the map on page 86.) To contain French ambitions, they ringed France with strong countries. In the north, they added Belgium and Luxembourg to Holland to create the kingdom of the Netherlands. To prevent French expansion eastward, they gave Prussia lands along the Rhine River. They also allowed Austria to reassert control over northern Italy. This policy of containment proved fairly successful in maintaining the peace.

**Stability.** To turn back the clock to 1792, the architects of the peace promoted the principle of legitimacy, restoring hereditary monarchies that the French Revolution or Napoleon had unseated. Even before the Congress began, they had put Louis XVIII on the French throne. Later, they restored "legitimate" monarchs in Portugal, Spain, and the Italian states.

To protect the new order, Metternich pushed to create the Concert of Europe, a peacekeeping organization. It included all of the major European states. Leaders pledged to maintain the balance of power and to suppress any uprisings inspired by the ideas of the French Revolution.

**Problems of the peace.** The Vienna statesmen achieved their immediate goals. However, they failed to foresee how powerful new forces such as nationalism would shake the foundations of Europe. They redrew national boundaries without any concern for national cultures.

In Germany, they created a loosely organized German Confederation with Austria as its official head. But Germans who had battled Napoleon were already dreaming of a strong united German nation. Their dream would not come true for more than 50 years, but the story of German unification began in this period.

**Looking ahead.** Many people inspired by revolutionary ideals condemned the Vienna settlement. Still, the general peace lasted for a hundred years. Europe would not see war on a Napoleonic scale until 1914.

Yet the ideals of the French Revolution were not destroyed. In the next decades, its slogan and goals would inspire people in Europe and Latin America to seek equality and liberty. (See Chapter 4.) The spirit of nationalism ignited by Napoleon remained a powerful force.

## SECTION 5 REVIEW

1. **Identify** (a) Waterloo, (b) Clemens von Metternich, (c) Concert of Europe.
2. **Define** (a) guerrilla warfare, (b) abdicate, (c) legitimacy.
3. How did Napoleon's success contain the seeds of his defeat?
4. (a) What were the chief goals of the Congress of Vienna? (b) Describe three actions taken to achieve these goals.
5. *Critical Thinking* **Drawing Conclusions** Do you agree that Napoleon was "the revolution on horseback"? Why or why not?
6. *ACTIVITY* Imagine that it is 1816 and you are Napoleon, Metternich, or a former French revolutionary. Write a letter in which you evaluate the events of the last 30 years.

## CHAPTER REVIEW

### REVIEWING VOCABULARY

Select *five* vocabulary words from the chapter. Write each word on a separate slip of paper. Then, write the definition for each word on other slips of paper. Scramble the slips and exchange them with another student. Match the words with their definitions, and then check each other's results.

### REVIEWING FACTS

1. Why was there discontent with the old regime in France?

2. Why did a crowd storm the Bastille?

3. What was the slogan of the French Revolution?

4. What happened to Louis XVI and Marie Antoinette in 1793?

5. What was the Reign of Terror?

6. List the reforms that Napoleon made as leader of France.

7. How did Napoleon try to increase French power in Europe?

8. What was the result of Napoleon's invasion of Russia?

9. How did the Congress of Vienna try to restore the balance of power in Europe?

## SKILLS FOR SUCCESS     IDENTIFYING RELEVANT FACTS

When researching a topic, students of history must wade through a large amount of information and decide what is relevant. Relevant information has a clear and important link to the subject under investigation.

Imagine that you are preparing a paper about the Reign of Terror. Look at the information below, and then answer the following questions.

1. **Look for *examples* and *details* relevant to your topic.** (a) Which statement illustrates that the Committee of Public Safety ruled with almost dictatorial powers? (b) Is statement B relevant to the topic? Explain.

2. **Look for information providing background and reasons relating to the topic.** (a) Which statements provide reasons why the Reign of Terror began and ended? (b) Is statement D relevant to the topic? Explain.

3. **Draw conclusions about the relevance of the information.** What are some key words, names, and dates that appear in the statements that are relevant to the Reign of Terror?

---

*TOPIC: The Reign of Terror*

A. By 1794, the supporters of the revolution began to question the need for constant executions. In July, Robespierre was arrested and executed.

B. The revolution transformed daily life in France.

C. In the face of domestic and foreign threats, the National Convention set aside the constitution and created a Committee of Public Safety with almost dictatorial powers.

D. With the help of troops loyal to him, Napoleon Bonaparte and two directors overthrew the government in 1799.

E. The National Assembly abolished feudalism and introduced sweeping religious reforms.

F. The campaign known as the Reign of Terror lasted from July 1793 to July 1794.

G. Maximilien Robespierre led the Committee of Public Safety during the Reign of Terror.

H. To uncover traitors, the Committee of Public Safety sent agents across France.

I. Between 20,000 and 40,000 French people were executed as traitors.

## REVIEWING CHAPTER THEMES

Review the "Focus On" questions at the start of this chapter. Then select *three* of those questions and answer them, using information from the chapter.

## CRITICAL THINKING

1. **Defending a Position** The Declaration of the Rights of Man has been called the "death certificate" of the old regime. Do you agree? Why or why not?

2. **Linking Past and Present** Most historians agree that the French Revolution was a great turning point in European history. What events and ideas that emerged during the French Revolution are still a part of our political and social views today?

## ANALYZING PRIMARY SOURCES

Use the quotations on pages 72 and 76 to answer the following questions.

1. What mood did Wordsworth express in the first passage?

2. What mood did he express in the second passage?

3. What accounts for the change in Wordsworth's attitude toward the French Revolution?

## FOR YOUR PORTFOLIO

CREATING A DOCUMENTARY Work with a group of four students to prepare a segment for a documentary series on the French Revolution. First, choose one of these topics: The Way It Was, The Outbreak of the Revolution, A Moderate Start, The Radicals Take Over, The Rise and Fall of Napoleon, or Peace Again. Then review the relevant pages in your textbook and consult outside sources for additional research on your segment. Note documents, maps, and other visuals to include in your segment. Work with your group to write your segment. Finally, present your segment to the class.

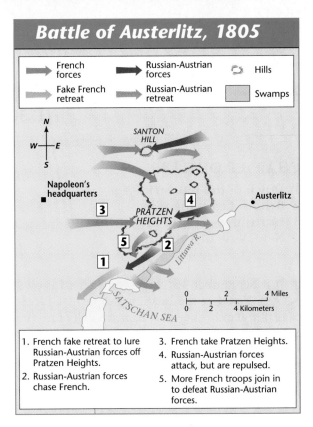

### Battle of Austerlitz, 1805

| | | | |
|---|---|---|---|
| → French forces | → Russian-Austrian forces | | Hills |
| → Fake French retreat | → Russian-Austrian retreat | | Swamps |

1. French fake retreat to lure Russian-Austrian forces off Pratzen Heights.
2. Russian-Austrian forces chase French.
3. French take Pratzen Heights.
4. Russian-Austrian forces attack, but are repulsed.
5. More French troops join in to defeat Russian-Austrian forces.

## ANALYZING MAPS

Use the map to answer the following questions.

1. In what direction from Austerlitz was Napoleon's headquarters located?

2. What was the result of the fighting at Santon Hill?

3. Which body of water did the Russian and Austrian troops cross in their retreat after the battle?

### INTERNET ACTIVITY

INTERPRETING HISTORICAL SYMBOLS
Use the Internet to research one of the symbols of the French Revolution or the French republic, such as the Bastille, the Tricolor, or "La Marseillaise." Then write a brief historical analysis of the symbol. Explain how it originated, what it represented to French citizens during the revolution, and, if possible, how it appears in France today.

# The Industrial Revolution Begins

## (1750–1850)

### CHAPTER OUTLINE

1 Dawn of the Industrial Age
2 Britain Leads the Way
3 Hardships of Early Industrial Life
4 New Ways of Thinking

On September 15, 1830, an excited crowd gathered at the bustling seaport of Liverpool, England. They had come to celebrate the opening of the Liverpool & Manchester, the world's first public steam-operated railway.

The 600 specially invited guests climbed aboard the gaily decorated trains. The engineer signaled that all was ready. Slowly, the shiny locomotives moved out of the station.

About halfway along the route, the locomotives stopped to take on water. Several passengers climbed down to get a closer look at the engines. Among them was William Huskisson, president of Britain's Board of Trade.

Suddenly, another locomotive steamed up the track. Startled guests clambered to safety. "Huskisson! For God's sake, get to your place!" shouted someone. But in his hurry, Huskisson stumbled and fell. The approaching engine ran him over and crushed his leg.

Stunned passengers lifted the injured man onto another train. The rescue locomotive roared to the nearest town. But despite a doctor's efforts, Huskisson died of his wounds.

The tragedy took the joy out of the occasion. Still, people noted the amazing speed attained by the engine carrying the wounded Huskisson. An astonished observer reported:

66The . . . engine conveyed the wounded body of the unfortunate gentleman a distance of about 15 miles in 25 minutes, or at the rate of 36 miles an hour. This incredible speed burst upon the world with the effect of a new and unlooked-for phenomenon.99

Despite the sad events of opening day, investors flocked to the new railroad. Soon railroads were sprouting everywhere, creating fabulous fortunes for builders and speeding people and goods to distant destinations.

Steam-powered railroads were part of the enormous transformation known as the Industrial Revolution. The Industrial Revolution refers to the shift of production from simple hand tools to complex machines, and from human and animal power to steam power.

The Industrial Revolution was a crucial turning point in history. The changes that began in Western Europe 250 years ago have spread around the globe. In this chapter we will look at the early Industrial Revolution in its birthplace in Britain, from about 1750 to 1850.

**FOCUS ON** these questions as you read:

■ **Continuity and Change**
How did the Industrial Revolution transform traditional ways of life?

■ **Economics and Technology**
What role did capital and technology play in the Industrial Revolution?

■ **Impact of the Individual**
How did individual contributions shape the industrial age?

■ **Political and Social Systems**
Why did new social and political philosophies develop during the industrial age?

### TIME AND PLACE

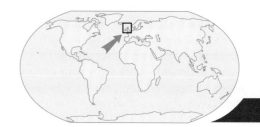

**An Industrial Town** Iron and coal were key ingredients of the Industrial Revolution. Coal powered the steam engines in Europe's new factories. Iron was used in railroads, bridges, and machines. Here, blast furnaces, used to purify iron ore, light up the sky of an early industrial town. **Continuity and Change** Based on this picture, how do you think the Industrial Revolution changed the European landscape? Explain.

## HUMANITIES LINK

**Art History** Joseph Wright, *An Iron Forge* (page 95).
**Literature** In this chapter, you will encounter passages from the following works of literature: Alfred, Lord Tennyson, "Ode Sung at the Opening of the International Exhibition" (page 94); Charles Dickens, *Hard Times* (page 100).

| **1760s** Watt improves steam engine | **1776** Smith's *Wealth of Nations* | **1800** Owen begins social reforms at New Lanark | **1830** Liverpool– Manchester Railroad opens | **1848** Marx and Engels publish *The Communist Manifesto* |

| 1750 | 1775 | 1800 | 1825 | 1850 |

# 1 Dawn of the Industrial Age

## Guide for Reading

- What factors contributed to a second agricultural revolution?
- Why did populations soar in Europe?
- What energy sources powered the Industrial Revolution?
- **Vocabulary** *enclosure*

For thousands of years after the rise of civilization, most people lived and worked in small farming villages. A chain of events set in motion in the mid-1700s changed that way of life forever.

The Industrial Revolution started in Britain. Unlike most political revolutions, it was neither sudden nor swift. Instead, it was a long, slow, uneven process in which production shifted from simple hand tools to complex machines. New sources of power replaced human and animal power. In the 250 years since it began, the Industrial Revolution has spread from Britain to the rest of Europe and North America, and then around the globe.

## A Turning Point in History

In 1750, most people worked the land, using simple handmade tools. They lived in simple cottages lit by firelight and candles. They made their own clothes and grew their own food. In nearby towns, they might exchange goods at a weekly outdoor market.

Like their peasant ancestors, these people knew little of the world that existed beyond their village. The few who left home traveled only as far as their feet or a horse-drawn cart could take them. Those bold adventurers who dared to cross the seas were at the mercy of winds that filled billowing sails.

Then the Industrial Revolution began. For growing numbers of people, the rural way of life began to disappear. By the 1850s, many country villages had grown into industrial towns and cities. Their inhabitants bought food and clothing in stores that offered a large variety of machine-made goods. They worked indoors behind a counter, desk, or factory machine. Their homes were multistory tenements.

Industrial-age travelers moved rapidly by train or steamship. Urgent messages flew along telegraph wires. New inventions and scientific "firsts" poured out each year. Between 1840 and 1855, for example, an American dentist used an anesthetic for the first time, a French physicist measured the speed of light, and a German chemist developed the Bunsen burner. Elias Howe made the first sewing machine, and a Hungarian doctor introduced antiseptic methods to reduce the risk of women dying in childbirth.

Still more stunning changes occurred in the next century, creating our familiar world of skyscraper cities and carefully tended suburbs. Cars and televisions, air travel and antibiotics, and a mass of other goods and services made their appearance.

How and why did these great changes occur? Historians point to a series of interrelated causes that helped trigger the industrialization of the West.

## A New Agricultural Revolution

Oddly enough, the Industrial Revolution was made possible in part by a change in the farming fields of Western Europe. Some 12,000 years ago, an agricultural revolution took place when people learned to farm and domesticate animals. About 300 years ago, a second agricultural revolution took place. It greatly improved the quality and quantity of farm products.

**Improved methods of farming.** The Dutch led the way in the new agricultural revolution. In the 1600s, they built earthen walls known as dikes to reclaim land from the sea. They combined smaller fields into larger ones to

The Industrial Revolution transformed the way people lived and worked. How does technology affect the way people live?

*This four Wheel Drill Plow, with a Seed and a Manure Hopper, was first Invented in the Year 1745, and is now in Use with W. Ellis at Little Gaddesden near Hempstead in Hertfordshire, where any person may View the same. It is so light that a man may Draw it, but Generally drawn by a pony or little Horse.*

**Improved Farm Machinery** *Jethro Tull's seed drill planted seeds in straight lines. Since crops planted this way grew in neat rows, they could be weeded with another new invention, the horse-drawn hoe, instead of by hand.* **Continuity and Change** *Does Tull's seed drill have anything in common with modern farm equipment? Explain.*

make better use of the land and used fertilizer from livestock to renew the soil.

In the 1700s, British farmers expanded on Dutch experiments. Some farmers mixed different kinds of soils to get higher crop yields. Others tried out new methods of crop rotation. Lord Charles Townshend won the nickname "Turnip Townshend" for urging farmers to grow turnips, which restored exhausted soil. Jethro Tull invented a mechanical device, the seed drill, to aid farmers. It deposited seeds in rows rather than scattering them wastefully over the land. Another pioneer, Robert Bakewell, bred stronger horses for farmwork and fatter sheep and cattle for meat.

Educated farmers exchanged news of experiments through farm journals. King George III himself, nicknamed "Farmer George," wrote articles about his model farm near Windsor Castle.

**Enclosure movement.** Meanwhile, rich landowners pushed ahead with enclosure, the process of taking over and fencing off land formerly shared by peasant farmers. In the 1500s, they had enclosed land to gain pastures for sheep and increased wool output. By the 1700s, they wanted to replace the strip farms of medieval times with larger fields that could be cultivated more efficiently.

As millions of acres were enclosed, farm output rose. Profits also rose because large fields needed fewer people to work them. But such progress had a human cost. Many farm laborers were thrown out of work. Small farmers were forced off their land because they could not compete with large landholders. Villages shrank as cottagers left in search of work.

In time, jobless farmworkers migrated to towns and cities. There, they formed a growing labor force that would tend the machines of the Industrial Revolution.

## The Population Explosion

The agricultural revolution contributed to a rapid growth of population. This population explosion has continued, although today, the center of growth has shifted from the western world to developing nations outside Europe.

Precise population statistics for the 1700s are rare, but those that do exist are striking. Britain's population, for example, soared from about 5 million in 1700 to almost 9 million in 1800. The population of France rose from 18 million in 1715 to 26 million in 1789. The population of Europe as a whole shot up from roughly 120 million to about 190 million in the same period. Such growth was unlike any in earlier history. Yet in the 1800s, populations would climb still higher.

The population boom of the 1700s was due more to declining death rates than to rising birthrates. The agricultural revolution reduced the risk of famine. Because they ate better, women were healthier and had stronger babies. Some deadly diseases, such as bubonic plague, had faded away. In the 1800s, better hygiene and sanitation along with improved medical care further slowed deaths from disease.

## An Energy Revolution

A third factor that helped trigger the Industrial Revolution was an "energy revolution."

From the beginning of human history, the energy for work was provided mostly by the muscles of humans and animals. In time, water mills and windmills were added to muscle power.

In the 1700s, inventive minds found ways to use water power more efficiently. Giant water wheels powered machines in the first factories. People also harnessed new sources of energy. Among the most important was coal, used to develop the steam engine. In 1712, inventor Thomas Newcomen had developed a steam engine powered by coal to pump water out of mines. About 1769, James Watt improved on Newcomen's engine. Watt's steam engines would become the vital power source of the early Industrial Revolution.

Watt linked up with a shrewd partner, Matthew Boulton, who saw the potential of steam engines. He told the king of England:

66Your Majesty, I have at my disposal what the whole world demands: something which will uplift civilization more than ever by relieving man of all undignified drudgery. I have *steam power*.99

# SECTION 1 REVIEW

1. **Identify** (a) Charles Townshend, (b) Jethro Tull, (c) Robert Bakewell, (d) Thomas Newcomen, (e) James Watt.
2. **Define** enclosure.
3. How did each of the following affect agriculture in the 1700s and 1800s: (a) new farming methods, (b) mechanical inventions, (c) enclosure?
4. Identify three causes of the population explosion in Europe in the 1700s and 1800s.
5. (a) What role did the steam engine play in the Industrial Revolution? (b) What energy source powered the steam engine?
6. *Critical Thinking* **Recognizing Causes and Effects** What were the immediate and long-term effects of the agricultural revolution?
7. *ACTIVITY* Keep a log of your activities for one week. Next to each activity, indicate how it might have been different if you lived in the pre-industrial world.

# 2 Britain Leads the Way

## Guide for Reading

- Why was Britain the first nation to industrialize?
- Why were coal and iron important to the industrial age?
- How did industrialization change the textile industry?
- **Vocabulary** *factory, turnpike*

Visitors crowded into London's Crystal Palace in 1851. The immense structure housed the Great Exhibition, a display of the "Works of Industry of all Nations." The palace itself was specially built for the occasion. A vast cavern of glass and iron, it symbolized the triumph of the industrial age.

This early world's fair, and a second one in 1862, offered an awesome array of machines, works of art, and other exhibits. Britain's leading poet, Alfred Tennyson, wrote:

66. . . lo! the giant aisles
Rich in model and design;
Harvest-tool and husbandry,
Loom and wheel and enginery,
Secrets of the sullen mine,
Steel and gold, and coal and wine,
Fabric rough or fairy-fine . . .
And shapes and hues of Art divine!
All of beauty, all of use
That one fair planet can produce.99

In the century before the exhibitions, Britain had been the first nation to industrialize. Its success became the model for others, in Europe and around the world.

## Why Britain?

Why did the Industrial Revolution begin in Britain? Historians have identified a number of key factors that helped Britain take an early lead in industry.

**Natural resources.** Though a relatively small nation, Britain had large supplies of coal to power steam engines. It also had plentiful iron to build the new machines.

**Human resources.** A large number of workers were needed to mine the coal and iron, build the factories, and run the machines. The agricultural revolution of the 1600s and 1700s freed many men and women in Britain from farm labor. The population boom that resulted further swelled the available work force.

**New technology.** Britain had been a center of the Scientific Revolution, which had focused attention on the physical world and developed new devices for managing it. In the 1700s, Enlightenment thinkers promoted the idea of progress through technology. The *Encyclopedia* compiled by the French philosophe Diderot, for example, included articles on technology as well as on social and political reform. In the 1700s, Britain had plenty of skilled mechanics who were eager to meet the growing demand for new, practical inventions.

Technology was an important part of the Industrial Revolution, but it did not cause it. After all, other societies, such as the ancient Greeks or Chinese, had advanced technology for their time but did not move on to industrialization. Only when other necessary conditions existed, including demand and capital, did technology pave the way for industrialization.

**Economic conditions—capital and demand.** In the 1700s, trade from a growing overseas empire helped the British economy prosper. The business class accumulated capital, or wealth to invest in enterprises such as mines, railroads, and factories. (See page 51.) A large number of these entrepreneurs were ready to risk their capital in new ventures.

**An Iron Forge** *In the late 1700s, most artists ignored the Industrial Revolution, which was changing the world around them. They thought that bleak factories and banging machinery were not proper subjects for art. But factory scenes fascinated English artist Joseph Wright, whose home town of Derby was a center of industry. In this painting, a giant hammer driven by a water wheel pounds a piece of white-hot iron. The red glow of the forge tints the faces of the master, his wife, and children.* **Art and Literature** *How are the children reacting to the sight of the forge?*

At home, the population explosion boosted demand for goods. However, a growing population alone would not have resulted in increased production. General economic prosperity was also needed to enable not only the middle and upper classes but also artisans and farmers to afford the new consumer goods.

**Political and social conditions.** Britain had a stable government that supported economic growth. It built a strong navy to protect its empire and overseas trade. Although members of the upper class tended to look down on business and business people, they did not reject the great wealth produced by the new entrepreneurs.

# Technology of the British Industrial Revolution

| Invention | Description | Impact | Connections Today |
|---|---|---|---|
| **Improved steam engine** (James Watt) 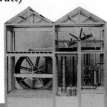 | Improved version of steam engine that used coal rather than water power. First used to pump water from mines and to forge iron. By the late 1780s, powered machines in cotton mills. | Steam engines provided power for early Industrial Revolution. They led to the factory system, early assembly lines, and rapidly growing production. | Steam engines are still used today to power giant ocean liners, pile drivers, and electric generators. |
| **Spinning mule** (Samuel Crompton)  | Spinning device that combined the features of the spinning jenny, which made it possible to spin many threads at one time, and the water frame, which could produce strong cotton threads. | Produced stronger, finer thread; helped create demand for factories; supply of thread exceeded weavers' ability to use; this spurred invention of better weaving machines. | Today's spinning machines use computers to ensure strong and even threads. They can spin even the coarsest natural fibers, such as hemp and flax. |
| **Steam-powered locomotive** (George Stephenson)  | Steam-powered vehicle used to pull a train. The "iron horse" moved faster and could haul heavier loads than a horse could. | Revolutionized transportation. Created demand for iron for rails and trains; created jobs building and running railroads; linked people far and wide. | Railroads, powered by electricity and diesel fuel, carry tons of freight and millions of passengers each year. High-speed passenger trains in Europe and Japan can reach 185 mph. |
| **Dynamo** (Michael Faraday) | Electric generator that worked by rotating a coil of wire between the poles of a magnet, which created electric current. | Development of electric power was critical to later industrial developments. By late 1800s, other inventors had found ways to use electric power to run machines and light up whole cities. | All electric generators and transformers work on the principle of Faraday's dynamo. In the 1990s, the U.S., Russia, and China together produced and used 42 percent of the world's total electric power. |

*Interpreting a Chart* Beginning in the mid-1700s, inventors in Britain applied scientific principles to practical problems. The technological advances that they made helped trigger the Industrial Revolution.
■ Review the definition of the Industrial Revolution on page 90. How does each of the inventions on the chart fit that definition?

Religious attitudes also played a role in the growth of British industry. Many entrepreneurs came from religious groups that encouraged thrift and hard work. At the same time, for many people, worldly problems had become more important than concern about life after death. Thus, inventors, bankers, and other risk-takers felt free to devote their energies to material achievements.

## The Age of Iron and Coal

New technologies in the iron industry were key to the Industrial Revolution. Iron was needed for machines and steam engines. Producing high-quality iron, however, required large quantities of fuel, which in the past had most often been wood. Over the centuries, Britain had cleared most of its trees. In the 1700s, the British turned to coal for fuel.

The Darby family of Coalbrookdale were leaders in developing Britain's iron industry. In 1709, Abraham Darby began to use coal instead of wood for smelting iron, that is, separating iron from its ore. When he discovered that coal gave off impurities that damaged the iron, Darby found a way to remove the impurities from coal.

Darby's experiments led him to produce better-quality and cheaper iron. His son and grandson improved on his methods. In 1779, his grandson, Abraham Darby III, made the world's first cast iron bridge. In the years that followed, high-quality iron found more and more uses, especially after the world turned to building railroads.

### GLOBAL CONNECTIONS

The Industrial Revolution in Britain had an unforeseen impact on the United States. American planters supplied raw cotton for the British textile industry. However, they could not keep up with demand until the invention of the cotton gin in 1793 speeded up the processing of the cotton. The "gin" changed everything. With enormous profits to be made, American planters wanted more slaves to plant and pick more cotton. A vicious cycle followed. Slaves planted cotton. Planters earned profits by selling the cotton and then bought more land and more slaves to earn more profits. In this way, slavery became entrenched in the American economy.

## Revolutionary Changes in the Textile Industry

Important changes also took place in Britain's largest industry—textiles. Indeed, it was in this industry that the Industrial Revolution first took hold.

**The early industry.** In the 1600s, cotton cloth imported from India had become increasingly popular. British merchants tried to organize a cotton cloth industry at home. They developed the putting out system. They distributed imported raw cotton to peasant families who spun it into thread and then wove the thread into cloth. Skilled artisans in the towns finished and dyed the cloth.

Under the putting out system, production was slow. As the demand for cloth grew, inventors came up with a string of remarkable devices that revolutionized the British textile industry. (See the chart on page 96.)

**Major inventions.** Among the inventions was John Kay's flying shuttle. Using Kay's device, weavers worked so fast that they soon outpaced spinners. James Hargreaves solved that problem by producing the spinning jenny in 1764, which spun many threads at the same time.

A few years later, Richard Arkwright invented the waterframe, using water power to speed up spinning still further. Arkwright, who had begun life as a barber, was typical of Britain's hard-working and highly disciplined entrepreneurs. An observer noted:

> [Arkwright] commonly labored in his [many] concerns from five o'clock in the morning till nine at night; and when considerably more than fifty years of age . . . he encroached upon his sleep, in order to gain an hour each day to learn English grammar.

**The first factories.** The new machines doomed the old putting out system of manufacturing. They were too large and expensive to be operated at home. Instead, manufacturers built long sheds to house the machines. At first, they located the sheds near rapidly moving streams, which provided water power to run the machines. Later, machines were powered by steam engines.

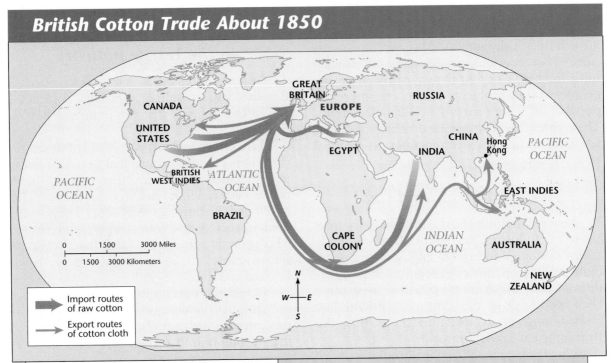

## British Cotton Trade About 1850

Import routes of raw cotton

Export routes of cotton cloth

## GEOGRAPHY AND HISTORY

As the textile industry grew, Great Britain needed ever-increasing supplies of raw cotton for its mills. It also sought out new markets for finished cotton cloth.

1. **Location** On the map, locate (a) Great Britain, (b) United States, (c) British West Indies.
2. **Movement** (a) Name two overseas sources that supplied raw cotton to Britain. (b) Name two overseas markets to which Britain exported its cotton cloth.
3. **Critical Thinking** **Predicting Consequences** What might have happened to the British cotton industry if Britain had lost control of its colony in India?

Spinners and weavers came each day to work in these first factories—as these places that brought together workers and machines to produce large quantities of goods came to be called. Early observers were awed at the size and output of these establishments. As a writer of the 1800s commented:

66 Those vast brick buildings, . . . towering to the height of 70 or 80 feet, . . . now perform labors which formerly employed whole villages. In the steam loom factories, the cotton is carded, roved, spun, and woven into cloth, and the same [amount] of labor is now performed in one of these structures which formerly occupied the industry of an entire district. 99

## Revolution in Transportation

As factories sprang up and production increased, entrepreneurs needed faster and cheaper methods of moving goods from place to place. In the 1700s, individuals made improvements in local systems of transportation. Some capitalists invested in turnpikes, which were privately built roads that charged a fee to travelers who used them. Others had canals dug to link rivers or connect inland towns to coastal ports. Engineers also built stronger bridges and upgraded harbors to help the rapidly expanding overseas trade.

**On land.** The great revolution in transportation, however, was the invention of the steam locomotive. It was this invention that made possible the growth of railroads.

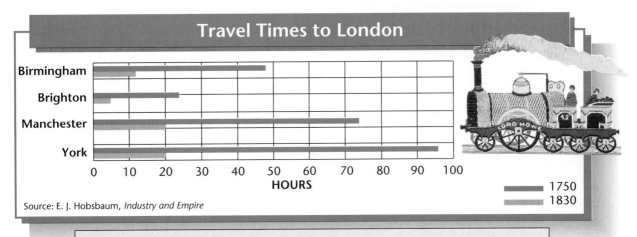

## Travel Times to London

**HOURS**

— 1750
— 1830

Source: E. J. Hobsbaum, *Industry and Empire*

**Interpreting a Graph** *Advances in transportation during the Industrial Revolution greatly reduced travel time between major cities.* ■ *About how long did it take to travel between London and Birmingham in 1750? In 1830? What invention made this increased speed possible?*

In the early 1800s, pioneers like George Stephenson developed steam-powered locomotives to pull carriages along rails. As we saw on page 90, the world's first major rail line, from Liverpool to Manchester in England, opened in 1830. In the following decades, railroads got faster and railroad building boomed. By 1870, rail lines crisscrossed Britain, Europe, and eastern North America.

**On sea.** Other inventors applied steam power to improve shipping. Scottish builders made the first paddle wheel steamboats to pull barges along canals. In 1807, an American, Robert Fulton, used Watt's steam engine to power the *Clermont* up the Hudson River. Fulton's steamboat traveled at a record-breaking speed of more than five miles an hour!

Designing steamships for ocean voyages was more difficult. The coal needed for the voyage took up much of the cargo space. But by the late 1800s, steam-powered freighters with iron hulls were carrying 10 to 20 times the cargo of older wooden ships.

### Looking Ahead

As the Industrial Revolution got under way, it triggered a chain reaction. In response to growing demand, inventors developed machines that could produce large quantities of goods more efficiently. As the supply of goods increased, prices fell. Lower prices made goods more affordable and thus created more consumers who further fed the demand for goods.

The Industrial Revolution did more than change the way goods were made. It affected people's whole way of life. In the 1800s, a tidal wave of economic and social changes swept the industrializing nations of the world.

## SECTION 2 REVIEW

1. **Identify** (a) Abraham Darby, (b) John Kay, (c) James Hargreaves, (d) Richard Arkwright, (e) Robert Fulton.
2. **Define** (a) factory, (b) turnpike.
3. Describe five factors that contributed to the Industrial Revolution in Britain.
4. Explain how each of the following was key to industrialization: (a) coal, (b) iron, (c) better methods of transportation.
5. How did the Industrial Revolution transform the textile industry?
6. *Critical Thinking* **Analyzing Information** Explain how each of the following helped contribute to demand for consumer goods in Britain: (a) population explosion, (b) general economic prosperity.
7. *ACTIVITY* Create a concept map that shows the major causes of the Industrial Revolution and how they were related.

# 3 Hardships of Early Industrial Life

## Guide for Reading

- How did the factory system change workers' lives?

- What problems did the industrial working class face?

- What were the costs and benefits of the Industrial Revolution?

- **Vocabulary** *urbanization*

The Industrial Revolution brought great riches to most of the entrepreneurs who helped set it in motion. For the millions of workers who crowded into the new factories, however, the industrial age brought poverty and harsh living conditions. In *Hard Times,* the British novelist Charles Dickens describes a typical factory town and the people who live in it:

> 66It was a town of machinery and tall chimneys, out of which interminable serpents of smoke trailed themselves forever and ever. . . . It had a black canal in it, and a river that ran purple with ill-smelling dye. [It was] inhabited by people . . . who all went in and out at the same hours, . . . to do the same work, and to whom every day was the same as yesterday and tomorrow, and every year the counterpart of the last and the next.99

In time, reforms would curb many of the worst abuses of the early industrial age in Europe and the Americas, and people at all levels of society would benefit from industrialization. Until then, working people could look forward only to lives marked by dangerous working conditions; unsafe, unsanitary, and overcrowded housing; and unrelenting poverty.

## The New Industrial City

The Industrial Revolution brought rapid **urbanization,** or a movement of people to cities. Changes in farming, soaring population growth, and an ever-increasing demand for workers led masses of people to migrate from farms to cities. Almost overnight, small towns around coal or iron mines mushroomed into cities. Other cities grew up around the factories that entrepreneurs built in once-quiet market towns. In these new, overcrowded urban centers, misery festered.

The market town of Manchester numbered 17,000 people in the 1750s. Within a few years, it exploded into a center of the textile industry. Its population soared to 40,000 by 1780 and 70,000 by 1801. Visitors described the "cloud of coal vapor" that polluted the air, the pounding noise of steam engines, and the filthy stench of its river "filled with waste dye-stuffs."

In Manchester, as elsewhere, a gulf divided the urban population. The wealthy and the middle class lived in pleasant neighborhoods. Vast numbers of poor, however, struggled to survive in foul-smelling slums. They packed into tiny rooms in tenement buildings. No light filtered through the dark, narrow alleys. They had no running water, only community pumps. There was no sewage or sanitation system, and wastes and garbage rotted in the streets. Cholera and other diseases spread rapidly. In time, reformers pushed for laws to improve conditions in city slums. (See Chapter 7.)

## The Factory System

The heart of the new industrial city was the factory. There, the technology of the machine age imposed a harsh new way of life on workers.

**Rigid discipline.** The factory system differed greatly from farmwork. In rural villages, people worked hard, but their work varied according to the season. In factories, workers faced a rigid schedule set by the factory whistle. "While the engine runs," said an observer, "people must work—men, women, and children are yoked together with iron and steam."

Working hours were long. Shifts lasted from 12 to 16 hours. Weary workers suffered accidents from machines that had no safety devices. They might lose a finger, a limb, or even their lives. Workers were exposed to other dangers, as well. Coal dust destroyed the lungs of miners, while textile workers constantly breathed air filled with lint. If workers were sick or injured, they lost their jobs.

**Women workers.** Women made up much of the new industrial work force. Employers often preferred women workers to men. They thought women could adapt more easily to machines and were easier to manage than men. More important, they were able to pay women less than men, even for the same work.

Factory work created special problems for women. Their new jobs took them out of their homes for 12 hours or more a day. They then returned to crowded slum tenements to feed and clothe their families, clean, and cope with sickness and other problems. Family life had been hard for poor rural cottagers. In industrial towns, it was even grimmer.

**Child labor.** Factories and mines hired many boys and girls. Nimble-fingered and quick-moving children changed spools in textile mills. Others clambered through narrow mine shafts, pushing coal carts.

Since children had helped with farmwork, parents accepted the idea of child labor. And the wages the children earned were needed to help support the family. One mother told investigators of her 10-year-old child who worked in the mines from six in the morning until eight at night. "It would hurt us," she said, "if children were prevented from working till [they were] 11 or 12 years old, because we've not jobs enough to live now as it is."

Employers often hired orphans, making deals with local officials who were glad to have the children taken off their hands. Orphans worked long hours for a minimum of food. Overseers beat children accused of idling. A few enlightened factory owners did provide basic education and a decent life for child workers. More often, though, children, like their parents, were slaves to the machines.

## Patience Kershaw's Life Underground

The horrors of child labor were slowly exposed in the 1830s and 1840s, when British lawmakers looked into abuses in factories and mines. Government commissions heard about children as young as five years old working in factories. Some died. Others were stunted in growth or had twisted limbs. Most remained uneducated.

**A 12-hour workday.** From 17-year-old Patience Kershaw, members of the Ashley Mines Commission heard about life in the coal mines:

“My father has been dead about a year. My mother is living and has 10 children, 5 lads and 5 lasses. The oldest is about 30, the youngest is 4. Three lasses go to mill. All the lads are [coal miners].”

Kershaw's sisters had started in the mines but switched to mill work. One changed jobs when her legs swelled from standing in the cold water that covered the mine floor.

Kershaw herself worked in the mines. Her job was "hurrying"—pushing carts of coal to the surface of the mine:

“I go to [the mine] at 5 o'clock in the morning and come out at 5 in the evening. . . . I hurry in the clothes I have now got on, trousers and ragged jacket. The bald place upon my head is made by [pushing] the corves [carts

*Working Underground Thousands of children worked in Britain's coal mines during the Industrial Revolution. In the cramped, narrow mine shafts, children crawled on all fours, pushing coal carts or dragging them behind. "Some places are scarcely fit for a dog to go in, not being more than from two feet and a half to a yard in height," one young miner said. **Economics and Technology** Why did many parents resist efforts to end child labor?*

full of coal]. . . . I hurry the corves a mile and more underground and back. . . . I wear a belt and chain . . . to get the corves out.**"**

Kershaw said that the men she worked with beat her if she did not work quickly enough. And "the boys sometimes pull me about. I am the only girl in the pit. There are about 20 boys and 15 men."

**Efforts at reform.** Like many other working poor, Kershaw had entered the mines as a small child. In a tangle of underground tunnels, men, women, and children mined coal to fuel the engines of the Industrial Revolution.

Kershaw probably never saw the Ashley Mines Commission report. Besides, since she had never attended school, she could not have read it in any case. But in 1842, her testimony shocked many people in Britain. Slowly, Parliament passed laws to regulate the employment of children in mines and factories. ▪

## The Working Class

In rural villages, farm families had ties to a community where they had lived for generations. When they moved to the new industrial cities, they felt lost and bewildered. In time, though, factory and mine workers developed their own sense of community.

**Protests.** As the Industrial Revolution began, weavers and other skilled artisans resisted the new "labor-saving" machines that were costing them their jobs. They smashed machines and burned factories. Such rioters in England were called Luddites after a mythical figure, Ned Ludd, who supposedly destroyed machines in the 1780s.

Protests met harsh repression. Luddites were hanged or sent to penal colonies in Australia. When workers held a rally in Manchester in 1819, soldiers charged the crowd, killing a dozen and injuring hundreds more. For years, workers were forbidden to form labor unions to bargain for better pay and working conditions. Strikes were outlawed.

**Spread of Methodism.** Many working-class people found comfort in a new religious movement. In the mid-1700s, John Wesley had been the leader of a religious revival and founded the Methodist Church. Wesley stressed the need for a personal sense of faith. He urged Christians to improve their lot by adopting sober, moral ways.

Methodist meetings featured hymns and sermons promising forgiveness of sin and a better life to come. Methodist preachers took this message of salvation into the slums. There, they sought to rekindle self-confidence and hope among the working poor. They set up Sunday schools where followers not only studied the Bible but also learned to read and write. Methodists helped channel workers' anger away from revolution and toward social reform.

*Worker Protests* On a hot August day in 1819, workers in the industrial city of Manchester gathered to hear several reformers speak. Suddenly, soldiers attacked the crowd, killing a dozen people and wounding hundreds more. *Art and Literature* Do you think the artist who created this cartoon sympathized with the workers or the soldiers? Explain.

# PARALLELS THROUGH TIME

## Frankenstein

In 1816, a teenager named Mary Shelley (below left) had a nightmare vision that "so possessed my mind that a thrill of fear ran through me." Shelley's nightmare inspired her to write *Frankenstein*, a novel about a scientist who tries to make a human being but creates a monster instead. The story reflected the fear of many Europeans during the Industrial Revolution that humans were using technology to tamper with nature.

**Linking Past and Present** Why did people during the Industrial Revolution worry that technology had gone too far? Are those concerns still valid today?

**PAST** In Shelley's novel, the monster is not a grunting brute. Instead, he is an intelligent but hideously ugly and evil creature who reads poetry and argues cleverly with Victor Frankenstein, his creator. "Why," he piteously asks, "did you form a monster so hideous that even you turned from me in disgust?"

**PRESENT** The story of Frankenstein and his monster has continued to capture the popular imagination. A silent movie based on the tale was made in 1910, and a film featuring Boris Karloff (above right) as the monster was one of the biggest hits of the 1930s. Mel Brooks made Young Frankenstein, a spoof on the original story, in the 1970s, and in 1994 still another version starring Robert De Niro was released.

FRANKENSTEIN,

BY

MARY W. SHELLEY.

## The New Middle Class

Those who benefited most from the Industrial Revolution were the entrepreneurs who set it in motion. This new middle class came from several groups. Some were merchants who invested their profits in factories. Others were inventors or skilled artisans who turned their technological know-how into a ticket to a better life. Some rose from "rags to riches," a pattern that the age greatly admired.

Middle-class families lived in solid, well-furnished homes. They dressed well and ate large meals. Middle-class men made their influence felt in Parliament, where they opposed any effort to regulate factories or legalize labor unions.

As a sign of their new standard of living, middle-class women were encouraged to become "ladies." They took up "ladylike" activities, such as drawing, embroidery, or playing the piano. A "lady" did not work outside the home. She was also discouraged from doing the physical labor of housework. The first thing a family's new wealth acquired was a maid servant. The family then set about educating their daughters to provide a happy, well-furnished home for their future husbands. Sons learned to become businessmen.

The new middle class valued hard work and the determination to "get ahead." They had confidence in themselves and often little sympathy for the poor. If they thought of the faceless millions in the factories and mines, they generally supposed the poor to be responsible for their own misery. Some believed the poor were so lazy or ignorant that they could not "work their way up" out of poverty.

## Benefits and Problems

Since the 1800s, people have debated whether the Industrial Revolution was a blessing or a curse. The hardships brought by the early industrial age were terrible. Said English writer Thomas Carlyle, "Something [ought] to be done."

In time, "something" would be done. Reformers pressed for laws to improve working conditions. (See Chapter 5.) Unions won the right to bargain with employers for better wages and hours. Eventually, working-class men gained the right to vote, which gave them political power. Some workers founded political parties and movements that sought swifter, more radical solutions.

Despite the social problems created by the Industrial Revolution—low pay, unemployment, dismal living conditions—the industrial age did bring material benefits. As demand for mass-produced goods grew, new factories opened, creating more jobs. Wages rose so that workers had enough left after paying rent and buying food to buy a newspaper or visit a music hall. As the cost of railroad travel fell, people could visit family in other towns. Horizons widened, opportunities increased.

Industrialization continues to spread around the world today. Often, it begins with great suffering. In the end, it produces more material things for more people.

## SECTION 3 REVIEW

1. **Identify** (a) Luddite, (b) John Wesley, (c) Methodism.
2. **Define** urbanization.
3. Describe working conditions in an early factory.
4. What special problems did factory work create for women?
5. How did the conditions of the early industrial age improve over time?
6. *Critical Thinking* **Comparing** Compare the life of a farmworker with that of a factory worker in the early industrial age.
7. *ACTIVITY* Write five questions for an interview with Patience Kershaw.

# 4 New Ways of Thinking

## Guide for Reading

- What economic ideas helped shape the industrial age?
- What reforms did individual thinkers urge?
- How was socialism linked to the Industrial Revolution?
- **Vocabulary** *utilitarianism, socialism, communism, proletariat*

Everywhere in his native England, Thomas Malthus saw the effects of the population explosion—crowded slums, hungry families, and widespread misery. After careful study, in 1798 he published an "Essay on the Principle of Population." Poverty and misery, he concluded, were unavoidable because the population was increasing faster than the food supply. Malthus wrote:

❝The power of population is [far] greater than the power of the Earth to produce subsistence for man.❞

Malthus was one of many thinkers who tried to understand the staggering changes taking place in the early industrial age. As heirs to the Enlightenment, these thinkers looked for natural laws that governed the world of business and economics. Their ideas would influence governments in the years ahead.

## Laissez-Faire Economics

During the Enlightenment, physiocrats argued that natural laws should be allowed to operate without interference. As part of this philosophy, they believed that government should not interfere in the free operation of the economy. In the early 1800s, middle-class business leaders embraced this laissez-faire, or "hands-off," approach.

**Legacy of Adam Smith.** The prophet of laissez-faire economics was Adam Smith. (See page 44.) Smith believed that a free market—

the unregulated exchange of goods and services—would eventually help everyone, not just the rich.

The free market, Smith said, would produce more goods at lower prices, making them affordable by everyone. A growing economy would also encourage capitalists to reinvest profits in new ventures. Supporters of this free enterprise capitalism pointed to the successes of the industrial age, in which government had played no part.

**Malthus on population.** Like Smith's *Wealth of Nations,* Thomas Malthus's writings on population shaped economic thinking for generations. As you have read on page 104, Malthus grimly predicted that population would outpace the food supply. The only checks on population growth, he said, were war, disease, and famine. As long as population kept increasing, he went on, the poor would suffer. He thus urged families to have fewer children.

In the early 1800s, many people accepted Malthus's bleak view. It was too pessimistic, however. Although the population boom continued, the food supply grew even faster. As the century progressed, living conditions for the western world also slowly improved. And then people did begin having fewer children. In the 1900s, population growth ceased to be a problem in western countries, though it still afflicted some nations elsewhere.

**Ricardo on wages.** Another influential British economist, David Ricardo, agreed with Malthus that the poor had too many children. In his "iron law of wages," Ricardo noted that when wages were high, families had more children. But more children increased the supply of labor, which led to lower wages and higher unemployment. Like Malthus, Ricardo held out no hope for the working class to escape poverty. Because of such gloomy predictions, economics became known as the "dismal science."

Neither Malthus nor Ricardo was a cruel man. Yet both opposed any government help for the poor. To these supporters of laissez-faire economics, the best cure for poverty was not government relief but the unrestricted "laws of the free market." Individuals, they felt, should be left to improve their lot through thrift, hard work, and limiting the size of their family.

### The Utilitarians

Others revised laissez-faire doctrines to justify some government intervention. By 1800, Jeremy Bentham was preaching utilitarianism, the idea that the goal of society should be "the greatest happiness for the greatest number" of its citizens. To Bentham, laws or actions should be judged by their "utility." Did they provide

*Overcrowding in a London Slum* Thomas Malthus warned that the population explosion was causing widespread misery throughout England. Here, French artist Gustave Doré captures the squalor and overcrowded conditions of a London slum. **Political and Social Systems** What did Malthus recommend as a solution to the problems of the early industrial age?

more pleasure (happiness) than pain? He strongly supported individual freedom, which he believed ensured happiness. At the same time, he saw the need for government to intervene under certain circumstances.

Bentham's chief follower, John Stuart Mill, also argued that actions are right if they promote happiness and wrong if they cause pain. He reexamined the idea that unrestricted competition in the free market was always good. Often, he said, it favored the strong over the weak.

Although he believed strongly in individual freedom, Mill wanted the government to step in to improve the hard lives of the working class. He further called for giving the vote to workers and women. These groups could then use their political power to win reforms. Mill and other utilitarians worked for reforms in many areas, from child labor to public health.

Most middle-class people rejected Mill's ideas. Only in the later 1800s were his views slowly accepted. Today's democratic governments, however, have absorbed many ideas from Mill and the utilitarians.

## Emergence of Socialism

While the champions of laissez-faire economics praised individual rights, other thinkers focused on the good of society in general. They condemned the evils of industrial capitalism, which they believed had created a gulf between rich and poor. To end poverty and injustice, they offered a radical solution—socialism. Under socialism, the people as a whole rather than private individuals would own and operate the "means of production"—the farms, factories, railways, and other large businesses that produced and distributed goods.

Socialism grew out of the Enlightenment faith in progress, its belief in the basic goodness of human nature, and its concern for social justice. The goal of socialists was a society that operated for the welfare of all the people. In a socialist society, one reformer predicted:

66There will be no war, no crime, no administration of justice, as it is called, no government. Besides there will be neither disease, anguish, melancholy,

nor resentment. Every man will seek . . . the good of all.99

**The Utopians.** Early socialists tried to build self-sufficient communities in which all work was shared and all property was owned in common. When there was no difference between rich and poor, they felt, fighting between people would disappear. These early socialists were called Utopians, after Thomas More's ideal community. The name implied that they were impractical dreamers. However, the Utopian Robert Owen did set up a model community to put his ideas into practice.

**Robert Owen.** A poor Welsh boy, Owen became a successful mill owner. Unlike most self-made industrialists at the time, he refused to use child labor. He campaigned vigorously for child labor laws and encouraged labor unions.

Owen insisted that the conditions in which people lived shaped their character. To prove his point, he set up his factory in New Lanark, Scotland, as a model village. He built homes for workers, opened a school for children, and generally treated employees well. He showed that an employer could offer decent living and working conditions and still run a profitable business. By the 1820s, many people were visiting New Lanark to observe Owen's reforms.

## The "Scientific Socialism" of Karl Marx

In the 1840s, Karl Marx, a German philosopher, condemned the ideas of the Utopians as unrealistic idealism. He put forward a new theory, "scientific socialism," which he claimed was based on a scientific study of history.

As a young man in Germany, Marx agitated for reform. Forced to leave his homeland because of his radical ideas, he lived first in Paris and then settled in London. He teamed up with another German socialist, Friedrich Engels, whose father owned a textile factory in England.

In 1848, Marx and Engels published a pamphlet, *The Communist Manifesto*. "A spectre is haunting Europe," it began, "the spectre of communism." Communism is a form of socialism that sees class struggle between employers and employees as inevitable.

**Marxism.** In the *Manifesto,* Marx theorized that economics was the driving force in history. The entire course of history, he argued, was "the history of class struggles" between the "haves" and "have-nots." The "haves" have always owned the means of production and thus controlled society and all its wealth. In industrialized Europe, Marx said, the "haves" were the bourgeoisie, or middle class. The "have-nots" were the proletariat, or working class.

According to Marx, the modern class struggle pitted the bourgeoisie against the proletariat. In the end, he predicted, the proletariat would triumph. It would then take control of the means of production and set up a classless, communist society. In such a society, the struggles of the past would end because wealth and power would be equally shared.

Marx despised capitalism. He believed it created prosperity for a few and poverty for many. He called for an international struggle to bring about its downfall. "Working men of all countries," he urged, "unite!"

**Impact.** At first, Marxist ideas had little impact. In time, however, they would have worldwide effects. In Western Europe, socialist political parties emerged. Many of them absorbed Marxist ideas, including the goal of a classless society.

In the late 1800s, Russian socialists embraced Marxism, and the Russian Revolution of 1917 set up a communist-inspired government. (See Chapter 11.) Later, revolutionaries around the world would adapt Marxist ideas to their own ends.

**Weaknesses.** Marx claimed his ideas were based on scientific laws. However, many of the assumptions on which he based his theories were wrong. He predicted that the misery of the proletariat would touch off a world revolution. Instead, by 1900, the standard of living of the working class improved. As a result, Marxism lost much of its appeal in industrially developed western countries.

Marx also predicted that workers would unite across national borders to wage class warfare. Instead, nationalism won out over working-class loyalty. In general, people felt stronger ties to their own countries than to the international communist movement.

***Champion of the Working Class*** *Karl Marx was a social philosopher and revolutionary. He argued that history was a struggle between the classes that would end with the victory of the working class.* ***Global Interaction*** *Marx was born in Germany but lived for more than 30 years in London. How might living in London during the industrial age have influenced Marx's ideas?*

## SECTION 4 REVIEW

1. **Identify** (a) Thomas Malthus, (b) "iron law of wages," (c) John Stuart Mill, (d) Utopians, (e) *The Communist Manifesto.*
2. **Define** (a) utilitarianism, (b) socialism, (c) communism, (d) proletariat.
3. (a) Which group of people supported the free-market ideas of Adam Smith? (b) Why?
4. How did Utopian socialists propose to end the miseries brought by the Industrial Revolution?
5. (a) Describe Karl Marx's view of history. (b) How have events challenged that view?
6. *Critical Thinking* **Linking Past and Present** Choose *one* economic or political theory discussed in this section. Then, analyze it in relation to life today.
7. *ACTIVITY* Make a chart outlining the main ideas of the individuals discussed in this section. Then, compare *two* of them.

# 3 | CHAPTER REVIEW AND SKILLS FOR SUCCESS

## CHAPTER REVIEW

### REVIEWING VOCABULARY

Review the vocabulary words in this chapter. Then, use *five* of these vocabulary words and their definitions to create a matching quiz. Exchange quizzes with another student. Check each other's answers when you are finished.

### REVIEWING FACTS

1. How did the enclosure movement affect people?
2. What new source of energy helped trigger the Industrial Revolution?
3. List three reasons why the Industrial Revolution began in Britain.
4. What inventions improved transportation on land and on sea?
5. Why did large numbers of people migrate to cities?
6. What benefits and problems did the Industrial Revolution create?
7. List the government reforms sought by John Stuart Mill.
8. Why did Marx's prediction of a proletarian revolution not come true?

## SKILLS FOR SUCCESS RECOGNIZING FAULTY REASONING

Whenever you participate in a discussion or a debate, you begin your argument with a **premise**, or statement that is the basis for your argument. You then build on your premise by adding specific arguments. You try to reach a **conclusion** that is so sound that the other side will agree with you.

Many people, however, employ faulty reasoning during discussions. Three common types of faulty reasoning are (1) attacking your opponents rather than their arguments, (2) incorrectly stating cause-and-effect relationships, and (3) using circular arguments, or giving a conclusion that simply restates your premise.

In the dialogue at right, several students are discussing the Industrial Revolution. Read the dialogue, and follow the steps to identify the faulty reasoning.

1. **Identify personal attacks.** (a) Which student is focusing on the person rather than on the argument? (b) Why is this faulty reasoning?

2. **Identify incorrect statements of cause-and-effect relationships.** (a) What argument does Student B use to criticize the Industrial Revolution? (b) Why is this faulty reasoning?

3. **Identify circular arguments.** (a) Which student uses circular reasoning to support his or her argument? (b) How is this circular reasoning?

> **Student A:** "I don't see how anyone can question the benefits of the Industrial Revolution. Without it, think of all the machines and scientific advances we wouldn't have today."
>
> **Student B:** "I don't agree. After all, the Industrial Revolution caused a lot of suffering. In 1860, shortly after the Industrial Revolution, the Civil War broke out in the United States. Later came World War I in Europe."
>
> **Student C:** "But the Industrial Revolution also produced labor unions and the middle class."
>
> **Student D:** "Your reasoning is all wrong. Those changes were produced by reformers who could see that all these new machines were just taking advantage of people."
>
> **Student E:** "I'd expect *you* to make a statement like that. After all, you still use a pencil and paper to do your homework. You just don't like machines!"

## REVIEWING CHAPTER THEMES

Review the "Focus On" questions at the start of this chapter. Then select *three* of those questions and answer them, using information from the chapter.

## CRITICAL THINKING

1. **Recognizing Causes and Effects** Why were the agricultural revolution and the energy revolution necessary to the Industrial Revolution?

2. **Analyzing Political Cartoons** Study the political cartoon on page 102. (a) What is the subject of the cartoon? (b) Who are the men on horseback? (c) Who are the people under attack? (d) What do you think was the artist's purpose in creating the cartoon?

3. **Defending a Position** Do you think that the negative social consequences of the Industrial Revolution could have been avoided? Use material from the chapter to defend your position.

## ANALYZING PRIMARY SOURCES

Use the quotations on pages 94, second column, and 100 to answer the following questions.

1. What is the mood of each quotation?

2. What picture did each writer present of the Industrial Revolution?

3. How might you account for the difference between the two views?

## FOR YOUR PORTFOLIO

**CONDUCTING A CLASS DEBATE** Work with classmates as part of a team to debate topics related to the chapter. Begin by reviewing the rules for formal debates. Assign two teams to each topic that the class wants to debate. Next, work with your team to prepare arguments for your side. As each pair of teams holds its debate, the rest of the class serves as an audience.

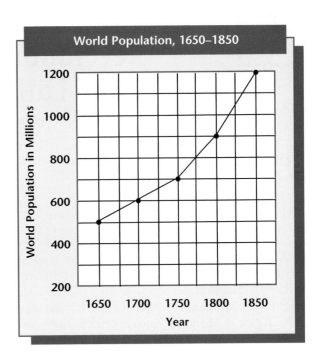

## ANALYZING GRAPHS

Use the graph as well as information from the chapter to answer the following questions.

1. What happened to world population during the period shown in the graph?

2. By how many people did world population rise between 1650 and 1700? Between 1800 and 1850?

3. By what year had the world population of 1700 doubled?

4. What were some causes of the population growth shown in the graph?

## INTERNET ACTIVITY

**WRITING AN OPINION PAPER** Use the Internet to research primary or secondary sources on the daily life of factory workers during the Industrial Revolution. Then write an opinion paper explaining why you do or do not think that the benefits of living in an industrialized nation today outweigh the negative social consequences of the Industrial Revolution.

# Revolutions in Europe and Latin America

## (1790–1848)

**CHAPTER OUTLINE**

1  An Age of Ideologies
2  To the Barricades!
3  Latin American Wars of Independence

Was it possible that an opera could spark a revolution? The answer was a resounding "Yes" in Brussels on August 25, 1830. That night, the audience at the opera house, the Théâtre de la Monnaie, eagerly settled into their seats. They had come to see a popular new opera, *La Muette de Portici*. But was their real interest in the opera's music or in its political content?

The opera is set in Naples, Italy. The year is 1647, and Naples is under Spanish rule. The hero, a young fisherman named Masaniello, yearns to free his country. In the second act, he sings of his love for his land:

66Sacred love of country
　　Restore to us our daring and
　　　our pride!
　　My country gave me life
　　And I shall give it liberty.99

The Belgian audience listened raptly to Masaniello's words. For 15 years, since the Congress of Vienna, Belgians had been forced to live under Dutch rule. As the tenor lingered over the last lines of the aria, the audience rose to their feet and joined their voices to his.

Outside, crowds of students and workers took up the patriotic song. Within hours, the demonstrations in Brussels turned into riots and then into a full-scale revolt against Dutch rule. Within days, the Belgians had successfully ejected the Dutch from their land. By year's end, they had won independence.

The Brussels revolt was part of a wave of violent uprisings that swept Western Europe in the first half of the 1800s. Across the continent, minor incidents flared into revolution. This "age of revolutions," as it is sometimes called, was fueled by the political ideas of the French Revolution and the economic problems caused by the Industrial Revolution.

In the aftermath of the Congress of Vienna, the great powers sought to silence liberal and nationalist demands. But simmering discontent erupted in three major revolutionary outbreaks—in the 1820s, 1830, and 1848. Rebels, divided by class interests, were soon crushed. Still, the uprisings sent a chilling message to rulers across Europe. The winds of liberalism and nationalism also swept across the Atlantic, igniting wars of independence in Latin America.

**FOCUS ON** these questions as you read:

■ **Political and Social Systems**
　How were revolutionaries seeking to change the European political and social system?

■ **Economics and Technology**
　How did economic changes contribute to revolutionary unrest in Europe?

■ **Continuity and Change**
　How were the revolutions of the early 1800s an outgrowth of the French Revolution?

■ **Global Interaction**
　How did events and ideas in Europe affect the people of Latin America?

**TIME AND PLACE**

**The Spirit of Revolution** *In 1830 and again in 1848, the streets of European cities seethed with rebellion. As in 1789, the revolts began in Paris and spread across the continent. In time, the revolutionary spark jumped the Atlantic and ignited uprisings in the Americas. Here, a French crowd storms the barricades.* **Art and Literature** *Do you think the painter supported the rebels? Explain.*

## HUMANITIES LINK

*Art History* Honoré Daumier, *"You Have the Floor"* (page 116).
*Literature* In this chapter, you will encounter passages from the following works of literature: Daniel Auber, Eugène Scribe, Germaine Delavigne, *La Muette de Portici* (page 110); Stendhal, *The Charterhouse of Parma* (page 112).

**1804**
Haiti declares independence from France

**1810**
Mexican Revolution begins

**1824**
Latin American wars for independence end

**1830**
Belgium begins fight for independence

**1848**
Revolutions take place throughout Europe

1790    1800    1810    1820    1830    1840    1850

#  An Age of Ideologies

## Guide for Reading

- How did the goals of conservatives and liberals differ?

- How did nationalism pose a challenge to the old order?

- Why was Europe plagued by constant unrest after 1815?

- **Vocabulary** *ideology, universal manhood suffrage, autonomy*

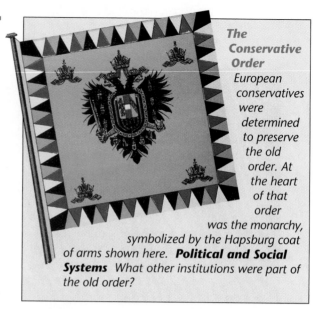

*The Conservative Order* European conservatives were determined to preserve the old order. At the heart of that order was the monarchy, symbolized by the Hapsburg coat of arms shown here. **Political and Social Systems** What other institutions were part of the old order?

A "revolutionary seed" had been planted in Europe, warned Prince Clemens von Metternich. The ideas spread by the French Revolution and Napoleon Bonaparte, he believed, not only threatened Europe's monarchs. They also undermined its basic social values:

> 66Kings have to calculate the chances of their very existence in the immediate future. Passions are let loose and [join] together to overthrow everything that society respects as the basis of its existence: religion, public morality, laws, customs, rights, and duties, all are attacked, confounded, overthrown, or called in question.99

At the Congress of Vienna, the European powers had sought to uproot that "revolutionary seed." Other voices, however, kept challenging the order imposed in 1815. The clash of people with opposing ideologies, or systems of thought and belief, plunged Europe into a period of turmoil that lasted more than 30 years.

## Preserving the Old Order

The Congress of Vienna was a clear victory for conservative forces. Who were these forces? And what did they want?

Conservatives included monarchs and members of their government, noble landowners, and church leaders. They supported the political and social order that had come under attack during the French Revolution. They had

benefited in many ways from the old order. Conservative ideas also appealed to peasants, who wanted to preserve traditional ways.

**Goals.** The conservatives in 1815 had very different goals from conservatives in the United States today. Conservatives of the early 1800s wanted to turn back the clock to the way things had been before 1789. They wanted to restore to power the royal families that had lost their thrones when Napoleon swept across Europe. They accepted the hierarchy of social classes. The lower classes, they felt, should respect and obey their social superiors. Conservatives also backed an established church—Catholic in Austria and the southern European countries, Orthodox in Eastern Europe, and Protestant in Britain, the Netherlands, Prussia, and the Scandinavian lands.

**Attitude toward change.** Conservatives believed that talk about natural rights and constitutional government could lead only to chaos, as it had in France in 1789. If change had to come, they argued, it must come slowly. A character in a novel by the French writer Stendhal expresses the conservative view:

> 66The words *liberty, justice,* and *happiness of the greatest number* are criminal. They give men's minds a habit of discussion. Man ends by distrusting . . . the authority of the princes set up by God.99

Conservatives equated their own interests with peace and stability for all people. Conservative leaders like Metternich opposed freedom of the press. They urged monarchs throughout Europe to suppress revolutionary ideas and crush protests in their own countries. Metternich also proposed that monarchs should step in to defeat successful revolutions in neighboring lands. ( ★ See *Skills for Success*, page 128.)

## The Liberal Challenge

Challenging the conservatives at every turn were the liberals. In the early 1800s, liberals embraced Enlightenment ideas spread by the French Revolution. They spoke out against divine-right monarchy, the old aristocracy, and established churches. They defended the natural rights of individuals to liberty, equality, and property.

Because liberals spoke mostly for the bourgeoisie, or middle class, their ideas are sometimes called "bourgeois liberalism." Liberals included business owners, bankers, and lawyers, as well as politicians, newspaper editors, writers, and others who helped to shape public opinion.

**Political ideas.** Liberals wanted governments to be based on written constitutions and separation of powers. They called for rulers elected by the people and responsible to them. Thus, most liberals favored a republican form of government over a monarchy, or at least wanted the monarch to be limited by a constitution.

The liberals of the early 1800s saw the role of government as limited to protecting basic rights such as freedom of thought, speech, and religion. They believed that only male property owners or others with a financial stake in society should have the right to vote. Only later in the century would liberals throw their support behind the principle of universal manhood suffrage, giving all adult men the right to vote, and social reforms. John Stuart Mill, an influential English liberal, was a notable exception, who urged equal rights for women.

**Economic views.** Liberals strongly supported the laissez-faire economics of Adam Smith and David Ricardo. (See page 44.) They saw the free market as an opportunity for capitalist entrepreneurs to succeed. As capitalists and often employers, liberals had different goals from those of workers laboring in factories, mines, and other enterprises of the early Industrial Revolution.

## Nationalist Stirrings

Another challenge to Metternich's conservative order came from nationalists. Like liberalism, nationalism was an outgrowth of the Enlightenment and the French Revolution. Also like liberalism, it ignited a number of revolts against established rule.

**Goals.** For centuries, European rulers had won or lost lands in war. They exchanged territories and the people who lived in them like pieces in a game. Regions also passed back and forth with various marriages between royal families. As a result of all this land swapping, by 1815 Europe had several empires that included many nationalities. The Austrian, Russian, and Ottoman empires, for example, each included diverse peoples.

Unifying and gaining independence for people with a common national heritage became a major goal of nationalists in the 1800s. Each national group, they believed, should have its own state.

While nationalism gave people with a common heritage a sense of identity and a goal—establishment of their own homeland—it also had negative effects. It often bred intolerance and led to persecution of national or ethnic minorities.

**Revolts in the Balkans.** The Balkans, in southeastern Europe, were home to many ethnic groups. In the early 1800s, several Balkan peoples rebelled against the Ottomans, who had ruled them for more than 300 years.

The first Balkan people to revolt were the Serbs. In two major rebellions between 1804 and 1817, the Serbs suffered terrible defeats. In the end, however, they achieved autonomy, or self-rule, within the Ottoman empire. The bitter

**ISSUES For TODAY** Conservatives in the 1800s tried to preserve the old social order by holding back the forces of change. How can the need for social and political change be balanced with the desire for a stable society?

struggle fostered a sense of Serbian identity. A revival of Slavic literature and culture added to the sense of nationhood.

**Independence for the Greeks.** In 1821, the Greeks, too, revolted, seeking to end centuries of Ottoman rule. At first, the Greeks were badly divided. But years of suffering in long, bloody wars of independence helped shape a national identity.

Leaders of the rebellion justified their struggle as "a national war, a holy war, a war the object of which is to reconquer the rights of individual liberty." They appealed for support to Western Europeans, who admired ancient Greek civilization.

The Greeks won sympathy in the West. In the late 1820s, Britain, France, and even conservative Russia forced the Ottomans to grant independence to some Greek provinces. By 1830, Greece was independent. The European powers, however, pressured the Greeks to accept a German king, a move meant to show that they did not support revolution. Still, liberals were enthusiastic, while nationalists everywhere saw reasons to hope for a country of their own.

## Challenges to the Old Order

Several other challenges to the Vienna settlement erupted in the 1820s. Revolts occurred along the southern fringe of Europe. In Spain, Portugal, and the Italian states, rebels demanded constitutional governments.

Metternich urged conservative rulers to crush the uprisings. A French army marched into Spain to suppress a revolt, while Austrian forces crossed the Alps to smash Italian rebels.

Troops dampened the fires of liberalism and nationalism in western and southern areas of Europe, but could not smother them. In the next decades, sparks would flare anew. Added to liberal and nationalist demands were the goals of the new industrial working class. By the mid-1800s, social reformers and agitators were urging workers to support socialism or some other way of reorganizing property ownership, further contributing to the unrest of this period.

*Greek Independence* *Inspired by the nationalism that was sweeping Europe, the Greeks proclaimed independence. For a decade, they battled their Ottoman rulers. At last, after the British, French, and Russians intervened, the Turks granted Greece independence. Here, a victorious Greek soldier raises the national flag over a defeated enemy.* **Art and Literature** *Compare this painting with that on page 111. How does each represent the spirit of nationalism?*

## SECTION 1 REVIEW

1. **Identify** (a) conservatives, (b) liberals, (c) nationalists.
2. **Define** (a) ideology, (b) universal manhood suffrage, (c) autonomy.
3. (a) Which groups backed conservative ideas? Why? (b) How did the political goals of conservatives differ from those of liberals?
4. How did nationalists threaten the system set up by Metternich?
5. *Critical Thinking* **Applying Information** How did ideologies like liberalism and nationalism contribute to unrest?
6. *ACTIVITY* Create a series of political cartoons expressing the point of view of each of the following groups: (a) conservatives, (b) liberals, (c) nationalists.

# To the Barricades!

## Guide for Reading

- Why did revolts break out in France in 1830 and 1848?

- How did revolutions in France affect other parts of Europe?

- Why did the revolts of 1830 and 1848 generally fail to achieve their goals?

The quick suppression of liberal and nationalist uprisings in the 1820s did not end Europe's age of revolutions. "We are sleeping on a volcano," warned Alexis de Tocqueville, a liberal French leader who saw widespread discontent. "Do you not see that the Earth trembles anew? A wind of revolution blows, the storm is on the horizon."

In 1830 and 1848, Europeans saw street protests explode into full-scale revolts. As in 1789, the upheavals began in Paris and radiated out across the continent.

### France After the Restoration

When the Congress of Vienna restored Louis XVIII to the French throne, he prudently issued a constitution, the Charter of French Liberties. It created a two-house legislature and allowed limited freedom of the press. Still, while Louis was careful to shun absolutism, the king retained much power.

**Efforts at compromise.** Louis's efforts at compromise satisfied few people. Ultraroyalists, supporters on the far right, despised constitutional government and wanted to restore the old regime. The "ultras" included many high clergy and emigré nobles who had returned to France after the Revolution.

The ultras faced bitter opposition from other factions. Liberals wanted to extend suffrage and win a share of power for middle-class citizens like themselves. On the left, radicals yearned for a republic like that of the 1790s. And in working-class slums, men and women wanted what they had wanted in 1789—a decent day's pay and bread they could afford.

**The July revolution.** When Louis XVIII died in 1824, his brother, Charles X, inherited the throne. Charles, a strong believer in absolutism, rejected the very idea of the charter. In July 1830, he suspended the legislature, limited the right to vote, and restricted the press.

Liberals and radicals responded forcefully to the king's challenge. In Paris, angry citizens threw up barricades across the narrow streets. From behind them, they fired on the soldiers and pelted them with stones and roof tiles. Within days, rebels controlled Paris. The revolutionary tricolor flew from the towers of Notre Dame cathedral. A frightened Charles X abdicated and fled to England.

With the king gone, radicals wanted to set up a republic. Moderate liberals, however, insisted on a constitutional monarchy. The Chamber of Deputies, the lower house of the French legislature, chose Louis Philippe as king. He was a cousin of Charles X and in his youth, had supported the revolution of 1789.

**The "citizen king."** The French called Louis Philippe the "citizen king" because he owed his throne to the people. Louis got along well with the liberal bourgeoisie. Like them, he dressed in a frock coat and top hat. Sometimes, he strolled the streets, shaking hands with well-wishers. Liberal politicians and professionals filled his government.

Under Louis Philippe, the upper bourgeoisie prospered. Louis extended suffrage, but only to France's wealthiest citizens. The vast majority of the people still could not vote. Louis Philippe's other policies also favored the middle class at the expense of the workers.

### The French Revolution of 1848

In the 1840s, discontent grew. Radicals formed secret societies to work for a French republic. Utopian socialists called for an end of private ownership of property. (See Chapter 3.) Even liberals denounced Louis Philippe's government for corruption and called for expanded suffrage.

Toward the end of the decade, an economic slump shut down factories. Harvests were poor. People lost their jobs and bread prices soared. Scandals involving high officials filled the newspapers. As in 1789, Paris was ripe for revolution.

## ART HISTORY

La Caricature (Journal) N° 446

*"You have the floor; explain yourself!"*

**"You Have the Floor"** The political cartoons of French artist Honoré Daumier combine masterful line drawings with a sharp wit. His works were immensely influential in calling attention to the social injustices of the time. In this drawing, Daumier depicts a court scene. The defendant, mouth gagged and arms pinned down by his prosecutors, stands before the judge. The judge snarls, "You have the floor; explain yourself!" **Art and Literature** What do the judge's words mean? Based on the cartoon, what is Daumier's view of the French justice system?

**"February Days."** In February 1848, when the government took steps to silence critics and prevent public meetings, angry crowds took to the streets. During the "February Days," iron railings, overturned carts, paving stones, and toppled trees again blocked the streets of Paris. Church bells rang alarms, while women and men on the barricades sang the revolutionary "La Marseillaise." A number of demonstrators clashed with royal troops and were killed.

As the turmoil spread, Louis Philippe abdicated. A group of liberal, radical, and socialist leaders proclaimed the Second Republic. (The First Republic had lasted from 1792 until 1804, when Napoleon became emperor.)

From the start, deep differences divided the new government. Middle-class liberals were interested in political reforms such as constitutions. Socialists wanted far-reaching social and economic change that would help hungry work-

ers. In the early days of the new republic, the socialists forced the government to set up national workshops to provide jobs for the unemployed.

**"June Days."** By June, however, upper- and middle-class interests had won control of the government. They saw the national workshops as a waste of money, and they shut them down.

Furious, workers took to the streets of Paris, rallying to the cry "Bread or Lead!" This time, however, bourgeois liberals turned violently against the protesters. Peasants, who feared that socialists might take their land, also attacked the rioting workers. At least 1,500 people were killed before the government crushed the rebellion.

The fighting of the "June Days" left a bitter legacy. The middle class both feared and distrusted the left, while the working class nursed a deep hatred for the bourgeoisie.

**Louis Napoleon.** Toward the end of the year, the National Assembly, dominated by forces who wanted to restore order, issued a constitution for the Second Republic. It created a strong president and a one-house legislature. But it also gave the vote to all adult men, the widest suffrage in the world at the time. Nine million Frenchmen now could vote, compared to only 200,000 who had that right before.

When elections for president were held, the overwhelming winner was Louis Napoleon, nephew of Napoleon Bonaparte. The "new" Napoleon attracted the working classes by presenting himself as a man who cared about social issues such as poverty. At the same time, his famous name, linked with order and authority as well as with France's past glories, helped him with conservatives.

Once in office, Louis Napoleon used his position as a steppingstone to greater power. By 1852, he had proclaimed himself emperor, taking the title Napoleon III. (He was the third Napoleon because the son of Napoleon I, Napoleon II, had died in his youth without ever ruling France.) Thus ended the short-lived Second Republic.

Like his celebrated uncle, Louis Napoleon used a plebiscite to win public approval for his seizure of power. A stunning 90 percent of voters supported his move to set up the Second Empire. Many saw a monarchy as more stable than a republic. Millions of French also recalled the glory days of Napoleon Bonaparte and hoped that his nephew would restore the magic. A few voters even thought he was the old Napoleon, miraculously still alive and returned from exile!

In fact, Napoleon III, like Louis Philippe, ruled at a time of rapid economic growth. For the bourgeoisie, the early days of the Second Empire brought prosperity and contentment. In time, however, Napoleon III would embark on foreign adventures that brought down his empire and ended France's long leadership in Europe.

## "Europe Catches Cold"

In both 1830 and 1848, the revolts in Paris inspired uprisings elsewhere in Europe. As Metternich said, "When France sneezes, Europe catches cold." Most uprisings were suppressed. But here and there, rebels did force changes on conservative governments. Even when they failed, they frightened rulers badly enough to encourage reform later in the century.

**Belgium.** The one notable success for Europe's revolutionaries in 1830 took place in Belgium. In 1815, the Congress of Vienna had united the Austrian Netherlands (present-day Belgium) and the Kingdom of Holland under the Dutch king. The Congress had wanted to create a strong barrier against French expansion.

The Belgians resented the new arrangement. The Belgians and Dutch had different languages, religions, and economic interests. The Belgians were Catholic, while the Dutch were Protestant. The Belgian economy was based on manufacturing; the Dutch, on trade.

In 1830, news of the Paris uprising that toppled Charles X ignited a revolutionary spark in Belgium. Students and workers threw up barri-

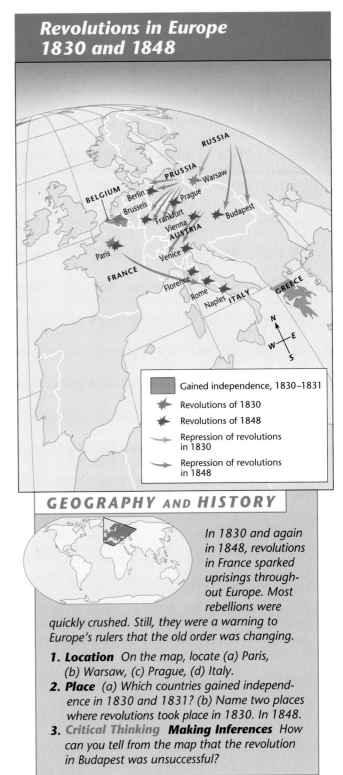

## Revolutions in Europe 1830 and 1848

Gained independence, 1830–1831

★ Revolutions of 1830

★ Revolutions of 1848

→ Repression of revolutions in 1830

→ Repression of revolutions in 1848

### GEOGRAPHY AND HISTORY

In 1830 and again in 1848, revolutions in France sparked uprisings throughout Europe. Most rebellions were quickly crushed. Still, they were a warning to Europe's rulers that the old order was changing.

1. **Location** On the map, locate (a) Paris, (b) Warsaw, (c) Prague, (d) Italy.
2. **Place** (a) Which countries gained independence in 1830 and 1831? (b) Name two places where revolutions took place in 1830. In 1848.
3. *Critical Thinking* **Making Inferences** How can you tell from the map that the revolution in Budapest was unsuccessful?

cades in Brussels, the capital. The Dutch king turned to the other European powers for help. Britain and France, however, believing they would benefit from the separation of Belgium and Holland, supported Belgian demands for independence. The conservative powers—Austria, Prussia, and Russia—were too busy putting down revolts of their own to become involved.

As a result, in 1831, Belgium became an independent state with a liberal constitution. Shortly after, the major European powers signed a treaty recognizing Belgium as a "perpetually neutral state." Protecting Belgian neutrality would be an important issue at the outset of World War I, in 1914. (See page 284.)

**Poland.** Nationalists in Poland also staged an uprising in 1830. But, unlike the Belgians, the Poles failed to win independence for their country.

In the late 1700s, Russia, Austria, and Prussia had divided up Poland among themselves. Poles had hoped that the Congress of Vienna would restore their homeland in 1815. Instead, the great powers handed most of Poland to Russia.

In 1830, Polish students, army officers, and landowners rose in revolt. They failed to gain widespread support, however, and were brutally crushed by Russian forces. Survivors fled to Western Europe and the United States, where they kept alive the dream of freedom. "Poland is not yet lost," they proudly declared, "while still we live."

## The Springtime of the Peoples

In 1848, revolts in Paris again unleashed a tidal wave of revolution across Europe. For opponents of the old order, it was a time of such hope that they called it the "springtime of the peoples." Michael Bakunin, a young Russian revolutionary, recalled the feeling of unlimited possibilities:

❝It seemed as if the entire world was turned upside down. The improbable became commonplace, the impossible possible. . . . If someone had said, 'God has been driven from heaven and a republic has been proclaimed there,' . . . no one would have been surprised.❞

**Sources of discontent.** Revolution in France was the spark that touched off the revolts. But grievances had been piling up for years.

Unrest came from many sources. Middle-class liberals wanted a greater share of political power for themselves, as well as protections for the basic rights of all citizens. Workers demanded relief from the miseries of the spreading Industrial Revolution. And nationalists of all classes ached to throw off foreign rule. By 1848, discontent was so widespread that it was only a matter of time before it exploded into full-scale revolution.

**Metternich falls.** In the Austrian empire, revolt first broke out in Vienna, taking the government by surprise. Metternich, who had dominated Austrian politics for more than 30 years, tried to suppress the students who took to the streets. But when workers rose up to support the students, Metternich resigned and fled in disguise. The Austrian emperor promised reform.

▲ Metternich flees in disguise

Revolution quickly spread to other parts of the empire. In Budapest, Hungarian nationalists led by Louis Kossuth demanded an independent government. They also called for an end to serfdom and a written constitution to protect basic rights. In Prague, the Czechs made similar demands. Overwhelmed by events, the Austrian government agreed to the reforms.

Any gains were short-lived, however. The Austrian army soon regained control of Vienna and Prague. With Russian help, Austrian forces also smashed the rebels in Budapest. Many were imprisoned or executed or forced into exile.

**Revolution in Italy.** Uprisings also erupted in the Italian states. Nationalists wanted to end domination of Italy by the Austrian Hapsburgs. As elsewhere, nationalist goals were linked to demands for liberal reforms such as constitutional government. Workers suffering economic hardships demanded even more radical changes.

From Venice in the north to Naples in the south, Italians set up independent republics. Revolutionaries even expelled the pope from Rome and installed a nationalist government. (See Chapter 6.)

Before long, however, the forces of reaction surged back here, too. Austrian troops ousted the new governments in northern Italy. A French army restored the pope to power in Rome. In Naples, local rulers betrayed their promises to the rebels, canceling the reforms they had reluctantly accepted.

**Turmoil in the German states.** In the German states, university students passionately demanded national unity and liberal reforms. Economic hard times and a potato famine brought peasants and workers into the struggle. Workers destroyed the machines that threatened their livelihood, while peasants burned the homes of wealthy landowners.

Women, too, plunged into the struggle. A German woman explained her reasons for fighting alongside her husband:

66You know it was not [enthusiasm for] war that called me, but love. Yet I must confess—hate, too, a burning hate generated in the struggle against tyrants and oppressors of sacred human rights.99

In Prussia, liberals forced King Frederick William IV to agree to a constitution written by an elected assembly. Within a year, though, he dissolved the assembly. Later, he issued his own constitution keeping power in his own hands or those of the upper classes.

**Frankfurt Assembly.** Throughout 1848, delegates from many German states met in the Frankfurt Assembly. "We are to create a constitution for Germany, for the whole land," declared one leader with boundless optimism.

Divisions soon emerged. Delegates debated endlessly on such topics as whether the new Germany should be a republic or a monarchy, and whether or not to include Austria in a united German state. Finally, the assembly offered Prussia's Frederick William IV the crown of a united Germany. To their dismay, the conservative king rejected the offer because it came not from the German princes but from the people— "from the gutter," as he described it. By early 1849, the assembly was dissolved, under threat from the Prussian military.

Outside the assembly, liberals clashed with workers whose demands were too radical for middle-class reformers to accept. Conservative forces rallied, dousing the last flames of revolt.

**GLOBAL CONNECTIONS**

The defeat of liberal forces in Europe in 1848 had a profound effect on the other side of the world. By the 1850s, Japan would begin to emerge from centuries of self-imposed isolation. Seeking to modernize, the new leaders of Japan looked to Europe for examples. The nation that they chose as a model was the conservative, militaristic Germany that had emerged after the defeat of the liberals in 1848. As a result, modern Japan, like Germany after 1848, was marked by political conservatism and emphasis on a strong military.

Hundreds were killed. Many more went to prison. And thousands of Germans left their homeland, most for the cities of the United States.

## Looking Ahead

By 1850, the flickering light of rebellion faded, ending the age of liberal revolution that had begun in 1789. Why did the uprisings fail? In general, revolutionaries did not have mass support. In Poland in 1830, for example, peasants did not take part in the uprising. In 1848, a growing gulf divided workers seeking radical economic change and liberals pursuing moderate political reform.

By mid-century, Metternich was gone from the European scene. Still, his conservative system remained in force. In the decades ahead, liberalism, nationalism, and socialism would win successes not through revolution but through political activity. Ambitious political leaders would unify Germany and Italy. Workers would campaign for reforms through unions and the ballot box, as they increasingly won the right to vote.

## SECTION 2 REVIEW

1. **Identify** (a) Charter of French Liberties, (b) Charles X, (c) Louis Philippe, (d) Louis Napoleon, (e) Louis Kossuth, (f) Frankfurt Assembly.
2. (a) What were the causes of the French revolution of 1830? (b) What were its effects?
3. How was the French revolution of 1848 really two revolutions?
4. Why did conservative leaders in Europe fear news of revolutions in France?
5. Why did most revolts in the 1830s and 1840s fail?
6. *Critical Thinking* **Identifying Alternatives** Do you think that European rulers could have prevented nationalist revolts by allowing reforms? Why or why not?
7. *ACTIVITY* Create a "docudrama" for television based on the "February Days" and "June Days" during the French revolution of 1848.

# 3 Latin American Wars of Independence

## Guide for Reading

- What were the long-term causes of the revolutions in Latin America?
- How did Haiti's struggle for freedom differ from independence fights in other parts of Latin America?
- How did Mexico and the nations of South America win independence?

Like many wealthy Latin American* creoles, young Simón Bolívar (boh LEE vahr) was sent to Europe to complete his education. There, he became a strong admirer of the ideals of the French Revolution.

One afternoon, Bolívar and his Italian tutor sat talking about freedom and the rights of ordinary people. Bolívar's thoughts turned to his homeland, held as a colony by Spain. He fell on his knees and swore a solemn oath:

  **"**I swear before God and by my honor never to allow my hands to be idle nor my soul to rest until I have broken the chains that bind us to Spain.**"**

In later years, Bolívar would fulfill his oath, leading the struggle to liberate northern South America from Spain. Elsewhere in Latin America, other leaders organized independence movements. By 1825, most of Latin America had been freed from colonial rule.

## Climate of Discontent

By the late 1700s, the revolutionary fever that gripped Western Europe had spread to Latin America. There, discontent was rooted in

---

*Latin America* refers to the regions in Middle and South America colonized by Europeans, especially the Spanish, French, and Portuguese, whose languages are rooted in Latin. It includes Spanish-speaking countries from Mexico to Argentina, Portuguese-speaking Brazil, and French-speaking Haiti.

the social, racial, and political system that had emerged during 300 years of Spanish rule.

**Ethnic and social hierarchy.** Spanish-born peninsulares dominated Latin American political and social life. Only they could hold top jobs in government and the Church. Many creoles—the European-descended Latin Americans who owned the haciendas, ranches, and mines—bitterly resented their second-class status. Merchants fretted under mercantilist policies that tied the colonies to Spain. "Commerce ought to be as free as air," declared one colonial merchant.

Meanwhile, a growing population of mestizos and mulattoes were angry at being denied the status, wealth, and power that were available to whites. Native Americans suffered economic misery under the Spanish, who had conquered the lands of their ancestors. In the Caribbean region and parts of South America, masses of enslaved Africans who worked on plantations longed for freedom.

Beyond dissatisfaction with Spanish rule, the different classes had little in common. In fact, they distrusted and feared one another. At times, they worked together against the Spanish. But once independence was achieved, the creoles, who had led the revolts, dominated the governments.

**Enlightenment ideas.** In the 1700s, educated creoles read the works of Enlightenment thinkers such as Voltaire, Rousseau, and Montesquieu. They watched colonists in North America throw off British rule. Translations of the Declaration of Independence and the Constitution of the United States even circulated among the creole elite.

Women actively participated in the exchange of ideas. In some cities, women hosted and attended salons, called *tertulias,* where independence and revolution were discussed.

During the French Revolution, young creoles like Simón Bolívar traveled in Europe and were inspired by the ideals of "liberty, equality, and brotherhood." Still, while Enlightenment ideas and revolutions in other lands touched off debates, most creoles were reluctant to act.

**Napoleon.** The spark that finally ignited widespread revolt in Latin America was Napoleon's invasion of Spain in 1808. Napoleon ousted the Spanish king and placed his brother

*Social Classes in Latin America* These portraits, both by Edouard Pingret, paint contrasting pictures of life in colonial Latin America. The wealthy women at top are probably peninsulares, Spanish-born settlers who dominated political and social life. At the opposite end of the social scale was the Native American woman, at bottom. This inequality between classes fed discontent and in time resulted in uprising. **Diversity** What other classes made up the social hierarchy in Latin America?

Joseph on the Spanish throne. Latin American leaders saw Spain's weakness as an opportunity to reject foreign domination and demand independence from colonial rule.

## Haiti's Struggle

Even before Spanish colonists hoisted the flag of freedom, revolution had erupted elsewhere in Latin America, in a French-ruled colony on the island of Hispaniola. Haiti, as it is now called, was France's most valued possession in the 1700s.

In Haiti, French planters owned great sugar plantations worked by nearly a half million enslaved Africans. The sugar trade was hugely profitable, but conditions for enslaved workers were horrendous. Many were cruelly overworked and underfed. Haiti also had a population of both free and enslaved mulattoes. Free mulattoes, however, had few rights and were badly treated by the French.

In the 1790s, revolutionaries in France were debating ways to abolish slavery in the West Indies. However, debating the issue in Paris did not help enslaved Haitians gain their freedom. Embittered by suffering and inspired by talk of liberty and equality, they took action. In 1791, a slave revolt exploded in northern Haiti. Under the able leadership of Toussaint L'Ouverture (too SAN loo vuhr TYOOR), Haitians would fight for freedom and pave the way for throwing off French rule.

## Toussaint L'Ouverture

Toussaint L'Ouverture was born into slavery in Haiti. But his father, the son of a noble West African family, had only recently been brought to the West Indian island. He taught the boy to take pride in his African heritage.

Toussaint learned to speak both French and the African language of his ancestors. Thanks to a kind master, he also learned to read. He pored over stories of slave revolts in ancient Rome and of military heroes like Julius Caesar.

In time, Toussaint read the works of the French philosophes. One passage, in particular, impressed him:

66 Nations of Europe, your slaves need neither your generosity nor your advice to break the . . . yoke that oppresses them. All they need is a brave leader. Who will he be? There is no doubt that he will appear. He will come and raise the sacred standard of liberty. 99

Toussaint determined to be that "brave leader" and bring his people to liberty.

**The uprising begins.** When a slave revolt broke out in 1791, Toussaint was nearly 50 years old. His intelligence and military skills soon earned him the position of leader.

The struggle was long and complex. Toussaint's army of former slaves faced many enemies. Mulattoes, promised high pay, joined French planters against the rebels. France,

*Toussaint L'Ouverture* A self-educated former slave, Toussaint L'Ouverture led Haitians in a revolt against French rule. Although Toussaint was captured and killed, his followers eventually won independence. In 1820, Haiti became a republic, the only nonslave nation in the Western Hemisphere. ***Impact of the Individual*** Compare this portrait with the portrait of Napoleon on page 79. What impression is each artist trying to create?

Spain, and Britain each sent armies to Haiti. The fighting took more lives than any other revolution in the Americas.

**An inspiring commander.** Although untrained, Toussaint was a brilliant general. He was also an inspiring commander. On the eve of one crucial battle, he issued this stirring call to his army:

66Do not disappoint me. Prove yourselves men who know how to value liberty and how to defend it. . . . We are fighting so that liberty—the most precious of all earthly possessions—may not perish. We are fighting to preserve it for ourselves, for our children, for our brothers, for our fellow citizens.99

**Rebuilding.** By 1798, Toussaint had achieved his goal—enslaved Haitians had been freed. And even though Haiti was still a French colony, Toussaint's forces controlled most of the island.

Toussaint set about rebuilding the country, which had been destroyed by long years of war. By offering generous terms, he won the support of French planters. He set out to improve agriculture, expand trade, and give Haiti a constitution. He even tried to heal rifts between classes by opening his government to whites and mulattoes as well as Africans.

**Renewed struggle.** In France, meantime, Napoleon Bonaparte rose to power. He determined to regain control over Haiti. In 1802, he sent a large army to the island.

Toussaint again took up arms, this time to fight for full independence. His guerrilla forces were aided by a deadly ally, yellow fever, which took a growing toll on the invaders. In April 1802, with soldiers dying at the rate of a hundred a day, the French agreed to a truce, or temporary peace.

*"The tree of black liberty."* Shortly after, a trusted French friend lured Toussaint to his house, where he betrayed him. Soldiers seized the Haitian leader and hustled him in chains onto a French warship. As the ship sailed, Toussaint told the captain:

66In overthrowing me, the French have only felled the tree of black liberty in

Haiti. It will shoot up again, for it is deeply rooted, and its roots are many.99

Ten months later, in a cold mountain prison in France, Toussaint died. But Haiti's struggle for freedom continued. In 1804, Haitian leaders declared independence. With yellow fever destroying his army, Napoleon abandoned Haiti. In the years ahead, rival Haitian leaders fought for power. Finally, in 1820, Haiti became a republic, the only nonslave nation in the Western Hemisphere. ▪

## *A Call to Freedom in Mexico*

The slave revolt in Haiti frightened creoles in Spanish America. While they wanted power themselves, most had no desire for economic or social changes that might threaten their way of life. In 1810, however, a creole priest in Mexico, Father Miguel Hidalgo (hih DAHL goh), raised a cry for freedom that would echo across the land.

**El Grito de Dolores.** Father Hidalgo presided over the poor rural parish of Dolores. On the morning of September 16, 1810, he rang the church bells summoning the people to prayer. When they gathered, he startled them with an urgent appeal. We do not know his exact words, but his message is remembered:

66My children, will you be free? Will you make the effort to recover the lands stolen from your forefathers by the hated Spaniards 300 years ago?99

Father Hidalgo's speech became known as "el Grito de Dolores"—the cry of Dolores. It called the people of Mexico to fight for "Independence and Liberty."

Poor Mexicans rallied to Father Hidalgo. A ragged army of poor mestizos and Native Americans marched to the outskirts of Mexico City. At first, some creoles supported the revolt. However, they soon rejected Hidalgo's call for an end to slavery and his plea for reforms to improve conditions for Native Americans. They felt that these policies would cost them power. They also believed that the Indians deserved their lot in life.

After some early successes, the rebels faced growing opposition. Less than a year after he

# PARALLELS THROUGH TIME

## National Flags

For most of history, flags were emblems of an army or a royal family. With the rise of nationalism, however, national flags began to emerge. Today, each nation has a flag whose design represents the ideals of its people.

**Linking Past and Present**  Why do you think designing a flag is often one of the first things a new nation does?

**PAST**  Each new nation of Latin America adopted its own flag. The yellow-blue-red flag of Venezuela symbolized the gold of the Americas separated from Spain by the blue ocean. Argentina borrowed its blue-white-blue flag from fleets that attacked Spanish ports during the colonial era.

**PRESENT**  These flags represent nations that gained independence since 1945. The Star of David on the Israeli flag symbolizes the quest for a Jewish homeland. The shield and crossed spears of Kenya's flag recall its proud struggle for independence.

---

issued the "Grito," Hidalgo was captured and executed, and his followers scattered.

**José Morelos.** Another priest picked up the banner of revolution. Father José Morelos was a mestizo who called for wide-ranging reform. He wanted to improve conditions for the majority of Mexicans, abolish slavery, and give the vote to all men. For four years, Morelos led rebel forces before he, too, was captured and shot in 1815.

Spanish forces, backed by conservative creoles, hunted down the surviving guerrillas. They had almost succeeded in ending the rebel movement when events in Spain had unexpected effects on Mexico.

**Independence achieved.** In Spain in 1820, liberals forced the king to issue a constitution. This alarmed Agustín de Iturbide (ee toor BEE day), a conservative creole in Mexico. Iturbide feared that the new Spanish government might impose liberal reforms on the colonies as well.

Iturbide had spent years fighting Mexican revolutionaries. Suddenly in 1821, he reached out to them. Backed by creoles, mestizos, and Native Americans, he overthrew the Spanish viceroy. Mexico was independent at last.

Iturbide took the title Emperor Agustín I. Soon, however, liberal Mexicans toppled the would-be monarch and set up the Republic of Mexico.

Although Mexico was free of Spanish rule, the lives of most people changed little. Military leaders dominated the government and ruled by force of arms. The next 100 years would see new struggles to improve conditions for Mexicans. These struggles would be even more complicated by the intervention of foreign powers, including the United States.

## New Republics in Central America

Spanish-ruled lands in Central America declared independence in the early 1820s. Iturbide tried to add these areas to his Mexican empire. After his overthrow, local leaders set up a republic called the United Provinces of Central America.

The union was short-lived. It soon fragmented into the separate republics of Guatemala, Nicaragua, Honduras, El Salvador, and Costa Rica. Like Mexico, the new nations faced many social and economic problems.

## Revolutions in South America

In South America, Native Americans had rebelled against Spanish rule as early as the 1700s. These rebellions had limited results, however. It was not until the 1800s that discontent among the creoles sparked a widespread drive for independence.

**An early challenge.** The strongest challenge by Native Americans was led by Tupac Amaru, who claimed descent from the Incan royal family. He demanded that the government end the brutal system of forced Indian labor. Spanish officials rejected the demand for reform.

In 1780, Tupac Amaru organized a revolt. A large army crushed the rebels and captured and killed their leader. But the revolt did have effects. The Spanish king ordered officials to look into the system of forced labor and eventually abolished it.

**A long struggle.** In the early 1800s, widespread discontent began to surface among other South Americans. Educated creoles like Simón Bolívar, whom you read about at the beginning of the section, had applauded the French and American revolutions. They dreamed of winning their own independence.

In 1808, when Napoleon Bonaparte occupied Spain, Bolívar and his friends saw it as a signal to act. Bolívar by then had returned to South America. In 1810, he led an uprising that established a republic in his native Venezuela.

Bolívar's new republic was quickly toppled by conservative

▲ Simón Bolívar

# CAUSE AND EFFECT

## Long-Term Causes

European domination of Latin America
Spread of Enlightenment ideas
American and French revolutions
Growth of nationalism in Latin America

## Immediate Causes

Creoles, mestizos, and Indians resent colonial rule
Revolutionary leaders emerge
Napoleon invades Spain and ousts Spanish king

## INDEPENDENCE MOVEMENTS IN LATIN AMERICA

## Immediate Effects

Toussaint leads slave revolt in Haiti
Colonial rule ends in much of Latin America
Attempts made to rebuild economies

## Long-Term Effects

18 separate republics set up
Continuing efforts to achieve stable democratic governments and to gain economic independence

## Connections Today

Numerous independent nations in Latin America
Ongoing efforts to bring prosperity and democracy to people in Latin America

*Interpreting a Chart* By 1825, most of Latin America had become independent. Growth of nationalism and discontent with colonial rule played a role in bringing about the independence movements. ■ What was one immediate effect of Latin American independence movements? Which effect of independence movements in Latin America continues to this day?

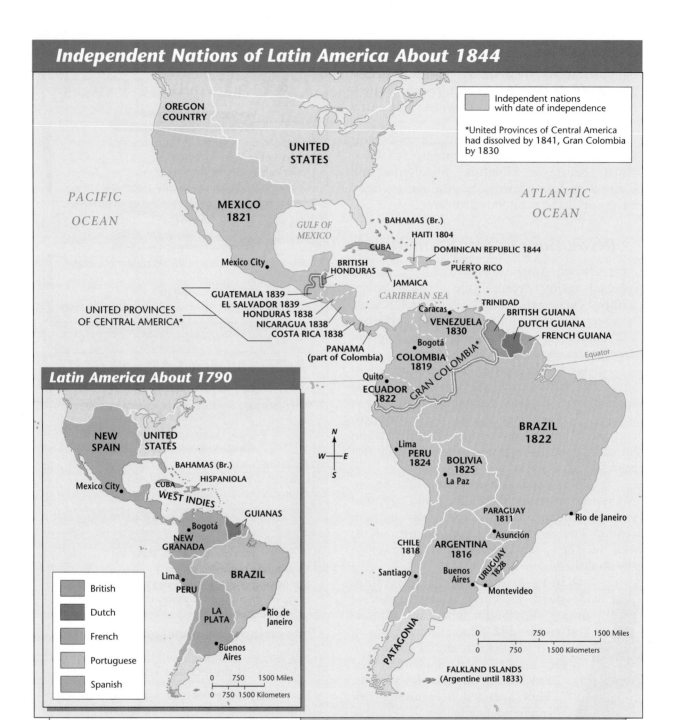

# Independent Nations of Latin America About 1844

Independent nations with date of independence

*United Provinces of Central America had dissolved by 1841, Gran Colombia by 1830

OREGON COUNTRY

UNITED STATES

PACIFIC OCEAN

ATLANTIC OCEAN

MEXICO 1821

Mexico City

GULF OF MEXICO

BAHAMAS (Br.)

HAITI 1804

CUBA

DOMINICAN REPUBLIC 1844

PUERTO RICO

BRITISH HONDURAS

JAMAICA

GUATEMALA 1839

EL SALVADOR 1839

HONDURAS 1838

NICARAGUA 1838

COSTA RICA 1838

UNITED PROVINCES OF CENTRAL AMERICA*

CARIBBEAN SEA

TRINIDAD

Caracas

BRITISH GUIANA

DUTCH GUIANA

FRENCH GUIANA

VENEZUELA 1830

PANAMA (part of Colombia)

Bogotá

COLOMBIA 1819

GRAN COLOMBIA*

Equator

Quito

ECUADOR 1822

BRAZIL 1822

Lima

PERU 1824

BOLIVIA 1825

La Paz

PARAGUAY 1811

Rio de Janeiro

Asunción

CHILE 1818

ARGENTINA 1816

URUGUAY 1828

Santiago

Buenos Aires

Montevideo

N
W — E
S

0     750     1500 Miles
0   750   1500 Kilometers

PATAGONIA

FALKLAND ISLANDS (Argentine until 1833)

## Latin America About 1790

NEW SPAIN

UNITED STATES

Mexico City

BAHAMAS (Br.)

HISPANIOLA

CUBA

WEST INDIES

GUIANAS

Bogotá

NEW GRANADA

BRAZIL

Lima

PERU

LA PLATA

Rio de Janeiro

Buenos Aires

British

Dutch

French

Portuguese

Spanish

0     750     1500 Miles
0   750  1500 Kilometers

## GEOGRAPHY AND HISTORY

In the late 1700s, Europeans controlled most of Latin America. Wars of independence erupted across the region, however, and by the mid-1800s, a number of new nations had been born.

1. **Location** (a) On the main map, locate the following: Mexico, Gran Colombia, Haiti. (b) On the inset map, locate the following: La Plata, New Spain.

2. **Place** (a) Which countries had been carved out of New Granada by 1844? (b) Which independent countries had been part of New Spain?

3. **Critical Thinking** **Synthesizing Information** In a sentence, summarize the information shown on these two maps. Then, explain why the mapmaker needed to include an inset map.

forces. For years, civil war raged in Venezuela. The revolutionaries suffered many setbacks, and twice Bolívar was forced into exile on the island of Haiti.

Then, Bolívar conceived a daring plan. He would march his army across the Andes and attack the Spanish at Bogotá, the capital of the viceroyalty of New Granada (present-day Colombia). First, he cemented an alliance with the hard-riding *llaneros,* or Venezuelan cowboys. Then in a grueling campaign, he led an army through swampy lowlands and over the snow-capped mountains. Finally, in August 1819, he swooped down to take Bogotá from the surprised Spanish.

Other victories followed. By 1821, Bolívar had freed Caracas, Venezuela. "The Liberator," as he was now called, then moved south into Ecuador, Peru, and Bolivia. There, he joined forces with another great South American leader, José de San Martín.

**San Martín.** Like Bolívar, San Martín was a creole. He was born in Argentina but went to Europe for military training. In 1816, this gifted general helped Argentina win freedom from Spain. He then joined the independence struggle in other areas. He, too, led an army across the Andes, from Argentina into Chile. He defeated the Spanish in Chile before moving into Peru to strike further blows against colonial rule.

Bolívar and San Martín tried to work together, but their views were too different. In 1822, San Martín stepped aside, letting Bolívar's forces win the final victories against Spain.

**Dreams and disappointments.** The wars of independence had ended by 1824. Bolívar now worked tirelessly to unite the lands he had liberated into a single nation, called Gran Colombia. Bitter rivalries, however, made that impossible. Before long, Gran Colombia split into three countries: Venezuela, Colombia, and Ecuador.

Bolívar faced another disappointment as power struggles among rival leaders triggered violent civil wars. Spain's former South American colonies faced a long struggle to achieve stable governments—and an even longer one for democracy. (See Chapter 9.) Before his death in 1830, a discouraged Bolívar wrote, "We have achieved our independence at the expense of

everything else." Contrary to his dreams, no social revolution took place. South America's common people had simply changed one set of masters for another.

## *Independence for Brazil*

No revolution or military campaigns were needed to win independence for Brazil. When Napoleon's armies conquered Portugal, the Portuguese royal family fled to Brazil. During his stay in Brazil, the Portuguese king introduced many reforms, including free trade.

When the king returned to Portugal, he left his son Dom Pedro to rule Brazil. "If Brazil demands independence," the king advised Pedro, "proclaim it yourself and put the crown on your own head."

In 1822, Pedro followed his father's advice. He became emperor of an independent Brazil. He accepted a constitution that provided for freedom of the press and religion as well as an elected legislature. Brazil remained a monarchy until 1889, when social and political turmoil led it to become a republic.

## SECTION 3 REVIEW

1. **Identify** (a) Toussaint L'Ouverture, (b) Miguel Hidalgo, (c) el Grito de Dolores, (d) José Morelos, (e) Agustín de Iturbide, (f) Tupac Amaru, (g) Simón Bolívar, (h) José de San Martín, (i) Dom Pedro.
2. How did the colonial class system contribute to discontent in Latin America?
3. (a) What was the first step on Haiti's road to independence? (b) What role did Toussaint L'Ouverture play in Haiti's struggle?
4. Why did creoles in Mexico refuse to support Hidalgo or Morelos?
5. (a) What was Bolívar's goal for South America? (b) Did he achieve his goal? Explain.
6. *Critical Thinking* **Comparing** Compare the ways Mexico and Brazil achieved independence.
7. *ACTIVITY* Imagine that you have been hired by the French government. Create a "wanted" poster for the capture of Toussaint L'Ouverture.

# 4 CHAPTER REVIEW AND SKILLS FOR SUCCESS

## CHAPTER REVIEW

### REVIEWING VOCABULARY

Review the following vocabulary from this chapter: *ideology, universal manhood suffrage, autonomy, nationalism, peninsular, creole, mulatto, mestizo.* Write sentences using each of these terms, leaving blanks where the terms would go. Exchange your sentences with another student and fill in the blanks on each other's lists.

### REVIEWING FACTS

1. What were the goals of the conservatives of the early 1800s?

2. What were the goals of the liberals of that period?

3. What was the goal of nationalists?

4. What sources of discontent led to revolts across Europe in 1848?

5. Describe the outcome of the 1848 rebellions.

6. How did Toussaint L'Ouverture aid the cause of Haitian independence?

7. When and how did Mexico gain independence from Spain?

8. How did Mexico's independence change the lives of its people?

## SKILLS FOR SUCCESS    IDENTIFYING IDEOLOGIES

An **ideology** is a system of thought that seeks to define the proper nature of government and society. Liberalism, conservatism, and capitalism are examples of ideologies.

The statements below reflect basic ideas of conservatism and liberalism, two opposing ideologies of the 1800s. Read the statements, and then follow the steps to identify the ideology each statement represents.

1. **Identify the subject of the statement.** (a) What is the main subject of Prince Metternich's statement? Of Jeremy Bentham's statement? (b) How are the two subjects related?

2. **List the major points of the statement.** (a) What rule does Metternich believe should guide change in government? (b) According to Bentham, what should be the goal of government?

3. **Identify the speaker's ideology.** (a) According to Metternich, from whom do kings get their power? (b) According to Bentham, from whom should a government get its power? (c) What ideology does each speaker represent? Explain.

---

*Prince Clemens von Metternich*

❝I am a true friend to order and public peace. As such . . . I am absolutely convinced that the governments ruled by kings must . . . stop the rioting and social unrest. By taking whatever steps are necessary, the kings will fulfill the duties which God . . . has given them power to do.

[O]ne rule guides how governments and citizens should behave when it comes to change. This rule declares 'that no one should ever dream of changing or reforming society when emotions are out of control.' ❞

Adapted from Prince Metternich, *Secret Memorandum for Alexander I*, December 15, 1820.

*Jeremy Bentham*

❝In every society, a government should work for the greatest happiness of the greatest number of citizens. . . . What we have now are governments by kings which work for the greatest happiness for themselves. . . . A king has no reason to see that his subjects are happy and content . . . since his subjects have no say in whether he will be ruler or not. . . . Under a representative democracy [in which men elect their government leaders], the goal is the greatest happiness of the greatest number. ❞

Adapted from Jeremy Bentham, *Constitutional Code for the Use of All Nations*, 1827, 1830.

## REVIEWING CHAPTER THEMES

Review the "Focus On" questions at the start of this chapter. Then select *three* of those questions and answer them, using information from the chapter.

## CRITICAL THINKING

1. **Recognizing Causes and Effects** How did ideologies like liberalism and nationalism contribute to unrest in Europe in the 1800s?

2. **Analyzing Information** You have read Metternich's comment, "When France sneezes, Europe catches cold." What did he mean?

3. **Synthesizing Information** (a) Identify the major goal of the following leaders: Toussaint L'Ouverture, Miguel Hidalgo, Simón Bolívar. (b) Did each achieve his goal? Explain.

## ANALYZING PRIMARY SOURCES

Use the quotation on page 112, first column, to answer the following questions.

1. Restate the first sentence of the excerpt in your own words.

2. What things, according to Metternich, were under attack?

3. From reading this excerpt, what do you think was Metternich's attitude toward public "passions"?

## FOR YOUR PORTFOLIO

**CREATING A HISTORICAL COMIC BOOK** Work with a group of classmates to produce a comic book about the age of revolution in Europe and Latin America. Begin by selecting an event from this chapter as the subject. Then assign some members to do research, others to write dialogue, and so on. With the group, outline the story you will tell. Then, after research is completed, have the writers and artists set down the story and assemble the comic book.

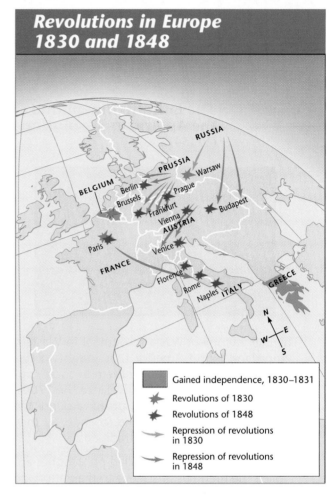

### Revolutions in Europe 1830 and 1848

| | |
|---|---|
| ■ | Gained independence, 1830–1831 |
| ✦ | Revolutions of 1830 |
| ✦ | Revolutions of 1848 |
| → | Repression of revolutions in 1830 |
| → | Repression of revolutions in 1848 |

## ANALYZING MAPS

Use the map to answer the following questions.

1. In which year was there a revolution in Warsaw?

2. Which city witnessed revolutions in both 1830 and 1848?

3. Were there revolutions in Great Britain in 1830 or 1848? How do you know?

### INTERNET ACTIVITY

**WRITING A SPEECH** Use the Internet to research the independence movement of a Spanish colony in Latin America. Then write a speech calling for that colony's independence from Spain.

# *Unit-in-Brief*

## Enlightenment and Revolution

**Chapter 1    The Enlightenment and the American Revolution (1715–1800)**

The Enlightenment was a movement in Western Europe and North America that sought to discover natural laws and apply them to social, political, and economic problems. Since the 1700s, Enlightenment ideas have spread around the world, creating upheaval and change as they have challenged established traditions.

- Enlightenment thinkers called philosophes applied the methods of science to their efforts to understand and improve society.
- The ideas of thinkers such as Locke, Montesquieu, and Rousseau would later justify revolutions and inspire principles of representative government.
- Physiocrats rejected mercantilism in favor of laissez-faire economics.
- Despite a growing middle class, most Europeans remained peasants who lived in small rural villages, untouched by Enlightenment ideas.
- England established a constitutional monarchy and built the most powerful commercial empire in the world.
- After years of growing dissent, Britain's North American colonies won independence in the American Revolution.
- Inspired by Enlightenment ideas, the United States adopted a constitution that would serve as a model for other democratic nations.

**Chapter 2    The French Revolution and Napoleon (1789–1815)**

Between 1789 and 1815, the French Revolution destroyed an absolute monarchy and disrupted a social system that had existed for over a thousand years. These events ushered in the modern era in European politics.

- France was burdened by an outdated social class system, a severe financial crisis, and a monarchy too indecisive to enact reforms.
- In 1789, dissatisfied members of the middle class called for a constitution and other reforms. Meanwhile, hunger and social resentment sparked rioting among peasants and poor city dwellers.
- In the first phase of the French Revolution, moderates attempted to limit the power of the monarchy and guarantee basic rights.
- In 1793, as enemies outside France denounced the revolution, radicals executed the king and queen and began a Reign of Terror.
- From 1799 to 1815, Napoleon Bonaparte consolidated his power within France and subdued the combined forces of the greatest powers of Europe.
- Under Napoleon, French armies spread the ideas of revolution across Europe.
- In 1815, the Congress of Vienna sought to undo the effects of the French Revolution and the Napoleonic era.

## Chapter 3 The Industrial Revolution Begins (1750–1850)

During the 1700s, production began to shift from simple hand tools to complex machines and new sources of energy replaced human and animal power. Known as the Industrial Revolution, this transformation marked a crucial turning point in history and changed the lives of people all over the world.

- An agricultural revolution contributed to a population explosion that, in turn, fed the growing industrial labor force.
- Abundant resources and a favorable business climate allowed Britain to take an early lead in industrialization.
- New sources of energy, such as coal and steam, fueled factories and paved the way for faster means of transporting people and goods.
- A series of remarkable inventions revolutionized the British textile industry and led to the creation of the first factories.
- Rapid urbanization and the rise of the factory system at first created dismal living and working conditions.
- Laissez-faire economists, utilitarians, and socialists put forth their own ideas for solving the problems of industrial society.
- Karl Marx promoted communism, a radical form of socialism that would have a worldwide influence.

## Chapter 4 Revolutions in Europe and Latin America (1790–1848)

With the Congress of Vienna, the great powers sought to return to the political and social order that had existed prior to 1789. However, in the early 1800s, a wave of violent uprisings swept across Western Europe and Latin America, fueled by the political ideas of the French Revolution and the economic problems of the Industrial Revolution.

- Two opposing ideologies emerged in Europe. Liberals embraced Enlightenment ideas about democracy and individual rights, while conservatives sought to preserve the old political and social order.
- Nationalism inspired independence movements among peoples with a shared heritage but also bred intolerance and persecution of minorities.
- In 1830 and 1848, ideological tensions and social inequalities sparked uprisings in France and elsewhere in Europe. Although most of these democratic revolutions were suppressed, they served to hasten reform later in the century.
- In Latin America, discontent with foreign domination led to a series of independence movements that freed most of the region from colonial rule by 1825.

# UNIT 1

# A Global View

## How Did the New Ideas of the Enlightenment Lead to a Wave of Democratic Revolutions?

During the later 1700s and the early 1800s, new ideas brought revolutionary changes in western society and government. The Enlightenment, the American and French revolutions, and the Industrial Revolution all made this period a turning point in western history.

### Ideas and Machines

Voltaire, Rousseau, and other thinkers of the French Enlightenment urged radical changes in government. They proposed limitations on governmental power and favored enlightened rule dedicated to the welfare of the people. Their ideas were partly inspired by the example of France's powerful neighbor across the English Channel. British monarchs actually shared power with Parliament, which included elected representatives of at least some of the people.

The Industrial Revolution also made key contributions to social change. In the beginning, industrialization created a poverty-stricken new working class. The demands of this class for improved living conditions would lead to major political changes in later years. At the same time, however, increased productivity would bring great material wealth.

### Revolutions in Europe

In the late 1700s, France, Europe's greatest power, confronted many economic, social, and political problems. These problems finally exploded in the French Revolution of 1789.

During the tumultuous years that followed, revolutionaries who were inspired by the ideas of the Enlightenment overthrew the French monarchy. They stripped the Church of its power and the ruling aristocracy of its land. Leaders like Robespierre also launched a savage Reign of Terror, which claimed the lives of thousands of people.

Out of this revolutionary chaos, a new ruler rose to power. Napoleon Bonaparte greatly strengthened the French government and conquered most of Europe. An alliance of all the other great powers finally

| 1750 | 1775 | 1800 |
|---|---|---|

**AFRICA**

**Late 1700s** Islamic revival in Africa

**1788** Futa Toro passes law against slave trade

**THE AMERICAS**

**1763** Britain wins control of Canada

**1775** American Revolution begins

**1789** United States Constitution takes effect

**ASIA AND OCEANIA**

**1756** Seven Years' War affects India

**1770** Cook claims Australia for Britain

**1793** Emperor Qianlong rejects British trade

**EUROPE**

**1751** Diderot publishes *Encyclopedia*

**1764** Spinning jenny invented

**1789** French Revolution begins

**132  UNIT 1**

defeated him at Waterloo in 1815.

Though the French Revolution had failed, the problems that had caused it persisted. As a result, Europeans rose in revolt in many lands in 1830 and 1848. Though most of these revolutions also failed, they made the need for reform clear.

## Revolutions in the Americas

More successful revolutions blazed up in Europe's American colonies. In both North and South America, Enlightenment ideas and economic grievances drove the colonists to revolt. Once free of European control, the former colonists established republics with elected governments rather than hereditary monarchies.

The first American revolution began in 1775 in Britain's North American colonies. After a hard struggle, George Washington and his colleagues freed the 13 colonies. The United States Constitution gave the new nation a republican government which guaranteed the rights of the people.

The United States experiment in democracy helped inspire revolutions in Spain's Latin American colonies. By 1825, a string of independent Spanish-speaking republics stretched from Argentina to Mexico. During this period, Haiti gained independence from France, while Brazil broke away from Portugal.

In the Americas as in Europe, most people did not yet have the right to vote. Still, most of two continents had been freed from European rule.

## Looking Ahead

By the mid-1800s, most of the world was still ruled by autocratic monarchs, and Europe's remaining overseas colonies had no democratic rights. Still, the "age of democratic revolutions" left a legacy of accelerating change. Enlightenment political ideas would develop further over the next two centuries. Europe and the Americas would continue to build increasingly democratic governments, and democratic ideas would begin to spread beyond the West.

**ACTIVITY** Choose two events and two pictures from the time line below. For each, write a sentence explaining how it relates to the themes expressed in the Global View essay.

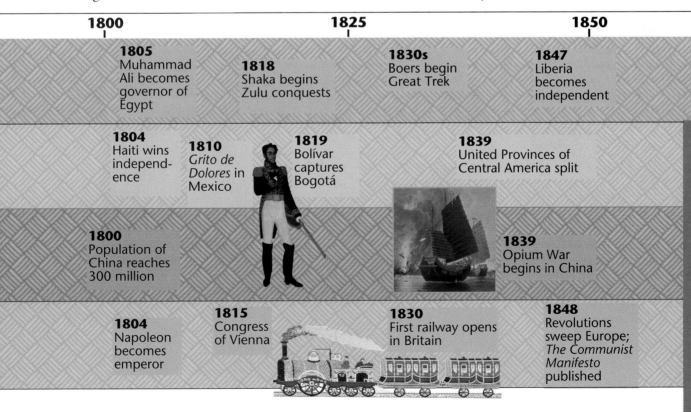

**1800**

**1825**

**1850**

**1805** Muhammad Ali becomes governor of Egypt

**1818** Shaka begins Zulu conquests

**1830s** Boers begin Great Trek

**1847** Liberia becomes independent

**1804** Haiti wins independence

**1810** *Grito de Dolores* in Mexico

**1819** Bolívar captures Bogotá

**1839** United Provinces of Central America split

**1800** Population of China reaches 300 million

**1839** Opium War begins in China

**1804** Napoleon becomes emperor

**1815** Congress of Vienna

**1830** First railway opens in Britain

**1848** Revolutions sweep Europe; *The Communist Manifesto* published

# You Decide

## Exploring Global Issues

### What Limits Should There Be on Freedom of Speech?

"I do not agree with a word that you say, but I will defend to the death your right to say it." Whether or not Voltaire said these exact words, he passionately believed in this idea. Since then, people everywhere have quoted these words to uphold the right to free speech.

But are there limits to freedom of speech? And, if so, what are they? To begin your investigation, examine these viewpoints.

In his influential work *On Liberty,* the philosopher John Stuart Mill stated his belief that democracy required the free exchange of ideas:

> "If all mankind minus one were of one opinion, and only one person were of the contrary opinion, mankind would be no more justified in silencing that one person, than he, if he had the power, would be justified in silencing mankind."

Supreme Court justice Oliver Wendell Holmes gave a famous definition of the limits of free speech in the case of *Schenck* v. *United States:*

> "The most stringent protection of free speech would not protect a man in falsely shouting fire in a theater and causing a panic."

During wartime, democratic governments have restricted free speech in the interests of security. "Silence," warns this poster from World War II. "The enemy hears your secrets." ▶

Mao Zedong founded a government in China based on the ideas of the communist philosopher Karl Marx:

> "What should our policy be towards non-Marxist ideas? As far as unmistakable counterrevolutionaries and saboteurs of the socialist cause are concerned, the matter is easy. We simply deprive them of their freedom of speech."

ENGLAND 1859 / UNITED STATES 1919 / FRANCE 1940 / CHINA 1957

SILENCE L'ENNEMI.. GUETTE VOS CONFIDENCES

UNIT 1

**IRAN**

**1979**

The same year he was overthrown, Shah Muhammad Reza Pahlavi had denounced the dangers of uncontrolled free speech:

66Freedom of thought, freedom of thought! Democracy, democracy! With five-year-old children going on strike and parading through the streets? That's democracy? That's freedom of thought?99

**SOUTH AFRICA**

**1980s**

In the face of protests from the black majority, the minority government of South Africa took many measures to limit free speech, including censoring news reports like this one. ▶

dela!'' echoed through the stadium as the wife of Nelson Mandela, the long-imprisoned black leader, arrived. ▇▇▇

▇▇▇▇ she told the workers. ▇▇▇

▇▇▇ Union leaders have asked miners to stay away from the pits this Wednesday as a gesture of protest and mourning.

**CANADA**

**1985**

The criminal code of Canada outlaws public remarks against religious, racial, or ethnic groups:

66Every one who, by communicating statements other than in private conversation, willfully promotes hatred against any identifiable group is guilty of . . . an indictable offense and is liable to imprisonment for a term not exceeding two years.99

### COMPARING VIEWPOINTS

**1.** Which of the viewpoints represented here seems to place the fewest restrictions on freedom of speech?

**2.** Mao Zedong and the shah of Iran were both authoritarian dictators. How are their viewpoints similar or different?

**3.** When should free speech in a democracy be restricted according to Holmes? According to the poster? According to the Canadian criminal code?

### YOUR INVESTIGATION

**1.** Find out more about other viewpoints related to this topic. You might investigate one or more of the following:

- The Alien and Sedition acts, enacted in the United States in 1798.
- Wartime censorship in Allied nations during World War I.
- Restrictions on free speech in Iran since the overthrow of the shah.
- The contrasting policies toward dissent of Soviet leaders Leonid Brezhnev and Mikhail Gorbachev.
- Recent debates in the United States about forms of "symbolic speech," such as flag burning.

**2.** Decide which viewpoint you agree with most closely and express it in your own way. You may do so in an essay, a cartoon, a poem, a drawing or painting, a song, a skit, a video, or some other way.

**ACTIVITY**

UNIT 1 THE BIG PICTURE

# UNIT 2 | INDUSTRIALISM AND A NEW GLOBAL AGE

### Political and Social Systems

**3**

*The Fifteenth Amendment granted voting rights to formerly enslaved African American men. The 1800s saw the extension of democratic rights in Britain and France as well as in the United States.*

**NORTH AMERICA**

**3**

ATLANTIC OCEAN

PACIFIC OCEAN

**SOUTH AMERICA**

### Impact of the Individual

**1**

*By 1871, nationalist leaders in Italy and Germany had forged new nations out of fragmented provinces. Otto von Bismarck, a master politician, was the architect of German unification.*

N
W — E
S

### Geography and History

**2**

*The waterways of Africa, such as these falls in Uganda, were a magnet for European explorers. But exploration paved the way for conquest, as European powers carved up the continent.*

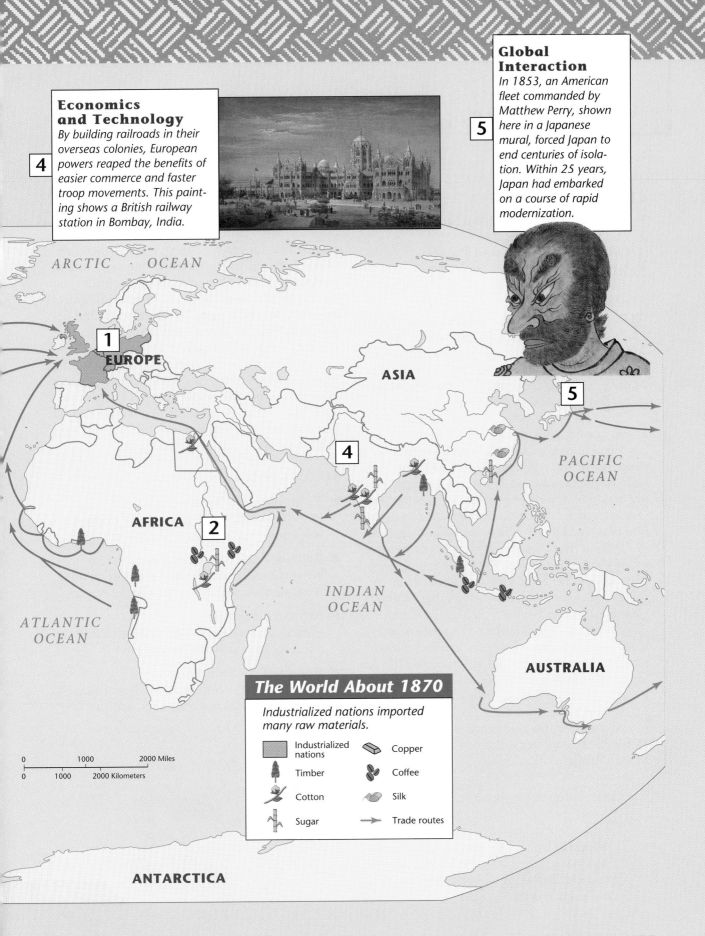

**Economics and Technology**

By building railroads in their overseas colonies, European powers reaped the benefits of easier commerce and faster troop movements. This painting shows a British railway station in Bombay, India.

4

**Global Interaction**

In 1853, an American fleet commanded by Matthew Perry, shown here in a Japanese mural, forced Japan to end centuries of isolation. Within 25 years, Japan had embarked on a course of rapid modernization.

5

ARCTIC   OCEAN

1

EUROPE

ASIA

5

PACIFIC OCEAN

4

AFRICA

2

INDIAN OCEAN

ATLANTIC OCEAN

AUSTRALIA

**The World About 1870**

Industrialized nations imported many raw materials.

Industrialized nations
Copper
Timber
Coffee
Cotton
Silk
Sugar
Trade routes

0   1000   2000 Miles
0   1000   2000 Kilometers

ANTARCTICA

# Life in the Industrial Age

## (1800–1910)

## CHAPTER OUTLINE

1 **The Industrial Revolution Spreads**
2 **The World of Cities**
3 **Changing Attitudes and Values**
4 **A New Culture**

The great French scientist Louis Pasteur (pas TOOR) was working in his laboratory on July 6, 1885. Suddenly, a woman rushed in, clutching her limping nine-year-old son. The mother explained that the boy had been savagely attacked by a dog two days before.

Though not a doctor, Pasteur agreed to examine the wounded child. He noted that the boy "had numerous bites . . . some of them very deep that made walking difficult." Still, the bites were not what worried Pasteur. The great danger was rabies, a deadly disease of the nervous system, which could be transmitted through the bite of a "mad dog." There was no known cure.

Pasteur had been studying rabies for five years. He had even saved the lives of some dogs. But he had never tried his treatment on humans. Still, two physicians agreed that, without treatment, the boy would die. Under Pasteur's direction, a doctor gave the boy a series of injections over 10 days. In great anxiety, Pasteur watched and waited. "All is going well," he wrote after five days. "If the lad keeps well during the following weeks, I think the experiment will be sure to succeed."

All summer, the boy continued to thrive. In October, Pasteur was able to report to the French Academy of Sciences:

> 66After I might say innumerable experiments, I have arrived at a preventive method, practical and prompt, the success of which has been so convincing in dogs that I have confidence of its general application in all animals and even in man.99

In the 1800s, medicine and other sciences stretched the frontiers of knowledge. Some discoveries, like Pasteur's rabies vaccine, helped people live longer, healthier lives. Others, applied to the growing world of industry, led to the development of thousands of inventions.

From the mid-1800s, industrialism spread rapidly across Europe to North America and beyond. During this second Industrial Revolution, the western world acquired greater wealth and power than any other society in the past. Big businesses emerged that dwarfed those of other eras. Economic and social changes transformed daily life. By the early 1900s, the western world had acquired much of the structure and patterns of life that are familiar to us today.

**FOCUS ON** these questions as you read:

- **Economics and Technology**
  How did science and new ways of doing business promote industrial growth?

- **Religions and Value Systems**
  What social, economic, and intellectual developments reshaped western social values?

- **Art and Literature**
  How did literature, music, and visual arts reflect changing attitudes and values?

- **Impact of the Individual**
  What important contributions were made by individuals in science, business, and the arts?

## TIME AND PLACE

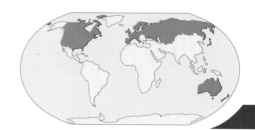

***The New Cities*** *The rapidly growing cities of the industrial world attracted people of all social classes. The well-to-do mother and daughter walking down this street lived a far different life from the flower seller or the men working on the pavement.* **Continuity and Change** *Compare this painting to the earlier engraving by Gustave Doré on page 105. How do they emphasize different aspects of city life?*

## HUMANITIES LINK

*Art History* Edvard Munch, *Spring Evening on Karl Johan Street, Oslo* (page 149).
*Literature* In this chapter, you will encounter passages from the following works of literature: Emile Zola, *Germinal* (page 145); Elizabeth Gaskell, *Cranford* (pages 151–152); William Wordsworth, "It is a beauteous evening, calm and free" (page 156); Charles Dickens, *Oliver Twist* (pages 159–160); Henrik Ibsen, *A Doll's House* (pages 162–163).

**1807**
Industrial Revolution spreads to Belgium

**1842**
Anesthesia first used in surgery

**1859**
*On the Origin of the Species* published

**1870s**
Impressionists develop new style of painting

**1903**
Wright brothers invent airplane

1800   1820   1840   1860   1880   1900   1920

# 1  The Industrial Revolution Spreads

## Guide for Reading

- How did the industrialized world expand in the 1800s?
- How was technology linked to economic growth?
- Why did big business emerge in the late 1800s?
- **Vocabulary** *interchangeable parts, assembly line, corporation, cartel*

The first phase of industrialism had largely been forged from iron, powered by steam engines, and driven by the British textile industry. By the mid-1800s, the Industrial Revolution entered a new phase. New industrial powers emerged. New factories powered by new sources of energy used new processes to turn out new products. And new forms of business organization led to the rise of giant new companies. As a new century—our century—dawned, this "second" Industrial Revolution transformed the economies of the western world.

## New Industrial Powers

In the early Industrial Revolution, Britain stood alone as the world's industrial giant. To protect its head start, Britain tried to enforce strict rules against exporting inventions.

For a while, the rules worked. Then, in 1807, a British mechanic, William Cockerill, opened factories in Belgium for the manufacture of spinning and weaving machines. Belgium thus became the first European nation outside Britain to industrialize. By the mid-1800s, other nations had joined the race, and several newcomers were challenging Britain's industrial supremacy.

**The new pacesetters.** Why did other nations catch up so quickly to Britain? First, nations such as Germany, France, and the United States had more abundant supplies of coal, iron, and other resources than did Britain. Also, they had the advantage of being able to follow Britain's lead. Like Belgium, latecomers often borrowed British experts or technology. The first American textile factory was built in Pawtucket, Rhode Island with plans smuggled out of Britain. American inventor Robert Fulton powered his steamboat with one of James Watt's steam engines.

Two countries in particular thrust their way to industrial leadership. Germany united into a powerful nation in 1871. (See Chapter 6.) Within a few decades, it became Europe's leading industrial power. Across the Atlantic, the United States advanced even more rapidly, especially after the Civil War. By 1900, American industry led the world in production.

**Uneven development.** Other nations industrialized more slowly, especially those in eastern and southern Europe. These nations often lacked natural resources or the capital to invest in industry. While Russia did have resources, social and political conditions slowed its economic development. Only in the late 1800s, more than 100 years after Britain, did Russia lumber toward industrialization.

In East Asia, however, Japan offered a remarkable success story. Although it lacked many basic resources, it industrialized rapidly after 1868. (See Chapter 9.) Canada, Australia, and New Zealand also built thriving industries.

**Impact.** Like Britain, the new industrial nations underwent social changes, such as rapid urbanization. Men, women, and children worked long hours in difficult and dangerous conditions. As you will read, by 1900, these conditions had begun to improve in many industrialized nations.

The factory system produced huge quantities of new goods at low-

New industrial products—a sewing machine (top) and a coffeemaker (bottom)

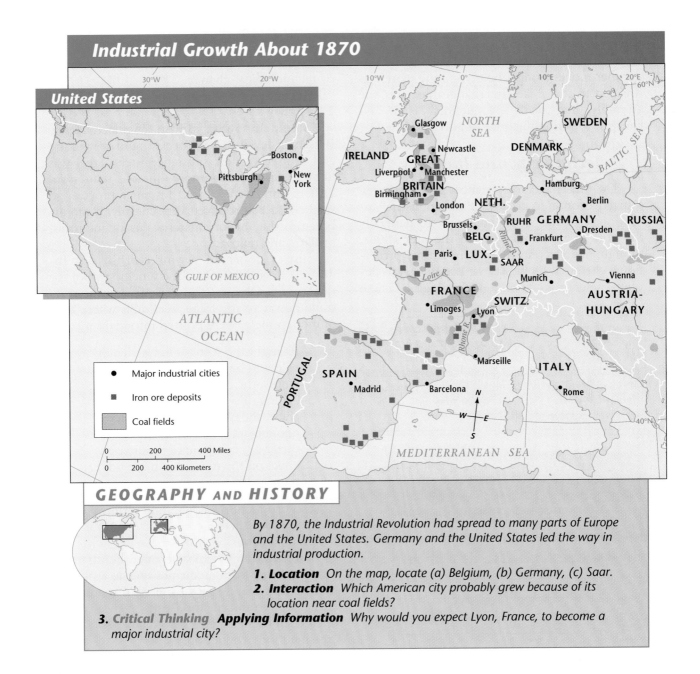

## Industrial Growth About 1870

**United States**

Boston
Pittsburgh
New York

GULF OF MEXICO

ATLANTIC
OCEAN

NORTH
SEA

SWEDEN

Glasgow
Newcastle

IRELAND    GREAT    DENMARK

Liverpool • Manchester

BRITAIN
Birmingham
London    NETH.    Hamburg
Berlin

Brussels    RUHR    GERMANY    RUSSIA

BELG.    Frankfurt    Dresden

Paris    LUX.
SAAR

Loire R.    Munich    Vienna

FRANCE    SWITZ.    AUSTRIA-
HUNGARY

Limoges    Lyon

Rhône R.

Marseille    ITALY

PORTUGAL    SPAIN    Rome

Madrid    Barcelona

N
W    E
S

• Major industrial cities

■ Iron ore deposits

▨ Coal fields

0        200        400 Miles
0    200    400 Kilometers

MEDITERRANEAN SEA

## GEOGRAPHY AND HISTORY

By 1870, the Industrial Revolution had spread to many parts of Europe
and the United States. Germany and the United States led the way in
industrial production.

**1. Location** On the map, locate (a) Belgium, (b) Germany, (c) Saar.
**2. Interaction** Which American city probably grew because of its
location near coal fields?
**3. Critical Thinking** **Applying Information** Why would you expect Lyon, France, to become a
major industrial city?

er prices than ever before. In time, workers were
buying goods that in earlier times only the
wealthy could afford. The demand for goods
created jobs, as did the building of cities, railroads, and factories. Politics changed, too, as
leaders had to meet the demands of an industrial
society.

Globally, industrial nations competed fiercely, altering patterns of world trade. Thanks to
their technological and economic advantage,
western powers came to dominate the world
more than ever before. (See Chapters 8 and 9.)

## New Methods of Production

The basic characteristics of the factory system remained the same. Factories still used large
numbers of workers and power-driven machines
to mass-produce goods. To improve the efficiency of the system, manufacturers designed
products with interchangeable parts, identical
components that could be used in place of one
another. Interchangeable parts simplified both
assembly and repair.

Later, manufacturers introduced another
new method of production, the assembly line.

Workers on an assembly line add parts to a product that moves along a belt from one work station to the next. Like interchangeable parts, the assembly line made production faster and cheaper, lowering the price of goods.

## Technology and Industry

The marriage of science and industry spurred economic growth. Early industrial inventions like the steam engine were generally the work of gifted tinkerers. By the later 1800s, though, many companies were hiring professional chemists, biologists, and engineers to develop new products and technologies. These

*Interpreting a Graph* Before the introduction of the Bessemer process, industrialized nations produced only a few thousand tons of steel a year. By the end of the 1800s, steel production was measured in the millions. ■ Which nation led in steel production in 1890? In 1900? How much steel did Germany produce in 1900?

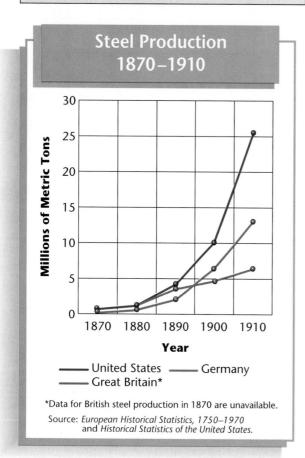

**Steel Production 1870–1910**

Millions of Metric Tons vs. Year (1870, 1880, 1890, 1900, 1910)

— United States — Germany
— Great Britain*

*Data for British steel production in 1870 are unavailable.

Source: *European Historical Statistics, 1750–1970* and *Historical Statistics of the United States.*

creative experts sped up the breathtaking pace of technological change. (■ See *You Decide,* "Is Technology a Blessing or a Curse?" pages 272–273.)

**Steel.** In 1856, British engineer Henry Bessemer developed a process to purify iron ore and produce a new substance, steel. Steel was lighter, harder, and more durable than iron. Others improved on the Bessemer process, so steel could be produced very cheaply. It rapidly became the major material used in tools, bridges, and railroads.

Just as steam was a symbol of the first Industrial Revolution, steel became a symbol for the second. Observers commented on the awesome power of the huge steel mills where tons of molten metal were poured into giant mixers:

66 At night the scene is indescribably wild and beautiful. The flashing fireworks, the terrific gusts of heat, the gaping, glowing mouth of the giant chest, the quivering light from the liquid iron, the roar of a nearby converter . . . combine to produce an effect on the mind that no words can translate. 99

As steel production soared, industrialized countries measured their success in steel output. (See the graph at left.)

**Chemicals.** Chemists created hundreds of new products, from medicines such as aspirin to new perfumes and soaps to margarine, the first artificially produced foodstuff. Newly developed chemical fertilizers played a key role in increasing food production.

The Swedish chemist Alfred Nobel invented dynamite, an explosive much safer than those used at the time. It became widely used in construction as well as in warfare—much to Nobel's dismay. Nobel earned a huge fortune from dynamite, which he willed to fund the Nobel prizes. (See page 278.)

**Electricity.** A new power source, electricity, was put to work in the late 1800s. Scientists like Benjamin Franklin had tinkered with electricity a century earlier. The Italian scientist Alessandro Volta developed the first battery about 1800. Later experimenters created the dynamo, which generated electricity. In the 1870s, the American inventor Thomas Edison

## Growth of Railroads, 1850–1914

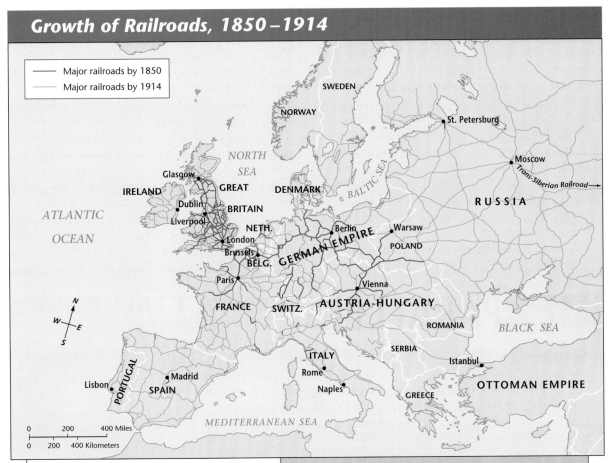

Major railroads by 1850
Major railroads by 1914

ATLANTIC OCEAN
NORTH SEA
BALTIC SEA
SWEDEN
NORWAY
St. Petersburg
Moscow
Trans-Siberian Railroad→
RUSSIA
IRELAND
Glasgow
GREAT BRITAIN
DENMARK
Dublin
Liverpool
NETH.
Berlin
London
Warsaw
Brussels
BELG.
GERMAN EMPIRE
POLAND
Paris
Vienna
FRANCE
SWITZ.
AUSTRIA-HUNGARY
ROMANIA
BLACK SEA
SERBIA
ITALY
Istanbul
Rome
PORTUGAL
Naples
OTTOMAN EMPIRE
Lisbon
Madrid
SPAIN
GREECE
MEDITERRANEAN SEA

0    200    400 Miles
0    200    400 Kilometers

### GEOGRAPHY AND HISTORY

*Improvements in transportation were an important part of the Industrial Revolution. By 1914, a web of railroad lines crisscrossed Europe as well as North America.*

1. **Location** *On the map, locate (a) Trans-Siberian Railroad, (b) Paris, (c) Berlin.*
2. **Place** *Which cities on the map appear to have been centers of railroad activity by 1850?*
3. **Critical Thinking** *Analyzing Information (a) Why do you think there were so many railroads in Germany? (b) What might be one reason that there were few railroads in northern Europe?*

made the first electric light bulb. Soon, Edison's "incandescent lamps" illuminated whole cities. The pace of city life quickened, and factories could remain productive after dark.

By the 1890s, cables carried electrical power from dynamos to factories. Electricity quickly replaced steam as the dominant source of industrial power.

### The Shrinking World

During the second Industrial Revolution, transportation and communications were trans-formed by technology. Steamships replaced sailing ships, and railroad building took off. In Europe and North America, rail lines connected inland cities and seaports, mining regions and industrial centers. In the United States, a transcontinental railroad provided rail service from the Atlantic to the Pacific. In the same way, Russians built the Trans-Siberian Railroad, linking Moscow in European Russia to Vladivostok on the Pacific. Railroad tunnels and bridges crossed the Alps in Europe and the Andes in South America. Passengers and goods rode on rails in India, China, Egypt, and South Africa.

**The horseless carriage.** The transportation revolution took a new turn when a German engineer, Nikolaus Otto, invented a gasoline-powered internal combustion engine. In 1887, his colleague Gottlieb Daimler (DĪM luhr) used Otto's engine to power the first automobile.

The French nosed out the Germans as early automakers. Then the American Henry Ford started making models that reached the breathtaking speed of 25 miles an hour. In the early 1900s, Ford began using the assembly line to mass-produce cars, making the United States a leader in the automobile industry.

**Conquest of the air.** The internal combustion engine powered more than cars. Motorized threshers and reapers boosted farm production. Even more dramatically, the internal combustion engine made possible the dream of human flight. In 1903, two American bicycle makers, Orville and Wilbur Wright, designed and flew a flimsy airplane at Kitty Hawk, North Carolina. Though their flying machine stayed aloft for only a few seconds, it ushered in the air age.

Soon, daredevils were flying across the English Channel and the Alps. Passenger travel, however, would not begin until the 1920s.

**Rapid communication.** A revolution in communications also made the world smaller. An American inventor, Samuel F. B. Morse, developed the telegraph, which could send coded

# PARALLELS THROUGH TIME

## Science Fiction

The dizzying rate of invention in the late 1800s led people to wonder what marvels might come next. Imaginative novelists like France's Jules Verne and England's H. G. Wells pioneered a new literary form—science fiction. Today, in print or on film, science fiction remains one of the most popular forms of entertainment.

**Linking Past and Present**  Why do you think science fiction has had such an enduring appeal? What inventions of today are creating new fantasies about the future?

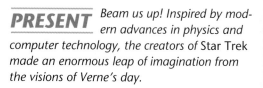

**PAST**  In his 1865 novel From the Earth to the Moon, Verne created one of the earliest pictures of space travel. Passengers on this rocket traveled in luxury, with padded walls for protection and a dog for companionship. The anchor would be tossed out the window to secure the vessel on the moon's surface. Verne also correctly predicted that space travelers would experience weightlessness.

**PRESENT**  Beam us up! Inspired by modern advances in physics and computer technology, the creators of Star Trek made an enormous leap of imagination from the visions of Verne's day.

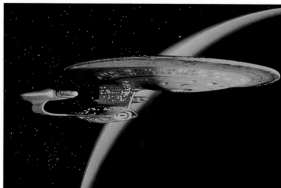

messages over wires by means of electricity. His first telegraph line went into service between Baltimore and Washington, D.C., in 1844. By the 1860s, an undersea cable was relaying messages between Europe and North America.

Communication soon became even faster. In 1876, the Scottish-born American inventor Alexander Graham Bell patented the telephone. By the 1890s, the Italian pioneer Guglielmo Marconi had invented the radio. In 1901, Marconi transmitted a radio message from Britain to Canada, using Morse's dot-and-dash code. He later recalled:

66 Shortly before mid-day I placed the single earphone to my ear and started listening. . . . The answer came at 12:30 when I heard, faintly but distinctly, *pip-pip-pip*. . . . The electric waves sent out into space from Poldhu had traversed the Atlantic—the distance, enormous as it seemed then, of 1,700 miles. . . . I now felt for the first time absolutely certain that the day would come when mankind would be able to send messages without wires not only across the Atlantic, but between the farthermost ends of the earth. 99

As Marconi foresaw, radio would become part of today's global communications network that links every corner of the world.

## New Directions for Business

New technologies required the investment of large amounts of money. To get the needed capital, entrepreneurs developed new ways of organizing businesses. Owners sold stock, or shares in their companies, to investors. Each stockholder thus became owner of a tiny part of a company.

**Rise of big business.** By the late 1800s, what we call "big business" came to dominate industry. Large-scale companies such as steel foundries needed so much capital that they sold hundreds of thousands of shares. These businesses formed giant corporations, businesses that are owned by many investors who buy shares of stock. Stockholders risk only the amount they invest in the company and cannot

be held personally responsible for any debts of the corporation.

With large amounts of capital, corporations could expand into many areas. In the novel *Germinal* by the French writer Emile Zola, two investors discuss the growth of a large coal mining company:

66 'And is your company rich?' asked Etienne. . . .

'Ah! yes. Ah! yes. . . . Ten thousand workers, concessions reaching over sixty-seven towns, an output of five thousand tons a day, a railway joining all the pits, and workshops, and factories! Ah! yes! Ah, yes! There's money there!' 99

**Move toward monopolies.** Powerful business leaders created monopolies and trusts, huge corporate structures that controlled entire industries or areas of the economy. In Germany, Alfred Krupp inherited a steelmaking business from his father. He bought up coal and iron mines as well as ore shipping lines that fed the steel business. Later, he and his son acquired plants that manufactured tools, railroad cars, and weapons. In the United States, John D. Rockefeller built Standard Oil Company of Ohio into an empire. By gaining control of oil wells, oil refineries, and oil pipelines, he dominated the American petroleum industry.

In their pursuit of profit, ruthless business leaders destroyed competing companies. Some lowered prices to force competitors out of business. Then, with the competition gone, they were free to raise prices to any level. Sometimes, a group of large corporations would form a cartel, an association to fix prices, set production quotas, or divide up markets. In Germany, a single cartel fixed prices for 170 coal mines. An international shipping cartel of British, German, French, Dutch, and Japanese shippers came close to setting freight rates on the sea lines of the world.

**Move toward regulation.** The rise of big business created a stormy debate. Some people saw the Krupps and Rockefellers as "captains of industry." Supporters praised their vision and skills. They pointed out that capitalists invested their great wealth in worldwide ventures, such

# CAUSE AND EFFECT

## Causes

Increased agricultural productivity
Growing population
New sources of energy, such as steam and coal
Growing demand for textiles and other mass-produced goods
Improved technology
Available natural resources, labor, and money
Strong, stable governments that promoted economic growth

## INDUSTRIAL REVOLUTION

## Immediate Effects

Rise of factories
Changes in transportation and communication
Urbanization
New methods of production using machines and steam power
Changes in workers' way of life and rise of urban working class
Growth of reform movements, including liberalism, socialism, and Marxism

## Long-Term Effects

Growth of labor unions
Increase in new, relatively inexpensive products
Spread of industrialization globally
Development of large corporations and other new ways of organizing businesses
Expansion of public education
Expansion of middle class
Fierce competition among industrialized nations for world trade
Progress in medical care and nutrition
Growth of women's movement

## Connections Today

Improvements in world health
Growth in population
Industrialization in developing nations
New sources of energy, including petroleum and nuclear power
Mass media and mass entertainment
Efforts to regulate world trade through international agreements

*Interpreting a Chart* Economics and technology sparked the Industrial Revolution. The long-term effects, however, touched nearly every aspect of life. ■ Identify two social and two economic effects of the Industrial Revolution.

as railroad building, that employed thousands of workers and added to general prosperity.

To others, the aggressive magnates were "robber barons." Any effort to destroy competition, critics argued, hurt the free-enterprise system. Reformers called for laws to prevent monopolies and regulate large corporations. By the early 1900s, some governments did move against monopolies. However, the political and economic power of business leaders often hindered efforts at regulation. ( ★ See *Skills for Success*, page 164.)

**Looking ahead.** By the late 1800s, European and American corporations were setting up operations around the world. Banks invested vast sums in undertakings such as building ports, railroads, and canals. As western capital flowed into Africa, Asia, and Latin America, western powers became increasingly involved in these regions, as you will read in Chapters 8 and 9.

## SECTION 1 REVIEW

1. **Identify** (a) Bessemer process, (b) Thomas Edison, (c) Gottlieb Daimler, (d) Henry Ford, (e) Wilbur and Orville Wright, (f) Guglielmo Marconi, (g) Alfred Krupp.
2. **Define** (a) interchangeable parts, (b) assembly line, (c) corporation, (d) cartel.
3. (a) How did the Industrial Revolution spread in the 1800s? (b) Why were other nations able to challenge Britain's leadership in industry?
4. How did science help industry expand? Give three examples.
5. How did the need for capital lead to new ways of organizing business?
6. *Critical Thinking* **Ranking** Which *three* technological advances in this section do you think were most important? Explain.
7. *ACTIVITY* Draw a political cartoon supporting or opposing laws against business monopolies in the late 1800s.

# The World of Cities

## Guide for Reading

- What was the impact of medical advances in the late 1800s?
- How did cities expand and change?
- Why did conditions for workers improve?

In the 1870s, a citizen of Berlin, Germany, boasted of his city's remarkable growth. "We have already 800,000 inhabitants, next year we shall have 900,000, and the year after that a million." He predicted that Berlin's population would soon compete with those of Paris and even London.

Cities grew as rural people streamed into urban areas. By the end of the century, European and American cities had begun to take on many of the features of cities today.

### Medicine and Population

The population explosion that had begun in the 1700s continued. Between 1800 and 1900, the population of Europe more than doubled. This rapid growth was not due to larger families. In fact, families in most industrializing countries had fewer children. Instead, populations soared because the death rate fell. People ate better and enjoyed longer lives, thanks in part to improved methods of farming, food storage, and distribution. Medical advances and improvements in public sanitation also slowed death rates.

**The fight against disease.** Since the 1600s, scientists had known of microscopic organisms, or microbes. Some scientists speculated that microbes might cause certain diseases. Yet most doctors scoffed at this "germ theory." Not until 1870 did Louis Pasteur clearly show the link between germs and disease. As you read, Pasteur developed a vaccine for rabies as well as a process, called pasteurization, to kill disease-carrying microbes in milk.

In the 1880s, the German doctor Robert Koch identified the bacteria that caused tuberculosis, a respiratory disease that claimed about 30 million human lives in the 1800s. The search

**Battling Disease?** This German cartoon from the 1830s shows a man trying to protect himself from cholera by wearing a skin of rubber, yards of flannel, and a copper plate over his heart. He carries with him juniper berries, peppercorns, camphor, smelling salts, a cigar, and other "medicines" supposed to prevent infection. **Economics and Technology** What point do you think this cartoonist was making?

for a tuberculosis cure, however, took half a century. By 1914, yellow fever and malaria had been traced to microbes carried by mosquitoes.

As people understood how germs caused disease, they bathed and changed their clothes more often. In western cities, better hygiene caused a marked drop in the rate of disease and death.

**In the hospital.** In 1846, a Boston dentist, William Morton, introduced anesthesia to relieve pain during surgery. The use of anesthetics allowed doctors to experiment with operations that had never before been possible.

Yet, throughout the century, hospitals could be dangerous places. Surgery was performed with dirty instruments in dank operating rooms. Often, a patient would survive an operation, only to die days later of infection. For the poor, being admitted to a hospital was often a death sentence. Wealthy or middle-class patients insisted on treatment in their own homes.

"The very first requirement in a hospital," said British nurse Florence Nightingale, "is that

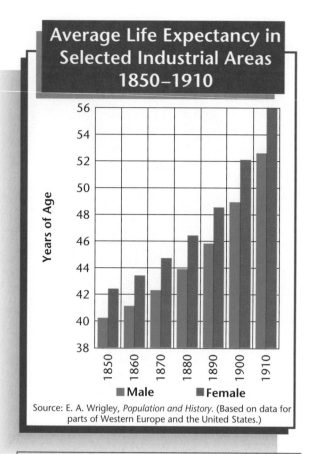

## Average Life Expectancy in Selected Industrial Areas 1850–1910

Years of Age

■ Male ■ Female

Source: E. A. Wrigley, *Population and History*. (Based on data for parts of Western Europe and the United States.)

**Interpreting a Graph** *The industrial world saw a steady increase in life expectancy. Sanitation played a major role in reducing death rates.* ■ *What was the average life expectancy for a man in 1850? In 1910? During what decade did women's average life expectancy increase the most?*

it should do the sick no harm." As an army nurse during the Crimean War, Nightingale insisted on better hygiene in field hospitals. Back home, she worked to introduce sanitary measures in British hospitals. She also founded the world's first school of nursing.

The English surgeon Joseph Lister discovered how antiseptics prevented infection. He insisted that surgeons wash their hands before operating and sterilize their instruments. Eventually, the use of antiseptics drastically reduced deaths from infection.

### The Life of the Cities

As industrialization progressed, cities came to dominate the West. City life, as old as civilization itself, underwent dramatic changes.

**The changing city landscape.** Growing wealth and industrialization altered the basic layout of European cities. City planners gouged out spacious new squares and boulevards. They lined these avenues with government buildings, offices, department stores, and theaters.

The most extensive urban renewal took place in Paris in the 1850s. Napoleon III's chief planner, Georges Haussmann, destroyed many tangled medieval streets full of tenement housing. In their place, he built wide boulevards and splendid public buildings. The project put many people to work, decreasing the threat of social unrest. The wide boulevards also made it harder for rebels to put up barricades and easier for troops to reach any part of the city.

As the century progressed, settlement patterns shifted. The rich developed pleasant residential neighborhoods on the outskirts of the city. The poor tended to crowd into slums near the city center, within reach of factories. Trolley lines made it possible to live in one part of the city and work in another.

**Sidewalks, sewers, and skyscrapers.** Paved streets made urban areas much more livable. First gas lamps, then electric street lights, increased safety at night. Cities organized police forces and expanded fire protection.

Beneath the streets and sidewalks, new sewage systems helped make cities healthier places to live. City reformers realized that clean water supplies were necessary to combat epidemics of cholera and tuberculosis. The massive new sewer systems of London and Paris were costly, but they cut death rates dramatically.

By the late 1800s, architects began using steel to construct soaring buildings. The metal Eiffel Tower became a symbol of Paris. In the United States, architects like Louis Sullivan pioneered a new structure, the skyscraper. In large cities, single-family middle-class homes gave way to multistory apartment buildings.

**Slums.** Despite urban improvements, city life remained harsh for the poor. Some working-class families could afford better clothing, newspapers, or tickets to a music hall. But they went home to small, cramped row houses or tenements in overcrowded neighborhoods.

In the worst tenements, whole families were often crammed into a single room. Unemployment or illness meant lost wages that could ruin

**Spring Evening on Karl Johan Street, Oslo** *This haunting street scene by the Norwegian painter Edvard Munch depicts the anonymous life of a big city. Munch was a pioneer in a style called expressionism. Expressionists used bold distortions and violent colors to explore complex, tortured emotional states.* **Art and Literature** *How does Munch express the idea of anonymity?*

a family. High rates of crime and alcoholism were a constant curse. Conditions had improved somewhat from the early Industrial Revolution, but slums remained a fact of city life.

**The lure of the city.** Despite their drawbacks, cities attracted millions of new residents. Many were drawn as much by the excitement as by the promise of work. Music halls, opera houses, and theaters provided entertainment for every taste. Museums and libraries offered educational opportunities. Sports, from tennis and horse racing to bare-knuckle boxing, drew citizens of all classes. Tree-lined parks offered a chance for fresh air, walks, and picnics.

The London *Times* described the hustle and bustle of holiday crowds in the late 1800s:

66Cyclists of both sexes covered the roads. River steamers and pleasure boats carried their thousands to Kew and the upper reaches of the Thames. The London parks were crowded. The Botanic Gardens and Zoological Gardens . . . and the flowers of Batersea Park drew large crowds all day.99

Few of these enjoyments were available in country villages. For residents and tourists alike, cities were magnetic centers of action.

## Working-Class Struggles

Workers tried to improve the harsh conditions of industrial life. They protested low wages, long hours, unsafe conditions, and the constant threat of unemployment. At first, employers and governments tried to silence protesters. Strikes and unions were illegal. Worker demonstrations were crushed.

**The Rise of Trade Unions** *Trade unions did more than fight for higher wages and better conditions. They also gave workers a sense of dignity and pride. This was the emblem for a trade union whose members were engineers, machinists, and metalworkers.* **Economics and Technology** *How do the images in this emblem glorify labor?*

By mid-century, workers slowly began to make progress. They formed mutual-aid societies to help sick or injured workers. Women as well as men joined socialist parties or organized unions. The revolutions of 1830 and 1848 left vivid images of worker discontent, which governments could not ignore.

**Steps to reform.** By the late 1800s, most western countries had granted all men the vote. Workers also won the right to organize unions to bargain on their behalf. Germany legalized labor unions in 1869. Britain, Austria, and France followed. Unions grew rapidly. In France, union membership grew from 140,000 in 1890 to over a million in 1912.

Pushed by unions, reformers, and working-class voters, governments passed laws regulating conditions in factories and mines. Early laws forbade employers to hire children under the age of 10. Later laws outlawed child labor entirely and banned the employment of women in mines. Other laws limited work hours and improved safety conditions. By 1909, British coal miners had won an eight-hour day, setting a standard for workers in other countries.

First in Germany, then elsewhere, western governments set up programs for old-age pensions, as well as disability insurance for workers who were hurt or became ill. These programs protected workers from dying in poverty once they were no longer able to work.

**Rising standards of living.** Wages varied across the industrialized world. Unskilled laborers earned much less than skilled workers. Women factory workers received less than half the pay of men doing the same work. Farm laborers lagged seriously behind. They barely scraped by during the economic slump of the late 1800s. Periods of unemployment brought desperate hardships to industrial workers and helped boost union membership.

Overall, the standard of living for workers improved. Families ate more varied diets, lived in better homes, and dressed in inexpensive, mass-produced clothing. Advances in medicine ensured healthier lives. Some workers even moved to the suburbs, traveling to work on cheap subways and trams. Still, the gap between workers and the middle class widened.

# SECTION 2 REVIEW

1. **Identify** (a) Louis Pasteur, (b) Robert Koch, (c) Florence Nightingale, (d) Joseph Lister.
2. Why did Europe's population grow in the late 1800s?
3. Describe three ways that city life changed in the later Industrial Revolution.
4. What laws helped workers in the late 1800s?
5. *Critical Thinking* **Linking Past and Present** How was city life in the 1800s similar to or different from city life today?
6. *ACTIVITY* Imagine that you have moved from a rural village to London or Paris in the late 1800s. Write a letter home describing your feelings about city life.

# 3 Changing Attitudes and Values

## Guide for Reading

- What new social hierarchy emerged in industrialized nations?
- What ideals shaped the middle class?
- What changes did some women seek?
- How did science challenge traditional beliefs?
- **Vocabulary** *women's suffrage, racism, social gospel*

> 66Once a woman has accepted an offer of marriage, all she has . . . becomes virtually the property of the man she has accepted as husband.99

This advice appeared in *The What-Not,* or *Ladies' Handbook* in 1859. Not all women, though, accepted such restrictions. Anna Mozzoni, a crusader for women's rights in Italy, denounced the legal status of women:

> 66For her, taxes but not an education; for her, sacrifices but not employment; for her, strict virtue but not honor; . . . for her, the capacity to be punished but not the right to be independent.99

The debate about women's rights was one of several challenges to traditional views in the late 1800s. At the same time, middle-class ways came increasingly to dominate western society.

## A Shifting Social Order

The Industrial Revolution slowly changed the old social order in the western world. For centuries, the two main classes were nobles and peasants. Their roles were defined by their relationship to the land. While middle-class merchants, artisans, lawyers, and officials played important roles, they still occupied a secondary position in society. With the spread of industry, a more complex social structure emerged.

By the late 1800s, Western Europe's new upper class included superrich industrial and business families as well as the old nobility. Wealthy entrepreneurs married into aristocratic families, gaining the status of noble titles. Nobles needed the money brought by the industrial rich to support their lands and lifestyle. By tradition, the upper class held the top jobs in government and the military.

Below this tiny elite, a growing middle class was pushing its way up the social ladder. Its highest rungs were filled with midlevel business people and professionals such as doctors, scientists, and lawyers. With comfortable incomes, they enjoyed a wide range of material goods. Next came the lower middle class, which included teachers, office workers, shopowners, and clerks. On much smaller incomes, they struggled to keep up with their "betters."

At the base of the social ladder were workers and peasants. In highly industrialized Britain, workers made up more than 30 percent of the population in 1900. In Western Europe and the United States, the number of farmworkers fell, but many families still worked the land. The rural population was even higher in eastern and southern Europe.

## Middle-Class Values

By mid-century, the modern middle class had evolved its own way of life. The nuclear family lived in a large house, or perhaps in one of the new apartment houses. Rooms were crammed with large overstuffed furniture, and paintings and photographs lined the walls. Clothing reflected middle-class tastes for luxury and respectability.

A strict code of etiquette governed social behavior. Rules dictated how to dress for every occasion, when to write letters, and how long to mourn relatives who died. In Elizabeth Gaskell's novel *Cranford,* a young woman is instructed about how to pay a social call:

> 66'It is the third day; I dare say your mamma has told you, my dear, never to let more than three days elapse between receiving a call and returning it; and also, that you are never to stay longer than a quarter of an hour.'

**Middle-Class Fashion**
*While fashions changed through the 1800s, clothing for women and men reflected middle-class values of luxury and respectability. The gentlemen on the left sport the latest French styles. Below, servants use tongs to lower a woman's dress over her many layers of petticoats.*
**Continuity and Change** *Compare these styles with clothing today. What details have remained the same? What has changed?*

'But am I to look at my watch? How am I to find out when a quarter of an hour has passed?'

'You must keep thinking about the time, my dear, and not allow yourself to forget it in conversation.'**"**

Parents strictly supervised their children, who were expected to be "seen but not heard." A child who misbehaved was considered to reflect badly on the entire family. Servants, too, were seen as a reflection of their employers. Even a small middle-class household was expected to have at least a cook and a housemaid.

**Courtship and marriage.** As in the past, middle-class families had a large say in choosing whom their children married. At the same time, young people had more freedom to choose a marriage partner. The notion of "falling in love" was more accepted than ever before.

Yet most women and men carefully considered the practical side of marriage. Mothers and daughters discussed the "likely prospects" of a possible husband. A young man was expected to court his bride-to-be with tender sentiments. But he also had to convince her father that he could support her in style. Until the late 1800s in most western countries, a husband controlled his wife's property, so marriage contracts were drawn up to protect a daughter's property rights.

**"Home, sweet home."** Within the family circle, the division of labor between wife and husband changed. In earlier times, middle-class women had often helped run family businesses out of the home. By the later 1800s, most middle-class husbands went to work in an office or shop. A successful husband was one whose income was enough to keep his wife at home. Women spent their working hours raising children, directing the servants, and perhaps doing religious or charitable service.

Books, magazines, and popular songs supported a "cult of domesticity" that idealized women and the home. Sayings like "home, sweet home" were stitched into needlework and hung on parlor walls. The ideal woman was seen as a tender, self-sacrificing caregiver who provided a nest for her children and a peaceful refuge for her husband.

This ideal rarely applied to the lower classes. Working-class women labored for low pay in garment factories or worked as domestic servants. Young women might leave domestic service after they married but often had to seek other employment. Despite long days working for wages, they were still expected to take full responsibility for child care and homemaking.

## Rights for Women

Some individual women and women's groups protested restrictions on women. Like earlier pioneers Olympe de Gouges (page 77) and Mary Wollstonecraft (page 44), they sought a broad range of rights. Across Europe and the United States, politically active women campaigned for fairness in marriage, divorce, and property laws. Women's temperance unions battled to combat the effects of alcoholism on family life.

These reformers faced many obstacles. In Europe and the United States, women could not vote. They were barred from most schools and had little, if any, protection under the law. A woman's husband or father controlled her property.

**Early voices.** Before 1850, some women had become leaders in the union movement. Others, mostly from the middle class, had campaigned for the abolition of slavery. In the process, they realized the severe restrictions on their own lives. In the United States, Elizabeth Cady Stanton and Susan B. Anthony crusaded against slavery before organizing a movement for women's rights.

Many women broke the barriers that kept them out of universities and professions. By the late 1800s, a few brave women overcame opposition to train as doctors or lawyers. Others became explorers, researchers, or inventors, often without recognition. For example, Julia Brainerd Hall worked with her brother to develop an aluminum-producing process. Their company became hugely successful, but Charles Hall received almost all of the credit.

**The suffrage struggle.** By the late 1800s, married women in some countries had won the right to control their own property. The struggle for political rights proved far more difficult. In the United States, the Seneca Falls Convention of 1848 demanded the right to vote for women. In Europe, groups dedicated to women's suffrage, or votes for women, emerged in the later 1800s.

Among men, some liberals and socialists supported women's suffrage. In general, though, suffragists faced intense opposition. Some critics claimed that women were too emotional to be allowed to vote. Others argued that women needed to be "protected" from grubby politics or that a woman's place was in the home, not in government. To such claims, Sojourner Truth, an African American campaigner for women's rights, replied:

> 66Nobody ever helps me into carriages, or over mudpuddles, or gives me any best place! And ain't I a woman? Look at me! Look at my arm! I have ploughed, and planted, and gathered into barns, and no man could head me! And ain't I a woman? I could work as much and eat as much as a man—when I could get it—and bear the lash as well! And ain't I a woman?99

On the edges of the western world, women made faster strides. In New Zealand, Australia, and some western territories of the United States, women won the vote before 1900. There, women who had "tamed the frontier" alongside men were not dismissed as weak and helpless. In Europe and most of the United States, however, the suffrage struggle succeeded only after World War I. You will read about the suffrage movement in various countries in Chapter 7.

## The Growth of Schools

By the late 1800s, reformers convinced governments to set up public schools and require basic education for all children. Teaching "the three Rs"—reading, writing, and 'rithmetic—was thought to produce better citizens. In addition, industrialized societies realized the need for a literate work force. Schools taught punctuality, obedience to authority, disciplined work habits, and patriotism. In European schools, children also received basic religious education.

**Public education.** At first, elementary schools were primitive. Many teachers had little schooling themselves. In rural areas, students attended class only when they were not needed on the farm or in their parents' shops.

By the late 1800s, more and more children were in school, and the quality of elementary education improved. Also, governments were expanding secondary schools, known as high schools in the United States. In secondary schools, students learned the "classical languages," Latin and Greek, along with history and mathematics.

In general, only middle-class families could afford to have their sons attend these schools, which trained students for more serious study or for government jobs. Middle-class girls were sent to school primarily in the hopes that they might marry well and become better wives and mothers.

**Higher education.** Universities expanded in this period, too. Most students were the sons of middle- or upper-class families. The university curriculum emphasized ancient history and languages, philosophy, religion, and law. By the late 1800s, universities added courses in the sciences, especially in chemistry and physics. At the same time, engineering schools trained students who would help build the new industrial society.

Some women sought greater educational opportunities. By the 1840s, a few small colleges for women opened, including Bedford College in England and Mount Holyoke in the United States. In 1863, the British reformer Emily Davies campaigned for female students to be allowed to take the entrance examinations for Cambridge University. She succeeded, but as late as 1897, male Cambridge students rioted against granting degrees to women. (See the picture on page 155.)

## The Challenge of Science

"Science moves, but slowly, slowly creeping on from point to point," wrote the British poet Alfred Tennyson. As you have seen, science in the service of industry brought great changes in

---

**GLOBAL CONNECTIONS**

Western schools encouraged physical fitness as well as learning. In the early 1800s, English schoolboys began playing a game that developed into soccer. School representatives drew up the first set of soccer rules in 1848. The game spread to the rest of Europe, then to Chile, Canada, and the United States. The first international soccer association formed in 1904, and the first World Cup match took place in 1930. Today, soccer is probably the most widely played sport in the world.

---

the later 1800s. At the same time, researchers advanced startling theories about the natural world. Their ideas challenged long-held ideas.

**Atomic theory.** A crucial breakthrough came in the early 1800s when the English Quaker schoolteacher John Dalton developed modern atomic theory. The ancient Greeks had speculated that all matter was made of tiny particles called atoms. Dalton showed how different kinds of atoms combine to make all chemical substances. In 1869, the Russian chemist Dmitri Mendeleyev (mehn duh LAY ehv) drew up a table that grouped elements according to their atomic weights. Mendeleyev's table became the basis for the periodic table of elements used by scientists today.

**The age of the Earth.** The new science of geology opened disturbing avenues of debate. In his *Principles of Geology* (1830–1833), Charles Lyell offered evidence to show that the Earth had formed over millions of years. His successors concluded that the Earth was at least two billion years old and that life had not appeared until long after Earth was formed. These ideas did not seem to agree with biblical accounts of creation.

Archaeology added other pieces to an emerging debate about the origins of life on Earth. In 1856, workers in the Neander valley of Germany accidentally uncovered the fossilized bones of prehistoric people, whom scientists called Neanderthal. Later scholars found fossils of other prehistoric humans and animals. These pioneering archaeologists had limited evidence and often drew mistaken conclusions. But as more discoveries were made around the world, scholars developed new ideas about early human life.

## The Darwin Furor

The most disturbing new idea came from the British naturalist Charles Darwin. In 1859, after years of research, he published *On the Origin of Species*. Darwin argued that all forms of life had evolved into their present state over millions of years. To explain the long, slow process of evolution, he put forward his theory of natural selection.

**Theory of natural selection.** Darwin adopted Malthus's idea that all plants and ani-

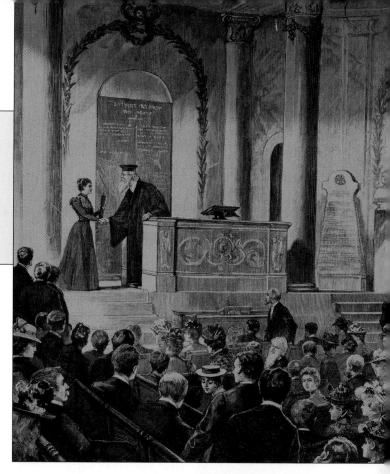

mals produced more offspring than the food supply could support. As a result, he said, members of each species constantly competed to survive. Natural forces "selected" those with physical traits best adapted to their environment. For example, short-necked giraffes, unable to reach the tender leaves at the top of trees, would starve. Longer-necked giraffes would survive and pass the trait on to their offspring. This process of natural selection later came to be called "survival of the fittest."

Over time, said Darwin, natural selection would give rise to entirely new species. He applied this theory to humans. "Man," he declared, "is descended from some less highly organized form." He claimed that humans, like all life forms, were still evolving.

**The uproar.** Like the ideas of Nicolaus Copernicus and Galileo Galilei in earlier times, Darwin's theory ignited a furious debate between scientists and theologians. To many Christians, the Bible contained the only true account of creation. It told how God created the world and all forms of life in six days. Darwin's theory, they argued, reduced people to the level of animals and undermined belief in God and the soul.

While some Christians eventually came to accept the idea of evolution, others did not. Controversy over Darwin's theory has continued to the present day.

**Social Darwinism.** Darwin himself never promoted any social ideas. However, some thinkers used Darwin's theories to support their own beliefs about society. Their ideas became known as Social Darwinism, applying the idea of survival of the fittest to war and economic competition. Industrial tycoons, argued Social Darwinists, earned their success because they were more "fit" than those they put out of busi-

ness. War brought progress by weeding out weak nations. Victory was seen as proof of superiority.

Social Darwinism encouraged racism, the belief that one racial group is superior to another. By the late 1800s, many Europeans and Americans claimed that the success of western civilization was due to the supremacy of the white race. Karl Pearson, a British mathematician, wrote:

66History shows me one way, and one way only, in which a high state of civilization has been produced, namely the struggle of race with race, and the survival of the physically and mentally fitter race.99

By the end of the century, such ideas would be used to justify the global expansion of European power. (See Chapter 8.)

## Christianity in the Industrial Age

Despite the challenge of new ideas, Christianity continued to be a major force in western society. Churches remained at the center of communities, and church leaders influenced political, social, and educational developments.

The grim realities of industrial life stimulated feelings of compassion and charity in many Christians. In Europe, Christian labor unions and political parties pushed for reforms. Individuals and church groups tried to help the working poor. Catholic priests and nuns set up schools and hospitals in urban slums.

In Europe and the United States, Protestant churches backed the social gospel, a movement that urged Christians to social service. They campaigned for reforms in housing, health care, and education. By 1878, William and Catherine Booth had set up the Salvation Army in London. It both spread Christian teachings and provided social services. Their daughter Evangeline Booth later helped bring the Salvation Army to the United States and Canada.

▲ *Evangeline Booth with two homeless children*

## SECTION 3 REVIEW

1. **Identify** (a) "cult of domesticity," (b) atomic theory, (c) Charles Lyell, (d) natural selection, (e) Salvation Army.
2. **Define** (a) women's suffrage, (b) racism, (c) social gospel.
3. Describe middle-class life in the late 1800s in terms of (a) social behavior, (b) marriage, (c) the home.
4. (a) What were the main goals of the women's movement? (b) Why did it face strong opposition?
5. Why did the ideas of Charles Darwin cause controversy?
6. *Critical Thinking* **Defending a Position** Why do you think reformers pushed for free public education?
7. *ACTIVITY* Create a diagram illustrating the new social hierarchy that emerged during the Industrial Revolution.

# 4 A New Culture

## Guide for Reading

■ What themes shaped romantic art, literature, and music?

■ How did realists respond to the industrial world?

■ How did the visual arts change?

■ **Vocabulary** *romanticism, realism, impressionism*

In the 1800s, many writers turned away from the harsh realities of industrial life to celebrate the natural world. The English poet William Wordsworth described the peace and beauty of sunset:

❝It is a beauteous evening, calm and
    free,
  The holy time is quiet as a Nun
  Breathless with adoration; the broad
    sun
  Is sinking down in its tranquillity;
  The gentleness of heaven broods o'er
    the Sea.❞

Other writers, however, took a different approach. They made the grim industrial world the subject of their work.

### *The Revolt Against Reason*

Wordsworth was part of a movement called romanticism. From about 1750 to 1850, romanticism shaped western literature and arts. Romantic writers, artists, and composers rebelled against the Enlightenment emphasis on reason. Using new verse forms, bold colors, or the swelling sounds of the orchestra, romantics sought to excite strong emotions.

**The romantic hero.** Romantic writers created a new kind of hero. He was a mysterious, melancholy figure who felt out of step with society. "My joys, my grief, my passions, and my powers,/Made me a stranger," wrote Britain's Lord Byron. Byron himself became a larger-than-life figure equal to those he created. After a rebellious, wandering life, he joined Greek forces battling for freedom. When he died of a fever in Greece, his legend bloomed. In fact, the moody, isolated romantic hero came to be described as "Byronic."

The romantic hero often hid a guilty secret and faced a grim destiny. Johann Wolfgang von Goethe (GEH tuh), Germany's greatest writer, recast an old legend into the dramatic poem *Faust*. The aging scholar Faust makes a pact with the devil, exchanging his soul for youth. After much agony, Faust wins salvation by accepting his duty to help others.

**Romance of the past.** Like Goethe, British and French writers combed history, legend, and folklore. Sir Walter Scott's novels and ballads evoked the turbulent history of Scottish clans or medieval knights. Alexandre Dumas (doo MAH) and Victor Hugo re-created France's past in novels like *The Three Musketeers* and *The Hunchback of Notre Dame*.

Architects, too, were inspired by old styles and forms. Churches and other buildings, including the British Houses of Parliament, were modeled on medieval Gothic styles. To people living in the 1800s, medieval towers and lacy stonework conjured up images of a glorious past.

**Romanticism in art.** Painters, too, broke free from the discipline and strict rules of the Enlightenment. Landscape painters like John Constable sought to capture the beauty and power of nature. Using bold brush strokes and colors, the brilliant landscape painter J.M.W. Turner showed tiny human figures struggling against sea and storm.

Romantics painted many subjects, from simple peasant life to medieval knights to current events. Bright colors conveyed violent energy and emotion. The French painter Eugène Delacroix (deh luh KRWAH) filled his canvases with dramatic action. In *Liberty Leading the People,*

**Romanticism in Art** This 1823 landscape by John Constable shows a view of England's Salisbury Cathedral. The painting transports the viewer far from the noise, poverty, and gloom of industrial London. **Art and Literature** Reread the lines by William Wordsworth on page 156. How do the poem and the painting convey similar romantic themes?

the Goddess of Liberty carries the revolutionary tricolor as French citizens rally to the cause.

**Music of the romantics.** Romantic composers also sought to inspire deep emotions. The piano music of the Hungarian Franz Liszt moved audiences to laugh or weep at the passion of his playing. Other composers wove traditional folk melodies into their works to glorify their nations' past. In his piano works, Frederic Chopin (SHOH pan) used Polish peasant dances to convey the sorrows and joys of people living under foreign occupation.

The orchestra as we know it today took shape in the early 1800s. The first composer to take full advantage of the broad range of instruments was a brooding genius who shared many traits of the romantic hero—Ludwig van Beethoven.

## A Tortured Musical Genius

It was Ferdinand Ries who brought the bad news to Beethoven. The brilliant composer had recently dedicated a new symphony to Napoleon Bonaparte. He had even inscribed the French general's name on the title page. Like many young Germans, Beethoven admired Napoleon as the heroic defender of "the rights of man."

But then, in 1804, Napoleon had declared himself emperor of France. Ries later recalled Beethoven's reaction:

> 66He broke into a rage and cried, 'So he is no more than a common mortal! And from now on he will trample on the rights of man and further only his own ambition. And from now on he will consider himself superior to everybody and become a tyrant!' Beethoven went to the table, snatched the title page of the manuscript, tore it in half and threw it on the floor.99

Despite his raging fury, Beethoven did not destroy his Bonaparte Symphony. Instead, he changed the title to *Eroica,* or "Heroic." To Beethoven, the music was far more important than the man.

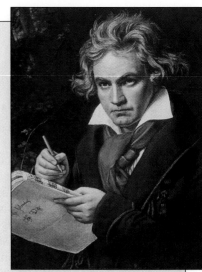

*Ludwig van Beethoven* Beethoven's wild hair and intense eyes have been immortalized in paintings and sculpture. You can almost sense the fury and inspiration that consumed him as he scribbled the lines, below right, from an 1808 composition. **Impact of the Individual** Why do you think Beethoven has been one of the most admired figures in world culture?

**A fiery talent.** Beethoven's life spanned the revolutionary era, from 1770 to 1827. His symphonies combined classical forms with the stirring range of sound favored by the romantics. He wrote from the heart, conveying intense emotional struggle.

Beethoven was a proud, difficult, extravagant man. In fact, he felt he had much in common with Napoleon. They were almost the same age. Through talent, energy, and ambition, each had risen from a lowly station to carve out his own destiny. These were the qualities that inspired the *Eroica.*

**Eroica.** At first, the new symphony did not please listeners. An early critic complained that, in spite of "startling and beautiful passages," the symphony had "too much that is glaring and bizarre." Beethoven, who conducted the first performance, angered the audience by refusing to nod in response to applause.

Some listeners, though, recognized the genius of the *Eroica.* Critics have suggested that it mirrors the spirit of both Beethoven and his ex-hero Napoleon. The first movement expresses a sweeping determination to succeed. Later, a funeral march expresses the power of the hero to survive death and despair. The symphony rushes on to a triumphant conclusion—the victory of the creative spirit.

**Triumph and tragedy.** After the *Eroica,* Beethoven went from masterpiece to masterpiece. In all, he produced nine symphonies, an opera, and dozens of shorter pieces. In the famous opening four notes of his Fifth Symphony, Beethoven captured the feeling of "Fate knocking at the door." His Ninth Symphony features the stirring choral "Ode to Joy," a favorite in both concert halls and churches.

Yet Beethoven's career was haunted by perhaps the greatest tragedy a musician can face. About 1798, he began to lose his hearing. Advancing deafness sparked outbursts of rage and depression. He alienated friends, lived in a chaotic, messy house, and once looked so ragged that he was arrested as a tramp. Late in life, he became totally deaf. Still, he continued to compose and conduct—music that he himself would hear only in his mind.

More than 20,000 admirers marched at Beethoven's funeral in 1827. A speaker summed up his tortured life:

>He withdrew from men after he had given them everything and received nothing in return. He remained solitary. . . . But even unto his grave he preserved a human heart for all who are human. . . . Thus he lived, thus he died, and thus he shall live forever.

The prediction came true. Today, audiences all over the world still buy recordings and flock to performances of Beethoven's works.

## The Call to Realism

By the mid-1800s, a new artistic movement, realism, took hold in the West. Realism was an attempt to represent the world as it was, without the sentiment associated with romanticism. Realists often looked at the harsher side of life in cities or villages. Many writers and artists were committed to improving the lot of the unfortunates whose lives they described.

**The novel.** The English novelist Charles Dickens vividly portrayed the lives of slum dwellers and factory workers, including children. In *Oliver Twist,* he told the story of a nine-

year-old orphan raised in a grim poorhouse. One day, Oliver asks for extra food:

>Child as he was, he was desperate with hunger, and reckless with misery. He rose from the table, and advancing on the master, basin and spoon in hand, said, somewhat alarmed at his own [boldness]:
>
>'Please, sir, I want some more.'
>
>The master was a fat, healthy man, but he turned very pale. He gazed in

*The World of Dickens* Dozens of beloved characters poured from the pen of Charles Dickens— from Oliver Twist and David Copperfield, to Ebenezer Scrooge and Tiny Tim in A Christmas Carol. *Dickens's novels were often published in installments. Families eagerly gathered to hear the latest chapters read out loud and find out what happened next.* **Continuity and Change** *Dickens's novels often shed light on social problems. What kinds of people might Dickens write about today?*

stupefied astonishment at the small rebel for some seconds. . . . 'What!' said the master at length, in a faint voice.

'Please, sir,' replied Oliver, 'I want some more.'

The master aimed a blow at Oliver's head with the ladle, pinioned him in his arms, and shrieked aloud.**99**

Later, Oliver runs away to London. There he is taken in by Fagin, a villain who trains homeless children to become pickpockets. *Oliver Twist* shocked middle-class readers with its picture of poverty and urban crime.

Victor Hugo moved from romantic to realistic novels. In *Les Miserables* (mih zehr AHB luh), he revealed how hunger drove a good man to crime and how the law hounded him ever after. Emile Zola's *Germinal* is a novel of class warfare in the mining industry. (See page 145.) To Zola's characters, neither the Enlightenment's faith in reason nor romantic feelings mattered at all.

**Drama.** The Norwegian dramatist Henrik Ibsen brought realism to the stage. His plays attacked the hypocrisy he saw around him. *A Doll's House* showed a woman caught in a straitjacket of social rules. In *An Enemy of the People,* a doctor discovers that the water in a local spa is polluted. Because the town's economy depends on its spa, the citizens denounce the doctor and suppress the truth. Ibsen's realistic dramas had a wide influence in Europe and the United States. ( See *World Literature,* "A Doll's House," pages 162–163.)

**Realism in art.** Painters also represented the realities of their time. Rejecting the romantic emphasis on imagination, they focused on ordinary subjects, especially working-class men and women. "I cannot paint an angel," said the French realist Gustave Courbet (koor BAY), "because I have never seen one." Instead, he painted works such as *The Stone Breakers,* which shows two rough laborers on a country road.

## Women Writers Win Recognition

By the mid-1800s, a growing number of women were getting their works into print. In northern England, the sisters Charlotte, Emily, and Anne Brontë lived quietly at home, the dutiful daughters of a country clergyman. But every day, they wrote. Using the names Currer, Ellis, and Acton Bell, they found a publisher for their poems and novels. Later, the publisher was shocked to discover his authors were women.

Charlotte Brontë's novel *Jane Eyre* follows the sufferings of an orphaned governess and her love for Mr. Rochester, a brooding, Byronic hero. In *Wuthering Heights,* Emily Brontë told a dramatic story of doomed love against the backdrop of the stormy Yorkshire moors.

In France, Aurore Dupin Dudevant (doo duh VAHN) published a highly successful novel, *Indiana,* under the name George Sand. Soon, critics were ranking her among the finest French writers. Sand defied convention by dressing like a man, complete with top hat and cigar.

In the United States, Harriet Beecher Stowe created a sensation with her first novel, *Uncle Tom's Cabin.* Its depiction of the lives of plantation slaves helped mold antislavery opinion. Kate Chopin's 1899 novel *The Awakening,* like Ibsen's *A Doll's House,* showed a wife rebelling against her restricted life. Yet Chopin's work was largely unappreciated until the 1960s.

## New Directions in the Visual Arts

By the 1840s, a new art form, photography, was emerging. Louis Daguerre (dah GAYR) in France and William Fox Talbot in England had improved on earlier technologies to produce successful photographs. At first, many photos were stiff-posed portraits of middle-class families or prominent people. Other photographs reflected the romantics' fascination with faraway places.

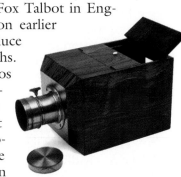

▲ *Camera, about 1845*

ISSUES *For* TODAY

Artists and writers responded in varying ways to the tremendous changes of the industrial era. How do you think literature and the arts reflect social and technological developments?

**Post-Impressionism** *Vincent van Gogh's unique brushwork lent a dreamlike quality to everyday subjects. His fields, flowers, and faces are some of the most recognized images in art today.* **Art and Literature** *Compare and contrast Van Gogh's cathedral to Constable's on page 157.*

In time, photographers used the camera to expose slum conditions and other social ills. Photographs provided shocking evidence to prod governments toward reform. Photographers also went to war. During the American Civil War, Mathew B. Brady preserved a vivid, realistic record of the corpse-strewn battlefields.

**The impressionists.** Photography posed a challenge to painters. Why try for realism, some artists asked, when a camera could do the same thing better? By the 1870s, a group of painters took art in a new direction, seeking to capture the first fleeting impression made by a scene or object on the viewer's eye. The new movement, known as impressionism, took root in Paris, capital of the western art world.

Since the Renaissance, painters had carefully finished their paintings so that not a brush stroke showed. But impressionists like Claude Monet (moh NAY) and Edgar Degas (day GAH) brushed strokes of color side by side without any blending. According to new scientific studies of optics, the human eye would mix these patches of color. (See the painting on page 163.)

By concentrating on visual impressions rather than realism, artists achieved a fresh view of familiar subjects. Monet, for example, painted the cathedral at Rouen (roo AHN), France, dozens of times from the same angle, capturing how it looked in different lights at different times of day.

**The post-impressionists.** Later painters, called post-impressionists, developed a variety of styles. Georges Seurat (suh RAH) arranged small dots of color to define the shapes of objects. The Dutch painter Vincent van Gogh experimented with sharp brush lines and bright color. Desperately poor, he sold few paintings in his short, unhappy life. Today, Van Gogh's masterpieces have sold for millions of dollars apiece.

Paul Gauguin (goh GAN) developed a bold, personal style. He rejected the materialism of Western life and went to live on the island of Tahiti. In his paintings, people look flat as in medieval stained-glass windows or "primitive" folk art. But his brooding colors and black outlining of shapes convey intense feelings and images.

## SECTION 4 REVIEW

1. **Identify** (a) Lord Byron, (b) Johann Wolfgang von Goethe, (c) Ludwig van Beethoven, (d) the Brontës, (e) George Sand, (f) Claude Monet, (g) post-impressionists.
2. **Define** (a) romanticism, (b) realism, (c) impressionism.
3. (a) How did romantics respond to industry? (b) Describe three subjects they favored.
4. How did each of the following explore realistic themes: (a) Charles Dickens, (b) Henrik Ibsen, (c) Gustave Courbet?
5. How did photography influence the development of painting in the late 1800s?
6. *Critical Thinking* **Linking Past and Present** Compare the ideal of a romantic hero of the 1800s to the ideal of a romantic hero today. How are they similar or different?
7. *ACTIVITY* Write a review of one of the paintings in this chapter. Consider such questions as: What style is used? What is the artist trying to do? What is your impression of the work?

# World Literature
## A Doll's House
### Henrik Ibsen

**Introduction** *By today's standards,* A Doll's House *is not a shocking play. In 1879, though, Henrik Ibsen's drama stunned audiences, first in Norway, then throughout Europe and the United States. Unlike the heroic or romantic dramas that were popular,* A Doll's House *presented a realistic picture of middle-class life. In addition, Ibsen challenged many accepted social ideas, especially about marriage.*

*At the start of the play, Torvald Helmer, a lawyer, and his wife, Nora, are happily married. But a crisis causes Nora to question her role. The following scene occurs near the end of the play.*

HELMER. *(Speaking to* NORA, *who is offstage)* How snug and nice our home is, Nora. You're safe here; I'll keep you like a hunted dove I've rescued out of a hawk's claws; I'll bring peace to your poor, shuddering heart. . . . For a man there's something indescribably sweet and satisfying in knowing he's forgiven his wife—and forgiven her out of a full and open heart. It's as if she belongs to him in two ways now: in a sense, he's given her fresh into the world again, and she's become his wife and his child as well. From now on that's what you'll be to me—you little, bewildered, helpless thing. Don't be afraid of anything, Nora; just open your heart to me, and I'll be conscience and will to you both— *(NORA enters in her regular clothes.)* What's this? Not in bed? You've changed your dress?

NORA. Yes, Torvald, I've changed my dress.

HELMER. But why now, so late? . . .

NORA. Sit down, Torvald; we have a lot to talk about.

HELMER. Nora—what is this? That hard expression—

NORA. Sit down. This'll take some time. I have a lot to say.

HELMER. You worry me, Nora. And I don't understand you.

NORA. No, that's exactly it. You don't understand me. And I've never understood you either—until tonight. No, don't interrupt. You can just listen to what I say. We're closing our accounts, Torvald.

HELMER. How do you mean that?

NORA. Doesn't anything strike you about our sitting here like this?

HELMER. What's that?

NORA. We've been married now eight years. Doesn't it occur to you that this is the first time we two, you and I, man and wife, have ever talked seriously together?

HELMER. What do you mean—seriously?

NORA. In eight whole years—longer even—right from our first acquaintance, we've never exchanged a serious word. . . .

HELMER. But dearest, what good would that ever do you?

NORA. That's the point right there: you've never understood me. I've been wronged greatly, Torvald—first by Papa, and then by you.

HELMER. What? By us—the two people who've loved you more than anyone else?

NORA. *(Shaking her head)* You never loved me. You've thought it fun to be in love with me, that's all.

HELMER. Nora, what a thing to say!

NORA. Yes, it's true now, Torvald. When I lived at home with Papa, he told me all his opinions, so I had the same ones too; or if they were different I hid them, since he wouldn't have cared for that. He used to call me his doll-child, and he played with me the way I played with my dolls. Then I came into your house—

HELMER. How can you speak of our marriage like that?

NORA. *(Unperturbed)* I mean, then I went from Papa's hands into yours. You arranged everything to your own taste, and so I got the same taste as you—or I pretended to; I can't remember. I guess a little of both, first one,

**Women at Work** *Working women were a favorite subject of the impressionist Edgar Degas. He showed women dancing at the ballet, scrubbing clothes in a laundry—or, in this painting, making hats in a Paris shop.* **Economics and Technology** *At the end of* A Doll's House, *Nora Helmer announces that she intends to find a job. Why do you think she considered this an important step?*

then the other. Now when I look back, it seems as if I'd lived here like a beggar—just from hand to mouth. I've lived by doing tricks for you, Torvald. But that's the way you wanted it. It's a great sin what you and Papa did to me. You're to blame that nothing's become of me.

HELMER. Nora, how unfair and ungrateful you are! Haven't you been happy here?

NORA. No, never. I thought so—but I never have.

HELMER. Not—not happy!

NORA. No, only lighthearted. And you've always been so kind to me. But our home's been nothing but a playpen. I've been your doll-wife here, just as at home I was Papa's doll-child. And in turn the children have been my dolls. I thought it was fun when you played with me, just as they thought it was fun when I played with them. That's been our marriage, Torvald.

HELMER. There's some truth in what you're saying—under all the raving exaggeration. But it'll all be different after this. Playtime's over; now for the schooling.

NORA. Whose schooling—mine or the children's?

HELMER. Both yours and the children's, dearest.

NORA. Oh, Torvald, you're not the man to teach me to be a good wife to you.

HELMER. And you can say that?

NORA. And I—how am I equipped to bring up children?

HELMER. Nora!

NORA. Didn't you say a moment ago that that was no job to trust me with?

HELMER. In a flare of temper! Why fasten on that?

NORA. Yes, but you were so very right. I'm not up to the job. There's another job I have to do first. I have to try to educate myself. You can't help me with that. I've got to do it alone. And that's why I'm leaving you now.

HELMER. *(Jumping up)* What's that?

NORA. I have to stand completely alone, if I'm ever going to discover myself and the world out there.

Source: Henrik Ibsen, *A Doll's House,* translated by Rolf Fjelde (New York: New American Library, 1965).

## Thinking About Literature

1. List five phrases or nicknames Torvald uses that reveal his attitude toward his wife.
2. (a) According to Nora, how was she "wronged" by her father and her husband? (b) What does she intend to do about it?
3. *Critical Thinking* **Synthesizing Information** Review the subsections Middle-Class Values on pages 151–152 and Rights for Women on page 153. (a) Does the Helmers' marriage fit the middle-class ideal of the time? Explain. (b) Nora expresses a need to educate herself. Why do you think many women in the late 1800s fought for the right to an education?

## CHAPTER REVIEW

### REVIEWING VOCABULARY

Review the vocabulary words in this chapter. Then, use *eight* of these words to create a crossword puzzle. Exchange puzzles with a classmate. Complete the puzzles and then check each other's answers.

### REVIEWING FACTS

1. Which two nations became industrial leaders in the late 1800s?
2. List three inventions that improved transportation and communication.

3. What arguments were made for and against the rise of big business?
4. How did city governments make cities cleaner and safer?
5. What kinds of attractions did cities offer their residents?
6. How did education change in the late 1800s?
7. Summarize Charles Darwin's theory of natural selection.
8. Name three important women writers of the 1800s and one famous work by each writer.

## SKILLS FOR SUCCESS  ANALYZING POLITICAL CARTOONS

Political cartoons express a person's point of view on a current event or issue. The purpose of the cartoon is to sway the opinions of others. To do this, the cartoonist often uses humor and exaggeration. Cartoonists also use a variety of symbols to convey their message.

The cartoon below appeared in the American magazine *The Verdict* in 1899. The title of the cartoon is "The Menace of the Hour." Examine the cartoon and then answer the following questions:

**1. Identify the symbols.**
(a) What does the octopus-like monster represent? (b) What is the monster doing to the city?

**2. Analyze the meaning of the cartoon.** (a) List three types of businesses that, according to the cartoon, are controlled by monopolies. (b) Explain the title of the cartoon. (c) How do you think this cartoonist probably felt about government regulation of big business? Explain your answer.

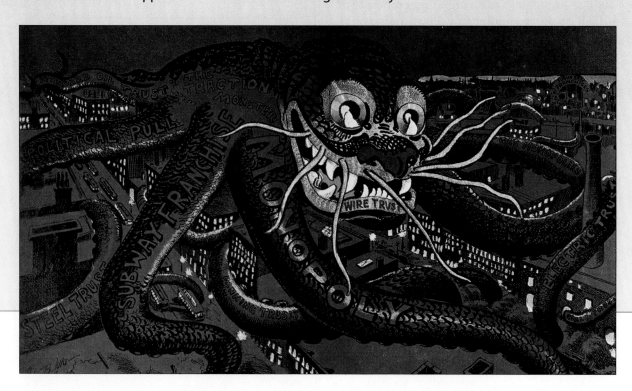

## REVIEWING CHAPTER THEMES

Review the "Focus On" questions at the start of this chapter. Then select *three* of those questions and answer them, using information from the chapter.

## CRITICAL THINKING

1. **Linking Past and Present** (a) How did the second phase of the Industrial Revolution differ from the first phase? (b) Some historians have suggested that we are now in the midst of a "third" Industrial Revolution. Do you agree or disagree? Explain.

2. **Recognizing Points of View** Review the discussion of laissez-faire economics on page 44. (a) Which side do you think Adam Smith would have taken in the debate over regulating monopolies? Explain. (b) Do you think David Ricardo would have favored the organization of labor unions? Explain.

## ANALYZING PRIMARY SOURCES

Use the quotation on page 153 to answer the following questions.

1. What activities did Truth claim she could perform as well as a man?

2. What does the repeated phrase, "And ain't I a woman?" mean?

3. Summarize Truth's argument in a sentence.

## FOR YOUR PORTFOLIO

**PRESENTING A DRAMATIZATION**   Work with a group of classmates to write a script for a dramatic presentation of some aspect of life in the Industrial Age. Begin by reviewing this chapter and deciding on an incident, invention, or person to feature. Discuss with your group what characters to include in your dramatization. Then research additional information for your script, outline the story you will present, and write the script. Finally, rehearse the script as a group and present it to the class.

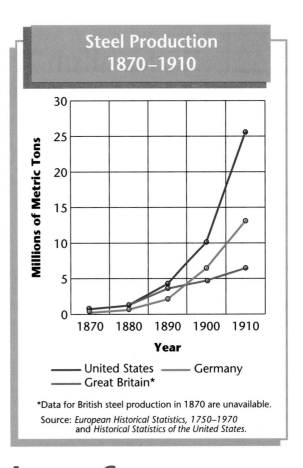

**Steel Production 1870–1910**

Millions of Metric Tons (y-axis)

Year (x-axis): 1870 1880 1890 1900 1910

—— United States  —— Germany
—— Great Britain*

*Data for British steel production in 1870 are unavailable.

Source: *European Historical Statistics, 1750–1970* and *Historical Statistics of the United States.*

## ANALYZING GRAPHS

Use the graph to answer the following questions.

1. For the year 1890, list the three countries shown in the graph in order from highest to lowest steel production.

2. How did the order of the three countries change between 1890 and 1900?

3. Which countries produced more steel in 1910 than in 1870?

## INTERNET ACTIVITY

**RESEARCHING FINE ART**   Use the Internet to research the Impressionist movement. Then write an art critique of an Impressionist painting or group of paintings. In your critique, explain what makes that artwork part of Impressionism.

# Nationalism Triumphs in Europe

## (1800–1914)

## CHAPTER OUTLINE

1 Building a German Nation
2 Strengthening Germany
3 Unifying Italy
4 Nationalism Threatens Old Empires
5 Russia: Reform and Reaction

The Prussian legislators waited restlessly for Otto von Bismarck, the king's new chancellor, to speak. They knew he wanted them to vote more money to build up the Prussian army. Liberal members of the parliament, however, opposed the move.

At last, Bismarck rose. He was a tall man with a bristling mustache and hard, unyielding eyes. In harsh tones, he dismissed the concerns of the liberal opposition:

66Germany does not look to Prussia's liberalism, but to her power. . . . The great questions of the day are not to be decided by speeches and majority resolutions—that was the mistake of 1848 and 1849—but by blood and iron!99

Bismarck delivered his "blood and iron" speech in 1862. It set the tone for his policies in the years ahead. Bismarck had no respect for representative government. He was determined to build a strong, unified German nation, led by his state of Prussia. He meant to do so with or without the help of parliament.

A master of power politics at home and abroad, Bismarck dominated European affairs from 1862 to 1890. Once, when he was warned that Britain might oppose him on a certain issue, he replied:

66What is England to me? The importance of a state is measured by the number of soldiers it can put into the field of battle. . . . *It is the destiny of the weak to be devoured by the strong.*99

The last half of the 1800s can be called the age of nationalism. In this period, a new political order emerged in Europe. Bismarck welded the German states into a powerful empire. A divided Italy found political unity. And throughout the European continent, strong leaders harnessed national feeling to encourage industrialism and modernization.

In some countries, nationalism was a divisive rather than a unifying force. It strained Austria's multinational empire. It led Russian czars to suppress the cultures of national minorities within their land. To this day, nationalism has remained a powerful force that has both unified countries and sparked rivalries, conflicts, and great bloodshed.

FOCUS ON these questions as you read:

- **Political and Social Systems**
  What effect did nationalism and demands for reform have on European governments?

- **Impact of the Individual**
  How did tough-minded political leaders contribute to the unification of Germany and of Italy?

- **Diversity**
  How did nationalism affect ethnically diverse empires in central and Eastern Europe?

- **Religions and Value Systems**
  How were religion and nationalism linked in the Russian empire?

## TIME AND PLACE

*Triumph of Nationalism* After stunning victories over Austria and France, German leaders met in the palace at Versailles in 1871 to proclaim William I emperor of a united Germany. Here, William (on steps) takes the oath of office. William's chancellor and the architect of German unification, Otto von Bismarck (at center, in white jacket), looks on. **Global Interaction** How does the scene mark a shift of European power and a triumph of nationalism?

## HUMANITIES LINK

*Art History* Photographs of German workers (page 173).
*Literature* In this chapter, you will encounter passages from the following works of literature: Ernst Morris Arndt, "The German's Fatherland" (page 168); Alexander Pushkin, "Ode to Freedom" (page 182).

| 1814 | 1831 | 1862 | 1871 | 1905 | 1914 |
|------|------|------|------|------|------|
| Congress of Vienna begins | Giuseppe Mazzini founds Young Italy | Otto von Bismarck named Chancellor of Prussia | Germany is united under Second Reich | Russian Revolution of 1905 | World War I begins |

| 1800 | 1820 | 1840 | 1860 | 1880 | 1900 | 1920 |
|------|------|------|------|------|------|------|

# 1 Building a German Nation

## Guide for Reading

- How did early German nationalism pave the way for unity?

- What role did Bismarck play in the unification of Germany?

- What were the immediate cause and the immediate results of the Franco-Prussian War?

German nationalism developed gradually. In the early 1800s, romantic writers spoke of a unique "German national character" shaped by ancient traditions. Philosophers and poets promoted the idea of a German nation. In a widely admired poem, "The German's Fatherland," poet Ernst M. Arndt tapped into this patriotic feeling:

66Where is the German's Fatherland?
Name me its farthest bound!
'Wherever rings the German tongue,
Wherever its hymns to God are sung,
There shall it be!
There, brave German, make your
   Germany!'99

The early calls to nationhood came mostly from students and intellectuals. Their efforts to unite Germans faltered in the face of Metternich's conservative ideas. In the mid-1800s, however, an aggressive leader named Otto von Bismarck imposed a Prussian brand of nationhood on all of Germany.

## First Steps

In the early 1800s, German-speaking people lived in a host of small and medium-sized states as well as in Prussia and the Austrian Hapsburg empire. (See the map on page 86.) Napoleon's invasions unleashed new forces in these territories.

**Impact of Napoleon.** Between 1807 and 1812, Napoleon made important territorial changes in the German-speaking lands. He added lands along the Rhine River to France. He dissolved the Holy Roman Empire and organized a number of German states into a French-controlled Rhine Confederation.

At first, some Germans welcomed the French emperor as a hero with enlightened, modern policies. He encouraged freeing of the serfs, made trade easier, and abolished laws against Jews.

At the same time, Napoleon's conquests sparked German nationalism. People who had fought to free their lands from French rule began to demand a unified German state.

At the Congress of Vienna, Metternich opposed nationalist demands. He pointed out that a united Germany would require dismantling the governments of the many separate German states. Instead, the conservative peacemakers created the German Confederation, a weak body headed by Austria.

**Prussian leadership.** In the 1830s, Austria's great rival, Prussia, took the lead in creating an economic union called the Zollverein (TSAWL fuh rīn). It dismantled tariff barriers between many of the German states. Still, despite this step toward economic unity, Germany remained politically fragmented.

In 1848, liberals meeting in the Frankfurt Assembly once more took up the demand for German political unity. (See page 119.) They offered the throne of a united German state to King Frederick William IV of Prussia. The Prussian ruler rejected the notion of a throne offered by "the people." Again, Germany remained divided, but the stage was set for Prussian leadership.

## Bismarck: Architect of German Unity

Otto von Bismarck succeeded where others had failed. He came from Prussia's Junker (YUNG ker) class, which was made up of conservative landowning nobles. Bismarck served Prussia as a diplomat in Russia and France before King William I made him chancellor, or prime minister, in 1862. Within a decade, the new chancellor had used his policy of "blood and iron" to unite the German states under Prussian rule.

**The Roots of German Nationalism** *In 1812, Jacob and Wilhelm Grimm published the first of a series of folk tales they had collected from peasant villages throughout Germany. They hoped that their work would help unify the German people by giving them a sense of their common heritage. An illustration from one of the most popular tales, "Hansel and Gretel," is shown here.* **Art and Literature** *What stories do Americans share as part of their cultural heritage?*

**Master of Realpolitik.** Bismarck's success was due in part to his strong will and his ability to manipulate others. He was a master of Realpolitik, or realistic politics based on a tough-minded evaluation of the needs of the state. In Bismarck's view, the ends justified the means. Power was more important than principles such as liberalism.

A contemporary of Bismarck reflected the ideas of Realpolitik when he explained why national leaders sometimes had to make ruthless decisions:

66For the state, in contrast to the individual, self-preservation is the supreme law. The state must survive at any price; it cannot go into the poorhouse, it cannot beg, it cannot commit suicide; in short, it must take wherever it can find the essentials of life.99

Oddly enough, Bismarck, the architect of German unity, was not really a German nationalist. His primary loyalty was to the Hohenzollerns, the ruling dynasty of Prussia. He regarded uniting Germany as a means to make the Hohenzollerns master of all the German states.

**Strengthening the army.** As chancellor, Bismarck moved first to build up the Prussian army. Despite his "blood and iron" speech (see page 166), the liberal legislature refused to vote funds for the military. Bismarck would not be thwarted. He simply used money that had been collected for other purposes to strengthen the army. With a powerful, well-equipped military, he was ready to pursue an aggressive foreign policy.

## Victory in Three Wars

In the next decade, Bismarck led Prussia into three wars. Each war increased Prussian prestige and power while paving the way for German unity.

**Schleswig and Holstein.** Bismarck's first maneuver was to form an alliance in 1864 with Austria. They then moved to seize the provinces of Schleswig and Holstein from Denmark. After a brief war, Prussia and Austria "liberated" the two provinces, which were largely inhabited by Germans, and divided up the spoils. Austria was to administer Holstein and Prussia was to administer Schleswig.

**War with Austria.** In 1866, Bismarck invented an excuse to attack Austria. The Austro-Prussian War lasted just seven weeks and ended in a decisive Prussian victory. Prussia then annexed, or added, not only Holstein but several other north German states.

Bismarck dissolved the Austrian-led German Confederation and created a new North German Confederation dominated by Prussia. But the master of Realpolitik did not enforce harsh terms of peace. Instead, he allowed Austria and four other southern German states to

## Unification of Germany, 1865–1871

DENMARK
BALTIC SEA
NORTH SEA
SCHLESWIG
HOLSTEIN
EAST PRUSSIA
POMERANIA
Hamburg
MECKLENBURG
WEST PRUSSIA
HANOVER
BRANDENBURG
Oder R.
Vistula R.
NETHERLANDS
Berlin
PRUSSIA
POSEN
RUSSIA
N
W
E
S
WESTPHALIA
Elbe R.
Rhine R.
BELGIUM
Ems
THURINGIA
SAXONY
SILESIA
Sedan
LUX.
Frankfurt
Prague
Sadowa
To Paris
Main R.
Metz
BAVARIA
AUSTRIA-HUNGARY
LORRAINE
WURTEMBERG
FRANCE
ALSACE
HOHENZOLLERN
Danube R.
Vienna
Munich
0
100
200 Miles
0
50
100 Kilometers
SWITZERLAND
Prussia, 1865
Added to Prussia, 1866
Added to Prussia, 1867
Added to form German empire, 1871
Boundary of German empire, 1871
Battle sites
Route of Prussian armies in Austro-Prussian War
Route of German armies in Franco-Prussian War

### GEOGRAPHY AND HISTORY

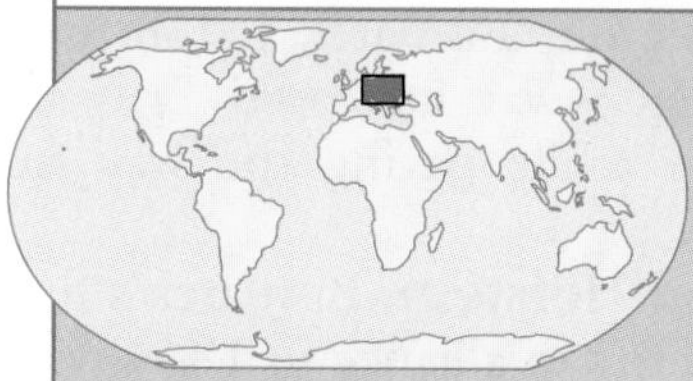

*In the early 1800s, most people living in German-speaking states had local rather than national loyalties. They considered themselves Silesians, Bavarians, and so on, rather than Germans. By the mid-1800s, however, local loyalties began to give way to a German national identity. This growth of national feeling helped make possible the unification of Germany in 1871.*

1. **Location** *On the map, locate (a) Prussia, (b) Silesia, (c) Bavaria, (d) Schleswig.*
2. **Region** *What area did Prussia add to its territory in 1866? In 1867?*
3. **Critical Thinking** **Analyzing Information** *Why do you think Austrian influence was greater among the southern German states than among the northern ones?*

remain independent. Bismarck's motives, as always, were strictly practical. "We had to avoid leaving behind any desire for revenge," he later wrote.

**The Franco-Prussian War.** The Prussian victory worried Napoleon III in France. A growing rivalry between the two nations led to the Franco-Prussian War of 1870. The immediate cause was a struggle over the vacant Spanish throne. When a relative of the Prussian king was offered the throne, France protested. It feared the spread of Prussian influence to its southern border.

Bismarck seized on the situation to rally all Germans—no matter where they lived—against Napoleon III. Germans recalled only too well the invasions of Napoleon I some 60 years earlier. Bismarck played up the image of the French menace to spur German nationalism. For his part, Napoleon III did little to avoid war, hoping to mask problems at home with military glory.

Bismarck helped the crisis along by rewriting and then releasing to the press a telegram that reported on a meeting between King William I and the French ambassador. Bismarck's editing of the "Ems dispatch" made it seem that William I had insulted the Frenchman. Furious, Napoleon III declared war on Prussia, as Bismarck hoped. Cries of "On to Berlin!" filled the streets of Paris. The fighting, however, quickly proved otherwise.

A superior Prussian force, helped by troops from other German states, smashed the badly organized, poorly supplied French soldiers. Napoleon III, old and ill, surrendered after a few weeks of fighting. France had to accept a humiliating peace. The French defeat led to the downfall of the Second Empire, as you will read in Chapter 7.

"The Great German Ogre" As part of his plan to unify Germany, Bismarck provoked the French into the disastrous Franco-Prussian War. This cartoon, titled "The Great German Ogre," shows the French view of the German chancellor. **Political and Social Systems** How does the cartoonist show his dislike of Bismarck?

N: 11.

LE GRAND ÔGRE ALLEMAND.

Les grands et petits seigneurs hobereaux des voisins pays s'étant permis de lui tenir tête et d'agir contre son gré ; il chaussa incontinent ses tant fameuses bottes de sept lieues, s'elança contre eux et les écrasa comme un tas de mouches. Comme avait moult grand appétit volontiers les voulaient tous dévorer tout crus avec leurs sujets ; mais craignant une indigestion... R* (Extrait d'une vieille légende.)

## The German Empire

Delighted by the victory over France, princes from the southern German states and the North German Confederation persuaded William I of Prussia to take the title kaiser (KĪ zer), or emperor. In January 1871, German nationalists celebrated the birth of the Second Reich, or empire. They called it that because they considered it heir to the Holy Roman Empire founded by King Otto the Great in the 900s and abolished by Napoleon I in 1806.

Success, as Bismarck had predicted, came from a policy of "blood and iron." He had dealt shattering blows to two great powers, Austria and France. The newly united Germany soon vaulted into a leading role in Europe. What an odd twist of fate that a conservative Prussian noble had created a united German nation, the goal set by liberals and nationalists in the early 1800s!

A constitution drafted by Bismarck set up a two-house legislature for the Second Reich. The Bundesrat, or upper house, was appointed by the rulers of the German states. The Reichstag, or lower house, was elected by universal male suffrage. Still, the new German nation was far from democratic, since the Bundesrat could veto any decisions of the Reichstag. Real power remained in the hands of the emperor and his chancellor.

## SECTION 1 REVIEW

1. **Identify** (a) Zollverein, (b) Realpolitik, (c) Schleswig and Holstein, (d) Austro-Prussian War, (e) North German Confederation, (f) Franco-Prussian War, (g) William I, (h) Second Reich.
2. What steps were taken toward German unity before 1850?
3. Describe the goals and policies of Otto von Bismarck.
4. Prussia fought three wars to unite Germany. Explain how each helped achieve that goal.
5. *Critical Thinking* **Applying Information** Identify three examples of Bismarck's use of Realpolitik.
6. *ACTIVITY* Create an illustrated map and time line showing the unification of Germany.

# Strengthening Germany

## Guide for Reading

■ What forces spurred the growth of the German economy?

■ What domestic policies did Bismarck pursue?

■ What were the goals of William II?

In January 1871, German princes gathered in the glittering Hall of Mirrors at the French palace of Versailles. (See the painting on page 167.) They had just defeated Napoleon III in the Franco-Prussian War and had chosen Louis XIV's palace to proclaim the new German empire. The symbolism was clear. French domination of Europe, dating from the age of Louis XIV, had ended. Germany, headed by William I and his chancellor, Otto von Bismarck, was the new power in Europe.

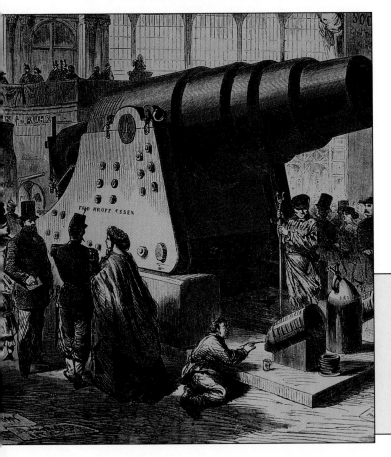

## The German Industrial Giant

In the aftermath of unification, the German empire emerged as the industrial giant of the European continent. By the late 1800s, German chemical and electrical industries set the standard worldwide. German shipping was second only to Britain's among the European powers.

**Economic progress.** Germany's spectacular growth was due in part to ample iron and coal resources, the basic ingredients for industrial development. A disciplined and educated work force also helped the economy, while a rapidly growing population—from 41 million in 1871 to 67 million by 1914—provided a huge home market and a highly skilled work force.

The new nation also benefited from earlier progress. During the 1850s and 1860s, Germans had founded large companies and built many railroads. The house of Krupp boomed after 1871, becoming an enormous industrial complex producing steel and weapons for a world market. (See page 145.) Between 1871 and 1914, the business tycoon August Thyssen built a small steel factory of 70 workers into a giant empire with 50,000 employees.

**Science, government, and industry.** German industrialists were the first to see the value of applied science in developing new products such as synthetic chemicals and dyes. They supported research and development in the universities and hired trained scientists to solve technological problems in their factories.

The German government promoted economic development. After 1871, it issued a single currency for Germany, reorganized the banking system, and coordinated railroads built by the various German states. When a worldwide depression hit in the late 1800s, it raised tariffs to protect home industries from foreign

*"Arsenal of the World"* Here, visitors to an international industrial exhibition admire a huge cannon produced by the Krupp works. By the time he died in 1887, Alfred Krupp had turned his family business into the "arsenal of the world." He had armed 46 different countries and was awarded military decorations by Russia, Belgium, Sweden, Spain, the Ottoman empire, Japan, and Brazil. ***Economics and Technology*** What advantages would a cannon like this one offer to an army?

competition. The new German empire was determined to maintain economic strength as well as military power.

## The Iron Chancellor

As chancellor, Bismarck pursued several foreign policy goals. He sought to keep France weak and isolated while building strong links with Austria and Russia. He respected British naval power but did not seek to compete in that arena. "Water rats," he said, "do not fight with land rats." Later, he took a more aggressive stand against Britain as the two nations competed for empire overseas. (See Chapter 8.)

On the domestic front, Bismarck applied the same ruthless methods he had used to achieve unification. The Iron Chancellor, as he was called, sought to erase local loyalties and crush all opposition to the imperial state. He targeted two groups, the Catholic Church and the socialists. In his view, both posed a threat to the new German state.

**Campaign against the Church.** After unification, Catholics made up about a third of the German population. The Lutheran Bismarck distrusted Catholics, especially the clergy, whose first loyalty, he believed, was to the pope.

In response to what he saw as the Catholic threat, Bismarck launched the Kulturkampf, or "battle for civilization." His goal was to make Catholics put loyalty to the state above allegiance to the Church. The chancellor had laws passed that gave the state the right to supervise Catholic education and approve the appointment of priests. Other laws closed some religious orders, expelled the Jesuits from Prussia, and made it compulsory for couples to be married by civil authority.

Bismarck's moves against the Catholic Church backfired. The faithful rallied behind the Church, and the Catholic Center party gained strength in the Reichstag. A realist, Bismarck saw his mistake and made peace with the Church.

**Campaign against the socialists.** Bismarck also saw a threat to the new Germany in the growing power of socialism. By the late 1870s, German Marxists had organized the Social Democratic party, which called for a true parliamentary democracy and laws to improve

*Photographs of German Workers* The invention of photography in the mid-1800s created a new art form. Photographers learned to use light and design to "paint" pictures. Soon, photos became a way to depict real life and to protest or comment about it. These photographic portaits are from a series depicting German workers at the beginning of the 1900s. **Art and Literature** What techniques did the photographer use to give the photographs an artistic quality? What do you think the photographer is trying to say about German workers?

conditions for the working class. Bismarck feared that socialists would undermine the loyalty of German workers and turn them toward revolution. He had laws passed that dissolved socialist groups, shut down their newspapers, and banned their meetings. Once again, repression backfired, unifying workers in support of the socialist cause.

Bismarck then changed course. He set out to woo workers away from socialism by sponsoring laws to protect them. By the 1890s, Germans had health and accident insurance as well as old-age insurance to provide retirement benefits. Thus, under Bismarck, Germany was a pioneer in social reform. Its system of economic safeguards became the model for other European nations.

Bismarck was frank about the goals of his social reforms:

66Give the workingman the right to work as long as he is healthy, assure him care when he is sick, and maintenance when he is old . . . then the socialists will sing their siren songs in vain, and the workingmen will cease to throng to their banner.99

Bismarck's plan was only partly successful. Although workers benefited from his measures, they did not abandon socialism. In fact, the Social Democratic party continued to grow in strength. By 1912, it had the most seats in the Reichstag. Yet Bismarck's program showed that workers could improve their condition without the upheaval of a revolution. Later, Germany and other European nations would build on Bismarck's social policies, greatly increasing government's role in providing for the needs of its citizens. (See Chapter 16.)

### A Confident New Kaiser

In 1888, William II succeeded his grandfather as kaiser. The new emperor was supremely confident of his abilities and wished to put his own stamp on Germany. In 1890, he shocked Europe by asking the dominating Bismarck to resign. "There is only one master in the Reich, and that is I," he said.

William II seriously believed in his divine right to rule. As he put it:

66My grandfather considered that the office of king was a task that God had assigned to him. . . . That which he thought I also think. . . . Those who wish to aid me in that task . . . I welcome with all my heart; those who oppose me in this work I shall crush.99

Not surprisingly, William resisted efforts to introduce democratic reforms. At the same time, his government provided services, from social welfare benefits to cheap transportation and electricity. An excellent system of public schools, begun under Bismarck, taught students obedience to the emperor along with the "three R's."

Like his grandfather, William II lavished funds on the German military machine, already the most powerful in Europe. He also launched an ambitious campaign to expand the German navy and win an overseas empire to rival those of Britain and France. You will see in later chapters how William's nationalism and aggressive military stance helped increase tensions on the eve of World War I.

▲ *Kaiser William II*

# SECTION 2 REVIEW

1. **Identify** Kulturkampf.
2. Why did Germany become an industrial giant in the late 1800s?
3. (a) Describe the social reforms adopted under Bismarck. (b) Why did he favor these reforms?
4. (a) Why did William II dismiss Bismarck as chancellor? (b) What policies did William introduce?
5. *Critical Thinking* **Recognizing Causes and Effects** Why do you think supporters of democratic government had little hope of success in Germany in the late 1800s?
6. *ACTIVITY* Write an obituary for Bismarck that evaluates his strengths and weaknesses.

# 3 Unifying Italy

## Guide for Reading

■ What forces hindered Italian unity?

■ How did individual leaders help forge the Italian nation?

■ What problems did Italy face after 1861?

■ **Vocabulary** *anarchist*

Sixteen-year-old Giuseppe Mazzini (joo ZEHP pee mah TSEE nee) was walking with his mother in Genoa in 1821. A few weeks earlier, Austrian forces had crushed a revolt in northern Italy. Mazzini later recalled how he and his mother were stopped by a "tall, black-bearded man":

❝He held out a white handkerchief, merely saying, 'For the refugees of Italy.' My mother . . . dropped some money into the handkerchief. . . . That day was the first in which a confused idea presented itself to my mind . . . an idea that we Italians could and therefore ought to struggle for the liberty of our country.❞

In time, Mazzini would become a revolutionary devoted to the cause of Italian unity. But when an Italian nation finally emerged, it was not the work of revolutionaries. Just as German unity was spearheaded by Prussia and Bismarck, Italian unification was brought about by the efforts of a single, powerful state—the kingdom of Sardinia—and of a shrewd and ruthless politician—Count Camillo Cavour.

## The Italian Peninsula

For centuries, Italy had been a battleground for ambitious foreign and local princes. Frequent warfare and foreign rule had led people to identify with local regions. The people of Florence considered themselves Tuscans, those of Venice Venetians, the people of Naples Neapolitans, and so on. But as in Germany, the invasions of Napoleon had sparked dreams of national unity.

The Congress of Vienna, however, ignored the demands of nationalists. To Metternich, Italy was merely a "geographical expression," not a nation. Moreover, a divided Italy suited Austrian interests. At Vienna, Austria took control of much of northern Italy, while Hapsburg monarchs ruled various other Italian states. In the south, a French Bourbon ruler was put in charge of Naples and Sicily.

In response, nationalists organized secret patriotic societies and focused their efforts on expelling Austrian forces from northern Italy. Between 1820 and 1848, nationalist revolts exploded across the region. Each time, Austria sent troops to crush the rebels.

**Mazzini's Young Italy.** In the 1830s, the nationalist leader Giuseppe Mazzini founded Young Italy. The goal of this secret society was "to constitute Italy, one, free, independent, republican nation."

*Verdi, an Italian Nationalist* Opera composer Giuseppi Verdi was an ardent Italian nationalist, and he used his music to rouse Italians to the nationalist cause. His opera I Lombardi told of Italian heroism during the Crusades. On opening night in 1843, its thinly disguised anti-Austrian themes whipped the audience into a riot. **Continuity and Change** Do people today use theater and music to promote a cause? Give examples to support your answer.

# PARALLELS THROUGH TIME

## The Red Cross

The International Red Cross operates in nearly every country of the world. It was founded in 1863 to provide relief in wartime. Participating governments agreed to care for victims whether they were from enemy or friendly countries. In later years, the Red Cross expanded to include many peacetime activities, such as first aid training, blood banks, child care, and water safety.

**Linking Past and Present** Why do you think a "neutral" organization was needed to care for war victims? Do you think the Red Cross is still needed today? Explain.

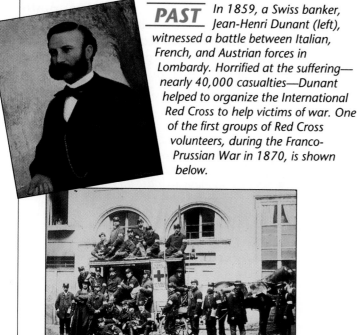

**PAST** In 1859, a Swiss banker, Jean-Henri Dunant (left), witnessed a battle between Italian, French, and Austrian forces in Lombardy. Horrified at the suffering—nearly 40,000 casualties—Dunant helped to organize the International Red Cross to help victims of war. One of the first groups of Red Cross volunteers, during the Franco-Prussian War in 1870, is shown below.

**PRESENT** Today, the Red Cross operates in more than 100 countries. A sister organizaton, the Red Crescent, above, is active in Muslim nations.

In 1849, Mazzini helped set up a revolutionary republic in Rome, but French forces soon toppled it. Like many other nationalists, Mazzini spent much of his life in exile, plotting and dreaming of a united Italy.

**The tide of nationalism.** "Ideas grow quickly," Mazzini once said, "when watered by the blood of martyrs." Although revolution had failed, nationalist agitation had planted seeds for future harvests.

To nationalists like Mazzini, a united Italy made sense not only because of geography but because of a common language and shared tra-

ditions. They reminded Italians of the glories of ancient Rome and the medieval papacy. To others, unity made practical economic sense. It would end trade barriers between the various Italian states, encourage railroad building, and stimulate industry.

### The Struggle for Italy

After 1848, leadership of the Risorgimento (ree sor jee MEHN toh), or Italian nationalist movement, passed to the small kingdom of Sardinia. (See the map on page 178.) Its constitutional monarch, Victor Emmanuel II, hoped to join other states to his own.*

**Cavour.** In 1852, Victor Emmanuel appointed Count Camillo Cavour as his prime minister. The new prime minister came from a noble family but favored liberal goals. He was a flexible, practical, crafty politician, willing to use almost any means to achieve his goals. Like Bismarck in Prussia, Cavour believed in Realpolitik. Also like Bismarck, he was a monarchist devoted to the interests of his royal master.

Once in office, Cavour moved first to reform Sardinia's economy. He improved agriculture, had railroads built, and encouraged commerce by supporting free trade. Cavour's long-term goal, however, was to expel Austrian power from Italy and add Lombardy and Venetia to Sardinia.

**Intrigue with France.** In 1855, led by Cavour, Sardinia joined Britain and France in the Crimean War against Russia. Although the fighting brought no rewards of territory, it did give Sardinia a voice at the peace conference. It also made Napoleon III take notice of the little Italian kingdom.

In 1858, Cavour negotiated a secret deal with Napoleon, who promised to aid Sardinia in case it faced a war with Austria. A year later, the shrewd Cavour provoked that war. With French help, Sardinia defeated Austria and annexed Lombardy. Meanwhile, nationalist groups overthrew Austrian-backed rulers in several other northern Italian states. These states then voted to join with Sardinia.

**Garibaldi's Red Shirts.** Next, attention shifted to the kingdom of the Two Sicilies in southern Italy. There, Giuseppe Garibaldi, a longtime nationalist and an ally of Mazzini, was ready for action. Like Mazzini, Garibaldi wanted to create an Italian republic. He did not, however, hesitate to accept aid from the monarchist Cavour. By 1860, Garibaldi had recruited a force of 1,000 red-shirted volunteers. Cavour provided weapons and allowed two ships to take Garibaldi and his "Red Shirts" south to Sicily.

With surprising speed, Garibaldi's forces won control of Sicily, crossed to the mainland, and marched triumphantly north to Naples. Later, Garibaldi recalled the Red Shirts' glorious campaign:

> **"**O noble Thousand! . . . I love to remember you! . . . 'Where any of our brothers are fighting for liberty, there all Italians must hasten!'—such was your motto, and you hastened to the spot without asking whether your foes were few or many.**"**

**Unity at last.** Garibaldi's success alarmed Cavour, who feared the nationalist hero would set up a republic in the south. To prevent this,

---

*The kingdom of Sardinia included Piedmont, Nice, and Savoy, as well as the island of Sardinia.

*Giuseppe Garibaldi* "I offer neither pay, nor quarters, nor provisions," Garibaldi warned his troops. "I offer hunger, thirst, forced marches, battles, and death. Let him who loves his country in his heart, and not with his lips only, follow me." His loyal Red Shirts did follow their beloved leader to victory. Garibaldi had learned techniques of guerrilla warfare during a 12-year exile in South America, where he joined wars of liberation in Brazil and Uruguay. **Impact of the Individual** What qualities might inspire people to follow a leader like Garibaldi?

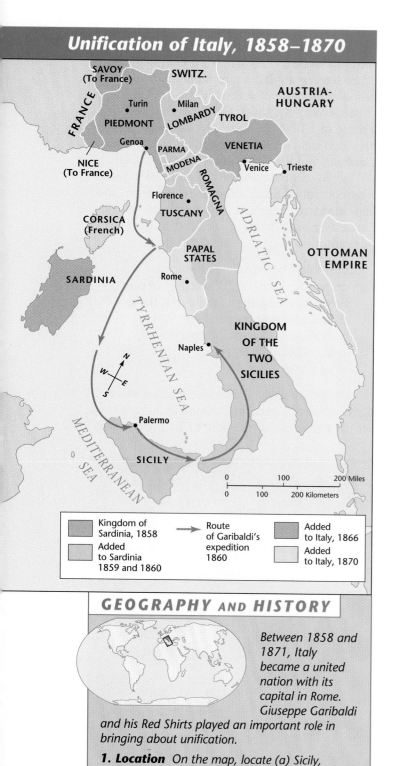

## Unification of Italy, 1858–1870

SAVOY (To France)
SWITZ.
FRANCE
Turin
Milan
PIEDMONT
LOMBARDY
TYROL
AUSTRIA-HUNGARY
Genoa
PARMA
VENETIA
NICE (To France)
MODENA
Venice
Trieste
ROMAGNA
Florence
CORSICA (French)
TUSCANY
ADRIATIC SEA
PAPAL STATES
OTTOMAN EMPIRE
SARDINIA
Rome
TYRRHENIAN SEA
KINGDOM OF THE TWO SICILIES
Naples
MEDITERRANEAN SEA
Palermo
SICILY

0        100        200 Miles
0        100        200 Kilometers

Kingdom of Sardinia, 1858
Added to Sardinia 1859 and 1860
Route of Garibaldi's expedition 1860
Added to Italy, 1866
Added to Italy, 1870

## GEOGRAPHY AND HISTORY

Between 1858 and 1871, Italy became a united nation with its capital in Rome. Giuseppe Garibaldi and his Red Shirts played an important role in bringing about unification.

1. **Location** On the map, locate (a) Sicily, (b) Naples, (c) Rome, (d) Venetia.
2. **Movement** Describe the route of Garibaldi's expedition in 1860.
3. **Critical Thinking** *Identifying Main Ideas* What is the main idea of this map? Explain.

Cavour sent Sardinian troops to deal with Garibaldi. The Sardinians overran the Papal States and linked up with Garibaldi in Naples.

In a patriotic move, Garibaldi turned over Naples and Sicily to Victor Emmanuel. Shortly after, southern Italy voted to approve the move, and in 1861, Victor Emmanuel II was crowned king of Italy.

Two areas remained outside the new Italian nation: Rome and Venetia. Cavour died in 1861, but his successors completed his dream. In a deal negotiated with Bismarck, Italy acquired Venetia in the peace treaty that ended the Austro-Prussian War in 1866. During the Franco-Prussian War in 1870, France was forced to withdraw its troops from Rome. Italian troops entered the city, and Rome became the capital of the new nation. For the first time since the fall of the Roman empire, Italy was a united land.

## Trials of the New Nation

Young Italy faced a host of problems. Like the many states Bismarck cemented into the German empire, Italy had no tradition of unity. Most Italians felt stronger ties to local areas than to the new nation. Regional disputes left Italy unable to solve critical national issues.

**Divisions.** The greatest regional differences were between Italians in the north and those in the south. The north was richer and had more cities than the south. For centuries, northern Italian cities had flourished as centers of business and culture. The south was rural and poor. Its population was booming, but illiterate peasants wrung a meager existence from the exhausted farmland.

Hostility between the state and the Roman Catholic Church further divided Italy. Popes bitterly resented the seizure of the Papal States and of Rome. The government granted the papacy the small territory of the Vatican. Popes, however, saw themselves as "prisoners" and urged Italian Catholics—almost all Italians—not to cooperate with their new government.

**Turmoil.** Under Victor Emmanuel, Italy was a constitutional monarchy with a two-house legislature. The king appointed members to the upper house, which could veto bills passed by the lower house. Although the lower house had elected representatives, only a small number of men had the right to vote.

In the late 1800s, unrest increased as radicals on the left struggled against a conservative government. Socialists organized strikes while anarchists, people who want to abolish all government, turned to sabotage and violence. Slowly, the government extended suffrage to more men and passed laws to improve social conditions. Still, the turmoil continued. To distract attention from troubles at home, the government set out to win an overseas empire. (See page 223.)

**Progress.** Despite its problems, Italy did develop economically, especially after 1900. Although it lacked important natural resources such as coal, industries did sprout up in northern Italy. Industrialization, of course, brought urbanization as peasants flocked to the cities to work in factories. Reformers campaigned to improve education and working conditions.

The population explosion of this period created tensions, but an important safety valve was emigration. Many Italians left for the United States, Canada, and Latin American lands.

**Looking ahead.** By 1914, the country was significantly better off than it had been in 1861. But it was hardly prepared for the great war that broke out in that year and into which it would soon be drawn.

## SECTION 3 REVIEW

1. **Identify** (a) Giuseppe Mazzini, (b) Risorgimento, (c) Victor Emmanuel II, (d) Camillo Cavour, (e) Giuseppe Garibaldi.
2. **Define** anarchist.
3. (a) What obstacles to unity did Italian nationalists face? (b) What conditions favored unity?
4. What steps did Cavour take to promote Italian unity?
5. Describe the problems Italians faced after unification.
6. *Critical Thinking* **Comparing** Compare the goals and methods of Cavour in Italy and Bismarck in Germany. (a) How are they similar? (b) How are they different?
7. *ACTIVITY* Create a comic strip showing the events leading to Italian unification.

# 4 Nationalism Threatens Old Empires

## Guide for Reading

- How was nationalism a divisive force in the Austrian empire?
- Why was the Dual Monarchy formed?
- Why did conflicts erupt in the Balkans?

While nationalism united people in Germany and Italy, it undermined old empires in Eastern Europe. The Austrian Hapsburgs and the Ottoman Turks ruled lands that included diverse ethnic groups. Nationalist feelings among these subject people contributed to tensions in Europe.

## *A Fading Power*

In 1800, the Hapsburgs were the oldest ruling house in Europe. Besides their homeland of Austria, they had acquired over the centuries Bohemia and Hungary, as well as parts of Romania, Poland, Ukraine, and northern Italy.

**Challenge of change.** Since the Congress of Vienna, the Austrian emperor Francis I and Metternich, his foreign minister, upheld conservative goals against liberal forces. "Rule and change nothing," the emperor told his son. Under Francis and Metternich, newspapers could not even use the word *constitution*. The government tried to limit industrial development, which would threaten traditional ways of life.

Austria, however, could not hold back the changes that were engulfing Europe. By the 1840s, factories were springing up, and the Hapsburgs were facing the familiar problems of industrial life—the growth of cities, worker discontent, and the stirrings of socialism.

**ISSUES For TODAY** During the 1800s, nationalism helped to reshape the map of Europe. How is nationalism both a unifying and a divisive force?

**A patchwork of people.** Equally disturbing to the old order were the urgent demands of nationalists. The Hapsburgs presided over a multinational empire. Of its 50 million people at mid-century, less than a quarter were German-speaking Austrians. Almost half belonged to different Slavic groups, including Czechs, Slovaks, Poles, Ukrainians, Serbs, Croats, and Slovenes. Often, rival groups shared the same region. The empire also included large numbers of Hungarians and Italians. ( ★ See *Skills for Success,* page 188.)

The Hapsburgs ignored nationalist demands as long as they could. "Peoples?" Francis I once exclaimed. "What does that mean? I know only subjects." As you have read, when nationalist revolts broke out across the empire in 1848, the government crushed them.

**Early reforms.** Amid the turmoil, 18-year-old Francis Joseph inherited the throne. He would rule until 1916, presiding over the empire during its fading days into World War I.

An early challenge came when Austria suffered its humiliating defeat by France and Sardinia in 1859. (See page 177.) Francis Joseph realized he needed to strengthen the empire at home and made some reforms. He granted a new constitution that set up a legislature. This body, however, was dominated by German-speaking Austrians. The reforms thus satisfied none of the empire's other national groups. The Hungarians, especially, were determined to settle for nothing less than self-government.

## The Dual Monarchy

Austria's disastrous defeat in 1866 in the war with Prussia brought renewed pressure from the Hungarians. A year later, Francis Deák (deh AHK), a moderate Hungarian leader, helped work out a compromise that created the Dual Monarchy of Austria-Hungary.

Under the agreement, Austria and Hungary were separate states. Each had its own constitution and parliament. Francis Joseph ruled as emperor of Austria and king of Hungary. The two states shared ministries of finance, defense, and foreign affairs but were independent of each other in all other areas.

While Hungarians welcomed the compromise, other subject people resented it. Restlessness increased among various Slavic groups, especially the Czechs in Bohemia. Some leaders called on Slavs to unite, insisting that "only through liberty, equality, and fraternal solidarity" could Slavs fulfill their "great mission in the history of mankind." By the early 1900s, nationalist discontent often left the government paralyzed in the face of pressing problems.

## Balkan Nationalism

Like the Hapsburgs, the Ottomans ruled a multinational empire. It stretched from Eastern Europe and the Balkans to North Africa and the Middle East. There, as in Austria, nationalist demands tore at the fabric of the empire. (You will

**Hub of the Hapsburg Empire**
*The Hapsburg empire boasted many fine cities, but none equaled Vienna at the turn of the century. With its great churches, Gothic palaces, fine museums, and stately tree-lined avenues, Vienna was a magnet that attracted many of the best minds and talents of Europe. Here, Vienna's leading citizens enjoy an evening of gaiety at an imperial ball.*
**Political and Social Systems**
*Based on this painting, make a generalization about the Hapsburg ruling class.*

In the late 1800s, the Balkans had become a powder keg, as various peoples and empires contended for power.

**1. Location** On the map, locate (a) Black Sea, (b) Ottoman empire, (c) Serbia, (d) Greece, (e) Russia.
**2. Place** Which countries in the Balkans were independent by 1878?
**3. Critical Thinking** **Linking Past and Present** Compare this map to the map on page 990. How is the political makeup of the Balkan region today different from its makeup in 1878?

read about Ottoman efforts to stem their decline in Chapter 9.)

In the Balkans, Serbia had won autonomy in 1817 and southern Greece won independence in the 1830s. (See Chapter 4.) But many Serbs and Greeks still lived in the Balkans under Ottoman rule. The Ottoman empire was home to other national groups, such as Bulgarians and Romanians. During the 1800s, various subject people revolted against the Ottomans, hoping to set up their own independent states.

Such nationalist stirrings became mixed up with the ambitions of the great European powers. In the mid-1800s, Europeans came to see the Ottoman empire as "the sick man of Europe." They eagerly scrambled to divide up Ottoman lands. Russia pushed south toward the Black Sea and Istanbul, which Russians still called Constantinople. Austria-Hungary took the provinces of Bosnia and Herzegovina, angering the Serbs who had hoped to expand there, too. Meanwhile, Britain and France set their sights on other Ottoman lands.

In the end, a complex web of competing interests contributed to a succession of crises and wars. Russia fought several wars against the Ottomans. France and Britain sometimes joined the Russians and sometimes the Ottomans. Germany supported Austrian authority over the national groups but encouraged the Ottomans, too, because of their strategic location at the eastern end of the Mediterranean. In between, the subject nationalities revolted and then fought among themselves. By the early 1900s, observers were referring to the region as the "Balkan powder keg." The explosion that came in 1914 helped set off World War I.

## SECTION 4 REVIEW

**1. Identify** Francis Joseph.
**2.** How did nationalism affect each of the following: (a) Austrian empire, (b) Ottoman empire?
**3.** (a) What was the Dual Monarchy? (b) Why did it fail to end nationalist demands?
**4.** Give two reasons why the Balkans were a trouble spot in the 1800s.
**5. Critical Thinking** **Solving Problems** Do you think that the Hapsburgs or Ottomans could have built a modern nation from their multinational empires? Explain.
**6. ACTIVITY** Create a concept map of nationalism as a positive and a negative force.

# 5 Russia: Reform and Reaction

## Guide for Reading

- Why did attempts to reform Russia often fail?

- How did Russia try to modernize and industrialize?

- What were the causes and results of the revolution of 1905?

- **Vocabulary** *zemstvo, pogrom, refugee*

The ideas of the French Revolution inspired Russia's great poet Alexander Pushkin to write his "Ode to Freedom":

66I will sing the freedom of the world,
And strike down the [evil] sitting on
 the throne,
Tyrants of the world tremble!
And you, fallen slaves, take heart
 and hear.
Arise!99

In the early 1800s, romantics like Pushkin dreamed of freeing Russia from autocratic rule, economic backwardness, and social injustice. But efforts to modernize Russia had little success. Between 1801 and 1914, repression outweighed reform, as czars imprisoned critics or sent them into icy exile in Siberia.

## The Russian Colossus

By 1800, Russia was not only the largest, most populous nation in Europe but also a great world power. Since the 1600s, explorers had pushed the Russian frontier eastward across Siberia to the Pacific Ocean. Peter and Catherine had added lands on the Baltic and Black seas, and czars in the 1800s had expanded into Central Asia. In this way, Russia acquired a huge multinational empire, part European and part Asian.

Other European nations looked on the Russian colossus, or giant, with wonder and misgiving. It had immense natural resources. Its vast size gave it global interests and influence. But Western Europeans disliked its autocratic government and feared its expansionist aims.

**Obstacles to progress.** Despite efforts by Peter and Catherine to westernize Russia, it remained economically undeveloped. By the 1800s, czars saw the need to modernize but resisted reforms that would undermine absolute rule. While they wavered, Russia fell further behind Western Europe in economic and social developments.

A great obstacle to progress was the rigid social structure. Landowning nobles dominated society and rejected any change that would threaten their privileges. The middle class was too small to have much influence. The majority of Russians were serfs, laborers bound to the land. While serfdom had almost disappeared in Western Europe by the 1700s, it survived and spread in Russia.

**The shame of serfdom.** Masters exercised almost total power over their serfs. In his autobiography, Peter Kropotkin, a noble who

*Russia's Diverse People* Dozens of ethnic groups and members of every major religion made up the population of Russia. Here, an 1812 engraving shows the variety of Russia's people. **Diversity** What role did conquest and colonization play in the development of Russia's multinational society?

became a revolutionary, described the brutal treatment of serfs:

> 66 I heard . . . stories of men and women torn from their families and their villages, and sold, or lost in gambling, or exchanged for a couple of hunting dogs, and then transported to some remote part of Russia to create a [master's] new estate; . . . of children taken from their parents and sold to cruel masters; . . . of flogging . . . that occurred daily with unheard-of cruelty. 99

The majority of serfs were peasants. Others might be servants, artisans, or soldiers forced into the czar's army. As industry expanded, masters sent serfs to work in factories but took much of their pay. Many enlightened Russians knew that serfdom was inefficient. As long as most people had to serve the whim of their masters, Russia's economy would remain backward. Landowning nobles had no incentive to improve agriculture and took little interest in industry.

▲ Russian serf

## Three Pillars of Russian Absolutism

For centuries, czars had ruled with absolute power, imposing their will on their subjects. The Enlightenment and French Revolution had almost no effect on Russian autocracy.

**Alexander I.** When Alexander I inherited the throne in 1801, he seemed open to liberal ideas. The new czar eased censorship and promoted education. He even talked about freeing the serfs.

By the time Napoleon invaded Russia in 1812, however, Alexander had drawn back from reform. Like earlier czars, he feared losing the support of nobles. At the Congress of Vienna, he joined the conservative powers in opposing liberal and nationalist impulses in Europe.

**Revolt and repression.** When Alexander I died in 1825, a group of army officers led an uprising, known as the Decembrist Revolt. They had picked up liberal ideas while fighting Napoleon in Western Europe and now demanded a constitution and other reforms. The new czar, Nicholas I, quickly suppressed the Decembrists and then cracked down on all dissent.

Nicholas used police spies to hunt out critics. He banned books from Western Europe that might spread liberal ideas. Only approved textbooks were allowed in schools and universities. Many Russians with liberal or revolutionary ideas were judged to be insane and shut up in mental hospitals. Up to 150,000 others were exiled to Siberia. The American humorist Mark Twain once quipped:

> 66 In Russia, whenever they catch a man, woman, or child that has got any brains or education or character, they ship that person straight to Siberia. It is admirable. . . . It keeps the general level of Russian intellect and education down to that of the Czar. 99

**"Orthodoxy, autocracy, and nationalism."** To bolster his regime, Nicholas I embraced the pillars of Russian absolutism symbolized in the motto: "Orthodoxy, autocracy, and nationalism." Orthodoxy referred to the strong ties between the Russian Orthodox Church and the government. Autocracy was the absolute power of the state. Nationalism involved respect for Russian traditions and suppression of non-Russian groups within the empire.

Still, Nicholas realized that Russia needed to modernize. He issued a new law code and made some economic reforms. He even tried to limit the power of landowners over serfs. But he could see no way to change the system without angering Russian nobles. Before he died, he told his son: "I am handing you command of the country in a poor state."

## Reforms of Alexander II

Alexander II came to the throne in 1855 during the Crimean War. The war had broken

**Orthodox Nuns** *The Orthodox Church was both a spiritual and a political force in Russia. Here, a group of Orthodox nuns proceeds to a ceremony for the blessing of the church bells.* **Political and Social Systems** *How did Nicholas I try to use the strength of the Orthodox Church to bolster his regime?*

out after Russia tried to seize Ottoman lands along the Danube. Britain and France stepped in to help the Turks, invading the Crimean peninsula that juts into the Black Sea. The war, which ended in a Russian defeat, revealed the country's backwardness. It had only a few miles of railroads, and the military bureaucracy was hopelessly inefficient.

**Emancipation.** A widespread popular reaction followed. Liberals demanded changes and students demonstrated for reform. Pressed from all sides, Alexander II finally agreed to reforms. In 1861, he issued a royal decree emancipating, or freeing, the serfs.

Freedom brought problems. Former serfs had to buy the land they had worked for so

Alexander's emancipation of the serfs came two years before Abraham Lincoln issued his Emancipation Proclamation. In the United States of the early 1800s, one sixth of the population were enslaved African Americans. While some Americans defended slavery, a growing number of citizens condemned it as immoral and called for its abolition. At last, in 1861, agitation over the issue involved the nation in a civil war. Not until after peace was restored in 1865 did slavery finally end.

long. Many were too poor to do so. Also, the lands allotted to peasants were often too small to farm efficiently or to support a family. As a result, peasants remained poor, and discontent festered.

Still, emancipation was a turning point. Many peasants moved to the cities, taking jobs in factories and building Russian industries. Equally important, freeing the serfs boosted the drive for further reform.

**Other reforms.** Along with emancipation, Alexander set up a system of local government. Elected assemblies, called zemstvos, were made responsible for matters such as road repair, schools, and agriculture. At the local level, at least, Russians gained some experience of open discussion and self-government.

The czar also introduced legal reforms based on ideas such as trial by jury. He eased censorship and tried to reform the military. A soldier's term of service was reduced from 25 years to 15, and brutal discipline was limited. Alexander also encouraged the growth of industry in Russia.

A movement to liberate women swept the urban centers of Russia. Since university education was denied them in Russia, hundreds of privileged young women left their homes and families to study abroad. Many became supporters of the goal of popular revolution.

## Return to Reaction

Alexander's reforms failed to satisfy many Russians. Peasants had freedom but not land. Liberals wanted a constitution and elected legislature. Radicals, influenced by socialist ideas from the West, demanded even more revolutionary changes. The czar, meantime, moved away from reform and toward repression.

**Revolutionary currents.** In the 1870s, some socialists carried the message of reform to the peasants. They went to live and work among the peasants, sometimes preaching rebellion. These educated young men and women had little success. The peasants scarcely understood them and sometimes turned them over to the police.

The failure of the "Go to the People" movement and renewed government repression sparked anger among radicals. Some turned to terrorism. A revolutionary group calling itself the People's Will assassinated officials and plotted to kill the czar. Their first attempts failed. Then, on a cold March day in 1881, terrorists hurled two bombs at Alexander's carriage. One struck down several guards. The second killed the "czar emancipator."

**Crackdown.** Alexander III responded to his father's assassination by reviving the harsh methods of Nicholas I. To wipe out liberals and revolutionaries, he increased the power of the secret police, restored strict censorship, and exiled critics to Siberia. He relied on his adviser and former tutor, Constantine Pobedonostsev (puh beh duh NAWS tsehv), who rejected all talk of democracy and constitutional government as "the lies of hollow and flabby people."

The czar also launched a program of Russification aimed at suppressing the cultures of non-Russian people within the empire. Alexander insisted on one language, Russian, and one church, the Russian Orthodox Church. Poles, Ukrainians, Finns, Armenians, and many others suffered persecution. The Russification campaign also targeted Jews and Muslim people throughout the empire.

**Persecution and pogroms.** Russia had acquired a large Jewish population when it carved up Poland and expanded into Ukraine. Under Alexander III, persecution of Russian Jews increased. He limited the number of Jews allowed to study in universities and practice professions such as law and medicine. He revived old laws that forced Jews to live in certain restricted areas.

Official persecution encouraged violent mob attacks on Jews, known as pogroms. Gangs beat and killed Jews and looted and burned their homes and stores. The police did nothing to stop the violence. Faced with savage persecution, many Jews escaped from Russia. They became refugees, or people who flee their homeland to seek safety elsewhere. Large numbers of Jews went to the United States. Though they often faced prejudice there, they were safe from pogroms and official persecution. Jewish immigrants sent joyful news back to Russia: "There is no czar in America!"

*A Jewish Village* The center of Russian Jewish life was the shtetl, or village. From day to day, Russia and the czar seemed far away from the village community. "The world was divided into two parts," recalled one Jewish woman, "Polotzk, the place where I lived, and a strange land called Russia." Yet, at any moment, a pogrom might shatter the peace of the shtetl. **Global Interaction** Why did many Jewish families flee to the United States?

## Building Russian Industry

Under Alexander III and his son, Nicholas II, Russia finally entered the industrial age. In the 1890s, Count Serge Witte, finance minister to Nicholas, made economic development a key goal. Witte encouraged railroad building to link iron and coal mines to factories and to transport goods across Russia. He secured foreign capital to invest in transportation and industry. Loans from France helped build the Trans-Siberian Railway. Begun in the 1890s, it stretched 5,000 miles (8,000 km) from European Russia to the Pacific Ocean.

The drive to industrialize increased political and social problems. Government officials and business leaders applauded and encouraged economic growth. Nobles and peasants opposed it, fearing the changes brought by the new ways.

Industrialization also created social ills as peasants flocked to cities to work in factories. There, they faced long hours and low pay in dangerous conditions. In the slums around the factories, poverty, disease, and discontent multiplied.

Radicals sought supporters among the new industrial workers. At factory gates, socialists handed out pamphlets that preached the revolutionary ideas of Karl Marx. Among the revolutionaries of the 1890s was young Vladimir Ulyanov, whose older brother had been executed for plotting to kill Alexander III. Like many revolutionaries, Ulyanov used an alias, or false name—Lenin. In 1917, Lenin would take power in a revolution that transformed Russia. (See Chapter 11.)

## The "Little Father" Betrays His People

War broke out between Russia and Japan in 1904. (See Chapter 9.) Nicholas II called on his people to fight for "the Faith, the Czar, and the Fatherland." But despite their efforts, the Russians suffered one humiliating defeat after another.

**A peaceful march.** News of the disasters unleashed pent-up discontent created by years of oppression. Protesters poured into the streets. Workers struck with demands for shorter hours and better wages. Liberals called for a constitution and reforms to overhaul an inefficient, corrupt government.

As the crisis deepened, a young Orthodox priest, Father George Gapon, organized a march for Sunday, January 22, 1905. He felt certain that the "Little Father," as Russians called the czar, would help his people if only he understood their sufferings.

The parade flowed through the icy streets of St. Petersburg toward the czar's Winter Palace. Chanting prayers and singing hymns, workers carried holy icons and pictures of the czar. They also brought a petition addressed to Nicholas:

> 66We, the workers of St. Petersburg, with our wives, our children, and our aged and feeble parents, have come to you, Sire, in search of justice and protection. We have fallen into poverty, we are oppressed, we are . . . treated as slaves. . . . Do not refuse to protect your people. Raise us from the grave of arbitrary power, poverty, and ignorance. . . . Free us from the intolerable oppression of officials. Destroy the wall between yourself and your people—and let us govern the country with you.99

**Bloody Sunday.** Fearing the marchers, the czar had fled the palace and called in soldiers. As the people approached, they saw troops lined up across the square. Suddenly, a crack of gunfire rang out, followed by another and another. Men and women reeled and fell. Hundreds lay dead in the snow. One marcher cried out: "How dare they shoot at a religious procession, at the portraits of the czar?"

A woman stumbling away from the scene of the massacre moaned: "The czar has deserted us! They shot away the orthodox faith." Indeed, the slaughter marked a turning point for Russians. "Bloody Sunday" killed the people's faith and trust in the czar. ■

## The Revolution of 1905

In the months that followed Bloody Sunday, discontent exploded across Russia. Strikes multiplied. In some cities, workers took over lo-

**Bloody Sunday** *The Russian people's faith in the czar was badly shaken by the events of Bloody Sunday. This illustration shows peaceful marchers being gunned down near the czar's Winter Palace in St. Petersburg. In the center stands Father Gapon, pleading vainly for mercy.* **Political and Social Systems** *How did the events of Bloody Sunday help spark the Revolution of 1905?*

cal government. In the countryside, peasants revolted, demanding land. Minority nationalities called for autonomy. Terrorists targeted officials, and some assassins were cheered as heroes by discontented Russians.

At last, the clamor grew so great that Nicholas was forced to announce sweeping reforms. In the October Manifesto, he promised "freedom of person, conscience, speech, assembly, and union." He agreed to summon a Duma, or elected national legislature. No law, he declared, would go into effect without approval by the Duma.

**Results of the revolution.** The manifesto won over moderates, leaving socialists isolated. Divisions between these groups helped the czar, who had no intention of letting strikers, revolutionaries, and rebellious peasants challenge him.

In 1906, the first Duma met, but the czar quickly dissolved it when leaders criticized the government. Nicholas then appointed Peter Stolypin (stuh LEE pihn), a conservative, as prime minister. Arrests, pogroms, and executions followed as Stolypin sought to restore order. Russians bitterly dubbed the hanging noose "Stolypin's necktie." A popular song mocked the czar's promises in the October Manifesto:

66The czar became frightened,
   He issued a manifesto:
   That the dead be given liberty,
   The living be arrested.99

Stolypin realized that Russia needed reform, not just repression. To regain peasant support, he introduced moderate land reforms. He strengthened the zemstvos and improved education before he was assassinated in 1911. Several more Dumas met during this period, but new voting laws made sure they were conservative. By 1914, Russia was still an autocracy, simmering with peasant and worker unrest.

## SECTION 5 REVIEW

1. **Identify** (a) Decembrist Revolt, (b) Crimean War, (c) Alexander II, (d) People's Will, (e) Russification, (f) Serge Witte, (g) Bloody Sunday, (h) October Manifesto, (i) Peter Stolypin.
2. **Define** (a) zemstvo, (b) pogrom, (c) refugee.
3. (a) Why was Russia a relatively backward country in the 1800s? (b) What reforms did Russia undertake?
4. What steps did Russia take to industrialize in the late 1800s?
5. (a) What were the causes of the revolution of 1905? (b) How did Nicholas II respond to the widespread turmoil?
6. *Critical Thinking* **Analyzing Information** Alexander II declared that it is "better to abolish serfdom from above than to wait until it will be abolished by a movement from below." What did he mean by this?
7. *ACTIVITY* Make a set of playing cards picturing each of the czars discussed in the section. On each card, list the goals and achievements of the czar. Color code the cards according to whether the czar was a reformer or a reactionary.

# 6 CHAPTER REVIEW AND SKILLS FOR SUCCESS

## CHAPTER REVIEW

### REVIEWING VOCABULARY

Review the following vocabulary from this chapter: *nationalism, Realpolitik, anarchist, serf, absolutism, autocracy, emancipation, zemstvo, pogrom, refugee.* Write sentences using each of these words, leaving blanks where the words would go. Exchange your sentences with another student, and fill in the blanks on each other's lists.

### REVIEWING FACTS

1. What three wars did Prussia fight to unify Germany?

2. What factors aided German economic growth in the late 1800s?

3. How did Bismarck try to convince workers not to support the socialists?

4. What was the goal of Mazzini's Young Italy society?

5. What regional difference divided Italians?

6. How did the Hapsburg leaders deal with the ethnic diversity of their empire?

7. How did European powers react to Ottoman weakness?

8. What reforms took place under Alexander II in Russia?

9. How did war with Japan help cause the Revolution of 1905 in Russia?

### REVIEWING CHAPTER THEMES

Review the "Focus On" questions at the start of this chapter. Then select *three* of those questions and answer them, using information from the chapter.

## SKILLS FOR SUCCESS  DRAWING INFERENCES FROM MAPS

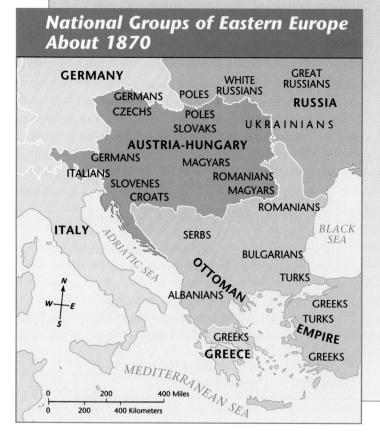

**National Groups of Eastern Europe About 1870**

Drawing inferences from a map usually involves (1) identifying information that the map presents indirectly, and (2) recalling and applying knowledge that you already have. Not everyone will draw the same inferences from a map.

The map at left and the map on page 181 show the Balkan region in about 1870 and 1878. Study the two maps. Then, follow the steps below to draw inferences about the Balkans.

1. **Identify information on the maps.** (a) What is the subject of the map at left? (b) What is the subject of the map on page 181?

2. **Decide what information is implied.** (a) List the national groups that lived in one of the multinational empires about 1870. (b) Did the country in which some national groups lived change between 1870 and 1878? How do you know?

3. **Combine prior knowledge with information from the maps.** (a) How did national groups encourage the drive for German unity? (b) How did national groups affect Austria-Hungary and the Ottoman empire?

## CRITICAL THINKING

1. **Analyzing Fine Art** Study the painting on page 167. (a) What is the subject of the painting? (b) Where does the scene take place? What was the special symbolism of that location? (c) Who seems to be the central figure of the painting? (d) What conclusions can you draw from this about the power structure in Germany at the time?

2. **Linking Past and Present** Is nationalism a force in the world today? Give examples to support your answer.

3. **Predicting Consequences** Based on your reading of the chapter, predict the consequences of the following: (a) German humiliation of France in the Franco-Prussian War, (b) growth of German nationalism and militarism in the late 1800s, (c) failure to satisfy nationalist ambitions in Austria-Hungary, (d) weakening of the Ottoman empire.

## ANALYZING PRIMARY SOURCES

Use the quotation on page 169 to answer the following questions.

1. What, according to Bismarck, was the "supreme law" for the state?

2. What was the state justified in doing to preserve itself?

3. How might this view of the state affect a leader's foreign policy decisions?

## FOR YOUR PORTFOLIO

**WRITING HISTORICAL FICTION** Write a short piece of historical fiction relating to people and events that you studied in the chapter. Begin by deciding on the time and place in which you will set your story and the characters you will include. Brainstorm a story plot. Use outside resources to research the events and people you will include. Then write a first draft. Ask a classmate to serve as an editor to help you review the story. Finally, revise your story as necessary and share it with the class.

## ANALYZING FINE ART

Use this image of Giuseppe Garibaldi, as well as information from the chapter, to answer the following questions.

1. What symbols of Italian nationalism appear in the painting?

2. How does the painting show that Garibaldi used military tactics to help unify Italy?

3. Does the painting portray Garibaldi as a successful leader? If so, how?

### INTERNET ACTIVITY

**COMPARING IDEAS** Use the Internet to research the theories of Realpolitik held by Henry Kissinger, a former American secretary of state. Then write a brief essay comparing Kissinger's version of Realpolitik to Bismarck's version. What goals do the two share? How do the two visions differ?

# CHAPTER 7

# Growth of Western Democracies

## (1815–1914)

**CHAPTER OUTLINE**

1 Britain Becomes More Democratic
2 A Century of Reform
3 Division and Democracy in France
4 Expansion of the United States

Charles Egremont is proud to be British. The son of a privileged family, he had grown up at a time when his nation's prosperity and prestige were soaring to remarkable heights. One day he boasts to some strangers that Victoria, the queen of England, "reigns over the greatest nation that ever existed."

"Which nation?" asks one of the strangers, "for she reigns over two":

> "Two nations: between whom there is no [communication] and no sympathy; who are as ignorant of each other's habits, thoughts, and feelings, as if they were dwellers in different zones or inhabitants of different planets; who are formed by a different breeding, are fed by a different food, are ordered by different manners, and are not governed by the same laws.'"

Surprised, Egremont wonders what these "two nations" are. The stranger replies, "THE RICH AND THE POOR."

Charles Egremont is the hero of Benjamin Disraeli's novel *Sybil*. Disraeli was familiar with Britain's "two nations." A leading political figure, he moved in the world of aristocratic luxury and elegance. In the 1840s, however, travels around Britain opened his eyes to the appalling poverty of factory towns and rural villages.

Disraeli did more than write about the gap between rich and poor. As prime minister and leader of the Conservative party, he worked to achieve many needed reforms.

The Industrial Revolution uprooted old ways of life. Prosperity offered unimagined opportunities. Left behind in this age of great material progress, however, masses of people were condemned to wretched poverty. In response to changing conditions, reformers demanded the vote and other rights. In Germany and Russia, repressive governments stemmed the tide of change. But Britain, France, and the United States slowly extended democratic rights.

In all three of these western democracies, many people struggled for social reform. Factory workers, farmers, women, and others slowly made gains. Their efforts paved the way for great improvements in the quality of life in our own century.

**FOCUS ON** these questions as you read:

- **Political and Social Systems**
  How did Britain, France, and the United States become more democratic?

- **Continuity and Change**
  How did western democracies adapt to the new demands of industrial society?

- **Religions and Value Systems**
  What role did nationalism play in the western democracies?

- **Diversity**
  How did women and members of religious and ethnic groups seek greater rights?

## TIME AND PLACE

The Victorian Age This 1887 plate honors Queen Victoria, the longest-ruling monarch in British history. She held little political power, but her strict code of behavior and morality set a standard for her time. For Britain, Victoria's reign was a time not only of power and prosperity but also of political reform. **Political and Social Systems** Review what you have learned about the British political system. Why did British monarchs hold little political power by the time of Victoria?

## HUMANITIES LINK

*Art History* Hannah Stokes, *Trade and Commerce Quilt* (page 210).
*Literature* In this chapter, you will encounter passages from the following works of literature: Benjamin Disraeli, *Sybil* (page 190); Emma Lazarus, "The New Colossus" (page 206).

| 1832 | 1845 | 1865 | 1894 | 1909 |
|------|------|------|------|------|
| Reform Bill becomes law in Britain | "Great Hunger" in Ireland | United States Civil War ends | Dreyfus affair begins | French Union for Women's Suffrage founded |

| 1815 | 1835 | 1855 | 1875 | 1895 | 1915 |
|------|------|------|------|------|------|

# 1 Britain Becomes More Democratic

## Guide for Reading

- Why did reformers seek to alter Parliament in the 1800s?

- What role did political parties play in the Victorian era?

- How did Britain achieve universal male suffrage?

Earl Grey, Britain's prime minister, must have felt nervous as he stood up in the House of Lords. His goal was to win support for a new election reform bill. Many Lords feared that the bill was a first step toward giving too much power to the "rabble"—the uneducated masses of common people.

Still, Grey proceeded boldly. The present system of elections, he declared, was desperately in need of reform. No one supported it. It was condemned "by all authority, by all reason . . . and by the common law of the land." Grey continued:

66The removal of this vicious and corrupt system, so far from tending to endanger the Constitution, in my opinion, will tend materially to improve and strengthen it.99

In the end, Grey won his point. Later historians agreed that the Reform Bill of 1832 was a turning point in British politics.

The British parliamentary system would face other challenges over the next 80 years. Again and again, Britain would show the way to achieve greater democracy through reform rather than revolution.

## Reforming Parliament

In 1815, Britain was a constitutional monarchy with a parliament and two political parties. Still, it was far from democratic. Parliament, you will recall, was made up of the House of Lords and the House of Commons. The Lords were hereditary nobles and high-ranking clergy in the Church of England. They had the right to veto any bill passed by the House of Commons.

Members of the Commons were elected. Still, less than five percent of the people could vote. Wealthy country squires and landowning nobles dominated politics and heavily influenced voters. In certain towns, local landowners even had the right to name members of Parliament. In addition, old laws banned Catholics and non-Anglican Protestants from voting or serving in Parliament.

**Pressure for change.** In the 1820s, reformers pushed to end religious restrictions. After fierce debate, Parliament finally granted Catholics and non-Anglican Protestants equal political rights.

An even greater battle was brewing to make Parliament more representative. During the Industrial Revolution, centers of population shifted. Some old rural towns lost so many people that there were few or no voters. Yet these so-called "rotten boroughs" still sent members to Parliament, chosen by powerful local landowners. At the same time, populous new industrial cities like Manchester and Birmingham had no seats in Parliament at all.

**Reform Bill of 1832.** In 1830, as revolts flared on the continent, Whigs and Tories* battled over a reform bill. In the streets, supporters of reform chanted, "The Bill, the whole Bill, and nothing but the Bill!" Their shouts seemed to echo the cries of revolutionaries on the continent.

Parliament finally passed the Great Reform Act in 1832. It redistributed seats in the House of Commons, giving representation to large towns and eliminating rotten boroughs. It also enlarged the number of voters by granting suffrage to men with a certain amount of property.

The Reform Bill of 1832 did not bring full democracy, but it did give a greater political voice to men in the middle class. Landowning nobles, however, remained a powerful force in the government and economy.

---

*The Whig party had increasingly come to represent middle-class and business interests. The Tory party spoke for nobles, landowners, and others whose interests and income were rooted in agriculture. (See Chapter 1.)

**Chartism.** Many workers rejected the reform bill and called for more radical change. In the 1830s, protesters drew up the People's Charter, a petition that demanded universal male suffrage, a secret ballot, annual parliamentary elections, and salaries for members of Parliament. Their movement became known as Chartism. (Although Chartists did not call for women's rights, women in the Chartist movement organized the first British association to work for women's suffrage.)

Twice the Chartists presented petitions with over a million signatures to Parliament. Both petitions were ignored. In 1848, as revolutions swept Europe, the Chartists prepared a third petition and organized a march on Parliament. Fearing violence, the government moved to suppress the march. Soon after, the unsuccessful Chartist movement declined. In time, however, Parliament would pass most of the major reforms proposed by the Chartists.

## The Victorian Age

By the mid-1800s, the great symbol in British life was Queen Victoria. Her reign, from 1837 to 1901, was the longest in British history. Although she exercised little real political power, she set the tone for what is today called the Victorian age.

**Symbol of a nation's values.** As queen, Victoria came to embody the values of her age. These Victorian ideals included duty, thrift, honesty, hard work—and, above all, respectability. Today, we associate most of these qualities with the Victorian middle class. (See pages 151–152.) However, people at all levels of society shared these ideals, even if they could not always live up to them. Victoria herself embraced a strict code of morals and manners. As a young woman, she married a German prince, Albert, and they raised a large family. Although she outranked Albert, she treated him with the devotion a dutiful wife was expected to have for her husband. When he died in 1861, Victoria went into deep mourning and dressed in black for the rest of her reign. A fond grandmother to her 38 grandchildren, she worried that manners were becoming far too loose and informal. "Young people," she fretted, "are getting very American I fear in their lives and ways."

**Queen of a changing nation.** Under Victoria, the British middle class—and many members of the working class—felt great confidence in the future. That confidence grew as Britain expanded its already huge empire. (See Chapter 8.) Victoria, the empress of India and ruler of some 300 million subjects around the world, became a revered symbol of British might.

As she aged from teenaged queen to grieving widow to revered national symbol, Victoria witnessed tremendous political changes. She herself commented on the growing agitation for social reform:

66The lower classes are becoming so well-informed, are so intelligent and earn their bread and riches so deservedly, that they cannot and ought not to be kept back.99

As the Victorian era went on, reformers continued the push toward greater democracy.

## Politics Transformed

In the 1860s, a new era opened in British politics. The old political parties regrouped under new leadership. Benjamin Disraeli, whom you read about at the beginning of this chapter, forged the old Tory party into the modern

# PARALLELS THROUGH TIME

## The Art of Caricature

A caricature is a portrait that exaggerates the subject's face and other features. In the hands of a political cartoonist, caricature can be a powerful weapon. A good-natured caricature, however, can bring a smile even to the face of the victim.

**Linking Past and Present**  Where would you be likely to find caricatures of famous people today?

**PAST**  *As the leading political figures of Victorian Britain, William Gladstone, right, and Benjamin Disraeli, below, were often the subject of caricatures.*

**PRESENT**

*Political figures are not the only people who are caricatured. These modern caricatures depict pop stars Stevie Wonder (above) and Bruce Springsteen (below).*

---

Conservative party. The Whigs, led by William Gladstone, evolved into the Liberal party. Between 1868 and 1880, as the majority in Parliament swung between the two parties, Gladstone and Disraeli alternated as prime minister. Both men fought for important reforms.

**Universal male suffrage.** In 1867, Disraeli's Conservative party pushed through a bill to give the vote to many working-class men. Conservatives backed the measure to win working-class support. The Reform Bill of 1867 almost doubled the size of the electorate.

In the 1880s, it was Gladstone and the Liberal party's turn to expand suffrage. Their reforms extended the vote to farmworkers and most other men. By century's end, almost-universal male suffrage, the secret ballot, and other Chartist ambitions had been achieved.

**Limiting the Lords.** In the early 1900s, Liberals in the House of Commons pressed ahead with social reforms. But many bills passed by the Commons met defeat in the House of Lords. In particular, the Lords used their veto power to block any attempt to increase taxes on the wealthy.

In 1911, a Liberal government passed measures to restrict the power of the Lords. For example, the new law would end their power to veto tax bills. Getting the Lords to approve the law was not easy. When the government threatened to have the king create enough new lords to approve the law, the Lords backed down.

People hailed the change as a victory for democracy. In time, the House of Lords, like the monarchy, became largely a ceremonial institution with little real power. The elected House of Commons would reign supreme.

## SECTION 1 REVIEW

1. **Identify** (a) rotten boroughs, (b) Chartism, (c) Victoria, (d) Benjamin Disraeli, (e) William Gladstone.
2. (a) In what ways was the British system of government not democratic in the early 1800s? (b) How did the Reform Bill of 1832 make Parliament more representative?
3. How did British political parties evolve in the 1800s?
4. (a) What groups gained the right to vote after 1860? (b) Why did reformers seek to limit the power of the House of Lords?
5. *Critical Thinking* **Drawing Conclusions** Why do you think the Chartists demanded (a) a secret ballot rather than public voting, (b) salaries for members of Parliament?
6. *ACTIVITY* Imagine that you are a land-owning aristocrat or a wealthy middle-class merchant. Write a letter to a friend of the same social class about the Reform Bill of 1832.

# 2 A Century of Reform

## Guide for Reading

- What social and economic reforms did Britain pass in the 1800s?
- How did British women work to win the vote?
- What were the goals of Irish nationalists?
- **Vocabulary** *home rule*

Lying in a British prison hospital, Lady Constance Lytton refused to eat voluntarily. Her hunger strike, she vowed, would go on until the government gave the vote to women. Lytton later recalled:

> ❝I was visited again by the Senior Medical Officer, who asked me how long I had been without food. I said I had eaten a buttered scone and a banana sent in by friends to the police station on Friday at about midnight. He said, 'Oh, then, this is the fourth day; that is too long, I shall feed you, I must feed you at once.'❞

In the end, the doctor—with the help of five prison matrons—force-fed Lytton through a tube. Yet the painful ordeal failed to weaken her resolve. "No surrender," she whispered.

Lytton's 1910 hunger strike was part of the long struggle for women's suffrage in Britain. Suffragists were not the only people to fight for reform. Between 1815 and 1914, Parliament responded to widespread discontent with a series of important laws.

## Economic and Social Reforms

During the 1800s, Parliament gradually passed a series of social and economic reforms. Many laws were designed to help the men, women, and children whose labor supported the new industrial society.

**Free trade.** Britain, like other European nations, taxed foreign imports in order to protect local economies. In the early 1800s, controversy erupted over the Corn Laws, which imposed high tariffs on imported grain. (In Britain, "corn" refers to all cereal grains, such as wheat and oats.) Farmers and wealthy landowners supported the Corn Laws because they kept the price of British grain high. Middle-class business leaders, however, fought to repeal the Corn Laws. Repeal, they argued, would make bread cheaper for city workers and would also open up trade in general.

Parliament finally repealed the Corn Laws in 1846. Liberals hailed the repeal as a victory for free trade and laissez-faire capitalism. However, economic hard times led Britain and other European countries to impose protective tariffs on many goods again by the early 1900s.

**Abolition of slavery.** Middle-class reformers also campaigned against slavery. Enlightenment thinkers had first turned the spotlight on the evils of the slave trade. The Congress of Vienna had condemned it but taken no action. In Britain, liberals preached the immorality of slavery. In 1833, Parliament passed a law banning slavery in all British colonies. Still, British textile manufacturers continued to import cheap cotton produced by enslaved African Americans in the United States.

**Crime and punishment.** Other reforms were aimed at the criminal justice system. In the early 1800s, more than 200 crimes were punishable by death. Such capital offenses included, not only murder, but also shoplifting, sheep stealing, or impersonating an army veteran. In practice, some juries refused to convict criminals because the punishments were so harsh. Executions were public occasions, and the hanging of a well-known murderer might attract thousands of curious spectators.

Victorian reformers began to reduce the number of capital offenses. By 1850, the death penalty was reserved for murder, piracy, treason, and arson. Many petty criminals were instead transported to penal colonies in the new British territories of Australia and New Zealand. (See Chapter 9.) In 1868, Parliament ended public hangings. Additional reforms improved prison conditions and outlawed imprisonment for debt.

**Victories for workers.** In Chapter 3, you read about harsh conditions for early industrial workers. Gradually, Parliament passed laws to regulate conditions in factories and mines. In 1842, for example, mineowners were forbidden to employ women or children under age 10. An 1847 law limited women and children to a 10-hour day. Later in the 1800s, the government regulated many safety conditions in factories and mines—and sent inspectors to see that the laws were enforced. Other laws set minimum wages and maximum hours of work.

Early in the Industrial Revolution, labor unions were outlawed. Under pressure, government and business leaders slowly accepted worker organizations. Trade unions were made legal in 1825. At the same time, though, strikes remained illegal.

Despite restrictions, unions spread, and gradually they won additional rights. Between 1890 and 1914, union membership soared. Besides winning higher wages and shorter hours for workers, unions pressed for other laws to improve the lives of the working class.

**Other reforms.** During the late 1800s, both political parties enacted reforms. Disraeli sponsored laws to improve public health and housing for workers in cities. Under Gladstone, an Education Act called for free elementary education for all children. Gladstone also pushed to open up government jobs based on merit rather than birth or wealth.

Another force for reform was the Fabian Society, a socialist organization founded in 1883. The Fabians promoted gradual change through legal means rather than by violence. Though small in number, the Fabians had a strong influence on British politics.

In 1900, socialists and union members backed the formation of a new political party, which became the Labour party. ("Labour" is the British spelling of "labor.") The Labour party would grow in power and membership until, by the 1920s, it surpassed the Liberal party as one of Britain's two major parties.

In the early 1900s, Britain began to pass social welfare laws modeled on those Bismarck had introduced in Germany. They protected workers with accident, health, and unemployment insurance as well as old-age pensions. One result of such reforms was that Marxism gained only limited support among the British working classes. The middle class hailed reforms as proof that democracy was working.

# Nineteenth-Century Reforms in Great Britain

| Area of Reform | Laws Enacted | Connections Today |
|---|---|---|
| **Representative government**  | **1832:** Reform Act gave representation to new industrial towns and eliminated many rotten boroughs. **1858:** Law ended property qualifications for members of Parliament. **1911:** Law restricted powers of House of Lords; elected House of Commons became supreme. | Britain combines centuries-old monarchy with democratic government. Majority party in elected House of Commons chooses cabinet and prime minister. House of Commons open to all citizens regardless of ethnic origin, creed, or gender. |
| **Voting rights**  | **1829:** Parliament gave Catholics the right to vote and hold most public offices. **1867:** Reform Act gave suffrage to many working-class men. **1884:** Law extended suffrage to most farmers and other men. **1918:** Women won the right to vote. | Today, all British citizens have the right to vote. |
| **Rights of workers**  | **1825:** Trade unions were legalized. **1840s to 1910s:** Parliament passed laws • limiting child labor • regulating work hours for women and children • regulating safety conditions in mines and factories • setting minimum wages • providing for accident and unemployment insurance • sending inspectors to enforce the laws | In 1900, trade unions founded and helped finance the Labour party, which has become one of the major political parties in Great Britain. Unions are still very influential in shaping the party's policies. |
| **Education**  | **1870:** Education Act set up local elementary schools run by elected school boards. **1902:** Law created a system of state-aided secondary schools. Industrial cities such as London and Manchester set up public universities. | Education from kindergarten through high school is free and compulsory. All British students who pass a series of demanding tests may attend one of Britain's 46 state universities for a minimal fee. |

*Interpreting a Chart  In the 1800s and early 1900s, Parliament passed dozens of reform measures. In addition to the acts listed here, new laws overhauled criminal justice, promoted public health, and set standards for housing.* ■ *Based on this chart, how is the British educational system similar to that of the United States? How is it different?*

## Votes for Women

In Britain, as elsewhere, women struggled for the right to vote against strong opposition. Just as Parliament had rejected the Chartist demand for universal male suffrage in 1848, so it resisted the demands of the women's suffrage movement. Women themselves were divided on the issue. Some women opposed suffrage altogether. Queen Victoria, for example, called the suffrage struggle "mad, wicked folly." Even women in favor of suffrage disagreed about how best to achieve it.

▲ *Emmeline Pankhurst*

**Suffragists revolt.** By the early 1900s, Emmeline Pankhurst, a leading suffragist, had become convinced that only aggressive tactics would bring victory. Radical suffragists interrupted speakers in Parliament, shouting, "Votes for women!" They collected petitions and organized huge public demonstrations. Describing one mass rally in London's Hyde Park, a newspaper wrote that "so many people have never before stood in one square mass anywhere in England."

When peaceful efforts brought no results, some women turned to violent protest. They smashed windows or burned buildings. Pankhurst declared:

66 There is something that governments care far more for than human life, and that is the security of property, so it is through property that we shall strike the enemy. 99

Pankhurst and other women, including her daughters Christabel and Sylvia, were arrested and jailed. As you read, some went on hunger strikes and were force-fed through tubes.

**A belated victory.** Many middle-class women disagreed with such radical actions. Yet they, too, spoke up in support of votes for women and equality under the law. Not until 1918, however, did Parliament finally grant suffrage to women over age 30. Younger women did not win the right to vote for another decade.

## "Ireland for the Irish"

Throughout the 1800s, Britain faced the ever-present "Irish question." The English had begun conquering Ireland in the 1100s. In the 1600s, English and Scottish settlers colonized Ireland, taking possession of much of the best farmland. (See pages 50–51.)

The Irish never accepted rule by the English. The Irish bitterly resented settlers, especially absentee landlords who held large tracts of land. Many Irish peasants lived in desperate poverty, while paying high rents to English landlords. In addition, the Irish, most of whom were Catholic, had to pay tithes to support the state Anglican church. Under these conditions, resistance and rebellion were common.

**Irish nationalism.** Like the national minorities in the Austrian empire, Irish nationalists campaigned vigorously for freedom in the 1800s. "My first object," said nationalist leader Daniel O'Connell, "is to get Ireland for the Irish."

Under pressure from O'Connell and other Irish nationalists, Britain slowly moved to improve conditions in Ireland. In 1829, Parliament passed the Catholic Emancipation Act, which allowed Irish Catholics to vote and hold political office. Yet many injustices remained. Absentee landlords could evict tenants almost at will. Other British laws forbade the teaching and speaking of the Irish language.

**The Great Hunger.** Under British rule, three quarters of Irish farmland was used to grow crops that were imported to England. The potato, introduced from the Americas, became the main source of food for most of the Irish people themselves. Still, potatoes were abundant and nutritious enough to support a growing population.

Then, in 1845, disaster struck. A blight, or disease, destroyed the potato crop. Other crops, such as wheat and oats, were not affected. Yet British landowners continued to ship these crops outside Ireland, leaving little for the Irish except the blighted potatoes. The result was a terrible famine that the Irish called the "Great Hunger."

Visitors to Ireland described many "scenes of frightful hunger." One man told of entering what he thought was a deserted village:

>"In the first [home], six famished and ghastly skeletons, to all appearances dead, were huddled in a corner on some filthy straw, their sole covering what seemed a ragged horsecloth. . . . I approached with horror, and found by a low moaning they were alive—they were in a fever, four children, a woman and what had once been a man. . . . In a few minutes I was surrounded by at least 200 such phantoms, such frightful spectres as no words can describe, either from famine or from fever."

In four years, at least one million Irish died of starvation or disease. Millions more emigrated to the United States and Canada. The Great Hunger left a legacy of Irish bitterness toward the English that still exists today.

**Struggle for home rule.** Throughout the century, Irish demands for self-rule intensified. The turmoil also disrupted English politics. At times, political parties were so deeply split over the Irish question that they could not take care of other business.

As prime minister, Gladstone pushed for reforms in Ireland. He ended the use of Irish tithe money to support the Anglican church and tried to ease the hardships of Irish tenant farmers. New laws prevented landlords from charging unfair rents and protected the rights of tenants to the land they worked.

In the 1870s, Irish nationalists found a rousing leader in Charles Stewart Parnell. He rallied Irish members of Parliament to press for home rule, or local self-government. The debate dragged on for decades. Finally, in 1914, Parliament passed a home rule bill. But it de-

***Erin Go Bragh*** *Portraits of leading Irish nationalists ring this patriotic banner. The banner includes many symbols of Irish pride, including the shamrock and the traditional Irish harp. The phrase* Erin Go Bragh *can be translated as "Ireland Forever!"* **Art and Literature** *What do you think the figures in the center of the wreath represent?*

layed putting the new law into effect when World War I broke out that year. As you will read in Chapter 13, the southern counties of Ireland finally became independent in 1921.

## SECTION 2 REVIEW

1. **Identify** (a) Corn Laws, (b) Fabian Society, (c) Emmeline Pankhurst, (d) Catholic Emancipation Act, (e) Great Hunger, (f) Charles Stewart Parnell.
2. **Define** home rule.
3. Describe three social reforms that helped the British working class.
4. What actions did women suffragists take to achieve their goals?
5. (a) Why did Irish nationalists oppose British rule? (b) Describe two reforms that improved conditions in Ireland.
6. *Critical Thinking* **Defending a Position** Do you agree that the tactics used by suffragists like Emmeline Pankhurst were necessary? Why or why not?
7. *ACTIVITY* Design a poster that an Irish nationalist of the 1800s might have used to win support for home rule.

**GLOBAL CONNECTIONS**

Americans rushed to the aid of the starving Irish. Quakers were the first to organize relief efforts. Catholic churches, Jewish synagogues, and women's groups worked to raise funds. The Choctaw Indians, still recovering from their own food shortages, contributed over $700—a large sum in the 1840s. The American government encouraged food shipments by announcing that no road or canal tolls would be charged on any supplies headed for Ireland.

# 3 Division and Democracy in France

## Guide for Reading

- What domestic and foreign policies did Napoleon III pursue?

- What steps toward democracy did the Third Republic take?

- What were the results of the Dreyfus affair?

- **Vocabulary** *coalition*

The news sent shock waves through Paris. An entire French army under the emperor Napoleon III had surrendered to the Prussians at the city of Sedan. Still worse, Prussian forces were about to advance on Paris. Could the city survive?

Georges Clemenceau (KLEHM uhn soh), a young doctor turned politician, passionately urged Parisians to resist the Prussian onslaught:

66Citizens, must France destroy herself and disappear, or shall she resume her old place in the vanguard of nations? . . . Each of us knows his duty. We are children of the Revolution. Let us seek inspiration in the example of our forefathers in 1792, and like them we shall conquer. Long live France!99

For four months, Paris did resist the German siege. Surrounded by Prussian troops, starving Parisians were reduced to catching rats and slaughtering circus animals for food. The siege did not end until January 1871, when the French government at Versailles accepted Prussia's terms.

The Franco-Prussian War ended the long period of unquestioned French domination of Europe that had begun under Louis XIV. Yet the nation survived its crushing defeat. The Third Republic rose on the ruins of Napoleon III's Second Empire. Economic growth, democratic reforms, and the fierce nationalism expressed by Clemenceau all played a part in shaping modern France.

## France Under Napoleon III

As you read in Chapter 4, Napoleon III rose to power after the revolution of 1848. His appeal cut across lines of class and ideology. The bourgeoisie saw him as a strong leader who would restore order. At the same time, his promise to end poverty gave hope to the lower classes. People of all classes were attracted by his magical name, a reminder of the days when France had towered over Europe. Unlike his famous uncle, however, Napoleon III would bring France neither glory nor an empire.

**Limits on liberty.** On the surface, the Second Empire looked like a constitutional monarchy. In fact, Napoleon III ruled almost like a dictator. He held the power to appoint his cabinet, the upper house of the legislature, and many officials. Although the assembly was elected by universal male suffrage, appointed officials "managed" elections so that supporters of the emperor would win. Debate was limited, and newspapers faced strict censorship.

In the 1860s, the emperor began to ease these controls. He lifted some censorship and gave the legislature more power. On the eve of his disastrous war with Prussia, he even issued a new constitution that extended democratic rights.

**Economic growth.** Like much of Europe, France prospered at mid-century. Napoleon promoted investment in industry and large-scale ventures such as railroad building. During this period, a French entrepreneur, Ferdinand de Lesseps (duh LEHS uhps), organized the building of the Suez Canal to link the Mediterranean with the Red Sea and thus the Indian Ocean.

Napoleon III sponsored huge public works programs, such as the rebuilding of Paris, that employed vast numbers of workers. (See page 148.) He also legalized labor unions, extended public education to girls, and created a small public health program. Apparently, the emperor was genuinely concerned over the hard lives of the poor. Yet in France, as in other industrializing nations, many people lived in shocking poverty.

**Foreign affairs.** Napoleon III's worst failures were in warfare and diplomacy. In the 1860s, he attempted to place Maximilian, an

Austrian Hapsburg prince, on the throne of Mexico. Through Maximilian, Napoleon hoped to turn Mexico into a French satellite. But after a large commitment of troops and money, the adventure failed. Mexican patriots resisted fiercely and the United States protested. After four years, France withdrew its army. Maximilian was overthrown and shot by Mexican patriots. (See page 258.)

Napoleon did enjoy some military successes. Yet they were almost as costly as his failures. He helped Italian nationalists defeat Austria, gaining Nice (NEES) and Savoy for France. This victory backfired when a united Italy emerged as a strong rival on the border of France. And, though France and Britain won the Crimean War against Russia, France had little to show for its terrible losses except a small foothold in the Middle East.

**A humiliating defeat.** At this time, France grew increasingly concerned about the rise of a great European rival, Prussia. The Prussian leader Otto von Bismarck shrewdly manipulated French worries to lure Napoleon into war in 1870.

As you read, the Franco-Prussian War was a disaster for France. After his humiliating surrender at Sedan, Napoleon III was overthrown. In 1871, the newly elected French National Assembly accepted a harsh peace with Germany. France had to surrender the provinces of Alsace and Lorraine and pay a huge sum to Germany. The bitter sting of defeat left the French burning to avenge their loss.

## The Paris Commune

The war brought another catastrophe. In 1871, while Prussians still occupied eastern France, an uprising broke out in the French capital. The rebels set up the Paris Commune. Like the radical government during the French Revolution, its goal was to save the Republic from royalist control.

Communards, as the rebels were called, included workers and socialists as well as bourgeois republicans. As patriots, they rejected the peace with Germany that the National Assembly had signed. Radicals dreamed of a new socialist order and hoped to rebuild France into a loose federation of communes.

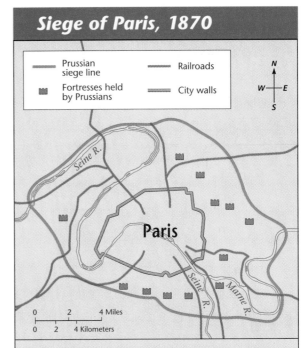

### Siege of Paris, 1870

Legend:
— Prussian siege line
🏰 Fortresses held by Prussians
— Railroads
═ City walls

Paris

Seine R.
Marne R.

0    2    4 Miles
0    2    4 Kilometers

*A Message to the Outside World* In the 1870 painting below, a Parisian woman, rifle in hand, salutes a balloon as it rises and drifts beyond the horizon. During the four-month siege, Prussian troops cut Paris off from the outside world. (See the map above.) Balloons were the only means of communication between Paris and the rest of Europe. **Art and Literature** How does the painting convey both pride and despair?

**History in Flames** Like much of Paris, the Tuileries Palace was burned during the Paris Commune of 1871. Built in 1564, the palace was later expanded by some of France's greatest architects. During the early years of the French Revolution, it was the residence of the king and queen. (See page 71.)
**Continuity and Change** Why do you think rebels tried to destroy a place of such cultural value to France?

The National Assembly ordered the Commune to disband. When it refused, the government sent troops to besiege Paris. For weeks, civil war raged. An English visitor described the scene:

66'Paris the beautiful' is Paris the ghastly, Paris the battered, Paris the burning, Paris the blood-spattered now. And this is the nineteenth century, and Europe professes civilization, and France boasts of culture, and Frenchmen are braining one another with the butt end of muskets, and Paris is burning.99

As government troops advanced, the rebels toppled great Paris monuments and slaughtered hostages. In the final blood bath, government forces butchered some 20,000 Communards. The suppression of the Paris Commune left bitter memories that deepened social divisions within France.

## The Third Republic

Born out of defeat and political chaos in 1871, the Third Republic remained in place for 70 years. The new Republic had a two-house legislature. The lower house, or Chamber of Deputies, was elected by universal male suffrage and had great influence. Together with the Senate, it elected the president of the Republic. He had little power and served mostly as a figurehead. The real political power was in the hands of the premier (prih MIR), or prime minister.

**Coalition governments.** Unlike Britain, with its two parties, France had many parties reflecting the wide splits within the country. Among them were divine-right royalists, constitutional monarchists, ultranationalists, moderate republicans, and radicals.

With so many parties, no single party could win a majority in the legislature. In order to govern, politicians had to form coalitions, or alliances of various parties. Once a coalition controlled enough votes, it could then name a premier and form a cabinet.

Multiparty systems and coalition governments are common in continental Europe. This system allows citizens to vote for a party that most nearly matches their own beliefs. Coalition governments, however, are often unstable. If one party deserts a coalition, the government might lose its majority in the legislature. The government then falls, and new elections must be held. In the first 10 years of the Third Republic, 50 different coalition governments were formed and fell.

**Scandals.** Despite frequent changes of governments, France made economic progress. It paid Germany the huge sum required by the peace treaty and expanded its overseas empire, as you will read in Chapter 8. But in the 1880s and 1890s, a series of political scandals shook public trust in the government.

One crisis erupted when a popular minister of war, General Georges Boulanger (boo lahn ZHAY), rallied royalists and ultranationalists eager for revenge on Germany. Accused of plotting to overthrow the Republic, Boulanger fled to Belgium and later committed suicide. In another scandal, members of the government were charged with bribery and corruption in connection with an attempt to build a canal across Panama. A nephew of the president was even caught selling nominations for the Legion of Honor, France's highest award. The president was forced to resign.

The most disturbing scandal began in 1894, when an army officer, Alfred Dreyfus, was unjustly convicted of spying. The Dreyfus affair scarred French politics and society for decades.

## The Dreyfus Affair

Under a leaden January sky, Captain Alfred Dreyfus stood at attention. "Alfred Dreyfus," declared his commanding general, "you are unworthy of your uniform. In the name of the French people, we degrade you."

The condemned man cried out, "I am innocent. I swear I am innocent. Long live France!" Ignoring the cry, a soldier approached. He ripped the gold braid from the captain's uniform, tore the buttons off his tunic, and broke his sword. The humiliating punishment was just one more horror in a tragic nightmare for Alfred Dreyfus.

**Charge of treason.** A few months earlier, in October 1894, Dreyfus had been arrested on charges of spying for Germany. A high-ranking member of the French army, Dreyfus had access to many military secrets. The military court that convicted Dreyfus claimed that there was plenty of written evidence against him. Yet the War Department kept that evidence in a "secret file." Even Dreyfus's own lawyers had not been al-

lowed to see the evidence against their client. The army claimed that secrecy was necessary to protect France.

There were more sinister reasons behind the army's eagerness to convict Dreyfus. Most of the military elite detested Dreyfus because he was the first Jew to reach a high position in the French army. He made a convenient scapegoat, or person chosen to take the blame, for the security leak in the high command.

After his conviction, Dreyfus was condemned to lifetime confinement on Devil's Island, a tiny tropical isle off the coast of South America. He left France still proclaiming his innocence.

**"I accuse."** The case might have faded from the headlines, but another man, Major Ferdinand Esterhazy, was soon charged as a spy. Dreyfusards, or supporters of Dreyfus, claimed that Esterhazy was guilty of the crime for which Dreyfus had been convicted. Esterhazy was a spendthrift and gambler. But he was also a member of the French nobility. Despite strong evidence, a secret military court cleared him of all charges. Esterhazy then fled the country.

Eventually, the case caught the attention of the novelist Emile Zola. (See page 160.) He began to untangle the web of official lies. Early in 1898, he put his pen into action.

"J'Accuse!" blazed the newspaper headline. "I Accuse!" In a blistering article, Zola charged the army and government officials with suppressing the truth and falsifying evidence. To protect "the honor of the army," said Zola, they had knowingly condemned an innocent man.

Zola knew he could be charged with libel. Indeed, he welcomed a trial:

> ❝I have but one passion—that of light. . . . Let them dare to bring me before the court of appeals and let an inquiry be made in broad daylight. I wait.❞

**A long struggle.** As the Dreyfus affair dragged on, it tore France apart. Ultranationalists, royalists, and Church officials charged the Dreyfusards with undermining France. Paris echoed with cries of "Long live the Republic!" "Long live the army!" "Death to traitors!" and "Down with the Jews!"

Dreyfusards were mostly liberals and republicans who upheld ideals of justice and equality. Few in number, they faced the wrath of an enraged public. Zola himself was convicted of libel and fled into exile.

Gradually, though, the Dreyfusards made progress. Under pressure, the army released evidence against Dreyfus. Much of it turned out to have been forged. In 1899, Esterhazy confessed to being both the forger and the spy.

**The fate of Dreyfus.** After almost five years in a hellish prison, Dreyfus was brought back to France for a new trial. The tropical climate, fevers, chains, and brutal treatment by guards had destroyed his health. Yet he still professed his faith in the army.

At his trial, the army again protected its honor by convicting Dreyfus. But this time, the president of France, convinced of the officer's innocence, pardoned Dreyfus.

For Dreyfus and his supporters, a pardon was not enough. It still implied that Dreyfus was guilty. Finally, in 1906, his conviction was overturned. Alfred Dreyfus was reinstated in the army and awarded the Legion of Honor. Emile Zola, though, did not witness this final triumph.

He had died four years earlier without ever having met Dreyfus.

The reinstatement of Dreyfus was, in the end, a victory for French justice and democracy. The political scars of the Dreyfus affair, however, took years to heal. ◼

## Calls for a Jewish State

The Dreyfus case reflected the rise of anti-Semitism in Europe. The Enlightenment and French Revolution had spread ideas about religious toleration. In Western Europe, some Jews—especially those who had converted to Christianity—had gained jobs in government, universities, and other areas of life. A few were successful in banking and business, though most struggled to survive in the ghettos of Eastern Europe or slums of Western Europe.

By the late 1800s, however, anti-Semitism was again on the rise. Anti-Semites were often members of the lower middle class who felt insecure in their social and economic position. Steeped in the new nationalist fervor, they adopted an aggressive intolerance for outsiders and a violent hatred of Jews.

*"J'Accuse!"* Before the Dreyfus affair, Emile Zola (right) was already known as a passionate defender of the underdog. On January 13, 1898, the newspaper Aurore printed Zola's stinging defense of Alfred Dreyfus (left). It sold 200,000 copies in one day. **Global Interaction** How did the world outside France react to the Dreyfus affair?

*A Home for Jews* Zionists met on this desert landscape in 1909 to make plans for the Jewish city of Tel Aviv. Today, nearly a quarter of Israel's population live in Tel Aviv and its surrounding metropolis. **Geography and History** Why did Jews want to make their home in a place that appeared so empty and forbidding?

The Dreyfus case and the pogroms in Russia (see Chapter 6) stirred Jewish leaders to action. In 1896, Theodor Herzl (HEHRT suhl), a Hungarian Jewish journalist living in France, published *The Jewish State*. In it, he called for Jews to form their own separate state, where they would have the rights and freedoms denied to them in European countries. Herzl helped launch the modern form of Zionism, the movement devoted to rebuilding a Jewish state in Palestine. Since the Romans had destroyed Jerusalem in A.D. 70, many Jews had kept alive this dream.

In 1897, Herzl organized the first world congress of Zionists in Basel, Switzerland. Afterward, he wrote in his diary:

❝At Basel, I founded the Jewish state. If I were to say this today, I would be greeted by universal laughter. In five years, perhaps, and certainly in 50, everyone will see it.❞

Just over 50 years later, Zionists in Palestine founded the modern nation of Israel.

## Reforms in France

Though shaken by the Dreyfus affair, the French government accomplished some serious reforms in the early 1900s. Like Britain, France adopted laws regulating wages, hours, and safety conditions for workers. It set up a system of free public elementary schools to provide basic education for all. Creating public schools was also a way to end the monopoly on education of the Roman Catholic Church.

**Separating church and state.** Like Bismarck in Germany, France tried to limit the power of the Church and end its involvement in government. Supporters of the French republic viewed the Church as a conservative force that opposed progressive policies. In the Dreyfus affair, it had backed the interests of the army and the ultranationalists.

The government therefore closed Church schools along with many monasteries and convents. In 1905, it passed a law to separate church and state and stopped paying the salaries for the clergy. Catholics, Protestants, and Jews enjoyed freedom of worship, but none had any special treatment from the government.

**Women's rights.** Under the Napoleonic Code, French women had few rights. Women could not even control their own property. By the 1890s, a growing women's rights movement sought legal reforms. Some gains were made, such as an 1896 law that gave married women the right to their own earnings.

In 1909, Jeanne-Elizabeth Schmahl founded the French Union for Women's Suffrage. She

**ISSUES For TODAY**

In the western democracies, reformers campaigned for wider suffrage and other rights. What rights should a democracy guarantee to its citizens?

argued that women should be allowed to vote because they had become better educated and more independent. Rejecting the radical tactics used in Britain, Schmahl and other women sought the vote through legal means. Yet even liberal men were reluctant to grant women suffrage. They feared that women would vote for Church and conservative causes. In the end, French women would not gain the right to vote until 1944.

**Looking ahead.** By 1914, France was the largest democratic country on the European continent, with a constitution that protected basic rights. A wide range of parties put up candidates for office. France's economy was generally prosperous, and its overseas empire was second only to that of Britain.

Yet the outlook was not all smooth. Coalition governments rose and fell at the slightest pressure. To the east across the Rhine River loomed the industrial might of Germany. Many French citizens were itching for a chance to revenge the defeat in the Franco-Prussian War and liberate the "lost provinces" of Alsace and Lorraine. That chance came in 1914, when all of Europe exploded into World War I. (See Chapter 10.)

## SECTION 3 REVIEW

1. **Identify** (a) Paris Commune, (b) Georges Boulanger, (c) Alfred Dreyfus, (d) Theodor Herzl, (e) Jeanne-Elizabeth Schmahl.
2. **Define** coalition.
3. (a) Describe the government of France during the Second Empire. (b) How did France become more democratic during the Third Republic?
4. Describe how each of the following heightened divisions within France: (a) the suppression of the Paris Commune, (b) the Dreyfus affair.
5. *Critical Thinking* **Solving Problems** (a) What solution did Zionists propose for the problem of widespread anti-Semitism? (b) Why do you think they felt it was the best solution?
6. *ACTIVITY* Draw a political cartoon about one of the domestic or foreign policies of Napoleon III.

# 4 Expansion of the United States

## Guide for Reading

■ How did the United States expand in the 1800s?

■ What changes made the United States more democratic?

■ What were the causes and effects of the Civil War?

■ **Vocabulary** *segregation, isolationism*

For many Irish families fleeing the Great Hunger, Russian Jews escaping pogroms, or poor Italian farmers seeking economic opportunity, the answer was the same—America! In "The New Colossus," Emma Lazarus expressed the hopes of millions of immigrants:

66 Give me your tired, your poor,
Your huddled masses yearning to
breathe free,
The wretched refuse of your teeming
shore.
Send these, the homeless, tempest-
tossed to me.
I lift my lamp beside the golden
door. 99

Lazarus's poem was later inscribed on the base of the Statue of Liberty.

In the 1800s, the United States was a beacon of hope for many people. At the same time, the nation grew rapidly in economic strength. Not everyone shared in the prosperity or the ideals of democracy. Still, by the turn of the century, Americans were increasingly proud of their status as an emerging world power.

## From Sea to Sea

In 1800, the United States extended from the Atlantic coast to the Mississippi River. A hundred years later, it had grown tremendously, reaching across the continent and beyond.

In 1803, President Thomas Jefferson bought the Louisiana territory from France. In

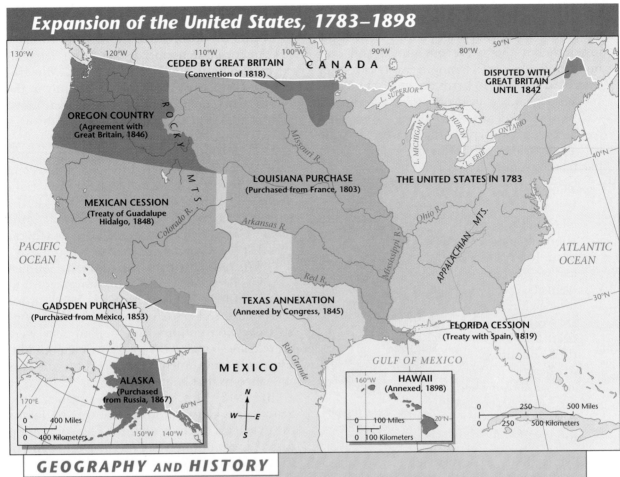

## Expansion of the United States, 1783–1898

CEDED BY GREAT BRITAIN
(Convention of 1818)

CANADA

DISPUTED WITH
GREAT BRITAIN
UNTIL 1842

OREGON COUNTRY
(Agreement with
Great Britain, 1846)

LOUISIANA PURCHASE
(Purchased from France, 1803)

THE UNITED STATES IN 1783

MEXICAN CESSION
(Treaty of Guadalupe
Hidalgo, 1848)

PACIFIC
OCEAN

ATLANTIC
OCEAN

GADSDEN PURCHASE
(Purchased from Mexico, 1853)

TEXAS ANNEXATION
(Annexed by Congress, 1845)

FLORIDA CESSION
(Treaty with Spain, 1819)

MEXICO

GULF OF MEXICO

ALASKA
(Purchased
from Russia, 1867)

HAWAII
(Annexed, 1898)

### GEOGRAPHY AND HISTORY

*The United States won independence in 1783. Over the next century, the nation expanded nearly to its present size through wars and treaties.*

1. **Location** On the map, locate (a) Louisiana Purchase, (b) Mexico, (c) Florida Cession, (d) Oregon Country.
2. **Region** (a) Which territories were acquired from Mexico? (b) Which were acquired from Great Britain?
3. **Critical Thinking** **Analyzing Information** Notice the scales of miles and kilometers on the main map and two inset maps. Why are the scales different on each map?

one stroke, the Louisiana Purchase virtually doubled the size of the nation. By 1850, the United States included other territories, such as Florida, Oregon, and the Lone Star Republic of Texas. The Mexican War of 1846 added California and the southwestern territories.

**Manifest destiny.** With growing pride and confidence, Americans talked of their "manifest destiny." The United States, they said, had a clear right to spread across the continent. Some people even urged expansion "from Panama to Hudson's Bay"—to include Canada and Mexico. In fact, the United States did go far afield. In 1867, it bought Alaska from Russia and in 1898 annexed the Hawaiian Islands.

During the 1800s, settlers flocked to newly acquired western lands. The discovery of gold in California drew floods of easterners. Other people, like the Mormons, sought a place to practice their religion freely. Still others headed west in the spirit of adventure.

**Native Americans.** The waves of settlers brought tragedy to Native Americans. The pattern begun in colonial days continued throughout the 1800s. Newcomers pushed the Indians off their lands, sometimes by treaty, but more often by force. In the 1830s, the Cherokees and other Indian nations were forced to leave their homes in the southeastern United States and move west of the Mississippi.

Some Native American nations resisted the invaders, but they were outgunned and outnumbered. As settlers moved westward, they destroyed the buffalo herds on which the Plains Indians depended. Survivors suffered spiritual as well as physical defeat. After a long, courageous resistance, Chief Joseph of the Nez Percé nation wearily surrendered to forces of the federal government in 1877:

▲ *Chief Joseph of the Nez Percé*

66Our chiefs are killed. . . . He who led the young men is dead. It is cold, and we have no blankets; the little children are freezing to death. . . . I am tired of fighting. My heart is sick and sad. From where the sun now stands I will fight no more forever.99

By the 1890s, most surviving Native Americans had been driven onto reservations, usually the least desirable parts of a territory. There, the first inhabitants of the continent suffered poverty and the further loss of their traditions.

## Expanding Democracy

In 1800, the United States had the most liberal suffrage in the world, but still only white men who owned property could vote. States slowly chipped away at requirements. By the 1830s, most white men had the right to vote. Democracy was far from complete, however. Women, Native Americans, and free blacks had no vote. Enslaved African Americans had no rights at all.

By mid-century, reformers were campaigning for many changes. Some demanded a ban on the sale of alcoholic beverages. Others called for better treatment of the mentally ill or pushed for free elementary schools. Two crusades, especially, highlighted the limits of American democracy—the abolition movement and the women's rights movement.

**Calls for abolition.** In the early 1800s, a few Americans denounced slavery and demanded its abolition. Frederick Douglass, who had himself escaped slavery, spoke eloquently in the North about the evils of slavery. William Lloyd Garrison pressed the antislavery cause through his newspaper, the *Liberator.*

By the 1850s, the battle over slavery intensified. As new states entered the union, pro- and antislavery forces met in violent confrontations to decide whether slavery would be legal in the new state. Harriet Beecher Stowe's novel, *Uncle Tom's Cabin,* helped convince many northerners that slavery was a great social evil.

**Women's rights movement.** Women worked hard in the antislavery movement. Lucretia Mott and Elizabeth Cady Stanton, for example, traveled to London for the World Antislavery Convention—only to find they were unwelcome because they were women. Gradually, American women began to protest the laws and customs that limited their lives.

In 1848, Mott and Stanton organized the Seneca Falls Convention in New York to discuss the problems faced by women. The convention passed a resolution, based on the Declaration of Independence. "We hold these truths to be self evident: that all men and women are created equal." The women's rights movement set as its goal equality before the law, in the workplace, and in education. Like women in Europe, American women also demanded the vote.

## Civil War and After

Economic differences, as well as the slavery issue, drove the North and South apart. The division reached a crisis in 1860 when Abraham Lincoln was elected president. Lincoln opposed extending slavery into new territories. Southerners feared that he would eventually abolish slavery altogether and that the federal government would infringe on their states' rights.

**The Civil War.** Soon after Lincoln's election, most southern states seceded from the Union and formed the Confederate States of America. This action sparked the Civil War. From 1861 to 1865, the agonizing ordeal divided families as well as a nation.

The South had fewer resources, people, and industry than the North. Still, southerners fought fiercely to defend their cause. They won many early victories. At one point, Confederate armies under General Robert E. Lee drove northward as far as Gettysburg, Pennsylvania. In a bloody three-day battle, the Union army turned back the southern advance for good.

In the last years of the war, Lincoln's most successful general, Ulysses S. Grant, used the massive resources of the North to launch a full-scale offensive against the South. After devastating losses on both sides, the Confederacy finally surrendered in 1865. The struggle cost more than 600,000 lives—the largest casualty figures of any American war. Although the war left a bitter legacy, it did guarantee that the nation would remain united.

**Challenges for African Americans.** During the war, Lincoln emancipated enslaved African Americans in the South. After the war, three amendments to the Constitution banned slavery throughout the country and granted political rights to African Americans. Under the Fifteenth Amendment, for example, African American men won the right to vote.

Despite these amendments, African Americans faced many restrictions. In the South, "Jim Crow" laws imposed segregation, or legal separation of the races, in hotels, hospitals, schools, and other public places. Other laws bypassed the Fifteenth Amendment to prevent African Americans from voting. Thus, in the United States, as in Europe, democracy remained a goal rather than a reality for many citizens.

African Americans also faced economic hardships. Freed from slavery but without land, many ended up working as tenant farmers. To escape the bleak poverty of the postwar South, some headed west. There, they became cowhands or farmed their own lands. Others migrated to the northern cities, seeking jobs in the factories that were springing to life.

## Economic Successes

Like Western Europe, the United States plunged into the Industrial Revolution. With seemingly unlimited natural resources and the help of European capital, the economy boomed. By 1900, the nation led the world in industrial and agricultural production.

Farm output soared as settlers flooded into the fertile farmlands of the Midwest. Inventions

*Fighting for Freedom* About 178,000 African Americans volunteered to serve in the Union Army during the Civil War. Of these, 21 were awarded the Medal of Honor. The secretary of war noted that the African American regiments "have proved themselves among the bravest of the brave, performing deeds of daring and shedding their blood with . . . heroism." **Diversity** Why do you think many African Americans were eager to fight for the Union cause?

**Trade and Commerce Quilt** This quilt, made around 1830 by Hannah S. Stokes, celebrates the bustling sea trade of that period. Its design includes rowboats, sailing ships, and the newly invented steamship. Quilting provided a creative outlet for women living in lonely stretches of rural America. A quilt like this one might take more than a year to complete. **Art and Literature** Art historians classify quilts as "folk art." What do you think this phrase means?

**Transportation.** A growing network of transportation and communication aided economic growth. In the early 1800s, canals and turnpikes helped farmers and entrepreneurs in the young nation. Later, railroads crisscrossed the country. The first transcontinental railroad was completed in 1869, opening up new opportunities for settlement and growth.

In the early 1900s, Americans took to the automobile faster than Europeans. Henry Ford's "Model T" became the symbol of the new automobile era. "When I'm through," Ford boasted, "everybody will be able to afford one, and about everybody will have one."

## Seeking Reform

In the United States, as in Europe, the growing prosperity was not shared by all. The Industrial Revolution brought urbanization as millions of people left the farms for jobs in the cities. In city slums, disease, poverty, and unemployment were daily threats. In factories, wages were low and conditions were often brutal.

**Labor unions.** By the late 1800s, American workers were organizing labor unions to defend their interests. Through unions such as the American Federation of Labor, they sought better wages, hours, and working conditions. Struggles with management sometimes erupted into violent confrontations. Slowly, however, workers made gains.

In the economic hard times of the late 1800s, farmers, too, organized to defend their interests. In the 1890s, they joined city workers to support the new Populist party. The Populists never became a major party, but their platform of reforms, such as an eight-hour workday, eventually became law.

**Immigrants.** The nation's population soared as millions of immigrants arrived in the 1800s and early 1900s. They represented nearly every nationality and ethnic group, including Irish, German, Chinese, Italian, Japanese, Eastern European Jews, and many others.

Typically, European immigrants settled first in cities on the Atlantic coast, while Asian immigrants filled cities on the Pacific coast. In time, newcomers spread out across the country. They worked in mines and factories, built canals and railroads, and opened up farmlands in the West.

like Cyrus McCormick's mechanical reaper increased production. Later, mechanical plows and threshers further revolutionized farming.

**Industrial output.** Industry grew even more rapidly. As in Europe, early progress came in the textile industry. Cotton mills used machines and cheap labor to turn out great quantities of mass-produced goods. Rich coal and iron resources fed other industries. A huge work force, swelled by waves of immigrants, labored in mines and factories.

After the Civil War, production and profits in many industries shot up. As in Europe, giant monopolies controlled whole industries. (See page 145.) Scottish-born Andrew Carnegie built the nation's largest steel company, while John D. Rockefeller's Standard Oil Company dominated the world's petroleum industry.

The newcomers made the United States "a nation of nations," with roots around the world.

Immigrants faced harsh conditions in crowded slum tenements. Often, newcomers suffered from prejudice and even violence from native-born Americans. In the West, whites hostile to Chinese workers pushed for laws to end immigration from China. For the first time, the United States began to close its "golden" door.

**Progressive movement.** By 1900, reformers known as Progressives again pressed for change. They sought laws to ban child labor, limit working hours, regulate monopolies, and give voters more power. Another major goal of the Progressives was votes for women. Copying the tactics used in Britain, American suffragists finally won the vote in 1920, when the Nineteenth Amendment went into effect.

## Becoming a World Power

By 1900, the United States was the world's leading industrial giant. It was also acquiring a new role—that of a global power. Its ships had opened up Japan to western trade. (See Chapter 9.) In the Spanish American War of 1898, the United States acquired overseas territories, including the Philippines, Guam, and Puerto Rico.

Many Americans wanted to maintain their tradition of isolationism, or limited involvement in world affairs. Expansionists, however,

urged the nation to pursue global economic and military interests. "Whether they will or no, Americans must now begin to look outward," wrote influential expansionist Alfred T. Mahan in 1890. "The growing production of the country demands it."

In 1914, rivalries among European nations exploded into global war. Although the United States was already a world power, it tried to stay out of the conflict. As you will read, World War I eventually forced the United States to take an even greater role on the world stage.

## SECTION 4 REVIEW

1. **Identify** (a) Louisiana Purchase, (b) manifest destiny, (c) Frederick Douglass, (d) Seneca Falls Convention, (e) Abraham Lincoln, (f) Fifteenth Amendment, (g) Progressives.
2. **Define** (a) segregation, (b) isolationism.
3. Give one example of how the United States grew in each of these areas in the 1800s: (a) territory, (b) population, (c) economy.
4. Describe two ways that reformers tried to make the United States more democratic.
5. (a) What issues divided the North and South? (b) Describe two results of the Civil War.
6. *Critical Thinking* **Recognizing Causes and Effects** Why do you think economic growth helped make the United States a world power?
7. *ACTIVITY* Write two four-line poems about the United States in the 1800s. Each poem should express the viewpoint of one of the following: a settler in the western United States, a Native American, a supporter of women's rights, a formerly enslaved African American, a business leader, an immigrant.

## CHAPTER REVIEW

### REVIEWING VOCABULARY

Review the following vocabulary from this chapter: *democracy, suffrage, free market, home rule, bourgeoisie, socialism, coalition, segregation, isolationism.* Write sentences using *six* of these terms, leaving blanks where the terms would go. Exchange your sentences with another student and fill in the blanks on each other's lists.

### REVIEWING FACTS

1. What were the effects of the Reform Bill of 1832?
2. How did British policy toward slavery change in 1833?
3. What was the "Great Hunger"?
4. How did the party system in France's Third Republic differ from the British party system?
5. What was the goal of the Zionist movement?
6. List the goals of the American progressives.

## SKILLS FOR SUCCESS    HOLDING A DEBATE

Formal debates follow a set format. In the most widely used format, the issue to be discussed is stated as a proposition, or a statement that can be answered yes or no. One side argues in favor of the proposition, and the other argues against it.

The debate is divided into two parts. During the constructive speeches, a debater on each side presents prepared arguments. During rebuttal, debaters try to refute the other side's arguments.

Imagine that you are going to debate the affirmative side of the following proposition: *RESOLVED, that a two-party political system is preferable to a multiparty system.* Read the following directions and answer the questions.

1. **Prepare a brief in favor of your position.** A brief is a written outline of the arguments on one side of the debate. What would the affirmative side in the debate need to prove?

2. **Locate factual information to support each of your arguments.** (a) What kinds of factual information would support your arguments? (b) Where might you look to find these facts?

3. **Prepare your speech.** A persuasive constructive speech has three parts: an introduction; a discussion of contentions, or points, and supporting evidence; and a conclusion. Why do you think it is important to practice and time your constructive speech?

Outline of an Affirmative Brief

Introduction

I. The cause for discussion is as follows:
   A.
   B.

II. The issues are as follows:
   A.
   B.

III. The affirmative will establish the following points:
   A.
   B.

Discussion

I. First contention states
   A. First supporting fact
   B. Second supporting fact

II. Second contention states
   A. First supporting fact
   B. Second supporting fact

Conclusion

I. Since...; (relate to contention I)

II. Since...; (relate to contention I)

Therefore,...(state proposition)

## REVIEWING CHAPTER THEMES

Review the "Focus On" questions at the start of this chapter. Then select *three* of those questions and answer them, using information from the chapter.

## CRITICAL THINKING

1. **Recognizing Causes and Effects** (a) List two long-term and two immediate causes of the Great Hunger. (b) List two immediate effects. (c) Why do you think the famine sparked lasting feelings of bitterness against Britain?

2. **Identifying Main Ideas** Reread the subsection "Expanding Democracy" on page 208. Then, write a sentence summarizing the main idea of this subsection.

3. **Linking Past and Present** The United States still continues to attract large numbers of immigrants from around the world. Do people come to the United States today for the same reasons that immigrants came in the late 1800s and early 1900s? Explain.

## ANALYZING PRIMARY SOURCES

Use the quotation on page 199 to answer the following questions.

1. What did the visitor first think the six figures were? What did they turn out to be?

2. Who were the "phantoms" the writer described?

3. Why did the "phantoms" have such a strange appearance?

## FOR YOUR PORTFOLIO

**CREATING A NEWSPAPER** Work with a group of classmates to publish a newspaper of events in the 1890s. First, decide who should fill each of the following roles: reporters, editors, feature writers, editorial writers, reviewers, and layout editors. Then assign articles for the paper. Set aside time to write, edit, and lay out the newspaper. Pass out copies of the newspaper to other world history classes.

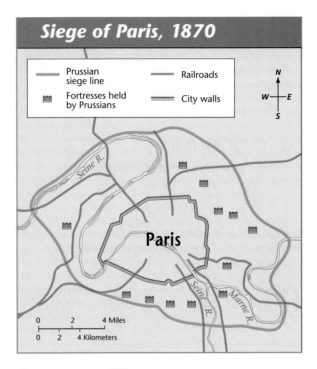

**Siege of Paris, 1870**

Prussian siege line
Fortresses held by Prussians
Railroads
City walls

Seine R.

Paris

Seine R.

Marne R.

0 2 4 Miles
0 2 4 Kilometers

## ANALYZING MAPS

Use the map to answer the following questions.

1. How does the map show that Parisians had no escape from the Prussian siege?

2. Were the Prussian-held fortresses inside or outside Paris's city walls?

3. Why did Parisians not use railroads to flee Paris?

## INTERNET ACTIVITY

**WRITING A TOUR PAMPHLET** Use the Internet to research Ellis Island, the site of an immigration center in New York harbor through which millions of immigrants to the United States passed beginning in the late 1800s. Then write a tour pamphlet of the museum now housed there. You may want to focus on how Ellis Island functioned when it was an immigration center, or on the history of groups of immigrants who arrived in the United States through Ellis Island.

# The New Imperialism

## (1800–1914)

## CHAPTER OUTLINE

In the late 1800s, Europeans seized almost the entire continent of Africa. A few critics opposed the expansion. But most Europeans applauded the move. As French statesman and historian Gabriel Hanotaux wrote of his nation's colonizing activities:

66I can think of nothing more heartening than the spectacle of the struggle waged for a century by the sons of civilized Europe against the sphinx that guards the mystery of Africa.99

Hanotaux's attitude was typical among westerners. The West, they believed, was modern and enlightened. It had to bring "civilization" to the "backward" people of Africa and Asia.

Europeans had other motives, as well, for expanding around the globe. In the words of British empire builder Frederick Lugard:

66There are some who say we have no *right* to Africa at all, that 'it belongs to the natives.' I hold that our right is the necessity that is upon us to provide for our ever-growing population—either by opening new fields for emigration, or by providing work and employment . . . and to stimulate trade by finding new markets.99

At the beginning of the 1800s, westerners had relatively little influence outside their own lands. With the Industrial Revolution, however, western nations gained extraordinary power. By the end of the century, they had carved out empires around the globe. During the "age of imperialism," from 1870 to 1914, they dominated other peoples and brought distant lands under their control.

In this chapter and the next one, we will look at how and why western industrial powers won global empires. We will also learn how people in the lands targeted for takeover fought to preserve their own cultures and traditions. When foreign powers pushed at their doors, they resisted, often in fierce but ultimately unsuccessful wars.

FOCUS ON these questions as you read:

■ **Economics and Technology**
How was the Industrial Revolution linked to imperialism?

■ **Global Interaction**
How did western powers gain global empires?

■ **Political and Social Systems**
What conditions in Africa and Asia helped western powers make inroads there?

■ **Continuity and Change**
How did people in Africa and Asia respond to western imperialism?

## TIME AND PLACE

***Growing European Empires*** *Europeans took control of much of Africa, Asia, and the Middle East in the 1800s. Early contacts between Europeans and local leaders were often polite, as in this meeting between a British naval officer and the king of Ambriz in Africa. Both sides knew, however, that behind the friendly gestures stood gunboats, cannons, and rifles that the Europeans would use to expand their imperialist rule.* **Continuity and Change** *Do foreign diplomats today conceal their nations' real motives and goals? Explain.*

## HUMANITIES LINK

*Art History* Indian miniature painting (page 232).
*Literature* In this chapter, you will encounter a passage from the following work of literature: Rudyard Kipling, "White Man's Burden" (page 217).

| 1805 | 1847 | 1857 | 1884 | 1911 |
|------|------|------|------|------|
| Muhammad Ali named governor of Egypt | Liberia becomes independent | Sepoy Rebellion breaks out | Berlin Conference meets | Sun Yixian becomes president of Chinese republic |

| 1800 | 1820 | 1840 | 1860 | 1880 | 1900 | 1920 |

# 1 A Western-Dominated World

## Guide for Reading

- Why did European imperialism grow in the late 1800s?

- What groups supported the new imperialism?

- How did Europeans rule their overseas empires?

- **Vocabulary** *imperialism, protectorate, sphere of influence*

When Edward VII inherited the British throne in 1901, his empire extended far beyond Britain. One writer boasted, "The sun never sets" on the British empire. In other words, since the empire circled the globe, the sun always shone on some part of it. Another writer noted:

> 66His Majesty rules over one continent, a hundred peninsulas, five hundred promontories, a thousand lakes, two thousand rivers, and ten thousand islands. . . . The empire to which [Queen] Victoria acceded in 1837 covered a sixth of the land of the world; that of King Edward covers nearly a quarter. The [British flag] has unfolded itself . . . over two acres of new territory every time the clock has ticked since 1800.99

Like Britain, other western powers built overseas empires in the late 1800s. The Industrial Revolution and the growth of science and technology had transformed the West. Armed with new economic and political power, western nations set out to dominate the world.

## The New Imperialism

European imperialism did not begin in the 1800s. Imperialism is the domination by one country of the political, economic, or cultural life of another country or region. As you have

read, European nations won empires in the Americas after 1492, established colonies in India and Southeast Asia, and gained toeholds on the coasts of both Africa and China. Despite these gains, between 1500 and 1800, Europe had little influence on the lives of the peoples of China, India, or Africa.

By the 1800s, Europe had developed politically and economically. Strong, centrally governed nation-states had emerged. The Industrial Revolution greatly strengthened European economies, and westerners had a new sense of confidence in themselves. Inspired by these changes, Europeans embarked on that path of aggressive expansion that today's historians call the "new imperialism." In just a few decades, from about 1870 to 1914, they brought much of the world under their control.

## Motives of the New Imperialists

Like other key developments in world history, the new imperialism exploded out of a combination of causes. They can be grouped into four main categories.

**Economic interests.** The Industrial Revolution created needs that spurred overseas expansion. Manufacturers wanted access to natural resources such as rubber, petroleum, manganese for steel, and palm oil for machinery. They also looked to expand their markets around the globe. Bankers sought ventures in far-flung parts of the world in which to invest their profits. Colonies also offered a valuable outlet for Europe's rapidly expanding population.

**Political and military interests.** Closely linked to economic motives were political and military issues. Steam-powered merchant ships and naval vessels needed bases around the world to take on coal and supplies. Industrial powers seized islands or harbors to satisfy these needs.

Nationalism played an important role, too. When France, for example, moved into West

**ISSUES** *For* **TODAY**

Advanced technology and a strong military enabled western nations to exert their will around the globe. What are the responsibilities of powerful nations toward those that are less powerful?

**Exploiting Natural Resources**
Tropical colonies supplied Europe with many valuable products. These workers in Ceylon (modern-day Sri Lanka) load crates of tea for shipment abroad. **Global Interaction** For what other purposes did European nations seek colonies?

Africa, rival nations like Britain and Germany seized lands nearby to halt further French expansion. Western leaders also claimed colonies were needed for national security. Sometimes, they were acquired for the prestige of ruling a global empire.

**Humanitarian and religious goals.** Many westerners felt a genuine concern for their "little brothers" beyond the seas. Missionaries, doctors, and colonial officials believed they had a duty to spread what they saw as the blessings of western civilization, including its medicine, law, and Christian religion. In his poem "White Man's Burden," Rudyard Kipling expressed this mission:

66Take up the White Man's Burden—
  Send forth the best ye breed—
  Go bind your sons to exile
  To serve your captives' need;
  To wait in heavy harness
  On fluttered folk and wild—
  Your new-caught, sullen peoples
  Half-devil and half-child.99

**Social Darwinism.** Behind the idea of a civilizing mission was a growing sense in the West of racial superiority. Many westerners had embraced the scientific-sounding ideas of Social Darwinism. They applied Darwin's ideas about natural selection and survival of the fittest to human societies and nations. European races, they argued, were superior to all others, and imperial conquest and destruction of weaker races were simply nature's way of improving the human species! As a result, millions of nonwesterners were robbed of their cultural heritage.

**Empire builders and critics.** Many people were involved in the new imperialism. Leading the way were soldiers, merchants, settlers, missionaries, and explorers. In Europe, imperial expansion found favor with all classes, from bankers and manufacturers to workers.

Yet critics did speak out. Some opponents argued that colonialism was a tool of the rich. Others said it was immoral. Westerners, they pointed out, were moving toward greater democracy at home but were imposing undemocratic rule on other people.

## Down the Barrel of a Gun

Western imperialism succeeded for a number of reasons. While European nations had grown stronger in the 1800s, several older civilizations were in decline, especially the Ottoman Middle East, Mughal India, and Qing China. In West Africa, wars among African peoples and the draining effect of the slave trade had undermined established empires, kingdoms, and city-states. Newer African states were not strong enough to resist the western onslaught.

**Western advantages.** Europeans had the advantages of strong economies, well-organized governments, and powerful armies and navies.

▼ *Maxim machine gun*

Superior technology and improved medical knowledge also played a role. Quinine and other new medicines helped Europeans survive deadly tropical diseases. And, of course, advances such as Maxim machine guns, repeating rifles, and steam-driven warships were very strong arguments in persuading Africans and Asians to accept western control. As an English writer sarcastically noted:

66Whatever happens, we have got
The Maxim gun, and they have not.99

**Resistance.** Africans and Asians strongly resisted western expansion. Some people fought the invaders, even though they had no weapons to equal the Maxim gun. As you will read, ruling groups in certain areas tried to strengthen their societies against outsiders by reforming their own Muslim, Hindu, or Confucian traditions. Finally, western-educated Africans and Asians organized nationalist movements to expel the imperialists from their lands.

## Forms of Imperial Control

The new imperialism took several forms. Among them were colonies, protectorates, and spheres of influence.

**Colonies.** In some areas, imperial powers established colonies. They sent out governors, officials, and soldiers to control the people and set up a colonial bureaucracy. Often, a handful of colonial officials ruled the local people and sought to transform their society.

France and Britain, the leading imperial powers, developed different kinds of colonial rule. The French practiced direct rule, sending officials from France to administer their colonies. Their goal was to impose French culture on their colonies and turn them into French provinces.

The British, by contrast, relied on a system of indirect rule. They used sultans, chiefs, or other local rulers as their agents in governing their colonies. They then encouraged the children of the local ruling class to get an education in Britain. In that way, a new generation was groomed to become agents of indirect rule—and of western civilization.

**Protectorates.** Sometimes, a western power established a protectorate. In a protectorate, local rulers were left in place. The ruler was, however, expected to accept the advice of European advisers on issues such as trade or missionary activity. A protectorate had certain advantages over a colony. It cost less to run than a colony did, and it did not require a large commitment of military or naval support unless a crisis occurred.

**Spheres of influence.** A third form of western control was the sphere of influence, an area in which an outside power claimed exclusive investment or trading privileges. Europeans carved out these spheres in China and elsewhere to prevent conflicts among themselves. The United States claimed Latin America as its sphere of influence.

## SECTION 1 REVIEW

1. **Identify** (a) new imperialism, (b) direct rule, (c) indirect rule.
2. **Define** (a) imperialism, (b) protectorate, (c) sphere of influence.
3. Describe three causes for the new imperialism.
4. What advantages did a protectorate have over a colony?
5. *Critical Thinking* **Analyzing Information** Review the poem on page 217. What is Kipling referring to when he uses the term "White Man's Burden"? Explain.
6. *ACTIVITY* Write a sentence offering a defense of the new imperialism that might have been offered by each of the following Europeans: (a) missionary, (b) merchant, (c) steel manufacturer, (d) banker.

**The Partition of Africa**

## Guide for Reading

- What forces were shaping Africa before 1880?

- Which European countries carved up Africa?

- How did Africans resist European imperialism?

In 1890, Chief Machemba of the Yao people in East Africa wrote in Swahili to a German officer:

&#x201C;I have listened to your words but can find no reason why I should obey you—I would rather die first. . . . If you desire friendship, then I am ready for it, today and always. But I cannot be your subject. If you desire war, then I am ready.&#x201D;

In the late 1800s, Germany and other European powers swept into Africa. Within about 20 years, they had carved up the continent and dominated its millions of people. Many, like the Yao, resisted. But despite their efforts, they could not hold back the tide of European conquest.

## On the Eve of the Scramble

In the early 1800s, westerners knew little about Africa. They called it the "dark continent," meaning the unknown land. Although they had built trading posts on the coasts, their maps of the interior were blank, or filled with imaginary features.

In the later 1800s, however, European nations sent explorers to Africa and later became involved in a "scramble" for African colonies. To understand the impact of European domination, we need to look at Africa in the early 1800s, before the scramble began.

**A diverse land.** Africa is a huge continent, four times the size of Europe. Across its many regions—the blank areas on European maps—people had evolved diverse cultures. They spoke hundreds of languages and had developed varied governments. Some people lived in large centralized states, others in village communities, still others in herding or food-gathering societies.

**North Africa.** North Africa includes the fertile land along the Mediterranean and the enormous Sahara. Since before 1800, the region has had close ties to the Muslim world. From the 1400s, much of North Africa, including Egypt, was ruled by the Ottoman empire. But by the 1800s, Ottoman control was weakening. You will read about Egypt and the Ottoman empire later in this chapter.

**West Africa.** On the grassy plains of West Africa, an Islamic reform movement had unleashed forces for change. Leaders like Usman dan Fodio preached jihad, a holy struggle, to revive and purify Islam. Under these leaders, several new Muslim states arose, built on trade, farming, and herding.

In the forest regions, strong states such as the Asante kingdom had grown up. The Asante traded with both Europeans and Muslims. Asante power was limited, however. They controlled many smaller states that felt no loyalty to the central government. These tributary states were ready to turn to other protectors who might help them defeat their overlords. The European imperialists would exploit that lack of unity.

**East Africa.** Islam had long influenced the region from the Red Sea down the coast of East Africa. Port cities like Mombasa and Kilwa had suffered setbacks when the Portuguese arrived in the early 1500s. Yet East Africans still sent trading ships to the Red Sea or Persian Gulf. Their cargoes were human captives marched from the interior to the coast to be shipped as slaves to the Middle East. Ivory and copper from Central Africa were also brought to the coast, where they were exchanged for Indian cloth and firearms.

**Southern Africa.** In the early 1800s, southern Africa was in turmoil. Shaka, you will recall, united the Zulu nation. His conquests, however, set off mass migrations and wars, creating chaos across much of the region. By the 1830s, the Zulus were also battling the Boers, who were migrating north from the Cape Colony.

## European Contacts Increase

In the 1500s and 1600s, Europeans traded along the coasts of Africa. Difficult geography and deadly diseases like malaria and sleeping sickness kept them from reaching the interior. Medical breakthroughs and river steamships changed all that in the 1800s.

**Impact of the slave trade.** For centuries, Europeans had taken enslaved Africans to work the plantations and mines of the Americas. Arabs and Africans had also traded in slaves.

Beginning in the early 1800s, European nations slowly outlawed the slave trade. In Britain and the United States, abolitionists promoted the idea of returning freed slaves to Africa. In 1787, the British organized Sierra Leone in West Africa as a colony for freed slaves. Later, some free blacks from the United States settled nearby Liberia. By 1847, after much hardship, Liberia became an independent republic.

Slavery still existed, however. Arab and African slave traders continued to send human beings from Central and East Africa to work as slaves in the Middle East and Asia well into the late 1800s. Thus, the demand for slaves remained, and the slave trade in Africa continued.

**Explorers.** In the early 1800s, European explorers began pushing into the interior of Africa. Daring adventurers like Mungo Park and Richard Burton set out to map the course and sources of the great African rivers such as the Niger, Nile, and Congo. Some explorers were self-promoters who wrote glowing accounts of their bold deeds. While they were fascinated by African geography, they had little understanding of the peoples they met. All, however, endured great hardships in pursuit of their dreams.

**Missionaries.** Catholic and Protestant missionaries followed the explorers. All across Africa, they sought to win souls to Christianity.

The missionaries were sincere in their desire to help Africans. They built schools and medical clinics alongside churches. They also focused attention on the evils of the slave trade.

Still, missionaries, like most westerners, took a paternalistic view of Africans. They saw them as children in need of guidance. To them, African cultures and religions were "degraded." They urged Africans to reject their own traditions in favor of western civilization.

**Livingstone.** The best known explorer-missionary was Dr. David Livingstone. For 30 years, he crisscrossed the African continent. He wrote about the many peoples he met with more sympathy and less bias than did most Europeans. He relentlessly opposed the slave trade, which remained a profitable business for some African rulers. The only way to end this cruel traffic, he believed, was to open up the interior of Africa to Christianity and trade.

Livingstone blazed a trail that others soon followed. In 1869, the journalist Henry Stanley trekked into Central Africa to find Livingstone, who had not been heard from for years. He finally tracked him down in 1871 in what is today Tanzania, greeting him with the now-legendary phrase "Dr. Livingstone, I presume?"

*King Njoya's Throne* King Njoya of Bamum, in modern-day Cameroon, impressed German colonizers with his orderly government and disciplined army. Njoya sent this ornate wooden throne as a gift to the German kaiser William II in 1908. **Political and Social Systems** How did Njoya's gift to Kaiser William suggest equality between the two rulers?

## The Great Scramble Begins

Shortly afterward, Stanley took a new assignment. King Leopold II of Belgium hired him to explore the Congo River basin and arrange trade treaties with African leaders. Publicly, Leopold spoke of a civilizing mission to carry the light "that for millions of men still plunged in barbarism will be the dawn of a better era." Privately, he dreamed of conquest and profit.

Leopold's activities in the Congo (present-day Zaire) set off a scramble by other European nations. Before long, Britain, France, and Germany were pressing rival claims to the region.

**Berlin Conference.** To avoid bloodshed, European powers met at an international conference in 1884. It took place not in Africa but in Berlin, Germany. No Africans were invited.

At the Berlin Conference, European powers recognized Leopold's private claims to the Congo Free State but called for free trade on the Congo and Niger rivers. They further agreed that a European power could not claim any part of Africa unless it had set up a government office there. This principle led Europeans to send officials who would exert their power over local rulers.

The rush to colonize Africa was on. With little understanding of or regard for traditional African patterns of settlement or ethnic boundaries, Europeans drew borders and set up frontiers as they carved out their claims. A British politician observed:

66We have been engaged in drawing lines upon maps where no white man's foot has ever trod. We have been giving away mountains and rivers and lakes to each other, only hindered by the small impediment that we never knew exactly where the mountains and rivers and lakes were.99

In the 20 years after the Berlin Conference, the European powers partitioned almost the entire continent. Only Ethiopia and Liberia remained independent. (See the map on page 222.)

**Horrors in the Congo.** Leopold and other wealthy Belgians, meantime, exploited the riches of the Congo, including its copper, rubber, and ivory. Soon, horrifying stories filtered out of the region. They told of Belgian overseers torturing and brutalizing villagers. Forced to work for almost nothing, unwilling laborers were savagely beaten or had hands and ears amputated. The population of some areas declined drastically.

Eventually, international outrage forced Leopold to turn over his colony to the Belgian government. It became the Belgian Congo in 1908. Under Belgian rule, the worst abuses of the state were ended. Still, the Belgians regarded the Congo as a possession to be exploited for their own enrichment, and African inhabitants were given little or no role in either the government or economy of the colony.

## Carving Up a Continent

In the 1800s, France took a giant share of Africa. In 1830, it had invaded and conquered Algeria in North Africa. The victory cost tens of thousands of French lives and killed many times more Algerians. Later, France extended its influence along the Mediterranean into Tunisia and won colonies in West and Central Africa. At their height, French holdings in Africa were as large as the continental United States.

Britain's share of Africa was smaller and more scattered than that of France. However, it included more heavily populated regions with many rich resources. Britain took chunks of West and East Africa. It gained control of Egypt, as you will read, and pushed south into the Sudan. It also ruled much of southern Africa.

**The Boer War.** Britain had acquired the Cape Colony in southern Africa from the Dutch in 1815. The Boers—Dutch farmers—resented British rule and had migrated north to found their own republics.

In the late 1800s, the discovery of gold and diamonds in the Boer republics set off the Boer War. The war, which lasted from 1899 to 1902, involved bitter guerrilla fighting. The British won, but at great cost.

In 1910, the British united the Cape Colony and the former Boer republics into the Union of South Africa. The new constitution set up a government run by whites and laid the foundation for a system of complete racial segregation that would remain in force until 1993. (See page 326.)

# Imperialism in Africa to 1914

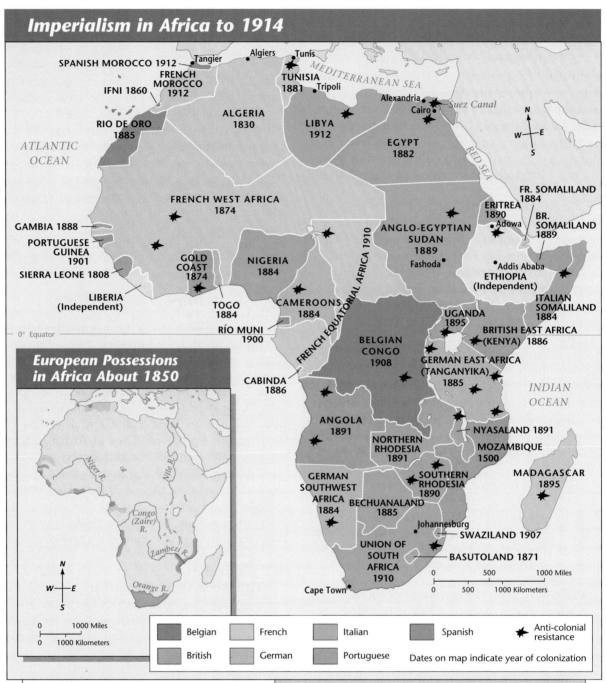

SPANISH MOROCCO 1912 — Tangier
Algiers
Tunis
FRENCH MOROCCO 1912
TUNISIA 1881
Tripoli
MEDITERRANEAN SEA
IFNI 1860
Alexandria
Cairo
Suez Canal
ALGERIA 1830
LIBYA 1912
RÍO DE ORO 1885
EGYPT 1882
RED SEA
ATLANTIC OCEAN
FR. SOMALILAND 1884
FRENCH WEST AFRICA 1874
ERITREA 1890
Adowa
BR. SOMALILAND 1889
GAMBIA 1888
ANGLO-EGYPTIAN SUDAN 1889
Fashoda
Addis Ababa
PORTUGUESE GUINEA 1901
SIERRA LEONE 1808
GOLD COAST 1874
NIGERIA 1884
ETHIOPIA (Independent)
ITALIAN SOMALILAND 1884
LIBERIA (Independent)
TOGO 1884
CAMEROONS 1884
UGANDA 1895
BRITISH EAST AFRICA (KENYA) 1886
RÍO MUNI 1900
FRENCH EQUATORIAL AFRICA 1910
0° Equator
CABINDA 1886
BELGIAN CONGO 1908
GERMAN EAST AFRICA (TANGANYIKA) 1885
INDIAN OCEAN
ANGOLA 1891
NYASALAND 1891
NORTHERN RHODESIA 1891
MOZAMBIQUE 1500
GERMAN SOUTHWEST AFRICA 1884
SOUTHERN RHODESIA 1890
MADAGASCAR 1895
BECHUANALAND 1885
Johannesburg
SWAZILAND 1907
UNION OF SOUTH AFRICA 1910
BASUTOLAND 1871
Cape Town
0    500    1000 Miles
0    500    1000 Kilometers

## European Possessions in Africa About 1850

Niger R.
Nile R.
Congo (Zaire) R.
Zambezi R.
Orange R.
N W E S
0    1000 Miles
0    1000 Kilometers

| | | | | |
|---|---|---|---|---|
| Belgian | French | Italian | Spanish | ★ Anti-colonial resistance |
| British | German | Portuguese | Dates on map indicate year of colonization | |

## GEOGRAPHY AND HISTORY

During the late 1800s, European countries took part in a scramble for Africa. They claimed control of nearly the whole continent by 1914. Only Ethiopia and Liberia remained independent.

1. **Location** On the main map, locate (a) Algeria, (b) Nigeria, (c) Angola, (d) Eritrea, (e) Cameroons, (f) Southern Rhodesia.

2. **Region** In which part of Africa were most of France's possessions located by 1914?

3. *Critical Thinking* **Making Inferences** How can you tell from the map that Africans did not willingly accept European domination?

**"Our place in the sun."** Other European powers joined the scramble, in part to bolster their national image, in part to further their economic growth and influence. The Portuguese carved out large colonies in Angola and Mozambique. Italy reached across the Mediterranean to occupy Libya and then pushed into the "horn" of Africa, at the southern end of the Red Sea. Italian efforts to conquer Ethiopia, however, ended in a stinging defeat.

The newly united German empire took lands in eastern and southwestern Africa. A German politician, trying to ease the worries of European rivals, explained, "We do not want to put anyone in the shade, but we also demand our place in the sun."

## Africans Fight Back

Europeans met armed resistance across the continent. The Algerians battled the French for years. Samori Touré fought French forces in West Africa, where he was building his own empire. The British battled the Zulus in southern Africa and the Asante in West Africa. When all seemed lost and their king exiled, the Asante put themselves under the command of their queen, Yaa Asantewaa. She led the fight against the British in the last Asante war.

Another woman who became a military leader was Nehanda, of the Shona in Zimbabwe. Although a clever tactician, Nehanda was captured and executed. However, her memory inspired later generations to fight for freedom.

In East Africa, the Germans fought wars against people like the Yao and Herero. Among some groups, resistance was weakened by an 1897 epidemic of rinderpest, a cattle disease that destroyed their herds. Still, they fought fiercely, especially in the Maji-Maji Rebellion of 1905. Only by using a scorched-earth policy that left thousands of local people to starve to death did the Germans triumph in the end.

**Ethiopia survives.** Successful resistance was mounted by Ethiopia. This ancient Christian kingdom had survived in the highlands of East Africa. But, like feudal Europe, it had been divided up among a number of rival princes who ruled their own domains.

In the late 1800s, a reforming ruler, Menelik II, began to modernize his country. He hired European experts to plan modern roads and bridges and set up a western school system. He imported the latest weapons and European officers to help train his army. Thus, when Italy invaded Ethiopia in 1896, Menelik was prepared. At the battle of Adowa (ah DUH wah), the Ethiopians smashed the Italian invaders. Ethiopia was the only African nation, aside from Liberia, to preserve its independence.

▲ *Emperor Menelik II*

**Impact.** During the age of imperialism, a western-educated African elite emerged. Some middle-class Africans admired western ways and rejected their own culture. Others valued their African traditions and condemned western societies that upheld liberty and equality for whites only. By the early 1900s, African leaders were forging nationalist movements to pursue self-determination and independence.

## SECTION 2 REVIEW

1. **Identify** (a) Sierra Leone, (b) Liberia, (c) David Livingstone, (d) Berlin Conference, (e) Congo Free State, (f) Boer War, (g) Nehanda, (h) Menelik II, (i) Adowa.
2. Describe one development in each region of Africa in the early 1800s.
3. How did Ethiopia maintain its independence?
4. Describe three examples of African resistance to European colonization.
5. *Critical Thinking* **Making Inferences** (a) Why do you think the Europeans held the Berlin Conference without inviting any Africans? (b) What might be the effect of this exclusion upon later African leaders?
6. *ACTIVITY* Imagine that you live in one of the African lands discussed in Section 2. Write a poem about the European colonization of your land.

# 3 European Challenges to the Muslim World

## Guide for Reading

- What problems did the Ottoman empire face?

- How did Egypt seek to modernize?

- Why did Iran become a focus of European interest?

- **Vocabulary** *genocide*

"Europe is a molehill," said Napoleon Bonaparte in 1797. He felt it offered too few chances for glory. "We must go to the East," he declared. "All great glory has been acquired there." Following through, in 1798 Napoleon invaded Egypt.

Napoleon's attack on Egypt opened a new era in European contacts with the Muslim world. It focused attention on the fading power of the Ottoman empire. By the early 1800s, European countries were nibbling at the fringes of the Muslim world. Before long, they would strike at its heartlands.

## Ferment in the Muslim World

The Muslim world extended from western Africa to Southeast Asia. During the 1500s, three giant Muslim empires ruled much of this world—the Mughals in India, the Ottomans in the Middle East, and the Safavids in Iran. By the 1700s, all three of these great powers were in decline.

The decay had many causes. Central governments had lost control over powerful groups such as landowning nobles, military elites, and urban craft guilds. Corruption was widespread. In some places, Muslim scholars and religious leaders were allied with the state. In other areas, they helped to foment discontent against the government.

**Islamic reform movements.** In the 1700s and early 1800s, reform movements sprang up across the Muslim world. Most stressed religious piety and obedience to strict rules of behavior. The Wahhabi movement in Arabia, for example, rejected the schools of theology and law that had emerged in the Ottoman empire. In their place, they wanted to recapture the purity and simplicity of Muhammad's original teachings. An Arab prince led the Wahhabis against Ottoman rule. Although the revolt was crushed, the Wahhabi movement survived. Its teachings are influential in the kingdom of Saudi Arabia today.

Islamic revivals rose in Africa, too. As you have read, Usman dan Fodio led the struggle to reform Muslim practices. In the Sudan, south of Egypt, Muhammad Ahmad announced that he was the Mahdi, the long-awaited savior of the faith. In the 1880s, the Mahdi and his followers fiercely resisted British expansion into the region. In modern Sudan, followers of the Mahdi still have great influence.

**European pressure.** Added to internal ferment and decay, the old Muslim empires faced western imperialism. Through a mix of diplomacy and military threat, European powers won treaties giving them favorable trading terms. They then demanded special rights for their citizens in the region and used excuses such as the need to protect those rights to intervene in local affairs. Sometimes, they took over an entire region.

## Challenges to the Ottoman Empire

At its height, the Ottoman empire had extended across the Middle East, North Africa, and parts of Eastern Europe. By 1800, however, it was facing serious challenges. Ambitious pashas, or provincial rulers, had increased their power. Economic problems and corruption also contributed to Ottoman decay.

**Nationalist revolts.** As ideas of nationalism spread from Western Europe, internal revolts posed constant challenges within the multi-ethnic Ottoman empire. Subject peoples in Eastern Europe, the Middle East, and North Africa threatened to break away. In the Balkans, Greeks, Serbs, Bulgarians, and Romanians gained their independence. (See pages 113–114.) Revolts against Ottoman rule also erupted in Arabia, Lebanon, and Armenia. The Ottomans suppressed these uprisings, but another valuable territory, Egypt, slipped out of their control.

**European involvement.** Britain, France, and Russia each sought to benefit from the slow crumbling of the Ottoman-held empire. France, which had seized Algeria in the 1830s, cast its eyes on other Ottoman-held territory. Russia schemed to gain control of the Turkish Straits— the Bosporus and Dardanelles—which would give it access to the Mediterranean Sea. Britain tried to thwart Russia's ambitions, which it saw as a threat to its own power in the Mediterranean and beyond it to India. And in 1898, the new German empire jumped onto the bandwagon, hoping to increase its influence in the region by building a Berlin-to-Baghdad railway.

During the Crimean War, which you read about in Chapter 6, the British and French had helped the Ottomans resist Russian expansion. By the late 1800s, however, France and Britain had extended their own influence over Ottoman lands.

## Efforts at Reform

Since the late 1700s, Ottoman rulers had seen the need for reform. Several sultans looked to the West for ideas. They reorganized the bureaucracy and system of tax collection. They built railroads, improved education, and hired European officers to train a modern military. Young men were sent to the West to study the new sciences and technology. Many returned home with western ideas about democracy and equality.

**Successes and failures.** The reforms brought better medical care and revitalized farming. These improvements, however, were a mixed blessing. Better living conditions resulted in a population explosion. The growing population increased pressure on the land, which led to unrest.

*A Crossroads of the World* Constantinople, at the crossroads of Europe and Asia, was the capital of the vast Ottoman empire. People from all over the world met and traded in the city. Here, Europeans mingle with Ottoman subjects from different parts of the empire on the banks of the Bosporus. In the background is Hagia Sophia, a giant Islamic mosque that was built originally as a Christian cathedral. **Diversity** How does the artist portray the diversity of the gathering?

The adoption of western ideas about government also increased tension. Many officials objected to changes that were inspired by a foreign culture. For their part, repressive sultans rejected reform and tried to rebuild the autocratic power enjoyed by earlier rulers.

**Young Turks.** In the 1890s, a group of liberals formed a movement called the Young Turks. They insisted that reform was the only way to save the empire. In 1908, the Young Turks overthrew the sultan. Before they could achieve their planned reforms, however, the Ottoman empire was plunged into the world war that erupted in 1914.

**Massacre of Armenians.** Meanwhile, Turkish nationalism had grown rapidly. In the 1890s, it took an ugly, intolerant course.

Traditionally, the Ottomans had let minority nationalities live in their own communities and practice their own religions. By the 1890s, however, nationalism was igniting new tensions, especially between Turks and minority peoples who sought their own states. These tensions triggered a brutal genocide of the Armenians, a Christian people concentrated in the mountainous eastern region of the empire. Genocide is a deliberate attempt to destroy an entire religious or ethnic group.

The Muslim Turks distrusted the Christian Armenians and accused them of supporting Russian plans against the Ottoman empire. When Armenians protested repressive Ottoman policies, the sultan had tens of thousands of them slaughtered. Survivors fled, many of them to the United States. Still, over the next 25 years, a million or more Armenians in the Ottoman empire were killed.

## Egypt Seeks to Modernize

Egypt in 1800 was a semi-independent Ottoman province. In the early 1800s, it made great strides toward reform. Its success was due to Muhammad Ali, an Albanian Muslim soldier who was appointed governor of Egypt in 1805.

**Muhammad Ali.** Muhammad Ali is sometimes called the "father of modern Egypt." He was an ambitious soldier who led an unsuccessful attempt to drive Napoleon from Egypt in 1799 and later conquered the neighboring lands of Arabia, Syria, and Sudan. To strengthen Egypt, he introduced a number of political and economic reforms.

Muhammad Ali improved tax collection, reorganized the landholding system, and backed large irrigation projects to increase farm output. By expanding cotton production and encouraging industry, he involved Egypt in world trade. Muhammad Ali also brought in western military experts to help him build a well-trained, modern army. Before he died in 1849, he had set Egypt on the road to becoming a complex industrialized society and made it a major Middle Eastern power.

**The Suez Canal.** Muhammad Ali's successors lacked his skills, and Egypt came increasingly under foreign control. In 1859, a French entrepreneur, Ferdinand de Lesseps, organized a company to build the Suez Canal. This 100-mile waterway links the Mediterranean and Red seas. (See the map on the next page.) Europeans hailed its opening in 1869 because it greatly shortened the sea route from Europe to South and East Asia. To Britain, especially, the canal was a "lifeline" to India.

In 1875, the ruler of Egypt found himself unable to repay loans he had contracted for the canal and other modernization projects. To pay his debts, he was forced to sell his shares in the canal. British prime minister Disraeli quickly bought them, giving Britain a controlling interest in the canal.

**A British protectorate.** Britain quickly expanded its influence over Egypt. When a nationalist revolt erupted in 1882, Britain made Egypt a protectorate. In theory, the governor of Egypt was an official of the Ottoman government. In fact, he followed policies dictated by Britain.

Under British influence, Egypt continued to modernize. At the same time, however, nationalist discontent simmered and flared into protests and riots well into the next century.

## Iran and the Western Powers

Like the Ottoman empire, Iran faced major challenges in the 1800s. The Qajar (kah JAHR) shahs, who ruled Iran from 1794 to 1925, exercised absolute power like the Safavids before them. Still, they did take steps to introduce reforms. The government improved finances and

# PARALLELS THROUGH TIME

## Shortcuts

Throughout history, people have taken advantage of new technology to create better and shorter ways of "getting there." The resulting works of engineering altered the face of the Earth, connecting oceans and continents and bringing people closer together.

**Linking Past and Present** Identify a structure that permits you to move easily from one place to another. How would your life be different without that structure?

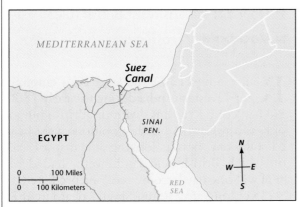

**PAST** The Suez Canal, which connects the Mediterranean and Red seas, opened in 1869. A French company headed by Ferdinand de Lesseps built the canal, but money and labor for the project came mainly from Egypt. The canal cut the distance between Europe and the East by thousands of miles and placed Egypt at the center of world trade routes. (See the map, left, and picture, below.)

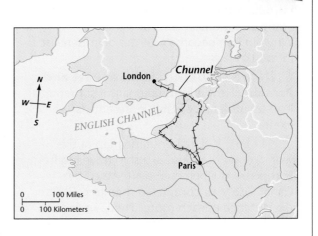

**PRESENT** The first plan to dig a tunnel under the English Channel was submitted to Napoleon Bonaparte in 1802. Almost 200 years later, work on the project finally began. The 31-mile tube, through which both trains and cars can travel, opened in 1994. (See the picture and map below.)

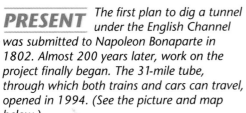

sponsored the building of telegraph lines and railroads. It even experimented with a liberal constitution.

Reform, however, did not save Iran from western imperialism. Both Russia and Britain battled for influence in the area. Russia wanted to protect its southern frontier and expand into Central Asia. Britain was concerned about protecting its interests in India.

For a time, each nation set up its own sphere of influence in Iran. Russia operated in the north and Britain in the south. The discovery of oil in the early 1900s upset the balance. Russia and Britain intrigued for control of Iranian oil fields. By 1914, Russia had sent troops into the region, giving it a dominant position.

Concessions, or economic rights granted to foreign powers, outraged Iranian nationalists. Nationalists included two very different groups. Some Iranians, especially the urban middle class, wanted to move swiftly to adopt western ways. Others, led by Muslim religious leaders, condemned the government and western influences. The religious leaders often spoke for the masses of the people who lived in rural poverty and resented government interference.

## SECTION 3 REVIEW

1. **Identify** (a) Mahdi, (b) Young Turks, (c) Muhammad Ali, (d) Suez Canal.
2. **Define** genocide.
3. Identify three causes of Ottoman decline.
4. (a) What reforms did Muhammad Ali introduce in Egypt? (b) How did Egypt come under British control?
5. Why did Iran become a center of imperialist interest?
6. *Critical Thinking* **Linking Past and Present** How might nationalism sometimes lead to intolerance? Give a present-day example .
7. *ACTIVITY* On an outline map of the world, draw the route of a ship traveling from Europe to Asia before and after the Suez Canal. Use your completed map to calculate the distance of each route. Then, write a sentence explaining why Europeans welcomed the canal.

# 4 The British Take Over India

## Guide for Reading

- What were the causes and results of the Sepoy Rebellion?
- What effects did British rule have on India?
- How did Indians resist British rule?
- **Vocabulary** *cash crop*

Ranjit Singh ruled the large Sikh empire in northwestern India during the early 1800s. He had cordial dealings with the British but saw only too well where their ambitions were headed. One day, he was looking at a map of India on which British-held lands were shaded red. "All will one day become red!" he predicted.

Not long after Ranjit Singh's death in 1839, the British conquered the Sikh empire. They added its 100,000 square miles to their steadily growing lands. As Singh had forecast, India was falling under British control, and the map of the subcontinent was almost entirely red.

## *The East India Company*

In the early 1600s, the British East India Company obtained trading rights on the fringe of the Mughal empire. As Mughal power declined, the company expanded its influence. By the mid-1800s, the Bristish East India Company controlled three fifths of India.

**A divided land.** How were the British able to conquer such a vast territory? The answer lies in the land's diversity. Even when Mughal power was at its height, India was home to many people and cultures. As Mughal power crumbled, India fragmented. Indians speaking dozens of different languages and with different traditions were not able to unite against the newcomers.

The British took advantage of this ferment by playing off rival princes against each other. Where diplomacy or intrigue did not work, their superior weapons overpowered local rulers.

**British policies.** The East India Company's main goal in India was to make money, and leading officials often got very rich. At the same time, the company did work to improve roads, preserve peace, and reduce banditry.

By the early 1800s, British officials introduced western education and legal procedures. Missionaries tried to convert Indians to Christianity, which they felt was far superior to Indian religions. The British also pressed for social change. They worked to end slavery and the caste system and to improve the position of women within the family. One law outlawed sati, a Hindu custom practiced mainly by the upper classes. It called for a widow to join her husband in death by throwing herself on his funeral fire.

## The Sepoy Rebellion

Indians from all social classes resented British interference and domination. Well-educated Indians were shut out of high posts. In line with mercantilist policy, the British kept Indians from engaging in large-scale manufacturing, which hurt the business class. Peasants felt the impact of the British-imposed economic policies and were angry at laws that violated ancient customs and traditions.

**Unpopular moves.** In the 1850s, the East India Company took several unpopular steps. First, it required sepoys—Indian troops—to serve anywhere, either in India or overseas. For high-caste Hindus, however, overseas travel was an offense against their religion. The second cause of discontent was a new law that allowed Hindu widows to remarry. Hindus viewed both moves as a Christian conspiracy to undermine their beliefs.

The final insult came in 1857, when the British issued new rifles to the sepoys. Troops were told to bite off the tips of cartridges before loading them into the rifles. The cartridges, however, were greased with animal fat—either from cows, which Hindus considered sacred, or from pigs, which were forbidden to Muslims. When the troops refused the order to "load rifles," they were dismissed without pay and sent home in disgrace.

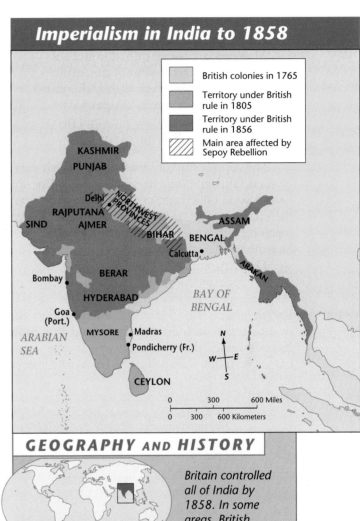

## Imperialism in India to 1858

British colonies in 1765

Territory under British rule in 1805

Territory under British rule in 1856

Main area affected by Sepoy Rebellion

KASHMIR
PUNJAB
Delhi
RAJPUTANA
NORTHWEST PROVINCES
SIND
AJMER
ASSAM
BIHAR
BENGAL
Calcutta
ARAKAN
Bombay
BERAR
HYDERABAD
BAY OF BENGAL
Goa (Port.)
ARABIAN SEA
MYSORE
Madras
Pondicherry (Fr.)
CEYLON

N S E W

0   300   600 Miles
0   300   600 Kilometers

### GEOGRAPHY AND HISTORY

Britain controlled all of India by 1858. In some areas, British officials ruled directly. In others, they governed through local Indian rulers.

1. **Location** On the map, locate (a) Punjab, (b) Delhi, (c) Hyderabad, (d) Madras.
2. **Region** Which region was most greatly affected by the Sepoy Rebellion?
3. *Critical Thinking* **Synthesizing Information** Kashmir is a mountainous area. How might this help explain why it was hard for Britain to gain control of that area?

**On to Delhi.** Angry sepoys rose up against their British officers. The Sepoy Rebellion swept across northern and central India. Several sepoy regiments marched off to Delhi, the old Mughal capital. There, they hailed the last Mughal ruler as their leader. Other sepoys issued a document calling on both Hindus and Muslims for their support:

> "It is well known to all, that in this age the people of [India], both Hindus and Muslims, are being ruined under the tyranny and oppression of the infidel and treacherous English. It is therefore the duty of all the wealthy people of India . . . to stake their lives and property for the well being of the public."

The sepoys brutally massacred British men, women, and children in some places. But the British soon rallied and crushed the revolt. They then took terrible revenge for their earlier losses, torching villages and slaughtering thousands of unarmed Indians.

**The aftermath.** The Sepoy Rebellion left a bitter legacy of fear, hatred, and mistrust on both sides. It also brought major changes in British policy. In 1858, Parliament ended the rule of the East India Company and put India directly under the British crown. It sent more troops to India, taxing Indians to pay the cost of these occupying forces. While it slowed the "reforms" that had angered Hindus and Muslims, it continued to develop India for its own economic benefit. ■

## The "Brightest Jewel"

After 1858, Parliament set up a system of colonial rule in India. A British viceroy in India governed in the name of the queen, and British officials held the top positions in the civil service and army. Indians filled most other jobs. With their cooperation, the British made India the "brightest jewel" in the crown of their empire.

British policies were designed to fit India into the overall British economy. At the same time, British officials felt they were helping India to modernize. In their terms, modernizing meant adopting not only western technology but also western culture.

**An unequal partnership.** Britain saw India both as a market and as a source of raw ma-

**The Sepoy Rebellion** *Resentment of foreign rule exploded in the Sepoy Rebellion. The uprising revealed deep-seated hostility toward British exploitation as well as anger at western attempts to change Indian society. Horrifying atrocities occurred on both sides before the uprising was suppressed.* **Diversity** *How was the Sepoy Rebellion a clash of cultures?*

terials. To this end, the British built roads and an impressive railroad network. Improved transportation let the British sell their factory-made goods across the subcontinent and carry Indian cotton, jute, wheat, and coal to coastal ports for transport to factories in England. New methods of communication, such as the telegraph, also gave Britain better control of India.

After the Suez Canal opened in 1869, British trade with India soared. But it remained an unequal partnership, favoring the British. The British flooded India with inexpensive, machine-made textiles, ruining India's once-prosperous hand-weaving industry.

Britain also transformed Indian agriculture. It encouraged nomadic herders to settle into farming and pushed farmers to grow cash crops, such as cotton and jute, that could be sold on the world market. Clearing new farmlands led to massive deforestation, or cutting of trees, and other environmental destruction.

**Population and famine.** The British introduced medical improvements. At the same time, new farming methods increased food production. The result was rapid population growth. The rising numbers, however, put a strain on the food supply, especially as farmland was turned over to growing cash crops instead of food. In the late 1800s, terrible famines swept India. Railroads could carry food to the stricken areas, but overall, millions of Indian peasants sank deeply into poverty.

**Benefits of British rule.** On the positive side, British rule brought peace and order to the countryside. The British revised the legal system to promote justice for Indians regardless of class.

The upper classes benefited from some British policies. They sent their sons to British schools, where they were trained for posts in the

GLOBAL CONNECTIONS

Economic developments in Great Britain had far-reaching effects in India. During the Civil War in the United States, Britain lost its source of cotton in the American South. To replace this important resource, Britain pressured Indian farmers to shift from growing food to growing cotton. This shift heightened the effects of a drought and led to widespread famine in India.

civil service and military. Indian landowners and princes, who still ruled their own territories, grew rich from exporting cash crops. Railroads helped Indians move around the country, while the telegraph and postal system let them communicate more easily than ever before. Greater contact helped bridge regional differences and opened the way for Indians to develop a sense of national unity.

## Indians and British: Viewing Two Cultures

During the age of imperialism, Indians and British developed different views of each other's culture. Educated Indians were divided in their opinion of the British. Some were impressed by British power and technology and urged India to follow a western model of progress. These mostly upper class Indians learned English and adopted western ways. Other Indians felt that the answer to change lay with their own Hindu or Muslim cultures.

**Ram Mohun Roy.** In the early 1800s, Ram Mohun Roy combined both views. A great scholar, he knew Sanskrit, Persian, and Arabic classics, as well as English, Greek, and Latin works. Roy felt that India could learn from the West. At the same time, he wanted to revitalize and reform traditional Indian culture.

Roy condemned some traditions, such as rigid caste distinctions, child marriage, sati, and purdah, the isolation of women in separate quarters. But he also set up learned societies that helped revive pride in Indian culture. Because of his influence on later leaders, he is often hailed today as the founder of Indian nationalism.

**Western attitudes.** The British disagreed among themselves about India. A few admired Indian theology and philosophy. As western scholars translated Indian classics, they acquired respect for India's ancient heritage. Western writers and philosophers borrowed ideas from Hinduism and Buddhism.

On the other hand, most British people knew little about Indian achievements and dismissed Indian culture with contempt. In an essay on whether Indians should be taught in English or their own languages, the English historian Thomas Macaulay wrote that "a single

**Indian Miniature Painting** Like India itself, Indian art blends the traditions of different cultures. The art of miniature painting was carried to Mughal India from Persia in the 1500s, part of the flow of ideas and customs within the Muslim world. The art form evolved in India, where painters often used the small paintings to tell a story. After the arrival of Europeans, Indian artists began to adopt western styles of perspective as well. This miniature painting, from about 1880, shows British colonel James Todd riding an elephant. **Art and Literature** Based on the painting, what was Colonel Todd's position in society? Explain.

shelf of a good European library is worth the whole native literature of India and Arabia."

## Growing Nationalism

During the years of British rule, a class of western-educated Indians emerged. In the view of Macauley and others, this elite class would bolster British power:

66We must at present do our best to form a class who may be interpreters between us and the millions whom we govern; a class of persons, Indian in blood and color, but English in taste, in opinions, in morals, and in intellect.99

As it turned out, exposure to European ideas had the opposite effect. By the late 1800s, western-educated Indians were spearheading a nationalist movement. Schooled in western ideals such as democracy and equality, they dreamed of ending imperial rule.

**Indian National Congress.** In 1885, nationalist leaders organized the Indian National Congress, which became known as the Congress party. Its members were mostly professionals and business leaders who believed in peaceful protest to gain their ends. They called for greater democracy, which they felt would bring more power to Indians like themselves. The Indian National Congress looked forward to eventual self-rule but supported western-style modernization.

Other Indian nationalists, however, took a more radical, anti-British stand. They wanted to restore Indian languages and Hindu and Muslim cultures.

**Muslim League.** At first, Muslims and Hindus worked together for self-rule. In time, however, Muslims grew to resent Hindu domination of the Congress party. They also worried that a Hindu-run government would oppress Muslims. In 1906, Muslims formed the Muslim League to pursue their own goals. Soon, they were talking of a separate Muslim state.

**Looking ahead.** By the early 1900s, protests and resistance to British rule increased. More and more Indians demanded not simply self-rule but complete independence. Their goal finally would be achieved in 1947, but only after a long struggle against the British and a nightmare of bloody conflict between Hindus and Muslims.

## SECTION 4 REVIEW

1. **Identify** (a) East India Company, (b) Sepoy Rebellion, (c) Ram Mohun Roy, (d) Indian National Congress, (e) Muslim League.
2. **Define** cash crop.
3. (a) What were the immediate causes of the Sepoy Rebellion? (b) What were the long-term causes?
4. (a) What were the goals of the East India Company in India? (b) What policies did the British government pursue in India after 1858?
5. How did British rule lead to growing Indian nationalism?
6. *Critical Thinking* **Applying Information** Review the definition of *racism* on page 155. Then, explain how the following statement by a British general serving in India in the mid-1800s reflects racism: "However well-educated and clever a native may be, and however brave he may prove himself, I believe that no rank we can bestow on him would cause him to be considered an equal of the British officer."
7. *ACTIVITY* Use the information in this chapter to create an illustrated time line of British rule in India.

# 5 China and the New Imperialism

## Guide for Reading

- What rights did westerners seek in China?
- How did internal problems weaken China?
- What were the goals of Chinese reformers?
- **Vocabulary** *balance of trade, trade deficit, indemnity, extraterritoriality*

By the 1830s, British merchant ships were arriving in China, loaded with opium to sell to the Chinese. Lin Zexu (LIHN DZEH SHOO), a Chinese official, complained bitterly to Britain's Queen Victoria. "I have heard that smoking opium is strictly forbidden in your country," he wrote. "Why do you let this evil drug be sent to harm people in other countries?"

For centuries, the Chinese had strictly controlled foreign trade, ensuring that it was in China's favor. By the 1800s, however, western nations were using their growing power to weave a web of influence over East Asia just as they were doing in the rest of the world.

## The Trade Issue

Chinese rulers placed strict limits on foreign traders. European merchants were restricted to a small area around the city of Guangzhou in southern China. China sold silk, porcelain, and tea to the merchants in exchange for gold and silver. Under this arrangement, China enjoyed a favorable **balance of trade,** exporting more than it imported. Westerners, on the other hand, had a **trade deficit** with China, buying more from the Chinese than they sold them. In 1793, the British requested increased trading rights. The emperor Qianlong refused, saying that there was nothing in the West that China needed.

By the late 1700s, two developments were underway that would transform China's relations with the western world. First, China

*A Shameful War* The Opium War began when Chinese officials tried to keep British ships from bringing the addictive drug into China. Here, a British warship sinks Chinese junks during the war. ***Economics and Technology*** *How does the picture convey Britain's superior technology in warfare?*

entered a period of decline. Second, the Industrial Revolution created a need for expanded markets for European goods. At the same time, it gave the West the military power to back its demands for such markets.

**The Opium War.** During the late 1700s, British merchants discovered that they could make huge profits by trading opium grown in India for Chinese tea, which was popular in Britain. Soon, many Chinese had become addicted to the drug. Silver flowed out of China in payment for the drug, disrupting the economy.

The Chinese government outlawed opium and executed Chinese drug dealers. They called on Britain to stop the trade. The British refused, insisting on the right of free trade.

In 1839, Chinese warships clashed with British merchants. The incident triggered what became known as the Opium War. During the war, Britain flexed its new industrial might. Its gunboats, equipped with the latest in firepower, bombarded Chinese coastal and river ports. With outdated weapons and fighting methods, the Chinese were easily defeated.

**Unequal treaties.** In 1842, Britain made China accept the Treaty of Nanjing. It was the first of a series of "unequal treaties" that forced China to give up rights to western powers. France and the United States soon signed similar treaties with China.

The treaty gave Britain a huge **indemnity,** or payment for losses in the war. The British also gained the island of Hong Kong, near Guangzhou. (See the map on page 236.) China had to open five ports to foreign trade and grant British citizens in China **extraterritoriality,** the right to live under their own laws and be tried in their own courts. Finally, the treaty included a "most favored nation clause." It said that if the Chinese granted rights to another nation, Britain would automatically receive the same rights.

The Opium War set a pattern for later encounters between China and the West. During the mid-1800s, western powers squeezed China to win additional rights, such as opening more ports to trade and letting Christian missionaries preach in China.

## Internal Pressures

By the 1800s, the Qing dynasty was in decline. Irrigation systems and canals were poorly maintained, leading to massive flooding of the Huang He Valley and its rich farmlands. The population explosion that had begun a century earlier created a terrible hardship for China's peasants. An extravagant court, widespread official corruption, and tax evasion by the rich added to the peasants' burden. Even the honored civil service system was rocked by bribery and cheating scandals.

**The Taiping Rebellion.** As poverty and misery increased, peasants rebelled. The Taiping Rebellion, which lasted from 1850 to 1864, was probably the most devastating peasant revolt in history. The leader, Hong Xiuquan (howng shyoo CHWAHN), was a village schoolteacher who had failed the civil service exams four times. Inspired by religious visions, he set himself up as a revolutionary prophet. He wanted to establish a "Heavenly Kingdom of Great Peace"—the Taiping (tī PIHNG).

Hong was influenced by the teachings of Christian missionaries, and he was disappointed when westerners refused to help his cause. Hong endorsed radical social ideas, including land reform, community ownership of property, equality of women and men, and strict morality. Above all, he called for an end to the hated Qing dynasty.

The Taiping rebels won control of large parts of China. They held out for 14 years. In the end, the government relied on regional governors and generals to crush the rebellion.

**Effects.** The Taiping Rebellion almost toppled the Qing dynasty. It is estimated to have caused the deaths of between 20 million and 30 million Chinese. The lower Yangzi basin, the heartland of the revolt, was largely destroyed. The Qing government survived, but it had to share power with regional commanders who rebuilt the region and their power base.

During the rebellion, Europeans kept up pressure on China. Russia seized lands along the Amur River in northern China. It then built the great port of Vladivostok on the Pacific coast.

## Reform Efforts

By the mid-1800s, educated Chinese were divided over the need to adopt western ways. Most scholar-officials saw no reason to foster new industries, since China's wealth—and taxes—came from land. Although Chinese merchants were allowed to do business, they were not seen as a source of economic prosperity.

Scholar-officials also disapproved of the ideas of western missionaries, whose emphasis on individual choice challenged the Confucian order. They saw western technology as dangerous, too, because it threatened Confucian ways that had served China successfully for so long.

The imperial court was a center of conservative opposition. By the late 1800s, the empress Ci Xi (tsee SHYEE) had gained power. A strong-willed ruler, she surrounded herself with advisers who were deeply committed to Confucian traditions.

**Self-strengthening movement.** Some Chinese wanted to adapt western ideas. But others worried that technology such as railroads and steamships would bring unwelcome changes. "One thing will lead to another," they said, "and we will not be able to refuse them." ( ★ See *Skills for Success,* page 238.)

In the 1860s, reformers launched what became known as the "self-strengthening movement." They imported western technology, setting up factories to make modern weapons. They developed shipyards, railroads, mining, and light industry. The Chinese translated not

**Empress Ci Xi** *The Empress Ci Xi ruled China from 1862 until her death in 1908. Through most of her reign, she blocked efforts to modernize the nation, accusing reformers of being traitors and having them jailed, exiled, or even executed.* **Political and Social Systems** *Why did conservative Chinese reject reform?*

only western works of science but also works by Europeans on government and the economy. The movement made limited progress, however, because the government did not rally behind it. Also, while China was undertaking a few selected reforms, the western powers—and nearby Japan—were moving ahead rapidly.

**War with Japan.** The island nation of Japan modernized rapidly after 1868. (See Chapter 9.) It then joined the western imperialists in the competition for global empire.

In 1894, Japanese pressure on China led to war. It ended in disaster for China, with Japan gaining the island of Taiwan off the coast of China. (See the map on page 236.) When the two powers met at the peace table, there was a telling difference. Japanese officials were dressed in western clothes, the Chinese in traditional robes.

**Spheres of influence.** The crushing defeat revealed China's weakness. Western powers moved swiftly to carve out spheres of influence along the Chinese coast. The British took the Yangzi Valley. The French acquired the territory near Indochina. Germany got the Shandong

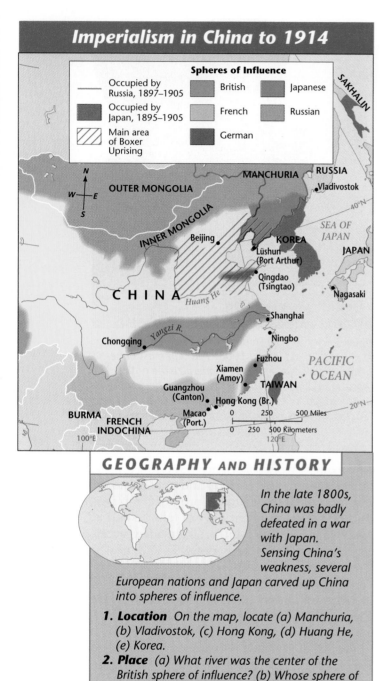

## Imperialism in China to 1914

**Spheres of Influence**

— Occupied by Russia, 1897–1905

■ Occupied by Japan, 1895–1905

▨ Main area of Boxer Uprising

■ British
■ French
■ German
■ Japanese
■ Russian

OUTER MONGOLIA
INNER MONGOLIA
MANCHURIA
RUSSIA
Vladivostok
SAKHALIN
40°N
Beijing
SEA OF JAPAN
KOREA
JAPAN
Lüshun (Port Arthur)
Qingdao (Tsingtao)
Nagasaki
CHINA
Huang He
Shanghai
Chongqing
Yangzi R.
Ningbo
Fuzhou
PACIFIC OCEAN
Xiamen (Amoy)
TAIWAN
Guangzhou (Canton)
Hong Kong (Br.)
BURMA
Macao (Port.)
FRENCH INDOCHINA
0    250    500 Miles
0    250    500 Kilometers
100°E
120°E
20°N

### GEOGRAPHY AND HISTORY

In the late 1800s, China was badly defeated in a war with Japan. Sensing China's weakness, several European nations and Japan carved up China into spheres of influence.

1. **Location** On the map, locate (a) Manchuria, (b) Vladivostok, (c) Hong Kong, (d) Huang He, (e) Korea.
2. **Place** (a) What river was the center of the British sphere of influence? (b) Whose sphere of influence included Lüshun (Port Arthur)?
3. **Critical Thinking** *Recognizing Causes and Effects* Use information on the map to list causes of the growth of nationalism in China.

Peninsula in northern China. Russia received the Liaotung Peninsula (which the European powers had forced Japan to return to China), also in northern China.

The United States, a longtime trader with the Chinese, did not take part in the carving up

of China. It feared that European powers might shut out American merchants. A few years later, in 1899, it called for a policy that would keep Chinese trade open to everyone on an equal basis. The imperial powers more or less accepted the idea of an Open Door Policy, as it came to be called. No one, however, consulted the Chinese about the policy.

**Hundred Days of Reform.** Defeated by Japan and humiliated by westerners, the Chinese looked for a scapegoat. Reformers blamed conservative officials for being "soundly asleep atop a pile of kindling." They argued that Confucius himself was a reformer and that China could not look to a golden age in the past but must modernize as Japan had.

In 1898, a young emperor, Guang Xu (gwawng SHYOO), launched the Hundred Days of Reform. New laws set out to modernize the civil service exams, streamline government, and encourage new industries. Reforms affected schools, the military, and the bureaucracy. Conservatives at court soon rallied. The emperor was imprisoned, and the aging empress Ci Xi reasserted control. Reformers fled for their lives.

### The Empire Crumbles

As the century ended, China was in turmoil. Anger against foreigners was growing. While the Chinese welcomed some western ideas, they resented Christian missionaries who belittled Chinese thinkers like Confucius. The presence of foreign troops was another source of discontent. Protected by extraterritoriality, foreigners could ignore Chinese laws and live in their own protected communities. In their parks, signs announced "Dogs and Chinese Not Allowed."

**Boxer Uprising.** Antiforeign feeling finally exploded in the Boxer Uprising. In 1899, a group of Chinese had formed a secret society, the Righteous Harmonious Fists. Westerners watching them train in the martial arts dubbed them Boxers. Their goal was to drive out the "foreign devils" who were polluting the land with their un-Chinese ways, strange buildings, machines, and telegraph lines. One group, called the Red Lantern, was made up primarily of young women. They carried red handkerchiefs and lanterns and were believed to have supernatural powers to stop foreign bullets.

**Father of Modern China** *Sun Yixian combined the ideas of Confucius with western ideas about religion, democracy, and socialism. His Three Principles of the People—nationalism, democracy, and economic security—became the guiding ideas of the Chinese republic.* **Global Interaction** *How did the thinking of Sun Yixian represent a global exchange of ideas?*

In 1900, the Boxers attacked foreign communities across China. In response, the western powers and Japan organized a multinational force. It crushed the Boxers and rescued foreigners besieged in Beijing. The empress Ci Xi had at first supported the Boxers but reversed her policy as they retreated.

**Aftermath.** China once again had to make concessions to foreigners. The defeat, however, forced even Chinese conservatives to support westernization. In a rush of reforms, China admitted women to schools and stressed science and mathematics in place of Confucian thought. More students were sent abroad to study.

China expanded economically, as well. Mining, shipping, railroads, banking, and exports of silk, tobacco, soybeans, and other commodities grew. With foreign capital, small-scale Chinese industry developed. A Chinese business class emerged, and a new urban working class began to press for rights as western workers had done.

**Three Principles of the People.** Although the Boxer Uprising failed, the flames of Chinese nationalism spread. Reformers wanted to strengthen China's government. By the early 1900s, they had introduced a constitutional monarchy. Some reformers called for a republic.

A passionate spokesman for a Chinese republic was Sun Yixian* (soon yee SHYAHN). Sun had studied and traveled in the West. In the early 1900s, he organized the Revolutionary Alliance. His goal was to rebuild China on "Three Principles of the People." The first principle was

nationalism, freeing China from foreign domination. The second was democracy, or representative government. The third was "livelihood," or economic security for all Chinese.

**Birth of a republic.** When Ci Xi died in 1908 and a two-year-old boy inherited the throne, China slipped into chaos. In 1911, uprisings in the provinces swiftly spread. Peasants, workers, students, local warlords, and even court politicians helped topple the dynasty and end China's 2,000-year-old monarchy.

Sun Yixian hurried home from a trip to the United States. In December 1911, he was named president of the new Chinese Republic. From the outset, the republic faced overwhelming problems. For the next 37 years, China was almost constantly at war with itself or fighting off foreign invasion.

## SECTION 5 REVIEW

1. **Identify** (a) Opium War, (b) Treaty of Nanjing, (c) Taiping Rebellion, (d) Ci Xi, (e) Open Door Policy, (f) Hundred Days of Reform, (g) Boxer Uprising, (h) Sun Yixian.
2. **Define** (a) balance of trade, (b) trade deficit, (c) indemnity, (d) extraterritoriality.
3. How did western powers gain rights in China?
4. What internal problems did the Qing dynasty face?
5. (a) What were the goals of Chinese reformers? (b) Why did they have a hard time putting their reforms into action?
6. *Critical Thinking* **Making Inferences** How was Britain's push into China linked to British imperialism in India?
7. *ACTIVITY* Organize a debate between a British merchant and a Chinese government official about the opium trade in China.

---

*In earlier history books, this name appears as Sun Yat-sen.

# CHAPTER REVIEW AND SKILLS FOR SUCCESS

## CHAPTER REVIEW

### REVIEWING VOCABULARY

Review the vocabulary words in this chapter. Then, use *six* of these words to create a crossword puzzle. Exchange puzzles with a classmate. Complete the puzzles and then check each other's answers.

### REVIEWING FACTS

1. List the four main motives of the new imperialists.

2. How did the Berlin Conference of 1884 affect Africa?

3. How did Ethiopia resist European colonization?

4. What is the Suez Canal? How did it affect world trade?

5. What caused the Sepoy Rebellion?

6. Name the two main reasons why China's policy of limiting trade with foreigners ended after the 1700s.

7. What was the goal of the Boxer Uprising?

## SKILLS FOR SUCCESS    IDENTIFYING ALTERNATIVES

To make choices about the future, leaders have to identify alternatives and project consequences. In the mid-1800s, for example, the Chinese were divided over a proposal to invite westerners to teach mathematics and astronomy. The excerpts below present two responses. The first was by Woren, the tutor to the emperor. The second was by the Zongli Yamen, a government board. Read the excerpts and follow the steps below.

1. **Identify the problem.** What is the issue that both excerpts addressed?

2. **Identify alternative solutions.** (a) What solution did Woren propose? (b) What solution did the Zongli Yamen propose?

3. **Evaluate the arguments.** Examine the arguments used in presenting an alternative for "loaded" language or bias. (a) What phrase did Woren use to describe westerners? What does this phrase tell about his attitude toward westerners? (b) What impression did the Zongli Yamen hope to convey by characterizing their plan as a "long-term policy"?

4. **Project the consequences.** Every alternative will, if put into action, produce consequences—negative, positive, or both. (a) According to Woren, what would be the effect of western mathematics on China? (b) What did the Zongli Yamen believe would result from adopting western technology and learning?

*Woren*
66If these subjects [astronomy and mathematics] are going to be taught by westerners as regular studies, the damage will be great. . . . If we seek trifling arts and respect barbarians as teachers, . . . all that can be accomplished is the training of mathematicians. . . . [I have] never heard of anyone who could use mathematics to raise the nation from a state of decline or to strengthen it in time of weakness.99

*The Zongli Yamen*
66While merely to get along with [westerners] for the time being is all right, it is not possible in this way to protect ourselves for . . . decades to come. Therefore [we] have pondered a long-term policy. . . . Proposals to learn . . . [western languages and science] represent nothing other than a struggle for self-strengthening. Woren considers our action a hindrance. . . . If he says [using righteousness as a shield] could accomplish diplomatic negotiations and be sufficient to control the life of our enemies, your ministers do not . . . believe it.99

Source: Ssu-yü and John K. Fairbank, *China's Response to the West* (Cambridge, MA: Harvard University Press, 1954).

## REVIEWING CHAPTER THEMES

Review the "Focus On" questions at the start of this chapter. Then select *three* of those questions and answer them, using information from the chapter.

## CRITICAL THINKING

1. **Recognizing Bias** Western imperialists viewed European culture as "modern" and the cultures of the rest of the world as "backward." How do you think nonwesterners might have responded to that view?

2. **Linking Past and Present** The opening of the Suez Canal in 1869 transformed world trade. Why do you think the canal might be less important today?

3. **Defending a Position** Do you think the British were right to try to outlaw traditions such as the caste system and sati? Defend your position.

## ANALYZING PRIMARY SOURCES

Use the quotation by Frederick Lugard on page 214 to answer the following questions.

1. According to Lugard, what gave Europeans the right to Africa?

2. What benefits could Europeans gain from Africa?

3. Do you agree that the need for a resource entitles a people to own that resource? Explain.

## FOR YOUR PORTFOLIO

**CREATING A HISTORICAL ATLAS** As a class, create a historical atlas covering the years 1800 to 1914. Begin by deciding what maps to include. Use your textbook, atlases, encyclopedias, and other resources to prepare the maps. Remember to include standard map devices such as a scale, directional arrow, and key. Place the completed atlas in a resource center where other students can use it.

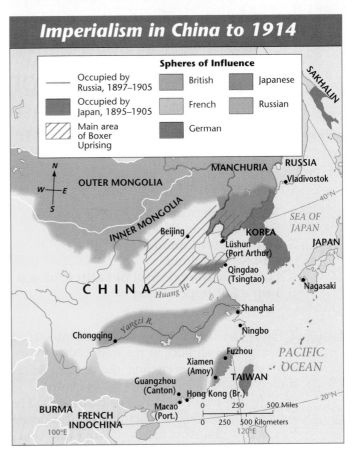

**Imperialism in China to 1914**

Spheres of Influence

- ——— Occupied by Russia, 1897–1905
- Occupied by Japan, 1895–1905
- Main area of Boxer Uprising
- British
- French
- German
- Japanese
- Russian

## ANALYZING MAPS

Use the map to answer the following questions.

1. What part of mainland Asia did Japan occupy as of 1905?

2. Describe the position of the French sphere of influence in relation to that of Britain.

3. Which nations' spheres of influence were affected by the Boxer Uprising?

## INTERNET ACTIVITY

**EXPLORING HISTORICAL EFFECTS** Use the Internet to research the influence of Victorian England on world culture, politics, or trade. Then write a brief essay explaining why you think the United States does or does not have a similar influence on the world today.

# New Global Patterns

## (1800–1914)

Siam—the land we now call Thailand—faced danger on all sides in the mid-1800s. Western powers were encircling the ancient kingdom, vying with one another for its control.

The burden of meeting this challenge fell to King Mongkut. Before inheriting the throne, he had been a Buddhist monk. During that time, he had studied foreign languages and read widely on modern science and mathematics. As king, he thus had a greater understanding of the West than many other Asian rulers. In a long letter to the Siamese ambassador in Paris, he mused on the problems facing their land:

    66Being, as we now are, surrounded on two or three sides by powerful nations, what can a small nation like us do? Supposing we were to discover a gold mine in our country, from which we could obtain [much] gold, enough to buy a hundred warships. Even with this, we would still be unable to fight them, because we would have to buy those very same warships and all the armaments from them.99

Besides, Mongkut added, western powers could refuse to sell arms to Siam, and the Siamese could not yet make the weapons themselves.

Mongkut's solution was to modernize his country. From 1851 to 1868, he cautiously introduced political, economic, and social reforms. Later, his son, Chulalongkorn, picked up the pace. While both had to grant some rights to western powers, Siam remained an independent kingdom during the Age of Imperialism.

In Chapter 8, you saw how Europeans competed for empire in Africa and parts of Asia. This chapter focuses on two related themes. First, how did people in different parts of the globe respond to western imperialism? Second, how did imperialism affect the cultures of these people?

**FOCUS ON** these themes as you read:

- **Continuity and Change**
  How did western domination threaten traditional cultures around the world?

- **Economics and Technology**
  How did imperialism create a new western-dominated world economy?

- **Political and Social Systems**
  Why did Latin American nations have a hard time achieving political stability?

- **Diversity**
  How did responses to imperialism differ in various parts of the world?

- **Geography and History**
  How did the migration of English-speaking people to Canada, Australia, and New Zealand shape their emergence as independent countries?

## TIME AND PLACE

*Influence of the West* Japan was one of the few nations to escape western domination. It did so by copying the West, transforming itself into a modern industrial power set on its own imperialist path. This painting shows the gaslights at Japan's first industrial fair, in 1877.
***Global Interaction*** What evidence of western influence can you find in the painting?

## HUMANITIES LINK

*Art History* Maori wood carving (page 255).
*Literature* In this chapter, you will encounter passages from the following works of literature: Fukuzawa Yukichi, *Autobiography* (pages 244 and 245); Rudyard Kipling, "The Ballad of East and West" (page 262).

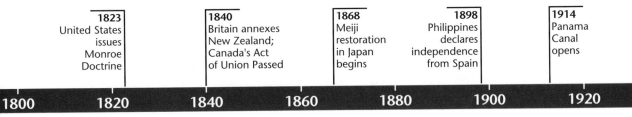

**1823**
United States issues Monroe Doctrine

**1840**
Britain annexes New Zealand; Canada's Act of Union Passed

**1868**
Meiji restoration in Japan begins

**1898**
Philippines declares independence from Spain

**1914**
Panama Canal opens

1800    1820    1840    1860    1880    1900    1920

# 1 Japan Modernizes

## Guide for Reading

- Why did Japan open its doors to western influences?

- Why was Japan able to modernize rapidly?

- How did Japan become an imperialist power?

- **Vocabulary** *zaibatsu, homogeneous society*

In 1853, the United States displayed its new military might, sending a naval force to make Japan open its ports to trade. Japanese leaders debated how to respond. Some resisted giving up their 215-year-old policy of seclusion. "We should . . . observe the ways of our ancestors, which is the safest and most dignified policy for the country," they said.

Other Japanese disagreed. Lord Ii, for example, pointed out:

66[Foreign states] have invented the steamship . . . and introduced radical changes in the art of navigation. They have also built up their armies . . . and are possessed of weapons of great power and precision. . . . If we cling to our [outdated] systems, heaven only knows what disaster may befall our Empire.99

In the end, Japan chose to abandon its centuries of isolation. As a defense against western imperialism, it decided to learn from the West. It swiftly transformed itself into a modern industrial power and then set out on its own imperialist path.

## Strains in Tokugawa Japan

The Tokugawa shoguns, who had gained power in 1600, imposed centralized feudalism, once again closed Japan to foreigners, and forbade Japanese to travel overseas. Their only window on the world was through Nagasaki, where the Dutch were allowed very limited trade.

For 215 years, Japan developed in near isolation. During that time, the economy expanded, especially internal commerce. But economic growth brought changes that put severe strains on the country.

Like China, Japan drifted into decline in the 1800s. Shoguns were no longer strong leaders, and corruption was common. Discontent simmered throughout Japanese society.

Daimyo suffered financial hardship because their wealth was in land. In a commercial economy, money was needed. Daimyo also had the heavy expense of maintaining households in both Edo and their own domains. Every other year, they traveled with their servants from one site to the other, a costly undertaking.

Lesser samurai were unhappy because they were no longer fighters. Many were government bureaucrats. Even though they were noble, they lacked the money to live as well as urban merchants.

For their part, merchants resented their place at the bottom of the social ladder. No matter how rich they were, they had no political power. Prestigious positions went only to nobles. Peasants, meanwhile, suffered under heavy taxes. Some fled to the cities. Others rose in rebellion.

The government responded by trying to revive old ways, emphasizing farming over commerce and extolling the virtues of simple moral values. Efforts at reform had scant success, which left many groups with little loyalty to the old system.

## Opening Up Japan

While the shogun faced troubles at home, disturbing news reached him from abroad. With alarm, he listened to reports of how the British had defeated China in the Opium War and how the imperialists had forced China to sign the unequal treaties. Surely, it would not be long before western powers began seeking trading rights in Japan.

**Foreign pressure.** Then, in July 1853, a fleet of well-armed American ships commanded by Commodore Matthew Perry sailed into Tokyo Bay. Perry had a letter from the President of the United States. It demanded that Japan open its ports to trade.

**Traditional Japan** *Before the 1850s, Japanese society developed largely in isolation from the western world. In this traditional Japanese painting, a woman inspects a piece of fine cloth.* **Global Interaction** *How do you think isolation might have affected Japanese attitudes toward foreigners?*

The shogun's advisers debated what to do. As Lord Ii noted, Japan did not have the ability to defend itself against the powerful United States Navy. In the Treaty of Kanagawa in 1854, the shogun agreed to open two Japanese ports to American ships, though not for trade.

The United States soon won trading and other rights, including the right of extraterritoriality and a "most favored nation" clause. (See page 234.) Britain, France, and Russia demanded and won similar rights. Like the Chinese, the Japanese deeply resented the humiliating terms of the unequal treaties. Some bitterly criticized the shogun for not taking a strong stand against the foreigners.

**Crisis and revolt.** Foreign pressure deepened the social and economic unrest. As the crisis worsened, many young, reform-minded samurai rallied around the emperor, long regarded as a figurehead. "Honor the emperor," "Expel the barbarian," were their cries.

In 1867, discontented daimyo and samurai led a revolt that unseated the shogun and "restored" the emperor to power. He moved from Kyoto, the old imperial capital, to the shogun's palace in Edo, which was renamed Tokyo, or "eastern capital."

**Meiji restoration.** The young emperor, just 15 years old, began a long reign. This period from 1868 to 1912, known as the Meiji (MAY jee) restoration, was a turning point in Japanese history.

Meiji means "enlightened rule." The Meiji reformers, who ruled in the emperor's name, were determined to strengthen Japan against the West. Their goal was summarized in their motto, "A rich country, a strong military."

The new leaders set out to study western ways, adapt them to Japanese needs, and eventually beat westerners at their own game. In 1871, members of the Meiji government traveled abroad to learn about western governments, economies, technology, and customs. The government brought western experts to Japan and sent young samurai to study in Europe and the United States.

## Fukuzawa Yukichi Travels Abroad

An early Japanese visitor to the West was Fukuzawa Yukichi. As a student, he had learned first Dutch and then English. In 1860, even before the Meiji restoration, he sailed on the first Japanese ship to cross the Pacific and visit California. Later, he traveled in Europe. In his *Autobiography,* he set out to explain western culture to the Japanese and Japanese culture to the West.

**Pride in Japan.** As the *Kanrin-Maru* set sail for the United States, Fukuzawa was filled with pride. The Japanese had seen their first steamship in 1853 when Commodore Perry arrived. Two years later, they began studying modern navigation. And in 1860, a Japanese steamship was crossing the Pacific. Fukuzawa marveled:

> ❝This means that about seven years after the first sight of a steamship, after only about five years of practice, the Japanese made a trans-Pacific crossing without help from foreign experts. I think we can without undue pride boast before the world of this courage and skill. . . . Even Peter the Great of Russia, who went to Holland to study navigation . . . could not have equalled this feat of the Japanese.❞

**Exploring a new world.** After 37 stormy days at sea, the *Kanrin-Maru* reached San Francisco. There, the Japanese visitors saw many unfamiliar sights. They were stunned to find the hotel floor covered with "valuable carpets that in Japan only the more wealthy could buy . . . at so much a square inch to make purses." Even more shocking, "Upon this costly fabric walked our hosts wearing shoes with which they had come in from the streets!" (At home, the Japanese, who highly value cleanliness, remove their shoes before entering a house.)

Among Fukuzawa's more confusing experiences were drinks served with "strange fragments floating in them." He told how "Some of the party swallowed these floating particles; others expelled them suddenly; others bravely chewed them." Upon closer inspection they

**A Japanese Student of Western Ways** *Fukuzawa Yukichi was an early student of western ways. Among other things, he became a strong supporter of equality for women. "Society should give women the same rank as men," he wrote. Here, Fukuzawa poses with an American girl during his visit to the United States.* **Global Interaction** *Why did the Meiji government send people abroad to study western ways?*

learned that the particles were ice. "Hardly did we expect to find *ice* in the warm spring weather," they said.

Among many bewildering American customs was a dancing party. "To our dismay, we could not make out what they were doing. The ladies and gentlemen seemed to be hopping about the room together. As funny as it was, we knew it would be rude to laugh, and we controlled our expressions with difficulty as the dancing went on."

**Modern ways.** The Japanese examined telegraphs and visited a sugar refinery. Fukuzawa, however, was more interested in American life than in industry, which he had read about in books. He was stunned at the "enormous waste of iron everywhere":

66In garbage piles, on the seashores—everywhere—I found lying old oil tins, empty cans, and broken tools. This was remarkable to us, for in [Tokyo] after a fire, there would appear a swarm of people looking for nails in the ashes.99

Later, on a visit to Europe, Fukuzawa had his first view of democratic politics. In London, he tried to figure out how Parliament worked. He had read about "bands of men called political parties . . . who were always fighting against each other in the government." But he found it hard to understand how they could be "fighting in peacetime" and how "enemies in the House" could share a table and friendly talk in a restaurant. "It took me a long time, and some tedious thinking, before I could gather a general notion of these separate mysterious facts."

Individuals like Fukuzawa introduced the Japanese to the West and westerners to Japan. In a few generations, their efforts would help Japan become a global power. ■

## Reforms Under the Meiji

The Meiji reformers faced an enormous task. They were committed to replacing the rigid old feudal order with a new political and social system and to building a modern economy. Change did not come easily. It involved setbacks and confusion. In the end, however, Japan adapted foreign ideas with amazing success.

**Government.** The reformers wanted to create a strong central government, equal to those of western powers. After studying various European governments, they adapted the German model. In 1889, the emperor issued the Meiji constitution. It set forth the principle that all citizens were equal before the law. Like the German system, however, it gave the emperor autocratic power. A legislature, or Diet, was formed, made up of one elected house and one house appointed by the emperor. But its powers were strictly limited. Suffrage, too, was limited.

Japan then established a western-style bureaucracy with separate departments to supervise finance, the army, the navy, and education. To strengthen the military, it turned to western technology and ended the special privilege of samurai. In the past, samurai alone were warriors. In modern Japan, as in the modern West, all men were subject to military service.

**The economy.** Meiji leaders made the economy a major priority. They encouraged Japan's business class to adopt western methods. The government set up a banking system, built railroads, improved ports, and organized a telegraph and postal system.

*A Textile Workshop* Japanese manufacturing grew rapidly in the late 1800s. As in Europe and the United States, women played a key role in Japan's industrial revolution. In this 1897 print, women make clothing in a Japanese workshop. ***Economics and Technology*** Which steps in the process seem to have been influenced by western technology?

To get industries started, the government typically built factories and then sold them to wealthy business families who developed them further. With such support, business dynasties like the Kawasaki family soon ruled over industrial empires that rivaled those of the Rockefellers in the United States or the Krupps in Germany. These powerful banking and industrial families were known as zaibatsu (ZĪ BAHT SOO).

By the 1890s, industry was booming. With modern machines, silk manufacturing soared. Shipyards, copper and coal mining, and steelmaking also helped make Japan an industrial powerhouse. As in other industrial countries, the population grew rapidly, and many peasants flocked to the growing cities for work.

**Social change.** The constitution, as you have seen, ended legal distinctions between classes, thus freeing people to build the nation. The government set up schools and a university. It hired westerners to teach the new generation modern technology.

Despite the reforms, class distinctions survived in Japan as they did in the West. Also, although literacy increased and some women gained an education, women in general were still assigned a secondary role in society.

The reform of the Japanese family system, and women's position in it, became the topic of major debates in the 1870s. Reformers wanted women to become full partners in the process of nation building and to learn skills that would allow them to live on their own. While the government agreed to some increases in education for women, it dealt harshly with other attempts at change. It passed laws reestablishing the most oppressive model of the family. It took away earlier political and legal rights that women had won. After 1898, Japanese women were forbidden any political participation and legally were lumped together with minors.

**Amazing success.** During the Meiji period, Japan modernized with amazing speed. Its success was due to a number of causes. It was a homogeneous society—that is, it had a common culture and language that gave it a strong sense of identity. Economic growth during Tokugawa times had set Japan on the road to development. Also, the Japanese had experience in learning from foreigners. Centuries before, they had selectively borrowed and adapted ideas from China.

Then, too, like other people faced with western imperialism, the Japanese were determined to resist foreign rule. In fact, in the 1890s, Japan was strong enough to force western powers to revise the unequal treaties. By then, it was already competing with the West and acquiring its own overseas empire.

## Competition for Empire

As with western industrial powers, Japan's economic needs fed its imperialist desires. A small island nation, Japan lacked many basic resources, including coal, essential for its industrial growth. Yet, spurred by nationalism and a strong ambition to equal the West, Japan built an empire. With its modern army and navy, it maneuvered for power in East Asia.

In 1894, rivalry between Japan and China over Korea led to war. Although China had far greater resources, Japan had benefited from modernization. To the surprise of China and the West, Japan won easily. It used its victory to gain treaty ports in China and rights to rule the island of Taiwan.

Ten years later, Japan successfully challenged Russia, its rival for power in Korea and Manchuria. (See the map on page 236.) During the Russo-Japanese War, Japan's armies defeated Russian troops in Manchuria, and its navy destroyed almost the entire Russian fleet. For the first time in modern history, an Asian power humbled a European nation. In the 1905 Treaty of Portsmouth, Japan gained control of Korea as well as rights in parts of Manchuria. This foothold on the mainland would fuel its ambitions in East Asia.

## Korea: A Focus of Competition

Imperialist rivalries put the spotlight on Korea. Located at a crossroads of East Asia, it was a focus of competition among Russia, China, and Japan.

**"A shrimp among whales."** Although Korea had long been influenced by its powerful Chinese neighbor, it had its own traditions and government. Like China and Japan, it had shut its doors to foreigners in early modern times. It

***Expanding in Asia*** *Japan tested its new strength in wars against China and Russia. Here, Japanese troops occupy Seoul, Korea, during the Russo-Japanese War.* **Geography and History** *Why was Korea a focus of competition?*

ever before, but most of it went to feed the Japanese.

The Japanese were as unpopular in Korea as western imperialists were elsewhere. They imposed harsh rule on their colony and deliberately set out to erase the Korean language and identity. Repression bred resentment. And resentment, in turn, nourished a Korean nationalist movement.

Nine years after annexation, a nonviolent protest against the Japanese began on March 1, 1919, and soon spread throughout Korea. The Japanese crushed the uprising and massacred many Koreans. The March First Movement became a rallying symbol for Korean nationalists.

**Looking ahead.** The Koreans would have to wait many years for freedom. By the early 1900s, Japan was the strongest power in Asia. In competition with western nations, it continued to expand in East Asia during the years ahead. In time, Japanese ambitions to control a sphere of influence in the Pacific would put it on a collision course with several western powers, especially Britain and the United States.

did, however, maintain relations with China and sometimes with Japan.

By the 1800s, Korea faced growing pressure from outsiders. As Chinese power declined, Russia expanded into East Asia. Then, as Japan industrialized, it too eyed Korea. Once again, Korea saw itself as "a shrimp among whales."

In 1876, Japan used its superior power to force Korea to open its ports to Japanese trade. Faced with similar demands from western powers, the Hermit Kingdom had to accept humiliating unequal treaties.

As Japan extended its influence in Korea, it came into conflict with China, which still saw Korea as a tributary state. After defeating China and then Russia, Japan made Korea a protectorate. In 1910, it annexed Korea outright, ending Korean independence and absorbing the kingdom into the Japanese empire.

**Japanese rule.** Japan ruled Korea for 35 years. Like western imperialists, the Japanese set out to modernize their possession. They built factories, railroads, and communications systems in Korea. Development, however, generally benefited the colonial power, Japan. Under Japanese rule, Koreans produced more rice than

## SECTION 1 REVIEW

1. **Identify** (a) Matthew Perry, (b) Treaty of Kanagawa, (c) Meiji restoration, (d) Russo-Japanese War.
2. **Define** (a) zaibatsu, (b) homogeneous society.
3. (a) What problems did Tokugawa Japan face in the early 1800s? (b) Why did Japan end 200 years of seclusion?
4. (a) List three ways in which Japan modernized. (b) Explain how each helped strengthen Japan so that it could resist western pressure.
5. Why did Japan want to build an overseas empire?
6. *Critical Thinking* **Predicting Consequences** What do you think might have happened if Japan had not rushed to modernize in the late 1800s? Give reasons for your answer.
7. *ACTIVITY* Write a dialogue between two advisers to the shogun giving arguments for and against opening up Japan to the West in the mid-1800s.

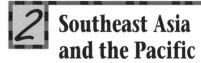

# 2 Southeast Asia and the Pacific

## Guide for Reading

- What effect did imperialist rivalries have on Southeast Asia?

- Why was Thailand able to remain independent?

- How did the United States expand in the Pacific?

A Vietnamese official, Phan Thanh Gian, faced a dilemma in 1867. The French were threatening to invade. As a patriot, Phan Thanh Gian wanted to resist. But as a devoted follower of Confucius, he was obliged "to live in obedience to reason." And based on the facts, he concluded that the only reasonable course was to surrender:

> 66 The French have immense warships, filled with soldiers and armed with huge cannons. No one can resist them. They go where they want, the strongest [walls] fall before them. 99

Phan Thanh Gian made his choice with a heavy heart. By avoiding a useless war that would hurt his people, he became a traitor to his king. For that decision, he wrote, "I deserve death."

Leaders throughout Southeast Asia faced the same dilemma during the Age of Imperialism. As they had in Africa, western industrial powers gobbled up the region in their relentless race for raw materials, new markets, and Christian converts.

## Colonizing Southeast Asia

Southeast Asia commanded the sea lanes between India and China and had long been influenced by both civilizations. In the 1500s and 1600s, European merchants gained footholds in the region, but most of the Southeast Asian peoples remained independent. When the Industrial Revolution set off the Age of Imperial-

ism in the 1800s, the situation changed. Westerners played off local rivalries and used their modern armies and technology to colonize much of Southeast Asia.

**Dutch colonies.** During the 1600s, the Dutch East India Company gained control of the fabled riches of the Moluccas, also called the Spice Islands. They then reached out to dominate the rest of Indonesia. The Dutch expected their Southeast Asian colonies to produce profitable crops of coffee and indigo as well as spices.

**British inroads.** In the early 1800s, rulers of Burma (present-day Myanmar) clashed with the British, who were expanding eastward from India. At first, the Burmese misjudged British strength. In several wars, they suffered disastrous defeats. By the 1880s, Britain had annexed Burma as part of its Indian empire. The Burmese, however, constantly resisted British rule.

The British also pushed south through the Malay Peninsula. The bustling port of Singapore, on the sea route between the Indian Ocean and the China Sea, grew up at the southern tip of Malaya. Soon, rubber and tin from Malaya along with profits from Asian trade were flowing through Singapore to enrich Britain.

**French Indochina.** The French meanwhile were building an empire on the Southeast Asian mainland. In the early 1800s, French missionaries began winning converts in what is today Vietnam. The region had long been influenced by Confucian traditions. Vietnamese officials tried to suppress Christianity by killing converts and missionary priests.

As with Burma and the British, the Vietnamese misjudged European power. In the 1860s, the French invaded and seized a chunk of Vietnam. Over the next decades, they added more lands, eventually seizing all of Vietnam, Laos, and Cambodia. The French and other westerners referred to these holdings as French Indochina.

**European rule.** By the 1890s, Europeans controlled most of Southeast Asia. They introduced modern technology and expanded commerce and industry. They set up new enterprises to mine tin and harvest rubber, brought in new crops of corn and cassava, and built harbors and railroads. But as you will read later in this chap-

ter, these changes benefited Europeans far more than the people of Southeast Asia.

Many Chinese migrated to Southeast Asia to escape hardship and turmoil at home and to benefit from growing economic opportunities. Despite local resentment, these communities of "overseas" Chinese formed vital networks in trade, banking, and other economic activities.

## Thailand Survives

Sandwiched between British-ruled Burma and French Indochina lay the kingdom of Siam. As you have read at the beginning of this chapter, Siam escaped becoming a European colony partly because its rulers did not underestimate western power and avoided incidents that might provoke invasion.

Although King Mongkut had to accept some unequal treaties, he set Siam on the road to modernization. He and his son, Chulalongkorn, who ruled from 1868 to 1910, reformed government, modernized the army, and hired western experts to train Thais in the new technology. They abolished slavery and gave women some choice in marriage. Thai students traveled abroad and spread western ways when they returned home. As Siam modernized, Chulalongkorn bargained to remove the unequal treaties.

In the end, both Britain and France saw the advantage of making Thailand a buffer, or neutral zone, between them. In the early 1900s, they guaranteed its independence. But then, to stop other imperialist powers from pushing into Siam, each set up its own sphere of influence there.

## Imperialism in Southeast Asia and the Pacific

**Possessions**
- British
- French
- Portuguese
- Dutch
- German
- United States

CHINA
TAIWAN (Japanese)
BURMA
LAOS
VIETNAM
INDOCHINA
SIAM
CAMBODIA
SOUTH CHINA SEA
PHILIPPINES
MARIANA IS. (Ger.)
GUAM (U.S.)
PACIFIC OCEAN
CAROLINE IS. (Ger.)
NORTH BORNEO
MALAYA
SARAWAK
SINGAPORE (Br.)
SUMATRA
BORNEO
CELEBES
JAVA
INDIAN OCEAN
TIMOR
NEW GUINEA
Equator
AUSTRALIA

0   600   1200 Miles
0   600   1200 Kilometers
100°E   110°E   130°E   140°E
30°N   20°N   10°N   10°S

### GEOGRAPHY AND HISTORY

The lure of spices first brought Europeans to Southeast Asia. Then the Industrial Revolution spurred European traders to search for raw materials to fuel the new industries. In Southeast Asia, they found such products as tin and rubber.

1. **Location** On the map, locate (a) New Guinea, (b) Siam, (c) Singapore, (d) Philippines (e) Indochina.
2. **Region** Which European countries claimed territory on the mainland?
3. **Critical Thinking** **Synthesizing information** Review the discussion of earlier encounters between Europeans and the peoples of Southeast Asia, on pages 32–33. Based on that information, why do you think the Dutch controlled the largest area in Southeast Asia around 1914?

## Imperialism and Nationalism in the Philippines

In the 1500s, Spain had seized the Philippines and extended its rule over the islands. Catholic missionaries spread Christianity among the Filipinos, and the Catholic Church gained enormous power and wealth. Many Filipinos accused the Church of abusing its position. By the late 1800s, their anger had fueled strong resistance to Spanish rule.

The United States became involved in the fate of the Philippines almost by accident. In 1898, war broke out between Spain and the United States over Cuba's independence from Spain. (See page 261.) During the Spanish-American War, American battleships destroyed the Spanish fleet which was stationed in the Philippines. Seizing the moment, Filipino leaders declared their independence from Spain. Rebel soldiers threw their support into the fight against Spanish troops.

In return for their help, the Filipino rebels had expected the Americans to recognize their independence. The peace settlement with Spain, however, placed the Philippines under American control.

Bitterly disappointed, Filipino nationalists renewed their struggle. From 1899 to 1901, Filipinos led by Emilio Aguinaldo (ah gee NAHL doh) battled American forces. Thousands of Americans and hundreds of thousands of Filipinos died. In the end, the Americans crushed the rebellion. The United States set out to modernize the Philippines, promising Filipinos self-rule some time in the future.

## Western Powers in the Pacific

In the 1800s, the industrial powers began to take an interest in the islands of the Pacific.* At first, American, French, and British whaling and sealing ships looked for bases to take on supplies. Missionaries, too, moved into the Pacific region. As in Africa, they opened the way for political involvement.

**Samoa.** In 1878, the United States secured an "unequal treaty" from Samoa, gaining rights such as extraterritoriality and a naval sta-

---

*The thousands of islands splashed across the Pacific are known as Oceania. Besides Australia and New Zealand, Oceania includes three regions: Melanesia, Micronesia, and Polynesia. (See the map on page 646.)

tion. Other nations gained similar agreements. As their rivalry increased, the United States, Germany, and Britain agreed to a triple protectorate over Samoa.

**Hawaii.** From the mid-1800s, American sugar growers pressed for power in Hawaii. When the Hawaiian queen Liliuokalani (lee lee oo oh kah LAH nee) tried to reduce foreign influence, American planters overthrew her in 1893. They then asked the United States to annex Hawaii, which it did in 1898. Supporters of annexation argued that if the United States did not take Hawaii, Britain or Japan might do so.

**Looking ahead.** By 1900, the United States, Britain, France, and Germany had claimed nearly every island in the Pacific. Japan, too, wanted a share of the region. Eventually, it would gain German possessions in the Pacific, setting the stage for a growing rivalry with the United States.

▲ Queen Liliuokalani

## SECTION 2 REVIEW

1. **Identify** (a) French Indochina, (b) Chulalongkorn, (c) Emilio Aguinaldo, (d) Queen Liliuokalani.
2. (a) Which European nations set up colonies in Southeast Asia? (b) What products did they take from these colonies?
3. What steps did Thailand take to preserve its independence?
4. How did the United States acquire each of the following: (a) Philippines, (b) Samoa, (c) Hawaii?
5. *Critical Thinking* **Comparing** Compare the partition of Southeast Asia to the partition of Africa during the Age of Imperialism. (a) How was it similar? (b) How was it different?
6. *ACTIVITY* Create a map and time line showing colonization of Southeast Asia and the Pacific during the Age of Imperialism.

# 3 Self-Rule for Canada, Australia, and New Zealand

## Guide for Reading

■ How did Canada achieve self-rule?

■ How did Australia and New Zealand emerge as independent nations?

■ What effects did colonization have on the Aborigines and Maoris?

■ **Vocabulary** *indigenous, penal colony*

The pattern of imperialism in the British colonies of Australia and New Zealand differed from that in other parts of the world. The **indigenous** (ihn DIHJ uh nuhs), or original, inhabitants of these regions were relatively few in number, and white settlers quickly subdued and replaced them. Still, the process of "replacement" was as deadly as it had been when Europeans settled the Americas some 200 years earlier.

These two English-speaking colonies, as well as Canada, won independence faster and with greater ease than England's territories in Africa or Asia. One reason was that nonwestern peoples had no cultural roots in western-style government. However, western racial attitudes also played a part. Imperialist nations like Britain felt that whites could govern themselves. Nonwhites in places like India were thought to be incapable of shouldering such responsibility.

## *The Canadian Pattern*

Canada's first European rulers, you will recall, were the French. When France lost Canada to Britain in 1763, thousands of French-speaking settlers remained there. After the American Revolution, an estimated 30,000 or more colonists who had remained loyal to Britain fled to Canada. Unlike the French-speaking Catholics, the newcomers were English-speaking and Protestant. Rivalries between the two groups have been an ongoing theme in Canada's history ever since.

*A Blending of Cultures* Canadian culture blends English, French, and Native American traditions. This is the symbol of the "Mounties," the Canadian mounted police, formed in 1873. The crown stands for the British monarchy, while the buffalo and maple leaves represent the Americas. **Diversity** How does the Mounties' symbol reflect Canada's French heritage?

Native Americans formed another strand of the Canadian heritage. In the 1790s, various Native American people still lived in eastern Canada. Others remained largely undisturbed by white settlers in the west and north.

**The two Canadas.** To ease ethnic tensions, Britain passed the Canada Act in 1791. It created two provinces: English-speaking Upper Canada (now Ontario) and French-speaking Lower Canada (now Quebec). Each had its own laws, legislature, and royal governor. French traditions and the Catholic Church were protected in Lower Canada, while English traditions and laws guided Upper Canada.

During the early 1800s, unrest grew in both colonies. The people of Upper Canada resented the power held by a small British elite. In Lower Canada, too, people felt that British officials ignored their needs. In 1837, discontent flared into rebellion in both Upper and Lower Canada. "Put down the villains who oppress and enslave our country," cried William Lyon Mackenzie, a leader of the Upper Canada revolt.

**The Durham Report.** The British had learned a lesson from the American Revolution. While they hurried to put down the disorder, they sent an able politician, Lord Durham, to study the causes of the unrest. In 1839, the Durham Report called for the two Canadas to be reunited and given control over their own affairs.

In 1840, Parliament passed the Act of Union, a major step toward self-government. It gave Canada an elected legislature to determine domestic policies. Britain kept control of foreign policy and trade.

**Dominion of Canada.** Like the United States, Canada expanded westward in the 1800s. Two Canadians, John Macdonald and George Etienne Cartier, urged confederation, or unification, of all Canada's provinces. Like many Canadians, Macdonald and Cartier feared that the United States might try to dominate Canada. A strong union, they felt, would strengthen Canada against American ambitions and help it develop economically.

Britain finally agreed. In 1867, it passed the British North America Act of 1867, creating the Dominion of Canada. It united four provinces in a self-governing nation. Six additional provinces joined the union in later years.

As a dominion, Canada had its own parliament, modeled on Britain's. By 1900 it had some control over its own foreign policy. Still, although self-governing, Canada maintained close ties with the British monarchy.

**Expansion.** John Macdonald, Canada's first prime minister, encouraged expansion across the continent. To unite the far-flung regions of Canada, he called for a transcontinental railroad. In 1885, the Canadian Pacific Railway opened, linking eastern and western Canada. Wherever the railroad went, settlers followed. It moved people and products, such as timber and manufactured goods, across the country.

As in the United States, westward expansion destroyed the way of life of Native Americans in Canada. Most were forced to sign treaties giving up their lands. Some resisted. Louis Riel led a revolt of the Métis, people of mixed Native American and European descent. Many were French-speaking Catholics who accused the government of stealing their land and trying to destroy their language and religion. Govern-

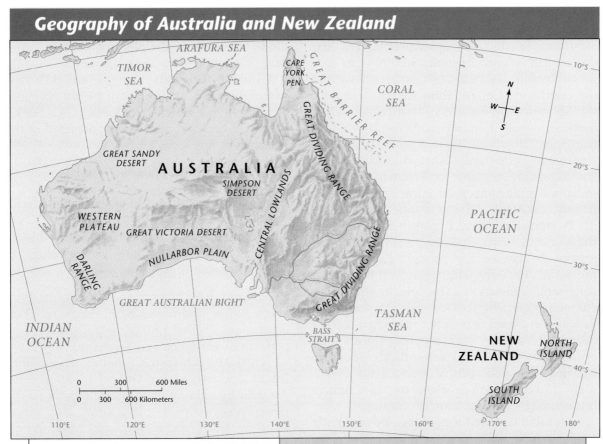

## Geography of Australia and New Zealand

ment troops put down the uprising and executed Riel.

**Immigration.** In the late 1800s and early 1900s, immigrants flooded into Canada from Europe and Asia. Newcomers from Germany, Italy, Poland, Russia, Ukraine, China, and Japan enriched Canada economically and culturally.

By 1914, Canada was a flourishing nation. Still, two issues plagued Canada. First, French-speaking Canadians desperately tried to preserve their separate heritage, making it hard for Canadians to create a single national identity. Second, the United States exerted a powerful economic and cultural influence that threatened to domi-

nate its neighbor to the north. Both issues have continued to affect Canada to the present day. (See Chapter 16.)

### Europeans in Australia

The Dutch in the 1600s were the first Europeans to reach Australia—the world's smallest continent. In 1770, Captain James Cook claimed Australia for Britain. For a time, however, it remained too distant to attract European settlers.

**The first settlers.** Like most regions claimed by imperialist powers, Australia had long been inhabited by other people. The first settlers had reached Australia 50,000 years ago, probably from Southeast Asia, and spread across the continent. Cut off from the larger world, the Aborigines, as Europeans later called them,* lived in small hunting and food-gathering bands, much as their Stone Age ancestors had. Aborigine groups spoke as many as 250 distinct languages. When white settlers arrived in Australia, the indigenous population suffered disastrously, just as it had in the Americas.

**A penal colony.** Events halfway around the world in North America and Britain ended Australia's isolation and brought Europeans to the island continent. During the 1700s, Britain had sent convicts to its North American colonies, especially to Georgia. The American Revolution closed that outlet just when the Industrial Revolution was disrupting British society. Prisons in London and other cities were jammed with poor people arrested for crimes such as stealing food or goods to pawn, agitating against the government, or murder.

To fulfill the need for prisons, Britain made Australia into a penal colony, a place to send people convicted of crimes. The first ships, carrying about 700 convicts, arrived in Botany Bay, Australia, in 1788. The men,

▼ Convicts arriving at an Australian penal colony

women, and children who survived the grueling eight-month voyage faced more hardships on shore. Many were city dwellers with no farming skills.

---

*Aborigine* was a word used by Europeans to denote the earliest people to live in a place. Today, many Australian Aborigines call themselves Kooris.

Under the brutal discipline of soldiers, work gangs cleared land for the settlement.

Among these first arrivals was Matthew Everingham, who at the age of 14 had been given a seven-year sentence for stealing two books. Despite illness and beatings, he dreamed of the future:

> 66 I have now two years and seven months to remain a convict and then I am at liberty to act as a free-born Englishman ought to. . . . I am yet but young, only 19. If my health is spared I shall not be one jot the worse for being transported. 99

Everingham later married another convict, Elizabeth Rimes, and remained in Australia. Their descendants carved out farms and some prospered in their rugged new homeland.

**Into the Outback.** In the early 1800s, Britain encouraged free citizens to emigrate to Australia by offering them land and tools. As the newcomers occupied coastal lands, they thrust aside or killed the Aborigines. After settlers found that sheep herding was suited to the land and climate, a prosperous wool industry grew up in Australia.

In 1851, gold was found in eastern Australia. The resulting gold rush brought a population boom. Many gold hunters stayed on to become ranchers and farmers. They pushed into the rugged interior known as the Outback. There, too, they displaced the Aborigines and carved out huge sheep ranches and wheat farms. By the late 1800s, Australia had won a place in a growing world economy.

**Achieving self-government.** Like Canada, Australia was made up of separate colonies scattered around the continent. During the Age of Imperialism, Britain worried about interfer-

**GLOBAL CONNECTIONS**

European nations often punished people convicted of crimes by sending them to far-off places. Russia sent convicts to Siberia. France created a penal colony on Devil's Island, off the coast of South America. Before they hit upon Australia, the British tried to make West Africa a dumping ground for "undesirable" citizens.

ence from other powers. To counter this threat and to boost development, it responded to Australian demands for self-rule. In 1901, Britain helped the colonies unite into the independent Commonwealth of Australia. The new country kept its ties to Britain by recognizing the British monarch as its head of state.

The Australian constitution drew on both British and American models. Like the United States Constitution, it set up a federal system that limited the power of the central government. Its Parliament has a Senate and House of Representatives, but its executive is a prime minister chosen by the majority party in Parliament. Unlike Britain and the United States, Australia quickly granted women the right to vote. It also was the first nation to introduce the secret ballot.

## New Zealand

Far to the southeast of Australia lies New Zealand. In 1769, Captain Cook claimed its islands for Britain. Missionaries landed there in 1814 to convert the local people, the Maoris, to Christianity.

**Maori struggles.** Unlike Australia, where the Aborigines were spread thinly across a large continent, the Maoris were concentrated in a smaller area. They were descended from seafaring people who had reached New Zealand from Polynesia in the 1200s. Unlike the nomadic Aborigines, the Maoris were settled farmers. They were also a warlike people, determined to defend their land.

Missionaries were followed by white settlers, attracted by the mild climate and good soil. They introduced sheep and cattle and were soon exporting wool, mutton, and beef. In 1840,

*Maori Wood Carving* Wood carving was a highly respected art among the Maoris. Carved figures served a religious function, affirming a community's ties to its gods and ancestors. The head was given special prominence because the Maoris believed that the soul resided in the head. The intricate curving surface designs imitate the tattoos worn by Maori people. This figure stood outside a Maori meeting house. **Art and Literature** Compare this carving with the Mayan clay figurine on page 14. How did Maori wood carvings and the Mayan figurine serve different functions? How did Maori wood carvings and Byzantine icons serve a similar function?

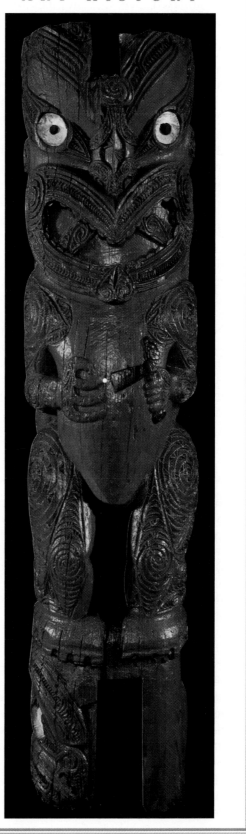

Britain annexed New Zealand. The move was designed in part to keep out other imperialist powers.

As colonists poured in, they took over more and more of the land, leading to fierce wars with the Maoris. Many Maoris died in the struggle. Still more perished from disease, alcoholism, and other misfortunes that came with European colonization.

By the 1870s, resistance crumbled. The Maori population had fallen drastically, from 250,000 to less than 50,000. Only in recent years has the Maori population started to grow once more.

**Self-government.** Like settlers in Australia and Canada, white New Zealanders sought self-rule. In 1907, they won independence, with their own parliament, prime minister, and elected legislature. They, too, preserved close ties to the British empire.

New Zealand pioneered in several areas of democratic government. In 1893, it became the first nation to give suffrage to women. Later, it was in the forefront of other social reforms, passing laws to guarantee old-age pensions and a minimum wage for all workers.

## SECTION 3 REVIEW

1. **Identify** (a) Upper Canada, (b) Lower Canada, (c) John Macdonald, (d) British North America Act, (e) Aborigines, (f) Maoris.
2. **Define** (a) indigenous, (b) penal colony.
3. (a) How did ethnic tensions affect Canada? (b) What steps led to Canadian self-rule?
4. (a) Who were the first white settlers in Australia? (b) What traditions influenced Australian government?
5. (a) Why did Maoris fight colonists in New Zealand? (b) What democratic advances were made by New Zealand?
6. *Critical Thinking* **Analyzing Information** Why might young nations like Australia and New Zealand have been willing to grant women the right to vote before European nations did so?
7. *ACTIVITY* Imagine you are a teenage prisoner who was transported to Australia. Write a short story about your experiences.

# 4 Economic Imperialism in Latin America

## Guide for Reading

- What problems did Latin American nations face in the 1800s?
- How were Latin American nations linked to the world economy?
- How did the United States gain influence in Latin America?
- **Vocabulary** *regionalism, caudillo, economic dependence, peonage*

During the Age of Imperialism, Latin American nations found their economies increasingly dependent on those of more developed countries. Britain, and later the United States, invested heavily in Latin America. Both then intervened to protect their interests there.

## Problems Facing the New Nations

Simón Bolívar had hoped to create strong ties among the nations of Latin America. After all, most people shared a common language, religion, and cultural heritage. But feuds among leaders, geographic barriers, and local nationalism shattered that dream. In the end, 20 separate nations emerged. (See the map on page 126.)

These new nations wrote constitutions modeled on that of the United States. They set up republics with elected legislatures. During the 1800s, however, most Latin American nations were plagued by revolts, civil war, and dictatorships.

**Colonial legacy.** Many problems had their origins in colonial rule. Spain and Portugal had kept tight control on their colonies, giving them little experience with self-government. The wars of independence barely changed the colonial hierarchy. Creoles simply replaced peninsulares as the new ruling class. The Roman Catholic Church kept its privileged position and still controlled huge amounts of land.

For most people—mestizos, mulattoes, blacks, and Indians—life did not improve after independence. The new constitutions guaranteed equality before the law, but deep-rooted inequalities remained. Voting rights were limited. Racial prejudice was widespread, and land remained in the hands of a few. Owners of haciendas ruled their great estates, and the peasants who worked them, like medieval European lords.

**Instability.** With few roads and no tradition of unity, the new nations were weakened by regionalism, loyalty to a local area. Local strongmen, called caudillos, assembled private armies to resist the central government. At times, popular caudillos gained national power. They looted the treasury and ignored the constitution. Supported by the military, they ruled as dictators.

Power struggles led to frequent revolts that changed little except the name of the leader. In the long run, power remained in the hands of a privileged few who had no desire to share it.

As in Europe, the ruling elite in Latin America was divided between conservatives and liberals. (See pages 120–121.) Conservatives defended the old social order, favored press censorship, and strongly supported the Catholic Church. Liberals backed laissez-faire economics, religious toleration, and freedom of the press. They wanted to weaken the Catholic Church by breaking up its landholdings and ending its

**The Caudillo**
*In many Latin American countries, caudillos won power by appealing to the masses. "I am one of you, poor and humble," one caudillo declared. Once in power, however, caudillos usually followed policies that helped the rich.* **Political and Social Systems** *What factors hindered growth of democratic self-government in Latin America?*

monopoly on education. Liberals saw themselves as enlightened supporters of progress but often showed little concern for the needs of the majority of the people.

## The Economics of Dependence

Under colonial rule, mercantilist policies made Latin America economically dependent on Spain and Portugal. Colonies sent raw materials such as sugar, cotton, or precious metals to the parent country and had to buy manufactured goods from them. Strict laws kept colonists from trading with other countries or building local industries that might compete with the parent country.

After independence, this pattern changed very little. The new republics did adopt free trade, welcoming all comers. Britain and the United States rushed into the new markets, replacing Spain as the chief trading partner in Latin America. But Latin America remained as economically dependent as before.

Economic dependence occurs when less developed nations export raw materials and commodities to industrial nations and import manufactured goods, capital, and technological know-how. The relationship is unequal because the more developed nation controls prices and the terms of trade.

**Foreign influence.** In the 1800s, foreign goods flooded into Latin America, creating large profits for foreigners and for a handful of local business people. At mid-century, an American diplomat described how British capital and goods were everywhere in Brazil. "British pottery, British articles of glass, iron or wood," he wrote, "are as common as woolens and cotton cloth." He then continued:

66Great Britain supplies Brazil with its steam and sailing ships, and paves and repairs its streets, lights its cities with gas, builds its railways, exploits its mines, is its banker, puts up its telegraph wires, carries its mail, builds its furniture, motors, and wagons.99

Foreign investment, which could yield enormous profits, was often accompanied by interference. British, American, or other investors might pressure their own governments to take action if political events or reform movements in a Latin American country seemed to threaten their interests.

**Economic growth.** After 1850, some Latin American economies did grow. With foreign capital, they developed mining and agriculture. Chile exported copper and nitrates, while Argentina expanded livestock and wheat growing. Brazil added coffee and rubber to its traditional export crop of sugar. By the early 1900s, Venezuela and Mexico were developing important oil industries.

Throughout the region, foreigners invested in modern ports and railroads to carry goods from the interior to coastal cities. As in the United States, European immigrants flooded into Latin America. The newcomers helped to promote economic activity, and a small middle class emerged.

Thanks to trade, investment, technology, and migration, Latin American nations moved into the world economy. Yet development was limited. Local industries grew slowly, in part because of the social structure. The tiny elite at the top benefited from the economic upturn. Their wealth grew, but very little trickled down to the masses of people at the bottom. The poor earned too little to buy consumer goods. Without a strong demand, many industries failed to develop.

## Mexico's Struggle for Stability

During the 1800s, each Latin American country followed its own course. In this section, we will explore the experiences of Mexico as an example of the challenges facing Latin American nations.

Large landowners, army leaders, and the Catholic Church dominated Mexican politics. However, bitter battles between conservatives and liberals led to revolts and the rise of dictators. Deep social divisions separated wealthy creoles from mestizos and Indians who lived in desperate poverty.

**Santa Anna.** Between 1833 and 1855, an ambitious and cunning caudillo, Antonio López de Santa Anna, gained and lost power many times. At first, he posed as a liberal reformer. Soon, however, he reversed his stand and crushed efforts at reform.

In Mexico's northern territory of Texas, discontent against Santa Anna grew. Settlers from the United States began an independence movement. In 1835, American settlers and some Mexicans in Texas revolted and the next year set up an independent republic. In 1845, the United States annexed Texas. Mexicans were outraged by this act, which they saw as a declaration of war. In the fighting that followed, the United States invaded Mexico. In Mexico City, young military cadets fought to the death rather than surrender.

Despite the bravery of these "boy heroes," Mexico lost the Mexican War. And in the treaty ending the war, it lost almost half its territory. This defeat shook the creole ruling class and triggered new violence between conservatives and liberals.

**La Reforma.** In 1855, Benito Juárez (WAHR ehz) and other liberals seized power, opening La Reforma, an era of reform. Juárez, a Zapotec Indian, offered hope to the oppressed people of Mexico. He and his fellow reformers revised the Mexican constitution to strip the military of power and end the special privileges of the Church. They ordered the Church to sell unused lands to peasants.

Conservatives resisted La Reforma, unleashing a civil war. In 1861, Juárez was elected president. He used his new office to expand reforms. His wealthy opponents turned to Europe for help. In 1863, Napoleon III sent troops to Mexico and set up Austrian archduke Maximilian as Mexican emperor. (See page 201.)

For four years, Juárez led Mexicans in battle against conservative and French forces. When France withdrew its troops, Maximilian was captured and shot. In 1867, Juárez was returned to power. Although he tried to renew reform, opponents resisted. Juárez, who died in office in 1872, never achieved all the reforms he envisioned. He did, however, help unite Mexico, bring mestizos into political life, and separate church and state.

**"Order and Progress."** After Juárez died, General Porfirio Díaz, a hero of the war against the French, gained power. From 1876 to 1880 and 1884 to 1911, he ruled as a dictator. In the name of "Order and Progress," he strengthened the army, local police, and central government. Any opposition was brutally crushed.

## Cowboys

In South America as in the western United States, cowboys became folk heroes. From Argentina to Mexico, *gauchos* and *vaqueros* herded cattle on the rugged frontier. The heyday of the cowboy was brief, but the cowboy lives on in songs, novels, films, and television shows.

**Linking Past and Present** Cowboy legends became popular at a time when the open frontier was disappearing in both South and North America. Why did cowboys become heroes at such a time? Why are they still popular?

**PAST** *The story of Martín Fierro fascinated the people of Argentina in the 1870s. The hero, a gaucho, told of his adventures on the vast plains of central Argentina.*

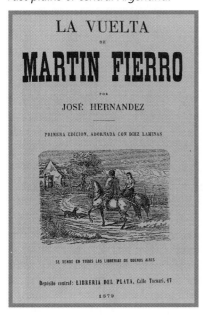

**PRESENT** *In the United States, "westerns" once dominated both movies and television. The Virginian was a best-selling novel at the turn of the century, a hit movie in 1929, and a popular television show in the 1960s. Westerns have made a comeback in recent years with the success of* Wyatt Earp, *below, and other movies.*

Under his harsh rule, Mexico made impressive economic advances. It built railroads, increased foreign trade, developed some industry, and expanded mining. Growth, however, had a high cost. Capital for development came from foreign investors, to whom Díaz granted special rights. He also let wealthy landowners buy up Indian lands.

The rich prospered, but most Mexicans continued in grinding poverty. Many Indians and mestizos fell into peonage to their employers. In the peonage system, hacienda owners would give workers advances on their wages and require them to stay on the hacienda until they had paid back what they owed. Wages remained low, and workers were rarely able to repay the hacienda owner. Many children died in infancy. Others worked 12-hour days and never learned to read or write.

In the early 1900s, pressure mounted for real change. Middle-class Mexicans demanded democracy. Urban and rural workers joined protests and strikes. In 1910, Mexico plunged into revolution. It was one of the world's major

## Imperialism in the Caribbean, 1898–1917

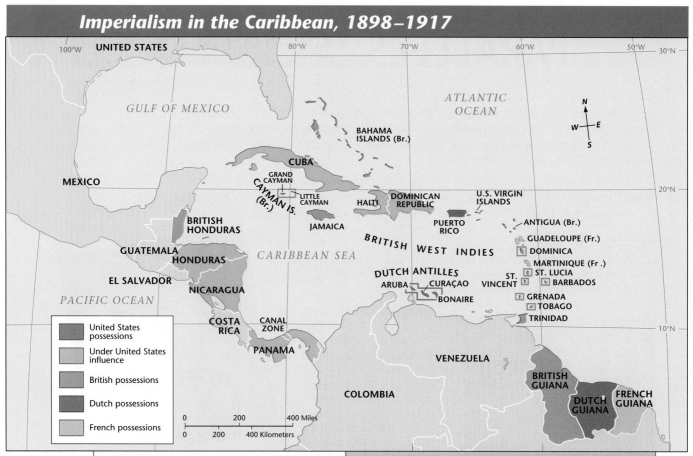

**GEOGRAPHY AND HISTORY**

In the early 1900s, much of the Caribbean was still under the influence of foreign powers. Foreign governments often intervened in the region to protect business investments there.

**1. Location** On the map, locate (a) Mexico, (b) Cuba, (c) Puerto Rico, (d) Canal Zone, (e) British West Indies.

**2. Place** (a) Which country controlled Martinique? Bahama Islands? (b) Name two United States possessions. (c) Which islands were controlled by the Dutch?

**3. Critical Thinking** **Applying Information** Why did the United States have a particularly strong interest in Caribbean affairs?

---

upheavals and the first true social revolution in Latin America. (See Chapter 12.)

### Colossus of the North

As nations like Mexico tried to build stable governments, a neighboring republic, the United States, was expanding across North America. At first, the young republics in the western hemisphere looked favorably on each other. Bolívar praised the United States as a "model of political virtues and moral enlightenment." In time, however, Latin American nations felt threatened by the "Colossus of the North," the

giant power that cast its shadow over the entire hemisphere.

**The Monroe Doctrine.** In the 1820s, Spain plotted to recover its American colonies. Britain opposed any move that might close the door to trade with Latin America. It asked the United States to join it in a statement opposing any new colonization of the Americas.

President James Monroe, however, wanted to avoid any "entangling alliance" with Britain. Acting alone, in 1823 he issued the Monroe Doctrine. "The American continents," it declared, "are henceforth not to be considered as subjects for future colonization by any European powers." The United States lacked the military power to enforce the doctrine. But knowledge that Britain was willing to use its strong navy to support the doctrine discouraged European interference. For more than a century, the Monroe Doctrine would be the key to United States policy in the Americas.

**Expansion.** As a result of the war with Mexico, in 1848 the United States acquired the thinly populated regions of northern Mexico, including the Colorado River valley and California. The victory fed dreams of future expansion. Boasted one journalist:

66 The North Americans will spread out far beyond their present bounds. New territories will be planted, declare their independence, and be annexed. We have New Mexico and California! We will have Old Mexico and Cuba! 99

For decades, Cuban patriots had battled to free their island from Spanish rule. As they began to make headway, the United States joined their cause, declaring war on Spain in 1898. The brief Spanish-American War ended in a crushing defeat for Spain.

In the peace treaty ending the war, the United States acquired Puerto Rico in the Caribbean and the Philippines and Guam in the Pacific. Cuba was granted independence, but in 1901 the United States forced Cubans to add the Platt Amendment to their constitution. It gave the United States naval bases in Cuba and the right to intervene in Cuban affairs.

**Intervention.** American investments in Latin America soared in the early 1900s. Citing the need to protect those investments, in 1904 the United States issued the Roosevelt Corollary to the Monroe Doctrine. Under this policy, the United States claimed "international police power" in the Western Hemisphere. When the Dominican Republic failed to pay its foreign debts, the United States sent in troops. It collected customs duties, paid off the debts, and remained there for years.

In the next decades, the United States sent troops to Cuba, Haiti, Mexico, Honduras, Nicaragua, and other countries. Like European powers in Africa and Asia, the United States intervened in the Caribbean to protect American lives and investments.

**Panama Canal.** From the late 1800s, the United States had wanted to build a canal across Central America. A canal would let the American fleet move swiftly between the Atlantic and Pacific oceans and protect its coastlines on either side of the continent. It would also greatly reduce the cost of trade between the two oceans.

Panama, however, belonged to Colombia, which refused to sell the United States land for the canal. In 1903, the United States backed a revolt by Panamanians against Colombia. The Panamanians quickly won independence and gave the United States land to build the canal.

The Panama Canal opened in 1914. It was an engineering marvel that boosted American trade and shipping worldwide. To people in Latin America, however, the canal was another example of "Yankee imperialism." In those years, nationalist feeling in the hemisphere was often expressed as anti-Americanism. (In 1978, the United States agreed to a series of treaties that would grant Panama control over the Canal Zone by the year 2000.)

## SECTION 4 REVIEW

1. **Identify** (a) Antonio López de Santa Anna, (b) Benito Juárez, (c) Porfirio Díaz, (d) Colossus of the North, (e) Monroe Doctrine, (f) Spanish-American War, (g) Roosevelt Corollary, (h) Panama Canal.
2. **Define** (a) regionalism, (b) caudillo, (c) economic dependence, (d) peonage.
3. (a) Why did Latin American nations have trouble building stable governments? (b) How did Mexico's experience in the 1800s reflect the problems facing Latin American nations?
4. (a) How did Latin America become part of the global economy? (b) Why was the region's economic growth limited?
5. Why did Latin American nations feel threatened by the United States?
6. *Critical Thinking* **Defending a Position** (a) Why do poor nations encourage foreign investment? (b) Do you think foreign investors should have the right to intervene to protect their investments? Why or why not?
7. *ACTIVITY* Imagine you are a Latin American in the late 1800s. Draw a political cartoon depicting the "Colossus of the North."

# 5 Impact of Imperialism

## Guide for Reading

- What were the main features of the new world economy?

- How did imperialism affect both western cultures and traditional cultures around the world?

- How did imperialism fuel tensions among industrial powers?

In 1900, Rudyard Kipling was among the most popular writers in the English-speaking world. Kipling was born in British-ruled India and, after being educated in England, returned to India as a journalist for a number of years. His stories and poems, such as "White Man's Burden," often glorified imperialism or presented it as a romantic adventure. (See page 217.)

Like most westerners, Kipling emphasized differences between what he saw as "exotic" India and his own English culture. In a famous poem, "The Ballad of East and West," however, he recounted a dramatic clash between equals: a gallant Afghan chief and a heroic British officer. Though enemies, the two men respect each other and act with nobility and courage. The poem begins and ends with these lines:

> **66**Oh, East is East, and West is West;
>     and never the twain shall meet,
> Till Earth and Sky stand presently at
>     God's great Judgment Seat;
> But there is neither East nor West,
>     Border, nor Breed, nor Birth,
> When two strong men stand face to
>     face, though they come from the
>     ends of the Earth!**99**

The Age of Imperialism brought confrontations between differing cultures "from the ends of the Earth." By 1900, western nations had unfurled their flags over much of the globe. That expansion set off radical changes that reshaped the lives of subject people from Africa to Southeast Asia and the Pacific. For their western rulers, too, imperialism would bring dramatic economic, political, and cultural changes.

## New Economic Patterns

During the Age of Imperialism, a truly global economy emerged. It was dominated by the industrialized nations of the West, especially the United States, Britain, France, and Germany. From these nations, machine-made goods, investment capital, and technology flowed to the rest of the world. In return, the people of Africa, Asia, and Latin America provided agricultural goods, natural resources, and cheap labor. Most profits from this global exchange went to the industrialized nations.

The demands of the new world economy disrupted traditional local economies in Africa and Asia. As in Europe before the Industrial Revolution, most people on these continents grew and produced goods by hand for local use. Under colonial rule, they were forced to supply products such as rubber, copper, and coffee needed by the industrial world.

**Money economy.** Western capitalists developed plantations and mines but relied on a steady supply of local labor to work them. At the same time, colonial rulers introduced a money economy that replaced the old barter system. To

▲ Colonial money

cover the expense of governing their colonies, colonial authorities imposed heavy taxes on their subjects. The only way that people could earn money to pay the taxes was by working on plantations, in mines, or on projects such as railroad building.

Families were disrupted as men left their homes and villages to work in distant mines or cities. In southern and eastern Africa, especially, many men became migrant workers. Their departure shattered families and undermined village life as women were left alone to grow food and support their children. In other parts of the world, such as Japan and Latin America, sons were kept at home to farm while daughters were sent to cities to find work as domestics or in the growing textile industry.

**Dependency.** Mass-produced goods from the industrialized world further disrupted traditional economies. India, for example, was seen by Britain as a great market for its goods. It flooded the subcontinent with cheap, factory-made cloth. The British textile industry flourished. Indian weavers who produced cloth by hand, however, could not compete and were ruined. Elsewhere, too, artisans and handcraft industries were destroyed.

Local economies that had once been self-sufficient became dependent on the industrial powers, which bought their raw materials and supplied them with manufactured goods. When the demand and prices for crops or minerals were high, colonies prospered. When demand and prices fell, people suffered. In addition, because many workers were producing export crops rather than food for local consumption, famines occurred in lands that had once fed themselves.

**Modernization.** Colonial rule did bring some economic benefits. Westerners laid the groundwork for modern banking systems. They introduced new technology and built modern communication and transportation networks. Capitalists invested huge sums in railroad building to boost the export economy. Railroads linked plantations and mines to ports, which developers also modernized.

From China to Chile, some local leaders and business people benefited from the new economic system. Countries like Argentina, Brazil, and Chile, for example, used export profits to develop industry, buy modern farm equipment, and promote growth.

## Cultural Impact

During the Age of Imperialism, Europeans were convinced of their own superiority and believed they had a mission to "civilize" the world.

# CAUSE AND EFFECT

### Causes

Industrial Revolution strengthens the West
Newly industrialized nations seek new markets and raw materials
European nations compete for power and prestige
Europeans feel duty to spread western culture

## NEW IMPERIALISM

### Immediate Effects

Europeans claim and conquer large empires in Africa and Asia
Ottoman and Qing empires attempt reforms to meet imperialist challenge
Local people resist European domination
Japan modernizes along western lines
Europeans pursue economic imperialism in Latin America
United States acquires territories in Caribbean and Pacific

### Long-Term Effects

New global economy emerges
Traditional cultures and economies disrupted around the world
Western culture spreads around the globe
Resistance to imperial rule evolves into nationalist movements
European competition for empire contributes to outbreak of two world wars

### Connections Today

Civil wars disrupt nations of Africa and Asia
Latin American nations struggle to build stable democracies

*Interpreting a Chart* At the beginning of the 1800s, westerners had little influence outside their own lands. But with the Industrial Revolution, they gained the power to carve out empires around the globe. ■ Identify two other causes for the "new imperialism." How are the effects of the new imperialism still felt in Africa and Asia today?

(See page 217.) Cecil Rhodes, a leading promoter of British imperialism, declared:

> 66The more of the world we inhabit the better it is for the human race. . . . If there be a God, I think what he would like me to do is to paint as much of the map of Africa British red as possible.99

**Westernization.** As westerners conquered other lands, they pressed subject people to accept "modern" ways. By this, they meant western ideas, government, technology, and culture. Thus, during the Age of Imperialism, modernization and westernization came to be seen as one and the same.*

Many nonwesterners, especially in conquered lands, came to accept a belief in western superiority. The successes of the western imperialist nations sapped their confidence in their own cultures. To share in the material advantages of western society, business and professional people and others who had contact with westerners learned western languages, wore western clothing, and embraced many western ways.

Other nonwesterners, however, had great misgivings about abandoning their own age-old traditions. They greatly resented—and often strongly resisted—western efforts to force new ways on them.

The new imperialism spread western culture around the world. Still, many regions were able to escape its influence. In Africa, the Middle East, and Asia, many farming villagers and nomadic herders had virtually no contact with westerners. As a result, their lives continued largely unchanged.

**Schools and hospitals.** Western culture was often spread by missionaries who built schools and hospitals. They taught children basic literacy and trained young men for jobs in colonial governments.

Western medicine brought benefits. Missionaries introduced medical breakthroughs such as vaccines and modern methods of hygiene that saved lives. At the same time, however, modern medicine undermined traditional herbalists and local healers.

**Religion.** Missionaries spread their Christian faith across the globe. They had great success in some areas. In southern Africa, for example, Christianity became widespread, although Africans adapted its teachings and beliefs to their own traditions. In regions where other world religions or belief systems such as Islam, Hinduism, Buddhism, and Confucianism were deeply rooted, Christian missionaries won fewer converts.

**Old and new ways.** The pressure to westernize forced people to reevaluate their traditions. In Asia, people were proud of their ancient civilizations. On the other hand, they did work to discourage some customs, such as sati in India or footbinding in China. In the end, many nonwestern cultures created a complex blend of old and new ways.

As people moved into cities that had become westernized, many still felt the pull of the past. "People come to the city because they want to live like Europeans," admitted one Nigerian, "but we still feel close to our village and always go back to visit it."

**Impact on western culture.** Western cultures changed, too, during the Age of Imperialism. The Columbian Exchange that had begun in 1492 picked up speed in the 1800s. Westerners drank coffee from Brazil and tea from Sri Lanka. They ate bananas from Honduras and pineapples from Hawaii. Their factories turned out products made from rubber harvested on plantations in Southeast Asia or South America.

Archaeologists and historians slowly unearthed evidence about ancient civilizations previously unknown to the West. Westerners who studied Hindu and Buddhist texts, Chinese histories, or Japanese poetry realized they had much to learn from other civilizations. The arts of Japan, Persia, Africa, and Southeast Asia influenced western sculptors and painters. West-

---

*The process of modernization along western lines has continued to the present. In today's world, however, modernization and westernization are often seen as separate and different courses. (See page 423.)

**ISSUES** *For* **TODAY** Western imperialist nations pressured their overseas colonies to adopt "modern" ways. How does modernization affect traditional cultures?

ern manufacturers also copied designs from other lands, launching fashions for Egyptian furniture, Japanese kimonos, and Chinese embroidery screens.

### New Political Tensions

Imperialism had global political consequences, as you have seen. Europeans claimed and conquered large empires in Africa and Asia. They disrupted traditional political units such as tribes and small kingdoms. Often, they united rival people under a single government, imposing stability and order where local conflicts had raged for centuries.

By the early 1900s, however, resistance to imperialism was taking a new course. In Africa and Asia, western-educated elites were organizing nationalist movements to end colonial rule.

At the same time, the competition for empire was fueling tensions among western powers. In the Sudan in 1898, British forces expanding south from Egypt and French forces

pushing east from West Africa met at Fashoda. An armed clash was barely avoided. Elsewhere, the British and Russians played a cat-and-mouse game in Central Asia. The Great Powers—Germany, Britain, France, and Russia—tried to thwart one another's ambitions in Ottoman lands. More than once, Germany and France teetered on the brink of war over Morocco in North Africa. In 1914 and again in 1939, imperialist ambitions would contribute to the outbreak of two shattering world wars.

## SECTION 5 REVIEW

1. (a) What did nonwestern lands contribute to the new global economy? (b) What did western nations contribute?
2. (a) What did westerners mean by modernization? (b) What are two ways that imperialism affected the cultures of subject people?
3. Why did imperialism lead to increased tensions among industrial powers?
4. *Critical Thinking* **Analyzing Information** List the benefits and disadvantages brought by colonial rule. Do you think subject people were better or worse off as a result of the Age of Imperialism? Explain.
5. *ACTIVITY* Create a flowchart showing the movement of goods and money in the global economy that emerged in the late 1800s. Be sure to include the effects that the new world economy had on the traditional economies of the unindustrialized nations. Use original drawings or pictures from magazines to illustrate your completed flowchart.

## CHAPTER REVIEW

### REVIEWING VOCABULARY

Review the vocabulary words in this chapter. Then, use *five* of these vocabulary words and their definitions to create a matching quiz. Exchange your quiz with another student. Check each other's answers when you are finished.

### REVIEWING FACTS

1. What factors helped account for Japan's success in modernizing?

2. Where in Southeast Asia did the French establish colonies?

3. Starting in the late 1700s, what use did Britain make of Australia?

4. When and why was the Panama Canal built?

5. Which nations dominated the global economy that emerged during the Age of Imperialism?

6. How did imperialism make some economies dependent on others?

## SKILLS FOR SUCCESS    USING CD-ROM

A CD-ROM (compact disc/read-only memory) may contain an encyclopedia, dictionary, atlas, or other reference works. The screens below are examples of what you might see when you use a CD-ROM for research. Study the screens and follow the steps to research the Australian Aborigines.

1. **Start your research.** Study Screen 1. Which source would you select to find the correct spelling of *Aborigine*?

2. **Narrow your search.** (a) Which subject would you choose to find out about the Aborigines' religion? (b) Which would you select to learn how the Aborigines arrived in Australia?

3. **Research your topic.** (a) What topic is being researched on Screen 3? (b) Where do most Aborigines live?

4. **Search for additional information.** Study Screen 4. Which topic would you select to find out the number of Aborigines who live in Australia?

**Screen 1**

You may begin your search with one of the following:

    BOOKSHELF
        Dictionary
        Roget's Thesaurus
        The World's Best Encyclopedia
        The World Almanac 1995
        Bartlett's Quotations
        Hammond Atlas

Enter your choice below:
>>

**Screen 2**

Your search: **The World's Best Encyclopedia**
Line
# ------------Subjects-------------
1    Aborigines -- Definition and Location
2    Aborigines -- Culture
3    Aborigines -- Early History
4    Aborigines -- Contemporary Life and
                    Challenges

Enter  line # to see information given on topic:
>>

**Screen 3**

**The World's Best Encyclopedia**
**Aborigines, Definition and Location**

Aborigine is the name given to those Australians whose ancestors  were the first people to settle in Australia. Aborigines make up about 1 percent of the Australian population and have Australian citizenship. Most live in Australian towns and settlements.

**Screen 4**

**The World's Best Encyclopedia**
Line #
            **Associated Topics**

    1        Population Figures
    2        Traditional Homelands, Map
    3        City Life
    4        Settlement Life
    5        Aboriginal Lands Regained From
             Government, Map

Enter line # for associated topic:  >>

## REVIEWING CHAPTER THEMES

Review the "Focus On" questions at the start of this chapter. Then select *three* of those questions and answer them, using information from the chapter.

## CRITICAL THINKING

1. **Synthesizing Information** How was imperialism the "child" of the Industrial Revolution?

2. **Comparing** Compare Japan's response to western imperialism with that of China. (a) How were they similar? (b) How were they different?

3. **Applying Information** (a) What principle did the United States put forth in the Monroe Doctrine? (b) How did the United States use the Monroe Doctrine to support its intervention in Latin America?

4. **Defending a Position** Mexican President Porfirio Díaz defended his regime: "We were harsh. Sometimes we were harsh to the point of cruelty. But it was necessary then to the life and progress of the nation." Do you agree or disagree with Díaz's view that the end justifies the means? Defend your position.

## ANALYZING PRIMARY SOURCES

Use the quotation on page 240 to answer the following questions.

1. What basic problem did the king describe?

2. Why, according to the king, would the discovery of wealth not solve his country's problem?

3. What would be a solution to the problem?

## FOR YOUR PORTFOLIO

**WRITING JOURNAL ENTRIES** Imagine that you are a world traveler during the 1800s. Write journal entries for visits that you make at two different times to a place discussed in this chapter. Consult library resources for additional information about the place you will visit. Then write your journal entries.

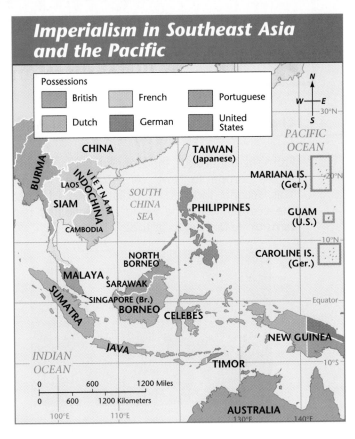

*Imperialism in Southeast Asia and the Pacific*

## ANALYZING MAPS

Use the map to answer the following questions.

1. Which three nations claimed parts of New Guinea?

2. Which nation controlled colonies located on the Equator?

3. Which nation controlled the island of Guam?

### INTERNET ACTIVITY

**CREATING A TABLE** Use the Internet to research the current level of imports of some of the nations in Latin America. Then create a table that shows what percentages of those nations' total imports come from the United States. Based on the data in your table, do you think the United States is still an economic "Colossus of the North" to the nations of Latin America? Why or why not? Write a report summarizing your findings.

# Unit-in-Brief

## Industrialism and a New Global Age

**Chapter 5**  Life in the Industrial Age
(1800–1910)

From the mid-1800s, industrialism spread rapidly across Europe to North America and beyond. This second Industrial Revolution transformed the economies of the world and solidified patterns of life familiar to us today.

- By the mid-1800s, other western nations, particularly Germany and the United States, were challenging Britain's position as the world's industrial giant.
- Steel, electricity, and advances in communications and transportation marked the second Industrial Revolution.
- By the late 1800s, "big business" came increasingly to dominate the industrial world.
- With the spread of industry, a more complex social structure, dominated by middle-class values, evolved. Although the poor continued to endure harsh conditions, the overall standard of living for workers improved.
- Artistic movements such as romanticism, realism, and expressionism reflected various responses to social and technological changes.

**Chapter 6**  Nationalism Triumphs
in Europe
(1800–1914)

The 1800s saw an upsurge of nationalism in Europe. Nationalism unified some countries and sparked divisiveness and conflict in others.

- Between 1862 and 1890, Otto von Bismarck molded the German states into a powerful empire. To strengthen the German state, Bismarck promoted economic development, aggressive foreign policy goals, and domestic reforms.
- Although nationalist forces unified Italy in 1870, a long history of fragmentation created a host of problems for the new state.
- Nationalist feelings among diverse ethnic groups in Eastern Europe created widespread unrest and helped hasten the decline of the Ottoman and Hapsburg empires.
- Reluctant to surrender absolute power, Russian czars of the 1800s swung between reform and repression.

**Chapter 7**  Growth of Western
Democracies
(1815–1914)

In Britain, France, and the United States, reformers struggled for an extension of democratic rights and social change. Although many inequalities persisted, these efforts paved the way for great improvements in the quality of life.

- The British Parliament passed a series of reforms designed to help those whose labor supported the new industrial society. Suffrage was extended to all male citizens, prompting women to seek the vote as well.

- Following its defeat in the Franco-Prussian War and a fierce internal revolt, France established the Third Republic, which instituted a series of important reforms.
- By 1900, the United States had become the world's leading industrial giant, a global power, and a magnet for immigrants seeking freedom and opportunity.

## Chapter 8   The New Imperialism
(1800–1914)

During the 1800s, European powers embarked on a period of aggressive expansion known as the Age of Imperialism. Despite fierce resistance, these powers brought much of the world under their control between 1870 and 1914.

- The Industrial Revolution gave western powers both the means and the motives to seek global domination.
- With little regard for traditional patterns of settlement, European powers partitioned almost the entire African continent.
- Taking advantage of the slowly crumbling Ottoman empire, Britain, France, and Russia competed to extend their influence over Algeria, Egypt, and other Ottoman lands.
- Britain set up a profitable system of colonial rule, controlling over 60 percent of India.
- Western powers carved out spheres of influence along the Chinese coast. China unsuccessfully tried to resist foreign influence with belated efforts at modernization and reform.

- By the early 1900s, leaders in many colonized regions were forging their own nationalist movements.

## Chapter 9   New Global Patterns
(1800–1914)

Imperialism resulted in a global exchange that profited industrial nations but disrupted local economies in Africa, Asia, and Latin America. Radical changes reshaped the lives of both subject peoples and westerners.

- As a defense against western imperialism, Japan transformed itself into a modern industrial power and set out on its own imperialist path.
- By 1900, western powers had claimed most islands in the Pacific and divided up most of Southeast Asia.
- The British colonies of Canada, Australia, and New Zealand won independence relatively quickly.
- Although Latin American nations struggled to set up stable governments and economies, a pattern of military rule and economic dependency emerged.
- The United States created its own sphere of influence in the Western Hemisphere.
- Europeans forced subject peoples to accept western ideas about government, technology, and culture.

# A Global View

## How Did Industrialization, Nationalism, and the Growth of Democracy Reshape the World?

As we saw in the review unit, the first global age began with European expansion in the late 1400s. In the 1800s, a second wave of expansion extended western power to almost all parts of the world. Forces that were reshaping the West itself thus took on a new global importance.

### The Age of Steam

During the early 1800s, the Industrial Revolution spread from Britain to Europe and the Americas. Modern industrial cities emerged, built around the new factories. In the cities, the middle classes lived in elegant neighborhoods, while most workers survived in slum tenements.

The citizens of this new industrial society began to develop new views and values. Many admired the middle-class virtues that made the system work. Others challenged established institutions.

### New Nations

Kindled by the Napoleonic wars, nationalism reshaped Europe. All peoples, nationalists insisted, had a right to their own countries. This call to nationhood was echoed by Irish nationalists seeking freedom from British rule and, later, by Zionists who sought a Jewish state.

Inspired in part by nationalism, two new European states emerged in the late 1800s. Led by the dynamic kingdom of Sardinia, most of the separate states of Italy were united by 1861. A decade later, Bismarck's Prussia, already one of Europe's great powers, forged a united German empire.

Elsewhere, nationalism was a threat to unity. Both Austria and the Ottoman empire faced disintegration as their multinational populations called for "national self-determination." Czarist Russia confronted this problem along with demands for economic, political, and social reforms.

### Spread of Democracy

In Western Europe and North America, democratic ideas were the main force for

| | 1800 | 1830 | 1860 |
|---|---|---|---|
| **AFRICA** | | **1805** Muhammad Ali becomes governor of Egypt | **1830** France conquers Algeria | |
| **THE AMERICAS** | **1803** Louisiana Purchase | **1823** Monroe Doctrine issued | **1840** Act of Union unites Canada | |
| **ASIA AND OCEANIA** | | **1814** Missionaries arrive in New Zealand | **1842** Treaty of Nanjing | **1857** Sepoy Rebellion |
| **EUROPE** | | **1807** Industrial Revolution spreads to Belgium | **1832** Reform Bill in Britain | **1845** Great Hunger in Ireland |

political change. In Britain, where Parliament had come to share royal power, genuine democracy began to emerge, as a series of reform bills gave the vote to most male citizens. People also demanded—and got—more social reforms, from child labor laws to public education.

Democratic reforms also came to France and the United States. The French Third Republic built on the foundation laid by the French Revolution of 1789. Despite such setbacks as the Dreyfus affair, France increasingly lived up to its democratic principles of liberty and equality.

Still, the United States was perhaps the world's most successful democracy. After the abolition of slavery, male suffrage was widespread. The economic boom of the "gilded age" of the late 1800s also made America the most productive of all industrial states.

## Expanding Empire

Democratic and nationalistic ideals, however, did not stop western powers from imposing their will on other peoples. Driven by a variety of motives, imperialists were now equipped with new weapons produced by the Industrial Revolution.

The New Imperialism seemed unstoppable. Its leaders included old colonial powers like Britain and France, as well as Germany, Belgium, and Japan. By 1900, imperialist powers had divided up almost all of Africa and dominated most of Asia. While Latin American nations retained their independence, they were subject to economic domination and, occasionally, military intervention.

## Looking Ahead

The forces that shaped the 1800s would continue into the next century. Industrial development would reach new heights. Nationalism would kindle wars, fragment empires, and forge new states. Democracy would survive challenges to spread to many new lands. And the effects of imperialism would last long after most colonies won independence.

*ACTIVITY* Choose two events and two pictures from the time line below. For each, write a sentence explaining how it relates to the themes expressed in the Global View essay.

1860

1890

1920

**1869** Suez Canal opens

**1884** Berlin Conference carves up Africa

**1896** Ethiopia defeats Italy at Battle of Adowa

**1861** Civil War begins

**1876** Diaz gains power in Mexico

**1898** Spanish-American War

**1914** Panama Canal opens

**1900** Boxer Uprising in China

**1908** Young Turks overthrow sultan

**1868** Meiji restoration begins

**1885** Indian National Congress formed

**1870** Italy unified

**1871** Germany unified

**1894** Dreyfus affair begins

**1905** Bloody Sunday in Russia

**1918** Women win suffrage in Britain

UNIT 2 THE BIG PICTURE

# *You Decide*

## Exploring Global Issues

### *Is Technology a Blessing or a Curse?*

To Mary Shelley, the Industrial Revolution sparked the nightmare of the Frankenstein monster. To Jules Verne, it inspired dreams of traveling to the moon or far beneath the sea. Today, these two visions still reflect people's hopes and fears about technology. Should we welcome all technological advances as signs of progress? Or do the dangers of technology far outweigh the benefits? To begin your investigation, examine these viewpoints:

**UNITED STATES**
**1867**

Industrial nations of the 1800s sponsored huge industrial expositions to show off the products of their technology. Here, visitors admire a gear-cutting machine at an exhibition in Philadelphia. ▶

**IRELAND**
**1895**

Writer and wit Oscar Wilde saw technology as a tool for cultural progress:

❝The fact is, that civilization requires slaves. . . . Unless there are slaves to do the ugly, horrible, uninteresting work, culture and contemplation become almost impossible. Human slavery is wrong, insecure, and demoralizing. On mechanical slavery, on the slavery of the machine, the future of the world depends.❞

**INDIA**
**1955**

As nations such as India gained independence, Prime Minister Jawaharlal Nehru commented on their need for technological development:

❝There can be no real well-being or advance in material standards in India without the big factory. I shall venture to say that we cannot even maintain our freedom and independence as a nation without the big factory and all that it represents.❞

**FRANCE**
**1964**

Writer Jacques Ellul commented on the effects of technology in his book *The Technological Society*:

❝The machine tends not only to create a new human environment, but also to modify man's very essence. . . . He must adapt himself, as though the world were new, to a universe for which he was not created. He was made to go six kilometers an hour, and he goes a thousand. He was made to eat when he was hungry and to sleep when he was sleepy; instead, he obeys a clock. He was made to have contact with living things, and he lives in a world of stone.❞

IRAN
1964

Ruhollah Khomeini, a Muslim reformer, belittled the technological progress of the western powers who dominated his country:

❝Let them go all the way to Mars or beyond the Milky Way; they will still be deprived of true happiness. . . . For the solution of social problems and the relief of human misery require foundations in faith and morals; merely acquiring material power and wealth, conquering nature and space, have no effect in this regard.❞

JAPAN
1984

Ikeda Daisaku spoke of the effects of technology from the viewpoint of a Buddhist philosopher:

❝The man who rides in a car all of the time loses the ability to walk long distances vigorously. Even when we employ mechanical devices, we must realize that it is we human beings who are at the controls and that whether the machine is a blessing or curse depends on what is inside us.❞

SOUTH
AFRICA
1986

This cartoon uses imagery borrowed from the pyramid builders of ancient Egypt to comment on modern technology. ▶

## COMPARING VIEWPOINTS

1. Which views represented here seem least critical of modern technology?
2. Both India and Iran sought to free themselves from western domination. How does Nehru's view of western technology differ from Khomeini's?
3. How is Ellul's view of technology similar to Ikeda's?
4. How do Wilde and the cartoonist use the same image to express different viewpoints?

## YOUR INVESTIGATION

ACTIVITY

1. Find out more about other viewpoints related to this topic. You might investigate one or more of the following:

■ The Luddite movement in early industrial Britain.

■ The view of technology depicted in a work of science fiction, such as the novel *The Shape of Things to Come* by H. G. Wells, the play *R.U.R.* by Karel Capek, or the American movie *War Games.*

■ Debates over the "rationing" of modern medical technology, such as kidney dialysis or organ transplants.

■ The history and effects of robotics in Japan.

■ Commentary on an industrial disaster, such as the chemical leakage at Bhopal, India, or the nuclear accident at Chernobyl, Ukraine.

2. Decide which viewpoint you agree with most closely and express it in your own way. You may do so in an essay, a cartoon, a poem, a drawing or painting, a song, a skit, a video, or in some other way.

UNIT 2   THE BIG PICTURE

# UNIT 3

# WORLD WARS AND REVOLUTIONS

**Impact of the Individual**

*Mohandas Gandhi led India's drive for independence from British rule. He urged Indians to use methods of non-violent protest, such as using home-spun rather than British cotton.*

**2**

UNITED STATES

**1**

ATLANTIC OCEAN

PACIFIC OCEAN

**Economics and Technology**

*The Great Depression began in 1929 in the United States. It quickly spread to the rest of the world, bringing hardship both to urban workers and to rural families, like this one.*

**1**

N
W — E
S

**Continuity and Change**

*African nationalists such as Jomo Kenyatta and Léopold Sédar Senghor called for a revival of traditional cultures. This staff was carried by a student of African languages.*

**3**

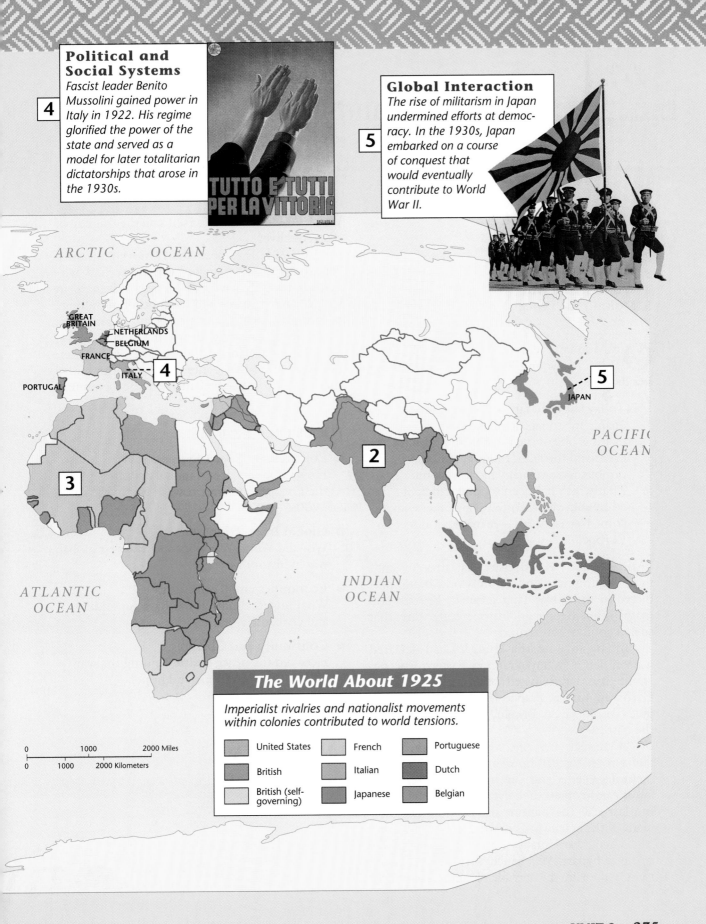

**Political and Social Systems**

**4** Fascist leader Benito Mussolini gained power in Italy in 1922. His regime glorified the power of the state and served as a model for later totalitarian dictatorships that arose in the 1930s.

TUTTO E TUTTI PER LA VITTORIA

**Global Interaction**

**5** The rise of militarism in Japan undermined efforts at democracy. In the 1930s, Japan embarked on a course of conquest that would eventually contribute to World War II.

ARCTIC OCEAN

GREAT BRITAIN
NETHERLANDS
BELGIUM
FRANCE
PORTUGAL
ITALY **4**

**2**

**3**

JAPAN **5**

PACIFIC OCEAN

ATLANTIC OCEAN

INDIAN OCEAN

### The World About 1925

*Imperialist rivalries and nationalist movements within colonies contributed to world tensions.*

- United States
- British
- British (self-governing)
- French
- Italian
- Japanese
- Portuguese
- Dutch
- Belgian

0   1000   2000 Miles
0   1000   2000 Kilometers

# World War I and Its Aftermath

## (1914–1919)

## CHAPTER OUTLINE

1 The Stage Is Set
2 The Guns of August
3 A New Kind of Conflict
4 Winning the War
5 Making the Peace

On Monday evening, August 3, 1914, Vera Brittain, a young English woman, wrote in her diary:

66Today has been far too exciting to enable me to feel at all like sleep—in fact it is one of the most thrilling I have ever lived through, though without doubt there are many more to come. That which has been so long anticipated by some and scoffed at by others has come to pass at last—Armageddon in Europe!99

"Armageddon" is a decisive, catastrophic conflict, like the fiery end-of-the-world battle predicted in the Bible. That summer, Brittain and many other people in Europe were sure that such a conflict had arrived.

In late July, Austria-Hungary had declared war on Serbia, a tiny nation in Eastern Europe. In the days that followed, other major powers—Germany, Russia, France—had joined the conflict. Would Great Britain, too, be drawn into the battle?

"One feels as if one were dreaming," Brittain wrote. "Every hour brings fresh and momentous events and one must stand still and await catastrophes each even more terrible than the last. All the nations of this continent are ready with their swords drawn."

When war finally came, Vera Brittain's world fell apart. Her fiancé, brother, and many friends died in the terrible slaughter of World War I. As a nurse, she herself saw the tragedy of shattered lives.

By 1914, Europeans had enjoyed almost a century without a major war. They had witnessed incredible changes. Rapid advances in science and industry had fed a belief in unlimited progress, peace, and prosperity. That confidence came crashing down in August 1914, buried in an avalanche of death and destruction. For Vera Brittain's generation—the ones who survived—World War I marked the beginning of a disturbing new age.

**FOCUS ON** these themes as you read:

- **Political and Social Systems**
  How did political and military rivalries push the European powers toward war in the early 1900s?

- **Global Interaction**
  Why did World War I become the first global war in history?

- **Economics and Technology**
  What impact did total war have on soldiers and civilians?

- **Continuity and Change**
  How did the peace treaties ending the war lead to both bitterness and hope?

## TIME AND PLACE

*A Vision of Destruction* German artist Ludwig Meidner painted this nightmarish landscape in 1913. The following year, Europe was embroiled in World War I. It would become the most destructive conflict in world history up to that time. **Art and Literature** Compare this painting with the excerpts from Vera Brittain's diary on page 276. What do the two sources tell you about the mood in Europe on the eve of World War I?

## HUMANITIES LINK

*Art History* C.R.W. Nevinson, *Return to the Trenches* (page 290).
*Literature* In this chapter you will encounter passages from the following works of literature: Vera Brittain, *Chronicle of Youth* (page 276); Siegfried Sassoon, "Suicide in the Trenches" (page 289).

| 1914 | 1915 | 1916 | 1917 | 1918 | 1919 |
|------|------|------|------|------|------|
| World War I begins | Sinking of *Lusitania* | Battle of Verdun | United States enters war | Treaty of Brest-Litovsk; armistice ends war | Versailles peace conference |

1914    1915    1916    1917    1918    1919

# 1 The Stage Is Set

## Guide for Reading

- Why did many people in the early 1900s believe that war was unlikely?
- What forces pushed Europe toward war?
- What were the causes and effects of European alliances?
- **Vocabulary** *militarism*

To many, war seemed far away in the decades before 1914. After a century of relative peace, idealists hoped for a permanent end to war. "The future belongs to peace," said French economist Frédéric Passy.

Others were far less hopeful. "I shall not live to see the Great War," warned German chancellor Otto von Bismarck, "but you will see it, and it will start in the east." It was Bismarck's prediction, rather than Passy's, that came true.

## Pressure for Peace

The late 1800s and early 1900s saw serious efforts to end the scourge of war. Alfred Nobel, the Swedish inventor of dynamite, came to regret the military uses of his invention. In his will, he set up the Nobel Peace Prize to reward each year the individual whose work advanced the cause of peace.

The struggle for women's suffrage throughout Europe supported the peace movement. Aletta Jacobs, the first woman doctor in the Netherlands, argued that if women won the vote, they would be able to prevent wars:

**GLOBAL CONNECTIONS**

Baron Pierre de Coubertin, a French educator, believed that international sports competition would be one way to promote world peace. In 1894, he proposed that the ancient Greek Olympic Games be revived. Two years later, the first modern Olympic Games were held in Athens. Today, athletes from around the world still compete every four years in the summer and winter Olympics.

"Yes, the women will do it. They don't feel as men do about war. They are the mothers of the race. Men think of the economic results, women think of the grief and pain."

Organizations such as the Women's International League for Peace and Freedom gave women a way to voice their concerns.

Governments, too, backed peace efforts. In 1899, the First Universal Peace Conference brought together leaders of many nations in The Hague in the Netherlands. There, they set up a world court to settle disputes between nations. The Hague Tribunal, as the court was called, could not force nations to submit their disputes, nor could it enforce its rulings. Still, it was a step toward keeping the peace.

At the same time, other powerful forces were pushing Europe to the brink of war. They included aggressive nationalism, economic competition, imperialism, an arms race, and rival alliance systems.

## Aggressive Nationalism

Nationalism can be a positive force, binding together a nation's people. People enjoy such patriotic celebrations as St. Patrick's Day in Ireland or Cinco de Mayo in Mexico. At the same time, national pride can fuel bitter conflicts. In the early 1900s, aggressive nationalism was a leading cause of international tension.

**Alsace and Lorraine.** Nationalism was strong in both Germany and France. Germans were proud of their new empire's military power and industrial leadership. France longed to regain its position as Europe's leading power.

The French were still bitter about their defeat in the Franco-Prussian War. (See page 201.) They especially resented German occupation of the border provinces Alsace and Lorraine. Patriotic French citizens longed for revenge against Germany and recovery of the "lost provinces."

**Pan-Slavism.** In Eastern Europe, Russia sponsored a powerful form of nationalism called Pan-Slavism. According to Pan-Slavism, all Slavic peoples shared a common nationality. As the largest Slavic country, Russia felt that it had a duty to lead and defend all Slavs. By 1914, it stood ready to support Serbia, an ambitious young Slavic nation, against any threat.

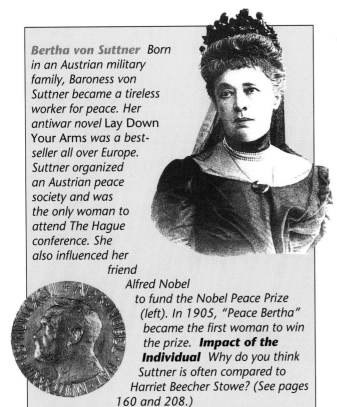

**Bertha von Suttner** Born in an Austrian military family, Baroness von Suttner became a tireless worker for peace. Her antiwar novel *Lay Down Your Arms* was a bestseller all over Europe. Suttner organized an Austrian peace society and was the only woman to attend The Hague conference. She also influenced her friend **Alfred Nobel** to fund the Nobel Peace Prize (left). In 1905, "Peace Bertha" became the first woman to win the prize. **Impact of the Individual** Why do you think Suttner is often compared to Harriet Beecher Stowe? (See pages 160 and 208.)

**Crises in the Balkans.** Two old multinational empires particularly feared rising nationalism in Eastern Europe. Austria-Hungary was worried that nationalism might foster rebellion among the many minority populations within its empire. Ottoman Turkey felt threatened by new nations on its borders, such as Serbia and Greece. Serbia was especially aggressive. It dreamed of creating and ruling a South Slav state.

In 1912, several Balkan states attacked Turkey. The next year, they fought among themselves over the spoils of war. These brief but bloody Balkan wars raised tensions to a fever pitch. By 1914, the Balkans were the "powder keg of Europe." A tiny spark might lead to an explosion.

## Economic and Imperial Rivalries

Economic rivalries further poisoned the international atmosphere. The British felt threatened by Germany's rapid economic growth. By 1900, Germany's new, modern factories increasingly outproduced Britain's older ones. Britain therefore had strong economic reasons to oppose Germany in any conflict. Germany, in turn, thought the other great powers did not give them enough respect.

Imperialism also divided European nations. In 1905 and again in 1911, competition for colonies brought France and Germany to the brink of war. Germany wanted to keep France from imposing a protectorate on the Muslim kingdom of Morocco. Although diplomats kept the peace, Germany gained some territory in central Africa. As a result of the two Moroccan crises, Britain and France began to form closer ties against Germany.

## Militarism and the Arms Race

The late 1800s saw a rise in militarism, the glorification of the military. Under militarism, the armed forces and readiness for war came to dominate national policy. Militarists painted war in romantic colors. Young men dreamed of blaring trumpets and heroic cavalry charges—not at all the sort of conflict they would soon face.

The rise in militarism grew partly out of the ideas of Social Darwinism. (See page 155.) Echoing the idea of "survival of the fittest," the German militarist Friedrich von Bernhardi claimed that war was "a biological necessity of the first importance."

**The arms race.** As international tensions grew, the great powers expanded their armies and navies. The result was an arms race that further increased suspicions and made war more likely.

The fiercest competition was the naval rivalry between Britain and Germany. To protect its vast overseas empire, Britain had built the world's most respected navy. When Germany began to acquire colonies, it began to build up its own navy. Kaiser William II boasted:

&6All the long years of my reign, my colleagues, the monarchs of Europe, have paid no attention to what I have to say. Soon, with my great navy to endorse my words, they will be more respectful.99

Suspicious of Germany's motives, Britain increased its naval spending. In a British cartoon of the time, one man warns another, "We must build a bigger navy than the enemy will build

## Toy Soldiers

Miniature soldiers have been found in the tombs of ancient Egypt. During the Middle Ages, noble children staged mock jousts with wooden knights. Later, young rulers like Louis XIV and Peter the Great learned military strategy by playing with toy armies. Not until the 1700s, though, were mass-produced toy soldiers widely available to ordinary children.

**Linking Past and Present**  Some parents today object to "war toys." Do you agree or disagree? Explain.

**PAST** *In the early 1900s, as world powers built up their armies, toymakers did the same. The British regiment at right came in a box that boasted of their worldwide exploits. Below, an Austro-Hungarian cavalry struts proudly. American marines, Japanese infantrymen, Zulu warriors, and Indian troops mounted on elephants—all were reproduced in miniature.*

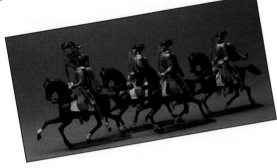

**PRESENT** *Plastic soldiers and posable "action figures," such as G.I. Joe™ (right), have largely replaced the tin or lead figurines of earlier times.*

when he hears we're building a bigger navy than he's building."

**Military leaders.** Fear of war gave military leaders more influence. On matters of peace and war, governments turned to military leaders for advice. German generals and British admirals enjoyed great respect and got more funds to build up their forces. As militarism and the arms race fed each other, tensions grew.

### A Tangle of Alliances

Fear and distrust led the great powers to protect themselves through alliances. Nations signed treaties pledging to defend each other. These alliances were intended to create powerful combinations that no one would dare attack. Gradually, two huge alliances emerged.

**The Central Powers.** The first alliances had their origins in Bismarck's day. He was aware that France longed to avenge its humiliating defeat in the Franco-Prussian War. Knowing that France would not attack Germany without help, Bismarck signed treaties with the other great powers. In 1872, Germany joined a weak alliance with Austria-Hungary and Russia. Ten years later, Germany formed the Triple Alliance with Austria-Hungary and Italy.

After Bismarck resigned, Kaiser William II pursued his own policies. He preserved the Triple Alliance. However, he allowed Bismarck's Reinsurance Treaty, made with Russia in 1887, to lapse. Thus, Russia was free to seek new allies.

In 1914, when war did erupt, Germany and Austria-Hungary fought on the same side. They became known as the Central Powers.

**The Allies.** A rival bloc took shape in 1894, when France and Russia signed an alliance. In 1904, France and Britain signed an *entente cordiale* (ahn TAHNT kawr DYAHL), or "friendly understanding." Though not as binding as a treaty, the entente led to close military and diplomatic ties. Three years later, Britain signed a similar agreement with Russia. When war began, these powers became known as the Allies.

**Consequences.** Other states were drawn into alliances. Germany signed a treaty with the Ottoman empire, while Britain drew close to Japan. Rather than easing tensions, the growth of rival alliance systems made governments increasingly nervous. A local conflict could easily mushroom into a general war. In 1914, that threat became a horrifying reality.

## SECTION 1 REVIEW

1. **Identify** (a) Alfred Nobel, (b) Pan-Slavism, (c) Central Powers, (d) Allies.
2. **Define** militarism.
3. (a) What was the purpose of the Hague Tribunal? (b) How was its power limited?
4. Describe how each of the following inflamed tensions in Europe: (a) nationalism, (b) imperialism, (c) militarism.
5. (a) Why did European nations form alliances? (b) How did the alliance systems increase fears of war?
6. *Critical Thinking* **Past and Present** Do you think the idea of going to war excites young people today in the same way it did in the early 1900s? Why or why not?
7. *ACTIVITY* Choose someone living today that you would nominate for the Nobel Peace Prize. Write a brief paragraph explaining why you think he or she deserves the honor.

# 2 The Guns of August

## Guide for Reading

- How did ethnic tensions in the Balkans spark a political assassination?
- How did conflict between Austria-Hungary and Serbia widen?
- Whom do historians blame for the outbreak of World War I?
- **Vocabulary** *ultimatum, mobilize, neutrality*

In April of 1913, Bertha von Suttner wrote a grim prediction in her diary:

❝All in all, it seems to me that the great European disaster is well on its way. If so many seeds have been sown, surely the weeds will sprout up soon and surely so much stockpiled gunpowder will explode.❞

"Peace Bertha" died on June 20, 1914. Eight days later, an assassin's bullet set off the "gunpowder" and ignited a war that engulfed much of the world for four bloody years.

## A Murder With Millions of Victims

On a spring night in 1914, a small group of young revolutionaries huddled around a cafe table in Belgrade, Serbia. By the light of a flickering gas lamp, they read a news article. It announced that Archduke Francis Ferdinand of Austria-Hungary would visit Sarajevo (sar uh YAY voh), the capital of neighboring Bosnia, on June 28.

The Serbians were outraged to learn about this. June 28 was the date on which Serbia had been conquered by the Ottoman empire in 1389. On the very same date in 1912, Serbia had at last freed itself from Turkish rule. But Bosnia, home to many Serbs, was still ruled by Austria-Hungary. Now Francis Ferdinand, heir to the Austrian throne, had chosen June 28 to come to Bosnia! "Our decision was taken almost immediately," recalled one of the group. "Death to the tyrant!"

**The killer.** Among the group was a youth of 19 named Gavrilo Princip (GAHV ree loh PREEN tseep). Princip's family were Serb farmers who made a meager living in Bosnia. Having grown up under Austrian rule, he felt that he must take action against the oppressors.

Princip joined Unity or Death, a terrorist group commonly known as the Black Hand. Organized by Bosnian Serbs, its goal was to organize all South Slav peoples into a single nation. On June 28, Princip would be waiting on the streets of Sarajevo.

**The victims.** June 28 was a special date for Francis Ferdinand as well. Exactly 14 years earlier, he had married Countess Sophie Chotek. The love match brought both joy and bitterness. The Hapsburg royal family snubbed Sophie, because of her lower social rank. Still, Francis Ferdinand sought ways to make sure she was acknowledged. When his duties took him to Sarajevo on their anniversary, he decided to bring his wife along.

Politically, Francis Ferdinand was not a supporter of democracy. Yet he recognized how nationalism was threatening the Hapsburg empire. He even anticipated making some concessions to the Slavs. This view made him unpopular with hardliners on both sides. Conservative Austrians saw him as too soft. Serbian radicals feared concessions might weaken their movement.

The archduke ignored warnings of anti-Austrian unrest in Sarajevo. On the morning of June 28, he dictated a telegram for his daughter:

66Mama and I are very well . . . We gave a large dinner party yesterday and this morning there is a big reception in Sarajevo. Another large dinner party after that and then we are leaving. . . . Dearest love to you all. Papa.99

▲ New York Times *headline of June 29, 1914*

**Murder in Sarajevo.** A few hours later, the royal motorcade drove through Sarajevo. Stationed along the route were seven members of the Black Hand. Several carried crude hand bombs and pistols. The first two conspirators lost their nerve as the cars passed. The third hurled his bomb. It missed the archduke's car but injured an officer in another car. After stopping to see what happened, the royal couple continued with the day's program.

Meanwhile, despite the failure of his co-conspirators, Gavrilo Princip held firm to his plan. He stayed near the route the motorcade would follow later in the day.

Leaving the town hall, the archduke asked to visit the officer who had been wounded in the bombing. But no one told the chauffeur to drive to the hospital. Instead, he followed the old route. When told to change directions, he stopped to put the car in reverse—right at the spot where Princip stood. Seizing his opportunity, he sprang toward the car and fired twice into the back seat.

Horrified guards hurled themselves upon the killer. It was too late—the royal couple had been struck. According to one witness, the archduke gasped, "Sophie, Sophie, don't die. Stay alive for the children!" Within minutes, both were dead.

**The punishment.** At his trial, Princip stood by his deed. His only regret, he said, was killing a woman. Because he was under 20 years of age, he was not executed. He died in prison of tuberculosis in 1918.

For Europe, the punishment was more severe. The archduke and his wife were the first victims of a war that killed millions. ▪

## Peace Unravels

News of his nephew's assassination shocked the aging Austrian emperor, Francis Joseph. He and his government in Vienna blamed Serbia. Serbia would stop at nothing, they believed, to achieve its goal of a South Slav empire. The Austrians

*"Who Did It?"* One by one, the major powers of Europe were drawn into the dispute between Serbia and Austria-Hungary. This cartoon appeared in an American newspaper in 1914, just after war broke out. **Global Interaction** What point is this cartoon making about the events leading up to the war?

decided that their only course was to punish Serbia.

**A harsh ultimatum.** Austria sent Serbia a sweeping ultimatum, or final set of demands. To avoid war, said the ultimatum, Serbia must end all anti-Austrian agitation and punish any Serbian official involved in the murder plot. It must even let Austria join in the investigation.

Serbia agreed to most, but not all, of the terms. This partial refusal gave Austria the opportunity to take decisive action. On July 28, Austria declared war on Serbia.

**Capital to capital.** A war between a major power and a small Balkan state might have been another "summer war," like most European wars of the past century. But as diplomats sent notes from capital to capital, larger forces drew the great powers deeper into conflict.

Austria might not have pushed Serbia into war without the backing of its longtime ally, Germany. In Berlin, Kaiser William II was horrified at the assassination of a royal heir. He advised Francis Joseph to take a firm stand toward Serbia and assured him of German support. Thus, instead of urging restraint, the kaiser gave Austria a "blank check."

Serbia meanwhile sought help from Russia, the champion of Slavic nations. From St. Petersburg, Nicholas II telegraphed William II. The czar asked the kaiser to urge Austria to soften its demands. When this plea failed, Russia began to mobilize, or prepare its military forces for war. Germany responded by declaring war on Russia.

Russia, in turn, appealed to its ally France. In Paris, nationalists saw a chance to avenge France's defeat in the Franco-Prussian War. Though French leaders had some doubts, they gave Russia the same kind of backing Germany offered Austria. When Germany demanded that France remain neutral, France refused. Germany then declared war on France. By early August, the battle lines were hardening.

**The Schlieffen Plan.** Italy and Britain remained uncommitted. Italy decided to remain neutral for the time being. Neutrality is a policy of supporting neither side in a war. Britain had to decide quickly whether or not to support its ally France. Then Germany's war plans suddenly made the decision for Britain.

Germany's worst fear was a war on two fronts, with France attacking from the west and Russia from the east. Years earlier, General Alfred von Schlieffen (SHLEE fuhn) had developed a strategy to avoid a two-front war. Schlieffen reasoned that Russia's lumbering military would be slow to mobilize. Under the Schlieffen Plan, Germany first had to defeat France quickly. Then it would fight Russia.

**ISSUES For TODAY**

The Balkan "powder keg" and the complex web of alliances were key ingredients in the outbreak of World War I. What conditions can increase the possibility of war?

## Europe, 1914

**Central Powers**

**Allies**

**Neutral nations**

**Neutral nations that later joined the Central Powers**

**Neutral nations that later joined the Allies**

### GEOGRAPHY AND HISTORY

By 1914, the major European powers formed rival alliances. Some neutral nations later joined one side or the other.

1. **Location** On the map, locate (a) Germany, (b) Austria-Hungary, (c) France, (d) Serbia.
2. **Place** (a) Which countries remained neutral throughout the war? (b) Which neutral nations eventually joined the Central Powers?
3. **Critical Thinking** *Predicting Consequences* What disadvantage did Germany face because of its location?

To ensure a quick victory in the west, the Schlieffen Plan required German armies to march through Belgium, then swing south behind French lines. On August 3, Germany invaded Belgium. However, Britain and other European powers had signed a treaty guaranteeing Belgian neutrality. Outraged by the invasion of Belgium, Britain declared war on Germany.

## Whose Fault?

How could an assassination lead to all-out war in just a few weeks? During the war, each side blamed the other. Afterward, the victorious Allies put the blame on Germany. Today, most historians agree that all parties must share blame for a catastrophe nobody wanted.

Each great power believed its cause was just. Austria wanted to punish Serbia for encouraging terrorism. Germany felt that it must stand by its one dependable ally, Austria. Russia saw the Austrian ultimatum to Serbia as an effort to oppress Slavic peoples. France feared that if it did not support Russia, it would have to face Germany alone later. Britain felt committed to protect Belgium but also feared the powerful German force just across the English Channel. ( See *You Decide*, "Is War Ever Justified?" pages 404–405.)

**"The lamps are going out."** Although leaders made the decisions, most people on both sides were equally committed to military action. Young men rushed to enlist, cheered on by women and their elders. Now that war had come at last, it seemed an exciting adventure.

British diplomat Edward Grey was less optimistic. As armies began to move, he predicted, "The lamps are going out all over Europe. We shall not see them lit again in our lifetime."

## SECTION 2 REVIEW

1. **Identify** (a) Francis Ferdinand, (b) Gavrilo Princip, (c) Black Hand, (d) Schlieffen Plan.
2. **Define** (a) ultimatum, (b) mobilize, (c) neutrality.
3. (a) Why did Serbian nationalists plot the assassination of Francis Ferdinand? (b) How did Austria react to the assassination?
4. Describe how each of the following nations got involved in the conflict: (a) Germany, (b) Russia, (c) France, (d) Britain.
5. **Critical Thinking** *Drawing Conclusions* Do you think that war could have been avoided in 1914? Why or why not?
6. *ACTIVITY* Choose one of the European powers involved in the outbreak of World War I. From that nation's point of view, draw a cartoon assigning blame for the war.

# 3 A New Kind of Conflict

## Guide for Reading

- Why did a stalemate develop on the western front?

- What forces made World War I different from earlier wars?

- How did the war become a global conflict?

"The Great War," as newspapers soon called it, was the largest war in history up to that time. The French mobilized almost 8.5 million men, the British 9 million, the Russians 12 million, and the Germans 11 million.

For those who fought, the statistics were more personal. "At least one in three of my generation in school died," recalled one survivor. Another young man wrote:

66One out of every four men who went out to the World War did not come back again, and of those who came back, many are maimed and blind and some are mad.99

The early enthusiasm for the war soon faded. There were no stirring cavalry charges, no quick and glorious victories. This was a new kind of war, far deadlier than any before.

## The Western Front

As the war began, German forces swept through Belgium toward Paris. German generals, however, soon violated the Schlieffen Plan. Russia mobilized more quickly than expected. After Russian forces won a few small victories in eastern Prussia, Germany hastily shifted some troops to the east. That move weakened German forces in the west. When British troops reached France, the German offensive stalled.

Both sides then dug in for the winter. They did not know that the battle lines in France and Belgium would remain almost unchanged for four years.

**Trench warfare.** On the Western Front, the warring armies burrowed into a vast system of trenches, stretching from the Swiss frontier to the English Channel. A war correspondent described the scene:

66To say where the trenches began and where they ended is difficult. . . . There were vast stretches of mud, of fields once cultivated, but now scarred with pits, trenches, rusty barbed wires. The roads were rivers of clay. They were lined with dugouts, cellars, and caves.99

An underground network linked bunkers, communications trenches, and gun emplacements. There, millions of soldiers roasted under the broiling summer sun or froze through the

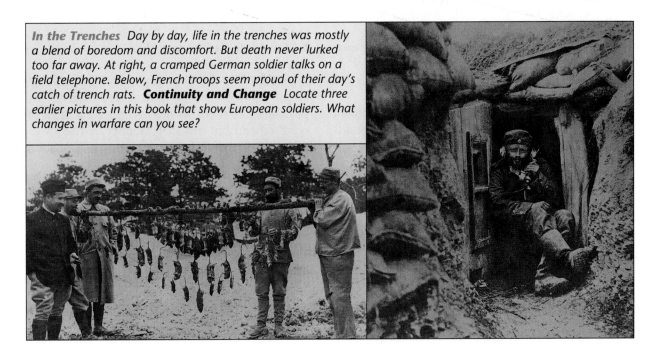

*In the Trenches* Day by day, life in the trenches was mostly a blend of boredom and discomfort. But death never lurked too far away. At right, a cramped German soldier talks on a field telephone. Below, French troops seem proud of their day's catch of trench rats. **Continuity and Change** Locate three earlier pictures in this book that show European soldiers. What changes in warfare can you see?

long winters. They shared their food with rats and their beds with lice.

Between the opposing trench lines lay "no man's land." In this empty tract, pocked with shell holes, every house and tree had long since been destroyed. Through coils of barbed wire, soldiers peered over the edge of their trenches, watching for the next attack. They themselves would have to charge into this man-made desert when officers gave the order.

Sooner or later, soldiers would obey the order to go "over the top." With no protection but their rifles and helmets, they charged across no man's land toward the enemy lines. With luck, they might overrun a few trenches. In time, the enemy would launch a counterattack, with similar results. Each side then rushed in reinforcements to replace the dead and wounded. The struggle continued, back and forth, over a few hundred yards of territory.

**Costly battles.** In 1916, both the Allies and Central Powers launched massive offensives to break the stalemate. German forces tried to overwhelm the French at Verdun (vuhr DUHN). The French sent up the battle cry "They shall not pass." The French defenders held firm, but the struggle cost more than a half-million casualties on both sides.

An Allied offensive at the Somme (SAHM) River was even more costly. In a single grisly day, 60,000 British soldiers were killed or wounded. In the five-month battle, over one million soldiers were killed, without either side winning an advantage.

**A war of machines.** Modern weapons added greatly to the destructiveness of the war. In 1914, German artillery could shell enemy lines from a distance of 15 miles away. By 1918, they were shelling Paris from battle lines 70 miles away.

World War I was truly the first mechanized war. The Quick Study Chart on page 287 details some of the technology that helped turn the war into a seemingly endless ordeal.

## Other European Fronts

On the Eastern Front, battle lines swayed back and forth, sometimes over large areas. Casualties rose even higher than in the west, but the results were just as indecisive.

**Disasters for Russia.** In August 1914, Russian armies pushed into eastern Germany. Then, at the battle of Tannenberg, they suffered one of the worst defeats of the war. Reeling, the Russians retreated. After Tannenberg, armies in the east fought on Russian soil.

As the least industrialized of the great powers, Russia was poorly equipped to fight a modern war. Troops sometimes lacked even rifles. Still, Russian commanders continued to fling masses of peasant soldiers into combat.

**War in the south.** Southeastern Europe was another battleground. In 1915, Bulgaria joined the Central Powers and helped crush its old rival Serbia. Italy, meanwhile, joined the Allies to gain Austrian-ruled lands inhabited by Italians. Caporetto, the major battle on the Italian front, was as disastrous for Italy as Tannenberg had been for Russia.

## The War Beyond Europe

Though most of the fighting took place in Europe, World War I was a global conflict. At sea, Britain blockaded Germany, while German U-boats sank ships crossing the Atlantic toward Allied ports. Such unrestricted submarine warfare outraged neutral countries, especially the United States.

**War and the colonies.** European colonies were drawn into the struggle. The Allies overran scattered German colonies in Africa and Asia. They also turned to their own colonies and dominions for troops, laborers, and supplies. Canada, Australia, and New Zealand sent troops to Britain's aid. Colonial recruits from British India and French West Africa fought on European battlefields.

People in the colonies had mixed feelings about serving. Many volunteered eagerly, expecting that their service would be a step toward citizenship or independence. Others were reluctant to serve the imperial powers. A South African man remarked:

66When we speak of joining . . . our women curse and spit at us, asking us whether the Government, for whom we propose to risk our lives, is not the one which sends the police to our houses at night.99

QUICK STUDY

# World War I: Technology Changes Warfare

| Invention | Description | Use in World War I | Connections Today |
|---|---|---|---|
| Automatic machine gun  | Mounted gun that fires a rapid, continuous stream of bullets. | Made it possible for a few gunners to mow down waves of soldiers. This helped create a stalemate by making it difficult to advance across no man's land. | Machine guns helped to make cavalry obsolete and to reduce the importance of infantry charges. |
| Tank  | Armored vehicle that travels on a track allowing it to cross many kinds of land. | Protected advancing troops as they broke through enemy defenses. Early tanks were not used often because they were slow and clumsy. | Tanks replaced cavalry as major means of ground advance. Some nations have used tanks to crush civilian unrest. |
| Submarine (in German, *Unterseeboot*, or U-boat) | Underwater ship that can launch torpedoes, or guided underwater bombs. | Used by Germany to destroy Allied shipping. U-boat attacks helped bring United States into war. | Modern nuclear submarines carry long-range atomic weapons. |
| Airplane  | One- or two-seat propeller plane equipped with machine gun. | At first, mainly used for observation. Later, flying "aces" engaged in individual combat, though such "dogfights" had little effect on the war. | Airplanes carry troops and supplies, bomb targets within enemy territory, and support ground action. |
| Poison gas; gas mask  | Various gases that cause choking, blinding, or severe skin blisters; gas masks protect soldiers from poison gas. | Lobbed by missile into enemy trenches, killing or disabling troops. Development of gas masks lessened the importance of poison gas. | Although outlawed by international agreement, poison gas was used in 1990s by Iraq against Kurdish rebels and by terrorists in Japan. |

*Interpreting a Chart  World War I was the first modern, fully industrialized war. Some weapons, such as machine guns, altered the nature of the fighting. Other new technology, such as tanks and airplanes, did not have their greatest impact until years later.  ■  Which invention on this chart do you think has done the most to change how wars are fought? Explain.*

## Europe at War, 1914–1918

Allies, 1918
Central Powers 1918
Neutral nations
Farthest advance by Central Powers
Battle sites

## GEOGRAPHY AND HISTORY

World War I was fought on many fronts, with massive losses of life and property.

1. **Location** On the map, locate (a) Sarajevo, (b) Verdun, (c) Somme River, (d) Tannenberg, (e) Caporetto, (f) the Dardanelles.
2. **Movement** How far into France did the Central Powers advance?
3. *Critical Thinking* **Comparing** Compare this map with the Time and Place map on page 276. Why do the two maps show different areas?

**Non-European powers.** The Ottoman empire joined the Central Powers in 1914. The Turks then closed off Allied ships from the Dardanelles, a strategic link to the Black Sea and Russia. (See the map above.) The Allies sent a massive force of British, Indian, Australian, and New Zealand troops to open up the strait. At the battle of Gallipoli (guh LIHP uh lee), Turkish

troops tied down the trapped Allies on the beaches. A British soldier described the futility of the struggle that followed:

❝On June 4th we went over the top. We took the Turks' trench and held it. It was called Hill 13. The next day we were relieved and told to rest for three hours, but it wasn't more than half an hour before the relieving regiment came running back. The Turks had returned and recaptured their trench. On June 6th my favorite officer was killed and no end of us butchered, but we managed to get hold of Hill 13 again. We found a great muddle, carnage and men without rifles shouting, 'Allah! Allah!,' which is God's name in the Turkish language. Of the 60 men I had started out to war from Harwich with, there were only three left. **99**

In January 1916, after 10 months and more than 200,000 casualties, the Allies finally withdrew from the Dardanelles. In turn, the Ottoman empire was hard hit in the Middle East. Arab nationalists, supported by the British, attacked Turkish outposts in their own struggle for freedom.

Japan, allied to Britain, used the war as an excuse to seize German outposts in China and islands in the Pacific. It also tried to impose a protectorate on China. The world's other great industrial power, the United States, tried to remain neutral. However, as you will read, it was eventually drawn into the war as well.

## SECTION 3 REVIEW

1. **Identify** (a) Western Front, (b) no man's land.
2. (a) Why did the war turn into a stalemate? (b) How was trench warfare conducted?
3. Describe how three new weapons affected the course of the war.
4. What role did Europe's overseas colonies play in World War I?
5. *Critical Thinking* **Predicting Consequences** Governments on both sides tried to keep full casualty figures and other bad news from reaching the public. What effect do you think disastrous defeats such as Tannenberg, Caporetto, or Gallipoli would have had on the attitude of people back home?
6. *ACTIVITY* With a partner, prepare an interview between a war correspondent and a soldier fighting on the Western Front during World War I.

# 4 Winning the War

## Guide for Reading

- How did World War I become a total war?
- What role did women play in the war effort?
- What impact did events in Russia and the United States have on the course of World War I?
- **Vocabulary** *total war, propaganda, atrocity, armistice*

By 1917, European societies were cracking under the strain of war. Instead of praising the glorious deeds of heroes, war poets began denouncing the leaders whose errors wasted so many lives. In "Suicide in the Trenches," the British poet and soldier Siegfried Sassoon captured the bitter mood:

**66**You smug-faced crowds with kindling eye
Who cheer when soldier lads march by,
Sneak home and pray you'll never know
The hell where youth and laughter go.**99**

Three years into the war, a revolution in Russia and the entry of the United States into the war would upset the balance of forces and finally end the long stalemate.

## *Effects of the Stalemate*

As the struggle wore on, nations realized that a modern, mechanized war required the total commitment of their whole society. The result was what we today call **total war,** the channeling of a nation's entire resources into a war effort.

**Economic impact.** Early on, both sides set up systems to recruit, arm, transport, and supply armies that numbered in the millions. All of the warring nations except Britain imposed universal military conscription, or "the draft,"

***Returning to the Trenches*** *British artist C.R.W. Nevinson painted in a new style called Futurism. The aim of Futurist art was to express a sense of motion and an increasingly mechanized world. In this painting, individual soldiers interlock like parts of a giant, impersonal machine. Nevinson saw trench warfare firsthand as a member of the British medical corps.* **Art and Literature** *Why was Futurism a fitting style for a painting about World War I?*

which required all young men to be ready for military or other service.

Governments raised taxes and borrowed huge amounts of money to pay the costs of war. They rationed food and other products, from boots to gasoline. In addition, they introduced other economic controls, such as setting prices and forbidding strikes.

**Propaganda war.** Total war meant controlling public opinion. Even in democratic countries, special boards censored the press. Their aim was to keep complete casualty figures and other discouraging news from reaching the people. Government censors also restricted popular literature, historical writings, motion pictures, and the arts.

Both sides waged a propaganda war. Propaganda is the spreading of ideas to pro-

mote a cause or damage an opposing cause. In Germany, people learned to sing a "Hymn of Hate" against the British:

66Hate by water and hate by land;
  Hate of the head and hate of the hand;
  We love as one, we hate as one;
  We have *one* foe and one alone—
  ENGLAND!99

Allied propaganda often played up Germany's invasion of Belgium as a barbarous act. The British and French press circulated tales of atrocities, horrible acts against innocent people. Often, these stories were greatly exaggerated versions of misreported incidents. Many were completely made up. ( ★ See *Skills for Success,* page 298.)

## Women at War

Women played a major part in total war. As millions of men left to fight, women took over their jobs and kept national economies going. Many women worked in war industries, manufacturing weapons and supplies. Others joined women's branches of the armed forces. When food shortages threatened Britain, volunteers in the Women's Land Army went to the fields to grow their nation's food.

**At the front.** Military nurses shared the dangers of the men whose wounds they tended. At aid stations close to the front lines, they worked around the clock, especially after a big "push" brought a flood of casualties. In her diary, Vera Brittain describes sweating through 90-degree days in France, "stopping hemorrhages, replacing intestines, and draining and reinserting innumerable rubber tubes" with "gruesome human remains heaped on the floor" around her feet.

Some women became national heroes. Edith Cavell, a British nurse, ran a Red Cross hospital in Belgium even after the German invasion. When the Germans discovered that she was helping Allied prisoners escape, they shot her as a spy. Allied propaganda made Cavell a symbol of German brutality, although women on both sides were executed as spies.

**Looking ahead.** War work gave women a new sense of pride and confidence. After the war, most women had to give up their jobs to men returning home. Still, they had challenged the idea that women were too "delicate" for demanding and dangerous jobs. In many countries, including Britain and the United States, women's support for the war effort helped them finally win the right to vote, after decades of struggle.

## Collapsing Morale

By 1917, the morale of both troops and civilians had plunged. Germany was sending 15-year-old recruits to the front. Britain was on the brink of bankruptcy. Long casualty lists, food shortages, and the failure of generals to win promised victories led to calls for peace.

As morale collapsed, troops mutinied in some French units. In Italy, many soldiers de-

**Serving Her Country** Posters like this one recruited thousands of women to serve in the Royal Air Force. Their work on the ground supported the exploits of daredevil flying aces in the air. **Continuity and Change** How does this poster both reinforce and challenge traditional notions of "women's work"?

serted after the defeat at Caporetto. In Russia, soldiers left the front to join in a full-scale revolution back home.

**Revolution in Russia.** Three years of war had hit Russia especially hard. Stories of incompetent generals and corruption destroyed public confidence. In March 1917, bread riots in St. Petersburg mushroomed into a revolution that brought down the Russian monarchy. (You will read more about the causes and effects of the Russian Revolution in Chapter 11.)

At first, the Allies welcomed the overthrow of the czar. They hoped Russia would institute a democratic government and become a stronger ally. But later that year, when V. I. Lenin came to power, he promised to pull Russian troops out of the war. Early in 1918, Lenin signed the Treaty of Brest-Litovsk (brehst lih TAWFSK) with Germany. The treaty ended Russian participation in World War I.

**Impact on the war.** Russia's withdrawal had an immediate impact on the war. With Russia out of the struggle, Germany could concentrate its forces on the Western Front. In the spring of 1918, the Central Powers stood ready to achieve the great breakthrough they had sought so long.

## The United States Declares War

Soon after the Russian Revolution began, however, another event altered the balance of forces. The United States, which so far had stayed out of the fighting, declared war on Germany. Why did the United States exchange neutrality for war in 1917?

**Unrestricted submarine warfare.** One major reason was German submarine attacks on merchant and passenger ships carrying American citizens. Many of these ships were carrying supplies to the Allies. But President Woodrow Wilson insisted that Americans, as citizens of a neutral country, had a right to safe travel on the seas.

In May 1915, a German submarine torpedoed the British liner *Lusitania*. Almost 1,200 passengers were killed, including 128 Americans. Germany justified the attack, arguing that the *Lusitania* was carrying weapons. When Wilson threatened to cut off relations with Germany, though, Germany agreed to restrict its submarine campaign. Before attacking any ship, U-boats would surface and give warning, allowing neutral passengers to escape to the lifeboats. In February 1917, however, Germany angered Wilson by resuming unrestricted submarine warfare.

**Cultural ties.** The United States had other reasons to support the Allies. Many Americans felt ties of culture and language to Britain. Americans were also sympathetic to France as another democracy. Still, some German Americans favored the Central Powers. So did many Irish Americans, who resented Britain's domination of Ireland, and Russian Jewish immigrants, who did not want to be allied with the czar.

**Zimmermann note.** In early 1917, the British intercepted a message from the German foreign minister, Arthur Zimmermann, to his ambassador in Mexico. Zimmermann promised that, in return for Mexican support, Germany would help Mexico "to reconquer the lost territory in New Mexico, Texas, and Arizona." Britain revealed the Zimmermann note to the American government. When the note became public, anti-German feeling intensified in the United States.

**"The Yanks are coming!"** In April 1917, Wilson asked Congress to declare war on Germany. "We have no selfish ends to serve," he stated. Instead, he painted the conflict idealistically as a war "to make the world safe for democracy" and as a "war to end war."

First, the United States needed months to recruit, train, supply, and transport a modern army across the Atlantic. By 1918, about two million of these fresh American soldiers had joined the war-weary Allied troops fighting on the Western Front. The confidence of these Americans was captured in "Over There," a popular song by George M. Cohan. "The Yanks are coming!" it promised. "And we won't come back/ Till it's over, over there!"

▲ Sheet music for "Over There"

Although relatively few American troops got into combat, they proved to be good fighters. Their arrival gave Allied troops a much-needed morale boost. Just as important to the debt-ridden Allies was the financial aid provided by the United States.

**The Fourteen Points.** Though he had failed to maintain American neutrality, Wilson still hoped to be a peacemaker. In January 1918, he issued the Fourteen Points, a list of his terms for resolving this and future wars. He called for an end to secret treaties, freedom of the seas, free trade, and large-scale reductions of arms. Wilson also favored self-determination, by which the peoples of Eastern Europe would choose their own form of government. All those issues, he felt, had helped cause the war. Finally, he urged the creation of a "general association of nations" to keep the peace in the future.

## *Campaign to Victory*

A final showdown got underway in early 1918. In March, the Germans launched a huge offensive that pushed the Allies back 40 miles by July. But the effort exhausted the Germans. The Allies then launched a counterattack, slowly driving German forces back across France and Belgium. In September, German generals told the kaiser that the war could not be won.

The German people showed their monarch their frustration as uprisings exploded among hungry city dwellers. German commanders advised the kaiser to step down, as the czar had done. William II did so in early November, fleeing into exile in the Netherlands.

By autumn, Austria-Hungary was also reeling toward collapse. As the government in Vienna tottered, the subject nationalities revolted, splintering the empire of the Hapsburgs.

The new German government sought an armistice, or agreement to end fighting, with the Allies. At 11 A.M. on November 11, 1918, the Great War at last came to an end.

## SECTION 4 REVIEW

1. **Identify** (a) Women's Land Army, (b) Edith Cavell, (c) Treaty of Brest-Litovsk, (d) Woodrow Wilson, (e) Fourteen Points.
2. **Define** (a) total war, (b) propaganda, (c) atrocity, (d) armistice.
3. How did wartime governments attempt to control (a) national economies, (b) public opinion?
4. Describe two ways that World War I affected women.
5. (a) Why did Russia withdraw from the Allies? (b) Why did the United States declare war on Germany?
6. *Critical Thinking* **Analyzing Information** Why is 1917 considered to be a turning point in the war?
7. *ACTIVITY* Imagine that you are a soldier fighting for the Allies or for the Central Powers. Write a letter home describing your feelings about the armistice.

## 5 | Making the Peace

### Guide for Reading

- What problems did Europeans face in 1918?
- How did the Big Three disagree over the peace?
- What were the results of the Paris Peace Conference?

- **Vocabulary** *reparations, mandate*

Just weeks after the war ended, President Wilson boarded the steamship *George Washington,* bound for France. He had decided to go in person to Paris, where Allied leaders would make the peace. Wilson was certain that he could solve the problems of old Europe. "Tell me what is right," Wilson urged his advisers, "and I'll fight for it."

Sadly, it would not be that easy. Europe was a shattered continent. Its problems, and those of the world, would not be solved at Paris, or for many years afterward.

### *The Costs of War*

The human and material costs of the war were staggering. More than 8.5 million people were dead. Double that number had been wounded, many handicapped for life. Famine threatened many regions. The devastation was made even worse in 1918 by a deadly epidemic

▲ *French war orphans*

## Casualties of World War I

| Allies | Deaths in Battle | Wounded in Battle |
|---|---|---|
| France | 1,357,800 | 4,266,000 |
| British empire | 908,371 | 2,090,212 |
| Russia | 1,700,000 | 4,950,000 |
| Italy | 462,391 | 953,886 |
| United States | 50,585 | 205,690 |
| Other | 502,421 | 342,585 |
| **Central Powers** | | |
| Germany | 1,808,546 | 4,247,143 |
| Austria-Hungary | 922,500 | 3,620,000 |
| Ottoman empire | 325,000 | 400,000 |

Source: R. E. Dupuy and T. N. Dupuy,
*The Encyclopedia of Military History*

*Interpreting a Chart* World War I resulted in far more casualties than any previous war. In countries such as Britain, France, and Germany, hardly a family emerged untouched. ■ Which nation suffered the most military deaths among the Allies? Among the Central Powers? Why did the United States suffer relatively few casualties?

of influenza. In just a few months, the flu swept around the world, killing more than 20 million people—twice as many as the war itself.

**Financial burdens.** In battle zones from France to Russia, homes, farms, factories, roads, and churches had been shelled into rubble. Rebuilding and paying huge national war debts would burden an already battered world.

Shaken and disillusioned, people everywhere felt bitter about the war. The Allies blamed the conflict on their defeated foes and insisted that the losers make reparations, or payments for war damage. The stunned Central Powers, who had viewed the armistice as a cease-fire rather than a surrender, looked for scapegoats on whom to blame their defeat.

**Political turmoil.** Under the stress of war, governments had collapsed in Russia, Germany, Austria-Hungary, and the Ottoman empire. Political radicals dreamed of building a new social order from the chaos, as revolutionaries in Russia seemed to be doing. Conservatives warned against the spread of bolshevism, or communism, as it came to be called.

Unrest also swept through Europe's colonial empires. African and Asian soldiers had discovered that the imperial powers were not as invincible as they seemed. Colonial troops returned home with a more cynical view of Europeans and renewed hopes for independence.

### The Paris Peace Conference

To a weary and angry world, Woodrow Wilson seemed a symbol of hope. His talk of democracy and self-determination raised expectations for a just and lasting peace, even in defeated Germany. As he rode along the broad Paris boulevards, crowds cheered wildly. Overhead, a giant banner proclaimed, "Honor to Wilson the Just."

**The Big Three.** Wilson was one of three strong personalities who dominated the Paris Peace Conference. A dedicated reformer, Wilson was so sure of his rightness that he could be hard to work with. Urging "peace without victory," he wanted the Fourteen Points to be the basis of the peace.

The other Allies had different aims. The British prime minister, David Lloyd George, knew that the British people demanded harsh treatment for Germany. He promised that he would build a postwar Britain "fit for heroes"—a goal that would cost money. The French leader, Georges Clemenceau, bore the nickname "the Tiger" for his fierce war policy. His chief goal was to weaken Germany so that it could never again threaten France. "Mr. Wilson bores me with his Fourteen Points," complained Clemenceau. "Why, God Almighty has only ten!"

**Difficult issues.** Crowds of other representatives circled around the "Big Three" with their own demands and interests. Among the most difficult issues were the secret agreements made by the Allies during the war. Italy had signed one such treaty. Its prime minister, Vittorio Orlando, insisted on gaining for Italy lands that were once ruled by Austria-Hungary. Such secret agreements violated Wilson's principle of self-determination.

Self-determination posed other problems. Many people who had been ruled by Russia, Austria-Hungary, or the Ottoman empire now demanded national states of their own. The territories claimed by these peoples often overlapped, so it was impossible to satisfy them all.

Faced with conflicting demands, Wilson had to compromise on his Fourteen Points. On one point, though, he stood firm. His dream was to create an international League of Nations to guarantee peace for the future. With the league in place, he felt sure that any mistakes made in Paris could be corrected in time.

## The Treaty of Versailles

In June 1919, the peacemakers summoned representatives of the new German Republic to the palace of Versailles outside Paris. The Germans were ordered to sign the treaty drawn up by the Allies.

The German delegates read the document with growing horror. It forced Germany to assume full blame for causing the war:

66 The Allied and Associated Governments affirm, and Germany accepts, the responsibility of Germany and her allies for causing all the loss and damage to which the Allied and Associated Governments and their nationals have been subjected as a consequence of the war imposed on them by the aggression of Germany and her allies. 99

The treaty also imposed huge reparations that would put an already damaged German economy under a staggering burden. The reparations covered not only the destruction caused by the war, but also pensions for millions of Allied soldiers or their widows and families. The total cost of German reparations would come to over $30 billion.

Other clauses were aimed at weakening Germany. The treaty severely limited the size of the once-feared German military machine. It returned Alsace and Lorraine to France, removed hundreds of square miles of territory from western and eastern Germany, and stripped Germany of its overseas colonies.

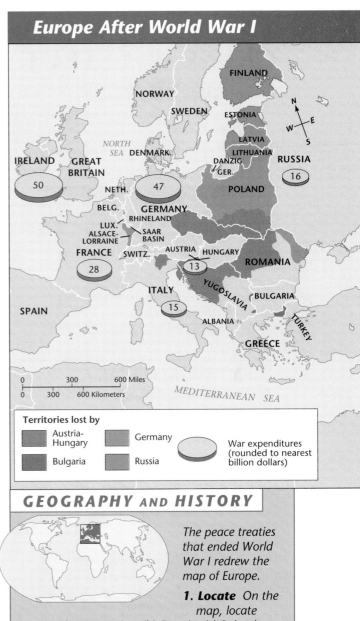

### Europe After World War I

Territories lost by
- Austria-Hungary
- Bulgaria
- Germany
- Russia

War expenditures (rounded to nearest billion dollars)

### GEOGRAPHY AND HISTORY

The peace treaties that ended World War I redrew the map of Europe.

**1. Locate** On the map, locate (a) Alsace-Lorraine, (b) Estonia, (c) Poland, (d) Hungary, (e) Yugoslavia.

**2. Region** Which of the Central Powers lost the most territory in Eastern Europe?

**3. Critical Thinking** Analyzing Information (a) How does the map show the cost of the war for the various countries? (b) Which country spent the most? (c) About how much did Italy spend?

The Germans signed because they had no choice. But German resentment of the Treaty of Versailles would poison the international climate for 20 years—and help spark an even more deadly world war. (See Chapter 14.)

# CAUSE AND EFFECT

### Long-Term Causes

Imperialist and economic rivalries among European powers
European alliance system
Militarism and arms race
Nationalist tensions in Balkans

### Immediate Causes

Austria-Hungary annexation of Bosnia and Herzegovina
Fighting in the Balkans
Assassination of Archduke Francis Ferdinand
German invasion of Belgium

## WORLD WAR I

### Immediate Effects

Enormous cost in lives and money
Russian Revolution
Creation of new nations in Eastern Europe
Requirement that Germany pay reparations
German loss of its overseas colonies
Balfour Declaration
League of Nations

### Long-Term Effects

Economic impact of war debts on Europe
Emergence of United States and Japan as important powers
Growth of nationalism in colonies
Rise of fascism
World War II

### Connections Today

Ethnic tensions in Balkans
International agreement banning poison gas
Use of airplanes and submarines for military purposes
Arab-Israeli conflict

## Other Settlements

The Allies drew up separate treaties with the other Central Powers. These treaties redrew the map of Eastern Europe.

**Self-determination in action.** A band of new nations emerged where the German, Austrian, and Russian empires had once ruled. These nations included the Baltic states of Lithuania, Latvia, and Estonia. (See the map on page 295.) Poland regained independence after more than 100 years of foreign rule.

Three new republics—Czechoslovakia, Austria, and Hungary—rose in the old Hapsburg heartland. In the Balkans, the peacemakers created a new South Slav state, Yugoslavia, dominated by Serbia. Eastern Europe, however, remained a center of conflict, as you will read.

**Mandate system.** European colonies in Africa, Asia, and the Pacific had looked to the Paris Peace Conference with high hopes. Many people from these lands had fought alongside Europeans. Colonial leaders expected that the peace would bring new respect and an end to imperial rule. They took up Wilson's call for self-determination.

However, the leaders at Paris applied the principle of self-determination only to parts of Europe. Outside Europe, the victorious Allies added to their existing overseas empires. The treaties created a system of mandates, or territories that were administered by western powers. Britain and France gained mandates over German colonies in Africa and Ottoman lands in the Middle East. In theory, mandates were to be held and modernized until they were able to "stand alone." In practice, they practically became European colonies. From Africa to the Middle East and across Asia, colonized peoples felt betrayed by the peacemakers.

**Unfulfilled goals.** Germany was not the only power dissatisfied by the peace. Italy was angry because it did not get all the lands promised in its secret treaty with the Allies.

*Interpreting a Chart* World War I grew out of rivalries among the nations of Europe. But its effects are still being felt around the world today. ■ What single event sparked the outbreak of World War I? Which long-term effect of World War I do you think is most important today? Why?

Conference at Versailles In this painting, the Big Three—Lloyd George, Wilson, and Clemenceau—sit together in the center, surrounded by dozens of other delegates. Standing left of center is Faisal, future king of Iraq, who had come to Paris seeking Arab independence. **Global Interaction** How do you think Faisal reacted when the peacemakers created the mandate system?

sioned with war and its consequences, the United States chose to play a lone hand in world affairs.

As time soon revealed, the league was powerless to prevent aggression or war. Still, it was a first step toward something genuinely new—an international organization dedicated to maintaining peace and advancing the interests of all peoples.

Japan protested the refusal of western nations to recognize its claims in China. At the same time, China was forced to accept Japanese control over some former German holdings. (See page 336.) Russia, excluded from the peace talks, resented the reestablishment of a Polish nation and three independent Baltic states on lands that had been part of the Russian empire.

All of these discontented nations bided their time. They waited for a chance to revise the peace settlements in their favor.

## Hopes for Global Peace

The Paris Peace Conference offered one beacon of hope in the League of Nations. In the aftermath of the war, millions of people looked to the league to ensure the peace. More than 40 nations joined the league. They agreed to negotiate disputes rather than resort to war. Members of the league promised to take common action, economic or even military, against any aggressor state.

Wilson's dream had become a reality. Yet his own Senate refused to ratify the treaty and the United States never joined the league. Disillu-

## SECTION 5 REVIEW

1. **Identify** (a) David Lloyd George, (b) Georges Clemenceau, (c) Treaty of Versailles, (d) League of Nations.
2. **Define** (a) reparations, (b) mandate.
3. Describe conditions in Europe after World War I.
4. (a) Explain three issues to be settled at the Paris Peace Conference. (b) How did Wilson's goals for the peace differ from those of other Allied leaders?
5. How did the treaties both follow and violate Woodrow Wilson's principle of self-determination?
6. *Critical Thinking* **Making Inferences** Wilson's closest adviser wrote, "Looking at the conference in retrospect, there is much to approve and much to regret." What do you think he might have approved? What might he have regretted?
7. *ACTIVITY* Write an editorial or draw a cartoon about the Treaty of Versailles that might have appeared in a German newspaper in 1919.

# 10 | CHAPTER REVIEW AND SKILLS FOR SUCCESS

## CHAPTER REVIEW

### REVIEWING VOCABULARY

Write sentences using *five* of the vocabulary words from this chapter, leaving blanks where the vocabulary words would go. Exchange your sentences with another student and fill in the blanks on each other's lists.

### REVIEWING FACTS

1. What arms race occurred in the years leading up to World War I?
2. Which nations made up the Central Powers and the Allies?
3. Why did Austria declare war on Serbia?
4. How did Germany's attack on France bring Britain into the war?
5. Describe trench warfare.
6. How did troops from European colonies become involved in the fighting in Europe?
7. What factors led the United States to enter the war?
8. What were the Fourteen Points?
9. Describe the terms of the Treaty of Versailles.
10. What was the League of Nations?

## SKILLS FOR SUCCESS   RECOGNIZING PROPAGANDA

MEN OF BRITAIN! WILL YOU STAND THIS?

Nº 2 Wykeham Street, SCARBOROUGH, after the German bombardment on Decr 16th. It was the Home of a Working Man. Four People were killed in this House including the Wife, aged 58, and Two Children, the youngest aged 5.

78 Women & Children were killed and 228 Women & Children were wounded by the German Raiders

ENLIST NOW

**Propaganda** consists of ideas or information that are spread deliberately to influence people's thoughts or actions. The information given may be true. However, it is usually only one side of an issue or may be presented in a distorted manner.

One technique that propagandists use is to present half-truths, or supplying only those facts that support a particular cause. A second technique is to engage in name-calling. A third technique is to identify a cause with a famous person or noble idea. A fourth technique is to show the other side in the worst possible light.

During World War I, both sides used posters to spread propaganda. The poster at left was printed in Britain in 1915. Examine the poster, then answer the following questions.

1. **Identify the use of propaganda techniques.** (a) Does the British poster contain any half-truths? Explain. (b) Does the poster make use of name-calling? Explain.
2. **Analyze the emotional appeal of the propaganda.** What emotions might this poster have stirred up in the British people? Why?
3. **Draw conclusions.** (a) Who was the intended audience of this poster? (b) What was the main goal of the poster?

## REVIEWING CHAPTER THEMES

Review the "Focus On" questions at the start of this chapter. Then select *three* of those questions and answer them, using information from the chapter.

## CRITICAL THINKING

1. **Linking Past and Present** (a) What efforts were made to promote world peace before and after World War I? (b) How do individuals and governments work for peace today?

2. **Analyzing Political Cartoons** Study the cartoon on page 283. (a) What attitude does the cartoonist seem to have toward the major powers of Europe? (b) How does the cartoon reflect the position of the United States at the beginning of the war? (c) Based on your reading, does this cartoon accurately depict the crisis leading up to World War I?

3. **Analyzing Information** What did Woodrow Wilson mean by "peace without victory"?

## ANALYZING PRIMARY SOURCES

Use the quotation on pages 288–289 to answer the following questions.

1. How many times did one side or the other capture Hill 13?

2. What statements suggest the high number of casualties in the fighting?

3. What do you think was the writer's attitude toward the war? Explain.

## FOR YOUR PORTFOLIO

**UNDERSTANDING PROPAGANDA** Imagine that it is 1917 and that you have been assigned to produce propaganda that will convince more Americans to support the Allies. Begin by making a list of reasons for the United States to support the Allies. Then decide what form your propaganda will take, such as a speech, poster, song, or skit. Finally, prepare your propaganda and present it to the class.

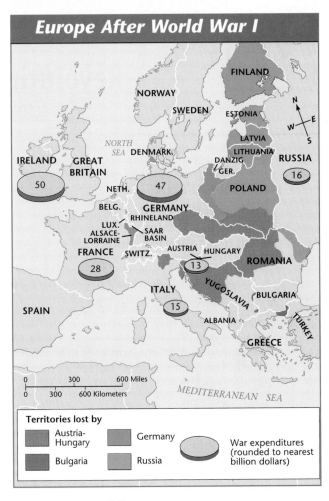

### Europe After World War I

Territories lost by

- Austria-Hungary
- Bulgaria
- Germany
- Russia

War expenditures (rounded to nearest billion dollars)

## ANALYZING MAPS

Use the map to answer the following questions.

1. How was Poland created?

2. Which nation formerly occupied Estonia, Latvia, and Lithuania?

3. Which side spent more on the war, the Allies or the Central Powers?

## INTERNET ACTIVITY

**CREATING A MAP** Use the Internet to research important battles, turning points, and changes in methods of warfare that took place during World War I. Then create an illustrated map of Europe during World War I that highlights some of those events and explains their significance.

# Revolution in Russia

## (1917–1939)

**CHAPTER OUTLINE**

1 Two Revolutions in Russia
2 From Lenin to Stalin
3 Life in a Totalitarian State

As he watched the Bolsheviks celebrate their victory in November 1917, N. N. Sukhanov (soo KAHN awf) was both excited and nervous. In just a few months, these radical revolutionaries had seized power in Russia. Their leader, Lenin, and his comrades rose before a cheering crowd, savoring their triumph. Everyone sang the "Internationale," the anthem for supporters of worldwide socialism. "The mass of delegates," recalled Sukhanov, "were permeated by the faith that all would go well in the future too."

Sukhanov was not so sure. Like many Russians, he had long dreamed of the moment when the czar would be gone and the government would undertake much-needed changes. Like the Bolsheviks, he, too, was a socialist. But he feared these determined revolutionaries:

66 Applause, hurrahs, caps flung up in the air . . . But I didn't believe in the success, in the rightness, or in the historic mission of a Bolshevik regime. Sitting in the back seats, I watched this celebration with a heavy heart. How I longed to join in and merge with this mass and with its leaders in a single feeling! But I couldn't. 99

Time would later justify Sukhanov's worst fears. In 1931, he himself would be arrested by the new government's secret police, to vanish like millions of others into a brutal forced-labor camp. The revolution that many Russians had welcomed in 1917 would have costs that they never anticipated.

Like the American and French revolutions, the Russian Revolution began with a small incident—bread riots in the capital. But it soon mushroomed into one of the most important events of the century. Leaders like Lenin were determined to create a new society based on the ideas of Karl Marx. Certain that capitalism was destined to fall, they harbored ambitions to spread communist revolution around the world.

The worldwide revolution that Marx had predicted never took place. But Lenin and his successors would transform czarist Russia into the communist Soviet Union. For almost 75 years, Soviet experiments in one-party politics and a state-run economy would serve as a model for revolutionaries from China to Cuba.

**FOCUS ON** these themes as you read:

- **Continuity and Change**
  How did political, social, and economic conditions in czarist Russia spark a revolution?

- **Impact of the Individual**
  What roles did Lenin and Stalin play in the emergence of the Soviet Union?

- **Economics and Technology**
  How did the Soviet economy develop?

- **Political and Social Systems**
  How did the Soviet Union become a totalitarian state?

**TIME AND PLACE**

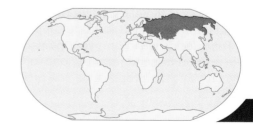

*A New Russia* The year 1917 saw two revolutions in Russia. The first overthrew the czar. The second led to the creation of the world's first communist nation, the Soviet Union. Here, the Soviet Red Army parades in Moscow past a statue of Lenin, leader of the communist takeover. The city is decorated in red, the color of the revolution. **Art and Literature** Do you think this painter admired the revolution? How can you tell?

## HUMANITIES LINK
*Art History* Sergei Eisenstein, *Battleship Potemkin* (page 312).
*Literature* In this chapter, you will encounter passages from the following works of literature: Mikhail Sholokhov, *And Quiet Flows the Don* (page 307); Vladimir Mayakovsky, "Vladimir Ilyich Lenin" (page 316); Anna Akhmatova, "Requiem" (page 316).

| **1917** | **1921** | **1924** | **1928** | **1934** | **1941** |
|---|---|---|---|---|---|
| Bolsheviks take over in Russia | Lenin adopts New Economic Policy | Lenin dies | Stalin proposes first five-year plan | Great Purge begins in Soviet Union | Germany invades Soviet Union |

| 1915 | 1920 | 1925 | 1930 | 1935 | 1940 |
|---|---|---|---|---|---|

# 1 Two Revolutions in Russia

## Guide for Reading

- Why did revolution break out in Russia in 1917?

- What were the goals of Lenin and the Bolsheviks?

- What problems did the Bolsheviks face?

- **Vocabulary** *soviet*

On Easter 1913, Czar Nicholas II gave his wife, Alexandra, a fabulous jeweled egg, made by the world-famous jewelry firm of Fabergé (fab uhr ZHAY). The egg's enamel shell held tiny portraits of all the Romanovs who had reigned since Michael Romanov was elected to rule Russia in 1613. Balls, parades, and other ceremonies marked the 300th anniversary of the Romanov dynasty. Everywhere, Russians cheered wildly for the czar and his family.

Years later, an exiled Russian noblewoman recalled the anniversary celebrations:

66Nobody seeing those
enthusiastic crowds
could have imagined that
in less than four years,
Nicky's very name would
be splattered with mud
and hatred.99

▲ *Fabergé egg given by Nicholas II to his wife*

After the Revolution of 1905, Nicholas had failed to solve Russia's basic problems. Discontent sparked new eruptions. In March 1917, the first of two revolutions would topple the Romanov dynasty and pave the way for even more radical changes.

## Revolutionary Rumblings

In 1914, the huge Russian empire stretched from Eastern Europe to the Pacific. Compared to industrialized Western Europe, it was a backward land dominated by landowning nobles, priests, and an autocratic czar. Much of its majority peasant population endured in stark poverty. A small middle class and an urban working class were emerging as Russia began to industrialize.

**Unrest.** Under pressure, czars had made some reforms, but too few to ease the nation's crisis. (See page 187.) The elected Duma set up after the Revolution of 1905 had no real power. Moderates pressed for a constitution and social change. But Nicholas II, a weak and ineffectual man, blocked attempts to limit his authority. Like past czars, he relied on his secret police and other enforcers to impose his will. Adding to the problems of the government were a corrupt bureaucracy and an overburdened court system.

Outside the government, revolutionaries hatched radical plots. Some hoped to lead discontented peasants to overthrow the czarist regime. Marxists tried to ignite revolution among the proletariat—the growing class of factory and railroad workers, miners, and urban wage earners. To outwit government spies and informers, revolutionaries worked in secrecy under rigid discipline. A revolution, they believed, would occur, but the time was not yet ripe.

**World War I.** The outbreak of war in 1914 fired national pride and united Russians. Armies dashed to battle with enthusiasm. But like the Crimean and Russo-Japanese wars, World War I quickly strained Russian resources. Factories could not turn out enough supplies. The transportation system broke down, delivering only a trickle of needed materials to the front. By 1915, soldiers had no rifles, no ammunition, and no medical care. Badly equipped and poorly led, they died in staggering numbers. In 1915 alone, Russian casualties reached two million.

In a patriotic gesture, Nicholas II went to the front to take personal charge. The decision proved a disastrous blunder. The czar was no more competent than many of his generals. Worse, he left domestic affairs to the czarina, Alexandra. Many Russians already distrusted Alexandra because she was German born. She also knew little about government. As corruption and intrigue flourished, Alexandra came to rely more and more on the advice of a notorious "holy man" named Gregory Rasputin.

## Death of the Mad Monk

An illiterate Siberian peasant, Rasputin was not actually a monk in the Russian Orthodox Church. In fact, he was amazingly corrupt and fond of worldly pleasures. But his powerful personality helped him gain a widespread reputation as a healer.

No one believed in his "miraculous" powers more than the czarina. Time and again, he eased the suffering of her only son, Alexis. The boy suffered from hemophilia, an inherited disorder in which any injury can lead to uncontrollable bleeding. When doctors were not able to help, Rasputin stopped the prince's bleeding, apparently through hypnosis.

**A threat to Russia?** By 1916, Rasputin's influence over Alexandra reached new heights. At his say-so, officials could be appointed or dismissed. Those who flattered him won top jobs for which they were wholly unqualified. Yet Alexandra chose to ignore all warnings about Rasputin's evil nature. She insisted that he had been sent by God to save Russia and the Romanov dynasty. At a time when wise leadership was desperately needed, Russia was in the hands of a shady character known to his enemies as the "mad monk."

Members of the Duma, nobles, and the czar's relatives saw the danger. To save the

Hemophilia was considered a "curse of kings" because it afflicted so many of the royal families of Europe. The disease is carried by the mother but is usually inherited by male children. Alexandra's grandmother, Queen Victoria, passed the gene for hemophilia to many of her 9 children and 34 grandchildren. Through royal marriages, it spread from Britain to the ruling houses of Russia, Spain, and Germany. Kaiser William II, another grandchild of Victoria, escaped the disease, but his uncle and two nephews were hemophiliacs.

**The Mad Monk** *Both nobles and ordinary Russians hated Rasputin for his influence over the czarina. "He is hated," complained Alexandra, "because we love him." Rasputin once boasted that "the czar and czarina bow down to me, kneel to me, kiss my hands."* **Impact of the Individual** *How might Rasputin's appearance have added to his reputation as a "holy man" and a magical healer?*

monarchy, a group of five men hatched a plot to destroy Rasputin.

**A hard man to kill.** On December 29, 1916, Prince Felix Yussoupov (yoo soo pawf), a nephew of the czar, lured Rasputin to his palace. The prince fed the "mad monk" cakes and wine laced with poison. Rasputin polished them off and talked on—for hours.

Yussoupov hurried upstairs to consult his nervous co-conspirators. He returned with a revolver and shot Rasputin. As the plotters examined the body, Rasputin suddenly leaped up and grabbed the prince, who fled in terror. One of the plotters described what happened next:

66What I saw would have been a dream if it hadn't been a terrible reality. Rasputin, who half an hour before lay dying in the cellar, was running quickly across the snow-covered courtyard toward the iron gate which led to the street.99

Another shot felled Rasputin, who was then clubbed into stillness. The conspirators dropped the body into the icy Neva River. Later when it was found, doctors discovered that neither poison nor bullets had killed Rasputin. He had died by drowning.

**Rasputin's final warning.** News of Rasputin's death caused rejoicing in the capital. Alexandra, though, was desolate. Just weeks before, Rasputin had written her a letter predicting his murder. If he were killed by nobles, he warned, "None of your children or relations will remain alive for more than two years. They will be killed by the Russian people."

Rasputin's prophecy would enhance his legend. In 1917, the Romanov dynasty indeed came to an end. Its downfall, though, was not due to Rasputin's murder, but to long unsolved problems and the strains of war. ▪

## The March Revolution

By March 1917,* disasters on the battlefield, combined with food and fuel shortages on the home front, brought the monarchy to collapse. In St. Petersburg (renamed Petrograd during the war), workers were going on strike. Marchers, mostly women, surged through the streets, shouting, "Bread! Bread!" Troops refused to fire on the demonstrators, leaving the government helpless. Finally, on the advice of military and political leaders, the czar abdicated.

Duma politicians then set up a provisional, or temporary, government. Middle-class liberals in the government began preparing a constitution for a new Russian republic. At the same time, they continued the war against Germany. That decision proved fatal. Most Russians were fed up with the war. Troops at the front were deserting and returning home in droves. Peasants wanted land. City workers demanded food and an end to the desperate shortages.

Outside the provisional government, revolutionary socialists plotted their own course. In Petrograd and other cities, they set up soviets,

---

*The revolutions of March and November 1917 are known to Russians as the February and October revolutions. In 1917, Russia still used an old calendar, which was 13 days behind the one used in Western Europe. Not until 1918 did Russia adopt the western calendar.

or councils of workers and soldiers. At first, the soviets worked democratically within the government. Before long, though, the Bolsheviks, a radical socialist group, took charge. The leader of the Bolsheviks was a determined revolutionary, V. I. Lenin.

## Lenin and the Bolsheviks

Lenin's real name was Vladimir Ilyich Ulyanov (ool YAHN awf). He was born in 1870 to a middle-class family. When he was 17, his older brother was arrested and hanged for plotting to kill Alexander III. The execution branded the entire family and instilled in young Vladimir a lifetime hatred for the czarist government. Still, he managed to finish his studies.

As a young man, he read the works of Karl Marx and participated in student demonstrations. He spread Marxist ideas among factory workers along with other socialists, including Nadezhda Krupskaya (nah DYEZH duh kroop SKĪ uh), the daughter of a poor noble family.

In 1895, Lenin and Krupskaya were arrested and sent to Siberia. During their imprisonment, they were married. After their release, they went into exile in Switzerland. There, they worked tirelessly to spread revolutionary ideas. A rival once described Lenin's total commitment to the cause:

66There is no other man who is absorbed by the revolution 24 hours a day, who has no other thoughts but the thought of revolution, and who, even when he sleeps, dreams of nothing but the revolution.99

**A new view of Marx.** Lenin adapted Marxist ideas to Russian conditions. Marx had predicted that the industrial working class would rise spontaneously to overthrow capitalism. But Russia did not have a large urban proletariat. Instead, Lenin called for an elite group to lead the revolution and set up a "dictatorship of the proletariat." Though this revolutionary party represented a small percentage of socialists, Lenin gave them the name Bolsheviks, meaning "majority."

In Western Europe, many socialists had come to think that socialism could be achieved through gradual reforms such as higher wages, increased suffrage, and social welfare programs. The Bolsheviks rejected this approach. To Lenin, reforms were merely capitalist tricks to repress the masses. Only revolution, he said, could bring about needed changes.

**An exile returns.** In March 1917, Lenin was still in exile. As Russia stumbled into revolution, Germany saw a chance to weaken its enemy by helping Lenin return home. In a sealed train, it rushed the Bolshevik leader across Germany to the Russian frontier.

On April 16, 1917, Lenin stepped off the train in Petrograd. A crowd of fellow exiles and activists recently released from the czar's prisons met him at the station. Lenin triumphantly addressed the crowd:

> 66Dear comrades, soldiers, sailors and workers, I am happy to greet in you the victorious Russian revolution, to greet you as the advance guard of the international proletarian army. . . . Any day may see the general collapse of European capitalism. The Russian revolution you have accomplished has dealt it the first blow and has opened a new epoch. . . . Long live the International Socialist Revolution!99

## The November Revolution

Lenin threw himself into the work of furthering the revolution, assisted by another committed Marxist revolutionary, Leon Trotsky. To the hungry, war-weary Russian people, Lenin and the Bolsheviks promised "Peace, Land, and Bread."

That summer, the provisional government launched yet another disastrous new offensive against Germany. As troops mutinied and another grim winter closed in, the Bolsheviks made their move.

**The Bolshevik takeover.** In November 1917, squads of Red Guards—armed factory workers—joined mutinous sailors from the Russian fleet in attacking the provisional government. In a matter of days, Lenin's forces overthrew a government that no longer had any support.

In Petrograd, members of the government were meeting in an inner room at the Winter Palace. Suddenly, a young cadet entered the room to announce that Bolsheviks were storming the palace. "What are the provisional government's orders?" he asked.

"It's no use," one politician announced. "We give up. No bloodshed!"

*The Death of Old Russia* In the March Revolution, angry workers confronted the czar's troops in Petrograd. Instead of firing, the soldiers turned against their officers and joined the rebellion. "Cars full of soldiers with rifles and red flags are driving through the streets," one woman reported. "The crowd rushes toward them and shouts 'Hurray!'" *Political and Social Systems* Why do you think soldiers turned against their officers and the czar?

**Revolutionary Genius** *An iron will and brilliant mind made Lenin the natural leader of the Bolsheviks. Once in power, however, Lenin found his revolution threatened by enemies inside and outside the country. "The capitalists of England, America, and France are leading a war against Russia," he railed in one speech. Lenin told soldiers that the Red Army was invincible "because it combines millions of active peasants and workers who have now learned how to fight."* **Impact of the Individual** *How does this painting convey the impression that Lenin was an energetic, commanding leader?*

A moment later, armed men flooded into the room. The provisional government had fallen without a struggle.

**Bolsheviks in charge.** The Bolsheviks quickly seized power in other cities. In Moscow, it took a week of fighting to blast the local government out of the walled Kremlin. Moscow became the Bolsheviks' capital, and the Kremlin their headquarters.

"We shall now occupy ourselves in Russia in building up a proletarian socialist state," declared Lenin. The Bolsheviks ended private ownership of land and distributed land to peasants. Workers were given control of the factories and mines. A new red flag with an entwined hammer and sickle symbolized union between peasants and workers.

Millions of Russians thought they had at last won control of their lives. In fact, the Bolsheviks—renamed Communists—would soon become their new masters.

## Under Siege

After the Bolshevik Revolution, Lenin quickly sought peace with Germany. Despite its high cost, Russia signed the Treaty of Brest-Litovsk in March 1918, giving up a huge chunk of its territory and its population. (See page 291.) But the Communists needed all their energy to defeat a battery of enemies at home.

For three years, civil war raged. The newly formed Red Army battled the Whites, counter-revolutionaries who remained loyal to the czar. National groups that the czars had conquered also took up arms against the Red Army. Poland, Estonia, Latvia, and Lithuania broke free, but nationalists in Ukraine, the Caucasus, and Central Asia were eventually subdued.

**Allied invasion.** Foreign powers intervened, too. Japan seized land in East Asia that czarist Russia had once claimed. The Allies—Britain, France, and the United States—sent forces to help the Whites, who wanted to continue the war against Germany. Although the Allied forces failed, their presence roused Russian nationalism. In the long run, the invasion fed Communist distrust of the West.

**A costly triumph.** Both sides took brutal measures to win the civil war. Counterrevolutionary forces slaughtered captured Communists and tried to assassinate Lenin. To crush their enemies, the Communists unleashed a reign of terror. They organized their own secret police, the Cheka. Ordinary citizens were executed if they were suspected of counterrevolutionary activities. The former czar and czarina and their five children were shot to keep them from becoming a rallying symbol for counterrevolutionary forces.

The Communists adopted a policy known as "war communism." They took over banks, mines, factories, and railroads. Peasants were forced to deliver "surplus" food to hungry people in the cities. Peasant laborers were drafted into the military or into factory work.

Meanwhile, Trotsky turned the Red Army into an effective fighting force, under the close watch of Communist officials. Trotsky's passionate speeches roused soldiers to fight. So did the order to shoot every tenth man if a unit performed poorly—a tactic borrowed from the armies of ancient Rome.

The great Russian writer Mikhail Sholokhov (SHAW luh kawf) described the civil war in his novel *And Quiet Flows the Don*. Here, a Red Army officer tells how he feels about executing Cossacks, peasants in the czar's cavalry:

66In real life there isn't a man who is
without fear in battle, and not a man
who can kill people without carrying—
without getting morally scratched.
I don't feel any regret for the officers.
. . . But yesterday I had to shoot three
Cossacks among the rest—three toilers.
I began to bind one. . . . I happened to
touch his hand, and it was as hard as
sole-leather, covered with calluses.
A black palm, all cuts and lumps.99

By 1921, the Communists had defeated their scattered foes. Although Lenin had triumphed, Russia was in chaos. Millions had died since the beginning of World War I. Famine stalked the land, killing millions. Lenin faced an immense job of rebuilding a nation and an economy in ruins.

## SECTION 1 REVIEW

1. **Identify** (a) Nicholas and Alexandra, (b) Gregory Rasputin, (c) Nadezhda Krupskaya, (d) Leon Trotsky, (e) Red Guard, (f) Whites, (g) Cheka, (h) Mikhail Sholokhov.
2. **Define** soviet.
3. (a) What was the immediate cause of the March Revolution? (b) What were the long-term causes?
4. (a) How did Lenin adapt Marxism to conditions in Russia? (b) Why were the Bolsheviks able to seize power in November 1917?
5. What problems did the Bolsheviks face after taking over the government?
6. *Critical Thinking* **Understanding Sequence** Make a list of entries for a time chart of key events in Russia in 1917. Your chart should clearly indicate how one event led to or influenced another.
7. *ACTIVITY* Write a letter that the czar might have written to the czarina, or the czarina to the czar, while he was away at the front during World War I.

# 2 From Lenin to Stalin

## Guide for Reading

■ What policies did Russia pursue under Lenin?

■ How did Stalin gain power?

■ What were Stalin's economic goals?

■ **Vocabulary** *command economy, collective, kulak*

In January 1924, tens of thousands of people lined up in Moscow's Red Square. They had come to view the body of Lenin, who had died a few days earlier.

Meanwhile, Lenin's party colleagues debated what to do with his corpse. His widow, Krupskaya, wanted him buried simply, next to his mother's grave in Petrograd. Communist party officials—including Joseph Stalin—had other ideas. They wanted Lenin preserved and put on permanent display. In the end, the party had its way. Lenin's body would remain on display in Red Square for more than 65 years.

By having Lenin preserved, Stalin wanted to show that he would carry on the goals of the revolution. In the years that followed, he used ruthless measures to win dictatorial power and impose a new order on Russia.

## Lenin Builds a Communist State

Lenin's first years as leader of Russia had been occupied in putting down civil war. Once his power was secure, he turned to his chief goal—building a classless society in which the means of production were in the hands of the people. As you will see, Lenin was never fully able to meet this Marxist goal.

**Government.** In 1922, the Communists produced a constitution that sounded both democratic and socialist. It set up an elected legislature, later called the Supreme Soviet, and gave all citizens over 18 the right to vote. All political power, resources, and means of production would belong to workers and peasants.

In practice, however, the Communist party, not the people, reigned supreme. Like the czars before them, the party used the army and secret police to enforce its will. The new government brought much of the old Russian empire under its rule. (See the map on page 309.) It then created the Union of Soviet Socialist Republics (USSR). Like the old Russian empire, the Soviet Union was a multinational state made up of diverse European and Asian peoples. In theory, each republic had certain rights. In reality, Russia, the largest republic, dominated the others.

**The NEP.** On the economic front, Lenin retreated from his policy of "war communism," which had brought the economy to near collapse. Under party control, factory and mine output had fallen. Peasants stopped producing grain, knowing it would only be seized by the government.

In 1921, Lenin adopted the New Economic Policy, or NEP. It allowed some capitalist ventures. While the state kept control of banks, foreign trade, and large industries, small businesses were allowed to reopen for private profit. The government also stopped squeezing peasants for grain. Under the NEP, they held on to small plots of land and freely sold their surplus crops.

Lenin's compromise with capitalism helped the Soviet economy recover and ended armed resistance to the new government. By 1928, food and industrial production had climbed back to prewar levels. The standard of living improved, too. But Lenin had always seen the NEP as a temporary retreat from communism. His successor would soon put the Soviet Union back on the road to "pure" communism.

## Stalin Gains Power

Lenin's sudden death in 1924 set off a power struggle among Communist leaders. The chief contenders were Trotsky and Joseph Stalin. Trotsky was a brilliant Marxist thinker, a skillful speaker, and an architect of the Bolshevik Revolution. Stalin, by contrast, was neither a scholar nor an orator. He was, however, a shrewd political operator and behind-the-scenes organizer.

**"Man of steel."** Stalin was born Joseph Djugashvili (joo guhsh VEE lee) to a poor family in Georgia, a region in the Caucasus Mountains. As a boy, he studied for the priesthood. But his growing interest in revolution brought him un-

der the seminary's harsh discipline. Once, he was confined to a punishment cell for reading a novel about the French Revolution.

By 1900, Djugashvili had joined the Bolshevik underground and had taken the name Stalin, meaning "man of steel." He organized robberies to get money for the party and spent time in prison and in Siberian exile. He played a far less important role in the revolution and civil war than Trotsky. But in the 1920s, he became general secretary of the party. He used that position to build a loyal following who owed their jobs to him.

**Stalin versus Trotsky.** As early as 1922, Lenin had expressed grave doubts about Stalin's ambitious nature:

66Comrade Stalin, having become general secretary, has concentrated an enormous power in his hands; and I am not sure that he always knows how to use that power with sufficient caution.99

To Lenin, Stalin was "too rude." He urged the party to choose a successor "more tolerant, more loyal, more polite, and more considerate to comrades."

At Lenin's death, Trotsky and Stalin jockeyed for position. They differed on most issues, including the future of communism. Trotsky, a firm Marxist, urged support for a worldwide revolution against capitalism. Stalin took a more cautious view. Efforts to foster Marxist revolutions in Europe after World War I had failed. Instead, he wanted to concentrate on building socialism at home first.

With political cunning, Stalin put his own supporters into top jobs and isolated Trotsky within the party. Stripped of party membership, Trotsky fled into exile in 1929. Later, he was murdered in Mexico by a Stalinist agent.

## The Five-Year Plans

Once in power, Stalin set out to make the Soviet Union into a modern industrial power. In the past, said Stalin, Russia had suffered defeats because of its economic backwardness. In 1928, therefore, he proposed the first of several "five-year plans" aimed at building heavy industry, improving transportation, and increasing farm output.

## Soviet Union, 1917–1938

EUROPE
LITHUANIA
LATVIA
FINLAND
ESTONIA
POLAND
•Leningrad
BELORUSSIAN SSR
•Archangel
UKRAINIAN SSR
•Moscow
BLACK SEA
TURKEY
Stalingrad•
Volga R.
GEORGIAN SSR
ARMENIAN SSR
AZERBAIJAN SSR
CASPIAN SEA
ARAL SEA
KAZAKH SSR
TURKMEN SSR
UZBEK SSR
IRAN
KIRGHIZ SSR
AFGHANISTAN
TADZHIK SSR
INDIA
CHINA

RUSSIAN SOVIET FEDERATED SOCIALIST REPUBLIC

Ob R.
Yenisei R.
L. BALKHASH
Lena R.
L. BAIKAL
MONGOLIA

ARCTIC OCEAN
PACIFIC OCEAN
SEA OF OKHOTSK
SAKHALIN
Amur R.
MANCHURIA
Vladivostok•
JAPAN
KOREA

0   500   1000 Miles
0   500   1000 Kilometers

Russian empire, 1914

Area controlled by Bolsheviks, 1919

Union of Soviet Socialist Republics 1938

## GEOGRAPHY AND HISTORY

*In the years following the Bolshevik Revolution, the Soviet Union extended control over many areas of the former Russian empire. It became the largest country in the world*

1. **Location** On the map, locate (a) Lithuania, (b) Georgian SSR, (c) Moscow, (d) Leningrad, (e) China.
2. **Region** Name three countries that had been part of the Russian empire in 1914 that were not part of the Soviet Union in 1938.
3. **Critical Thinking** **Applying Information** How does the map help explain why Russia became the most influential republic in the Soviet Union?

To achieve this economic growth, he brought all economic activity under government control. The Soviet Union developed a command economy, in which government officials made all basic economic decisions. Under Stalin, the government owned all businesses and allocated financial and other resources. By contrast, in a capitalist economy, the free market controls most economic decisions. Businesses are privately owned and operated by individuals for profit.

**Industrial growth.** Stalin's five-year plans set high production goals, especially for heavy industry and transportation. The government pushed workers and managers to meet these goals by giving bonuses to those who succeed-

ed—and by punishing those who did not. Between 1928 and 1939, large factories, hydroelectric power stations, and huge industrial complexes rose across the Soviet Union. Oil, coal, and steel production grew. Mining expanded, and new railroads were built.

**Mixed results.** Despite the impressive progress in some areas, Soviet workers had little to show for their sacrifices. Some former peasants did improve their lives, becoming skilled factory workers or managers. Overall, though, standards of living remained poor. Wages were low and consumer goods were scarce. Also, central economic planning was often inefficient, causing shortages in some areas and surpluses in others. Many managers, concerned only with meeting production quotas, turned out large quantities of low-quality goods.

During and after the Stalin era, the Soviet Union continued to produce well in heavy industry, such as the manufacture of farm machinery. But its planned economy failed to match the capitalist world in making consumer goods such as clothing, cars, and refrigerators.

## Revolution in Agriculture

Stalin also brought agriculture under government control. Under the NEP, peasants had held on to small plots of land. But Stalin saw that system as inefficient, as well as being a threat to state power. He forced peasants to give up their private plots and live on either state-owned farms or on collectives, large farms owned and operated by peasants as a group. Peasants were allowed to keep their houses and personal belongings, but all farm animals and implements were to be turned over to the col-

lective. The state set all prices and controlled access to farm supplies.

On collectives, the government planned to provide tractors, fertilizers, and better seed, and to teach peasants modern farm methods. The government needed increased grain output to feed workers in the cities. Surplus grain would also be sold abroad to earn money to invest in industrial growth.

**A ruthless policy.** Peasants resisted collectivization by killing farm animals, destroying tools, and burning crops. The government responded with brutal force. An army officer described his horror at the orders he received:

66 I am an Old Bolshevik. . . . I worked in the underground against the czar and I fought in the civil war. Did I do all that in order that I should now surround villages with machine guns and order my men to fire indiscriminately into crowds of peasants? Oh, no, no!99

*Lunch Break* During the revolution, the Communists had promised to give land to peasants. But under Stalin, the Soviet government forced peasants to give up their land and work on large, state-run farms. Workers on the collective farm shown here eat lunch together in the fields. **Economics and Technology** What does this photograph suggest about discipline on a collective farm?

Stalin sought to destroy the kulaks, or wealthy peasants. The government confiscated kulaks' land and sent them to labor camps. Thousands were killed or died from overwork.

**Effects.** Collectivization took a horrendous toll. Angry peasants often grew just enough to feed themselves. In response, the government seized all the grain, leaving the peasants to starve. This ruthless policy, combined with poor harvests, led to a terrible famine. Between five and eight million people died in Ukraine alone.

Although collectivization increased Stalin's control, it did not improve farm output. During the 1930s, grain production inched upward, but meat, vegetables, and fruits remained in short supply. Feeding the population would remain a major problem in the Soviet Union.

## The Great Purge

Even though Stalin's power was absolute, he harbored obsessive fears that rival party leaders were plotting against him. In 1934, he launched the Great Purge. In this reign of terror, Stalin and his secret police cracked down especially on Old Bolsheviks, party activists from the early days. His net soon widened to target army heroes, industrial managers, writers, and ordinary citizens. They were charged with a wide range of crimes, from counterrevolutionary plots to failure to meet production quotas.

Between 1936 and 1938, Stalin staged a series of spectacular public "show trials" in Moscow. Former Communist leaders confessed to all kinds of crimes after prolonged torture or to save family or friends. Many purged party members were never tried but were sent to forced-labor camps in Siberia and elsewhere. Others were executed. Secret police files reveal that at least four million people were purged during the Stalin years.

The purges replaced the older generation of revolutionaries with young party members who owed absolute loyalty to Stalin. He thus increased his own power while impressing upon the Soviet people the dangers of disloyalty.

The victims of the purges included most of the nation's military officers. This vacuum in military leadership would come back to haunt Stalin in 1941, when Germany invaded the Soviet Union. (See Chapter 14.)

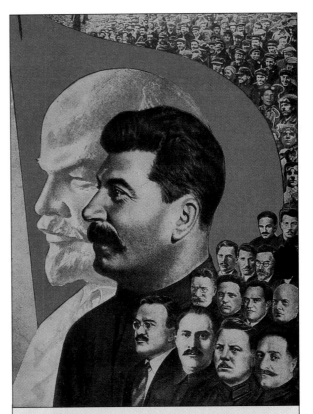

**Stalin's Dictatorship** *This propaganda poster presents Stalin as Lenin's heir. Many of the other Communist leaders shown here later became victims of Stalin's Great Purge.* **Political and Social Systems** *How did glorification of Stalin contradict the original goals of the Russian Revolution?*

## Foreign Policy

Between 1917 and 1939, the Soviet Union pursued contradictory foreign policy goals. As communists, both Lenin and Stalin wanted to bring about the worldwide revolution that Marx had predicted. But as Russians, they wanted to guarantee their nation's security by winning the support of other countries.

Lenin formed the Communist International, or Comintern. It aided revolutionary groups around the world and urged colonial peoples to rise up against imperialist powers. Yet the Soviet Union also sought to join the League of Nations and to improve diplomatic and trade relations with many western governments.

Comintern propaganda against capitalism made western powers highly suspicious of the Soviet Union. In the United States, fear of Bolshevik plots led to the Red Scare in the early 1920s. Britain broke off relations with the Soviet

***Battleship Potemkin*** *Motion pictures were the most original new art form of the twentieth century. Soviet director Sergei Eisenstein pioneered a technique called montage, cutting back and forth between clashing images. Eisenstein's 1925 silent film* Battleship Potemkin *dramatized the 1905 revolution. (See page 186.) This sequence shows a protest on a wide outdoor staircase in Odessa. In rapid succession, we see imperial troops firing on the crowd, a mother carrying her wounded son, and a baby carriage bouncing wildly down the steps. Although Eisenstein passionately supported the revolution, Stalin had many of his later films edited or banned.* **Art and Literature** *How did Eisenstein choose images that would shock and anger audiences? Give two examples.*

Union when evidence revealed Soviet schemes to turn a 1926 strike into a revolution.

The Soviet Union slowly won recognition from western powers and increased trade with capitalist countries. Eventually, it joined the League of Nations. Mistrust still poisoned relations, especially after the Great Purge.

## Impact of Three Revolutions

Historians often compare the Russian, French, and American revolutions. The American was in many ways the least radical of the three. American leaders did not order mass executions or seize property. French revolutionaries executed thousands and nationalized the lands of the church and aristocracy. In Russia, Stalin seized even the lands of the peasant masses. His policies caused millions of deaths.

All three revolutions had a worldwide impact. The Declaration of Independence and the Constitution served as models of democratic government. The French Revolution inspired revolts across Europe. As you will see, the Soviet Union supported revolts in many lands and became a model for other socialist and communist governments. Yet today, Russia and most of its allies have abandoned the goals of Lenin and Stalin. Democratic nations continue to build on the principles preached during the American and French revolutions.

## SECTION 2 REVIEW

1. **Identify** (a) USSR, (b) NEP, (c) Great Purge, (d) Comintern.
2. **Define** (a) command economy, (b) collective, (c) kulak.
3. How did Lenin's economic policies change?
4. (a) How did Stalin differ from Trotsky? (b) Why was he able to gain power?
5. What were the goals and results of Stalin's five-year plans?
6. *Critical Thinking* **Defending a Position** Do you think western nations were justified in being suspicious of the Soviet Union in the 1920s and 1930s? Explain.
7. *ACTIVITY* Draw a political cartoon about the Great Purge from the viewpoint of one of the Old Bolsheviks.

# 3 Life in a Totalitarian State

## Guide for Reading

- How did the Communists promote their ideas?
- How did communism shape Soviet society?
- What policy did Stalin impose on the arts?
- **Vocabulary** *totalitarian state, socialist realism*

Stalin's propaganda mills created a fatherly image of the Soviet leader. Poets wrote hymns of praise to "the new Lenin" or "dear Comrade Stalin." Wrote one poet:

> 66We receive our sun from Stalin,
> We receive our prosperous life
>     from Stalin. . . .
> Even the good life in the tundras filled
>     with snowstorms
> We made together with him,
> With the Son of Lenin,
> With Stalin the Wise.99

From the 1930s until his death in 1953, Stalin tried to boost morale and faith in the communist system by making himself into a godlike figure. This "cult of personality" was one more pillar to support his absolute power.

## An "Iron Age" of Totalitarian Control

Marx had predicted that under communism the state would wither away. The opposite occurred under Stalin. He turned the Soviet Union into a totalitarian state. In this form of government, a one-party dictatorship attempts to regulate every aspect of the lives of its citizens. You have already seen how Stalin purged political rivals and imposed central government control over industry and agriculture.

To ensure obedience, Stalin's Communist party used secret police, censorship, and terror.

Police spies did not hesitate to open private letters or plant listening devices. Nothing appeared in print without official approval. Grumblers or critics were rounded up and sent to brutal labor camps, where many died.

**Propaganda.** Using modern technology, the party bombarded the public with relentless propaganda. Radios and loudspeakers blared into factories and villages. In movies, theaters, and schools, citizens heard about communist successes and the evils of capitalism. Newsreels and newspapers showed bumper harvests and new hydroelectric dams opening up, or proclaimed the misery of workers in the capitalist West. Billboards and posters urged workers to meet or exceed production quotas.

Stalinist propaganda also revived extreme nationalism. Headlines in the Communist party newspaper, *Pravda,* or "Truth," linked enemies at home to foreign agents:

**❝SPIES SOUGHT TO BREAK UP OUR COUNTRY AND RE-ESTABLISH POWER OF LAND-OWNERS AND CAPITALISTS IN U.S.S.R.—SHOOT THEM!❞**

Those who supported Stalin's aims were often glorified as heroes. For example, the government put up statues honoring a 14-year-old boy who turned his own father over to the secret police for associating with kulaks.

**War on religion.** In accordance with the ideas of Marx, atheism became the official policy of the state. Early on, the Communists targeted the Russian Orthodox Church, which had strongly supported the czars. The party seized most religious property, converting many churches into offices and museums. Many priests and other religious leaders were killed or died in prison camps. Government-run museums set up exhibits discrediting miracles and other religious teachings.

ISSUES For TODAY

The Russian Revolution began with the overthrow of a monarchy but resulted in a totalitarian dictatorship. Why is it often difficult to establish democracy in a country without a tradition of democratic government?

Other religions were persecuted as well. At one show trial, 15 Roman Catholic priests were charged with "counterrevolutionary activities," such as teaching religion to the young. The state seized Jewish synagogues and banned the use of Hebrew. Stalin used anti-Semitic propaganda in his campaign against the Old Bolsheviks, many of whom were Jewish.

Islam was also officially discouraged. However, Muslims living in the Soviet Union generally faced fewer restrictions, partly because the Communists hoped to win support among colonized peoples in the Middle East.

**Communist ideology.** The Communists replaced religion with their own ideology. Like a religion, communist ideology had its own "sacred" texts—the writings of Marx and Lenin—and its own shrines, such as the tomb of Lenin. Portraits of Stalin replaced religious icons in Russian homes.

## Changes in Soviet Society

The Communists transformed Russian life. They destroyed the old social order of landowning nobles at the top and serfs at the bottom. But instead of creating a society of equals, as they promised, they created a society where a few elite groups emerged as a new ruling class.

**The new elite.** At the head of society were members of the Communist party. Only a small fraction of Soviet citizens were allowed to join the party. Many who did so were motivated by a desire to get ahead, rather than a belief in communist ideology.

The Soviet elite also included industrial managers, military leaders, scientists, and some artists and writers. The elite enjoyed benefits denied to most people. They had the best apartments in the cities and vacation homes in the country. They could shop at special stores for scarce consumer goods. Good shoes, noted one western visitor, distinguished the elite from the common citizen.

**Social benefits and drawbacks.** Although excluded from party membership, most people did enjoy benefits unknown before the revolution. Free education was offered to all. The state also provided free medical care, day care for children, inexpensive housing, and public transportation and recreation.

While these benefits were real, the standard of living remained low. As elsewhere, industrial growth led millions of people to migrate to cities. Although the state built massive apartment complexes, housing was scarce. Entire families might be packed into a single room. Bread was plentiful, but meat, fresh fruit, and other foods were in short supply.

**Education.** After the Russian Revolution, the Communists built schools everywhere and required all children to attend. Other schools taught adults to read and write, an opportunity few had enjoyed in czarist Russia. The state supported technical schools and universities as well.

Schools served important goals. Educated workers were needed to build a modern industrial state. In addition to basic skills, schools taught communist values, such as atheism, the glory of collective farming, and love of Stalin.

The Communist party also set up programs for students outside school. The youth organization Komsomol provided sports programs, cultural activities, and political classes to train teenagers for party membership. Sometimes, these young Communists would be sent to help harvest crops or participate in huge parades.

**Women.** Long before 1917, women such as Lenin's wife, Krupskaya, worked for the

# PARALLELS THROUGH TIME

## Fighting Illiteracy

Most ordinary people throughout history did not learn to read or write. Widespread literacy became a goal of industrialized nations only in the 1800s. Today, it is a major goal of developing nations. Illiteracy keeps individuals from reaching their full potential and also hinders economic growth.

**Linking Past and Present**   Why do you think the Soviet government wanted people to learn to read? Why do democratic governments today want citizens to be educated?

### PAST

Before the revolution, few Russian peasants could read. The Soviet government built schools and launched campaigns to increase adult literacy. The Soviet poster at left proclaims, "Knowledge Will Break the Chains of Serfdom." Above, women in the Soviet republic of Turkmenistan attend classes.

### PRESENT

Today, about 20 million adult Americans are functionally illiterate, unable to read well enough to carry out basic, day-to-day tasks. The poster at right encourages adults to join a government-sponsored literacy program. Below, an insurance company provides literacy training for workers.

revolution, spreading radical ideas among peasants and workers. Some urged fellow Socialists to pay attention to women's needs. In 1905, Alexandra Kollontai (kawl uhn TĪ) noted "how little our party concerned itself with the fate of women of the working class and how meager was its interest in women's liberation." After the revolution, Kollontai became the only high-ranking woman to serve in Lenin's government. She vigorously campaigned for women's rights.

Under the Communists, women won equality under the law. They gained access to education and a wide range of jobs. By the 1930s, many Soviet women were working in medicine, engineering, or the sciences.

By their labor, women contributed to Soviet economic growth. They

▲ Soviet women working in a laboratory

worked in factories, in construction, and on collectives. Within the family, their wages were needed because men earned low salaries. The government provided day nurseries for children.

Despite new opportunities, women were expected to shoulder a double load. They spent a full day on the job, followed by a second shift caring for children and doing housework.

## The Arts and the State

The Bolshevik Revolution at first meant greater freedom for Russian artists and writers. They welcomed the chance to experiment with ideas and forms. The poet Vladimir Mayakovsky (mah yuh KAWF skee) exalted in the new society and praised revolutionary heroes:

66Revolutions
    are the business of peoples;
  for individuals
    they're too heavy to wield,

yet Lenin
  ranked foremost
    among his equals
by his mind's momentum,
  his will's firm steel.99

**Socialist realism.** "Art must serve politics," Lenin had insisted, but he generally did not interfere in artistic freedom. Under Stalin, however, the heavy hand of state control gripped the arts. Stalin forced artists and writers to conform to a style called socialist realism. Its goal was to boost socialism by showing Soviet life in a positive light. Artists and writers could criticize the bourgeois past or even, to a limited degree, point out mistakes under communism. Their overall message, though, had to promote hope in the socialist future. Popular themes for socialist-realist artists were peasants, workers, heroes of the revolution—and, of course, Stalin.

**Censorship.** Government controlled what books were published, what music was heard, and which works of art were put on display. Artists who ignored socialist-realist guidelines could not get materials, work space, or jobs.

Under Stalin, writers, artists, and composers faced persecution. The Jewish poet Osip Mandelstam was imprisoned, tortured, and exiled for composing a satirical verse about Stalin. Out of fear for his wife's safety, Mandelstam gave in and wrote an "Ode to Stalin."

Anna Akhmatova (ahk MAH taw vuh), one of Russia's greatest poets, fell out of favor because her poetry did not stress communist ideas. She went on writing poetry in secret. In "Requiem," she described the daily ordeal of trying to visit her 20-year-old son, imprisoned during the Stalinist terrors:

66For seventeen long months my pleas,
  My cries have called you home.
I've begged the hangman on my knees,
  My son, my dread, my own.
My mind's mixed up for good, and I'm
  No longer even clear
Who's man, who's beast, nor how
    much time
Before the end draws near.99

Although Akhmatova could not publish her works, friends memorized them to preserve her genius for future generations.

*Socialist Realism* Bold, heroic images were the trademark of socialist realism. Here, workers and farmers hold aloft the hammer and sickle, symbol of the Soviet Union. Bright sunbeams suggest a glorious future just ahead. (The letters CCCP stand for USSR in the Cyrillic alphabet.) **Religions and Value Systems** What Soviet values does this painting uphold?

Despite restrictions, some Soviet writers produced magnificent works. *And Quiet Flows the Don,* by Mikhail Sholokhov, passed the censor. (See page 307.) The novel tells the story of a man who spends years fighting in World War I, the Russian Revolution, and the civil war. Sholokhov later became one of the few Soviet writers to win the Nobel Prize for literature.

## *Looking Ahead*

Strict censorship, massive propaganda, and terror were instruments used by Stalin to ensure personal power and to push the Soviet Union toward modernization. By the time he died in 1953, the Soviet Union was a world leader in heavy industry, steel, and oil production. Along with the United States, it was one of the world's two military superpowers. Yet Stalin's efforts exacted a brutal toll.

The Soviet Union was not the only totalitarian state to emerge in the decades after World War I. In Western Europe, the 1920s and 1930s brought turmoil and economic hardship. As you will read in Chapter 13, dictators in Italy and Germany imposed their own ideologies that differed from Soviet communism. They, too, created one-party states and cults of personality to impose dictatorial rule on their people.

## SECTION 3 REVIEW

1. **Identify** (a) Komsomol, (b) Alexandra Kollontai, (c) Vladimir Mayakovsky, (d) Osip Mandelstam, (e) Anna Akhmatova.
2. **Define** (a) totalitarian state, (b) socialist realism.
3. How did Stalin make propaganda into a powerful weapon?
4. (a) How did the Communists attack religion? (b) What alternative did they offer to faith?
5. Describe three ways in which life under communism differed from life under the czars.
6. *Critical Thinking* **Applying Information** One historian has said that Soviet arts policy was "communism with a smiling face." What do you think he meant?
7. *ACTIVITY* Write a dialogue between a Russian peasant woman and her daughter who has become a factory worker. The two women might discuss religion, work, or the changing lives of women since the Russian Revolution.

## CHAPTER REVIEW

### REVIEWING VOCABULARY

Review the vocabulary words in this chapter. Then, use *five* of these vocabulary words and their definitions to create a matching quiz. Exchange your quiz with another student. Check each other's answers when you are finished.

### REVIEWING FACTS

1. How did World War I contribute to the collapse of the Russian monarchy in March 1917?

2. How and when did the Bolsheviks take power in Russia?

3. What was the final outcome of the Russian civil war?

4. Describe Stalin's policy toward Soviet agriculture.

5. What was the Great Purge?

6. What was the Soviet government's policy toward religion?

7. According to Stalin, what purpose should art serve?

## SKILLS FOR SUCCESS    DOCUMENTING YOUR SOURCES

Every research report you do must contain a **bibliography,** or list of the sources you consulted. A bibliography helps your readers determine whether the information in your report is accurate, current, and reliable. It also gives them additional references that they can use to learn more about the subject.

Bibliographies are written in a standard form:

*For a book,* include author's name (last name first), title (underlined or italic), place of publication, name of the publisher, and date of publication.

*For a magazine article,* include author's name, title (in quotation marks), name of the publication (underlined or in italics), date of the publication, and page numbers.

*For a newspaper,* include headline of the article (in quotation marks), author (if given), name of newspaper (underlined or italic), date, edition, section, and page numbers.

Imagine that you are writing a paper about Lenin. Look at the list of sources below. Then, answer the following questions:

1. **Make a bibliography entry for each source.** What would you list first in a bibliography entry for Source A?

2. **Arrange the entries in alphabetical order.** Sources are listed by the authors' last names; unsigned articles are listed according to the first word of the title. Which of the sources below should appear first in the bibliography? Why?

3. **Review the entries for correct style and punctuation.** Use periods between the parts of each entry, such as author's name and title. (a) Write a bibliography entry for Source C. (b) Write a bibliography entry for Source D.

---

*Sources*

A. An unsigned magazine article entitled "Lenin's Curse" that appeared in the magazine *The Economist* on April 27, 1991, on pages 11 and 12.

B. A book by Robert Service entitled *Lenin, a Political Life,* published in 1985 by Indiana University Press in Bloomington, Indiana.

C. A newspaper article written by the Associated Press entitled "Thousands Pay Respects to Lenin" that appeared in the first section of the newspaper *The Oregonian* in Section A, page 8, on April 24, 1994.

D. A book by Robert Payne entitled *The Life and Death of Lenin,* published in 1964 by Simon and Schuster in New York.

## REVIEWING CHAPTER THEMES

Review the "Focus On" questions at the start of this chapter. Then select *three* of those questions and answer them, using information from the chapter.

## CRITICAL THINKING

1. **Comparing** Review Chapter 1. **(a)** Compare the Russian Revolution to the American Revolution in terms of causes and effects. **(b)** Why do you think the American Revolution has had a longer-lasting impact than the Russian Revolution?

2. **Linking Past and Present** In the 1990s, the breakup of the Soviet Union led to a revival of open religious practices. Why do you think the Soviets were unsuccessful in their attempt to destroy religion?

## ANALYZING PRIMARY SOURCES

Use the quotation on page 313 to answer the following questions.

1. For what gifts, according to the poet, should the Soviet people thank Stalin?

2. What message was the poet sending when he referred to Stalin as "the Son of Lenin"?

3. How did poems such as this help Stalin maintain his power?

## FOR YOUR PORTFOLIO

**CONDUCTING AN INTERVIEW** Prepare a list of questions that you would ask if you were able to interview a figure from Russian or Soviet history. Start by deciding whom you would like to interview. Then review the role that this person played in Russian or Soviet history. Use outside resources, such as encyclopedias and biographies, to gain further information. Then prepare a list of interview questions. Finally, submit your questions to the class without identifying the person they are addressed to. Can your classmates guess the person's identity?

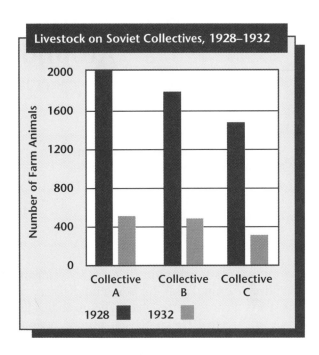

Livestock on Soviet Collectives, 1928–1932

## ANALYZING GRAPHS

Use the graph as well as information from the chapter to answer the following questions.

1. Stalin's first five-year plan began in 1928. How did the five-year plan affect the number of farm animals on the collectives?

2. Which collective farm experienced the greatest loss in number of farm animals?

3. Based on this graph, what can you conclude about the effect of the first five-year plan? Why?

## INTERNET ACTIVITY

**ANALYZING PROPAGANDA** Use the Internet to research propaganda from the Soviet Union. You can look at posters, speeches, book excerpts, or film clips. Then write a brief essay explaining the techniques used in the propaganda to influence the public's view of the Soviet Union or its leaders.

# Nationalism and Revolution Around the World

## (1914–1939)

In his gold-embroidered coat and elegant headdress, Emir Faisal cut a splendid figure at the Paris Peace Conference. The Arab leader went to Paris in 1919 to persuade the victorious Allies to stand by agreements they had made during World War I. Britain, he said, had promised to recognize Arab independence if the Arabs helped fight the Turks. In the meanwhile, however, Britain and France had secretly agreed to divide up Arab lands between themselves, canceling the promises "that were made to us before all the world." Angrily, Faisal continued:

66We have paid a heavy price for our liberty, but we are not exhausted. We are ready to fight on, and I cannot believe that the great rulers here assembled will treat us as did our former oppressors [the Ottoman Turks]. I think they will act from higher, nobler motives, but—if not—they should remember how badly it has turned out for our former oppressors.99

Faisal spoke to the Allies of Arab nationalism and of the Arabs' desire for unity. He pointed to Woodrow Wilson's principle of self-determination, to the splendors of Arab civilization, and to Arab contributions during the war. But even as Faisal spoke, British and French diplomats were working behind the scenes to create mandates over the Arab provinces of the shattered Ottoman empire.

Angry and frustrated, Faisal returned home empty-handed. He was not alone. Outside the Arab world, nationalists in Africa and Asia were also disappointed by the terms of the peace.

The postwar years from 1919 to 1939 saw a surge of hope around the world. They also brought great turmoil. Desire for democracy and self-determination contributed to explosive struggles in many regions. In Mexico and China, revolutions toppled governments and triggered civil wars. In Latin America, Africa, and Asia, continued western imperialism fueled the forces of nationalism. Everywhere, new leaders were slowly forging liberation movements that would change the face of the world.

**FOCUS ON** these questions as you read:

■ **Political and Social Systems**
How did nationalism and a desire for modernization affect countries around the world?

■ **Impact of the Individual**
How did nationalist leaders bring people together to change their countries?

■ **Economics and Technology**
How did the Great Depression affect world economies?

■ **Global Interaction**
What forces did anti-imperialism movements awaken?

## TIME AND PLACE

**A Wave of Nationalism** *The years after World War I saw dramatic changes in many parts of the world. The war had loosened the grip of European nations on their colonies. In Asia, Africa, and the Middle East, nationalists fought for independence. Nationalists in China faced internal divisions as well as foreign invaders. This poster celebrates the victory of the nationalist Guomindang over local Chinese warlords in the 1920s.* **Global Interaction** *Why do you think World War I encouraged nationalist movements in the developing world?*

## HUMANITIES LINK

*Art History* Diego Rivera, *The History of Mexico* (page 324).
*Literature* In this chapter, you will encounter passages from the following works of literature: Léopold Senghor, "Black Woman" (page 328); Rabindranath Tagore, "We Crown Thee King" (page 342).

| 1917 | 1920s | 1923 | 1930 | 1934 | 1937 |
|------|-------|------|------|------|------|
| Mexico adopts constitution | Pan-Africanism grows | Atatürk begins modernizing Turkey | Gandhi leads Salt March | Mao Zedong leads Long March | Japan invades China |

| 1915 | 1920 | 1925 | 1930 | 1935 | 1940 |

# 1 Struggle for Change in Latin America

## Guide for Reading

■ Why did revolution erupt in Mexico in 1910?

■ What were the effects of the Mexican Revolution?

■ How did nationalism grow in Latin American countries?

■ **Vocabulary** *nationalization*

The winds of revolution swept through Mexico between 1910 and 1920. "It is like a hurricane," says a peasant fighter in Mariano Azuela's novel *The Underdogs*. "If you're in it, . . . you're a leaf . . . blown by the wind." Azuela, a doctor, had fought with the rebel army of Pancho Villa. His novel captures the turmoil of the Mexican Revolution and details its effects on millions of Mexican men and women.

The Mexican Revolution unleashed radical forces. As the revolution spread, Indian peasants battled to end centuries of oppression and to win land. A century after Miguel Hidalgo raised the "cry of Dolores" (see page 123), the Mexican Revolution finally opened the door to social and economic reform.

## The Mexican Revolution

By 1910, the dictator Porfirio Díaz had ruled Mexico for almost 35 years, winning reelection as president again and again. On the surface, Mexico enjoyed peace and economic growth. Díaz welcomed foreign investors who developed mines, built railroads, and drilled for oil. (See pages 258–259.)

**Sources of discontent.** Prosperity benefited wealthy landowners, business people, and foreign investors. But most Mexicans were peasants who lived in desperate poverty. Without land or education, they had no hope for improvement. Their demands for land were ruthlessly crushed by the police or military.

Discontent rippled through Mexico in the early 1900s. Peasant land hunger could not be stifled forever. Factory workers and miners earning meager wages were restless and angry. And middle-class liberals, who embraced the ideals of democracy, opposed the Díaz dictatorship.

**The battle begins.** The unrest boiled over when Francisco Madero, a liberal reformer, demanded free elections in 1910. After being imprisoned by Díaz, he hoisted the flag of revolt. Soon, revolutionaries all across Mexico joined Madero's cause.

Faced with rebellion in several parts of the country, Díaz resigned in 1911. "Madero has unleashed a tiger, now let us see if he can control it," declared the dictator as he left Mexico. Díaz's taunt proved well founded. Madero became president of Mexico but within two years was murdered, probably on the orders of one of his generals, Victoriano Huerta. Huerta, himself, was soon forced to flee Mexico.

**A complex upheaval.** During the power struggle that followed, several radical leaders emerged. Among them was Francisco "Pancho" Villa, a hard-riding rebel from the north. He fought mostly for personal power but won the intense loyalty of his peasant followers.

In southern Mexico, Emiliano Zapata led a peasant revolt. Zapata, himself an Indian tenant farmer, understood the misery of peasant villagers who "own only the ground on which they stand. They suffer the horrors of poverty," he declared, because "the lands, woods, and water are monopolized by a few." The battle cry of the Zapatistas, as the rebels who followed Zapata were called, was *"Tierra y Libertad!"*—Land and Liberty!

◀ *A soldadera, or female soldier*

Fighting flared across Mexico for a decade, killing as many as a million Mexicans. Peasants, small farmers, ranchers, and urban workers were drawn into the violent struggle. *Soldaderas,* women soldiers, cooked, tended the wounded, and even fought alongside the men. Women marched with regular army units or joined hit-and-run guerrilla bands.

## Reforms

In 1917, Venustiano Carranza, a conservative, was elected president of Mexico. That year, he reluctantly approved a new constitution. With amendments, it is still in force today.

**A new constitution.** The Constitution of 1917 addressed three major issues: land, religion, and labor. It permitted the breakup of large estates, placed restrictions on foreigners owning land, and allowed nationalization, or government takeover, of natural resources. Church land was made "the property of the nation." The constitution set a minimum wage for workers and protected their right to strike.

Although the constitution gave suffrage only to men, it did give women some protection. Women doing the same job as men were entitled to the same pay. In response to pressures from women activists, Carranza also passed laws allowing married women to draw up contracts, to take part in legal suits, and to have equal authority with men in spending family funds.

**Social change.** At first, the constitution was just a set of goals to be achieved sometime in the future. But in the 1920s, as the government finally restored order after years of civil war, it began to carry out reforms.

The government helped some Indian communities regain lands that had been taken from them illegally in the past. It supported labor unions and launched a massive effort to combat illiteracy. Schools and libraries were set up. For the first time, Mexicans in rural areas who grew up speaking various Indian languages learned Spanish.

Dedicated teachers, often young women, worked for low pay. While they taught basic skills, they spread ideas of nationalism that began to bridge the gulf between the regions and the central government. As the revolutionary era ended, Mexico became the first Latin American nation to pursue real social and economic reforms for the majority of its people.

**The PRI.** In 1929, government leaders organized what later became the Institutional Revolutionary party (PRI). It has dominated Mexican politics ever since. The PRI managed to accommodate all groups in Mexican society, including business and military leaders, peasants, and workers. Its leaders backed social reform but suppressed political opposition. It also boosted industry. In 1938, the government nationalized foreign oil holdings, part of a program to reduce foreign influence.

## Rising Tide of Nationalism

Mexico's move to reclaim its oil fields from foreign investors reflected a growing spirit of nationalism in Latin America. It was directed largely at ending economic dependence on the industrial powers, especially the United States. (See page 257.)

**Economic nationalism.** During the 1920s and 1930s, world events affected Latin American economies. After World War I, trade fell off with Europe. New products such as synthetic textiles and nitrates competed with Latin American exports. The Great Depression that struck the United States in 1929 spread around the world in the 1930s. Prices for Latin American exports plunged as demand dried up. At the same time, the cost of imported consumer goods rose.

A tide of economic nationalism swept Latin American countries. They were determined to develop their own economies and end foreign economic control. Since consumers could no longer afford costly imports, local entrepreneurs set up factories to produce goods. They urged their governments to raise tariffs to protect the new industries. And, following Mexico's lead, some nations also nationalized resources or took over foreign-owned industries.

 **ISSUES** *For* **TODAY**

In the 1920s, feelings of nationalism surged in the nations of Latin America. What conditions fuel the forces of nationalism?

**The History of Mexico** *As a young man, Diego Rivera studied painting in Europe. But after a while, his imitations of European art seemed "like a collection of masks and disguises." On his return to Mexico, Rivera began to paint in a bold, new style that drew on Mexican folk art. "It was as if I were being born anew," he wrote. "In everything I saw a potential masterpiece—the crowds, the markets, the festivals." In this mural, Rivera uses bright colors and bold forms to tell the story of Mexico. The mural moves from the Spanish conquest at the base to the victory of the Mexican Revolution at the top.* **Art and Literature** *How does Rivera's mural communicate a political message?*

The drive to create domestic industries had limited success. In Mexico, Argentina, Brazil, and a few other countries, some areas of manufacturing grew. Mexico and Venezuela also benefited from a growing demand for oil. But most Latin American nations did not have oil and lacked the resources to build large industries. As in the past, the unequal distribution of wealth hampered economic development.

**Cultural nationalism.** By the 1920s, an upsurge of national feeling led Latin American writers, artists, and thinkers to reject European influences. Instead, they took pride in their own unique culture, which blended western and Indian traditions. A Brazilian urged:

66Let us forget the marble of the Acropolis and the towers of the Gothic cathedrals. We are the sons of the hills and the forests. Stop thinking of Europe. Think of America!99

In Mexico, cultural nationalism was reflected in the revival of mural painting, a major art form of the Aztecs. In the 1920s and 1930s, Diego Rivera, José Clemente Orozco (oh RAHS koh), David Alfaro Siqueiros (sih KAY rohs), and other muralists created magnificent works that won worldwide acclaim. On the walls of public buildings, they portrayed the struggles of the Mexican people for liberty. They captured the desire of Indian peasants to regain land taken from them first by Spanish conquerors and later by foreigners during the Díaz era. The murals have been a great source of national pride ever since.

## The "Good Neighbor" Policy

During and after World War I, investments by the United States in the nations of Latin America soared, especially as British influence declined. The United States continued to play the role of "international policeman," intervening to restore order when it felt its interests were threatened.

During the Mexican Revolution, the United States supported leaders who it thought would protect American interests. In 1914, it bombarded the port of Vera Cruz to punish Mexico for imprisoning several American sailors. In 1916, it invaded Mexico after Pancho

Villa killed 17 Americans in New Mexico. Although the United States felt justified in these actions, they stirred up violent anti-Yankee sentiment in Mexico.

During the 1920s, anti-American feeling grew. In Nicaragua, Augusto César Sandino led a guerrilla movement against United States forces occupying his country. Many people throughout Latin America saw Sandino as a hero.

In the 1930s, President Franklin Roosevelt took a new approach to Latin America. He abandoned the Roosevelt Corollary, which had been used to justify military intervention. In its place, he pledged to follow "the policy of the good neighbor."

Under the Good Neighbor Policy, the United States withdrew troops it had stationed in Haiti and Nicaragua. It also lifted the Platt Amendment, which had limited Cuban independence. When Mexico nationalized foreign oil holdings, Roosevelt resisted demands by some Americans to intervene. The Good Neighbor Policy survived until 1945, when global tensions led the United States to intervene once again in the region.

## SECTION 1 REVIEW

1. **Identify** (a) Porfirio Díaz, (b) Zapatistas, (c) Diego Rivera, (d) Good Neighbor Policy.
2. **Define** nationalization.
3. Describe three causes of the Mexican Revolution.
4. Explain how the Constitution of 1917 addressed each of these issues: (a) land, (b) religion, (c) labor.
5. Give two examples of how nationalism helped shape Latin American republics in the 1920s and 1930s.
6. *Critical Thinking* **Analyzing Information** (a) How did world events affect the economy of Latin American nations during the 1920s and 1930s? (b) Do you think that a nation can avoid the effects of global events? Explain.
7. *ACTIVITY* Study the mural on page 324. Then, create a mural that illustrates an event in the Mexican Revolution.

# Nationalist Movements in Africa and the Middle East

## Guide for Reading

- How did African nationalism grow after World War I?

- How did nationalism help Turkey and Iran modernize?

- What were the goals of Arab nationalists?

- **Vocabulary** *apartheid*

The Kikuyu people of Kenya were outraged. Not only had the British taken their land, but they also treated the Kikuyu like second-class citizens. Jomo Kenyatta, a young Kikuyu leader, explained their anger in this way:

66If you woke up one morning and found that somebody had come to your house, and had declared that house belonged to him, you would naturally be surprised, and you would like to know by what arrangement. Many Africans found that, on land that had been in the possession of their ancestors from time immemorial, they were now working as squatters or as laborers.99

The Kikuyu were among many African people who resented colonial rule. During the 1920s and 1930s, a new generation of leaders like Kenyatta, proud of their unique heritage, struggled to stem the tide of imperialism and restore Africa for Africans.

## Movements for Change in Africa

During the early 1900s, more and more Africans felt the impact of colonial rule. In Kenya and Rhodesia, for example, white settlers forced Africans off the best land. Those who were lucky enough to keep their land were forbidden to grow the most profitable crops—only Europeans could grow these. In Kenya, too, the

British made all Africans carry identification cards and restricted where they could live or travel.

Everywhere, Africans were forced to work on European-run plantations or in mines to earn money to pay taxes. Farmers who had kept their land had to grow cash crops. Increasingly, they lost their self-sufficiency and became dependent on European-made goods. Also, land converted to cash crops no longer produced food, which led to famines in some regions.

**Resistance.** Opposition to imperialism grew among Africans. Resistance took many forms. Those who had lost their lands to Europeans sometimes squatted, or settled illegally, on white-owned plantations. In cities, workers began to form unions, even though such activity was illegal.

Many western-educated Africans criticized the injustice of imperial rule. Although they had trained for professional careers, the best jobs went to Europeans. Inspired by President Woodrow Wilson's call for self-determination, they condemned the system that excluded Africans from the political life of their own lands. Some eagerly read Lenin's writings that claimed imperialism was the final stage of a corrupt and dying capitalist society. In Africa, as elsewhere around the world, socialism had a growing appeal.

**Protests.** While large-scale revolts were rare, protests were common. In Kenya, the Kikuyu protested the loss of their land, forced labor, heavy taxes, and the hated identification cards. The British jailed the Kikuyu leaders, but protests continued.

In West Africa, women had traditionally controlled the marketplaces and the farmland. In the 1920s, Ibo women in Nigeria denounced British policies that threatened their rights. They demanded a voice in decisions that affected them. The "Women's War," as it was called, became a full-fledged revolt. Women armed with machetes and sticks mocked British troops and shouted down officials who ordered them to disperse. In the end, the British silenced demonstrators with gunfire.

**South Africa.** Between 1910 and 1940, whites strengthened their grip on South Africa. They imposed a system of racial segregation that became known as apartheid (uh PAHRT hīt). Their goal was to ensure white economic power. New laws, for example, restricted better-paying jobs in mines to whites only. Blacks were pushed into low-paid, less-skilled work. As in Kenya, South African blacks had to carry passes at all times. They were evicted from the best land, which was set aside for whites, and forced to live on crowded "reserves," which were located in dry, infertile areas.

*Racial "Apartness"*
After 1910, whites in South Africa imposed a system of apartheid, or "apartness." The system did not just separate the races, it reserved the best jobs, houses, and schools for whites. It also strictly controlled travel by blacks, who had to carry pass books like the one shown here. **Political and Social Systems** What were the economic effects of the system of apartheid on South Africa's black population?

NON-WHITES ONLY
NET NIE-BLANKES

# PARALLELS THROUGH TIME

## Pride in Heritage

People all over the world share the desire to preserve their language, customs, religion, and culture. Often, they have to resist pressure to give up their heritage and assimilate. Immigrants to the United States, for example, become American citizens but still keep up ties to Mexico, China, Cuba, or Italy.

**Linking Past and Present** Why do you think people want to preserve their heritage? Do you think Americans today are more aware of ethnic pride? Explain.

**PAST** After World War I, Pan-Africanism and négritude asserted the value of African culture. In the United States, artists and writers of the Harlem Renaissance rediscovered African traditions, as shown by Nancy Elizabeth Prophet's sculpture of a male head, at left. In Africa, nationalists like Jomo Kenyatta used cultural pride as a weapon against imperialism. Kenyatta's book Facing Mount Kenya expresses that pride.

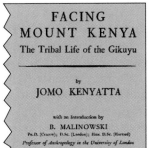

FACING
MOUNT KENYA
The Tribal Life of the Gikuyu

by
JOMO KENYATTA

with an Introduction by
B. MALINOWSKI
Ph.D. (Cracow); D.Sc. (London); Hon. D.Sc. (Harvard)
Professor of Anthropology in the University of London

**PRESENT**
Today, people continue to celebrate their heritage throughout the world. Above, artist John Lightfoot uses traditional Native American colors and designs in his modern paintings. At left, a young Canadian of Scottish origin performs a traditional dance from the highlands of Scotland.

---

Other laws further chipped away at the rights of blacks. In one South African province, educated blacks who owned property had been allowed to vote in local elections. In 1936, the government abolished that right. The system of segregation set up at this time would become even more restrictive after 1948. (See page 523.)

Yet South Africa was also home to a vital nationalist movement. African Christian churches and African-run newspapers demanded rights for black South Africans. In 1912, educated Africans organized a political party, later known as the African National Congress (ANC). Its members worked through legal means, protesting laws that restricted the freedom of black Africans. Their efforts, however, had no effect on the white government of South Africa. Still, the ANC did build a framework for later political action.

## Growing Self-Confidence

During the 1920s, a movement known as Pan-Africanism began to nourish the nationalist spirit. Pan-Africanism emphasized the unity of Africans and people of African descent around the world. Among its most inspiring leaders was

Jamaican-born Marcus Garvey. He preached a forceful message of "Africa for Africans" and demanded an end to colonial rule. Although he never visited Africa, his ideas influenced a new generation of African leaders.

**Pan-African Congress.** Led by the African American W.E.B. DuBois (doo BOIS), Pan-Africanists tried to forge a united front. DuBois organized the first Pan-African Congress in 1919. It met in Paris, where the victorious Allies were holding their peace conference. Delegates from African colonies, the West Indies, and the United States called on the Paris peacemakers to approve a charter of rights for Africans. Although the western powers ignored their demands, the Pan-African Congress established a tradition of cooperation among African leaders.

**Négritude.** French-speaking writers in West Africa and the Caribbean further awakened self-confidence among Africans. They expressed pride in their African roots through the *négritude* movement. Best known among them was the Senegalese poet Léopold Senghor, who celebrated Africa's rich cultural heritage. He fostered African pride by rejecting the negative views of Africa spread by colonial rulers. In his poem "Black Woman," he uses the image of an African woman to reflect on the beauty of Africa:

> 66Black woman,
> Clothed in your color which is life,
>     your form which is beauty!
> I grew up in your shadow, the
>     sweetness of your hands bandaged
>     my eyes,
> And here in the heart of summer and
>     of noon, I discover you, promised
> land from the height of a burnt
>     mountain,
> And your beauty strikes my heart,
>     like the lightning of an eagle.99

Later, Senghor would take an active role in Senegal's drive to independence and would serve as its first president.

**Egypt.** African nationalism brought little political change, except to Egypt. During World War I, Egyptians had been forced to provide food and workers to help Britain. Simmering resistance to British rule flared as the war ended.

Western-educated officials, peasants, landowners, Christians, and Muslims united behind the Wafd (WAHFT) party, which launched strikes and riots.

In 1922, the British finally agreed to declare Egypt independent. In fact, however, British troops stayed in Egypt to guard the Suez Canal, and Britain remained the real power behind Egypt's King Faud.

In the 1930s, young Egyptians were attracted to the Muslim Brotherhood. This group fostered a broad Islamic nationalism that rejected western culture and denounced widespread corruption in the Egyptian government.

## Modernization in Turkey and Iran

Nationalism brought immense changes to the Middle East in the aftermath of World War I. The defeated Ottoman empire collapsed in 1918. Its Arab lands, as you read at the beginning of the chapter, were divided up between Britain and France. In Asia Minor, however, Turks resisted western control and fought to build a modern nation.

**Atatürk.** Led by the determined and energetic Mustafa Kemal, Turkish nationalists overthrew the sultan, defeated western occupation forces, and declared Turkey a republic. Kemal later took the name Atatürk, meaning "father of the Turks." Between 1923 and his death in 1938, Atatürk forced through an ambitious program of radical reforms. His goals were to modernize Turkey along western lines and create a secular state that separated religion from government.

**Westernization.** In a move that swept away centuries-old traditions, Atatürk replaced Islamic law with a new law code based on European models. He discarded the Muslim calendar in favor of the western (Christian) calendar and moved the day of rest from Friday, traditional with Muslims, to Sunday, in line with Christian practice.

Like Peter the Great in Russia, Atatürk forced his people to wear western dress. He replaced Arabic script with the western (Latin) alphabet, stating it was easier to learn. He closed religious schools but opened thousands of state schools to prepare young Turks for the challenges of modern society.

**A New Turkey** *Mustafa Kemal, known as Atatürk, pushed radical reforms to make Turkey a modern nation. "Surviving in the world of modern civilization depends upon changing ourselves," he declared. One change that he introduced was the replacement of Arabic with western script. Here, Atatürk reveals the new Turkish alphabet to a crowd in an Istanbul park.* **Impact of the Individual** *Why do you think Atatürk introduced the new alphabet himself in a public ceremony?*

Other reforms transformed the lives of women. They no longer had to veil their faces and were allowed to vote. Polygamy—the custom allowing men to have more than one wife—was banned. Given freedom to work outside the home, women became teachers, doctors, lawyers, and even politicians.

Under Atatürk, the government helped industry expand. It built roads and railroads, set up factories, and hired westerners to advise on how to make Turkey economically independent.

To achieve the reforms he wanted, Atatürk ruled with an iron hand. To many Turks, he was a hero who was transforming Turkey into a strong, modern power. Some Turkish Muslims, however, rejected his secular government. To them, the Quran and Islamic customs provided all needed guidance, from prayer and behavior to government, commerce, and education.

**Nationalism and reform in Iran.** Atatürk's reforms inspired nationalists in neighboring Iran. They greatly resented the British and Russians, who had won spheres of influence in their land. In 1925, an ambitious army officer, Reza Khan, overthrew the shah. He set up his own Pahlavi dynasty, with himself as shah.

Like Atatürk, Reza Khan rushed to modernize Iran and make it fully independent. He built factories, roads, and railroads and strengthened the army. He, too, adopted the western alphabet, forced Iranians to wear western clothing, and set up modern, secular schools. In addition, he moved to replace Islamic law with secular law and encouraged women to take part in public life. While the shah had the support of wealthy urban Iranians, Muslim religious leaders fiercely condemned his efforts to introduce western ways.

As Iran modernized, it won better terms from the British company that controlled its oil industry. It persuaded the British to give it a larger share of the profits and insisted that Iranian workers be hired at all levels. In the decades ahead, oil would become a major factor in Iranian economic and foreign affairs.

## Arab Nationalism and European Mandates

Arab nationalism blossomed after World War I and gave rise to Pan-Arabism. This nationalist movement built on the shared heritage of Arabs who lived in lands from the Arabian Peninsula through North Africa.* Pan-Arabism emphasized their common history and language and recalled the golden age of Arab civilization. Pan-Arabism sought to free Arabs from foreign domination and unite them in

---

*The Arab Middle East included lands from the Arabian Peninsula through North Africa. Today, this area includes nations such as Syria, Jordan, Iraq, Egypt, Algeria, and Morocco.

## The Middle East, 1920s

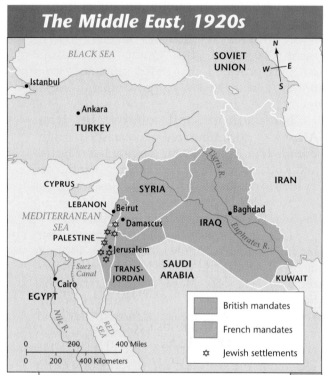

Map legend:
- British mandates
- French mandates
- ✡ Jewish settlements

## GEOGRAPHY AND HISTORY

After World War I, European nations sought to increase their influence in the Middle East. The League of Nations awarded Great Britain and France mandates in parts of the former Ottoman empire. In theory, a mandated territory was to be held until it was able to "stand alone." In practice, however, mandates became indistinguishable from European colonies.

1. **Location** On the map, locate (a) Syria, (b) Palestine, (c) Trans-Jordan, (d) Saudi Arabia, (e) Egypt, (f) Jerusalem, (g) Damascus, (h) Lebanon, (i) Suez Canal, (j) Mediterranean Sea.
2. **Place** (a) Which Middle Eastern countries became French mandates after World War I? (b) Which Middle Eastern countries became British mandates? (c) What was the status of Iran in the 1920s?
3. **Critical Thinking** **Applying Information** (a) Is this map a useful source of information about the European mandates in the Middle East? Why or why not? (b) Is it a useful source of information about the origins of the Arab-Jewish conflict in the Middle East? Explain your answer.

their own state. An Arab student spoke of this mission:

> 66 I am an Arab, and I believe that the Arabs constitute one nation. The sacred right of this nation is to be sovereign in her own affairs . . . to liberate the Arab homeland, to unite all its parts and to found [distinctively Arab] political, economic, and social institutions. 99

**Betrayal at the peace conference.** The mandates—territories administered by European nations—set up by the Paris Peace Conference outraged Arabs. During World War I, they had helped the Allies against the Central Powers, especially the Ottomans. In return, they had been promised independence. Instead, the Allies carved up the Ottoman lands, giving France mandates in Syria and Lebanon and Britain mandates in Palestine and Iraq. Later, Trans-Jordan was added to the British mandate.

Arabs felt betrayed by the West—a feeling that has endured to this day. During the 1920s and 1930s, their anger erupted in frequent protests and revolts against western imperialism. A major center of turmoil was the British mandate of Palestine. There, Arab nationalists faced European Zionists, or Jewish nationalists, with their own dreams of creating a Palestinian homeland.

**Promises in Palestine.** Since Roman times, Jews had dreamed of returning to Palestine. In 1897, Theodor Herzl (HER tsuhl) responded to growing anti-Semitism in Europe by founding the modern Zionist movement. His goal was to rebuild a Jewish state in Palestine, "our ever-memorable historical home." Soon, a few Eastern European Jews migrated to Palestine. There they joined the small Jewish community that had survived there since biblical times.

During World War I, the Allies made two vague sets of promises. First, they promised Arabs their own kingdoms in former Ottoman lands, including Palestine. Then, in 1917, the British issued the Balfour Declaration to win support of European Jews. In it, Britain supported the idea of setting up "a national home for the Jewish people" in Palestine. The declaration noted, however, that "nothing shall be done which may prejudice the civil and religious rights of existing non-Jewish communities in Palestine." Those communities were Arab. The stage was thus set for conflict between Arab and Jewish nationalists.

**A bitter struggle.** In the 1930s, anti-Semitism in Germany and Eastern Europe forced many Jews to seek safety in Palestine. Despite great hardships, they set up factories, built new towns, and turned arid desert into irrigated farmland.

At first, some Arabs welcomed the money and modern technical skills that the newcomers brought with them. But as Jews poured into the land of Palestine, tensions between the two groups developed. Sometimes, Jewish settlers bought land from Arab landowners and then forced Arab tenants off the land. In the cities, Jewish factory owners often refused to hire Arabs. Angry Arabs attacked Jewish settlements, hoping to oust the Jews. For the rest of the century, Arab nationalists battled Zionists over a land that Arabs called Palestine and Jews called Israel. (See page 491.)

## SECTION 2 REVIEW

1. **Identify** (a) "Women's War," (b) négritude, (c) Léopold Senghor, (d) Atatürk, (e) Reza Khan, (f) Pan-Arabism, (g) Balfour Declaration.
2. **Define** apartheid.
3. (a) Why did Africans resent colonial rule? (b) How was Pan-Africanism an expression of African nationalism?
4. (a) How did Turkey and Iran seek to modernize? (b) How was modernization linked to nationalism?
5. (a) Why did Arabs resent the mandate system? (b) Why did Palestine become a center of conflict?
6. *Critical Thinking* **Analyzing Information** Why do you think leaders in Turkey and Iran tried to modernize their countries using western models?
7. *ACTIVITY* Imagine you are a member of the Pan-African movement in the 1920s. Use what you have learned about African culture in this and earlier chapters to write a speech extolling your unique heritage.

## 3 India Seeks Self-Rule

### Guide for Reading

- How did World War I strengthen Indian nationalism?
- How did Gandhi become a national hero?
- What goals did Muslims in India pursue?
- **Vocabulary** *civil disobedience*

Tensions were running high in Amritsar, a city in northern India. Protests against British rule had sparked riots and attacks on British residents. On April 13, 1919, a large but peaceful crowd jammed into a walled field in the heart of the city. The British commander, General Reginald Dyer, had banned public meetings, but Indians either ignored or had not heard the order.

As Indian leaders addressed the crowd, Dyer arrived with 50 soldiers. To clear the field, they opened fire on the unarmed men, women, and children. For 10 minutes, they rained death on the people trapped in the field, killing 379 and wounding more than 1,100. Dyer later claimed he had acted "to make a wide impression" and produce "a sufficient moral effect" on Indian protesters.

The Amritsar massacre was a turning point for many Indians. It convinced them of the evils of British rule. For Jawaharlal Nehru, a leading Indian nationalist, the incident made him realize "more vividly than I had ever done before, how brutal and immoral imperialism was and how it had eaten into the souls of the British upper classes." ( See *World Literature*, "We Crown Thee King," page 342.)

### Moves Toward Independence

The tragedy at Amritsar was linked to Indian frustrations after World War I. During the war, more than a million Indians had served overseas, suffering heavy casualties. As thousands died on distant battlefields, Indian nationalists grew increasingly angry that they had no freedom at home.

To quiet nationalist demands, the British promised India greater self-government after the war. But when the fighting ended, Britain proposed only a few minor reforms. Meanwhile, Britain's crackdown on protesters triggered riots and the brutal slaughter in Amritsar.

Since 1885, the Congress party had pressed for self-rule within the British empire. (See page 232.) After Amritsar, it began to call for full independence. But party members were mostly a middle-class, western-educated elite who had little in common with the masses of Indian peasants. In the 1920s, a new leader emerged, Mohandas Gandhi. He united all Indians behind the drive for independence. Adoring Indians dubbed him Mahatma, or "Great Soul."

## Mohandas Gandhi

Mohandas Gandhi came from a middle-class Hindu family. At age 19, he went to England to study law. After returning to India, he tried to set up his own law practice but soon joined an Indian law firm in South Africa. Thousands of Indians had gone to South Africa as indentured servants and then settled there. Some had prospered, but many were poor. All faced racial prejudice under South Africa's white rulers.

For 20 years, Gandhi fought laws that discriminated against Indians in South Africa. In his struggle against injustice, he adopted the weapon of nonviolent (passive) resistance. He called it *satyagraha,* or "soul-force." In 1914, Gandhi returned to India and joined the Congress party. His ideas inspired Indians of all religions and ethnic backgrounds and encouraged them to resist British rule.

### GLOBAL CONNECTIONS

Gandhi's philosophy of nonviolence won him a small but devoted following in the United States. Among those he inspired was Martin Luther King, Jr. King organized a campaign of nonviolent resistance against racism and discrimination in the American South. Like Gandhi, King and his followers did not try to evade unjust laws. Rather, they openly defied them and proudly went to jail when they were challenged. King's civil rights movement helped bring sweeping changes to the United States, just as Gandhi's *satyagraha* did in India.

**Nonviolence.** While leaders like Atatürk adopted western solutions to national problems, Gandhi embraced Hindu traditions. Above all, he preached the ancient doctrine of ahimsa, or nonviolence and reverence for all life. He applied this idea to the fight against British rule. By using the power of love, he believed, people could convert even the worst wrongdoer to the right course of action. As Gandhi explained, passive resistance involved sacrifice and suffering:

❝Passive [nonviolent] resistance is a method of securing rights by personal suffering. It is the reverse of resistance by arms. . . . If I do not obey [an unjust] law and accept the penalty for its breach, I use soul-force.❞

**Western influence.** Gandhi's philosophy reflected western as well as Indian influences. He admired Christian teachings about love and had read the works of Henry David Thoreau, an American philosopher of the 1800s who believed in civil disobedience, the refusal to obey unjust laws.

Gandhi also embraced western ideas of democracy and nationalism. He rejected the inequalities of the caste system and fought hard to end the harsh treatment of untouchables. He urged equal rights for all Indians, women as well as men.

**Gandhi sets an example.** Abandoning western-style clothing, Gandhi dressed in the *dhoti,* the simple white garment traditionally worn by village Indians. During the 1920s and 1930s, he launched a series of nonviolent actions against British rule. He called for boycotts of British goods, especially textiles, and urged Indians to wear only cotton grown and woven in India. He worked to restore pride in India's traditional spinning and weaving industries, making the spinning wheel a symbol of the nationalist

*Woman spinning* ▶

movement. Women joined the self-sufficiency movement in large numbers, learning to spin and weave their own clothes and producing as much as they could in their homes.

Through his own example, Gandhi inspired Indians to "get rid of our helplessness." His campaigns of civil disobedience attracted wide support. But when protests led to violent riots, Gandhi was deeply upset. He would fast, pray, and call on patriots to practice self-control.

## The Salt March

 To mobilize mass support, Gandhi offered a daring challenge to Britain in 1930. He set out to end the British salt monopoly. Like earlier rulers in India, the British claimed the sole right to produce and sell salt. By taxing those sales, they collected money to maintain their government in India.

**The challenge.** To Gandhi, the government salt monopoly was an evil burden on the poor and a symbol of British oppression. Every-

*A Protest March*
*The Salt March focused the attention of all India on Gandhi's challenge to the British. As Gandhi and his supporters walked from village to village, his message of opposition to British rule spread like wildfire. "If the awakening of the people in the country is true and real," Gandhi said, "the salt law is as good as abolished." When the marchers arrived at the sea, Gandhi lifted a lump of salt over his head and declared, "With this, I am shaking the foundations of the British empire."* **Impact of the Individual** *In what ways do you think Gandhi's personal example was important to the Indian independence movement?*

one needed salt to survive. But while natural salt was available in the sea, Indians were forbidden to touch it. They could only buy salt sold by the government.

Early in 1930, Gandhi wrote to the British viceroy in India, explaining his motives and goals. He stated his intention to break the law and condemned British rule as "a curse":

66[British rule] has impoverished the dumb millions by a system of progressive exploitation. . . . It has reduced us politically to serfdom. It has sapped the foundations of our culture . . . and degraded us spiritually.99

**While the world watched.** On March 12, Gandhi made good on his challenge. With 78 followers, he set out on a 240-mile march to the sea. As the tiny band passed through villages, crowds listened eagerly to Gandhi's message. They prayed for the protest's success, and some even joined the procession. By the time they reached the sea, the marchers numbered in the thousands.

Each day, reporters wired news of Gandhi's "salt march" to newspapers in India and around the globe. The world wondered what would happen when the small man in his simple white loin cloth broke the law. On April 6, Gandhi waded into the surf and picked up a lump of sea salt. A young woman marcher and poet, Sarojini Naidu, cried out: "Hail, law breaker!"

Gandhi urged Indians to follow his lead. Even though he was soon arrested and jailed, coastal villagers started collecting salt. Congress party leaders sold salt on city streets, displayed it to huge rallies—and went to jail. As Gandhi's campaign gained force, tens of thousands of Indians were dragged off to prison.

**An effective tool.** All around the world, newspapers thundered against Britain. Stories revealed how police brutally clubbed peaceful marchers who tried to occupy a government saltworks. "Not one of the marchers even raised an arm to fend off the blows," wrote an outraged American reporter.

The Salt March embarrassed Britain, which took pride in its democratic traditions. But in India, its officials were jailing thousands who asked only for basic freedoms that the British enjoyed in their own country.

**Toward freedom.** Gandhi's campaign of nonviolence and the self-sacrifice of his followers slowly forced Britain to agree to hand over some power to Indians and to meet other demands of the Congress party. Complete independence, however, would not be achieved until 1947, one year before the Mahatma's death. (See page 484.) ■

### Looking Ahead

As India came closer to independence, Muslim fears of the Hindu majority increased. While millions of Muslims responded to Gandhi's campaigns, tensions between Hindus and Muslims often erupted into violence.

**A separate Muslim state.** During the 1930s, the Muslim League gained an able leader in Muhammad Ali Jinnah. Like Gandhi, Jinnah came from a middle-class background and had studied law in England. At first, he represented Muslim interests within the Congress party. Later, he threw his support behind the idea of a separate state for Muslims. It would be called Pakistan, meaning "land of the [ritually] pure."

**World War II.** India was moving toward independence when a new world war exploded in 1939. Britain outraged Indian leaders by postponing further action on independence and then bringing India into the war without consulting them. Angry nationalists launched a campaign of noncooperation and were jailed by the British. Millions of Indians, however, did help Britain during the war.

When the war ended in 1945, independence could no longer be delayed. But a new tragedy unfolded as Hindu-Muslim violence raged on the Indian subcontinent. (See Chapter 18.)

## SECTION 3 REVIEW

1. **Identify** (a) Amritsar, (b) Salt March, (c) Muhammad Ali Jinnah.
2. **Define** civil disobedience.
3. (a) How did World War I strengthen Indian resentment of British rule? (b) How did the Amritsar massacre change Indian goals?
4. (a) How did Gandhi revive Indian pride? (b) Describe Gandhi's method for resisting British rule.
5. How did the goal of Muslims in India change during the 1930s?
6. *Critical Thinking* **Analyzing Information** Why do you think civil disobedience is an effective weapon?
7. *ACTIVITY* Review the discussion of the Amritsar massacre on page 331. Then, write a headline about the event for (a) an Indian newspaper, (b) a British newspaper.

# Upheavals in China

## Guide for Reading

- What problems did the new republic of China face?

- What were the goals of the May Fourth Movement?

- Why did civil war erupt between the Guomindang and the Communists?

Sun Yixian, "father" of the Chinese revolution, painted a grim picture of China after the overthrow of the Qing dynasty. "In comparison with other nations," he wrote, "we have the greatest population and the oldest culture, of 4,000 years' duration." Yet China, he noted, was "the poorest and weakest state in the world." Other countries were "the carving knife and the serving dish," and China was "the fish and the meat."

As the new Chinese republic took shape, nationalists like Sun Yixian set the goal of "catch-ing up and surpassing the powers, east and west." But that goal would remain a distant dream as China suffered the turmoil of civil war and foreign invasion.

## The Chinese Republic

In China, as you recall, the Qing dynasty collapsed in 1911. Sun Yixian hoped to rebuild China on the Three Principles of the People. (See page 237.) But he made little progress. China quickly fell into chaos.

**Internal problems.** In 1912, Sun Yixian stepped down as president in favor of a powerful general, Yuan Shikai. Sun hoped that Yuan would restore order and create a strong central government. But the ambitious general had other ideas. He tried to set up a new ruling

*A Chinese City* China in the early 1900s was on the edge of major change. This picture shows the business district of Hangzhou, a major Chinese trading city for over 800 years. Hangzhou was opened to foreign trade in 1896. By the 1930s, it was a major railway hub and the site of China's first modern roads. *Political and Social Systems* What problems did China face in the early 1900s?

dynasty, with himself as emperor. When Yuan died in 1916, China plunged into still greater disorder.

In the provinces, local warlords seized power. As rival armies battled for control, the economy collapsed and millions of peasants suffered terrible hardships. Warlords forced them to pay taxes to support their armies. The constant fighting ravaged the land. Bandits and famine added to their misery. A foreign observer compared the plight of China's peasants to "that of a man standing permanently up to his neck in water, so that even a ripple is enough to kill him."

**Foreign imperialism.** During this period of upheaval, foreign powers increased their influence over Chinese affairs. Foreign merchants, missionaries, and soldiers dominated the ports China had opened to trade. They also exerted influence inland.

In 1915, Japan put new pressure on its once-powerful neighbor. While western powers were distracted by World War I, Japan presented Yuan Shikai with Twenty-one Demands, which sought to make China a Japanese protectorate. Too weak to resist, Yuan gave in to some of the demands.

Then, in 1919, at the Paris Peace Conference, the victorious Allies gave Japan control over German possessions in China. That news infuriated Chinese nationalists, who blamed their leaders for "selling out" at Versailles.

**May Fourth Movement.** On May 4, 1919, student protests erupted in Beijing and later spread to cities across China—a startling event in those days. "China's territory may be conquered," they declared, "but it cannot be given away! The Chinese people may be massacred, but they will not surrender." Students organized boycotts of Japanese goods.

Student protests set off a cultural and intellectual ferment known as the May Fourth Movement. Like earlier reform movements, its goal was to strengthen China. Western-educated leaders blamed the imperialists' successes on China's own weakness. As in Meiji Japan, Chinese reformers wanted to learn from the West and use that knowledge to end foreign domination. Most reformers rejected Confucian traditions and many turned to western science and ideas such as democracy and nationalism to solve China's problems.

Women played a key role in the May Fourth Movement, as they had in earlier uprisings. They joined marches and campaigned to end arranged marriages, footbinding, and the seclusion of women within the home. Their work helped open doors for women in education and the economy.

**The appeal of Marxism.** Some Chinese turned to the revolutionary ideas of Marx and Lenin. The Russian Revolution seemed to offer a model of how a strong, well-organized party could transform a nation. And Soviet Russia was more than willing to train Chinese students and military officers to become the vanguard—or elite leaders—of a communist revolution. By the 1920s, a small group of Chinese communists had formed their own party.

## Leaders for a New China

In 1921, Sun Yixian and his Guomindang (gwoh meen DAWNG), or Nationalist, party established a government in south China. Sun planned to raise an army, defeat the warlords, and spread his government's rule over all of China. When western powers ignored pleas for help in building a democratic China, Sun decided "that the one real and genuine friend of the Chinese Revolution is Soviet Russia." Russian experts helped the Nationalists plan and carry out their campaign against the warlords.

**Jiang Jieshi.** After Sun's death in 1925, an energetic young army officer, Jiang Jieshi* (jyawng jeh SHEE), took over the Guomindang. He had received military training in Japan. While he was determined to reunite China, Jiang had little interest in either democracy or communism.

In 1926, Jiang Jieshi began a march into northern China, crushing local warlords as he advanced and capturing Beijing. In mid-campaign, he stopped to strike at the Chinese Communist party, which he saw as a threat to his power. While Jiang had the support of landlords and business leaders, the Communists were winning converts among the small proletariat in cities like Shanghai.

Early in 1927, on orders from Jiang, Guomindang troops slaughtered Communist party

---

*In earlier textbooks, this name is spelled Chiang Kai-shek.

**The Young Mao** *As a youth, Mao Zedong avidly read the works of Voltaire, Thomas Jefferson, and Karl Marx. He had been a librarian and was a school principal at the time he helped found China's Communist party. This portrait of the young Mao was painted in 1968, after he had ruled China for almost 20 years.* **Art and Literature** *How does the artist convey Mao's strength and determination?*

members and the workers who supported them. In Shanghai and elsewhere, thousands of people were killed. Anger over the massacre would fuel a bitter civil war for the next 22 years.

**Mao Zedong.** Among the Communists who escaped Jiang's attack was a young revolutionary of peasant origins, Mao Zedong. Unlike earlier Chinese Communists, Mao believed the Communists should seek support not among the small urban working class but among the large peasant masses.

Although the Communists were pursued at every turn by Guomindang forces, Mao was optimistic of eventual success. "A single spark can start a prairie fire," he once observed. For a time, Mao and the Communists organized the peasants in southeastern China. They redistributed land to peasants and offered them schooling and health care.

**The Long March.** Jiang Jieshi, however, was determined to destroy the "Red bandits," as he called the Communists. He led the Guomindang in a series of "extermination campaigns" against them.

In 1934, in an epic retreat known as the Long March, Mao and about 100,000 of his followers fled the Guomindang. During the next year, they trekked more than 6,000 miles, facing daily attacks as they crossed rugged mountains, deep gorges, and mighty rivers. Only about 20,000 people survived the ordeal. For decades, the Long March stood as a symbol of Communist heroism to Chinese opposed to the Guomindang.

During the Long March, the Communists enforced strict discipline. Soldiers had to follow three main rules: Obey orders, "do not take a single needle or a piece of thread from the people," and turn in everything you capture. Further, they were to treat peasants politely, pay for goods they wanted, and avoid damaging crops. Such behavior made Mao's forces welcome among peasants who had suffered at the hands of the Guomindang.

At the end of the Long March, the Communists set up a new base in remote northern China. There, Mao rebuilt his forces and plotted new strategies. He claimed the great retreat as a victory. As he observed:

66The Long March is also a seeding-machine. It has sown many seeds in eleven provinces, which will sprout, grow leaves, blossom into flowers, bear fruit, and yield a crop in future.99

## China, 1925–1935

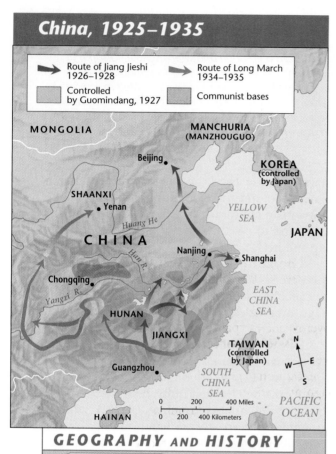

| | |
|---|---|
| → Route of Jiang Jieshi 1926–1928 | → Route of Long March 1934–1935 |
| ▢ Controlled by Guomindang, 1927 | ▢ Communist bases |

MONGOLIA
MANCHURIA (MANZHOUGUO)
Beijing
KOREA (controlled by Japan)
SHAANXI
Yenan
YELLOW SEA
*Huang He*
CHINA
JAPAN
*Han R.*
Nanjing
Shanghai
Chongqing
EAST CHINA SEA
*Yangzi R.*
HUNAN
JIANGXI
TAIWAN (controlled by Japan)
Guangzhou
SOUTH CHINA SEA
N W E S
HAINAN
PACIFIC OCEAN

0    200    400 Miles
0    200    400 Kilometers

## GEOGRAPHY *AND* HISTORY

Beginning in 1925, the Guomindang and the Communists waged a long and bitter battle for control of China.

1. **Location** On the map, locate (a) Beijing, (b) Nanjing, (c) Jiangxi.
2. **Movement** Describe the route of the Long March.
3. *Critical Thinking* **Synthesizing Information** What natural features made the Long March difficult?

## Japanese Invasion

While Jiang was pursuing the Communists across China, the country faced another danger. In 1931, Japan invaded Manchuria in northeastern China, adding it to the growing Japanese empire. (See the map on page 340.) As Japanese aggression increased, some of Jiang's own generals began to doubt him. Why, they demanded, did he waste valuable resources fighting other Chinese instead of mobilizing against the foreign invaders? In the end, Jiang was forced to form a united front with the Communists against Japan.

In 1937, the Japanese struck again. This time, they attacked China proper. As airplanes bombed Chinese cities, highly disciplined and well-equipped Japanese troops overran eastern China, including Beijing and Guangzhou. Jiang Jieshi retreated to the interior and set up his capital at Chongqing (chawng CHIHNG). The Japanese set up their puppet government in Nanjing, the former Nationalist capital. The killing and brutality that accompanied their entry into the city became known as the "rape of Nanjing."

**Looking ahead.** From 1937 to 1945, the Guomindang, the Communists, and the Japanese were locked in a three-sided struggle. The bombing of Pearl Harbor in 1941 brought the United States not only into the war against Japan but into an alliance with the Chinese, as well. After Japan's defeat, the United States tried to prevent renewed civil war in China, but with no success. Within a few years, the Communists would triumph, and Mao would move to impose revolutionary change on China.

## SECTION 4 REVIEW

1. **Identify** (a) Yuan Shikai, (b) Twenty-one Demands, (c) May Fourth Movement, (d) Guomindang, (e) Jiang Jieshi, (f) Mao Zedong, (g) Long March, (h) rape of Nanjing.
2. Why did the new republic of China fall into chaos after 1912?
3. (a) What western ideas appealed to Chinese reformers? (b) How did these reformers plan to end the growth of foreign influence in China?
4. Describe the goals of each of the following: (a) Sun Yixian, (b) Jiang Jieshi, (c) Mao Zedong.
5. *Critical Thinking* **Recognizing Causes and Effects** How did the actions of foreign imperialist powers help to strengthen nationalism in China?
6. *ACTIVITY* Review Mao's statement about the Long March as a "seeding-machine." Draw a cartoon illustrating this statement.

# Empire of the Rising Sun

## Guide for Reading

- How did Japanese democracy grow during the 1920s?

- Why did the Great Depression undermine Japanese democracy?

- What policies did Japanese militarists pursue?

Solemn ceremonies marked the start of Emperor Hirohito's reign. A few honored participants gathered in the Secret Purple Hall. Other high-ranking guests sat in an outer chamber, able to hear but not to see the emperor.

In the hall, the new emperor sat stiffly on the ancient throne of Japan. Beside him sat his wife, the empress Nagako. With great care, he performed sacred purification rituals going back thousands of years. Calling on the spirits of his ancestors, he pledged "to preserve world peace and benefit the welfare of the human race."

The prime minister then made his own brief speech, ending with a ringing cry: "May the Lord Emperor live 10,000 years!" Instantly, the words echoed across Japan. "May the Lord Emperor live 10,000 years!" shouted millions of voices, invoking the traditional wish for a long and successful reign.

In fact, Hirohito reigned from 1926 to 1989—an astonishing 63 years. During those decades, Japan experienced remarkable successes and appalling tragedies. In this section, we will focus on the 1920s and 1930s, when the pressures of extreme nationalism and economic upheaval set Japan on a militaristic and expansionist path that would eventually engulf all of Asia.

## Liberal Changes of the 1920s

In the 1920s, Japan moved toward greater democracy. Political parties grew stronger, and elected members of the Diet—the Japanese parliament—exerted their power. By 1925, all adult men had won the right to vote. Western ideas about women's rights had brought a few changes. Overall, however, Japanese women remained subordinate to men, and they would not win suffrage until 1947.

**Economic growth.** During World War I, the Japanese economy enjoyed phenomenal growth. Its exports to the Allies soared. Also, while western powers battled in Europe, Japan expanded its influence in East Asia. As you have seen, it sought additional rights in China with the Twenty-one Demands.

By the 1920s, the powerful business leaders known as the zaibatsu strongly influenced politics through donations to political parties. They pushed for policies to favor international trade and their own interests. At the same time, in the spirit of world peace, Japan signed an agreement with the United States and Britain to limit the size of its navy. The government reduced military spending, signaling support for commercial over military expansion.

**Serious problems.** Behind this seeming well-being, Japan faced some grave problems. The economy grew more slowly in the 1920s than at any time since Japan had modernized. Rural peasants enjoyed none of the prosperity of city-dwellers. In the cities, factory workers earning low wages were attracted to the socialist ideas of Marx and Lenin. As they won the right to vote, socialists were elected to the Diet.

In the cities, too, the younger generation was in revolt against tradition. They adopted western fads and fashions and rejected family authority for the western notion of individual freedom.

During the 1920s, tensions between the government and the military simmered not far below the surface. Conservatives, especially military officers, blasted government corruption, including payoffs by powerful zaibatsu. They also condemned western influences for undermining basic Japanese values of obedience and respect for authority.

## The Nationalist Reaction

In 1929, the Great Depression rippled across the Pacific, striking Japan with devastating force. Trade, Japan's economic lifeline, suffered as foreign buyers could no longer afford Japanese silks and other exports. Prices for all exports plummeted. Unemployment in the

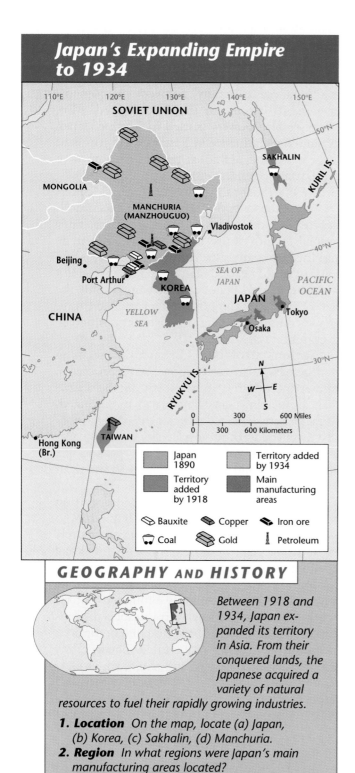

## Japan's Expanding Empire to 1934

**SOVIET UNION**

110°E · 120°E · 130°E · 140°E · 150°E

50°N

SAKHALIN

KURIL IS.

MONGOLIA

MANCHURIA (MANZHOUGUO)

Vladivostok

40°N

Beijing

Port Arthur

KOREA

SEA OF JAPAN

PACIFIC OCEAN

CHINA

YELLOW SEA

JAPAN

Tokyo

Osaka

30°N

RYUKYU IS.

N
W—E
S

0    300    600 Miles
0    300    600 Kilometers

TAIWAN

Hong Kong (Br.)

| Legend | |
|---|---|
| Japan 1890 | Territory added by 1934 |
| Territory added by 1918 | Main manufacturing areas |

Bauxite · Copper · Iron ore
Coal · Gold · Petroleum

### GEOGRAPHY AND HISTORY

Between 1918 and 1934, Japan expanded its territory in Asia. From their conquered lands, the Japanese acquired a variety of natural resources to fuel their rapidly growing industries.

1. **Location** On the map, locate (a) Japan, (b) Korea, (c) Sakhalin, (d) Manchuria.
2. **Region** In what regions were Japan's main manufacturing areas located?
3. *Critical Thinking* **Identifying Main Ideas** (a) What resources did Japan acquire in Manchuria? (b) From where did Japan acquire petroleum? (c) How could Japan use that resource to help its economy?

cities soared, while in the countryside peasants were only a mouthful from starvation.

**A worsening crisis.** Economic disaster fed the discontent of the military and extreme nationalists, or ultranationalists. They condemned politicians for agreeing to western demands to stop overseas expansion. Western industrial powers, they pointed out, had long ago grabbed huge empires. By comparison, Japan's empire was tiny.

Japanese nationalists were further outraged by racial policies in the United States, Canada, and Australia that shut out Japanese immigrants. The Japanese took great pride in their achievements as a modern industrial power and bitterly resented being treated as second-class citizens of the world.

As the crisis worsened, nationalists demanded renewed expansion. An empire in Asia, they argued, would provide much-needed raw materials and an outlet for Japan's rapidly growing population. They set their sights on the Chinese province of Manchuria. (See the map at left.) It was rich in natural resources, and Japanese businesses had already invested heavily there.

**The Manchurian incident.** In 1931, a group of Japanese army officers provoked an incident that would provide an excuse to seize Manchuria. They blew up tracks on a Japanese-owned railroad line and claimed the Chinese had done it. In "self-defense," they then attacked Chinese forces. Without consulting their own government, the Japanese army conquered all of Manchuria and set up a puppet state there that they called Manzhouguo (mahn joh GWOH).

When the League of Nations condemned Japanese aggression, Japan simply withdrew from the League. When politicians in Tokyo objected to the army's high-handed actions, public opinion sided with the military. In the years ahead, the military would increase its power at home and expand Japan's empire abroad.

### Militarists in Power

By the early 1930s, ultranationalists were winning popular support for foreign conquests and a tough stand against the western powers. Members of "patriotic" societies assassinated a number of politicians and business leaders who opposed military expansion. Military leaders

**Militarists Rule Japan** *Japan's military steadily increased their power over the government during the 1930s. The navy used propaganda, like this poster, to win public support.* **Art and Literature** *How did this poster appeal to Japanese patriotism?*

plotted to overthrow the government and, in 1936, briefly occupied the center of Tokyo.

**Traditional values revived.** Civilian government survived, but by 1937 it had been forced to accept military domination. To please the ultranationalists, it cracked down on socialists and ended most democratic freedoms. It revived ancient warrior values and built a cult around the emperor, who was believed to be descended from the sun goddess.

To spread its nationalistic message, the government focused on the schools. Students had to study *The Way of the Emperor's Subjects*. This government pamphlet deplored the Japanese adoption of western ideas:

66With the influx of European and American culture into this country, . . . individualism, liberalism, utilitarianism, and materialism began to assert themselves, with the result that the traditional character of the country was much impaired and the virtuous habits and customs bequeathed by our ancestors were affected unfavorably.99

To practice "the way of the emperor's subjects," students were taught absolute obedience to the emperor and service to the state.

**Renewed expansion.** During the 1930s, Japan took advantage of China's civil war to increase its influence there. In 1937, as you have read, its armies invaded the Chinese mainland. They committed terrible atrocities as they overran eastern China.

Japan expected to complete its conquest of China within a few years. But in 1939, while the two nations were locked in deadly combat, World War II broke out in Europe. That conflict swiftly spread to Asia, where France and Britain had large empires.

By 1939, Japan had joined with two aggressive European powers, Germany and Italy. That alliance, combined with renewed Japanese conquests, would turn World War II into a brutal, wide-ranging conflict waged not only across the continent of Europe but across Asia and the Pacific, as well.

## SECTION 5 REVIEW

1. **Identify** (a) Hirohito, (b) Manzhouguo.
2. How did Japan become more democratic in the 1920s?
3. (a) How did the Great Depression affect Japan's economy? (b) What political effects did it have on Japan?
4. (a) What goals did Japanese militarists pursue at home? (b) What goals did they pursue overseas?
5. *Critical Thinking* **Recognizing Causes and Effects** Why do you think a nation might turn to military leaders and extreme nationalists during a time of crisis?
6. *ACTIVITY* Review the discussion of the Manchurian incident on page 340. Then, write two telegrams reporting the incident, one by a Japanese soldier and the other by a Chinese soldier.

# World Literature
## "We Crown Thee King"
### Rabindranath Tagore

**Introduction** *Rabindranath Tagore was probably the most important Indian writer of this century. He produced numerous poems, short stories, plays, novels, essays, and travel books. One of his poems became India's national anthem. In 1913, Tagore became the first writer outside Europe to win the Nobel Prize for literature.*

*Like many educated Indians of his time, Tagore had an uneasy association with the Anglo-Indians, or the British living in India. In 1915, he accepted a knighthood from the British government. After the Amritsar massacre of 1919, however, he renounced his knighthood in protest. Tagore's 1916 short story "'We Crown Thee King'" explores the relationship between the British* sahibs, *or ruling class, and the Indian elite.*

Pramathanath was a Bachelor of Arts, and in addition was gifted with common sense. But he held no high official position; he had no handsome salary; nor did he exert any influence with his pen. There was no one in power to lend him a helping hand, because he desired to keep away from the Englishmen, as much as they desired to keep away from him. So it happened that he shone only within the sphere of his family and friends, and excited no admiration beyond it.

Yet this Pramathanath had once sojourned in England for some three years. The kindly treatment he received during his stay there overpowered him so much that he forgot the sorrow and humiliation of his own country, and came back dressed in European clothes. This rather grieved his brothers and his sisters at first, but after a few days they began to think that European clothes suited nobody better, and gradually they came to share his pride and dignity.

On his return from England, Pramathanath resolved that he would show the world how to associate with Anglo-Indians on terms of equality. Those of our countrymen who think that no such association is possible, unless we bend our knees to them, showed their utter lack of self-respect, and were also unjust to the English—so thought Pramathanath.

He brought with him letters of introduction from many distinguished Englishmen at home, and these gave him some recognition in Anglo-Indian society. He and his wife occasionally enjoyed English hospitality at tea, dinner, sports and other entertainments. Such good luck intoxicated him, and began to produce a tingling sensation in every vein of his body.

About this time, at the opening of a new railway line, many of the town, proud recipients of official favor, were invited by the Lieutenant-Governor to take the first trip. Pramathanath was among them. On the return journey, a European Sergeant of the Police expelled some Indian gentlemen from a railway-carriage with great insolence. Pramathanath, dressed in his European clothes, was there. He, too, was getting out, when the Sergeant said: "You needn't move, sir. Keep your seat, please."

At first Pramathanath felt flattered at the special respect shown to him. When, however, the train went on, the dull rays of the setting sun, at the west of the fields, now ploughed up and stripped of green, seemed in his eyes to spread a glow of shame over the whole country. Sitting near the window of his lonely compartment, he seemed to catch a glimpse of the downcast eyes of his Motherland, hidden behind the trees. As Pramathanath sat there, lost in reverie, burning tears flowed down his cheeks, and his heart burst with indignation.

He now remembered the story of a donkey who was drawing the chariot of an idol along the street. The wayfarers bowed down to the idol, and touched the dusty ground with their foreheads. The foolish donkey imagined that all this reverence was being shown to him. "The only difference," said Pramathanath to himself,

"between the donkey and myself is this: I understand today that the respect I receive is not given to me but to the burden on my back."

Arriving home, Pramathanath called together all the children of the household, and lighting a big bonfire, threw all his European clothes into it one by one. The children danced round and round it, and the higher the flames shot up, the greater was their merriment. After that, Pramathanath gave up his sip of tea and bits of toast in Anglo-Indian houses, and once again sat inaccessible within the castle of his house, while his insulted friends went about from the door of one Englishman to that of another, bending their turbaned heads as before.

[*A few years later, Nabendu Sekhar, a young Indian with political ambitions, marries one of Pramathanath's daughters. Nabendu tries to impress his new in-laws by showing off his connections with the British.*]

As if by mistake, he would often hand to his sisters-in-law sundry letters that his late father had received from Europeans. And when the cherry lips of those young ladies smiled sarcastically, and the point of a shining dagger peeped out of its sheath of red velvet, the unfortunate man saw his folly, and regretted it.

Labanyalekha, the eldest sister, surpassed the rest in beauty and cleverness. Finding an auspicious day, she put on the mantel-shelf of Nabendu's bedroom two pairs of English boots, daubed with vermilion, and arranged flowers, . . . incense, and a couple of burning candles before them in true ceremonial fashion. When Nabendu came in, [she] said with mock solemnity: "Bow down to your gods, and may you prosper through their blessings."

The third sister Kiranlekha spent many days in embroidering with red silk one hundred common English names such as Jones, Smith, Brown, Thomson, etc., on a cloth. When it was ready, she presented this [cloth] to Nabendu Sekhar with great ceremony.

The fourth, Sasankalekha, of tender age and therefore of no account, said: "I will make you a string of rosary beads, brother, with which to tell the names of your gods—the sahibs." Her sisters reproved her, saying: "Run away, you saucy girl."

Source: Rabindranath Tagore, *The Hungry Stones and Other Stories* (New York: The Macmillan Company, 1916).

## Thinking About Literature

1. **Vocabulary** Use the dictionary to find the meanings of the following words: sojourned, intoxicated, recipients, insolence, inaccessible, sundry, auspicious, vermilion, saucy.
2. How does the fable of the donkey and the idol remind Pramathanath of his own situation?
3. (a) Why do Pramathanath's daughters tease Nabendu Sekhar? (b) What point are they making?
4. *Critical Thinking* **Drawing Conclusions** (a) How does this story illustrate a cultural conflict within Indian society? (b) Judging by the story, how do you think Tagore felt about British rule in India?

## CHAPTER REVIEW

### REVIEWING VOCABULARY

Review the following vocabulary from this chapter: *nationalization, nationalism, imperialism, apartheid, mandate, ahimsa, civil disobedience, warlord, zaibatsu, ultranationalist.* Write sentences using each of these terms, leaving blanks where the terms would go. Exchange your sentences with another student and fill in the blanks on each other's lists.

### REVIEWING FACTS

1. What was the Good Neighbor Policy?
2. How did Atatürk try to transform Turkey into a western, secular state?
3. How did World War I affect relations between India and Britain?
4. What three-sided struggle took place in China from 1937 to 1945?
5. How did the Great Depression affect the influence of ultranationalists in Japan?

## SKILLS FOR SUCCESS    INTERPRETING GRAPHS

A graph shows numerical facts in picture form. Bar graphs, like the one below, are useful for showing changes in data over a period of time.

Study the bar graph below. Then follow the steps to interpret the graph.

1. **Identify the subject of the graph.** (a) What is the title of the graph? (b) What do the bars represent?

2. **Read the data on the graph.** (a) What was the value of Japan's imports in 1920? In 1940? (b) What was the value of Japan's exports in 1920? In 1940?

3. **Interpret the graph.** (a) What happened to Japan's trade between 1925 and 1930? (b) What worldwide economic event might explain that change?

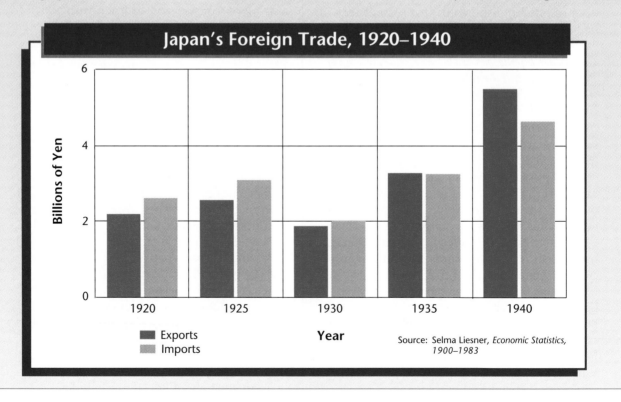

**Japan's Foreign Trade, 1920–1940**

Exports
Imports

Year

Source: Selma Liesner, *Economic Statistics, 1900–1983*

## REVIEWING CHAPTER THEMES

Review the "Focus On" questions at the start of this chapter. Then select *three* of those questions and answer them, using information from the chapter.

## CRITICAL THINKING

1. **Making Inferences** (a) What were the three main issues addressed by the Mexican Constitution of 1917? (b) What groups do you think welcomed the constitution? (c) What groups might have opposed the constitution? Explain.

2. **Linking Past and Present** (a) Describe Gandhi's methods of nonviolence and civil disobedience. (b) How were the methods used by the Reverend Martin Luther King, Jr., in the United States similar to Gandhi's?

3. **Drawing Conclusions** Do you think the rise of the militarists in Japan could have been avoided? Why or why not?

## ANALYZING PRIMARY SOURCES

Use the quotation on page 325 to answer the following questions.

1. What comparison did Kenyatta make to describe the position of Africans?

2. What do you think Kenyatta hoped to achieve by making this comparison?

3. How might a supporter of European imperialism have responded to this argument?

## FOR YOUR PORTFOLIO

**WRITING A BIOGRAPHY** Write a biography of a foreign leader for students in sixth grade. Begin by choosing a leader to write about. Then use the chapter text and outside resources to research your biography. Outline your biography and write a first draft using that outline. Ask a classmate to read the draft and make suggestions. Finally, revise your biography and present it to students in a sixth-grade class.

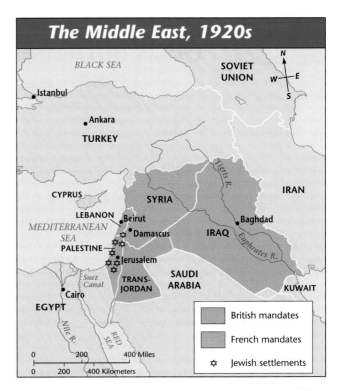

*The Middle East, 1920s*

## ANALYZING MAPS

Use the map as well as information from the chapter to answer the following questions.

1. Which European nation controlled the territory in which Jewish settlements were located?

2. What did Syria and Lebanon have in common?

3. What did Trans-Jordan and Iraq have in common?

4. Which independent nation emerged from the former Ottoman empire?

### INTERNET ACTIVITY

**CREATING ARTWORK** Use the Internet to research the nationalist movement of Mexico, China, or an African nation during the early 1900s. Then create a piece of artwork that reflects the ideals of that movement. You may want to create a sculpture or painting or design a small mural.

# Crisis of Democracy in the West

## (1919–1939)

## CHAPTER OUTLINE

1 The Western Democracies
2 A Culture in Conflict
3 Fascism in Italy
4 Hitler and the Rise of Nazi Germany

World War I ended in November 1918. Battlefields littered with debris were gradually cleared. Farms sprouted anew where tens of thousands had died. Restless heroes, who had survived the slaughter, tried to return to civilian life. For them, war had no romance. Erich Maria Remarque (ray MAHRK), a German survivor of the trenches, captured their disillusionment in his 1929 novel *All Quiet on the Western Front*.

In the novel's last chapter, Paul Bäumer, a young German soldier, sits alone in a garden, recovering from a poison gas attack. At the age of 21, he is already a veteran of three years of combat. His friends are gone, killed by bullets, shrapnel, artillery explosions, or poison gas.

Now, in the autumn of 1918, he knows that the war is almost over. "The armistice is coming soon, I believe it now too. Then we will go home." But Bäumer cannot even imagine peace. He wonders how he can return to civilian life feeling used up, dead inside:

> &#x66;&#x66;Had we returned home in 1916, out of the suffering and the strength of our experience we might have unleashed a storm. Now if we go back we will be weary, broken, burnt out, rootless, and without hope. We will not be able to find our way any more.**

In fact, he never lives to see peace. He is killed in the last month of the war.

*All Quiet on the Western Front* captured the bitterness of survivors on both sides. Remarque dedicated the novel to "a generation of men who, even though they may have escaped its shells, were destroyed by the war."

After World War I ended, western nations worked to restore prosperity and ensure peace. But in the 1920s and 1930s, political and economic turmoil challenged democratic traditions. In Italy and Germany, people turned to dictators, whose seemingly simple solutions offered an escape from despair. Extremists pushed their own brand of ultranationalism and created scapegoats to blame for all their ills.

Today, we can see the mistakes and failures made between 1919 and 1939. As you read this chapter and the next one, though, think about why people responded as they did to each new crisis. Above all, why did the "war to end all wars" and Wilson's goal to create a "just and lasting peace" result in only a 20-year truce?

**FOCUS ON** these questions as you read:

- **Economics and Technology**
  What were the causes and effects of the Great Depression?

- **Art and Literature**
  How did writers and artists reflect the mood of postwar Europe and the United States?

- **Political and Social Systems**
  Why did some countries turn to authoritarian governments in the postwar era?

- **Religions and Value Systems**
  What values did fascism uphold?

## TIME AND PLACE

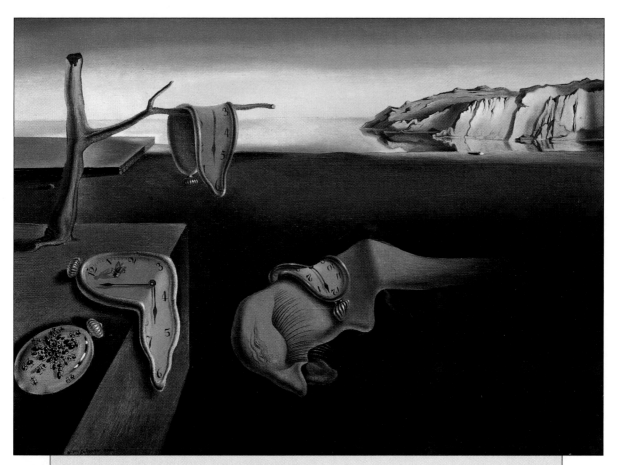

***An Uncertain World*** *The horrors of World War I shook many people's faith in human reason. Some artists turned instead to exploring the irrational world of dreams. This 1931 painting,* The Persistence of Memory, *by the Spanish artist Salvador Dali seems to suggest a dream world where nothing is solid, even time. In the face of postwar confusion, others looked to powerful dictators for security.* **Art and Literature** *Can you think of ways that melting watches make sense as symbols of the postwar world?*

## HUMANITIES LINK

*Art History* Käthe Kollwitz, *War* (page 349).
*Literature* In this chapter, you will encounter passages from the following works of literature: Erich Maria Remarque, *All Quiet on the Western Front* (page 346); William Butler Yeats, "The Second Coming" (page 354); Thomas Hardy, "Drinking Song" (page 354).

| 1916 Easter Rising in Ireland | 1922 Mussolini takes power in Italy | 1925 Locarno treaties signed | 1929 Great Depression begins | 1933 Hitler becomes chancellor of Germany | 1938 Kristallnacht |
|---|---|---|---|---|---|
| **1915** | **1920** | **1925** | **1930** | **1935** | **1940** |

**The Western Democracies**

## Guide for Reading

- How did the postwar world try to ensure the peace?

- What challenges faced Britain, France, and the United States?

- How did the Great Depression affect western nations?

- **Vocabulary** *general strike*

"The belief in Progress," remarked a British clergyman in the early 1900s, "has been the working faith of the West for about a hundred and fifty years." Enlightenment thinkers had encouraged the belief that problems could be solved through reason. The Industrial Revolution bolstered confidence in technological and economic progress.

The catastrophe of World War I shattered this sense of optimism. People added up the staggering costs—10 million dead, more than 20 million wounded, unimaginable property losses. Economic and political crises would only add to the growing pessimism of the 1920s and 1930s.

### Postwar Problems

In 1919, three western democracies—Britain, France, and the United States—appeared powerful. They had ruled the Paris Peace Conference and boosted hopes for the spread of democracy to the new nations of Eastern Europe. Beneath the surface, however, postwar Europe faced grave problems.

At first, the most pressing issues were finding jobs for returning veterans and rebuilding war-ravaged lands. Many nations also owed huge debts because they had borrowed heavily to pay for the war. In the early postwar years, economic problems fed social unrest and made radical ideas more popular. The Russian Revolution unleashed fears of the spread of communism. (See Chapter 11.) Some people saw socialism as the answer to hardships. Others embraced nationalistic political movements.

Other troubles clouded the international scene. As you have read, the peace settlements dissatisfied many Europeans, especially in Germany and among various ethnic groups in Eastern Europe. Finally, Europe lacked strong leaders just when they were most needed. The war had killed many of those who might have helped solve critical problems.

### Pursuing Peace

During the 1920s, diplomats worked hard for peace. Many shared the fears of British prime minister Stanley Baldwin. "One more war in the West," he warned, "and the civilization of the ages will fall with as great a shock as that of Rome."

**The "spirit of Locarno."** Hopes soared in 1925 when representatives from seven European nations signed a series of treaties at Locarno, Switzerland. The treaties settled Germany's borders with France, Belgium, Czechoslovakia, and Poland. The Locarno treaties became the symbol of a new era. "France and Germany Ban War Forever," trumpeted a *New York Times* headline.

The "spirit of Locarno" was echoed in the Kellogg-Briand Pact of 1928. Almost every independent nation in the world signed onto this agreement, promising to "renounce war as an instrument of national policy." In this hopeful spirit, the great powers pursued disarmament. The United States, Britain, France, Japan, and other nations signed treaties to reduce the size of their navies. However, they failed to agree on limiting the size of their armies.

Despite grumblings about the Versailles treaty, people around the world put their hope in the League of Nations. From its headquarters in Geneva, Switzerland, the League encouraged cooperation and tried to get members to make a commitment to stop aggression. In 1926, after signing the Locarno agreements, Germany joined the League. Later, the Soviet Union was also admitted.

**Disturbances to the peace.** Although the Kellogg-Briand Pact outlawed war, there was no way of enforcing the ban. The League of Nations, too, was powerless to stop aggressors. It had also been damaged by the American refusal to join. In 1931, for example, the League

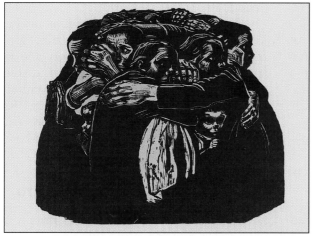

**War** *Käthe Kollwitz, one of Germany's leading postwar artists, used her art to comment on injustice. In 1923, she produced a striking series of woodcuts titled* War. *The two shown here—*The Mothers, *left, and* The Parents, *right—reflect Kollwitz's own grief at the death of her son in World War I. Woodcuts, the world's oldest form of printing, are made by pressing ink images from designs carved on a block of wood.*
**Art and Literature** *How do these prints make a universal statement about war?*

vigorously condemned the Japanese invasion of Manchuria, but to no effect. (See page 338.) Other ambitious powers noted the League's weakness. In Chapter 14, you will see how ambitious dictators rearmed their military forces and pursued aggressive foreign policies.

## Recovery and Collapse

During the 1920s, Europe made a shaky recovery. Economies returned to peacetime manufacturing and trade. Veterans gradually found jobs. Middle-class families generally enjoyed a rising standard of living, with money to buy new products such as cars, refrigerators, and radios.

The United States emerged from the war as the world's leading economic power. American banks and businesses controlled a global network of trade and finance. American loans and investments backed the recovery in Europe. As long as the American economy was healthy, the global economy remained relatively prosperous.

**A dangerous imbalance.** Both the American and the world economy had weak spots, however. Oddly enough, a major problem was overproduction. The war had increased demand for raw materials from Africa, Asia, and Latin America. Improved technology and farm-

ing methods also contributed to higher output. When demand dwindled after the war, prices fell. Consumers benefited from the lower prices. But farmers, miners, herders, and other suppliers of raw materials suffered severe hardships.

At the same time, industrial workers won higher wages, which raised the price of manufactured goods. An imbalance emerged. Because farmers' earnings had fallen, they could afford fewer manufactured goods. Despite the slowing demand, factories kept pouring out goods. This imbalance, combined with other problems, undermined industrial economies. By the late 1920s, conditions were ripe for disaster.

**The crash.** Few people saw the looming danger. In the United States, prices on the New York Stock Exchange soared. Eager investors acquired stocks on margin, that is, they paid only part of the cost and borrowed the rest from brokers. In the autumn of 1929, jitters about the economy caused brokers to call in these loans. When investors were unable to repay, financial panic set in. Stock prices crashed, wiping out the fortunes of many investors.

**Spiraling disaster.** The stock market crash triggered the Great Depression of the 1930s, a painful time of global economic collapse. The crash created financial turmoil in the

*Chapter 13* **349**

industrial world as American banks stopped making loans abroad and demanded repayment of foreign loans.

In the United States and elsewhere, banks failed and businesses closed, throwing millions out of work. The cycle spiraled steadily downward. The jobless could not afford to buy goods, so more factories had to close, which in turn increased the numbers of unemployed.

In once-prosperous western cities, people slept on park benches and lined up to eat in charity soup kitchens. Former business leaders sold apples in the street. In one of Britain's richest coal-mining regions, writer George Orwell observed poor families scrambling through the slag heaps:

> ❝The dumpy, shawled women, with their sacking aprons and their heavy black clogs, [were] kneeling in the cindery mud and the bitter wind searching for tiny chips of coal. . . . In winter they are almost desperate for fuel. It is more important almost than food.❞

**Global impact.** In desperation, governments tried to protect their economies from foreign competition. The United States imposed the highest tariffs in its history. The policy backfired because other nations retaliated by raising their tariffs. In the end, all countries lost access to the larger global market. As you read in Chapter 12, the Great Depression spread misery outside the industrial world.

As the depression dragged on, many people lost faith in the ability of democratic governments to solve the problems. Misery and hopelessness created fertile ground for extremists who promised radical solutions. Communists gloated over the failure of capitalism. Right-wing extremists played on themes of intense nationalism, the failure of democracy, the virtues of authoritarian rule, and the need to rearm.

## Britain in the Postwar Era

Even before the depression, Britain faced economic problems. Although it emerged victorious from the war, much of its overseas trade was lost. German U-boats had wreaked havoc on British shipping. The nation was deeply in debt, and its factories were out of date.

During the 1920s, unemployment was severe. Wages remained low, leading to worker unrest and frequent strikes. In 1926, a **general strike,** or strike by workers in many different industries at the same time, lasted nine days and involved some three million workers.

**Economics and politics.** During the 1920s, the Labour party surpassed the Liberal party in strength. (See page 196.) Labour leaders gained support among workers by promoting a gradual move toward socialism. The middle class, however, firmly backed the Con-

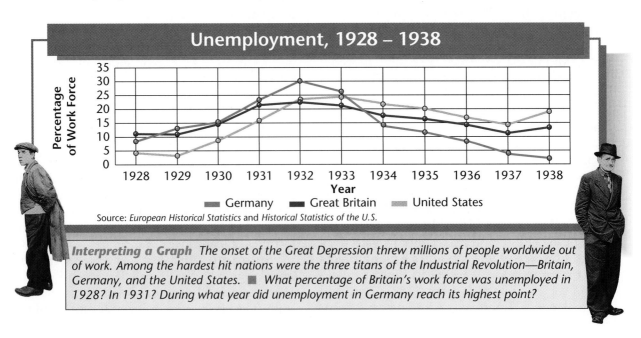

**Unemployment, 1928 – 1938**

Germany ■ Great Britain ■ United States

Source: *European Historical Statistics* and *Historical Statistics of the U.S.*

*Interpreting a Graph* The onset of the Great Depression threw millions of people worldwide out of work. Among the hardest hit nations were the three titans of the Industrial Revolution—Britain, Germany, and the United States. ■ What percentage of Britain's work force was unemployed in 1928? In 1931? During what year did unemployment in Germany reach its highest point?

servative party, which held power during much of this period. Widespread fear of communism contributed to a drift toward the right. After the general strike, Conservatives passed legislation limiting the power of workers to strike.

The Great Depression intensified the nation's economic woes. As the crisis worsened, Britain set up a coalition government with leaders from all three major parties. The government provided some unemployment benefits to ease the worst problems, but millions of people suffered great hardships.

**Irish independence.** At the war's end, Britain still faced the "Irish question." In 1914, you will recall, Parliament passed a home rule bill that was shelved when the war began. (See page 199.) Militant Irish nationalists, however, were unwilling to wait. On Easter 1916, a small group launched a revolt against British rule. Although the Easter Rising was quickly suppressed, the execution of 15 rebel leaders stirred wider support for their cause.

When Britain again failed to grant home rule in 1919, civil war erupted in Ireland. Members of the Irish Republican Army (IRA) carried on a guerrilla war against British forces and their supporters. Civilians were often caught in the middle of the violence.

In 1922, moderate leaders in Ireland and England finally reached an agreement. Most of Ireland became the independent Irish Free State, later called Eire. The largely Protestant northern counties (Ulster) remained under British rule. That settlement ended the worst violence. However, the IRA and many other nationalists never accepted the division of Ireland. In years to come, too, Catholics in the north faced discrimination. The status of Northern Ireland remained a thorny issue. (See page 439.)

**Commonwealth and empire.** Abroad, Britain took steps to satisfy the demands of Canada, Australia, New Zealand, and South Africa. In 1931, all four former colonies became fully self-governing dominions within the newly formed British Commonwealth of Nations. Although linked by economic and cultural ties, each member of the Commonwealth pursued its own course.

Despite challenges from nationalist groups, Britain's colonial empire still stretched around the globe. To the British, their empire remained

**A Change of Government** *After years of struggle, the Irish Free State finally won independence in 1922. Here, a statue of Queen Victoria is lowered from the roof of the building where Ireland's new parliament met.* **Continuity and Change** *How does this picture capture a symbolic moment?*

a source of wealth and pride. At the same time, Britain worked to improve agriculture, education, and medical care in its colonies while planning for gradual independence at some uncertain date.

**Foreign policy.** Britain's postwar foreign policy created tensions with its ally France. Almost from the signing of the Treaty of Versailles, British leaders wanted to relax the treaty's harsh treatment of Germany. They feared that if Germany became too weak, the Soviet Union would be able to expand and France might gain too much control on the continent. Britain's leniency toward Germany helped push France in the opposite direction.

## France Pursues Security

Like Britain, France emerged from World War I both a victor and a loser. Fighting on the Western Front had devastated northern France. The French had suffered enormous casualties. Survivors felt battered and insecure.

# CAUSE AND EFFECT

### Long-Term Causes

Worldwide interrelationship of governments, financial institutions, and industries

Huge debts resulting from costs of World War I

European dependence on American loans

Widespread use of credit

Overproduction of goods while demand was falling

Rising wages for industrial workers while farmers' earnings were falling

### Immediate Causes

New York stock market crash ruins investors who have borrowed and speculated on credit

Farmers who have purchased large machinery on credit are unable to make payments

Banks demand repayment of loans

American loans to other countries dry up

Without capital, businesses and factories fail

## WORLDWIDE ECONOMIC DEPRESSION

### Immediate Effects

Vast unemployment and misery

Growth of economic nationalism, with tariffs imposed to protect industries

Loss of faith in capitalism and democracy

Authoritarian leaders gain support

### Long-Term Effects

Nazis take control in Germany

Fascist leaders win support in Eastern Europe

Governments experiment with social programs

People blame scapegoats for economic woes

World War II begins

### Connections Today

Government monitoring of or control of national economies

Stricter controls on banks, credit, stock market

Continuation of social programs set up during depression

Monitoring of worldwide economic developments by international agencies

The French economy recovered fairly rapidly, thanks in part to German reparations and to territories gained from Germany, including Alsace and Lorraine. Later, the Great Depression did not hurt France as much as it did some countries. French industry was not as centralized in the hands of big business. Small workshops served local regions and were less affected by global trends.

**Coalition governments.** Still, economic swings did occur, adding to an unstable political scene. Political divisions and financial scandals continued to plague the Third Republic. (See Chapter 7.) Many parties—from conservatives to communists—competed for power. During the postwar years, France was again ruled by a series of coalition governments.

In 1936, several parties on the left united behind the socialist leader Leon Blum. His Popular Front government tried to solve labor problems and passed some social legislation. But it could not satisfy more radical leftists whose strikes soon brought down Blum's government. Thus, France, like Britain, muddled through a series of crises. Democracy survived, but the country lacked strong leadership that could respond to the clamor for change.

**The Maginot Line.** The chief French concern after the war was securing its borders against Germany. France deeply distrusted its neighbor across the Rhine, which had invaded in 1870 and 1914. To prevent a third invasion, it built massive fortifications along the border. The Maginot (MA zhee noh) Line, as this defensive "wall" was called, offered a sense of security—a false one. The line would be of little use when Germany again invaded in 1940.

In its quest for security, France strengthened its military and sought alliances with other countries, including the Soviet Union. It insisted on strict enforcement of the Versailles treaty and complete payment of reparations, hoping to keep the German economy weak.

*Interpreting a Chart* Today, economists still debate the causes and effects of the Great Depression. For most people at the time, however, the effects seemed simple—unemployment and misery. ■ *What measures do governments today take to deal with the conditions that caused the Great Depression?*

## Prosperity and Depression in the United States

The United States emerged from World War I in excellent shape. A late entrant into the war, it had suffered relatively few casualties and little loss of property. It led the world in industrial and agricultural output and helped finance the European recovery.

**Avoiding foreign entanglements.** As you have read, the United States stayed out of the League of Nations. Many Americans feared that joining the League might lead to involvement in future foreign wars. They insisted that the nation maintain its free hand in foreign affairs. Still, during the 1920s, the United States took a leading role in international diplomacy. It sponsored the Kellogg-Briand Pact, pressed for disarmament, and worked to reduce German reparations.

**Closing the door.** At the same time, the government moved to limit immigration from overseas. Millions of immigrants had poured into the United States between 1890 and 1914. (See page 211.) Some native-born Americans sought to exclude these newcomers, whose cultures differed from those of earlier settlers from northern Europe. In response, Congress passed laws limiting immigration from Europe. Earlier laws had already excluded Chinese immigrants and strictly limited Japanese immigration.

Fear of bomb-throwing radicals and the Bolshevik Revolution in Russia set off a "Red Scare" in 1919 and 1920. Police rounded up suspected foreign-born radicals, and a number were expelled from the United States.

**Boom and bust.** Communism had little appeal in the boom years of the 1920s. Middle-class Americans were enjoying the benefits of capitalism, stocking their homes with radios, refrigerators, and automobiles. Most Americans agreed with President Calvin Coolidge's slogan that "the business of America is business."

The 1929 stock market crash burst this bubble of prosperity. Banks failed, thousands of businesses closed, and unemployment spread misery everywhere. President Herbert Hoover firmly believed that the government should not intervene in private business matters. However, an angry public prompted him to try a variety of limited measures to solve the crisis.

**The New Deal.** In 1932, Americans elected a new President, Franklin D. Roosevelt, who projected an air of energy and optimism. "FDR" argued that government had to take an active role in combating the Great Depression. He introduced the New Deal, a massive package of economic and social programs.

Under the New Deal, the federal government became more directly involved in people's everyday lives than ever before. New laws regulated the stock market and protected bank depositors' savings. Government programs created jobs for the unemployed or gave aid to poverty-stricken farmers. The United States also set up a social security system. It provided old-age pensions and other benefits that major European countries had introduced years earlier.

The New Deal did not end the Great Depression, but it did ease the suffering for many. Still, some critics fiercely condemned the New Deal because it expanded the role of government so sharply. As a result of Roosevelt's policies, many Americans came to expect the government to intervene directly to promote their economic well-being. As you will read in Chapter 16, the debate about the role of government continues to influence American politics.

## SECTION 1 REVIEW

1. **Identify** (a) Locarno agreements, (b) Kellogg-Briand Pact, (c) IRA, (d) Commonwealth of Nations, (e) Leon Blum, (f) Maginot Line, (g) New Deal.
2. **Define** general strike.
3. (a) What steps did the major powers take to protect the peace? (b) Why did these moves have limited effects?
4. Explain how each of the following contributed to the Great Depression: (a) overproduction, (b) margin buying.
5. How did the Great Depression affect political developments in the United States?
6. *Critical Thinking* **Applying Information** How did Britain and France emerge from World War I as both victors and losers?
7. *ACTIVITY* Draw a political cartoon showing how the Great Depression undermined confidence in democracy.

# 2 A Culture in Conflict

## Guide for Reading

- What new ideas revolutionized science and thought?

- What artistic and literary trends emerged in the 1920s?

- How did women's lives change after World War I?

- **Vocabulary** *stream of consciousness, flapper*

In his poem "The Second Coming," the Irish poet William Butler Yeats summed up the feelings of many postwar writers and artists:

66Things fall apart; the centre cannot hold;
Mere anarchy is loosed upon the world,
The blood-dimmed tide is loosed, and
    everywhere
The ceremony of innocence is
    drowned.99

It was not only the war and the Great Depression that fostered a sense of uncertainty. New ideas and scientific discoveries were challenging long-held ideas about the nature of the world.

### New Views of the Universe

The ancient Greeks were the first to propose that all matter is composed of tiny, indivisible atoms. Over the centuries, most scientists came to accept this idea. But discoveries made in the late 1800s and early 1900s showed that the atom was more complex than anyone suspected.

**Radioactivity.** By the early 1900s, the Polish-born French scientist Marie Curie and other scientists were experimenting with a process called radioactivity. They discovered that the atoms of certain elements, such as radium and uranium, spontaneously release charged particles. As scientists investigated radioactivity further, they discovered that it could change atoms of one element into atoms of another element. Such findings proved that atoms were not solid and indivisible.

**Relativity.** By 1905, the German-born physicist Albert Einstein advanced his theories of relativity. Einstein argued that space and time measurements are not absolute but are determined by many factors, some of them unknown. This idea raised questions about Newtonian science, which compared the universe to a machine that operated according to absolute laws.

In the postwar years, many scientists came to accept the theory of relativity. To much of the general public, however, Einstein's ideas seemed impossible to understand. And what they did understand disturbed them. Many feared that all the old certainties were crumbling. British writer Thomas Hardy echoed this mood of uncertainty:

66And now comes Einstein with a
    notion—
        Not yet quite clear
        To many here—
    That's there's no time, no space,
        no motion, . . .
    But just a sort of bending ocean.99

*A Fatal Discovery* Along with her husband, Pierre, Marie Curie won a Nobel prize for her ground-breaking research on radioactivity. But she paid a high price for knowledge. Curie's fingertips were often burned from handling deadly radioactive material. Although she shrugged off the danger to her health, she died in 1934 from radiation poisoning. Curie is shown here with her daughter Irene, who also went on to win a Nobel prize for her work with radioactive materials. **Impact of the Individual** Why do you think Curie ignored the health risks of her experiments?

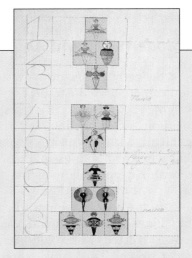

Modern science seemed to reinforce the unsettling sense of a universe whirling beyond the understanding of human reason.

**Probing the mind.** The Austrian physician Sigmund Freud (FROID) also challenged faith in reason. He suggested that the unconscious mind drives much human behavior. Freud said that, in civilized society, learned values such as morality and reason help people repress, or check, powerful urges. But an individual feels constant tension between repressed drives and social training. This tension, argued Freud, may cause psychological illness or physical symptoms, such as paralysis or blindness.

Freud pioneered psychoanalysis, the study and treatment of the human mind. He analyzed dreams for clues to subconscious desires and developed ways to treat mental illnesses. His ideas had an impact far beyond medicine. Freud's work led writers and artists to explore the subconscious mind.

### The New Literature

In the 1920s, war novels, poetry, plays, and memoirs flowed off the presses. Works like Remarque's *All Quiet on the Western Front* exposed the grim horrors of modern warfare. Other writers heaped scorn on blundering military and political leaders. Their works reflected a powerful disgust with war that would color the European scene for decades.

**A loss of faith.** To many postwar writers, the war symbolized the moral breakdown of western civilization. In 1922, the American-born English poet T. S. Eliot published *The Waste Land*. This long poem portrays the modern world as spiritually empty and barren. In *The Sun Also Rises*, American novelist Ernest Hemingway shows the rootless wanderings of young people who lacked deep convictions. "I did not care what it was all about," says the narrator. "All I wanted to know was how to live in it."

**Literature of the inner mind.** As Freud's ideas became popular, some writers experimented with stream of consciousness. In this technique, a writer probes a character's random thoughts and feelings without imposing any logic or order. In novels like *To the Lighthouse* and *Mrs. Dalloway*, British novelist Virginia Woolf used stream of consciousness to explore the hidden thoughts of people as they go through the ordinary actions of their everyday lives.

The Irish novelist James Joyce went even further. In *Finnegan's Wake*, he explores the mind of a hero who remains sound asleep throughout the novel. To convey the freedom and playfulness of the unconscious mind, Joyce invented many words—including some, like bababadalgharaghtakamminarronnkonnbronnt-onnerronntuonnthunntrovarrhounawnskawnto-ohoohoordenenthurnuk, 100 letters long!

## Modern Art and Architecture

In the early 1900s, many western artists rejected earlier styles. Instead of trying to reproduce the real world, they explored other dimensions of color, line, and shape. Painters like Henri Matisse (mah TEES) outraged the public with their bold use of color and odd distortions. He and fellow artists were dubbed Fauves (FOHVZ), or Wild Beasts.

**Cubism.** Before the war, the Spanish artist Pablo Picasso and his friend Georges Braque (BRAHK) created a revolutionary new style, called Cubism. They broke three-dimensional objects into fragments and composed them into complex patterns of angles and planes. By redefining objects into separate shapes, they offered a new view of reality. (See page 265.)

Later artists, like the German Paul Klee (KLAY) and the Russian Vasily Kandinsky, moved even further from representing reality. They created abstract works—compositions of line, color, and shape with no recognizable subject matter at all.

**Dada and surrealism.** During and after the war, Dada burst onto the Paris art world. Dada was a revolt against civilization. Its goal was to "give the bourgeois a whiff of chaos." One Dadaist declared, "Dada is life without discipline or morality and we spit on humanity." Paintings by artists like Hans Arp and Max Ernst shocked, haunted, and disturbed viewers.

Cubism and Dada helped inspire surrealists like Salvador Dali. His dreamlike landscapes suggested Freud's notion of the chaotic unconscious mind. (See the painting on page 347.)

**Architecture.** Architects, too, rejected classical traditions and invented new styles to match an industrial, urban world. The famous Bauhaus school in Germany influenced architec-

# PARALLELS THROUGH TIME

## Stars and Their Fans

Since ancient times, crowds have cheered winning athletes, great actors, and other popular heroes. The relationship between stars and their fans got a big boost from technology in the 1920s. Radio and film brought people closer to their heroes than ever before.

**Linking Past and Present** What might be some negative effects of admiring stars?

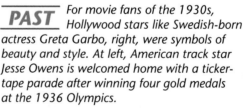

**PAST** For movie fans of the 1930s, Hollywood stars like Swedish-born actress Greta Garbo, right, were symbols of beauty and style. At left, American track star Jesse Owens is welcomed home with a ticker-tape parade after winning four gold medals at the 1936 Olympics.

**PRESENT** Fans of Elvis Presley, who died in 1977, still show their devotion to "the King" by flocking to his Tennessee home, Graceland. At the far right, fans of the Dallas Cowboys crowd to get an autograph.

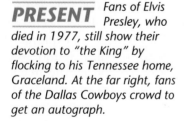

ture by blending science and technology with design. Bauhaus designers used glass, steel, and concrete but little ornamentation.

The American architect Frank Lloyd Wright reflected the Bauhaus belief that the function of a building should determine its form. In designing houses, he used materials and forms that fit their environment.

## Popular Culture

New technologies helped create a mass culture shared by millions in the world's developed countries. Affordable cars gave middle-class people greater mobility. Movie stars made famous by Hollywood, such as Charlie Chaplin, had fans on every continent. Radios brought news, music, and sports into homes throughout the western world.

Many radios were tuned to the sounds of jazz. Jazz was pioneered by African American musicians who combined western harmonies with African rhythms. Jazz musicians, like trumpeter Louis Armstrong, took simple melodies and improvised endless subtle variations in beat and rhythm. They produced music that was both original and popular.

Europeans embraced American popular culture, with its greater freedom and willingness to experiment. The nightclub and the sound of jazz were symbols of that freedom. In fact, the 1920s are often referred to as the Jazz Age.

## A Changing Society

In the aftermath of World War I, many people yearned to return to "normalcy"—to life as it had been before 1914. But rebellious young people rejected the moral values and rules of the Victorian Age and chased after excitement. Gertrude Stein, an American writer living in Paris, called them the "lost generation." Others saw them as immoral pleasure-seekers.

**The flapper.** The reigning queen of the Jazz Age was the liberated young woman called the flapper. The first flappers were American, but their European sisters soon adopted the fashion. Flappers rejected old ways. Shocking their elders, they bobbed their hair and wore skirts far shorter than prewar fashions. They went out on dates unchaperoned, enjoyed wild

**Flappers and Homemakers** *These two advertisements reflect contrasting images of women in the 1920s. Above, young flappers shop for the latest clothing styles. At right, a homemaker takes advantage of a new labor-saving device.* **Continuity and Change** *How do these ads reflect actual social changes?*

new dance fads such as the Charleston, smoked, and drank in nightclubs.

**Women's lives.** For most women, the postwar period brought limited progress. During the war, women had held a wide range of jobs. While most returned to the home when the war ended, women's war work helped them win the vote in many western countries. A few women were elected to public office, such as Texas governor Miriam Ferguson or Lady Nancy Astor, the first woman to serve in the British Parliament.

Women continued to push open the doors to higher education. A few succeeded in what were considered "men's" fields. Even before the war, Marie Curie had won two Nobel prizes for her work in chemistry and physics. Still, like many other women, Curie had to balance her work with home duties. "I have a great deal of work," she lamented, "what with the housekeeping, the children, the teaching, and the laboratory, and I don't know how I shall manage it all."

By the 1920s, labor-saving devices were common in middle-class homes. Washing machines, vacuum cleaners, and canned foods freed women from many time-consuming household chores. Some women found paid work outside the home. Others took volunteer jobs, providing social services or raising funds for charities.

In the new atmosphere of emancipation, women pursued careers in many arenas—from sports to the arts. Women golfers, tennis players, swimmers, and pilots set new records. Women worked as newspaper reporters, published best-selling novels, and won recognition for their artwork. Most professions, though, were still dominated by men. Women doing the same work as men earned much less.

## SECTION 2 REVIEW

1. **Identify** (a) Marie Curie, (b) T. S. Eliot, (c) Virginia Woolf, (d) James Joyce, (e) Cubism, (f) Dada, (g) Bauhaus, (h) Jazz Age.
2. **Define** (a) stream of consciousness, (b) flapper.
3. Describe how the ideas of each of the following contributed to a sense of uncertainty in the postwar world: (a) Albert Einstein, (b) Sigmund Freud.
4. (a) What themes did postwar writers stress? (b) How did artists challenge older western traditions?
5. Describe three ways that women's lives changed in the postwar period.
6. *Critical Thinking* **Linking Past and Present** (a) How did technology shape popular culture in the 1920s? (b) What technologies are shaping popular culture today?
7. *ACTIVITY* Create flashcards for *six* individuals discussed in this section. On one side of each card, write the name of the person. On the other side, write a sentence describing his or her impact on postwar culture.

## 3 Fascism in Italy

### Guide for Reading

- How did conditions in Italy favor Mussolini's rise to power?
- How did Mussolini reshape Italy?
- What were the values and goals of fascism?

Italo Balbo was disgusted with life back home in Italy. He had gone off to war in a spirit of patriotism. He returned to a land of economic chaos and political corruption:

&&I hated politics and politicians, who, in my opinion, had betrayed the hopes of soldiers, reducing Italy to a shameful peace. . . . Better to deny everything, destroy everything, in order to renew everything from the foundations.??

Embittered and angry, Balbo joined a new movement, called fascism. Italy's Fascist party was led by a fierce nationalist, Benito Mussolini, who in the 1920s made himself dictator. His rise to power served as a model for ambitious strongmen elsewhere in Europe.

### Rise of Mussolini

In 1919, Italian nationalists were outraged by the Paris peace treaties. As one of the victorious Allies, Italy had expected to gain territory on the Adriatic. Instead, these lands became part of the newly created Yugoslavia. At the same time, disorders multiplied at home. Inspired in part by the Russian Revolution, peasants seized land and workers went on strike or took over factories. Their actions frightened the landowners and industrialists who had traditionally held power.

Amid the chaos, returning veterans faced unemployment. Trade declined and taxes rose. The government, split into feuding factions, seemed powerless to end the crisis.

**A fiery speaker.** Into this seething conflict stepped Benito Mussolini. The son of a socialist blacksmith and a devoutly religious schoolteacher, Mussolini had been a socialist in his youth. During the war, however, he switched loyalties, exchanging belief in class struggle for intense nationalism.

In 1919, he organized veterans and other discontented Italians into the Fascist party. They took their name from the Latin *fasces,* a bundle of sticks wrapped around an ax—a symbol of authority in ancient Rome. In fiery speeches, Mussolini spoke of reviving Roman greatness. He promised to end corruption and replace turmoil with order. With his jutting jaw and slashing phrases, Mussolini commanded attention.

**Seizing power.** Mussolini organized his supporters into "combat squads." These gangs, uniformed in black shirts, rejected the democratic process in favor of violent action. They broke up socialist rallies, smashed leftist presses, and attacked farmers' unions and cooperatives. Through terror and intimidation, "Black Shirts" ousted elected officials in northern Italy. Many Italians accepted these moves because they, too, had lost all faith in constitutional government.

In 1922, the Fascists made a bid for power. At a rally in Naples, they announced a "march on Rome" to demand that the government make changes. "On to Rome," chanted tens of thousands of Fascists who swarmed into the capital. Fearing civil war, King Victor Emmanuel III bowed to pressure. He asked Mussolini to form a government as prime minister. Without firing a shot, Mussolini thus obtained a legal appointment from the king.

## Mussolini's Italy

At first, Fascists held only a few cabinet posts. By 1925, though, Mussolini had assumed more power and taken the title *Il Duce* (EEL DOO chay), "The Leader." He suppressed rival parties, muzzled the press, limited the number of voters, and rigged elections. In provinces and towns, he replaced elected officials with Fascist supporters.

In theory, Italy remained a parliamentary monarchy. In fact, it was a dictatorship upheld by Fascist violence and terror. Critics were thrown into prison, forced into exile, or murdered outright. Secret police and propaganda bolstered the regime.

**Economic policy.** To encourage economic growth and end conflicts between owners and workers, Mussolini brought the economy under state control. Unlike socialists, though, he preserved capitalism. Under Mussolini's "corporate state," representatives of business, labor, government and the Fascist party controlled industry, agriculture, and trade. This policy did help business, and production increased. This success came, though, at the expense of workers, who were forbidden to strike and whose wages lagged.

FERROVIE DELLO STATO

LE PIU' RECENTI CARROZZE DI 3ª CLASSE

*Fascist Propaganda* Mussolini prided himself on making the state more efficient. When he came to power, he fired thousands of bureaucrats who did little but collect their paychecks. He also strove to make Italy's notoriously slow trains run on time. This poster celebrates the introduction of new railroad cars for passengers. **Political and Social Systems** How does the image stress the fascist ideal of the "great man"?

**Social policies.** To Fascists, the individual was unimportant except as a member of the state. Men, women, and children were bombarded with slogans glorifying the state and Mussolini. "Believe! Obey! Fight!" loudspeakers blared and posters proclaimed. Men were urged to be ruthless, selfless warriors for the glory of Italy. "A minute on the battlefield," they were told, "is worth a lifetime of peace."

Women were called on to "win the battle of motherhood." Those who bore more than 14 children were given a medal by Il Duce himself. Women were valued as wives and mothers but not as workers. "Machines and women," declared Mussolini, "are the two major causes of unemployment." Under the Fascists, women were pushed out of paid jobs or earned much less than men for the same work.

Still, Mussolini expected women to make sacrifices for the nation. He once asked them to donate their gold wedding bands to the treasury, handing out iron ones in exchange. The iron symbolized their contribution to a stronger nation.

**Fascist youth.** Shaping the young was a major Fascist goal. Fascist youth groups toughened children and taught them to obey strict military discipline. Boys and girls learned about the glories of ancient Rome. Young Fascists marched in torchlight parades, singing patriotic hymns and chanting "Mussolini is always right." By the 1930s, a generation of young soldiers stood ready to back Il Duce's drive to expand Italian power.

## What Is Fascism?

Historians still debate the real nature of fascist ideology. Mussolini coined the term, but

▲ *Benito Mussolini*

fascists had no single unifying set of beliefs, as Marxists did. Today, we generally use the term to describe any authoritarian government that is not communist. In the 1920s and 1930s, though, fascism meant different things in different countries.

All forms of fascism, however, shared some basic features. It was rooted in extreme nationalism. Fascists glorified action, violence, discipline, and, above all, blind loyalty to the state. According to Mussolini:

> 66 Fascism conceives of the State as an absolute, in comparison with which all individuals or groups are relative, only to be conceived of in their relation to the State. 99

Fascists were antidemocratic. They rejected the Enlightenment emphasis on reason and the concepts of equality and liberty spread by the French Revolution. To them, democracy led to greed, corruption, and weakness. They claimed it put individual or class interests above national goals and destroyed feelings of community. Instead, fascists emphasized emotion and the need for the citizen to serve the state.

Fascists also pursued aggressive foreign expansion. Their ideas were linked to Social Darwinism, with its notion of "survival of the fittest." (See page 155.) Fascist leaders glorified warfare as a necessary and noble struggle for survival. "War alone," said Mussolini, "brings up to its highest tension all human energy and puts the stamp of nobility upon peoples who have the courage to face it."

**Compared to communism.** Fascists were the sworn enemy of socialists and communists. While communists called for world revolution of the proletariat, fascists pursued nationalist goals. Fascists found allies among business leaders and wealthy landowners, as well as the lower middle class. Communists won support among the urban working class.

Despite these basic differences, there are significant similarities between these two ideolo-

**ISSUES** *For* **TODAY**

In Italy, supporters of fascism turned from democracy to one-party dictatorship. Under what circumstances might people be willing to sacrifice democratic rights and ideals?

## Features of Totalitarian States

1. **Single-party dictatorship**

2. **State control of economy**

3. **Police spies and state terrorism**

4. **Strict censorship and government control of media**

5. **Use of schools and media to indoctrinate and mobilize citizens**

6. **Unquestioning obedience to single ruler**

*Interpreting a Chart* *Stalin's Soviet Union was on the opposite end of the political scale from Mussolini's Italy and Hitler's Germany. Yet all three totalitarian governments had important characteristics in common.* ■ *Why is control of the media important in a totalitarian state? How did Mussolini use schools to indoctrinate young Fascists?*

gies. Both flourished during economic hard times by promoting extreme programs of social change. In both communist Russia and fascist Italy, dictators imposed totalitarian governments in order to bring about their social revolutions. In both, the party elite claimed to rule in the name of the national interest.

**Totalitarian rule.** Mussolini built the first totalitarian state, which served as a model for others. Fascist rule in Italy was never as absolute as Stalin's in the Soviet Union or the government Adolf Hitler would impose on Germany. All three governments, however, had some basic features in common. (See the chart above.)

**Appeal.** Given its restrictions on individual freedom, why did fascism appeal to many Italians? First, it promised a strong, stable government and an end to the political feuding that

had paralyzed democracy. Mussolini's intense nationalism also struck a chord among ordinary Italians. He revived national pride, pledging to make the Mediterranean Sea a "Roman lake" once more. Finally, Mussolini projected a sense of power and confidence at a time of disorder and despair.

At first, Il Duce received good press outside Italy, too. Newspapers in Britain, France, and North America applauded Mussolini. "He made the trains run on time," they said, giving an approving nod to the discipline and order of the new government. Only later, when Mussolini embarked on a course of foreign conquest, did western democracies protest his actions.

**Looking ahead.** Three systems of government competed for influence in postwar Europe. Democracy endured in Britain and France but faced an uphill struggle in economic hard times. Communism emerged in Russia and won support elsewhere, but many people saw it as a dangerous threat. In Italy, fascism offered a different formula. Its chest-thumping calls for action, national unity, and dedication to the state ignited patriotic feeling. As the Great Depression spread, other nations looked to leaders who preached fascist ideology.

## SECTION 3 REVIEW

1. **Identify** (a) Black Shirts, (b) Il Duce.
2. (a) What problems did Italy face after World War I? (b) How did these problems help Mussolini win power?
3. Describe two economic or social goals of Mussolini, and explain the actions he took to achieve each goal.
4. (a) What values did fascism promote? (b) List two similarities and two differences between fascism and communism.
5. *Critical Thinking* **Analyzing Information** Why do you think the fascists blamed democracy for problems in Italy?
6. *ACTIVITY* Many people today use the word *fascist* in discussing politics. Take a poll of several voters and ask what they think the word means. Then, write a paragraph or make a chart comparing these definitions to what fascism meant under Mussolini.

# 4 Hitler and the Rise of Nazi Germany

## Guide for Reading

- Why did the Weimar government fail?
- How did Hitler turn Germany into a totalitarian state?
- How did fascist leaders gain power in Eastern Europe?

- **Vocabulary** *concentration camp*

In November 1923, a German army veteran and leader of an extremist party, Adolf Hitler, tried to take a page from Mussolini's book. His brown-shirted thugs burst into a beer hall in Munich, Germany, where a political meeting was set to start. Hitler climbed onto a table and fired his pistol. "The National Socialist revolution has begun!" he shouted.

The coup failed, and Hitler was soon behind bars. But Hitler was a force that could not be ignored forever. Within a decade, he made a new bid for power. This time, he succeeded by legal means.

Hitler's rise to power is one of the most significant events of our century. His success raised disturbing questions that we still debate today. How did Germany, which had a liberal democratic government in the 1920s, become a totalitarian dictatorship in the 1930s? Why did Hitler gain the enthusiastic support of many Germans?

## Struggles of the Weimar Republic

In November 1918, as World War I was drawing to a close, Germany tottered on the brink of chaos. Under the threat of a socialist revolution, Kaiser William II abdicated. Moderate leaders signed the armistice and later, under protest, the Versailles treaty.

In 1919, the new German Republic drafted a constitution in the city of Weimar (vī mahr). It created a democratic government known as the Weimar Republic. The constitution set up a parliamentary form of government led by a prime minister, or chancellor. It gave both women and men the vote, and included a bill of rights.

**Unrest.** The Weimar government faced severe problems from the start. Politically, it was weak because Germany had many small parties. Like the French premier, the German chancellor had to form coalitions that easily fell apart.

The government came under constant fire from both the left and right. Communists demanded revolutionary changes like those Lenin had brought to Russia. Conservatives—including the old Junker nobility, military officers, and wealthy bourgeois—attacked the government as too liberal. To many conservatives, democracy meant weakness. They longed for another strong leader like Bismarck or the kaiser.

Germans of all classes blamed the government for the hated Versailles treaty, with its war-guilt clause and heavy reparations. (See Chapter 10.) In their bitterness, they looked for scapegoats. Many accused Marxists and Jews of an imaginary conspiracy to betray Germany.

**Inflation.** Economic disaster fed unrest. In 1923, when Germany fell behind in reparations payments, France occupied the coal-rich Ruhr Valley. Ruhr Germans turned to passive resistance, refusing to work. To support them, the government printed huge quantities of paper money. This move set off terrible inflation that spiraled out of control. The German mark became almost worthless. An item that cost 100 marks in July 1922 cost 944,000 marks by August 1923. A newspaper or loaf of bread cost tens of thousands of marks.

Inflation spread misery and despair. Salaries rose by billions of marks, but they still could not keep up with skyrocketing prices. Many middle-class families saw their savings wiped out.

**Recovery.** With help from the western powers, the government did bring inflation under control. In 1924, the United States won British and French approval for a plan to reduce German reparations payments. Under the Dawes Plan, France withdrew its forces from the Ruhr and American loans helped the German economy recover.

Germany began to prosper, but memories of the miseries of 1923 revived when the Great Depression hit. Germans turned to an energetic leader, Adolf Hitler, who promised to solve the economic crisis and restore German greatness.

## Adolf Hitler

Hitler was born in Austria in 1889. When he was 18, he went to Vienna, hoping to enter art school, but he was turned down. At this time, Vienna was the capital of the multinational Hapsburg empire. Austrian Germans were a minority, but they felt superior to Jews, Serbs, Poles, and other ethnic or religious groups. During his stay in Vienna, Hitler developed the fanatical anti-Semitism that would later play a major role in his rise to power.

Hitler later moved to Germany and fought in the German army during World War I. Like many ex-soldiers, he despised the Weimar government. In 1919, he joined a small group of right-wing extremists. Within a year, he was the unquestioned leader of the National Socialist German Workers, or Nazi, party. Like Mussolini, Hitler organized his supporters into fighting squads. Nazi "Storm Troopers" battled in the streets against communists and others they saw as enemies.

**Mein Kampf.** In 1923, as you have read, Hitler made a failed attempt to seize power in Munich. While in prison, he wrote *Mein Kampf* (My Struggle), the "holy book" of Nazi goals and ideology. *Mein Kampf* reflected Hitler's obsessions—extreme nationalism, racism, and anti-Semitism. Germans, he said, belonged to a superior "master race" of Aryans, or light-skinned Europeans, whose greatest enemy were the Jews. Hitler viewed Jews not as members of a religion but as a separate race. Echoing a familiar theme, he claimed that Germany had not lost the war but had been betrayed by Marxists, Jews, corrupt politicians, and business leaders.

In his recipe for revival, Hitler urged Germans wherever they lived to unite into one great nation. Germany must expand, he said, to gain *Lebensraum,* or living space, for its people. Slavs and other inferior races must bow to Aryan needs. To achieve its greatness, Germany needed a strong leader, or *Führer* (FYOO ruhr). Adolf Hitler was determined to become that leader.

**The road to power.** After leaving prison, Hitler renewed his table-thumping speeches. He found enthusiastic followers among veterans and lower-middle-class people who felt frustrated about the future. The Great Depression played into Hitler's hands. As unemployment

*"Yes! Leader, We Follow You!"* Nazi propaganda used simple slogans and images. The intelligence of ordinary people is small, Hitler said. Therefore, "all effective propaganda must be limited to a very few points and must harp on these in slogans until the last member of the public understands what you want him to understand." The pin above shows the swastika, symbol of the Nazi party. **Religions and Value Systems** Compare this poster to the one on page 359. How do they promote similar values?

rose, Nazi membership grew to almost a million. Hitler's program appealed to workers and business people alike. He promised to end reparations, create jobs, and rearm Germany.

With the government paralyzed by divisions, both Nazis and Communists won more seats in the Reichstag, or lower house of the legislature. Finally, in 1933, other conservative politicians decided Hitler must become chancellor. They despised him as a vulgar rabble-rouser but planned to use him for their own ends. Thus, like Mussolini in Italy, Hitler became head of state through legal means.

Within a year, Hitler was master of Germany. He suspended civil rights, destroyed the Communists, and disbanded other political parties. Germany became a one-party state. Nazi flags, with their black swastikas, waved across the country. Like Stalin in Russia, Hitler purged his own party, brutally executing Nazis he felt were disloyal. Nazis learned that the Führer demanded unquestioning obedience.

## Hitler's Third Reich

Once in power, Hitler moved to build a new Germany. Like Mussolini, Hitler appealed to nationalism by recalling past glories. Germany's First Reich, or empire, was the medieval Holy Roman Empire. The Second Reich was the empire forged by Bismarck in 1871. Under Hitler's new Third Reich, he boasted, the German master race would dominate Europe for 1,000 years.

Hitler soon repudiated the hated Versailles treaty. He began scheming to unite Germany and Austria. "Today Germany belongs to us," sang young Nazis. "Tomorrow, the world."

**A totalitarian state.** To achieve his goals, Hitler organized a brutal system of terror, repression, and totalitarian rule. Nazis controlled all areas of German life—from government to religion to schools. Elite, black-uniformed SS troops enforced the Führer's will. His secret police, the Gestapo, rooted out opposition.

Few Germans saw or worried about this terror apparatus taking shape. Instead, they cheered Hitler's accomplishments in ending unemployment and reviving German power.

**Economic policy.** To combat the Great Depression, Hitler launched large public works programs (as did Britain and the United States). Tens of thousands of people were put to work building highways and housing or replanting forests. Hitler also began a crash program to rearm Germany, in violation of the Versailles treaty. Demand for military hardware stimulated business and helped eliminate unemployment.

Like Mussolini, Hitler preserved capitalism but brought big business and labor under government control. Few objected to this loss of freedom because their standard of living rose. Nazi propaganda highlighted the improvements. Workers joined "Strength Through Joy" programs, which offered vigorous outdoor vacations that also made them physically fit for military service.

**Social policy.** Like Italian Fascists and Russian Communists, the Nazis indoctrinated young people with their racist ideology. In passionate speeches, the Führer urged young Ger-

▲ *Marchers at a Nazi rally*

mans to destroy their so-called "enemies" without mercy:

>  **66**Extremes must be fought by extremes. Against the infection of [Marxism], against the Jewish pestilence, we must hold aloft a flaming ideal. And if others speak of the World and Humanity, we must say the Fatherland—and only the Fatherland!**99**

On hikes and in camps, the "Hitler Youth" pledged absolute loyalty to Germany and undertook physical fitness programs to prepare for war. (★ See *Skills for Success,* page 368.)

Like Fascists in Italy, Nazis sought to limit women's roles. Women were dismissed from upper-level jobs and turned away from universities. "National Socialism will restore her to her true profession—motherhood." To raise the birthrate, Nazis offered "pure-blooded Aryan" women rewards for having more children. Hitler's goal to keep women in the home applied mainly to the privileged. As German industry expanded, women workers were needed.

## Purging German Culture

Nazis used the arts and education as propaganda tools. They denounced modern art and music, saying it was corrupted by Jewish influences. Instead, they sought to purge, or purify, German culture. The Nazis glorified old German myths such as those re-created in the operas of Richard Wagner.

School courses and textbooks were rewritten to reflect Nazi racial views. "We teach and learn history," said one Nazi educator, "not to say how things actually happened but to instruct the German people from the past." At huge public bonfires, Nazis burned books of which

The swastika, which the Nazi party adopted in 1920, is actually one of the oldest symbols in the world. It has been found on ancient Mesopotamian and Greek coins, as well as on Mayan monuments. In India, Hindus and Jains use it as a good-luck symbol on doorways and elsewhere. Swastikas may appear with the arms rotating either clockwise, as in the Nazi swastika, or counterclockwise.

they disapproved. *All Quiet on the Western Front* was one of many works that went up in flames. The Nazis viewed Remarque's novel as an insult to the German military.

**Nazism and the churches.** Hitler despised Christianity as "weak" and "flabby." He sought to replace religion with his racial creed. In an attempt to control the churches, the Nazis combined all Protestant sects into a single state church. They closed Catholic schools and muzzled the Catholic clergy.

Martin Niemoller, a German Protestant minister, was jailed for trying to help Jews. He later commented on the results of not speaking out against Nazism:

>  **66**The Nazis came first for the Communists. But I wasn't a Communist, so I didn't speak up. Then they came for the Jews, but I wasn't a Jew so I didn't speak up. Then they came for the trade unionists, but I wasn't a trade unionist so I didn't speak up. Then they came for the Catholics, but I was a Protestant so I didn't speak up.
>  Then they came for me. By that time, there was no one left to speak up.**99**

**Campaign against the Jews.** In his fanatical anti-Semitism, Hitler set out to drive Jews from Germany. In 1935, the Nuremberg Laws placed severe restrictions on Jews. They were prohibited from marrying non-Jews, attending or teaching at German schools or universities, holding government jobs, practicing law or medicine, or publishing books. Nazis beat and robbed Jews and roused mobs to do the same. Many Jews, including Albert Einstein, fled the growing menace.

In November 1938, a German diplomat in Paris was shot by a young Jew whose parents had been mistreated in Germany. Hitler used the incident as an excuse to attack all Jews.

## Night of the Broken Glass

"Dead silence—not a sound to be heard in the town. The lamps in the street, the lights in the shops and in the houses are out. It is 3:30 A.M." In the German town of Emden, a small

A Vicious Campaign "We are going to destroy the Jews," Hitler said privately two months after Kristallnacht. In the picture above, Jewish-owned stores are marked with the word Jude, or Jew—a warning to "Aryans" not to shop there. Later, every Jew was required to wear a yellow Star of David in public. Yet the worst was still to come. **Diversity** Why do you think Hitler's campaign required that Jews be publicly identified?

Jewish boy was sleeping peacefully in his bed. Then, he recalled, the peace was shattered:

66Of a sudden noises in the street break into my sleep, a wild medley of shouts and shrieks. I listen, frightened and alarmed, until I distinguish words: 'Get out, Jews! Death to the Jews!'99

For this boy and for other Jews all over Germany, it was the beginning of a nightmare. This was *Kristallnacht* (krihs TAHL nahkt), or "Night of the Broken Glass."

**Two nights of terror.** The Kristallnacht riots took place on the nights of November 9 and 10, 1938. Nazi-led mobs attacked Jewish communities all over Germany. They smashed windows, looted shops, and burned synagogues. The boy in Emden recalled:

66Fists are hammering at the door. The shutters are broken open. We can hear the heavy cupboards crashing to the floor. Two Storm Troopers run upstairs, shouting at the top of their voices: 'Out with the Jews!'99

As the family stumbled downstairs, a gun was fired. "I am hit!" cried the boy's father. Still, the Storm Troopers forced the injured man and his family into the street. There, they watched in terror as other homes were plundered and Jews were beaten.

In Dusseldorf, a rabbi answered his phone at midnight. A terrified voice cried, "Rabbi, they're breaking up the synagogue hall and smashing everything to bits, they're beating the men, we can hear it from here." Before the rabbi could reply, fists pounded at his own door. Voices shouted, "Revenge for Paris! Down with the Jews!" Glass shattered, wood splintered, and footsteps thundered upstairs. The rabbi was dragged into the street. His books and typewriter were thrown out the windows onto the cobblestones below.

**Aftermath.** Kristallnacht brought such bad publicity to Hitler's Germany that it was not repeated. Yet Hitler made the Jewish victims pay for the damage. Tens of thousands of Jews were later sent to concentration camps, detention centers for civilians considered enemies of a state. Before long, Hitler and his henchmen were making even more sinister plans for what they would call the "final solution"—the extermination of all Jews. ■

## Looking Ahead

In the 1930s, Germany became Europe's second fascist state. Germans of all classes responded to Hitler's hypnotic speeches and programs, which restored their national pride. Despite the warnings of some courageous Germans who realized what was happening, most individuals ignored the ugly side of Nazi rule. Those who opposed Nazism were not united and were soon silenced or sent to concentration camps.

While Hitler won absolute power at home, he moved boldly to expand Germany's power in Europe. As you will read in Chapter 14, Nazi aggression set the stage for the largest war the world has yet seen.

## Authoritarian Rule in Eastern Europe

Like Germany, most new nations in Eastern Europe slid from democratic to authoritarian rule in the postwar era. In 1919, a dozen countries were carved out of the old Russian, Hapsburg, Ottoman, and German empires. (See the map on page 295.) Though they differed from one another in important ways, they faced some common problems. They were small countries whose rural agricultural economies lacked capital to develop industry. Social and economic inequalities separated poor peasants from wealthy, semifeudal landlords. None had much experience in democracy.

**Ethnic nationalism.** Old rivalries between ethnic and religious groups created severe tensions. In Czechoslovakia, for example, Czechs and Slovaks were unwilling partners, while some Germans living in Czechoslovakia itched to become part of Germany itself. Serbs dominated the new state of Yugoslavia, but restless Slovenes and Croats living there pressed for autonomy or independence. In Poland, Hungary, and Romania, conflict flared among various ethnic minorities.

**Democracy retreats.** Economic problems and ethnic tensions contributed to instability, which in turn helped fascist rulers gain power. In Hungary, military strongman Nicholas Horthy (HOHR tee) overthrew a communist-led government in 1919. By 1926, Joseph Pilsudski (peel SOOT skee) had become dictator of Poland. Eventually, right-wing dictators emerged in every Eastern European country except Czechoslovakia and Finland. Like Hitler, they promised order and won the backing of the military and wealthy. They also turned to anti-Semitism, using Jews as scapegoats for many national problems.

In the 1930s, Franklin Roosevelt tried to explain why so many nations had rejected democracy:

> 66 Democracy has disappeared in several great nations, not because the people of those nations dislike democracy, but because they have grown tired of unemployment and insecurity, of seeing their children hungry while they sat helpless in the face of government confusion and government weakness. . . . Finally, in desperation, they chose to sacrifice liberty in the hope of getting something to eat. 99

**Looking ahead.** While dictators in Eastern Europe could impose harsh regimes on their own lands, they could not change the region's political geography. As in earlier centuries, strong, aggressive neighbors eyed these small, weak states as tempting targets. Before long, Eastern Europe would fall into the orbit first of Hitler's Germany and then of Stalin's Soviet Union.

## SECTION 4 REVIEW

1. **Identify** (a) Ruhr Valley, (b) Dawes Plan, (c) *Mein Kampf,* (d) Third Reich, (e) Gestapo, (f) Nuremberg Laws, (g) Kristallnacht, (h) Nicholas Horthy, (i) Joseph Pilsudski.
2. **Define** concentration camp.
3. How did the failures of the Weimar Republic pave the way for the rise of Hitler?
4. (a) How did Hitler create a one-party dictatorship? (b) What racial and nationalistic ideas did Nazis promote?
5. Why did dictators gain power in much of Eastern Europe?
6. *Critical Thinking* **Defending a Position** Do you think that there are any circumstances when a government would be justified in banning books or censoring ideas? Explain.
7. *ACTIVITY* Draw a poster, write a poem, or compose a song about Kristallnacht from the point of view of a teenaged Jewish victim.

## CHAPTER REVIEW

### REVIEWING VOCABULARY

Review the following vocabulary from this chapter: *general strike, stream of consciousness, flapper, ideology, dictator, nationalism, inflation, racism, anti-Semitism, concentration camp.* Write sentences using each of these words, leaving blanks where the words would go. Exchange your sentences with another student and fill in the blanks on each other's lists.

### REVIEWING FACTS

1. What imbalance helped cause the Great Depression of the 1930s?
2. What was the Maginot Line?
3. How did the literature of the 1920s reflect the influence of World War I?
4. Why did the ideology of fascism appeal to many Italians?

## SKILLS FOR SUCCESS    ANALYZING PHOTOGRAPHS

Photographers make many choices—such as subject, lighting, and camera angle—that influence how you perceive a photo. They may want you to appreciate the beauty of a scene or be shocked or moved by their photographs.

The photographs below were taken in Germany in 1938. Study the photographs and answer the following questions.

1. **Identify the subject matter of the photographs.**
   (a) How old do the boys in each picture seem to be?
   (b) What kind of organization do the boys on the left belong to? (c) What are the boys on the right doing?
   (d) How do you think they feel about their actions?

2. **Analyze the reliability of the photographs.** How do these photographs support the information given on page 365?

3. **Use the photographs to draw conclusions about the historical period.** (a) What impression do the two pictures give you about the lives of youth in Nazi Germany? (b) Why do you think the Nazis encouraged activities like these?

5. What were Hitler's racist theories about Aryans and Jews?

6. Describe the economic policies that Hitler pursued as German leader.

## REVIEWING CHAPTER THEMES

Review the "Focus On" questions at the start of this chapter. Then select *three* of those questions and answer them, using information from the chapter.

## CRITICAL THINKING

1. **Synthesizing Information**  Review what you read about Adam Smith in Chapter 1 and about the liberal philosophy of the 1800s in Chapter 4. How did the New Deal challenge traditional free-market capitalism?

2. **Identifying Main Ideas**  Reread Martin Niemoller's words about Nazism on page 365. Then, restate Niemoller's main point in your own words.

## ANALYZING PRIMARY SOURCES

Use the quotation on page 358 to answer the following questions.

1. Why did Balbo feel betrayed by politicians?

2. What was Balbo's attitude toward Italy's postwar problems?

3. What sort of political leaders would a person like Balbo support?

## FOR YOUR PORTFOLIO

CREATING A MUSEUM EXHIBIT  Work with classmates to prepare an annotated catalog for a museum exhibit representing the years between the world wars. Make a list of the topics you will include in the catalog and the way in which you will represent each topic. Divide into teams and write the descriptions of the catalog entries. Then compile the completed entries into a catalog.

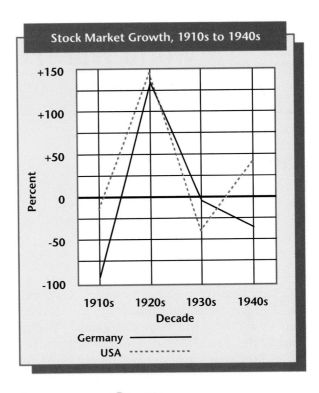

**Stock Market Growth, 1910s to 1940s**

Percent / Decade

Germany ———
USA  - - - - - - -

## ANALYZING GRAPHS

Use the graph as well as information from the chapter to answer the following questions.

1. What happened to both stock markets between the 1910s and the 1930s?

2. What world event helps explain why the German stock market's growth was much less than the American stock market's growth in the 1910s?

3. What world event helps explain what happened to both the German and the American stock markets in the 1930s?

**INTERNET ACTIVITY**

COMPARING ECONOMIC AND POLITICAL SYSTEMS  Use the Internet to research *either* the economic systems of capitalism, socialism, and communism *or* the political systems of democracy and totalitarianism. Then make a graphic organizer that compares and contrasts the systems you chose.

# World War II and Its Aftermath

## (1931–1949)

## CHAPTER OUTLINE

1 **Aggression, Appeasement, and War**
2 **The Global Conflict: Axis Advances**
3 **The Global Conflict: Allied Successes**
4 **Toward Victory**
5 **From World War to Cold War**

Here and there along the quiet Normandy beach, German officers peered through binoculars into the English Channel. Behind them, the French coast bristled with barbed wire. Metal tank traps spiked out of the sand. From dunes and cliffs, machine-gun nests and artillery pointed toward the sea.

Suddenly, through the thinning morning mist, a warship appeared. Soon, a dozen such silhouettes loomed into view, then a hundred, then more. It was dawn on June 6, 1944, and the largest naval invasion in history had just begun. As German guns roared into action, thousands of ships, carrying 176,000 American, British, Canadian, and French troops, began the assault on Nazi-controlled Europe. Cornelius Ryan, a war correspondent, later recalled the landing:

66 The noise was deafening as the boats . . . churned steadily for shore. In the slopping, bouncing [landing] craft, the men had to shout to be heard over the diesels. . . . There were no heroes in these boats, just cold, miserable, anxious men.99

Despite heavy German resistance, the operation was a success. Allied troops were soon marching inland, through France to Germany. The "D-Day" invasion, as it is known, marked the beginning of the end of World War II.

World War II was the most costly conflict in history. It also had enormous impact on world politics, shifting the balance of power away from Western Europe into the hands of the United States and the Soviet Union. Finally, like all wars, World War II had a purely human dimension. For millions of people, it was not a page in history, but a daily struggle between life and death.

**FOCUS ON** these questions as you read:

- **Continuity and Change**
  Why was the world plunged into a second global conflict just two decades after World War I?

- **Economics and Technology**
  How did technology affect the nature of the fighting and the extent of destruction in World War II?

- **Political and Social Systems**
  How did totalitarian regimes carry out their goals during the war?

- **Global Interaction**
  How did World War II change the balance of world power?

- **Geography and History**
  How did geography influence the war in Eastern Europe and Russia?

## TIME AND PLACE

*World War II* After only 20 years of peace, war engulfed Europe and the world once more in 1939. World War II was very different from World War I. Instead of a static war of trenches, it was mobile, high speed, and deadly. Airplanes, tanks, and warships moved troops quickly to the front. Battle lines shifted from tiny Pacific islands to the deserts of North Africa, from the steppes of Russia to the skies above London. The conflict killed tens of millions of men, women, and children. From its ashes arose a new world dominated by two superpowers, the United States and the Soviet Union. Here, Allied paratroopers land on a French beach on D-Day, June 6, 1944. *Economics and Technology* What does this painting suggest about fighting during World War II?

## HUMANITIES LINK

*Art History* Pablo Picasso, *Guernica* (page 374).
*Literature* In this chapter, you will encounter passages from the following works of literature: Cornelius Ryan, *The Longest Day* (page 370); W. H. Auden, "In Memory of W. B. Yeats" (page 376).

| 1935 | 1939 | 1941 | 1945 | 1949 |
|---|---|---|---|---|
| Italy invades Ethiopia | Germany invades Poland; World War II begins | Japan bombs Pearl Harbor; U.S. enters war | World War II ends; world learns of Holocaust | NATO founded |

| 1930 | 1935 | 1940 | 1945 | 1950 |
|---|---|---|---|---|

# 1 Aggression, Appeasement, and War

## Guide for Reading

■ How did dictators undermine the peace in the 1930s?

■ How was the Spanish Civil War a dress rehearsal for World War II?

■ Why were the western democracies unable to stop aggressive dictators?

■ **Vocabulary** *sanction, appeasement, pacifism*

In the last chapter, you saw how the western democracies tried to strengthen the framework for peace during the 1920s. In the 1930s, that structure crumbled. Dictators in Italy and Germany along with militarists in Japan pursued ambitious goals for empire. They scorned peace and glorified war. "In constant struggle," said Germany's Adolf Hitler, "mankind has become great—in eternal peace it must perish."

Unlike these dictators, leaders of the western democracies were haunted by memories of the Great War. Spurred by voters who demanded "no more war," the leaders of Britain, France, and the United States tried to avoid conflict through diplomacy. During the 1930s, the two sides tested each other's commitment and will.

## Early Challenges to World Peace

Challenges to peace followed a pattern throughout the 1930s. Dictators took aggressive action but met only verbal protests and pleas for peace from the democracies. Mussolini and Hitler viewed that desire for peace as weakness and responded with new acts of aggression. With hindsight, we can see the shortcomings of the democracies' policies. We must remember, however, that these policies were the product of long and careful deliberation. People at the time strongly believed that they would work.

**Japan on the move.** One of the earliest tests was posed by Japan. Japanese military leaders and ultranationalists felt that Japan should have an empire equal to those of the western powers. In pursuit of this goal, Japan seized Manchuria in 1931. (See page 340.) When the League of Nations condemned the aggression, Japan withdrew from the organization.

Japan's easy success strengthened the militarists. In 1937, Japanese armies overran much of eastern China. (See page 341.) Once again, western protests had no effect.

**Italy invades Ethiopia.** In Italy, Mussolini used his new, modern military to pursue his own imperialist ambitions. He looked first to Ethiopia, in northeastern Africa. Italy's defeat by the Ethiopians at the battle of Adowa in 1896 still rankled. (See page 223.)

In 1935, Italy invaded Ethiopia. Although the Ethiopians resisted bravely, their outdated weapons were no match for Mussolini's tanks, machine guns, poison gas, and airplanes. The Ethiopian king Haile Selassie (HĪ lee suh LAS ee) appealed to the League of Nations for help. The league voted sanctions, or penalties, against Italy for having violated international law. League members agreed to stop selling weapons or other war materials to Italy. But the sanctions did not extend to petroleum, which fueled modern warfare. Besides, the sanctions were not enforced. By early 1936, Italy had conquered Ethiopia.

**Hitler's challenge.** By then, Hitler, too, had tested the will of the western democracies and found it weak. First, he built up the German military in defiance of the Versailles treaty. Then, in 1936, he sent troops into the Rhineland—another treaty violation. The area belonged to Germany, but it lay on the frontier with France. (See the map on page 375.) In 1919, France had insisted that the Rhineland be a "demilitarized" zone, off-limits to German troops.

Hitler's successful challenge of the hated Versailles treaty increased his popularity in Germany. Western democracies denounced his moves but took no real action. Instead, they adopted a policy of appeasement, giving in to the demands of an aggressor in order to keep the peace.

**Why appeasement?** The policy of appeasement evolved for various reasons. France was demoralized, suffering from political divisions at home. It needed British support for any move against Hitler.

The British, however, had no desire to confront the German dictator. Some Britons thought that Hitler's actions were a justified response to the Versailles treaty, which they believed had been too harsh.

In both Britain and France, many saw Hitler as a defense against a worse evil—the spread of Soviet communism. Also, the Great Depression sapped the energies of the western democracies. Finally, widespread pacifism, or opposition to all war, and disgust with the last war pushed governments to seek peace at any price.

**Reaction in the United States.** As war clouds gathered in Europe in the mid-1930s, the United States Congress passed a series of Neutrality Acts. One law forbade the sale of arms to any nation at war. Others outlawed loans to warring nations and prohibited Americans from traveling on ships of warring powers. The fundamental goal of American policy, however, was to avoid involvement in a European war, not to prevent such a conflict.

**Rome-Berlin-Tokyo Axis.** In the face of the democracies' apparent weakness, Germany, Italy, and Japan formed what became known as the Rome-Berlin-Tokyo Axis. The three nations agreed to fight Soviet communism. They also agreed not to interfere with one another's plans for expansion. The agreement cleared the way for these anti-democratic, aggressor powers to take even bolder steps to bring other nations under their sway.

## The Spanish Civil War

In 1936, Spain plunged into civil war. Although the Spanish Civil War was a local struggle, it soon drew other European powers into the fighting.

**From monarchy to republic.** In the 1920s, Spain was a monarchy dominated by a landowning upper class, the Catholic Church, and the military. Most Spaniards were poor peasants or urban workers. In 1931, popular unrest against the old order forced the king to leave Spain. A republic was set up with a new, more liberal constitution.

The republican government passed a series of controversial reforms. It took over some

**No Help for Ethiopia** *Ethiopian king Haile Selassie, shown here, asked the League of Nations for help after Italy invaded his country in 1935. The league's weak response encouraged Mussolini to pursue the war in Ethiopia and gave a green light to the expansionist plans of other dictators.* **Impact of the Individual** *Do you think Haile Selassie was right to ask for help from the League of Nations? Explain.*

Church lands and ended Church control of education. It redistributed some land to peasants, gave women the vote, and ended some privileges of the old ruling class. These moves split the people of Spain. Communists and other leftists demanded more radical reforms. On the right, conservatives backed by the military rejected change. Clashes between leftists and rightists created chaos. Any moderate voices were drowned out.

**Nationalists versus Loyalists.** In 1936, a right-wing general, Francisco Franco, led a revolt that touched off a bloody civil war. Franco's forces, called Nationalists, rallied conservatives to their banner. Supporters of the republic, known as Loyalists, included communists, socialists, supporters of democracy, and others.

Several European powers quickly took sides. Hitler and Mussolini sent forces to help Franco. Like them, he was a nationalist and a foe of democracy and socialism. The Soviet Union and a handful of volunteers from the western democracies gave some support to the Loyalists. Britain, France, and the United States, however, remained neutral.

**A dress rehearsal.** Both sides committed unbelievable atrocities. The ruinous struggle took almost one million lives. Among the worst

**Guernica** *The bombing and strafing of the Spanish town of Guernica inspired one of Pablo Picasso's greatest works of art. The huge canvas, completed in 1937, is over 11 feet tall and 25 feet wide. By the 1930s, Picasso had moved beyond Cubism in his style of painting. (See page 356.) The distorted human and animal figures that in Cubist works were just images here symbolize the violent effects of war.* **Art and Literature** *Why do you think Picasso included horses and other animals in* Guernica? *What might be the symbolism of the oil lamp and the electric light?*

horrors was a German air raid on Guernica, a small Spanish market town of no military value. One April morning in 1937, German bombers streaked over the market square. They dropped their load of bombs and then swooped low to machine-gun people in the streets. An estimated 1,600 people were killed.

To Nazi leaders, the attack on Guernica was an "experiment" to see what their new planes could do. To the world, it was a grim warning of the destructive power of modern warfare, as well as a "dress rehearsal" for what was to come. Later, the Spanish artist Pablo Picasso created a massive painting, *Guernica,* shown above, that captured the brutality and terror of that day.

By 1939, Franco had triumphed. Once in power, he created a fascist dictatorship like those of Hitler and Mussolini. He rolled back earlier reforms, killed or jailed enemies, and used terror to promote order.

## German Aggression Continues

In the meantime, Hitler pursued his goal of bringing all German-speaking people into the Third Reich. He also took steps to gain "living space" for Germans in Eastern Europe. (See page 363.) Hitler, who believed in the superiority of the German, or Aryan, "race," thought that Germany had a right to conquer the inferior Slavs to the east. "Nature is cruel," he claimed, "so we may be cruel, too. . . . I have a right to remove millions of an inferior race that breeds like vermin."

**Austria annexed.** From the outset, Nazi propaganda had found fertile ground in Austria. By 1938, Hitler was ready to engineer the Anschluss, or union of Austria and Germany. Early that year, he forced the Austrian chancellor to appoint Nazis to key cabinet posts. When the Austrian leader balked at other demands, Hitler sent in the German army "to preserve order."

The Anschluss violated the Versailles treaty and created a brief war scare. But Hitler quickly silenced any Austrians who opposed the German takeover. And since the western democracies took no action, Hitler easily had his way.

**The Czech crisis.** Hitler's next victim was Czechoslovakia. At first, he insisted that the three million Germans in the Sudetenland in

## Aggression in Europe to 1939

### GEOGRAPHY AND HISTORY

Between 1936 and 1939, Germany and Italy repeatedly threatened the peace in Europe.

1. **Location** On the map, locate (a) Germany, (b) Italy, (c) Sudetenland, (d) Rhineland, (e) Albania, (f) Dachau.
2. **Region** Locate the region called the Polish Corridor. Why is that an appropriate name for the region?
3. **Critical Thinking** **Applying Information** (a) What example of Italian aggression in the 1930s is not shown on the map? (b) What changes on the map would be required in order to show that aggression?

western Czechoslovakia be given autonomy. The demand set off new alarms among the democracies.

Czechoslovakia was one of two remaining democracies in Eastern Europe (Finland was the other). Still, Britain and France were not willing to go to war to save it. As British and French leaders searched for a peaceful solution, Hitler increased his price. The Sudetenland, he said, must be annexed to Germany.

At the Munich Conference in September 1938, British and French leaders again chose appeasement. They caved in to Hitler's demands and then persuaded the Czechs to surrender the Sudetenland without a fight. In exchange, Hitler assured Britain and France that he had no further plans for expansion.

**"Peace for our time."** Returning from Munich, the British prime minister Neville Chamberlain told cheering crowds that he had achieved "peace for our time." In the House of Commons, he declared that the Munich Pact had "saved Czechoslovakia from destruction and Europe from Armageddon." The French

WONDER HOW LONG THE HONEYMOON WILL LAST?

*Nazi-Soviet Pact* *In 1939, a shocked world learned that Nazi Germany and the Soviet Union had signed a nonaggression treaty. As this cartoon suggests, the honeymoon between Hitler and Stalin would be short-lived. Less than two years later, Hitler launched a surprise attack on the Soviet Union.* **Political and Social Systems** *Why did two sworn enemies, Hitler and Stalin, join together in a pact?*

leader Edouard Daladier had a different reaction to the joyous crowds that greeted him in Paris. "The fools, why are they cheering?" he asked.

The Czech crisis revealed the Nazi menace. British politician Winston Churchill, who had long warned of the Nazi threat, judged the diplomats harshly: "They had to choose between war and dishonor. They chose dishonor; they will have war."

## The Plunge Toward War

As Churchill predicted, Munich did not bring peace. Instead, Europe plunged rapidly toward war. In March 1939, Hitler gobbled up the rest of Czechoslovakia. The democracies finally accepted the fact that appeasement had failed. At last thoroughly alarmed, they promised to protect Poland, most likely the next target of Hitler's expansion.

**Nazi-Soviet Pact.** In August 1939, Hitler stunned the world by announcing a nonaggres-

sion pact with his great enemy—Joseph Stalin, head of the Soviet Union. Publicly, the Nazi-Soviet Pact bound Hitler and Stalin to peaceful relations. Secretly, the two agreed (1) not to fight if the other went to war and (2) to divide up Poland and other parts of Eastern Europe between them.

The pact was based not on friendship or respect but on mutual need. The Nazis feared communism as Stalin feared fascism. But Hitler wanted a free hand in Poland. Also, he did not want to fight a war with the western democracies and the Soviet Union at the same time.

For his part, Stalin had sought allies among the western democracies against the Nazi menace. Mutual suspicions, however, kept them apart. By joining with Hitler, Stalin bought time to build up Soviet defenses. He also saw a chance for important territorial gains.

**Invasion of Poland.** On September 1, 1939, a week after the Nazi-Soviet Pact, German forces stormed into Poland. Two days later, Britain and France honored their commitment to Poland and declared war on Germany. World War II had begun. There was no joy at the news of war as there had been in 1914. The British poet W. H. Auden caught the mood of gloom in these lines:

> **"**In the nightmare of the dark
> All the dogs of Europe bark
> And the living nations wait
> Each sequestered in its hate.**"**

## Why War Came

Many factors contributed to World War II. You have learned some of the reasons behind Axis aggression. You have also seen why western democracies adopted a policy of appeasement. Today, historians often see the war as an effort to revise the 1919 peace settlement. The Versailles treaty had divided Europe into two camps—those who were satisfied with its terms and those who were not. Germany, Italy, Japan,

**ISSUES** *For* **TODAY**

Aggression by the Axis powers resulted in World War II. How can countries stop aggression by other nations?

and the Soviet Union all felt betrayed or excluded by the settlement and wanted to change it.

Since 1939, people have debated issues such as why the western democracies failed to respond forcefully to the Nazi threat and whether they could have stopped Hitler if they had responded. Dreading war, the democracies hoped that diplomacy and compromise would right old wrongs and prevent further aggression. They were distracted by political and economic problems and misread Hitler's intentions. A few people warned of the danger, but most disregarded even Hitler's declared goals in *Mein Kampf*. (See page 363.)

Many historians today think that Hitler might have been stopped in 1936, before Germany was fully rearmed. If Britain and France had taken military action then, they argue, Hitler would have had to retreat. But the French and British were unwilling to risk war. The experience of World War I and awareness of the destructive power of modern technology made the idea of renewed fighting unbearable. Unfortunately, when war came, it proved to be even more horrendous than anyone had imagined.

## SECTION 1 REVIEW

1. **Identify** (a) Haile Selassie, (b) Rome-Berlin-Tokyo Axis, (c) Guernica, (d) Anschluss, (e) Munich Conference, (f) Neville Chamberlain, (g) Nazi-Soviet Pact.
2. **Define** (a) sanction, (b) appeasement, (c) pacifism.
3. (a) List three acts of aggression by Italy, Germany, and Japan during the 1930s. (b) How did the western democracies respond to each?
4. How did the Spanish Civil War become a battleground for the competing political forces in the western world?
5. (a) Why did the western democracies follow a policy of appeasement? (b) How did the aggressor nations respond to appeasement?
6. *Critical Thinking* **Recognizing Causes and Effects** How was the Munich Conference a turning point in the road toward war?
7. *ACTIVITY* Make an illustrated time line titled "The Road to World War II."

# The Global Conflict: Axis Advances

## Guide for Reading

- How did new technologies affect the fighting in World War II?
- What goals did the Axis powers pursue in Europe and Asia?
- Why did Japan attack the United States?
- **Vocabulary** *blitzkrieg*

"Hitler will collapse the day we declare war on Germany," predicted a confident French general on the eve of World War II. He could not have been more wrong. World War II, the costliest war in history, lasted six years—from 1939 to 1945. It pitted the Axis powers, chiefly Germany, Italy, and Japan, against the Allied powers, which eventually included Britain, France, the Soviet Union, China, the United States, and 45 other nations.

Unlike World War I, with its dug-in defensive trenches, the new global conflict was a war of aggressive movement. In the early years, things went badly for the Allies as Axis forces swept across Europe, North Africa, and Asia, piling up victories.

## *The First Onslaught*

In September 1939, Nazi forces stormed into Poland, revealing the enormous power of Hitler's **blitzkrieg,** or "lightning war." First, German planes bombed airfields, factories, towns, and cities, and screaming dive bombers fired on troops and civilians. Then fast-moving tanks and troop transports roared into the country. The Polish army fought back but could not stop the motorized onslaught.

While Germany attacked from the west, Stalin's forces invaded from the east, grabbing areas promised under the Nazi-Soviet Pact. Within a month, Poland ceased to exist.

With Poland crushed, Hitler passed the winter without much further action. Stalin's armies, however, pushed on into the Baltic states of

Estonia, Latvia, and Lithuania. They also seized part of Finland, which put up stiff but unsuccessful resistance.

**Early Axis triumphs.** During that first winter, the French hunkered down behind the Maginot Line. (See page 352.) Britain sent troops to wait with them. Some reporters dubbed this quiet time the "phony war."

Then, in April 1940, the war exploded into action. Hitler launched a blitzkrieg against Norway and Denmark, both of which soon fell. Next, his forces slammed into the Netherlands and Belgium. Within weeks, Germany had overrun them, too.

**Miracle of Dunkirk.** By May, German forces were pouring into France. Retreating Allied forces were soon trapped between the advancing Nazis and the English Channel. In a desperate gamble, the British sent every available naval vessel, merchant ship, and even every pleasure boat across the choppy channel to pluck stranded troops off the beaches of Dunkirk and Ostend.

Despite German air attacks, the improvised armada ferried more than 300,000 troops to safety. This heroic rescue, dubbed the "miracle of Dunkirk," greatly raised British morale.

**France falls.** Meanwhile, German forces headed south toward Paris. Sensing an easy victory, Italy declared war on France and attacked from the south. Overwhelmed and demoralized, France surrendered.

On June 22, 1940, in a forest clearing in northeastern France, Hitler avenged the German defeat of 1918. He forced the French to sign the surrender documents in the same railroad car in which Germany had signed the armistice ending World War I. A young American reporter described the scene:

&6I observed [Hitler's] face. It was grave, solemn, yet brimming with revenge. There was also in it . . . a note of the triumphant conqueror, the defier of the world. There was something else, difficult to describe, in his expression; a sort of scornful, inner joy at being present at this great reversal of fate—a reversal he himself had wrought.99

Following the surrender, Germany occupied northern France. In the south, the Germans set up a "puppet state," with its capital at Vichy (VIHSH ee). Some French officers escaped to England, where they set up a government-in-exile. Led by Charles de Gaulle, these "free French" worked to liberate their homeland. Inside France itself, resistance fighters turned to guerrilla tactics to harass the occupying German forces.

**The technology of modern warfare.** The whirlwind Nazi advance revealed the awesome power of modern warfare. Air power took a prominent role. After its tryout in Spain, the Luftwaffe, or German air force, perfected methods of bombing civilian as well as military targets. Hitler also used fast-moving armored tanks and troop carriers along with parachute troops to storm through Europe.

Technology created a war machine with even greater destructive power. Scientists and engineers working for the Axis and Allied governments improved the design and effectiveness of airplanes and submarines. They produced ever more deadly bombs and invented hundreds of new devices, such as radar to detect airplanes and sonar to detect submarines. At the same time, research also led to medical advances to treat the wounded and new synthetic products to replace scarce strategic goods.

## The Battle of Britain

With the fall of France, Britain stood alone. Hitler was sure that the British would sue for peace. But Winston Churchill, who had replaced Neville Chamberlain as prime minister, had other plans. For many years, Churchill had been a lone voice against the Nazi threat. In 1940, he rallied the British to fight on:

&6We shall defend our island, whatever the cost may be. We shall fight on the beaches, we shall fight on the landing grounds, we shall fight in the fields and in the streets, we shall fight in the hills; we shall never surrender.99

Faced with this defiance, Hitler ordered preparation of Operation Sea Lion—the invasion of Britain. First, however, he set out to weaken Britain's air power and break the British will to resist. To achieve this goal, he launched massive air strikes against the island nation.

**The battle begins.** On August 12, 1940, the first wave of German bombers appeared over England's southern coast. The Battle of Britain had begun.

Racing to their planes, British Royal Air Force (RAF) fighter pilots rose into the air. They scrambled after the Germans until their fuel ran low. Landing, they snatched a few hours' sleep, refueled, and took off to fight again. A local resident commented on their bravery:

> ❝I'd seen our RAF boys spiraling down. I'd also seen them do a victory roll when they shot a German airplane down. These boys went up day and night, in these Spitfires, almost stuck together with chewing gum.❞

For a month, the RAF valiantly battled the German Luftwaffe. Then the Germans changed their tactics, turning their attention from military targets to the bombing, or blitz, of London and other cities.

**The London blitz.** Late on the afternoon of September 7, German bombers appeared over London. All through the night, until dawn the next day, relays of aircraft showered high explosives and firebombs on the sprawling capital. For the next 57 nights, the bombing went on. German Stukas and Messerschmitts pounded docks and railways, buildings and homes. Much of the city was destroyed, and some 15,000 people lost their lives.

For Londoners, the blitz became a fact of life. Each night, they waited for the howl of air raid sirens that warned of the latest Luftwaffe assault. As searchlights swept the sky in search of the enemy, people took refuge wherever they could. Some hid in cellars under their homes, others in special shelters built in backyards. Thousands took shelter in cold subways, deep underground.

The city did not break under the blitz. Parliament continued to sit in defiance of the enemy. Citizens carried on their daily lives, seeking protection in shelters and then emerging when the all-clear sounded to resume their routine. One mother marveled at her own response to the nightly raids:

**London in Flames**
The Nazi blitz of London raged for two months in 1940. Each night, German bombers dropped tons of bombs, igniting fires that burned out of control. Each morning, Londoners picked through the rubble and counted the dead. The blitz destroyed some of the city's most precious buildings, but it failed to break the will of the English people. At right, a woman surveys the results of a raid. At far right, Londoners escape the bombs by bedding down in a subway station. **Religions and Value Systems** Why do you think the blitz failed to destroy British morale?

&#x66;&#x66;I never thought I could sit and read to children, say about Cinderella, while you could hear the German planes coming. Sometimes a thousand a night came over, in waves. We had a saying, 'I'm gonna getcha, I'm gonna getcha.' That's how the planes sounded. You'd hear the bomb drop so many hundred yards that way. And you'd think, Oh, that missed us. You'd think, My God, the next one's going to be a direct hit. . . . But you bore up. And I wasn't the bravest of people, believe me.&#x99;

The Germans continued to bomb London and other cities off and on until June 1941. But contrary to Hitler's hopes, British morale was not destroyed. In fact, the bombing brought the British closer together in their determination to turn back the enemy.

**A German defeat.** The Battle of Britain showed that terror bombing could not defeat a determined people. By June 1941, Hitler had abandoned Operation Sea Lion in favor of a new campaign. This time, he targeted the Soviet Union. The decision to invade Russia helped save Britain. It also proved to be one of Hitler's most costly mistakes.

## Charging Ahead

While the Luftwaffe was blasting Britain, Axis armies were pushing into North Africa and the Balkans. In September 1940, Mussolini sent forces from Italy's North African colony of Libya into Egypt. When the British repulsed the invaders, Hitler sent a brilliant commander, General Erwin Rommel, to North Africa. The "Desert Fox," as he was nicknamed, chalked up a string of successes in 1941 and 1942. He pushed the British back across the desert toward Cairo, in Egypt. The British worried that he would seize the Suez Canal, thus severing their lifeline to India.

In 1940, Italian forces invaded Greece. When they met stiff resistance, German troops once again came to the rescue, and both Greece and Yugoslavia were added to the Axis empire. Even after the Axis triumph, however, Greek and Yugoslav guerrillas plagued the occupying forces.

Meanwhile, both Bulgaria and Hungary had joined the Axis alliance. By 1941, the Axis powers or their allies controlled most of Western Europe. (See the map on page 386.)

## Operation Barbarossa

In June 1941, Hitler embarked on Operation Barbarossa—the conquest of the Soviet Union.* Hitler's motives were clear. He wanted to gain "living space" for Germans and to win control of regions rich in resources. "If I had the Ural Mountains with their incalculable store of treasures in raw materials," he declared, "Siberia with its vast forests, and the Ukraine with its tremendous wheat fields, Germany under National Socialist leadership would swim in plenty." He also wanted to crush communism and defeat his powerful rival Joseph Stalin.

**The German advance.** In Operation Barbarossa, Hitler unleashed a new blitzkrieg. About three million Germans poured into Russia. They caught Stalin unprepared, his army still suffering from the purges that had wiped out many of its top officers. (See page 311.)

The Russians lost two and a half million soldiers trying to fend off the invaders. As they were forced back, they destroyed factories and farm equipment and burned crops to keep them out of enemy hands. But they could not stop the German war machine. By autumn, the Nazis had smashed deep into Russia and were poised to take Moscow and Leningrad. "The war is over," declared Hitler's propaganda minister Joseph Goebbels.

There, however, the German drive stalled. Like Napoleon's Grand Army in 1812, Hitler's forces were not prepared for the fury of Russia's "General Winter." By early December, temperatures plunged to –20 degrees Celsius. Thousands of German soldiers froze to death.

**Siege of Leningrad.** The Russians, meanwhile, suffered appalling hardships. In September 1941, the two-and-a-half-year siege of Leningrad began. Food was soon rationed to two pieces of bread a day. Desperate Leningraders ate almost anything. They chewed paper or boiled wallpaper scraped off walls because its paste was said

---

*The plan took its name from the Holy Roman emperor Frederick Barbarossa, who had won great victories in the East.

**War on Many Fronts** *In sharply contrasting conditions, the German army made rapid advances during the early years of the war. At left, a tank division advances through the Russian snow during Operation Barbarossa. At right, German troops ride over the desert sands of North Africa.* **Geography and History** *What problems would an army face trying to maneuver in the desert? How did Russia's geography make it difficult to conquer?*

to contain potato flour. Owners of leather briefcases boiled and ate them—"jellied meat," they called it.

More than a million Leningraders died during the German siege. The survivors, meanwhile, struggled to defend their city. Hoping to gain some relief for the exhausted Russians, Stalin urged Britain to open a second front in Western Europe. Although Churchill could not offer much real help, the two powers did agree to work together.

### Growing American Involvement

When the war began in 1939, the United States declared its neutrality. Although isolationist feeling remained strong, many Americans sympathized with the Poles, French, British, and others who battled the Axis powers. Later, President Roosevelt found ways around the Neutrality Acts to provide aid, including warships, to Britain as it stood alone against Hitler.

**The arsenal of democracy.** In early 1941, FDR convinced Congress to pass the Lend-Lease Act. It allowed him to sell or lend war materials to "any country whose defense the President deems vital to the defense of the United States." The United States, said Roosevelt, would not be drawn into the war, but it would

become "the arsenal of democracy," supplying arms to those who were fighting for freedom.

**Atlantic Charter.** In August 1941, Roosevelt and Churchill met secretly on a warship in the Atlantic. The two leaders issued the Atlantic Charter, which set goals for the war—"the final destruction of the Nazi tyranny"—and for the postwar world. They pledged to support "the right of all peoples to choose the form of government under which they will live" and called for a "permanent system of general security."

### Japan Attacks

In December 1941, the Allies gained a vital boost when a surprise action by Japan suddenly pitched the United States into the war. From the late 1930s, Japan had been trying to conquer China. (See pages 340 and 341.) Although Japan occupied much of eastern China, the Chinese would not surrender. When war broke out in Europe in 1939, the Japanese saw a chance to grab European possessions in Southeast Asia. The rich resources of the region, including oil, rubber, and tin, would be of immense value in fighting the Chinese war.

**Growing tensions.** In 1940, Japan advanced into French Indochina and the Dutch East Indies (present-day Indonesia). To stop Japanese aggression, the United States banned

*Pearl Harbor* By November 1941, American officials knew that Japan was planning an attack somewhere in the Pacific. Still, they were stunned by the bombing of the naval base at Pearl Harbor. Said one navy commander, "I didn't believe it when I saw the planes, and I didn't believe it when I saw the bombs fall." Here, an American battleship burns in Pearl Harbor. ***Political and Social Systems*** *Why was the bombing of Pearl Harbor a turning point in World War II?*

the sale to Japan of war materials, such as iron, steel, and oil for airplanes. This move angered the Japanese.

Japan and the United States held talks to ease the growing tension. But extreme militarists such as General Tojo Hideki were gaining power in Japan. They did not want peace. Instead, they hoped to seize lands in Asia and the Pacific. The United States was interfering with their plans.

**Attack on Pearl Harbor.** With talks at a standstill, General Tojo ordered a surprise attack on the American fleet at Pearl Harbor, Hawaii. Early on December 7, 1941, Japanese airplanes struck. They damaged or destroyed 19 ships, smashed American planes on the ground, and killed more than 2,400 people.

The next day, a grim-faced President Roosevelt told the nation that December 7 was "a date which will live in infamy." He asked Congress to declare war on Japan. Three days later, Germany and Italy, as Japan's allies, declared war on the United States.

**Japanese victories.** In the long run, the Japanese attack on Pearl Harbor would be as serious a mistake as Hitler's invasion of Russia. But the months after Pearl Harbor gave no such hint. Instead, European and American possessions in the Pacific and in Southeast Asia fell one by one to the Japanese. They drove the Americans out of the Philippines and seized other American islands across the Pacific. They over-

ran the British colonies of Hong Kong, Burma, and Malaya, pushed deeper into the Dutch East Indies, and completed the takeover of French Indochina.

By the beginning of 1942, the Japanese empire stretched from Southeast Asia to the western Pacific Ocean. (See the map on page 389.) The Axis powers had reached the high point of their successes.

## SECTION 2 REVIEW

1. **Identify** (a) "phony war," (b) Dunkirk, (c) Winston Churchill, (d) Battle of Britain, (e) Operation Barbarossa, (f) Lend-Lease Act, (g) Atlantic Charter, (h) Pearl Harbor.
2. **Define** blitzkrieg.
3. How did new technologies make World War II a war of rapid movement?
4. What successes did the Axis have in Europe?
5. (a) What goals did Japan pursue in Asia? (b) Why did General Tojo order an attack on the United States?
6. *Critical Thinking* **Identifying Alternatives** Do you think that the United States could have stayed out of the war? Why or why not?
7. *ACTIVITY* Imagine that you are a teenager during the London blitz. Write a series of diary entries describing your experiences.

# 3 The Global Conflict: Allied Successes

## Guide for Reading

- How did the Axis powers treat the people they conquered?
- How did nations mobilize for total war?
- What battles were turning points in the war?
- **Vocabulary** *collaborator*

World War II was fought on a larger scale and in more places than any other war in history. It was also more costly in human life than any earlier conflict. Civilians were targets as much as soldiers. In 1941, a reporter visited a Russian town that had 10,000 people before the German invasion. The reporter found a lone survivor:

66[She was] a blind old woman who had gone insane. She was there when the village was shelled and had gone mad. I saw her wandering barefooted around the village, carrying a few dirty rags, a rusty pail, and a tattered sheepskin.99

From 1939 until mid-1942, the Axis ran up a string of successes. During those years, the conquerors blasted villages and towns and divided up the spoils. Then the Allies won some key victories. Slowly, the tide began to turn.

## Occupied Lands

While the Germans rampaged across Europe, the Japanese conquered an empire in Asia and the Pacific. Each set out to build a "new order" in the occupied lands.

**Nazi Europe.** Hitler's new order grew out of his racial obsessions. He set up puppet governments in Western European countries that were peopled by "Aryans" or related races. The Slavs of Eastern Europe were viewed as an inferior race. They were shoved aside to provide "living space" for Germans.

To the Nazis, occupied lands were an economic resource to be plundered and looted. One of Hitler's high officials bluntly stated his view:

66Whether nations live in prosperity or starve to death interests me only insofar as we need them as slaves for our culture.99

The Nazis systematically stripped countries of works of art, factories, and other resources. They sent thousands of Slavs and others to work as slave laborers in German war industries. As resistance movements emerged to fight German tyranny, the Nazis took savage revenge, shooting hostages and torturing prisoners.

**Nazi genocide.** The most savage of all policies was Hitler's program to kill Jews and others he judged "racially inferior," such as Slavs, Gypsies, and the mentally ill. At first, the Nazis forced Jews in Poland and elsewhere to live in ghettos. By 1941, however, Hitler and his supporters had devised plans for the "final solution of the Jewish problem"—the genocide, or deliberate destruction, of all European Jews.

To accomplish this goal, Hitler had "death camps" built in Poland and Germany, at places like Auschwitz and Bergen Belsen. The Nazis shipped Jews from all over occupied Europe to the camps. There, Nazi engineers designed the most efficient means of killing millions of men, women, and children.

As Jews reached the camps, they were stripped of their clothes and valuables. Their heads were shaved. Guards separated men from women and children from their parents. The young, old, and sick were targeted for immediate killing. Within a few days, they were herded into "shower rooms" and gassed. The Nazis worked others to death or used them for perverse "medical" experiments. By 1945, the Nazis had massacred more than six million Jews in what became known as the Holocaust. Almost as many other "undesirable" people were killed as well.

Jews resisted the Nazis even though they knew their efforts could not succeed. In October 1944, for example, a group of Jews in the Auschwitz death camp destroyed one of the gas chambers. The rebels were all killed. One woman, Rosa Robota, was tortured for days before

she was hanged. "Be strong and have courage," she called out to the camp inmates who were forced by the Nazis to watch her execution.

In some cases, friends, neighbors, or others concealed or protected Jews from the Holocaust. Italian peasants, for example, hid Jews in their villages, and Denmark as a nation saved almost all its Jewish population. Most often, however, people pretended not to see what was happening. Some were collaborators, helping the Nazis hunt down the Jews or, like the Vichy government in France, shipping tens of thousands of Jews to their death.

The scale and savagery of the Holocaust have been unequaled in history. The Nazis deliberately set out to destroy the Jews for no other reason than their religious and ethnic heritage. Today, the record of that slaughter is a vivid reminder of the monstrous results of racism and intolerance.

**The Co-Prosperity Sphere.** On the other side of the world, Japan wrapped itself in the mantle of anti-imperialism. Under the slogan "Asia for Asians," it created the Greater East Asia Co-Prosperity Sphere. Its self-proclaimed mission was to help Asians escape western colonial rule. In fact, its goal was a Japanese empire in Asia.

The Japanese treated the Chinese and other conquered people with great brutality, killing and torturing civilians everywhere. They seized food crops and made local people into slave laborers. Whatever welcome the Japanese had at first met as "liberators" was soon turned to hatred. In the Philippines, Indochina, and elsewhere, nationalist groups waged guerrilla warfare against the Japanese conquerors.

## The Allied War Effort

After the United States entered the war, the Allied leaders met periodically to hammer out their strategy. In 1942, the Big Three—Roosevelt, Churchill, and Stalin—agreed to finish the war in Europe first before turning their attention to the Japanese in Asia.

From the outset, the Allies distrusted one another. Churchill thought Stalin wanted to dominate Europe. Roosevelt felt that Churchill had ambitions to expand British imperial power. Stalin believed that the western powers wanted to destroy communism. At meetings and in writing, Stalin urged Roosevelt and Churchill to relieve the pressure on Russia by opening a second front in Western Europe. Not until 1944, however, did Britain and the United States make such a move. The British and Americans argued that they did not have the resources before then. Stalin saw the delay as a deliberate policy to weaken the Soviet Union.

**Total war.** Like the Axis powers, the Allies were committed to total war. Democratic governments in the United States and Britain increased their political power. They directed economic resources into the war effort, ordering factories to stop making cars or refrigerators and to turn out airplanes or tanks instead. Governments rationed consumer goods, from shoes to sugar, and regulated prices and wages. On the positive side, while the war brought shortages and hardships, it ended the unemployment of the depression era.

Under pressure of war, even democratic governments limited the rights of citizens. They censored the press and used slick propaganda to win public support for the war. In the United States and Canada, many citizens of Japanese descent lost their civil rights. On the West Coast, Japanese Americans even lost their freedom, as they were forced into internment camps after the government decided they were a security risk. The British took similar action against German refugees. Some 40 years later, the United States government would apologize to Japanese Americans for its wartime policy.

**Women help win the war.** As men joined the military and war industries expanded, millions of women replaced them in essential jobs. Women built ships and planes, produced munitions, and staffed offices. A popular British song recognized women's contributions:

66She's the girl that makes the thing that
  drills the hole that holds the spring
That drives the rod that turns the knob
  that works the thingumebob. . . .
And it's the girl that makes the thing
  that holds the oil that oils the ring
That works the thingumebob THAT'S
GOING TO WIN THE WAR!99

British and American women served in the armed forces in auxiliary roles—driving trucks and ambulances, delivering airplanes, decoding

# PARALLELS THROUGH TIME

## Women in Wartime

As they have since ancient times, women in this century played key roles in times of war. On farms and in factories, women workers produced the food, weapons, and other supplies needed for the war effort. Other women served as translators, spies, nurses, and bomb experts.

**Linking Past and Present** What opportunities did wartime service offer women during World War II? What opportunities do the armed forces offer women today?

**PAST** *Although the British and American armies did not allow women to serve in combat positions in World War II, women did serve in uniform as auxiliaries. In England, volunteers in the Women's Auxiliary Air Force (WAAF) worked alongside Royal Air Force pilots. Women also did dangerous work in the anti-Nazi resistance in occupied Europe. The Dutch woman below risked her life to distribute an anti-Nazi newspaper in Amsterdam.*

**PRESENT**
*Today, women play even more active roles in the armed forces. At right, women serve as soldiers in Operation Desert Storm. The Vietnam Women's Memorial, below, honors the women who lost their lives working in war zones as nurses and in other support positions.*

## World War II in Europe and North Africa

| | | | |
|---|---|---|---|
| ■ | European Axis Powers, 1942 | ■ | Allied territory, 1942 |
| ■ | Maximum extent of Axis control, 1942 | → | Allied advances |
| ■ | Neutral nations 1942 | ■ | Concentration camps 1939–1945 |

## GEOGRAPHY AND HISTORY

Axis power reached its height in Europe in 1942. Then the tide began to turn. The Allies scored successes in North Africa and went on to invade Europe through Italy and France.

**1. Location** On the map, locate (a) Vichy France, (b) Soviet Union, (c) El Alamein, (d) Berlin, (e) Normandy, (f) Palermo.

**2. Movement** (a) Describe the extent of the Axis advance to the east by 1942. (b) In what year did the Allies advance into Italy? (c) When did they advance through Romania?

**3. Critical Thinking** **Linking Past and Present** If you lived in Germany today, what do you think would be an appropriate way to commemorate the end of World War II?

messages, assisting at anti-aircraft sites. In occupied Europe, women fought in the resistance. Marie Fourcade, a French woman, directed 3,000 people in the underground and helped downed Allied pilots escape to safety.

Many Soviet women saw combat. Soviet pilot Lily Litvak, for example, shot down 12 German planes before she herself was killed.

## Turning Points

During 1942 and 1943, the Allies won several victories that would turn the tide of battle. The first turning points came in North Africa and Italy.

**El Alamein.** In Egypt, the British under General Bernard Montgomery finally stopped Rommel's advance during the long, fierce Battle of El Alamein. They then turned the tables on the Desert Fox, driving the Axis forces back across Libya into Tunisia.

Later in 1942, American general Dwight Eisenhower took command of a joint Anglo-American force in Morocco and Algeria. Advancing from the west, he combined with the British forces to trap Rommel's army, which surrendered in May 1943.

**Invasion of Italy.** Victory in North Africa let the Allies leap across the Mediterranean into Italy. In July 1943, a combined British and American army landed first in Sicily and then in southern Italy. They defeated the Italian forces there in about a month.

Italians, fed up with Mussolini, overthrew the Duce. The new Italian government signed an armistice, but the fighting did not end. Hitler sent German troops to rescue Mussolini and stiffen the will of Italians fighting in the north. For the next 18 months, the Allies pushed slowly up the Italian peninsula, suffering heavy losses against stiff German resistance. Still, the Italian invasion was a decisive event for the Allies because it weakened Hitler by forcing him to fight on another front.

## The Red Army Resists

Another major turning point in the war occurred in the Soviet Union. After their triumphant advance in 1941, the Germans were stalled outside Moscow and Leningrad. In 1942, Hitler launched a new offensive. This time, he aimed for the rich oil fields of the south. His troops, however, got only as far as the city of Stalingrad.

**Stalingrad.** The Battle of Stalingrad was one of the costliest of the war. Hitler was determined to capture Stalin's namesake city. Stalin was equally determined to defend it.

The battle began when the Germans surrounded the city. The Russians then encircled their attackers. As winter closed in, a bitter street-by-street, house-by-house struggle raged. Soldiers fought for two weeks for a single building, wrote a German officer. Corpses "are strewn in the cellars, on the landings and the staircases," he said.

Trapped, without food or ammunition and with no hope of rescue, the German commander finally surrendered in early 1943. The battle cost the Germans approximately 300,000 killed, wounded, or captured soldiers.

**Counterattack.** After the Battle of Stalingrad, the Red Army took the offensive. They lifted the siege of Leningrad and drove the invaders out of the Soviet Union. Hitler's forces suffered irreplaceable losses of troops and equipment. By early 1944, Soviet troops were advancing into Eastern Europe.

## Invasion of France

By 1944, the Allies were at last ready to open the long-awaited second front in Europe—the invasion of France. General Dwight Eisenhower was made the supreme Allied commander. He and other Allied leaders faced the enormous task of planning the operation and assembling troops and supplies. To prepare the

*Chapter 14*   **387**

way for the invasion, Allied bombers flew constant missions over Germany. They targeted factories and destroyed aircraft that might be used against the invasion force. They also destroyed many German cities.

The Allies chose June 6, 1944—D-Day, they called it—for the invasion of France. ( ★ See *Skills for Success*, page 398.) About 176,000 Allied troops were ferried across the English Channel. From landing craft, they fought their way to shore amid underwater mines and raking machine-gun fire. They clawed their way inland through the tangled hedges of Normandy. Finally, they broke through German defenses and advanced toward Paris. Meanwhile, other Allied forces sailed from Italy to land in southern France.

In Paris, French resistance forces rose up against the occupying Germans. Under pressure from all sides, the Germans retreated. On August 25, the Allies entered Paris. Joyous crowds in the "city of light" welcomed the liberators. Within a month, all of France was free. The next goal was Germany itself.

## SECTION 3 REVIEW

1. **Identify** (a) Holocaust, (b) Auschwitz, (c) Greater East Asia Co-Prosperity Sphere, (d) Battle of El Alamein, (e) Dwight Eisenhower, (f) Battle of Stalingrad, (g) D-Day.
2. **Define** collaborator.
3. (a) What was Hitler's "new order" in Europe? (b) How did the Japanese treat the people they conquered?
4. (a) How did democratic governments mobilize their economies for war? (b) How did they limit the rights of citizens?
5. How was each of the following battles a turning point in the war: (a) El Alamein, (b) Stalingrad?
6. *Critical Thinking* **Defending a Position** Do you think that democratic governments should be allowed to limit their citizens' freedoms during wartime? Defend your position.
7. *ACTIVITY* Write a poem or design a memorial commemorating the millions who died in the Holocaust.

# 4 Toward Victory

## Guide for Reading

- What battles were turning points in the Pacific war?
- How did the Allied forces defeat Germany?
- Why did the United States use the atomic bomb on Japan?
- **Vocabulary** *kamikaze*

While the Allies battled to liberate Europe, fighting against the Japanese in Asia raged on. The war in Southeast Asia and the Pacific was very different from that in Europe. Most battles were fought at sea, on tiny islands, or in deep jungles. At first, the Japanese won an uninterrupted series of victories. By mid-1942, however, the tide began to turn.

## War in the Pacific

A major turning point in the Pacific war occurred just six months after the bombing of Pearl Harbor. In May and June 1942, American warships and airplanes severely damaged two Japanese fleets during the battles of the Coral Sea and Midway Island. These victories greatly weakened Japanese naval power and stopped the Japanese advance.

After the Battle of Midway, the United States took the offensive. That summer, under the command of General Douglas MacArthur, United States Marines landed at Guadalcanal in the Solomon Islands, the first step in an "island-hopping" campaign. The goal of the campaign was to recapture some Japanese-held islands while bypassing others. The captured islands served as stepping stones to the next objective. In this way, American forces gradually moved north from the Solomon Islands toward Japan itself. (See the map on page 389.)

On the captured islands, the Americans built air bases to enable them to carry the war closer to Japan. By 1944, American ships were blockading Japan, while American bombers pounded Japanese cities and industries.

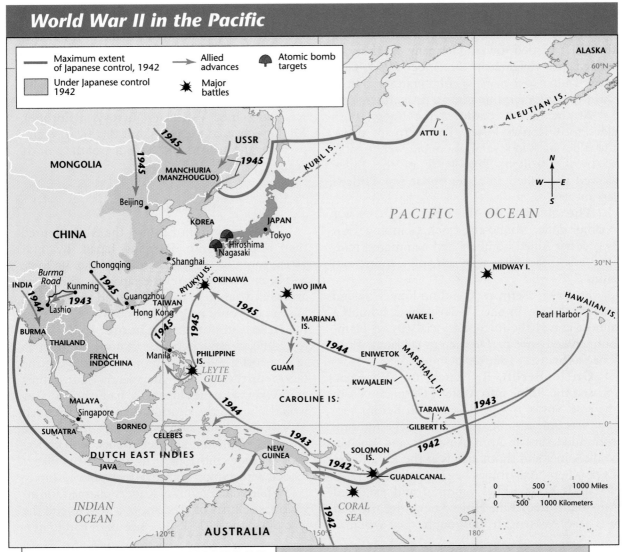

# World War II in the Pacific

**Legend:**
- Maximum extent of Japanese control, 1942
- Under Japanese control 1942
- Allied advances
- Major battles
- Atomic bomb targets

ALASKA
60°N
ALEUTIAN IS.
ATTU I.
KURIL IS.
USSR
MONGOLIA
MANCHURIA (MANZHOUGUO)
1945
1945
1945
Beijing
KOREA
JAPAN
Tokyo
Hiroshima
Nagasaki
PACIFIC OCEAN
CHINA
Chongqing
Shanghai
MIDWAY I.
30°N
Burma Road
INDIA
Kunming
1945
RYUKYU IS.
OKINAWA
IWO JIMA
HAWAIIAN IS.
1944
Lashio
1943
Guangzhou
TAIWAN
Hong Kong
1945
1945
1945
MARIANA IS.
WAKE I.
Pearl Harbor
BURMA
THAILAND
FRENCH INDOCHINA
Manila
PHILIPPINE IS.
LEYTE GULF
GUAM
ENIWETOK
MARSHALL IS.
1944
MALAYA
Singapore
BORNEO
CELEBES
1944
KWAJALEIN
CAROLINE IS.
TARAWA
1943
SUMATRA
1943
GILBERT IS.
0°
DUTCH EAST INDIES
JAVA
NEW GUINEA
1942
SOLOMON IS.
1942
GUADALCANAL
0    500    1000 Miles
0    500    1000 Kilometers
INDIAN OCEAN
CORAL SEA
1942
AUSTRALIA
120°E
150°E
180°

## GEOGRAPHY AND HISTORY

*For six months after the bombing of Pearl Harbor, the Japanese won a series of uninterrupted victories. After the Battle of Midway, however, the Allies took the offensive in the Pacific. Their goal was to recapture the Philippines and invade Japan.*

**1. Location** On the map, locate (a) Japan, (b) Midway Island, (c) Pearl Harbor, (d) Iwo Jima, (e) Hiroshima, (f) Burma Road, (g) Manchuria.

**2. Movement** (a) Did Japan ever gain control of New Guinea? Explain. (b) When did the Allies advance into Manchuria? (c) When did they reach the Philippines?

**3. Critical Thinking Making Inferences** How did geography make it difficult for Japan to keep control of its empire?

In October 1944, MacArthur began to retake the Philippines. The British meanwhile were pushing the Japanese back in the jungles of Burma and Malaya. Despite such setbacks, the militarists who dominated the Japanese government rejected any suggestions of surrender.

## The Nazis Defeated

Hitler, too, scorned talk of surrender. "If the war is to be lost," he declared, "the nation also will perish." To win the assault on "Fortress Europe," the Allies had to use devastating force.

**Battle of the Bulge.** After freeing France, the Allies battled toward Germany. As they advanced into Belgium in December 1944, Germany launched a massive counterattack. Hitler was throwing everything into a final effort.

At the bloody Battle of the Bulge, both sides took terrible losses. The Germans drove the Allies back in several places but were unable to break through. The Battle of the Bulge slowed the Allied advance, but it was Hitler's last success.

**The air war.** By this time, Germany was reeling under round-the-clock bombing. For two years, Allied bombers had hammered military bases, factories, railroads, oil depots, and cities.

By 1945, Germany could no longer defend itself in the air. In one 10-day period, bombing almost erased the huge industrial city of Hamburg. Allied raids on Dresden in February 1945 killed as many as 135,000 people.

**On to Berlin.** By March, the Allies had crossed the Rhine into western Germany. From the east, Soviet troops closed in on Berlin. Victory was only months away, but savage fighting continued. In late April, American and Russian soldiers met and shook hands at the Elbe River. Everywhere, Axis armies began to surrender.

In Italy, guerrillas captured and executed Mussolini. In Berlin, Hitler knew that the end was near. As Soviet troops fought their way into the city, Hitler committed suicide in his underground bunker. After just 12 years, Hitler's "thousand-year Reich" was a smoldering ruin.

On May 7, Germany surrendered. Officially, the war in Europe ended the next day, which was proclaimed V-E Day (Victory in Europe). Millions cheered the news, but the joy was tempered by the horrors and tragedies of the past six years.

## Defeat of Japan

With war won in Europe, the Allies poured their resources into defeating Japan. By mid-1945, most of the Japanese navy and air force had been destroyed. Yet the Japanese still had an army of two million men. The road to victory, it appeared, would be long and costly.

**Invasion versus the bomb.** Some American officials estimated that an invasion of Japan would cost a million or more casualties. At the bloody battles to take the islands of Iwo Jima and Okinawa, the Japanese had shown they would fight to the death rather than surrender. To save their homeland, young Japanese became kamikaze (kah mih KAH zee) pilots, who undertook suicide missions, crashing their planes loaded with explosives into American warships.

While Allied military leaders planned for invasion, scientists offered another way to end the war. Since the early 1900s, scientists had under-

**Meeting of the "Big Three"** The three main Allied leaders—(left to right) Churchill, Roosevelt, and Stalin—met several times during the war. Their last meeting, shown here, took place at the Soviet city of Yalta in February 1945. There, they planned "the whole shape and structure of post-war Europe." As German authority ended, the Soviets were the de facto rulers in eastern Europe. The three leaders agreed that Stalin would oversee free elections. This concession would become a key factor in the Cold War that began after 1945. **Global Interaction** Why do you think the Big Three went to the trouble to meet in person?

stood that matter, made up of atoms, could be converted into pure energy. (See page 354.) In military terms, this meant that, by splitting the atom, scientists could create an explosion far more powerful than any yet known. During the war, Allied scientists, some of them refugees from Hitler's Germany, raced to harness the atom. In July 1945, at Alamogordo, New Mexico, they successfully tested the first atomic bomb.

News of the test was brought to the new American President, Harry Truman. Truman had taken office after FDR died unexpectedly on April 12. Truman knew that the atomic bomb was a terrible new force for destruction. Still, after consulting with his advisers, he decided to use the new weapon.

At the time, Truman was meeting with Allied leaders in the city of Potsdam, Germany. They issued a warning to Japan to surrender or face "utter and complete destruction." When the Japanese ignored the deadline, the United States took action.

**The Atomic Bomb** *In August 1945, the world entered the atomic age. On August 6 and August 9, American airplanes dropped single atomic bombs on the Japanese cities of Hiroshima and Nagasaki. The force of the explosions vaporized glass, metal, concrete, and human flesh. The center of Hiroshima, shown here, became a barren wasteland. Japan surrendered a few days after the second bombing.*
**Religions and Value Systems** *What were some of the arguments for and against dropping the atomic bomb on Japan?*

**Hiroshima.** On August 6, 1945, an American plane dropped an atomic bomb on the mid-sized city of Hiroshima. Residents saw "a strong flash of light"—and then, total destruction. The bomb flattened four square miles and instantly killed more than 70,000 people. In the months that followed, many more would die from radiation sickness, a deadly after-effect from exposure to radioactive materials.

Truman warned the Japanese that if they did not surrender, they could expect "a rain of ruin from the air the like of which has never been seen on this Earth." And on August 8, the Soviet Union declared war on Japan and invaded Manchuria. Still, Japanese leaders did not respond. The next day, the United States dropped a second atomic bomb, on Nagasaki, killing more than 40,000 people.

Some members of the Japanese cabinet wanted to fight on. Other leaders disagreed. Finally, on August 10, Emperor Hirohito intervened—an action unheard of for a Japanese emperor—forcing the government to surrender. On September 2, 1945, the formal peace treaty was signed on board the American battleship

After learning that American scientists had developed an atomic bomb, President Truman had jotted in his diary, "It's a good thing that Hitler's crowd or Stalin's did not discover this atomic bomb." Four years later, the Soviets had the bomb, too. Other nations soon joined the nuclear club. Britain conducted its first nuclear test in Australia in 1952. France followed suit in 1960. China was next. By the 1990s, Argentina, Brazil, India, Pakistan, and South Africa were all close to possessing a workable nuclear bomb.

*Missouri*, which was anchored in Tokyo Bay. The war had ended.

**An ongoing controversy.** Dropping the atomic bomb on Japan brought a quick end to World War II. It also unleashed terrifying destruction. Ever since, people have debated whether or not the United States should have used the bomb.

Why did Truman use the bomb? First, he was convinced that Japan would not surrender without an invasion that would cost an enormous loss of both American and Japanese lives. Growing differences between the United States and the Soviet Union may also have influenced his decision. Truman may have hoped the bomb would impress the Soviets with American power. At any rate, the Japanese surrendered shortly after the bombs were dropped, and World War II was ended.

## *Looking Ahead*

After the surrender, American forces occupied the smoldering ruins of Japan. In Germany, meanwhile, the Allies had divided Hitler's fallen empire into four zones of occupation—French, British, American, and Russian. In both countries, the Allies faced difficult decisions about the future. How could they avoid the mistakes of 1919 and build the foundations for a stable world peace?

## SECTION 4 REVIEW

1. **Identify** (a) Battle of the Coral Sea, (b) Battle of the Bulge, (c) V-E Day, (d) Harry Truman.
2. **Define** kamikaze.
3. How did the United States bring the war closer to Japan?
4. (a) How did the Allies weaken Germany? (b) Why was the Battle of the Bulge significant?
5. *Critical Thinking* **Making Decisions** Imagine that you are President Truman. What information would you want before making the decision to drop an atomic bomb on Japan?
6. *ACTIVITY* Write a series of newspaper headlines reporting the final months of the war in Europe.

# 5 From World War to Cold War

## Guide for Reading

- ■ What were the human and material costs of World War II?
- ■ How did World War II change the global balance of power?
- ■ What were the origins of the Cold War?
- ■ **Vocabulary** *containment*

"Give me ten years and you will not be able to recognize Germany," said Hitler in 1933. His prophecy was correct—although not in the way he intended. In 1945, Germany was an unrecognizable ruin. Poland, Russia, Ukraine, Japan, and many other lands also lay in ruins. Total war had gutted cities, factories, harbors, bridges, railroads, farms, homes—and lives. Millions of refugees, displaced by war or liberated from prison camps, wandered the land. Amid the devastation, hunger and disease took large tolls for years after the fighting ended.

## *Aftermath of War*

While the Allies celebrated victory, the appalling costs of the war began to emerge. The global conflict had raged in Asia since Japan invaded China in 1937 and in Europe since 1939. It had killed as many as 75 million people worldwide. In Europe, about 38 million people lost their lives, many of them civilians. The Soviet Union suffered the worst casualties—more than 22 million dead.

Numbers alone did not tell the story of the Nazi nightmare in Europe or the Japanese brutality in Asia. In the aftermath of war, new atrocities came to light.

**Horrors of the Holocaust.** During the war, the Allies knew about the existence of Nazi concentration camps. But only at war's end did they learn the full extent of the Holocaust and the tortures and misery inflicted on Jews and others in the Nazi camps. General Dwight Eisenhower, who visited the camps, was stunned

## Casualties in World War II

| | Military Dead* | Military Wounded* | Civilian Dead* |
|---|---|---|---|
| **Allies** | | | |
| Britain | 389,000 | 475,000 | 65,000 |
| France | 211,000 | 400,000 | 108,000 |
| Soviet Union | 7,500,000 | 14,102,000 | 15,000,000 |
| United States | 292,000 | 671,000 | † |
| **Axis** | | | |
| Germany | 2,850,000 | 7,250,000 | 5,000,000 |
| Italy | 77,500 | 120,000 | 100,000 |
| Japan | 1,576,000 | 500,000 | 300,000 |

Source: Henri Michel, *The Second World War*

*All figures are estimates.
†Very small number of civilian dead

**Interpreting a Chart** *World War II resulted in enormous casualties. Because planes carried destruction far beyond the battlefield, civilians suffered more than in World War I, and civilian deaths reached record numbers.* ■ *Which nation suffered the greatest number of both civilian and military casualties?*

to come "face to face with indisputable evidence of Nazi brutality and ruthless disregard of every sense of decency."

Walking skeletons stumbled out of the death camps with tales of mass murder. The Nazi Rudolf Hoess, commander at Auschwitz, would admit that he had supervised the killing of two and a half million people, not counting those who died of disease or starvation.

**War crimes trials.** At wartime meetings, the Allies had agreed that Axis leaders should be tried for "crimes against humanity." In Germany, the Allies held war crimes trials in Nuremberg, where Hitler had staged mass rallies in the 1930s. A handful of top Nazis received death sentences. Others were imprisoned. Similar war crimes trials were held in Japan and Italy. The trials showed that political and military leaders could be held accountable for actions in wartime.

**Allied occupation.** The war crimes trials served another purpose. By exposing the savagery of the Axis regimes, they further discredited the Nazi, fascist, and militarist ideologies that had led to the war.

Yet disturbing questions haunted people then, as now. How had the Nazi horrors happened? Why had ordinary people in Germany, Poland, France, and elsewhere accepted and even collaborated in Hitler's "final solution"? How could the world prevent dictators from again terrorizing Europe or Asia?

The Allies tried to address those issues when they occupied Germany and Japan. The United States felt that strengthening democracy would ensure tolerance and peace. The western Allies built new governments with democratic constitutions to protect the rights of all citizens. In German schools, for example, Nazi textbooks and courses were replaced with a new curriculum that taught democratic principles.

### The United Nations

As in 1919, the World War II Allies set up an international organization to secure the peace. In April 1945, delegates from 50 nations met in San Francisco to draft a charter for the United Nations. The UN would last longer and play a much greater role in world affairs than its predecessor, the League of Nations.

Under the UN Charter, each member nation had one vote in the General Assembly, where members could debate issues. The much smaller Security Council was given greater power. Its five permanent members—the United States, the Soviet Union (today Russia), Britain, France, and China—all have the right to veto any council decision. The goal was to give these great powers the authority to ensure the peace. Often, however, differences among these powerful nations kept the UN from taking action on controversial issues.

The UN's work would go far beyond peacekeeping. The organization would take on many world problems—from preventing disease and improving education to protecting refugees and aiding nations to develop economically. UN agencies, like the World Health Organization and the Food and Agricultural Organization, have provided help for millions of people around the world. You will read more about the activities of the United Nations in later chapters.

## The Crumbling Alliance

Amid the rubble of war, a new power structure emerged that would shape events in the postwar world. In Europe, Germany was defeated. France and Britain were drained and exhausted. Two other powers, the United States and the Soviet Union, had brought about the final victory. Before long, these two nations would become superpowers with the economic resources and military might to dominate the globe. They would also become tense rivals in an increasingly divided world.

**Growing differences.** During the war, the Soviet Union and the nations of the West had cooperated to defeat Nazi Germany. By 1945, however, the wartime alliance was crumbling. Conflicting ideologies and mutual distrust divided the former Allies and soon led to the conflict known as the Cold War. The Cold War was a state of tension and hostility among nations without armed conflict between the major rivals. At first, the focus of the Cold War was Eastern Europe, where Stalin and the western powers had very different goals.*

---

*Stalin was deeply suspicious of other powers. Russia had been invaded by Napoleon's armies and by Germans in World Wars I and II. Also, the United States and Britain had both sent troops into Russia during World War I. (See page 306.)

**Origins of the Cold War.** Stalin had two goals in Eastern Europe. First, he wanted to spread communism into the area. And second, he wanted to create a buffer zone of friendly governments as a defense against Germany, which had invaded Russia during World War I and again in 1941.

As the Red Army had pushed German forces out of Eastern Europe, it left behind occupying forces. At wartime conferences, Stalin tried to get the West to accept Soviet influence in the region. He bluntly claimed:

66Whoever occupies a territory also imposes his own social system. Everyone imposes his own system as far as his armies can reach. It cannot be otherwise.99

The Soviet dictator pointed out that the United States was not consulting the Soviet Union about peace terms for Italy or Japan, defeated and occupied by American and British troops. In the same way, Russia would determine the fate of the Eastern European lands overrun by the Red Army on its way to Berlin.

Roosevelt and Churchill rejected Stalin's view, making him promise "free elections" in Eastern Europe. Stalin ignored that pledge. Backed by the Red Army, local communists in Poland, Czechoslovakia, and elsewhere destroyed rival political parties and even assassinated democratic leaders. By 1948, Stalin had installed pro-Soviet communist governments throughout Eastern Europe.

**"An iron curtain."** Churchill had long distrusted Stalin. As early as 1946, on a visit to the United States, he warned of the new danger facing the war-weary world:

66A shadow has fallen upon the scenes so lately lighted by the Allied victories. . . . From Stettin in the Baltic to Trieste in the Adriatic, an iron curtain has descended across the Continent. Warsaw, Berlin, Prague, Vienna, Budapest, Belgrade, Bucharest, and Sofia, all these famous cities and populations around them lie in what I must call the Soviet sphere and all are subject to a very high and, in many cases, increasing measure of control from Moscow.99

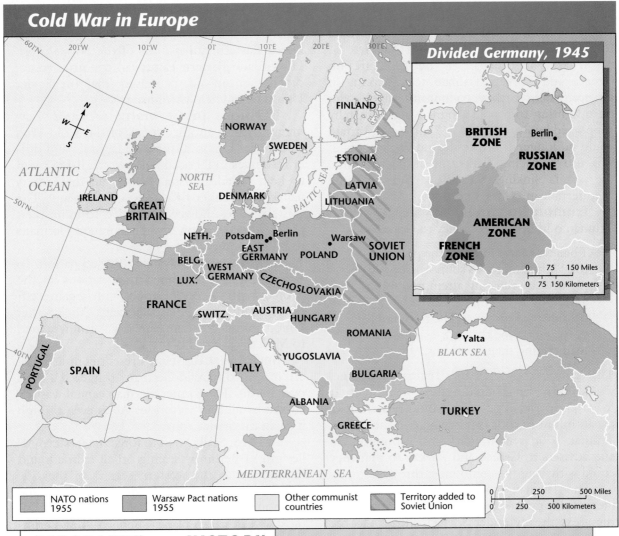

# Cold War in Europe

**Divided Germany, 1945**

BRITISH ZONE
Berlin
RUSSIAN ZONE
AMERICAN ZONE
FRENCH ZONE

0    75    150 Miles
0    75    150 Kilometers

FINLAND
NORWAY
SWEDEN
ESTONIA
LATVIA
LITHUANIA
ATLANTIC OCEAN
NORTH SEA
IRELAND
GREAT BRITAIN
DENMARK
BALTIC SEA
NETH.
Potsdam  Berlin
EAST GERMANY
Warsaw
SOVIET UNION
BELG.
WEST GERMANY
POLAND
LUX.
CZECHOSLOVAKIA
FRANCE
SWITZ.
AUSTRIA
HUNGARY
ROMANIA
Yalta
BLACK SEA
PORTUGAL
SPAIN
ITALY
YUGOSLAVIA
BULGARIA
ALBANIA
GREECE
TURKEY
MEDITERRANEAN SEA

NATO nations 1955 | Warsaw Pact nations 1955 | Other communist countries | Territory added to Soviet Union

0    250    500 Miles
0    250    500 Kilometers

## GEOGRAPHY AND HISTORY

By 1955, the Cold War was well underway in Europe. Western nations had joined to form NATO. In response, the Soviet Union formed the Warsaw Pact. Meanwhile, Germany, as well as the city of Berlin, was divided into communist and non-communist zones of occupation.

1. **Location** On the main map, locate (a) West Germany, (b) East Germany, (c) Lithuania, (d) Warsaw Pact nations.
2. **Region** Use the inset map to identify the occupation zone in which Berlin was located.
3. **Critical Thinking** **Synthesizing Information** Why would Turkey be a likely locale for a Cold War conflict?

In the West, Churchill's "iron curtain" became a symbol of the Cold War. It expressed the growing fear of communism. More important, it described the division of Europe into an "eastern" and "western" bloc. In the East were the Soviet-dominated, communist countries of Eastern Europe. In the West were the western democracies, led by the United States.

## Containing Communism

Like Churchill, President Truman saw communism as an evil force creeping across Europe and threatening countries around the world, including China. To deal with that threat, the United States abandoned its traditional isolationism. Unlike after World War I, when it withdrew from global affairs, it took a leading role on the world stage after World War II.

When Stalin began to put pressure on Greece and Turkey, Truman took action. In Greece, Stalin backed communist rebels who were fighting to topple a right-wing monarchy supported by Britain. By 1947, however, Britain could no longer afford to defend Greece. Stalin was also menacing Turkey in the Dardanelles, the straits linking the Black Sea and the Mediterranean.

**Truman Doctrine.** On March 12, 1947, Truman outlined a new policy to Congress:

> ❝I believe that it must be the policy of the United States to support free people who are resisting attempted subjugation by armed minorities or by outside pressures. . . . The free peoples of the world look to us for support in maintaining their freedoms.❞

This policy, known as the Truman Doctrine, would guide the United States for decades. It made clear that Americans would resist Soviet expansion in Europe or elsewhere in the world. Truman soon sent military and economic aid and advisers to Greece and Turkey so that they could withstand the communist threat.

The Truman Doctrine was rooted in the idea of containment, limiting communism to the areas already under Soviet control. George Kennan, the American statesman who first proposed this approach, believed that communism would eventually destroy itself. With "patient but firm and vigilant containment," he said, the United States could stop Soviet expansion. Stalin, however, saw containment as "encirclement" by the capitalist world that wanted to isolate the Soviet Union.

**The Marshall Plan.** Postwar hunger and poverty made Western European lands fertile ground for communist ideas. To strengthen democratic governments, the United States offered a massive aid package, called the Marshall Plan. Under it, the United States funneled food and economic assistance to Europe to help countries rebuild. Billions in American aid helped war-shattered Europe recover rapidly and reduced communist influence there.

President Truman also offered aid to the Soviet Union and its satellites in Eastern Europe. Stalin, however, saw the plan as a trick to knock Eastern Europe out of the Soviet orbit. He forbade Eastern European countries to accept American aid, promising that the Soviet Union would help them instead.

**Divisions in Germany.** Defeated Germany became another focus of the Cold War. The Soviet Union dismantled factories and other resources in its occupation zone, using them to help rebuild Russia. Above all, the Soviets feared the danger of a restored Germany. The western Allies, however, decided to unite their zones of occupation and encouraged Germans to rebuild industries.

Germany thus became a divided nation. In West Germany, the democratic nations let the people write a constitution and regain self-government. In East Germany, the Soviet Union installed a communist government tied to Moscow.

**Berlin airlift.** Stalin's resentment at western moves to rebuild Germany triggered a crisis over Berlin. The former German capital was occupied by all four victorious Allies even though it lay in the Soviet zone.

In 1948, Stalin tried to force the western Allies out of Berlin by sealing off all railroads and highways into the western sectors of the city. The western powers responded to the blockade by mounting a round-the-clock airlift. For almost a year, cargo planes supplied West Berliners with food and fuel. Their success forced the Soviets to end the blockade. The West had won a victory in the Cold War, but the crisis deepened the hostility between the two camps.

**Military alliances.** In 1949, as tensions grew, the United States, Canada, and nine Western European countries formed a military alliance. It was called the North Atlantic Treaty Organization (NATO). Members of NATO pledged to help one another if any one of them was attacked.

In 1955, the Soviet Union responded by forming its own military alliance, the Warsaw Pact. It included the USSR and seven satellite states in Eastern Europe. Unlike NATO, however, the Warsaw Pact was a weapon used by the Soviets to keep its satellites in order.

**The arms race.** Each side in the Cold War armed itself to withstand an attack by the other. At first, the United States, which had the atomic

**The Arms Race** *World War II and the Cold War changed American society. Before the war, the United States had spent less on the military than many European countries. After the war, military spending remained high, and the military became increasingly important to the economy. This postwar cartoon shows a toy store filled with missiles and other weapons.* **Art and Literature** *What point is the cartoonist making about postwar American society?*

bomb, held an advantage. But Stalin's top scientists were under orders to develop an atomic bomb. When they succeeded in 1949, the arms race was on.

For four decades, the superpowers spent fantastic sums to develop new, more deadly nuclear and conventional weapons. They invested still more to improve "delivery systems"—the bombers, missiles, and submarines to launch these terrifying weapons of mass destruction. Soon, the global balance of power became, in Churchill's phrase, a "balance of terror."

**The propaganda war.** Both sides campaigned in a propaganda war. The United States spoke of defending capitalism and democracy against communism and totalitarianism. The Soviet Union claimed the moral high ground in the struggle against western imperialism. Yet linked to those stands, both sides sought world power.

**Looking ahead.** In 1945, the world hoped for an end to decades of economic crisis, bloody dictators, and savage war. Instead, it faced new tensions.

The Cold War would last for more than 40 years. Rivalry between the hostile camps would not only divide Europe but would also fuel crises around the world. It would drain the resources of the United States and exhaust those of the Soviet Union. Though it would not erupt into large-scale fighting between the two superpowers, many small wars broke out, with the superpowers championing opposite sides. Meanwhile, the spread of ominous new weapons would more than once raise the specter of global destruction.

## SECTION 5 REVIEW

1. **Identify** (a) UN, (b) "iron curtain," (c) Truman Doctrine, (d) Berlin airlift, (e) NATO, (f) Warsaw Pact.
2. **Define** containment.
3. (a) Describe conditions that total war had created in Europe and Asia following World War II. (b) How did the Allies try to hold the Axis leaders responsible for the suffering they caused during the war?
4. (a) Who were the superpowers that emerged after World War II? (b) What were the main differences between them?
5. State two causes of the Cold War.
6. *Critical Thinking* **Recognizing Causes and Effects** Some historians argue that the Cold War began in 1918 when the World War I Allies, including the United States, sent forces to Russia to topple the Bolsheviks there. How might they support this position?
7. *ACTIVITY* Use Churchill's "iron curtain" image to create a political cartoon about the Cold War.

## CHAPTER REVIEW

### REVIEWING VOCABULARY

(a) Classify each of the vocabulary words introduced in this chapter under one of the following themes: Economics and Technology, Political and Social Systems, Global Interaction. (b) Choose one word in each category and write a sentence explaining how that word relates to the theme.

### REVIEWING FACTS

1. What happened at the Munich Conference of 1938?

2. What event started World War II? When did it occur?

3. What event brought the United States into World War II? When did it occur?

4. What means did Nazi Germany use in its attempt to murder all European Jews?

5. Why was the Battle of Stalingrad important?

6. Explain the American "island-hopping" campaign.

7. When and why was the United Nations established?

8. What was the Truman Doctrine?

## SKILLS FOR SUCCESS    MAKING DECISIONS

Decisions involve choices between alternatives. You have already learned how to identify alternatives and project their consequences. (See page 238.) In this lesson, you will build on that skill in order to learn how to make decisions.

During World War II, General Dwight Eisenhower had the task of preparing the invasion of France. The excerpt below is from his memoir, *Crusade in Europe.* Read the excerpt and follow the steps to analyze how and why Eisenhower chose June 6, 1944, for D-Day.

1. **Identify the alternatives.** (a) What date had originally been set for the Normandy landing? (b) What other date did Eisenhower consider? Why?

2. **Project the consequences for each alternative.** (a) What were possible consequences of a landing on June 5? (b) What were possible consequences of a landing on June 6?

3. **Make the decision.** (a) What did Eisenhower decide? (b) Why?

*Dwight D. Eisenhower*
66The final conference for determining the feasibility of attacking on the selected day, June 5, was scheduled for 4:00 A.M. on June 4. However, some of the attacking [groups] had already been ordered to sea. . . .

When the commanders assembled on June 4 . . . the report we received was discouraging. . . . The meteorologists said that air support would be impossible, naval gunfire would be inefficient, and even the handling of small boats would be rendered difficult. . . . Weighing all factors, I decided that the attack would have to be postponed. . . .

[The next morning] . . . the first report was that . . . if we had persisted in the attempt to land on June 5 a major disaster would almost surely have resulted. [They told us] that by the following morning a period of relatively good weather . . . would ensue, lasting probably 36 hours. . . .

The prospect was not bright because of the possibility that we might land the first several waves successfully and then find later build-up impracticable, and so have to leave the isolated original attacking forces easy prey to German counteraction. However, the consequences of the delay justified great risk and I quickly announced the decision to go ahead with the attack on June 6.99

## REVIEWING CHAPTER THEMES

Review the "Focus On" questions at the start of this chapter. Then select *three* of those questions and answer them, using information from the chapter.

## CRITICAL THINKING

1. **Analyzing Information** Why do you think some historians call the period from 1919 to 1939 the 20-year armistice?

2. **Linking Past and Present** What lessons does the Holocaust have for us today?

3. **Analyzing Information** Explain the following statement: World War II brought down several dictatorships but at the same time increased the power of the world's largest totalitarian state.

## ANALYZING PRIMARY SOURCES

Use the quotation by Winston Churchill on page 378 to answer the following questions.

1. What was Churchill's basic message?

2. What phrase is repeatedly used in this excerpt?

3. Why do you think Churchill used the technique of repetition?

## FOR YOUR PORTFOLIO

**CONDUCTING AN INTERVIEW** Interview someone who lived during World War II. Begin by locating a person who was born before World War II. Explain your assignment and request permission to tape an oral history. Hold a preliminary meeting with the interviewee, at which you can share the topics you plan to cover. (Possible topics include life on the home front and memories of critical events, such as the Japanese attack on Pearl Harbor.) Offer the interviewee the chance to refresh his or her memory of the events. Then set the date and time for the interview. Finally, tape record the interview and share it with your class.

### Key Events of World War II

| Event | Outcome |
|---|---|
| 1939: German invasion of Poland | Britain and France declare war on Germany |
| 1941: Japanese attack on Pearl Harbor | United States declares war on Japan |
| 1942: Battle of Midway | United States forces take the offensive in the Pacific |
| 1942–1943: Battle of Stalingrad | Red Army takes the offensive in the Soviet Union |
| 1944: Allied invasion of France (D-Day) | Allied troops take the offensive in Western Europe |
| 1945: Fall of Berlin | Germany surrenders |
| 1945: Atomic bombing of Hiroshima and Nagasaki | Japan surrenders |

## ANALYZING TABLES

Use the table and information from the chapter to answer the following questions.

1. What event caused the United States to enter the war?

2. What events marked turning points that led to an Allied victory in the war?

3. What event or events marked the end of World War II?

4. If you could add one key event to this list, which event would you choose? Why?

## INTERNET ACTIVITY

**MAKING A TIME LINE** Use the Internet to research some important events of World War II. Then create a time line that shows the progression of the war. Use a special color or other design to present especially important dates, such as the war's beginning and end and major turning points.

# Unit-in-Brief

UNIT

3

# World Wars and Revolutions

**Chapter 10** World War I
and Its Aftermath
(1914–1919)

Many forces—including nationalism, militarism, and imperialist rivalries—propelled Europe into World War I. This massive conflict engulfed much of the world for four years and ushered in a new age of modern warfare.

- Two huge alliances emerged in Europe: the Central Powers, dominated by Germany and Austria-Hungary, and the Allies, led by France, Britain, and Russia.
- Although the assassination of Archduke Francis Ferdinand in 1914 ignited World War I, historians agree that all the major powers share blame for the conflict.
- Trench warfare and new weapons contributed to a stalemate on the Western Front.
- In 1917, the United States entered the war, allowing the Allies to achieve victory.
- The Paris peace conference imposed heavy penalties on Germany and redrew the map of Eastern Europe.

**Chapter 11** Revolution in Russia
(1917–1939)

V. I. Lenin and his successors transformed czarist Russia into the communist Soviet Union. This experiment in single-party politics and a state-run economy would exert a powerful influence over the modern world for almost 75 years.

- In March 1917, political, social, and economic conditions in Russia sparked a revolution that overthrew the czar and paved the way for more radical changes.
- After leading the Bolsheviks to power in October 1917, Lenin hoped to build the classless, communist state envisioned by Karl Marx.
- Lenin's successor, Stalin, imposed "five-year plans" to build industry and farm output.
- Stalin created a totalitarian state, employing censorship, propaganda, and terror to ensure personal power and push the Soviet Union toward modernization.

**Chapter 12** Nationalism and
Revolution Around
the World (1914–1939)

Between 1919 and 1939, the desire for democracy and self-determination contributed to explosive struggles in many regions. New leaders in Africa, Latin America, and Asia built liberation movements that would change the world.

- The Mexican Revolution opened the door to social and economic reforms.
- Latin American leaders promoted economic nationalism, seeking to end dependence on the industrial powers.

- In Africa, a new generation of leaders called for an end to imperialism and reaffirmed traditional cultures.
- Arab nationalism gave rise to Pan-Arabism, a movement which sought to end foreign domination and unite Arabs in their own state.
- In India, Gandhi led a campaign of nonviolent resistance to British rule.
- In China, foreigners extended their spheres of influence. Later, communists and nationalists engaged in civil war.
- During the 1920s and 1930s, extreme nationalism and economic upheaval set Japan on a militaristic and expansionist path.

### Chapter 13 Crisis of Democracy in the West
(1919–1939)

After World War I, western nations worked to restore prosperity and ensure peace. At the same time, political and economic turmoil in the 1920s and 1930s challenged democratic traditions and led to the rise of powerful dictators.

- The Great Depression of the 1930s created financial turmoil and widespread suffering throughout the industrialized world.
- Scientific discoveries, new trends in literature and the arts, and social changes all contributed to a sense of uncertainty.
- Three systems of government—democracy, communism, and fascism—competed for influence in postwar Europe.
- In Italy, Mussolini and his Fascist party took advantage of economic and political unrest to win power in the 1920s.

- In Germany, Hitler rose to power by appealing to extreme nationalism, anti-Semitism, anti-communism, and resentment of the Treaty of Versailles. In the 1930s, he turned Germany into a totalitarian Nazi dictatorship.

### Chapter 14 World War II and Its Aftermath
(1931–1949)

Between 1939 and 1945, nations all over the globe fought World War II, the largest and most costly conflict in history. The war shifted the balance of world power from Western Europe to the United States and the Soviet Union.

- The Axis powers—Germany, Italy, and Japan—embarked on a course of aggression in the late 1930s. At first, France and Britain adopted a policy of appeasement but finally declared war when Hitler invaded Poland.
- The Axis at first enjoyed an unbroken string of victories in Europe.
- During the Holocaust, the Nazis systematically killed more than six million Jews, as well as millions of other people the Nazis considered undesirable.
- The Soviet Union and the United States joined the war on the Allied side. Allied victories in North Africa and Europe eventually led to the defeat of Germany.
- To force a Japanese surrender, the United States employed a powerful new weapon, the atomic bomb.
- World War II was followed by the Cold War, which pitted the western democracies, led by the United States, against the communist bloc, dominated by the Soviet Union.

# A Global View

## How Did World Events Reflect Growing Interaction?

Future historians may view the first half of the twentieth century as a giant step backward in human history. The events that swept the globe between 1900 and 1945 pitted many peoples around the world against one another or against their own governments.

The two world wars revealed a world that was violently divided. Revolutions tore through some of the world's largest nations. Cruel dictatorships arose in others. We might conclude that, at this point in history, people simply could not live together in harmony.

### A World Drawn Together

Amid such division, it is hard to see evidence of a world moving together. Yet these terrible events were also signs of a movement toward the globalization of history. The major events, trends, and even disasters of the period were, after all, increasingly global in scope.

World War I was fought mostly in Europe between European armies. But, as we have seen, non-Europeans also fought in that war, and there were battles beyond the continent. Certainly, the causes and consequences of World War I were global in scale.

The world economy in the early part of the century was still dominated by the West— German factories, American farms, stock exchanges in New York and London. But Japan was quickly joining the ranks of leading economic powers. In addition, ties of trade or empire linked Asia, Africa, and Latin America to the dominant economies.

Such economic connections meant that all regions were affected by the prosperity of the 1920s. But, by the same token, the Great Depression of the 1930s, which began in the United States, quickly escalated into a global disaster.

### Political Upheavals

The early 1900s also saw the longest and bloodiest revolutions in a century. Unlike the democratic revolutions that took place in Europe and Latin

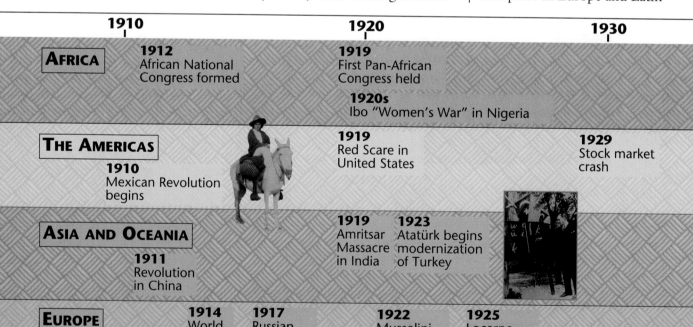

**1910**    **1920**    **1930**

**AFRICA**
1912
African National
Congress formed

1919
First Pan-African
Congress held

1920s
Ibo "Women's War" in Nigeria

**THE AMERICAS**
1910
Mexican Revolution
begins

1919
Red Scare in
United States

1929
Stock market
crash

**ASIA AND OCEANIA**
1911
Revolution
in China

1919
Amritsar
Massacre
in India

1923
Atatürk begins
modernization
of Turkey

**EUROPE**
1914
World
War I
begins

1917
Russian
Revolution

1922
Mussolini
gains power
in Italy

1925
Locarno
agreements

America in the early 1800s, the revolutions of the twentieth century were global in scope.

The Russian Revolution under Lenin, the Chinese Revolution that climaxed with Mao's victory, and the long Mexican Revolution all served as inspirations or warnings to the rest of the world. At least in part because of these revolutions, rebellion against imperialism would soon boil up around the globe.

The brutal decade of the 1930s was an age of tyranny and aggression in Europe. This was the age of Hitler and Stalin and the beginning of the Nazi campaign against Jews that led to the Holocaust. But it was also the decade of Japanese militarism and aggression in East Asia, of Mussolini's invasion of Ethiopia, and of military regimes in Latin America. The brutality of the 1930s was not confined to the West.

Finally, World War II was beyond doubt a global conflict. Its major combatants included great powers of all continents except South America. Its theaters of war included Europe, Asia, Africa, and large sections of the Atlantic and Pacific oceans. Literally, no part of the globe escaped unscathed. The ruins that littered half the world in 1945 were grim evidence of the continuing globalization of history.

## Looking Ahead

More global confrontations waited in the second half of the century. During the decades after 1945, the old European empires collapsed and the Cold War divided the world between two global alliances. During the second half of the century also, the globe was drawn more closely together by closer economic ties, social contacts, and bonds of communications and culture. Today, no nation is farther from any other than the nearest television set—and Macdonald's, not even a dream in 1945, spans the globe.

All of these developments lay ahead as the world dug out of the ruins of World War II. The year 1945 thus marked the beginning of a new wave of global interdependence.

***ACTIVITY*** Choose two events and two pictures from the time line below. For each, write a sentence explaining how it relates to the themes expressed in the Global View essay.

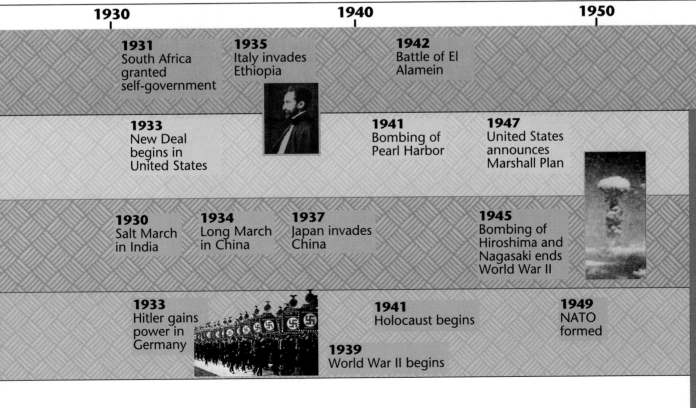

**1930**

**1940**

**1950**

**1931**
South Africa granted self-government

**1935**
Italy invades Ethiopia

**1942**
Battle of El Alamein

**1933**
New Deal begins in United States

**1941**
Bombing of Pearl Harbor

**1947**
United States announces Marshall Plan

**1930**
Salt March in India

**1934**
Long March in China

**1937**
Japan invades China

**1945**
Bombing of Hiroshima and Nagasaki ends World War II

**1933**
Hitler gains power in Germany

**1941**
Holocaust begins

**1949**
NATO formed

**1939**
World War II begins

# You Decide

UNIT **3**

## Exploring Global Issues

### *Is War Ever Justified?*

"Everlasting peace is a dream," declared the German military leader Helmuth von Moltke, "and war is a necessary part of God's arrangement of the world." Moltke spoke for militarists of all nationalities in the decades before World War I.

At the other extreme were the pacifists, who denounced war utterly. "A Christian cannot consistently uphold, and actively support, a government based on the sword," argued American pacifist Lucretia Mott.

Today, the debate continues. Should the risk of war be avoided at all costs? Or are there times when it may even be morally wrong to keep out of a conflict? To begin your investigation, examine these viewpoints:

**CHINA**

**300s B.C.**

The warrior-philosopher Sun Tzu wrote *The Art of War*, an influential handbook of military strategy:

> ❝A government should not mobilize an army out of anger, military leaders should not provoke a war out of wrath. Act when it is beneficial, desist when it is not. Anger can revert to joy, wrath can revert to delight, but a nation destroyed cannot be restored to existence, and the dead cannot be restored to life.❞

**AZTEC EMPIRE**

**1400s**

Like other world empires, the Aztecs glorified military might. This statue shows an elite Eagle Warrior, whose conquests kept the empire supplied with tribute money and sacrificial victims. ▶

**RUSSIA**

**1700s**

The empress Catherine the Great, whose conquests greatly increased Russian territory, wrote of the value of war:

> ❝The only way to save our empires from the encroaching of the people is to engage in war, and thus substitute national passions for social aspirations.❞

Poet and revolutionary José Martí was a leader of his nation's fight against Spanish rule:

> ❝Anyone is a criminal who promotes an avoidable war. And so is he who does not promote an inevitable civil war.❞

**CUBA**

**late 1800s**

**INDIA**

**1948**

Mohandas Gandhi, who led a nonviolent campaign to free India from British rule, denounced all forms of warfare and violence:

66What difference does it make to the dead, the orphans and the homeless, whether the mad destruction is wrought under the name of totalitarianism or the holy name of democracy and liberty?99

**UNITED STATES**

**1970s**

The women's group Another Mother Against War created this poster and slogan, which became popular on T-shirts, bumper stickers, and pins. ▶

war is not healthy for children and other living things

**ZIMBABWE**

**1978**

Bishop Abel Muzorewa joined the struggle for majority rule in his nation and later served as prime minister:

66I question whether God himself would wish me to hide behind the principles of nonviolence while innocent persons were being slaughtered.99

## COMPARING VIEWPOINTS

**1.** Which statements or pictures do you think represent the most militaristic point of view? Which represent a pacifist viewpoint?

**2.** How is Sun Tzu's viewpoint similar to that of Martí?

**3.** Martí, Gandhi, and Muzorewa were all involved in movements to free their nations from colonial rule. Compare their views on the need for military action.

## YOUR INVESTIGATION

**ACTIVITY**

**1.** Find out more about other viewpoints related to this topic. You might investigate one or more of the following:

■ The feudal military ideals of chivalry (Europe) and bushido (Japan).

■ The history and philosophy of Quakerism.

■ President Woodrow Wilson's war message to Congress in 1917.

■ The life and work of a Nobel Peace Prize winner, such as Jane Addams of the United States, Albert Luthuli of South Africa, Mairead Corrigan and Betty Williams of Northern Ireland, or Oscar Arias Sanchez of Costa Rica.

■ Contrasting positions on the appeasement of Hitler in the 1930s.

■ Debates in the 1990s about the use of UN or American troops in the Persian Gulf, Haiti, Bosnia, or another trouble spot.

**2.** Decide which viewpoint you agree with most closely and express it in your own way. You may do so in an essay, a cartoon, a poem, a drawing or painting, a song, a skit, a video, or in some other way.

# THE WORLD TODAY

**Global
Interaction**
*Today, millions of
refugees live in various
countries around the
world. Here, at a camp
in Zaire (Congo), the
International Red
Cross gives aid to
refugees from a civil
war in Rwanda.*

2

**Political and Social
Systems**
*Chile was one of several nations
that experienced a period of
harsh military rule. After 16
years, civilian government was
finally restored in 1989.*

1

1

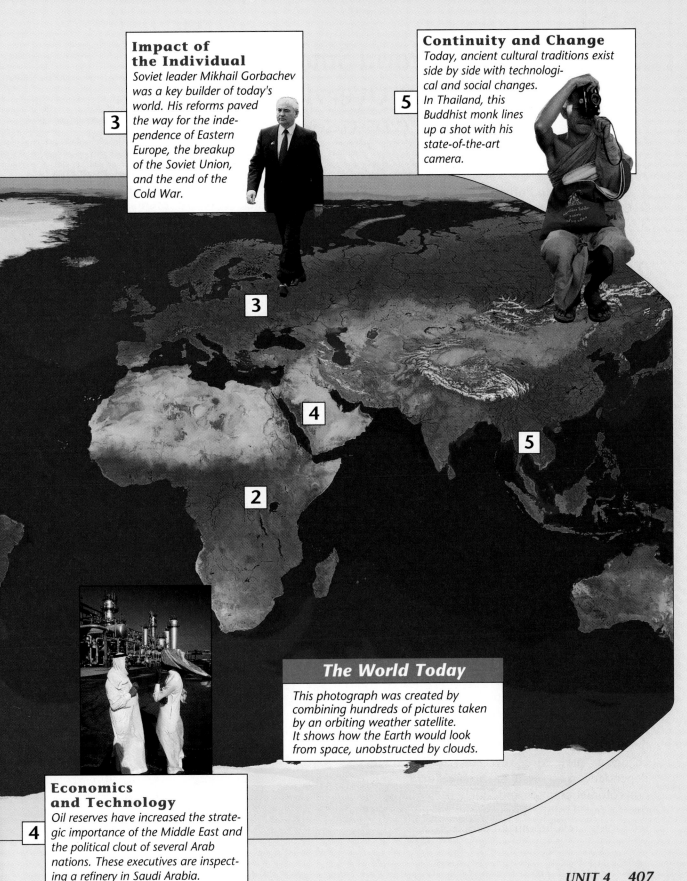

## Impact of the Individual

**3** Soviet leader Mikhail Gorbachev was a key builder of today's world. His reforms paved the way for the independence of Eastern Europe, the breakup of the Soviet Union, and the end of the Cold War.

## Continuity and Change

Today, ancient cultural traditions exist side by side with technological and social changes.
**5** In Thailand, this Buddhist monk lines up a shot with his state-of-the-art camera.

### The World Today

This photograph was created by combining hundreds of pictures taken by an orbiting weather satellite. It shows how the Earth would look from space, unobstructed by clouds.

## Economics and Technology

**4** Oil reserves have increased the strategic importance of the Middle East and the political clout of several Arab nations. These executives are inspecting a refinery in Saudi Arabia.

# The World Since 1945: An Overview

## (1945–Present)

## CHAPTER OUTLINE

1 **The Changing Political Climate**
2 **Global Economic Trends**
3 **Changing Patterns of Life**

In her short story "The Lake of Nothingness," Saudi writer Fawziyya al-Bakr describes the life of an unnamed business executive. He has carved out a successful career making deals with foreign companies. The rewards include a "luxurious American car. . . . First-class hotels. Luxurious seats in the planes, flying in and out of the capitals of money and business." Yet he is filled with a strange emptiness. He compares his new life to the world of his childhood:

&&He remembered, tenderly, the mud hut he'd lived in when he was a boy. He'd gone barefoot and things had seemed friendlier then, even the insects and the dirt. And the neighbors, those good people, used to exchange smiles and food with them.99

This fictional executive happens to be an Arab. But his story might have struck a familiar note in Singapore, Nigeria, or Bolivia. In the developing world, millions of people have flocked from small villages to growing cities. Some, like the man in the story, have prospered materially. Many more live poverty-stricken existences in crowded shantytowns. All, however, have had to adjust to a rapidly changing world.

In this unit, we are no longer looking at events that occurred centuries ago but at recent developments. Since 1945, the world has changed rapidly. More than 100 nations won independence as a result of the breakup of western colonial empires and, later, the collapse of the Soviet Union. Populations boomed, and technology revolutionized people's lives.

The recent past presents special problems for students of history. While we can see the immediate results of recent events, we cannot know their long-term impact. We lack the perspective of historians studying the distant past.

This chapter explores political, economic, and social trends and issues that have shaped the world since World War II. Some of those patterns will still be important 20, 50, or 100 years from now. Others may be less crucial. In the chapters that follow, we will look at how postwar trends affected individual regions.

**FOCUS ON** these questions as you read:

■ **Political and Social Systems**
  What postwar developments have helped or hindered the spread of democracy?

■ **Global Interaction**
  How has global interdependence increased in recent decades?

■ **Economics and Technology**
  How does the gap between rich and poor nations affect the world?

■ **Geography and History**
  Why have environmental issues attracted global attention?

■ **Continuity and Change**
  How have modernization and westernization brought rapid social and cultural change?

## TIME AND PLACE

*An Urban Township* In the 1960s and 1970s, painter Jo Maseko depicted life in the black townships around Johannesburg, South Africa. The effects of urban poverty were heightened by the government's policy of apartheid. But the tin-roofed shacks and bustling streets of this township mirrored slums in other developing nations. Rapid urbanization has been a major feature of the world since 1945. **Continuity and Change** Review Chapter 3. What were the effects of rapid urbanization in Europe during the Industrial Revolution?

## HUMANITIES LINK

*Art History* Jean Tinguely, *M.K. III* (page 427).
*Literature* In this chapter, you will encounter passages from the following works of literature: Fawziyya al-Bakr, "The Lake of Nothingness" (page 408); Nguyen Sa, "No Time" (page 421).

| 45 rld II ds | 1960s Green Revolution | 1975 Helsinki Agreement defines basic human rights | 1980s Computers become essential tools | 1992 United Nations Conference on Environment | 1997 Adult mammal cloned for first time |
|---|---|---|---|---|---|

| 1945 | 1960 | 1975 | 1990 | PRESENT |
|---|---|---|---|---|

▲ *Postage stamps from newly independent countries*

# 1 The Changing Political Climate

## Guide for Reading

- Why did European overseas empires crumble after World War II?

- How did the Cold War affect all regions of the world?

- Why did new nations have problems building stable governments?

- Why have ties among nations increased?

- **Vocabulary** *nonaligned, interdependence, terrorism*

In 1972, President Julius Nyerere (nyuh RAIR ay) of Tanzania in East Africa spoke of the goals of struggling new nations:

66There is a world movement now against being pushed around. . . . This movement will succeed. Eventually, imperialism and racialism will become merely a chapter in the history of man—we shall hear about it in museums.99

The balance of world power changed dramatically after 1945. European influence declined while the United States and the Soviet Union emerged as superpowers locked in a tense Cold War. Perhaps the greatest change, however, was the collapse of western overseas empires and the emergence of dozens of new countries.

## The Great Liberation

The postwar decades brought a major turning point in world history when the colonial empires built by western powers during the Age of Imperialism crumbled. In Asia and Africa, people demanded and won freedom.

**Nationalism and independence.** Resistance to colonial rule had begun long before. By the 1930s, nationalist movements had taken root in Africa, Asia, and the Middle East. (See Chapter 12.) After World War II, nationalist

leaders like Gandhi in India insisted on independence.

At first, Britain, France, and other powers tried to hold on to their empires. But the war had exhausted their military and financial resources. With subject peoples ready to fight for freedom, many war-weary Europeans had no desire for further conflict.

The Cold War, too, undermined imperialism. The United States backed the right of people everywhere to self-determination. Its rival, the Soviet Union, also had long condemned western imperialism. Soon, both superpowers were seeking allies among emerging nations.

**Global impact.** Altogether, nearly 100 new countries emerged during this "great liberation." Some, such as India and Nigeria, were large in area or population. Many others, such as Nepal, Kuwait, or Lesotho, were small.

The new nations of Africa and Asia, as well as the countries of Latin America, became known as the developing world.* Although these nations differed greatly from one another, they shared common goals. All were determined to pursue modernization, which meant building stable governments and developing their countries economically. They followed different paths toward modernization, but many experienced similar challenges.

The needs and goals of developing nations transformed the postwar world. Most joined the United Nations, where they have become an important voice by uniting their interests and often voting as a bloc. Individually and in regional groups, a number of them have played significant roles in global political and economic affairs.

---

*During the Cold War, the term *Third World* was used to refer to these nations with less-advanced technology than the First World (the western industrial powers and Japan) or the Second World (the communist bloc nations).

## The Cold War Goes Global

The new nations emerged into a world dominated and divided by the Cold War. The United States and the Soviet Union competed for influence by offering economic and military aid to developing nations. Each superpower wanted new countries to adopt its ideology—either capitalism or socialism. Many new nations favored socialism, in part because their old colonial rulers had been capitalist. Other nations were attracted by the greater prosperity of the West.

**Nonaligned nations.** To avoid superpower rivalry, many new nations chose to remain nonaligned, that is, not allied to either side in the Cold War. The goal of the nonaligned movement was to reduce world tensions and promote economic policies that would benefit developing nations. India, which blended a democratic government with a socialist economy, was a leader in the nonaligned movement.

**Hot spots.** In Africa, Latin America, and Asia, local conflicts took on a Cold War dimension. Often, the United States and the Soviet Union supported opposite sides. Through such struggles, the superpowers confronted each other indirectly rather than head to head.

On occasion, the Cold War did erupt into "shooting wars," especially in Asia. Both Korea and Vietnam were torn by brutal conflicts in which the United States and the Soviet Union played crucial roles. (You will read about these wars in more detail in Chapter 17.)

**The Cold War ends.** The Cold War ended suddenly in 1991 when the Soviet Union collapsed. (See Chapter 16.) With this dramatic change, tensions eased and some long-standing conflicts were resolved. Many people hoped for a more peaceful world. But troubling local, regional, and global problems remained.

Within many nations—from Russia to Indonesia to Rwanda—ethnic groups pushed for autonomy, or independence. They wanted their own states to protect their identity. Other clashes occurred between rival religious groups or different clans. Often, however, economic or political struggles were at the root of ethnic clashes.

## New Nations Seek Stability

While new nations had high hopes for the future, they faced immense problems. In Africa, especially, nations inherited random colonial borders that mixed together people with different languages, religions, and ethnic identities. Colonial rulers, using a "divide and conquer" strategy, had often exploited ethnic rivalries. At independence, people in nations like Nigeria had few ties to unite them. (See page 518.)

The new nations wrote constitutions modeled on those of western democracies. Only a few, however, like India, were able to sustain democratic rule. In general, colonial rulers had done little to prepare the people for self-government in a postwar world. Many new nations were shaken by revolution or civil war. Often, a wealthy, western-educated elite controlled the government and economy. The great majority of people remained poor.

As problems multiplied, the military or authoritarian leaders often took over. Many times, these were the same people who had led the fight for liberation. They imposed order by

**The Nonaligned Ark** This cartoon from a Bombay newspaper shows Indira Gandhi, longtime prime minister of India, sending out a dove of peace. India had assumed leadership of the nonaligned movement under Gandhi's father, Jawaharlal Nehru. **Political and Social Systems** According to this cartoon, what dangers did emerging nations face in the Cold War world? What was their goal?

building one-party dictatorships. They banned other political parties, claiming that a multiparty system threatened stability. Leaders waved the banner of nationalism, hoping to overcome ethnic, religious, or regional divisions.

Despite setbacks, democracy did make some progress in the late 1980s and early 1990s. In Africa, Asia, and Latin America, nations that had been ruled by dictators or by a single party held multiparty elections. The outcome of these experiments in democracy remains uncertain given the problems that face developing nations and their lack of experience with forms of representative government.

## The Shrinking Globe

Since 1945, transportation and communications systems have made the world increasingly interdependent. Interdependence is the dependence of countries on goods, resources, and knowledge from other parts of the world. Political, economic, cultural, and other links have created both problems and opportunities. A number of international organizations deal with issues of global concern.

**The UN.** The United Nations was set up as a forum for settling disputes. (See page 393.) Its responsibilities, like its membership, have expanded greatly since 1945. The UN played a vital role in decolonization. Since then, it has tried to act as peacekeeper from Cambodia and the Middle East to Africa and the Balkans. Some UN interventions have been successful. Others have failed, often from an inability of members to agree on goals and methods.

UN agencies provide services for millions of people worldwide. The World Health Organization (WHO), for example, helped wipe out smallpox through its program of vaccinations. Today, WHO works with other groups to seek a solution to the AIDS crisis. Other UN programs spearhead campaigns to reduce malnutrition or ensure access to safe drinking water. The UN has also sponsored global summits on issues such as the environment and population.

**Other organizations.** Many nations formed regional groups to promote trade or meet other common needs. Powerful regional trading blocs have emerged. In later chapters, you will see how such groups as the European Community, the North American Free Trade Association, and the Association of Southeast Asian Nations have worked to lower trade barriers and promote the free exchange of goods and services.

The importance of global trade was recognized by a series of international agreements known as the General Agreement on Tariffs and Trade (GATT). It tried to establish fair trade policies for all nations. At the highest levels, the Group of Seven, which represents the seven most productive economies—the United States, Canada, Japan, Germany, France, Britain, and Italy—has met annually to discuss common economic problems.

The World Bank and the International Monetary Fund (IMF) make loans to developing nations. Many other types of nongovernmental organizations have forged valuable global networks, including the International Olympic Committee and the International Red Cross.

## Enduring Issues

Many issues pose a challenge to world peace. Since the United States first exploded an atomic bomb in 1945, nations have poured resources into building nuclear weapons. The number of nuclear weapons grew from 3 in 1945 to over 50,000 in the 1980s.

**Nuclear weapons.** During the Cold War, efforts to curb the arms race had only limited success. In 1968, a number of nations signed the Nuclear Non-Proliferation Treaty (NPT), agreeing to halt the spread of nuclear weapons. As the treaty came up for renewal in the 1990s, though, some nations were unwilling to sign. They asked why a few countries like the United States and Russia could keep nuclear weapons and they could not. Still, in 1995, the NPT was renewed indefinitely.

**Arms trade.** Despite the end of the Cold War, military spending in many countries has

ISSUES *For* TODAY

Interdependence has created strong ties among rich and poor nations around the world. Do the benefits of increasing political and economic ties with other nations outweigh the dangers?

*Games for a Changing World* In 1896, the first modern Olympic Games featured 311 male athletes from 13 nations. In 1996, the Olympic Games in Atlanta, shown above, featured more than 10,000 male and female athletes from nearly 200 nations. **Global Interaction** Why are the Olympic Games a symbol of the interdependence of the world's nations?

continued to grow. In nations split by ethnic or other conflicts, arms dealers traffic in deadly weapons. Some people have condemned the international arms trade. Others defend the economic right of arms makers to produce and sell their goods on the free market.

**Terrorism.** Since the 1960s, the world has seen a rise in terrorist activity. Terrorism is the deliberate use of random violence, especially against civilians, to exact revenge or achieve political goals. Through bombings, kidnappings, airplane hijackings, and shootings, terrorists focused attention on their causes and tried to force governments to give in to their demands.

Militants on both sides of the conflict in Northern Ireland murdered civilians. In 1972, a radical group killed Israeli athletes at the Olympic Games to push its demands for a Palestinian state. In the 1990s, separate terrorist groups assassinated India's leader Rajiv Gandhi, bombed New York's World Trade Center, and released deadly nerve gas in the subways of Tokyo. The random and secret nature of terrorist activities makes them hard to prevent. To combat terrorism, some governments passed tough laws and stepped up vigilance.

Some governments have been suspected of "state-sponsored terrorism," training and arm-ing extremists to carry out attacks abroad. Human rights groups and others also claim that governments engaged in terrorism when they used torture, murder, and illegal arrests against their own citizens.

**Human rights.** In 1948, UN members approved the Universal Declaration of Human Rights. The first article states:

66All human beings are born free and equal in dignity and rights. They are endowed with reason and conscience and should act towards one another in a spirit of brotherhood.99

The document goes on to state that all people are entitled to basic rights and freedoms "without distinction of any kind, such as race, color, sex, language, property, birth or other status." These human rights include "the right to life, liberty, and security of person."

In 1975, 35 nations signed the chief agreement of the Helsinki Accords. It guaranteed the basic rights of freedom of speech, religion, and the press. The rights to a fair trial, to earn a living, and to live in safety were also guaranteed.

Despite such agreements, human rights abuses such as torture and arbitrary arrest occurred around the world. At times, the world community pressed countries to stop those abuses. World pressure and economic sanctions, for example, helped push South Africa to end its system of apartheid. (See Chapter 19.)

Still, some leaders accused the West of trying to impose its own ideas about individual freedom. Some claim that their cultures value the community over the individual. Chinese leaders, for example, argued that national economic goals, such as improving the standard of living for its people, were more important than individual political freedoms.

**The question of intervention.** The human rights debate raises tough issues. Does the world community have a responsibility to intervene to end abuses? For example, the UN Charter forbids any action that violates the independence of a member nation. Yet in the 1990s, the UN sent peacekeepers to northern Iraq to protect the Kurds, an ethnic minority that was being persecuted by the government.

In the 1990s, Serbs in Bosnia killed or drove Muslims from their homes. (You will read about this conflict in Chapter 16.) World opinion was outraged, but for complex political reasons, the UN and western powers were reluctant to take military action against the Serbs. As ethnic conflict rose around the world, intervention continued to stir debate.

## SECTION 1 REVIEW

1. **Identify** (a) GATT, (b) NPT, (c) International Monetary Fund, (d) Universal Declaration of Human Rights, (e) Helsinki Agreement.
2. **Define** (a) nonaligned, (b) interdependence, (c) terrorism.
3. (a) Why did European nations lose their colonial empires after World War II? (b) What was one effect of the great liberation?
4. How did the Cold War become global?
5. Why did political instability plague many Third World nations?
6. *Critical Thinking* **Predicting Consequences** Is interdependence likely to make the world more peaceful? Why or why not?
7. *ACTIVITY* Design an invitation to an international conference on nuclear arms, terrorism, or human rights.

 # Global Economic Trends

## Guide for Reading

- How is today's world divided along economic lines?

- Why have developing nations made limited economic progress?

- How are environmental and economic issues linked?

- **Vocabulary** *multinational corporation, privatization, acid rain*

In 1969, Pope Paul VI expressed what he saw as a troubling mix of successes and failures in the modern age:

> 66Ours is a time of problems, of gigantic problems. Everything is being transformed under the magic influence of science and technology. And every day, if we want to live with open eyes, we have a problem to study, to resolve.99

As new nations won independence, they aspired to the high standard of living in the industrial world. Since the 1950s, however, a growing gulf has divided the world into rich and poor nations. A few developing nations have done well. Many others have not. In today's interdependent world, the stories of rich and poor nations are closely linked.

### *The Global North and South: Two Worlds of Development*

The Cold War created an ideological split between the communist East and the capitalist West. Today, an economic gulf divides the world into two spheres—the relatively rich nations of the global North and the relatively poor nations of the global South.

**Rich nations.** The global North includes the industrial nations of Western Europe and North America, as well as Japan and Australia. Most are located in the temperate zone north of the Equator. They control most of the world's wealth. Although pockets of poverty exist, the

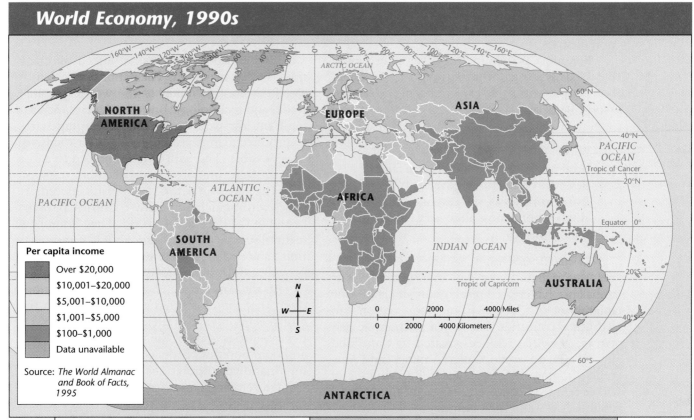

## World Economy, 1990s

**Per capita income**
- Over $20,000
- $10,001–$20,000
- $5,001–$10,000
- $1,001–$5,000
- $100–$1,000
- Data unavailable

Source: *The World Almanac and Book of Facts, 1995*

## GEOGRAPHY AND HISTORY

Per capita income is one measure of a country's wealth. By comparing the per capita income of different countries, you can make inferences about the well-being of people in those countries.

**1. Location** On the map, locate (a) South America, (b) Europe, (c) Asia, (d) Africa, (e) North America.

**2. Region** (a) In which region do you find most of the countries with per capita income under $1,000? (b) In which region do you find most of the countries with per capita income over $10,000?

**3. Critical Thinking** **Applying Information** How does this map illustrate the idea of the global North and global South?

standard of living in the North is generally high. Most people are literate, earn adequate wages, and have basic health services. Rich nations have a lower birthrate and higher life expectancy than do the nations of the global South. ( ★ See *Skills for Success,* page 428.)

With a few exceptions, such as socialist Sweden, most rich nations have basically capitalist economies. Economic decisions about what to produce and for whom are generally regulated by the free market, not by the government. Still, their governments support economic growth through transportation and communication systems, public education, and social services.

**Poor nations.** The global South refers to the developing world. Most of these nations lie in Asia, Africa, and Latin America in the zone between the tropics of Cancer and Capricorn. (See the map above.) The South has three quarters of the world's population and much of its natural resources. Some nations have enjoyed strong growth, especially the Asian "tigers"—Taiwan, Hong Kong, Singapore, and South Korea—and the oil-exporting nations of the Middle East. Overall, though, the global South remains generally poor and underdeveloped. Unlike the nations that industrialized in the 1700s and 1800s, newer nations have not had enough time to build up their capital, resources, or industries.

For most people in the developing world, life is a daily struggle for survival. About one billion people worldwide live in extreme poverty. A World Bank report noted:

&&A disproportionate number of [the poor]—perhaps two in five—are children under ten, mainly in large families. More than three quarters of them live in rural areas, the rest in urban slums—but almost all in very crowded conditions.99

**Migration.** Despite some growth, the gap between rich and poor nations is growing. The imbalance has created resentment and led to the migration of people from poor regions to wealthier countries. Every year, economic refugees, as well as refugees created by war, flood into Western Europe, North America, and Australia, hoping to find a better life. Millions of other refugees, however, remain in Third World countries close to their homes.

*Looking for a Home* By the 1990s, there were more than 18 million refugees around the world. Here, a Vietnamese child peers out from behind the barbed wire at a crowded refugee camp in Hong Kong. **Global Interaction** What conditions cause people to flee their homelands?

## Economic Interdependence

Rich and poor nations are linked by many trade and financial ties. The nations of the global North control much of the world's capital, trade, and technology. But they depend increasingly on low-paid workers in developing states to produce manufactured goods as inexpensively as possible. This shift in labor has led to a loss of manufacturing jobs in many western nations.

Huge multinational corporations, enterprises with branches in many countries, have invested in the developing world. They bring new technology to mining, agriculture, transportation, and other industries. Rich nations also provide aid, technical advisers, and loans.

At the same time, however, poor nations claim that the North has a stranglehold on the global economy. With their great buying power, rich countries control the prices of most goods and commodities produced by the South. Also, multinational corporations remove many profits from developing countries and often limit workers' attempts to seek higher wages. As a result, some emerging nations see interdependence as a new form of imperialism.

**The oil crisis.** In an interdependent world, events in one country or region can affect people everywhere. A drastic example of this was the oil crisis of the early 1970s. All nations use oil for transportation and for products ranging from plastics to fertilizers. This demand has allowed nations with oil resources—from Venezuela to Britain—to seek the most favorable prices on the world market.

Much of the world's oil comes from the Middle East. In 1973, a political crisis in the Middle East led the Organization of Petroleum Exporting Countries (OPEC) to halt oil exports and then raise oil prices. (You will read more about the roots of this crisis in Chapter 18.) Oil shortages and soaring oil prices set off economic shock waves in industrialized nations. Suddenly, people in the United States and other nations realized how much they depended on imported oil. While some efforts were made to find other fuels or to conserve energy use, the energy crisis showed what impact a single vital product could have on the world economy.

**The debt crisis.** The oil crisis fed into another global economic development. Higher oil

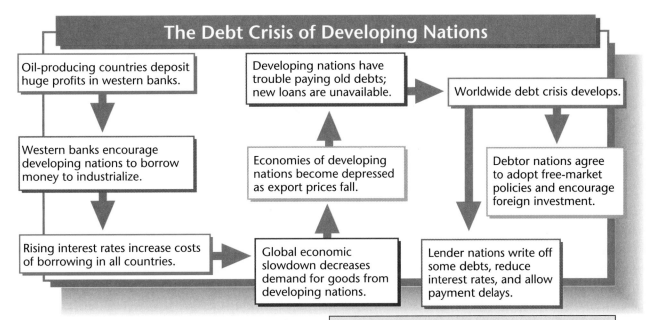

## The Debt Crisis of Developing Nations

Oil-producing countries deposit huge profits in western banks.

Western banks encourage developing nations to borrow money to industrialize.

Rising interest rates increase costs of borrowing in all countries.

Developing nations have trouble paying old debts; new loans are unavailable.

Economies of developing nations become depressed as export prices fall.

Global economic slowdown decreases demand for goods from developing nations.

Worldwide debt crisis develops.

Debtor nations agree to adopt free-market policies and encourage foreign investment.

Lender nations write off some debts, reduce interest rates, and allow payment delays.

*Interpreting a Chart* The effects of the debt crisis varied from country to country. In general, though, the pressure of falling prices and high interest rates had a devastating effect on developing economies.
■ *According to the flowchart, why did debtor nations have trouble repaying their loans?*

prices brought riches to OPEC members. They deposited their oil earnings in western banks, which in turn invested the money to earn high interest.

Poor nations, needing capital to modernize, took loans offered by western banks. In the 1980s, however, bank interest rates rose, while the world economy slowed down. As demand for many of their goods fell, poor nations were unable to repay their debts or even the interest on their loans. Their economies stalled as they spent all their income from exports on payments to their foreign creditors.

The debt crisis hurt rich nations, too, as banks were stuck with billions of dollars of bad debts. The losses threatened the whole world financial system. To ease the crisis, the International Monetary Fund, the World Bank, and private banks worked out agreements with debtor nations. Lenders lowered interest rates or gave some nations more time to repay the loans. In some cases, debts were even canceled altogether.

In return, debtor nations had to agree to adopt free-market policies. Many turned from socialism to privatization, selling off state-owned industries to private investors. Nations hoped that more efficient private enterprises would produce higher-quality goods in the long run. Still, the immediate effects of privatization often hurt the poor, as debtor nations cut social programs. The imposed reforms sparked resentment against the IMF and the West.

## Obstacles to Development

While some developing nations have made progress toward modernization, others have not. Why have they failed to achieve their economic goals? The answers vary from country to country, but many shared problems in five general areas: (1) geography, (2) population and poverty, (3) economic dependence, (4) economic policies, (5) political instability.

**Geography.** In parts of Africa, Asia, and Latin America, geography has posed an obstacle to progress. For example, some newly created African countries are tiny and have few natural resources. Difficult climates, uncertain rainfall, lack of good farmland, and disease have added to the problems of some nations.

**Population and poverty.** The population boom that began in the 1700s has continued. Better medical care and increased food supplies have reduced death rates and led to explosive population growth. In the developing world, though, rapid growth is linked to poverty. Each year, the populations of countries like Nigeria, Egypt, and India increase by millions. All those people need food, housing, education, jobs, and medical care. Meeting the needs of so many people puts a staggering burden on developing nations.

Another result of the population boom is that the world's population has become younger. About half the people alive today are under the age of 25. In developing nations, the percentage can be even higher. Each year, tens of thousands of people in these countries begin looking for work. Often, there are not enough jobs. At the same time, these young people begin raising new families.

Across the developing world, people are caught in a cycle of poverty. Many suffer hunger. An estimated 35 million people die each year from illnesses related to hunger. Children are the most vulnerable. According to the UN, 35,000 children die each day from malnutrition, disease, and other effects of poverty.

Many developing nations have tried to slow population growth. But few countries, except China, want to force people to limit family size. In many cultures, having children is a status symbol. In farming societies, children are a source of labor. They are seen as an insurance policy to support their parents in old age. Religious traditions often encourage large families. Also, despite education efforts, many people still lack information about or access to family planning.

**Economic dependence.** The economic patterns established during the Age of Imperialism did not change after 1945. Most new nations remained dependent on their former colonial rulers. As you read, they sold agricultural products and raw materials to the industrial world. In turn, they relied on the West for manufactured goods, technology, and investment. Also, many new nations had only a single export crop or commodity, such as sugar, cocoa, or copper. Their economies prospered or fell depending on world demand for the product.

As you have read, developing nations borrowed heavily from foreign banks. These funds were intended for development. Once in debt, though, nations had to spend much of their resources to pay interest.

**Economic policies.** After independence, many new nations expected that socialism, rather than capitalism, would help them modernize quickly. They modeled their economic policies on those of China or the Soviet Union,

which had made rapid gains in a short period. Under socialism, the government controls the economy. Since these nations had little private capital, only the government could raise the money—through loans, taxes, and controlling profits from labor—to finance large-scale development projects.

Emerging nations made some gains in the 1950s and 1960s. But in the long run, socialism frequently hindered economic growth. As you have read, under international pressure, many emerging nations introduced free-market policies in the 1980s.

**Political instability.** Civil wars and other struggles prevented economic development. El Salvador in Central America, Lebanon in the Middle East, Cambodia in Southeast Asia, and Mozambique in Africa are among a number of nations devastated by civil wars. Military dictators or other authoritarian leaders spent huge sums on weapons and warfare instead of on education, housing, or health care.

War created millions of refugees living in camps both inside and outside their home countries. The loss of their labor has further hurt war-torn countries.

## Economic Development and the Environment

For both rich and poor nations, economic development has been achieved at great cost to the natural environment. Modern industry and agriculture have gobbled up natural resources and polluted the world's water, air, and soil.

**Growing threats.** Since earliest times, people everywhere have taken what they wanted from their environment. In the past, damage was limited because the world's population was relatively small and technology was simple. With the Industrial Revolution and the population explosion, the potential for widespread environmental damage grew.

By the 1970s, conservationists raised the alarm about threats to the planet's fragile environment. Strip mining provided vital ores for industry but destroyed much land. Chemical fertilizers and pesticides produced more food crops but harmed the soil and water. Oil spills polluted oceans, lakes, and rivers. Gases from power plants and factories produced acid rain, a

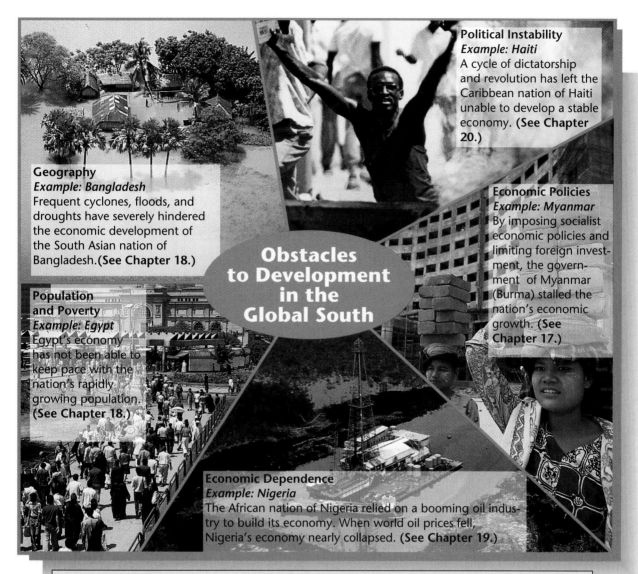

**Geography**
*Example: Bangladesh*
Frequent cyclones, floods, and droughts have severely hindered the economic development of the South Asian nation of Bangladesh.**(See Chapter 18.)**

**Political Instability**
*Example: Haiti*
A cycle of dictatorship and revolution has left the Caribbean nation of Haiti unable to develop a stable economy. **(See Chapter 20.)**

**Obstacles to Development in the Global South**

**Economic Policies**
*Example: Myanmar*
By imposing socialist economic policies and limiting foreign investment, the government of Myanmar (Burma) stalled the nation's economic growth. **(See Chapter 17.)**

**Population and Poverty**
*Example: Egypt*
Egypt's economy has not been able to keep pace with the nation's rapidly growing population. **(See Chapter 18.)**

**Economic Dependence**
*Example: Nigeria*
The African nation of Nigeria relied on a booming oil industry to build its economy. When world oil prices fell, Nigeria's economy nearly collapsed. **(See Chapter 19.)**

*Interpreting a Chart* This chart gives just one example for each of the five obstacles to development described in this chapter. In Chapters 16–20, you will read about these examples and others in more detail. ■ How can political instability contribute to economic instability?

form of pollution in which toxic chemicals in the air come back to the Earth as rain, snow, or hail. Acid rain damaged forests, lakes, and farmland, especially in industrial Europe and North America. The chart on page 420 outlines other challenges to the world's environment.

Some scientists warned of "global warming" caused by the increased emission of gases into the upper atmosphere. Global warming, they thought, could change the Earth's climate, melting the polar icecaps. This would flood low-lying areas, including most major coastal cities. Not all scientists, however, accepted the global warming theory.

**Industrial accidents.** Major accidents focused attention on threats to the environment. In Bhopal, India, a leak from a pesticide plant in 1984 killed 3,600 people and injured 100,000. In 1986, an accident at the Chernobyl nuclear power plant in the Soviet Union exposed people, crops, and animals to deadly radiation—from Ukraine into other parts of Europe and Turkey. An American oil tanker spill in 1989 destroyed much marine life off the coast of Alaska.

In response to such disasters, technicians have developed measures to increase safety. However, such measures do not always succeed, and companies often resist the expense.

# Global Environmental Challenges

| | Causes | Effects | Outlook for the Future |
|---|---|---|---|
| **Air and Water Pollution**  | Auto and factory emissions; dumping of waste; leeching of pesticides into ground water; release of chlorofluorocarbons (CFCs) | Thinning ozone layer; acid rain; poisoned water supplies; human diseases | Although there are few internationally recognized guidelines, nations are seeking ways to reduce pollution while containing costs. Recycling, treatment, and new technologies are promising approaches. |
| **Deforestation**  | Overforesting to harvest trees or to build roads, farms, and cities | Change in local weather; less absorption of carbon dioxide; soil erosion; extinction of plants and animals | Balancing economic needs with preservation of forests is a global challenge that requires research and cooperation among local peoples, businesses, governments, and the international community. |
| **Desertification** 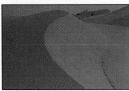 | Overfarming, overgrazing, and climate shifts that have caused deserts, such as the Sahara, to grow | Reduced arable land; hunger | Famines in Africa have brought the problem to international attention. New farming methods, including improved irrigation, may slow the process of desertification. |
| **Endangered Plants and Animals**  | Human alterations to landscape through land clearing, river damming, and building; pollution; overfishing; hunting animals for profit; slash-and-burn agriculture | Ecosystem imbalance; loss of resources for food and medicines | International agreements have banned shipment and sale of endangered species. Some people favor preserving habitats as a way of protecting endangered and other species. |
| **Waste Disposal**  | Proliferation of waste because of population growth and industrial production; use of nuclear power; overuse of packaging on consumer goods | Pollution of ground water and oceans; health hazards; endangering of plant and animal species; full landfills | Solutions include conservation, recycling, waste reduction, new landfills, and incineration. Cooperation among people can help reduce unnecessary waste. |

*Interpreting a Chart* Identifying environmental problems has been easier than solving them. Often, the long-term effects must be measured against short-term goals, such as preserving jobs or feeding the population. ■ Describe how rapid population growth has contributed to two of the problems shown on the chart.

**Protecting the environment.** Rich nations, the greatest consumers of natural resources, produce much of the world's pollution. At the same time, they have also led the campaign to protect the environment. They have passed some laws to control pollution and ensure conservation in their own countries.

In 1992, the UN sponsored the Conference on the Environment, or Earth Summit, in Rio de Janeiro, Brazil. World leaders discussed how to clean up and preserve the planet. They agreed to restrain damage but disagreed over who was responsible and who should pay for it. Many other issues were hotly debated. Should economic development take priority over protecting the environment? Are people, especially in rich nations, willing to do with less in order to preserve the environment? How can emerging nations afford costly safeguards?

As the twentieth century neared its end, many people agreed that permanent damage to the planet was too high a price to pay for economic progress. Agreeing on solutions, however, is a challenge for present and future generations. ( ☑ See *You Decide*, "What Is the Relationship Between People and the Environment?" pages 564–565.)

## SECTION 2 REVIEW

1. **Identify** (a) OPEC, (b) Chernobyl, (c) Earth Summit.
2. **Define** (a) multinational corporation, (b) privatization, (c) acid rain.
3. How do the global North and global South differ?
4. Why have emerging nations had difficulty reaching their goals?
5. How has economic development increased the potential for widespread damage to the environment? Give two examples.
6. *Critical Thinking* **Applying Information** Describe how each of the following showed interdependence: (a) the oil crisis of the 1970s, (b) the debt crisis of the 1980s.
7. *ACTIVITY* Design a board game on economic development. Spaces on the board might indicate rewards and pitfalls.

# 3 Changing Patterns of Life

## Guide for Reading

■ Why has urbanization disrupted older ways of life?

■ How has modernization affected the lives of women?

■ What are the benefits and limits of modern science and technology?

■ How has technology helped shape a new global culture?

■ **Vocabulary** *liberation theology*

In recent decades, hundreds of millions of people have migrated from rural villages to urban centers. For many, the anonymity and fast pace of city life required difficult adjustments. The Vietnamese poet Nguyen Sa wrote:

&6I must get far away from this city
with its soot-streaked curbs
and people who pass each other
of a Monday morning
without a smile or a word.
'No time! I have no time!'99

Urbanization has transformed the lives of people in the developing world just as it did in Europe during the Industrial Revolution. First, though, we will look at how the village continues to shape the lives of millions of people.

## The Village: Continuity and Change

The village is close-set houses made of stones, clay bricks, or sticks plastered over with mud, roofed with thatch, palm leaves, tile, or tin. It is hard-packed earthen paths crossed by bare feet, sandals, or perhaps a bicycle or two. It is water from a village well, vegetables from a back garden, chickens or goats in the yard. It is

**Village Life** *In villages around the world, economic activities often reflect centuries-old patterns. At right, potters display their wares at an outdoor market in the South Asian kingdom of Nepal. Above, a Peruvian Indian weaves a mat in the doorway of her cottage.* **Continuity and Change** *What forces are changing village life?*

dust, heat, and insects. It is also families, neighbors, and an enduring way of life.

Village people continue to form the largest part of the world's population—about 3.3 billion of the 5.7 billion people on Earth. Most of them live in the global South. Their lives vary widely, depending on climate, geographic isolation, or other factors. Still, similar patterns link village people from Uruguay to Malaysia.

**Enduring ways.** The day may begin before sunrise, with the sound of a rooster crowing. If the village is in a Muslim land, a muezzin may call villagers to predawn prayer. Or the church bells of a Latin American village may announce the start of early mass.

As the morning goes on, children in school uniforms race toward the crossroads to catch the bus, their books swinging behind them in straps or satchels. At the stream, women who do not yet own washing machines slap wet clothes against a rock and lay them out on the grass to dry. Other young women and men labor in fields, workshops, or markets. Many will have sore backs by noon.

Later, people gather at small open-fronted shops around the village square. In tropical regions, lizards may crawl along the walls and ceiling—a welcome addition because each lizard eats several times its weight in flies and mosquitoes. Customers look among the various goods piled here and there. One jokes with the clerk. Another gives news of his daughter attending a

university in a far-off city. In times of crisis, villagers gather anxiously around the storekeeper's radio.

**Changing patterns.** Many village ways have endured for centuries. But decades of urbanization, westernization, and new technology have left their mark. Indian writer Prafulla Mohanti noted:

> ❝My village is changing. A straight road was built in the mid-1960s to carry iron ore from the mines to the port of Paradip, 40 miles away. . . . Nylon, stainless steel, plastic, fizzy drinks have reached the village. Electricity has come, too . . . there is a cinema and video hall.❞

While such changes enrich village life, they also weaken traditional cultures. Supermarkets—efficient but impersonal—threaten village grocers. Worse, more and more young people are leaving the village for the wider vistas of the city.

Still, the village goes on. Life is not easy. Sometimes it is cruelly harsh. Yet for millions of market women and teachers, healers and matchmakers, children and old people, the village remains a vital center of existence. ◼

## Old Ways and New

In the western world, industrialization and urbanization began more than 200 years ago during the Industrial Revolution. Since 1945, the rest of the world has experienced similar upheavals.

**Urbanization.** People in the developing world have flocked to the cities to find jobs and escape rural poverty. Cities offer not only economic opportunities but also attractions such as pop music concerts, stores, and sports.

With no money and few jobs, some newcomers cannot afford to ride buses or go to movies. Instead, most settle in shantytowns that ring the cities. These slums are as crowded and dangerous as European cities were in the 1800s. They lack even basic services such as paving, running water, or sewage. Drugs and crime are ever-present threats. Today, millions of people struggle to survive in these conditions.

In cities, the traditional extended family of rural villages is giving way to the nuclear family. As urban children attend school and become literate, they often reject their parents' ways. Without the support of the village and extended family, older beliefs and values are undermined by urban values such as material wealth, education, and job status. People who move from villages to cities frequently suffer a sense of overwhelming stress and isolation, often called culture shock.

**Westernization.** In the cities, people adopted western fashions and ideas. During the Age of Imperialism, you will recall, westerners taught that their civilization was superior. Even after independence, many people in emerging nations felt that the way to modernize was to follow western models.

Some early nationalists, such as Mohandas Gandhi, rejected the rush to abandon traditional ways. Today, leaders in some Muslim lands

have called for modernization without westernization. Although they welcome modern technology, they want to preserve older traditions and religious beliefs. They reject western emphasis on material success and the individual, which they feel undermines the community and family.

**Religious influences.** Despite revolutionary changes, many traditions remain strong. The major world religions and their offshoots still shape modern societies. (See the pictures on page 424.) Since the 1980s, religious revivals have swept many regions. Christian, Muslim, Buddhist, and Hindu reformers have offered their own solutions to the problems of today's world. Some of these reformers have been called fundamentalists because they stress what they see as the fundamental, or basic, values of their religions. Many have sought increased political power in an effort to resist changes that they feel threaten their beliefs.

In the West, evangelical Protestant sects have emphasized salvation through faith and preaching, offering spiritual guidelines in a rapidly changing world. In the 1960s, the Second Vatican Council gave Roman Catholics more freedom to discuss issues and promoted cooperation with other Christian faiths. In Latin America, some Roman Catholic clergy adopted a movement called liberation theology. They urged the Church to take a more active role in opposing the social conditions that contributed to poverty. Conservative Catholic forces have often opposed such political activities. (You will read more about the role of the Church in Latin America in Chapter 20.)

In Muslim countries, too, religious reformers called on governments to work for social improvements. Some Muslim leaders rejected westernization and secular goals. Instead, they insisted that government and society should be based on strict obedience to the Sharia, or Islamic religious law. (See Chapter 18.)

## New Rights and Roles for Women

After 1945, women's movements brought changes to both the western and developing worlds. The UN Charter included a commitment to work for "equal rights for men and women." By 1950, women had won the right to

**GLOBAL CONNECTIONS**

Urbanization and other changes are threatening many of the world's languages. About 6,000 different languages are spoken in the world today. Many are spoken only in isolated rural areas or remote islands. As families migrate to cities or other countries, their children often grow up speaking a dominant tongue, such as English, Hindi, or Spanish. In the next century, 90 to 95 percent of all current languages may become extinct. Scholars are now working to preserve many of these disappearing languages.

vote in most European nations, as well as in Japan, China, Brazil, and other nations. In most African nations, women and men won the vote at the same time, at independence.

A small but growing number of women won elected office. Women headed democratic governments in Britain, Israel, India, Pakistan, the Philippines, and other countries. Yet in 1985, a report to a UN Conference on Women noted that while women represent half of the world's people, "they perform nearly two thirds of all working hours, receive only one tenth of the world's income, and own less than one percent of world property."

**The West.** In the industrial world, more and more women worked outside the home and gradually won equal access to education. By the 1970s, a strong feminist movement sought equal access to jobs and promotions, equal pay for equal work, and an end to sexual harassment on the job. Women moved into high-profile jobs as business owners and executives, astronauts, scientists, or technicians.

Yet new roles for women raised difficult social issues. Working women had to balance jobs outside the home with child rearing and household work. A growing need emerged for affordable day care. Some critics charged that the growth in the female work force was partly responsible for rising divorce rates and a decline in family life. Others responded that many families required two incomes.

**Developing nations.** In emerging nations, women worked actively in the nationalist struggles. Their constitutions spelled out equality between women and men, at least on paper.

While women still had less education than men, the gap was narrowing. Women from the middle and elite classes entered the work force in growing numbers. Their skills and labor contributed to their nations' wealth.

At the same time, women generally shouldered a heavy burden of work inside and around the home. In many places, religious and cultural traditions kept women confined to the home or segregated men and women in the workplace.

In rural areas, especially in Africa, women have traditionally done much of the agricultural work along with household tasks. In recent years, men have gone to the cities to find work, leaving women with added responsibilities. According to one report on Kenya, one third of all rural households are headed by women:

66Everywhere one sees women walking to market with basketloads of vegetables on their heads, infants strapped to their backs, and older children following behind. Even while they walk to market, these women often are weaving baskets or fashioning other handiwork . . . to exchange for cash needed for the family's support or the children's education.99

In other regions, such as Southeast Asia, it is often the women who leave home to work. Their wages go to keep the family on the farm or pay for the education of their brothers.

## Science and Technology

Since 1945, technology has transformed human life and thought. Instant communication via satellites has shrunk the globe. New forms of energy, especially nuclear power, have been added to the steam power, electricity, and gasoline energy of the first industrial age.

**The computer revolution.** The computer is among the most revolutionary developments of the past 50 years. The first electronic computers, built in the 1940s, were huge, slow machines. Later, the computer was miniaturized thanks to inventions like the silicon chip.

Computers led to an information revolution. By the 1990s, a growing computer network linked individuals, governments, and businesses around the world. Computerized robots operated in factories, while computers appeared in more and more homes and schools. Multinational electronics and software companies often depended on labor in developing nations. Still, access to computers added to the gap between the global North and South.

**The space age.** In October 1957, the space age began when the Soviet Union launched *Sputnik*, a tiny satellite, into orbit. *Sputnik* set off a frantic "space race" between the superpowers. In 1969, the United States landed the first man on the moon. Both superpowers explored the military uses of space and sent spy satellites to orbit the Earth. In the post–Cold War world, however, the United States and Russia turned to cooperation and launched joint space ventures.

Other European nations, as well as Japan and China, launched their own satellites. By then, satellites had many peaceful uses. They mapped weather and tracked droughts, livestock diseases, and plagues. In the weightlessness of space, scientists experimented with promising new drugs and vaccines.

**Medical breakthroughs.** In the postwar era, medicine achieved amazing successes. Scientists developed new antibiotics to treat illnesses. Vaccines wiped out some diseases like

**The View From Outer Space** *High above the Earth's atmosphere, American astronauts repair the Hubble Space Telescope in December 1993. Once fixed, the orbiting observatory sent astonishingly clear pictures of faraway galaxies back to scientists on Earth.* **Economics and Technology** *Do you think countries should spend large sums of money learning about outer space? Why or why not?*

smallpox and prevented the spread of others. In the 1980s and 1990s, however, new challenges arose with the spread of deadly new diseases such as ebola and AIDS.

In the 1970s, surgeons learned to transplant organs to save lives. Lasers made surgery safer. Scientists also made headway in treating some cancers. Yet advances in medicine were costly and usually limited to people and nations that could afford them.

A controversial area of research is genetic engineering. It involves altering the chemical codes carried by all living things. In medicine, such research has produced important drug therapies to treat diseases. Still, genetic engineering has raised ethical issues about how far science should go to create and change life.

**The Green Revolution.** Scientists applied new technology to increasing food production for the world's growing population. During the 1960s, they touched off the Green Revolution, developing new kinds of rice and other grains that yielded more food per acre than older strains. In India, Indonesia, and elsewhere, the Green Revolution doubled food output.

The Green Revolution had limits, however. It succeeded only in areas with regular moisture. Also, it required chemical fertilizers and pesticides as well as irrigation systems, which only wealthy farmers with large acreage could afford. Thus, many poor peasants did not benefit from the new technology. Many were forced off their small farms, unable to compete with larger, more efficient agricultural enterprises.

**Enduring issues.** Technology has improved life for people everywhere. Many people, especially in the industrial world, pin their hopes on technology to solve a variety of economic, medical, and environmental problems. Yet it has not solved such basic problems as hunger or poverty. Also, while technology has created many new kinds of jobs, it has threatened others. For example, a single computer can process thousands of telephone calls that were once handled by human operators.

## A New International Culture

"Radio has changed everything," noted Egyptian leader Gamal Abdel Nasser in the 1950s. "Today, people in the most remote villages hear of what is happening and form their opinions." Modern communications technology has indeed created "a new world." Radio, television, satellites, fax machines, and computer networks have put people everywhere in touch and helped create a global culture.

**A westernized popular culture.** The driving force behind this new global culture has been the United States. Since World War II, American fads, fashions, music, and entertainment have captured the world's imagination. American movies and television programs play to audiences in Moscow, Beijing, Buenos Aires, and Cairo. Blue jeans, soft drinks, and fast foods

# PARALLELS THROUGH TIME

## Television

The first public television broadcasts were transmitted in 1936. Since then, television has become the most influential form of communication in the world.

**Linking Past and Present** Today, more people get their news from television than from newspapers. What do you think are the advantages and disadvantages of television over earlier sources of information?

**PAST** *In 1949, there were a million television sets in the United States. By 1953, there were over 20 million. That same year, the very first issue of* TV Guide *(left) had a cover story on television's most popular program,* I Love Lucy.

**PRESENT** *Today, television reaches almost every corner of the world. Below, an Egyptian family watches a religious program. At right, French television listings include such American programs as* The Simpsons *and* Dr. Quinn, Medicine Woman.

first popularized in the United States are marketed around the world. English has become the leading language of international business.

In some countries, critics have compared this westernization of culture to a foreign invasion. Yet the new global culture sometimes balanced western and nonwestern traditions. From Latin America, popular music such as calypso and reggae gained international popularity. Movie makers like Japan's Akira Kurosawa and India's Satyajit Ray adapted western techniques to express their own distinct traditions.

**The arts.** Global exchanges have influenced literature and the visual arts for hundreds of years. By the 1700s, Europeans were copying Turkish carpets and Chinese pottery. A century later, European painters adapted Japanese printmaking traditions. About the same time, however, Japanese artists were studying the styles of European painters. More recently, writers from Africa to the Middle East to India have adapted western literary forms, such as the novel.

In the twentieth century, the western world gained a new appreciation for the arts of other civilizations. Western artists studied African and Southeast Asian sculptures, dances, and music. Collectors valued Persian or Chinese paintings as well as ancient Mayan or Incan works.

**Preserving ancient cultures.** Global interest in the arts has made nations realize the value of ancient cultural treasures. The UN and other groups are helping countries preserve and restore temples, palaces, manuscripts, and other artifacts. Museums, too, preserve the heritage of past cultures. Traveling exhibits of Egyptian jewelry, Russian icons, Native American carvings, Indian sculpture, or African masks help modern audiences understand cultures from other times and places.

## Looking Ahead

Many current trends and issues emerged long before 1945 and will continue beyond 2000. At the same time, new issues and conflicts will almost certainly take shape in the new millennium, or thousand-year period, that begins after the year 2000.

The next five chapters trace how the trends discussed in this chapter have affected different regions. As you read, notice how two contradic-

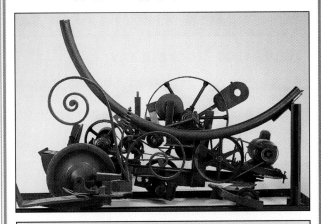

ART HISTORY

**M.K. III** *The modern fascination with technology led to a new art form called kinetic, or moving, sculpture. Using parts found in junkyards, Swiss artist Jean Tinguely created elaborate, machinelike constructions like this one. Powered by electric motors, Tinguely's sculptures moved, made noise, or even produced abstract paintings. Others were designed to self-destruct!* **Art and Literature** *How do sculptures like this poke fun at modern machines?*

tory trends are shaping the world. Nationalism is on the rise. Yet global interdependence has become an inescapable fact of life. In many nations and regions, people must reconcile local and global interests.

## SECTION 3 REVIEW

1. **Define** liberation theology.
2. How has urbanization affected people in developing nations?
3. Describe two ways in which women's lives have changed in recent decades.
4. Describe how three developments in science or technology have affected the modern world.
5. How have American influences helped shape a new global culture?
6. *Critical Thinking* **Predicting Consequences** What do you think might be some major global issues of the next century?
7. *ACTIVITY* Imagine that you are a scholar, a business leader, or a teenager in a Third World nation. Draw a cartoon or poster expressing your feelings about westernization.

## CHAPTER REVIEW

### REVIEWING VOCABULARY

Choose *four* vocabulary words from this chapter. Then, write a sentence for each word in which you define the word and describe its relation to the postwar world.

### REVIEWING FACTS

1. Why did many new nations emerge in the years after World War II?

2. What was the Universal Declaration of Human Rights?

3. Explain what is meant by the terms "global North" and "global South."

4. What were the causes of the debt crisis faced by many poor nations?

5. How has urbanization affected life in the developing world?

6. List some of the medical breakthroughs of the postwar era.

## SKILLS FOR SUCCESS    INTERPRETING STATISTICAL TABLES

Statistics, or numerical data, can be arranged in a table for quick, easy interpretation. However, you must be very careful when drawing conclusions from statistics. Though the data appear clear and concise, they can prove misleading.

The table below contains health statistics for 10 countries. Study the table, then answer the following questions.

1. **Study the statistical data in the table.** (a) What kinds of information does the chart provide for each country? (b) Which country has the most physicians relative to the population?

2. **Compare the data and look for relationships.** (a) What is the apparent relationship between the number of physicians per person and life

expectancy? (b) Which statistics might have a relationship to infant mortality? Why? (c) Look at the map on page 415. Which countries on this chart are part of the global North? The global South?

3. **Interpret the information.** Make two generalizations about the global North and the global South based on this table.

### Health Statistics of Selected Countries, 1996

| Country | Population (thousands) | Life Expectancy at Birth (male/female) | Hospital Beds (per 1,000 people) | Physicians (per 1,000 people) | Infant Mortality (deaths per 1,000) |
|---|---|---|---|---|---|
| Argentina | 34,673 | 68/75 | 4.4 | 2.7 | 28 |
| Australia | 18,261 | 76/83 | 5.0 | 2.3 | 6 |
| Guatemala | 11,278 | 63/68 | * | 0.8 | 51 |
| Japan | 125,450 | 77/83 | 13.5 | 1.8 | 4 |
| Jordan | 4,212 | 71/75 | 1.1 | 1.7 | 32 |
| Myanmar | 45,976 | 55/58 | 0.6 | 0.3 | 81 |
| Netherlands | 15,568 | 75/81 | 5.7 | 2.6 | 5 |
| Poland | 38,643 | 68/76 | 5.6 | 2.2 | 12 |
| United States | 265,563 | 73/79 | 4.5 | 2.6 | 7 |
| Zaire | 46,498 | 45/49 | 2.1 | 0.1 | 108 |

Source: *World Almanac and Book of Facts.*                    * *Data unavailable*

## REVIEWING CHAPTER THEMES

Review the "Focus On" questions at the start of this chapter. Then select *three* of those questions and answer them, using information from the chapter.

## CRITICAL THINKING

1. **Analyzing Information** (a) Why might lack of experience with representative government be a problem for developing nations? (b) Do you think democracy will help them solve their problems?

2. **Linking Past and Present** Review pages 57 and 69–70. How does the idea of universal human rights echo the French Declaration of the Rights of Man and the Citizen and the American Bill of Rights?

## ANALYZING PRIMARY SOURCES

Use the quotation on page 416 to answer the following questions.

1. According to the report, roughly what percentage of the poor are children?

2. Do most of these poor children live in cities or on farms?

3. What is true about the living conditions for almost all poor children?

## FOR YOUR PORTFOLIO

**WRITING A MAGAZINE FEATURE** Imagine that you are a staff writer on a magazine for teens and that your editor has asked you to write a two-page feature showing how fashions, foods, music, art, and other aspects of lifestyle have helped create a global culture. Do outside research to find current articles on this subject, as well as photographs, charts, and other visuals to illustrate your feature. Use your research notes to outline your article. Then draft your article. Ask a classmate to act as your editor and make comments. Finally, prepare your revised article for publication.

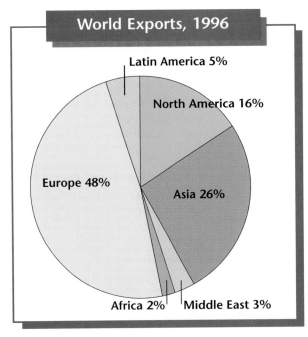

**World Exports, 1996**

- Latin America 5%
- North America 16%
- Europe 48%
- Asia 26%
- Africa 2%
- Middle East 3%

## ANALYZING GRAPHS

Use the graph and information from the chapter to answer the following questions.

1. Which region had the largest share of world exports in 1996?

2. Are the regions with the smallest shares of world exports in the global North or the global South?

3. Compare the information in the graph with the map on page 415. What link do these two graphics suggest between exports and per capita income?

**INTERNET ACTIVITY**

**REPORTING ON CURRENT EVENTS**
Use the Internet to research one of the present-day issues mentioned in the chapter, such as science and technology, global warming, urbanization, or human rights. Then write a report on the status of that issue today. You may want to include photos, diagrams, graphs, or charts to illustrate your topic.

# CHAPTER
# 16

# Europe and North America

## (1945–Present)

## CHAPTER OUTLINE

An East German farm woman told a visitor of her daring adventure in November 1989:

66One day last week, I took my bike and—just went over. I had to stop and laugh! I felt so strange. For 40 years we couldn't do something so simple. I just had to stop and laugh.99

All she had done was to ride a short distance across the border from East Germany into West Germany. But that simple action would have been impossible just a few weeks earlier. For decades, grim-faced guards and police dogs had patrolled the wasteland of barbed wire, mine fields, and concrete that divided east from west.

In the divided city of Berlin, a giant concrete wall kept East Berliners "at home." Time and again, East German guards obeyed orders to "shoot to kill" anyone trying to cross into West Berlin. Then, in November 1989, the unthinkable suddenly happened. As a wave of change engulfed the communist world, a million East Germans protested their communist government. "We are the people!" they chanted. "Democracy, now or never!"

Under growing pressure, the East German government opened the border. Families from both sides clambered up "the Wall" before hammers smashed its weather-pitted concrete into history. (See the picture on page 433.)

For almost a half century after World War II, the Cold War loomed over Europe. Under its shadow, Western Europe and North America enjoyed their most rapid and sustained economic growth since the Industrial Revolution. On both sides of the Atlantic, governments pushed through broad new social programs.

Communist Eastern Europe also rebuilt under the iron hand of Stalin. In the Soviet Union, economic growth slowed and then stagnated in the 1980s. Efforts at major reform unleashed forces that brought the collapse of communism and an end to the Soviet Union. In the post-Cold War world, Europe faced new challenges.

## FOCUS ON these questions as you read:

- **Economics and Technology**
  How are global economic changes affecting the industrial West?

- **Continuity and Change**
  Why is Western Europe struggling with the issue of unity?

- **Impact of the Individual**
  How did individual leaders in Europe and North America reshape their nations?

- **Political and Social Systems**
  Why did communism collapse in the Soviet Union and Eastern Europe?

- **Diversity**
  Why have ethnic tensions in Europe increased since the end of the Cold War?

## TIME AND PLACE

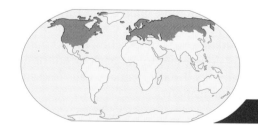

***Western Prosperity*** *The western world we know today took shape after World War II. In Europe and North America, as well as in Japan, rapid economic growth transformed cities into shimmering temples of glass and steel. Television, satellites, and computers sped up the pace of life. As the world's richest and most powerful nation, the United States strongly influenced the cultures of other nations. American artist Richard Estes captures the look and feel of a modern city in his painting* Central Savings. ***Economics and Technology*** *How does the painting suggest the complexity of modern life?*

## HUMANITIES LINK

***Art History*** Roy Lichtenstein, *Preparedness* (page 443).
***Literature*** In this chapter, you will encounter passages from the following works of literature: Martin Luther King, Jr., "I Have a Dream" (page 445); Yevgeny Yevtushenko, "The Heirs of Stalin" (page 447).

| **1954**<br>*Brown* v. *Board of Education* | **1957**<br>European Community formed | **1973**<br>Worldwide oil crisis | **1990**<br>Germany reunited | **1991**<br>Soviet Union collapses | **1997**<br>NATO expands into Eastern Europe |

| 1945 | 1960 | 1975 | 1990 | PRESENT |

# 1 The Western World: An Overview

## Guide for Reading

- How did the Cold War pose a threat to Europe?

- How have economic cycles affected Europe?

- How did European nations pursue cooperation and peace?

- **Vocabulary** *détente, welfare state, service industry*

Western Europe rebounded out of the rubble of World War II. During the postwar years, standards of living rose dramatically. People earned higher wages, bought homes with central heating and running water, and enjoyed luxuries unheard of in earlier times. Amid these comforts, many other changes were shaping the western world.

## The Cold War in Europe

For more than 40 years, the Cold War divided Europe into two hostile military alliances. The communist nations of Eastern Europe, dominated by the Soviet Union, formed the Warsaw Pact. The western democracies, led by the United States, formed NATO. (See the map on page 395.) In general, the superpowers avoided direct confrontation in Europe. Yet several incidents brought the continent to the brink of war.

**The Berlin Wall.** Berlin remained a focus of Cold War tensions. The city was divided between democratic West Berlin and communist East Berlin. In the 1950s, West Berlin became a showcase for West Germany, whose economy boomed. Thousands of low-paid East Germans, many of them professionals who were discontented with communism, slipped across the border into prosperous West Berlin.

To stop its citizens from fleeing, the East German government built a wall in 1961 that separated the two sectors of the city. The Berlin

Wall grew into a massive concrete barrier, topped with barbed wire and patrolled by guards. It became an ugly symbol of the Cold War and a propaganda defeat for the Soviets. It showed that workers, far from enjoying a communist paradise, had to be forcibly restrained from fleeing. As you will see, revolts in Eastern Europe further shone a negative light on Soviet rule.

**The nuclear peril.** Over a 40-year period, the Cold War sometimes heated up and then cooled off. Each crisis triggered a new round in the arms race. Both sides produced huge arsenals of nuclear weapons. Europe, especially Germany, sat in the middle of this deadly weapons storehouse. If a "shooting" war erupted, it could be destroyed.

Critics denounced the buildup. A nuclear war, they said, would destroy both sides. Yet the superpowers argued that they dared not stop because each side wanted to have the power to deter the other from launching its nuclear weapons. The result was a "balance of terror."

**Disarmament and détente.** Both sides tried to avoid a nuclear showdown by holding disarmament talks. But mutual distrust often blocked progress. In 1963, the superpowers signed the Nuclear Test Ban Treaty, which prohibited the testing of nuclear weapons in the atmosphere. Underground testing was still permitted, however.

By the 1970s, American and Soviet leaders promoted an era of détente (day TAHNT), or relaxation of tensions. Détente brought new agreements to reduce nuclear stockpiles. Détente faced a severe setback, however, when the Soviet Union invaded Afghanistan in 1979.

The arms race had a huge cost. Both superpowers invested fantastic sums of money in

**GLOBAL CONNECTIONS**

In 1959, the United States and the Soviet Union joined 10 other nations—including Argentina, Australia, Japan, France, and South Africa—in signing the Antarctic Treaty. It forbade all parties from building military bases, testing nuclear weapons, or disposing of radioactive wastes on or around Antarctica. It also encouraged cooperation among scientists from all nations who conduct research on the continent. Other nations later agreed to the treaty.

building weapons systems. The Soviet Union spent a large portion of its budget on the military, which meant cutbacks in other areas of the economy. The United States, too, paid a large price to support its military preparedness. In 1953, President Dwight Eisenhower had warned:

> 66Every gun that is made, every warship launched, every rocket fired, signifies, in the final sense, a theft from those who hunger and are not fed, those who are cold and are not clothed. . . . The cost of one modern heavy bomber is this: a modern brick school in more than 30 cities.99

**A new era.** By the 1990s, as you will read, a new Soviet leader, Mikhail Gorbachev (mee kī EEL gor bah CHAWF), loosened the Soviet grip on Eastern Europe. One after another, communist governments collapsed, setting the stage for the ultimate collapse of the Soviet Union itself.

As the Cold War ended, nations in Western and Eastern Europe sought normal relations. Germany was reunited. The Warsaw Pact dissolved. NATO, originally formed to defend the West against communism, had to redefine its role in a post-Cold War world.

Even as Europeans celebrated the end of the Cold War, new issues arose. Many Eastern Europeans fled economic hardships to find work in the West. The newcomers were not always welcomed. Ethnic clashes, especially in the Balkans, created new tensions that threatened the peace of Europe.

## Recovery and Growth in Western Europe

With Marshall Plan aid, Western European countries recovered fairly quickly from World War II. They rebuilt industries, farms, and transportation networks destroyed by the war. In the 1950s, western economies boomed.

On the political front, right-wing parties, which had supported fascism, were discredited. In France, Italy, and Germany, communists and socialists had often led the resistance against the Nazis. Many postwar governments thus adopted policies favored by the left.

**The welfare state.** A major goal of leftist parties was to extend the welfare state. Under this system, a government keeps most features of a capitalist economy but takes greater responsibility for the social and economic needs of its people. The welfare state had its roots in the late 1800s, when governments passed reforms to ease the hardships of the industrial age. Germany, Britain, and other nations banned child labor, regulated mine safety, and set up public schools, unemployment insurance, and old-age pensions. (See Chapter 5.)

*Chapter 16* **433**

After 1945, governments expanded these programs. Both the middle class and the poor benefited from national health care, unemployment insurance, old-age pensions, and new policies that let any qualified student go to college. Other programs gave aid to the poor and created an economic cushion to help people through hard times. Still, the welfare state was costly, involving many new taxes and greater government regulation.

Socialists supported the welfare state and a larger role for government in the economy. In Britain, France, and elsewhere, governments nationalized basic industries such as railroads, airlines, banks, coal, steel, and nuclear power. Conservatives condemned the drift away from free enterprise toward socialism.

**The oil shock.** As you read in Chapter 15, the West was tied into a complex global economy. In 1973, the West suffered an economic jolt when OPEC cut oil production and raised prices. (See page 416.) Since most Western European countries used imported oil to fuel industries, the higher prices hurt. The oil crisis slowed economic growth. In 1979, OPEC again raised prices, triggering a severe recession. Factories and businesses cut back, and unemployment rose.

**Economic shifts.** At the same time, the West faced growing competition from other parts of the world. For 200 years, western factories had exported basic goods to the world. By the 1980s, however, the pattern changed. Japan, already an industrial power, enjoyed dra-

# PARALLELS THROUGH TIME

## When Leaders Meet

No Roman emperor ever met an emperor of China face to face. Queen Elizabeth I of England never sat down to dinner with the Ottoman sultan Suleiman. But today, leaders of great powers often get together to discuss war, peace, and the challenges of an interdependent world.

**Linking Past and Present** Why is direct contact between world leaders easier today than in the past?

**PAST** After World War I, the leaders of the three most powerful nations—David Lloyd George of Britain, Georges Clemenceau of France, and Woodrow Wilson of the United States—met at the Paris peace conference (right). At the height of the Cold War, leaders of the two superpowers held infrequent summit meetings to ease tensions. Below right, President John Kennedy shakes hands with Soviet leader Nikita Khrushchev.

**PRESENT** The Group of Seven (G-7), leaders of the seven most prosperous capitalist nations, meet annually to discuss economic issues. Above, the leaders of Germany, France, Britain, the United States, Canada, Japan, and Italy pose at a G-7 meeting. Russia has since joined the G-7.

matic growth after World War II. Other countries, such as China and India, also expanded their industries. In addition, western-based multinational corporations set up factories in the developing world, where labor was cheap. From there, they exported goods to the West.

Older industries in the West could not compete with those cheaper production costs. Many factories had to close, throwing workers out of their jobs. Western nations remained rich and powerful, but their economies changed. Most new jobs at home were created not in manufacturing but in service industries. A service industry is one that provides a service rather than a product. Service industries include health care, finance, sales, education, and recreation.

The economic slowdown of the 1970s and 1980s forced governments to cut costs. Some moved away from the welfare state, reducing benefits. Conservative governments privatized state-owned industries. In the new economic climate, the gap between rich and poor grew, but most people still enjoyed a relatively high standard of living.

## Toward European Unity

Europe's recovery from World War II was helped by economic cooperation. In 1952, six nations—France, West Germany, Belgium, Italy, the Netherlands, and Luxembourg—set up the European Coal and Steel Community. This independent agency set prices and otherwise regulated the coal and steel industries of member states. This cooperation spurred economic growth across Western Europe.

**The Common Market.** In 1957, the same six nations signed a treaty to form the European Community (EC), or Common Market, to expand free trade. Over the next decades, the Common Market gradually ended tariffs on goods and allowed labor and capital to move freely across national borders. It set up the European Parliament, a multinational body elected by citizens of the Common Market countries. Its powers were limited, however, since member states remained independent.

**European Union.** Despite disputes between members, the Common Market prospered. In 1973, after much debate, Britain was admitted, along with Denmark and Ireland. In

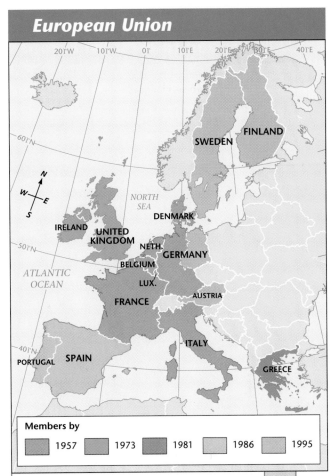

## European Union

Members by
1957 | 1973 | 1981 | 1986 | 1995

## GEOGRAPHY AND HISTORY

The European Union, formerly known as the Common Market, created a vast free-trade zone across most of Western Europe.

1. **Location** On the map, locate (a) United Kingdom, (b) France, (c) Germany, (d) Denmark, (e) Ireland, (f) Belgium.
2. **Region** (a) How many nations belonged to the European Union by 1973? (b) Which nations shown on the map joined most recently?
3. *Critical Thinking* **Synthesizing Information** Compare this map to the map on page 642. (a) Which European nations were not members of the European Union by 1995? (b) Based on your reading, why were most of these nations not included?

the 1980s and 1990s, it expanded still further and took the name the European Union (EU). With the end of communism, some Eastern European nations were eager to join the EU.

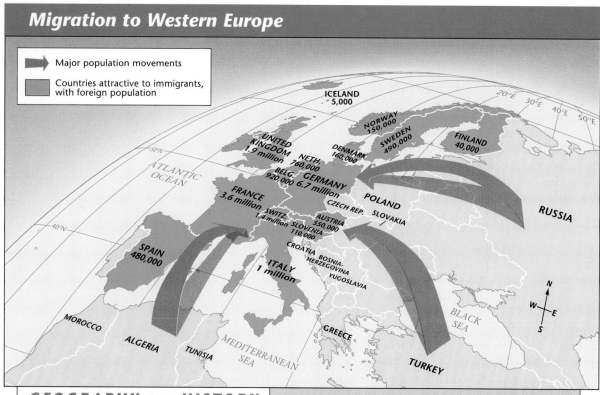

## Migration to Western Europe

**Legend:**
- Major population movements
- Countries attractive to immigrants, with foreign population

ICELAND 5,000

NORWAY 150,000

SWEDEN 490,000

FINLAND 40,000

UNITED KINGDOM 1.9 million

DENMARK 160,000

NETH. 760,000

BELG. 920,000

GERMANY 6.7 million

FRANCE 3.6 million

SWITZ. 1.4 million

AUSTRIA 550,000

SLOVENIA 110,000

SPAIN 480,000

ITALY 1 million

ATLANTIC OCEAN

POLAND

CZECH REP.

SLOVAKIA

RUSSIA

CROATIA

BOSNIA HERZEGOVINA

YUGOSLAVIA

GREECE

BLACK SEA

TURKEY

MOROCCO

ALGERIA

TUNISIA

MEDITERRANEAN SEA

## GEOGRAPHY AND HISTORY

Today, as in the past, nations with higher income tend to attract immigrants from poorer countries. By the 1990s, Western European nations were receiving more than two million new immigrants a year.

1. **Location** On the map, locate (a) France, (b) Algeria, (c) Germany, (d) Turkey, (e) Russia.
2. **Movement** (a) Which three countries had the largest foreign populations? (b) What was the foreign-born population of Austria? Italy? Iceland?
3. **Critical Thinking** **Linking Past and Present** Why has France become a major destination of immigrants from Algeria?

The EU became a powerful economic force. With just over 6 percent of the world's population, it controlled 37 percent of the world's trade. The EU also promoted regional peace by replacing destructive competition with an amazing degree of cooperation.

**Nationalism versus unity.** By the late 1990s, the EU was pushing for complete economic unity, a single currency, and greater political unity. EU members welcomed the benefits of cooperation. Still, nationalist feelings remained strong. Many British leaders, such as Margaret Thatcher, opposed increased links with Europe. In Denmark, too, voters opposed changes that they feared would destroy their unique identity. Thus, a United States of Europe seemed unlikely to emerge any time soon.

## Social Trends

The pace of social change speeded up after 1945. Class lines blurred as prosperity spread. For most of western history, a tiny wealthy class had dominated the majority of the people. By the 1950s, more and more people in the West belonged to the middle class. As wages rose, working-class people bought homes and cars, and their children could qualify to study at state-funded universities. Although grim pockets of poverty remained, most people had opportunities unknown in earlier times.

**Ethnic diversity.** Since the 1950s, many immigrants from former colonies in Asia, Africa, and the Caribbean settled in Europe. In Germany and elsewhere in Europe, "guest workers"

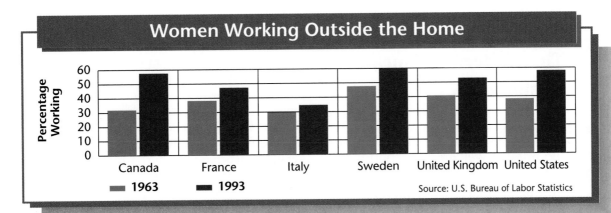

## Women Working Outside the Home

Percentage Working

Canada | France | Italy | Sweden | United Kingdom | United States
■ 1963   ■ 1993

Source: U.S. Bureau of Labor Statistics

*Interpreting a Graph* The number of women working outside the home varied from country to country. In general, though, all western nations saw a dramatic rise in the female work force after World War II. ■ What percentage of Canadian women worked outside the home in 1963? In 1993? In which countries were fewer than half the women working outside the home by 1993?

from Turkey and the Middle East provided low-wage labor for booming economies. Most lived in segregated areas and faced discrimination.

During later economic recessions, Europeans resented newcomers who competed with them for scarce jobs. In some countries, ultranationalists and racist thugs attacked and sometimes killed foreign workers and immigrants.

**Women.** In 1949, French writer Simone de Beauvoir (boh VWAHR) analyzed the status of women in western society:

66The two sexes have never shared the world in equality. And even today woman is heavily handicapped, though her situation is beginning to change. Almost nowhere is her legal status the same as man's, and frequently it is much to her disadvantage.99

Since then, women in Europe and North America have made progress toward legal and economic equality. (See page 424.) A growing number of women worked outside the home. Despite efforts to ensure equality, however, women's pay lagged behind that of men. Women in many careers ran into a "glass ceiling," an invisible barrier that kept them from promotion to top jobs.

A woman's income helped improve her family's standard of living. But while ideals about families survived, family life itself changed. Western families had fewer children than in the past. Children remained in school longer to get skills needed in advanced industrial societies.

Family stability, however, seemed to decline. The divorce rate rose. In cases where a divorced father separated himself from his financial responsibilities, women and children suffered. Dependent only on a mother's income, a growing number of woman-headed families found themselves living in poverty.

## SECTION 1 REVIEW

1. **Identify** (a) Berlin Wall, (b) Nuclear Test Ban Treaty, (c) Common Market, (d) European Union.
2. **Define** (a) détente, (b) welfare state, (c) service industry.
3. (a) Describe two effects of the Cold War on Europe. (b) What were two results of the end of the Cold War?
4. Describe how each of the following affected western economies: (a) oil crisis of 1973, (b) shift of manufacturing jobs to other parts of the world.
5. How did Western European nations achieve greater unity after World War II?
6. *Critical Thinking* **Predicting Consequences** (a) Why did European nations move toward the welfare state? (b) What benefits and drawbacks might this policy have for individuals and nations?
7. *ACTIVITY* Draw a political cartoon about the Berlin Wall, the nuclear arms race, or another Cold War issue from the viewpoint of a small nation in Western Europe.

# 2 The Western European Democracies

## Guide for Reading

- How did Britain's welfare state change in the 1980s?

- What problems did France overcome in the postwar period?

- How did Germany achieve unity?

In July 1994, an army of bicycles snaked through the English countryside, cheered on by a million spectators. The event was the famous Tour de France bicycle race. The cyclists had crossed from France through the new Channel tunnel, nicknamed Chunnel. For the first time since the ice age, a land route linked Britain and continental Europe.

To an English spectator, the Chunnel was an important symbol. "It's all about the future," he said, "about being part of Europe." The Chunnel reflected increased ties between Britain and France as well as improved relations among European nations generally.

After 1945, the Western European democracies operated within a growing framework of regional and global cooperation, including the Common Market, NATO, and the UN. Each nation, however, faced its own problems and made its own contributions to postwar freedom and prosperity.

## Britain: Government and the Economy

World War II left Britain physically battered and economically drained. In 1945, voters put the Labour party in power. The war had helped change old attitudes toward the working class. A Labour official noted that if a working-class boy "can save us in a Spitfire, the same brain can be turned to produce a new world."

That "new world" gave government an ever-larger role in the economy. It nationalized major industries and expanded social welfare bene-fits such as unemployment insurance and old-age pensions. The government built housing for the poor and opened new state-funded universities. A national health service extended free or low-cost medical care to all citizens. To pay for all these benefits, taxes rose tremendously.

**Welfare rollback.** Later governments generally accepted the welfare state. By 1979, however, Britain, like the rest of Europe, was reeling under economic hard times. The Conservative party won power from the Labour party. Led by Margaret Thatcher, Conservatives denounced the welfare state as costly and inefficient. During 11 years as Britain's prime minister, Thatcher worked to replace government social and economic programs with what she called an "enterprise culture" that promoted individual initiative.

Thatcher privatized government-run industries. She curbed the power of labor unions, reduced the size of the government bureaucracy, and cut back welfare services. These changes did help to slow government spending but did not revive the British economy as much as Thatcher had hoped. And many people who faced unemployment and declining services reacted with demonstrations, strikes, and general unrest.

▲ Margaret Thatcher

**A new world role.** After the war, Britain adjusted to a new world role. The British empire shrank as colonies in Asia and Africa won independence. (See page 410.) Still, many former colonies preserved their ties to Britain by joining the Commonwealth of Nations. Immigrants from former British colonies—such as India, Pakistan, and the West Indies—surged into Britain. Increased diversity sometimes led to social tensions.

Weakened by the war and its loss of empire, Britain reluctantly gave up global leadership to its close ally, the United States. Yet it remained a major player in the UN and was active in NATO efforts to resist Soviet power. Britain also sought closer ties within Western Europe. In

1973, it joined the Common Market. By the 1990s, however, surging British nationalism led some people to reject greater European unity.

**Northern Ireland.** When Ireland won independence in 1922, Britain retained control of six northern counties. (See page 351.) Northern Ireland remained a source of bitter conflict. In the face of widespread discrimination, many Catholics demanded civil rights and pressed for the reunification of Ireland. Protestants wanted to remain part of Britain.

Violence escalated in the early 1970s. Extremists on both sides turned to terrorism, killing many people. Betty Williams, co-founder of a joint Catholic-Protestant peace league, described the atmosphere of violence:

> 66Last week I had a bomb scare. They [radical IRA members] rang me up at one o'clock in the morning and said they were going to come and bomb the house. And me with my cheeky attitude, I said, 'You'd better hurry up, because I want to get to sleep.' Then I sat up all night, because I have two kids and I was really frightened that they would hurt the children.99

British soldiers were stationed throughout Northern Ireland to keep order. But their presence inflamed tensions, especially as they jailed IRA members and violated their civil rights.

Outbreaks of violence continued for more than 20 years. A cease-fire declared in 1995 did not hold. Talks were held on and off, leading many people on both sides to hope for a lasting peace.

## France: Revival and Prosperity

Like Britain, France was greatly weakened by World War II. The Fourth French Republic, set up in 1946, did little to renew confidence. Ineffective cabinets drew criticism from both communists and conservatives. Bloody colonial wars in Vietnam and Algeria further drained and demoralized France.

**De Gaulle.** In Algeria, longtime French settlers and the French military opposed Algerian nationalists who wanted independence. France itself was so divided over the issue that civil war threatened. Amid the deepening crisis,

**Hope for Peace** Conflict between Catholics and Protestants in Northern Ireland exploded in the 1970s. The Irish Republican Army, or IRA, attacked British troops and Protestant groups. Protestant militias targeted the IRA and Catholic civilians. Hopes for peace rose in the mid-1990s after the IRA announced a cease-fire. Peace talks were held, but violence broke out anew. This poster from Northern Ireland supports peace and the withdrawal of British troops. **Continuity and Change** Why do you think the conflict in Northern Ireland has lasted so long?

voters turned to General Charles de Gaulle, who had led the Free French during the war.

In 1958, de Gaulle set up the Fifth Republic. Its constitution gave him, as president, great power. Although a staunch nationalist, de Gaulle realized that France must give up Algeria. In 1962, he made peace with the Algerians. Other French colonies in Africa soon won freedom without bloodshed. (See Chapter 19.)

De Gaulle worked hard to restore French prestige and power. He forged new ties with West Germany, ending the long hostility between the two nations. He developed a French nuclear force and challenged American dominance in Europe. For example, he opposed the Cold War stance of the United States and opened talks with communist nations such as China and Cuba.

In 1968, youth revolts shook France. The next year, de Gaulle resigned. Although he was widely disliked by the left, he had successfully asserted French leadership in Europe.

**Economic revival.** Like Britain, France nationalized some industries and expanded social welfare benefits after the war. With government help, industry and business modernized, leading to new prosperity by the 1970s.

French Socialists, led by François Mitterrand, won power in the early 1980s, just as a global economic recession hit. Mitterrand's efforts to nationalize more industries and expand welfare benefits deepened the crisis. A practical man, he then took a more moderate course and encouraged the growth of private business. His successor, Jacques Chirac, set out to cut government spending. His policies sparked protests by students, farmers, and other groups.

## Germany: Reunited at Last

The early years after World War II were a desperate time for Germany. People were starving amid a landscape of destruction. German cities lay in ruins. "Nothing is left in Berlin," wrote an American reporter:

66There are no homes, no shops, no transportation, no government buildings. Only a few walls. . . . Berlin can now be regarded only as a geographical location heaped with mountainous mounds of debris.99

By 1949, feuds among the Allies divided Germany. (See page 394.) West Germany was a member of the western alliance. East Germany lay in the Soviet orbit. Over the next decades, differences between the two Germanies widened, and the Soviet Union opposed a unified Germany that might pose a new threat to its security.

**West Germany's "economic miracle."** As the Cold War began, the United States rushed aid to its former enemy. It wanted to strengthen West Germany against the communist tide sweeping Eastern Europe. From 1949 to 1963, West Germany was guided by a strong-minded chancellor, Konrad Adenauer (AD ehn ow er). During this time, West Germans rebuilt their cities, factories, and trade. Despite high taxes to pay for the recovery, West Germany created a booming industrial economy.

This "economic miracle" raised European fears of a German revival. But West German leaders worked closely with France and the United States. West Germany also played a key role in NATO and the European Community.

While West Germany remained a capitalist country, later chancellors belonged to the Socialist party. They expanded the welfare state. German workers won unemployment benefits, pensions, and long summer vacations.

**East Germany.** The postwar decades brought no economic miracle to East Germany. Under communist rule, its economy rebuilt but stagnated. The Soviet Union exploited East German workers and industry for its own benefit. Still, unemployment was low, and East German workers did have some basic benefits, such as health care, housing, and free education.

Lured by glittering views of the West, however, many East Germans fled. As you have read, this mass exodus led to the building of the

Berlin Wall in 1961. Overnight, the migration ended. Occasionally, an East German made a dramatic escape. Many died in the attempt.

**Ostpolitik.** In 1969, West German chancellor Willy Brandt tried to ease tensions with communist neighbors to the east. He called his policy *Ostpolitik,* or "eastern policy." While he kept close ties with the West, Brandt signed treaties with the USSR and Poland. He opened economic doors to Eastern Europe and signed a treaty of mutual recognition with East Germany. But Brandt's long-term goal—the reunification of Germany—seemed impossible in the Cold War world.

**Reunification.** By 1989, the decline of communism in the Soviet Union at last made reunification possible. Without Soviet power to back them up, East German communist leaders were forced out of office. The Wall was dismantled, as you read, and Germans set about reuniting their divided land.

West German chancellor Helmut Kohl was the architect of unity. He assured both the Soviet Union and the West that a united Germany would pose no threat to peace. In 1990, German voters approved reunification, and Kohl became chancellor of a united Germany.

**New challenges.** While Germans welcomed unity, the change brought a number of serious problems. Prosperous West Germans had to pay higher taxes to finance the rebuilding of the east. At the same time, East Germans faced a difficult transition to a market economy. As old government-run factories closed, unemployment rose.

The economic shock fed social problems. A few right-wing extremists revived Nazi ideology. Seeing the answer to hard times in racism and hatred, these neo-Nazis viciously attacked foreign workers. Most Germans condemned such actions and worked instead to fulfill the hopes of unity.

## Other Democratic Nations of the West

Other parts of Western Europe slowly recovered from the war. The Scandinavian countries of Norway, Sweden, and Denmark created extensive socialist welfare programs. By the 1990s, rising costs revived debate about how much people were willing to pay for the welfare state. Yet many people saw these social programs as essential to a democratic society.

**Italy.** Postwar Italy was economically divided. In the urban north, industries rebuilt and prospered. In the rural south, the largely peasant population remained much poorer.

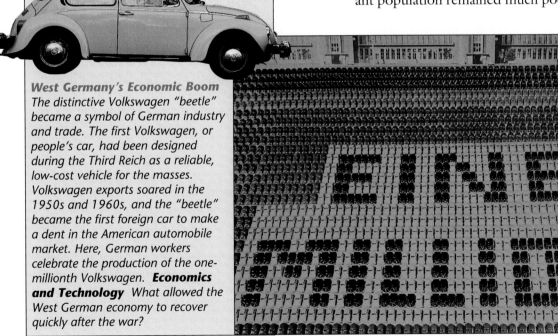

*West Germany's Economic Boom*
*The distinctive Volkswagen "beetle" became a symbol of German industry and trade. The first Volkswagen, or people's car, had been designed during the Third Reich as a reliable, low-cost vehicle for the masses. Volkswagen exports soared in the 1950s and 1960s, and the "beetle" became the first foreign car to make a dent in the American automobile market. Here, German workers celebrate the production of the one-millionth Volkswagen.* **Economics and Technology** *What allowed the West German economy to recover quickly after the war?*

Politically, Italy's multiparty system led to instability, as one coalition government succeeded another. The Italian Communist party was strong, although it never won enough votes to become a majority. Corruption and financial scandals shook the major political parties. The Mafia, a violent criminal syndicate, defied government efforts to end its power, especially in the south. Despite these problems, Italy made impressive economic gains and joined the powerful Group of Seven.

**Democratic gains.** Change came more slowly to three other countries of southern Europe: Spain, Portugal, and Greece. In 1945, all were economically undeveloped with large peasant populations. In Spain and Portugal, dictators clung to power for decades. Finally, in the 1970s, both Spain's Francisco Franco and Portugal's Antonio Salazar died. Their authoritarian governments soon collapsed. Both countries adopted democratic governments and eventually won admission to the Common Market. Their economies have grown rapidly.

After World War II, communist rebels unleashed a civil war in Greece. With American aid, the government won. Later military rulers imposed a right-wing government. In 1975, however, Greece returned to civilian rule.

## SECTION 2 REVIEW

1. **Identify** (a) Konrad Adenauer, (b) Ostpolitik, (c) Helmut Kohl, (d) neo-Nazis.
2. What impact did Margaret Thatcher's policies have on Britain's welfare state?
3. Describe two steps Charles de Gaulle took to reassert French power in Europe.
4. (a) How did the experiences of West Germany and East Germany differ after World War II? (b) Why was Germany finally able to reunify?
5. *Critical Thinking* **Defending a Position** Some people, especially in France, worried that a reunited Germany would pose a danger to Europe. Using historical evidence, explain why you agree or disagree.
6. *ACTIVITY* Design a banner or write a song about *either* the cease-fire in Northern Ireland or the reunification of Germany, from the viewpoint of someone living there.

# 3 North American Prosperity

## Guide for Reading

■ What world role did the United States take on after World War II?

■ How did economic prosperity and social reforms change American life?

■ What issues have shaped Canada?

■ **Vocabulary** *deficit*

❝Let every nation know that we shall pay any price, bear any burden, meet any hardship, support any friend, oppose any foe to assure the survival and the success of liberty.❞

John F. Kennedy made this vow when he became President in 1961. In the postwar era, the United States sought to contain communism, extend civil rights, and ensure economic prosperity. To the north, Canada also built democracy and prosperity.

## *The United States and the Cold War*

In 1945, the United States was the world's greatest military power and the only country with the atomic bomb. Yet it felt threatened by communist expansion, especially after the Soviet Union developed its own atomic bomb. For this and other reasons, the United States gave up its tradition of avoiding foreign alliances. During the Cold War, it used its vast economic and military resources to protect its interests and the security of the free, or non-communist, world.

**Global commitments.** The United States built bases overseas and organized military alliances from Europe to Southeast Asia. Its fleets patrolled the world's oceans and its air power provided a "nuclear umbrella" over its allies. American troops fought in major wars to stop the spread of communism in Korea and Vietnam. They joined UN peacekeeping missions in the Middle East and elsewhere.

**Preparedness** *This painting reflects the position of the United States as the world's dominant military and industrial power. The artist, Roy Lichtenstein, was a leading figure in the 1960s movement known as "pop" art. Pop artists used techniques and images drawn from the mass media and popular culture. Lichtenstein used bold colors, dots, and strong lines to imitate the style of a color comic strip.* **Art and Literature** *Identify three images that Lichtenstein uses to symbolize American might.*

Along with military efforts to contain communism, the United States funneled economic aid to help Europe rebuild and, later, to assist emerging nations. At times, American aid went to nations, such as Zaire and Iran, that were ruled by anti-communist dictators. Yet Presidents such as Jimmy Carter also pressed other countries to end human rights abuses.

**The Cold War at home.** Early in the Cold War, extreme anti-communists in the United States warned that Soviet agents were operating everywhere. Between 1950 and 1954, Senator Joseph McCarthy charged many Americans with harboring communist sympathies. Government probes, however, produced little evidence of subversion. Eventually, the Senate condemned McCarthy's reckless behavior, but not before his unjust charges had ruined the careers of thousands of Americans.

McCarthy's campaign took place while the United States was embroiled in a war to stop communist expansion in Korea. (See pages 472–473.) As the Korean War wound down,

President Eisenhower began to aid another Asian country that seemed threatened by a communist uprising, South Vietnam.

**Turmoil over Vietnam.** American involvement in Vietnam increased under Eisenhower's successors. Between 1964 and 1968, President Lyndon Johnson sent massive aid and a growing number of troops to Southeast Asia. Eventually, American forces there numbered half a million.

By 1967, Americans at home were bitterly divided over the Vietnam War. Many opposed supporting an unpopular regime in South Vietnam. Antiwar protesters disrupted college campuses and filled city streets. In 1968, Richard Nixon, a vigorous anti-communist, was elected President and promised to end American involvement in Vietnam. At first, Nixon widened the war. Actions such as the bombing of Cambodia sparked further protests at home. By 1974, though, Nixon finally negotiated an American withdrawal. The divisions within the nation, though, would take decades to heal.

*Chapter 16* **443**

**The post-Cold War world.** The end of the Cold War did not bring world peace. Instead, conflicts erupted in many places. As the sole superpower, the United States tried to resolve some of them. In 1991, it led a multinational force against Iraqi invaders of Kuwait. American forces restored Haiti's elected leader to power. After years of bloody civil war in Bosnia, the United States and its NATO allies imposed at least a temporary peace.

## Economy and the Role of Government

Unlike Europe, the United States emerged from World War II with its cities and industries undamaged. In 1945, it produced 50 percent of the world's manufactured goods. Factories soon shifted from tanks and bombers to peacetime production. With the Cold War looming, however, government military spending increased, creating many jobs in defense industries.

By the early 1950s, the American economy was booming. At home, a growing population demanded homes, cars, refrigerators, and thousands of other products. Overseas, American businesses were investing in Europe's recovery and expanding into markets around the globe.

**A wider role for government.** In the United States, as in Western Europe, government's role in the economy grew. Under President Harry Truman, Congress created generous benefits that helped veterans attend college or buy homes. Other Truman programs expanded FDR's New Deal, providing greater security for the elderly and poor.

Truman's successor, Dwight Eisenhower, tried to reduce the government's role in the economy. At the same time, he approved government funding to build a vast interstate highway system. This program spurred the growth of the auto, trucking, and related industries. Highways and home building changed the face of the nation. Many middle-class Americans moved out of cities to the booming suburbs, while inner-city neighborhoods deteriorated.

**The Great Society.** Reformers urged bold new programs to help the poor and disadvantaged. During the 1960s, the government expanded social programs. President Kennedy wanted to provide health care to the elderly. Af-

ter his assassination in 1963, Lyndon Johnson pressed ahead with a broad new program, which he called the Great Society. It funded Medicare for the elderly, job training and low-cost housing for the poor, and support for education. Many Americans came to rely on these programs in the next decades.

**The conservative response.** In the 1980s, conservatives challenged costly social programs and the growth of government. Like Margaret Thatcher in Britain, President Ronald Reagan called for cutbacks in government spending on social programs. Congress did end some welfare programs, reduce government regulation of the economy, and cut taxes. At the same time, military spending increased.

Government spending and tax cuts greatly increased the national deficit, the gap between what a government spends and what it takes in through taxes and other sources. As the deficit continued to grow in the 1990s, conservatives crusaded for deeper cuts in social and economic programs. Debate raged about how far to cut spending on programs ranging from education and welfare to environmental protection.

## The Civil Rights Movement

The 1950s seemed a peaceful time at home. Yet major changes were underway that would reshape American society. Among the most far-reaching was the civil rights movement.

**Equality under the law.** Although African Americans had won freedom nearly a century before, many states, especially in the South, denied them equality. Segregation was legal in education and housing. African Americans also faced discrimination in jobs and voting. In the 1950s and 1960s, the civil rights movement renewed earlier efforts to end racial injustice.

In 1954, the Supreme Court issued a landmark ruling in *Brown* v. *Board of Education of Topeka*. It declared that segregated schools were unconstitutional. Some southern states tried to resist court-ordered desegregation, but President Eisenhower and his successors used federal power to uphold the law.

**Martin Luther King, Jr.** By 1956, a gifted preacher, Dr. Martin Luther King, Jr., emerged as a leader of the civil rights movement. Inspired by Gandhi's campaign of civil disobedience in

**I Have a Dream** *Martin Luther King, Jr., was arrested dozens of times for breaking segregation laws. He explained that a person who willingly goes to jail "in order to arouse the conscience of the community over its injustice is in reality expressing the highest respect for law." This 1988 quilt by noted artist Faith Ringgold celebrates King and several women of the civil rights movement.* **Religions and Value Systems** *Do you think the fact that King was a minister made him a more effective spokesman for civil rights?*

India, King organized boycotts and led peaceful marches throughout the 1960s to end segregation in the United States.

Many black and white Americans joined the civil rights movement. Their courage in the face of sometimes brutal attacks stirred the nation's conscience. In 1963, at a huge civil rights rally in the nation's capital, King declared:

> ❝I have a dream that one day this nation will rise up and live out the true meaning of its creed: 'We hold these truths to be self-evident, that all men are created equal.'❞

**Progress and problems.** In time, Congress responded. It outlawed segregation in public accommodations, protected the rights of black voters, and required equal access to housing and jobs. Despite these victories, racial prejudice survived, and African Americans faced many economic obstacles. They earned less than whites. Poverty and unemployment plagued

African American communities in urban areas. Still, the civil rights movement provided wider opportunities. Many African Americans won elected offices or gained top jobs in business and the military.

**Other groups.** The civil rights movement inspired other groups, such as Native Americans and Hispanics, to campaign for equality. Women, too, renewed their efforts to gain equal rights. The new civil rights laws banned discrimination based on gender as well as race in hiring and promotion. More women ran successfully for political office, and many had begun to make progress toward high positions in business.

## The United States and the Global Economy

In the postwar decades, the United States profited greatly from the growing global economy. But interdependence also brought problems. In the 1970s, OPEC price hikes fed inflation and showed how much Americans relied on imported oil. Inflation also contributed to the Third World debt crisis, which involved American banks. (See Chapter 15.)

American industries faced stiff competition from Asian and other nations. Like Western Europe, the United States lost manufacturing jobs to the developing world. Some American corporations even moved operations to Mexico or Asia to take advantage of lower wages.

Still, the United States remained a rich nation and a magnet for immigrants. Unlike the immigrants of the late 1800s and early 1900s, these newcomers came largely from Latin America and Asia. By the 1990s, however, Americans were calling for tough laws to stop illegal immigration and to restrict benefits allowed to legal immigrants.

## Postwar Canada

Like the United States, Canada was a nation shaped by immigrants. After gaining independence, it charted its own course but still maintained links with Britain through the Commonwealth of Nations.

Canada ranked among the major democratic, industrial powers. It sided with the Allies in both world wars and was a staunch member of

NATO. Through quiet diplomacy, Canada often worked behind the scenes to ease Cold War tensions. Its troops served in UN peacekeeping missions around the world.

**Economic growth.** Canada, too, enjoyed a postwar economic boom, due in part to rich oil and gas deposits found in the western provinces. In 1959, Canada and the United States completed the St. Lawrence Seaway. It opened the Great Lakes to ocean-going ships and linked the interior of both countries to the Atlantic Ocean.

With a population only a tenth that of the United States, Canada encouraged immigration. Since the 1950s, Canada's population has grown increasingly diverse, with newcomers from Europe, Asia, Africa, Latin America, and the Caribbean.

**Quebec separatism.** Defining a national identity has remained a challenge for Canada. Quebec's French-speaking population saw themselves as a "distinct society." To protect their culture, Quebec demanded more autonomy within Canada.

Government leaders tried hard to meet those demands. But other provinces resisted any solutions that gave Quebec special treatment. Meantime, some people in Quebec wanted to separate from Canada and become an independent nation. In the 1990s, Quebec's future remained a subject of heated debate.

**United States influence.** Another challenge for Canada has been the immense impact of the United States. Although the two nations enjoyed close ties, many Canadians resented their neighbor's cultural domination. Economic competition led to disputes over trade and tariffs. A key step toward solving those issues was a treaty that created a vast free-trade zone between the two nations. NAFTA later extended this zone to Mexico. (See page 547.)

Other issues between Canada and the United States concerned the environment. Chemical pollution from American smokestacks, for example, contributed to acid rain that fell on northeastern Canada. The two nations agreed to work together for a common solution. (See page 418.)

## SECTION 3 REVIEW

1. **Identify** (a) Joseph McCarthy, (b) Great Society, (c) Ronald Reagan, (d) *Brown* v. *Board of Education of Topeka,* (e) Martin Luther King, Jr., (f) St. Lawrence Seaway.
2. **Define** deficit.
3. How did the Cold War affect the role of the United States in the postwar era?
4. What were the goals of the civil rights movement?
5. Give one example of cooperation and one example of conflict between Canada and the United States.
6. *Critical Thinking* **Comparing** How is the situation of French-speaking Canadians similar to or different from that of minority groups within the United States?
7. *ACTIVITY* Interview someone you know who was born before World War II about American life during the postwar years. Topics might include the Cold War era, the civil rights movement, the changing role of women, the Vietnam War and antiwar protests, and economic changes. Prepare eight to ten questions.

# 4 The Soviet Union: Rise and Fall of a Superpower

## Guide for Reading

- What policies did Soviet leaders pursue?
- What were the strengths and weaknesses of the Soviet economy?
- What were the causes and effects of the collapse of the Soviet Union?
- **Vocabulary** *dissident, glasnost, perestroika*

"We shall bury you," Soviet leader Nikita Khrushchev (KROOSH chawf) told the West during the Cold War. His statement was not, he later explained, a military threat. Rather, he believed that capitalism was doomed and Soviet communism was the wave of the future.

Khrushchev's prediction never came true. Instead, in the 1980s, the Soviet economy began to crumble. Efforts at reform led the Soviet empire to disintegrate with stunning speed.

### Stalin's Successors

The Soviet Union emerged from World War II a superpower. Stalin forged a Soviet sphere of influence from the Baltic to the Balkans.

Victory, however, brought few rewards to the Soviet people. Stalin returned to his ruthless prewar policies. He filled slave labor camps with "enemies of the state." He seemed ready to launch a new wave of purges when he died in 1953.

**Khrushchev.** Nikita Khrushchev emerged as the new Soviet leader. In 1956, he shocked top Communist party members when he publicly denounced Stalin's abuse of power. Khrushchev then pursued a policy of de-Stalinization. He did not change Soviet goals but did free many political prisoners and eased censorship. He sought a thaw in the Cold War, calling for "peaceful coexistence" with the West.

The thaw had limits, though. When Hungarians revolted against communist rule in 1956, Khrushchev sent tanks to smash them. When critics at home grew too bold, he clamped down. Soviet poet Yevgeny Yevtushenko (yehv GAY nee yehv tuh SHEHN koh) warned that a return to Stalinism was always a danger:

> "But how do we remove Stalin
>     from Stalin's heirs?
> Some of his heirs . . .
>     from platforms rail against Stalin,
> but,
>     at night,
>         yearn for the old days."

**Brezhnev.** In 1964, economic and foreign policy setbacks resulted in Khrushchev's removal from office. In time, Leonid Brezhnev (BREHSH nehf) took over the Soviet Union, holding power until his death in 1982. Brezhnev rigorously suppressed dissidents, people who spoke out against the government. Critics faced arrest and imprisonment. Some were locked away in insane asylums, a policy once used by czarist Russia.

*Andrei Sakharov* In the 1950s, Andrei Sakharov was known as a brilliant physicist, the "father of the Soviet hydrogen bomb." By the 1980s, though, he was even better known as a leading Soviet dissident. He campaigned to limit nuclear testing and spoke out against human rights abuses. His efforts won him a Nobel Peace Prize but also angered the repressive Brezhnev government. In 1980, Sakharov was exiled to a remote city. Six years later, as the Soviet Union entered an era of growing freedom, Sakharov was finally released from exile. **Impact of the Individual** Why did it take courage for Sakharov and other dissidents to defy the Soviet government?

## The Soviet Economy

After the war, Stalin rebuilt shattered Soviet industries, using factories and other equipment stripped from Germany. As in the 1930s, he and his successors focused on industries such as steel, coal, and heavy machinery. They also poured resources into science, technology, and weapons.

**Successes.** In 1957, the Soviets launched *Sputnik I*, the first artificial satellite to orbit the Earth. Khrushchev trumpeted *Sputnik* as a victory in the propaganda war against the West. The Soviets claimed other advantages as well. Citizens enjoyed benefits such as low rents, cheap bread, free health care, and day care for their children. Although wages were low, unemployment was almost nonexistent.

**Problems.** Neither Khrushchev nor Brezhnev, however, was able to solve basic Soviet economic problems. The state-run economy could produce impressive results when it poured resources into major projects such as weapons manufacture or the space race. But collectivized agriculture remained so unproductive that the Soviet Union frequently had to import grain to feed its people. Nor could Russia's command economy match the free-market economies of the West in producing consumer goods. Soviet shoes, suits, and television sets were far inferior to those made in the West, and luxuries like frozen food, clothes washers, or automobiles remained rare. People spent many hours of their lives waiting in line to buy food and other goods. The average person might spend years on a waiting list to buy a car.

Low output was due to inefficiencies in central economic planning. A huge bureaucracy, rather than supply and demand, decided what to produce, how much, and for whom. Government planners in Moscow often had little knowledge of the local conditions. Sometimes, factories were forced to shut down because needed supplies never arrived. At the local level, workers set out to meet production quotas, regardless of quality. Since workers had lifetime job security, they had little incentive to produce better-quality goods.

Still, for decades, the system supported the Soviet Union as a superpower. In the late 1980s, however, with military costs skyrocketing, the economy faced major obstacles.

## Foreign Policy Issues

Stalin and his successors forcefully asserted Soviet control over Eastern Europe. In 1955, Khrushchev set up the Warsaw Pact, in theory to defend the communist bloc against NATO. In practice, as you will read, it would be used to suppress dissent within Eastern Europe.

**The developing world.** As nations emerged from colonial rule, the Soviet Union, like the United States, supplied them with military and economic aid. Local conflicts sometimes flared into major Cold War confrontations. In two bitter wars, Soviet-backed governments in North Korea and North Vietnam battled American-backed governments in South Korea and South Vietnam. (See Chapter 17.)

**Rivalry with the United States.** As you saw, Soviet-American relations swung back and forth between confrontation and détente. In 1961, the building of the Berlin Wall increased Cold War tensions. A year later, Khrushchev tried to build nuclear missile bases in Cuba, triggering the dangerous Cuban missile crisis. (See page 540.) The nuclear war that everyone feared almost took place.

Brezhnev invested in a huge military buildup. In the Brezhnev Doctrine, he asserted that the Soviet Union had a right to intervene militarily in any Warsaw Pact nation. At the same time, he also pursued détente and disarmament with the United States.

Détente came to an abrupt end in 1979, after the Soviets invaded Afghanistan to ensure Soviet influence in that neighboring nation. Like the Vietnam War for the United States, the Afghan War drained the Soviet economy and provoked a crisis in morale at home.

▲ *Moscow citizens lining up to buy food*

## Collapse of the Soviet Empire

As the fighting in Afghanistan dragged on, the Soviet economy stagnated. In 1985, an energetic new leader, Mikhail Gorbachev, took up the reins of power. Gorbachev was eager to reform inefficiencies in government and the economy. The changes he unloosed, however, spiraled out of his control, swamping him and the Soviet Union.

**The Gorbachev revolution.** In foreign policy, Gorbachev sought an end to costly Cold War tensions. He renounced the Brezhnev Doctrine, signed arms control treaties with the United States, and eventually pulled Soviet troops out of Afghanistan.

At home, Gorbachev launched a two-pronged effort at reform. First, he called for glasnost, or openness. He ended censorship and encouraged people to discuss publicly the country's problems. Second, he urged the restructuring of government and the economy, called perestroika (pehr uh STROI kuh). Streamlining government and reducing the size of the bureaucracy, he hoped, would boost efficiency and output. He backed some free-market ideas, including limited private enterprise, but wanted to keep the essence of communism.

Corrupt or incompetent officials were dismissed. To produce more and higher-quality consumer goods, factory managers, instead of central planners, were made responsible for decisions. To increase food supplies, farmers were allowed more land on which to grow food to sell on the free market.

**Unexpected results.** Such rapid change brought economic turmoil. Shortages grew worse and prices soared. Factories that could not survive without government help closed, throwing thousands out of work. Old-line Communists and bureaucrats whose careers were at stake denounced the reforms. At the same time, other critics, like the popular Russian leader Boris Yeltsin, demanded even more radical changes.

Gorbachev faced a host of other problems. Glasnost encouraged unrest in the multinational Soviet empire. The Baltic republics of Estonia, Latvia, and Lithuania had been seized by Stalin in 1940. In 1991, they regained full independence. In Eastern Europe, countries from

**Freedom for the Baltic States** As the Soviet Union weakened, the small republics of Latvia, Estonia, and Lithuania declared independence. In a tense standoff, Soviet troops threatened to crush the independence movements. These demonstrators at the United Nations demanded that Gorbachev recognize the independence of the Baltic states. In the end, the Soviet army withdrew. **Geography and History** Look at the map on page 642. Why are Latvia, Estonia, and Lithuania called the Baltic states?

Poland and East Germany to Romania and Bulgaria broke out of the Soviet orbit.

In mid-1991, hardliners tried to overthrow Gorbachev and restore the old order. Their coup failed, but it further weakened Gorbachev. By year's end, as other Soviet republics declared independence, Gorbachev resigned as president. After 74 years, the Soviet Union ceased to exist.

## The Russian Republic

Russia, the largest republic in size and population, had dominated the Soviet Union. After the breakup, Russia and its president, Boris Yeltsin, faced a difficult future.

**Political problems.** Russians approved a new constitution, but they had no democratic traditions. In the 1990s, economic hardships and political turmoil increased. Many Russians feared the growing chaos and longed for a return to order.

Yeltsin clashed repeatedly with parliament. Many members were former Communists who

## The Former Soviet Union

| Country | Major Ethnic Groups | Major Religions |
|---|---|---|
| Armenia | Armenian 93% | Armenian Orthodox Church 94% |
| Azerbaijan | Azeri 83%, Russian 6%, Armenian 6% | Mostly Muslim |
| Belarus | Belarusian 80%, Russian 13% | Mostly Belarusian Orthodox |
| Estonia | Estonian 62%, Russian 30% | Mostly Lutheran |
| Georgia | Georgian 70%, Armenian 8%, Russian 6% | Georgian Orthodox 65%, Muslim 11%, Russian Orthodox 10% |
| Kazakhstan | Kazakh 42%, Russian 37%, Ukrainian 5%, German 4% | Muslim 47%, Russian Orthodox 44% |
| Kyrgyzstan | Kirghiz 52%, Russian 22%, Uzbek 13% | Muslim 70% |
| Latvia | Latvian 52%, Russian 34% | Lutheran, Roman Catholic, Russian Orthodox |
| Lithuania | Lithuanian 80%, Russian 9%, Polish 8% | Mostly Roman Catholic |
| Moldova | Moldovan/Romanian 65%, Ukrainian 14%, Russian 13% | Eastern Orthodox 99% |
| Russia | Russian 82%, Tatar 4% | Russian Orthodox 25%, nonreligious 60% |
| Tajikistan | Tajik 65%, Uzbek 25%, Russian 4% | Mostly Sunni Muslim |
| Turkmenistan | Turkmen 73%, Russian 10%, Uzbek 9% | Muslim 87% |
| Ukraine | Ukrainian 73%, Russian 22% | Orthodox 76%, Ukrainian Catholic 13.5%, Muslim 8.2% |
| Uzbekistan | Uzbek 71%, Russian 8% | Mostly Sunni Muslim |

Source: *The World Almanac and Book of Facts, 1996*

*Interpreting a Chart* The powerful Soviet government had held together a diverse population of European and Asian peoples. When the Soviet Union collapsed in 1991, it left behind 15 independent states. ■ Why do you think Russians are a major ethnic group in almost every nation shown here? Which former Soviet republic seems to have the most diverse population?

wanted to turn the clock back. Others were extreme nationalists who rejected western ideas and called for a revival of the Russian empire. Whether democracy would survive the turmoil remains to be seen.

Further troubles arose when minorities within Russia sought greater autonomy or independence. In 1994, Yeltsin brutally crushed a revolt in Chechnya (CHAYCH nee ah), a region in the Caucasus Mountains. The conflict revealed divisions within the army and government.

**Economic problems.** To solve Russia's economic problems and gain western aid, Yeltsin had to privatize more state-run industries and collective farms. The changeover to a market economy was painful. Unemployment soared. Without government controls, prices skyrocketed. Older people on fixed pensions were especially hard hit. Unlike East Germany, which got massive aid from West Germany, Russia got relatively little aid from the West.

Some Russians succeeded in the new economy. Their success, however, fanned resentment among poorer Russians. Criminals also flourished, and ruthless gangs preyed on the new business class. In an atmosphere of uncertainty, ultranationalists and old Communists won support at the polls.

**A world power.** Russia reduced its nuclear stockpile after the breakup of the Soviet Union. Still, with its large military and nuclear arsenal, Russia exercised influence as a world power. Its old rival, the United States, hoped Russia might work to resolve global problems. Yet Eastern European nations were alarmed when Russian nationalists and former Communists called for Russia to reassert its power. At the same time, Russia objected to efforts by Eastern European nations to join NATO, fearing a threat to its own security.

## The Other Republics

Like Russia, the other former Soviet republics wanted to build stable governments and improve their standard of living. They, too, faced unrest and divisions between the pro-communist and pro-democracy groups. Ethnic violence erupted in republics that included a mix of national groups. Other conflicts arose over disputed borders. Armenia, for example, tried to seize a small area in neighboring Azerbaijan, where many Armenians lived. The republic of Georgia was torn by a bloody civil war.

These new nations endured hard times as they switched to market economies. In the Central Asian republics, many skilled Russian workers left, causing a shortage of trained managers and technicians. With help from the UN, the World Bank, and the International Monetary Fund, the new nations worked to increase trade and build economic ties with the rest of the world. The republics of Ukraine, Kazakhstan, and Belarus gave up the nuclear weapons left on their soil in return for trading privileges or investments from the West.

## SECTION 4 REVIEW

1. **Identify** (a) Nikita Khrushchev, (b) Leonid Brezhnev, (c) Boris Yeltsin, (d) Chechnya.
2. **Define** (a) dissident, (b) glasnost, (c) perestroika.
3. Give three examples of how Stalin's successors both eased and inflamed Cold War tensions.
4. What problems did the Soviet economy face?
5. (a) What were Mikhail Gorbachev's goals? (b) How did his reforms contribute to the collapse of Soviet communism?
6. *Critical Thinking* **Predicting Consequences** (a) How have former Communist hardliners challenged democracy in the former Soviet republics? (b) What do you think might happen if they came to power again?
7. *ACTIVITY* Using obituaries in a local newspaper as models, write an obituary for the Soviet Union.

## 5 A New Era in Eastern Europe

### Guide for Reading

- How were Eastern European nations tied to the Soviet Union during the Cold War?
- How did Eastern European nations achieve democracy?
- Why did civil war break out in Yugoslavia?

For centuries, the peoples of Eastern Europe lived in the shadow of larger powers. Before 1914, most of the region was divided up among the old German, Russian, Austrian, and Ottoman empires. Many small nations gained independence after World War I, only to be overrun by the Nazis. After the war, the region fell under Soviet domination.

Finally, in 1989, Eastern European nations again won independence. Vaclav Havel, a playwright and the first president of the Czech Republic, spoke about the challenges of freedom:

> **❝**Independence is not just a state of being. It is a task. And fresh independence, such as ours, is a particularly complex task. We must . . . ensure that it will not merely be a new burden but that, on the contrary, it will bring benefits to all its citizens, who should experience independence as something worth fighting for, something worth defending, and something worth holding dear.**❞**

### In the Soviet Orbit

In 1945, Soviet armies occupied much of Eastern Europe. Backed by Soviet power, local Communist parties from Hungary to Bulgaria destroyed rival parties, silenced critics, censored the press, and campaigned against religion. As in the Soviet Union, Communist leaders in Eastern Europe ended private ownership of businesses and turned to central economic planning.

Despite Soviet domination, each country kept its own culture and identity. Poland, Hungary, Romania, and other nations also differed in economic wealth.

Stalin forced his satellites to contribute to the rebuilding of Soviet industry. They had to sell natural resources to the Soviet Union on favorable terms and provide troops and money to finance the Warsaw Pact.

**Unrest and repression.** As the Cold War deepened, the Soviet Union tightened its grip on its satellites. More than 30 divisions of Soviet troops were stationed throughout Eastern Europe. Yet in East Germany, Poland, Hungary, and elsewhere, unrest simmered. Despite some economic progress, many people despised the communist monopoly on power. Nationalists resented Moscow's domination.

By 1956, Imre Nagy (NOJ), a communist reformer and strong nationalist, gained power in Hungary. He ended one-party rule, ejected Soviet troops, and withdrew from the Warsaw Pact. Khrushchev responded to this challenge with tanks and troops. Hungarian "freedom fighters" resisted the Soviet advance and called on the West for help. None came. Thousands died in the fighting, and Nagy himself was executed. Many others fled to the West. The failure of western powers to intervene showed that they had accepted the Soviet sphere of influence in Eastern Europe.

A dozen years later, Alexander Dubçek introduced liberal reforms in Czechoslovakia. In easing controls, he called for "socialism with a human face." Once again, the Soviets responded with force. Warsaw Pact troops ousted Dubçek and restored a communist dictatorship. As you have read, under the Brezhnev Doctrine, the Soviet Union claimed the right to intervene in the affairs of any communist nation.

**Tito's independence.** Soviet power did not extend to Yugoslavia. During World War II, a fierce guerrilla leader, Josip Tito, had battled German occupying forces. Later, Tito set up a communist government in Yugoslavia, but he pursued a path independent of Moscow. He refused to join the Warsaw Pact and claimed to be neutral in the Cold War.

## Poland's Struggle Toward Democracy

Poland was the Soviet Union's most troublesome satellite. Like Hungarians and Czechs, Poles wanted greater freedom within the Soviet bloc. Stalin had clamped down hard on Poland. Communist persecution of the Roman Catholic Church, however, backfired. The Church became a rallying point for Poles opposed to the regime.

In 1956, economic woes touched off riots and strikes. To end the turmoil, the Polish government made some reforms. Dissatisfaction with communism, however, would continue to surface.

**Solidarity.** In 1980, economic hardships ignited strikes of shipyard workers in the port of Gdansk. Led by Lech Walesa (vah LEHN sah),

*Hungarian Uprising* In 1956, hundreds of thousands of Hungarians took to the streets to protest Soviet domination. An entire people, one Hungarian said, "rose up without weapons in defense of truth and freedom." Here, Hungarians stand beside a gigantic statue of Stalin, toppled during the revolt. **Art and Literature** What does the size of the statue suggest about the symbolic importance of Stalin?

## Revolution and Freedom

By late 1989, a "democracy movement" was sweeping Eastern Europe. Everywhere, people took to the streets, demanding reform. One by one, communist governments fell. A dissident writer and human rights activist, Vaclav Havel, was elected president of Czechoslovakia. In East Germany, as you have read, the Berlin Wall was toppled and the country reunited.

Most changes came peacefully. Only Romania's brutal longtime dictator, Nicolae Ceausescu (chah SHEHS koo), refused to step down. He was overthrown and executed.

For the first time since 1945, Eastern European countries were free to settle their own affairs. They withdrew from the Warsaw Pact and requested that Soviet troops leave. By then, Soviet power itself was crumbling.

**New struggles.** Like Russia and the former Soviet republics, Eastern European nations set out to build stable governments and free-market economies. Although the experiences of each nation differed, all faced similar challenges.

To attract western investment, governments had to push radical economic reforms. They privatized industries and stopped keeping prices for basic goods and services artificially low. As in Russia, the changes brought high unemployment, soaring prices, and crime waves. Consumer goods were more plentiful, but many people could not afford them.

By the mid-1990s, governments ended many benefits from the old days, such as generous maternity leave and free tuition at universities. Some people became disillusioned with reform. "I don't know why," observed a young Hungarian woman, "but even though we knew that we were a backward country—way behind Western Europe—it somehow felt better then." In some countries, former Communists won seats in the parliaments.

**Return to Europe.** In the 1990s, Eastern European nations looked to the West for aid, and many hoped to join the European Union and NATO. This idea was controversial. Russia opposed NATO's expansion into a region once within its sphere of influence. Some in the West were reluctant to assume the responsibility of protecting Eastern European nations. Still, in 1997 NATO invited Poland, Hungary, and the

*A Pope From Poland* In 1978, Polish cardinal Karol Wojtyla became Pope John Paul II—the first non-Italian pope in 456 years. From the Vatican, the pope gave cautious but firm encouragement to anti-communist forces in Eastern Europe. On visits to Poland in 1979 and 1983, he criticized the country's communist rulers. The pope's support inspired Lech Walesa and other members of Solidarity. Here, Walesa holds a photograph of the pope. **Impact of the Individual** Why do you think John Paul II was important to Polish nationalists?

they organized an independent trade union called Solidarity. It soon claimed 10 million members, who pressed for political change.

Under pressure from the Soviets, the Polish government cracked down on Solidarity. It outlawed the union and arrested its leaders, including Walesa. Still, unrest simmered. Walesa became a national hero. Pressure from the world community further strained the communist government.

**Peaceful transition.** In the late 1980s, Gorbachev declared he would not interfere in Eastern Europe. By then, Poland was introducing radical economic reforms similar to Gorbachev's changes in the Soviet Union. It also legalized Solidarity and, in 1989, sponsored the first free elections in 50 years. Solidarity candidates outpolled those of the Communist party. A year later, Lech Walesa was elected president of Poland. The new government began a difficult, but peaceful, transition from socialism to a market economy. It was the beginning of the end for Soviet domination of Eastern Europe.

***Troubled Waters*** After the fall of communism, many East Europeans hoped to enjoy higher wages and new consumer goods right away. In practice, though, the transition to a market economy proved slow and painful. This cartoon shows the dangerous economic waters that Eastern Europe must navigate. ***Economics and Technology*** *What does the boat represent? What dangers does it face? What does the cartoon suggest about its destination?*

Czech Republic to join the organization. Other Eastern European nations were expected to be invited at a later date.

**Ethnic tensions.** Centuries of migration and conquest left most Eastern European countries with ethnically diverse populations. Most countries had a majority population, but with one or more ethnic minorities asserting their own identity. Nationalism has helped unite countries like Poland and Hungary, but it has also been a divisive force. Hungarians in Romania demanded autonomy. Faced with ethnic tensions, Czechoslovakia peacefully split into two countries, the Czech Republic and Slovakia. In 1991, ethnic conflict tore Yugoslavia apart in a long and tragic civil war.

### War Comes to Sarajevo

"I'm trying to concentrate so I can do my homework," 11-year-old Zlata Filipovic wrote in her diary on April 5, 1992. "But I simply can't. Something is going on in town. You can hear gunfire from the hills." Zlata was right. In just a few days, war would come to the beautiful, peaceful city where Zlata lived—Sarajevo.

**Breakup of Yugoslavia.** While Zlata was growing up, Sarajevo was part of Yugoslavia. Its three main ethnic groups were Croats, who were Roman Catholics; Serbs, who were Orthodox Christians; and Muslims. The groups had distinct customs and religions, but they had lived side by side peacefully for years. They all spoke the same language, Serbo-Croatian.

After Tito's death and the fall of communism, however, a wave of nationalism tore Yugoslavia apart. Ambitious extremists, such as Serb leader Slobodan Milosevic, stirred ethnic unrest for their own ends. Croats created the separate countries of Croatia and Slovenia. Sarajevo became the capital of a new nation called Bosnia-Herzegovina. Serbia and Montenegro kept the name Yugoslavia.

**Bosnia.** Although Bosnia, where Zlata lived, became independent, it was still divided. Muslims made up the majority, but there were also many Serbs and Croats. Bosnian Serbs got money and arms from nearby Serbia. As Serbs conquered more and more of Bosnia, neighbors and friends turned against one another.

Serbs practiced "ethnic cleansing," forcibly removing other ethnic groups from the areas they controlled. Hundreds of thousands of Bosnians became refugees, living on food sent by the United Nations and by charities. Others were brutalized or killed. To many, ethnic cleansing recalled the horrors of Nazi Germany and the Holocaust.

**A record of terror.** Zlata watched in horror as shelling and snipers killed thousands of people. On May 7, she wrote:

    ❝Today a shell fell on the park in front of my house, the park where I used to play and sit with my girlfriends. A lot of people were hurt. . . . AND NINA IS DEAD. A piece of shrapnel lodged in her brain and she died. She was such a sweet, nice little girl.❞

Ethnic conflict has taken many forms—from violence against guest workers in Western Europe to the Quebec separatist movement to "ethnic cleansing" in Bosnia. How can nations encourage harmony among diverse peoples within their borders?

Conditions in Sarajevo became almost unbearable. Serbian troops shelled schools, hospitals, and libraries. They cut off electricity and water supplies for long periods. "I've forgotten what it's like to have water pouring out of a tap, what it's like to shower," Zlata wrote.

Zlata tried to understand what was causing the war. "I keep asking why? What for? Who's to blame?" She was especially upset about the violence among ethnic groups:

    66Among my girlfriends, among our friends, in our family, there are Serbs and Croats and Muslims. It's a mixed group and I never knew who was a Serb, a Croat or a Muslim. Now politics has started meddling around. . . . Of course, I'm 'young,' and politics are conducted by 'grown ups.' But I think we 'young' would do it better. We certainly wouldn't have chosen war.99

After enduring many months of war, Zlata and her parents finally left Sarajevo for Paris in 1993. Not everyone could flee the battle. The struggle went on. 🔳

## Looking Ahead

In 1995, the United States finally brought the warring parties to Dayton, Ohio. There, they hammered out a series of agreements, called the Dayton Accords. NATO forces were sent to Bosnia to implement the agreements. Progress in making the agreements work was slow and often unsatisfactory to Muslims, Serbs, or Croats. The Dayton Accords seemed the best hope for peace in a wartorn land. But no one could predict whether the peace would survive over the long term.

In the 1990s, Bosnia became a test case for western powers in the post-Cold War world. When the civil war in Yugoslavia began, United Nations forces tried but failed to restore peace. As Serb forces advanced, the United States and its European allies were uncertain whether or not to intervene militarily or arm the Muslims or Croats. While they debated, the war raged on. Finally, they imposed at least a temporary peace. Meantime, an international court at the Hague held trials for those accused of war crimes in Bosnia.

## SECTION 5 REVIEW

1. **Identify** (a) Imre Nagy, (b) Alexander Dubçek, (c) Josip Tito, (d) Lech Walesa.
2. How did the Soviet Union come to dominate Eastern Europe?
3. (a) What events led to democracy in Poland? (b) Why are some people in Eastern Europe dissatisfied with democracy and free-market economics?
4. Why did civil war break out in Yugoslavia?
5. *Critical Thinking* **Recognizing Causes and Effects** To what extent did Eastern Europe owe its independence to Mikhail Gorbachev?
6. *ACTIVITY* With a classmate, prepare a dialogue between two people in an Eastern European nation. Discuss the changes in your country and the outlook for the future.

## CHAPTER REVIEW

### REVIEWING VOCABULARY

Select *five* vocabulary words from the chapter. Write each word on a separate slip of paper. Then, write the definition of each word on other slips of paper. Scramble the slips and exchange them with another student. Match the words with their definitions, and then check each other's results.

### REVIEWING FACTS

1. What were the effects of the Cold War arms race between the superpowers?
2. What conflict caused violence in Northern Ireland?

3. What event made the reunification of Germany possible?
4. What was the source of tension between Quebec and the Canadian government?
5. Why was the Soviet economy less efficient than western capitalist economies?
6. What was the largest and most powerful country formed from the breakup of the Soviet Union?
7. What economic changes did Eastern European nations make after the fall of communism?
8. How did the breakup of Yugoslavia differ from the breakup of Czechoslovakia?

## SKILLS FOR SUCCESS PLANNING A MULTIMEDIA PRESENTATION

Multimedia presentations communicate information in a variety of forms, both audio and visual. The preproduction, or planning, stage of a presentation is the most important part. Here you draft an outline and script, decide what media to use and where, arrange interviews or photography sessions, select images, and choose music.

Imagine that you have been assigned to produce a multimedia presentation on some aspect of cultural diversity in the United States. Use the preproduction topic analysis sheet at right and the following steps to prepare your presentation.

1. **Plan your content.** (a) What possible topics might you focus on? (b) What segments might you use for each topic?
2. **Plan a script.** You must decide whether to use a running commentary by a single narrator, comments by interviewees, or a combination. What are the advantages and disadvantages of using a single narrator?
3. **Make a list of interviews, images, and music.** (a) What images would fit the content and mood of each segment? (b) What kinds of people could you interview? (c) What pieces or types of music would best enhance the mood of your presentation?

**Preproduction Topic Analysis Sheet**

**Assignment:** An aspect of United States cultural diversity

**Possible topics:**
1. _____
2. _____
3. _____

**Sources for topic information:**
_____

Intended audience: _____
Information to be presented:
_____

**Segment description and sequence:**
1. _____
2. _____
3. _____
Mood: _____
Type of narration: _____

**Graphics/Illustrations, Interviews, Music**
Segment #1 _____ _____
_____ _____

Segment #2 _____ _____
_____ _____

## REVIEWING CHAPTER THEMES

Review the "Focus On" questions at the start of this chapter. Then select *three* of those questions and answer them, using information from the chapter.

## CRITICAL THINKING

1. **Defending a Position** If you lived in a Western European country, would you support moves toward a "United States of Europe"? Why or why not?

2. **Analyzing Information** In Germany and other nations, extremist groups attacked foreign refugees and guest workers. Why do you think attacks on immigrants and minorities often increase during hard times?

3. **Linking Past and Present** List three ways the civil rights movement of the 1950s and 1960s helped shape American life today.

## ANALYZING PRIMARY SOURCES

Use the quotation on page 442 to answer the following questions.

1. Restate the quotation in your own words.

2. Did this statement suggest that American commitments would be limited or unlimited? Explain your answer.

3. List two different ways in which Soviet leaders might have reacted to Kennedy's words.

## FOR YOUR PORTFOLIO

**PREPARING A DATA FILE** Work with a group of classmates to prepare a data file on one of the decades from 1950 to the present. First, meet with your team to choose the decade you will research. Then review the material in this chapter for information about your decade. Use outside resources to learn more about important events in this time period. Decide how to organize your decade file. Work with your group to prepare the file on your decade. Finally, present your decade file to the class.

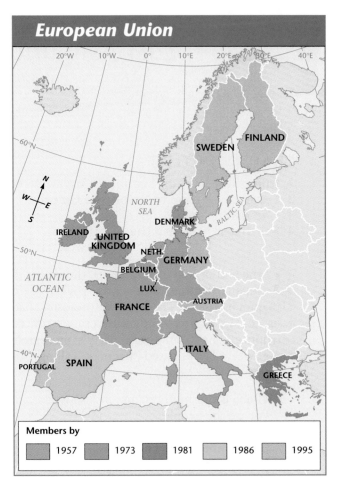

**European Union**

Members by
| 1957 | 1973 | 1981 | 1986 | 1995 |

## ANALYZING MAPS

Use the map to answer the following questions.

1. Who were the original members of the EU?

2. Between which two years did the northernmost members join the EU?

3. Why does Germany show two colors, representing two different times of membership?

**INTERNET ACTIVITY**

**WRITING A NEWS REPORT** Use the Internet to research an important post–World War II event in North America or Europe. Then write a news report describing the event as if you were a television, newspaper, or radio reporter on the scene.

# East Asia and Southeast Asia

## (1945–Present)

## CHAPTER OUTLINE

**1  Japan Becomes an Economic Superpower**
**2  From Revolution to Reform in China**
**3  The Asian Tigers**
**4  Southeast Asia and the Pacific Rim**

By the end of May 1989, tens of thousands of student demonstrators had packed into Tiananmen Square. The youthful protesters had a list of grievances—inflation, crime, official corruption, the Communist party's monopoly on power. They raised banners calling for democracy:

66China is our motherland.
  We are the people.
  The government should be our
    government.99

Across the world, people watched this historic moment. How would China's totalitarian government respond? Would it agree to political reforms?

The answer came on June 4, with a brutal crackdown. Tanks rolled through Tiananmen Square, followed by armed troops. Soldiers killed hundreds of demonstrators and wounded many more. The Tiananmen Square massacre showed that China's leaders would not allow their authority to be challenged. But it also became a symbol for Chinese who hoped one day to achieve democracy.

Over the past 50 years, China and other nations in East Asia and Southeast Asia have transformed themselves. They cast off foreign control and set out to modernize. In some nations, like China, a totalitarian government remade the economy and society. Other nations made economic progress under authoritarian rule. With its democratic government, Japan was an exception. After a spectacular recovery from the war, Japan claimed a place among the world's top industrial nations.

For decades, Asia was a battleground in the Cold War. As the superpowers jockeyed for position, they fought shooting wars through third parties—Korea and Vietnam. By the 1990s, the Cold War was over. For the first time in years, the major powers in Asia and the United States were at peace. Growing trade and other ties linked the nations of the Pacific Rim from Asia to the Americas.

**FOCUS ON** these questions as you read:

■ **Continuity and Change**
   How did the Cold War affect the nations of East Asia and Southeast Asia?

■ **Economics and Technology**
   How did technology and trade contribute to the success of Japan and the Asian "tigers"?

■ **Political and Social Systems**
   How is the new China created by the communist revolution changing again today?

■ **Impact of the Individual**
   How did leaders like Mao Zedong and Ho Chi Minh remake their nations?

■ **Global Interaction**
   Why did the Pacific Rim become a dynamic center of growth?

## TIME AND PLACE

夺丰收 广积粮

人民公社好

*A New Path for China*  In 1949, the Communists won control of China. They proclaimed three main goals for their revolution. They promised a better life for the poor. They called for development of a modern economy. And they pledged to restore China's position as a major world power. Here, a propaganda poster urges the Chinese to "win a good harvest, increase grain production." **Art and Literature**  *What image of China's farmworkers does this poster present?*

## HUMANITIES LINK

*Art History*  Indonesian batik (page 478).
*Literature*  In this chapter, you will encounter a passage from the following work of literature: Yuan Kejia, "Labor is joy" (page 466).

| 1949 | 1950s | 1975 | 1987 | 1997 |
|------|-------|------|------|------|
| People's Republic of China founded | Japanese "economic miracle" begins | North defeats South in Vietnam War | South Korea holds elections | Hong Kong reverts to China |

**1945**        **1960**        **1975**        **1990**        **PRESENT**

# 1 Japan Becomes an Economic Superpower

## Guide for Reading

- What were the goals of American occupation forces in Japan?
- How did Japan become an economic superpower?
- What challenges does Japan face today?
- **Vocabulary** *gross domestic product*

"The wise bamboo sways with the wind," says a Japanese proverb. In 1945, for the first time in its history, Japan had to accept foreign occupation. As in the past, the Japanese learned from outsiders. They selectively borrowed western ideas and technology and put them to their own use. By the 1960s, Japan had emerged as an economic superpower equal to the United States and the Soviet Union.

## On the Road to Recovery

In 1945, Japan lay reeling. It had suffered perhaps the most devastating property damage of any nation involved in World War II. Hiro-shima and Nagasaki were leveled. Other Japanese cities were burned-out ruins. Tens of thousands of Japanese were homeless and hungry.

**Occupation goals.** Under General Douglas MacArthur, the American military government set two main goals for the occupation of Japan: to destroy militarism and to ensure democratic government. Japan's armed forces were disbanded. As in Germany, trials were held to punish those responsible for wartime atrocities. Along with Japan's defeat, the trials further discredited the military.

In 1946, a new constitution provided that "the Japanese people forever renounce war as a sovereign right of the nation." Japan, it said, would never maintain military forces except for its own defense.

The constitution stripped the emperor of power. Instead, power was vested in the people, who elected representatives to the Diet, or parliament. The constitution also protected basic rights such as freedom of thought, press, and assembly.

**Social and economic reforms.** To help build Japanese democracy, American occupying forces backed social change. They reformed Japan's education system to open it to all people. They emphasized legal equality for women. Women gained the right to vote and hold office. Marriages had to be based on mutual consent, with equal rights for wife and husband.

*Postwar Japan* When American troops arrived in Japan at the end of World War II, their first job was to provide emergency food and shelter for their former enemies. Here, village leaders distribute food from the United States in rural Japan. **Political and Social Systems** Why do you think the American occupiers used local leaders to give out food?

The Americans introduced economic reforms designed to promote democracy. The constitution protected the right of workers to organize unions. A sweeping land-reform program divided up large estates among tenant farmers. The former owners received payment, while peasants owned land for the first time. This change erased lingering traces of feudalism in Japan.

Although the Americans tried to disband the zaibatsu, or giant business combines, the Japanese resisted. They felt that large firms were needed to compete internationally.

**The Cold War.** By 1950, Japan was on the road to recovery. At the same time, the Cold War was making the United States eager to end the occupation and turn its World War II enemy into an ally. As the Cold War erupted into an armed conflict in nearby Korea (see Section 3), the United States and Japan signed a peace treaty. In 1952, the occupation ended.

Japan and the United States preserved close ties during the Cold War. The American military operated out of bases that they set up in Japan, while Japan enjoyed the protection of the American "nuclear umbrella." The two nations were also trading partners and, in time, competitors for global markets.

## Japanese Successes

Between 1950 and 1975, Japan produced its own economic miracle, even more spectacular than Germany's. It chalked up huge jumps in gross domestic product (GDP). GDP refers to the total value of all goods and services produced by a nation.

**Manufacturing.** The Japanese success story was built on producing goods for export. At first, Japan manufactured textiles. When other Asian nations entered that field, it shifted to making steel for shipbuilding and machinery.

By the 1970s, Japanese cars, cameras, and television sets found eager buyers on the world market. Its companies also moved into high technology. Soon, Japanese electronic goods—from computers to robots—were competing with western, especially American, products.

**Trade and investment.** As a small island nation with few resources, Japan depended on trade. It had to import oil and other raw materials like iron ore, but it exported the more profitable finished goods, such as steel. It marketed its products so successfully that it built a favorable balance of trade, exporting more goods than it imported. So many Americans bought Japanese-made cars, for example, that American automakers felt a threat to their decades-old dominance.

As Japan's economy expanded, it invested in ventures around the world. The Japanese financed and operated mines and plantations. They built airports and chemical plants. When a tire factory was to be built in East Africa or a dam in Central America, the engineers were as likely to be Japanese as American. Japan's presence everywhere showed that it had not only caught up with the West but was rapidly moving ahead of it.

**Reasons for success.** With few natural resources, how did Japan enjoy such enormous success? After the war, Japan—like Germany—had to rebuild from scratch. Also like Germany, it had the advantage of having successfully industrialized in the past. Now, it quickly built efficient, modern factories that outproduced older industries in the West. It adapted the latest technology from the West to create its own high-quality products.

Japan also benefited from a well-educated and skilled work force. Thanks to the postwar educational reforms, almost all Japanese went to high school and almost 40 percent continued through higher education.

Japanese workers saved much of their pay, which gave banks the capital to invest in industrial growth. Management and labor also tended to work together. Until recently, many large companies guaranteed Japanese workers lifetime employment. In return, workers gave the company total loyalty.

Ironically, Japan also benefited from the restrictions on military development that were forced on it after World War II. Unlike most industrial nations, it spent very little on defense. The government could therefore invest generously in the economy. It helped business and industry develop new products, open new overseas markets, and meet foreign competition. Its high tariffs and many regulations kept foreign imports to a minimum, which in turn gave Japanese products a boost at home.

tween the two nations stumbled along for years, with only limited success.

## A New World Role

Economic success allowed Japan to benefit from the modern global economy. Yet Japan felt the negative effects of interdependence as well, especially because of its need for imported raw materials.

**Dependence on oil.** Nothing brought home Japan's dependence on world markets more than OPEC's price hikes in the 1970s. (See page 416.) Japan's booming industries had fed on cheap imported oil. Higher energy costs sent shock waves through its economy.

In response, Japan sought better relations with oil-producing nations of the Middle East. It also tried to reduce energy use by building more efficient power plants and expanding and improving public transportation. Still, its modern economy required oil.

**Japan and its neighbors.** As Japan sought economic openings in Asia, it had to deal with nations that still held bitter memories of World War II. China, Korea, and parts of Southeast Asia had suffered terribly under Japanese occupation. Japan was slow to apologize for its wartime actions, but it did work hard to regain the trust of neighboring peoples. By the 1980s, Japan was a major investor in China and the emerging nations of Southeast Asia. In the 1990s, Japanese leaders finally offered public regrets for the death and destruction of the war years.

**International politics.** Although Japan was an economic superpower, it took a back seat in international politics. During the Cold War, it supported the western alliance led by the United States. More recently, it has edged toward a larger world role. For decades, it has given huge amounts of foreign aid to emerging

**The trade issue.** Japan's protectionist policies angered its trading partners, who were concerned about their trade deficit with Japan. This trade deficit existed because Japan exported more goods to these nations than it imported from them.

The United States, for example, claimed that Japanese trade barriers deprived American corporations of a fair chance to sell their goods in Japanese markets. To reduce its trade deficit with Japan, the United States threatened to raise tariffs on Japanese imports, making them more expensive for American consumers. That threat was designed to force Japan to open its door to more American imports. Trade talks be-

nations. Today, it ranks as the world's largest donor nation. In 1990, it provided money, but no soldiers, for the Gulf War. (See page 503.) Two years later, its soldiers joined a UN peace-keeping force for the first time.

The United States has urged Japan to rearm and assume more of the costs for its own defense. Asian neighbors oppose Japan's rearmament, and the Japanese themselves are divided on the issue. Some think Japan's status as a world power requires rearmament. Most prefer to avoid the hazards and expense of becoming a military power.

## Changing Patterns

In the past 50 years, Japan has enjoyed many economic successes. In the 1990s, however, Japan faced its worst economic depression since the 1930s. Companies had to make cutbacks, and many workers lost the security of guaranteed lifetime employment.

**Political stresses.** Japan's democracy has survived many crises. The Liberal Democratic party (LDP) has dominated the government since the 1950s. But Japanese political parties differ from those in the United States. The LDP is, in fact, a coalition of conservative factions that compete behind the scenes for top government positions. In the 1990s, charges of corruption greatly weakened the LDP. Some younger, reform-minded politicians broke with the LDP, threatening its monopoly on power.

**Crowded cities.** Today, 80 percent of the Japanese population live in cities, which are hugely overcrowded. Housing is expensive, and space is scarce. Most people live in tiny, cramped apartments. Many space-hungry Japanese move to the suburbs but then face long commutes to work.

In 1995, a severe earthquake badly damaged the city of Kobe (KOH BEE). It also shook Japanese faith in modern "quake-proof" technology. Japan lies in a region often rocked by

# PARALLELS THROUGH TIME

## The Classroom

Public education has changed greatly over the centuries. Until the late 1800s, even in industrialized countries few people got more than an elementary school education. In this century, schools have gone from providing the three R's—reading, 'riting, and 'rithmetic—to offering students a wide variety of specialized and technical courses.

**Linking Past and Present** What subjects that you study in school were taught 50 years ago? What subjects were introduced in recent years?

**PAST** These Japanese students in the late 1940s are learning English. The traditional classroom setting did not differ very much from schools in Africa, Europe, or the Americas.

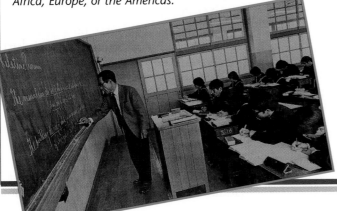

**PRESENT** Modern classrooms like this one in Japan give students a chance to work with the latest technology. Here, students in a language lab use computers to practice English.

earthquakes, and Japanese highways and other structures were supposed to be designed to withstand such quakes. The disaster in Kobe raised questions about just how much technology can protect against natural forces.

**Women.** Japanese women have legal equality and often control the family finances. But traditional attitudes toward women keep them in subordinate positions in the workplace. About half the adult women work outside the home, but most are in low-paying jobs or in family-run businesses. Fewer women than men get a university education, and only a handful have moved into higher-level jobs in business or government.

**Weakening work ethic.** For decades, the Japanese sacrificed family life to work long hours. They also saved large portions of their earnings. Younger Japanese, however, want more time to enjoy the benefits of economic success. Some older Japanese worry that the old work ethic is weakening.

## SECTION 1 REVIEW

1. **Identify** (a) Douglas MacArthur, (b) Diet, (c) Liberal Democratic party.
2. **Define** gross domestic product.
3. (a) What were the main goals of the occupation forces after World War II? (b) Describe three ways that they tried to achieve these goals.
4. (a) How did the Japanese economy grow in the postwar years? (b) What were three reasons for Japan's economic success?
5. What role has Japan played in world affairs in recent years?
6. *Critical Thinking* **Recognizing Points of View** Japan's trading partners complained that unfair Japanese policies caused their large trade deficits with Japan. To the Japanese, however, the trade deficits of these foreign nations were Japan's trade *surplus*. Explain the two points of view. How might these differing perspectives affect efforts to resolve the trade issue?
7. *ACTIVITY* Imagine that you are a Japanese teenager. Write a letter to the prime minister supporting or opposing the rearming of Japan.

# 2 From Revolution to Reform in China

## Guide for Reading

- Why did Mao's forces triumph in China?
- How did the Communists revolutionize China?
- What policies did Mao's successors pursue?
- **Vocabulary** *commune*

On October 1, 1949, to cheering crowds in Beijing, Mao Zedong announced the birth of the People's Republic of China. "The Chinese people have stood up, and the future of our nation is infinitely bright," declared the Communist leader. The government, he pledged, would call on "the great collective strength of the masses . . . to build a new China, independent, democratic, peaceful, unified, prosperous and strong."

In 1911, the collapse of the Qing dynasty marked the end of Confucian China. Mao's triumph in 1949 signaled the start of an even more intense upheaval. China's revolution ranks with Russia's as one of the major revolutionary struggles of our century.

### Triumph of Communism

After World War II, Mao Zedong's Communist forces and Jiang Jieshi's Nationalists resumed the bitter struggle for power that had begun in the 1920s. (See Chapter 12.) Civil war raged until Mao's forces swept to victory and set up the People's Republic of China (PRC) in 1949. The defeated Jiang Jieshi and his supporters fled to the island of Taiwan. After decades of struggle, China was finally united, with the Communists in control.

**Reasons for success.** Why did the Communists triumph? There were a number of reasons for their success.

Mao won the support of China's huge peasant population. Peasants had long suffered from brutal landlords and crushing taxes. The Communists pledged to distribute land to poor peasants and end oppression by landlords.

Women also threw their support behind Mao. The Nationalists had done little to improve their harsh lives. Women were still seen as inferior to men and were often cruelly mistreated. The Communists rejected the inequalities of the old Confucian society. "Women hold up half the sky," Mao said.

Finally, Mao's army was superior to Jiang's. With the guerrilla tactics they had perfected against the Japanese in World War II, they outfought Jiang's armies.

While Mao's support grew, Nationalist popularity dwindled. Chinese of all classes grew disgusted as they watched corrupt officials enrich themselves instead of working to solve China's problems. Peasant-soldiers drafted into the army had little desire to defend a government that oppressed them. Many educated Chinese saw Jiang's government as morally and politically bankrupt. They were drawn to the Communist program for a new China and an end to domination by foreigners who had humiliated their country for so long.

## Remaking Chinese Life

Once in power, the Communists set out to turn China from a backward peasant society into a modern industrial nation. First, however, they had to overcome hunger, poverty, disease, and illiteracy.

**Rebuilding the economy.** To build socialism and repair the economy, China nationalized all businesses. The government also drew up five-year plans designed to increase coal and steel output and develop heavy industry. With Soviet help, the Chinese built hydroelectric plants, railroads, and canals.

To boost agriculture, Mao distributed land to peasants. He encouraged peasants to "speak bitterness" against landlords. Tens of thousands of landlords were attacked and killed. The government urged peasants to pool their land and labor on more efficient cooperative farms.

**Remolding society.** Like Lenin in the Soviet Union, Mao Zedong built a one-party totalitarian state, with the Communist party supreme. Communist ideology replaced Confucian beliefs and traditional religions. The gov-

**Transforming China** *China set out in a new direction in 1949. Led by Mao Zedong, the Chinese Communists launched revolutionary new programs to change China from a peasant society to a modern, industrial nation. This poster shows peasants hailing the takeover by Mao's Communists.* **Impact of the Individual** *Do you think that a strong leader is needed to bring about major change? Explain.*

ernment attacked crime and corruption. It did away with the old landlord and business classes. In their place, peasants and workers were honored as the builders of the new China.

To increase literacy, reformers simplified Chinese characters, making it easier to learn to read and write. Schools were opened for young and old. The emphasis was on political education. Students learned to praise the "Great Helmsman," Mao Zedong, who could do no wrong.

The Communists sent health-care workers to remote rural areas. Although many of these "barefoot doctors" had limited training, they did help to reduce disease and teach better hygiene.

**Equality for women.** Under China's new constitution, women won equality under the law. They were expected to work alongside men in fields and factories. State-run nurseries were set up to care for the children. These changes weakened the old ideal of the extended family dominated by the oldest male. In China's cities, as elsewhere in the developing world, the nuclear family became increasingly common.

Although Chinese women made real progress, they did not enjoy full equality. Only a few won promotion to top jobs in government and industry. Women were often paid less than men for the same work. Also, after working at paid jobs, they still were responsible for cleaning, cooking, and child care.

**The Great Leap Forward.** In 1958, Mao launched the Great Leap Forward. He urged people to make a superhuman effort to increase farm and industrial output. In an attempt to make agriculture more efficient, he created communes. A typical commune included several villages, thousands of acres of land, and up to 25,000 people. It had its own schools, factories, housing, and dining halls.

Each commune had production quotas. Communes also mobilized labor brigades to build dams and irrigation systems. Rural communes set up "backyard" industries to produce steel and other products. Poet Yuan Kejia (yoo AHN kuh JYAH) praised the virtues of hard work and self-sacrifice for the new China:

> 66Labor is joy, how joyful is it?
>   Bathed in sweat and two hands
>     full of mud,
>   Like sweet rain, my sweat waters
>     the land
>   And the land issues scent,
>     better than milk.99

The Great Leap Forward was a dismal failure. Backyard industries turned out low-quality, useless goods. The commune system slowed food output. Bad weather added to the problems and led to a terrible famine. Between 1959 and 1961, up to 30 million Chinese are thought to have starved to death. In response, China turned to more moderate policies.

**The Cultural Revolution.** China slowly recovered from the Great Leap Forward. Mao, however, feared that bureaucrats and technicians were slowly replacing revolutionaries in running the country. In 1966, he launched the Great Proletarian Cultural Revolution. Its goal was to purge China of "bourgeois," or nonrevolutionary, tendencies. He urged young Chinese to experience revolution firsthand, as his generation had.

In response, teenagers formed bands of Red Guards. Waving copies of the "Little Red Book" of Mao's sayings, Red Guards attacked those they claimed were counterrevolutionaries. They targeted people in authority, from party leaders and factory managers to teachers, writers, and artists. The accused were publicly humiliated or beaten—sometimes even killed.

The Cultural Revolution convulsed China. Schools and universities closed. Millions of people were driven from their jobs. Government offices ceased to function, the economy slowed, and civil war threatened.

At last, Mao had the army restore order. Many Red Guards were sent to work on communes. They became a lost generation, undereducated and cut off from normal family life and careers. In the end, many became disillusioned with communism.

## China and the Cold War

The Communist victory in China dominated the Cold War in 1949. The United States had supported Jiang Jieshi. After he fled to Taiwan, the Americans continued to support the Nationalist government. They refused to recognize the People's Republic of China, or, as they called it, "Red China."

**Relations with the United States.** The rift between China and the United States deepened when they supported opposing sides in the Korean War. (See Section 3.) For years, the United States tried to isolate China, which it saw as an aggressive communist power expanding across Asia.

In 1971, however, China won admission to the United Nations. A year later, United States President Richard Nixon visited Mao in Beijing,

opening the door to improved relations. Both leaders used this occasion to strengthen their position with the Soviet Union. Formal diplomatic recognition of China by the United States finally came in 1979.

**Split with the Soviet Union.** Despite a treaty of friendship between China and the Soviet Union, the two communist giants were uneasy allies. In the 1950s, Stalin sent economic aid and technical experts to help China modernize. But he and Mao disagreed on many issues, especially ideology.

Mao had adapted Marxism to Chinese conditions. Marx, for example, had predicted that the industrial working class—the proletariat—would lead the revolution. Since China had little industry, Mao relied on peasants rather than factory workers to make the revolution. Stalin rejected Mao's views. Mao, for his part, thought the Soviets were too conservative and accused them of being too willing to "coexist" with the capitalist powers.

China and the Soviet Union were also rivals for influence in the Third World. In addition, border disputes triggered tensions between the two. Their border on the Amur River dated from czarist times, when Russia had seized territory from China. In 1960, border clashes and disputes over ideology led the Soviets to withdraw all aid and advisers from China, thus ending the alliance.

## China After Mao

Mao Zedong died in 1976. Despite disastrous mistakes, he remained the revolutionary hero who had restored order, ended foreign domination, and made China a world power once again.

After Mao, more moderate leaders controlled China. By 1981, Deng Xiaoping (duhng show PIHNG) had set China on a new path. Deng was a practical reformer, more interested in raising output than in political purity. "I don't care if a cat is red [socialist] or white [capitalist]," he declared, "as long as it catches mice."

**Economic reforms.** Deng backed a program called the Four Modernizations. It emphasized agriculture, industry, science, and defense.

◀ Nixon and Mao

**A Call for Democracy** *In May 1989, Chinese students and workers rallied for democracy in Beijing's Tiananmen Square. The demonstrators, shown here, carried banners and paraded a statue of the Goddess of Liberty. Hundreds died and many more were injured when the Chinese government sent in troops to put down the protest.* **Global Interaction** *How did the statue reflect global interaction?*

China. The government set up special enterprise zones where foreigners could own and operate industries.

Deng's reforms brought a surge of growth and a better standard of living for some Chinese. They were soon buying motor scooters, televisions, and tape decks. On the down side, crime and corruption grew. Inequalities grew again as a new wealthy class emerged. A gap also grew between poor rural farmers and city dwellers on the coast who were exposed to western influences.

**Tiananmen Square massacre.** By the late 1980s, some Chinese were demanding greater political freedom. In Beijing and other cities, students, workers, and others supported a democracy movement like those sweeping Eastern Europe and the Soviet Union. Unlike Gorbachev in the Soviet Union, however, Deng allowed only economic, not political, reform.

In May 1989, as you have read, demonstrators occupied Tiananmen Square. They built a huge plaster statue called the Goddess of Liberty and waved banners proclaiming, "Give us freedom or give us death." When they refused to disperse, the government sent in troops and tanks. Thousands of demonstrators were killed or wounded. Many others were arrested and tortured, some put to death.

The crackdown showed that China's Communist leaders were determined to maintain control. To them, order was more important than political freedom. During the 1990s, efforts to push China to end human rights violations had limited effects.

## Looking Ahead

By the mid-1990s, China was a major industrial power. Its economy ranked among the fastest growing in the world, and it was building major trade ties with countries worldwide. Yet it faced many unresolved issues. With its leadership in transition, no one knew what direction it would take.

**Population policies.** Population growth posed a challenge for the future. Since 1949, China's population has more than doubled, to 1.2 billion. Such rapid growth strained the economy. In the 1980s, the government instituted a one-child-per-family policy. Parents

As part of the Four Modernizations, Deng introduced economic reforms, including some private ownership of property and free-market policies. In agriculture, the responsibility system replaced the communes. Under it, peasant families were allotted plots of farmland. The government took a share of their crops, but the family could sell the rest on the free market. Entrepreneurs were allowed to set up their own businesses. Managers of state-run factories were given more freedom but were expected to make their plants more efficient.

Deng welcomed foreign capital and technology. Investors from Japan, Hong Kong, Taiwan, and the West organized joint ventures with

who had only one child were given rewards, such as better housing or improved medical benefits. Those who had more children faced fines and other penalties.

The campaign to slow the birthrate worked better in cities, where the government had more control, than in rural areas. Farm families, who wanted children to work the land, often paid fines rather than obey the policy. The one-child policy had a tragic effect in a country that still valued boys over girls. Female infanticide, or the killing of girl babies, increased despite efforts to prevent it.

**Economic and political challenges.** China continued to grapple with economic problems. State-run industries were often inefficient, but could not be closed without risking high unemployment and economic chaos. Cities were bursting at the seams as millions of peasants poured in to seek new opportunities.

Across China, communist ideology was weakening. Many Chinese—from party officials on down—were more interested in profit than in socialism. For some, Deng Xiaoping's death in 1997 marked the end of an era of stunning change. Yet more changes seemed likely. As economic reforms continued, pressure for political reforms would grow, too.

## SECTION 2 REVIEW

1. **Identify** (a) People's Republic of China, (b) Great Leap Forward, (c) Cultural Revolution, (d) "Little Red Book," (e) Four Modernizations, (f) Tiananmen Square massacre.
2. **Define** commune.
3. Why were the Communists able to win power in China in 1949?
4. Describe three ways that communism transformed Chinese life.
5. What economic reforms did Deng Xiaoping introduce?
6. *Critical Thinking* **Predicting Consequences** Do you think China can continue to push economic reforms without making political reforms? Why or why not?
7. *ACTIVITY* Imagine that you are an artist working for the Chinese government. Create a poster supporting one of the programs introduced by the People's Republic.

# 3 The Asian Tigers

## Guide for Reading

- How are Taiwan and Hong Kong linked to China?
- Why are the Asian tigers an economic success story?
- How do North Korea and South Korea differ?

At a university in Taiwan, Professor Xu Wen-xing worked on what he called a "futuristic dream." After 10 years, he proudly unveiled a computerized fingerprint-recognition device. Xu's invention has many possible uses—it may one day replace passports—and his university set up a company to market the device. To Xu, however, the most satisfying aspect of his success was that "the technology involved was developed in Taiwan."

Taiwan is one of four small Asian lands that have vaulted into the class of "newly industrialized countries." Besides Taiwan, Hong Kong, Singapore, and South Korea are also known for their aggressive growth. The four are often called the "Asian tigers." Although they differ in important ways, all have followed similar roads to modernization since 1945.

## *Taiwan and Hong Kong*

The four Asian tigers were all influenced to some degree by China and Confucian traditions. The island of Taiwan was once ruled by the mainland. Today, the People's Republic still considers it part of China. Hong Kong was returned to China in 1997 after more than a century under British colonial rule. Neither Taiwan nor Hong Kong experienced Mao's Communist revolution. Still, they are linked through history and culture to China.

**Taiwan.** Taiwan fell to Japan in 1895 during the Age of Imperialism. The Japanese built some industry, providing a foundation for later growth. In 1945, Taiwan reverted to China. But when Jiang Jieshi fled the mainland in 1949, he set up his Nationalist government on

Taiwan. Despite Jiang's autocratic rule, Taiwan's economy grew rapidly.

Taiwan first set up light industries such as textiles. Later, it developed heavy industry. In the 1960s, the Green Revolution (see page 425) helped Taiwan's agriculture become more productive. Trade boomed, industrial cities grew, and in time Taiwan's standard of living rose to one of the highest in Asia. Backed by economic success, the government slowly allowed people more freedom.

Hostility between Taiwan and the mainland eased somewhat as the Cold War wound down. Taiwanese businesses took advantage of Deng Xiaoping's economic reforms to invest in the mainland. They financed projects in China's foreign enterprise zones along the coast. In addition, extensive trade—some of it illegal—took place between Taiwan and the mainland.

Most residents of Taiwan welcome closer links with the mainland. Yet some have warned against Beijing acquiring too much power over the island's economy. Beijing's long-term goal is still to reunite Taiwan with China.

**Hong Kong.** Britain gained the tiny island of Hong Kong after the Opium War. (See page 234.) Under British rule, Hong Kong and nearby territories grew into a center of trade. In 1949, refugees from Mao's Communist revolution crowded into Hong Kong. They provided labor and capital to help develop the territory.

Hong Kong's economy today is based on trade and light industry such as electronics and textiles. It is also a major financial center with many foreign banks and a busy stock market. Wealth from these profitable industries helped Hong Kong modernize.

Hong Kong's amazing growth was also due in part to its location on China's doorstep. Hong Kong Chinese built commercial ties to the mainland at a time when the People's Republic was largely isolated from the world community. For years, it was the chief link between the PRC and the rest of the world.

In 1997, Britain returned Hong Kong to China. The People's Republic had earlier agreed not to change Hong Kong's social or economic system for 50 years and to allow its people self-government. China stood to profit from Hong Kong's bustling free-market economy. But many Hong Kong residents remain nervous about the future. They fear the PRC's power and use of repression against protests. But as one Hong Kong resident noted:

66We don't believe we have any control over events. So we just wait and see what happens.99

**Singapore.** The smallest Asian tiger is the city-state of Singapore. It sits on a tiny island at the tip of the Malay Peninsula in Southeast Asia. Its 200 square miles have a population of about 2 million.

In 1819, British empire-builder Sir Stamford Raffles leased the island from a local ruler. Raffles recognized its ideal location on the

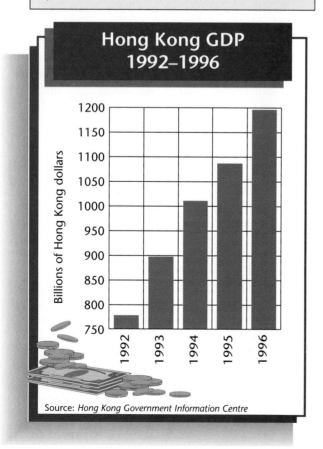

*Interpreting a Graph* Under the British, Hong Kong became a major center of trade, manufacturing, shipping, and finance. As the graph shows, in the 1990s its economy was booming. ■ What was Hong Kong's GDP in 1992? In 1996? Approximately what percentage increase was that? What event did Hong Kong residents fear might hurt their economy? Explain.

**Hong Kong GDP 1992–1996**

Billions of Hong Kong dollars

1200
1150
1100
1050
1000
950
900
850
800
750

1992 1993 1994 1995 1996

Source: *Hong Kong Government Information Centre*

*Rising Singapore* Modern office towers symbolize the prosperity of Singapore, one of the Asian tigers. Singapore's deep, natural sheltered harbor and location along Asian trade routes helped make it a thriving center of trade. Though Singapore is Southeast Asia's smallest country, its standard of living is the region's highest. **Impact of the Individual** What policies of Lee Kwan Yew promoted prosperity in Singapore?

Malacca Straits, halfway between China and India. He and his successors turned the island's fishing villages into one of the most prosperous and corrupt seaports in Asia.

Under British rule, Singapore grew to include not only Malayans and British merchants and sailors but also Chinese and Indian immigrants. All were eager to make money in the booming "lion city" of Singha Pura, soon shortened to Singapore. The British brought in Chinese workers to process tin and rubber from Malaya. In time, the Chinese became the dominant ethnic group and their Confucian traditions shaped the local culture.

### Lee Kwan Yew's Singapore

Among the Chinese who settled in Singapore were the parents of Lee Kwan Yew. They taught Lee to aim high and succeed at any cost. They also made sure that he got a fine education, including a law degree from Cambridge University in Britain.

**Order and prosperity.** Lee joined Singapore's struggle for independence first from Britain in 1959 and then from nearby Malaya in 1963.

For 30 years, Lee was Singapore's prime minister and remade the city-state. Every resident, he said, "must live up to our motto—From Each His Best." He set high standards for Singapore in short rules and slogans such as:

> 66Rule One, Work Hard. Rule Two, Be Fit. Rule Three, Be Clean. Work is an obligation. Nobody owes us our living.99

Lee was an autocratic ruler. In elections, he claimed to win 99 percent of the vote. He jailed those who opposed him too strongly. One story tells how Lee treated an independent-minded critic and newspaper owner. Lee leaned across his desk, seized the man's collar, and said: "I'm a thug, you're a thug, and as one thug to another, you'll do what I say!"

Yet under Lee, Singapore was transformed into an economic powerhouse, one of the "tiger economies" of the Asian Pacific rim. First, Lee's government expanded the seaport inherited from the British into one of the world's busiest harbors. Then it had a modern airline and airport built.

The government supported a free-market economy. It welcomed foreign investors, invited immigrants with needed skills to settle there, and insisted on education for all—in both English and Chinese. Lee's government backed the growth of high-tech industries, manufacturing, finance, and tourism.

As Singapore's economy grew, its standard of living rose. The government organized an outstanding public housing program. Almost all married couples are home owners, thanks to government loans.

Lee turned one of the dirtiest, most crime-ridden cities in the world into one of the cleanest and safest. The new Singapore is a garden city with flowers, fountains, and parks. Crime is low. Even today, years after Lee retired, it is still illegal to litter, smoke, or chew gum in public. Vandals can be punished by caning. Drug dealers are executed.

Lee traveled the world encouraging other nations to follow Singapore's example. He preached what he called "Confucian values." He urged such virtues as hard work, loyalty toward family, and respectful obedience to authority.

**Outlook for the future.** Singapore is often seen as a model of successful development. Yet because it depends heavily on trade, its economy can be affected by events around the world. Critics note limits on individual rights, including censorship of the press. To these criticisms, the government answers with the Confucian argument that order is more important than individual freedom.

Still, Singapore faces demands for more freedom from its younger well-educated citizens. It also has to deal with ethnic tensions between the Chinese majority and Malay and Indian minorities. ▪

## The Two Koreas

The fourth Asian tiger is South Korea. It emerged amid Cold War tensions and a devastating "hot" war that involved not only Korea but also China and the United States.

**A Cold War division.** In 1910, Japan annexed Korea and imposed a brutal regime on the peninsula. After the Allied victory in World War II, the Soviet Union and the United States agreed to a temporary division of Korea, along the 38th parallel of latitude. American forces occupied the south. The Soviets held the north.

During the Cold War, Korea's division—like Germany's—seemed to become permanent. North Korea, ruled by Kim Il Sung, became a communist ally of the Soviet Union. In South Korea, the United States backed an authoritarian but noncommunist leader, Syngman Rhee.

**The Korean War.** In 1950, North Korean forces invaded the south, seeking to unify the country. They almost overran the peninsula. Backed by the UN, the United States organized an international force to help South Korea.

UN forces, mostly Americans and South Koreans, were commanded by United States general Douglas MacArthur. After landing troops behind enemy lines, he drove the invaders back across the 38th parallel. He continued to push northward toward the Yalu River on the border of China.

MacArthur's success moved China into action. Mao Zedong feared an American invasion. He sent Chinese troops to help the North Koreans. Together, they pushed the UN forces back to the 38th parallel.

**The long truce.** Fighting continued until an armistice was signed in 1953. That cease-fire has held for more than 40 years. More than a million North Korean and South Korean troops dug in along the truce line. American forces, too, remained in South Korea to guarantee the peace.

## Differences North and South

After the war, the two Koreas slowly rebuilt economies destroyed by the fighting and by years of Japanese occupation. Both remained centers of Cold War rivalry. The United States funneled aid to South Korea, while the Soviets helped the north.

**An economic powerhouse.** Economically, South Korea leaped ahead of the north after the mid-1960s. At first, it exported textiles and

**ISSUES** *For* **TODAY**

Singapore's rulers claimed that they needed to restrict individual freedom in order to achieve economic prosperity for their people. Can developing nations promote economic growth without sacrificing political freedom?

## Korean War, 1950–1953

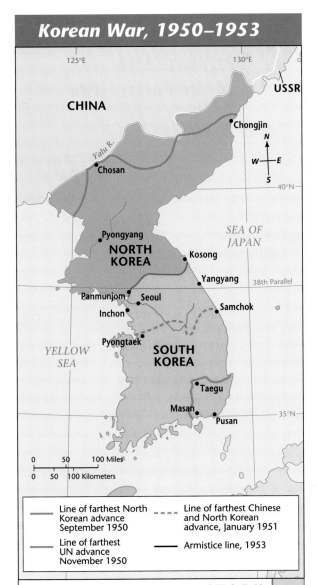

Legend:
- Line of farthest North Korean advance September 1950
- Line of farthest UN advance November 1950
- Line of farthest Chinese and North Korean advance, January 1951
- Armistice line, 1953

### GEOGRAPHY AND HISTORY

After North Korean troops stormed across the 38th parallel into South Korea, the UN sent an army to aid South Korea. Fighting continued for three years, until a cease-fire was signed in 1953.

1. **Location** On the map, locate (a) North Korea, (b) South Korea, (c) 38th parallel, (d) Yalu River, (e) China.
2. **Movement** Which nation gained territory as a result of the armistice?
3. **Critical Thinking** **Making Inferences** Based on the map, why do you think the UN advance across the 38th parallel worried the Chinese?

inexpensive goods. Then, it shifted to higher-priced exports such as automobiles. Its strong growth was due in part to international loans and investment and in part to low wages paid to workers. By the 1990s, South Korea was an economic powerhouse. As prosperity increased, workers demanded better pay, and South Korea's standard of living rose remarkably.

For decades, dictators backed by the military ruled South Korea. By 1987, however, growing prosperity and fierce student protests forced the government to hold direct elections. The moves toward democracy increased in the 1990s, as former presidents were indicted for crimes committed while in office.

**The totalitarian north.** Under Kim Il Sung, North Korea recovered from the war. State-owned industries and collective farms increased output. By the late 1960s, however, growth slowed. Kim's emphasis on self-reliance kept North Korea isolated from much of the world. Yet when its old partners, the Soviet Union and China, tried out economic reforms in the 1980s, North Korea clung to hardline communism.

In North Korea, propaganda constantly glorified Kim as the "Great Leader." After Kim's death in 1994, his son Kim Jong Il, the "Dear Leader," took over. He faced growing problems. North Korea's longtime ally, China, had not only reached out to the capitalist world but also set up economic ties with South Korea. Then failed government policies and terrible floods destroyed harvests, bringing widespread hunger. By 1997, North Korea had to accept food aid from the United States and other nations to prevent mass starvation. Some observers wondered if the disaster could undermine Kim's power.

**The nuclear issue.** Like several emerging nations, North Korea tried to develop nuclear power plants and weapons. Under intense pressure from the United States, North Korea agreed to end its nuclear weapons program. In exchange the United States was to supply North Korea with oil and start the process of diplomatic recognition of North Korea.

**Looking ahead.** Despite differences between the two Koreas, most Koreans want to see their country reunited. After all, they share the same language, culture, and heritage. Reunification on the German model seemed unlikely as long as North Korea insisted on its policy of

**The Great Leader** *During his nearly 50 years in power, Kim Il Sung fostered a powerful cult of personality. Here, a giant portrait of the "Great Leader" looms over a student gathering in Pyongyang.* **Impact of the Individual** *How do you think North Korea's isolation helped to strengthen Kim Il Sung's power?*

isolation. South Korea's growing prosperity also created an economic gulf between the countries. Resolving the issue was of global interest because of Korea's strategic location between three Asian giants—China, Russia, and Japan.

## SECTION 3 REVIEW

1. **Identify** (a) Asian tigers, (b) Lee Kwan Yew, (c) Syngman Rhee, (d) Kim Jong Il.
2. (a) How is Taiwan linked to China today? (b) Why is Hong Kong's future uncertain?
3. (a) Describe Singapore's development as an Asian tiger. (b) What challenges does Singapore face today?
4. (a) How was the division of Korea related to the Cold War? (b) What was one immediate and one long-term result of the Korean War?
5. *Critical Thinking* **Analyzing Information** Why might Korea be harder to reunify than Germany?
6. *ACTIVITY* Singapore leader Lee Kwan Yew argues that economic development is more important than political freedom for developing countries. Write a letter to Lee expressing your opinion on this issue.

# 4 Southeast Asia and the Pacific Rim

### Guide for Reading

■ What problems did developing nations of Southeast Asia face after World War II?

■ Why was Vietnam plunged into decades of war?

■ Why is the Pacific Rim an economic powerhouse today?

Today, more than 50 years after the end of World War II, Southeast Asia has emerged as a key player in the global economy. In the immediate postwar years, however, the region was shaped by the nationalist drive for independence. Some nations won freedom easily, without much violence. Others, like Vietnam, fought long wars of liberation.

## Sources of Conflict

After World War II, local nationalists rejected European efforts to reclaim their colonial empires in Southeast Asia. Ho Chi Minh, a Vietnamese nationalist, echoed the view of people throughout the region when he declared:

❝The whole Vietnamese people, animated by a common purpose, are determined to fight to the bitter end against any attempt by the French colonialists to reconquer their country.❞

Cold War tensions complicated the drive for freedom. The United States supported independence for colonial people in principle. But the West was anxious to stop the spread of communism. As a result, the United States helped noncommunists gain power in Southeast Asia even though they had little popular support.

Other problems occurred because emerging Southeast Asian nations lacked experience in self-government. Many faced years of instability as they set out to modernize. Efforts to modernize were further hampered by complex ethnic and regional conflicts.

## Decades of War in Vietnam

In mainland Southeast Asia, an agonizing liberation struggle tore apart the region once known as French Indochina. It affected the emerging nations of Vietnam, Cambodia, and Laos. The 30-year conflict had two major phases: the battle against the French and the Cold War conflict.

**Battle against the French.** The first phase of the struggle lasted from 1946 to 1954. During World War II, Ho Chi Minh, the Vietnamese communist, had organized guerrillas to resist the Japanese. At war's end, Ho controlled much of northern Vietnam.

In 1946, the French set out to regain Indochina. Like Mao in China, however, Ho "swam in the peasant sea." With peasant support, Ho's guerrilla fighters slowly wore down the French and finally forced them to leave.

**Vietnam divided.** By this time, the struggle in Vietnam had become part of the Cold War. At a 1954 conference in Geneva, Switzerland, western and communist powers agreed to a temporary division of Vietnam. Ho and the communists ruled North Vietnam. A noncommunist government, supported by the United States and headed by Ngo Dinh Diem, ruled South Vietnam. Cambodia and Laos became independent nations.

The agreement called for elections to be held in 1956 to reunite Vietnam. The elections never took place, however, largely because the Americans and Diem feared that the communists might win. American officials believed in the "domino theory." It held that a communist victory in South Vietnam would cause noncommunist governments across Southeast Asia to fall to communism, like a row of dominos. To prevent such a disaster, as the French withdrew from Vietnam, the United States stepped in to shore up the Diem government.

**American involvement.** The second phase of the Vietnam War raged from 1959 to 1975. Ho Chi Minh wanted to unite Vietnam under northern rule. He supported the Viet Cong, communist rebels trying to overthrow Diem in South Vietnam.

At first, the United States sent only military advisers and supplies to Diem. Under Presidents Kennedy and Johnson, however, the American

## Vietnam War, 1968–1975

Legend:
→ Tet Offensive, 1968
■ American bases
▨ National Liberation Front base areas
- → North Vietnam's final offensive, 1975

## GEOGRAPHY AND HISTORY

In Vietnam, what started as a struggle against colonialism ended up as a major contest of the Cold War. The United States threw its support behind South Vietnam against the communist north. But despite this intervention, the war ended with a North Vietnamese victory.

1. **Location** On the map, locate (a) North Vietnam, (b) South Vietnam, (c) Cambodia, (d) Laos, (e) Saigon, (f) Ho Chi Minh Trail.
2. **Movement** How did North Vietnam's use of the Ho Chi Minh Trail as a supply route help to spread the war beyond Vietnam?
3. *Critical Thinking* **Applying Information** Use the map to describe the "domino theory."

**Generations of Soldiers** *The people of Vietnam were at war for more than 30 years. Generations of young people grew up expecting to fight. These young boys served in the South Vietnamese army.* **Global Interaction** *How did Vietnam's struggle for independence become part of the Cold War?*

involvement increased, and a local struggle became a major Cold War conflict.

In 1964, the United States began bombing targets in North Vietnam. When air raids failed to force Ho to abandon the war, the United States committed more troops. By 1969, more than 500,000 Americans were serving in Vietnam. Meantime, the Soviet Union and China sent aid but no troops to help North Vietnam.

Even with massive American help, South Vietnam could not defeat the communist guerrillas and their North Vietnamese allies. At the same time, the bombing of North Vietnam and growing American casualties on the ground inflamed antiwar opinion in the United States. Under increasing pressure, President Nixon finally arranged a cease-fire and began withdrawal of American forces in 1973. Two years later, the North Vietnamese captured Saigon, capital of the south, and reunited the country.

**Why the communists won.** Ever since, Americans have debated why the communists won. In some ways, the Vietnam War mirrored

the civil war in China that had brought Mao to power in 1949. Diem and his successors in South Vietnam were unpopular leaders of a corrupt government. Ho Chi Minh was widely admired as a hero who had fought the Japanese and the French. Many Vietnamese saw the United States as another foreign power seeking to dominate their land. Also, despite American air power and advanced technology, guerrillas fought well in the jungle terrain.

**Vietnam today.** The communist victors imposed harsh rule on the south. Tens of thousands of Vietnamese fled in small boats. Many of these "boat people" drowned. Survivors landed in refugee camps. Eventually, some were accepted into the United States or other countries.

Vietnam itself had to rebuild a land destroyed by war. Recovery was slow due to government inefficiency and an American-led boycott of Vietnam. For years, the country was mired in poverty, unable to attract foreign capital.

In the early 1990s, however, Vietnam introduced some free-market reforms, opening the door to investors. Some children of the "boat people" who had fled Vietnam went back to begin businesses there. Diplomatic relations with the United States were also normalized. Today, Vietnam seems ready for economic growth.

## Tragedy in Cambodia

During the Vietnam War, fighting spilled over into neighboring Cambodia. The North Vietnamese sent supplies through Cambodia to guerrilla forces in South Vietnam. In 1970, the United States bombed that route and then invaded Cambodia. After the Americans left, Cambodian communist guerrillas, the Khmer Rouge, overthrew the government.

**GLOBAL** ⊕ **CONNECTIONS**

Ho Chi Minh lived in France for six years, between 1917 and 1923. In 1919, he addressed a petition to the representatives of the Great Powers at the Versailles peace conference that ended World War I. He demanded that the French colonial power grant its subjects in Indochina equal rights with the French rulers. This act brought no response from the peacemakers, but it made him a hero to the Vietnamese.

Led by Pol Pot, the Khmer Rouge unleashed a reign of terror. To destroy all western influences, they drove people from the cities and forced them to work in the fields. They slaughtered or caused the death of more than a million Cambodians, perhaps a third of the population.

In 1979, Vietnam invaded and occupied Cambodia. Pol Pot and his forces retreated to remote areas. In 1993, UN peacekeepers supervised elections. Despite guerrillas who still terrorized parts of the country, a new government began to rebuild Cambodia.

## Independence for the Philippines

In 1946, the island nation of the Philippines gained freedom peacefully after almost five decades of American rule. The United States, however, exerted a strong influence on the country through military and economic aid.

**Rebellions.** Although the Filipino constitution set up a democratic government, a wealthy elite controlled politics and the economy. The peasant majority, meanwhile, was desperately poor. Many peasants threw their support behind the Huks, local communists who promised land reform. With American help, the government crushed the Huks, but new rebellions kept erupting.

In 1965, Ferdinand Marcos was elected president. Marcos had promised reform but instead made himself dictator. He cracked down on free speech and forced opponents into exile. He even had Benigno Aquino (beh NEE nyoh ah KEE noh), a popular rival politician, murdered.

*"People power."* Under heavy pressure, Marcos finally held elections in 1986. At the polls, Corazon Aquino, widow of the slain Benigno, defeated Marcos. When Marcos tried to overturn the results, the people of Manila forced him to leave in what was called the "people power" revolution.

Under Aquino and her successors, the fragile Filipino democracy survived. In

◄ *Corazon Aquino*

the early 1990s, it also saw some economic growth. But the government failed to make the major changes needed to improve life for the poverty-stricken majority. With the election of a new president, Fidel Ramos, who had served in both the Marcos and Aquino governments, there was renewed optimism for the future.

## Developing Nations of Southeast Asia

Other Southeast Asian nations emerged from colonial rule after brief struggles. All pursued the same goal, modernization, but their paths differed. Here, we will look at the experiences of two developing nations: Myanmar (formerly Burma) and Indonesia.

**Myanmar.** Ethnic tensions also plagued Burma after independence. Burmans, who make up the majority of the population, dominated the country. For years, repressive military rulers battled rebel ethnic minorities who wanted autonomy. In 1989, the military renamed the country Myanmar, meaning "the People's Country." By taking that name, the government recognized that other groups besides Burmans lived there.

The military government isolated the country from the world, thus limiting trade and foreign investment. It tried to develop the economy by imposing state socialism modeled on China's system. Its policies brought little improvement in the standard of living.

Under mounting pressure from students and other young people, the government held elections in 1990. The opposition party won. It was led by Aung San Suu Kyi (AWNG SAHN SOO SHEE), whose father had helped Burma win independence. The military rejected the election results and jailed, killed, or exiled many opponents. Suu Kyi was held under house arrest. In 1991, while still a prisoner, she was awarded the Nobel Peace Prize for her "nonviolent struggle for democracy and human rights." Suu Kyi was finally released in 1995 and vowed to continue to fight for democracy in Myanmar.

**Indonesia.** Geography is an obstacle to unity in Indonesia, as in many Third World nations. Indonesia includes more than 13,000 islands splashed across 3,200 miles of ocean—a distance equal to the width of the United States.

**Indonesian Batik** *Indonesians have long been known for their beautiful batik fabrics. Following a centuries-old method, the artist paints a design on cloth with melted wax, then dyes the cloth. The coated areas do not absorb the color, and when the wax is removed the design is revealed. Remains of cloth found on Indonesia's main island of Java indicate that the same or similar designs have been in use for about 1,000 years. A contemporary Indonesian artist created the imaginative batik design shown here.* **Art and Literature** *What mood does the artist convey with this design? Explain.*

Its large population is ethnically diverse. The Javanese dominate, but about 300 other groups, with their own languages or dialects, also live in Indonesia. Despite this diversity, about 90 percent of Indonesians are Muslims.

Since independence, an authoritarian government has suppressed rebellions. In 1965, it crushed what looked like a communist uprising and massacred hundreds of thousands of suspected communists. Mobs killed many Chinese whose ancestors had settled in Indonesia. More recently, the government has silenced protests in East Timor, an island whose Roman Catholic population wanted autonomy. In 1996, two activists from East Timor, Bishop Carlos Ximenes Belo and Jose Ramos-Horta, won the Nobel Peace Prize.

Under military rule, Indonesia made great economic progress. It benefited from exporting oil, tin, rubber, spices, and coffee. The rise and fall of world oil prices, however, meant that income was uncertain. Still, the government increased literacy and in the 1990s, introduced economic reforms that attracted more foreign capital.

**Regional cooperation.** Demands for political freedom and social justice remained an issue in Southeast Asia. Some government leaders, however, asserted that order and economic development must take priority over democracy.

To achieve prosperity and improve regional self-reliance, six Southeast Asian countries formed the Association of Southeast Asian Nations (ASEAN) in 1967. Since then, Singapore, Malaysia, Thailand, the Philippines, Indonesia, and Brunei have worked to promote economic and cultural cooperation. Besides lowering trade barriers, they have increased contacts with other Southeast Asian nations, including Vietnam.

## The Pacific Rim

In the modern global economy, Southeast Asia and East Asia are part of a vast region known as the Pacific Rim. It includes countries in Asia and the Americas that border the Pacific Ocean. (See the map on page 479.)

The Pacific first became an artery for world trade in the 1500s. By the mid-1900s, links across the Pacific had grown dramatically. The end of the Cold War fed a new surge of trade and other contacts.

By the 1990s, the volume of trade across the Pacific was greater than that across the Atlantic. Some analysts predicted that the 2000s will be the "Pacific century" because of this region's potential for further growth.

**Population and markets.** Countries on the Asian Pacific Rim formed a huge market that lured investors, especially multinational corporations. With more than 1.2 billion people, China has a fifth of the world's population. Indonesia, with 190 million people, and Japan,

## Pacific Rim

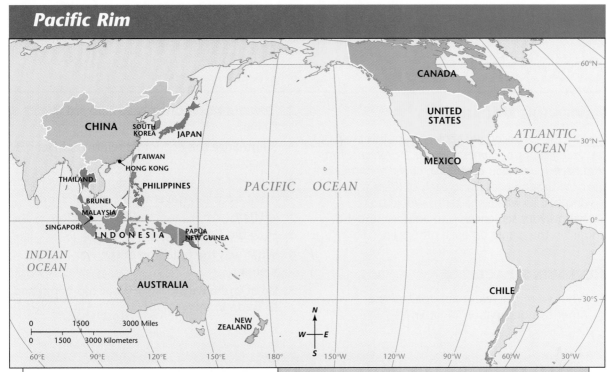

### GEOGRAPHY AND HISTORY

The nations shown here belong to the Asia-Pacific Economic Cooperation group (APEC). The goal of APEC is to promote trade across the Pacific Rim region.

**1. Location** On the map, locate (a) Pacific Ocean, (b) Hong Kong, (c) Japan, (d) China, (e) United States, (f) Chile, (g) Indonesia, (h) Australia.

**2. Movement** What might be some of the effects of trade among the nations of the Pacific Rim?

**3. Critical Thinking Synthesizing Information** The nations of the Pacific Rim are spread out across the globe. What unites them as a region?

with 125 million, are also among the world's most populous nations. Vietnam is just emerging as a new market in the region.

Since the 1960s, Japan has dominated the Asian Pacific Rim economically. By the 1990s, however, China was challenging Japan's economic empire. American companies, too, sought a place on the Asian Pacific Rim.

**Cultural exchanges.** Countries on the Pacific Rim are enormously diverse. Indian, Hindu, Buddhist, and Confucian traditions, you will recall, helped shape Southeast Asian cultures. Later, Islam took root in some areas, while the Age of Imperialism brought western and Christian influences.

Today, cultural exchanges occur rapidly as radio and television programs are beamed by satellite throughout Asia. Businesses and tourists aid the exchange of technology and ideas. The development of the Pacific Rim promises to bring the Americas and Asia into closer contact.

## SECTION 4 REVIEW

1. **Identify** (a) Ho Chi Minh, (b) domino theory, (c) Khmer Rouge, (d) Corazon Aquino, (e) Aung San Suu Kyi, (f) ASEAN.
2. How did the Cold War affect Southeast Asia?
3. (a) Describe the two phases of the Vietnam War. (b) Why did North Vietnam triumph?
4. Why is the Pacific Rim seen as an important link in the global economy?
5. *Critical Thinking* **Drawing Conclusions** Why might a country like Indonesia have a hard time creating a national identity?
6. *ACTIVITY* Imagine that you are Aung San Suu Kyi of Myanmar. Prepare a speech accepting the Nobel Peace Prize. Be sure to include remarks about the present state of your nation and your hopes for its future.

## CHAPTER REVIEW

### REVIEWING VOCABULARY

Review the following vocabulary from this chapter: *zaibatsu, gross domestic product, protectionism, trade deficit, ideology, commune, guerrilla, entrepreneur.* Write sentences using each of these terms, leaving blanks where the terms would go. Exchange your sentences with another student and fill in the blanks on each other's lists.

### REVIEWING FACTS

1. What were the two main goals of the American occupation of Japan?

2. How did Mao's Great Leap Forward affect China?

3. Summarize the economic reforms of Deng Xiaoping.

4. Why did Taiwan create a separate government from the government of mainland China?

5. How did Korea become divided?

6. What was the outcome of the war in Vietnam?

7. What is the Pacific Rim? What has happened to trade in this region?

## SKILLS FOR SUCCESS   SYNTHESIZING INFORMATION

**Synthesizing** means putting together and analyzing various pieces of information in order to form a complete picture. The more evidence you synthesize, the more accurate your conclusions will be.

Below are three pieces of evidence about education in South Korea. Study them and then follow the steps to synthesize the information.

1. **Identify the evidence.**
(a) What is the subject of the graph? (b) What is the subject of the chart? (c) What is the third piece of evidence?

2. **Analyze each piece of evidence.** (a) According to the circle graph, what percentage of South Korea's total budget is spent on education? (b) According to the table, what percentage of

students who applied to a university in 1990 were accepted? (c) What does the slogan tell you about the difficulty of South Korean high schools?

3. **Synthesize the information and draw conclusions.** Based on this evidence, what conclusion can you draw about the importance of education in South Korea?

*Slogan among South Korean high school students:*

"You'll pass with three hours of sleep but you'll fail with four."

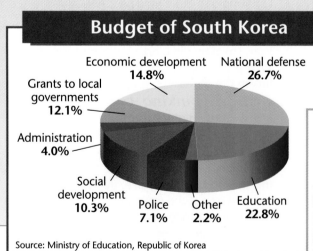

### Budget of South Korea

- Economic development **14.8%**
- National defense **26.7%**
- Grants to local governments **12.1%**
- Administration **4.0%**
- Social development **10.3%**
- Police **7.1%**
- Other **2.2%**
- Education **22.8%**

Source: Ministry of Education, Republic of Korea

### Applications to Universities in South Korea

| Year | Number of Applicants | Openings | Percentage Accepted |
|------|----------------------|----------|---------------------|
| 1987 | 732,931 | 271,745 | 37.1 |
| 1988 | 765,604 | 296,820 | 38.8 |
| 1989 | 803,140 | 310,220 | 38.6 |
| 1990 | 889,148 | 334,855 | 38.8 |

Source: *Education Indicators in Korea*

## REVIEWING CHAPTER THEMES

Review the "Focus On" questions at the start of this chapter. Then select *three* of those questions and answer them, using information from the chapter.

## CRITICAL THINKING

1. **Recognizing Causes and Effects** (a) List the reasons for Japan's economic success after World War II. (b) How might its emergence as an economic superpower threaten some of the values that brought success?

2. **Comparing** Compare Deng's reforms in China to those of Gorbachev in the Soviet Union. (a) How were the reforms similar? (b) How were they different?

3. **Linking Past and Present** What effects of the Vietnam War can still be seen in the United States today?

## ANALYZING PRIMARY SOURCES

Use the quotation on page 474 to answer the following questions.

1. What was the "common purpose" that Ho Chi Minh referred to?

2. Why do you think Ho used the term "reconquer" instead of "reoccupy"?

3. What might Ho have said if he had been told that the United States would later send troops to Vietnam?

## FOR YOUR PORTFOLIO

**WRITING A MEETING AGENDA** Imagine that you work for an Asian trade organization. You have been asked to prepare an agenda for an upcoming meeting on international trade. Begin by reviewing the information on economics and trade in this chapter. Then use outside resources to update your information. Identify the main issues that Asian nations might wish to discuss with western nations. Draw up your agenda. Finally, share your agenda with the class and explain your choices.

### Korean War, 1950–1953

## ANALYZING MAPS

Use the map to answer the following questions.

1. Which side had nearly won the war in September 1950? In November 1950?

2. Why was the Yalu River an important landmark in the Korean War?

### INTERNET ACTIVITY

**RESEARCHING CURRENT EVENTS** Use the Internet to research current events in a nation of East Asia or Southeast Asia. Then select one of the sections in the chapter and write an update that describes some recent events in that country.

# South Asia and the Middle East

## (1945–Present)

## CHAPTER OUTLINE

1 **Nations of South Asia**
2 **Forces Shaping the Modern Middle East**
3 **Nation Building in the Middle East: Three Case Studies**
4 **The Middle East and the World**

August 15, 1947, was a joyful day in India. Everywhere, parades and mass meetings filled the streets with huge crowds. Speeches hailed Mohandas Gandhi as "father of the nation." Bands played, flags waved, and fireworks exploded. At the stroke of midnight, after decades of struggle, power had passed from British colonial governors to India's own chosen leaders. This was India's Independence Day.

Jawaharlal Nehru, India's first prime minister, greeted the day with hope for the future:

66The Appointed Day has come, the day appointed by destiny, and India stands forth again after a long slumber and struggle, awake, vital, free, and independent. A new star rises, the star of freedom in the East. . . . May the star never set and that hope never be betrayed.99

Sadly, independence would bring tragedy along with joy. Soon, bloody riots exploded between Hindus and Muslims, while Gandhi himself would fall victim to assassination. Less than a year after the celebrations, Nehru wrote:

66Freedom came to us, our long-sought freedom, and it came with a minimum of violence. But immediately after, we had to wade through oceans of blood and tears.99

India and its neighbors on the subcontinent emerged from colonial rule to face many challenges—from religious strife and border conflicts to poverty and limited rights for women.

Developing nations in the Middle East also cast off western rule and set out to modernize. Some had the advantage of great oil wealth. Most did not. In the Middle East, as elsewhere, modernization was linked to a population explosion, urbanization, and disturbing social and economic problems. Nations responded differently to those challenges. In Muslim societies, many people looked for answers in a renewed commitment to Islamic traditions.

FOCUS ON these questions as you read:

■ **Diversity**
What impact did diversity have on challenges to nations in South Asia and the Middle East?

■ **Economics and Technology**
How did emerging nations use technology to develop economically?

■ **Geography and History**
Why was geography a significant force in shaping the modern Middle East?

■ **Continuity and Change**
How did modernization pose a challenge to older cultural values and traditions?

■ **Religions and Value Systems**
Why did the Islamic revival have a strong appeal to many Muslims?

## TIME AND PLACE

***Profession of Faith*** *This ceramic by Iraqi artist Wasma'a K. Chorbachi repeats the central belief of Islam: "There is no God but God, and Muhammad is his prophet." Like many artists in former European colonies, Chorbachi at first followed western styles. But then, she wrote, "I suddenly felt that these paintings were not me, the Arab and the Muslim. . . . I had not been trained in an artistic language that would enable me to express the inner identity I so strongly felt."* ***Religions and Value Systems*** *Islam has continued to be a major force in both South Asia and the Middle East. What other religions have shaped these regions?*

## HUMANITIES LINK

***Art History*** Igael Tumarkin, *War Memories* (page 500).
***Literature*** In this chapter, you will encounter passages from the following works of literature: R. K. Narayan, *The Tale of Nagaraj* (page 486); The First Book of Maccabees (page 500); Liyana Badr, "A Land of Rock and Thyme" (page 502).

**1947**
Independent India and Pakistan created; UN partitions Palestine

**1971**
Bangladesh breaks away from Pakistan

**1979**
Egypt makes peace with Israel; Iranian revolution begins

**1991**
Second Persian Gulf War

**1994**
Palestinians gain limited self-rule

| 1945 | 1960 | 1975 | 1990 | PRESENT |

# Nations of South Asia

## Guide for Reading

- Why was India partitioned in 1947?

- What goals did independent nations of South Asia pursue?

- What obstacles to progress did South Asian nations face?

- What role have India and Pakistan played in world affairs?

In 1950, a new constitution set lofty goals for India:

> 66 . . . to secure to all its citizens: JUS-TICE, social, economic, and political; LIBERTY of thought expression, belief, faith and worship: EQUALITY of status and opportunity; and to promote among them all FRATERNITY assuring the dignity of the individual and the unity of the Nation. 99

Achieving those goals would prove difficult. In 1950, most Indians were poor and uneducated. They were divided by caste, region, language, and ethnic background. Yet India did make progress toward the promises made at independence. Two other new nations on the subcontinent, Pakistan and Bangladesh, grappled with similar challenges.

### Independence and Partition

As you read in Chapter 12, Indian nationalists had demanded independence since the late 1800s. After World War II, Britain finally agreed to these demands. As independence neared, a long-simmering issue surfaced. What would happen to the Muslim minority in a Hindu-dominated India?

**Two states.** Muhammad Ali Jinnah, leader of the Muslim League, insisted that Muslims have their own state, Pakistan. Riots between Hindus and Muslims helped convince Britain to partition, or divide, the subcontinent. In 1947, British officials hastily drew borders to create Hindu India and Muslim Pakistan. Pakistan was made up of two widely separated areas that had large Muslim populations. (See the map on page 485.)

**A tragedy unfolds.** Drawing fair borders was impossible because Hindus and Muslims lived side by side. In 1947, therefore, millions of Hindus and Muslims crossed the borders of India and Pakistan in both directions. During the mass migration, centuries of mistrust—which the British had exploited to keep the population divided—plunged northern India into savage violence. Hindu and Sikh mobs massacred Muslims fleeing into Pakistan. Muslims slaughtered Hindu and Sikh neighbors. An estimated 10 million refugees fled their homes. As many as a million or more, mostly Muslims, may have died.

Horrified at the partition and the violence, Gandhi turned once more to satyagraha. (See page 332.) On January 30, 1948, he was shot and killed by a Hindu extremist. Jawaharlal Nehru told a stricken nation, "The light has gone out of our lives and there is darkness everywhere." Gandhi's death discredited the extremists and helped end the worst violence. Still, Hindu-Muslim tensions persisted.

*An Extraordinary Family* This family photograph shows three prime ministers of India. Jawaharlal Nehru, center, led India for 17 years after independence. His daughter Indira Gandhi and his grandson Rajiv Gandhi would in turn succeed Nehru as prime minister. Both would die at the hands of assassins. **Impact of the Individual** Why do you think the sons and daughters of political leaders often become politicians themselves?

The partition of India created two populous new states in South Asia. It also uprooted millions of people and led to widespread violence.

1. **Location** On the map, locate (a) India, (b) West Pakistan, (c) East Pakistan, (d) Kashmir, (e) Ceylon, (f) Afghanistan.
2. **Movement** Using this map, describe the movement of Hindus and Muslims across the India-West Pakistan border during the 1947 partition.
3. *Critical Thinking* **Linking Past and Present** Compare this map to the map on page 608. What has happened to Pakistan since 1947?

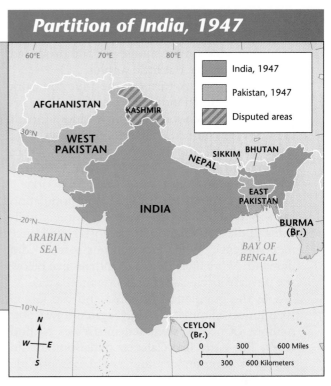

## Partition of India, 1947

India, 1947
Pakistan, 1947
Disputed areas

## The World's Largest Democracy

India built on the legacy of British rule, including its system of law and government. Today, with a population of more than 900 million, it is the world's largest democracy.

**Unity and diversity.** Indians had united behind the Congress party in its drive to independence. Still, the new nation was deeply divided. It included hundreds of princely states that had survived British rule. Indians spoke a wide variety of languages and dialects. While most Indians were Hindu, millions of others were Muslim, Christian, Sikh, or Buddhist.

India's constitution set up a federal system, like that of the United States, with powers divided between a strong central government and smaller local governments. In time, the government reorganized the princely states into a smaller number of states. It recognized 15 official languages and 35 major regional languages.

**The Nehru "dynasty."** For 40 years after independence, India was led by members of the Nehru family. As prime minister from 1947 until his death in 1964, Jawaharlal Nehru worked to build a modern, secular state dedicated to promoting social justice.

After he died, his daughter Indira Gandhi, and later his grandson Rajiv Gandhi, served as prime minister. Both were popular, energetic leaders, but their high-handed policies sometimes eroded goodwill. In the end, both fell victim to violence, as you will read. Today, many

Indians hope that Rajiv's young son will someday enter politics.

## Economic Growth

Like other developing nations, India wanted to apply modern technology to expand agriculture and industry. The government adopted the socialist model, drawing up five-year plans to set economic goals and manage resources.

**Industrial growth.** British-built railroads gave India a basic transportation network. After independence, Nehru had dams built to produce hydroelectric power and poured resources into heavy industries such as steel. Within a few decades, India edged toward becoming an industrial power. Development, however, remained uneven. India lacked oil and natural gas—two resources essential to economic growth. As a result, it had to rely on costly imported oil.

**Green Revolution.** Seeking to make India self-sufficient in food production, Nehru took advantage of the Green Revolution. (See page 425.) New seeds, chemical fertilizers, and irrigation methods boosted crop output. Still, only farmers with enough land and money could grow the new crops. Most farmers, as in the past, depended on the monsoons and produced enough to survive but little surplus.

**Education.** To turn out the educated work force needed in an industrial economy, the government built schools and universities. India's literacy rate climbed, but unevenly. Boys were more likely to attend school than girls. Also, children from poor families often got little schooling because they were needed to work.

**The population issue.** Rapid population growth hurt efforts to improve living conditions. India's population has almost tripled since independence. While food output rose, so did demand. More than a third of Indians live below the poverty level, eating only one meal a day.

As the population boomed and the Green Revolution eliminated many agricultural jobs, millions of people streamed into cities to find work. But cities like Calcutta and Bombay did not have enough jobs and could not provide even basic services such as water or sewage. To help the urban poor, a Roman Catholic nun named Mother Teresa founded a religious order called the Missionaries of Charity, which has branches across India and elsewhere.

The government encouraged family planning but did not impose harsh population control measures as China did. (See page 468.) To many Indians, especially in rural areas, children were seen as an economic resource to work the land and care for parents in old age.

**Economic reforms.** An economic slowdown and pressure from international lenders forced India to undertake major reforms. Moving away from the socialist model of development, it looked to the successes of the Asian tigers. (See Chapter 17.) It privatized some industries and made foreign investment easier. By the 1990s, India had a significant role in textiles, software, and other industries.

## Social Change

In India, as elsewhere, urbanization eroded ancient ways. Still, most Indians continued to live in villages, where traditional attitudes and values remained strong.

**The caste system.** In the 1930s, Gandhi had begun a campaign to end the inhuman treatment of the untouchables, or harijans. At independence, India's constitution banned discrimination against untouchables. The government set aside jobs and places in universities for these long-mistreated groups.

Despite such programs, deep prejudice persisted. Higher-caste Hindus still received better schooling and jobs. In the 1990s, a reform-minded government tried to open more jobs to untouchables. Violent protests by higher-caste Hindus who feared losing their jobs forced the government to back off from its plan.

**Women.** At independence, women gained the right to vote along with other legal rights. A few educated women, like Indira Gandhi, won elected office or entered the professions. In the cities, upper- and middle-class families sought to educate their daughters as a sign of modernization and accomplishment. In R. K. Narayan's novel *The Tale of Nagaraj*, a father brags about his daughter's achievements:

66 She is singing a famous song from the latest Hindi film. She has learnt it by herself. . . . Gramophone companies want her to record but I say, 'Not yet.' She must complete her M.A. [graduate degree] first. 99

*Slow Change* As this cartoon shows, the grip of India's caste system has kept untouchables from getting ahead. The government has introduced programs to make up for centuries of discrimination. But when the government announced plans to set aside places in universities for untouchables, some upper-caste students burned their diplomas in protest. *Political and Social Systems* Why do you think upper-caste Indians resented efforts to help untouchables?

## Love and Marriage

Marriage, like other institutions, has undergone change over the years. Until recently, arranged marriages were common in most of the world. By choosing partners for their children, parents could form alliances with other families, control property, and guide their children's future.

**Linking Past and Present** Why do you think arranged marriages are less common than in the past?

**PAST** Traditionally, Indian parents selected a child's marriage partner based on the reputation and economic status of the partner's family. Often, the bride and groom were still children—sometimes six years old or younger. They usually did not meet until their wedding day. In the marriage portrait below, the couple pose with the bride's parents, who arranged the match.

**PRESENT** As India modernizes, marriage customs are changing. Child marriages, left, still take place, especially in rural areas, but they are much rarer than in the past. And, although most marriages are still arranged, couples usually meet before the wedding. They may even refuse their parents' choice. Men and women living in cities, or even abroad, have found new ways to meet, such as through personal ads like the ones below.

Punjabi Hindu parents invite correspondence for their handsome, well mannered son, 231/2/5'11". Pharmacy graduate. Send biodata with returnable photograph. 40010-M.

Brother invites matrimonial correspondence from an educated U.S. citizen girl for 26 years old handsome, caring, tall and sophisticated Industrial Engineer (presently residing in India). Caste no bar. Biodata/Photo to Dr. S.M.

---

Yet, because of class and caste differences, many girls from poor families receive little or no education. Women on the lower rungs of society cluster in menial, low-paying jobs. In rural areas, women make up a majority of the work force, but few receive wages for their labor.

Indian women have formed organizations and movements to meet their needs. For example, the Self-Employed Women's Association (SEWA) created production and marketing cooperatives, opened banks, and provided classes and legal advice for poor women. Women's groups have also fought violence against women, protested dowry laws, and worked for environmental protection.

### Enduring Issues

As India approached its fiftieth year of independence, it had a record of political and economic achievement in many areas. Yet difficult religious and regional divisions persisted.

**Hindu fundamentalism.** In India, as elsewhere, religious fundamentalism increased in response to the problems of modernization. In the early 1990s, the Bharata Janata party (BJP) won growing support. Unlike the Congress party, which wanted to separate religion and government, the BJP called for a government guided by Hindu principles.

In 1992, the BJP supported calls for the destruction of a mosque in Ayodhya (uh YOHD yuh). Hindu fundamentalists claimed it stood on a sacred Hindu site seized by Muslim invaders centuries ago. The BJP wanted to build a Hindu temple there instead. The conflict touched off rioting at Ayodhya and the mosque was destroyed.

**Sikh separatism.** In the prosperous Punjab region of northern India, some Sikhs demanded a state of their own. In 1983, Sikh separatists occupied the Golden Temple in Amritsar to push their demands. When talks failed, Indira Gandhi sent troops to clear the temple.

Thousands of Sikhs died in the fighting. A few months later, Gandhi was killed by two of her own Sikh bodyguards. The assassination ignited battles between Hindus and Sikhs.

## Pakistan's Road to Modernization

At independence, Pakistan faced severe problems. Early on, military leaders seized power and ruled as dictators. The country lacked many natural resources for industry. Ethnic rivalries also fueled conflicts.

**A divided nation.** West and East Pakistan were separated by a wide swath of Indian territory. Although the people of both regions were Muslim, their languages and cultures differed. Bengalis in the east outnumbered Punjabis in the west, but Punjabis dominated the government and economy.

As tensions flared, Bengalis broke away. In 1971, they declared independence for Bangladesh, or "Bengal Nation." Pakistan's military ruler ordered the army to crush the rebels. To escape the bloodbath, millions of Bengalis fled into India. India responded by attacking and defeating the Pakistani army in Bangladesh.

**Politics.** Defeat discredited Pakistan's ruling general. A civilian politician, Zulfikar Ali Bhutto, became president. He promised to "pick up the pieces" and make a "prosperous and progressive Pakistan." But Bhutto was later overthrown, tried, and executed by the military.

In 1988, Pakistan again had a civilian government, with Bhutto's daughter Benazir as prime minister. She was the first woman to head a modern Muslim state. She served as prime minister twice between 1988 and 1996, working for economic and social reforms. But in the upheavals of Pakistani politics, she also was ousted from power twice.

**Economic choices.** Pakistan moved to improve agriculture. It distributed unused lands to landless farmers, experimented with new high-yield crops, and financed irrigation projects. Building dams and clearing land helped boost food output, but at a high cost to the environment. Deforestation caused terrible floods when monsoon rains were very heavy.

To modernize, Pakistan nationalized major industries. More recently, however, the government has encouraged private or mixed government and private ownership of businesses.

## Trials of Bangladesh

Since 1971, Bangladesh has struggled to rise out of poverty, but geography often stands in the way. The large population is crowded on a low-lying coastal plain. Cyclones are a frequent peril. The region is also subject to devastating floods when monsoon rains are too heavy or to droughts if the rains are too light.

Explosive population growth has strained resources still further. More than 50 million people live below the poverty level, many of them women and children. Large amounts of foreign aid have brought little improvement, in part because various military governments misused the assistance.

In the early 1990s, a civilian government encouraged foreign investment. Foreign businesses took advantage of cheap labor costs to make clothes in Bangladesh for export to Japan and the West. Human rights groups, however, showed how textile workers, often young children, were treated like slaves. Development in Bangladesh seemed to mirror the miseries of the early Industrial Revolution in the West.

## South Asia and the World

Fear and mistrust have often guided relations between India and Pakistan. At independence, border conflicts ignited a war over Kashmir, a princely state in the Himalayas. Its Hindu prince signed Kashmir over to India, but its majority Muslim population wanted to be a part of Pakistan. Since then, the two nations have fought several wars over Kashmir.

**The nuclear issue.** The stakes for conflict rose after India tested a nuclear device in 1974. While India was proud of its status as a nuclear power, Pakistan felt threatened. It tried to acquire its own nuclear technology.

**Child Labor** Despite laws against it, child labor is common in India, Pakistan, and Bangladesh. Young children work up to 10 hours a day in mines, farms, and factories. One 12-year-old rug weaver said, "Whether I like it or not, I have to do this for the rest of my life." **Continuity and Change** Why do you think child labor is difficult to stop in the developing world?

Today, India and Pakistan deny having nuclear weapons. But both nations refused to sign the Non-Proliferation Treaty. (See page 412.) Some people in the world community thought wealthy nations should cut off aid to India and Pakistan if they did not sign the NPT.

**The Cold War.** During the Cold War, India and Pakistan took different paths. Nehru welcomed economic aid from both superpowers but otherwise embraced neutrality. Pakistan, feeling threatened both by India and by the Soviet Union to the north, accepted United States military aid. Partly to counter this alliance, Indira Gandhi signed a treaty of friendship with the Soviet Union in the 1970s.

**Afghanistan.** In 1979, the Soviet Union invaded Afghanistan and set up a puppet government. (See page 448.) Millions of Afghan Muslim refugees crossed into Pakistan. The United States funneled weapons and aid to Afghan guerrillas based in Pakistan. Guerrilla attacks and dissent at home eventually forced the Soviets to withdraw. Conflict dragged on, however, among rival rebel factions.

**Sri Lanka.** In the 1970s, ethnic tensions sparked guerrilla war in Sri Lanka (formerly Ceylon), an island nation off the south coast of India. Most Sri Lankans were Buddhists who spoke Singhalese. A Tamil-speaking Hindu minority charged the government with discrimination. When efforts to win equality failed, Tamil rebels waged war to set up a separate nation.

India at first favored Tamil separatists and then opposed them. In the 1980s, Rajiv Gandhi sent troops in an unsuccessful attempt to smash the rebels. His action outraged Tamil extremists, who assassinated him in 1991. Fighting eventually eased, but tensions remained high.

## SECTION 1 REVIEW

1. **Identify** (a) "Nehru dynasty," (b) BJP, (c) Golden Temple, (d) Bhutto family, (e) Kashmir.
2. (a) Why was India divided into two nations? (b) Describe two effects of the partition.
3. (a) What economic goals did India pursue? (b) Why has progress been limited?
4. How has geography affected Bangladesh?
5. Why have India and Pakistan fought several wars?
6. *Critical Thinking* **Applying Information** "The past clings to us still," said Nehru. (a) What do you think he meant? (b) Give two examples that support his view.
7. *ACTIVITY* Design a banner that untouchables might use in their campaign to win full equality.

## GLOBAL CONNECTIONS

Under Nehru, nonaligned India took a major role in world affairs. India was an active member of the UN and the British Commonwealth. In 1953, India negotiated prisoner-of-war exchanges during the Korean War. Indian troops joined a UN peacekeeping force trying to end a civil war in Zaire. India also led other nonaligned nations—such as Egypt, Ghana, Indonesia, and Yugoslavia—in calling for disarmament talks between Soviet and American leaders.

# 2 Forces Shaping the Modern Middle East

## Guide for Reading

■ How have diversity and nationalism shaped the Middle East?

■ What resources have had a powerful impact on the region?

■ What social and religious forces influence the Middle East today?

In the Arab world, as in South Asia, nations sought to free themselves from the legacy of imperialism. "We are eradicating the traces of the past," declared Egyptian president Gamal Abdel Nasser in the 1950s. "We are building our country on strong and sound bases."

Leaders of Nasser's generation embarked on ambitious reforms. Their policies, however, often failed to bring promised improvements. By the 1970s, Islamic reformers began to offer another route to modernization.

## A Region of Diversity

What do we mean when we speak of the Middle East? Western colonial powers first used the term to refer to the region between Europe and what they called the "Far East"—China, Japan, and Southeast Asia. To avoid this western bias, some people now call the region Southwest Asia. Yet the UN and many experts continue to use the term Middle East.

**Location.** Experts also differ on what areas are part of the Middle East. In this chapter, we refer to the region from Egypt in the west to Iran in the east and from Turkey in the north to the Arabian Peninsula in the south. (See the map on page 640.) Some historians also include Muslim North Africa and Afghanistan.

Throughout history, location has made the Middle East a bridge between Asia, Africa, and Europe. As a world crossroads and a hub of civilization, it became a region of great diversity.

**Diversity.** Judaism, Christianity, and Islam all emerged in the Middle East. Today, most people there are Muslim, but the region is home to Jews and Christians. Different sects within these religions add to the diversity.

Middle Eastern peoples speak more than 30 different languages, including Arabic, Turkish, Persian, Hebrew, Kurdish, and Armenian. Every country has its minority groups—some as many as a dozen. The Kurds, for example, are an ethnic group divided by modern borders among Turkey, Iraq, and Iran. Their efforts to win autonomy have led to repression.

Like Christians in Europe, Muslims share the same faith but belong to different national groups. Arabs, Turks, and Iranians have their own cultures and histories. Often, such differences have created divisions.

## Nationalism and Independence

In the Middle East, as elsewhere, nationalism and imperialism continued to have a strong impact. In the 1920s and 1930s, Arab nationalists opposed European mandates. (See page 330.) Iraq won freedom from Britain in 1932. After World War II, British and French mandate territories won complete independence as the nations of Lebanon, Syria, and Jordan.

The Pan-Arab dream of a united Arab state foundered as nations pursued individual goals. Yet their shared heritage linked Arabs across borders. Pan-Arabism survived in the Arab League, which promoted Arab solidarity in times of crisis and worked for common economic goals.

**Colonial legacy.** Even after independence, Arab nations remained economically dependent on the West. Westerners owned banks and industries. They provided the capital and technology needed for development, as well as the principal market for exports. Ending western economic domination would become a goal of governments in the Middle East.

Imperialism left another legacy. Britain and France had drawn borders to serve their own interests. At independence, Arab nations inherited these borders, leading to disputes. For example, British mapmaking created Iraq, a nation that had never existed before. Within its borders were various groups who had no reason to call themselves Iraqis and were sometimes hostile to one another. Colonial borders also limited Iraq's access to the Persian Gulf. Religious and

ethnic tensions, plus a desire for outlets on the gulf, have fueled conflicts in Iraq to the present.

**The birth of Israel.** The legacy of Britain's Balfour Declaration fueled a conflict over Palestine. (See page 330.) Both Jews and Palestinian Arabs claimed a historical right to the land. Jewish migration to Palestine, which began in the late 1800s, accelerated after World War II. In the United States, the horrors of the Holocaust created strong support for a Jewish homeland. But increased migration and conflicting British policies led to violent clashes.

As the turmoil increased, Britain turned over its mandate to the UN. In 1947, the UN drew up a plan to partition Palestine into an Arab and a Jewish state. Jews accepted the plan, but Arabs rejected it. To them, it was a plan to relocate European Jews on Arab territory.

When Britain withdrew in 1948, Jews proclaimed the independent state of Israel. The United States and Soviet Union both recognized the new nation. Arab states, however, assembled military forces and attacked Israel. Israeli forces fought well against the badly equipped and badly led Arabs, whose governments were not all independent. In the end, Israel almost doubled its territory. Other wars would follow, as you will see.

The nation of Israel developed rapidly after 1948. The government built towns for settlers and provided many services. American aid and high taxes gave Israel the capital to invest in industry and agriculture. Despite scarce natural resources, a skilled work force made rapid progress. Israelis built factories and developed methods to farm their arid land. Kibbutzim, or collective farms, produced crops for export.

**The refugee issue.** The 1948 war uprooted 700,000 Arabs from Palestine. The UN set up temporary shelters for Palestinian refugees. As the Arab-Israeli conflict dragged on, the shelters became permanent homes. In these poverty-stricken camps, new generations of Palestinians grew up bitterly determined to win a homeland of their own.

## Impact of Oil

Parts of the Middle East sit atop the world's largest reserves of oil. Concern over this essential resource has led the United States and other powers to increase their political and military presence in the Middle East. At the same time, the 1973 OPEC oil embargo showed that oil could be a powerful diplomatic weapon. (See page 416.)

Oil is unevenly distributed. Only a few countries, mostly on the Persian Gulf, have large oil reserves. Oil-rich nations include Saudi Arabia and Kuwait, which have small populations. Turkey and Egypt, with much larger populations, have little oil.

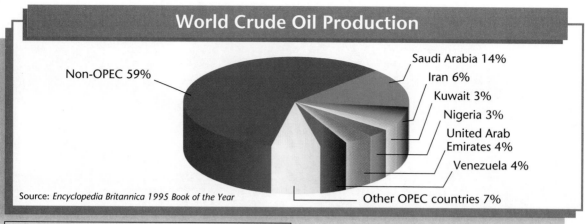

## World Crude Oil Production

Non-OPEC 59%

Saudi Arabia 14%

Iran 6%

Kuwait 3%

Nigeria 3%

United Arab Emirates 4%

Venezuela 4%

Other OPEC countries 7%

Source: *Encyclopedia Britannica 1995 Book of the Year*

**Interpreting a Graph** *In the 1970s, OPEC nations produced more than half of the world's oil. Today, that figure is much lower, but many nations still depend on imported OPEC oil to fuel their industries and transportation.* ■ *Which OPEC nation produces the largest share of the world's oil? Which OPEC nations shown on this graph are located outside the Middle East?*

Differences between "haves" and "have-nots" contributed to resentments within the region. Oil-rich nations were able to build roads, hospitals, and schools. Poorer countries lacked the capital needed for development.

### Political and Economic Patterns

Middle Eastern nations have worked to modernize their governments and economies. In Egypt and Iraq, revolutionary military leaders toppled monarchs who were closely tied to western powers. In other countries, such as Jordan and Saudi Arabia, hereditary monarchs remained in power but took steps to adapt to the modern world.

**Governments.** Most Middle Eastern nations developed authoritarian governments. Jordan and Saudi Arabia were ruled by hereditary monarchs. In Iraq and Syria, a single party won power. Dictators like Iraq's Saddam Hussein brutally suppressed opponents but enjoyed some popular backing because their social and economic policies improved life for many.

Only Israel and Turkey formed multiparty, democratic systems. In both countries, however, minority groups—Kurds in Turkey and Arabs in Israel—faced restrictions.

**Economic policies.** In the 1950s, some Arab nations turned to socialism as a way to end foreign economic control and modernize rapidly. They nationalized banks, oil companies, and factories. Despite those moves, they still depended on the industrial world for much of their technology.

Governments raised capital with foreign loans. They then used these funds to finance large projects in industry and agriculture, especially irrigation projects. In some countries, they redistributed land to peasants. But small farmers did not produce efficiently, and food output could not keep pace with rapid population growth.

By the 1990s, under pressure from the International Monetary Fund and western banks, many governments eased restrictions on foreign ownership and privatized some state-run enterprises. (See page 417.) The Middle East, like other developing regions, faced grave economic challenges. While nations had built some industry and bustling modern cities, large segments of the people lived in poverty.

### Keep the Water Flowing

A fleet of well over 1,500 trucks and earthmovers crawled across southeastern Anatolia in Turkey. Where Hittites, Persians, and Romans once built forts and palaces, an army of modern workers erected the 600-foot-high (180 m) Atatürk Dam. It was one of 22 dams that Turkey built in the late 1980s to harness the waters of the Tigris and Euphrates rivers.

The goal of this massive project was to turn the region into a breadbasket. Kamren Inan, a Turkish official, noted:

"These rivers have been here for millions of years. We want to put the water to use, to benefit the children of this country. . . . Turkey is increasing by 1.3 million people every year. The requirements are enormous, but if intelligently used, our resources are more than enough to cover these demands."

**A vital resource.** Water is vital to people the world over. But nowhere is it more valued than in areas like the Middle East, where rainfall is limited and water is often scarce. Since ancient times, farmers have adapted to arid conditions. They planted crops in river valleys and coastal plains, irrigating their fields with water from streams, rivers, and underground springs.

In modern times, growing populations and rising standards of living have increased demands for water. Farmers in the Middle East can produce good crops—if they can get water. Farming accounts for 80 percent of water use in the region.

For Turkey and other nations, the key to irrigation was building dams. Developing nations take pride in such projects that not only water crops but also supply hydroelectric power.

**Whose water is it?** At the same time, dam building has sparked explosive debates over water rights. Many rivers in the Middle East run through several countries. The Nile flows through Ethiopia and Sudan before reaching Egypt. Israel, Jordan, and Syria all have claims on the waters of the Jordan River. The Euphrates rises in Turkey but flows through Syria and Iraq before emptying into the Persian Gulf.

Turkey opened its dams in 1990. For several weeks, they siphoned off 75 percent of the Euphrates water that usually flowed through Syria and Iraq. These nations protested furiously. Turkey's president promised, "We will never use the control of water to coerce or threaten our neighbors."

Today, nations that share river systems seek ways to use water cooperatively. "In the coming decades," predicted Inan, "the most important resource in the Middle East will be water, much more valuable than oil."

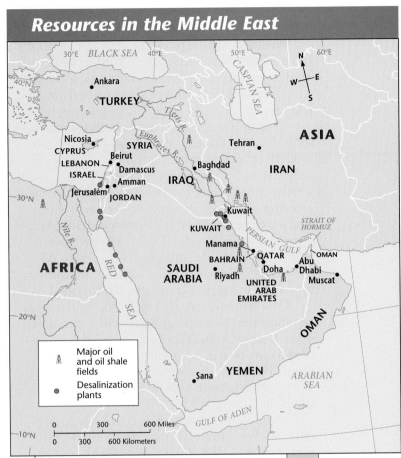

## Resources in the Middle East

## GEOGRAPHY AND HISTORY

Oil wealth has allowed some Middle Eastern nations to ease an age-old problem: scarcity of fresh water. Nations have used new technology to build desalinization plants, which remove the salt from seawater.

1. **Location** On the map, locate (a) Saudi Arabia, (b) Kuwait, (c) Iraq, (d) Iran.
2. **Place** (a) Which countries in the Middle East have major oil fields? (b) Which countries have built desalinization plants?
3. *Critical Thinking* **Applying Information** Why might an oil spill in the Persian Gulf pose a threat to desalinization efforts?

## Islamic Revival

Islam has been a shaping force in the Middle East for more than 1,300 years. As in the past, the Quran and Sharia provide guidance to all aspects of life—from government to family relationships.

**Western influences.** During the Age of Imperialism, westerners urged Muslim lands to modernize. To the West, modernization meant adopting western forms of secular government and law.

After nearly a century of western influence, some Middle Eastern leaders adopted western models of development, promising economic progress and social justice. In the 1950s and 1960s, western cultural influences grew. In the growing cities, people wore western-style clothing, watched American television programs, and bought foreign products. Yet despite government promises, life improved very little. With the failure of their leaders to solve mounting problems, many people became disillusioned.

**Call for reform.** By the 1970s, in the face of failed development and repressive regimes, many Muslim leaders and writers called for a return to the Sharia. They blamed social and economic ills on blind imitation of western models and applied Islamic principles to the search for solutions.

Islamic reformers (often called fundamentalists by westerners) did not reject modernization, but they did reject westernization. They argued that a renewed commitment to Islam was the only way out of their current problems. Offering Islam as an inspiration, the movement appealed to poor and educated Muslims alike.

**Impact.** By the 1990s, the Islamic revival had spread across the Muslim world—from Morocco to Indonesia. Its impact varied from country to country. In Iran, revolutionaries overthrew an unpopular shah. In Algeria, voters supported members of a party that pledged to restore the Sharia. In Egypt and elsewhere, some extremists justified terrorist acts as a

weapon against authoritarian governments. Other Muslim groups worked within the system for political reforms and social programs.

Across the Muslim world, the Islamic revival sparked heated debates between reformers and secularists. Issues included science, alcohol use, advertising, teenage crime, and the role of women.

## Women in the Middle East

Conditions for women vary greatly from country to country in the modern Middle East. Since the 1950s, women in most countries have won voting rights and equality before the law. They attend schools and universities in growing numbers. Middle- and upper-class women have entered professions such as law, engineering, and medicine.

The changes have taken place at different rates in different places. In Turkey, Syria, and Egypt, many urban women gave up long-held practices such as wearing *hejab*, or cover.\* On the other hand, conservative countries like Saudi Arabia opposed the spread of many western secular influences among women.

**Return to hejab.** In recent decades, many educated Muslim women led a return to wearing hejab. For some women, the movement symbolized resistance to unpopular governments or a refusal to imitate western culture. An Egyptian student said:

> 66I think of Muslim dress as a kind of uniform. It means I am serious about myself. . . . I can sit in class with men and there is no question of attraction and so on—we are all involved in the same business of learning.99

Most important, women who elected to return to hejab saw it as an expression of sincere loyalty to Muslim values and practices.

**Issues.** Some women in Muslim countries were dismayed by social and political forces that put severe limits on their lives. Under Sharia

▼ *Muslim children studying the Quran*

---

\*The Arabic word *hejab* means following Islamic guidelines for women's dress in public. The practice includes a variety of head coverings as well as a long, loose-fitting garment. In English, the word is often translated as "veiling," though only a small fraction of Muslim women cover their faces.

**Wearing Hejab** With the growing popularity of hejab, fashionable new forms of Muslim dress have appeared next to traditional styles. Here, a group of Iranian women enjoy an afternoon of boating. **Continuity and Change** How does the renewed popularity of traditional dress show continuity in the Muslim world?

law, women traditionally held powerful positions in the family and played important economic roles. In some countries, however, laws and traditions limited women's right to vote, to work, and to drive. Many Muslim and non-Muslim women spoke out on the need for women to realize their full potential and contribute to national life.

## SECTION 2 REVIEW

1. **Identify** (a) Kurds, (b) Arab League, (c) kibbutzim, (d) hejab.
2. Give one example of how diversity has caused tensions in a Middle Eastern nation.
3. (a) What forces have linked Arab nations? (b) What forces have blocked Arab unity?
4. How was the Islamic revival linked to social and political development?
5. *Critical Thinking* **Defending a Position** (a) How has oil shaped the economies of some Middle Eastern nations? (b) Do you agree that water is "much more valuable than oil" as a resource? Why or why not?
6. *ACTIVITY* Write a four-line verse about hejab from the viewpoint of a Muslim woman.

## 3 Nation Building in the Middle East: Three Case Studies

### Guide for Reading

- What issues posed challenges to Turkey?
- How have Egyptian leaders tried to modernize their country?
- What were the causes and effects of the revolution in Iran?

Ruhollah Khomeini (roo HOH luh koh MAY nee), an Iranian religious leader, angrily denounced the evils of the government. While the shah lived off the riches of the land, claimed Khomeini, most people lived in misery:

66When you enter Tehran, you see all the cars and that deceptive exterior, but you haven't gone to the other side of Tehran. . . . Take a look south of the city. Look at those pits, those holes in the ground where people live, dwellings you reach by going down a hundred steps into the ground, homes people have built out of rush matting or clay so their poor children can have somewhere to live.99

Khomeini's fiery speeches against the shah and his American backers helped spur an Iranian revolution in 1979.

In this section, we will see how three nations pursued modernization. Turkey, Egypt, and Iran are the most populous nations in the Middle East. While they have faced similar issues, each followed its own course.

### Turkey Moves Toward Democracy

Turkey had been an independent republic since the 1920s, while its Arab neighbors were still under European control. Kemal Atatürk pushed to build a modern secular state like those in the West. (See Chapter 12.)

After World War II, the Soviets tried to expand southward into Turkey to gain control of the Bosporus. With American military and economic aid, Turkey held off the Soviet threat. In the 1950s, it joined NATO and remained an important western ally in the Mediterranean.

**Government and economy.** Turkey struggled to build a stable government. At first, the military seized power in times of unrest. Later, a multiparty democracy emerged. In the 1990s, Muslim reformers gained support and played a larger role in Turkish politics.

Turkey transformed its economy, building dams and expanding industry. It exported crops and manufactured goods to Europe and even sought to join the European Union. (See page 435.) While the EU agreed to form closer ties, it denied full membership to Turkey.

*Without a Country* Although Kurds were promised a homeland during World War I, postwar treaties failed to create a Kurdish nation. Since the 1920s, Kurds in Turkey and Iraq have fought for their own nation. That struggle has brought violent reprisals. In the 1980s, Iraq dropped poison gas on Kurdish villages, killing thousands of civilians. The Turkish government has also waged war against Kurdish rebels in eastern Turkey. As a result, thousands of Turkish Kurds like these have become refugees, taking with them only what they can carry.
*Political and Social Systems* Why do you think Turkey and Iraq oppose a separate Kurdish nation?

As elsewhere, modernization and urbanization brought social upheaval. Istanbul could not provide jobs for millions of newcomers. The jobless and the poor lived in shantytowns, where desperate conditions fed unrest.

**Conflicts.** For decades, Turkey tried to force Kurds within its borders to abandon their identity. They were forbidden to speak, broadcast, or publish books in their language. Kurdish revolts were fiercely suppressed. Gradually, the Turkish government agreed to abolish laws against Kurdish culture. Still, that move was unlikely to satisfy Kurdish nationalists who sought autonomy.

Turkey also waged a long struggle over Cyprus, an island in the eastern Mediterranean. The conflict had complex roots dating to Ottoman times. In the 1970s, clashes between the Greek majority and Turkish minority led Turkey to invade. The island was then partitioned. Today, UN peacekeepers monitor the dividing line between Turkish and Greek communities.

## Egypt: A Leader in the Arab World

Egypt has roots both in Africa, where it is located, and in the Arab world, the source of its majority religion. Today, as in the past, geography influences Egypt's destiny. Its location between the Red Sea and the Mediterranean, where Asia and Africa meet, has always been strategically important. Today, it is the most populous Arab state, shares a long border with Israel, and controls the Suez Canal. As in the past, it is a rich agricultural region. But, since most of Egypt is desert, 99 percent of its people live on 4 percent of the land in the fertile Nile Valley.

**Nasser.** In the 1950s, Gamal Abdel Nasser emerged as a towering figure in the Middle East. Like Atatürk, Nasser was a military officer who came to power after the overthrow of a ruler who had allowed foreigners to dominate his country.

Nasser was determined to modernize Egypt and, at the same time, end foreign domination. In 1956, he nationalized the Suez Canal, ending British control. Nasser proclaimed:

66This money is ours. This Canal is the property of Egypt. . . . The Canal was dug by Egypt's sons and 120,000 of them died while working. The Suez Canal Company in Paris is an impostor company.**"**

Britain and France threatened to invade, but Nasser's defiance of the West boosted his prestige in the Arab world. He later formed a union of Egypt and Syria, a step toward the Pan-Arab goal of a United Arab Republic. But the union did not last.

An outspoken enemy of Israel, Nasser led two wars against the Zionist state. Although defeated each time, he remained a symbol of Arab independence and pride.

**Economic development.** Like leaders of other developing nations, Nasser turned to socialism. He nationalized banks and businesses and undertook sweeping land reforms. Large estates were broken up, and land was given to peasant farmers.

In the 1960s, with Soviet help, Nasser built the huge Aswan High Dam on the upper Nile. About 17 times larger than Egypt's Great Pyramid, the dam created a huge reservoir, Lake Nasser, plus more than 2 million acres of new farmland. It also controlled the Nile floodwaters and made year-round irrigation possible.

Like many such projects, however, the blessings of the Aswan High Dam came at a high price. It increased the salt content of the Nile, caused erosion of the delta, and destroyed fish hatcheries in the eastern Mediterranean. Even Egypt's ancient past was threatened. As Lake Nasser rose, many ancient temples had to be relocated to higher ground.

**New directions.** Nasser's economic policies had only limited success. After Nasser's death in 1970, the new president, Anwar Sadat, turned to a policy of *infitah*, or "opening." His goal was to encourage foreign investment and private business.

In foreign affairs, Sadat moved away from the Soviet camp and closer to the United States. In 1979, he became the first Arab leader to make peace with Israel. Although that move angered other Arab states, Sadat promised Egyptians that peace would have economic benefits. It did bring American aid but did not improve life for most Egyptians.

**Unresolved issues.** In 1981, Sadat was assassinated. His successor, Hosni Mubarak, reaf-

*Gamal Abdel Nasser* *In the 1950s and 1960s, Egyptian president Nasser, below, was the foremost spokesman of the Arab world. He used his prominence to promote unity among Arabs living in different nations. Perhaps Nasser's boldest move was to nationalize the Suez Canal, right, giving Egypt control of one of the world's most strategic waterways. Today, more than 50 ships a day pass through the canal.* ***Impact of the Individual*** *How did Nasser pursue both Pan-Arab and nationalist goals?*

firmed the peace with Israel but mended fences with his Arab neighbors. At home, Mubarak faced serious problems. Although farm output and industry expanded, the economy could not keep pace with the population boom. Most rural families who streamed into cities like Cairo ended up in crowded slums, barely managing to survive. Many families set up homes in the City of the Dead, a Cairo cemetery.

Muslim reformers denounced the government's failure to solve social and economic ills. Their emphasis on Islamic solutions seemed to offer a vision for change that Mubarak's government lacked. Islamic organizations developed schools, medical services, and relief for the poor, providing social services for which tight government budgets could no longer pay. A fringe of extremists turned to terrorism against a government they called corrupt and antireligious. Harsh government crackdowns, though, tended to increase support for the dissenters.

## Iran: Goals of the Revolution

Iran is the most ethnically diverse country in the Middle East. About half the people are Iranians, while the rest come from many groups. Unlike their neighbors, most Iranians are Shiite, not Sunni, Muslims and speak Persian, not Arabic or Turkish.

**Nationalism and oil.** The discovery of vast oil fields made Iran a focus for British, Soviet, and American interests. In 1945, the young shah, Muhammad Reza Pahlavi, had western backing but faced opposition from many groups at home. Iranian nationalists wanted to end British control of Iran's oil wealth and limit the shah's dictatorial powers.

Led by Muhammad Mosaddiq (MOH sah dehk), nationalists in the Iranian parliament voted to nationalize the oil industry. That action touched off a long, complex crisis involving the shah, Mosaddiq, Britain, and the United States.

In 1953, the United States helped the shah oust Mosaddiq, an action that angered many Iranians. The United States wanted the anticommunist shah as a solid ally against Soviet influence in the region. For the next 25 years, American weapons and experts helped the shah remain in power.

**Reform from above.** To strengthen Iran and quiet widespread discontent, the shah continued the modernization program begun by his father. He used oil wealth to build roads and industries, redistributed some land to peasants, and granted rights to women. In an attempt to separate religion and government, he reduced the power of the *ulama,* or Islamic scholars, teachers, and legal experts. The shah's "reform from above" was supported by the army, the westernized elite, and others who prospered under the shah. Opposition came from landowners, merchants, students, and religious leaders.

As unrest grew, the shah became more repressive. Savak, his dreaded secret police, arrested, tortured, or executed opponents, especially members of left-wing political groups. Others were forced into exile. The army crushed Kurds and other ethnic minorities who demanded autonomy.

**Revolution.** In the 1970s, the shah's enemies rallied around Shiite leaders, especially the exiled Ayatollah* Ruhollah Khomeini. He accused the shah of violating Islamic law and undermining morality. The ulama also opposed the distribution of land from religious foundations to peasants.

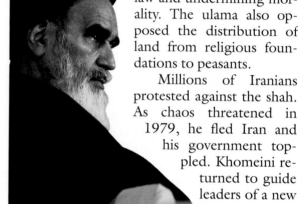
▲ *Ayatollah Ruhollah Khomeini*

Millions of Iranians protested against the shah. As chaos threatened in 1979, he fled Iran and his government toppled. Khomeini returned to guide leaders of a new Islamic republic that would restore the Sharia to a central place in Iranian life. Revolutionaries attacked corruption and banned western books, music, and movies. The Khomeini government abolished all previous legislation favoring women's rights. Still, many women backed the revolution, seeking ways to contribute to national life while following religious law.

At first, the new government allowed some open discussion. Before long, however, like the shah they replaced, the revolutionaries suppressed opponents.

**Foreign policy.** The new leaders bitterly denounced the West. After the shah was allowed into the United States for medical treatment, revolutionaries seized the American embassy in Tehran, holding 53 hostages for over a year. They also tried to export their revolution, urging Muslims in countries like Egypt and Turkey to overthrow secular governments. Although the revolution seemed to strengthen the Islamic revival, it was not reproduced in other Muslim lands.

---

*Ayatollah is a title given to the most learned Shiite legal experts.

# CAUSE AND EFFECT

## Long-Term Causes

Oil fields discovered in Iran in early 1900s
Oil rights sold to foreigners; Britain and Russia set up spheres of influence in Iran
Iranian nationalists resent western interference
Modernization efforts fail to benefit common people
Muslim religious leaders condemn modernization efforts
Iran becomes focus of Cold War rivalries
Islamic revival begins in 1970s

## Immediate Causes

Shah introduces "reform from above"
As opposition to shah grows, he becomes more repressive
Exiled Ruhollah Khomeini speaks out forcefully against the shah and his American backers
Iranians protest shah's policies

## REVOLUTION IN IRAN

## Immediate Effects

Shah flees Iran
Khomeini returns to Iran to guide leaders of new government
Revolutionaries take 53 Americans hostage
Government imposes strict code of behavior, bans western books and music, and overturns women's rights legislation

## Long-Term Effects

Iran tries to encourage revolution in other Muslim countries
Iran is isolated by international community
Living conditions do not improve a great deal; poverty and unemployment continue
War with Iraq drains resources

## Connections Today

Iran works to improve relations with the West and with other Muslim nations
Debate continues in Iran about how to modernize while remaining loyal to Islamic principles

*Interpreting a Chart  In 1979, a revolution in Iran brought down the shah and set the nation on a new course. The Iranian revolution had worldwide consequences.* ■ *Why was the discovery of oil fields a long-term cause of the revolution? Why do you think the revolution isolated Iran from the West and from other Muslim nations?*

In 1980, as you will read, neighboring Iraq took advantage of the turmoil to invade Iran. In Iran, the war helped rally support for the new government even though the ordeal took a huge economic and human toll.

**Effects.** Since Khomeini's death in 1989, more moderate voices have steered Iran. President Hashemi Rafsanjani (hah SHAY mee  rahf sahn JAH nee) worked to rebuild the economy and restore more normal relations with western powers.

The revolution changed Iran's foreign policy and some forms of public behavior. It did not, however, improve life greatly for most people. Corruption resurfaced. Poverty, unemployment, and other problems remained. Still, some reforms did improve conditions in rural areas.

By the mid-1990s, moderates and radicals debated the future of the revolution. They continued seeking ways to achieve modernization while upholding Islamic principles.

## SECTION 3 REVIEW

1. **Identify** (a) Aswan High Dam, (b) Anwar Sadat, (c) Hosni Mubarak, (d) Muhammad Mosaddiq, (e) Ruhollah Khomeini.
2. Describe one step each of these nations took toward modernization: (a) Turkey, (b) Egypt, (c) Iran.
3. How did Nasser challenge the West?
4. (a) Why did discontent spread under the shah? (b) Describe two effects of the Iranian revolution.
5. *Critical Thinking*  **Recognizing Points of View** (a) Who might consider the Iranian revolution a success? Why? (b) Who might criticize it? Why?
6. *ACTIVITY* Create a chart comparing the three nations discussed in this section in terms of population, government, economy, and critical issues.

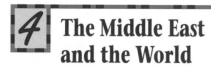

# 4 The Middle East and the World

## Guide for Reading

- Why was the Arab-Israeli conflict difficult to resolve?
- What forces plunged Lebanon into civil war?
- Why did the Persian Gulf become a battleground?
- **Vocabulary** *intifada*

66The land whereto we have returned to inherit it, it is the inheritance of our fathers and within it no stranger has part or parcel. . . . We have taken unto us our fathers' inheritance and have dwelt in it.99

With this biblical quotation, David Ben-Gurion, Israel's first prime minister, greeted the birth of modern Israel in 1948. To Arabs then living on the land called Palestine, though, the creation of Israel was an illegal outrage. An official Arab proclamation stated:

66Palestine is the homeland of the Arab Palestinian people. It is an indivisible part of the Arab homeland, and the Palestinian people are an integral part of the Arab nation.99

These conflicting claims touched off repeated violence. The Arab-Israeli struggle was one of many issues that focused world attention on the Middle East.

## The Cold War and the Middle East

As in other regions, Cold War rivalries touched the Middle East. The region commanded vital oil resources, as well as strategic waterways such as the Bosporus, the Suez Canal, and the Persian Gulf.

In their global rivalry, each superpower lined up allies in the Middle East. The United States sent aid to stop a communist threat to

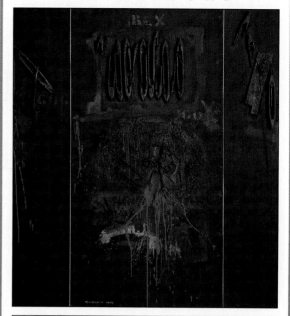

**War Memories** *Israeli abstract artist Igael Tumarkin saw the effects of war first in Germany, where he was born, and then through four wars in Israel. In works like* War Memories, *Tumarkin uses splashes of paint and fragments of everyday objects to suggest the psychological damage inflicted by war.* **Art and Literature** *Why have many modern painters experimented with abstract styles instead of reproducing reality?*

Turkey in 1947 and backed the anti-communist shah of Iran. The Soviets found an ally in Egypt during the Nasser years. Iraq, Syria, and Libya joined the Soviet camp, too. They mistrusted their former colonial rulers in the West and condemned western support for Israel.

Each superpower sold arms to its allies in the region. In the Arab-Israeli conflict, the United States helped Israel, while the Soviet Union aided the Arabs. After each Arab-Israeli war, the superpowers rearmed their allies with expensive new weapons.

## The Arab-Israeli Conflict

After the 1948 war, Israel and its Arab neighbors faced off again in 1956, 1967, and 1973. (See the map on page 502.) Between wars, Israel was a center of guerrilla warfare and terrorist activity.

**The occupied territories.** In 1967, Israeli forces won the Golan Heights from Syria, East Jerusalem and the West Bank from Jordan, and the Gaza Strip and Sinai Peninsula from Egypt. In 1973, Arabs attacked Israel but failed to regain the occupied lands.

Israel refused to give up the territories until Arab nations recognized Israel's right to exist. Later, Israel annexed East Jerusalem and the Golan Heights. The government helped Jewish settlers build homes in the occupied territories, displacing more Palestinian Arabs.

**Palestinian resistance.** The number of Palestinians in refugee camps had grown since 1948. Many supported the Palestine Liberation Organization (PLO), headed by Yasir Arafat. The PLO waged guerrilla war against Israelis at home and abroad. PLO bombings, airplane hijackings, and the massacre of Israeli athletes at the 1972 Olympics brought Palestinian demands to the attention of the world.

In 1987, resistance to Israel took another form. Young Palestinians in the occupied territories mounted the intifada, or uprising. Teenage boys openly defied Israeli soldiers, throwing rocks and disobeying curfews. When soldiers cracked down on the violence, they were accused of human rights violations. The intifada deepened divisions within Israel. Some Israelis wanted to give up the occupied territories in exchange for peace. Others became even more determined to keep the lands they had won.

**Peace efforts.** During the Cold War, efforts to solve the Arab-Israeli conflict had little success. However, as you have read, Anwar Sadat did take a courageous first step. After the 1979 peace treaty, Israel returned the Sinai Peninsula to Egypt. The collapse of the Soviet Union in 1991 sped up the peace process. Without Soviet aid, some Arab governments accepted the need to negotiate with Israel.

In 1994, Jordan and Israel signed a peace agreement. Talks between Israel and Syria stalled on the issue of the Golan Heights. The status of Jerusalem was another thorny issue. Israel claimed the city as its capital. Arabs insisted that Jerusalem, a holy city to Muslims as well as to Jews and Christians, must be part of any final agreement.

**A historic accord.** In 1993, direct talks were held for the first time between Israel and the PLO. Yasir Arafat and Israeli prime minister Yitzhak Rabin (rah BEEN) signed a historic agreement that gave Palestinians in Gaza and the West Bank city of Jericho limited self-rule in 1994. The following year, a new pact further extended Palestinian self-rule.

The accords raised hopes. But both sides knew that peace would not come quickly. "A bloody conflict, which has been raging for 100 years," warned Rabin, "can only be resolved by means of a process—not a stopwatch."

Some Palestinians were dissatisfied because the agreement promised only limited self-rule, not the independent Palestinian homeland they wanted. The continuing growth of Israeli settlements in the occupied lands also fed Palestinian anger. Radical Palestinian groups, such as Hamas, denounced Arafat as a puppet of Israel and launched new attacks.

*The Intifada* In 1987, Palestinians rebelled against Israeli military rule in a rebellion called the intifada. Young people and even children took to the streets, demanding an end to the 20-year Israeli occupation of the West Bank and the Gaza Strip. "Whatever measures the Israelis take," swore one young Palestinian, "the intifada will not end. The Palestinians have a strong will." *Religions and Value Systems* Why do you think young people led the intifada?

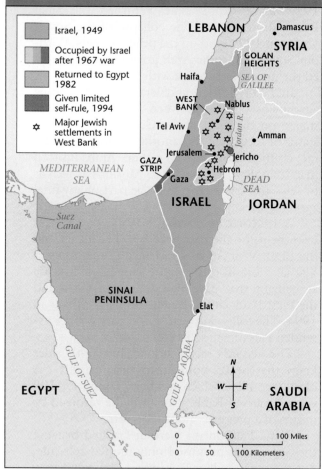

## Arab-Israeli Conflict 1948–1995

**Legend:**
- Israel, 1949
- Occupied by Israel after 1967 war
- Returned to Egypt 1982
- Given limited self-rule, 1994
- ✡ Major Jewish settlements in West Bank

LEBANON
SYRIA • Damascus
GOLAN HEIGHTS
Haifa •
SEA OF GALILEE
WEST BANK
Nablus
Tel Aviv •
Jordan R.
Amman •
Jerusalem •
Jericho
GAZA STRIP
Hebron
Gaza
DEAD SEA
MEDITERRANEAN SEA
ISRAEL
JORDAN
Suez Canal
SINAI PENINSULA
Elat •
GULF OF SUEZ
GULF OF AQABA
EGYPT
SAUDI ARABIA

N W E S

0    50    100 Miles
0    50    100 Kilometers

### GEOGRAPHY AND HISTORY

Israel and its Arab neighbors have fought four wars since 1948. Conflict between Jews and Palestinians in the occupied territories has been an even more explosive issue.

1. **Location** On the map, locate (a) Israel, (b) Egypt, (c) Jordan, (d) Syria, (e) West Bank, (f) Gaza Strip, (g) Sinai Peninsula.
2. **Movement** What territories did Israel gain in the 1967 war?
3. **Critical Thinking** *Drawing Conclusions* Why do you think Israel returned the Sinai to Egypt?

(a Christian sect), Sunni and Shiite Muslims, Druze (a sect derived from Islam), and others. Maronites held the most power, but local political bosses ran their own districts backed by private armies. Increasing numbers of Palestinian refugees crossed the border, straining resources. As the Muslim population grew to outnumber Maronites, unrest spread. Adding to the tensions, the PLO became an important presence in Palestinian refugee camps. Israel, seeking to end the PLO threat to its security, sought influence in southern Lebanon.

**Tragic violence.** In 1975, Lebanon was plunged into a seemingly endless civil war. Christian and Muslim militias battled for villages and the capital city of Beirut. Israel invaded PLO bases in the south and occupied parts of Lebanon as far as the capital. Syria occupied the east. Lawlessness led to brutal massacres on all sides. At one point, a UN peacekeeping force tried to restore order but withdrew after French and American troops were killed in suicide bombings.

The victims included thousands of Palestinian refugees. Palestinian writer Liyana Badr described life in a besieged refugee camp:

❝There was one young man, I remember, who said, 'When I die, put me in this coffin.' They made coffins from cupboard doors and there was a door ready. 'I'll measure it against my body,' the young man said. A moment later a splinter of shrapnel struck him in the

Many Israelis, too, bitterly criticized the peace accords. They distrusted Arafat, who in the past had worked to destroy Israel. Some called Rabin a traitor for giving up any part of the Jewish "promised land." In November 1995, Rabin was killed by a Jewish law student who opposed his policies. The following year Benjamin Netanyahu, a critic of Rabin's peace policies, became prime minister, and the peace process slowed.

## Civil War in Lebanon

In the 1970s, the Arab-Israeli conflict fueled tensions in nearby Lebanon. After independence, Lebanon had become a thriving center of international commerce. People of diverse ethnic and religious groups lived mostly in harmony. But prosperity masked problems.

**Growing tensions.** The government depended on a delicate balance among Maronites

back and killed him on the spot. So they did put him in the coffin he'd measured himself for."

By 1990, Lebanese leaders finally restored a measure of order. The PLO was forced out of southern Lebanon, private armies began to disarm, and businesses in the devastated city of Beirut rebuilt. Divisions remained, though, and both Syria and Israel still operated in Lebanon.

## Two Wars in the Persian Gulf

Border disputes, oil wealth, foreign intervention, and ambitious rulers fed tensions along the Persian Gulf. In 1980, Iraqi dictator Saddam Hussein took advantage of turmoil in Iran to occupy a disputed border area and then pushed deeper into Iran. Iran launched a counterattack amid calls to spread its revolution to Iraq.

Iraq used its superior weapons, tanks, airplanes, and even poison gas to stop waves of Iranian soldiers. When both sides attacked tankers and oil fields, the United States took steps to protect shipping lanes in the Persian Gulf and the Strait of Hormuz. (See the map on page 493.) The eight-year Iran-Iraq War drained both sides.

**A second Gulf war.** In 1990, Hussein invaded oil-rich Kuwait. He claimed Kuwait was a creation of Britain and belonged to Iraq. Control of Kuwait would also expand Iraq's access to the Persian Gulf.

The United States saw the invasion as a threat both to its ally Saudi Arabia and to the oil flow from the Persian Gulf. President George Bush organized a coalition of European and Arab powers to drive Iraqi forces out of Kuwait. In the 1991 Gulf War, American missiles and bombers destroyed targets in Iraq, while ground forces swiftly freed Kuwait.

**Looking ahead.** Defeated and diplomatically isolated, Hussein still held onto power. He managed to suppress revolts by Kurdish and

*Environmental Disaster* During the Persian Gulf War of 1991, retreating Iraqi soldiers blew up hundreds of oil wells in Kuwait. It took crews of firefighters 10 months to put out the oil fires and cap more than 700 wells. **Global Interaction** Why did the burning of the oil fields raise worldwide concern?

Shiite minorities who had suffered brutally under his rule. Although UN and coalition forces eventually took steps to protect the Kurds, their future remained bleak.

After the war, UN economic sanctions kept Iraq from selling oil abroad. The goal was to force Hussein to stop his chemical and nuclear weapons programs. Without oil income and under an import embargo, Iraq suffered great hardships. In the late 1990s, the UN allowed some oil sales after Hussein agreed to dismantle more weapons. Yet with Hussein still in power, Iraq remained a potentially dangerous force.

## SECTION 4 REVIEW

1. **Identify** (a) PLO, (b) Yasir Arafat, (c) Yitzhak Rabin, (d) Saddam Hussein.
2. **Define** intifada.
3. (a) Why were the occupied territories a source of tension? (b) What steps were taken toward resolving the conflict?
4. Why did civil war break out in Lebanon?
5. What were the effects of the 1991 Gulf War?
6. *Critical Thinking* **Solving Problems** If you were organizing a Middle East peace conference, whom would you invite and what issues would you put on the table?
7. *ACTIVITY* Draw a cartoon about the role of oil in fueling tensions on the Persian Gulf.

ISSUES *For* TODAY

The Arab-Israeli conflict, the civil war in Lebanon, and the Iraqi invasion of Kuwait became the focus of worldwide concern. When should the world community intercede in local conflicts to promote peace?

## CHAPTER REVIEW

### REVIEWING VOCABULARY

Review the following vocabulary from this chapter: *refugee, secular, caste, nonaligned, guerrilla warfare, ethnic group, autonomy, terrorism, annex, intifada*. Write sentences using each of these terms, leaving blanks where the terms would go. Exchange your sentences with another student and fill in the blanks on each other's lists.

### REVIEWING FACTS

1. Why did Britain decide to divide the Indian subcontinent into the separate nations of India and Pakistan?

2. What led to the creation of an independent Bangladesh?

3. What were the results of the 1948 war between Israel and the Arab nations?

4. How did Iran's policy toward the United States change after the revolution of 1979?

5. When and how did Israel gain control of the Sinai Peninsula, the Gaza Strip, and the West Bank?

6. What was the outcome of the 1991 Gulf War?

### REVIEWING CHAPTER THEMES

Review the "Focus On" questions at the start of this chapter. Then select *three* of those questions and answer them, using information from the chapter.

## SKILLS FOR SUCCESS    REVISING YOUR WRITING

During the revision stage of the writing process, you examine the content, organization, tone, and language of your first draft. You check to make sure that what you have written matches your original thesis. Revision also includes a mechanics check, including grammar, spelling, and punctuation.

Look at the sample composition and the thesis statement at right. Then, follow these revision steps.

1. **Check your introductory paragraph against your original thesis.** (a) What is the original thesis? (b) Is there any detail in the original thesis that the writer omitted in the first paragraph?

2. **Examine each sentence to be sure that content and structure are clear.** Delete unnecessary words or sentences. You many choose to combine simple sentences or rewrite long, unclear sentences. How could you condense the three circled sentences in paragraph B?

3. **Correct any mistakes in spelling, punctuation, and grammar.** (a) Why are *Iran* and *United States* capitalized? (b) What word is misspelled in paragraph E?

---

**ORIGINAL THESIS:**

   The Iranian Revolution of 1979 was a reaction against earlier changes in that country.

**A.** After years of secular rule, Iran experienced an Islamic Revolution ‸in 1979 that brought a new government to power. That revolution had its roots in earlier events.

**B.** Iran's oil wealth made it important to western nations. *In 1953 the United States helped the shah take power. He overthrew Muhammad Mosaddiq. Mosaddiq had supported nationalizing the oil industry.*

> Condense into one sentence

**C.** The shah, ~~as leader of Iran,~~ ruled Iran with military and other kinds of help from the United States.

> Combine paragraphs C and D

**D.** The shah modernized the country. He also reduced the power of the Muslim leaders. His policies were opposed by ~~many opponents among~~ the Iranians. The shah's secret police arrested and tortured those who opposed his rule.

**E.** ~~Then events moved forward.~~ In the 1970s Muslim leaders such as Ayatollah Ruhollah Khomenei became leaders in the fight against the shah. The shah fled the country. Khomenei became the head of the new Islamic goverment.

---

## CRITICAL THINKING

1. **Linking Past and Present** Give three examples of how the legacy of western imperialism influenced recent developments in South Asia and the Middle East.

2. **Comparing** Review pages 444–445. How is India's attempt to reform the caste system similar to the civil rights movement in the United States? How is it different?

3. **Applying Information** Review the subsection "Old Ways and New" from Chapter 15, pages 422–423. Give two examples of how the changes described there apply to the Middle East.

4. **Recognizing Points of View** Reread the statement by the Egyptian woman on page 494. According to her, is hejab a restricting or a liberating force? Explain.

## ANALYZING PRIMARY SOURCES

Use the two quotations on page 482 to answer the following questions.

1. Contrast the mood of the two excerpts.

2. In the first excerpt, what was Nehru referring to when he spoke of India's "long slumber and struggle"?

3. What events caused the "oceans of blood and tears" Nehru described in the second excerpt?

## FOR YOUR PORTFOLIO

**ASSEMBLING QUOTATIONS** Work with a partner to compile a book of collectible quotations from prominent figures of South Asia and the Middle East. Begin by rereading the chapter to list the people mentioned. Then add to your list by using outside resources. Do research to find an appropriate quotation from each person on your list. Finally, compile your quotations into a book, organized chronologically or by topic, and share it with the class as a social studies resource.

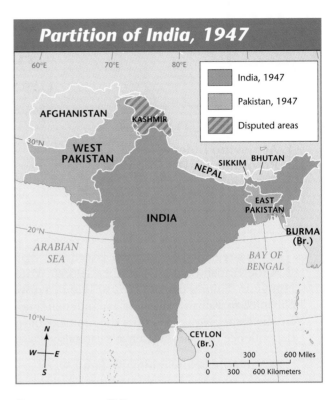

### Partition of India, 1947

- India, 1947
- Pakistan, 1947
- Disputed areas

AFGHANISTAN
KASHMIR
WEST PAKISTAN
NEPAL  SIKKIM  BHUTAN
INDIA
EAST PAKISTAN
BURMA (Br.)
ARABIAN SEA
BAY OF BENGAL
CEYLON (Br.)

0    300    600 Miles
0   300   600 Kilometers

## ANALYZING MAPS

Use the map as well as information from the chapter to answer the following questions.

1. Which nation bordered West Pakistan to the north? To the South?

2. What body of water did East Pakistan border?

3. How would you change the labels for West Pakistan and East Pakistan to reflect events of 1971?

## INTERNET ACTIVITY

**TAKING A "VIRTUAL VACATION"** Use the Internet to research modern-day life in one of the countries of South Asia or the Middle East. Then imagine you are touring that country and write a letter home describing what you have seen. Be sure to include descriptions of sites you have visited, as well as comments on the climate and natural features of the country.

# CHAPTER

## 19

# Africa

## (1945–Present)

## CHAPTER OUTLINE

1 Achieving Independence
2 Programs for Development
3 Four Nations: A Closer Look
4 Struggles in Southern Africa
5 Africa: Past and Present

"Kenya regained her *Uhuru* [freedom] from the British on 12 December 1963," writes Ngugi wa Thiong'o in *A Grain of Wheat,* a novel chronicling Kenya's struggle for independence. In one scene, Ngugi describes the moment of independence in Nairobi, Kenya's capital:

66A minute before midnight, lights were put out at the Nairobi stadium. . . . In the dark, the Union Jack was quickly lowered. When next the lights came on the new Kenya flag was flying and fluttering, and waving, in the air. The . . . band played the new National Anthem and the crowd cheered continuously. . . . The cheering sounded like one intense cracking of many trees, falling on the thick mud in the stadium.99

In villages throughout Kenya, men, women, and children celebrated the occasion. Still, people had many questions. In Ngugi's novel, the villagers wonder about the future:

66Men stood or talked in groups about the prospects opened up by Uhuru. . . . Would the government now become less stringent on those who could not pay tax? Would there be more jobs? Would there be more land?99

In the decades after World War II, nationalists across Africa demanded freedom and the power to control their own destinies. Slowly at first and then in rapid succession, African nations emerged from colonial rule. Since 1945, more than 50 new nations have been born.

Leaders of the new nations set out to build strong central governments, achieve economic growth, and raise standards of living to match those in the developed world. Modernization, however, would not be easy. Nations faced a string of problems—from lack of technology, drought, and other natural disasters to economic dependency, political instability, and ethnic rivalries.

Despite repeated setbacks, African nations did not lose hope. They continued to search for workable solutions.

**FOCUS ON** these questions as you read:

- **Diversity**
  How did diversity pose problems for emerging African nations?

- **Impact of the Individual**
  What challenges did liberation leaders face in the struggle for freedom?

- **Economics and Technology**
  Why did developing nations of Africa remain economically dependent on the industrialized world?

- **Political and Social Systems**
  What kinds of governments did the new nations of Africa develop?

- **Continuity and Change**
  Why have many Africans called for their nations to seek African solutions to African problems?

## TIME AND PLACE

**506    Chapter 19**

*Independent Africa* After World War II, dozens of former colonies in Africa emerged as independent nations. The new countries made economic growth a priority. They invested in schools, roads, dams, factories, and other modernization projects. The Kenyatta Center in Nairobi, Kenya, shown here, symbolizes the new Africa at the same time it echoes traditional African designs. ***Global Interaction*** In what ways does the Kenyatta Center reflect a blend of cultural influences?

## HUMANITIES LINK

***Art History*** Voyiya, *Rhythm in 3/4 Time* (page 522).
***Literature*** In this chapter, you will encounter passages from the following works of literature: Ngugi wa Thiong'o, *A Grain of Wheat* (page 506); Sembene Ousmane, *God's Bits of Wood* (page 508); John Pepper Clark, "The Casualties" (page 517).

**Late 1940s**
Nationalist movements intensify throughout Africa

**1964**
Nyerere becomes president of Tanzania

**1970**
Nigerian civil war ends

**1980s**
Zimbabwe begins economic and land reforms

**1994**
Nelson Mandela is elected president of South Africa

1945     1960     1975     1990     PRESENT

# 1 Achieving Independence

## Guide for Reading

■ How did African nations win independence?

■ How did the colonial legacy hamper development?

■ How did nationalist leaders guide the independence movements?

From the town of Thiès, the women march on Dakar, capital of French-ruled Senegal. They want to add their voices to those of their men—railroad workers on strike for equal pay. As they approach the city, they are warned that a column of soldiers has orders not to let them pass. One of their leaders, Penda, speaks up:

66 'The soldiers can't eat us!' she cried. 'They can't even kill us; there are too many of us! Don't be afraid—our friends are waiting for us in Dakar! We'll go on!' 99

Suddenly, shots ring out, and Penda falls. The women, however, continue their march toward the city, where they are welcomed as heroes.

That scene, from *God's Bits of Wood* by Senegalese writer and filmmaker Sembene Ousmane (suhm BEH neh us MAH neh), is based on a real event in 1947. Eventually, the French forced an end to the Senegalese strike. Still, the bravery of the strikers and the women who supported them spurred further campaigns for reform and justice.

By the 1950s, strikes and protests were multiplying. Across the continent, Africans demanded more than reform. They called for freedom from foreign rule.

### The Nationalist Tide

In 1945, four European powers—Britain, France, Belgium, and Portugal—controlled almost all of Africa. (See the map on page 509.) Only Egypt, Ethiopia, Liberia, and white-ruled South Africa were independent nations. The ris-

ing tide of nationalism, however, soon swept over European colonial empires, bringing a great liberation in Africa and around the world.

**Impact of World War II.** World War II sharpened the edges of nationalist movements in Africa. Japanese victories in Asia shattered the West's reputation as an unbeatable force. Also, African troops had fought Axis armies in Africa, the Middle East, and other parts of the world. When they returned home to discrimination and second-class citizenship, these ex-soldiers became easy recruits for the growing nationalist movements. Nationalists also found support among workers who had migrated to the cities to work in defense industries during the war.

**The global setting.** After the war, most Europeans were reluctant to fight to hold onto overseas colonies. Faced with growing nationalist demands, Britain and France, the largest imperialist powers, adopted new policies toward their African colonies. They introduced political reforms that would gradually lead to independence. They soon discovered, however, that they could not dictate either the terms or the pace of change.

Pressures for independence built up both within and outside Africa. The two superpowers, you will recall, rejected colonialism. (See page 410.) After India won independence from Britain in 1947, African leaders grew impatient. Everywhere rose the cry "Freedom Now."

**Nationalist leaders.** Most nationalist leaders were western educated. Many were powerful speakers whose words inspired supporters. Kwame Nkrumah in Gold Coast, Jomo Kenyatta in Kenya, and Léopold Senghor in Senegal, to name but a few, were skilled political organizers.

In colonies throughout Africa, leaders organized political parties. In the cities, parties published newspapers, held mass rallies, and mobilized popular support for independence. Demonstrations,

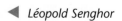

◀ *Léopold Senghor*

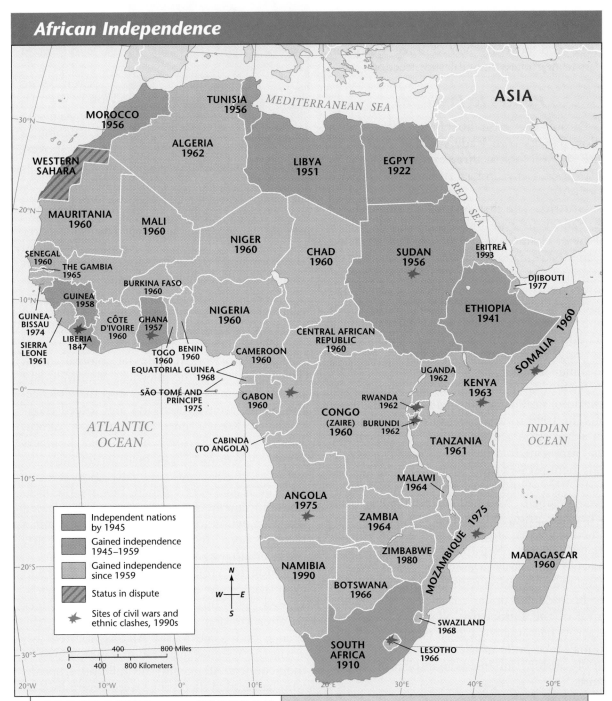

# African Independence

MOROCCO 1956
TUNISIA 1956
ALGERIA 1962
LIBYA 1951
EGPYT 1922
WESTERN SAHARA
MAURITANIA 1960
MALI 1960
NIGER 1960
CHAD 1960
SUDAN 1956
ERITREÀ 1993
SENEGAL 1960
THE GAMBIA 1965
BURKINA FASO 1960
DJIBOUTI 1977
GUINEA 1958
GUINEA-BISSAU 1974
CÔTE D'IVOIRE 1960
GHANA 1957
NIGERIA 1960
ETHIOPIA 1941
SIERRA LEONE 1961
LIBERIA 1847
TOGO 1960
BENIN 1960
CAMEROON 1960
CENTRAL AFRICAN REPUBLIC 1960
EQUATORIAL GUINEA 1968
SÃO TOMÉ AND PRÍNCIPE 1975
GABON 1960
SOMALIA 1960
UGANDA 1962
KENYA 1963
RWANDA 1962
CONGO (ZAIRE) 1960
BURUNDI 1962
CABINDA (TO ANGOLA)
TANZANIA 1961
MALAWI 1964
ANGOLA 1975
ZAMBIA 1964
MOZAMBIQUE 1975
ZIMBABWE 1980
MADAGASCAR 1960
NAMIBIA 1990
BOTSWANA 1966
SWAZILAND 1968
SOUTH AFRICA 1910
LESOTHO 1966

MEDITERRANEAN SEA
ASIA
RED SEA
ATLANTIC OCEAN
INDIAN OCEAN

Legend:
- Independent nations by 1945
- Gained independence 1945–1959
- Gained independence since 1959
- Status in dispute
- Sites of civil wars and ethnic clashes, 1990s

N
W—E
S

0    400    800 Miles
0    400    800 Kilometers

# GEOGRAPHY AND HISTORY

A great liberation took place in Africa following World War II. Slowly at first, and then with increasing speed, the people of Africa regained their independence.

1. **Location** On the map, locate (a) Egypt, (b) Angola, (c) Tanzania, (d) Zaire, (e) South Africa.

2. **Place** (a) Which nations were independent before 1945? (b) Which nations regained independence before 1960? (c) When did Zimbabwe gain independence?

3. **Critical Thinking** **Drawing Conclusions** Based on the map, what conclusion can you draw about the fate of European colonial empires in Africa?

strikes, and boycotts helped force European rulers to negotiate timetables for freedom.

## Routes to Freedom

During the great liberation, each African nation had its own leaders and it own story. Here, we will look at three examples: Ghana in West Africa, Kenya in East Africa, and Algeria in North Africa.

**Ghana.** The first African nation south of the Sahara to win freedom was the British colony of Gold Coast. In the late 1940s, young Kwame Nkrumah (kwah MEE ehn KROO muh) was impatient with Britain's policy of gradual movement toward independence. Nkrumah had spent time in the United States, where he was inspired by the Pan-Africanist Marcus Garvey and other civil rights leaders. He also studied the nonviolent methods of Mohandas Gandhi, the Indian leader.

Back in Gold Coast, Nkrumah organized a radical political party. Through strikes and boycotts, he tried to win concessions from Britain. But when mass actions led to riots, Nkrumah was imprisoned. Still, his "Positive Action" movement pressed on.

In 1957, Gold Coast finally won independence. Nkrumah, who had emerged from prison to become prime minister of the new nation, named it Ghana, after the ancient West African empire.* The symbolism was clear. *Gold Coast* reflected European interests in Africa. *Ghana* linked the new nation with the African past that had been denied under colonialism. Before the arrival of the Europeans, Nkrumah said, "our ancestors had attained a great empire. . . . Thus we may take pride in the name of Ghana, not out of romanticism, but as an inspiration for the future."

**Kenya.** In Kenya, freedom came only with armed struggle. White settlers had carved out farms in the fertile highlands, where they displaced African farmers, mostly Kikuyu (kih KOO yoo). Settlers considered Kenya their homeland and had passed laws to ensure their domination. They feared giving up any power to the African majority.

◀ *Jomo Kenyatta*

Even before World War II, Jomo Kenyatta had become a leading spokesman for the Kikuyu. "The land is ours," he said. "When Europeans came, they kept us back and took our land." Kenyatta supported nonviolent methods to end oppressive laws.

Other, more radical leaders turned to guerrilla warfare. They burned farms and destroyed livestock, hoping to scare whites into leaving. By 1952, they began to attack settlers and Africans who worked with the colonial rulers. The British called the guerrillas Mau Mau and pictured them as savages. To stop the violence, the British arrested Kenyatta and forced thousands of Kikuyu into concentration camps. Kikuyu casualties rose when British bombers pounded Mau Mau fighters armed mostly with swords.

The rebels were crushed, but not the freedom movement. Eventually, the British released Kenyatta, whose years in prison had made him a national hero. In 1963, he became the first prime minister of an independent Kenya.

**Algeria.** From 1954 to 1962, a longer and even costlier war of liberation raged in Algeria. During the 1800s France had conquered Algeria after a brutal struggle. Over the years, the French had come to see Algeria, located just across the Mediterranean from France, as part of their country. Along with the million Europeans who had settled there, they were determined to keep the Arab-Berber people of Algeria from winning independence.

Muslim Algerian nationalists set up the National Liberation Front (FLN). In 1954, it turned to guerrilla warfare to win freedom. France, which had just lost Vietnam, was unwilling to retreat from Algeria. As the fighting escalated, a half-million French troops went to Algeria. Thousands were killed, but hundreds of thousands of Algerians died during the long war that followed.

---

*Ancient Ghana was located to the north and west of modern Ghana.

Eventually, public opinion in France turned against the war. After Charles de Gaulle, France's World War II leader, became president in 1958, he began talks to end the war. Four years later, Algeria celebrated its freedom.

### *High Expectations, Dashed Hopes*

More than 50 new nations were born in Africa during the great liberation. Throughout the continent, Africans had great hopes for the future. Karari Njama, a Kenyan, wrote how different people had their own ideas about what freedom meant:

> 66All the old people think of freedom as the old lives they had prior to the coming of the European . . . while many ignorant young people interpret the freedom as casting down all the present laws with a replacement of liberty to do what he personally wishes.99

People looked forward to rapid political and economic development. African leaders knew they had much to do to build modern nations, but they welcomed the chance to deal on an equal footing with the nations of the world. After 70 years of colonial rule, Africans were again in control of their destinies.

During the early decades after independence, the new nations took different paths to modernization. Some made progress despite huge obstacles. Many others were plunged into crisis by civil war, natural disasters, military rule, and corrupt dictators. Projects for economic development failed, and standards of living fell. In many countries, a small elite enjoyed wealth and privileges, while the majority lived in poverty.

### *The Colonial Heritage*

Scholars trace many of Africa's recent problems to the colonial experience. Western imperialism had a complex and contradictory impact

# PARALLELS THROUGH TIME

## Patterns of Migration

Migration has taken place throughout human history. Beginning in the 1500s, European colonists settled in the Americas, Africa, and Asia. Recently, the flow has reversed, as West Indians, Africans, and Asians moved to Europe. But while European colonists enjoyed many privileges, newcomers to Europe often face discrimination and hardship.

**Linking Past and Present**  Why did Europeans set up colonies in Africa, the Americas, and Asia? Why do you think people from former colonies have moved to Europe?

**PAST**  *France conquered Algeria, in North Africa, in the 1830s. By the 1950s, more than a million French colonists lived in Algeria. The French dominated the economy and granted Algerians few political rights. After a bloody war for independence, most French settlers left Algeria.*

**PRESENT**

*Since World War II, several million Algerians and Moroccans have crossed the Mediterranean to live in France. Although the newcomers speak French, they have held onto their Muslim faith and North African customs. Many have found it difficult to integrate themselves into the mainstream of French life. These children of Algerian-born parents live outside Paris.*

**The Cold War in Africa** *Rivalry between the United States and the Soviet Union had devastating effects in Africa. Both sides armed their allies, fueling regional conflicts and civil wars that claimed millions of lives. One of the bloodiest struggles took place in the Horn of Africa, where the United States backed Somalia and the Soviet Union aided Ethiopia. In this cartoon, American and Soviet advisers rushing to help their African allies head for a collision.* **Political and Social Systems** *Why do you think the United States and the Soviet Union cared about which political system African nations adopted?*

ROTHCO

on Africa. Some changes could be considered gains. Others had a destructive effect on African life that is felt down to the present.

**Economic changes.** Colonial rulers introduced new crops, technologies, and cash economies. They built roads, railroads, harbors, and cities. The new forms of transportation were meant to make the colonies profitable by linking plantations and mines to ports. Exporting raw materials and cash crops from Africa helped pay for European rule. For the majority of Africans, who were subsistence farmers, there was little benefit from these facilities.

After liberation, the pattern of economic dependence continued. To pay for expensive development projects, African nations exported minerals and agricultural goods to the industrial world. But most profits flowed out of Africa because the new nations had to buy expensive manufactured goods and technology from the West. Also, many large farms and mines were still owned by westerners.

**Political changes.** During the colonial period, Europeans undermined Africa's traditional political systems. Even when they left African rulers in place, they dictated laws and told Africans how to govern. White officials shared the racial views of their day. They saw Africans as children who needed guidance, overlooking the fact that Africans had ruled themselves for centuries. Europeans denied educated Africans top jobs in colonial governments.

Suddenly, at independence, colonial powers expected African leaders to transform authoritarian colonies into democratic nations. They seemed to forget that western nations themselves had achieved democracy only after centuries of turmoil and with the help of strong industrial economies.

**Education and health care.** In parts of Africa, colonial rulers had paid little attention to schools and health care. Instead, those services were provided by missionary groups. Western doctors, however, did develop vaccines for yellow fever and smallpox and helped to reduce deaths from malaria.

By the 1950s, in response to nationalist demands, colonial rulers built more hospitals and schools. But they emphasized elementary education. There were few secondary schools and only a handful of universities.

**Artificial borders.** The map of Africa after independence was itself a legacy of colonial rule. New nations inherited borders drawn by colonial powers, which caused great problems.

Africa is a continent of enormously diverse societies with more than 1,000 languages and dialects. Colonial borders had forced together people from diverse ethnic groups and with different, even conflicting interests into the same

**GLOBAL CONNECTIONS**

Millions of people of African descent are scattered around the world. The slave trade created the African diaspora, carrying Africans across the Atlantic to the Americas. In Brazil, the Caribbean, and North America, especially, many people identify with aspects of African culture. In the United States, African Americans make up about one eighth of the population.

country. To herders and traders, such artificial borders were meaningless. Even farming people migrated regardless of lines drawn on a map. Thus, leaders of the new nations often had to create a sense of national unity where there had been none before.

## The Cold War and Africa

Although many African nations supported the nonaligned movement (see page 411), the continent could not avoid the pressures of the Cold War. Leaders who were strongly anti-communist received western aid and support. Those who embraced socialism were looked on with suspicion by the West.

The rival superpowers were drawn into African conflicts. As you will read in Section 4, Soviet- and American-supported forces took part in the liberation struggles in southern Africa. In the Horn of Africa, along the Red Sea, the superpowers became involved in a long, drawn-out war between Ethiopia and Somalia. Elsewhere, the superpowers supplied arms to governments they favored. In the process, they helped increase the power of the military, thus adding to an already unstable situation.

## SECTION 1 REVIEW

1. **Identify** (a) Kwame Nkrumah, (b) Jomo Kenyatta, (c) Mau Mau, (d) National Liberation Front.
2. (a) How did World War II influence nationalist movements in Africa? (b) Why were most African nations able to win freedom peacefully?
3. Describe three ways in which the legacy of colonial rule hampered development after independence.
4. Describe the role of each of the following leaders in winning independence for his country: (a) Kwame Nkrumah, (b) Jomo Kenyatta.
5. *Critical Thinking* **Recognizing Points of View** Many Europeans viewed the Mau Mau as terrorists. Africans viewed them as freedom fighters. How would you explain these different points of view?
6. *ACTIVITY* Select one nation highlighted in this section. Design a logo that might have been used by its independence movement.

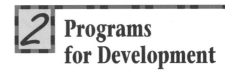

# 2 Programs for Development

## Guide for Reading

- What were the main goals of new African nations?
- What obstacles hindered development?
- What political and economic choices did African nations face?
- **Vocabulary** *mixed economy*

"Independence is the beginning of a real struggle," declared one liberation leader in Africa. The new nations faced two critical issues. They needed to create unified states with stable governments, and they needed to build productive economies that would improve the standard of living of their people. Meeting those challenges would be a long, complex process—a process that is still incomplete.

Making accurate generalizations about Africa is difficult. Every nation is different. Some nations have rich resources to help finance progress. Others are poor in resources. Each has its own set of problems and its own history.

In the decades since independence, African governments experimented with various programs. They made some progress but also took some wrong turns. In this section, we will look at the political and economic challenges faced by several new African nations.

## Seeking Unity and Stability

At independence, African nations set up governments modeled on those of departing colonial rulers. But parliamentary systems did not work in Africa as they had in Europe, where they had evolved over centuries.

**Divisions and civil war.** Colonial borders left most African nations a patchwork of people with diverse cultures, languages, and histories. Nationalism had united Africans against colonial rule. But once freedom was won, many Africans felt their first loyalty was to their own people, not to a faceless national government.

Like Eastern European nations, African nations were plagued by ethnic and regional conflict. In Sudan, for example, the majority, Arabic-speaking Muslims, in the north dominated and persecuted the minority, mostly Christian groups, in the south. Southerners tried to break away, which led to civil war.

Westerners often blamed African civil wars on ancient "tribal" rivalries.* But most conflicts were more complex. Some were rooted in colonial history. Britain, for example, found it convenient to rule its African colonies through what it called "tribal" leaders. It assigned Africans in each colony to tribes and then chose one tribe to rule others. The ill-will that was thus fostered lasted long after independence.

Civil wars also resulted when liberation leaders monopolized political and economic power for their own group. In Nigeria and Zaire, civil war erupted when economically successful groups tried to set up their own nations. Civil wars unleashed terrible violence in African societies.

**One-party rule.** Faced with divisions that threatened national unity, many early leaders turned to one-party systems. Multiparty systems, they declared, encouraged disunity. In Tanzania, Julius Nyerere (nyuh RAIR ay) claimed that a one-party system could be democratic and offered voters a choice of candidates within the party.

In fact, most one-party nations became authoritarian states. Some nationalist leaders who had led the struggle for freedom became dictators supported by a privileged elite. Some used their position to enrich themselves, allowed corruption to thrive, and failed to provide justice. Others used force to hold onto power.

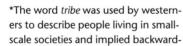

▲ *Julius Nyerere*

*The word *tribe* was used by westerners to describe people living in small-scale societies and implied backwardness. The term is misleading, however. Like societies elsewhere, Africans in precolonial times belonged to ethnic or social groups that shared a common culture or loyalty. But these groups changed over time and continue to change today.

**Military rule.** When bad government led to unrest, the military often seized power. More than half of all African nations suffered military coups. Military leaders claimed that they—unlike greedy politicians—were motivated by a sense of duty to their country. Some military rulers, like Idi Amin, who murdered thousands of citizens in Uganda, were brutal tyrants. Others, like Nyerere, sought to end abuses and improve conditions.

Military leaders usually promised to restore civilian rule once they had cleaned up the government. In many cases, however, they gave up power only when they were toppled by other military coups.

**New solutions.** Political and economic woes brought Africa to the brink of crisis in the 1980s. Demands for change came from inside and outside the continent. African thinkers looked for African solutions to their problems. They studied precolonial African societies that had limited a ruler's power and allowed people a share in decision making. Although they did not propose returning to the past, they did hope to build on traditions that had worked in Africa before.

The call of Africans for "people participation" was matched by demands for democratic reforms from external sources. Western governments and the World Bank often refused badly needed loans without such reforms. Under this pressure, some governments eased autocratic policies, legalized opposition parties, and lifted censorship. In some places, multiparty elections unseated long-ruling leaders.

## Economic Development

African nations, like other developing regions of the world, faced serious obstacles to development. These obstacles fell into five general areas: geography, population and poverty, economic dependence, economic policies, and political instability. (See pages 414–421 for an

**ISSUES** *For* **TODAY** Some leaders believed African nations should find unique "African" patterns for development. How can developing nations achieve their full potential while preserving their traditions?

overview of the problems facing developing nations in the post-colonial era.)

Developing modern economies meant improving agriculture and developing industry. To achieve those goals, African nations had to build transportation systems, develop resources, increase literacy, and solve problems of rural poverty left by colonial governments. Many had little capital to invest in such projects. As a result, they had to make difficult choices.

**Socialism or capitalism.** At independence, many African nations chose socialism, with an emphasis on government direction of the economy, over the capitalism of colonial rulers. The socialist governments wanted to control scarce resources, using them where they were most needed. They hoped to end foreign economic influence and prevent inequalities between rich and poor. But to regulate the economy, socialism created large, inefficient bureaucracies. Often, the laws imposed by the national government were poorly suited to local farming communities.

Some African nations set up mixed economies, with both private and state-run enterprises. They, too, had problems. These nations relied heavily on foreign aid from the UN, the World Bank, and countries of the global North—as you recall, the industrial nations of Europe, North America, and Japan. Foreign capital was used to build airports, hydroelectric plants, and factories and to improve farming. Some programs succeeded. Many others, like Ghana's Akosombo Dam, were costly failures, due partly to mistakes by government planners or western advisers.

Although African nations did build some industries, they remained dependent on imports. Because most people were subsistence farmers, there was too little demand for goods to make local industries prosper.

Sadly, too, corrupt officials and powerful elites often used aid money to line their own pockets. Bloated bureaucracies and corruption are found in governments everywhere, including the industrial world. In Africa, however, where economies were fragile, waste and greed meant losses to desperately needed development programs.

**Cash crops or food.** In the early years, governments pushed programs to increase earn

**Building Independent Economies** *After independence, African nations struggled to modernize. They invested in transportation links, agricultural projects, new industries, and education. This railroad station was part of a development project in the highlands of Kenya.* **Economics and Technology** *How would a railroad network contribute to economic growth?*

ings by growing more cash crops for export. But land used for cotton, tea, coffee, or sisal did not produce food. As a result, African countries that had once fed their people from their own land had to import food.

**Urban or rural needs.** The food dilemma had another aspect. City dwellers who earned low wages needed cheap food to survive. Farmers, however, would grow food crops only if they received good prices for them. Many governments kept food prices artificially low to satisfy poor city people. As a result, farmers either used their land for export crops or produced only for themselves.

In general, many early government programs neglected rural development in favor of industrial projects. By the 1980s, however, governments realized they must pay more attention to farmers' needs. In Zimbabwe, for example, the government helped small farmers buy tools, fertilizer, and seed. Equally important, it made sure farmers received higher prices for their crops. The policy paid off in higher food output.

**The debt crisis.** Soaring oil prices in the 1970s crushed developing economies. In 1975, a ton of cotton could buy 111 barrels of oil. By 1980, it bought only 60 barrels. As oil prices went up, the world economy slowed down. Prices for African exports fell, plunging the young nations deep into debt. Governments had to pay so much interest on loans that they had little money for development.

The debt crisis led the World Bank and other lenders to require developing nations to make tough economic reforms before granting them new loans. African governments had to privatize businesses and cut spending on development projects. In the long term, the reforms were designed to help economies grow. In the short term, however, they increased unemployment and hurt the poor.

## People and the Environment

The population explosion put a staggering burden on Africa's developing economies. In 1965, Africa's population was about 280 million. By 1990, it had reached 640 million. That number was expected to double before 2020.

**Hardships for farmers.** Rapid population growth worsened rural poverty as more people competed for land. Family land was divided into smaller plots, which made it harder for people to produce enough food.

Today, as in the past, African farmers face harsh conditions, such as irregular rainfall, poor soils, and tropical diseases. Now, as then, when soil is exhausted, farmers migrate to other areas. Because of the growing population, however, many move onto less desirable land in arid steppe regions.

**Drought and famine.** In the early 1970s and again in the 1980s, prolonged drought caused famine in parts of Africa. Livestock died, farmland turned to dust and blew away, and millions of people became refugees. The Sahel was especially hard hit. This semidesert region stretches across Africa just south of the Sahara. There, overgrazing and farming speeded up desertification.

In countries like Ethiopia and Sudan, civil war intensified the effects of drought and famine. Each side in the conflict tried to keep relief supplies from reaching the other. On several occasions, huge international efforts helped save millions of people facing starvation.

**Deforestation.** Rain forests, too, came under attack. To boost badly needed export earnings, African governments allowed hardwood trees to be cut for shipment to the global North. When forests were cleared, heavy tropical rains washed nutrients from the soil, destroying its fertility. In Kenya, Wangari Maathi challenged government policy by starting the Greenbelt movement. Her aim was to restore the environment while opening up opportunities for women in jobs such as rearing seedlings, planting, marketing, and forestry.

**AIDS.** By the 1990s, many African nations, especially Uganda and Tanzania, were reeling from the staggering effects of the AIDS epidemic. Experts lacked adequate information, but the World Health Organization estimated that up to 20 million Africans would be infected by 2000. Many victims were young people in their twenties and thirties as well as children born to mothers infected with AIDS.

## Outlook and Gains

Despite many setbacks since independence, African nations have made progress in every field. As independent nations, they claimed an equal place on the world scene and won the power to shape their own future. Within each nation, the process of building a national identity went slowly. But education and urbanization did begin to break the localism of the past.

**Education and health care.** As governments sponsored increased schooling, literacy rates rose. Every year, millions of young Africans attended high school. Universities trained a new generation of leaders to provide guidance for a promising future.

Countries that promoted female education, such as Ghana, created the first generation of university-educated women. Those women who achieved university degrees went on to participate at high levels in the modern economy.

Most African nations improved health care and created family planning programs. Governments saw that controlling the rate of population growth was an essential step toward improving standards of living.

**Economic growth.** Despite often depressing economic news, Africa remains a region with enormous potential for growth. By the 1990s,

***Improving Health Care*** *Providing medical care, especially in rural areas, has been a main goal of African nations. In much of the countryside, doctors are scarce and hospitals nonexistent. As a result, health projects often focus on prevention. Doctors at this rural clinic in Nigeria teach women the importance of good nutrition in raising healthy children.* **Political and Social Systems** *Why is preventive medicine especially important in areas with few doctors or hospitals?*

many nations had learned from failed policies of the past. With free-market reforms, countries like Ghana enjoyed a surge of economic growth. Other nations expanded mining and manufacturing and improved transportation. Some built factories to process agricultural products for export and expanded communication and transportation networks.

## SECTION 2 REVIEW

1. **Define** mixed economy.
2. Describe two goals of the emerging nations of Africa.
3. Why did many African countries have trouble building stable governments?
4. (a) What were two economic obstacles to modernization? (b) Describe two areas in which African nations have made progress since independence.
5. *Critical Thinking* **Applying Information** According to an African saying, "Cotton is the mother of poverty." To what economic problem does this saying apply? Explain.
6. *ACTIVITY* Design a magazine cover highlighting one of the problems facing young African nations. Then, write a short "Message From the Publisher" describing the problem and some possible solutions.

## 3 Four Nations: A Closer Look

### Guide for Reading

- What problems did Nigeria face at independence?
- Why has the Congo suffered setbacks in development?
- What were Nyerere's goals for Tanzania?
- How did Zimbabwe achieve majority rule?

Nigerian poet John Pepper Clark saw his nation torn by civil war. In "The Casualties," he chronicled both the obvious effects and unseen costs of the war:

66The casualties are not only those who
   are dead;
   They are well out of it.
   The casualties are not only those who
   are wounded,
   Though they await burial by
   installment. . . .
   The casualties are not only those led
   away by night;
   The cell is a cruel place . . .
   The casualties are many, and a good
   number well
   Outside the scenes of ravage and
   wreck; . . .

We fall,
All casualties of the war,
Because we cannot hear each
   other speak
Because eyes have ceased to see the
   face from the crowd.99

Nigeria was only one of many African nations that suffered a disastrous civil war after independence. In this section, we will take a closer look at Nigeria, the Congo, Tanzania, and Zimbabwe. Their experiences, resources, populations, and leaders differed. But their efforts to modernize illustrate the patterns that were common during the post-independence years.

## Pressures for Change in Nigeria

When Nigeria won independence in 1960, it hoped to develop rapidly. This large West African nation had rich resources, especially oil. Its population was the largest in Africa south of the Sahara, giving it a potentially strong internal market. Its fertile farming areas produced exports of cocoa and palm oil as well as food crops. The Niger and Benue rivers provided a good transportation network.

**A diverse population.** Following borders drawn in colonial times, Nigeria lumped together 250 different ethnic groups. At independence, several large regional groups competed for power. In the north were the Muslim Hausa and Fulani, who had forged a strong empire in the early 1800s. In the oil-rich southeast, the Christian Ibo were a bustling, energetic people. The Yoruba of the southwest were also mainly Christian.

**Civil war.** After independence, Nigeria drew up a federal constitution to protect the various regional interests. The system did not work well, however.

At first, the Hausa dominated the government. Ethnic rivalries continued, however, and in 1966, after 20,000 Ibo living in the north were massacred, the nation erupted into civil war. In 1967, Ibo leaders in the southeast seceded, declaring the region the independent state of Biafra. For two and a half years, war raged. It ended only after Nigeria imposed a blockade on Biafra, causing countless deaths from starvation. By 1970, when Biafra surrendered, the conflict had taken almost a million lives.

**Economic recovery.** The 1970s oil boom helped Nigeria recover from the war. The government spent lavishly on development projects. It set up industries, including a steel mill, auto assembly plant, and petrochemical works. To pay for prestige projects like a new capital, it borrowed heavily from the West.

Rural people flooded into the cities, hoping to share in the boom. Between 1960 and 1985, Lagos, the capital city, grew from 500,000 to more than six million. But while cities boomed, the government paid little heed to farmers. Nigeria, once a food exporter, bought expensive imported grain. Local food production fell, and rural poverty grew.

**The debt crisis.** Later, when world oil prices fell, the economy came close to collapse. A huge debt burden, combined with waste, mismanagement, and corruption, strangled the young nation. A small elite continued to profit enormously, but the majority of people suffered. A Nigerian editor expressed disgust with the self-serving wealthy class:

66It is the elites who have chosen their own narrow interests over everything else. Now the whole place is twisted because you cannot expect justice, and you cannot expect your fair share. They have robbed the country and ruined it.99

**Military rule.** Since independence, Nigeria has often lived under military rule. The military usually took over in the name of reform,

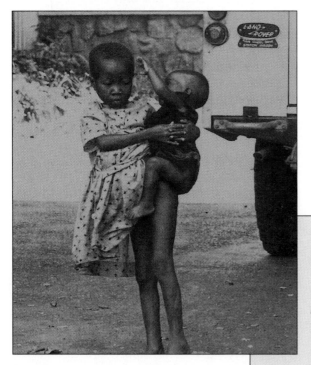

*Tragedy in Biafra* Ethnic conflicts have taken a heavy toll in some parts of Africa. In 1967, the Ibo people of Nigeria tried to create their own nation, called Biafra. To crush the independence movement, Nigeria blockaded Biafra. In the famine that resulted, nearly a million people died, including hundreds of thousands of children. *Political and Social Systems* Why do you think the Nigerian government violently suppressed the independence of Biafra?

arguing that something needed to be done to end the lavish lifestyle and corrupt practices of civilian politicians. Many citizens welcomed the military as a force for order and honest government even though it imposed censorship and other restrictions.

During Nigeria's debt crisis in the 1980s, General Ibrahim Babangida imposed harsh economic reforms to restore economic stability. He declared war on corruption, inefficiency, and waste. He banned most imports and refocused attention on agriculture, paying farmers higher prices for their crops.

Babangida promised to return the government to civilian rule. Elections were held in 1993, but he and his military successors set aside election results and cracked down on critics. Despite international appeals, the government executed Ken Saro-Wiwa, a renowned writer and critic of the regime.

## The Congo: A Dictator's Legacy

After World War II, Belgium was determined to hang on to the Congo, its huge colony in Central Africa. As a result, it did nothing to prepare the colony for freedom. Then, in 1960, fearing a struggle like the French war in Algeria, Belgium suddenly rushed the Congo to independence. The unprepared young nation soon plunged into civil war.

**Freedom—and war.** Physically, the Congo had many advantages. It had rich resources, including vast tropical forests, plantations, and great mineral wealth. And the immense Zaire River and its tributaries flowed from the interior to the coast.

Yet the new nation, made up of some 200 ethnic groups, had no sense of unity. At independence, more than 100 political parties sprang up. They represented diverse regional and ethnic groups. Within months after independence, the nation split apart.

**Mobutu gains power.** Civil war raged for almost three years before United Nations peacekeeping troops ended the worst fighting in 1963. Two years later, an army general, Mobutu Sese Seko, seized power and imposed some kind of order. He renamed the nation Zaire, meaning "big river."

For the next 30 years, Mobutu built an increasingly brutal dictatorship in Zaire. He

▲ Mobutu Sese Seko

bilked the treasury of billions, slaughtered rivals, and ran the economy into the ground. The country's roads were left to rot. By 1990, fewer than 10 percent of the nation's roads were passable. Copper and diamond mines closed, and agriculture declined. Zaire's national currency became worthless, and its people resorted to a barter economy. Lawlessness reigned, and most people lived in miserable poverty.

Mobutu survived in power in part because his strong anti-communism won favor in the West during the Cold War. Also, he represented order. A western official noted: "He maintains stability. What would happen without him?" When he was eventually forced to hold elections, Mobutu won an unbelievable 99.9 percent of the vote. In a country where critics seldom lived long, few doubted the reason for his success.

**A new leader.** Despite economic misery and bad government, Mobutu clung to power. In the late 1990s, ethnic violence in neighboring Rwanda and Burundi spilled over into eastern Zaire. Finally, in 1997, rebels led by Laurent Kabila forced Mobutu from power. Kabila renamed Zaire the Democratic Republic of the Congo.

## Tanzania's Experiment in Socialism

In sharp contrast to Zaire's greedy and corrupt dictator, Tanzania's first president, Julius Nyerere, set out on a high-minded crusade. Nyerere's ambitious goals included improving rural life, building a classless society, and creating a self-reliant economy.

To carry out his program, Nyerere embraced what he called "African socialism." This system was not a western import, he declared, but was based on African village traditions of cooperation and shared responsibility. Nyerere was a strong supporter of women's rights, claiming

**On the Socialist Road** *Many Africans identified capitalism with the colonial system that had drained Africa of its resources for many years. Socialism seemed to offer a road to development without exploitation. Under Julius Nyerere, Tanzania became a laboratory for socialist policies. Like Mao Zedong in China, Nyerere made collective farms the centerpiece of his program. Here, women prepare the soil for planting on a collective farm in Tanzania.* **Economics and Technology** *Based on the picture, what obstacles did these women face in developing their farm?*

that their subservient position was "inconsistent with our socialist conception of the equality of all human beings."

In the 1960s, Nyerere introduced a command economy, nationalizing all banks and foreign-owned businesses. He emphasized the idea that Tanzania was "a rural society where improvement will depend largely upon the efforts of the people in agriculture and village development." He tried to prevent the rise of a wealthy elite through laws that forbade politicians to accumulate riches.

**One-party rule.** At independence, Tanzania was a large country with plenty of land and labor but very little capital or technology. Its main exports were coffee, cotton, tea, and tobacco. Most people were farmers or herders.

Tanzania included about 120 ethnic groups. Most groups were small, however, and the country escaped the worst rivalries that ravaged Nigeria and Zaire.

To promote unity, Nyerere set up a one-party democracy. Several candidates could run for each office. They could debate any topic except those related to ethnic or regional issues.

**Mutual cooperation.** Nyerere promoted the idea of *ujamaa*, a Kiswahili word meaning familyhood or mutual cooperation. Rural farmers were encouraged to live in large villages and to farm the land collectively. The government pledged to build roads and provide technical advice, tools, clean water, health care, and schools. Under this arrangement, Nyerere believed, agricultural output would increase. The govern-

ment would sell the surplus crops to towns or export them to other nations.

Nyerere's bold experiment did not work as planned. Many families refused to leave land they had farmed for generations, and the government had to force them to move to the *ujamaa* villages. Those farmers who did relocate resented experts who tried to teach them to farm. In the end, farm output did not rise.

**Disasters and reforms.** High oil prices, inflation, and a bloated bureaucracy plunged Tanzania into debt. In 1985, Nyerere resigned. His successor, Ali Hassan Mwinyi, introduced reforms. He cut government spending by reducing bureaucracy and privatized some businesses. These moves toward a market economy brought some improvement.

**Successes.** Although it faced serious problems, Tanzania did have some successes. Unlike many African nations, its food output did not decline. With foreign aid, the government provided basic services such as clean water, schools, and health care to its rural villages.

## Zimbabwe and Majority Rule

Southern Rhodesia was a British colony in southern Africa. It had a mild climate and fertile farmland. White settlers had carved out prosperous farms that produced food crops like corn and profitable cash crops such as tea, tobacco, and cotton. Equally valuable were mines that produced gold, copper, nickel, chrome, and coal.

Whites made up only five percent of Rhodesia's population but owned half the land and controlled the government. As the tide of nationalism swept through Africa in the 1960s, white Rhodesians flatly rejected any move to give up power to the black majority. When Britain supported demands for majority rule, conservative whites led by Ian Smith declared independence in 1965.

**Armed struggle.** Smith's white-minority government faced fierce resistance from guerrilla forces led by Robert Mugabe (moo GAH beh) and Joshua Nkomo (uhn KOH moh). The 15-year armed struggle that followed created much suffering in Rhodesia and nearby countries.

By the late 1970s, guerrillas held most of Rhodesia. Many whites had fled, and the UN had imposed economic sanctions that hurt the economy. At last, Smith was forced to accept a negotiated settlement that ensured black majority rule.

**Economic and political challenges.** In 1980, Rhodesia became the independent state of Zimbabwe. The new nation faced severe challenges. Years of war and sanctions had ravaged the economy. Droughts caused further problems. Recovery was also slowed by a bitter power struggle between Mugabe and Nkomo, which pitted the majority Shona people against the minority Ndebele (ehn duh BEH leh).

In the end, Mugabe won, becoming the elected president of Zimbabwe. He pressed for a one-party system, claiming it would promote national unity. Although he did not ban other parties, Mugabe tolerated little opposition.

During the 1980s, Mugabe worked to rebuild agriculture and industry. He encouraged white settlers to stay in Zimbabwe and contribute to its recovery. At the same time, he began to reverse the unequal land arrangement set up in colonial times, transferring some land held by whites to black farmers. To encourage food production, he provided support and higher prices to farmers. The policy helped black farmers increase output, although droughts and other forces could still endanger harvests.

**Rhodesia Becomes Zimbabwe** *When Rhodesia's white minority refused to share power, black nationalists launched a guerrilla war to oust the government led by Ian Smith. After years of bitter fighting, Smith was forced to seek a compromise. In 1980, Rhodesia became the republic of Zimbabwe, under black majority rule.* **Political and Social Systems** *What problems did Zimbabwe face after independence?*

## SECTION 3 REVIEW

1. **Identify** (a) Biafra, (b) Ibrahim Babangida, (c) Mobutu Sese Seko, (d) Julius Nyerere, (e) *ujamaa,* (f) Ian Smith, (g) Robert Mugabe.
2. (a) List four problems Nigeria has experienced since independence. (b) Why did some Nigerians welcome military rule?
3. (a) Why did civil war erupt in the Congo after independence? (b) How did Mobutu's policies affect Zaire?
4. (a) Describe Nyerere's program of African socialism. (b) Did it succeed? Why or why not?
5. (a) Why did Africans wage guerrilla war in Zimbabwe? (b) How has Mugabe tried to promote economic growth in Zimbabwe?
6. *Critical Thinking* **Defending a Position** (a) What arguments can be made in favor of authoritarian or military rule for a country like Nigeria or the Congo? (b) What arguments can be made against such a system of government?
7. *ACTIVITY* Select one of the nations studied in Section 3. Then, prepare a script for a TV program profiling that nation since independence. You might include interviews with both the nation's leaders and with "people on the street."

**Struggles in Southern Africa**

## Guide for Reading

■ How did apartheid affect South Africans?

■ What steps led to the end of apartheid?

■ How did the Cold War affect Angola and Mozambique?

Nelson Mandela stood erect and proud before a crowd of more than 50,000 black and white South Africans. Their cheers hailed the historic moment. It was May 1994, and Mandela had just been inaugurated as South Africa's first president elected by voters of all races.

For 342 years, whites had dominated South Africa, denying blacks the most basic civil rights. Mandela's election set the country on a new track. In his inauguration speech, he spoke of reconciliation, not of revenge for the losses suffered by black South Africans:

66 The time for the healing of wounds has
come. . . . We enter into a covenant
that we shall build a society in which all
South Africans, both black and white,
will be able to walk tall, without any
fear in their hearts, assured of their
inalienable right to human dignity—a
rainbow nation at peace with itself and
the world. 99

The crowd sang "Nkosi Sikelel' iAfrika" (God Bless Africa)—the anthem that had come to symbolize South Africa's struggle for freedom. In the years ahead, South Africa's successful transition to democratic rule would serve as a beacon to other African nations.

## *Crusade for Majority Rule in South Africa*

In 1910, South Africa won self-rule from Britain. Freedom, however, was limited to white settlers. Whites also controlled the vast mineral resources and fertile land that made South Africa the richest nation on the African conti-

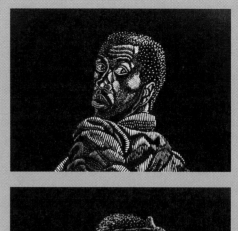

*Rhythm in 3/4 Time* Traditionally, artists in Africa have produced works to be enjoyed by the whole community, not sold to private collectors or placed in museums. During the struggle to end apartheid in South Africa, the connection between artists and ordinary people was reinforced. "There can be no line separating the artist from his community," one young South African painter said. In this linocut, Vuyile Cameron Voyiya shows a political prisoner who had been severely beaten by the South African police. In prison, the man lived in fear of more beatings and often raised his arms "like he's evading blows." **Art and Literature** How can art like this linocut by Voyiya help to bring about change?

nent. After independence, the white minority passed racial laws to keep the black majority in a subordinate position.

**Afrikaner nationalism.** After World War II, thousands of blacks moved to towns and cities. There, as elsewhere in Africa, black nationalism stirred demands for rights. In response, Afrikaners, who were descended from Dutch settlers, demanded severe new limits on blacks.

In 1948, the Afrikaner National party won a majority in a "whites-only" parliament. They then extended the system of racial segregation that had grown up over the years, creating what was known as apartheid, or the separation of the races.

Under apartheid, all South Africans were registered by race: Black, White, Colored (people of mixed descent), and Asian. Afrikaners claimed that apartheid would allow each race to develop its own culture. In fact, it was designed to give whites control over South Africa.

**Apartheid in action.** For nonwhites, apartheid meant a life of restrictions. Blacks were treated like foreigners in their own land. They had to get permission to travel and had to carry passbooks or face arrest. The pass laws were an especially heavy burden for women, who had to get permission from their parents, guardian, or husband, as well as from the authorities, in order to move from one district to another.

All blacks were assigned to "homelands," based on their ethnic group. Homelands were located in arid, unproductive parts of the country. More than 80 percent of South Africa, including the richest farmland, mines, and cities, was reserved for the fewer than 20 percent of the population who were white.

Apartheid laws banned mixed marriages and set up segregated restaurants, beaches, schools, and other facilities. Although blacks were needed to work in factories, mines, and other jobs, they were paid less than whites for the same work. Black schools received less funding than white schools. Low wages and inferior schooling condemned blacks to poverty.

**Black resistance.** From the beginning, black South Africans protested apartheid. In 1912, an organization, later called the African National Congress (ANC), was set up to oppose white domination. In the 1950s, as Afrikaner nationalists imposed ever-harsher laws, the ANC organized marches, boycotts, and strikes.

As protests continued, government violence increased. In 1960, police gunned down 69 men, women, and children taking part in a peaceful demonstration in Sharpeville, a black township outside Johannesburg. Another 180 were wounded. In the wake of the incident, the government outlawed the ANC and cracked down on trade unions and other groups opposed to apartheid.

The massacre at Sharpeville stunned the world. At home, it pushed some young ANC activists to shift from nonviolent protest to armed struggle. Some leaders left South Africa to wage the battle for freedom from abroad. Others went underground. Among this last group was a young lawyer, Nelson Mandela.

## Nelson Mandela

Rolihlahla (raw lee LAH luh) Mandela was born in 1918 among the fertile valleys of the Transkei. His father was related to the ruler of the Thembu, a Xhosa-speaking people. As a boy, Mandela enjoyed stories told by the elders about the days before the whites came:

66Then our people lived peacefully, under the democratic rule of their kings and their councillors, and moved freely and confidently up and down the country. . . . Then the country was ours. We . . . operated our own government, we controlled our own armies, and we organized our own trade and commerce.99

At school, the boy heard tales not of his own people, who were dismissed as savages, but of white warriors. One day, he told his family, "My name is Nelson!" The teacher had given him that name, after Britain's bold admiral Lord Nelson. The boy gave up his Xhosa name Rolihlahla, which means "stirring up trouble." Both names, in fact, would suit Mandela.

**"Stirring up trouble."** Mandela grew up at a time when whites were imposing harsher laws on blacks. Outraged by the plundering of black lands and the restricting of black freedoms, he helped organize the ANC Youth League. With other league leaders, he mobilized young South Africans to take part in acts of civil disobedience against apartheid laws. In time, as government suppression grew, Mandela joined the ANC militants who called for armed struggle against the white regime.

**"An ideal for which I am prepared to die."** By 1964, Mandela had been arrested, tried, and condemned to life in prison for conspiracy against the government. At his trial, he declared:

▲  *Nelson Mandela*

66During my lifetime I have dedicated myself to the struggle of the African people. . . . I have cherished the ideal of a democratic and free society in which all persons live together in harmony and with equal opportunities. It is an ideal which I hope to live for and to achieve. But, if needs be, it is an ideal for which I am prepared to die.99

**A powerful symbol.** Mandela would remain in prison for 27 years. During much of that time, he was permitted only one half-hour visit and one incoming and one outgoing letter every six months. He could not talk to members of the press, and his writings could not be published.

Despite his enforced isolation, Mandela remained a popular leader and a powerful symbol of the struggle against apartheid. Just as he had listened to tales of ancient African warriors as a boy, so young South African children were raised on stories of Nelson Mandela, fighter for freedom. Inspired by his example, these young Africans carried on the struggle in his absence. Both in South Africa and abroad, demands grew for the release of Mandela and an end to apartheid. ▨

## A New South Africa

Over the decades, world attention was increasingly focused on South Africa. During the 1980s, a number of countries, including the United States, imposed economic sanctions on the white-ruled nation. They refused to trade with or invest in businesses there. South African athletes were banned from international sports events such as the Olympic Games. In 1984, the black Anglican bishop Desmond Tutu won the Nobel Peace Prize for his nonviolent opposition to apartheid.

Foreign boycotts hurt South Africa's economy. Even worse, protests and growing violence at home forced the government to impose a state of emergency in 1985. Many South African whites questioned the oppressive measures used by the government and began to call for reform.

**Reform.** By 1989, F. W. de Klerk, newly elected president of South Africa, boldy accepted the need for reform. He abandoned apartheid, repealed the segregation and pass laws, and held talks with the imprisoned Mandela. After lifting the ban on the ANC, he finally freed Mandela in 1990.

For the next four years, Mandela and de Klerk negotiated the terms on which South Africa would move from white rule to majority rule. In 1992, white voters overwhelmingly supported reforms that would allow equal rights for all.

**"Free at last!"** By 1994, Mandela and de Klerk had worked out an arrangement for the nation's first multiracial elections. While the world watched, black South Africans—long barred from voting—lined up with white voters to cast their ballots. They elected Nelson Mandela as the first president of a new democratic South Africa. In a speech to supporters, he echoed a phrase made famous by the African American leader Martin Luther King, Jr.: "We can loudly proclaim from the rooftops: free at last!"

Mandela offered a striking example to other African nations when he welcomed longtime political enemies into his government. If he could work with Afrikaners who had once tyrannized the black majority, perhaps other African leaders could learn to accept opposition and democratic, multiparty systems.

## Looking Ahead

The new government faced the difficult task of meeting its people's high expectations for change. Mandela had promised a better life to the black majority, which had so long been kept in poverty. Once in office, he had a hard time delivering looked-for improvements.

South Africa was a rich country with a strong industrial base. But it could afford only a limited amount of spending for new programs. Mandela soon realized that change would take decades, not just a few years.

The gap in income and education between blacks and whites remained large. Middle-class blacks welcomed the new era of equality, but millions of poor blacks lacked economic power.

Mandela enjoyed great prestige among black and white South Africans. But he would serve only one term as president. People wondered who could succeed a leader who had not only helped end apartheid but had gone on to unite black and white South Africans.

## Freedom for Southern Africa

The colonies of southern Africa were among the last to win independence. From the 1960s to the 1980s, the white-minority government of South Africa interfered to prevent neighboring colonies from gaining their freedom.

**Independence for Namibia.** In 1920, South Africa received German Southwest Africa as a mandate from the League of Nations. After World War II, the UN asked South Africa to prepare the territory for independence. South Africa refused. Instead, it backed the white minority, who imposed an oppressive apartheid regime.

By the 1960s, the Southwest African People's Organization (SWAPO) had turned to armed struggle to win independence. For years, SWAPO guerrillas battled South African troops. The struggle became part of the Cold War, with the Soviet Union and Cuba lending their support to SWAPO.

As the Cold War ground to a halt, an agreement was finally reached to hold free elections. In 1990, Namibia—as the new country was called—celebrated independence.

**Freedom for Portuguese colonies.** As Britain and France bowed to nationalist demands in their African possessions, Portugal clung fiercely to its colonies in southern Africa. During the 1960s, the Portuguese dictator António Salazar had no intention of letting Africans win freedom.

In Angola and Mozambique, nationalists turned to guerrilla warfare. Portugal responded by sending almost its entire army to defend its empire. After 15 years of fighting, however, many Portuguese army officers realized that the struggle could not be won. In Portugal, an army coup toppled the dictatorship of Salazar's successor, Marcelo Caetano, in 1974. A year later, Angola and Mozambique celebrated independence.

*Freedom for Namibia* Like many African peoples, Namibians waged a long armed struggle to win independence. Here, a group of Namibian women celebrate the birth of their nation in 1990. **Global Interaction** How did the Cold War affect Namibia's struggle for independence?

**Wars continue.** Independence did not end the fighting in Angola and Mozambique. Bitter civil wars, fueled by Cold War rivalries among the superpowers, raged for years in both countries.

Both South Africa and the United States had seen the struggles for freedom in southern Africa as a threat because liberation leaders were socialists. To undermine the new governments, South Africa aided rebel groups in both countries that wanted power themselves.

From 1975 to 1992, rebels in Mozambique starved and massacred tens of thousands of civilians. They killed teachers, burned health clinics, and destroyed schools in an effort to topple the government.

In Angola, a complicated power struggle dragged on for years. The Soviet Union helped one side in the struggle by financing more than 50,000 Cuban troops that went to fight in Angola. South Africa supported a rival group and even sent in its own troops. The United States, too, tried to undermine the Soviet-backed government. The war staggered to a halt in 1987. By 1990, both Cuban and South African troops had withdrawn. In both Mozambique and Angola, the end of the Cold War and of apartheid in South Africa helped bring peace after long, agonizing civil wars. Ahead lay the struggle to rebuild.

## SECTION 4 REVIEW

1. **Identify** (a) Nelson Mandela, (b) ANC, (c) Sharpeville, (d) Desmond Tutu, (e) F. W. de Klerk, (f) SWAPO.
2. Describe three effects of apartheid on South Africa.
3. Why did the South African government end apartheid?
4. (a) Why did Portuguese colonies in Africa have a hard time winning independence? (b) What role did Cold War rivalries play in southern Africa?
5. *Critical Thinking* **Recognizing Causes and Effects** Why do you think economic sanctions helped pressure South Africa to end apartheid?
6. *ACTIVITY* Create a mural portraying the struggle for majority rule in South Africa.

# 5 Africa: Past and Present

## Guide for Reading

- How have African nations helped to shape the UN?
- How are urbanization and modernization affecting social patterns?
- What role do Christianity and Islam play in African societies?

Since the 1950s, Africa has experienced extraordinary changes. It has thrown off the yoke of colonialism and given birth to dozens of new nations. Outside the political sphere, Africans felt the impact of modernization, with its accompanying social upheavals. With independence, noted Kofi Awoonor, a writer from Ghana, "We have had to rediscover ourselves as people."

## African Nations and the World Community

African nations emerged into a world dominated by powerful blocs. As new nations, however, they hoped to carve out their own position in the world. They did so in part through regional and global organizations.

**Organization of African Unity.** At independence, African nations maintained links with the Pan-African movement. While they did not pursue the Pan-Africanist idea of a United States of Africa, African leaders did try to build bridges among their nations.

In 1963, Africans set up the Organization of African Unity (OAU). It encouraged cooperation among members and supported independence for areas still under colonial rule. Members pledged to respect one another's borders and to seek peaceful settlement of disputes.

*Interpreting a Chart* African writers have won world acclaim. Many write about the conflict between traditional and western ways. Others have challenged the corruption of the new African elite or exposed the evils of apartheid. ■ *Which authors wrote in African languages? How would this help promote Africans' pride in their heritage?*

# Modern African Writers

| Writer | Career Highlights | Major Works | Major Themes or Subjects | Influence Today |
|---|---|---|---|---|
| **Chinua Achebe**<br>Nigeria<br> | Writer, radio broadcaster, university professor | **Novels**<br>*Things Fall Apart,*<br>*A Man of the People* | Encounters between people of different cultures; effects of imperialism | His use of Ibo in his writings encouraged other Africans to write in African languages |
| **Nadine Gordimer**<br>South Africa<br>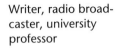 | Published first story at age 15; Nobel Prize for Literature (1991) | **Novels**<br>*The Lying Days,*<br>*Burger's Daughter,*<br>*My Son's Story*<br>**Short Stories**<br>*Friday's Footprint and Other Stories* | Impact of world events on individuals; injustice of apartheid | Helped raise world consciousness to evils of apartheid |
| **Naguib Mahfouz**<br>Egypt<br> | Government official, journalist; Nobel Prize for Literature (1988) | **Novels**<br>*Midaq Alley,*<br>*Cairo Trilogy,*<br>*Miramar* | Sensitivity to human suffering; opposition to repressive governments; struggles for freedom and independence | Popularized novel as literary form in Arab world; used fiction as political commentary |
| **Sembene Ousmane**<br>Senegal<br> | Fisherman, plumber, stevedore, union leader, filmmaker | **Novels**<br>*God's Bits of Wood,*<br>*Tribal Scars*<br>**Films**<br>*Black Girl,*<br>*The Money Order,*<br>*Ceddo* | Need for political and social change; conflict between tradition and modernism; tensions among African groups | His use of African languages in films encouraged other African filmmakers to do the same; set the example of using films to fight for reform |
| **Okot p'Bitek**<br>Uganda<br> | Teacher, member Ugandan national soccer team, professor, director of Uganda National Theater and Cultural Center | **Poetry**<br>*Song of Lawino*<br>**Nonfiction**<br>*African Religions and Western Scholarship*<br>**Folk Tales**<br>*Hare and Hornbill* | Clash between African and western values; need to preserve traditional culture | Uganda's best-known poet; founded Gulu Arts Festival; helped preserve traditional songs and poetry |
| **Wole Soyinka**<br>Nigeria<br> | Journal editor, actor, founder of national theater; first African writer to win Nobel Prize for Literature (1986) | **Poetry**<br>*Poems from Prison*<br>**Plays**<br>*The Trials of Brother Jero, Kongi's Harvest, Requiem for a Futurologist* | Need for social change and human rights; conflict between traditional and western values | Leading Nigerian writer; uses his influence to work for justice and political reform |

In the OAU, African nations discussed and tried to settle common problems. The OAU set up the African Development Bank to channel much-needed investment capital from foreign sources into development programs. Its impact was limited, however, because it had no power to enforce decisions and opposed interfering in the internal affairs of member states.

**The UN.** New African nations took pride in joining the United Nations. They contributed to and benefited from the UN and its many agencies. Africans served in UN peacekeeping missions around the world.

Along with other emerging countries, African nations focused world attention on issues important to them, including health care, literacy, and economic development. They also called for an end to racism and imperialism. They pressed nations of the global North to deal with problems such as the unequal distribution of wealth and technology. For example, they sought higher prices for their exports, lower tariffs against their agricultural goods, and more investment capital.

**Disaster relief.** The UN—along with rich industrial nations and private agencies like the International Red Cross, Britain's Oxfam, and the French organization Doctors Without Borders—has responded to famine and other crises in Africa. In the early 1960s, UN peacekeepers helped stop the fighting in Zaire. Later UN efforts helped save millions from starvation in Biafra during Nigeria's civil war.

Some international efforts had limited success. In the early 1990s, UN forces, with massive American help, brought food to Somalians caught up in a civil war. Outsiders, however, could not restore peace. In the end, the UN and most foreigners withdrew, concluding that only Somalians could solve their own problems. In Burundi and Rwanda, the UN again fed refugees of civil wars but could not stop bloody massacres or bring peace.

## Old and New Patterns

In Africa, as elsewhere, modernization and urbanization disrupted traditional ways of life. Colonial rule had also undermined African traditions by promoting westernization. Today, people across Africa are faced with hard choices.

On the one hand, they want the high standard of living, advanced technology, and other benefits of modern societies. On the other, they value and want to preserve their own traditions.

**Urbanization.** By 1990, a quarter of all Africans lived in towns and cities. That number was expected to double by 2000.

City life weakened traditional cultures. It ruptured the ethnic and kinship ties that held together rural communities. Young urban dwellers who returned to their villages often scorned village customs and traditions. At the same time, many educated Africans looked to their past with pride. Some scholars were urging governments to base policies on African experiences and solutions rather than on western models.

**Women.** Women took part in the great migration to the cities. There, an educated few joined the elite, winning civil service jobs or entering modern professions. Most urban women, however, struggled to feed and keep their families together in poverty-stricken urban slums.

The majority of African women continue to live in rural areas, where they make up the bulk of the population. With the migration of men to cities, these rural women took on sole responsibility for caring and providing for their children. They planted and harvested food crops, collected wood and water, and prepared food. In some areas, they also found work growing cash crops on large farms. In West Africa, their historical role as market traders allowed some women to gain considerable economic power.

After independence, most African nations drafted constitutions that were generous in the area of women's rights. Often, however, these rights have not been enforced, and many aspects of women's lives are still controlled by traditional laws. A small but powerful group of highly educated women have worked to make governments more responsive to women's issues.

In the area of education, tremendous strides were made in providing girls with elementary school education. But few girls continued on to high school. Instead, they were required to stay at home to help their mothers with farm work and household chores. Illiteracy among African women stands at more than 70 percent on the average—and more than 90 percent in rural areas.

**Diverse Traditions** *Diversity marks the religious practices of Africa's people. Sometimes, religious practices intermingle, as in this Catholic church in Ivory Coast, where dancers in traditional dress take part in the service.* **Religions and Value Systems** *How might the incorporation of traditional practices help to strengthen the Catholic Church in a nation such as Ivory Coast?*

**Religion.** Today, as in the past, Africa is home to diverse religious traditions. Colonialism and modernization disrupted many traditional practices, but in rural areas, people remain faithful to their old religious beliefs. They seek the help of ancestors and others in the spirit world who serve as intermediaries for the Creator God.

Centuries ago, Christianity and Islam took root in parts of Africa. Since the population boom of the 1950s, both faiths have grown. The Catholic Church accounts for almost three fourths of African Christians. However, many other Africans belong to Orthodox or Protestant sects.

At independence, African clergy replaced white Christian missionaries. Church leaders have risked their lives to stand up to dictators like Mobutu in Zaire and Idi Amin in Uganda. In South Africa, as you have read, Bishop Desmond Tutu preached against apartheid.

**Islamic revival.** Islam has long influenced the northern half of Africa and linked it to the Middle East. From North Africa, Islam also spread along trade routes into both East and West Africa. Nigeria has the largest Muslim population south of the Sahara.

In recent years, Muslim African nations have taken part in the Islamic revival that began in the Middle East. (See Chapter 18.) Its message of reform and call for social justice won a wide welcome. So, too, did its rejection of western influences.

Algeria's Islamic party did well in elections in 1992. The secular party that had ruled Algeria since independence feared an Islamic revolution like Iran's. It encouraged the military to seize power. The government then waged war on Islamic extremists whose attacks on politicians, scholars, and others created turmoil. More than 30,000 people were killed in the fighting, which brought the country to the brink of civil war.

## SECTION 5 REVIEW

1. **Identify** Organization of African Unity.
2. (a) How have African nations influenced the goals of the UN? (b) What role has the UN played in Africa?
3. (a) What effects did urbanization have on African traditions? (b) How have women's lives changed since independence?
4. (a) How have African Christian leaders worked for reform since independence? (b) How did Muslim African nations respond to the Islamic revival of recent years?
5. *Critical Thinking* **Analyzing Information** How does the OAU help to keep alive the idea of Pan-Africanism?
6. *ACTIVITY* Imagine that you are an African farm woman. Write a letter to the leaders of your government explaining why the government should provide you with education and technical training.

## CHAPTER REVIEW

### REVIEWING VOCABULARY

Review the following vocabulary from this chapter: *cash crop, ethnic group, socialism, capitalism, mixed economy, subsistence farmer, desertification, urbanization, apartheid.* Write sentences using each of these terms, leaving blanks where the terms would go. Exchange your sentences with another student and fill in the blanks on each other's lists.

### REVIEWING FACTS

1. What happened to the number of independent African nations following World War II?

2. How did artificial colonial borders create problems for newly independent African nations?

3. What caused the growth in foreign debt among many African nations?

4. Describe the cause and outcome of the civil war that began in the 1960s in Nigeria.

5. What events led to the end of white-minority rule in Rhodesia?

6. How did apartheid affect where black South Africans lived?

7. Describe the important event that occurred in South Africa in 1994.

# SKILLS FOR SUCCESS  ANALYZING CARTOGRAMS

### Relative Population of African Nations, 1990

= 5.4 million people

The cartogram does not show Africa's smallest nations.

Source: *The New State of the World Atlas*

A **cartogram** is a special-purpose map used to present statistics geographically. In most maps, the size of a country corresponds to its physical dimensions. In a cartogram, the size of a country is determined by a statistical feature, such as population.

Study the cartogram at left. Then, follow the steps to read and analyze the cartogram.

1. **Identify the subject of the cartogram.** As with any map, look first at the title and key. (a) What is the title of the cartogram? (b) In your own words, what information does the cartogram present? (c) What is the relationship between the size of a country and its population?

2. **Compare the cartogram with a conventional map.** A cartogram distorts the size and shape of countries. To recognize the distortion of a cartogram, you will need to compare it to a conventional land area map. Compare the cartogram to the map on page 606. Name one country that appears bigger on the cartogram than on the map, and one country that appears smaller on the cartogram than on the map.

3. **Analyze relationships among the data.** How might the problems faced by a country with small area and large population differ from those faced by a country with large area and large population?

## REVIEWING CHAPTER THEMES

Review the "Focus On" questions at the start of this chapter. Then select *three* of those questions and answer them, using information from the chapter.

## CRITICAL THINKING

1. **Recognizing Causes and Effects** Young African nations faced many difficult problems. (a) Which problems were related to internal forces? (b) Which problems were caused by external forces? Explain.

2. **Linking Past and Present** "We have to rediscover ourselves as people," said Ghanaian writer Kofi Awoonor. What did he mean by this? Give three examples from the chapter to illustrate the statement.

3. **Making Inferences** Why were ample resources not a guarantee of a healthy economy in some African nations?

## ANALYZING PRIMARY SOURCES

Use the quotation on page 517 to answer the following questions.

1. Which three groups of casualties did Clark mention in the first stanza?

2. Restate the second stanza in your own words.

3. Would this poem apply to wars other than the Nigerian civil war? Explain.

## FOR YOUR PORTFOLIO

**CREATING AN ALMANAC** Work with classmates to research and write an Almanac of African Nations. Begin by holding a meeting to select the nations to include. Then find almanacs in the library and study them. Decide which statistics you will include in your almanac. Use outside sources to compile the information. Then write up each entry. Finally, assemble the pages in your almanac and place it in the classroom where other students can use it.

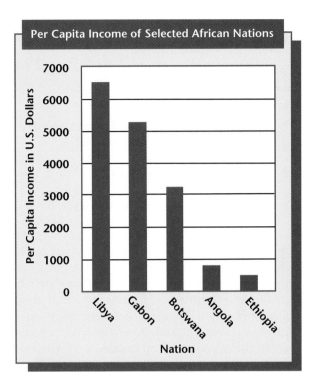

Per Capita Income of Selected African Nations

## ANALYZING GRAPHS

Use the graph and information from the chapter to answer the following questions.

1. Which nation on the graph has the highest per capita income? The lowest?

2. What political problems help explain the low per capita incomes of Ethiopia and Angola?

3. The economies of Libya and Gabon depend heavily on oil exports. How would a drop in the world price of oil affect per capita income in those two nations?

### INTERNET ACTIVITY

**EVALUATING ECONOMIC POLICIES**
Use the Internet to research how African nations today are working to improve their economies and standards of living. Then write a brief analysis of a particular nation's economic plan. Explain why you think that plan will or will not be successful, and why.

# Latin America

## (1945–Present)

## CHAPTER OUTLINE

Pablo Neruda was outraged. He had worked to help Gabriel González Videla get elected president of Chile in 1946. González Videla had pledged to promote economic and social justice. Once in office, though, he went back on his promises. He cracked down on workers, censored the press, and even persecuted former supporters like Neruda.

Neruda was a highly respected poet and political activist. He wanted to improve the lot of the poor, end injustice, and reduce foreign domination. Faced with González Videla's betrayal, Neruda took an unusual revenge. He included the Chilean president among the villains in his *Canto general*.

In this series of poems, Neruda created an epic for the Americas. He recounts a series of betrayals—from the Spanish conquest to the broken promises of independence that denied equality to the majority. Finally, his accusing finger comes around to González Videla:

> "He has *betrayed* everything.
>   He climbed like a rat to my
>     people's shoulders
>   and there, gnawing on my country's
>     sacred
>   flag, he twitches his rodent's tail
>   telling landowners and foreigners,
>     the owners
>   of Chile's subsoil: 'Drink all this
>     nation's blood.'"

Neruda goes on to deliver a ringing call to the people of Chile:

> "Break the bonds, open the walls
>     that enclose you!
>   Crush the ferocious passage
>     of the rat that governs
>   from the Palace."

Neruda's poem points up a cycle of dictatorship shared by many Latin American nations.

Like other world regions, Latin America does not lend itself to easy generalizations. Its 33 countries are a complex mosaic of people and cultures. Still, Latin American nations have shared similar problems. They have tried to sustain economic growth and overcome a legacy of repression and poverty.

**FOCUS ON** these questions as you read:

■ **Economics and Technology**
  How did Latin American nations evolve economic policies to meet changing needs?

■ **Political and Social Systems**
  Why did Latin American nations have trouble preserving democratic governments?

■ **Continuity and Change**
  How did colonialism and independence influence present-day Latin America?

■ **Global Interaction**
  How did the Cold War affect Latin America?

■ **Impact of the Individual**
  How did leaders like Juan Perón and Fidel Castro reshape their nations?

## TIME AND PLACE

***Enduring Folkways of Rural Life*** *Latin American folk traditions have deep roots that can be seen in music, dance, handicrafts, clothing, and religious festivals. This handmade miniature from Mexico shows a bride and groom in a wedding cart being serenaded by a band. Like other centuries-old rural customs, the wedding cart is still used in parts of modern Mexico. But in Latin America, as in other developing regions, older ways of life are increasingly giving way to modern, urban conditions.* **Continuity and Change** *Why do you think that customs change as people move to urban areas?*

## HUMANITIES LINK

***Art History*** Marisol, *The Family* (page 538).
***Literature*** In this chapter, you will encounter passages from the following works of literature: Pablo Neruda, *Canto general* (page 532); Carolina Maria de Jesus, *Child of the Dark* (page 534); Marta Traba, *Mothers and Shadows* (pages 556–557).

| 1948 Organization of American States formed | 1962 Cuban missile crisis | 1973 Augusto Pinochet comes to power in Chile | 1980s Debates over Brazilian rain forest | 1993 NAFTA signed |

| 1945 | 1960 | 1975 | 1990 | PRESENT |

# 1 Forces Shaping Modern Latin America

## Guide for Reading

- What conditions contributed to unrest in Latin America?

- How did the military, the Catholic Church, and Marxist ideology influence political developments in the region?

- How did governments try to promote economic development?

- What forces have contributed to social change in Latin America?

- **Vocabulary** *import substitution, agribusiness*

Like millions of poor people, Carolina Maria de Jesus migrated from the country to the city in the postwar era. For her, life in the slums of São Paulo, Brazil, was filled with hardship. Sometimes she found a job to earn money to feed her family. At other times she combed garbage for paper and other goods to sell. In her published diary, *Child of the Dark*, De Jesus described her daily struggle to move her family out of poverty:

66May 26. At dawn it was raining. I only have four cruzeiros [coins], a little food left over from yesterday, and some bones. I went to look for water to boil the bones. There is still a little macaroni and I made a soup for the children. I saw a neighbor washing beans. How envious I became. It's been two weeks that I haven't washed clothes because I haven't any soap.99

After years of war and economic dependence, Latin American nations often faced problems that mirrored those of emerging nations in Africa or Asia—rapid population growth, hunger, illiteracy, political instability, and authoritarian governments. In Latin America, as elsewhere, each country pursued its own course toward modernization.

## A Diverse Region

Latin America stretches across a geographically diverse region from Mexico, Central America, and the Caribbean through South America. (See the map on page 644.) It includes 33 independent countries that range from tiny island nations like Grenada and Haiti to giant Brazil, a nation almost as large as the United States.

Conquest, immigration, and intermarriage made Latin America culturally diverse. After 1492, Europeans imposed their civilization on Native Americans and later brought millions of Africans to the region. As these populations mingled, they created vital new cultures. Since the late 1800s, immigrants from Europe and Asia have further contributed to the diversity. Today, people of Indian descent are still the majority population in Mexico, Guatemala, Peru, and Bolivia. Brazil has more people of African descent than any other nation in Latin America. While Spanish is the dominant language of the region, Portuguese, French, English, Creole, and hundreds of Native American languages and African dialects are also spoken.

Most Latin American nations won freedom in the 1800s. However, many Caribbean islands and a few mainland areas—including Jamaica and Belize—did not gain independence until after 1960. (See page 410.) Despite vast differences, many Latin American nations shared common problems as they pushed to modernize.

## Sources of Unrest

In the decades after World War II, uprisings and revolution shook much of Latin America. They grew in part out of changes brought by modernization and reflected the failure of governments to reform deep-rooted inequalities.

**Gulf between rich and poor.** Since colonial days, a key feature of Latin America has been the uneven distribution of wealth. In most

**ISSUES** *For* **TODAY**

The gulf between rich and poor has fed unrest in many Latin American nations. How can a country reduce poverty without threatening its economic stability?

countries, a tiny elite controlled the land, mines, businesses, and factories. The wealthy few opposed reforms that threatened their economic power. A growing gulf between rich and poor fueled discontent in the postwar era.

**Social classes.** Poverty was linked to the social structure that had survived since colonial times. The upper classes were mostly descended from Europeans. The great majority of the population—the urban and rural poor—were a combination of mestizos, Native Americans, or African Americans.

By the mid-1900s, two social classes were emerging as important forces. As Latin American cities grew, the middle class and urban working class expanded. These classes were less tied to particular ethnic groups than the old aristocracy and peasantry. Both had their own hopes for progress and prosperity.

**Population and poverty.** In Latin America, as elsewhere around the world, the population grew as more people gained access to medical services. The population explosion contributed to poverty. Between 1930 and 1985, for example, the populations of Brazil, the Dominican Republic, and Mexico increased by more than four times. Venezuela's population rose from 3 million to more than 17 million. Growth rates in some countries slowed during the 1980s, but overall populations kept climbing because a large proportion of the people were young and just starting their own families.

Latin America's population, which reached 400 million in 1990, was expected to top 600 million by the year 2000.

In rural areas, where most people were peasant farmers, rapid population growth put stress on the land. A family might own a small plot for growing food. But the majority worked for low wages on the estates of wealthy landlords who held the best land. Although the entire family worked hard, many had to borrow money from their landlords just to get by from harvest to harvest. Burdened by this so-called debt slavery, they were tied to the land unless they ran away to the cities. In Central America and the Andes region, many Indians practiced traditional subsistence farming in isolated villages.

**Urbanization.** Pressure on the land was one cause for the great migration that sent millions of peasants to the cities. Today, 70 percent of Latin Americans live in cities.

Some newcomers found jobs in factories, offices, or stores. Many more survived by working odd jobs such as doing laundry or mending shoes. Others scavenged at the city garbage dump. In the shantytowns that ringed Latin American cities, people lived in tin-roofed shacks without electricity, sewage, or other services. Yet because they were near urban centers, they were more likely to attend school or have access to health care than the rural poor. As a result, the children of the city poor were often in a better position to move ahead than rural children.

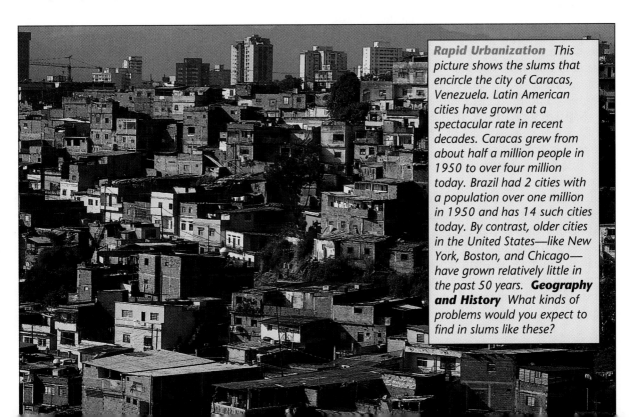

*Rapid Urbanization* This picture shows the slums that encircle the city of Caracas, Venezuela. Latin American cities have grown at a spectacular rate in recent decades. Caracas grew from about half a million people in 1950 to over four million today. Brazil had 2 cities with a population over one million in 1950 and has 14 such cities today. By contrast, older cities in the United States—like New York, Boston, and Chicago—have grown relatively little in the past 50 years. **Geography and History** What kinds of problems would you expect to find in slums like these?

## Reform, Repression, or Revolution?

Most Latin American countries had constitutions modeled on those of the United States or France. On paper, they protected the rights of individuals. Yet building real democracy was difficult in countries plagued by poverty and inequality.

**Competing ideologies.** In the postwar era, various groups pressed for economic and social reforms. They included liberals, socialists, students, labor leaders, peasant organizers, and Catholic priests and nuns. While differing over how to achieve their goals, all wanted to improve conditions for the poor. Most called for schools, housing, health care, and land reform.

Conservative forces, however, resisted reforms that would undermine their power. Among those who supported the status quo were the military, the traditional landed aristocracy, and the growing business middle class. These elite groups were often allied to foreign investors and multinational corporations. Conflict between conservatives and reformers contributed to political instability in many nations.

**Military regimes.** In the mid-1900s, military leaders ruled much of South and Central America. Like the caudillos of the 1800s, military rulers most often served conservative interests. However, some supported modest social and economic reforms, in part because an increasing number of officers came from the lower middle or working classes.

In the 1960s and 1970s, as social unrest increased, military governments seized power in Argentina, Brazil, Chile, Uruguay, and elsewhere. Claiming the need to restore order, they imposed harsh regimes. They outlawed political parties, censored the press, and closed down universities. In Argentina and Chile, the military imprisoned and executed thousands of dissidents. In both these countries, as well as other places such as El Salvador, regimes organized illegal "death squads" to murder opponents.

Military rulers tried to boost growth and solve economic problems by sponsoring capitalism. In Chile, General Augusto Pinochet (pee noh SHAY), who ruled from 1973 to 1990, promoted foreign investment and appointed economists trained in the United States to increase efficiency. The Chilean economy did expand. In general, however, most military regimes were unable to solve basic problems.

**The threat of revolution.** During the 1960s and 1970s, guerrillas and urban terrorists battled military governments in many Latin American countries. Revolutionary groups used bombings, kidnappings, and assassinations as tools against military regimes.

The leaders of many of these revolutionary groups supported Marxist goals. Only a socialist revolution, they said, would be able to end inequalities. Marxism won support among both peasants and urban workers, as well as intellectuals. Still, many revolutionaries were

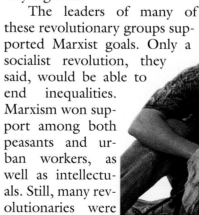

▶ *Leftist guerrilla in El Salvador*

**536   Chapter 20**

The Power of the Military  Military officers ruled many Latin American nations in the 1960s and 1970s. In other countries, elected leaders stayed in power only with the army's support. In this painting, The Parrots, Colombian artist Beatriz González uses the repeating image of a civilian president flanked by generals. **Art and Literature**  What point do you think the artist is making by repeating the images of the president and his military supporters?

motivated more by nationalism and local concerns than by the theories of Karl Marx. They condemned economic and cultural domination by the United States.

During the Cold War, the spread of Marxism complicated moderate reform efforts. Conservatives tended to view any effort at reform as a communist threat.

**Revival of democracy.**  By the mid-1980s, the debt crisis, inflation, and unpopularity led military leaders to step aside. Argentina, Brazil, Chile, and other countries held multiparty elections to restore civilian governments. Still, elections alone could not solve underlying problems. Since the 1980s, some elected governments have made modest progress, but world economic forces often affected successes. Whether stable democratic governments would survive remained to be seen.

## Economic Development

Except during the Great Depression of the 1930s, most Latin American nations experienced economic growth between 1900 and the 1960s. Their economies were tied into the global economic order, dependent on the industrial world. Many relied on the export of a single crop or commodity, so they were especially hard hit if harvests failed or demand declined. By the 1960s, Latin America faced increased competition from emerging nations elsewhere seeking to export their crops and commodities.

**Economic nationalism.**  The trend toward economic nationalism continued after World War II. (See Chapter 12.) To reduce dependence on imported goods, many Latin American governments had begun to set up

their own industries in the 1940s. Under this policy, known as import substitution, governments encouraged local manufacturers to produce goods at home to replace imports. In time, many nations produced consumer goods such as textiles or refrigerators. They also set up auto assembly plants, although the parts were mostly imported from overseas.

Efforts to promote industry had mixed success. The middle class prospered, but life did not improve for most people. Many new industries were inefficient and needed government help or foreign capital to survive. Some home products were expensive or poorly made compared to imported products. Also, industry did not expand rapidly enough to produce new jobs for a rapidly growing population. Eventually, governments returned to promoting agricultural exports.

**Expanding agriculture.**  In the past 50 years, large amounts of land have been opened up for farming through irrigation and clearing forests. Much of the best farmland belonged to agribusinesses, or large commercial farms that were owned by multinational corporations. They used modern technology, tractors, and irrigation to develop the land and set up food-processing plants. In Brazil and Central America, developers cleared tropical forests and opened new lands for farming and grazing. As you will read, this development had environmental and human costs.

Commercial agriculture also changed the food habits of many people. Advertisers encouraged people to eat hamburgers instead of tortillas and beans. Many traditional foods were no longer grown, as much land was turned over to growing crops for export. As a result, more food had to be imported, at a high cost.

**Crisis and reform.** In the 1980s, Latin American nations were buffeted by economic storms, including higher oil costs, rising interest rates, and a worldwide recession. Nations that had borrowed to develop industry were hurt when interest rates rose. (See Chapter 15.)

To dig out of the debt crisis, nations like Mexico and Brazil had to swallow bitter economic reforms. They cut spending on social programs, raised prices on goods, stopped financing local businesses, and opened their markets to foreign companies. Eventually, most governments got their debt payments under control.

By the 1990s, many nations were enjoying renewed economic growth. Still, for most people, standards of living had fallen. Foreign investments did bring new business, but wages remained low. After all, the chief reason multinational corporations built factories in Latin America was to benefit from cheap labor.

## Changing Social Patterns

In Latin America, as elsewhere, urbanization brought social upheaval. City life weakened the extended family of rural villages, replacing it with the smaller nuclear family. Family members no longer worked the land for food but had to earn cash. To support their families, women

**The Family** The Venezuelan artist Marisol has become world famous for mixed media, that is, using a mix of three-dimensional materials to create a single image. In her 1961 work The Family, members of a poor family are painted on separate slabs of wood and set against the backdrop of an actual door. Although the work reflects the makeshift shanties common in slums, the expressions on the children's faces suggest a sense of hope for the future. **Art and Literature** How does Marisol suggest the strength of the mother?

took jobs outside the home. Often, families sent their daughters to the city to work as maids, while their sons stayed home to work on the family farm.

In the struggle to survive in the city, some families fell apart. In large cities like Rio de Janeiro, thousands of runaway or abandoned children roamed the streets. Many were caught up in crime and violence.

**Women.** The wars of independence had not improved the status of women during the 1800s. Their role in public life was limited, and they had few legal rights. In this century, women campaigned for equality, including the right to vote. By 1961, they had won the vote throughout the Americas. By the 1990s, women moved into the political arena in small but growing numbers. Both Argentina and Nicaragua had had women as presidents, while Benedita da Silva became the first black woman elected to the Brazilian congress. The fact that "the daughter of a washwoman from a shantytown" could be elected to congress, Da Silva said, was a hopeful sign of change.

Women's status varied according to class and race. All women had responsibilities in the home and for child care. Upper-class women, though, had access to education and professional careers and could hire servants to care for their homes and children. Rural women of Indian or African descent faced prejudice and poverty. They lacked schooling and basic health care, and often labored for low pay.

A peasant woman from El Salvador described her life in the fields. She began harvesting crops when she was 16 years old. Part of each year, she and other women picked coffee. Then, she explained, they would move on to the cotton fields:

66The poisons they use in the fields are very strong and we're always having to take people off to the hospital. They'd give you two and a half sacks as a quota for every day and if you didn't manage it, they didn't pay you anything. Men have always been paid 5 colones more than women or children and we all do exactly the same work.99

When women organized, they became an effective force for change. To protect their families and communities, some peasant women campaigned successfully for schools and health care. In Argentina and elsewhere, women banded together to protest human rights violations by brutal military governments. (See page 553.) Some set up mutual aid networks. During the harsh Pinochet years in Chile, poor women in Santiago organized food kitchens that collected food and served meals to their community. Other groups protested violence against women or challenged the subordinate position of women within the family.

**Religion.** The Catholic Church remained a major influence throughout Latin America. Traditionally, it was a conservative force tied to the ruling class. During the Mexican Revolution, for example, the Church denounced changes that threatened its traditional position and wealth.

Within the Church, however, some people had always spoken up for the poor. During the 1960s and 1970s, a number of priests, nuns, and church workers crusaded for social justice and an end to poverty. Their movement became known as liberation theology. (See page 423.) These activists saw Jesus as a "liberator of the poor." They urged the Church to become a force for reform. Many joined the struggle against oppressive governments. Some became the object of violence themselves. In El Salvador, for example, Archbishop Oscar Romero was assassinated by right-wing death squads.

Some evangelical Protestant groups won a growing following among the poor. Their message, which emphasized the power of faith, had an especially strong appeal among women, who then brought other family members into the faith.

## SECTION 1 REVIEW

1. **Define** (a) import substitution, (b) agribusiness.
2. Describe four conditions that fed unrest in Latin America.
3. (a) What led the military leaders to take control in many Latin American nations? (b) Why did Marxism appeal to some people?
4. (a) Describe two policies Latin American governments adopted to build their economies. (b) Were these policies successful? Why or why not?
5. What were the goals of liberation theology?
6. *Critical Thinking* **Applying Information** Women's movements in Latin America have adopted the slogan "Democracy in the country and in the home." How have women worked for these twin goals?
7. *ACTIVITY* Organize a debate around the following proposition: "In the long run, the rise of agribusiness will probably be a positive development."

# 2 Latin America, the United States, and the World

## Guide for Reading

- What was the impact of the Cuban Revolution?

- What policies did the United States pursue in Latin America?

- What issues have linked Latin America to the world?

"The duty of every revolutionary is to make revolution," declared Cuban dictator Fidel Castro in 1962. After bringing sweeping changes to his island nation, he vowed to export his communist revolution to other nations in Latin America. During the Cold War, Castro's call for revolution had an enormous impact on relations between Latin American nations and their powerful neighbor the United States.

Throughout the century, Latin American nations tried to limit United States influence and exercise greater independence. By the time the Cold War ended, they had carved out new relations in the larger global arena.

## Impact of the Cold War

Between 1933 and 1945, the United States pursued the Good Neighbor Policy, greatly improving relations in the Western Hemisphere. (See page 324.) During the Cold War, however, the United States often saw Latin American reform movements as communist threats. It backed right-wing, anti-communist dictators. At times, it even helped topple leftist leaders.

In Guatemala, for example, a leftist, Jacobo Arbenz, won election in 1950. When his land-reform program threatened United States-owned businesses, the United States helped the army oust Arbenz in 1954. Latin American nations, opposed to foreign intervention, protested this action.

Despite the furor, the United States intervened elsewhere in the hemisphere when it felt its interests were in danger. During the Cold War, Cuba became the chief focus of United States concern.

## Revolution in Cuba

In 1898, Cuba won independence from Spain but was occupied by United States forces until 1902. Over the years, the United States became the chief purchaser of Cuba's major export, sugar, and United States investors bought up Cuban sugar plantations and mills. By the 1930s, the Cuban economy was heavily dependent on the United States. The United States also influenced Cuban politics and for years supported the dictator Fulgencio Batista.

**Castro.** In the 1950s, a young lawyer, Fidel Castro, rallied forces opposed to the corrupt Batista regime. By 1959, Castro had led his tiny guerrilla army to victory. Cubans cheered the bearded young rebel as a hero. For many, the joy soon wore off as Castro introduced radical reforms that turned Cuba into a communist state. He nationalized foreign-owned sugar plantations and businesses. He put most land under government control and distributed the rest to peasant farmers.

While Castro imposed harsh authoritarian rule, he did improve conditions for the poor. During the 1960s, Cuba raised its literacy rate, provided basic health care for all, and backed equality for women. But Castro's revolution angered middle-class Cubans. As in other communist countries, critics were jailed or silenced. Hundreds of thousands of Cubans fled to the United States. Castro's own sister, in exile in Miami, called Cuba "a prison surrounded by water."

**Bay of Pigs disaster.** The Cuban Revolution alarmed the United States, especially as Castro denounced "Yankee imperialism" and turned to the Soviet Union for support. In 1961, the United States backed a plot by anti-Castro exiles to invade Cuba and lead an uprising against Castro.

The poorly planned plot was a disaster. An invasion force landed at the Bay of Pigs in Cuba but was quickly crushed. News of the plot helped Castro rally Cuban popular opinion against foreign interference, and the defeat hurt the reputation of the United States.

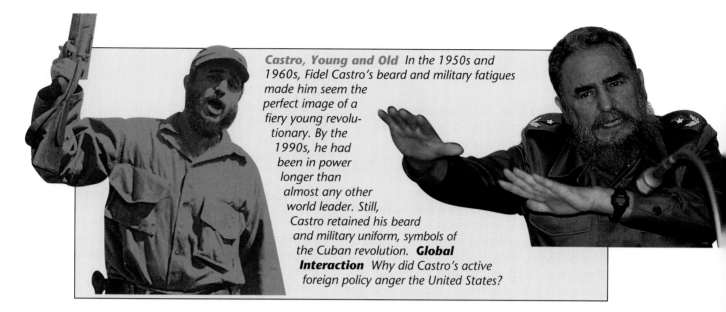

**Castro, Young and Old** In the 1950s and 1960s, Fidel Castro's beard and military fatigues made him seem the perfect image of a fiery young revolutionary. By the 1990s, he had been in power longer than almost any other world leader. Still, Castro retained his beard and military uniform, symbols of the Cuban revolution. **Global Interaction** Why did Castro's active foreign policy anger the United States?

**Cuban missile crisis.** In 1962, the United States imposed a trade embargo on Cuba. The embargo and the Bay of Pigs incident led Castro to seek even closer ties to the Soviet Union. Castro let the Soviets build nuclear missile bases in Cuba, just 90 miles (145 km) off the Florida coast. The threat of Soviet nuclear bases almost in its backyard outraged the United States and touched off a dangerous crisis.

In October 1962, President John Kennedy declared a naval blockade of Cuba. He demanded that the Soviets remove the weapons. For several days, the superpowers stood on the brink of nuclear war. In the end, Soviet leader Nikita Khrushchev backed down. He agreed to remove the missiles from Cuba but won a secret pledge from Kennedy not to invade Cuba. The United States retained its naval base at Guantánamo Bay, Cuba—the only United States military base on communist soil during the Cold War.

**Exporting revolution.** Over the next decades, the Soviets provided massive economic and military aid to Cuba and became its chief trading partner. Castro meanwhile tried to encourage revolution in other Latin American nations. Cuba also sent troops to Africa to help the socialist government of Angola. In response to Castro's policies, the United States continued its efforts to isolate Cuba and undermine Castro. Vowing to prevent "another Cuba," the United States aided anti-communist regimes elsewhere in Latin America.

**After the Cold War.** With the collapse of communism in the Soviet Union and Eastern Europe, Cuba lost its chief allies and trading partners. Even with the Cuban economy in shambles, however, Castro vowed to preserve communism. He encouraged tourism, allowed some features of a market economy, and welcomed foreign investment.

The UN urged the United States to end its embargo. But after years of suspicion and hostility, the United States was unwilling to negotiate with Cuba. Many Latin American leaders who disagreed with Castro's policies nevertheless criticized the United States for its position. They argued that Cuba no longer posed a threat to the hemisphere and that the United States had opened relations with communist governments in China and Vietnam.

## Colossus of the North

A complex network of ties linked Latin America and the United States. Like powerful nations in many times and places, the United States developed a sphere of influence that included a number of smaller neighboring states. The United States was the leading investor and trading partner for most nations in the hemisphere. Profits from United States-owned companies flowed from Latin America to the north. Many cultural influences drifted both north and south.

Still, the United States and its neighbors had very different views of one another. The United States saw itself as the defender of democracy and capitalism and the source of humanitarian aid. Many Latin Americans, however, felt that they lived under the shadow of the "colossus of the north." Mexican poet Octavio Paz wrote:

> 66North Americans are always among us, even when they ignore us or turn their back on us. Their shadow covers the whole hemisphere. It is the shadow of a giant.99

While Latin Americans admired the wealth and technology of the United States, they often resented its political, economic, military, and cultural influence.

**Regional organizations.** Despite disagreements, Latin American nations and the United States did work together. The Organization of American States (OAS) was formed in 1948 to promote democracy, economic cooperation, and human rights. Members pledged not to interfere "directly or indirectly, for any reason whatever, in the internal or external affairs of any other State." Although the United States often used its power to dominate the OAS, Latin American members did at times pursue an independent line.

The Castro revolution and other Cold War tensions led President Kennedy to launch the ambitious Alliance for Progress in 1961. The United States pledged billions in loans and investments. Latin American governments were to cooperate by introducing genuine reform programs. Jointly, their efforts would promote education and land reform, reduce inequality and poverty, weaken dictatorships, and help countries withstand revolutions.

The alliance accomplished little. Landowners and the business community in many countries opposed basic reforms. Over the decades, the United States did provide economic and other aid to Latin America, but never on the scale originally proposed by Kennedy.

**Intervention.** The United States did invest much aid in training and equipping the military in Latin America. It also returned to a policy of intervention, sending troops to the Dominican Republic in 1965, Grenada in 1983, and Panama in 1989. During the Cold War, it often used secret operations to preserve its power in the hemisphere.

After Salvador Allende (ah YEHN day), a socialist, was elected president of Chile, President Richard Nixon told officials to "make the [Chilean] economy scream." When a military coup overthrew Allende in 1973, the United States quietly lent its support to the coup. Later, it helped the military in Central American countries battle guerrillas. Such undercover operations aroused fierce resentments.

## Regional and Global Issues

By the end of the Cold War, many Latin American nations had reduced their dependence on the United States, although it remained their chief trading partner. They became increasingly tied to the global economy. Oil-rich Venezuela joined Arab nations in OPEC, while Brazil worked with coffee-exporting nations of Africa to support coffee prices.

Many Latin American nations increased trade and cultural links to European countries. Some exported food or minerals to Asian Pacific Rim nations. Japanese investments in Latin America, especially in Brazil, increased.

**Regional ties.** In Latin America, as elsewhere around the world, regional trading blocs gained importance in the 1990s. Such groups created larger markets by lowering trade barriers among neighboring countries.

In 1993, Mexico linked its economy to those of the United States and Canada through NAFTA. (See page 446.) Two years later, a new South American trading bloc, Mercosur, paved the way for increased trade among Argentina, Brazil, Paraguay, and Uruguay. The new groups operated alongside older blocs that linked Andean, Caribbean, or Central American nations. There was even talk of a hemisphere-wide free-trade zone by the year 2005.

**The drug wars.** Regional cooperation played an essential role in efforts to control the illegal drug trade. Indians in Colombia, Peru, and Bolivia had for centuries grown coca for their own uses. As drug use increased in the United States and elsewhere during the 1970s, criminal gangs began producing and smuggling ever-larger quantities of cocaine and other drugs for export.

In the 1980s, the United States declared a "war on drugs" and set out to halt the flow of drugs into the country. It pressed governments in Colombia, Bolivia, and Peru to destroy coca crops and move against drug lords who reaped huge profits from drug trafficking.

Latin American governments recognized the evils of the drug trade. After all, drug lords were bribing government officials and hiring assassins to kill judges, journalists, and others who spoke out against them. But many people in Latin America argued that the root of the problem was not the *supply* of drugs but the growing *demand* for illegal drugs in the United States. Still, countries from Mexico to Colombia accepted aid and cooperated with the United States in the antidrug fight.

**Migration.** Immigration from Latin America to the United States increased rapidly after the 1970s. Poverty, civil war, and repressive governments led many people to flee their homelands. Like earlier immigrants, they sought freedom and economic opportunity.

By the 1990s, the United States had more than 8 million immigrants from Mexico, Central America, the Caribbean, and South America. Many immigrants entered the United States legally and eventually became citizens. A large number, however, were illegal immigrants, which created resentment in the United States. In the 1990s, pressure increased in the United States to halt illegal immigration, deny services to illegal aliens, and return aliens to their country of origin.

### Development Versus the Environment: No Easy Answers

Environmental protection also raised troubling issues for Latin America and the world. Developing nations insisted that they needed to exploit their land and other resources if they wanted economic growth. "You cannot talk ecology to people who are struggling to survive," said a Brazilian delegate to the Earth Summit. (See page 421.) Leaders of developing nations pointed out that western powers had long since cleared many of their forests and mined their lands. What right, they asked, did industrial nations have to tell them to stop developing their resources?

The most widely publicized issue was the rapid destruction of the Amazon rain forest, which occupies more than a million square miles in the heart of Brazil. It is rich in mineral re-

**Drug Wars** *Efforts to stop the drug trade have met many obstacles. Often, drug traffickers are able to bribe judges, police, and army officers. At other times, they have murdered officials outright. Still, governments have made a major effort to halt the flow of illegal drugs. Above, a Colombian soldier guards a luxurious house seized from a drug trafficker. Below, Colombian troops burn more than two tons of captured cocaine.* **Global Interaction** *What does the drug trade show about global interaction?*

sources for economic growth. It also could provide land to millions of landless peasants. Since the 1930s, Brazil has tried to open up this vast area to development. By the 1970s and 1980s, vast tracts of tropical forest were being bulldozed and burned for farms, cattle ranches, highways, and even newly planned cities.

Environmentalists argued that deforestation had enormous costs. They called the Amazon rain forest "the lungs of the world" because it plays a key role in absorbing poisonous carbon dioxide from the air and releasing essential oxygen. It has been home to 15 million species of plants and animals, which have been threatened by development. Some forms of plant life might even hold cures for diseases.

***Another Rain Forest*** *Some countries have made strong efforts to preserve their rain forests. Costa Rica, in Central America, has had some success by turning its rain forest areas into tourist attractions. With ecological tourism, or "ecotourism," visitors hike through rain forests led by a knowledgeable guide without damaging the fragile environment.* **Geography and History** *Describe one way in which the United States has tried to preserve natural environments.*

Rapid development has also meant disaster for many indigenous peoples. Isolation had protected bands of self-sufficient forest dwellers for centuries. Land-hungry farmers, speculators, or foreign mining companies converged on the forest, threatening these ancient ways of life. Many Indians died of strange diseases introduced by the newcomers or were killed in conflicts provoked by impatient developers.

Debate on the rain forest heated up in the 1980s. In 1988, a murder in a small Brazilian village revealed the explosive nature of the issue.

## A Man of Courage

The night was hot and muggy in Xapuri, a town along the Amazon River in northern Brazil. Francisco "Chico" Mendes, a leader of the local rubber tappers union, had just finished playing dominoes with friends. Dinner was ready. But first, he wanted to cool off at an outdoor water tap.

Mendes never got his dinner. As he stepped out of his small house, he was felled by a shotgun blast.

The murder of Chico Mendes in December 1988 was just another in a series of violent attacks on union activists. In fact, Mendes, like other union leaders, had been living for months under a death threat. But reaction to the murder of this once-obscure rubber tapper was worldwide. Mendes had become a hero to those struggling to save the world's largest remaining tropical rain forest.

**Saving a way of life.** Mendes was an unlikely hero for environmentalists. His chief interest was his small union. Rubber tappers collected raw latex from trees in the rubber plantations of the Amazon rain forest. They worked long hours for low pay. Because Brazil's rubber industry was no longer profitable, ranchers wanted to clear the land for cattle or farming. They tried to buy or push out the rubber tappers. When the tappers would not leave, ranchers hired gunmen to terrorize or kill them.

To save the tappers' way of life, Mendes worked to stop the destruction of the forest. To do so meant standing up to the ranchers. As the conflict raged, environmentalists took up the cause of Mendes and the rubber tappers. They had already sounded the alarm about the burning of the forest by developers. A 1987 satellite photo had shown a smoky haze over the entire Amazon.

Environmentalists praised Mendes as a hero. At the same time, however, he remained clear about his own goals:

Development has threatened indigenous peoples in other parts of the world. The Penan, a nomadic group of hunter-gatherers, live in the rain forest of Borneo, an island in Malaysia. Commercial logging is destroying their ancient way of life. Many Penan have barricaded logging roads and used other forms of nonviolent protest. International environmental groups have asked the Malaysian government to stop logging in areas of the forest where the Penan live.

"I'm not protecting the forest because I'm worried that in 20 years the world will be affected. I'm worried about it because there are thousands of people living here who depend on the forest—and their lives are in danger every day."

"I want to live." Along with environmentalists, however, Mendes wanted to create "extractive reserves," protected areas of the forest that tappers and others could use for its resources without destroying it. That goal did not sit well with a local rancher, who issued a death threat against Mendes.

The union leader was brave but not foolhardy. He accepted protection from the police.

"If a messenger came down from heaven and guaranteed that my death would strengthen our struggle, it would even be worth it. But experience teaches us the opposite. . . . I want to live."

Police protection did not save Mendes. Still, his murder helped to focus attention on an issue that has become increasingly important—not only to Brazil but to the world. ◼

## SECTION 2 REVIEW

1. **Identify** (a) Bay of Pigs, (b) Cuban missile crisis, (c) OAS, (d) Alliance for Progress, (e) Salvador Allende, (f) Chico Mendes.
2. What were three results of Castro's revolution in Cuba?
3. (a) Describe two ways the United States intervened in Latin American affairs. (b) How did Latin Americans respond?
4. Why did Latin American nations join regional trading blocs?
5. *Critical Thinking* **Identifying Alternatives** Experts disagree about whether the fight against illegal drugs should focus on supply or demand. List some arguments for and against each approach.
6. *ACTIVITY* Draw a political cartoon about the conflict between economic development and environmental protection from the viewpoint of a developing nation.

# 3 Mexico, Central America, and the Caribbean

## Guide for Reading

- What economic successes did Mexico achieve?
- Why did Central American countries experience civil wars?
- What problems did democracy face in Haiti?

- **Vocabulary** *ejidos, maquiladoras*

"Today we must fight for a better world, without poverty, without racism, with peace." This message of hope and resolve was delivered at the city hall in Oslo, Norway, by a woman dressed simply in the traditional striped garments of a Guatemalan Indian. Rigoberta Menchu had come to accept the Nobel Peace Prize for her work on behalf of human rights.

Menchu had traveled a difficult road to this moment. From before her birth, the Central American nation of Guatemala had been locked in a struggle between the government and the Indian majority. Tens of thousand of Indians were killed, including Menchu's own parents and brother. Menchu became a leader in the Indians' fight to retain their farmland.

When it was announced that Menchu had won the Nobel Peace Prize in 1992, the Guatemalan government was outraged. To them, Menchu was a revolutionary. To Menchu, however, the award meant that the world recognized her people's cause:

"I consider this prize not as an award to me personally, but rather as one of the greatest conquests in the struggle for peace, for human rights, and for the rights of the indigenous people."

In the postwar era, Guatemala and several other Central American countries were battered by civil wars. To the north, their larger and richer neighbor, Mexico, weathered those decades with relatively little turmoil.

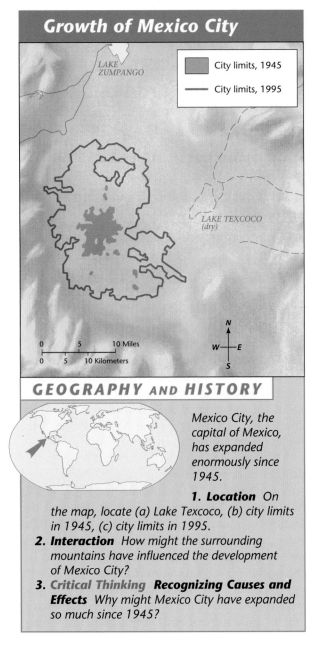

## Growth of Mexico City

LAKE ZUMPANGO

City limits, 1945
City limits, 1995

LAKE TEXCOCO (dry)

0    5    10 Miles
0    5    10 Kilometers

N
W — E
S

### GEOGRAPHY AND HISTORY

Mexico City, the capital of Mexico, has expanded enormously since 1945.

**1. Location** On the map, locate (a) Lake Texcoco, (b) city limits in 1945, (c) city limits in 1995.
**2. Interaction** How might the surrounding mountains have influenced the development of Mexico City?
**3. Critical Thinking** *Recognizing Causes and Effects* Why might Mexico City have expanded so much since 1945?

## Mexico on the Move

As you read in Chapter 12, Mexico had already endured a long, violent revolution. Its government was committed—at least in theory—to improving conditions for the poor.

**The rural poor.** In the 1930s, Mexico's president, Lázaro Cárdenas, had taken steps to fulfill the promises of the Mexican Revolution, especially land reform. He distributed some 44 million acres of land to peasants. Most was given to *ejidos* (eh HEE dohs), or peasant cooperatives. Some families also received small plots to farm themselves.

Much of the land was arid. It needed to be irrigated and fertilized to be productive. As rural populations grew, the land was subdivided and exhausted from overfarming. Presidents after Cárdenas, however, paid less attention to Mexico's rural poor. Instead, they favored agri-businesses that produced cash-earning export crops.

As conditions worsened, many peasants migrated to towns and cities, especially to Mexico City. The population of Mexico's capital mushroomed—from 1.5 million in 1940 to 20 million in 1995—making it the world's largest city. By the year 2000, that number is expected to reach 30 million.

**Politics.** Since the Mexican Revolution, a single party—the Institutional Revolutionary Party (PRI)—has dominated Mexican politics. It claimed to represent all groups—from workers and peasants to business-industrial interests and the military. Although a few small political parties did exist, PRI bosses moved forcefully against any serious opposition.

In part, the PRI held on to power by responding to social ills with programs for education, welfare, and health. As a result, it generally kept discontent from exploding into violence. Yet, in 1968, student protests shook Mexico as they did other western countries. Riot police and the army brutally suppressed the turmoil. The riots and the government's response received worldwide attention because the summer Olympic Games were held in Mexico City that year. Although much criticized, the PRI remained in power.

From time to time, the government also faced guerrilla movements. In 1994, for example, armed Indian rebels in the southern state of Chiapas challenged the government, demanding social and economic reforms. By skillfully using the media, the Chiapas rebels became international heroes. Yet they failed to achieve their goals.

Under pressure from all sides, the PRI made some election reforms. Then, in elections in 1997, an opposition candidate was elected mayor of Mexico City, and the PRI lost its majority in the legislature. These results suggested that the PRI's monopoly on power had finally ended.

**Economic ups and downs.** After World War II, Mexico pushed ahead with efforts to foster import substitution, reduce foreign influence, and expand agriculture. To promote industry, the government worked closely with private businesses. It invested in building roads, dams, and ports and encouraged tourism.

Between 1940 and 1982, both manufacturing and agriculture made huge gains. Mexico became the second largest economy in Latin America after Brazil. That growth turned Mexico from an agricultural economy into a mostly urban, industrial society.

In the late 1970s, new oil discoveries and rising oil prices spurred an economic boom. Mexico borrowed heavily to fund development projects. Then the worldwide recession of the 1980s, falling oil prices, and rising interest rates plunged the country deeply into debt. Like other debtor nations, Mexico was forced to cut spending on social and other programs. (See page 417.) The government also reduced barriers to foreign businesses and privatized some industries.

**Poverty and prosperity.** Mexico remained a disturbing mix of prosperity and poverty. During the 1980s, a system of *maquiladoras* (mah kee luh DOHR uhs), or assembly plants, began to flourish along Mexico's northern border. Maquiladoras, which were owned by multinational corporations, used cheap Mexican labor to assemble imported parts for cars and electronic goods. Finished products were then exported to the United States, Japan, and elsewhere. The maquiladoras system provided jobs for many Mexicans—most of them women. Still, environmental problems in the plants, plus the government's refusal to allow the workers to organize, resulted in a series of worker demonstrations.

Despite economic successes, most Mexicans remained poor. The economy could not produce enough jobs to keep up with rapid population growth. Wealth continued to be unequally distributed. The top 10 percent of the people controlled over 40 percent of the wealth, while the poorest 20 percent earned less than 2 percent of national income.

**Links to the United States.** Mexico has felt the powerful economic and political influence of its northern neighbor. In the 1930s, it set out to reduce economic influence through import substitution. Yet Mexico has continued to rely on investment capital from the United States. In 1995, a $20 billion loan from the United States bailed Mexico out of an economic crisis.

In 1993, Mexico, the United States, and Canada signed NAFTA. Supporters claimed it would boost prosperity by lowering trade barriers, opening up a huge regional market. In its first years, NAFTA did bring some business and investment to Mexico. At the same time, it hurt Mexican manufacturers who could not compete with a flood of goods from the United States.

Issues such as illegal immigration and drug smuggling have created tension between Mexico and the United States. Some employers in the United States, especially commercial farmers, relied on Mexicans to harvest crops

*Earthquake in Mexico City* Many regions of the world—from Japan to Iran—have experienced devastating earthquakes. In September 1985, a powerful quake struck Mexico City. Over a hundred buildings collapsed, and thousands more were damaged. The earthquake killed more than 20,000 people. **Geography and History** Why do you think the effects of an earthquake would be worse in a developing country?

**Factories on the Border** *During the 1980s, more than 1,500 maquiladoras sprang up along the United States-Mexican border. Today, these plants employ nearly half a million Mexicans. Many workers in the border factories are women, like those shown here assembling electronic goods.* **Economics and Technology** *What benefits do the maquiladoras offer Mexico and the United States?*

for low wages. But when a growing number of Mexicans crossed the border illegally, many people in the United States came to resent the newcomers. Despite differences, both nations have cooperated on solving issues such as environmental problems.

## War and Peace in Central America

In Central America, unrest threatened the traditional ruling elite of military, business, and landowning interests. Discontent grew in the cities and among rural Indian communities that had long suffered from poverty and oppression. Fearing the spread of communism, the United States intervened repeatedly in the region.

**Nicaragua.** Along with Mexico and Cuba, Nicaragua was the only other Latin American country to have a genuine revolution in this century. From 1936 to 1979, the Somoza family ruled—and looted—Nicaragua. Because of their strong anti-communist stand, they gained United States backing.

In the 1970s, various groups opposed to Anastasio Somoza joined forces. They called themselves Sandinistas after Augusto Sandino, a revolutionary of the 1930s. Like Sandino, they were reform-minded nationalists, including a large number of women and leftist students.

In 1979, the Sandinistas ousted Somoza and set out to reshape Nicaragua. Under Sandinista president Daniel Ortega, they introduced land reform and instituted other socialist policies. Fearing that Nicaragua would become "another Cuba," President Ronald Reagan secretly backed the *contrarevolucionarios,* or contras—guerrillas who opposed the Sandinistas. This pro-contra policy violated OAS policy, sparking bitter debate both within the United States and throughout Latin America.

The long civil war weakened the economy but did not unseat the Sandinistas. Other Central American countries finally helped both sides reach a compromise to stop fighting and hold elections. In 1990, Violeta Chamorro, a moderate, won election as president. The Sandinistas peacefully handed over power, although they kept control of the army. Nicaragua then began the difficult job of rebuilding its economy.

**Guatemala.** The United States helped topple Guatemala's reform government in 1954. The military and landowners then regained power. In the next decades, however, they faced constant challenges from leftist guerrilla movements. During the grueling civil war, the government routinely tortured and murdered critics, including student and labor leaders.

The chief victims were the indigenous Indian majority. An estimated 30,000 died during the 1980s alone. Some were killed fighting for the land they tilled but did not own. Others were shot as military forces exterminated whole villages.

Although a civilian government took power in the mid-1980s, the military remained a powerful force behind the scenes. The 30-year civil war ended in 1996, when the government and guerillas signed a peace agreement.

**El Salvador.** In El Salvador, too, reformers and left-wing revolutionaries challenged the wealthy landowners and the military. During a vicious 12-year civil war, right-wing death squads slaughtered student and labor leaders, church workers, and anyone else thought to sympathize with leftists. Although the United States pressed the government to make some re-

*An Outspoken Priest* Oscar Romero was a conservative member of El Salvador's elite until he became archbishop. Then he began to condemn government death squads that were killing students and peasants. Romero's outspokenness cost him his life. On March 24, 1980, as he said mass, shots rang out. Moments later, Romero lay dead, a victim of the death squads he had denounced. These signs and flowers honored Romero on the fourth anniversary of his death. **Religions and Value Systems** *The sign under Romero's picture says, "If you silence a prophet, he will speak out through his people." What do you think the saying means?*

forms, it provided weapons and other aid to help the military battle guerrillas.

Eventually, it became clear that neither side could win. In 1991, both agreed to a UN-brokered peace. In the next few years, former enemies met in the congress, not in battle. Joaquín Villalobos, once a guerrilla leader, was grateful to the UN for its help:

66This is a new country. After all we have seen in Bosnia and Rwanda and Somalia, it is good for the world to know there is at least one place where a peace process has been successful.99

Despite the return to peace, many problems remained unsolved, leaving democracy on a shaky footing.

## Struggle in Haiti

The first Latin American country to win independence was the Caribbean nation of Haiti. (See Chapter 4.) But after 1804, this impoverished land endured a stormy history. It was often ruled by dictators who were overthrown by rebellions. A small upper class of mulattoes (people of mixed African and European heritage) controlled the economy and ruled over the majority of the black rural poor.

**A pattern of dictatorship.** From 1957 to 1971, Dr. François Duvalier (doo vahl YAY) ruled Haiti. "Papa Doc," as he was called, created a brutal secret police force that crushed opposition and terrorized the people. After his death in 1971, his son, Jean-Claude Duvalier, took over. "Baby Doc" continued to loot the country until he was driven into exile in 1986. A succession of military leaders then ruled the island nation.

Finally, in 1990, Haiti held its freest elections ever. Jean-Bertrand Aristide (ar ih STEED), a priest and supporter of liberation theology, won 70 percent of the vote. A hero to the poor, Aristide proclaimed, "Our primary objective is to move from misery to dignified poverty." Just months after Aristide took office in 1991, a military coup forced him into exile, and power returned to the wealthy elite. They then launched a reign of terror against Aristide's supporters. Many tried to flee to the United States, where few were accepted.

**Democracy Returns to Haiti** *After the overthrow of Jean-Bertrand Aristide, the United States spearheaded international pressure to restore democracy to Haiti. Aristide's support among poor Haitians was so great that his movement took the name Lavalas, meaning "the flood." Here, Haitians celebrate Aristide's return in 1994.* **Global Interaction** *Why do you think the United States favored the restoration of democracy in Haiti?*

For three years, Aristide sought international help to return democracy to Haiti. When economic pressure failed, the United States used the threat of military action to force the army from power. United States and, later, UN forces helped Aristide's efforts to build a functioning democracy.

**An uncertain future.** On his return to Haiti, an optimistic Aristide declared:

66This is a day on which the sun of democracy rises, never to set. A day of national reconciliation, a day for the eyes of justice to open and never close again. Never, never, never again will blood be shed in this country.99

Despite Aristide's pledge, Haiti's outlook has remained clouded. It is the poorest state in the Western Hemisphere. Past rulers had looted the country, which lacked roads, electricity, and other basic services. Armed gangs, including some former military henchmen, roamed the capital city, Port-au-Prince.

Aristide had little success in reconciling the old ruling elite to his goals for social and economic justice. He stepped down in 1996, and a new president was elected. Haiti's fragile democracy survives but faces many problems.

## SECTION 3 REVIEW

1. **Identify** (a) Lázaro Cárdenas, (b) PRI, (c) Chiapas, (d) Somoza family, (e) Sandinistas, (f) contras, (g) François Duvalier, (h) Jean-Bertrand Aristide.
2. **Define** (a) *ejidos,* (b) *maquiladoras.*
3. (a) How did Mexico develop its economy? (b) What problems did it face?
4. (a) What were the goals of revolutionaries in Nicaragua? (b) How did El Salvador's civil war end?
5. Why did democracy have a hard time taking root in Haiti?
6. *Critical Thinking* **Predicting Consequences** How might the collapse of the Soviet Union and the end of the Cold War affect the prospects for peace in Central America?
7. *ACTIVITY* Write two slogans for a Mexican election—one that might be used by the PRI and one that might be used by a small opposition party.

## Focus on Argentina and Brazil

### Guide for Reading

- Why was Juan Perón a popular dictator?
- How did economic swings affect Argentina and Brazil?
- What successes and setbacks did democracy experience in Argentina and Brazil?

At carnival every year in Rio de Janeiro, Brazil, groups compete for the best float. In 1991, Joaozinho Trinta helped create a winning entry based on *Alice's Adventures in Wonderland*. Early in her adventures, Alice first shrinks to tiny size, then grows very tall. Later, a caterpillar asks her, "Who are you?" Alice replies:

> 66 I no longer know who I am. First, I was small like Brazil, underdeveloped, with many problems. Suddenly I grew, became a giant, a great power, but with many problems, a huge foreign debt. I don't know what else I can do. 99

But the caterpillar reassures Alice. "I am a caterpillar, but I turn myself into a butterfly," he says. "This could happen to you." Trinta's float expressed his optimism about his native land. Like Alice, Brazil, too, had experienced disturbing changes. But Trinta was convinced that Brazil would emerge stronger than ever.

Brazil is one of a dozen independent nations of South America, a richly diverse region. Here we will look at the two largest South American republics—Argentina and Brazil. History, geography, and other powerful forces have shaped each country's efforts to develop a stable government and a strong, modern economy.

### Argentina's Drive to Modernize

Argentina fills much of southern South America. In area, it is the largest Spanish-speaking nation in the world.

## Economic Activity in Argentina

- Meatpacking and food processing
- Textiles
- Metals
- Chemicals
- Car assembly
- Wheat
- Corn

## GEOGRAPHY AND HISTORY

Since the 1980s, Argentina has regained its position as the most stable economy in Latin America. Its economic success stems from a wide variety of resources and industries.

1. **Location** On the map, locate (a) Buenos Aires, (b) Falkland Islands, (c) Chile.
2. **Region** Using longitude and latitude, describe the major agricultural region of Argentina.
3. *Critical Thinking* **Making Inferences** Based on this map, name two cities that you might expect to attract a great many workers from rural areas.

By 1900, Argentina was the richest nation in Latin America, with a fairly stable government dominated by the wealthy elite. Its economy was booming, fed by exports of beef and wheat, mostly to Britain. Like the United States at the time, Argentina was a land of promise to millions of immigrants. Many worked in food-processing plants or in other factories being built in Buenos Aires.

Argentina seemed poised to equal the economic giants of Europe and North America. Then the Great Depression shattered its prosperity and led to a military coup. For the next 50 years, Argentina was plagued by economic crises, unrest, and military rule. Since the 1980s, it has worked to rebuild democracy and recover prosperity.

**Perón in power.** In 1946, a former army colonel, Juan Perón, was elected president. He appealed to Argentine nationalism by limiting foreign-owned businesses and pushing ahead with import substitution. By boosting wages, strengthening labor unions, and promoting social reforms, Perón won the loyalty of the working classes. For the first time, the urban poor, whom Perón called the *descamisados,* or "shirtless ones," felt a sense of belonging.

Perón was helped greatly by his glamorous wife Eva Duarte Perón. She had risen from poverty to fame as an actress. She used her position as Perón's chief aide and adviser to help the poor. She once said:

66I, a humble woman of the people, understood that it was my duty to take my place with the workers, with the descamisados.99

She had clinics and child-care centers built and gave money to the sick and unemployed. To secure more votes for her husband, she helped women gain the right to vote. At the same time, she lined her own pockets and lived an extravagant lifestyle. Still, the descamisados adored their "Evita." "You, too, will have clothes as rich as mine," she promised the poor women of Argentina.

While Juan Perón wooed the urban poor, his authoritarian government stifled opposition. Many educated people fled the repression. Perón increased government power by nationalizing many industries, but his policies led to a huge debt and soaring inflation. After Evita died of cancer in 1952, Perón's power declined. Within three years, he was ousted by a military coup and forced into exile.

**The military takeover.** For two decades, the military was in and out of power, while Perónistas, or supporters of Perón, continued to demand a return to his policies. In 1973, after 21 years in exile, an aging Perón was finally allowed to return. He was again elected president, and his new wife, Isabel, was chosen vice president. When he died the next year, Isabel Perón became president—the first woman head of state in the Western Hemisphere.

Lacking the popularity of Perón's first wife, Isabel Perón also faced a worsening economic and political crisis. Terrorists on the left and right were disrupting the country. In 1976, the military took power and set out to destroy Perón's legacy.

To combat leftist guerrillas, the army waged a "dirty war," terrorizing people they claimed were enemies of the state. They kidnapped, tortured, and murdered thousands of citizens. As many as 20,000 people simply "disappeared" after being taken from their homes. Many more fled the country to escape persecution. ( See *World Literature,* "Mothers and Shadows," pages 556–557.)

**War and defeat.** In 1982, the military hoped to mask economic troubles by seizing the British-ruled Falkland Islands. Argentina had long claimed these islands, which it called the Malvinas. The military believed that Britain would not fight to keep the islands. But in a brief but decisive war, the British recaptured the Falklands. Defeat undermined the military's prestige, and it was forced to hold free elections.

◀ *Juan and Eva Perón*

The "Mothers of the Plaza de Mayo" Argentina's military kidnapped thousands of opponents, mostly young people. Mothers of the desaparecidos, or the disappeared, marched silently in the Plaza de Mayo in Buenos Aires every Thursday, holding up pictures of their children. Only recently has the military admitted that nearly all the disappeared were murdered—often by being thrown into the ocean from airplanes or helicopters. **Political and Social Systems** Why do you think some of the Mothers of the Plaza de Mayo wore masks?

**Democracy restored.** In 1983, a newly elected government restored democracy to Argentina. Many people wanted the government to investigate and prosecute military leaders for atrocities committed during the "dirty war." Only when people learned the full story of the military's abuses, they insisted, could Argentina heal divisions.

Despite economic setbacks and scandals of corruption, democratic rule survived. Still, like many nations, Argentina was caught up in the debt crisis and took tough measures to reduce inflation and government spending.

In the 1990s, Argentina's economy again grew. The country had strong human resources, including the highest literacy rate in Latin America, and many natural resources. Yet its wealth was still concentrated in the hands of a few. It seemed unlikely to reach its goal of being recognized as a fully developed nation until more people shared in the nation's prosperity.

## Brazil—A Country of the Future

Brazil occupies almost half the continent of South America. Its varied landscapes include the world's largest tropical forest and the mighty Amazon River, fed by thousands of tributaries. Northeastern Brazil, however, is an arid plain.

Brazil's rich resources include minerals, timber, and fertile farmlands that produce cash crops such as coffee, sugar, and cocoa. Size, climate, and differences in resources have contributed to regionalism and uneven settlement patterns. About 90 percent of Brazilians live within 200 miles of the Atlantic coast, many in the fertile, temperate south. To draw settlers in-

land, the government has encouraged development of the interior.

**Population.** Unlike its South American neighbors, Brazil was settled by Portugal, not Spain. With a population over 155 million, Brazilians outnumber their Spanish-speaking neighbors. Brazil is a melting pot. A Brazilian patriot, Afonso Celso, considered diversity to be a source of national strength:

66Three elements contributed to the formation of the Brazilian people: the American Indian, the African, and the Portuguese. . . . Any one of these elements . . . possesses qualities of which we should be proud.99

In this century, many Japanese settled in Brazil, adding to its cultural mix.

Most Brazilians are Roman Catholic, but a growing number embrace evangelical Protestant faiths. Others practice Candomblè, which blends African and Christian beliefs.

Rapid population growth and class divisions have contributed to poverty in Brazil. In the cities, where more than 75 percent of Brazilians live, the contrast between rich and poor is seen everywhere. Teeming, garbage-strewn *favelas,* or slums, ring the cities, which boast luxurious high-rise apartments and wealthy shopping areas. ( ★ See *Skills for Success,* page 558.)

**An unstable giant.** Unlike other South American republics, Brazil won independence peacefully. (See Chapter 4.) Like its neighbors, however, Brazil has had its share of dictators and military rulers. They pursued modernization under the motto "order and progress."

# PARALLELS THROUGH TIME

## Parades

Nearly all societies celebrate holidays or special occasions with public parades. Often, parades express the values and hopes of a society. But mostly, they are a way to have fun.

**Linking Past and Present** Describe a parade you have participated in or seen. Do you think that the parade reflected the values of your country or community? Explain.

**PRESENT** In the 1990s, Brazil's carnival reflected popular interest in science fiction, as a colorful astronaut floated above the crowd, below. People in the United States enjoy parades, too, such as the Tournament of Roses in Pasadena, California, or Macy's Thanksgiving Day Parade in New York City, above.

**PAST** In Brazil, as well as in many Caribbean nations, millions celebrate carnival just before the start of Lent. Originally a religious holiday, carnival now gives marchers a chance to construct huge, ornate floats and to put on outrageous costumes. Above, a float from a 1940s carnival celebrates Latin American unity.

---

Between 1930 and 1945, the dictator Getúlio Vargas allied himself with the working poor. Like Juan Perón in Argentina, he improved wages and benefits, favored labor unions, and gave women the vote. The military eventually toppled Vargas but permitted elected presidents to rule for almost two decades. By 1964, economic problems and fear of communism led the military to take over again.

Backed by the middle and upper classes, the generals ruled with a heavy hand. They tortured and jailed critics, censored the press, and ignored calls for social reform. In the mid-1980s, they gradually eased their grip on power. In 1989, Brazilians were finally able to vote directly for a president for the first time in 29 years.

**Economic development.** "Brazil is a country of the future, and always will be." That familiar saying suggests both Brazil's potential and its many setbacks. In the past century, it has weathered many boom-and-bust cycles.

By 1910, the huge demand for Brazilian rubber suddenly fell off, causing economic hardships. Coffee exports then replaced rubber. But again and again, unstable prices or natural disasters wreaked havoc on the economy.

In the 1930s, Brazil diversified its economy. Vargas encouraged industry. He built highways, dams for hydroelectric power, and schools. During and after World War II, industry continued to expand. In the 1950s, president Juscelino Kubitschek (zhoo suh LEE nuh KOO bih chehk) promised "fifty years of progress in five." He opened up the interior to settlers by carving out a new capital, Brasília, in the wilderness, hundreds of miles from the Atlantic coast.

**"Economic miracle."** Despite their repressive rule, military leaders pushed for economic growth. "Power in the world," said one, "is a great nation that has territory, population, wealth, financial resources, technology, material goods, minerals." Brazil had almost all of these.

Brazil is the fifth largest country in the world in area. Yet its population is very unevenly distributed.

**1. Location** On the map, locate (a) Rio de Janeiro, (b) São Paulo, (c) Brasília, (d) Amazon River.

**2. Interaction** (a) What is the population density of the area around the city of Salvador? (b) What is the density of the area 1,000 miles west of Salvador?

**3. Critical Thinking** *Drawing Conclusions* Why do you think Brazil's population density is heaviest along the Atlantic coast?

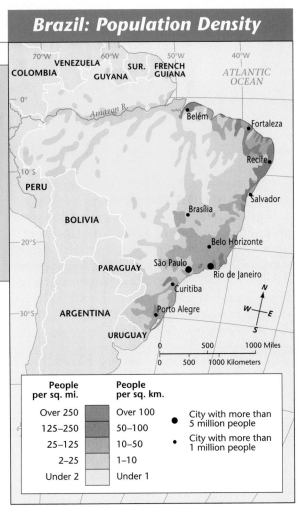

### Brazil: Population Density

| People per sq. mi. | People per sq. km. |
|---|---|
| Over 250 | Over 100 |
| 125–250 | 50–100 |
| 25–125 | 10–50 |
| 2–25 | 1–10 |
| Under 2 | Under 1 |

● City with more than 5 million people

• City with more than 1 million people

Under the military, experts ran the economy, which for a time chalked up impressive growth. Brazil began producing everything from steel and cars to shoes. People talked of Brazil's "economic miracle," like those in postwar Germany or Japan. The miracle enriched a few. To most Brazilians, however, it brought little or no benefits.

**People on the move.** By the 1980s, Brazil, like other developing nations, faced a host of economic problems—from inflation fed by higher oil prices to a staggering foreign debt. Rapid population growth, too, strained services to the limit. In the 1970s alone, more than 30 million people flooded into cities. (Unlike other Latin American countries that have only one major city, Brazil has more than a dozen.) In the favelas that surrounded São Paulo and Rio de Janeiro, thousands of children survived on the streets without families or education.

By 1990, the government had to curb spending, which further hurt the poor. To spur growth, it again pushed to develop the Amazon region. As you have read, the movement of people into the interior posed problems for the environment.

**Looking ahead.** As world economic conditions improved, so did Brazil's. In the 1990s, it numbered among the top 10 world economies. With ample human and natural resources, this giant of South America was determined to take its place among the world's economic superpowers—and become the country of the future today.

## SECTION 4 REVIEW

1. **Identify** (a) Isabel Perón, (b) "dirty war," (c) Falklands, (d) Getúlio Vargas.

2. (a) Why were Juan and Eva Perón popular figures to many people in Argentina? (b) Describe two policies they pursued.

3. Explain why the military seized power in (a) Argentina, (b) Brazil.

4. (a) Describe the Brazilian economic miracle. (b) Why did it falter?

5. *Critical Thinking* **Analyzing Information** What benefits and drawbacks might result from building a "cult of personality" around figures like Juan and Eva Perón?

6. *ACTIVITY* Review the section opener story on page 551. Then, design a carnival pageant float that captures some aspect of the current political or economic situation in Brazil.

# *World Literature*

## Mothers and Shadows

### Marta Traba

**Introduction** *During the early 1980s, a group of determined women assembled each week at the Plaza de Mayo in Buenos Aires, demanding that the government account for their missing sons and daughters. The relentless struggle of the "Mothers of the Plaza de Mayo" inspired Marta Traba's novel* Mothers and Shadows. *In this passage, Irene, an Argentine actress, attends her first demonstration in the Plaza de Mayo.*

**S**omething felt wrong. She looked and looked again, trying to work out what was out of place in that provincial square whose every detail she knew so well. . . . Everything was as it had always been, drab, bare, and ugly. And then it hit her: apart from the groups of women arriving for the demonstration, there was nobody in the square. No sightseers were standing around, no school children or men going about their daily business were hurrying across it, no old people were sunning themselves on the park benches. There were no street vendors anywhere to be seen. . . .

A woman dashed past with a bundle of duplicated lists and handed her one. It went on for twenty-three pages; she felt an urge to count the names and started to run her forefinger down the columns to work out how many names were on each page. She'd got to the forty-fifth line when someone stopped at her elbow and said: "You needn't bother to count them, sister, there are about a thousand names down here, but the actual number who've disappeared is much higher than that. We've only just started compiling the lists. The job is complicated by the fact that a lot of people are unwilling to give the full names and ages, or the parents' names and phone numbers."

She shrugged her shoulders and walked on. She felt annoyed with the woman for calling her "sister" and poking her nose into what was none of her business, but she took another glance at the list. Only now did she notice the ages: they mostly ranged from fifteen to twenty-five; she went on going through it page by page. A woman of sixty-eight, another of seventy-five. She shuddered. A four-month-old baby, a two-year-old girl, another of five, a brother and sister of three and four. The list in her hand began to quiver. How can a four-month-old baby disappear? The entry read: Anselmo Furco, four months, disappeared on . . . Parents: Juan Gustavo Furco, 23, Alicia, 20, also missing. It was followed by the name, address, and telephone number of the grandparents. A violent lurch in the pit of her stomach made her grope for the nearest wall to lean against.

Someone came up to her and said: "Come on, now, you musn't give up." They steered her back to the square. She felt better in the open air and looked around her. So these were the Madwomen of the Plaza de Mayo. . . .

The number of women was incredible and so was the silence; apart from the rapid footsteps and muffled greetings, there was not a sound. Not a single prison van, not a single policeman, not a single army jeep was in sight. The Casa Rosada looked like a stage set, with thick curtains drawn across its windows. There were no grenadier guards on sentry duty at the gates either. It was the realization that the grenadier guards were not there that gave her a sudden, terrifying insight into the enemy's machinations: *every Thursday, for the two or three hours during which the demonstration took place, the Plaza de Mayo was wiped off the map.* They couldn't fire on the women or lock them all up. It would have undermined the concerted effort they'd made to project a carefree image of "the Argentina I love." Their ploy was simply to ignore them; to ignore the existence of the square and of the madwomen stamping their feet. . . .

**A Tribute to Motherhood** *This sculpture of a mother and baby, by the Mexican artist Francisco Zuniga, is titled* Maternity. *Like Marta Traba in* Mothers and Shadows, *Zuniga celebrates the strength of mothers and their role in keeping the family together. The fact that mothers, rather than a political organization, led protests about the "disappeared" in Argentina won widespread sympathy for their cause.* **Art and Literature** *Do you think the sculpture presents a positive image of motherhood? Explain.*

[*Irene narrates what happens next.*]

Without a word or command being uttered, the women raised the photographs above their heads. Why, when there was no one there to see them? I expected that, with so much handling and fondling, those childlike faces would soon be disfigured past the point of recognition. Near me, an old woman was holding up a cheap studio portrait with both hands. The girl was smiling stiffly, her head tilted to one side, no doubt obeying the photographer's instructions. She was sitting with her legs crossed, an organdie dress covering her knees. . . . A woman right next to me took out of her handbag a tiny picture in an oval frame. She looked at me and smiled apologetically. The only photos she had of him were taken when he was a child, if only she'd known. . . . I asked her how old he was now. "He'll be twenty next month. We were so proud of him. We were going to hold a party to celebrate." She could barely finish the sentence, but she pulled herself together, sighed and raised the tiny frame as high as she could, along with all the other photographs. I started to feel uncomfortable just standing there with nothing to hold up. I raised the list with both hands and waited expectantly. Was that it? Just this coming together to share one's silent grief with the silent grief of others?

And that was when it started, Dolores. I can't explain to you what it was that happened. How can I find the words? I could say that suddenly someone started to shout and everyone started shouting and in a matter of minutes the whole square was one single shout. But that wouldn't begin to tell you what it was like. . . .

The crowd of women surged forward like a tide. They continued to advance, we knocked into one another, stumbling over each other's feet. The chaos was indescribable as hundreds of sheets of paper were tossed into the air. I did exactly the same as the madwomen, and I couldn't begin to tell you what I felt; it was as if someone was trying to rip my insides out and I was clinging on to them for all I was worth. . . .

I thought I glimpsed a snatch of Elena's jacket in the middle of a circle of women and I elbowed my way toward her. She was part of a chorus chanting in unison, and this time I could clearly hear the words "Where are they? Where are they?"

Source: Marta Traba, *Mothers and Shadows*, translated by Jo Labanyi (Mexico City: Readers International, 1985).

## Thinking About Literature

1. **Vocabulary** Use the dictionary to find the meanings of the following words: *provincial, grenadier, sentry, machinations, concerted.*
2. (a) What surprises Irene when she arrives at the plaza? (b) How does she explain it?
3. Describe how each of the following affects Irene: (a) the list, (b) the photographs, (c) the shouting.
4. *Critical Thinking* **Making Inferences** (a) Why are the Mothers of the Plaza de Mayo called "madwomen"? (b) Why do they represent a threat to the dictatorship?

*Chapter 20* **557**

## CHAPTER REVIEW

### REVIEWING VOCABULARY

Review the following vocabulary from this chapter: *caudillo, guerrilla warfare, terrorism, import substitution, agribusiness, multinational corporation, liberation theology, blockade, indigenous, ejidos, maquiladoras, regionalism.* Write sentences using each of these terms, leaving blanks where the terms would go. Exchange your sentences with another student and fill in the blanks on each other's lists.

### REVIEWING FACTS

1. How did Latin America's distribution of wealth cause problems after World War II?
2. How did military regimes in nations such as Argentina and Chile affect those nations?
3. Why did relations between the United States and Cuba worsen after 1959?
4. Describe the *maquiladoras* and their effect on Mexico.
5. Who forced Jean-Bertrand Aristide from power in Haiti? Who returned him to power?
6. What step did Argentina take toward democratic rule in the 1980s?

### REVIEWING CHAPTER THEMES

Review the "Focus On" questions at the start of this chapter. Then select *three* of those questions and answer them, using information from the chapter.

## SKILLS FOR SUCCESS  PREDICTING CONSEQUENCES

To predict consequences, or results, you must analyze what has happened in the past and compare it to the present situation. You must also study similar situations in other areas. Then you must synthesize this information and draw appropriate conclusions.

The article at right describes the effects of rapid population growth on Rio de Janeiro, one of Brazil's largest cities. Read the article, then follow these steps.

1. **Identify trends and developments.** (a) According to the article, what long-term population trend has been occurring? (b) What was happening to the city's industry during this time?
2. **Analyze the available information.** (a) How has Rio de Janeiro coped with the new arrivals? (b) How is the population trend related to the industrial trend?
3. **Predict possible future developments.** What might be the effects if the trends continue unchanged?

From an October, 1990 article in the São Paulo, Brazil, news magazine *Veja:*

66Rio de Janeiro, known for its beaches and climate, has been called 'Brazil's treasury of natural beauty.' . . . But Rio has changed a lot—into one of the tragedies of the twentieth century. In 1980, the belt of slums at the edge of Rio was officially recognized by the United Nations as the world's most violent place. More than 2,500 people are murdered there every year. . . .

Since the beginning of the century, Rio has played a decreasing role in the nation's development. . . . Rio's factories are increasingly out of date. . . . 'The problem of investment in Rio is very simple,' says Congressman Francisco Dornelles. 'No company wants to invest in a city where you never know whether the lights will come on in the morning, or whether your workers can get decent transportation to bring them to work.'

Over the past 25 years, the city's population has increased from 4 million to 6 million. Of these 2 million new inhabitants, 400,000 live in real houses or apartments, made of concrete or bricks, with lights that turn on and water that runs. The others—1.6 million people—have moved into the . . . slums.

'When the police do their duty,' says one professor, 'investments will return.' 99

## CRITICAL THINKING

1. **Drawing Conclusions** How can a wide gap between rich and poor make it difficult for democracy to flourish?

2. **Identifying Alternatives** Environmentalists, many of them from industrialized nations, have called on Brazil to stop the destruction of the Amazon rain forest. (a) What possible courses of action can Brazil take? (b) What are the possible consequences of each course?

3. **Linking Past and Present** Review pages 322–323. How were the causes of the Mexican Revolution of 1910 similar to the later revolutions in Cuba and Nicaragua?

4. **Recognizing Causes and Effects** What do you think is the relationship between political stability and economic growth? Explain your reasoning, using examples from the chapter.

## ANALYZING PRIMARY SOURCES

Use the quotation on page 539 to answer the following questions.

1. Why were workers regularly taken to the hospital?

2. What happened to workers who did not pick the required amount on a certain day?

3. Why would employers treat workers the way this woman describes?

## FOR YOUR PORTFOLIO

**FORMING AN ACTION PLAN** Work with a small group to describe an action plan for a Latin American country. Begin by deciding which country you will address and identifying this nation's past and likely future problems. Then brainstorm with your group to come up with solutions to these problems. Use outside resources to learn more about the needs and problems of the nation you have picked. Then decide on a plan for your nation. Finally, share your plan with the class. Be prepared to defend your recommendations.

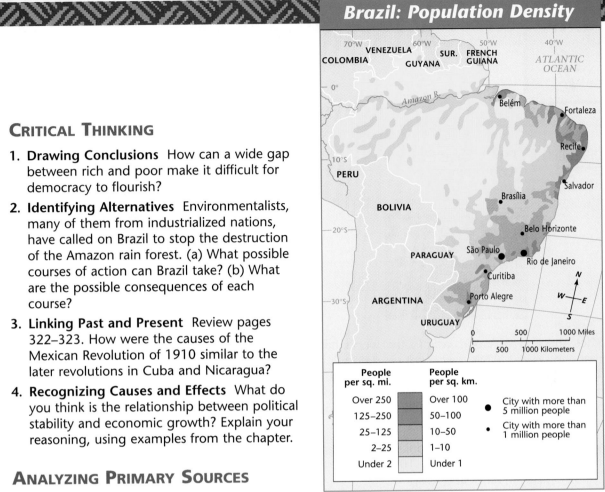

### Brazil: Population Density

| People per sq. mi. | People per sq. km. | |
|---|---|---|
| Over 250 | Over 100 | ● City with more than 5 million people |
| 125–250 | 50–100 | • City with more than 1 million people |
| 25–125 | 10–50 | |
| 2–25 | 1–10 | |
| Under 2 | Under 1 | |

## ANALYZING MAPS

Use the map to answer the following questions.

1. Why do you think the land along the Amazon River has a higher population density than other nearby areas?

2. What are the two largest cities in Brazil? How can you tell?

3. What is the westernmost city on the map?

## INTERNET ACTIVITY

**CREATING A CITY GUIDE** Use the Internet to research a Latin American city of your choice. Then create a tourist guide to that city that includes historical and cultural information, illustrated maps, and photos. Your guide should also list the language and currency of the city you chose.

# *Unit-in-Brief*

## The World Today

### Chapter 15  The World Since 1945: An Overview
(1945–Present)

Since the end of World War II, the world has changed rapidly. While we cannot yet determine the long-term impact of events of the recent past, we can identify political, social, and economic trends that have shaped the postwar years.

- The collapse of western colonial empires led to the emergence of nearly 100 new countries, mostly in Africa and Asia.
- Nuclear weapons, terrorism, and human rights are enduring issues in an increasingly interdependent world.
- Complex economic ties link the rich nations of the global North and the poor nations of the global South.
- Urbanization, modernization, women's movements, and technology have brought dramatic social changes.
- Technology has revolutionized agriculture and medicine and helped create a global, westernized popular culture.

### Chapter 16  Europe and North America
(1945–Present)

Within a framework of growing regional cooperation, Western Europe enjoyed tremendous economic growth after World War II. At the same time, the Cold War pitted the West, led by the United States, against the Soviet Union and its allies.

- In the postwar era, Western European nations expanded social programs and introduced the welfare state. By the 1980s, an economic slowdown forced cuts in social programs.
- The United States led world opposition to communism, extended civil rights, and pursued economic prosperity.
- Efforts to reform inefficiencies in government and the economy led to the collapse of the Soviet Union.
- After shaking off Soviet domination, nations of Eastern Europe faced economic challenges and ethnic conflicts.

### Chapter 17  East Asia and Southeast Asia
(1945–Present)

China, Japan, and other Asian nations have achieved varying degrees of success in their efforts to modernize. Several of these nations enjoy growing trade and other ties, linking the nations of the Pacific Rim from Asia to the Americas.

- After World War II, Japan introduced democratic reforms and by the 1960s had emerged as an economic superpower.
- Under communist rule, the People's Republic of China achieved modest economic gains while sacrificing individual political freedoms.

- The "Asian tigers"—Taiwan, Hong Kong, Singapore, and South Korea—vaulted into the class of newly industrialized nations.
- Cold War tensions sparked long, devastating conflicts in Korea, Vietnam, and Cambodia.

## Chapter 18 South Asia and the Middle East
### (1945–Present)

In South Asia and the Middle East, nations cast off western rule and set out to modernize. They have often confronted similar challenges—from religious strife and border conflicts to urbanization and population growth.

- Upon achieving independence, India built on the legacy of British rule to create the world's largest democracy.
- Ethnic and religious rivalries have fueled ongoing conflict among people of South Asia.
- When secular governments in the Middle East did not yield promised improvements, some reformers rejected western models and called for a reaffirmation of Islamic values.
- The long Arab-Israeli struggle and other conflicts have focused world attention on the Middle East.

## Chapter 19 Africa
### (1945–Present)

Leaders of new African nations set out to build strong central governments, achieve economic growth, and raise standards of living. They have faced a variety of obstacles, including economic dependency and political instability.

- After independence, many new nations experienced military or one-party rule but have since introduced multiparty democracy.
- African nations experimented with different economic systems, including socialism and mixed economies.

- After decades of conflict, South Africa abandoned its system of apartheid in the 1990s and made a transition to democratic rule.
- In Africa, as elsewhere, modernization and urbanization have disrupted traditional cultures and ways of life.

## Chapter 20 Latin America
### (1945–Present)

Despite setbacks, Latin American nations have tried to sustain economic growth and overcome a legacy of poverty and social inequality. Marxism, military rule, and the Roman Catholic Church have been continuing influences in the region.

- In the postwar period, poverty and uneven distribution of wealth fed social unrest in many nations.

- Latin America was a focus of Cold War politics, especially after a communist revolution in Cuba in 1959.
- Through trade, investment, and military intervention, the United States was a dominant force in Latin America.
- Although Mexico enjoyed economic gains in agriculture and manufacturing, most people remained in poverty.
- Argentina and Brazil experienced economic growth and long periods of military rule.

# UNIT 4

# A Global View

## What Trends Are Influencing the Direction of World History Today?

The world in the second half of the twentieth century has faced many problems and seen many changes. The trends and currents of the past half century will also powerfully influence the shape of things to come.

Three major political trends were the Cold War, the collapse of overseas empires, and the creation of global political organizations, such as the UN. Economic trends included the interdependence of developed and developing countries, as well as the pollution of the global environment.

Social changes were also clear. Conflicts flared between ethnic groups and between old and new ways of life. Urbaniza-

tion, rights for women, and the impact of science also shaped twentieth-century society.

### The Developed World

After World War II, two highly industrialized superpowers dominated world politics. The West, led by the United States, defended democratic government and free-enterprise economies. The eastern bloc, dominated by the Soviet Union, dreamed of a world politically controlled by Communist parties and economically run by government planners.

Economically, the period from the 1940s to the 1970s saw a long boom in Western Europe, North America, and Japan. These prosperous years

brought more material goods to more people than ever before in history. The eastern bloc, however, fared less well. In 1989, the Soviet alliance collapsed, and in the early 1990s, both communist dictatorships and state-run economies disappeared from Europe.

### The Developing World

The story of many developing nations begins with the "great liberation" following World War II. Newly liberated nations of Africa and Asia, as well as the already independent nations of Latin America, followed different paths, linked only by a common concern for economic development.

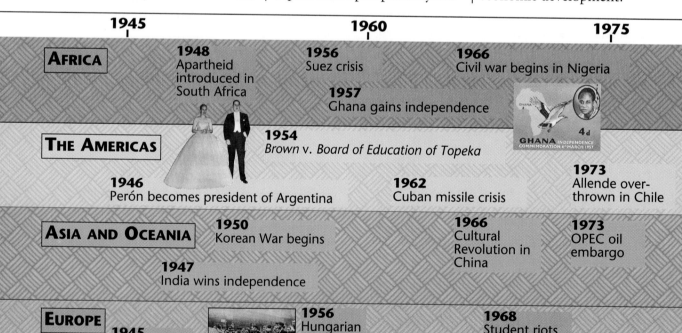

| | 1945 | 1960 | 1975 |
|---|---|---|---|

**AFRICA**
- **1948** Apartheid introduced in South Africa
- **1956** Suez crisis
- **1966** Civil war begins in Nigeria
- **1957** Ghana gains independence

**THE AMERICAS**
- **1954** Brown v. Board of Education of Topeka
- **1946** Perón becomes president of Argentina
- **1962** Cuban missile crisis
- **1973** Allende overthrown in Chile

**ASIA AND OCEANIA**
- **1950** Korean War begins
- **1966** Cultural Revolution in China
- **1973** OPEC oil embargo
- **1947** India wins independence

**EUROPE**
- **1945** Labour party gains power in Britain
- **1956** Hungarian uprising
- **1968** Student riots in France
- **1957** European Community formed

562    UNIT 4

Some nations prospered, to varying degrees. A group of Asian "tiger" economies flourished. Oil made the fortunes of a number of Middle Eastern states. Brazil, Argentina, and Mexico were often put in a category of "nearly developed" states.

For other nations—from Bangladesh to Tanzania to Bolivia—the road to development was strewn with obstacles. Foreign economic domination, population pressures, and a worldwide debt crisis were among many factors that hindered growth.

Politically, wars and unrest buffeted the developing world. The United States joined major wars against communist regimes in Korea and Vietnam and supported anti-communist governments in struggles around the world. The Jewish state of Israel was repeatedly locked in combat with its Arab Muslim neighbors. The black majority population of South Africa struggled against the racial system of apartheid.

## Looking Ahead

As the year 2000 drew near, the world seemed to be at a turning point. The peoples of Earth still faced many challenges. Yet some pressing problems had been solved. The collapse of the Soviet Union ended the Cold War. Nelson Mandela's victory in South Africa signaled the end of apartheid. And there were hopes for more advances—from democracy and economic growth in South America and Eastern Europe to peace accords in the Middle East.

Looking ahead to a future that has not yet happened is as hard for a historian as it is for a history student. Studying the past may help you understand how world history works. But it will be up to you to shape the history that is yet to come.

**ACTIVITY** Choose two events and two pictures from the time line below. For each, write a sentence explaining how it relates to the themes expressed in the Global View essay.

---

**1975**

**1990**

**PRESENT**

**1975**
Angola and Mozambique gain independence

**1980**
Rhodesia becomes Zimbabwe

**1994**
Mandela wins first multiracial election in South Africa

**late 1970s**
Mexican oil boom

**1993**
Canada, United States, and Mexico sign NAFTA agreement

**2000**
Panama Canal to be turned over to Panama

**1980s**
Debate over Brazilian rain forest

**1979**
Revolution in Iran

**1993**
Israel and PLO sign peace accord

**1997**
Hong Kong returned to China

**1975**
Vietnam War ends

**1975**
Greece restores civilian rule

**1989**
Berlin Wall falls

**1995**
Cease-fire in Northern Ireland

**1991**
Breakup of Soviet Union, Yugoslavia

UNIT 4 THE BIG PICTURE

# You Decide

## Exploring Global Issues

### What Is the Relationship Between People and the Environment?

In 1972, a team of loggers arrived in a forest in northern India. To their amazement, they were confronted by a group of women who were shielding the trees with their bodies. The women were members of the Chipko, or "Hug-the-Tree," movement. Their admirers saw the Chipko women as heroic defenders of the environment. To critics, however, *tree hugger* became a scornful term for an environmental extremist who stood in the way of economic progress.

Today, environmental issues are getting worldwide attention. Is it more important for a poor nation to protect its environment or to develop its resources? How much right do people have to alter the environment in the first place? To begin your investigation, examine these viewpoints:

The scientist and philosopher Aristotle used logic to explain relationships in the natural world:

66 Plants exist for the sake of animals, and animals exist for the sake of man—the tame for use and food, the wild, if not all, at least the greater part of them, for food and for the provision of clothing and various instruments. Now, if nature makes nothing in vain, [it follows] that she has made all animals for the sake of man. 99

The traditions of Zen Buddhism stressed closeness to and respect for nature, as in this print by the artist Hokusai. ▼

President Getúlio Vargas vowed to build Brazil's economy by subduing its mightiest resource—the Amazon River:

66 Nothing will prevent us from accomplishing . . . the highest task of civilized man: the conquest and domination of great valleys of equatorial torrents, transforming their blind force and extraordinary fertility into disciplined energy. The Amazon with the impulse of our will, of our effort, and of our work . . . will become a chapter in the history of civilization. 99

**KENYA**

**1960s**

Perez Olindo, a zoologist, explained why he resigned from the Kenya Game Department:

❝I resigned in protest at having been assigned the duties of 'elephant control' work which, in effect, involved shooting elephants considered to be in conflict with economic activities. . . . I held, and still hold, the view that elephants and other animals have a right to live, and no human has any control over that right.❞

**INDONESIA**

**1980s**

Dr. Sumitro Djojohadikusumo, former minister of trade and industry, gave economic reasons for managing and protecting the environment:

❝We certainly need a healthy natural environment. . . . If we are to make further progress we need the natural resources, we need the timber, we need the water, we need the fish. We can apply science to manage nature so that everyone benefits, even the animals.❞

**UNITED STATES**

**1992**

American cartoonist Tom Toles commented on protecting biodiversity, the wide variety of plant and animal species on the planet. ▶

---

## COMPARING VIEWPOINTS

1. How does Aristotle's view of the relationship between people and animals differ from those of Olindo and Toles?
2. Both Vargas and Djojohadikusumo were government officials in developing nations. Compare their views on the environment.
3. What relationship between people and nature is expressed in the Hokusai print? Which other viewpoints seem similar to Hokusai's?

## YOUR INVESTIGATION

**ACTIVITY**

1. Find out more about one of the viewpoints above or another viewpoint related to this topic. You might investigate:
   - The biblical story of creation in the book of Genesis.
   - The teachings of the Indian prophet Mahavira, founder of Jainism.
   - The view of nature in Native American literature.
   - Poems about nature by British Romantic poets such as William Wordsworth.
   - The views of an American conservationist such as John Muir, Theodore Roosevelt, or Rachel Carson.
   - Opposing sides in a recent environmental controversy, such as the damming of the Narmada River in India or the cutting of rain forests in Brazil.
2. Decide which viewpoint you agree with most closely and express it in your own way. You may do so in an essay, a cartoon, a poem, a drawing or painting, a song, a skit, a video, or in some other way.

UNIT 4   THE BIG PICTURE

# CASE STUDIES ON CONTEMPORARY ISSUES: PORTFOLIO PROJECTS

**D**uring your study of world history, you may have worked on many projects and activities. In this unit, you have an opportunity to work on a final project. This final project is a **case study on a contemporary issue.** In this project you can apply the knowledge and the skills you have developed while studying world history to a topic of current interest. Then you can demonstrate what you know in a presentation to the class.

# CASE STUDY PROJECT
# OVERVIEW

The Project Overview tell how to analyze and research a case study topic. It also tells how you can present your case study as a project. Refer to the Project Overview as you work on your case study project.

## The Case Study Project

What is a case study? A case study is an in-depth analysis of an issue or topic carried out by looking carefully at specific cases, or examples. In this unit, the topics range from the fall of communism in Europe to the future of democracy in the world. The specific examples are countries that illustrate the topic.

### CHOOSING A TOPIC

In this unit you will find seven case study topics. Your teacher may assign one or more of the case study topics to you. Or your teacher may want you to choose one or more topics.

Because these projects deal with large topics, your teacher might want you to share the work with other students. You may, however, develop your case study as an individual project if your teacher approves.

### ANALYZING YOUR TOPIC

How will you begin to work on your case study project? The first step is to analyze your topic. This means breaking it down into smaller pieces or subtopics. Later you will put these pieces back together to create a presentation based on your research.

#### General Categories of Human Activity

You might begin by looking at your topic in terms of five general categories of human activity. They are shown in the diagram below. If you are part of a team, one member might be responsible for gathering information on each of these categories and then sharing that information with the rest of the group.

### General Categories of Human Activity

The first step in working on your case study project is to analyze your topic. To do this, look at the topic in terms of the five general categories. Depending on the topic, not all factors may apply. For example, if your topic is comparing two countries' economic development, you would examine economic factors and political factors.

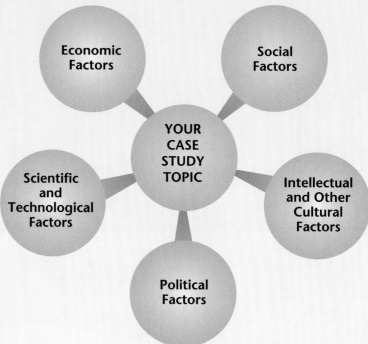

**Geographic Factors** As you get deeper into your subject, focus on some of the geographic factors that underlie the five categories of human activity. These include:

- natural and political boundaries
- scarcity or abundance of natural resources
- problems with bordering states
- industrial development
- transportation and communication systems

**Historical Factors** Also try to look at the historical factors that relate to your subject. What events that happened long ago still have an impact on what is going today? What recent changes or developments are important to your case study? Have they created new problems? Have they made old problems better or worse?

Finally, think about how these long-range historical factors and recent developments interact. Can you spot any trends or patterns that are likely to have an impact on the future?

## Putting Your Project Together

Your case study project will have three parts:

- a **PRESENTATION** of your topic based on your research
- an **INTERVIEW** or question and answer period following the presentation
- a **PROJECT JOURNAL** that can be added to your world history portfolio

## THE PRESENTATION

In your presentation you will present what you learned from your case study to an audience. This presentation should:

- introduce the topic of your case study
- show the impact of this topic in the countries you studied
- draw some conclusions as to the importance of this topic to those countries and the rest of the world.

On page 573 you will find a table of different methods of presentation. Read the table and choose one presentation method. Be sure to get your teacher's approval. You may want to illustrate your presentation with visuals such as maps, time lines, graphs, pictures, and videos.

## THE INTERVIEW

After your presentation, be prepared to answer questions from your audience. Your audience will probably be made up mainly of students and your teacher. It might also include parents, school staff, and representatives from your community.

The purpose of the interview is twofold. First, it provides audience members with an opportunity to find out more about issues of special interest to them. Second, it gives you and your team members a chance to demonstrate your knowledge. During the interview you will be able to share stories, facts, reactions, or conclusions that were not part of your more formal presentation.

## THE PROJECT

The project journal will be a record of your own research and reflections on your case study. It should include the following:

- **A brief overview of your case study.** The overview should define your topic and briefly describe the countries in your case study.

- **A research record.** Your research record should list all of the resources you used for your case study.

- **A short essay.** In this essay describe what you think is important about your case study from the following two points of view.

**A local citizen's perspective.** First, look at your case study from the point of view of a citizen who lives in one of the nations you are studying. Ask yourself: "If I were a citizen of this country, what would my greatest concerns about this topic be? My greatest hopes?"

**An American perspective.** Second, look at your case study from an American perspective. Ask yourself: "Why should Americans be interested in this topic? The countries I studied? How might developments in these countries affect the United States? What have I learned that might make me a better citizen?"

# METHODS OF PRESENTATION

Your case study can be presented in any one of the following ways.

- **POSTER DISPLAY:** A large visual display of the sort you might find in a museum, library. or information kiosk. Your intended audience would be the general public.

- **EXPERT BRIEFING:** A live presentation of your case study to a group with a professional interest in your topic. Your audience might be the President of the United States and his cabinet, a government agency, or group of business leaders.

- **NEWSPAPER OR NEWS MAGAZINE REPORT:** A special feature or section in a newspaper or news magazine devoted an in-depth report on your topic. Your intended audience would be readers of that periodical.

- **VIDEO DOCUMENTARY:** A film or video based on your case study. Your audience might be movie-goers or television viewers.

- **TELEVISION NEWS FEATURE:** An in-depth television news feature based on your case study. It might appear on the nightly news or one of the television news programs. You can present your story live or prerecord it on video. Your audience would be the general television-viewing public.

- **WEB SITE OR MULTIMEDIA PROJECT:** A computer-based multimedia presentation that could be published on a computer disk or the World Wide Web. Your audience would be computer users and web browsers around the globe.

# Researching Your Topic

Each case study includes a list of resources for you to use as you research your topic. Your research, however, should go beyond the list. You will also want to study recent new stories, interview experts, talk with foreign students, and locate people who have visited the countries in your case study. You can find these resources by using the library, the Internet, and the organizations listed on the next page.

## IN YOUR LIBRARY

Your library is a good starting point for research. You may want to begin by consulting print or electronic encyclopedias, atlases, almanacs, and factbooks such as the *Central Intelligence Agency World Fact Book*.

Look for recent magazine and newspaper stories on your subject. You can find more in-depth articles in such journals as *Foreign Affairs, The National Interest, Journal of Democracy,* and *World Politics*. To locate such articles, use *The Reader's Guide to Periodical Literature,* newspaper indexes, and electronic indexes to periodicals such as Infotrac. Your reference librarian will show you how to use these guides.

## ON THE INTERNET

The Internet will connect you to a treasure trove of information, experts, and illustrations such as maps, pictures, and film clips. You can launch your search using one of the standard search engines such as Yahoo, Alta Vista, Lycos, or Infoseek. From there you can link to web sites created by government agencies, scholars, trade groups, and students from around the world.

The Internet can also link you to a vast array of electronic news sources including on-line newspapers, radio and television news providers, and on-line magazines.

## PROJECT SCORING GUIDE

Your case study project will be evaluated according to how well you demonstrated the following:

### 1. Knowledge of history, geography, and your research data

In your presentation and interview did you:

- demonstrate a thorough knowledge and understanding of your topic?
- use quotations and statistics to support your main points?
- present information that is clear, well-organized, and factually accurate?
- answer questions accurately?

### 2. Ability to communicate ideas

In your presentation and interview did you:

- combine information from many sources into an interesting and informative story?
- take clear positions and support them in an organized and persuasive manner?
- use visuals effectively to enhance your key points?

### 3. Research, writing, and thinking skills

In your project journal did you:

- clearly define your case study?
- provide a written record of your research?
- analyze information on your topic from multiple perspectives?
- pay attention to grammar and spelling rules?

### 4. Teamwork skills

In your group did you:

- stay on task?
- divide up the work fairly?
- listen to and express ideas and views?
- allow for and accept differing opinions?
- resolve conflicts satisfactorily to all members?

# ORGANIZATIONS TO HELP YOU RESEARCH

The following world affairs organizations may help you locate information and experts to interview as part of your research. Like any organization, each of these groups has its own purpose, perspective on the world, and political point of view. You will want to pay attention to any possible biases as you evaluate any materials these organizations provide.

**Asia Foundation**, P.O. Box 193223, San Francisco, CA 94119-3223. The Asia Foundation assists economic, political, and social development in Asia, and supports exchange programs between Asia and the United States.

**Foreign Policy Association**, 470 Park Avenue, S., New York, NY 10016-6819. This organization provides education materials on foreign policy issues, including its magazine *Headline.*

**Foreign Policy Research Institute**, 1528 Walnut Street, Suite 610, Philadelphia, Pennsylvania. The Institute produces education materials on international affairs including its magazine *Orbis* and newsletter *Footnotes.*

**Goethe Institute**, German Cultural Center, 1014 5th Avenue, New York, NY 10028. This institute provides information on cultural life in Germany and German language instruction.

**Hoover Institution on War, Revolution and Peace**, Stanford University, Stanford, CA 94305-6010. The Hoover Institution is an international research center for the study of political, economic, and social change in the twentieth century.

**Institute for Contemporary Studies**, 720 Market Street, 4th Floor, San Francisco, CA 94102. This research center prepares studies on domestic and foreign policy issues.

**Institute of the Americas**, 10111 North Torrey Pines Road, La Jolla, CA 92037. This institution encourages economic, political, and social reform in the Americas by strengthening relations between Latin America, the United States, and Canada, as well as through the publication of its periodical *Hemisfile.*

**Japan Society**, 333 E. 47th Street, New York, NY 10017. The Japan Society is dedicated to furthering understanding and cultural exchange between the peoples of Japan and the United States.

**Korea Society**, 950 3rd Avenue, 8th Floor, New York, NY 10022. The Korea Society works to increase understanding and cultural exchange between the peoples of Korea and the United States.

**Pan American Society of California**, 312 Sutter Street, Suite 506, San Francisco, CA 94108. This organization promotes mutual understanding among peoples of the Americas.

**Population Reference Bureau (PRB)**, 1875 Connecticut Avenue NW, Suite 520, Washington, DC 20009. PRB gathers and publishes information about United States and international population trends.

**Society for International Development (SID)**, San Francisco Bay Area Chapter, c/o Asia Foundation, P.O. Box 3223, San Francisco, CA 94119-3223. SID is an international organization of people who are interested in international economic, political, and social development.

**World Resources Institute (WRI)**, 1709 New York Avenue NW, Washington, DC 20006. WRI provides research and technical assistance on global environmental and economic development issues.

**World Trade Centers Association**, World Trade Center, Suite 7701, New York, NY 10048. This association encourages global commerce and helps citizens develop international business.

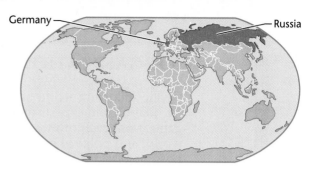
Germany ——                    —— Russia

# Russia and Germany: After Communism

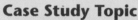

## Case Study Topic

The fall of communism in Europe led to the breakup of the Soviet Union and also to the reunification of Germany. In this case study, you will report on the changes brought to Russia and Germany by the fall of communism.

## How to Complete Case Study 1

■ Be sure to read or review the **Project Overview** on pages 568–573. It describes how to complete a case study.

■ Then read the **background information** on this page and on page 575. It will provide a starting point for your research.

■ Next, study the **map and charts** on the next page for additional data.

■ Finally, on page 576, you will find "**Voices and Views,**" a collection of quotations. Analyze them and add them to your research.

■ On page 577 is a list of **what you need to include** in your case study presentation. Also provided is a list of **resources** for your research.

### BACKGROUND INFORMATION

If you looked at a map of Europe before 1987 and compare it with one created in 1992, you would notice some big differences. The 1987 map would show the Soviet Union, East Germany, and West Germany. The 1992 map would show Russia, a united Germany, and a number of new nations that formerly were Soviet republics.

What brought about these changes? First, communism came to an abrupt end in Europe. Second, the Cold War between East and West ended. These two developments caused the Soviet Union to break apart and Germany to reunite.

### THE COLLAPSE OF COMMUNISM IN EUROPE

Few people expected communism in Europe to collapse when it did. Fewer still would have predicted that the end would begin in Poland. In the early 1980s, however, Polish workers, students, and dissidents came together with one goal: to destroy the communist system Poland had lived under since World War II.

From Poland across Eastern Europe, communist leaders tried to cling to power by promising reforms. However, people did not want a new and improved totalitarian system. In one country after another, they poured into the streets demanding democracy. One by one, communist governments fell.

### THE FEDERAL REPUBLIC OF GERMANY

On October 3, 1990, East and West Germany were legally reunited for the first time since the end of World War II. With reunification came new questions and new challenges.

■ What was to be done with all the state-owned homes, farms, and businesses in East Germany?

■ What should be done with the secret files of the *Stasi*, East Germany's secret police? The *Stasi* had collected information on more than six million East Germans. Should those files be opened? Should the files be destroyed, even though this would mean destroying evidence of how East Germany's totalitarian system worked?

■ What should be done to bring East and West Germans together as one people? While both *Ossis* (East Germans) and *Wessis* (West Germans) speak the same language and share a

## Russia: Political

**Data for Your Case Study**

Use the map and charts below as you research your case study project. You may also use the data in your case study presentation.

## Russia and Germany at a Glance

| | RUSSIA | GERMANY |
|---|---|---|
| Total land area | 6,520,660 mi² (16,888,418 km²) | 134,850 mi² (349,260 km²) |
| Population (1997 estimate) | 147.3 million | 82 million |
| Number of people per square mile | 23 (60 per km²) | 608 (1,575 per km²) |
| Urban population | 73% | 84% |
| Per capita GDP (in U.S. dollars) | $2,240 | $27,510 |

## One Germany, Two Peoples?

| | WEST GERMANS | EAST GERMANS |
|---|---|---|
| Percent unemployed | 8% | 14% |
| Household financial assets in German marks (DM) | 100,000 | 20,000 |
| Living space per person | 36 mi² | 27 mi² |
| Women in the work force | 51% | 91% |
| Favor more spending on the environment | 87% | 82% |
| Want more police presence to deal with rising crime | 25% | 65% |
| Are proud to be Germans | 2 out of 3 | 2 out of 3 |

common history, they come from very different political and economic backgrounds. Misunderstandings and prejudices are common on both sides.

### RUSSIA

In December 1991, a startling announcement came out of Russia: "The Soviet Union has ceased to exist." In August 1991, supporters of democracy led by Boris Yeltsin seized power in Moscow. One of Yeltsin's first acts was to outlaw the Communist Party. After 74 years, the communist era had come to an end. Just weeks later, nine of the 15 republics that made up the USSR had declared their independence.

As Russia made the transition from communism toward democracy, the country faced many changes and challenges. Some of these follow:

- Although Russia is a federation, the balance of power between the federal government and the regional authorities is still developing. A big challenge for the future is for Russia to build a genuine federal system in which Moscow shares power with the rest of the country.

- Russia's labor force is well-educated and skilled, but mismatched to the needs of the economy. As a result, in 1997 millions of Russian workers were underemployed or out of work.

- The move from a centrally planned economy toward a free market has placed a strain on Russia's economy. Russia's gross domestic product fell by about 38 percent between 1992 and 1997.

Analyze the quotations below as you research your case study. You may
also use the quotations in your case study presentation.

# VOICES and VIEWS

## ON THE TRANSFORMATION OF RUSSIA

"The Russian Federation—Russia shall be a democratic, federative, law-based state with a republican form of government."
*Article I, Russian Constitution*

"In the place of a totalitarian state which terrorized the world for 45 years, a civilized Commonwealth of Independent States has been formed."
*Russian Foreign Minister Andrei Kozyrev*

"We have given you freedom of enterprise. You can determine your own wages. We are setting prices free. We are forming a free market. . . . Now it is up to you to show us what you are worth."
*Boris Yeltsin to the Russian people, 1991*

"It will be a healthy society with healthy youth. . . . We'll have hippies and Yuppies, just like the rest of the world."
*Ilya Reznikov, Moscow university student*

"For many years we couldn't speak about anything. Now we can suddenly talk. It's all very strange, but great. Things are getting better."
*Ann Goodenko, teenager in the city of Stavrobol*

"Maybe things will be better for our children. But not for us. It's chaos here. It will take 10 or 20 years for my country to improve."
*Sergei Kalina, St. Petersburg student*

"Once you've tasted this freedom, it's impossible to go back."
*Moscow high school student*

## ON GERMAN REUNIFICATION

"Wir sind wieder wer."
("We are somebody again.")
*Slogan seen across Germany in 1990.*

"This is not unification, it's an annexation."
*Margit Venner, East German psychologist*

"We Jews cannot contemplate a united Germany without feelings of inner resistance."
*Elie Wiesel, Holocaust survivor, author, and human rights activist*

"I fear the superpatriotism of nationalism again. We still haven't worked out our history yet. We haven't come to terms with Nazism. East Germans have thought even less about it."
*Thorsten Laute, West Berlin university student*

"We Germans got married in a hurry and enjoyed it. Now we must get to know each other. Normally it is the other way around, but, then, what is normal in Germany?"
*Egon Bohn, West German politician*

An *Ossi* meets a *Wessi* and says, "We are one people!" To which the *Wessi* replies, "So are we!"
*Joke told by German Foreign Minster Hans-Dietrich Genscher to illustrate the difficulty of uniting East and West Germans*

"The Germans are being given a second chance. That is the rarest of gifts, and one can only hope that they will do justice to it. The Germans deserve friends who feel the burden of the past, as so many of them do, but who have compassion for a people who have had so rich and terrifying a history."
*Fritz Stern, professor of history, Columbia University*

▲ *Shown above is the construction site of the Reichstag, which will become the seat of the German Parliament by the end of the century.*

# Researching and Presenting Case Study 1

## RESEARCHING

As you research *Russia and Germany: After Communism,* remember that your case study project will have three parts:

- a **presentation** based on your research and reflection on the topic
- an **oral interview** to follow your presentation
- a **project journal** that will include a case study overview, research log, and an essay on the significance of your topic

See pages 568–573 for a detailed description of these elements.

## PRESENTING

Your presentation on this topic should include the following:

- a **brief overview or time line** of key events leading up to the fall of communism in Europe
- a **description** of the immediate impact of the fall of communism on Germany and Russia
- an **examination** of the problems Russians face as they make the transition from dictatorship to democracy and from a command economy to a free enterprise system
- a **concluding statement** on the significance of these historic changes for the peoples of Germany and Russia and for the United States

## RESOURCES

### IN YOUR WORLD HISTORY TEXTBOOK

To locate useful background information on this topic in your textbook, check the index under the following headings: **communism, Marxism, socialism, Germany, East Germany, West Germany, Russia, Soviet Union**

### IN YOUR LIBRARY

✔Daniels, Robert V.
*A Documentary History of Communism from Lenin to Gorbachev*
Hanover, NH: University Press of New England, 1993. Also, *Soviet Communism from Reform to Collapse.* Lexington, MA: D.C. Heath., 1995.

✔Darnton, Robert
*Berlin Journal*
New York: W. W. Norton, 1993.

✔Fischer, Marc
*After the Wall: Germany, the Germans, and the Burdens of History*
New York: Simon & Schuster, 1995.

✔Fulbrook, Mary
*The Divided Nation: A History of Germany , 1918-1990*
Oxford: Oxford University Press, 1992.

✔Lapidus, Gail W., ed.
*The New Russia: Troubled Transformation*
Boulder, CO: Westview Press, 1994.

✔Remick, David
*Lenin's Tomb: The Last Days of the Soviet Empire*
New York: Random House, 1994.

✔Shlaes, Amity
*Germany: the Empire Within*
New York: Farrar, Strauss, & Giroux, 1991.

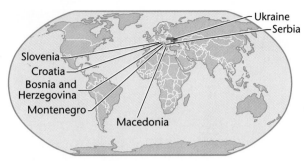

Ukraine
Serbia
Slovenia
Croatia
Bosnia and
Herzegovina
Montenegro
Macedonia

# Ukraine and Yugoslavia: The Resurgence of Nationalism

## Case Study Topic

In this case study, you will examine why nationalism led to a peaceful independence movement in Ukraine and a violent break-up of Yugoslavia.

## How to Complete Case Study 2

■ Be sure to read or review the **Project Overview** on pages 568–573. It describes how to complete a case study.

■ Then read the **background information** on this page and on page 579. It will provide a starting point for your research.

■ Next, study the **map and chart** on the next page for additional data.

■ Finally, on page 580, you will find "**Voices and Views**," a collection of quotations. Analyze them and add them to your research.

■ On page 581 is a list of **what you need to include** in your case study presentation. Also provided is a list of **resources** for your research.

## BACKGROUND INFORMATION

Events in the past help shed light on why nationalism had different results in Ukraine and the former Yugoslavia. Reviewing these events is critical to understanding the present situation.

### THE REPUBLIC OF UKRAINE

Ukrainians trace their history back to the 700s and the founding of the first Russian state. Later Ukraine was ruled by Lithuania and Poland.

In the early 1600s, Ukraine allied itself with Russia as it fought for independence from Poland and Lithuania. As a result of that struggle, Ukraine became part of the Russian empire. After that, Ukraine remained under Russian, and later Soviet domination until the late 1980s.

Soviet rule left a bitter legacy in Ukraine. Joseph Stalin's collective farming campaign brought immense suffering and even famine to this rich agricultural region. According to some historians, Stalin also launched a campaign of terror designed to stamp out Ukrainian language and culture.

The collapse of the Soviet Union encouraged Ukrainians to dream about nationhood. In 1991, ninety percent of all Ukrainians voted in favor of independence. Since 1994, the goverment has worked to enact economic reforms and remove almost all controls over prices and foreign trade. These measures were taken to stablize the economy and achieve economic growth.

### YUGOSLAVIA, OLD AND NEW

In contrast with Ukraine, Yugoslavia has existed only since World War I. The peace settlement ending that war created Yugoslavia to unite several Balkan peoples into one kingdom. Yugoslavia began its existence as one of the world's most divided nations. It had two alphabets, three religions, four languages, and many different ethnic groups divided into six republics and two provinces.

This patchwork nation was held together by its royal rulers until the Nazis took it over during World War II. After the war, communists led by Marshal Josip-Broz Tito seized power and declared Yugoslavia to be a Federal People's Republic. Tito managed to keep ethnic rivalries under control. After his death in 1980, however, one

Use the map and chart as you research your case study project. You may also use the data in your case study presentation.

## Ethnic Groups in the Former Yugoslavia

SLOVENIA

CROATIA

BOSNIA AND HERZEGOVINA

SERBIA

ADRIATIC SEA

MACEDONIA

Legend:
- Slovenes
- Croats
- Serbs
- Bosnians (Muslims)
- Montenegrins
- Macedonians
- Hungarians
- Albanians
- Ethnic mixture

As of the 1980 census

0   50   100 Miles
0   50   100 Kilometers

Lambert Azimuthal Equal Area Projection

## Ukraine and Yugoslavia at a Glance

| | **UKRAINE** | **YUGOSLAVIA** |
|---|---|---|
| **Total land area** | 233,090 mi² (603,700 km²) | 39,449 mi² (102,173 km²) |
| **Population** (1996 estimate) | 52.5 million | 10.9 million |
| **Number of people per square mile** | 225 (87 per km²) | 277 (107 per km²) |
| **Urban population** | 67% | 47% |
| **Per capita GDP** (in U.S. dollars; 1995 estimate) | $3,370 | $2,000 |
| **Ethnic divisions** | Ukrainian, 73%; Russian, 22%; Jewish, 1%; other, 4% | Serbs, 63%; Albanians, 14%; Montenegrins, 6%; Hungarians, 4%; other, 13% |
| **Religions** | Ukrainian Orthodox, Ukrainian Catholic, Protestant, Jewish (figures not available) | Orthodox, 65%; Muslim, 19%; Roman Catholic, 4%; Protestant, 1%; other, 11% |

group after another began to complain of unfair treatment by the others and to call for independence. Some leaders stirred up ethnic rivalries to gain political power.

In 1991, the old Yugoslavia fell apart. Four of the six republics declared their independence. The remaining two, Serbia and Montenegro, proclaimed themselves the new Federal Republic of Yugoslavia. An ethnic map of the area is shown above.

The breakup of Yugoslavia fueled years of brutal fighting between Serbs and other groups. The struggle for control of territory also spawned a new form of genocide called "ethnic cleansing." American intervention brought an uneasy peace to the region at the end of 1995.

Analyze the quotations below as you research your case study. You may also use the quotations in your case study presentation.

# VOICES and VIEWS

## ON UKRAINIAN INDEPENDENCE

"Ukraine is as big as France, and this year we produced as much grain—50 million tons, or one ton for everyone living in the republic. But France does not have food shortages and we do."

*Ivan Plusch, Ukrainian official, before independence vote*

"All our people really want is to speak their own language, worship in their own churches, have something to buy in the shops, and live at peace—without having to ask for these rights."

*Vasili Shpitser, Ukrainian mayor, before independence vote*

"A great historic event has occurred, which I am confident will change not only the life of the Ukrainian people but the face of the world. . . ."

"The Soviet Union has disintegrated. . . . An independent Ukraine is born."

*Leonid Krachuck, first president of Ukraine, after independence vote*

"To lose Ukraine would be like cutting off a limb for many Russians. It is very difficult for them to accept."

*Oles Donji, Ukrainian student leader, before independence vote*

"The Ukrainians have in their hands the fate of the nation, that of the other republics of the former Soviet Union and our neighbors in Europe. . . . They have enjoyed their nationalism, but let them think hard about what they say and do. Much depends on it."

*Russian official, after 1991 independence vote*

## ON THE BREAKUP OF YUGOSLAVIA

"By their oppression the Communists created this longing among the people to express their religious and national identity. Perhaps in four or five years we shall have passed through the mine field to the horizon of a civil society."

*Alija Izetbegovic, Bosnian Muslim leader, 1990*

"What we want is to preserve our people's unity. . . . The Serbs do not want to accept being broken apart. Enough of breaking the Serbs apart! . . . We cannot accept that."

*Radovan Karadzic, Bosnian Serb leader and indicted war criminal, 1992*

"Searching for the one who started it is a waste of time. Once it had started, the massacres were unstoppable."

*Macedonian officer fighting in Croatia*

"Yugoslavia did not deteriorate suddenly, but gradually and methodically, step by step through the 1980s, becoming poorer and meaner and more hate-filled by the year. That's why every conversation I had was so sad. We were shouting to the outside world about a coming catastrophe, but no one wanted to hear our awful secret. No one was interested."

*Robert D. Kaplan, American journalist*

"I want to see my parents again. . . . I love everyone: Serbs, Muslims, Croats, they are all my brothers. This is what my parents taught me. Why were they killed?"

*Nerimina Guso, 13-year-old Bosnian Muslim*

"My imagination does not go far enough to see Serbs, Moslems, Croats co-existing again for as long as the children and the people who can remember this terrible Bosnian war are alive."

*Dobrica Cosic, President of Yugoslavia*

▲ *Ukrainians at a pro-independence rally in 1991*

## Researching and Presenting Case Study 2

### RESEARCHING

As you research *Ukraine and Yugoslavia: The Resurgence of Nationalism,* remember that your case study project will have three parts:

■ a **presentation** based on your research and reflection on the topic

■ an **oral interview** to follow your presentation

■ a **project journal** that will include a case study overview, research log, and an essay on the significance of your topic

See pages 568-573 for a detailed description of these elements.

### PRESENTING

Your presentation on this topic should include the following:

■ a **brief overview or time line** of the key events that led to independence for Ukraine and the breakup of Yugoslavia

■ a **description** of how nation-building has proceeded in Ukraine since independence

■ a **summary** of the ethnic conflict that followed the breakup of Yugoslavia

■ a **comparison** of the effects of nationalism in the Ukraine and the former Yugoslavia

■ a **concluding statement** on the significance of these historic changes for the peoples of Ukraine, the former Yugoslavia, and the United States

# RESOURCES

## *IN YOUR WORLD HISTORY TEXTBOOK*

To locate useful background information on this topic in your textbook, check the index under the following headings: **nationalism, Ukraine, Russia, Soviet Union, Yugoslavia, Balkans, Bosnia, Serbia**

## *IN YOUR LIBRARY*

✔Conquest, Robert. *Harvest of Sorrow: Soviet Collectivism and the Terror-Famine.* New York: Oxford University Press, 1986.

✔Dink, Nadia & Adrian Karatnychy. *The Hidden Nations: The People Challenge the Soviet Union.* New York: Morrow, 1991.

✔Glenny, Misha. *The Fall of Yugoslavia: The Third Balkan War.* New York: Penguin Books, 1993.

✔Kaplan, Robert D. *Balkan Ghosts: A Journey Through History.* New York: St. Martin's Press, 1993.

✔Kuzio, Taras & Andrew Wilson. *Ukraine from Perestroika to Independence.* New York: St. Martin's Press, 1994.

✔Malcolm, Noel. *Bosnia: A Short History.* New York: New York University Press, 1994.

✔Moynihan, Patrick. *Pandaemonium: Ethnicity in International Politics.* New York: Oxford University Press, 1993.

✔Ramet, Sabrina P. *Nationalism and Federalism in Yugoslavia,* 1962-1991. Bloomington: Indiana University Press, 1992.

✔Sjelten, Tom. *Sarajevo Daily: A City and Its Newspaper Under Siege.* New York: HarperCollins, 1995.

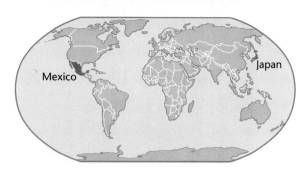

## CASE STUDY 3

# Japan and Mexico: Paths to Prosperity

## Case Study Topic

In this case study, you will compare and contrast the means by which Japan and Mexico have worked to achieve economic prosperity.

## How to Complete Case Study 3

■ Be sure to read or review the **Project Overview** on pages 568–573. It describes how to complete a case study.

■ Then read the **background information** on this page and on page 583. It will provide a starting point for your research.

■ Next, study the **graphs and chart** on the next page for additional data.

■ Finally, on page 584, you will find **"Voices and Views,"** a collection of quotations. Analyze them and add them to your research.

■ On page 585 is a list of **what you need to include** in your case study presentation. Also provided is a list of resources for your research.

### BACKGROUND INFORMATION

The twentieth century has been a testing ground for different paths to economic development. One path is capitalism, under which most economic decisions are made in a free market. The opposite path is communism, under which almost all economic decisions and enterprises are controlled by the government.

Other nations have sought a middle path between capitalism and communism. This approach generally involves three things: (1) heavy government planning and regulation of the economy, (2) the nationalization of key resources and in-

dustries, and (3) trade barriers designed to protect domestic industries from foreign competition. Both Japan and Mexico have followed this middle path in different ways and with different results.

### JAPAN

The economic development of Japan began with the Meiji Restoration in 1868. Reformers took control of the government. Their goal was to industrialize and modernize their country. By the early twentieth century, Japan had largely achieved this goal.

The Great Depression of 1929 hit Japan with devastating force. In response, economic nationalists joined with militarists to promote territorial expansion as the key to renewed wealth. Instead of wealth, however, Japan's empire-building resulted in years of brutal warfare. By the time World War II ended in 1945, the country lay in ruins.

Japan's recovery from World War II was so rapid that it has been called an "economic miracle." Guided by the dominant Liberal Democratic Party (LDP), Japanese businesses invested heavily in new plants and technologies. The results were stunning. When the American occupation of Japan ended in 1952, Japan's gross domestic product (GDP) was little more than one third of that of France or Britain. By the late 1970s, Japan's GDP equaled that of both those countries combined. Today, Japan's economy ranks second in size only to that of its most important trading partner, the United States. In recent years, however, there have been setbacks. Political corruption scandals combined with a deep recession have shaken the confidence of the Japanese in their government and economy.

## Data for Your Case Study

Use the graphs and chart as you research your case study project. You may also use the data in your case study presentation.

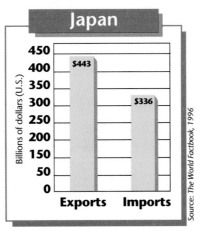

### Japan

Billions of dollars (U.S.)

Exports $443
Imports $336

Source: The World Factbook, 1996

Japan's chief trading partners: Southeast Asia, United States, Western Europe, China

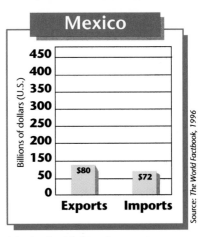

### Mexico

Billions of dollars (U.S.)

Exports $80
Imports $72

Source: The World Factbook, 1996

Mexico's chief trading partners: United States, Japan, Western Europe

## Japan and Mexico at a Glance

| | MEXICO | JAPAN |
|---|---|---|
| **Total land area** | 756,066 mi$^2$ (1,958,201 km$^2$) | 145,870 mi$^2$ (377,801 km$^2$) |
| **Population** (1996 estimate) | 95.4 million | 126.3 million |
| **Number of people per square mile** | 126 (49 per km$^2$) | 886 (334 per km$^2$) |
| **Urban population** | 75% | 78% |
| **Per capita GDP** (in U.S. dollars; 1995 estimate) | $7,700 | $21,300 |
| **Natural resources** | petroleum, silver, copper, gold, lead, zinc, natural gas, timber | negligible mineral resources, fish |
| **Percentage of arable land** | 12% | 13% |
| **Adult literacy** (age 15 and over can read and write) | 89.6% | 99% |

## MEXICO

Like Japan, Mexico was also rocked by economic recession and political scandals in the 1990s. Like the Japanese, many Mexicans have responded by calling for fundamental changes in the way their government and economy work.

Mexico's approach to economic development was forged in the revolution that raged across Mexico from 1910 to 1920. This struggle pitted the nation's poverty-stricken peasants and workers against the powerful landowners and business owners. It ended with the adoption of a new constitution that is still in force today. This constitution gave the government considerable control of economic resources such as land, minerals, and oil.

The Great Depression was as hard on Mexico as on Japan. Mexico's answer, however, was not to expand militarily. Instead, under the ruling Institutional Revolutionary Party (PRI), Mexico adopted a program of economic nationalism. Its economy was closed to both foreign trade and investment.

Recently the PRI has faced mounting challenges to its political monopoly and economic control. In response, the government has reformed Mexico's election system. By adopting the North American Free Trade Agreement (NAFTA), it also opened up the economy to foreign investment and competition.

Analyze the quotations below as you research your case study. You may
also use the quotations in your case study presentation.

# VOICES and VIEWS

## ON JAPAN'S ECONOMIC MIRACLE

"Workers will find true happiness through work,
for work will always be the basis of society."
*Slogan on Toyota factory wall*

"We're no longer satisfied simply with working
hard. . . . We need to keep a good balance between work and something else, like families."
*Norio Gomi, 1989*

"We're more interested today in consuming
than working. And you know what we're most
interested in consuming? Leisure."
*Japanese Finance Ministry worker, 1989*

"Japan may be the world's richest nation, but
something is terribly wrong when white collar
workers in top firms cannot afford to buy a house,
or even pay for their children's education."
*Hidezo Inaba, Chairman,
Industrial Policy Research Institute, 1987*

"Despite the recession, people are still happy with
continued job security. . . . Job security is so sacred."
*Shijuro Ogata, 1997*

"As Japan searches for a path to take into the next
century, the challenges of building a modern market
economy—and the resulting anxiety—are disconcert-
ingly similar to those in the former communist world.
In Japan almost as much as in Russia, there is a con-
sensus that the old economic and political system was
ill-suited for the future, and that society must move
several steps in the direction of American-style capitalism, but that this will be as painful as it is inevitable."
*New York Times, 1997*

"They'll have to work harder and harder just to
stay in place. I wonder what it will be like in 20 or
30 years."
*Japanese employee Toshi-yuki Hozawa,
on his sons' future, 1997*

## ON POLITICAL FERMENT IN MEXICO

"Our elections are so sophisticated that we can
tell who won hours before the polls close," boasts
an American. "So what?" replies his Mexican
friend. "Here we can tell months before."
*Old Mexico joke*

"The government is not a place for amassing
wealth."
*Ernesto Zedillo Ponce de León, PRI leader,
elected President of Mexico, 1994*

"We will never know if Mexico is a democracy
until the presidency falls to the opposition."
*Sergio Sarmento, television news director*

"Those who bleed the country are those who
have the most: the governors, deputies, senators,
and presidents. . . . The majority of our people
are poor. Of the 70 million people in our country

I think only 100 or 500 are millionaires. If our
country is a democracy, this isn't right—*ricos*
[rich people] with castles on the coasts, while in
some pueblos the parents don't have food to put
in their children's mouths."
*Augustin Peréz, Mexican worker*

"Every week I have to go to Mexico City to find
work because PRI corruption has left this town
with no money for jobs. . . . I don't know if the
opposition will change that, but I'm sure not going
to vote for what doesn't work for my parents."
*Joaquin Bermeo, 21, during 1997 election*

"It simply was no longer logical for a Mexican to
vote for the PRI, a party that has a dark complicity
[involvement] with corruption."
*Cuauhtemoc Cardenas, opposition party leader,
elected mayor of Mexico City, 1997*

▲ *A worker inspects a car at a Japanese automobile factory.*

# Researching and Presenting Case Study 3

## RESEARCHING

As you research *Japan and Mexico: The Path to Prosperity*, remember that your case study project will have three parts:
- a **presentation** based on your research and reflection on the topic
- an **oral interview** to follow your presentation
- a **project journal** that will include a case study overview, research log, and an essay on the significance of your topic

See pages 568–573 for a detailed description of these elements.

## PRESENTING

Your presentation on this topic should include the following:
- a **brief overview or time line** of key events in the economic and political development of Japan since the Meiji Restoration and Mexico since the Mexican Revolution
- an **examination** of Japan's post-war economic miracle and the challenges Japan faces today
- an **analysis** of Mexico's path toward prosperity under the PRI and recent efforts to open the Mexican economy to foreign trade and investment
- a **comparison** of one-party rule in Japan and Mexico, and of efforts to open each nation's political system to more competition
- a **concluding statement** on the importance to the United States of a prosperous and peaceful Japan and Mexico

# RESOURCES

## IN YOUR WORLD HISTORY TEXTBOOK

To locate useful background information on this topic in your textbook, check the index under the following headings:
**economy, economic nationalism, debt crisis, trade, North American Free Trade Association (NAFTA), Association of Southeast Asian Nations (ASEAN), Japan, Mexico**

## IN YOUR LIBRARY

✔Casteneda, Jorge.
*The Mexican Shock: Its Meaning for the United States.* New York: New Press, 1995.

✔Irokawa, Daikichi.
*The Age of Hirohito: In Search of Modern Japan.* Free Press, 1995.

✔Krauze, Enrique.
*Mexico, Biography of Power: A History of Modern Mexico.* New York: HarperCollins, 1997.

✔Lincoln, Edward.
*Japan's New Global Role.* Washington, DC: Brookings Institution, 1995.

✔Pastor, Robert A., and Jorge Castaneda.
*Limits to Friendship: The United States and Mexico.* New York: Random House, Inc., 1989.

✔Ross, John.
*Rebellion at the Roots: Indian Uprising in Chiapas.* Monroe, ME: Common Courage Press, 1994.

✔Sato, Ryuzo.
*The Chrysanthemum and the Eagle: The Future of U.S.-Japan Relations.* New York: New York University Press, 1995.

✔Schlesinger, Jacob M.
*Shadow Shoguns: The Rise and Fall of Japan's Postwar Political Machine.* New York: Simon & Schuster, 1997.

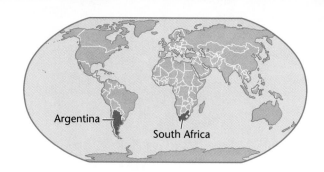

Argentina
South Africa

## CASE STUDY 4

# Argentina and South Africa: The Road to Democracy

### Case Study Topic

In this case study, you will examine how Argentina and South Africa moved from authoritarian rule toward democratic government.

### How to Complete Case Study 4

- Be sure to read or review the **Project Overview** on pages 568–573. It describes how to complete a case study.

- Then read the **background information** on this page and on page 587. It will provide a starting point for your research.

- Next, study the **chart** on the next page for additional data.

- Finally, on page 588, you will find **"Voices and Views,"** a collection of quotations. Analyze them and add them to your research.

- On page 589 is a list of **what you need to include** in your case study presentation. Also provided is a list of **resources** for your research.

### BACKGROUND INFORMATION

Not long ago, it was hard to find a country in Latin America or Africa that was not ruled by an authoritarian government or by the military. Today, in contrast, most Latin American countries and a growing number of African nations have elected governments. In some of these nations, the road to democracy was relatively peaceful. More often, however, that transition has been marked by violence and bloodshed. Such was the case in both Argentina and South Africa.

### ARGENTINA

In the 1920s, Argentina ranked among the world's ten richest nations and was ruled by a democratically elected government. The Great Depression, however, shattered Argentina's prosperity and its leaders' commitment to democracy. Since 1930, some 25 governments have come to power in that country, more than half of them following military coups.

After the last military coup in 1976, the ruling generals declared war on "enemies of the state." Over the next few years, tens of thousands of people disappeared in what Argentines called their "dirty war." Public outrage forced the generals to turn over power to an elected government in 1983. Since then, Argentina's fragile democracy has survived coup attempts, runaway inflation, corruption scandals, and widespread social unrest.

Many Argentine citizens have demanded justice for the victims of the "dirty war." Of some 7,000 possible defendants in cases involving the disappeared, however, only 60 or so people were charged with crimes. Fewer still were brought to trial, convicted, and jailed.

In 1991, saying that he wanted to "close a black chapter" in Argentina's history, newly elected President Carlos Saul Menem pardoned even those few. Still, for many that "black chapter" could not be closed so easily. Nearly 50,000 people filled the streets of Buenos Aires to protest the pardons.

### SOUTH AFRICA

South Africa is the richest nation in Africa. Until recently, it was also the most racially divided as well. Under the system of apartheid, South Africans were

# Data for Your Case Study

Use this chart as you research your case study project. You may also use this data in your case study presentation.

## Argentina and South Africa at a Glance

| | ARGENTINA | SOUTH AFRICA |
|---|---|---|
| **Total land area** | 1, 073, 519 mi² (2,780,400 km²) | 471,445 mi² (1,221,037 km²) |
| **Population** | 35.3 million | 43.7 million |
| **Number of people per square mile** | 33 (13 per km²) | 93 (36 per km²) |
| **Urban population** | 88% | 51% |
| **Per capita GDP** (in U.S. dollars; 1995 estimate) | $8,100 | $4,800 |
| **Adult literacy** (age 15 and over can read and write) | 96.2% | 81.8% |
| **Life expectancy at birth** | 71.7 years | 59.5 years |
| **Ethnic divisions** | white, 85%; mestizo, Indian, or other nonwhite, 15% | black, 75.2%; white, 13.6%; Colored, 8.6%; Indian, 2.6% |
| **Natural resources** | fertile plains of the Pampas, lead, zinc, tin, copper, iron ore, manganese, petroleum, uranium | gold, chromium, antimony, coal, iron ore, manganese, nickel, phosphates, tin, uranium, gem diamonds, platinum, copper, vanadium, salt, natural gas |

rigidly segregated on the basis of race, with whites dominating all other racial groups.

The harshness of the apartheid regime brought South Africa worldwide condemnation backed by economic sanctions. It also led to ever-increasing unrest and violence at home. In 1990, newly elected President F.W. de Klerk called for an end to apartheid. Four years later, South Africans of all races went to the poles to elected Nelson Mandela as their country's first black president. Since that historic election, South Africa's government has worked hard to heal the wounds of apartheid by exposing them to the light of truth.

In 1996, a Truth and Reconciliation Commission was created in South Africa to investigate murders and other human rights abuses committed during the apartheid era. Those who agreed to tell the truth were promised amnesty, or pardons, in exchange for their confessions.

In all, about 8,000 people applied for amnesty. As they and their victims testified before the commission, South Africans learned of the horrible deeds done to defend—and fight—apartheid. Police told of assassinations. Politicians confessed to bombings. Anti-apartheid activists admitted to murders.

Confronting the past has not been easy for South Africans. Many agree, however, that it is necessary. "If you look at history," said one white apartheid opponent who was severely injured in a terrorist bomb attack, "some countries try to bury the past. No nation has ever succeeded. If we try to ignore or bury the past, it will haunt us, even destroy us."

Analyze the quotations below as you research your case study. You may also use the quotations in your case study presentation.

# VOICES and VIEWS

## ON ARGENTINA'S FRAGILE DEMOCRACY

"There is no democracy without voting, but voting in and of itself is not sufficient. Democracy is a form of governing and of organizing a society [based on] respect for the dignity of man. It is inconceivable without justice."

*President Raúl Alfonsín*

"Twenty years later, more than nine thousand Argentine families still do not know exactly what happened to the person who was once yanked away from his or her home by agents of the state, never to be seen again. At the time, the military authorities told them they could not know and would never know. . . . Now democratically elected leaders . . . tell them that they should not want to know."

*Juan Méndez, Human Rights Watch*

"One of the things that I simply will not do now is shut up. The women of my generation in Latin America have been taught that the man is always in charge and the woman is silent even in the face of injustice. . . . Now I know that we have to speak about the injustices publicly. If not, we are accomplices."

*Maria del Rosario de Cerruti,*
*Mother of the Plaza de Mayo*

"I've often gone to the Plaza de Mayo, like an idiot, like a coward, hiding behind the trees, to watch the mothers walking around the plaza on behalf of the disappeared, knowing that I had thirty disappeared persons on my conscience."

*Francisco Sciligo, first to break the military's pact*
*of silence on crimes of the "dirty war"*

## ON SOUTH AFRICA AFTER APARTHEID

"The people who structured apartheid and put it on the law books were not evil people. . . . Apartheid was, in its idealist form, a plan to make all the people of South Africa free."

*F. W. de Klerk, last white president of South Africa*

"While we were desperately holding on to our mad little system, we never dared participate in the intellectual life of the 20th century. Now all those debates are opening up to us. We have rejoined the human race."

*Ken Owen, white newspaper editor*

"My school used to be all-white. Now, it's open to all races. The school is two-thirds white and one-third other races. . . . Now I have friends from all races. Three years ago, you were never around them; you didn't even know about them. Now you learn to not judge someone just by how they look."

*Marianneke Zondstra, 15, white student*

"We're able to go to far better schools now that apartheid has been abolished. . . . Everything is better, and it happened because for the first time we are able to choose the schools we want to attend."

*Carmen Fernandis, 14, colored student*

"The images of South Africans going to the polls that day are burned in my memory. Great lines of patient people snaking through the dirt roads and streets of towns and cities; old women who have waited half a century to cast their first vote saying they felt like human beings for the first time in their lives; white men and women saying they were proud to live in a free country at last. . . . it was as if we were a nation reborn."

*Nelson Mandela on first all-race elections*

▲ *Two women vote in South Africa's first all-race elections in 1994.*

# Researching and Presenting Case Study 4

## RESEARCHING

As you research *Argentina and South Africa: The Road to Democracy*, remember that your case study project will have three parts:

■ a **presentation** based on your research and reflection on the topic

■ an **oral interview** to follow your presentation

■ a **project journal** that will include a case study overview, research log, and an essay on the significance of your topic

## PRESENTING

Your presentation on this topic should include:

■ a **brief overview or time line** of key events leading up to the transition to democracy in Argentina and South Africa

■ an **examination** of the social and economic challenges confronting Argentina's government

■ an **analysis** of challenges facing South Africa's majority government as it seeks to overcome the legacy of apartheid

■ a **comparison** of efforts by both countries to seek justice for victims of the former regime

■ a **concluding statement** on the importance of these transitions to democracy for Argentines, South Africans, and Americans

# RESOURCES

## IN YOUR WORLD HISTORY TEXTBOOK

To locate useful background information on this subject in your textbook, check the index under the following headings:
**democracy, apartheid, Argentina, Latin America, South Africa**

## IN YOUR LIBRARY

✔Bouvard, Marguerite Guzman. *Revolutionizing Motherhood: The Mothers of the Plaza de Mayo.* Wilmington, DE: Scholarly Resources, 1994.

✔Crassweller, Robert D. *Peron and the Enigmas of Argentina.* New York: W.W. Norton, 1987.

✔Mandela, Nelson. *Long Walk to Freedom: The Autobiography of Nelson Mandela.* Boston: Little, Brown, 1994.

✔Poneman, Daniel. *Argentina: Democracy on Trial.* New York: Paragon House Publishers, 1987.

✔Sparks, Allister. *Tomorrow is Another Country: The Inside Story of South Africa's Road to Change.* Chicago: University of Chicago Press, 1995.

✔Suzman, Helen. *In No Uncertain Terms: A South African Memoir.* New York: Alfred A. Knopf, 1993.

✔Timmerman, Jacobo. *Prisoner Without a Name, Cell Without a Number.* New York: Random House, 1988.

✔Thompson, Leonard. *A History of South Africa.* Princeton: Yale University Press, 1996.

✔Waldmeir, Patti. *Anatomy of a Miracle: The End of Apartheid and the Birth of the New South Africa.* New York: W.W. Norton, 1997.

Czech
Republic

South
Korea

## CASE STUDY 5

# The Czech Republic and South Korea: Democracy and Economic Development

## Case Study Topic

The Czech Republic has a democratic government that is determined to foster economic development. South Korea became an economic powerhouse under an authoritarian government. In this case study, you will report on the state of democracy and economic development in these two countries.

## How to Complete Case Study 5

■ Be sure to read or review the **Project Overview** on pages 568–573. It describes how to complete a case study.

■ Then read the **background information** on this page and on page 591. It will provide a starting point for your research.

■ Next, study the **maps and chart** on the next page for additional data.

■ Finally, on page 592, you will find **"Voices and Views,"** a collection of quotations. Analyze them and add them to your research.

■ On page 593 is a list of **what you need to include** in your case study presentation. Also provided is a list of **resources** for your research.

### BACKGROUND INFORMATION

Is political freedom essential to economic development? Not necessarily, or at least not at first, say some economists and historians. Apart from the United States and Great Britain, few of the world's wealthiest democracies developed their modern economies entirely under democratic rule.

Still, many economists agree that there is a strong link between economic development and democracy. Once people get used to some measure of economic freedom, they often begin to work for political rights and freedoms as well. Some economists believe that as a nation becomes more prosperous, it also becomes more democratic.

### THE CZECH REPUBLIC

After World War I, Czechoslovakia was one of the most prosperous and democratic nations in Europe. It might still be so had it not been taken over by communists after World War II. Under communist rule, the freedoms that had once been part of Czech life became distant memories.

Following the example of the USSR, Czechoslovakia's communist rulers stressed the building of heavy industry in their economic development plans. Agriculture and the production of consumer goods were neglected. Rather than create prosperity, this lopsided approach to development produced food shortages, scarce housing, and poor-quality consumer goods.

In 1989 Czechoslovakians staged mass protests to oust their communist rulers in what human rights activist Vaclav Havel has called the "velvet revolution." Less than three years later, Czechs and Slovaks agreed to a "velvet divorce." In 1993 the country was divided to form two new nations, the Czech Republic and Slovakia.

Under the direction of Prime Minister Vaclav Klaus, the Czech Republic privatized the economy by the mid-1990s. *Privatization* is the selling off of state-owned industries to private investors. Unemployment stayed low at only 3.3 percent.

## Data for Your Case Study

Use the maps and the table below as you research your case study project. You may also use the data in your case study presentation.

**Czechoslovakia, Before 1993**

0 100 200 Mi.
0 100 200 Km

⊕ Prague
CZECHOSLOVAKIA
• Bratislava

Elbe R.
Danube R.

⊕ National capital
• Other city

Lambert Azimuthal Equal Area Projection

**Czech Republic and Slovakia**

0 100 200 Mi.
0 100 200 Km

⊕ Prague
CZECH REPUBLIC
SLOVAKIA
⊕ Bratislava

Elbe R.
Danube R.

⊕ National capital

Lambert Azimuthal Equal Area Projection

## Czech Republic and South Korea at a Glance

| | Czech Republic | South Korea |
|---|---|---|
| **Total land area** | 30,450 mi² (78,864 km²) | 38,230 mi² (99,016 km²) |
| **Population** (1996 estimate) | 10.5 million | 45.5 million |
| **Number of people per square mile** | 344 (133 per km²) | 1,188 (459 per km²) |
| **Urban population** | 63% | 78% |
| **Per capita GDP** (in U.S. dollars; 1995 estimate) | $10,200 | $13,000 |
| **Adult literacy** (age 15 and over can read and write) | 99% | 98% |
| **Natural resources** | hard coal, soft coal, kaolin | coal, tungsten, graphite, moybdenum, lead, hydropower |
| **Industries** | fuels, ferrous metallurgy, machinery and equipment, coal, motor vehicles, glass, armaments | electronics, automobile production, chemicals, shipbuilding, steel, textiles, clothing, footwear, food processing |
| **Trading partners** | Germany, Slovakia, Austria, Poland, Italy, Russia, Netherlands, France, United Kingdom, Hungary, United States, Belgium | United States, Japan, European Union |

## SOUTH KOREA

Fifty years ago, South Korea was one of the world's poorest nations with a per capita GDP of $100. Today the Republic of Korea is a major industrial power with a GDP of about $10,000 per person. In that period, South Korea transformed itself from an agrarian society that could not even produce a bicycle to the world's seventh largest automobile maker and a leading producer of semiconductors and high-tech electronics.

For most of those years, South Koreans lived under a dictatorship dominated by the military. Under military rule, the government launched an ambitious program of industrial and economic development. Economic planners used loans and favors to promote the growth of one industry af-

ter another. These industries were dominated by huge, octopus-like corporations known as *chaebol*.

In 1987, a wave of pro-democracy protests and riots rocked South Korea. Unable to quell the unrest, the government finally agreed to democratic reforms (see page 473).

In 1995, South Korea's government was rocked by scandal when it was charged with taking $307 million in bribes from businessmen. In early 1996, former presidents Roh Tae Woo and Chun Doo Hwan were both charged with treason in connection with the deaths of about 200 pro-democracy demonstrators. Some Korea watchers pointed out that, although shocking, the former presidents' downfall was evidence of the development of democratic principles and rule of law.

## Data for Your Case Study

Analyze the quotations below as you research your case study. You may also use the quotations in your case study presentation.

# VOICES and VIEWS

## ON THE CZECHS' TRANSITION FROM TOTALITARIANISM

"The behavior of people during this transition from totalitarianism is quite similar to that of someone who had just been released from prison. . . . We were used to being in prison. There were only a few rules, but they were very strong rules. And now we have freedom. But what to do with it?"

*Dana Nemcova, sociologist*

"If we want a democracy, we need an economy that works. And in order to have an economy that works, we need a democracy"

*Ivan Havel, computer scientist*

"It wasn't so bad under communism, and now it's much worse."

*Complaint of older Czechs*

"The majority of people is willing to sell freedom for social security. There is a real danger that they will be tempted to follow any leader who will promise them this security."

*Juraj Mesik, environmentalist*

"Communists, we forgive you. Please come back!"

*Half-serious Czech joke*

"I am convinced that we will never build a democratic state based on the rule of law if we do not at the same time build a state that is . . . humane, moral, intellectual and spiritual, and cultural. The best laws . . . will not in themselves guarantee legality or freedom or human rights."

*President Vaclav Havel*

## ON DEMOCRACY IN SOUTH KOREA

"Democracy is the founding principle of our country. . . . Democracy alone is the road to freedom, the road to economic equality, and the road to social welfare. Democracy alone is the road for the people of the Republic of Korea to feel purposeful and proud."

*Kim Dae Jung, political leader*

"The two groups that had wielded the most power in Korea over the last 30 years are the military and the *chaebol*. The military may be said to have gone back to their barracks, but the *chaebol* have become even more powerful."

*Chung Un-chan, Korean economist*

"After ten years of democratization, many people increasingly feel a sense of crisis that Korean democracy is adrift, if not on the verge of running aground."

*Jaung Hoon, Korean political scientist*

"Politics that is controlled by money is not democracy. Democracy gives an equal vote to all people, and everyone—the learned and the unlearned, the rich and poor—has the right to exercise his or her vote. . . . In reality, however, this basic principle of democracy is being greatly undermined in Korea. Money sways politics."

*Lee Young-hee, Korean law professor*

"I was active in politics for a long time, and I have always believed that the way politics was conducted in this country was wrong. I firmly believe that politics should be free of the yoke of money."

*President Kim Young Sam*

▲ *The business district of Seoul, South Korea's capital*

## Researching and Presenting Case Study 5

### RESEARCHING

As you research *The Czech Republic and South Korea: Democracy and Economic Development*, remember that your case study project will have three parts:

- a **presentation** based on your research and reflection on the topic
- an **oral interview** to follow your presentation
- a **project journal** that will include a case study overview, research log, and an essay on the significance of your topic

### PRESENTING

Your presentation on this topic should include the following:

- a **brief overview** or **time line** of key events leading up to the transition to democracy in the Czech Republic and South Korea
- an **examination** of the challenges facing the Czech Republic as it tries to establish a democratic government and a market economy at the same time
- an **analysis** of the strengths and weaknesses of South Korea's democratic government
- a **comparison** of the impact of corruption in both nations
- a **concluding statement** on what we can learn from the experiences of the Czech Republic and South Korea about the prospects of the world's newest democracies

# RESOURCES

## IN YOUR WORLD HISTORY TEXTBOOK

To locate useful background information on this subject in your textbook, check the index under the following headings: **democracy, developing nations, economy, Czechoslovakia, Czech Republic, Eastern Europe, Korea, South Korea**

## IN YOUR LIBRARY

✔Cummings, Bruce. *Korea's Place in the Sun: A Modern History.* New York: W.W. Norton, 1997.

✔Lee, Kenneth B. *Korea and East Asia: The Story of Phoenix.* New York: Praeger, 1997.

✔MacDonald, Donald Stone & Donald N. Clark, Eds. *The Koreans: Contemporary Politics and Society.* Boulder: Westview Press, 1996.

✔*Mini Dragons: South Korea.* PBS Video, 1995.

✔Nagorski, Andrew. *The Birth of Freedom: Shaping Lives and Societies in the New Eastern Europe.* New York: Simon & Schuster, 1993.

✔Pridham, Geoffrey & Paul Lewis, Eds. *Stabilizing Fragile Democracies: New Party Systems in Southern and Eastern Europe.* New York: Routledge, 1995.

✔Sommer, Mark. *Living in Freedom: The Exhilaration and Anguish of Prague's Second Spring.* San Francisco: Mercury House, 1992.

✔Wheaton, Bernard & Zdenek Kavan. *The Velvet Revolution: Czechoslovakia, 1988-1991.* Boulder: Westview Press, 1992.

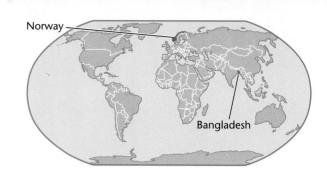

Norway

Bangladesh

## CASE STUDY 6

# Women in National Development: Bangladesh and Norway

### Case Study Topic

Women worldwide have challenged and begun to change their political and economic roles as citizens. In this case study, you will report on how women in two countries—Bangladesh and Norway—have taken an active role in government and economic development.

### How to Complete Case Study 6

■ Be sure to read or review the **Project Overview** on pages 568–573. It describes how to complete a case study.

■ Then read the **background information** on this page and on page 595. It will provide a starting point for your research.

■ Next, study the **picture and chart** on the next page for additional data.

■ Finally, on page 596, you will find **"Voices and Views,"** a collection of quotations. Analyze them and add them to your research.

■ On page 597 is a list of **what you need to include** in your case study presentation. Also provided is a list of **resources** for your research.

## BACKGROUND INFORMATION

Women today play increasingly important roles in the economic development of their nations. Worldwide, women are the sole breadwinners in one in three households. Seventy percent of all small businesses are run by women. In Asia and Africa, women farmers raise from 60 to 80 percent of the food grown in their countries.

Women are also increasing their participation in political life. In the world's newest democracies, such as South Africa, women have gained the right to vote and run for public office at the same time as men. In the older democracies, women are running for office—and winning—in greater numbers than ever before. Another measure of women's progress in political life is the growing number of women who have served as prime ministers or presidents—in countries as different as Bangladesh and Norway.

### BANGLADESH

Bangladesh is one of the world's poorest and most densely populated nations. Since gaining its independence from Pakistan in 1971, the people of Bangladesh have endured famines, devastating storms, and political turmoil.

Traditionally, the status of women has been low in this country. Today, however, Bangladeshi women are gaining new respect and economic independence thanks to the work of Muhammad Yunus, founder of the Grameen ("Village") Bank. The Grameen Bank lends small amounts of money to the poorest of the poor—landless women—on the basis of trust. The women then use this money to start businesses and earn enough not only to repay the loans, but to improve their lives.

Women in Bangladesh have also become more active politically. In 1991, Begum Khalida Zia became Bangladesh's first female prime minister.

Yunus's idea of "microcredit"—lending small amounts to poor people so that they can help themselves out of poverty—has spread from Bangladesh to more than 50 nations, including

## Data for Your Case Study

Use the chart below as you research your case study project. You may also use the data in your case study presentation.

### Bangladesh and Norway at a Glance

| | Bangladesh | Norway |
|---|---|---|
| **Total land area** | 55,598 mi² (144,000 km²) | 149,405 mi² (386,958 km²) |
| **Population** (1996 estimate) | 117.9 million | 4.4 million |
| **Number of people per square mile** | 2,121 (819 per km²) | 29 (11 per km²) |
| **Urban population** | 20% | 77% |
| **Per capital GDP** (in U.S. dollars; 1995 estimate) | $1,130 | $24,500 |
| **Natural resources** | natural gas, arable land, timber | petroleum, copper, natural gas, pyrites, nickel, iron ore, zinc, lead, fish, timber, hydropower |
| **Arable land** | 67% | 3% |
| **Life expectancy** | 55.9 years | 77.5 year |
| Men | 56 years | 74.6 years |
| Women | 55.7 years | 80.6 years |
| **Adult Literacy** | 38.1% | 99% |
| Men | 49.4% | 99% |
| Women | 26.1% | 99% |
| **Women in labor force** | 67% | 60% |
| **Parliamentary seats held by women** | 10% | 39% |
| **Women in administrative and management jobs** | 5% | 31% |
| **Salaries of women as a percent of men's incomes** | 23% | 41% |

▲ *A Grameen Bank borrower in Bangladesh uses a cellular telephone to run her business. Under a program set up by the Grameen Bank, the telephones were provided exlusively to bank borrowers in villages without telephone service.*

the United States. "These millions of small people with their millions of small pursuits," says Yunus, "can add up to create the biggest development wonder."

## NORWAY

In contrast to Bangladesh, Norway is one of the world's richest and least densely populated nations. After World War II, Norway discovered large deposits of oil and natural gas off its coast.

Today it is the world's third largest oil exporter.

Norway also leads the world in the percentage of women in top government and political positions. Norwegian women won the right to vote in 1907. By 1990, not only were its prime minister, Dr. Gro Harlem Bruntland, and half her cabinet women, but three of the country's major political parties were headed by women. Women held nearly 40 percent of the seats in the parliament as well.

## Data for
## Your Case Study

Analyze the quotations below and the chart on the next page as you research your case study. You may also use the quotations and the chart in your case study presentation.

# VOICES and VIEWS

## ON WOMEN AND ECONOMIC DEVELOPMENT

"Everyone, without discrimination, has the right to equal pay for equal work."
*United Nations Universal Declaration of Human Rights, 1948*

"Women make up half the world, are responsible for nearly two thirds of all working hours, yet they earn one tenth of the world's income and own less than one percent of the world's property."
*United Nations Report on the Status of Women, 1985*

"I can assure you that if the right environment and incentives were created for women farmers, and the problems facing them now were addressed, the sustainable end of hunger would be a reality."
*Dr. Ester Afua Ocloo, entrepreneur, Ghana*

"We found that many positive things could be achieved by lending to women. Because when a woman's income increases, the immediate beneficiaries are the children. A woman looks to the future with a planned strategy to improve the family situation. Men don't pay attention to such things."
*Muhammad Yunus, founder of Bangladesh's Grameen Bank*

"These women have become a lot braver because of the Grameen Bank. Previously, if any strange man came, they would go into their houses. . . . Now they come out and talk."
*Oirashibala Dhor, Grameen Bank borrower in Bangladesh*

## ON WOMEN IN POLITICS

"In no country do women have political status, access, or influence equal to men."
*Barbara Nelson, American professor of public affairs and Najma Chowdhury, Bangladeshi political scientist*

"To be successful, a woman has to be much better at her job than a man."
*Golda Meir, Prime Minister of Israel from 1969 to 1974*

"The biggest asset for a woman candidate is being a woman, and the biggest liability is not being a man."
*Barbara Curran, former New Jersey Assemblywoman*

"Democracy minus women is not democracy."
*Slogan of Russia's First Independent Women's Forum*

"The feminists have become far too strident [harsh-sounding] and have done damage to the cause of women by making us out to be something we're not. You get on because you have the right talents."
*Margaret Thatcher, Prime Minister of Britain from 1979 to 1990*

"I was elected by the women of Ireland, who instead of rocking the cradle, rocked the system."
*Mary Robinson, elected president of Ireland in 1990 and Ireland's first woman president*

"You no longer think: these are three women talking. Where are the men?"
*Bernt Aardal, Norwegian researcher, after a televised debate by three female party leaders*

## Women Heads of State Since 1960

**Corazon Aquino,** president of the Philippines, 1986–1992

**Sirimavo Bandaranaike,** became prime minister of Sri Lanka in 1994

**Benazir Bhutto,** prime minister of Pakistan, 1988–1990 and 1993–1996

**Violeta Barrios de Chamorro,** president of Nicaragua, 1990–1997

**Indira Gandhi,** prime minister of India, 1966–1977 and 1980–1984

**Chandrika Kumaratunge,** became president of Sri Lanka in 1994

**Golda Meir,** prime minister of Israel, 1969–1974

**Isabel Peron,** president of Argentina, 1974–1976

**Margaret Thatcher,** prime minister of the United Kingdom, 1979–1990

**Mary Robinson,** president of Ireland, 1990–1997

**Sheikh Hasina Wajed,** became prime minister of Bangladesh in 1996

# Researching and Presenting Case Study 6

## RESEARCHING

As you research *Women in National Development: Bangladesh and Norway,* remember that your case study project will have three parts:

- a **presentation** based on your research and reflection on the topic

- an **oral interview** to follow your presentation

- a **project journal** that will include a case study overview, research log, and an essay on the significance of your topic

## PRESENTING

Your presentation on this topic should include the following:

- a **brief overview** of the economies of Bangladesh and Norway

- a **description** of how the Grameen Bank has improved women's lives in Bangladesh

- a **survey** of the political gains women have made in Norway

- a **comparison** of the barriers to political and economic equality faced by women in each country

- a **concluding statement** on the significance of women's changing political and economic roles to the people of Bangladesh and Norway as well as to Americans

## RESOURCES

### IN YOUR WORLD HISTORY TEXTBOOK

To locate useful background information on this topic in your textbook, check the index under the following headings:
**women, economy, welfare state, Bangladesh, South Asia, Norway**

### IN YOUR LIBRARY

✔Baxter, Craig.
*Bangladesh: From a Nation to a State.* Boulder: Westview, 1997.

✔Bornstein, David.
*The Price of a Dream: The Story of the Grameen Bank.* New York: Simon & Schuster, 1996.

✔Langley, Winston E., Ed.
*Women's Rights in International Documents: A Sourcebook with Commentary.* Jefferson, NC: McFarland, 1991.

✔Liswood, Laura.
*Women World Leaders: Fifteen Great Politicians Tell Their Stories.* New York: HarperCollins, 1997.

✔Nelson, Barbara J. & Najma Chowdhury.
*Women and Politics Worldwide.* New Haven: Yale University Press, 1994.

✔Todd, Helen.
*Women at the Center: Grameen Bank Borrowers After One Decade.* Boulder: Westview, 1997.

✔Wahid, Abu N.M., Ed.
*The Grameen Bank: Poverty Relief in Bangladesh.* Boulder: Westview, 1993.

✔Wahid, Abu N.M. & Charles E. Weis, Eds.
*The Economy of Bangladesh: Problems and Prospects.* New York: Praeger, 1996.

✔World Bank.
*Bangladesh: Strategies for Enhancing the Role of Women in Economic Development.* World Bank, 1990.

# Civic Participation: Australia and the United States

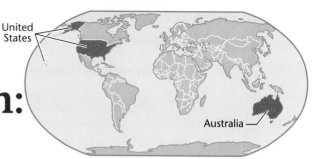

United States

Australia

## Case Study Topic

A key component in a representative democrary is the electorate—the body of voters who elect those who govern. Although voter turnout is critical to the future of democratic governments, voter participation is declining in some countries. In this case study, you will investigate the decline in civic participation in two democracies—the United States and Australia. You will also report on what must be done to revitalize civic life in the United States.

## How to Complete Case Study 7

■ Be sure to read or review the **Project Overview** on pages 568–573. It describes how to complete a case study.

■ Then read the **background information** on this page and on page 599. It will provide a starting point for your research.

■ Next, study the **map and chart** on the next page for additional data.

■ Finally, on page 600, you will find **"Voices and Views,"** a collection of quotations. Analyze them and add them to your research.

■ On page 601 is a list of **what you need to include** in your case study presentation. Also provided is a list of **resources** for your research.

## BACKGROUND INFORMATION

From El Salvador in Central America to Poland in Eastern Europe to the Philippines in East Asia, democracy is on the rise. The number of people living under governments they have chosen themselves has increased dramatically in the past two decades. Worldwide, the future of democracy has never looked brighter.

In many older democracies, however, some people are worried. From Switzerland in Western Europe to Australia in the Western Pacific to the United States in North America, more and more people are choosing not to participate in politics and government, sometimes not even bothering to vote. Growing public apathy has caused concerned citizens to ask two questions: Why are people "dropping out" of politics and civic life? What can be done to reverse this disturbing trend?

### AUSTRALIA

Australia has been a democracy since it gained its independence from Great Britain in 1901. In 1924, its parliament adopted a system of compulsory voting for national elections. Under Australia's election law, individuals over the age of 18 are required by law to register to vote and to cast ballots at every federal election. Failure to register or to vote can be punished by fines and even imprisonment.

As a result of this system, Australia has one of the highest voter turnout rates in the world, usually well above 90 percent. However, while Australians vote in large numbers, there are signs of growing political apathy. A recent study by a parliamentary committee revealed "a remarkable level of ignorance in the Australian population about even quite elementary aspects of politics and government."

Concern about the health of Australian democracy has led to a renewed debate over compulsory voting. Supporters of the system argue that democratic government means rule by the people. Therefore elections should be decided by all of the people. In their view, voting is a civic duty— the same as jury service or paying taxes.

Critics of compulsory voting make two main arguments. The first is that in a democracy, the right to vote should also include the right not to vote. The second is that compulsory voting allows politicians to take voters for granted. Because

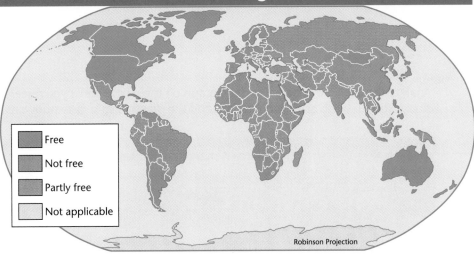

### Data for Your Case Study

Use the map and chart below as you research your case study project. You may also use the data in your case study presentation.

Free

Not free

Partly free

Not applicable

Robinson Projection

## Australia and the United States at a Glance

| | **AUSTRALIA** | **UNITED STATES** |
|---|---|---|
| **Total land area** | 2,978,147 mi² (7,713,364 km²) | 3,615,292 mi² (9,363,563 km²) |
| **Population** (1996 estimate) | 18.1 million | 264 million |
| **Number of people per square mile** | 6 (2 per km²) | 73 (28 per km²) |
| **Urban population** | 85% | 75% |
| **Per capita GDP** (in U.S. dollars; 1995 estimate) | $22,100 | $27,500 |
| **Adult literacy** (age 15 and over can read and write) | 100% | 97% |
| **Life expectancy at birth** | 79.4 years | 76 years |
| **Ethnic divisions** | Caucasian, 95%; Asian, 4%; aboriginal and other, 1% | white, 83%; black, 12.4%; Asian, 3.3%; Native American, .8% |
| **Religion** | Anglican, 26.1%; Roman Catholic, 26%; other Christian, 24.3% | Protestant, 56%; Roman Catholic, 28%; Jewish, 2%; other, 4%; none, 10% |

politicians do not have to convince voters to vote, the critics argue, they are not as sensitive to the interests and needs of the people as they should be.

### THE UNITED STATES

In the United States, one of the world's oldest democracies, voting has always been voluntary. Early in the twentieth century, the right to vote was broadened to include women. More recently, the Fifteeth Amendment, the Twenty-sixth Amendment, and the Voting Rights Act have eliminated barriers that had kept minorities and young people from voting. Today any qualified American over the age of 18 can register to vote.

While the number of people eligible to vote has increased, voter participation in national elections has been steadily decreasing—from 63 percent in the early 1960s to under 50 percent in 1996. Equally disturbing is a drop in civic participation. The number of Americans reporting that "in the past year" they "attended a public meeting on town or school affairs" fell by more than a third between 1973 and 1993.

Analyze the quotations below and the graph on the next page as you research your case study. You may also use the quotations and the graph in your case study presentation.

# VOICES and VIEWS

## ON COMPULSORY VOTING IN AUSTRALIA

❝It shall be the duty of every elector to record a vote at each election.❞

*Commonwealth Electoral Act*

❝I am one who believes a system where 95 percent of adults vote is more democratic that one in which 50 percent vote. That voting is analogous to [like] other citizen's duties: paying taxes, jury and military service, and sending children to school.❞

*Laurie Oakes*

❝Surely it is a fundamental human right to be left alone, to be allowed to live one's own life within the law but otherwise unmolested, and to take no interest in politics at all except by choice.❞

*Padraic McGuinness, newspaper columnist*

❝Insisting that citizens vote encourages everyone to think about the issues.❞

The Courier Mail, *an Australian newspaper*

❝Compulsory voting keeps down the cost of campaigns. The most expensive part of a campaign where there is not compulsory voting is having to 'turn out the vote.'❞

*Chris Puplick, Australian politician*

❝Recent figures show that many did not vote in the last State election and were not fined. This shows what an unenforceable, wasteful use of taxpayer's money compulsory voting is.❞

*Letter to the editor of the* Adelaide Advertiser, *Adelaide, Australia*

## ON VOLUNTARY VOTING IN THE UNITED STATES

❝No right is more precious in a free country than that of having a voice in the election of those who make the laws under which . . . we must live. Other rights . . . are illusionary . . . if the right to vote is undermined.❞

*United States Supreme Court in* Wesberry v. Sanders

❝Nobody will ever deprive the American people of the right to vote but the American people themselves—and the only way they could is by not voting.❞

*President Franklin Delano Roosevelt*

❝Americans hate politics as it is now practiced because we have lost all sense of the public good. . . . They understand instinctively that politics these days is not about finding solutions. It is about discovering postures that offer short-term political benefits.❞

*E.J. Dionne, Jr., journalist*

❝Democracy is not a thing, it is a process. Self-government cannot be put on automatic pilot.❞

*League of Women Voters*

❝The probability that a lone vote will actually affect an election outcome is minuscule. . . . Quite simply, for many Americans voting just doesn't seem worth the effort.❞

*Ruy A. Teixeira, Economic Policy Institute*

❝People often say, with pride, 'I'm not interested in politics.' They might as well say, 'I'm not interested in my standard of living, my health, my job, my rights, my freedoms, my future or any future. . . . If we mean to keep any control over our world and lives, we must be interested in politics."

*Martha Gellhorn, journalist*

## Voter Turnout

▲ Voter turnout in presidential elections dropped from 55 percent in 1992 to 49 percent in 1996.

# Researching and Presenting Case Study 7

## RESEARCHING

For this case study, your focus should be on voter participation in your community. To learn more about what can be done to increase voter participation where you live, you will want to interview the following:

■ elected officials and local political party leaders

■ local chapter of the League of Women Voters

As you research *Civic Participation: Australia and the United States*, remember that your case study project will have three parts:

■ a **presentation** based on your research and reflection on the topic

■ an **oral interview** to follow your presentation

■ a **project journal** that will include a case study overview, research log, and an essay on the significance of your topic

## PRESENTING

Your presentation on this topic should include the following:

■ a **brief review** of voter participation rates in Australia and the United States since World War II

■ a **summary** of Australia's compulsory voting laws and the main arguments for and against this system

■ an **opinion** of why you think voter turnout has dropped in the United States since the 1960s

■ **recommendations** on reversing this trend

■ a **concluding statement** on the importance of informed and involved citizens to the future of democracy, both in the United States and worldwide

## RESOURCES

### IN YOUR WORLD HISTORY TEXTBOOK

To locate useful background information on this topic in your textbook, check the index under the following headings: **democracy, social contract, suffrage, Australia, United States**

### IN YOUR LIBRARY

✔Dionne, E.J, Jr. *Why Americans Hate Politics.* New York: Simon & Schuster, 1992.

✔Ravitch, Diane & Abigail Thernstrom, Eds. *The Democracy Reader: Classic and Modern Speeches, Essays, Poems, Declarations, and Documents on Freedom and Human Rights Worldwide.* New York: HarperCollins, 1993.

✔Smith, Sam. *Sam Smith's Great American Political Repair Manual: How to Rebuild Our Country So the Politics Aren't Broken and Politicians Aren't Fixed.* New York: W.W. Norton, 1997.

✔Tipp, Stacey L. & Carol Wekesser, Eds. *Politics in America: Opposing Viewpoints.* San Diego: Greenhaven Press, 1992.

### ON THE WORLD WIDE WEB

For information on U.S. voting trends, you might begin by going to the League of Women Voters' web site and reading its 1997 report titled *Charting the Health of American Democracy.*

For information on Australia's election laws and voter turnout, look for the web sites of the Australian Electoral Commission and Australia's Parliamentary Education Office.

# REFERENCE

## Contents

# *SECTION*

# Historical Documents

# The World: Political

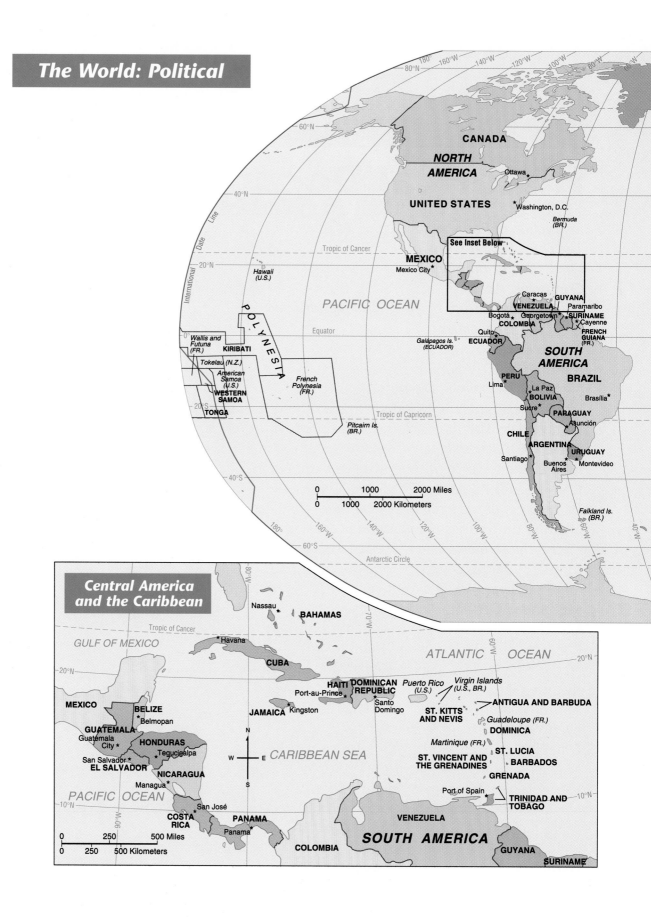

CANADA

**NORTH AMERICA**

Ottawa ★

**UNITED STATES**

★ Washington, D.C.

Bermuda (BR.)

Tropic of Cancer

**MEXICO**

Mexico City ★

*PACIFIC OCEAN*

Hawaii (U.S.)

See Inset Below

Caracas ★  **GUYANA**
**VENEZUELA** ★  Paramaribo
Bogotá ★  Georgetown ★ ★  **SURINAME**
**COLOMBIA**  Cayenne ★
**FRENCH GUIANA (FR.)**

Equator

Quito ★
Galápagos Is. (ECUADOR)  **ECUADOR**

**SOUTH AMERICA**

Wallis and Futuna (FR.)

0

**KIRIBATI**

Tokelau (N.Z.)

American Samoa (U.S.)

**WESTERN SAMOA**

**TONGA**

*POLYNESIA*

French Polynesia (FR.)

**PERU**

Lima ★

La Paz ★
**BOLIVIA**

Sucre ★

**BRAZIL**

Brasília ★

**PARAGUAY**

Asunción ★

Tropic of Capricorn

Pitcairn Is. (BR.)

**CHILE**

**ARGENTINA**  **URUGUAY**

Santiago ★

Buenos Aires ★  ★ Montevideo

0    1000    2000 Miles
0    1000    2000 Kilometers

Falkland Is. (BR.)

Antarctic Circle

International Date Line

## Central America and the Caribbean

Nassau ★
**BAHAMAS**

Tropic of Cancer

*GULF OF MEXICO*

Havana ★

*ATLANTIC OCEAN*

**CUBA**

**MEXICO**

**BELIZE**
★ Belmopan

**GUATEMALA**
Guatemala City ★

**HAITI**  **DOMINICAN REPUBLIC**
Port-au-Prince ★  ★ Santo Domingo

**JAMAICA**  Kingston

Puerto Rico (U.S.)

Virgin Islands (U.S., BR.)

**ANTIGUA AND BARBUDA**

**ST. KITTS AND NEVIS**

Guadeloupe (FR.)

**DOMINICA**

Martinique (FR.)

**ST. LUCIA**

**HONDURAS**
★ Tegucigalpa

San Salvador ★
**EL SALVADOR**

**NICARAGUA**

Managua ★

*CARIBBEAN SEA*

**ST. VINCENT AND THE GRENADINES**

**BARBADOS**

**GRENADA**

N
W   E
S

*PACIFIC OCEAN*

San José ★
**COSTA RICA**

**PANAMA**

Panama ★

Port of Spain ★

**TRINIDAD AND TOBAGO**

**VENEZUELA**

**SOUTH AMERICA**

**COLOMBIA**

**GUYANA**

**SURINAME**

0    250    500 Miles
0    250    500 Kilometers

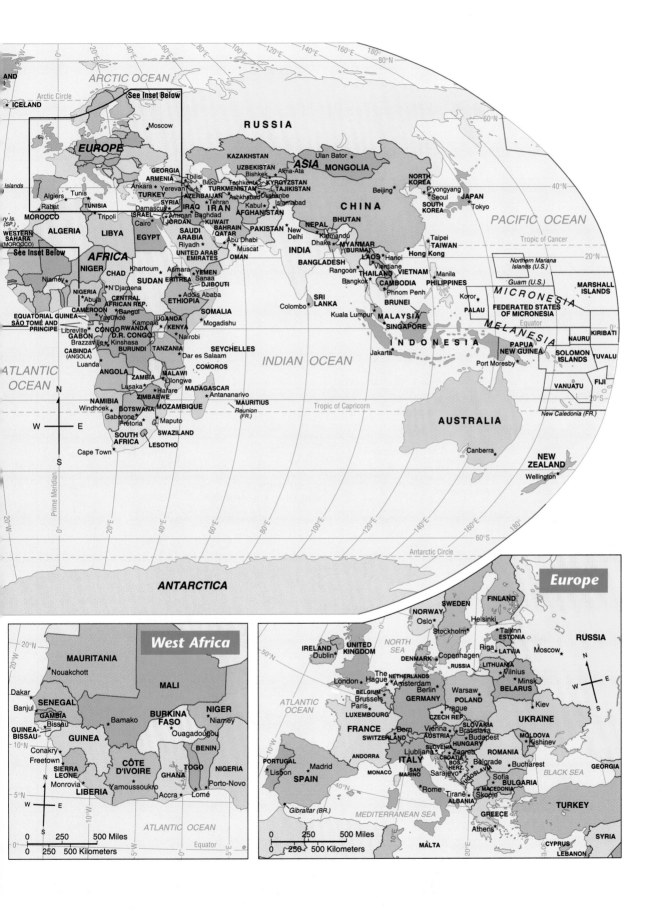

ARCTIC OCEAN

Arctic Circle

ICELAND

EUROPE   See Inset Below

Moscow

RUSSIA

60°N

Islands

Algiers   Tunis

Rabat   TUNISIA

MOROCCO

WESTERN
SAHARA
(MOROCCO)

ALGERIA   LIBYA

EGYPT

See Inset Below

AFRICA

NIGER   CHAD

Niamey

NIGERIA

Abuja

CENTRAL
AFRICAN REP.

CAMEROON   Bangui

EQUATORIAL GUINEA
SÃO TOMÉ AND
PRINCIPE

Libreville   Yaoundé

GABON   CONGO   D.R. CONGO   RWANDA

Brazzaville   Kinshasa   BURUNDI

CABINDA
(ANGOLA)

Luanda

ANGOLA   ZAMBIA   MALAWI

Lusaka   Lilongwe

Harare

NAMIBIA   ZIMBABWE   MOZAMBIQUE

Windhoek   BOTSWANA

Gaborone   Maputo

Pretoria   SWAZILAND

SOUTH
AFRICA   LESOTHO

Cape Town

ATLANTIC
OCEAN

GEORGIA   Tbilisi   Baku

ARMENIA

Ankara   Yerevan

TURKEY   AZERBAIJAN

SYRIA   Tehran

Damascus   IRAQ   IRAN

ISRAEL   Amman   Baghdad

Cairo   JORDAN   KUWAIT

BAHRAIN   QATAR

SAUDI   Abu Dhabi

ARABIA   Riyadh   Muscat

UNITED ARAB   OMAN

EMIRATES

Khartoum   Asmara   YEMEN

SUDAN   ERITREA   Sanaa

DJIBOUTI

ETHIOPIA

Addis Ababa

SOMALIA

UGANDA   Kampala

Mogadishu

Kinshasa   KENYA

Nairobi

TANZANIA

Dar es Salaam

SEYCHELLES

COMOROS

MADAGASCAR

Antananarivo

MAURITIUS

Reunion
(FR.)

Tropic of Capricorn

KAZAKHSTAN   Ulan Bator

UZBEKISTAN   ASIA   MONGOLIA

Bishkek   Alma-Ata

Tashkent   KYRGYZSTAN

TURKMENISTAN   TAJIKISTAN

Ashkhabad   Dushanbe   Beijing

Kabul   Islamabad   CHINA

AFGHANISTAN

NEPAL   BHUTAN

New   Katmandu

PAKISTAN   Delhi   Dhaka   MYANMAR

BANGLADESH   (BURMA)

INDIA   LAOS   Hanoi

Rangoon   Vientiane

Colombo   THAILAND   VIETNAM

SRI   Bangkok

LANKA   CAMBODIA

Phnom Penh

BRUNEI

Kuala Lumpur   MALAYSIA

SINGAPORE

I N D O N E S I A

Jakarta

INDIAN OCEAN

NORTH
KOREA

P'yongyang   JAPAN

Seoul   Tokyo

SOUTH
KOREA

Taipei   TAIWAN

Hong Kong

Manila

PHILIPPINES

Koror

PALAU

PACIFIC OCEAN

Tropic of Cancer

Northern Mariana
Islands (U.S.)

Guam (U.S.)

MICRONESIA

FEDERATED STATES
OF MICRONESIA

MELANESIA

PAPUA
NEW GUINEA

Port Moresby

New Caledonia (FR.)

AUSTRALIA

Canberra

MARSHALL
ISLANDS

NAURU   KIRIBATI

SOLOMON
ISLANDS   TUVALU

VANUATU   FIJI

NEW
ZEALAND

Wellington

Antarctic Circle

ANTARCTICA

N
W   E
S

## West Africa

MAURITANIA

Nouakchott

Dakar

SENEGAL

Banjul

GAMBIA

Bissau

GUINEA-
BISSAU

Conakry

GUINEA

Freetown

SIERRA
LEONE

Monrovia

LIBERIA

MALI

Bamako

BURKINA
FASO

Ouagadougou

NIGER

Niamey

BENIN

CÔTE
D'IVOIRE   TOGO

Yamoussoukro   GHANA

Accra   Lomé

NIGERIA

Porto-Novo

N
W   E
S

ATLANTIC   OCEAN

Equator

| 0 | 250 | 500 Miles |
| 0 | 250 | 500 Kilometers |

## Europe

SWEDEN   FINLAND

NORWAY   Helsinki

Oslo   Stockholm   Tallinn

ESTONIA

IRELAND   UNITED   DENMARK   Copenhagen   Riga   LATVIA   Moscow

Dublin   KINGDOM   RUSSIA   LITHUANIA

NORTH   The   NETHERLANDS   Vilnius   Minsk

London   Hague   Amsterdam   Berlin   Warsaw   BELARUS

BELGIUM   GERMANY   POLAND

Paris   Brussels   Prague   Kiev

LUXEMBOURG   CZECH REP.   UKRAINE

FRANCE   SLOVAKIA

Bern   Vienna   Bratislava   MOLDOVA

SWITZERLAND   AUSTRIA   Budapest   Kishinev

ANDORRA   Ljubljana   HUNGARY   ROMANIA

SLOVENIA   Zagreb   Bucharest   GEORGIA

PORTUGAL   ITALY   CROATIA   Belgrade

Madrid   BOS.   Sofia   BLACK SEA

MONACO   SAN   HERZ.   Sarajevo   BULGARIA

Lisbon   MARINO   YUGOSLAVIA   MACEDONIA

SPAIN   Rome   Tiranë   Skopje   TURKEY

Gibraltar (BR.)   ALBANIA   GREECE

ATLANTIC
OCEAN

MEDITERRANEAN SEA

Athens

SYRIA

MALTA   CYPRUS   LEBANON

| 0 | 250 | 500 Miles |
| 0 | 250 | 500 Kilometers |

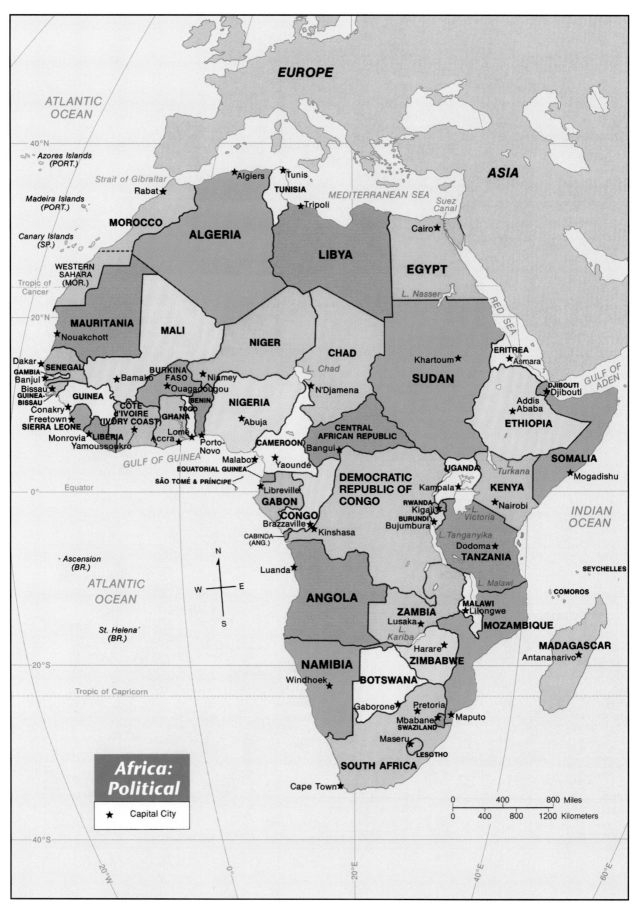

**EUROPE**

ATLANTIC OCEAN

40°N

Azores Islands (PORT.)

Strait of Gibraltar

Madeira Islands (PORT.)

★Algiers ★Tunis
Rabat★ **TUNISIA**

MEDITERRANEAN SEA

★Tripoli

Suez Canal

Cairo★

**ASIA**

Canary Islands (SP.)

**MOROCCO**

**ALGERIA**

**LIBYA**

**EGYPT**

Tropic of Cancer

WESTERN SAHARA (MOR.)

L. Nasser

RED SEA

GULF OF ADEN

20°N

**MAURITANIA**

★Nouakchott

**MALI**

**NIGER**

**CHAD**

Khartoum★

**ERITREA**
★Asmara

**SUDAN**

Dakar★
**GAMBIA** **SENEGAL**
Banjul★
Bissau★
**GUINEA-BISSAU** **GUINEA**
Conakry★
Freetown★
**SIERRA LEONE**
Monrovia★
**LIBERIA**
Yamoussoukro★

★Bamako
**BURKINA FASO**
★Niamey
★Ouagadougou
**BENIN**
**TOGO**
**CÔTE D'IVOIRE (IVORY COAST)** **GHANA**
★Lomé
Accra★
Porto-Novo★

L. Chad

N'Djamena★

**NIGERIA**
★Abuja

**CENTRAL AFRICAN REPUBLIC**
Bangui★

**DJIBOUTI**★Djibouti
Addis Ababa★
**ETHIOPIA**

GULF OF GUINEA

Malabo★
**EQUATORIAL GUINEA**
**SÃO TOMÉ & PRÍNCIPE**

**CAMEROON**
★Yaounde

**UGANDA**
Kampala★

**SOMALIA**
★Mogadishu

**KENYA**
★Nairobi

Equator 0°

Libreville★
**GABON**
**CONGO**
Brazzaville★

**DEMOCRATIC REPUBLIC OF CONGO**

L. Turkana

**RWANDA**
Kigali★
**BURUNDI**
Bujumbura★

L. Victoria

INDIAN OCEAN

Kinshasa★

L. Tanganyika

Dodoma★

**SEYCHELLES**

·Ascension (BR.)

ATLANTIC OCEAN

CABINDA (ANG.)

★Luanda

**TANZANIA**

L. Malawi

**COMOROS**

St. Helena (BR.)

**ANGOLA**

**ZAMBIA**
Lusaka★
L. Kariba

**MALAWI**
★Lilongwe

**MOZAMBIQUE**

**MADAGASCAR**
Antananarivo★

20°S

**NAMIBIA**
Windhoek★

**BOTSWANA**

Harare★
**ZIMBABWE**

Tropic of Capricorn

Gaborone★
Pretoria★
Mbabane★
**SWAZILAND**

★Maputo

Maseru★
**LESOTHO**
**SOUTH AFRICA**

N
W E
S

0  400  800 Miles
0  400  800  1200 Kilometers

Cape Town★

**Africa: Political**

★ Capital City

40°S

20°W    0°    20°E    40°E    60°E

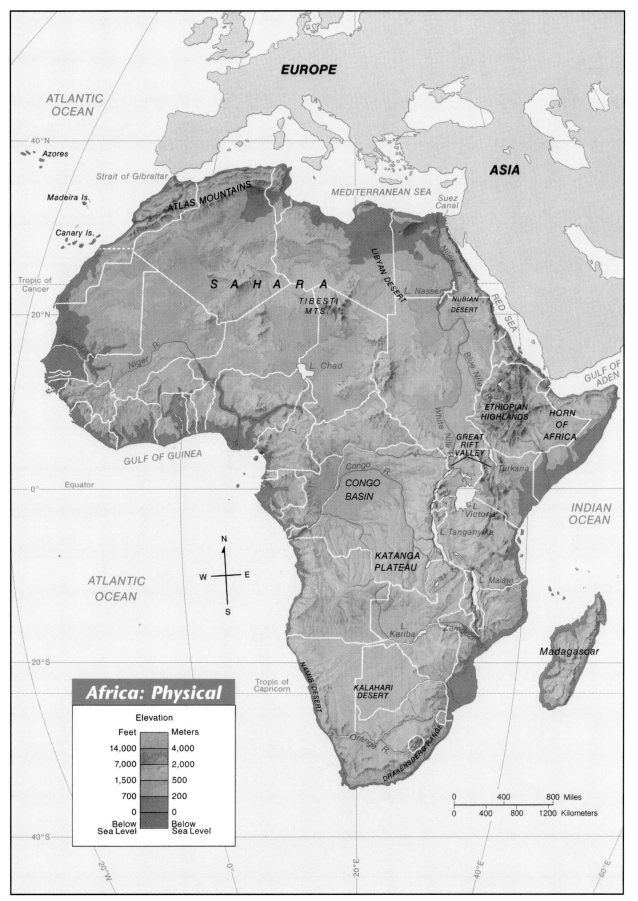

EUROPE

ATLANTIC
OCEAN

ASIA

40°N

Azores

Strait of Gibraltar

MEDITERRANEAN SEA

Suez
Canal

Madeira Is.

ATLAS MOUNTAINS

Canary Is.

Tropic of
Cancer

S  A  H  A  R  A

LIBYAN DESERT

L. Nasser

NUBIAN
DESERT

RED SEA

20°N

TIBESTI
MTS.

Niger R.

Senegal R.

Niger R.

L. Chad

Blue Nile

GULF OF
ADEN

White Nile

ETHIOPIAN
HIGHLANDS

HORN
OF
AFRICA

GULF OF GUINEA

Congo R.

CONGO
BASIN

GREAT
RIFT
VALLEY

Turkana

0°    Equator

N

L.
Victoria

INDIAN
OCEAN

L. Tanganyika

ATLANTIC
OCEAN

W            E

KATANGA
PLATEAU

L. Malawi

S

Madagascar

L.
Kariba

Zambezi

20°S

Tropic of
Capricorn

NAMIB DESERT

KALAHARI
DESERT

**Africa: Physical**

Elevation

| Feet | Meters |
|---|---|
| 14,000 | 4,000 |
| 7,000 | 2,000 |
| 1,500 | 500 |
| 700 | 200 |
| 0 | 0 |
| Below Sea Level | Below Sea Level |

Orange R.

DRAKENSBERG RANGE

0        400        800  Miles

0    400    800   1200  Kilometers

40°S

20°W

0°

20°E

40°E

60°E

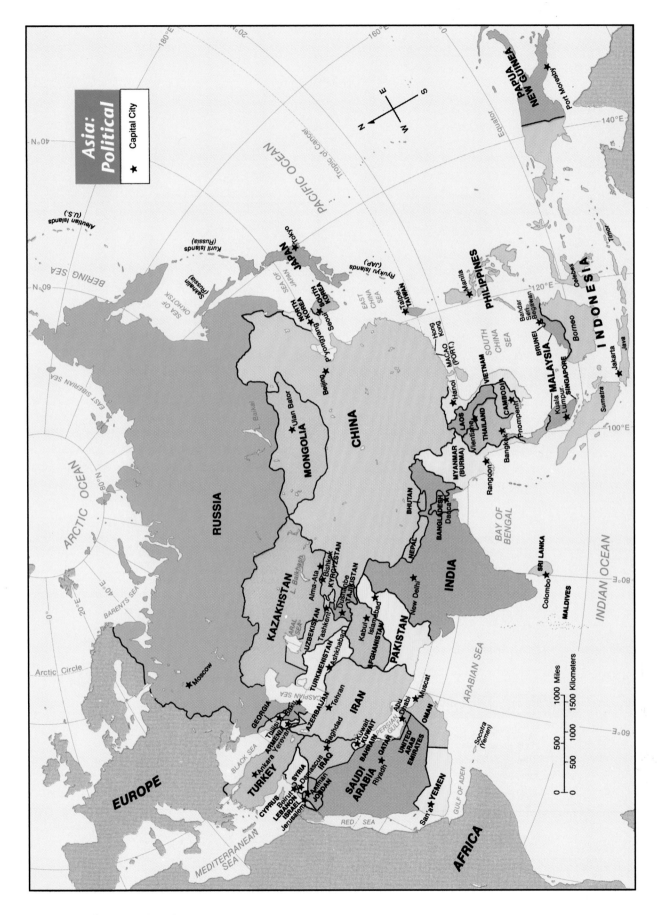

**Asia: Political**

★ Capital City

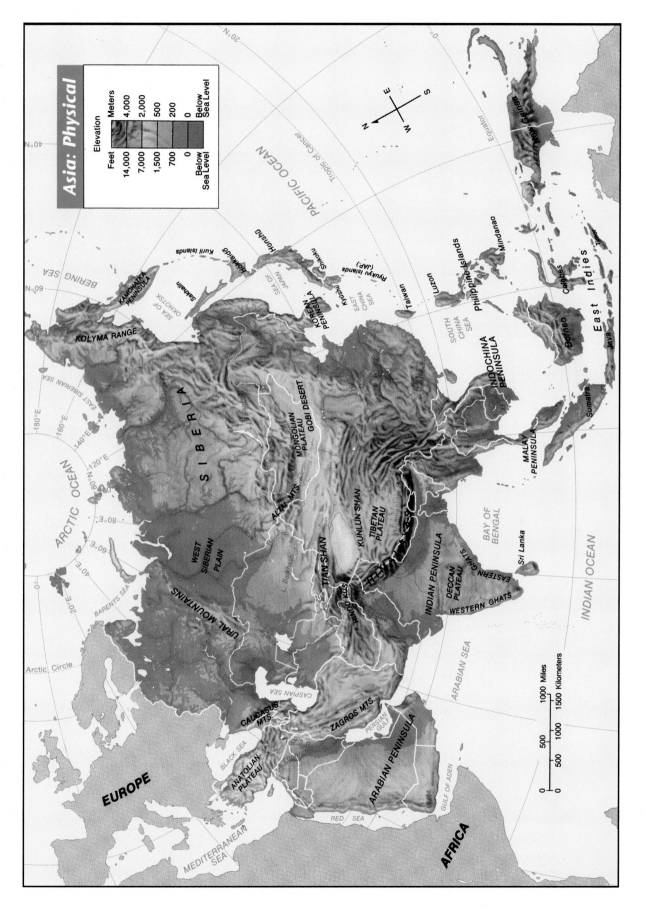

Asia: Physical

Elevation

| Feet | Meters |
|------|--------|
| 14,000 | 4,000 |
| 7,000 | 2,000 |
| 1,500 | 500 |
| 700 | 200 |
| 0 | 0 |
| Below Sea Level | Below Sea Level |

PACIFIC OCEAN

Tropic of Cancer

Equator

New Guinea

E
N — S
W

Mindanao

RyuKyu Islands (JAP.)

Philippine Islands

Luzon

Celebes

East Indies

Timor

Borneo

Java

Sumatra

Kuril Islands

Hokkaido

Honshu

Shikoku

Kyushu

SEA OF JAPAN

Taiwan

EAST CHINA SEA

SOUTH CHINA SEA

KOREAN PENINSULA

INDOCHINA PENINSULA

MALAY PENINSULA

BAY OF BENGAL

Sri Lanka

INDIAN OCEAN

BERING SEA

KAMCHATKA PENINSULA

KOLYMA RANGE

SEA OF OKHOTSK

Sakhalin

EAST SIBERIAN SEA

SIBERIA

ARCTIC OCEAN

180°E

160°E

140°E

120°E

100°N

80°E

60°N

40°N

20°N

60°E

MONGOLIAN PLATEAU

GOBI DESERT

ALTAI MTS.

WEST SIBERIAN PLAIN

TIAN SHAN

KUNLUN SHAN

TIBETAN PLATEAU

HIMALAYAS

HINDU KUSH

L. Balkhash

INDIAN PENINSULA

DECCAN PLATEAU

WESTERN GHATS

EASTERN GHATS

URAL MOUNTAINS

BARENTS SEA

Arctic Circle

20°E

40°E

CASPIAN SEA

CAUCASUS MTS.

ZAGROS MTS.

PERSIAN GULF

ARABIAN PENINSULA

ARABIAN SEA

1000 Miles

1500 Kilometers

1000

500

500

0

0

BLACK SEA

ANATOLIAN PLATEAU

EUROPE

MEDITERRANEAN SEA

RED SEA

GULF OF ADEN

AFRICA

Europe: Political

★ Capital City
• Major City

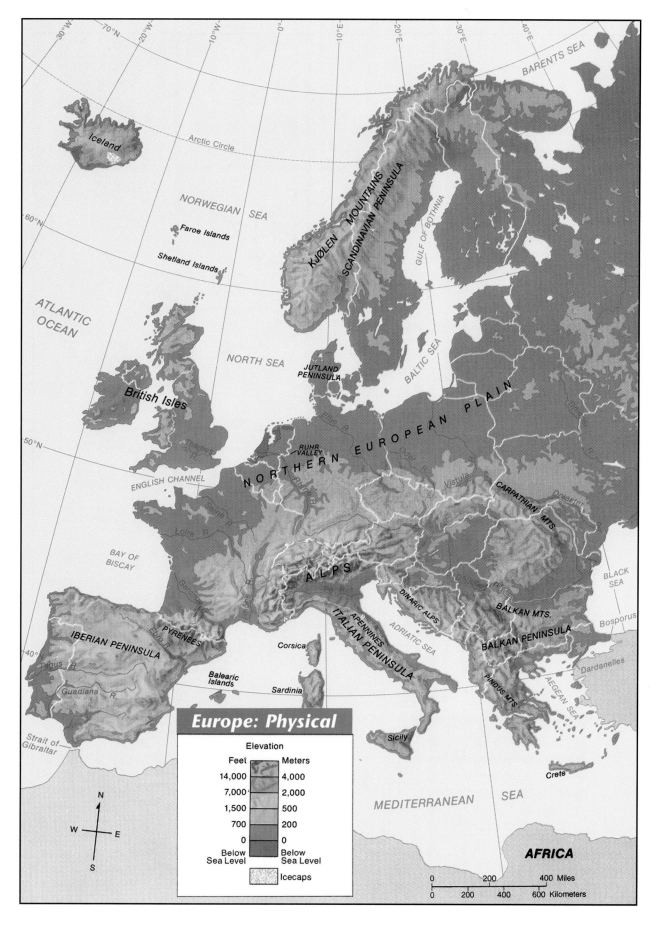

ATLAS

**Europe: Physical**

Elevation

| Feet | | Meters |
|---|---|---|
| 14,000 | | 4,000 |
| 7,000 | | 2,000 |
| 1,500 | | 500 |
| 700 | | 200 |
| 0 | | 0 |
| Below Sea Level | | Below Sea Level |

Icecaps

N
W — E
S

0        200        400 Miles
0     200     400     600 Kilometers

BARENTS SEA

NORWEGIAN SEA

Iceland

Arctic Circle

Faroe Islands

Shetland Islands

KJØLEN MOUNTAINS
SCANDINAVIAN PENINSULA

GULF OF BOTHNIA

ATLANTIC OCEAN

NORTH SEA

BALTIC SEA

JUTLAND PENINSULA

British Isles

NORTHERN EUROPEAN PLAIN

Elbe R.

RUHR VALLEY

Oder R.

Vistula R.

CARPATHIAN MTS.

Dniester

ENGLISH CHANNEL

Seine R.

Loire R.

BAY OF BISCAY

ALPS

DINARIC ALPS

ADRIATIC SEA

BALKAN MTS.

BLACK SEA

Bosporus

APENNINES
ITALIAN PENINSULA

BALKAN PENINSULA

Dardanelles

Garonne R.

Ebro R.

PYRENEES

IBERIAN PENINSULA

Tagus R.

Guadiana R.

Corsica

Balearic Islands

Sardinia

Sicily

PINDUS MTS.

AEGEAN SEA

Crete

Strait of Gibraltar

MEDITERRANEAN          SEA

AFRICA

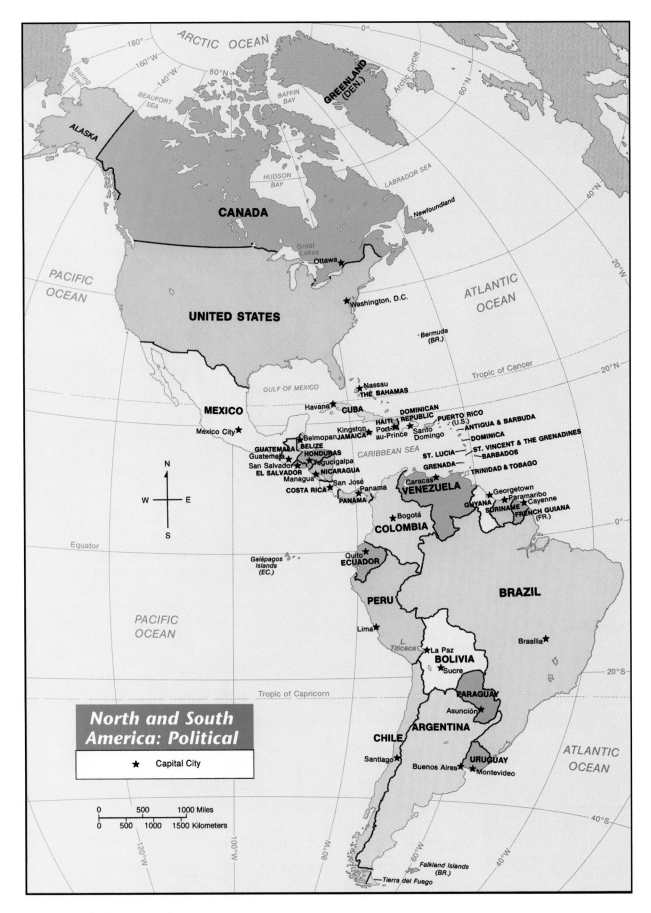

North and South
America: Political

★ Capital City

0    500    1000 Miles
0  500  1000  1500 Kilometers

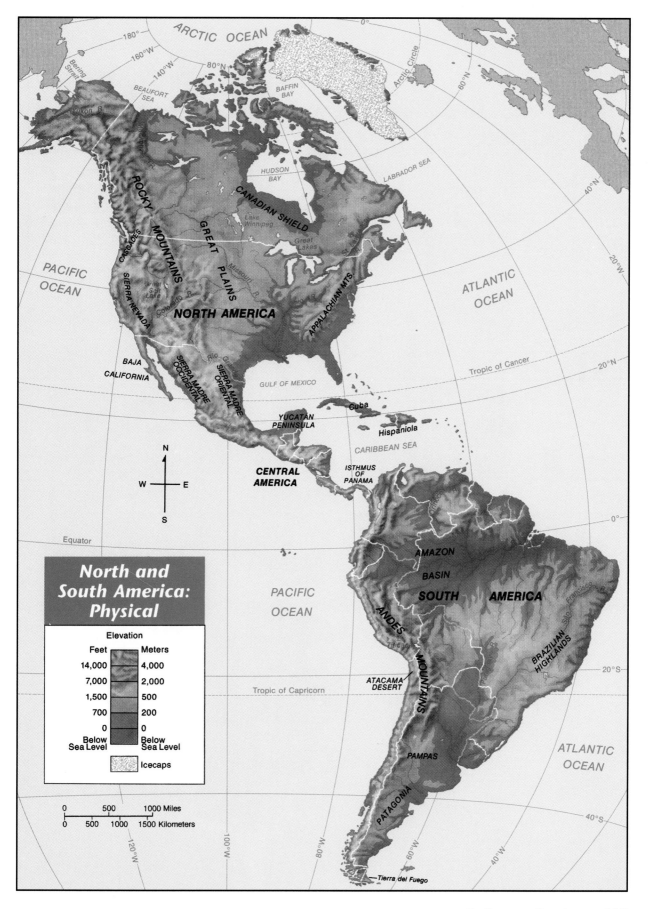

ARCTIC OCEAN

BEAUFORT
SEA

BAFFIN
BAY

Arctic Circle

HUDSON
BAY

LABRADOR SEA

CANADIAN SHIELD

ROCKY MOUNTAINS

GREAT PLAINS

CASCADES

SIERRA NEVADA

Great
Salt
Lake

Lake
Winnipeg

Great
Lakes

St. Lawrence R.

Missouri R.

APPALACHIAN MTS.

NORTH AMERICA

PACIFIC
OCEAN

ATLANTIC
OCEAN

BAJA
CALIFORNIA

SIERRA MADRE OCCIDENTAL

SIERRA MADRE ORIENTAL

Rio Grande

Colorado R.

GULF OF MEXICO

Tropic of Cancer

YUCATAN
PENINSULA

Cuba

Hispaniola

CARIBBEAN SEA

N

W            E

S

CENTRAL
AMERICA

ISTHMUS
OF
PANAMA

Equator

**North and
South America:
Physical**

AMAZON

BASIN

SOUTH        AMERICA

PACIFIC
OCEAN

ANDES MOUNTAINS

BRAZILIAN HIGHLANDS

São Francisco R.

Elevation

| Feet | | Meters |
|---|---|---|
| 14,000 | | 4,000 |
| 7,000 | | 2,000 |
| 1,500 | | 500 |
| 700 | | 200 |
| 0 | | 0 |
| Below
Sea Level | | Below
Sea Level |

Icecaps

ATACAMA
DESERT

Tropic of Capricorn

PAMPAS

PATAGONIA

ATLANTIC
OCEAN

0        500       1000 Miles
0    500   1000   1500 Kilometers

Tierra del Fuego

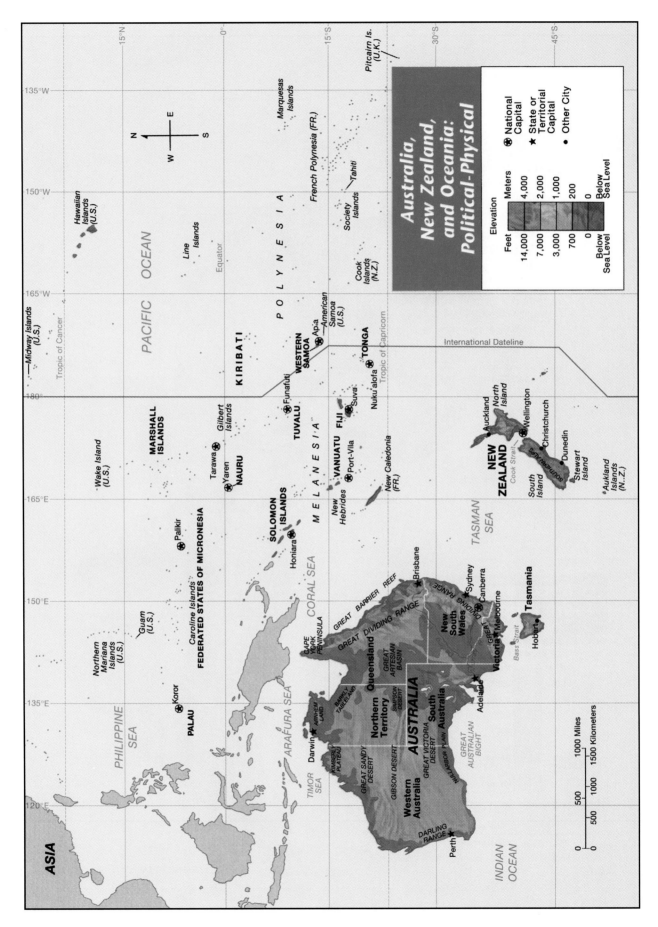

Australia, New Zealand, and Oceania: Political-Physical

Legend:
- ⊛ National Capital
- ★ State or Territorial Capital
- • Other City

Elevation

| Feet | Meters |
|---|---|
| 14,000 | 4,000 |
| 7,000 | 2,000 |
| 3,000 | 1,000 |
| 700 | 200 |
| 0 | 0 |
| Below Sea Level | Below Sea Level |

15°N

135°W

150°W

165°W

180°

165°E

150°E

135°E

120°E

N
W E
S

Midway Islands (U.S.)

Hawaiian Islands (U.S.)

PACIFIC OCEAN

Tropic of Cancer

Equator

Line Islands

Marquesas Islands

French Polynesia (FR.)

Society Islands

Tahiti

Pitcairn Is. (U.K.)

Cook Islands (N.Z.)

P O L Y N E S I A

American Samoa (U.S.)

Apia

WESTERN SAMOA

TONGA

Nuku'alofa

Tropic of Capricorn

International Dateline

KIRIBATI

Funafuti

TUVALU

Suva

FIJI

VANUATU

Port-Vila

New Caledonia (FR.)

M E L A N E S I A

New Hebrides

Wake Island (U.S.)

MARSHALL ISLANDS

Tarawa

Gilbert Islands

Yaren

NAURU

SOLOMON ISLANDS

Honiara

Palikir

Caroline Islands

FEDERATED STATES OF MICRONESIA

Guam (U.S.)

Northern Mariana Islands (U.S.)

Koror

PALAU

PHILIPPINE SEA

ASIA

Auckland

North Island

Wellington

Christchurch

Dunedin

South Island

Cook Strait

NEW ZEALAND

Stewart Island

Aukland Islands (N.Z.)

TASMAN SEA

CORAL SEA

GREAT BARRIER REEF

CAPE YORK PENINSULA

ARNHEM LAND

Darwin

KIMBERLEY PLATEAU

GREAT SANDY DESERT

GIBSON DESERT

Western Australia

GREAT VICTORIA DESERT

NULLARBOR PLAIN

GREAT AUSTRALIAN BIGHT

Perth

DARLING RANGE

INDIAN OCEAN

TIMOR SEA

ARAFURA SEA

Queensland

GREAT DIVIDING RANGE

BARKLY TABLELAND

Northern Territory

SIMPSON DESERT

GREAT ARTESIAN BASIN

AUSTRALIA

South Australia

Adelaide

Brisbane

New South Wales

Sydney

Canberra

Victoria

Melbourne

GREAT DIVIDING RANGE

Bass Strait

Tasmania

Hobart

1000 Miles

1500 Kilometers

500

1000

500

0

0

30°S

45°S

# UNDERSTANDING MAP PROJECTIONS

Geographers and historians use globes and maps to represent the Earth. A globe is like a small model of the Earth. It shows major geographic features, representing the landmasses and bodies of water accurately. However, a globe is not always convenient to use. A map, on the other hand, which can be printed on a piece of paper or in a book, is a more convenient way to show the Earth. Unfortunately, no map can be an exact picture of the Earth because all maps are flat and the Earth's surface is curved.

Mapmakers have developed many ways of showing the curved Earth on a flat surface. Each of these ways is called a map projection. The three maps on this page show different types of map projections—each with its advantages and disadvantages.

The Robinson projection shows correct shapes and sizes of landmasses for most parts of the world. They are commonly used today by geographers. You will find numerous Robinson projections in this book. They appear at the beginning of each unit, beside the time line at the beginning of each chapter, and as a locator map beneath most other maps in the book.

The Mercator projection, one of the earliest projections developed, accurately shows the directions north, south, east, and west. As you can see, the parallels and meridians are straight lines intersecting each other at right angles. This makes it easy to plot distances on the map. As a result, Mercator projections are useful for showing sailors' routes and ocean currents. Sizes become distorted, however, as you move farther away from the equator.

The Interrupted projection shows the sizes and shapes of landmasses accurately. However, the interruptions in the oceans make it difficult to measure distances and judge directions across water.

## Map Projections

**Robinson Projection**

**Mercator Projection**

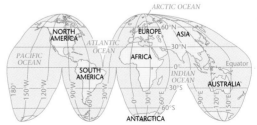

**Interrupted Projection**

---

## GEOGRAPHY AND HISTORY

*Map projections enable mapmakers to show the curved Earth on a flat page. Each of the projections shown here has its advantages and disadvantages.*

1. **Location** *On the maps, locate (a) North America, (b) Africa, (c) Australia.*
2. **Region** *(a) On an Interrupted projection, which continent is divided into sections? Why is it divided? (b) List three pages in this textbook on which you can find a Robinson projection.*
3. **Critical Thinking** **Comparing** *Locate Antarctica on the Robinson and Mercator projections. On which map is its size shown more accurately? Explain why this is so.*

## DOCUMENT IN BRIEF

In this letter Ptah-hotep describes rules of behavior that he believes will help his son live a successful life.

# Instruction of Ptah-hotep

Ptah-hotep, who lived around 2450 B.C. in Egypt, was a vizier, or chief minister, to a pharaoh during the Old Kingdom. In the excerpt below, Ptah-hotep describes some practical rules for behavior that he believes will help his son live a successful life.

*Be not arrogant because of your knowledge, and be not puffed up because you are a learned man. Take counsel with the ignorant as with the learned, for the limits of art cannot be reached, and no artist is perfect in his skills. . . .*

*If you are a leader, commanding the conduct of many, seek out every good aim, so that your policy may be without error. A great thing is truth, enduring and surviving; it has not been upset since the time of Osiris. He who departs from its laws is punished. It is the right path for him who knows nothing. Wrongdoing has never brought its venture safe to port. Evil may win riches, but it is the strength of truth that it endures long. . . .*

*If you want your conduct to be good, free from every evil, then beware of greed. It is an evil and incurable sickness. No man can live with it; it causes divisions between fathers and mothers, and between brothers of the same mother; it parts wife and husband; it is a gathering of every evil, a bag of everything hateful. A man thrives if his conduct is right. He who follows the right course wins wealth thereby. But the greedy man has no tomb. . . .*

*If you are a worthy man sitting in the council of his lord, confine your attention to excellence. Silence is more valuable than chatter. Speak only when you know you can resolve difficulties. He who gives good counsel is an artist, for speech is more difficult than any craft. . . .*

*If you listen to my sayings, then all your affairs will go forward. . . . If the son of a man accepts what his father says, no plan of his will fail. . . . Failure follows him who does not listen. . . .*

▲ Egyptian tomb painting

## ANALYZING THE DOCUMENT

Use the excerpt above to answer the following questions.

1. Which of the following is the best summary of the fourth paragraph?

   A Speak only when you have something helpful to say.

   B Achieve excellence so that you may council the lord.

   C Remain silent while in the council of the lord.

   D Give good counsel in order to gain wealth.

2. The author wishes his son to listen to his advice so that he will —

   A be greedy.

   B be sick.

   C be successful.

   D be arrogant.

3. *Critical Thinking:* **Making Inferences**
   What does Ptah-hotep mean by the phrase, "the greedy man has no tomb"?

# The Epic of Gilgamesh

**DOCUMENT IN BRIEF**

In this epic poem Gilgamesh comes to realize that death is the common lot of all people, even fearless heroes.

DOCUMENTS

The Epic of Gilgamesh is a collection of tales about a hero named Gilgamesh written about 2000 B.C. The main themes of the poem are the unpredictability of the gods and the inevitability of death. These themes may be a reflection of life in Sumer, where the flooding of the Tigris and Euphrates was both unpredictable and devastating.

*U*tnapishtim says to him, to Gilgamesh. . . .
    *"About a plant I will tell thee. . . .*
*Its thorns will prick thy hands just as does the rose.*
*If thy hands obtain the plant, thou wilt attain [eternal] life."*
*No sooner had Gilgamesh heard this, . . .*
*He tied heavy stones to his feet.*
*They pulled him down into the deep and he saw the plant.*
*He took the plant, though it pricked his hands.*
*He cut the heavy stones from his feet.*
*The sea cast him up upon its shore.*
*Gilgamesh says to him, to Urshanabi, the boatman:*
*"Urshanabi, this plant is a plant apart,*
*Whereby a man my regain his life's breath. . . .*
*Its name shall be 'Man Becomes Young in Old Age.'*
*I myself shall eat it*
*And thus return to the state of my youth."*
*Gilgamesh saw a well whose water was cool.*
*He went down into it to bathe in the water.*
*A serpent snuffed the fragrance of the plant;*
*It came up from the water and carried off the plant,*
*Going back to shed its slough [skin].*
*Thereupon Gilgamesh sits down and weeps.*
*His tears running down over his face.*
*He took the hand of Urshanabi, the boatman:*
*"For whom, Urshanabi, have my hands toiled?*
*For whom is being spent the blood of my heart?*
*I have not obtained a boon [benefit] for myself.*
*For the serpent have I effected a boon!"*

▲ Gilgamesh holding a lion

## ANALYZING THE DOCUMENT

Use the excerpt above to answer the following questions.

1. What does Utnapishtim tell Gilgamesh about?
    A a boatman named Urshanabi
    B a plant that brings eternal life
    C a well with cool water
    D a serpent who carries away youth

2. At the end of the poem, Gilgamesh weeps because—

    A the serpent has shed its skin.
    B he has toiled with his hands for too long.
    C he has failed to find everlasting life and must accept death.
    D he has eaten all of the plant.

3. *Critical Thinking:* **Synthesizing Information** What physical characteristic of snakes leads the author to choose it as the creature who benefits from the plant?

# The Code of Hammurabi

Hammurabi's Code, written about 1750 B.C., is a series of 282 laws decreed by Hammurabi, the ruler of the city of Babylon. The laws were written down so that people and judges would have a consistent set of rules to follow in settling disputes and imposing penalties. Although some of the penalties seem cruel by today's standards, they did provide a more orderly system of government than unrestricted personal vengeance.

1. *If a man bring an accusation against another man, charging him with murder, but cannot prove it, the accuser shall be put to death.*

22. *If a man practice robbery and is captured, that man shall be put to death.*

23. *If the robber is not captured, the man who has been robbed shall, in the presence of god, make an itemized statement of his loss, and the city and the governor in whose province and jurisdiction the robbery was committed shall compensate him for whatever was lost.*

53. *If a man neglects to maintain his dike and does not strengthen it, and a break is made in his dike and the water carries away the farmland, the man in whose dike the break has been made shall replace the grain which has been damaged.*

117. *If a man be in debt and sell his wife, son, or daughter, or bind them over to service, for three years they shall work in the house of their purchaser or master; in the fourth year they shall be given their freedom.*

195. *If a son strike his father, they shall cut off his hand.*

196. *If a man destroy the eye of another man, they shall destroy his eye.*

199. *If he destroy the eye of a man's slave or break a bone of a man's slave, he shall pay one-half his price.*

200. *If a man knock out the tooth of a man of his own rank, they shall knock out his tooth.*

206. *If a man strike another man in a quarrel and wound him, he shall swear, "I struck him without intent," and he shall pay for the physician.*

229. *If a builder build a house for a man and does not make its construction sound, and the house which he has built collapses and causes the death of the owner of the house, the builder shall be put to death.*

▲ Babylon's King Hammurabi

## ANALYZING THE DOCUMENT

Use the excerpts above to answer the following questions.

1. Which of the following statements best describes the penalties in Hammurabi's Code?

    A Punishment should be equal to the crime or offense.

    B Punishment should be greater than the crime or offense.

    C Punishment should be decided by the judge and the victim.

    D Punishment should be swift.

2. According to the excerpts above, which of the following statements was true of the society in which these laws were written?

    A Children were required to be obedient to their fathers.

    B Builders were not responsible for their work.

    C Governors were not responsible for robberies in their cities.

    D People could not be sold as slaves or servants.

3. *Critical Thinking:* **Drawing Conclusions** In what ways do you think law number 23 above would influence a governor's actions?

# Confucius: *Analects*

The *Analects* are a collection of 497 verses recorded by Confucius' followers long after his death (perhaps in the fourth century B.C.). Confucius' teachings emphasize duty and responsibility as a means of ensuring social order and good government.

DOCUMENT IN BRIEF

The *Analects* are a collection of sayings that emphasize education and self-sacrifice as the keys to becoming a superior person.

DOCUMENTS

*T*he Master said, He who rules by moral force is like the pole-star, which remains in its place while all the lesser stars do homage to it.

The Master said, If out of the three hundred Songs I had to take one phrase to cover all my teaching, I would say 'Let there be no evil in your thoughts.'

Mêng Wu Po asked about the treatment of parents. The Master said, Behave in such a way that your father and mother have no anxiety about you, except concerning your health.

Tzu-kung asked about the true gentleman. The Master said, He does not preach what he practices till he has practiced what he preaches.

The Master said, A gentleman can see a question from all sides without bias. The small man is biased and can see a question only from one side.

The Master said, Yu, shall I teach you what knowledge is? When you know a thing, to recognize that you know it, and when you do not know a thing, to recognize that you do not know it. That is knowledge.

Chi K'ang-tzu asked whether there were any form of encouragement by which he could induce the common people to be respectful and loyal. The Master said, Approach them with dignity, and they will respect you. Show piety towards your parents and kindness towards your children, and they will be loyal to you. Promote those who are worthy, train those who are incompetent; that is the best form of encouragement.

▲ Confucius and his students

## ANALYZING THE DOCUMENT

Use the excerpts above to answer the following questions.

1. According to the excerpts, which one saying did Confucius pick to best summarize his teachings?

   A Be kind to your father and mother.

   B Let there be no evil in your thoughts.

   C Do not preach what you do not practice.

   D A gentleman can see a question from all sides without bias.

2. Confucius describes a gentleman as one who—

   A is knowledgeable.

   B is respectful and loyal.

   C can understand more than one point of view on a question or issue.

   D can distinguish those who are worthy from those who are incompetent.

3. *Critical Thinking:* **Identifying Main Ideas** Use your own words to describe Confucius' definition of knowledge.

◆ DOCUMENT IN BRIEF

This speech by the Athenian leader Pericles is one of the most famous defenses of democracy of all time.

# Thucydides: *History of the Peloponnesian War*

This excerpt from Thucydides' *History of the Peloponnesian War* records a speech made by the Athenian leader Pericles in honor of those who died fighting Sparta in the first year of the war (431 B.C.). In the speech, Pericles describes the superior qualities of Athenian democracy as compared to life in Sparta.

*For our government is not copied from those of our neighbors: we are an example to them rather than they to us. Our constitution is named a democracy, because it is in the hands not of the few but of the many. But our laws secure equal justice for all in their private disputes, and our public opinion welcomes and honors talent in every branch of achievement, not for any sectional reason but on grounds of excellence alone. And as we give free play to all in our public life, so we carry the same spirit into our daily relations with one another . . .*

*We are lovers of beauty without extravagance, and lovers of wisdom without unmanliness. Wealth to us is not mere material for vainglory but an opportunity for achievement; and poverty we think it no disgrace to acknowledge but a real degradation to make no effort to overcome. Our citizens attend both to public and private duties, and do not allow absorption in their own various affairs to interfere with their knowledge of the city's. We differ from other states in regarding the man who holds aloof from public life not as 'quiet' but as useless; we decide or debate, carefully and in person, all matters of policy, holding, not that words and deeds go ill together, but that acts are foredoomed to failure when undertaken undiscussed. For we are noted for being at once adventurous in action and most reflective beforehand. Other men are bold in ignorance, while reflection will stop their onset. But the bravest are surely those who have the clearest vision of what is before them, glory and danger alike, and yet notwithstanding go out to meet it. . . . In a word I claim that our city as a whole is an education to Greece, and that her members yield to none, man by man, for independence of spirit, many-sidedness of attainment, and complete self-reliance in limbs and brain.*

▲ Athena, goddess of wisdom

## ANALYZING THE DOCUMENT

Use the excerpt above to answer the following questions.

1. Pericles defines democracy as a system based on—

    A equal justice for all.

    B the say of all people, not just a few.

    C beauty and wisdom.

    D free play in public life.

2. According to Pericles, a good citizen is one who—

    A participates fully in public debate.

    B is quiet during public debate.

    C acts boldly without being delayed by discussion.

    D attends exclusively to his own business.

3. *Critical Thinking:* **Synthesizing Information** What does Pericles mean when he states that Athens is "an education to Greece"?

# Aristotle: *The Politics*

**DOCUMENT IN BRIEF**

*The Politics* describes the characteristics of an ideal state as well as practical matters relating to the preservation and improvement of government.

DOCUMENTS

The Greek philosopher Aristotle (384–322 B.C.), was a student of Plato. Like Plato, Aristotle was suspicious of democracy, which he thought could lead to mob rule. Instead, Aristotle favored rule by a single strong and virtuous leader. In this excerpt from *The Politics*, Aristotle outlines the forms of government and discusses the strengths and weaknesses of each form.

*First let us consider what is the purpose of a state and how many forms of government there are by which human society is regulated. We have already said, earlier in this treatise . . . that man is by nature a political animal. And therefore men, even when they do not require one another's help, desire to live together all the same, and are in fact brought together by their common interests. . . . Well-being is certainly the chief end of individuals and of states. . . .*

*The conclusion is evident: governments which have a regard to the common interest are constituted in accordance with strict principles of justice, and are therefore true forms; but those which regard only the interest of the rulers are all defective and perverted forms. For they are despotic, whereas a state is a community of free men. . . .*

*We call that form of government in which one rules, and which regards the common interest, kingship or royalty; that in which more than one, but not many, rule, aristocracy. It is so called, either because the rulers are the best men, or because they have at heart the best interest of the state and of the citizens. But when the citizens at large administer the state for the common interest, the government is called by the generic name—constitutional government. . . .*

*Of the above-mentioned forms, the perversions are as follows: of royalty, tyranny; of aristocracy, oligarchy; of constitutional government, democracy. For tyranny is a kind of monarchy which has in view the interest of the monarch only; oligarchy has in view the interest of the wealthy; democracy, of the needy; none of them the common good of all.*

▲ Democracy crowning the people of Athens

## ANALYZING THE DOCUMENT

Use the excerpt above to answer the following questions.

1. The form of government in which more than one, but not many, rule is known as—

   A kingship or royalty.

   B aristocracy.

   C constitutional government.

   D tyranny.

2. Which of the following does Aristotle describe as the corrupt form of aristocracy?

   A tyranny

   B oligarchy

   C monarchy

   D democracy

3. *Critical Thinking:* **Identifying Main Ideas**
   What does Aristotle mean when he states that "man is by nature a political animal"?

▲ Pillar of Asoka

# Asoka: *Edicts*

During his rule of Maurya India beginning in 268 B.C., Asoka converted to Buddhism, rejected violence, and resolved to rule by moral example. Asoka had stone pillars set up across India announcing laws, or edicts, and describing the just actions of his government. The following are excerpts from several of the pillars.

*This world and the other are hard to gain without great love of Righteousness, great self-examination, great obedience, great circumspection, great effort. Through my instruction respect and love of Righteousness daily increase and will increase. . . . For this is my rule— to govern by Righteousness, to administer by Righteousness, to please my subjects by Righteousness, and to protect them by Righteousness.*

*Whoever honors his own [religion] and disparages another man's, whether from blind loyalty or with the intention of showing his own [religion] in a favorable light, does his own [religion] the greatest possible harm. Concord is best, with each hearing and respecting the other's teachings. It is the wish of the [king] that members of all [religions] should be learned and should teach virtue.*

*All the good deeds that I have done have been accepted and followed by the people. And so obedience to mother and father, obedience to teachers, respect for the aged, kindliness . . . to the poor and weak, and to slaves and servants, have increased and will continue to increase. . . . And this progress of Righteousness . . . has taken place in two manners, by enforcing conformity to Righteousness, and by exhortation [urging or pleading]. I have enforced the law against killing certain animals and many others, but the greatest progress of Righteousness . . . comes from exhortation in favor of noninjury to life and abstention from killing living beings.*

*I have done this that it may endure . . . as long as the moon and sun, and that my sons and my great-grandsons may support it; for by supporting it they will gain both this world and the next.*

## ANALYZING THE DOCUMENT

Use the excerpt above to answer the following questions.

1. The excerpt provides evidence that Asoka favored—

   A animal sacrifices.

   B war.

   C daily rituals.

   D religious tolerance.

2. Based on the passage you can tell that Asoka was probably—

   A a vegetarian.

   B a monk.

   C a dictator.

   D a judge.

3. *Critical Thinking:* **Drawing Conclusions** Which of his actions does Asoka view as the best promotion of Righteousness? Why do you think this is so?

# *Magna Carta*

A group of barons forced King John of England to sign the Magna Carta at Runnymede in 1215. The barons were tired of the king's military campaigns and heavy taxes. The purpose of the document was to limit the power of the monarch and to secure rights such as trial by jury, due process of law, and protection against the arbitrary taking of life, liberty, or property. Below are excerpts from 5 of its 63 articles.

◆ DOCUMENT IN BRIEF

The Magna Carta— or Great Charter— established the principle that the king or queen must obey the law.

DOCUMENTS

2. *We also have granted to all the freemen of our kingdom, for us and for our heirs [those who inherit a title or property] forever, all the underwritten liberties, to be had and holden by them and their heirs, of us and our heirs forever. . . .*

12. *No scutage [tax] or aid shall be imposed in our kingdom, unless by the general council of our kingdom; except for ransoming our person, making our eldest son a knight and once for marrying our eldest daughter; and for these there shall be paid no more than a reasonable aid.*

14. *And for holding the general council of the kingdom concerning the assessment of aids, except in the three cases aforesaid, and for the assessing of scutage, we shall cause to be summoned the archbishops, bishops, abbots, earls, and greater barons of the realm, singly by our letters. And furthermore, we shall cause to be summoned generally, by our sheriffs and bailiffs all others who hold of us in chief, for a certain day, that is to say, forty days before their meeting at least, and to a certain place. And in all letters of such summons we will declare the cause of such summons. And summons being thus made, the business shall proceed on the day appointed, according to the advice of such as shall be present, although all that were summoned come not.*

39. *No freeman shall be taken or imprisoned, or diseised [deprived], or outlawed, or banished, or in any way destroyed . . . unless by the lawful judgment of his peers, or by the law of the land.*

40. *We will sell to no man, we will not deny to any man, either justice or right.*

▲ King Edward I and the Great Council

## ANALYZING THE DOCUMENT

Use the excerpt above to answer the following questions.

1. In article 2 the king grants the rights described in the document to—

   A only those freemen who have heirs.

   B his own heirs.

   C all freemen and their heirs for all time.

   D all freemen currently living in England.

2. Article 14 forces the king to consult a great council before raising new taxes. The article also prevents the king from—

   A holding unannounced meetings or meetings on short notice.

   B summoning the general council to make laws regarding taxation.

   C consulting with the general council before calling a meeting.

   D summoning the sheriffs and bailiffs.

3. *Critical Thinking:* **Making Inferences**
   What does article 40 imply about royal corruption during this period of English history?

In his *Discourses*,
Machiavelli describes
methods for estab-
lishing and preserv-
ing republics.

# Niccolò Machiavelli:
# *Discourses*

Niccolò Machiavelli (1469-1527) is best known for a system of power politics in which "the ends justify the means," as described in his book *The Prince*. How-ever, in his book *Discourses on the First Ten Books of Titus Livy*, Machiavelli con-cludes that the best-governed state is ruled by the people rather than by a ruthless prince.

*In short, to bring this topic to conclusion, I say that, just as princely forms of government have endured for a very long time, so, too, have republican forms of government; and that in both cases it has been essen-tial for them to be regulated by laws. For a prince who does what he likes is a lunatic; and a populace which does what it likes is unwise. If, there-fore, it be a question of a prince subservient to the laws and of a populace chained up by laws, more virtue will be found in the populace than in the prince; and if it be a question of either of them loosed from control by the law, there will be found fewer errors in the populace than in the prince, and these of less moment and much easier to put right. For a licentious [disregarding rules] and turbulent populace, when a good man can obtain a hearing, can easily be brought to behave itself; but there is no one to talk to a bad prince, nor is there any remedy except the sword. . . .*

*When the populace has thrown off all restraint, it is the not the mad things it does that are terrifying, nor is it of present evils that one is afraid, but of what may come of them, for amidst such confusion there may come to be a tyrant. In the case of bad princes it is just the opposite: it is present evils that are terrifying, but for the future there is hope, since men are convinced that the evil ways of a bad prince may make for freedom in the end. . . . The reason why people are prejudiced against the populace is because of the populace anyone may speak ill without fear and openly, even when the populace is ruling. But of princes people speak with the utmost trepidation and the utmost reserve.*

▲ Lorenzo de' Medici,
Renaissance Prince

## ANALYZING THE DOCUMENT

Use the excerpt above to answer the following questions.

1. Machiavelli states that the only way to bring an unruly prince under the law is to—

   A obtain a hearing.

   B use physical combat.

   C discuss the people's legal rights.

   D choose a tyrant.

2. Machiavelli concludes that the greatest threat posed by an unlawful populace is—

   A the rise of a dictator.

   B the violence of the mob.

   C the loss of a prince.

   D the destruction of property.

3. *Critical Thinking:* **Making Inferences** Why do you think Machiavelli believes that the populace is more subject to criticism than a prince?

# King Affonso I:
# *Letter to King John of Portugal*

**DOCUMENT IN BRIEF**

In his letter to the king of Portugal, King Affonso of Kongo pleads with the king to end the slave trade.

In 1490, the Portuguese converted the son of a Kongo king to Christianity and then helped him to assume his father's throne. The king, born Nzinga Mbemba, was renamed Affonso. King Affonso soon realized that his relationship with Portugal had extremely negative consequences, as can be seen from his letter in 1526 to King John of Portugal.

*Sir, Your Highness of Portugal should know how our Kingdom is being lost in so many ways. This is caused by the excessive freedom given by your officials to the men and merchants who are allowed to come to this Kingdom to set up shops with goods and many things which have been prohibited by us. Many of our vassals, whom we had in obedience, do not comply because they have the things in greater abundance than we ourselves. It was with these things that we had them content and subjected under our jurisdiction, so it is doing a great harm not only to the service of God, but to the security and peace of our Kingdoms and State as well.*

*And we cannot reckon how great the damage is, since the mentioned merchants are taking every day our natives, sons of the land and the sons of our noblemen and vassals and our relatives. The thieves and men of bad conscience grab them wishing to have the things and wares of this Kingdom which they are ambitious of; they grab them and get them to be sold. And so great, Sir, is the corruption and licentiousness that our country is being completely depopulated, and your Highness should not agree with this nor accept it as in your service. And to avoid it we need from those your Kingdoms no more than some priests and a few people to teach in schools, and no other goods except wine and flour for the holy sacrament.*

*That is why we beg of Your Highness to help and assist us in this matter, commanding your factors that they should not send here either merchants or wares, because it is <u>our will that in these kingdoms there should not be any trade of slaves nor outlet for them.</u> Concerning what is referred to above, again we beg of Your Highness to agree with it. . . .*

▲ West African ivory carving of Portuguese soldiers

## ANALYZING THE DOCUMENT

Use the excerpt above to answer the following questions.

1. Which of the following best describes the author's purpose for writing this letter?

   A to ask the king for money to help in ending the slave trade

   B to inform the king of the abuses taking place and to ask for his help in ending them

   C to inform the king about the extent of trade taking place in the kingdom

   D to ask the king for an explanation for why people are being enslaved

2. What does Affonso request of King John in the last paragraph?

   A that he not send any merchants or wares

   B that he send teachers

   C that he send priests

   D that he pray for Affonso

3. *Critical Thinking:* **Recognizing Causes and Effects** According to King Affonso, how have the Portuguese affected his kingdom and state?

DOCUMENT IN BRIEF

Bernal Díaz's history provides an account of the Aztec capital of Tenochtitlán before the Spanish conquest.

DOCUMENTS

# Bernal Díaz: *The True History of the Conquest of New Spain*

Bernal Díaz del Castillo (c. 1492-1581) accompanied Hernan Cortés on his conquest of the Aztecs in present-day Mexico. Díaz wrote his history many years later to refute what he viewed as inaccurate accounts of the conquest. The following excerpt describes a meeting between Cortés and Moctezuma, the Aztec king, in the Aztec city of Tenochtitlán.

*When we climbed to the top of the great [temple] there was a kind of platform, with huge stones where they put the poor Indians to be sacrificed, and an image like a dragon and other evil figures, with a great deal of blood that had been shed that day. Moctezuma, accompanied by two priests, came out from an oratory dedicated to the worship of his cursed idols. . . .*

*Then Moctezuma took him [Cortés] by the hand and bade him look at his great city and at all the other cities rising from the water, and the many towns around the lake. . . .*

*There we stood looking, for that large and evil temple was so high that it towered over everything. From there we could see all three of the causeways that led into Mexico. . . .*

*We saw the fresh water that came from Chapultepec, which supplied the city, and the bridges on the three causeways, built at certain intervals so the water could go from one part of the lake to another, and a multitude of canoes, some arriving with provisions and others leaving with merchandise. We saw that every house in this great city and in the others built on the water could be reached only by wooden drawbridges or by canoe. We saw temples built like towers and fortresses in these cities, all white-washed; it was a sight to see. . . .*

*After taking a good look and considering all that we had seen, we looked again at the great square and the throngs of people, some buying and others selling. The buzzing of their voices could be heard more than a league away. There were soldiers among us who had been in many parts of the world, in Constantinople and Rome and all over Italy, who said that they had never before seen a market place so large and so well laid out, and so filled with people.*

▲ Tenochtitlán

## ANALYZING THE DOCUMENT

Use the excerpt above to answer the following questions.

1. The scene described in this excerpt is of—

    A a view of Tenochtitlán's market and surroundings from the top of a tall temple.

    B an indoor temple with many statues.

    C a view of Tenochtitlán's temple from the market place.

    D a view of the markets in Rome.

2. Which of the following best describes the author's view of the Aztecs?

    A generous and busy

    B evil and prosperous

    C loving and kind

    D athletic and loud

3. *Critical Thinking:* **Recognizing Points of View** Which words and phrases in the excerpt above reveal the author's opinion of the Aztec's religion?

# The English Bill of Rights

**DOCUMENT IN BRIEF**

The English Bill of Rights ensured the superiority of Parliament over the king and queen.

When the Catholic king, James II, was forced from the English throne in 1688, Parliament offered the crown to his Protestant daughter Mary and her husband William of Orange. But Parliament insisted that William and Mary submit to a Bill of Rights. This document, a continuation of the struggle between the crown and Parliament, sums up the powers that Parliament had been seeking since the Petition of Right in 1628.

*Whereas, the late King James II. . .did endeavor to subvert and extirpate [eliminate] the Protestant religion and the laws and liberties of this kingdom. . .and whereas the said late King James II having abdicated the government, and the throne being vacant. . . .*

*The said lords [Parliament] . . . being now assembled in a full and free representative [body] of this nation . . . do in the first place . . . declare:*

1. *That the pretended power of suspending of laws or the execution of laws by regal authority without consent of Parliament is illegal. . . .*

4. *That levying money for or to the use of the crown by pretense of prerogative [right] without grant of Parliament . . . is illegal;*

5. *That it is the right of the subjects to petition the king, and all commitments and prosecutions for such petitioning are illegal.*

6. *That . . . raising or keeping a standing army within the kingdom in time of peace, unless it be with consent of Parliament, is against law. . . .*

8. *That election of members of Parliament ought to be free. . . .*

9. *That the freedom of speech and debates or proceedings in Parliament ought not to be impeached [challenged] or questioned in any court or place out of Parliament. . . .*

10. *That excessive bail ought not to be required, nor excessive fines imposed, nor cruel and unusual punishments inflicted. . . .*

13. *And that, for redress of all grievances and for the amending, strengthening, and preserving of the laws, Parliaments ought to be held frequently. . . .*

## ANALYZING THE DOCUMENT

Use the excerpts above to answer the following questions.

1. This Bill of Rights required the monarch to—

    A raise money for paying the members of Parliament.

    B summon Parliament regularly.

    C cancel laws he or she considered unjust.

    D keep a standing army to defend the country.

2. Which of the following statements best summarizes these excerpts from the Bill of Rights?

    A The King's powers are limited by the Parliament.

    B The Parliament's powers are limited by the monarch.

    C The Parliament's duty is to amend laws.

    D The King's powers are unlimited.

3. *Critical Thinking:* **Making Inferences** Why do you think the members of Parliament included item 9 above? Why do you think this item was important?

In this essay Locke states that the primary purpose of government is to protect the natural rights of people.

# John Locke:
## *Two Treatises on Government*

English philosopher John Locke (1632-1704) published *Two Treatises on Government* in 1690. In the writings Locke holds that all people possess natural rights, including property and personal freedom. Locke also states that governments hold their power only with the consent of the people. Locke's ideas heavily influenced revolutions in America and France.

*But though men, when they enter into society give up the equality, liberty, and executive power they had in the state of Nature into the hands of society . . . the power of the society or legislative constituted by them can never be supposed to extend farther than the common good. . . . [W]hoever has the legislative or supreme power of any commonwealth, is bound to govern by established standing laws, promulgated and known to the people, and not by extemporary decrees, by indifferent [unbiased] and upright judges, who are to decide controversies by those laws; and to employ the force of the community at home only in the execution of such laws, or abroad to prevent or redress foreign injuries and secure the community from inroads and invasion. And all this to be directed to no other end but the peace, safety, and public good of the people. . . .*

*The reason why men enter into society is the preservation of their property; and the end while they choose and authorize a legislative is that there may be laws made, and rules set, as guards and fences to the properties of all the society, . . .*

*Whensoever, therefore, the legislative [power] shall transgress this fundamental rule of society, and either by ambition, fear, folly, or corruption, endeavor to grasp themselves, or put into the hands of any other, an absolute power over the lives, liberties, and estates of the people, by this breach of trust they forfeit the power the people had put into their hands for quite contrary ends, and it devolves [passes] to the people; who have a right to resume their original liberty, and by the establishment of a new legislative (such as they shall think fit), provide for their own safety and security, which is the end which they are in society. . . .*

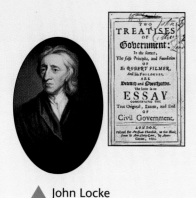

▲ John Locke

## ANALYZING THE DOCUMENT

Use the excerpts above to answer the following questions.

1. Which of the following groups has the final authority of government in Locke's opinion?

   A the legislature

   B the prince

   C the people

   D the judges

2. Which of the following statements best summarizes the excerpts above?

   A People should give up their fundamental rights in order to establish absolute monarchies.

   B People establish governments in order to set and enforce laws. If a government does not do this, the people may abolish it.

   C Most legislative powers are corrupt.

   D Judges may need to act outside the law.

3. ***Critical Thinking:* Making Inferences**
   According to Locke, what do people give up when they enter into a society? Why do you think people do this?

# Jean-Jacques Rousseau: *The Social Contract*

## DOCUMENT IN BRIEF

In consenting to form a government, Rousseau says, individuals choose to give up their self-interest in favor of the common good.

In *The Social Contract*, Rousseau (1712-1778) proposes an ideal society formed through a "social contract," and based on the natural will of the people. Rousseau believed that people in their natural state were basically good but were corrupted by the evils of society. The first lines of *The Social Contract*, "Man is born free, but is everywhere in chains," reflect this idea.

"*F*ind a form of association that defends and protects the person and goods of each associate with all the common force, and by means of which each one, uniting with all, nevertheless obeys only himself and remains as free as before." This is the fundamental problem which is solved by the social contract. . . .

[F]irst of all, since each one gives his entire self, the condition is equal for everyone, and since the condition is equal for everyone, no one has an interest in making it burdensome for the others. . . .

If, then, everything that is not the essence of the social compact is set aside, one will find that it can be reduced to the following terms: Each of us puts his person and all his power in common under the supreme direction of the general will; and in a body we receive each member as an indivisible part of the whole.

Instantly, in place of the private person of each contracting party, this act of association produces a moral and collective body, composed of as many members as there are voices in the assembly, which receives from this same act its unity, its common self, its life, and its will. This public person, formed thus by the union of all the others, formerly took the name <u>City</u>, and now takes that of <u>Republic</u> or <u>body politic</u>, which its members call <u>State</u> when it is passive, <u>Sovereign</u> when active, <u>Power</u> when comparing it to similar bodies. As for the associates, they collectively take the name <u>People</u>; and individually are called <u>Citizens</u> as participants in the sovereign authority, and <u>Subjects</u> as subjects to the laws of the State. . . .

▲ Jean-Jacques Rousseau

## ANALYZING THE DOCUMENT

Use the excerpt above to answer the following questions.

1. The "social contract" provides a solution to the problem of finding a form of government in which—

    A people's differences can be solved peacefully.

    B people remain as free as they were without government.

    C people are not subject to unjust laws.

    D minorities are protected.

2. The *Republic* or *body politic* is defined as the—

    A assembly.

    B collective body that comes into being when people dissolve the social contract.

    C collective body that comes into being when private persons enter the social contract.

    D moral and collective body appointed by the king.

3. ***Critical Thinking:*** **Drawing Conclusions** Why does Rousseau believe that people are safe putting themselves under the direction of the "general will"?

# Declaration of the Rights of Man and of the Citizen

The French National Assembly issued this document in 1789 after having overthrown the established government in the early stages of the French Revolution. The document was modeled in part on the English Bill of Rights and on the American Declaration of Independence.

*Therefore the National Assembly recognizes and proclaims, in the presence and under the auspices of the Supreme Being, the following rights of man and of the citizen:*

1. *Men are born and remain free and equal in rights. Social distinctions may be founded only upon the general good.*

2. *The aim of all political association is the preservation of the natural and imprescriptible [inviolable] rights of man. These rights are liberty, property, security, and resistance to oppression.*

4. *Liberty consists in the freedom to do everything which injures no one else. . . .*

5. *Law can only prohibit such actions as are hurtful to society. . . .*

6. *Law is the expression of the general will. Every citizen has a right to participate personally, or through his representative, in its formation. It must be the same for all, whether it protects or punishes. All citizens, being equal in the eyes of the law, are equally eligible to all dignities and to all public positions and occupations, according to their abilities, and without distinction except that of their virtues and talents.*

7. *No person shall be accused, arrested, or imprisoned except in the cases and according to the forms prescribed by law.*

9. *As all persons are held innocent until they shall have been declared guilty, if arrest shall be deemed indispensable, all harshness not essential to the securing of the prisoner's person shall be severely repressed by law.*

11. *The free communication of ideas and opinions is one of the most precious of the rights of man. Every citizen may, accordingly, speak, write, and print with freedom. . . .*

13. *A common contribution is essential for the maintenance of the public [military] forces and for the cost of administration. This should be equitably distributed among all the citizens in proportion to their means.*

▲ Declaration of Rights

## ANALYZING THE DOCUMENT

Use the excerpts above to answer the following questions.

1. Which article above specifically protects citizens from police brutality and torture?

   A 5          B 6

   C 9          D 11

2. Which of the following describes the tax policy set forth in this document?

   A All citizens pay the same amount of tax.

   B Only citizens in the military pay taxes.

   C All citizens pay taxes in proportion to their wealth.

   D There should be no taxes imposed on citizens.

3. *Critical Thinking:* **Applying Information** Give one real-life example of each of the four natural rights listed under article 2 above.

# Olympe de Gouges: *Declaration of the Rights of Woman and the Female Citizen*

**DOCUMENT IN BRIEF**

In this document French journalist Olympe de Gouges demands equal rights for women.

Born Marie Gouze, Olympe de Gouges did not believe the Declaration of the Rights of Man had gone far enough. In 1791 she wrote the Declaration of the Rights of Woman demanding equal rights for women. De Gouges was guillotined in 1793 in part because of her royalist politics and in part because of her ideas about women's rights.

1. *Woman is born free and lives equal to man in her rights. . . .*

2. *The purpose of any political association is the conservation of the natural and imprescriptible rights of woman and man; these rights are liberty, property, security, and especially resistance to oppression.*

6. *The law must be the expression of the general will; all female and male citizens must contribute either personally or through their representatives to its formation. It must be the same for all. . . .*

7. *No woman is an exception; she is accused, arrested, and detained in cases determined by law. Women, like men, obey this rigorous law.*

9. *Once any woman is declared guilty, complete rigor is [to be] exercised by the law.*

10. *No one is to be disquieted for his very basic opinions; woman has the right to mount the scaffold; she must equally have the right to mount the rostrum, provided that her demonstrations do not disturb the legally established public order.*

16. *No society has a constitution without the guarantee of rights and the separation of powers; the constitution is null if the majority of individuals comprising the nation have not cooperated in drafting it.*

17. *Property belongs to both sexes whether united or separate. . . . Woman, wake up; the tocsin [alarm bell] of reason is being heard throughout the whole universe; discover your rights. . . . When will you cease to be blind? What advantage have you received from the Revolution? A more pronounced scorn, a more marked disdain. . . . The reclamation of your patrimony [inheritance], based on the wise decrees of nature—what have you to dread from such a fine undertaking?*

▲ Women's march on Versailles

## ANALYZING THE DOCUMENT

Use the excerpts above to answer the following questions.

1. Which of the above articles specifically states a woman's right to speak publicly?

   A 2          B 6

   C 7          D 10

2. Why does de Gouges state that the constitution is not valid?

A Women have not cooperated in drafting it.

B It does not guarantee property rights to women.

C Women are not treated with respect.

D Women are subject to unjust arrest.

3. *Critical Thinking:* **Recognizing Causes and Effects** Why do you think de Gouges included article 9 above which implies that women should not be given special treatment if found guilty of a crime?

In this decree Miguel Hidalgo calls for an end to slavery and an end to heavy taxes on the poor in Mexico.

# Miguel Hidalgo:
## *Decree of Hidalgo*

Father Miguel Hidalgo of Mexico called for freedom from Spanish rule in 1810. The following decree, also issued in 1810 from Guadalajara, Jalisco, was an attempt to gain additional support for the uprising from Native Americans, blacks, and mestizos. In the end, Hidalgo's rebellion failed because creoles feared that more rights for Native Americans and an end to slavery would cost them power. Less than one year after the start of the uprising, Hidalgo was captured and executed, and his followers scattered.

*From the happy moment that the valiant American nation took up arms to shake off the heavy yoke that has oppressed it for three centuries, one of the principal objectives has been to extinguish such duties that cannot advance its fortune, especially those which in these critical circumstances do not well serve that end or provide for the real need of the kingdom in meeting the costs of the struggle, so therefore there is now put forward here the most urgent remedy in the following declarations:*

1. *That all owners of slaves shall give them their freedom before the end of ten days, under penalty of death, which shall be applied to those who violate this article.*

2. *That from now on the collection of tributes according to caste [race] shall cease, as shall exactions that are demanded of the Indians.*

3. *That all legal business, documents, letters and actions can be on common paper, with the requirement of the seal totally abolished.*

▲ Mural by Diego Rivera (Hidalgo is the white-haired man at the center)

## ANALYZING THE DOCUMENT

Use the excerpt above to answer the following questions.

1. Item 2 above calls for an end to—

   A slavery.

   B collection of any taxes.

   C collection of taxes based on race.

   D all business transactions with Indians.

2. What does "the seal" probably symbolize in item 3 above?

   A approval from Spanish authorities

   B a postage stamp

   C a special type of paper

   D Native American traditions

3. *Critical Thinking:* **Defending a Position** Describe some of the "natural rights" Hidalgo could have listed in his decree as explanations for why he wished to abolish slavery, taxes based on race, and the requirement of the seal.

# Simón Bolívar:
## *Address to the Congress of Venezuela*

**DOCUMENT IN BRIEF**

In this address Simón Bolívar offers the Venezuelan Congress advice on what type of government to establish in Venezuela.

Encouraged by the revolutions in British North America and France, colonists in Spanish South America soon began to create a force for independence. Simón Bolívar was one of the leaders of this movement. The excerpt below, from Bolívar's Address to the Second National Congress of Venezuela, was given in 1819.

*Subject to the threefold yoke of ignorance, tyranny, and vice, the American people have been unable to acquire knowledge, power, or [civic] virtue. The lessons we received and the models we studied, as pupils of such pernicious teachers, were most destructive. . . .*

*If a people, perverted by their training, succeed in achieving their liberty, they will soon lose it, for it would be of no avail to endeavor to explain to them that happiness consists in the practice of virtue; that the rule of law is more powerful than the rule of tyrants, because, as the laws are more inflexible, everyone should submit to their beneficent austerity; that proper morals, and not force, are the bases of law; and that to practice justice is to practice liberty. Therefore, Legislators, your work is so much the more arduous, inasmuch as you have to reeducate men who have been corrupted by erroneous illusions and false incentives. Liberty, says Rousseau, is a succulent morsel, but one difficult to digest. . . .*

*Legislators, meditate well before you choose. Forget not that you are to lay the political foundation for a newly born nation which can rise to the heights of greatness that Nature has marked out for it if you but proportion this foundation in keeping with the high plane that it aspires to attain. Unless your choice is based upon the peculiar . . . experience of Venezuelan people—a factor that should guide you in determining the nature and form of government you are about to adopt for the well-being of the people . . . the result of our reforms will again be slavery.*

▲ Simón Bolívar

## ANALYZING THE DOCUMENT

Use the excerpt above to answer the following questions.

1. According to Bolívar, the people of Latin America—

   A have not been well prepared for self-government by the Spanish.

   B have been well prepared for self-government by the Spanish.

   C have been ruled well by the Spanish.

   D have little desire for self-government.

2. Bolívar states that a government will be most effective if it—

   A adheres closely to theories of good government.

   B imitates the structure of other successful governments.

   C is molded to fit the character of the nation for which it is built.

   D is based on the rule of law.

3. *Critical Thinking:* **Defending a Position**
   Would you describe Bolívar as practical or idealistic? Use examples from the excerpt to defend your opinion.

**DOCUMENT IN BRIEF**

In this interview Gandhi explains the ideas behind his nonviolent method of passive resistance.

# Mohandas Gandhi: *Hind Swaraj*

Mohandas Gandhi led a successful, peaceful revolution in India against British rule. In the following excerpt from his book *Hind Swaraj (Indian Home Rule)*, published in 1938, Gandhi explains the ideas behind his nonviolent method of passive resistance in the form of an imaginary conversation between an editor and a reader.

**EDITOR:** *Passive resistance is a method of securing rights by personal suffering; it is the reverse of resistance by arms. When I refuse to do a thing that is repugnant to my conscience, I use soul-force. For instance, the Government of the day has passed a law which is applicable to me. I do not like it. If by using violence I force the Government to repeal the law, I am employing what may be termed body-force. If I do not obey the law and accept the penalty for its breach, I use soul-force. It involves sacrifice of self.*

*Everybody admits that sacrifice of self is infinitely superior to sacrifice of others. Moreover, if this kind of force is used in a cause that is unjust, only the person using it suffers. He does not make others suffer for his mistakes. . . . No man can claim that he is absolutely in the right or that a particular thing is wrong because he thinks so, but it is wrong for him so long as that is his deliberate judgment. It is therefore meet [proper] that he should not do that which he knows to be wrong, and suffer the consequence whatever it may be. This is the key to the use of soul-force.*

**READER:** *You would then disregard laws—this is rank disloyalty. We have always been considered a law-abiding nation. You seem to be going even beyond the extremists. They say that we must obey the laws that have been passed, but that if the laws be bad, we must drive out the lawgivers even by force.*

**EDITOR:** *Whether I go beyond them or whether I do not is a matter of no consequence to either of us. We simply want to find out what is right and to act accordingly. The real meaning of the statement that we are a law-abiding nation is that we are passive resisters. When we do not like certain laws, we do not break the heads of law-givers but we suffer and do not submit to the laws.*

▲ Mohandas Gandhi

## ANALYZING THE DOCUMENT

Use the excerpt above to answer the following questions.

1. What is the goal of a person who practices passive resistance?

   A to bring about peaceful reform or change

   B to gain support for violence

   C to discover truth

   D to injure wrongdoers

2. The author defines soul-force as—

   A weapons used for peaceful purposes.

   B refusal to obey a law that is unjust and accepting the penalty.

   C obeying all laws while working to overthrow the lawmakers.

   D trying to determine what is right.

3. ***Critical Thinking:*** **Understanding Sequence** What does Gandhi mean when he says that a person using soul force "does not make others suffer for his mistakes"?

# Franklin D. Roosevelt:
## *The Four Freedoms*

In this speech
Franklin D. Roosevelt
describes the four
"essential human
freedoms": freedom
of speech and wor-
ship, and freedom
from want and fear.

DOCUMENTS

Franklin D. Roosevelt delivered the following address to Congress in January 1941 after having been elected to a third term as president of the United States. In the speech he described the "four freedoms" which he hoped would be secured throughout the world. As he spoke, most of Europe had already fallen to Hitler's tyranny and Great Britain was struggling against the threat of German invasion.

*In the future days, which we seek to make secure, we look forward to a world founded upon four essential human freedoms.*

*The first is freedom of speech and expression—everywhere in the world.*

*The second is freedom of every person to worship God in his own way—everywhere in the world.*

*The third is freedom from want—which translated into world terms, means economic understandings which will secure to every nation a healthy peace time life for its inhabitants—everywhere in the world.*

*The fourth is freedom from fear—which translated into world terms, means a worldwide reduction of armaments to such a point and in such a thorough fashion that no nation will be in a position to commit an act of physical aggression against any neighbor—anywhere in the world. . . .*

*Since the beginning of our American history we have been engaged in change—in a perpetual peaceful revolution—a revolution which goes on steadily, quietly adjusting itself to changing conditions—without the concentration camp or the quick-lime in the ditch. The world order which we seek is the cooperation of free countries, working together in a friendly civilized society.*

*This nation has placed its destiny in the hands and heads and hearts of its millions of free men and women; and its faith in freedom under the guidance of God. Freedom means the supremacy of human rights everywhere. Our support goes to those who struggle to gain those rights or keep them. Our strength is in our unity of purpose.*

*To that high concept there can be no end save victory.*

▲ Franklin D. Roosevelt

## ANALYZING THE DOCUMENT

Use the excerpt above to answer the following questions.

1. Being able to make a living and support one's family is an example of—

   A freedom of speech.

   B freedom of worship.

   C freedom from want.

   D freedom from fear.

2. Roosevelt thinks the nation's strength comes from—

   A citizens worshipping together.

   B citizens working together for a common purpose.

   C its support for other nations.

   D carrying out peaceful revolutions.

3. *Critical Thinking:* **Applying Information**
   Describe some of the specific actions that would be necessary to secure Roosevelt's description of "freedom from fear."

# The Universal Declaration of Human Rights

The General Assembly of the United Nations adopted this declaration on December 10, 1948. They hoped that it would become a standard by which liberty and freedom could be judged throughout the world.

*Article 1*    *All human beings are born free and equal in dignity and rights. They are endowed with reason and conscience and should act towards one another in a spirit of brotherhood.*

*Article 2*    *Everyone is entitled to all the rights and freedoms set forth in this Declaration, without distinction of any kind, such as race, colour, sex, language, religion, political or other opinion, national or social origin, property, birth or other status. . . .*

*Article 3*    *Everyone has the right to life, liberty and security of person.*

*Article 4*    *No one shall be held in slavery or servitude. . . .*

*Article 5*    *No one shall be subjected to torture or to cruel, inhuman or degrading treatment or punishment.*

*Article 9*    *No one shall be subjected to arbitrary arrest, detention or exile.*

*Article 13*    *Everyone has the right to freedom of movement. . . .*

*Article 18*    *Everyone has the right to freedom of thought, conscience and religion. . . .*

*Article 19*    *Everyone has the right to freedom of opinion and expression. . . .*

*Article 20*    *Everyone has the right to freedom of peaceful assembly and association. . . .*

*Article 23*    *Everyone has the right to work, to free choice of employment, to just and favourable conditions of work and to protection against unemployment.*

*Article 25*    *Everyone has the right to a standard of living adequate for the health and well-being of himself and of his family, including food, clothing, housing and medical care and necessary social services, and the right to security in the event of unemployment, sickness, disability, widowhood, old age or other lack of livelihood. . . .*

*Article 26*    *Everyone has the right to education. Education shall be free, at least in the elementary and fundamental stages.*

▲ Vietnamese refugee

## ANALYZING THE DOCUMENT

Use the excerpts above to answer the following questions.

1. Which of the following articles grants a person the right to leave and return to their country?

A Article 4

B Article 5

C Article 13

D Article 18

2. Which of the following articles grants a person the right to live free from hunger?

A Article 1

B Article 9

C Article 23

D Article 25

3. *Critical Thinking:* **Drawing Conclusions** In what ways might the existence of this declaration benefit people living under an oppressive government?

# Mao Zedong:
## *The People's Democratic Dictatorship*

In this speech, given in 1949 on the anniversary of the founding of the Communist Party, Mao Zedong explains the philosophy that guided China under his leadership. Mao's ideas were heavily influenced by the communist philosopher Karl Marx.

### DOCUMENT IN BRIEF

In this speech Mao states that only "the people" have the right to vote, and the freedoms of speech, assembly, and association.

*W*ho are the "people"? At the present stage in China, they are the working class, the peasantry, the petty bourgeoisie and the national bourgeoisie.

*Under the leadership of the working class and the Communist Party, these classes unite to create their own state and elect their own government so as to enforce their dictatorship over the henchmen of imperialism—the landlord class and bureaucratic capitalist class. . . . The people's government will suppress such persons. It will only permit them to behave themselves properly. It will not allow them to speak or act wildly. Should they do so, they will be instantly curbed and punished. The democratic system is to be carried out within the ranks of the people, giving them freedom of speech, assembly and association. The right to vote is given only to the people, not to the reactionaries.*

*These two things, democracy for the people and dictatorship for the reactionaries, when combined, constitute the people's democratic dictatorship.*

*Why must things be done in this way? Everyone is very clear on this point. If things were not done like this, the revolution would fail, the people would suffer and the state would perish. . . .*

*Our present task is to strengthen the people's state apparatus— meaning principally the people's army, the people's police and the people's courts—thereby safeguarding national defence and protecting the people's interests. Given these conditions, China, under the leadership of the working class and the Communist Party, can develop steadily from an agricultural into an industrial country and from a New Democratic into a Socialist and, eventually, Communist society, eliminating classes and realizing universal harmony.*

▲ Mao Zedong

## ANALYZING THE DOCUMENT

Use the excerpt above to answer the following questions.

1. Who are the "reactionaries"?

   A the peasants

   B the bourgeoisie

   C the landlords and capitalists

   D the working class

2. According to Mao, the Communist Party represents the interests of—

   A the landlords.

   B the capitalists.

   C the imperialists.

   D the working class.

3. *Critical Thinking:* **Making Inferences** Why do you think the "people's government" denies some groups of people the right to free speech?

**DOCUMENT IN BRIEF**

In this excerpt Nkrumah describes his goal of political freedom for the Gold Coast and the work of building an independent economy.

# Kwame Nkrumah: *Autobiography*

Kwame Nkrumah led the people of Gold Coast in their quest for independence from Britain. After succeeding in 1957, Nkrumah became the first prime minister and renamed the country Ghana. In this excerpt from his *Autobiography*, Nkrumah speaks of the need to establish economic independence as a means of maintaining political independence.

*Independence for the Gold Coast was my aim. It was a colony, and I have always regarded colonialism as the policy by which a foreign power binds territories to herself by political ties, with the primary object of promoting her own economic advantage. No one need be surprised if this system has led to disturbances and political tension in many territories. There are few people who would not rid themselves of such domination if they could. . . .*

*I saw that the whole solution to [our] problem lay in political freedom for our people, for it is only when a people are politically free that other races can give them the respect that is due them. It is impossible to talk of equality of races in any other terms. No people without a government of their own can expect to be treated on the same level as people of independent sovereign states. It is far better to be free to govern or misgovern yourself than to be governed by anybody else. . . .*

*Once freedom is gained, a greater task comes into view. All dependent territories are backward in education, in science, in agriculture, and in industry. The economic independence that should follow and maintain political independence demands every effort from the people, a total mobilization of brain and manpower resources. What other countries have taken three hundred years or more to achieve, a once dependent territory must try to accomplish in a generation if it is to survive.*

## ANALYZING THE DOCUMENT

Use the excerpt above to answer the following questions.

1. How does the author define colonialism?

   A a balanced political alliance

   B a balanced economic alliance

   C a ruling country helping residents of a colony

   D a ruling country interested in its own economic gain

2. Nkrumah viewed political independence as a means of gaining—

   A respect from other sovereign states.

   B great personal wealth.

   C a better system of education.

   D better resources.

3. **Critical Thinking: Recognizing Causes and Effects** Nkrumah states that newly independent countries must establish economic independence with great speed if they are to survive. Give reasons to support this statement.

# Andrei Sakharov:
## *Nobel Peace Prize Lecture*

Andrei Sakharov was a Soviet physicist and a leading Soviet dissident. He was awarded the Nobel Peace Prize in 1975 for his efforts to limit nuclear testing, end human rights abuses, and protect intellectual freedom. Because of his outspokenness he was exiled in a remote Soviet city from 1980 to 1986.

⬥ **DOCUMENT IN BRIEF**

In this lecture Sakharov states that intellectual freedom is essential to progress and human rights.

*Peace, progress, human rights—these three goals are indissolubly linked: it is impossible to achieve one of them if the others are ignored. This idea provides the main theme of my lecture. . . .*

*I am convinced that international trust, mutual understanding, disarmament, and international security are inconceivable without an open society with freedom of information, freedom of conscience, the right to publish, and the right to travel and choose the country in which one wishes to live. I am also convinced that freedom of conscience, together with other civic rights, provides both the basis for scientific progress and a guarantee against its misuse to harm mankind, as well as the basis for economic and social progress. . . .*

*We cannot reject the idea of a spreading use of the results of medical research or the extension of research in all its branches, including bacteriology and virology, neurophysiology, human genetics, and gene surgery, no matter what potential dangers lurk in their abuse and the undesirable social consequences of this research. . . . It is quite clear that in the hands of irresponsible bureaucratic authorities operating secretly, all this research may prove exceptionally dangerous, but at the same time it may prove extremely important and necessary to mankind, if it is carried out under public supervision and discussion and socio-scientific analysis. . . .*

▲ Andrei Sakharov

*Freedom of conscience, the existence of an informed public opinion, a pluralistic system of education, freedom of the press, and access to other sources of information—all these are in very short supply in the socialist countries. . . . At the same time these conditions are a vital necessity, not only to avoid all witting or unwitting abuse of progress, but also to strengthen it.*

## ANALYZING THE DOCUMENT

Use the excerpt above to answer the following questions.

1. Sakharov states that scientific research must continue despite the risks that its findings may be misused because—

    A it may prove to be extremely important to people.

    B it is human nature to want to explore the unknown.

    C bureaucratic authorities depend on it.

    D it may lead to mutual international understanding.

2. In this excerpt, an "open society"—

    A encourages optimism.

    B allows a free flow of ideas.

    C allows authorities to operate secretly.

    D sees progress as a vital necessity.

3. *Critical Thinking:* **Identifying Main Ideas** What roles do public opinion, freedom of the press, and access to information play in protecting against the misuse of technology?

▲ Lech Walesa

# Lech Walesa:
## *Nobel Peace Prize Lecture*

Lech Walesa organized an independent trade union in Poland known as Solidarity. After a successful strike by Solidarity members in 1980, the Communist Polish government granted the workers many new rights and higher wages. A year later, however, the gains were withdrawn and Solidarity was outlawed. Lech Walesa was awarded the Nobel Peace Prize in 1983 for his work promoting freedom in Poland. This lecture was delivered at a time when Solidarity was still illegal.

*May I repeat that the fundamental necessity in Poland is now understanding and dialogue. I think that the same applies to the whole world: we should go on talking, we must not close any doors or do anything that would block the road to an understanding. And we must remember that only peace built on the foundations of justice and moral order can be a lasting one.*

*In many parts of the world the people are searching for a solution which would link the two basic values: peace and justice. The two are like bread and salt for mankind. Every nation and every community have the inalienable right to these values. No conflicts can be resolved without doing everything possible to follow that road. Our times require that these aspirations which exist the world over must be recognized.*

*Our efforts and harsh experiences have revealed to the world the value of human solidarity. Accepting this honourable distinction I am thinking of those with whom I am linked by the spirit of solidarity.*

*—first of all, of those who in the struggle for the workers' and civic rights in my country paid the highest price—the price of life;*

*—of my friends who paid for the defence of "Solidarity" with the loss of freedom, who were sentenced to prison terms or are awaiting trial;*

*—of my countrymen who saw in the "Solidarity" movement the fulfillment of their aspirations as workers and citizens, who are subjected to humiliations and ready for sacrifices, who have learn[ed] to link courage with wisdom and who persist in loyalty to the cause we have embarked upon;*

*—of all those who are struggling throughout the world for workers' and union rights, for the dignity of a working man, for human rights.*

## ANALYZING THE DOCUMENT

Use the excerpt above to answer the following questions.

1. Walesa feels that the Polish workers' efforts have taught the world the value of—

   A justice.

   B peace.

   C human solidarity.

   D hard work.

2. What were the members of Solidarity struggling for?

   A government loyalty

   B shorter prison terms

   C workers' and civic rights

   D bread and salt

3. *Critical Thinking:* **Defending a Position**
   Do you agree with the idea that the only way to build a lasting peace is to establish justice?

# Octavio Paz:
# *Latin America and Democracy*

Octavio Paz, a Mexican poet, philosopher, and diplomat, won the Nobel Prize for Literature in 1990. The following excerpt is from his book, *One Earth, Four or Five Worlds: Reflections on Contemporary History.*

◆ DOCUMENT IN BRIEF

In this essay Paz states that democracy is necessary for social and economic reform in Latin America.

DOCUMENTS

*Latin American democracy was a late arrival on the scene, and it has been disfigured and betrayed time and time again. It has been weak, hesitant, rebellious, its own worst enemy, all too eager to worship the demagogue, corrupted by money, riddled with favoritism and nepotism [appointing relatives]. And yet almost everything good that has been achieved in Latin America in the last century and a half has been accomplished under democratic rule, or, as in Mexico, a rule heading toward democracy. A great deal still remains to be done. Our countries need changes and reforms, at once radical and in accord with the tradition and the genius of each people. In countries where attempts have been made to change the economic and social structures while at the same time dismantling democratic institutions, injustice, oppression, and inequality have become stronger forces than ever. The cause of the workers requires, above all else, freedom of association and the right to strike, yet this is the very first thing that their liberators strip them of. Without democracy, changes are counterproductive; or, rather, they are not changes at all.*

*To repeat again, for on this point we must be unyielding: changes are inseparable from democracy. To defend democracy is to defend the possibility of change; in turn, changes alone can strengthen democracy and enable it to be embodied in social life. This is a tremendous, twofold task. Not only for Latin Americans: for all of us. The battle is a worldwide one. What is more, the outcome is uncertain, dubious. No matter: the battle must be waged.*

## ANALYZING THE DOCUMENT

Use the excerpt above to answer the following questions.

1. The author states that workers need—

   A higher wages.

   B. democracy.

   C change.

   D freedom of association and the right to strike.

2. Which of the following is the *best summary* of the passage?

A Democracy is the best system for change.

B Democracy is too flawed to be successful.

C Democratic institutions cannot be dismantled.

D Reforms must be made in keeping with the people's traditions.

3. *Critical Thinking:* **Recognizing Causes and Effects** According to the author, how have nondemocratic attempts at reform influenced Latin America?

# Mikhail Gorbachev: *Perestroika*

Mikhail Gorbachev's economic and political reforms paved the way for the independence of Eastern Europe, the breakup of the Soviet Union, and the end of the Cold War. In the following speech delivered in 1989, Gorbachev asks the people of the Soviet Union to maintain confidence in the changes brought about by perestroika despite the difficulties and criticisms of the program.

*Good evening, comrades, I am here to talk to you about our current affairs. The situation in the country is not simple. We all know and feel this. Everything has become entangled in a tight knot: Scarcity on the consumer goods market, conflicts in ethnic relations, and difficult and sometimes painful processes in the public consciousness, resulting from the overcoming of distortions and from the renewal of socialism. People are trying to understand where we have found ourselves at the moment, evaluating the pluses and minuses of the path we have covered during the last four-plus years, the development of democracy and the pace of the economic and political reforms. . . .*

*Some are ready to give up perestroika and return to the past. Others, who consider themselves "active reformers," want to head perestroika onto the path of rash decisions and hasty projects, prompted by ambition rather than concern for real progress. . . .*

*True, perestroika is meeting with many difficulties. But it is radical change, a revolution in the economy and in policy, in the ways of thinking and in people's consciousness, in the entire pattern of our life. Besides, we have not been able to avoid mistakes in our practical actions in the course of perestroika. But perestroika has opened up realistic opportunities for society's renewal, for giving society a new quality and for creating truly humane and democratic socialism. It has returned to the great nation a sense of dignity and given the Soviet people a sense of freedom. It is a powerful source of social, spiritual, and, I should say, patriotic energy for decades to come.*

*That is why we must do everything to continue perestroika on the basis of the ideas and principles proclaimed by the party. And we must not allow those who are using the difficulties we have met to impose on society doubts about the correctness of the path we have chosen.*

▲ Mikhail Gorbachev

## ANALYZING THE DOCUMENT

Use the excerpt above to answer the following questions.

1. Gorbachev states that the "active reformers" want to—

   A return to the past.

   B end the policy of perestroika.

   C speed up the pace of reforms under perestroika.

   D further debate the policy of perestroika.

2. Which of the following statements best *summarizes* this excerpt?

   A Perestroika imposes too many reforms on society.

   B Perestroika is a great source of dignity.

   C Perestroika must continue despite mistakes and criticism.

   D Perestroika does not allow for enough freedom.

3. *Critical Thinking:* **Recognizing Bias** How does Gorbachev discredit the ideas of "active reformers" in this excerpt?

# Vaclav Havel:
## *New Year's Address*

DOCUMENT IN BRIEF

In this speech Havel calls citizens to be active participants in their new democracy.

Vaclav Havel was a leading dissident and human rights activist in communist-led Czechoslovakia. When the "democracy movement" swept through Eastern Europe in 1989, Havel was elected president. In the following speech delivered on January 1, 1990, Havel asks the citizens of Czechoslovakia to accept responsibility for their past and to move forward in building a democracy.

> *Our country is not flourishing. The enormous creative and spiritual potential of our nations is being wasted. Entire branches of industry produce goods that are of no interest to anyone, while we lack the things we need. . . . We now have the most contaminated environment in all of Europe. . . .*
>
> *But all this is not even the main problem. The worst thing is that we live in a contaminated moral environment. We have fallen morally ill because we became used to saying one thing and thinking another. We have learned not to believe in anything, to ignore each other, to care only about ourselves. Notions such as love, friendship, compassion, humility, or forgiveness have lost their depth and dimensions. . . . Only a few of us managed to cry out loud that the powers-that-be should not be all-powerful. . . .*
>
> *We have all become used to the totalitarian system and accepted it as an immutable fact, thus helping to perpetuate it. In other words, we are all . . . responsible for the creation of the totalitarian machinery. . . .*
>
> *Why do I say this? It would be very unwise to think of the sad legacy of the last forty years as something alien or something inherited from a distant relative. On the contrary, we have to accept this legacy as something we have inflicted on ourselves. If we accept it as such, we will understand that it is up to all of us, and only us, to do something about it. We cannot blame the previous rulers for everything—not only because it would be untrue, but also because it could weaken our sense of duty, our obligation to act independently, freely, sensibly, and quickly. Let us not be mistaken: even the best government in the world, the best parliament, and the best president cannot do much on their own. And in any case, it would be wrong to expect a cure-all from them alone. Freedom and democracy, after all, require everyone to participate and thus to share responsibility.*

## ANALYZING THE DOCUMENT

Use the excerpt above to answer the following questions.

1. What does Havel mean by "contaminated moral environment"?

   A People are dishonest and disinterested.

   B People are disrespectful of the environment.

   C People are unwise and unruly.

   D People have no respect for the law.

2. According to Havel, why must everyone participate in the new democracy?

   A to correct the wrongs of the past

   B to share responsibility

   C to prevent totalitarianism

   D to prevent environmental pollution

3. *Critical Thinking:* **Recognizing Causes and Effects** Why does Havel want people to accept responsibility for the totalitarian machinery of the past?

*Historical Documents* **643**

DOCUMENTS

## DOCUMENT IN BRIEF

In this speech Vargas Llosa describes what is needed to sustain democracy in Latin America.

# Mario Vargas Llosa: *Latin America, The Democratic Option*

In this speech delivered in 1990, Peruvian writer Mario Vargas Llosa (1936– ) describes the changes that are needed to maintain and extend democracy in Latin America.

*The democratization of Latin America, even though it has today an unprecedented popular base, is very fragile. To maintain and extend this popular base, governments will have to prove to their citizens that democracy means not only the end of political brutality but progress—concrete benefits in areas such as labor, health, and education, where so much remains to be done. But, given Latin America's current economic crisis, when the prices of its exports are hitting record lows and the weight of its foreign debt is crushing, those governments have virtually no alternative but to demand that their citizens—especially the poor—make even greater sacrifices than they've already made. . . . A realistic and ethically sound approach that our creditors could take would be to demand that each debtor nation pay what it can without placing its stability in jeopardy. . . .*

*If we want democracy to take hold in our countries, our most urgent task is to broaden it, give it substance and truth. Democracy is fragile in so many countries because it is superficial, a mere framework within which institutions and political parties go about their business in their traditionally arbitrary, bullying way. . . .*

*Perhaps the hardest struggle we Latin Americans will have will be against ourselves. Centuries of intolerance, of absolute truths, of despotic governments, weigh us down—and it won't be easy to shake that burden off. The tradition of absolute power that began with our pre-Columbian empires, and the tradition that might makes right that the Spanish and Portuguese explorers practiced, were perpetuated in the nineteenth century, after our independence, by our caudillos [military dictators] and our oligarchies, often with the blessing or direct-intervention of foreign powers.*

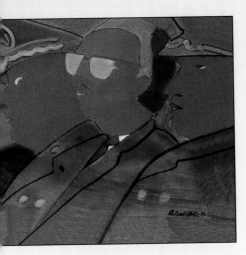

▲ *The Parrots*, by Colombian artist Beatriz González

## ANALYZING THE DOCUMENT

Use the excerpt above to answer the following questions.

1. The author states that democratic governments in Latin America have to provide—

    A real improvements in labor, health, and education.

    B higher incomes.

    C less bureaucracy.

    D greater income from exports.

2. The author states that many democratic governments are fragile because—

    A they lack authoritative governments.

    B they do not always act democratically.

    C they lack international support.

    D they lack strong political parties.

3. *Critical Thinking:* **Identifying Main Ideas** In the last paragraph the author describes what he thinks may be the greatest obstacle to democracy in Latin America. Restate the main idea of that paragraph in your own words.

# Aung San Suu Kyi:
## *Freedom from Fear*

DOCUMENT IN BRIEF

In this essay Aung San Suu Kyi describes the roles of fear and courage when living under an oppressive government.

Aung San Suu Kyi, leader of Burma's National League for Democracy and winner of the Nobel Peace Prize, has worked courageously for human rights and democracy in Burma. Because of her opposition to Burma's ruling military junta, she was held under house arrest from 1989 to 1995 and again in 1997.

*Fearlessness may be a gift but perhaps more precious is the courage acquired through endeavour, courage that comes from cultivating the habit of refusing to let fear dictate one's actions, courage that could be described as 'grace under pressure'—grace which is renewed repeatedly in the face of harsh, unremitting pressure.*

*Within a system which denies the existence of basic human rights, fear tends to be the order of the day. Fear of imprisonment, fear of torture, fear of death, fear of losing friends, family, property or means of livelihood, fear of poverty, fear of isolation, fear of failure. A most insidious [more dangerous than seems evident] form of fear is that which masquerades as common sense or even wisdom, condemning as foolish, reckless, insignificant or futile the small, daily acts of courage which help to preserve man's self-respect and inherent human dignity. It is not easy for a people conditioned by fear under the iron rule of the principle that might is right to free themselves from the enervating [weakening] miasma [pollution] of fear. Yet even under the most crushing state machinery courage rises up again and again, for fear is not the natural state of civilized man.*

*The wellspring [source] of courage and endurance in the face of unbridled power is generally a firm belief in the sanctity of ethical principles combined with a historical sense that despite all setbacks the condition of man is set on an ultimate course for both spiritual and material advancement. . . . It is man's vision of a world fit for rational, civilized humanity which leads him to dare and to suffer to build societies free from want and fear. Concepts such as truth, justice and compassion cannot be dismissed as trite [meaningless] when these are often the only bulwarks [defenses] which stand against ruthless power.*

## ANALYZING THE DOCUMENT

Use the excerpt above to answer the following questions.

1. According to the author, why do people work against all odds to build societies free from want and fear?

   A because they have a dream of a just world

   B because they dismiss truth and justice as trite

   C because they are powerless

   D because they wish to gain courage

2. What are the sources of courage according to the author?

   A power and history

   B belief in ethical principles and a sense that progress is inevitable

   C belief in truth and compassion

   D power and endurance

3. *Critical Thinking:* Applying Information
   Describe one or more examples of a person refusing to let fear dictate his or her actions.

◆ DOCUMENT
IN BRIEF

In this speech
Mandela calls the
people of South
Africa to build a new
nation based on jus-
tice and peace, and
free from sexism and
racism.

# Nelson Mandela:
## *Glory and Hope*

Nelson Mandela delivered this speech after having been elected president in South Africa's first multiracial elections in 1994. Knowing that the injustices of apartheid would not be easily erased, Mandela asked the people to work together for peace and justice.

*Today, all of us do, by our presence here, and by our celebrations . . . confer glory and hope to newborn liberty.*

*Out of the experience of an extraordinary human disaster that lasted too long must be born a society of which all humanity will be proud.*

*Our daily deeds as ordinary South Africans must produce an actual South African reality that will reinforce humanity's belief in justice, strengthen its confidence in the nobility of the human soul and sustain all our hopes for a glorious life for all. . . .*

*The time for the healing of the wounds has come. . . .*

*The time to build is upon us.*

*We have, at last, achieved our political emancipation. We pledge ourselves to liberate all our people from the continuing bondage of poverty, deprivation, suffering, gender and other discrimination.*

*We have triumphed in the effort to implant hope in the breasts of the millions of our people. We enter into a covenant that we shall build the society in which all South Africans, both black and white, will be able to walk tall, without any fear in their hearts, assured of the inalienable right to human dignity—a rainbow nation at peace with itself and the world. . . .*

*We understand it still that there is no easy road to freedom.*

*We know it well that none of us acting alone can achieve success.*

*We must therefore act together as a united people, for national reconciliation, for nation building, for the birth of a new world.*

*Let there be justice for all. Let there be peace for all. Let there be work, bread, water, and salt for all. . . . The sun shall never set on so glorious a human achievement!*

▲ Nelson Mandela

## ANALYZING THE DOCUMENT

Use the excerpt above to answer the following questions.

1. In this speech Mandela is celebrating—

   A the birth of a new, free nation.

   B decades of peace and justice in South Africa.

   C years of racial justice.

   D the end of violence.

2. Which of the following best summarizes the excerpt?

   A We must find work for all South Africans.

   B We must not take the path of violence.

   C We must now finish the work of freedom that we have started.

   D We must correct the evils of the past through severe punishments.

3. *Critical Thinking:* **Making Inferences**
   Having achieved political freedom, what further "freedoms" does Mandela call for in his speech?

# Harry Wu: *The Outlook for China, Human Rights*

**DOCUMENT IN BRIEF**

In this speech Wu describes the state of communism in China and the country's system of forced labor camps.

Author and human rights activist Harry Wu was imprisoned in China for 19 years because of his criticisms of the Communist regime. The excerpt below is from a speech Wu delivered in 1996.

*Sometimes people ask me, "What are you fighting for?" And my answer is quite simple. I want to see the word* laogai *in every dictionary in every language in the world; I want to see the laogai ended. . . .*

*The economic boom made possible by capitalism makes profits for both the West and China. But despite the huge profits earned by China's external trade, ordinary people enjoy only a tiny part. The communist government puts most of the profits into upgrading its weapons systems, into internal and external political activities, and into maintaining the nation's political stability. . . .*

*Today, a specter is hovering over Mainland China—capitalism. Communism is dead; it is no longer believed in by the Chinese in general nor even by the majority of Communist Party members. The "capitalistic" economic boom has made the superstructure of the communist regime appear pretty on the outside, but its pillars are heavily damaged. Looming in front of China are some huge crises.*

*At the core of the human rights question in China today is China's fundamental machinery for crushing human beings physically, psychologically and spiritually: the laogai camp system, of which we have identified 1,100 camps. It is also an integral part of the national economy. Its importance is illustrated by some basic facts: one third of China's tea is produced in laogai camps; 60 percent of China's rubber vulcanizing chemicals are produced in a single laogai camp in Shanghai; the first and second chain hoist works in the country to receive direct export authority are laogai camps in Zhejiang Province; one of the largest and earliest exporters of hand tools is a camp in Shanghai; an unknown but significant amount of China's cotton crop is grown by prisoners. I could go on and on and on. . . . The laogai is not simply a prison system, it is a political tool for maintaining the Communist Party's totalitarian rule.*

▲ A call for democracy in China

## ANALYZING THE DOCUMENT

Use the excerpt above to answer the following questions.

1. What is a laogai?

    **A** a labor camp for prisoners

    **B** a warehouse for exports

    **C** a chemical plant

    **D** a tea or cotton plantation

2. The "damaged pillars" described in the second paragraph are a symbol of—

    **A** the noncommunist leadership.

    **B** the communist regime's lack of true support by the people.

    **C** the economy of the country.

    **D** the Chinese prison system.

3. *Critical Thinking:* **Synthesizing Information**
   Why do you think the author describes the laogai as "a political tool for maintaining the Communist Party's totalitarian rule"?

# GLOSSARY

This Glossary defines many important terms and phrases. Some terms are phonetically respelled to aid in pronunciation. See the Pronunciation Key below for an explanation of the respellings. The page number following each definition is the page on which the term or phrase is first discussed in the text. All terms that appear in blue type in the text are included in this Glossary. Other useful world history terms are also included. Also included are helpful social studies terms. No page references are given for these.

**PRONUNCIATION KEY** When difficult terms or names first appear in the text, they are respelled to aid in pronunciation. A syllable in small capital letters receives the most stress. The key below lists the letters used for respelling. It includes examples of words using each sound and shows how they are respelled.

| SYMBOL | EXAMPLE | RESPELLING |
|--------|---------|------------|
| a | hat | (hat) |
| ay | pay, late | (pay), (layt) |
| ah | star, hot | (stahr), (haht) |
| ai | air, dare | (air), (dair) |
| aw | law, all | (law), (awl) |
| eh | met | (meht) |
| ee | bee, eat | (bee), (eet) |
| er | learn, sir, fur | (lern), (ser), (fer) |
| ih | fit | (fiht) |
| ī | mile | (mīle) |
| ir | ear | (ir) |
| oh | no | (noh) |
| oi | soil, boy | (soil), (boi) |
| oo | root, rule | (root), rool) |
| or | born, door | (born), (dor) |
| ow | plow, out | (plow), (owt) |
| u | put, book | (put), (buk) |
| uh | fun | (fuhn) |
| yoo | few, use | (fyoo), (yooz) |
| ch | chill, reach | (chihl), (reech) |
| g | go, dig | (goh), (dihg) |
| j | jet, gently, bridge | (jeht), (JEHNT lee), (brihj) |
| k | kite, cup | (kīt, kuhp) |
| ks | mix | (mihks) |
| kw | quick | (kwihk) |
| ng | bring | (brihng) |
| s | say, cent | (say), (sehnt) |
| sh | she, crash | (shee), (krash) |
| th | three | (three) |
| y | yet, onion | (yeht), (UHN yuhn) |
| z | zip, always | (zihp), (AWL wayz) |
| zh | treasure | (TREH zher) |

# A

**abdicate** to give up a high office (p. 304)

**absolute monarch** ruler with complete authority over the government and lives of the people he or she governs (p. 34)

**acid rain** form of pollution in which toxic chemicals in the air come back to the Earth as rain, snow, or hail (p. 418)

**acropolis** (uh KRAHP uh lihs) hilltop fortress of an ancient Greek city-state (p. 10)

**agribusiness** large commercial farm owned by a multinational corporation (p. 537)

**ahimsa** (uh HIM sah) Hindu belief in nonviolence (p. 748)

**anarchist** person who wants to abolish all government (p. 179)

**annex** to add a territory onto an existing state or country (p. 81)

**anti-Semitism** prejudice against Jews (p. 203)

**apartheid** policy of strict racial separation in South Africa; abolished in 1989 (p. 326)

**appeasement** policy of giving in to an aggressor's demands in order to keep the peace (p. 372)

**aqueduct** in ancient Rome, bridgelike stone structure that carried water from the hills into the cities (p. 13) ▲

**archaeology** (ahr kee AHL uh jee) study of the lives of early people through examination of their physical remains

**archipelago** (ahr kuh PEHL uh goh) chain of islands

**aristocracy** in Greek city-states, government headed by a privileged minority or upper class (p. 10)

**armistice** agreement to end fighting in a war (p. 293)

**artifact** object made by human beings

**artisan** skilled craftworker (p. 3)

**assembly line** production method that breaks down a complex job into a series of smaller tasks (p. 141)

**astrolabe** instrument used to determine latitude by measuring the position of the stars (p. 30) ▲

**atrocity** brutal act (p. 290)

**autocrat** ruler who has complete authority (p. 514)

**autonomy** self-rule (p. 113)

# B

**balance of power** distribution of military and economic power that prevents any one nation from becoming too strong (p. 34)

**balance of trade** difference between how much a country imports and how much it exports (p. 233)

**baroque** ornate style of art and architecture popular in the 1600s and 1700s (p. 48)

**barter economy** system in which one set of goods or services is exchanged for another

**bias** prejudice for or against someone or something

**bishop** in the Christian Church, a high-ranking Church official with authority over a local area, or diocese (p. 524)

**blitzkrieg** lightning war (p. 377)

**blockade** the shutting off of a port to keep people or supplies from moving in or out (p. 82)

**bourgeoisie** (boor zhwah ZEE) the middle class (p. 65)

**brahman** according to Aryan belief, the single spiritual power that resides in all things (p. 7)

**bureaucracy** system of managing government through departments run by appointed officials (p. 3)

# C

**caliph** successor to Muhammad as political and religious leader of the Muslims (p. 22)

**capital** money for investment

**capitalism** economic system in which the means of production are privately owned and operated for profit (p. 33)

**caravel** improved type of sailing ship in the 1400s (p. 30)

**cartel** association of large corporations formed to fix prices, set production quotas, or divide up markets (p. 145)

**cartographer** mapmaker (p. 30)

**cash crop** crop raised to be sold for money on the world market (p. 231)

**caste** in traditional Indian society, unchangeable social group into which a person is born (p. 7)

**cataract** waterfall

**caudillo** military dictator in Latin America (p. 257)

**charter** in the Middle Ages, a written document that set out the rights and privileges of a town

**chivalry** code of conduct for knights during the Middle Ages (p. 17)

**circumnavigate** to travel all the way around the Earth

**city-state** political unit made up of a city and the surrounding lands (p. 4)

**civil disobedience** refusal to obey unjust laws (p. 332)

**civil law** body of law dealing with private rights of individuals

**coalition** temporary alliance of various political parties (p. 202)

**collaborator** person who cooperates with an enemy (p. 384)

**collective** large farm owned and operated by workers as a group (p. 310)

**colony** territory settled and ruled by people from another land (p. 54)

**command economy** system in which government officials make all basic economic decisions (p. 309)

**common law** system of law based on court decisions that became accepted legal principles (p. 18)

**commune** community in which property is held in common, living quarters are shared, and physical needs are provided in exchange for work at assigned jobs (p. 466)

**communism** form of socialism advocated by Karl Marx; according to Marx, class struggle was inevitable and would lead to the creation of a classless society in which all wealth and property would be owned by the community as a whole (p. 106)

**concentration camp** detention center for civilians considered enemies of a state (p. 366)

**conquistador** (kahn KEES tuh dor) name for the Spanish explorers who claimed lands in the Americas for Spain in the 1500s and 1600s (p. 32)

**constitutional government** a government whose power is defined and limited by law (p. 51)

**containment** Cold War policy of limiting communism to areas already under Soviet control (p. 396)

**corporation** business owned by many investors who buy shares of stock and risk only the amount of their investment (p. 145)

**creole** person in Spain's colonies in the Ameri-cas who was an American-born descendant of Spanish settlers (p. 536)

**crusade** holy war (p. 19)

**cultural diffusion** the spread of ideas, customs, and technologies from one people to another (p. 4)

**cuneiform** (kyoo NEE uh form) wedge-shaped writing of the ancient Sumerians and other ancient peoples (p. 5) ▲

**czar** title of the ruler of the Russian empire (p. 21)

# D

**daimyo** (DĪ myoh) warrior lords directly below the shogun in feudal Japan (p. 27)

**deficit** gap between what a government spends and what it takes in through taxes and other sources (p. 444)

**deficit spending** situation in which a government spends more money than it takes in (p. 65)

**delta** triangular area of marshland formed by deposits of silt at the mouth of some rivers

**democracy** government in which the people hold ruling power (p. 10)

**desertification** process by which fertile or semi-desert land becomes desert (p. 516)

**détente** easing of tensions between the United States and the Soviet Union in the 1970s (p. 432)

**diaspora** (dī AS puh ruh) the scattering of the Jewish people from their homeland in Palestine (p. 5); the scattering of African peoples as a result of the slave trade (p. 512)

**dictator** ruler who has complete control over a government (p. 258)

**direct democracy** system of government in which citizens participate directly rather than through elected representatives (p. 10)

**dissident** someone who speaks out against the government (p. 447)

**divine right** belief that a ruler's authority comes directly from God (p. 34)

**dynastic cycle** rise and fall of Chinese dynasties according to the Mandate of Heaven (p. 7)

**dynasty** ruling family (p. 7)

# E

**economic dependence** economic relationship, controlled by a developing nation, in which a less-developed nation exports raw materials to the developed nation and imports manufactured goods, capital, and technological know-how (p. 257)

**ejido** (eh HEE doh) Mexican peasant cooperative (p. 546)

**émigré** (EHM ih gray) person who flees his or her country for political reasons (p. 72)

**empire** group of states or territories controlled by one ruler (p. 5)

**enclosure** in England in the 1700s, the process of taking over and fencing off public lands (p. 93)

**encomienda** right the Spanish government granted to its American colonists to demand labor or tribute from Native Americans (p. 32)

**enlightened despot** absolute ruler who uses his or her power to bring about political and social change (p. 47)

**entrepreneur** person who assumes financial risks in the hope of making a profit (p. 33)

**ethics** moral standards of behavior (p. 5)

**ethnic group** large group of people who share the same language and cultural heritage (p. 21)

**excommunication** exclusion from the Roman Catholic Church as a penalty for refusing to obey Church laws (p. 19)

**extraterritoriality** right of foreigners to be protected by the laws of their own nation (p. 234)

# F

**factory** place in which workers and machines are brought together to produce large quantities of goods (p. 98)

**feudalism** (FYOOD uhl ihz uhm) loosely organ-ized system of government in which local lords governed their own lands but owed military service and other support to a greater lord (p. 16)

**fief** (FEEF) in the Middle Ages, an estate granted by a lord to a vassal in exchange for service and loyalty (p. 16)

**filial piety** respect for parents (p. 9)

**flapper** in the United States and Europe in the 1920s, a rebellious young woman (p. 357)

**free market** market in which goods are bought and sold without restrictions (p. 44)

# G

**general strike** strike by workers in many different industries at the same time (p. 350)

**genocide** deliberate attempt to destroy an entire religious or ethnic group (p. 226)

**geography** study of people, their environments, and their resources (p. 466)

**glacier** thick sheet of ice that covered parts of the Earth during the ice age

**glasnost** policy of openness instituted by Soviet leader Mikhail Gorbachev in the 1980s (p. 449)

**gravity** force that tends to pull one mass or object to another (p. 29)

**griot** (GREE oh) professional storyteller in early West Africa (p. 25)

**gross domestic product** total value of all goods and services produced by a nation (p. 461)

**guerrilla warfare** fighting carried on through hit-and-run raids (p. 83)

**guild** in the Middle Ages, association of merchants or artisans who cooperated to protect their economic interests (p. 17)

# H

**habeas corpus** principle that a person cannot be held in prison without first being charged with a specific crime

**hajj** pilgrimage to Mecca that all Muslims are expected to make at least once in their lifetime (p. 22)

**heliocentric** based on the belief that the sun is the center of the universe (p. 29)

**hierarchy** (HĪ uhr ahr kee) system of ranks (p. 4)

**hieroglyphics** (hī er oh GLIHF ihks) form of picture writing developed by the ancient Egyptians (p. 79)

GLOSSARY

**historian** person who studies how people lived in the past

**home rule** local self-government (p. 199)

**homogeneous society** society that has a common culture and language (p. 246)

**humanism** intellectual movement at the heart of the Italian Renaissance that focused on worldly subjects rather than on religious issues (p. 28)

# I

**ideology** system of thought and belief (p. 112)

**imperialism** domination by one country of the political, economic, or cultural life of another country or region (p. 216)

**import substitution** government policy of encouraging local manufacturers to produce goods that would replace imports (p. 537)

**impressionism** school of painting of the late 1800s and early 1900s that tried to capture fleeting visual impressions (p. 161)

**indemnity** payment for losses in war (p. 234)

**indigenous** original or native to a country or region (p. 251)

**inflation** economic cycle that involves a rise in prices linked to a sharp increase in the amount of money available

**interchangeable parts** identical components that can be used in place of one another in manufacturing (p. 141)

**interdependence** mutual dependence of countries on goods, resources, and knowledge from other parts of the world (p. 412)

**intifada** mass uprising mounted in 1987 by Palestinians in territory held by Israel (p. 501)

**isolationism** policy of limited involvement in world affairs (p. 211)

# J

**jury** group of people sworn to make a decision in a legal case (p. 18)

# K

**kamikaze** Japanese pilot who undertook a suicide mission (p. 390)

**kiva** large underground chamber used by the Anasazi for religious ceremonies (p. 15)

**knight** noble in Europe who served as a mounted warrior for a lord in the Middle Ages (p. 16)

**kulak** wealthy peasant in the Soviet Union in the 1930s (p. 311)

# L

**laissez faire** policy allowing business to operate with little or no government interference (p. 44)

**latitude** distance north or south of the Equator

**legislature** lawmaking body (p. 473)

**legitimacy** the principle by which monarchies that had been unseated by the French Revolution or Napoleon were restored (p. 87)

**liberation theology** in Latin America, movement urging the Roman Catholic Church to take a more active role in changing the social conditions that contribute to poverty and oppression (p. 423)

**limited monarchy** government in which a constitution or legislative body limits the monarch's powers (p. 35)

**loess** fine windblown yellow soil

**longitude** distance east or west of the Prime Meridian

GLOSSARY

# M

**mandate** after World War I, a territory that was administered by a western power (p. 296)

**manor** during the Middle Ages in Europe, a lord's estate, which included one or more villages and the surrounding lands (p. 17)

**maquiladora** (mah kee luh DOR uh) foreign-owned industrial plant in Mexico in which local workers assemble imported parts into finished goods (p. 547)

**matrilineal** term for a family organization in which kinship ties are traced through the mother

**mercantilism** policy by which a nation sought to export more than it imported in order to build its supply of gold and silver (p. 470)

**mercenary** soldier serving in a foreign army for pay

**messiah** savior sent by God (p. 13)

**mestizo** person in Spain's colonies in the Americas who was of Native American and European descent (p. 121)

**militarism** glorification of the military (p. 279)

**minaret** slender tower of a mosque, from which Muslims are called to prayer

**mixed economy** economic system with both private and state-run enterprises (p. 515)

**mobilize** to prepare military forces for war (p. 283)

**monarchy** government in which a king or queen exercises central power (p. 10)

**monopoly** complete control of a product or business by one person or group (p. 145)

**monotheistic** believing in one God (p. 5)

**monsoon** seasonal wind; in India, the winter monsoon brings hot, dry weather and the summer monsoon brings rain

**mosque** Muslim house of worship (p. 23)

**mulatto** person in Spain's colonies in the Americas who was of African and European descent (p. 121)

**multinational corporation** enterprise with branches in many countries (p. 416)

**mummification** (muhm mih fih KAY shuhn) practice of preserving the bodies of the dead

**mystic** person who devotes his or her life to seeking spiritual truths (p. 7)

# N

**nationalism** feeling of pride in and devotion to one's country (p. 77)

**nationalization** takeover of property or resources by the government (p. 323)

**natural laws** rules that govern human nature (p. 40)

**natural rights** rights that belong to all humans from birth (p. 41)

**neutrality** policy of supporting neither side in a war (p. 283)

**nirvana** in Buddhism, union with the universe and release from the cycle of rebirth (p. 8)

**nomad** person who moves from place to place in search of food (p. 2)

**nonaligned** not allied with either side in a conflict, such as the Cold War (p. 411)

**nuclear family** family unit consisting of parents and children (p. 25)

# O

**oligarchy** government in which ruling power belongs to a few people (p. 10)

**oral history** collection of people's remembrances about a time or an event

# P

**pacifism** opposition to all war (p. 373)

**patriarchal** describing a family headed by the father or oldest male

**patrician** member of the landholding upper class in ancient Rome (p. 12)

**patrilineal** term for a family organization in which kinship ties are traced through the father

**patron** person who provides financial support for the arts (p. 48)

**penal colony** place where people convicted of crimes are sent (p. 254)

**peninsular** member of the highest class in Spain's colonies in the Americas (p. 121)

**peonage** system by which workers owe labor to pay their debts (p. 259)

**perestroika** restructuring of the Soviet government and economy in the 1980s (p. 449)

**pharaoh** (FAIR oh) title of the rulers of ancient Egypt (p. 4)

**philosophe** member of a group of Enlightenment thinkers who tried to apply the methods of science to the improvement of society (p. 41)

**physiocrat** an Enlightenment thinker who searched for natural laws to explain economics (p. 44)

**pictogram** drawing used to represent a word (p. 3)

**plantation** large estate run by an owner or overseer and worked by laborers who live there (p. 32)

**plebeian** (plee BEE uhn) member of the lower class in ancient Rome, including farmers, merchants, artisans, and traders (p. 12)

**plebiscite** ballot in which voters have a direct say on an issue (p. 79)

**pogrom** violent attack on a Jewish community (p. 185)

**polis** city-state in ancient Greece (p. 10)

**polytheistic** believing in many gods (p. 7)

**pope** head of the Roman Catholic Church (p. 487)

**prehistory** period of time before writing systems were invented

**primary source** firsthand information about people or events of the past, such as that found in a diary or legal document

**prime minister** head of the cabinet in a parliamentary government; usually the leader of the largest party in the legislature (p. 53)

**privatization** the selling off of state-owned industries to private investors (p. 417)

**proletariat** the working class (p. 107)

**propaganda** the spreading of ideas to promote a certain cause or to damage an opposing cause (p. 290)

**prophet** spiritual leader believed to be interpreting God's will (p. 5)

**protectorate** country with its own government but under the control of an outside power (p. 218)

# R

**racism** belief that one racial group is superior to another (p. 155)

**realism** artistic movement whose aim was to represent the world as it is (p. 159)

**refugee** person who flees his or her homeland to seek safety elsewhere (p. 185)

**regionalism** loyalty to a local area (p. 257)

**reincarnation** in Hinduism, belief in the rebirth of the soul in another bodily form (p. 8)

**reparations** payment for war damages (p. 294)

**republic** system of government in which officials are chosen by the people (p. 12)

**romanticism** nineteenth-century artistic move-ment that appealed to emotion rather than reason (p. 156)

# S

**sacrament** sacred ritual of the Roman Catholic Church (p. 19)

**salon** informal social gathering at which writers, artists, and philosophers exchanged ideas; originated in France in the 1600s (p. 46)

**samurai** member of the warrior class in Japanese feudal society (p. 27)

**sanction** penalty (p. 372)

**sans-culottes** (sanz kyoo LAHTZ) working-class men and women who called for radical action in France during the French Revolution (p. 73)

**savanna** grassy plain with irregular patterns of rainfall

**schism** permanent division in a church (p. 20)

**scribe** in ancient civilizations, specially trained person who knew how to read and write and kept records (p. 5)

**secondary source** information about the past that is not based on direct experience

**sect** small religious group (p. 13)

**secular** having to do with worldly, rather than religious, matters (p. 17)

**segregation** separation of the races (p. 209)

**sepoy** Indian soldier who served in an army set up by the French or English East India company (p. 229)

**serf** in medieval Europe, peasant bound to the lord's land (p. 17)

**service industry** industry that provides a service rather than a product (p. 435)

**shogun** in Japanese feudal society, supreme military commander who held more power than the emperor (p. 27)

**silt** rich soil carried by flooding rivers

**slash-and-burn agriculture** farming method in which forest and brush are cut down and burned to create planting fields

**social contract** agreement by which people give up their freedom to a powerful government in order to avoid chaos (p. 40)

**social gospel** movement of the 1800s that urged Christians to do social service (p. 156)

**socialism** system in which the people as a whole rather than private individuals own all property and operate all businesses (p. 106)

**socialist realism** artistic style whose goal was to promote socialism by showing Soviet life in a positive light (p. 316)

**soviet** council of workers and soldiers set up by Russian revolutionaries in 1917 (p. 304)

**sphere of influence** area in which an outside power claims exclusive investment or trading privileges (p. 218)

**steppe** sparse, dry grassland

**strait** narrow water passage connecting two bodies of water

**stream of consciousness** literary technique that probes a character's random thoughts and feelings (p. 355)

**subcontinent** large landmass that juts out from a continent

**suffrage** the right to vote (p. 74)

**sultan** Muslim ruler (p. 23)

# T

**tariff** tax on imported goods (p. 44)

**technology** tools and skills people use to meet their basic needs (p. 142)

**terrorism** the deliberate use of random violence, especially against civilians, to achieve political goals (p. 413)

**theocracy** government run by church leaders

**theology** the study of religion

**total war** the channeling of a nation's entire resources into a war effort (p. 289)

**totalitarian state** government in which a one-party dictatorship regulates every aspect of citizens' lives (p. 313)

**trade deficit** situation in which a country imports more than it exports (p. 233)

**tributary state** independent state that has to acknowledge the supremacy of another state and pay tribute to its ruler (p. 27)

**tribute** payment that conquered peoples were forced to make to their conquerors (p. 14)

**turnpike** privately built road that charges a fee to travelers who use it (p. 98)

# U

**ultimatum** final set of demands (p. 283)

**universal manhood suffrage** right of all adult men to vote (p. 113)

**urbanization** movement of people from rural areas to cities (p. 100)

**utilitarianism** idea that the goal of society should be to bring about the greatest happiness for the greatest number of people (p. 105)

# V

**vassal** in medieval Europe, a lord who was granted land in exchange for service and loyalty to a greater lord (p. 16)

**vernacular** everyday language of ordinary people (p. 19)

**veto** power to block a government action

**viceroy** representative who ruled in the king's name (p. 230)

# W

**welfare state** system in which the government takes responsibility for its citizens' social and economic needs (p. 433)

**women's suffrage** right of women to vote (p. 153)

# Z

**zaibatsu** (ZĪ BAHT SOO) since the late 1800s, powerful banking and industrial families in Japan in the late 1800s (p. 246)

**zemstvo** local elected assembly set up in Russia under Alexander II (p. 184)

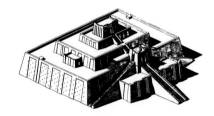

**ziggurat** (ZIHG oo rat) pyramid-temple dedicated to the chief god or goddess of an ancient Sumerian city-state (p. 4) ▲

GLOSSARY

# CONNECTIONS WITH PRENTICE HALL LITERATURE

CONNECTIONS CHARTS

## Unit 1 Enlightenment and Revolution

| | | | |
|---|---|---|---|
| A World of Progress and Reason, page 40 | Jonathan Swift | A Modest Proposal (satirical essay) | page 801 |
| Liberty, Equality, Fraternity, pages 69–70 | Victor Hugo | The Expiation (poetry) | page 890 |
| France After the Restoration, page 115 | Charles Baudelaire | The Albatross (poetry) | page 905 |

## Unit 2 Industrialism and a New Global Age

| | | | |
|---|---|---|---|
| The Revolt Against Reason, pages 156–158 | Alexander Pushkin | The Bridegroom (poetry) | page 880 |
| A Call to Realism, pages 159–160 | William Wordsworth | Ode: Intimations of Immortality (poetry) | page 896 |
| The Struggle for Italy, pages 176–178 | Luigi Pirandello | A Breath of Air (short story) | page 1134 |
| Opening Up Japan, pages 242–243 | Mori Ōgai | Under Reconstruction (short story) | page 1174 |
| The Economics of Dependence, pages 257–258 | Rubén Darío | Sonatina (poetry) | page 1162 |

## Unit 3 World Wars and Revolutions

| | | | |
|---|---|---|---|
| Revolutionary Rumblings, pages 302–303 | Anna Akhmatova | Everything Is Plundered (poetry) | page 1114 |
| Moves Toward Independence page 331–332 | Rabindranath Tagore | The Artist (short story) | page 1192 |
| The Chinese Republic, pages 335–336 | Lu Hsun | My Old Home (short story) | page 1182 |
| France Pursues Security, pages 351–352 | Colette | The Bracelet (short story) | page 1122 |
| Hitler's Third Reich, pages 364–365 | Thomas Mann | Mann's Stand Against the Nazis (letter) | page 1050 |
| The Spanish Civil War, pages 373–374 | Federico García Lorca | The Guitar (poetry) | page 1143 |

## Unit 4 The World Today

| | | | |
|---|---|---|---|
| Decades of War in Vietnam, pages 475–476 | Nguyen Thi Vinh | Thoughts of Hanoi (poetry) | page 1436 |
| Egypt: A Leader in the Arab World, pages 496–498 | Naguib Mahfouz | The Happy Man (short story) | page 1334 |
| Pressures for Change in Nigeria, pages 518–519 | Wole Soyinka | Civilian and Soldier (poetry) | page 1363 |
| A New South Africa, page 524 | Nadine Gordimer | The Ultimate Safari (short story) | page 1366 |
| Reform, Repression, or Revolution? pages 536–537 | Pablo Neruda | Ode to My Socks (poetry) | page 1250 |

CONNECTIONS CHARTS

# CONNECTIONS WITH PRENTICE HALL SCIENCE

| Topic | See Prentice Hall *Biology* or Prentice Hall *Chemistry*: Connections to Our Changing World |
|---|---|
| **Part I Early Civilizations** | |
| Agriculture, pages 2–3 | *Biology*, Seed Development, pages 540–542 |
| Geography: The Nile Valley, page 4 (deserts) | *Biology*, Deserts, page 1015 |
| **Part II Empires of the Ancient World** | |
| Golden Age of the Guptas, page 9 (vaccinations) | *Biology*, Immunity, pages 973–975 |
| Hellenistic Civilization, page 11 (illnesses and cures) | *Biology*, What Is a Disease? pages 953–954 |
| **Part III Regional Civilizations** | |
| Bubonic plague, page 19 | *Biology*, How Is Infectious Disease Spread? page 954 |
| **Part IV Early Modern Times** | |
| The Scientific Revolution, pages 28–29 (scientific method) | *Chemistry*, Scientific Method, pages 7–13 |
| **Unit 1 Enlightenment and Revolution** | |
| A New Agricultural Revolution, pages 91–92 (soils) | *Biology*, Types of Soil, pages 487–488 |
| The Age of Iron and Coal, page 97 (coal) | *Chemistry*, The Energy Crisis, pages 59–60 |
| **Unit 2 Industrialism and a New Global Age** | |
| The Shrinking World, pages 143–145 (internal combustion engines) | *Chemistry*, Exothermic Reactions, pages 382–383 |
| The Challenge of Science, page 154 (atomic theory) | *Chemistry*, Atomic Theory, pages 102–111 |
| **Unit 3 World Wars and Revolutions** | |
| New Views of the Universe, pages 354–355 (radioactivity) | *Chemistry*, Radioactivity, pages 99–100 |
| **Unit 4 The World Today** | |
| Economic Development and the Environment, pages 418–421 (global warming) | *Biology*, Air Pollution, pages 1055–1059 |
| Old Ways and New, pages 422–423 (overcrowded living conditions) | *Biology*, Density-Dependent Limiting Factors, pages 1036–1040 |

CONNECTIONS CHARTS

# INDEX

INDEX

women march on Versailles, 70–71, *p71*
Louis XVIII, king of France, 85, 87, 115
Louisiana Territory, *m56*, 86, 206–207, *m207*
Loyalists (American Revolution), 55
Loyalists (Spain), 373–374
Luddites, 102
Lugard, Frederick, 214
*Lusitania*, 292
Luther, Martin, 29
Luxembourg, 87, 435–436, *m435*
Lyell, Charles, 154
Lytton, Constance, 195
Maathi, Wangari, 516
Macao, 31
MacArthur, Douglas, 388–389, 460, 472
Macaulay, Catherine, 44
Macaulay, Thomas, 231–232
Macdonald, John, 252
Machemba, chief of the Yao people, 219
Machiavelli, Niccolò, 624
Mackenzie, William Lyon, 252
Madero, Francisco, 322
Maginot Line, 352, 378
Magna Carta, 18, 51, 623
Magyars, 21
Mahan, Alfred T., 211
Mahfouz, Naguib, *c527*
Maji-Maji Rebellion, 223
Malaria, 147, 220, 512
Malaya, 248, *m250*, 382, 389, *m389*
Malaysia, 478
Mali, 24, *m25*
Malthus, Thomas, 104, 105, 154
Malvinas, 552
Manchester, 100, 102, *p102*
Manchuria, 338, 340, *m340*, 372
Mandate of Heaven, 7
Mandate system, 296, 329–330, *m330*, 490
Mandela, Nelson, 522, 523–525, *p524*, 587, 588, 646
Mandelstam, Osip, 316
Manifest destiny, 207, *m207*
Manor system, 17
Mansa Musa, 24

Manufacturing. *See* Industry; *specific industries.*
Manzhouguo, 340
Mao Tse-tung. *See* Mao Zedong.
Mao Zedong, 134, 337, *p337*, 338, 464–467, *p467*, 470, 472, 475, 637
Maori people of New Zealand, 255–256, *p255*
*Maquiladoras*, 547, *p548*
Marconi, Guglielmo, 145
Marcos, Ferdinand, 477
Maria Theresa, 47
Marie Antoinette, 70–71, *p70*, 72, 74, 81
Marisol, *(The Family)*, *p538*
Maronites, 502
Marseilles, 77
Marshall Plan, 396, 433
Martín, San, 127
Martinique, 534
Marx, Karl, 106–107, *p107*, 300, 304, 336
Marxism: in China, 336, 467, 637; in Latin America, 536–537; in Russia/Soviet Union, 107, 300, 302, 304. *See also* Communism; Socialism.
Mary, queen of England, 35
Mathematics: Renaissance, 29
Matisse, Henri, 356
Maurya empire, 8–9
Maurya, Chandragupta, 8
Maximilian, 200–201, 258
May Fourth Movement, 336
Mayakovsky, Vladimir, 316
Mayan civilization, 14, *p14*
Mazzini, Giuseppe, 175–176, 177
McCarthy, Joseph, 443
McCormick, Cyrus, 210
Mecca, 22
Medicine: African, *p517*; anesthesia, 147; genetic engineering, 425; health statistics, *c428*; Industrial Revolution, 92, 93; Islamic, 23; modern, 264, 425; psychoanalysis, 355; quinine, 218; rabies vaccine, 138; Scientific

Revolution, 29
Mediterranean Sea, Suez Canal, 227, *m227*, 496, 500. *See also specific nations.*
Meidner, Ludwig, *p277*
Meiji restoration, 243, 245–246, *p245*, 336, 582
*Mein Kampf* (Hitler), 363, 377
Meir, Golda, 596, *c597*
Melanesia, *n250, m614*
Menchu, Rigoberta, 545
Mendeleyev, Dmitri, 154
Mendes, Chico, 544
Menelik II, 223, *p223*
Menem, Carlos Saul, 586
Menes, 4
Mercantilism, British, 54; English, 50, 51; vs. laissez-faire policy, 44; overseas colonies and, 54
Mercosur, 542
Meroe, 24
Mesopotamia, 4–5
*Messiah, The* (Handel), 48
Mestizo, 121, 123, 258, 535
Methodist Church, 102
Metternich, Clemens von, 87, *p118*; on European revolutions, 112, 113, 114, 117, 179; fall of, 118; ideology of, 128; on nationalist Germany, 168; on nationalist Italy, 175
Mexican War, 207, 258, 261
Mexico: anti-American sentiment, 324–325; art, *p14, p324*; Aztecs, 14, 324, *p324*; case studies, 582–585; cultural nationalism, *p324*; culture, *p533*; economic development, 258, 323, 324, 546–547, 582, 583, *c583*, 584–585; foreign debt, 417, 538, 547; government, 323, 546; Great Depression, 583; independence, 123–124, *m126*; land reform, 546; Maximilian, 200–201, 258; Mayas, 14, *p14*; Mexican Revolution, 322–323, *p322*, 539; Mexican War, 207, 258, 261; of Middle America,

14; modernization, 546–548, *m546, p547, p548*, 583; nationalism, 583; Native Americans, 534; North American Free Trade Agreement (NAFTA), 583 oil, 547; population increase, 535; reforms, 323; revolution, 259–260; society, *p36*, 323, 547; Spanish settlement, *n120, m126*; struggle for stability, 258–260; United States and, 257, 261, 323, 324–325, 542–543, 547–548, *p548*
Mexico City: growth of, 546, *m546*; Mexican War, 258
Michelangelo, 28
Microcredit, 594–595
Micronesia, *n250, m614*
Middle Ages: agriculture, 16, 17; Charlemagne, 16, 18; Christianity, 16, 17, 18–19, *p19*; decline of, 19; economy during, 16–17; education, 16; feudalism, 16–17, 18; Germanic kingdoms, 16; government, 18, *p18*; guilds, 17; learning, 16, 19; noblemen, noblewomen, 64; religion, church, 17, 18–19, *p19*, 20, *p20*, 21; social structure, 16–17; trade, commerce, 17, 20, 30; women, 19
Middle America, 14–15
Middle class: British, 53; communism, socialism, 106–107; Enlightenment, 45, *p45*, 46, *p46*, 48; of European 1800s, 113, 116, 118–119; French revolution of 1830, 115; higher education, 154; Industrial Revolution, 103–104, 105–106, 151–152, *p152*; Latin American, 259, 535, 536; in Mexico, 259; under Napoleon, 80; Russian, 182; Victorian England, 151–152, 193; after World War II, 436

INDEX

INDEX

**INDEX**

*(continued from page ii)*

from "The Second Coming" is reprinted with the permission of **Simon & Schuster, Inc. and A. P. Watt Ltd.** from *The Poems of W. B. Yeats: A New Edition*, edited by Richard J. Finneran. Copyright © 1924 by Macmillan Publishing Company, renewed 1952 by Bertha Georgia Yeats. Excerpts from *Mothers and Shadows* (Readers International, 1985), translated by Jo Labanyi from *Conversación al sur* (Mexico City: Siglo XXI, 1981). Reprinted by permission of **Siglo XXI Editores.** Excerpts from "Gonzalez Videla," from *Canto General* by Pablo Neruda, translated/ edited by Jack Schmitt. Copyright © 1991 Fundacion Pablo Neruda, Regents of the University of California. Used by permission of the publisher, the **University of California Press.** Excerpt from "Black Woman," by Léopold Senghor. Copyright © 1964, 1973, 1979, 1984, and 1990 by Éditions du Seuil, by permission of **George Borchardt, Inc.** Reprinted from *The Collected Poetry* by Léopold Sédar Senghor, translated with an Introduction by Melvin Dixon (**The University Press of Virginia,** Charlottesville, Virginia, 1991). Excerpts from *The Metamorphoses* by Publius Ovidius Naso, translated by Horace Gregory. Translation copyright © 1958 by The Viking Press, Inc., renewed 1986 by Patrick Bolton Gregory. Used by permission of **Viking Penguin, a division of Penguin Books USA Inc.**

Note: Every effort has been made to locate the copyright owner of material reprinted in this book. Omissions brought to our attention will be corrected in subsequent printings.

## ART CREDITS

**Cover Design:** Bruce Bond
**Design Services:** Margaret-Ann Rice, Future Design
**Visual Research:** Photosearch, Sue McDermott
**Contributing Artists:** Alfred G. Assin, Tammara L. Newnam, Carol Richmond
**Freelance desktop page layout:** Gabriela Pérez Fiato

## PHOTOGRAPHIC CREDITS

**Front Cover:** Matthew Weinreb/The Image Bank
**Back Cover:** Matthew Weinreb/The Image Bank
**Interior: v** top Dez & Jen Bartlett/Bruce Coleman, Inc.; middle © Archiv/Photo Researchers, Inc.; bottom Archivo Fotographico Oronoz, Madrid **vi** top Courtesy of the Peabody Essex Museum, Salem, Mass.; middle, top Musée Carnavalet, Paris/ Giraudon/The Bridgeman Art Library, London; middle,bottom Archiv für Kunst und Geschichte, Berlin; bottom © Jean-Loup Charmet **vii** left The Royal Collection © Her Majesty Queen Elizabeth II; top, right Library of Congress; bottom, right Archiv Für Kunst und Geschichte, Berlin **viii** top Staatliche Museen zu Berlin - Preussischer Kulturbesitz Museum für Volkerkunde; middle, top © Branger-Viollet; middle,bottom The Bettmann Archive; bottom Forbes Magazine Collection/The Bridgeman Art Library, London **ix** top Nehru Memorial Museum and Library, New Delhi; middle © The London Transport Museum; bottom NASA **x** top Reuters/Bettman; middle ©Michael Coyne/Black Star; bottom Minick/Jiao **xi** top © Emory Kristof/National Geographic Image Collection; middle © Mireille Vautier/Woodfin Camp & Associates **xii** top, left AP/Wide World Photos; top, right Courtesy Télégrama. Photo Ken Karp; bottom, left Courtesy of Gaslight Antiques; bottom, right © Josef Polleross/JB Pictures, Ltd. **xiii** New York State Historical Association, Cooperstown **xxi** top, left Board of Trustees of the National Museums and Galleries on Merseyside (Lady Lever Art Gallery, Port Sunlight); top, right Archiv für Kunst und Geschichte, Berlin; bottom, left JB/Keystone/Hulton Deutsch Collection Ltd.; bottom, right © Tomas Muscionico/Contact Press Images **xxii** top © Michael Fogden/Animals Animals; bottom © Tom Owen Edmunds/The Image Bank **xxiii** top © Michael Holford; middle © Buu-Hires/Gamma Liaison International; bottom © Palomo/

Cartoonists & Writers Syndicate **xxiv** top, left © André Held; top, middle © Liu Heung Shing/Contact Press Images; top, right (detail) From the collection of Hebrew Union College Skirball Museum, Eric Hockley Photographer; bottom, left Lauros-Giraudon/Art Resource, NY; bottom, middle (detail) Copyright British Museum (PS 192184); bottom, right © Esaias Baitel/Gamma Liaison International **xxv** top, left © Michael Holford; top, right © Jonathan Wallen/ Harry N. Abrams, Inc.; middle, left The Science Museum/Science & Society Picture Library; middle, right Whipple Museum of the History of Science; bottom, left Imperial War Museum/E.T. Archive; bottom, right © Somerville/ Cartoonists & Writers Syndicate **xxvi** top, left © Michael Holford; top, middle University of British Columbia/The Bridgeman Art Library, London; top, right Library of Congress; bottom, left © Justin Kerr/Brooklyn Museum; bottom,middle Copyright British Museum; bottom, right Werner Forman Archive, Smithsonian Institution, Washington/Art Resource, NY **xxvii** top, left (detail) The Louvre/The Bridgeman Art Library, London; top, middle Photo Bibliothèque Nationale, Paris; top, right © Hulton Deutsch Collection Ltd; middle, left Bibliothèque Nationale/The Bridgeman Art Library, London; middle, right New York Daily News; bottom, left © John Moss/Black Star; bottom,middle Diplomatic Reception Rooms, United States Department of State; bottom, right (detail) Collection: Congreso Nacional, Salón Eliptico. Photographer: Carlos German Rojas. Courtesy of the Foundation Gallery of National Art, Republic of Venezuela **xxviii** top © Punch/Rothco; bottom, left Nationalmuseet, Copenhagen/The Bridgeman Art Library, London; bottom, right Atkinson Art Gallery/The Bridgeman Art Library, London **xxix** top, left Victoria & Albert Museum/Art Resource, NY; top, right Scala/Art Resource, NY; bottom © Elke Walford/Hamburger Kunsthalle, Hamburg **xxx** top Dragon Head, late Zhou dynasty. Courtesy of the Freer

Gallery of Art, Smithsonian Institution, Washington, DC (32.14); bottom © Boltin Picture Library **1** top © Boltin Picture Library; bottom left Archivo Fotographico Oronoz, Madrid; bottom right Bibliothèque Nationale de Cartes et Plans/The Bridgeman Art Library, London **2** top Art Resource, NY; bottom left © Jehangir Gazdar/Woodfin Camp & Associates, Inc.; bottom right Photo: Wan-go Weng Inc. Archive **3** top © Boltin Picture Library; bottom left G Michael Holford; bottom right Scala/Art Resource, NY **4** © Archiv/Photo Researchers, Inc. **7** Dragon Head, late Zhou dynasty. Courtesy of the Freer Gallery of Art, Smithsonian Institution, Washington, DC (32.14) **8** top Copyright British Museum (PS 133392); bottom left © Boltin Picture Library; bottom right Robert Harding Picture Library **9** top (detail) Otis Imboden, © National Geographic Society; bottom left © Michael Holford; bottom right SEF/Art Resource, NY **11** © Boltin Picture Library **12** (detail) © Michael Holford **13** © André Held **14** © Boltin Picture Library **16** top © Boltin Picture Library; middle Peabody Museum, Harvard University. Photo: Hillel Burger; bottom Scala/Art Resource, NY **17** top (detail) Photo Bibliothèque Nationale, Paris; bottom left Photo Bibliothèque Nationale, Paris; bottom right The Metropolitan Museum of Art, Gift of Robert E. Tod, 1937 (37.191.1) **18** top The Royal Collection © 1994 Her Majesty Queen Elizabeth II; bottom © Meyer/Kunsthistorisches Museum, Vienna **19** © Jose Fuste Raga/The Stock Market **20** (detail) Scala/Art Resource, NY **22** (detail) Topkapi Sarayi Museum, Istanbul/Ergun Cagatay/Tetragon **23** Top Topkapi Sarayi Museum, Istanbul/Ergun Cagatay/Tetragon; bottom Topkapi Sarayi Museum, Istanbul/Ergun Cagatay/Tetragon **24** top © Boltin Picture Library; bottom © Boltin Picture Library **26** top, Collection of the National Palace Museum. Taipei, Taiwan, Republic of China; bottom The Metropolitan Museum of Art, Gift of Robert E. Tod, 1937 (37.191.1) **28** top left Museum

Geschichte, Berlin; bottom, right Ligue des Societes de la Croix-Rouge **177** Risorgimento Museum, Turin, Italy. David Lees/Time-Life Picture Syndication **181** Museum der Stadt Wien/E.T. Archive **182** Library of Congress **183** Free Library of Philadelphia. Photo: Will Brown **184** Museo Statale Russo/Art Resource, NY **185** Marilyn D. Davis. Courtesy of The Chicago Historical Society **187** © Jean-Loup Charmet **191** The Royal Collection © Her Majesty Queen Elizabeth II **193** © Museum of London **194** top, far left The Bettmann Archive; top, left The Bridgeman Art Library, London; top, right © Jay Blakesberg/Retna, Ltd.; top, far right © Robert Risko; Bottom, far left Archiv für Kunst und Geschichte, Berlin; bottom, left The Bridgeman Art Library, London; bottom, right © Mick Hutson/ Redferns/ Retna, Ltd.; bottom, far right Copyright 1986, Taylor Jones. Disrtibuted by Los Angeles Times Syndicate **197** top (detail) Bridgeman/Art Resource, NY; middle, top © Hulton Deutsch Collection Ltd; middle bottom James Klugmann Collection. Photo, Ken Karp; bottom © Hulton Deutsch Collection Ltd **198** London Musuem/ E.T. Achive **199** The Bettmann Archive **201** *The Balloon*, Pierre Puvis de Chavannes © Photo Réunion des Musées Nationaux **202** Archiv für Kunst und Geschichte, Berlin **204** top Snark/Art Resource, NY; bottom, left © Jean-Loup Charmet; bottom, right Bibliothèque Nationale/ Giraudon/Art Resource, NY **205** From the Library of the YIVO Institute for Jewish Research **208** Smithsonian National Anthropological Archives **209** Library of Congress **210** New York State Historical Association, Cooperstown **211** International Museum of Photography at George Eastman House **215** © National Maritime Museum, London **217** left © Hulton Deutsch Collection Ltd; right Courtesy of Thomas J. Lipton **218** The Bettmann Archive **220** Staatliche Museen zu Berlin - Preussischer Kulturbesitz Museum für Volkerkunde **223** © Hulton Deutsch Collection Ltd

**225** Atkinson Art Gallery/The Bridgeman Art Library, London **227** left AP/Wide World Photos; right © Jean-Loup Charmet **230** National Army Museum/The Bridgeman Art Library, London **232** Victoria & Albert Museum/E. T. Archive **234** E.T. Archive **235** E.T. Archive **237** © Jean-Loup Charmet **241** Gallery Kabutoya, Japan **243** Victoria & Albert Museum/Art Resource, NY **244** Fukuzawa Memorial Center for Modern Japanese Studies, Keio University, Tokyo **245** Museum of Fine Arts, Boston/Laurie Platt Winfrey, Inc. **247** Mary Evans Picture Library, London **249** left © Branger-Viollet; right © Roger-Viollet **251** The Bettmann Archive **252** North West Mounted Police, Ottawa **254** The Granger Collection, New York **255** Museum of New Zealand Te Papa Tongarewa (B19095) **257** Museo Historico Nacional, Buenos Aires/The Bettmann Archive **259** left Rare Books and Manuscripts Division. The New York Public Library. Astor, Lenox and Tilden Foundations; top, right © Archive Photos; bottom, right The Everett Collection **262** top The American Numismatic Society; bottom Board of Commissioners of Currency, Singapore **265** *Head of a Woman or a Sailor*, Pablo Picasso. Musée Picasso © Photo Réunion des Musées Nationaux © 1996 Artists Rights Society (ARS), New York/SPADEM, Paris **268** left Bury Art Gallery & Museum, Lancs./The Bridgeman Art Library, London; top, right Archiv für Kunst und Geschichte, Berlin; bottom, right The Royal Collection © Her Majesty Queen Elizabeth II **269** left © National Maritime Museum, London; right Gallery Kabutoya, Japan **270** top, left Museum of New Zealand Te Papa Tongarewa (B19095); top, right National Army Museum/The Bridgeman Art Library, London; bottom © Museum of London **271** top, left Library of Congress; bottom, left Risorgimento Museum, Turin, Italy. David Lees/Time-Life Picture Syndication; right © Hulton Deutsch Collection Ltd **272** The Bettmann Archive **273** © Berry, 1986 Cartoonists & Writers Syndicate **274** top ©

Archive Photos; bottom, left Courtesy of the Dorothea Lange Collection, © The City of Oakland, The Oakland Museum, 1990; bottom, right © Doran H. Ross **275** left The Library of Congress; right AP/Wide World Photos **277** © Rudolf Wakonigg/ Landesmuseum für Kunst und Kultergeschichte, Münster **279** left © The Nobel Foundation; right Archiv für Kunst und Geschichte, Berlin **280** left New Cavendish Books, London; top, right New Cavendish Books, London; bottom, right Kenner Toys, courtesy Edelman **282** The Bettmann Archive **283** © John McCutchson/The Chicago Tribune, 1914 Photo: Ken Karp **285** left René Dazy Collection, Paris; right Archiv für Kunst und Geschichte, London **287** top Imperial War Museum/E.T. Archive; top-2 Imperial War Museum, London; middle © James A. Bryant; bottom-2 Salamander Books Ltd., London; bottom Musée de Verdun/Luc Joubert/Tallandier **290** National Gallery of Canada, Ottawa, Gift of the Massey Collection of English Painting, 1946 **291** Imperial War Museum, London **292** Library of Congress **293** National Archives **297** National Portrait Gallery, Smithsonian Institution/Art Resource, NY **298** Imperial War Museum, London **301** Scala/Art Resource, NY **302** Forbes Magazine Collection/The Bridgeman Art Library, London **303** Archiv für Kunst und Geschichte, London **305** The Bettmann Archive **306** Museo Statale Russo/Art Resource, NY **310** The Bettmann Archive **311** Archiv für Kunst und Geschichte, Berlin **312** top, left Itar-Tass/Sovfoto; top, right Archiv für Kunst und Geschichte, London; middle Itar-Tass/Sovfoto; bottom, left Sovfoto; bottom, right The Kobal Collection, NY **315** top, left Sovfoto; top, right © Bronx Educational Services; bottom, left Itar-Tass/Sovfoto; bottom, right © Hank Morgan/Photo Researchers, Inc. **316** Itar-Tass/Sovfoto **317** Scala/Art Resource, NY **321** Thames and Hudson, London **322** UPI/Bettmann **324** (detail) Photograph © The Detroit Institute of Arts, 1995. Palacio Nacional

stairway, Mexico City. © Dirk Bakker, photographer. **326** left © David Turnley/Black Star; right JB/Keystone/Hulton Deutsch Collection Ltd. **327** top, left Museum of Art, Rhode Island School of Design; Gift of Miss Eleanor B. Green; top, right Courtesy Suzanne Brown Gallery; bottom, left Schomburg Center for Research in Black Culture, New York Public Library; bottom, right © John de Vissar/Black Star **329** Turkish Culture and Information Office, NYC **332** Nehru Memorial Museum and Library, New Delhi **333** top © Archive Photos/Express Newspapers; bottom (inset) By permission of The British Library (F839) **335** © Topham/Image Works **337** China Stock/Liu Ligun artist **341** Courtesy of Ted Cook **343** Victoria & Albert Museum, London/Art Resource, NY **347** *The Persistence of Memory*, Salvador Dali, The Museum of Modern Art, New York © 1996 Demart Pro Arte, Geneva/Artists Rights Society (ARS), New York **349** left © Elke Walford/Hamburger Kunsthalle, Hamburg; right © Elke Walford/Hamburger Kunsthalle, Hamburg **350** left and right Mary Evans/Thurston Hopkins **351** © *The Irish Times*, July 22, 1948. Courtesy of the National Library of Ireland, Dublin. (R.26.837) **354** New York Daily News **355** top © 1995 The Oskar Schlemmer Theatre Estate/Photo Archive C. Raman Schlemmer, Oggebbio, Italy; bottom © 1995 The Oskar Schlemmer Theatre Estate/Photo Archive C. Raman Schlemmer, Oggebbio, Italy **356** top, left AP/Wide World Photos; top, right The Kobal Collection, NY; bottom, left © Dod Kusel/Sipa Press; bottom, right © Bob Daemmrich/ Stock Boston, Inc. **357** top © The London Transport Museum; bottom Mary Evans Picture Library **359** © by Giancarlo Costa/ Ferrovie Dello Stato, 1940 **360** The Bettmann Archive **363** top Bildarchiv Preussischer Kulturbesitz; bottom Archiv für Kunst und Geschichte, Berlin **364** © Keystone/The Image Works **366** top © Topham/The Image Works; bottom Jewish Historical Museum, Amsterdam **368** left

## HISTORICAL DOCUMENT ACKNOWLEDGMENTS

# Stop the Presses

**Visit Prentice Hall on the Internet at**

*http://www.phschool.com*

**for the Prentice Hall Social Studies Update.**

There you will find periodic updates in the following areas:

- ★ **United States History**
- ★ **World Studies**
- ★ **American Government**

Each update topic provides you with background information as well as carefully selected links to guide you to related content on the Internet.